Global Guide
to
International Education

GLOBAL GUIDE TO INTERNATIONAL EDUCATION

David S. Hoopes, Editor

Kathleen R. Hoopes, Assistant Editor

Advisory Committee

James M. Becker,
   Indiana University
Henry Ferguson,
   New York State
   Education Department
Henry M. Halsted,
   The Johnson Foundation

Richard D. Lambert,
   University of Pennsylvania
Cassandra A. Pyle,
   American Council on Education
Andrew F. Smith,
   Global Perspectives
   in Education

Facts On File Publications
New York, New York ● Bicester, England

Global Guide to International Education

Library of Congress Cataloging in Publication Data

Hoopes, David S.
   Global guide to international education.
   Includes index.
   1. Education—Directories.   2. Education—Information
services—Handbooks, manuals, etc.   I. Title.
L900.H66   016.37   82-1545
ISBN 0-87196-437-6   AACR2

Printed in the United States of America

10 9 8 7 6 5 4 3 2 1

Composition by Centennial Graphics
Printed by Maple-Vail

ACKNOWLEDGMENTS

The first people to whom I want to pay tribute here are the men and women who run the offices of international education programs and organizations around the United States. Just before going to press we asked virtually every organization, academic program and publisher listed in this book to make a last minute entry check to make sure that the data we had was as accurate and up-to-date as possible. The response was tremendous. We heard from nearly 1,000 people. Their replies ranged from giving us information on changes in critical data to suggesting ways of improving our style (it is a challenge to the imagination of the author of a reference work to wake up in the morning with fresh ways of saying things). Many just wrote back with notes saying, "Looks great. Thanks for including us."

Our thanks to you for your help and encouragement.

My advisory committee was invaluable. I did not call on them often, but when I did their reactions were immediate and perceptive. They were particularly helpful in the beginning when I was structuring the book and establishing criteria for inclusion.

Finally, in addition to my assistant editor (my wife) and my secretary Jan Field, both of whose efforts I recognized in the first volume of the Global Guide series, I would like to offer a special thank-you to Toby Frank. Ms. Frank was my assistant during the years in Pittsburgh when I was a field officer in the fight to establish international and intercultural studies as an integral part of the educational experience of all Americans. Much of the knowledge and commitment needed to sustain us in compiling and writing this book was generated during those years of partnership with Ms. Frank.

CONTENTS

INTRODUCTION

The word *Guide* in the title of this book is somewhat deceptive. It is indeed a guide to international education in the United States. Principally, however, it is a *sourcebook*, providing information on international education organizations, academic programs, and printed and other resources currently available that will enable you to pursue more effectively your own particular interests in the field. At the same time, in a number of areas of international education (international studies in higher education, for instance), it also constitutes a *directory*—in which you can find the names, addresses and phone numbers of most of the programs, organizations or institutions involved.

But the GLOBAL GUIDE TO INTERNATIONAL EDUCATION is also more. If you examine it carefully, you will find a wealth of information about the state of the field, its strengths and weaknesses, its needs and potentials. It thus constitutes a kind of overview of international education in the United States and should give us all a better sense of the context in which we work.

While the materials gathered are as comprehensive as possible within the confines of the criteria we used for inclusion, there are some areas in which we felt we had to place limits—as follows:

1. Foreign language programs, departments, degrees, etc. While foreign language instruction is certainly at the heart of international education (and is carefully noted in the context of the area studies programs listed), we knew we could not possibly list all the Spanish, French, etc., degree programs in the country. Also, through the Modern Language Association, the Association of Departments of Foreign Languages, the American Council on the Teaching of Foreign Languages and other sources, there is ample access to such information. Therefore, at least in this first edition, we decided not to include traditional language and literature programs. In the chapter on foreign languages we have concentrated on listing general sources of information along with other selected resources that emphasize self-instructional language learning. Emphasis has also been placed to some degree on the less commonly taught languages, especially in the area studies and country chapters.

2. Standard undergraduate international relations programs with a political science orientation have not been included (except those offered at large graduate centers and schools). Most larger and many smaller institutions offer an international relations major or something comparable. As is the case with majors in Spanish, French, etc., there were simply too many too much alike to make it feasible or very useful to include them. Our efforts were directed instead toward ferreting out the plethora of international *studies* programs that have burgeoned in recent years (and that take almost as many forms as there are programs) but for which there is no adequate listing anywhere, including college catalogues; a thorough search of such catalogues revealed no more than half of those programs that we eventually identified.

3. Our initial intention was to include a listing of all study-abroad programs currently available to American students. Foolish thought! Some weeks later, awash in a chaotic collection of bewilderingly ephemeral information, we thought better of the idea. Study-abroad programs appear, disappear and change spots daily, making it almost impossible to catalogue them in an orderly fashion. Besides, to the degree it can be done, the Institute of International Education (IIE) already does it in their excellent *Guide to U.S.-Sponsored Programs Abroad.* We decided to limit ourselves to listing nonuniveristy sponsors of overseas study programs and to mentioning programs specifically cited by international and area studies program directors.

4. Organizations that serve only a local audience were, in general, not included. There are literally thousands of local organizations involved in some way in international education; we felt we had to limit inclusion to those that provide resources of some kind at the national level.

5. You will find that the embassies or consulates of some countries are listed and those of some others are not. We asked each embassy, in many cases several times, to indicate to us what information they are willing to provide educators and others about their countries. When, after repeated inquiries, we received no reply, we decided to leave them out entirely since we suspected our readers might have the same experience, and we did not want to direct them to unreliable sources.

6. The list of funding organizations and programs is limited to those that offer grants or awards to individuals and groups in the United States—principally American sources, though in some cases Canadian—and that are primarily international in scope. There are many grant programs that accept proposals and applications international in substance but which are not intrinsically "international." We did not feel such programs belonged in this book.

7. In the third section of Chapter 4, under the heading "International Program Offices," we listed for the most part only those that are multipurpose in function. The purposes include any combination of the following: advising on study abroad and faculty and research abroad, foreign student advising, and instructional and cocurricular educational activity falling outside major or degree programs. Since offices mainly concerned with administering contracts for overseas projects are generally engaged in *development assistance* rather than international education (despite the educational implications), they were not included.

8. Some people may argue that the chapter on foreign students and visitors should have been omitted, since providing assistance to foreign students in getting an education in the United States is not "international education," at least as the term is used in this volume. Most people in the profession, however, strongly believe that the presence of foreign students on American campuses substantially furthers the international education of Americans—a belief that we share. We limited our entries on English-as-a-second language (ESL) programs to proprietary programs with multiple centers. As with study abroad, IIE publishes an excellent annual directory of campus-based ESL programs.

9. We have only listed publications that are currently in print and, with some exceptions, available from a source in the United States.

10. The vast majority of programs in international and area studies include language study as a requirement. We therefore do not normally mention that fact (though we do list languages offered in area studies entries). Most of the programs not requiring language study are either general international studies programs at smaller institutions, or African studies programs in which there is a significant emphasis on Afro-American studies.

On the subject of African studies, many programs include strong components of Afro-American studies (concerned with the descendants of Africans in the Western Hemisphere) that we felt quite appropriate for inclusion. On the other hand, Black Studies programs, which focus primarily on black culture in the United States, were not included. They would seem more appropriate in a volume on ethnic education in the United States.

Programs in which the study of language and literature is the sole component are not listed, even when called area studies. The exceptions are those language and literature programs closely associated with an area studies program.

You will notice that the Western European Studies chapter is organized somewhat differently from the other area studies chapters. Western European studies present a problem.

Major segments of the humanities and social sciences as taught in American universities could justifiably be called Western European studies. At what point can they be defined as "area studies?" In most cases we accepted the title of the program, looking especially for those programs that attempt to integrate various disciplines in European studies. In the process, Scandinavia and the European Community emerged as two significant themes or organizing foci.

We had many terminology problems, not the least of which was "Middle East," which we finally decided to employ (1) because of the prevalence of its use in the academic world, (2) because it seems to us a little bit less ethnocentric than "Near East" (near to what?), and (3) because the more accurate alternative "Southwest Asia" is not widely used and might be confusing, especially when North Africa has to be included.

We covered Jewish studies somewhat sparsely, primarily because many of the programs fall more appropriately into the categories of religious and/or ethnic studies than international studies. Also, programs of "Near Eastern Studies," when confined primarily to ancient history and/or religious or biblical studies, were not included.

HOW TO USE THIS SOURCEBOOK

Please read the following paragraphs carefully. They will help you find your way more easily through what may sometimes appear to be a maze of data.

In each section that lists programs, centers or offices in institutions of higher education are organized alphabetically by state; then within each state the institutions are listed alphabetically. Such listings occur in Chapters 4–6 and 12–18.

The area studies and country sections do not include published resources for teaching area and country subjects at the elementary, secondary and undergraduate level. Such materials are found in Chapter 2.

Large academic outreach programs that constitute a national resource are included in Chapter 2. Most academic outreach programs, however, are described within the framework of the program descriptions given in Chapters 4–6 and 12–18.

In using Chapter 4, take particular care in distinguishing the kinds of programs, centers and offices included in each section: (1) Degree- or Certificate-Granting Programs and Centers; (2) Research Centers (including some not campus-based); (3) International Program Offices (noninstructional; normally providing only services); and (4) Academic Associations and Agencies Concerned with International Education (not academic institutions as such).

Remember that Chapter 7 only includes organizations that give *general* international grants and awards. Other sources of funding are listed under area studies and individual countries. Don't give up too easily.

Finally, there are three indexes at the end of the book: one listing every organization mentioned in the book; another listing every publication; and the third organized topically, i.e., according to subject.

Welcome to the GLOBAL GUIDE TO INTERNATIONAL EDUCATION.

1

General Sources of Information on International Affairs, Cultural Relations and World Issues

Selected International Affairs Organizations

1.001
The Atlantic Council of the United States
1616 H St. NW
Washington, DC 20006
(202) 347-9353

Contact(s):
James R. Huntley, President

Nonprofit educational organization designed to foster the security and economic growth and promote closer relationships among North Atlantic nations through existing and new international institutions; U.S. affiliate of the Atlantic Treaty Association; supported by tax-free contributions

• Organizes seminars and working groups and conducts studies focusing on economic, governmental and educational issues and on how Atlantic institutions (NATO, OECD, etc.) further the security and prosperity of the North Atlantic nations

• Provides fellowships to select government officers, sponsors a young political leaders program and offers internships to students for the summer or an academic term to assist working groups in their research

• Publishes *Atlantic Community Quarterly* (dealing with current issues affecting European-North Atlantic relations), a monthly newsletter and a series of policy papers resulting from the efforts of the working groups and focusing on a broad range of international economic and political issues especially as they affect U.S. foreign policy; also publishes policy papers in cooperation with the Westview Press (see 11.034)

1.002
Council on Foreign Relations, Inc.
The Harold Pratt House
58 East 68th St.
New York, NY 10021
(212) 734-0400
BRANCH: Washington, DC

Contact(s):
Winston Lord, President

Prestigious membership organization providing a forum for foreign policy study, discussion and debate among academics, business-persons, professionals and government leaders; approximately 2,000 members; meetings normally off the record

• Publishes *Foreign Affairs* (five times per year) and extensive list of foreign policy studies, reports, documents and bibliographies

• Conducts meetings primarily for

members to discuss current major foreign policy issues and sponsors seminars on foreign policy and international business issues for approximately 200 subscribing U.S. multinational corporations (Corporation Service Program)

　　• Offers a number of research fellowships (see 7.006)

　　• Provides speakers and arranges programs for affiliated Committees on Foreign Relations in 37 U.S. cities

1.003
Council on Religion and International Affairs
Merrill House
170 East 64th St.
New York, NY 10021
(212) 838-4120

Contact(s):
Robert J. Myers, President

Nonprofit, nonsectarian educational organization concerned with applying ethical and religious insights to international affairs, international business, and the formulation of foreign policy

　　• Conducts meetings among policymakers and public and private leaders; sponsors study groups, the Hans J. Morgenthau Memorial Lecture, and seminars on international economic development

　　• Publishes monthly *Worldview* (see 1.102) and reports of activities

1.004
English-Speaking Union of the United States
16 East 69th St.
New York, NY 10021
(212) 879-6800
BRANCHES: 88 in cities throughout the country

Contact(s):
John D. Walker, National Director

Individual and corporate membership organization designed to create and maintain cultural ties between the U.S. and other English-speaking countries

　　• Sponsors "English-in-Action" programs (see 10.031) and awards scholarships and travel grants (see 7.009)

　　• Sponsors reciprocal book exchange program among the U.S., Australia, Uganda, India, New Zealand and the United Kingdom

　　• Sponsors speakers and arranges seminars and symposia

　　• Maintains 8,700-volume library at New York office

1.005
Global Tomorrow Coalition
1525 New Hampshire Ave. NW
Washington, DC 20036
(202) 328-8222

Contact(s):
Donald R. Lesh, Executive Director

Nonprofit association of U.S. organizations concerned with natural resources, the environment, development and population growth as global issues

　　• Provides information to government and other policy-makers, sponsors public educational activities and publishes *Interaction* (a quarterly newsletter in tabloid newspaper format) and the *GTC Bulletin* (which reports on legislative developments), all designed to focus attention on the potential dangers of ignoring global issues and to encourage active U.S. leadership

1.006
Overseas Development Council
1717 Massachusetts Ave. NW, Suite 501
Washington, DC 20036
(202) 234-8701

Contact(s):
John W. Sewell, President

Nonprofit research and education organization concerned with development issues and questions of U.S. policy toward developing countries.
    • Publishes annual evaluation of U.S. relations with the developing countries: *U.S. Foreign Policy and the Third World: Agenda 19--*, various development papers, and shorter pieces; testifies before Congress; conducts seminars for executive and legislative officers, non-governmental organizations, corporate officials, and the press on trade and industrial policy, international finance, development strategies, and development assistance

1.007
United States National Commission for UNESCO
U.S. Department of State
Washington, DC 20520
(202) 632-2761 or 2804

Contact(s):
Bernard Engel, Executive Secretary

U.S. government-sponsored Commission of which some 60 non-governmental organizations in the U.S. are members; designed to promote an understanding of UNESCO within the U.S.
    • Sponsors UNESCO meetings and conferences

    • Answers inquiries about UNESCO and publishes and distributes materials about UNESCO including the brochure *UNESCO: What It Is, What It Does, How It Works*

1.008
The U.S. Association for the Club of Rome
1525 New Hampshire Ave. NW
Washington, DC 20036
(202) 745-7715

Contact(s):
Linda Kovan, Executive Administrator

Association of individuals concerned with understanding and seeking solutions to contemporary global problems; supports aims but is independent of the international Club of Rome; membership limited to 500
    • Sponsors meetings and conferences, disseminates reports and studies and publishes newsletter

1.009
Worldwatch Institute
1776 Massachusetts Ave. NW
Washington, DC 20036
(202) 452-1999

Contact(s):
Lester R. Brown, President

Nonprofit research organization which tracks international issues and world problems
    • Publishes *Worldwatch Papers* (approximately 50, @ $2) on a wide range of global issues including resources, pollution, population, technology, status of women, energy, etc.

Guides, Directories and Reference Books

1.010
ABC POL SCI: A Bibliography of Contents: Political Science and Government
Lloyd W. Garrison, Editor
ABC-Clio Information Services
Riviera Campus
2040 Alameda Padre Serra
Box 4397
Santa Barbara, CA 93103
5 issues per year plus a cumulative annual index; approx. 320 pages; subscription price established on service basis

• Compiles tables of contents of over 300 journals worldwide, including approximately 10,000 articles per year; covers international affairs, law, government, political science, sociology and economics; each issue indexed (uses Subject Profile Index system that provides a profile of each article cited and comprises two or more descriptors; descriptors are rotated and the complete article profile is repeated under each term

1.011
American Art Directory
Edited by Jacques Cettell Press
R. R. Bowker Co.
1180 Ave. of the Americas
New York, NY 10036
hardbound; 721 pages; $70

• Comprehensive directory of art museums, galleries and collections in the U.S.; entries briefly identify types of collections and include a large number in African, American Indian, Asian, Oriental and pre-Columbian art and a smaller number in Latin and Mexican art and in Canadian, Japanese, Polish and Russian painting (along with painting collections of Europe as a whole and specific countries of Western Europe); includes listings of U.S. and Canadian art organizations and art schools, major museums and schools in other countries and other listings such as magazines, scholarships, booking agencies, etc.; subject index to American collections

1.012
American Library Resources
Robert B. Downs
American Library Association
50 East Huron St.
Chicago, IL 60611
1981; cloth; 209 pages; $30

• Comprehensive bibliographical guide listing 4,200 new, annotated bibliographic aids; supplements original volumes and two earlier supplements

1.013
American Library Resources Cumulative Index, 1870–1970
Clara Keller
American Library Association
50 East Huron St.
Chicago, IL 60611
1981; hardbound; 96 pages; $25

• Identifies by subject and library all special collections acquired by American libraries through 1970

1.014
The Annual Register: A Record of World Events
H. V. Hodson, Editor
Gale Research Co.
Book Tower
Detroit, MI 48226
annual; hardbound; 544 pages; $100

• Articles chronicle leading events of the year concerning every country, the UN and other international organizations; they also discuss social and economic trends and major developments in all fields; includes statistics, texts of important documents, a chronology of events, charts and photographs; indexed

1.015
Bibliographic Index
H. W. Wilson Co.
950 University Ave.
Bronx, NY 10452
3 times per year; hardbound; $145 per
    volume

• Identifies current bibliographies in print (including those which appear as parts of books or in periodicals) under most headings relevant to international studies, world areas and individual countries, languages, etc.

1.016
Careers in International Affairs
School of Foreign Service
Georgetown University
Washington, DC 20057
1982; paperbound; 252 pages; $7.50

• Comprehensive overview of the international employment scene; discusses the job market in international affairs and then lists and describes agencies and organizations that operate internationally; includes sections on the U.S. government, international organizations, banks and businesses, consulting firms, trade and professional associations and research, education and nonprofit organizations; includes a discussion of women in international affairs and a bibliography

1.017
Congressional Information Service, Inc.
4520 East-West Highway
Washington, DC 20014
(301) 654-1550

• Comprehensive reference service for all documents produced by the U.S. Congress and all statistical data produced by the U.S. government; includes *CIS/Index to Publications of the United States Congress* (CIS/Index) and *American Statistics Index: A Comprehensive Guide to the Statistical Publications of the United States Government* (ASI); access to CIS and ASI services and documents may be obtained through any reference library subscribing to them or from CIS Customer Service Representative at address above.

1.018
Countries of the World and Their Leaders Yearbook
Gale Research Co.
Book Tower
Detroit, MI 48226
annual; hardbound; 2 volumes, 1,400 pages;
    $58

• Compilation of the most recent edition of the State Department Series "Background Notes on Countries of the World" (see 2.188); covers 168 countries with a brief factual overview of the land, people, history, government, political condition, economy, foreign relations, and relevant U.S. policies; the volume also includes lists of key U.S. overseas officers, information on newly independent nations, foreign chiefs of state and cabinet ministers, reports on five international agencies (OAU, NATO, OECD, the UN and the European Community), and long sections on health information for the traveler and foreign travel in general (the last providing visa, passport, customs and duty information for each country)

1.019
The International Relations Dictionary
Jack C. Plano and Roy Olton
ABC-Clio, Inc.
Riviera Campus
2040 Alameda Padre Serra
Box 4397
Santa Barbara, CA 93103
1982; 488 pages; hardbound, $37.50;
    paperbound $15.00

• Provides definitions and commentary on the significance of terms, concepts, institutions and events central to international political relations; arranged topically and sequenced parallel to most related texts under such headings as role of foreign policy, nationalism, ideology, communication, war and military policy, international law, etc.

1.020
Diplomatic List
Office of Protocol
U.S. Department of State
Washington, DC 20520
updated quarterly; paperbound; 77 pages;
    $4.75 per copy

Available from the Superintendent of Documents, U.S. Government Printing Office, Washington, DC 20402
• Provides current list of foreign embassies in the United States and their principal officers (does not list consulates outside of Washington); includes Delegation of the Commission of the European Communities

1.021
The Directory of Directories
James M. Ethridge, Editor
Gale Research Co.
Book Tower
Detroit, MI 48226
1984; hardbound; approx. 1,000 pages; $100

• Lists approximately 9,000 mostly U.S. directories (including organizational membership directories) under such headings as science, education, social sciences, humanities, biography, arts, ethnic affairs, travel, business and finance; extensive listing of directories on international subjects; also offers Directory Information Service, periodical listings of additional directories ($75)

1.022
Directory of Special Libraries and Information Centers
Brigitte T. Darnay, Editor
Gale Research Co.
Book Tower
Detroit, MI 48226
1983; hardbound; Volume I, in two parts,
    1,640 pages, $260 per set; Volume II, 836
    pages, $230; Volume III, periodical
    supplements, $240

• Volume I lists approximately 15,000 special libraries and information centers and services, including computerized services, networks and consortia in the U.S. and Canada; Volume II lists by state or province the institutions described in Volume I; Volume III is a supplement provided periodically; contains cumulative indexes

1.024
The Directory of World Museums
Kenneth Hudson and Ann Nicholls
Facts on File, Inc.
460 Park Ave. South
New York, NY 10016
1981; hardbound; 678 pages; $75

• Comprehensive country-by-country listing of museums of the world (includes approximately 30,300 museums); information includes name of museums, address and brief description of contents, and identifies special exhibits (excludes zoos and botanical gardens, historical houses and sites, propagandistic collections, museums without a permanent collection or collections without a serious theme)

1.025
Economics and Foreign Policy
Mark R. Amstutz, Editor
Gale Research Co.
Book Tower
Detroit, MI 48226
1977; hardbound; 265 pages; $40

• Bibliographic information about works on international political-economic relationships

1.026
Encyclopedia of Associations, Volume I
Mary Wilson Pair, Editor
Gale Research Co.
Book Tower
Detroit, MI 48226
annual; hardbound; 1,600 pages; $135

• Major compilation of information on most trade, professional and other nonprofit associations and organizations in the U.S., including extensive listing of those involved in international activities; gives address, phone number, principal officer, size of staff, number of members, description of aims and activities and principal publications

1.027
Encyclopedia of Information Systems and Services
John Schmittroth, Jr., Editor
Gale Research Co.
Book Tower
Detroit, MI 48226
1982; hardbound; 1,248 pages; $285

• Comprehensive compilation of information on data bases, telecommunications, information networks and services, data collection and analysis centers, information retrieval software and similar resources in the U.S. and abroad; describes the systems and gives information on staff, scope, input sources, holdings, microform computer-based products and services, clientele, availability and contact; listings included under the following internationally oriented headings: Africa, Arab Countries, Asia, Australia, Bilingualism, Canada, Caribbean Area, Developing Nations, Europe, European Economic Community, France, Germany, Great Britain, International Development, International Relations, Italy, Japan, Languages, Latin America, Linguistics, Middle East, the Netherlands, the Pacific Islands, the Soviet Union, Terrorism, Travel, Treaties and the United Nations

1.028
The Encyclopedia of Political Systems and Parties of the World
George G. Delury, Editor
Facts on File, Inc.
460 Park Ave. South
New York, NY 10016
1982; hardbound in 2 volumes; 1,200 pages;
    $120 per set

• Describes in detail the political system and government, including the executive, legislative and judicial branches, of each of over 130 countries and discusses the leadership, structural organization, history, constituency, financing and prospects of major and minor political parties; includes charts, tables and a bibliography for each country; indexed

1.029
Encyclopedia of the Third World
George Thomas Kurian
Facts on File, Inc.
460 Park Ave. South
New York, NY 10016
1983; hardbound in 3 volumes; 2,128 pages;
    $145 per set

• Describes, country by country and in substantial detail with supporting statistics, current conditions in 142 of the world's less developed and/or nonaligned nations, including many of the smallest; all principal social, economic and political aspects are reviewed for each country including such special areas as colonial experience, freedom/human rights, civil service, law enforcement, etc.; each section includes a glossary, chronology and bibliography; also describes 40 international and regional organizations in which Third World countries play major roles; appendices contain tables and statistics relative to economic and business activity in the Third World

1.030
Encyclopedias and Dictionaries of the World
Pergamon Press, Inc.
Fairview Park
Elmsford, NY 10523
1983; paperbound; 154 pages; free to
   libraries

• Provides information on approximately 4,300 modern subject and language encyclopedias and dictionaries and approximately 500 atlases and handbooks

1.031
Ethnic Information Sources of the U.S.
Paul Wasserman and Jean Morgan, Editors
Gale Research Co.
Book Tower
Detroit, MI 48226
1983; hardbound; 850 pages; $95

• Lists live and print sources of information on 89 American ethnic groups; indexed

1.032
The Europa Year Book: A World Survey
Europa Publications Ltd.
18 Bedford Square
London WC1B 3JN, England
annual; hardbound in 2 volumes; 3,645
   pages; $195 per set

Available from Gale Research Co., Book Tower, Detroit, MI 48226
• Very comprehensive yearbook, survey and compilation of data, statistics and directory-type information
• Includes entries for approximately 190 countries or political entities grouped alphabetically in Europe and rest-of-the-world sections; for each country there is a brief survey of historical and cultural background, and then extensive compilations of data, statistics, lists of names and descriptive materials in the following areas: economics, principal characteristics, social structure, government offices and officers, judicial system, media, publishers, financial institutions, trade and industrial entities, transportation, tourism, atomic energy, defense, education and dependencies
• Covers approximately 90 international organizations, principally economic, though including those with political and cultural functions; provides a list of member countries and a description of the structure, activities and policies, along with identification of principal personnel.
• Europa also publishes yearbooks for Africa south of the Sahara (see 12.071), the Middle East and North Africa (see 17.067), and the Far East and Australasia (see 13.149)

1.033
Facts On File
Facts On File, Inc.
460 Park Ave. South
New York, NY 10016
weekly; 20 pages; $385 per year

• Digest and index of current national and foreign news including sections on world affairs, U.S. affairs and foreign nations; information derived from major U.S. and foreign newspapers and periodicals and current commercial, educational and government documents; cumulative computer index provided twice monthly; also includes binder and color atlas

1.034
Foreign Affairs Bibliography, 1962–1972
Janis N. Koreslins, Editor
R. R. Bowker Co.
1180 Ave. of the Americas
New York, NY 10026
1976; hardbound; 921 pages; $49.50

• One of a series of bibliographies prepared every 10 years; covers works under general headings (political processes, economics, etc.), chronologically and by world regions; lists books and provides brief abstracts

1.035
Foreign Consular Offices in the U.S.
U.S. Department of State
Washington, DC 20520
semiannual; paperbound; 215 pages; $7.50;
    available from the Superintendent of
    Documents, U.S. Government Printing
    Office, Wash., D.C. 20402

• Lists consulates general, consulates and honorary consulates throughout the U.S. for all countries which maintain them; includes names and ranks of personnel and jurisdiction of office, address and phone number

1.036
Guide to Reference Books
Eugene P. Sheehy, Editor
American Library Association
50 East Huron St.
Chicago, IL 60611
1976; hardbound; 1,015 pages; $30;
    supplement; 1980, (305 pages) $15 2d
    supplement, 1982

• Lists and describes major world reference books including bibliographies, encyclopedias, dictionaries (in English and foreign languages) and periodical and other directories in the principal disciplines and world areas, including listings country by country

1.037
Handbook of the Nations
Gale Research Co.
Book Tower
Detroit, MI 48226
1981; hardbound; 225 pages; $35

Reprint of the CIA publication *The World Factbook—1981*
• Provides up-to-date economic, political, military, geographic, communications and governmental data on 188 of the world's political entities; maps

1.038
Historical Abstracts
Eric H. Boehm, Editor
Gail A. Schlachter, Executive Editor
ABC-Clio, Inc.
Riviera Campus
2040 Alameda Padre Serra
Box 4397
Santa Barbara, CA 93103
annual; 8 issues per year; issued in 2 parts;
    each 250 to 300 pages; subscription price
    established on service basis

• Abstracts and annotates articles from over 2,000 journals; includes listings of selected new books and dissertation citations; comes in two parts (four issues each): (1) Modern History Abstracts 1450 to 1914 and (2) Twentieth Century Abstracts 1914 to the Present; cumulative five-year indexes available in library editions (uses Subject Profile Index system that provides a profile of each article cited and comprises two or more descriptors; descriptors are rotated and the complete article profile is repeated under each term)

1.039
Directory of United Nations Information Systems
United Nations Publications
Palais des Nations
1211 Geneva 10, Switzerland

1980; 350 pages in 2 volumes; Volume I, $22 and Volume II, $13

Available from United Nations Publications, New York, NY 10017; Volume I is printed in separate English, French, Spanish and Chinese editions; specify edition when ordering
• Volume I describes in detail approximately 300 UN information systems in over 30 specialized agencies including libraries, referral centers, clearinghouses, data banks, statistical-information systems and other systems both computerized and manual; provides address, conditions of access and types of services available; indexed
• Volume II (in English, French and Spanish in a single volume) lists for each country the organizations from which data from the UN information systems may be obtained; includes 2,500 addresses in 167 countries

1.040

Information Sources of Political Science
Frederick L. Holler
ABC-Clio, Inc.
Riviera Campus
2040 Alameda Padre Serra
Box 4397
Santa Barbara, CA 93103
1981; hardbound; 278 pages; $65

• Basic guide to reference works in the political science field providing 1,750 detailed citations of printed or computerized sources; major section devoted to international relations and organizations and comparative and area studies

1.041

The International Almanac of Electoral History
Thomas T. Mackie and Richard Rose
Facts On File, Inc.
460 Park Ave. South
New York, NY 10016
1983; hardbound; 450 pages; $35

• Contains election data for 24 different countries including the U.S., Canada, Australia and many countries in Western Europe from their first competitive national elections to the present; each country's entry has a description of the electoral process, the form of government and voting procedure, a list of all political parties and the dates of all elections ever held; includes charts and tables; indexed

1.042

International Bibliography, Information, Documentation: Publications of International Organizations
UNIPUB
205 East 42d St.
New York, NY 10017
quarterly service; paperbound; 50 pages;
　$42 per year

• Lists and describes all publications, periodicals, microforms and audiovisual materials issued by 95 intergovernmental organizations, including annotations, ordering sources and the tables of contents for periodicals with signed articles

1.043

International Cultural Exchange
Center for Arts Information, Inc.
625 Broadway
New York, NY 10012
booklet; 12 pages; $3.50; periodically
　updated

Available from the Center for Arts Information at the above address
• Lists organizations which engage in, fund or support international cultural exchange; gives name, address, organizational director and brief description of activities with emphasis on its relevance to the arts

1.044

International Directory of Arts
Verlag Müller GMB and Co.
16 Grosse Eschenheimer Strasse
D-6000 Frankfurt/Main, West Germany
bi-annual, 2 volumes; hardbound; Volume I,
    802 pages; Volume II, 948 pages

Available from R. R. Bowker, 205 East 42d
St., New York, NY 10017; $120
    • Lists, country by country, museums
and galleries, art schools, associations, restor-
ers, names of experts, dealers, commercial
galleries, auctioneers, publishers, periodicals, booksellers, artists and collectors; museum entries include address, names of directors and curators and general identification
of the nature of the collection; headings in
German, English, French and Italian; listings in language of the country or one of the
four principal languages; not indexed

1.045

**International Directory of Scholarly
Publishers**
The UNESCO Press
7 Place de Fontenoy
75700 Paris, France
1977; pamphlet; 65 pages; $8.50

Available from UNIPUB, 345 Park Ave. South,
New York, NY 10010
    • Lists and provides information on
scholarly (mostly noncommercial, academic)
publishers worldwide

1.046

**The International Encyclopedia of Higher
Education**
Asa S. Knowles, Editor-in-Chief
Jossey-Bass, Inc., Publishers
433 California St.
San Francisco, CA 94104
1977; hardbound; 10 volumes; 6,000 pages;
    $550

    • Large compendium of information on
all aspects of education worldwide, including
systematic data on higher education in each
of the nations of the world; contains approximately 1,000 substantive articles in six areas:
general topics, national systems of higher education, fields of study, educational associations, research centers, and education reports; extensively cross-referenced

1.047

International Organizations
Alexine L. Atherton, Editor
Gale Research Co.
Book Tower
Detroit, MI 48226
1976; hardbound; 350 pages; $40

    • Bibliographic information about works
on international and intergovernmental organizations

1.048

**MLA Directory of Periodicals: A Guide to
Journals and Series in Languages and
Literatures**
Modern Language Association
62 Fifth Ave.
New York, NY 10011
1979; hardbound; 692 pages; $90

    • Provides data on the 3,000 journals
and series indexed in the *MLA International
Bibliography* (see 1.049), including subscription and article submission information (paperbound edition covering U.S. and Canadian
titles only, forthcoming)

1.049

MLA International Bibliography
Modern Language Association
62 Fifth Ave.
New York, NY 10011
1981; hardbound; 5 volumes, 754 pages;
    $500

• Major bibliographic guide available in most reference/research libraries; covers books and articles on virtually all modern languages and literatures, including foreign language pedagogy and, for the years 1969 to 1972, linguistics

1.050
Museums of the World
K. G. Sauer
Munich, West Germany
1981; hardbound; 623 pages; $195

Distributed by Gale Research Co., Book Tower, Detroit, MI 48226
• Lists approximately 18,000 museums in 163 countries giving name, address, type, founding date and subject descriptions of collections and facilities; appendix lists national and international museum associations of the world; indexed

1.051
The New York Times Information Service, Inc.
Mead Data Control
9333 Springboro Pike
Dayton, OH 45401
(1-800) 543-6862

Contact(s):
Paul Nezi

Computerized information service
• Provides online access to time-shared information storage and retrieval systems containing data bases of bibliographic information in index, abstract and full-text formats accessible through controlled vocabulary or free-text search techniques; includes The Information Bank, a general resource based on 56 major American and foreign newspapers and periodicals, and the Key Issues Tracking Service, focusing on selected key social, political and economic issues and based on approximately 40 general and specialized publications

• Provides abstracts on microfiche or in printed form for all Information Bank abstracts made from the New York Times

1.052
Online Bibliographic Databases: A Directory and Sourcebook
James L. Hall and Marjorie J. Brown, Editors
Aslib
3 Belgrave Square
London SW1X 8 PL, England
1983; hardbound; 383 pages; $90

Available from Gale Research Co., Book Tower, Detroit, MI 48226
• Provides detailed descriptions, including sample printouts, file data, access charges, etc., of 179 databases worldwide which are available through some 40 online service suppliers; relevant listings under education, information, language, current affairs, social science and others; includes introductory chapter covering the processes involved in using data bases, the addresses of online service suppliers, a bibliography and several indexes

1.053
Political Parties of the World
Alan J. Day and Henry W. Degenhart, Editors
Gale Research Co.
Book Tower
Detroit, MI 48226
and
Longman Group Ltd.
Harlow, Essex, England
1980; hardbound; 432 pages; $110

• Provides information country by country on the world's political parties including a narrative introduction, brief history, results of recent elections, and various other data; covers approximately 1,000 active political parties; indexed

1.054
Public Affairs Information Service Bulletin
Lawrence J. Woods, Editor
Public Affairs Information Service, Inc.
11 West 40th St.
New York, NY 10018
semimonthly; paperbound; $200 per year

• Provides an extensive subject index to books, pamphlets, government publications, agency reports and articles published throughout the world in English relating to economics, business, finance, banking, government, public administration, demography, public policy, sociology, court decisions, statistics, political science, and international relations, education and travel; listings include brief explanatory notes where needed; covers 800 journals and 6,000 books, monographs and reports annually; issued semimonthly with three quarterly cumulations and an annual bound volume with author index; can get quarterly and/or annual separately as well as back volumes to 1915

1.055
Public Affairs Information Service, Foreign Language Index
Lawrence J. Woods, Editor
Public Affairs Information Service, Inc.
11 West 40th St.
New York, NY 10018
quarterly; $220 per year (including annual bound volume) back volumes to 1968 also available

• Provides an extensive subject index to books, pamphlets, government publications, agency reports and articles published in French, Italian, Spanish, German and Portuguese throughout the world relating to economics, business, finance, banking, government, public administration, demography, public policy, sociology, court decisions, statistics, political science, international relations, education and travel; subject headings in English; citations in language of publication with occasional explanatory notes in English

1.056
Reference Guide to the United Nations
David Dull and Harvey William Greisman, Project Editors
United Nations Association of the United States of America
300 East 42d St.
New York, NY 10017
1978; looseleaf notebook; 100 pages; $7.50

• Includes basic descriptions and statistics (budget, staff size, etc.), including name of director, address and phone number of each of the major organs and agencies of the UN

1.057
Research Centers Directory
Mary Michelle Watkins and James A. Ruffner, Editors
Gale Research Co.
Book Tower
Detroit, MI 48226
1983; hardbound; 1,083 pages, 6314 entries; $225

• Lists and describes university-related and other nonprofit research organizations in the U.S. and Canada; provides information on governance, research fields and activities and publications and services; includes centers involved in research in area studies and other international subjects; indexed

1.058
Statesman's Year-Book: Statistical & Historical Annual of the States of the World
The Macmillan Press Ltd.
Little Essex St.
London WC2R 3LF, England
annual; paperbound; 1,684 pages; £13.75

• Covers international organizations as well as all nations of the world; discusses history, government, geography, religion, education, welfare, justice, finance, defense, economy, industry, trade, communications, banking and foreign relations; includes names of major government offices and officials

1.059
Statistics—Europe
Joan M. Harvey, Editor
CBD Research, Ltd.
Beckenham, England
1981; hardbound; 508 pages; $150

Distributed by Gale Research Co., Book Tower, Detroit, MI 48226
• Provides extensive listing of sources of statistical data for each country of Europe including Turkey and the USSR; includes central statistical office and other important statistics collection agencies, principal libraries containing statistics, libraries and information services in other countries which supply statistics on each country, principal bibliographies of statistical compilations, and major statistical publications with full address and/or bibliographic information

1.060
The Study of International Relations
Robert L. Pfaltzgraff, Jr., Editor
Gale Research Co.
Book Tower
Detroit, MI 48226
1977; hardbound; 155 pages; $40

• Bibliographic information about works on international relations with emphasis on works written since World War II

1.061
Subject Collections: A Guide to Special Book Collections and Subject Emphases as Reported by University, College, Public and Special Libraries and Museums in the U.S. and Canada
Lee Ash, Editor
R. R. Bowker Co.
205 E. 42d St.
New York, NY 10017
1984; hardbound, c. 1,300 pages; $160

• Comprehensive list of library collections organized by subject including world areas, individual countries, cultures and languages, international relationships and activities, etc.; provides address, librarian, budget and description of collection

1.062
Subject Index to Sources of Comparative International Statistics
F. C. Pieper, Editor
CBD Research, Ltd.
Beckenham, England
1978; hardbound; 745 pages; $225

Distributed by Gale Research Co., Book Tower, Detroit, MI 48226
• Indexes statistics available from 350 serials worldwide; 53,000 citations under 4,000 subject headings; information includes how statistics are presented, in what units, how frequently and for which countries

1.063
Ulrich's International Periodicals Directory
Gary Ink, Editor
R. R. Bowker Co.
1180 Ave. of the Americas
New York, NY 10028
biennial; hardbound; 2,200 pages in 2 volumes; $64.50

• Major periodicals directory; lists, with extensive information, approximately 60,000 periodicals published currently worldwide; arranged by subject and indexed by titles

1.064
U.S. Department of State Telephone Directory
U.S. Department of State
Washington, DC 20520
quarterly; paperbound; 160 pages; $3.95;
   available from Superintendent of
   Documents, U.S. Government Printing
   Office, Washington, DC 20402

• Includes numbers for the State Department, Arms Control and Disarmament Agency, International Development Cooperation Agency, the Agency for International Development, Board for International Broadcasting and the Overseas Private Investment Corporation; lists personnel by name and office; includes complete list of country desk officers

1.065
University Microfilms International
300 North Zeeb Road
Ann Arbor, MI 48106
(313) 761-4700 or (800) 521-3042

Contact(s):
Laura J. Klein, Account Executive

• Catalogues and makes available on microfilm over 1.5 million volumes of current and historical books, periodicals, documents, manuscripts, dissertations and theses from collections in the U.S., Great Britain and elsewhere in the world; offers approximately 13,000 serial titles, 100,000 books and 800,000 doctoral dissertations and theses; publishes abstracts, indexes and other research information and bibliographic access tools including online and offline computer searching; also offers Books-on-Demand reprinting services for out-of-print books

1.066
The World in Figures
The Economist Newspaper, Ltd.
25 St. James's St.
London SW1A 1HG England
1981; hardbound; 294 pages; $55;

Available from Gale Research Co., Book Tower, Detroit, MI 48226
• Comprehensive compilation of data for virtually every country in the world as of 1979 or 1980; presents comparative world figures and rankings in such areas as population, national income, standard of living, energy, manufacturing, education, transportation, labor, world trade, tourism and finance; country entries include data on geography, political status, economy, population, religions, culture, language, labor, education, standard of living, resources, agriculture, transportation, energy, ports, equipment, vehicles, GDP products and production, traffic, finance, budget, balance of payments, reserves and debt, trade, etc.; includes illustrative charts, graphs and maps as well as historical data back to 1960; indexed by country and subject focus; designed for use in making inter-country comparisons

1.067
World Guide to Libraries
Helga Lengenfelder, Editor
K. G. Saur
Munich, West Germany
1980; hardbound; 1,030 pages; $225

Distributed by Gale Research Co., Book Tower, Detroit, MI 48226
• Describes 42,000 libraries in 167 countries, listed by world region and country

and arranged by type: national libraries, general resource libraries, religious libraries, business and corporate libraries and special libraries; information includes main departments and special collections

1.068
World Guide to Special Libraries
Helga Lengenfelder, Editor
K. G. Saur
Munich, Germany
1983; hardbound; 990 pages; $120

Available in the U.S. exclusively from Gale Research Co., Book Tower, Detroit, MI 48226
  • Covers approximately 32,000 special libraries located in nearly 160 countries of the world; includes independent subject-oriented national libraries, public libraries with a subject focus, special libraries at institutions of higher learning, government and administrative libraries, law libraries, libraries of professional schools, libraries at government-sponsored or private research institutions, industrial and business libraries, libraries in museums and archives, libraries maintained by learned societies and professional associations, and libraries of religious bodies and churches; excludes libraries with fewer than 3,000 volumes, national and state libraries, public libraries, central university libraries, and general libraries at institutions of higher education; gives name of library in native language, address, telephone, director's name, special holdings and collections, statistics and other useful information

1.069
Worldmark Encyclopedia of the Nations
Moshe Y. Sachs, Editor
John Wiley & Sons, Inc.
605 Third Ave.
New York, NY 10016
1976; hardbound; 1,750 pages in 5 volumes;
  $99.50 per set

  • Practical guide to the geographic, historical, political, social and economic status of 162 nations and 90 dependencies and their international relations, including coverage of the UN system; separate volumes for the Americas, Europe, Africa, Asia and Australasia, and the UN; includes 172 maps and 600 tables

1.070
The Year Book of World Affairs
George W. Keeton and Georg
  Schwarzenberger, Editors
Westview Press
5500 Central Ave.
Boulder, CO 80301
annual; hardbound; 270 pages; $42

  • Contains articles on major topics of current international political concerns accessed through an analytical index

1.071
Yearbook of International Organizations
Union of International Associations
1 Rue aux Laines
1000 Brussels, Belgium
annual; hardbound; 1,120 pages; $105

Available from Gale Research Co., Book Tower, Detroit, MI 48226
  • Lists and provides extensive information on approximately 8,000 organizations worldwide which are actively international (engaged in activities in three or more countries)

Periodicals

1.072
Alternatives
Saul H. Mendlovitz and Rajni Kothari,
  Editors
Centre for the Study of Developing
  Societies
29 Rajpur Road
Delhi 110054, India
quarterly journal; approx. 150 pages; $30
  per year, institutions; $16 per year,
  individuals (inquire for different prices for
  overseas subscribers)

Order from World Policy Institute, 777 UN
Plaza, New York, NY 10017
  • Provides analyses of major global issues and presents alternative worldviews,
processes and strategies for confronting problems such as militarism, underdevelopment,
dependency, exploitation and ecological de-
terioration

1.073
**The Annals of the American Academy of
Political and Social Science**
Sage Publications, Inc.
275 South Beverly Drive
Beverly Hills, CA 90212
5 issues per year; hardbound; approx. 75
  pages; $7.50 (paperbound, $6)

  • Each edition focuses on a major issue
in political and social affairs, often international in scope, and brings to bear a variety
of perspectives on it

1.074
Atlantic Community Quarterly
Atlantic Council of the United States
1616 H St. NW
Washington, DC 20006
quarterly journal; individuals, $15;
  institutions, $18

  • Articles on foreign policy and political
relationships among individual nations and
between them, the Soviet bloc and the Third
World

1.075
Cultures
The UNESCO Press
7 Place de Fontenoy
75700 Paris, France
continuing series; approx. 200 pages; per
  number; $11.00 $27.50

Order from UNIPUB, 205 East 42d St., New
York, NY 10017
  • Reviews literature, art, crafts, religion, cinema, music and other aspects of culture, examining traditional forms of expression from a contemporary point of view and
exploring their transnational impact

1.076
Dance Research Journal
Congress on Research in Dance
Dance and Dance Education Department
New York University
35 West 4th St., Room 675
New York, NY 10003
biannual; journal; paperbound; Volumes 4–
  6, $4.25; Volumes 11 and 14 (double
  volumes) $8.50; all other volumes $5.25

Also publishes *Dance Research Annual*
  • Articles on dance history, research and
resources worldwide, conference reports, book
reviews, and bibliographies

1.089
International Studies Quarterly
Terrence Hopmann, Managing Editor
Institute of International Studies
University of Minnesota
Minneapolis, MN 55455
quarterly journal; approx. 80 pages; $40 per
   year for institutions; free to members of
   the International Studies Association,
   University of South Carolina, Columbia,
   SC 29208

Available to institutions through Butterworth
Scientific, Ltd., Westbury House, Bury St.,
Box 63, Guildford GU2 5BH England
   • Contains articles on international issues and on international studies and research from a variety of disciplines and perspectives

1.090
Journal of Cross-Cultural Psychology
Roy S. Malpass, Editor
Sage Publications, Inc.
275 South Beverly Drive
Beverly Hills, CA 90212
quarterly journal; approx. 75 pages; $18 per
   year

   • Scholarly articles on the results of scientific and empirical cross-cultural research
on psychological subjects and issues

1.091
Journal of International Affairs
Joshua D. Katz, Editor
School of International and Public Affairs
Columbia University
420 West 118th St.
New York, NY 10027
semiannual journal; approx. 220 pages;
   individuals, $11 per year; institutions, $22
   per year

   • Contains scholarly and more general
articles and essays on current issues in international relations; each issue focuses on a broad
area of interest (Japan's New World Role, A
New World Information Order, Politics of Labor Migration, etc.)

1.092
New Internationalist
New Internationalist
113 Atlantic Ave.
Brooklyn, NY 11201
monthly; magazine; $19

   • Provides hard-hitting reports on world
issues and problems especially in the areas of
development, poverty, human rights and in-
justice; each month includes a profile on the
status of these and other issues in a neglected
country

1.093
Planet Earth
Gordon Feller, Editor
Planetary Citizens
777 UN Plaza
New York, NY 10017
semiannual; approx. 32 pages; on newsprint
   in booklet form; $15 per year

   • Includes articles on the development
of global perspectives through individual, organizational and educational initiatives

1.094
Review
Immanuel Wallerstein, Editor
Sage Publications, Inc.
275 South Beverly Drive
Beverly Hills, CA 90212
quarterly journal; approx. 50 pages; $36 per
   year, institutions; $18 per year,
   individuals

Prepared by the Fernand Braudel Center for the Study of Economics, Historical Systems, and Civilization

• Contains articles that take an integrated global or "world system" perspective on international economic and social issues

1.095
Third World Quarterly
Altaf Gauhar, Editor
Third World Foundation
New Zealand House
Haymarket
London SW1Y 4TS, England
quarterly journal; approx. 780 pages; $30 per year

• Covers political, social and economic issues relative to Third World countries with particular emphasis on relations between developed and developing countries (North-South relations); includes book reviews and notes

1.096
The UNESCO Courier
The UNESCO Press
7 Place de Fontenoy
75700 Paris, France
monthly magazine; approx. 50 pages; $14 per year

Should be ordered from UNIPUB, 205 East 42d St., New York, NY 10017
• Articles on a wide range of contemporary world issues, themes and problems

1.097
The Washington Papers
Walter Laquer and Robert G. Neumann, Editors
Center for Strategic and International Studies
Georgetown University
Washington, DC 20057

8 issues per year; paperbound; $30 per year, institutions; $20 per year, individuals

Available from Sage Publications, Inc., P.O. Box 5024, Beverly Hills, CA 90210
• Series of papers prepared by the Center which appraise major issues affecting or affected by developments in the U.S., in U.S. foreign policy or in world affairs in general

1.098
World Affairs: A Quarterly Review of World Problems
American Peace Society
4000 Albemarle St. NW
Washington, DC 20016
quarterly journal; $20 per year

• Contains substantive articles on wide range of issues, especially involving East-West relations

1.099
The World of Music
Ivan Vandor, Editor
International Institute for Comparative
   Music Studies and Documentation
Winklerstrasse 20, D-1000
Berlin 33, West Germany
and
International Music Council
1 Rue Miollis, F-75737
Paris Cedex 15, France
3 times a year; journal; approx. 122 pages; $19, individuals; $24, institutions

Subscriptions should be sent to Edition Heinrichshofen, Postfach 620, D-2940 Wilhelmshaven, West Germany
• Articles in English on research on world music and musical traditions with summaries in French and German; includes book and record reviews, and a section on the UNESCO International Music Council

1.100
World Paper
Mark Gerzon, Managing Editor
Crocker Snow, Jr., President
World Times, Inc.
8 Arlington St.
Boston, MA 02116
8 issues per year; approx. 20 pages; $12 per
   year

Subtitled "A Global Community Newspaper"; also delivered as insert in other newspapers in nine cities abroad and one in the U.S.
   • Includes articles written from a global perspective by associate editors and established writers from many different countries; subjects include futurology, energy, economics, politics, population, hunger and other major world issues; includes cartoons, poetry and classifieds

1.101
World Politics
Elisbeth G. Lewin, Executive Editor
Princeton University Press
Princeton, NJ 08540

quarterly journal; approx. 160 pages;
   individuals, $16.50 per year; institutions,
   $25 per year

Journal of the Princeton University Center of International Studies (see 4.175)
   • Contains scholarly and theoretical articles on major world political issues

1.102
Worldview
John Tessitore, Editor
Council on Religion and International Affairs
170 East 64th St.
New York, NY 10021
monthly; newsprint magazine; approx. 35
   pages; $19.95 per year

   • Articles on aspects of contemporary international relations with an emphasis on values and moral and ethical issues; book reviews; takes advertising

Publishers

1.103
ABC-CLIO, Inc.
Riviera Campus
2040 Alameda Padre Serra
Box 4397
Santa Barbara, CA 93103
(805) 963-4221

   • Publishes reference books (especially bibliographies) on international and comparative politics, war/peace studies, library and art reference works and area studies (African, Asian, Eastern European and Latin American); includes *Historical Abstracts* (abstracts current periodical literature on history, see

1.038), *ABC POL SCI* (abstracts current periodical literature on the social sciences, see 1.010), *Information Sources of Political Science* (see 1.040), *The Study of International Politics* (sourcebook), *Soviet and East European Foreign Policy* (bibliography, see 14.068), *Modern Revolutions and Revolutionists* (a bibliography), *World Hunger* (bibliography), *Arms Control and Disarmament* (bibliography), *World Treaty Index* (index referencing 44,500 treaties from Treaty Research Center, University of Washington), *Latin American Political Dictionary* (see 16.141), *The International Relations Dictionary* (see 1.019), *Soviet and East European Political Dictio-*

nary (see 14.069), *Middle East Political Dictionary* (see 17.068), *East European Languages and Literatures* (index to articles in English language journals, see 14.065), *East, Central and Southeast Europe* (Library and Archival Resources, see 14.064), *Latin America: Social Science Information Sources*), a number of books in African, Asian and Latin American studies, and the *World Bibliographical Series* (see 2.198)

1.104
Ablex Publishing Corporation
355 Chestnut St.
Norwood, NJ 07648
(201) 767-8450

• Publishes books on international and intercultural communication

1.105
Archon Books
P.O. Box 4327
995 Sherman Ave.
Hamden, CT 06514
(203) 248-6307

• Publishes extensive list of books on international relations, diplomatic history, defense and military affairs; also *People of the Cape Verde Islands* (see 18.065)

1.106
Beekman Publishers, Inc.
P.O. Box 888
Woodstock, NY 12498
(914) 679-2300

Commercial publishing house
• Publishes extensive list of Marxist/socialist (British) titles on politics and economics; also publishes *Canadian Almanac and Directory* (see 18.059)

1.107
California Institute of Public Affairs
P.O. Box 10
Claremont, CA 91711
(714) 624-5212

Nonprofit research and publishing organization specializing in reference books
• Publishes guides, directories, and sourcebooks on current international, national and California-oriented subjects; includes *Foreign Area Programs at North American Universities: A Directory* (see 2.129), *California and the World: A Directory of California Organizations Concerned with International Affairs* and world directories of organizations and information sources on environmental issues, nuclear power, population and the world food crisis

1.108
Facts On File, Inc.
460 Park Ave. South
New York, NY 10016
(212) 683-2244

Commercial publishing house
• Publishes reference books and "fact" and other information resource books and publications in, among other areas, history, international relations, current affairs, business, economics, politics and world cultures; includes the Facts on File weekly digest and index of the news (see 1.033), a series of cultural, historical and political atlases, *The Encyclopedia of the Third World*, (see 1.029), *The Encyclopedia of Political Systems and Parties of the World* (see 1.028), *The International Almanac of Electoral History* (see 1.041) and a "Political Facts" series for Africa, Europe and the British Commonwealth

1.109
Hammond, Inc.
515 Valley St.
Maplewood, NJ 07040
(201) 763-6000

Commercial publishing house specializing in maps, atlases and globes

• Publishes a series of world atlases at a range of prices; most comprehensive is *Medallion World Atlas* with 672 pages of foreign and domestic maps ($60); others are *Ambassador World Atlas* ($34.95) and *Citation World Atlas* ($19.95 hardcover; $15.95 softcover); also publishes *World Atlas, International Edition* ($14.95) including additional information on the countries of the world

• Distributes Bartholomew Road and World Travel Maps ($6.95 each) covering most of the world regions and many individual countries (see countries for indication of availability); Bartholomew also produces maps for classroom use

1.110
Harvard University Press
79 Garden St.
Cambridge, MA 02138
(617) 495-2600

University publishing house

• Publishes extensive list of books in area studies including over 150 on China, 50 on Russia, and significant numbers on Japan, Asian studies, Latin American studies, Middle Eastern studies, and African studies; also a substantial list in comparative and international economics and international politics; includes catalogues of books contained in the Harvard Library world areas collections and audiovisual courses on Japan and China

1.111
Hoover Institution Press
Stanford University
Department C-79
Stanford, CA 94305
(415) 497-3373

University publishing house

• Publishes books, bibliographies and other reference works on international political affairs covering all world areas, particular emphasis on the world communist movement; includes annual *Yearbook on International Communist Affairs*, a number of research handbooks and guides, a wide selection of bibliographies (China, the Soviet Union and Africa), *Handbook of American Resources for African Studies* (see 12.081) and *Guide to Hungarian Studies* (see 18.196)

1.112
Human Relations Area Files, Inc.
P.O. Box 2054 Yale Station
New Haven, CT 06520
(203) 777-2334

Scholarly research and educational publisher; most conventional books published under the HRAF imprint

• Publishes books and multimedia resource materials for teaching and research in the social sciences; includes area and country anthropological surveys, bibliographies (especially *Annotated Bibliography of Afghanistan;* see 18.004), comparative and cross-cultural studies and various guides and resources for the use of the Human Relations Area Files (anthropological information about the cultures of the world)

1.113
Interbook, Inc.
611 Broadway, Room 227
New York, NY 10012
(212) 677-9201

• Publishes books on international relations and on current African affairs and African arts (see 12.120)

1.114
Intercultural Press, Inc.
Box 768
Yarmouth, ME 04096
(207) 846-5168

Contact(s):
Margaret D. Pusch, President

Publishing house specializing in books and materials on international and intercultural subjects for trainers, educators, professionals, business executives and others engaged in cross-cultural operations or activities
 • Publishes and distributes books on intercultural communication, overseas adjustment, cross-cultural training and intercultural analysis, along with descriptive information on specific countries; includes UPDATE Series (see 2.197), INTERACT Series (see Australia, Mexico and Thailand), *Survival Kit for Overseas Living* (see 8.039), *American Cultural Patterns: A Cross-cultural Perspective* and *Living in the USA* (see 10.049)

1.115
International Publishers
381 Park Ave. South
New York, NY 10016
(212) 685-2864

Commercial publishing house
 • Publishes books on social sciences with emphasis on Marxist theory

1.116
International Review Service
UN Bureau: Room 301
United Nations, NY 10017
(212) 754-7127

Contact(s):
A. G. Mezerik, Editor

 • Publishes books on international political and economic issues, particularly as they relate to the UN; also maintains subscription services that provide monthly reports on worldwide developments in economics and energy including *Trade and Economic Development* and *Energy Developments*

1.117
The Johns Hopkins University Press
Baltimore, MD 21218
(301) 338-7875

 • Publishes books on international economic and political affairs, history, law, language and country and area studies (Eastern and Western Europe, Latin America and the Middle East); includes *Yemen: Search for a Modern State* (see 18.586) and the *Persian Gulf States: A General Survey* (see 17.070) along with economic studies and periodicals prepared by the World Bank and other organizations including *MLN-Modern Language Notes* and *The Human Rights Quarterly*

1.118
Lexington Books
125 Spring St.
Lexington, MA 02173
(617) 862-6650 (customer service [800] 428-8071)

 • Publishes extensive list of books on the political aspects of international trade and economic relations, multinational business, developing economies, the oil crisis, nuclear energy, security, public policy, international communism and economic studies of developing countries

1.119
Micro Photo Division
Bell & Howell
Old Mansfield Road
Wooster, OH 44691
(800) 321-9881

Commercial microform publisher
 • Makes an extensive list of periodicals available on microfiche; includes a number of journals and magazines on world areas and other international subjects

1.120
The MIT Press
28 Carleton St.
Cambridge, MA 02142
(617) 253-5646

University publishing house
  • Publishes extensive list of titles on economics, economic development and international trade

1.121
Monthly Review Press
62 West 14th St.
New York, NY 10011
(212) 691-2555

Small commercial publishing house
  • Publishes books on world affairs concentrating on analysis of contemporary political, social and economic developments from a revolutionary socialist perspective

1.122
Nichols Publishing Co.
P.O. Box 96
New York, NY 10024
(212) 580-8079

Commercial publishing house
  • Publishes books on international relations emphasizing transnational relations, interdependence, international organization and management; includes bibliographies on international relations theory and the Atlantic Alliance

1.123
OECD Publications and Information Center
1750 Pennsylvania Ave. NW
Washington, DC 20006
(202) 724-1857

HEADQUARTERS: France
BRANCH CENTERS: Bonn, Tokyo
SALES AGENTS: in 35 countries

Publications and information arm in the U.S. of the Organization for Economic Cooperation and Development; members include Australia, Austria, Belgium, Canada, Denmark, Finland, France, Germany, Greece, Iceland, Ireland, Italy, Japan, Luxembourg, the Netherlands, New Zealand, Norway, Portugal, Spain, Sweden, Switzerland, Turkey, the United Kingdom, the U.S. and Yugoslavia (special status)
  • Answers inquiries about the work of OECD and distributes OECD publications on the following subjects: general economic issues, developing countries, environment, employment, energy, industry, agriculture, fisheries, tourism, inland and maritime transport, education, science and technology; standing orders for publications may be placed in each of these categories

1.124
Pergamon Press, Inc.
Maxwell House
Fairview Park
Elmsford, NY 10523
(914) 592-7700

Large commercial publishing house
  • Publishes a number of titles on international and transnational relations, military affairs and national security, cross-cultural psychology, intercultural communication and training, the Soviet Union/Eastern Europe and the Middle East, as well as publications produced by the East-West Center Culture Learning Institute (see 13.035); includes an annual *America and the World* series in which well-known analysts examine and review the state of American political and economic relations with the rest of the world; also distributes Haack Wall Maps (in English) for all

principal world areas, designed for classroom use

1.125
Praeger Publishers
521 Fifth Ave.
New York, NY 10017
(212) 599-4800

Commercial publishing house with strong academic list
• Publishes extensive list of books on international politics, development and economics covering all areas of the world; includes studies on specific countries and regions and a series "Studies in Influence in International Relations"

1.126
Princeton University Press
Princeton, NJ 08540
(609) 452-4900

University publishing house
• Publishes an extensive list of titles on international economics, military affairs, politics and political relations; on the history and politics of Asia, Eastern Europe, Africa, Latin America and the Middle East; and on Asian and African literatures, including an Asian-writers-in-translation series; particular strength in materials on China, India, Japan, the USSR and Eastern Europe

1.127
Rand McNally & Co.
International Division
P.O. Box 7600
Chicago, IL 60680
(312) 673-9100

Publishing house specializing in maps and atlases

• Publishes *The New International Atlas* ($75) and a variety of other world atlases as well as pocket guides to 13 Western European countries and cities; also publishes a series of guides to Chinese (PRC) cities and wall maps of a number of countries and regions
• Distributes Kummerly and Frey road maps ($7.95 each) covering major regions and countries of the world; see individual countries for indication of availability

1.128
Sage Publications, Inc.
275 South Beverly Drive
Beverly Hills, CA 90212
(213) 274-8003

• Publishes extensive list of titles analyzing current international political and economic issues; also publishes the following periodicals: *Washington Papers* (see 1.097), *Journal of Conflict Resolution* (see 5.034), *International Studies Quarterly* (see 1.089) and *Review* (on inter-American relations, see 16.157)

1.129
St. Martin's Press
175 Fifth Ave.
New York, NY 10010
(212) 674-5151 (customer service [800] 221-7945)

• Publishes extensive list of books in world politics, international relations and arms issues, as well as a number of books on historical and contemporary affairs in specific countries, including Afghanistan, Iraq, Laos and Libya (see under individual countries)

1.130
Stanford University Press
Stanford, CA 94305
(415) 497-9434

Large university publishing house
 • Publishes extensive list of books on international politics, culture, revolution and current affairs

1.131
Taylor & Francis, Inc.
International Publications Service Division
242 Cherry St.
Philadelphia, PA 19106-1906
(215) 238-0939

Contact(s):
Joel Packman, President, Taylor & Francis

Imports and distributes books published abroad in the fields of education and library reference materials
 • Imports and distributes English-language publications from all over the world; large number of titles stocked include serials and reference books in a wide range of subject areas including bibliography, language, literature, development and international organizations; catalogue available

1.132
Transaction Books
Rutgers University
New Brunswick, NJ 08903
(201) 932-2280

 • Publishes extensive list of titles on international economics and politics and a smaller list on military affairs and on Israeli, Asian, Middle Eastern, African and Latin American affairs

1.133
UNIPUB
205 East 42d St.
New York, NY 10017
(212) 916-1650
Customer Service
Box 1222
Ann Arbor, MI 48106
(313) 761-4700
(800) 521-8110

Large commercial publishing house
 • Publishes and distributes extensive list of books, reports, reference works and periodicals on international development, and on economic, political and cultural subjects including its own and those of a number of major organizations, e.g., UNESCO (complete catalogue available) and other UN agencies and 15 additional organizations and publishing houses; among the publications carried are UNESCO's *Study Abroad* (see 8.036), a country-by-country cultural policies series, a variety of bibliographic and library sourcebooks including *International Bibliography, Information, Documentation: Publications of International Organizations* (see 1.042) and *Directory of Educational Documentation and Information Services*

1.134
United Nations Publications
United Nations
Room A-3315
New York, NY 10017
(212) 754-8303

Titles may be ordered through UNIPUB (see 1.133).
 • Publishes approximately 2,000 titles, including documents, studies, guides, periodicals, bibliographies, yearbooks and statistical compilations related to the activities of the UN and to the areas of particular UN political, economic and social concern, especially economic development, trade, finance, public administration, international law, narcotics, cartography, human rights, demography, population, energy, disarmament and treaties; includes *Yearbook of the United Nations* (overview of the work of the UN), *Directory of Libraries and Documentation Centers in the United Nations*, *Your United Nations* (the official guidebook), *UNDOC: Current Index—United Nations Documents Index* (periodical providing information on all UN documents as they are prepared), the

UN Chronicle (magazine covering UN activities and areas of concern), *Statistical Yearbook*, *World Statistics in Brief* (a condensation of statistical information on population, trade, finance, communication, education and many other social phenomena in the world as a whole), *Statistical Yearbook for Latin America*, *Statistical Yearbook for Asia and the Pacific*, and *Demographic Yearbook;* comprehensive list of titles available

1.135
University Press of America, Inc.
Box 19101
Washington, DC 20036
(301) 459-3366

Large publishing house
   • Extensive list of books on international relations and world politics along with a limited selection on international cultural subjects

1.136
Westview Press
5500 Central Ave.
Boulder, CO 80301
(303) 444-3541

Commercial publishing house
   • Publishes extensive list of books on current international affairs in the following areas: Africa, Asia (especially on China), the Caribbean, Latin America, Western Europe, Eastern Europe and the Soviet Union, development, international economic and political relationships, international law, military and national security affairs, foreign policy, peace and terrorism; includes titles on major worldwide issues such as energy, food, communications, arms control, environment, futuristics, health, etc., along with a series of basic studies of the nations of the world focusing on current affairs within a historical context, designed for both the student and general reader (see individual countries)

1.137
John Wiley & Sons, Inc.
605 Third Ave.
New York, NY 10158
(212) 850-6000

Commercial publishing house
   • Extensive list of titles on international business and economics, basic texts for French, German and Spanish, and a selection on international political relations; also the following titles: *The Study of the Middle East* (see 17.072), *The Pinyin Chinese-English Dictionary* (see 18.102), *Chinese/English Phrasebook for Travellers* and accompanying cassette (see 9.042) and *Worldmark Encyclopedia of the Nations* (see 1.069)

2

Resources for Elementary, Secondary and Undergraduate International Studies and Global Education

Outreach, Consulting and Resource Organizations: General

See Chapter 5 (Peace and Conflict Resolution Studies) and Chapter 9 (Foreign Language Learning) for additional sources of teaching materials

2.001
Academy of World Studies
2820 Van Ness Ave.
San Francisco, CA 94109
(415) 441-1404 or 1405

Contact(s):
Ernest-Alexei d'Anjoux, Assistant to the
  President, Director of World Studies

Educational institution promoting world education with an emphasis on global affairs, future studies and language training
  • Conducts "World Ombudsman Training Program," an internship for students preparing for world service
  • Provides resources for global (synoptic) research and maintains library on global issues, especially world government and peacekeeping
  • Offers courses in language and future studies
  • Prepares and publishes world studies curricula, newsletter and other materials
  • Sponsors seminars on world studies and the UN University

2.002
American Association of Colleges of Teacher Education
One Dupont Circle NW, Suite 610
Washington, DC 20036
(202) 293-2450

Contact(s):
Frank H. Klassen, Associate Director

  • Provides information, conducts workshops, training programs and conferences, publishes educational materials and in other ways assists its approximately 760 members (which have schools or departments of teacher education) in developing and improving international and multicultural educational programs

2.003
American Association of State Colleges and Universities (AASCU)
1 Dupont Circle, NW Suite 700
Washington, DC 20036
(202) 293-7070

Contact(s):

Frank Klassen, Vice President for
  International Programs (alternate phone
  number: [202] 293-2450)

Association of educational institutions
  • The Office of International Programs
fosters the improvement of international
studies among AASCU members and represents their international interests to national
and international agencies and organizations
  • Conducts workshops, offers consultation, administers educational exchanges,
sponsors studies and prepares reports; publications include *International and Intercultural Education in Selected State Colleges and
Universities* (see 2.103) and *Trends and Issues in Globalizing Higher Education* (a summary of opinions expressed at a series of
AASCU workshops held in 1977; 20 pages;
$2 per copy)

2.004
American Federation of Teachers
11 Dupont Circle
Washington, DC 20036
(202) 797-4461 or 4449

Contact(s):

Carolyn Trice, Educational Issues
  Department

Labor union for educators
  • Maintains International Education
Teacher Center Network which provides information and consultation on global education, develops in-service global education
training programs and prepares model resource library lists; publications include *International Awareness Brochure* (free), *International Education Packet* (free), *World
Study and Travel for Teachers* ($4) and *Inter-
national Education: Values and Perspectives*
(free)

2.005
American Friends Service Committee
1501 Cherry St.
Philadelphia, PA 19102
(215) 241-7100
REGIONAL OFFICES: Atlanta, Baltimore,
Cambridge, Chicago, Dayton, Des Moines,
New York, Pasadena, San Francisco, Seattle,
Washington, DC

Contact(s):

Asia Bennett, Executive Secretary

International relief, service, peace, education and community relations organization of
the Religious Society of Friends (a Quaker
organization, interdenominationally staffed);
concerned with issues of peace, human rights,
international development and nonviolent social change
  • Sponsors programs and conducts seminars for students, teachers, parents and the
general public in support of international re-
construction and development, human rights,
disarmament and other peace and international relations activities
  • Publishes extensive list of inexpensive
educational materials suitable for classroom
use in the following major categories: disarmament, U.S. military support in the Third
World, human rights and global justice,
Southern Africa, the Middle East, Indochina, Latin America, the Caribbean and the
UN; also makes available several cassette/slide
shows, such as *Sharing Global Resources* and
other audiovisual materials
  • Makes AFSC staff with overseas experience available for speaking engagements

2.006
Anthropology Resource Center
37 Temple Place, Room 521
Boston, MA 02111
(617) 426-9286

Contact(s):
Shelton H. Davis, Director

Nonprofit membership organization designed to develop a public interest perspective in the anthropological profession; principal current orientation is toward fostering research, educational programs and policy development helpful to indigenous Indian populations of North and South America in pursuing their own political, social and economic aims
  • Conducts studies, promotes research and publishes reports on the effect of public policy on local cultures, particularly Native American cultures in North and South America
  • Publishes *The Global Reporter* (see 1.081) and other reports and studies
  • Sponsors Citizens Information Center, which maintains resource files and provides information for social scientists, journalists, students (at all levels) and others on a variety of subjects and issues including indigenous peoples in the western hemisphere, Australia and the Pacific

2.007
Anti-Defamation League of B'nai B'rith
823 United Nations Plaza
New York, NY 10017
(212) 490-2525

Contact(s):
Frances M. Sonnenschein, National
  Education Director

  • Develops curriculum materials and consults with schools on educational programs in the fields of human relations, human rights, prejudice reduction, multicultural education, Israel and the Middle East (see 2.084), Jews and Judaism, and the problems of Jewry as minority groups; free catalogue of materials available

2.008
Art Resources for Teachers and Students, Inc.
32 Market St.
New York, NY 10002
(212) 962-8231

Educational resource organization
  • Prepares and distributes resource materials on the cultures, arts and folklore of China and the Spanish Caribbean for children, parents and educators

2.009
Association for Childhood Education International
1141 Georgia Ave., Suite 200
Wheaton, MD 20902
(301) 942-2443

Contact(s):
James S. Packer, Executive Director

Professional association with international membership concerned with maintaining and increasing the quality of childhood education worldwide
  • Publishes wide range of materials on childhood education, including several publications on international and intercultural subjects
  • Sponsors educational travel and overseas conferences oriented toward international education

2.010
Association for Supervision and Curriculum Development
225 North Washington St.
Alexandria, VA 22314
(703) 549-9110

Contact(s):
Jean Hall, Associate Director

Educational association dedicated to the improvement of elementary and secondary supervision, instruction and curriculum
• Provides information, develops innovative curriculum and publishes books and pamphlets on global, multicultural and other educational subjects; publications include *Global Studies: Problems and Promises for Elementary Teachers* (see 2.168) and *The International Dimension of Education* (Leonard Kenworthy, $7)

2.011
Association for World Education
P.O. Box 589
Huntington, NY 11743
(516) 549-4143
OFFICES IN: Ahmedebad, India, Bogota, Colombia, Thy, Denmark (headquarters) Wollongong, N.S.W., Australia

Contact(s):
Melba Reiss, Executive Officer

International, nongovernmental membership association
• Publishes *Journal of World Education*, a quarterly newsletter providing practical information about international, intercultural and global education organizations, innovative programs, books, periodicals, teaching materials, training opportunities and general developments in the field; principally oriented toward higher education
• Sponsors annual international world education conference, normally outside the U.S.

2.012
Bay Area Global Education Program
World Affairs Center
312 Sutter St., Suite 200
San Francisco, CA 94108
(415) 982-2541

Contact(s):
Joyce Buchholz, Robert Freeman, David Grossman and Ronald Herring, Directors

• Project of the Stanford Program on International and Cross-Cultural Education (SPICE, see 2.061), the School Program of the World Affairs Council of Northern California, and Global Perspectives in Education (see 2.033)—West Coast office
• Works with teams of teachers, administrators and community members to develop global education materials, further staff and curriculum development and bring community international resources to bear as educational resources
• Conducts introductory, intermediate and advanced workshops and institutes for teachers, maintains a Resource Center and Teacher Library and provides consultation and speakers on a wide range of subjects and world areas
• Publishes newsletter and a variety of materials for the classroom teacher including *An Annotated Bibliography of Contemporary Middle Eastern and North African Literature* (see 2.112) and the following comprehensive curriculum guides ($10 each): *Understanding Our Cultural Diversity, Contemporary Issues, World Literature, Language, World Cultures* and *A Global Approach to U.S. History*

2.013
Center for International Programs
New York State Education Department
Cultural Education Center
Albany, NY 12230
(518) 474-5801

Contact(s):
Henry Ferguson, Director

Center for management of international and global studies in the New York State educational system

• Administers Educational Resources Center in India and develops educational and instructional materials on world issues and area studies

• Publishes educational resource materials especially on India, including *Learning about India* (see 2.178), *Your India Trip: An Orientation Guide* (see 18.211), *A Buyer's Guide to Indian Periodicals and Books for American Schools and Colleges* (see 2.114) and *Children's Books on India: An Annotated Bibliography* (see 2.117); also publishes *Human Rights and Citizenship* and selected war/peace materials and has prepared for the U.S. Department of Education *A Study with Recommendations of Outreach Educational Activities of Title VI National Resource Centers in International Studies*

2.014
Center for Public Education in International Affairs
University of Southern California
School of International Relations
VKC 330
University Park
Los Angeles, CA 90089-0043
(743) 8624 or 4214

Contact(s):
Steven L. Lamy, Director

Local, regional and national outreach education program of the USC School of International Relations

• Conducts K–12 in-service workshops and curriculum development programs; administers Resources in Global Studies (RIGS) program which compiles and disseminates bibliographies, articles, teaching materials, syllabi and lists of consultants and educational resources; conducts seminars, conferences and other community education programs

2.015
Center for Teaching International Relations
University of Denver
Denver, CO 80208
(303) 753-3106

Contact(s):
Ronald Schukar, Director
Steven Clarke, Director of Publications

Graduate center for research and training in global awareness education; established in 1968

• Develops and offers courses in teaching cultural awareness, ethnic heritage, comparative studies, communication, and world issues at the elementary and secondary levels

• Consults with schools and school districts on the improvement of global awareness teaching; serves as a National Service Center to assist in the planning and development of global education programs

• Publishes extensive list of and constitutes major resource on global education teaching materials for elementary and secondary levels; emphasis on global awareness, perceptual differences, diversity, ethnic and comparative studies, conflict and other global issues such as food, hunger, energy and population; most publications are in series: global awareness, cultural studies, environmental education, comparative studies and ethnic studies

2.016
Citizenship Development and Global Education
The Ohio State University
The Mershon Center
199 West 10th Ave.
Columbus, OH 43201
(614) 422-1681

Contact(s):
Richard Remy, Director
Robert B. Woyach, Associate Director

Research and public education program of The Mershon Center (see 4.183)

• Conducts research, sponsors programs and publishes educational materials designed to expand public understanding of world affairs; principal foci of the program have been the use of the local community as a resource in global education (based on the Columbus in the World Project, see 2.017), the expansion of the role of global issues in precollege education and the development of alternative approaches to the high school world studies curriculum

• Conducts regular in-service workshops for teachers and educational leaders

• Publications include the "Bringing A Global Perspective Series" (five volumes of lessons designed to introduce a global perspective into traditional social studies courses. American government, American history, economics, world geography and world history, each volume $5.), other curricula and reports published by Columbus World Affairs Council and the National Council for the Social Studies (see 2.047); has also edited special "Global Education" issue of the journal *Theory into Practice* (149 Arps Hall, 1945 North High St., Columbus, OH 43210-1120) and *Citizenship Education Software: A Selective Annotated Bibliography of Microcomputer Programs for the Social Studies* (a special issue of *Social Education* distributed free in single copies by the Center)

2.017
Columbus in the World Program
The Mershon Center
199 West 10th Ave.
Columbus, OH 43201
(614) 422-1681

Contact(s):
Chadwick Alger, Director

Outgrowth of a research project designed to examine the entire range of connections between an American city and the rest of the world and to explore ways in which these connections constitute resources for learning about international issues; part of the Mershon Center (see 4.183).

• Publishes a variety of materials designed (1) to assist other communities in studying their international relations and (2) to aid teachers in using community international relations as a resource for international education activities; includes *Foreign Policy in Local Communities* (a filmstrip); *You and Your Community in the World* (a series of college-level classroom exercises), *Your Community in the World/The World in Your Community* (a research guide), *Summaries* (a packet of 20 pamphlets summarizing the international contacts of the Columbus metropolitan community across all sectors of life) and *The City in International Systems: An Annotated Bibliography* ($1)

2.018
Consortium for International Studies Education
The Ohio State University
The Mershon Center
199 West 10th Ave.
Columbus, OH 43201
(614) 422-1681

Contact(s):
James E. Harf, Director

Program of the International Studies Association (see 4.257) headquartered at The Mershon Center (see 4.183)

• Generates instructional materials and course designs for college and high school international and global studies and sponsors workshops to train faculty in their use

2.019
Council for the Advancement of Experiential Learning (CAEL)
10598 Marble Faun Court
Columbia, MD 21044
(301) 997-3535

Contact(s):
Morris T. Keeton, President

Educational organization promoting the improvement and expanded use of experiential learning methods
  • Provides information and assistance to institutions in developing experiential educational programs and to individuals in locating suitable programs, including those which are international and/or cross-cultural
  • Sponsors research and publishes extensive list of books and materials, including *Cross-Cultural Learning* (see 2.095)

2.020
Council of Chief State School Officers
379 Hall of the States
400 North Capitol St. NW
Washington, DC 20001
(202) 624-7702

Contact(s):
Jerome N. Bluestein, Director, International
  Education

Association of school administrators
  • Sponsors projects designed to aid school officers in expanding international and global education in their school systems; publishes *Civic Literacy for Global Interdependence* (outlines rationale for improved international education)

2.021
Council for Intercultural Studies and Programs
777 UN Plaza
New York, NY 10017
(212) 972-9877

Contact(s):
Allen Yates, Executive Secretary

Nonprofit association of educational institutions designed to assist members in promoting international intercultural studies; membership consists of educational consortia, educational associations and individual colleges and universities
  • Consults with members on finding financial support for intercultural studies, sponsors conferences and workshops on intercultural studies in undergraduate education and conducts studies of and develops curriculum in intercultural education
  • Publishes the *Intercultural Studies Information Service* (see 2.205), *The CISP International Studies Funding Book* (see 7.037), and various reports, bibliographies, course syllabi and other educational materials (distributed through Learning Resources in International Studies, see 2.227)

2.022
Council on International and Public Affairs, Inc.
777 UN Plaza
New York, NY 10017
(212) 972-9877

Contact(s):
Ward Morehouse, President

Nonprofit research and educational organization of loosely associated programs aimed at expanded public awareness and comprehension of international issues
  • Sponsors activities and offers resources through four programs:
  • Policy Studies Associates (Box 337, Croton-on-Hudson, NY 10520), which conducts workshops and develops learning resources designed to help students to strengthen policy analysis skills and apply them to public issues
  • Citizens Participation in World Affairs

(Box 337, Croton-on-Hudson, NY 10520), which is engaged in the study of the citizen role in international affairs
  • Program in International Science and Technology Affairs (777 UN Plaza, New York, NY 10017), which fosters study and analysis of international flows of science and technology
  • International Literature and Arts Program (see 2.040)
  • Publishes materials resulting from or related to these programs which are distributed through Learning Resources in International Studies (see 2.227)

2.023
Curriculum Design for Tomorrow's World, Inc.
P.O. Box 326
Hillsdale, NY 12529
(518) 325-3046

Contact(s):
David C. King, Director

Association of professional writers and educators concerned with the quality of education in the U.S.
  • Develops curricula in the social studies, social sciences, history and language arts at elementary, middle and high school levels; produces supplementary materials that update text-based courses; conducts workshops, consults with schools and compiles special training packages to prepare students, teachers and business executives for cross-cultural contact

2.024
Curriculum Inquiry Center
University of California
405 Hilgard Ave.
Los Angeles, CA 90024
(213) 825-8311

Contact(s):
Jonathan Friedlander, Director of Outreach Programs

Local and national resource center and curriculum clearinghouse for international and multicultural education
  • Develops and disseminates resource guides and teaching materials for international and multicultural education; includes the film *Arabs in America*, the *Middle East Curriculum and Resource Unit* (five components; free; consult with the Center before ordering), *Teacher's Resource Handbook for Area Studies* (five volumes: Asia, Eastern Europe, Middle East, Latin America and the Soviet Union; see 2.151), *Film Strips for Area Studies* (see 2.128), *Teacher's Resource Manual on Worldmindedness* (see 2.155) and *The Middle East: Image and Reality* (see 2.181)

2.025
Educational Film Library Association
43 West 61st St.
New York, NY 10023
(212) 246-4533

Contact(s):
Nadine Covert, Executive Director
Lisa Flanzraich, Information Specialist
Judith Trojan, Editorial Coordinator

Nonprofit association designed to promote the use of films and other audiovisual materials in education and community programs; serves as a national clearinghouse on 16mm nontheatrical film and video
  • Answers inquiries concerning (1) independent filmmakers, (2) 16mm nontheatrical films and video (contents, distribution sources), (3) films and tapes on specific subjects, (4) distribution sources on theatrical and foreign films, and (5) evaluations of specific films
  • Publishes *Sightlines* (quarterly magazine), *EFLA Bulletin* (quarterly newsletter) and *EFLA Evaluations* (five times per year)

• Sponsors the annual American Film Festival and publishes Festival catalog

2.026
Educational Resources Information Center (ERIC)
ERIC Document Reproduction Service
　　(EDRS)
P.O. Box 190
Arlington, VA 22210
(703) 841-1212
and
ERIC Processing and Reference Facility
4833 Rugby Ave., Suite 301
Bethesda, MD 20814

Major U.S. government information resource on all aspects of education managed by the National Institute of Education, Washington, DC 20208

• Provides documents, articles, monographs, books and other materials on education collected and distributed through 16 ERIC clearinghouses (adult, career and vocational; counseling and personal; elementary and early childhood; etc.); extensive collections of international materials included in the Social Studies/Social Science Clearinghouse (see 2.058), the Languages and Linguistics Clearinghouse and the Teacher Education Clearinghouse

• May be ordered through ERIC Document Reproduction Service (EDRS) and through the individual clearinghouses; all documents abstracted in the journal *Resources in Education* and subject to computer searches; also retrievable online via the following vendors: Bibliographical Retrieval Service, Dialog Information Services and System Development Corporation

• Documents available in print and/or in microfiche form, except where restricted by publisher (order information provided)

• ERIC microfiche collections and search services are widely available in the U.S. and are identified in *Directory of ERIC Micro-*

fiche Collections and *Directory of ERIC Search Services*, both available from the ERIC Processing and Reference Facility

• Answers written and telephone inquiries regarding ERIC documents and services; inquiries should be directed as follows:
　　Specific identified documents—ERIC Processing and Reference Facility
　　Subject-oriented　　questions—ERIC Clearinghouse responsible for the subject area into which the question falls
　　Computer searches—nearest service point identified in *Directory of ERIC Search Services*
　　Publications of the clearinghouses—the appropriate clearinghouse

• Also makes available Information Analysis Products which are syntheses or interpretive studies of topics in education of high current interest; prepares periodic bibliographies of information analyses products and other major publications

• Those wishing to contribute documents should send them to the appropriate clearinghouse or the ERIC Processing and Reference Facility

• Publishes *All about ERIC*, a complete guide for using ERIC sources (available from the ERIC Processing and Reference Facility)

2.027
Foreign Policy Association
205 Lexington Ave.
New York, NY 10016
(212) 481-8450
BRANCH: 1800 K St. NW
Washington, DC 20006
(202) 833-2030

Contact(s):
Thetis Reavis, Vice President for Public
　　Affairs
Mary Soley, Social Studies Education
　　Specialist, Social Studies School Services

Large national, non-partisan, nonprofit organization designed to increase public understanding of and involvement in U.S. foreign policy concerns

• Conducts extensive program for the study and discussion of current foreign policy issues, including radio and television broadcasts, lectures, speeches, panels and roundtables, a young professionals group, off-the-record luncheons and a series of Washington meetings; includes Social Studies School Services which works with educators to develop programs and curriculum materials to improve the teaching of U.S. foreign policy issues

• Centers much activity around the annual Great Decisions program through network of community groups and educational organizations and institutes focusing on active discussion and debate of eight of the most pressing international issues of the year

• Publishes *Great Decisions* (see 2.202), a *Headline Series* of five booklets a year on major issues in world affairs written by well-known authors and a Special Reports Series on critical areas and aspects of current U.S. foreign policy; also publishes *Guide to Careers in World Affairs,* a practical handbook that lists organizations and companies and their requirements for recruits in international operations

2.028
Foundation for Ethnic Dance, Inc.
17 West 71st St.
New York, NY 10023
(212) 877-9565

Contact(s):
Matteo, Artistic Director

Educational organization promoting wider understanding of worldwide ethnic dance via the Matteo EthnoAmerican Dance Theatre

• Provides information, answers questions, makes referrals to other ethnic dance sources, helps develop curricula, offers training, presents concerts of various ethnic (multiracial) dances and conducts residencies

2.029
Global Development Studies Institute
Millbrook School
Millbrook, NY 12545
(914) 677-5606

Contact(s):
John P. Rorke, Advisory Committee

Educational resource organization

• Provides consultation and conducts pre- and in-service workshops for training teachers in secondary and undergraduate schools and colleges on global development education; maintains resource center and will provide assistance to students working on development studies projects; particular interest in world food and energy supplies

• Publishes books, pamphlets and teaching materials including model curricula, case studies and *Does It Work? Evaluation Guidelines for Global Studies Teachers*

2.030
Global Education Associates
552 Park Ave.
East Orange, NJ 07017
(201) 675-1409

Contact(s):
Jerry Mische, President

Nonprofit educational organization designed to promote the tenets of a new "human world order" through educational activity and the development of a network of active associates

• Conducts institutes, workshops and conferences on global interdependence and world order in the U.S. and other countries

• Consults with educational, community and religious organizations on furthering their work relative to global interdependence and world order

• Publishes basic statement *Toward a Human World Order* and short, inexpensive papers suitable for classroom use on various issues involved in pursuing a "human world order"; also makes available on loan a film-strip on the subject ($10 mailing and maintenance charges)

2.031
Global Learning, Inc.
40 South Fullerton Ave.
Montclair, NJ 07042
(201) 783-7616

Contact(s):
Jeffrey L. Brown, Executive Director

Educational organization which promotes global education at elementary and secondary levels
• Conducts workshops and graduate level institutes in global education subjects and teaching approaches (including conflict resolution, world hunger, cross-cultural awareness, human rights, alternative futures, etc.) for school teachers and for church and community groups, particularly in New Jersey
• Evaluates and consults on global education programs in the schools and develops curriculum
• Distributes computer games for school and home use (Global Learning Software; $19.95 each)

2.032
Global Learning Opportunities in Basic Education
P.O. Box 7421
Madison, WI 53707
(608) 839-4267

Contact(s):
Henry Bucher, President

Small private consulting firm
• Provides consulting and educational services to government and private agencies and institutions on global education, including curriculum development, teacher workshops, orientation for working abroad, intercultural education methodologies and grant proposal writing

2.033
Global Perspectives in Education, Inc.
218 East 18th St.
New York, NY 10003
(212) 475-0850

Contact(s):
Andrew F. Smith, President
Charles Roebuck, Publications Director
Patricia Margolf, Editor, *Access*

Nonprofit educational organization concerned with global perspectives education at all levels, but especially oriented toward pre-college
• Provides information and advice on global and international education programs and curriculum and maintains resource center
• Administers Global Perspectives Information Exchange Network designed to facilitate the exchange of ideas and information among educators, schools and organizations concerned with global, international and foreign language education; publishes newsletter *Access* (see 2.199) and develops and distributes resource lists and bibliographies
• Sponsors and administers local and national meetings and conferences
• Publishes the periodical *Intercom* (see 2.204) and a wide variety of curriculum and source materials in global education; curriculum materials (many of which are contained in back issues of *Intercom*) are grouped in the following categories: culture and area studies, humanities and language arts, U.S. history, environmental studies, legal studies, global issues and trends, and a group of materials designed specifically for elementary and middle grades; also publishes occasional papers which examine some of the broader

issues of global education, including *An Attainable Global Perspective* (see 2.091), the resource directory *The Global Yellow Pages* (see 2.132), *Moving Toward a Global Perspective: Social Studies and Second Languages* and *Education for a World of Change: A Report* (see 2.098)

2.034
IEP Clearinghouse
Office of the Director
International Education Programs
U.S. Department of Education
Washington, DC 20202
(202) 245-7804

Contact(s):
Marguerite Follette, Acting Director

• Provides or assists inquirers in locating sources of information about international education in general and prepares and distributes informational material about Department of Education and other international education programs

2.035
The Information Center on Children's Cultures
United States Committee for UNICEF
331 East 38th St.
New York, NY 10016
(212) 686-5522

Contact(s):
Melinda Greenblatt, Chief Librarian

Affiliated agency of the UN which gathers educational and cultural materials in English on children of the world
• Answers questions, provides information or directs inquirers to other sources of information relative to children in any country in the world regarding aspects of their culture, how to contact them, pictures and

photos of them, games they play, ways to teach about them, etc.; mail requests should be accompanied by a stamped self-addressed envelope; provides a variety of lists of books and teaching materials available, including a bibliography *Sources of Children's Books from Other Countries*
• Also conducts research on most effective materials for cross-cultural learning about children and prepares and circulates exhibits in the U.S.

2.036
Information Consulting Associates
303 West Pleasantview Ave.
Hackensack, NJ 07601
(201) 343-8833

Contact(s):
Muriel Wall, Director

Small research and consulting firm
• Offers workshops in language and cross-cultural adaptation for persons going abroad to work; conducts "Training Travel Tours" for teachers and others to expand cross-cultural awareness
• Publishes books on intercultural subjects including *Directory of Intercultural Newsletters* (see 2.123)

2.037
International Classroom
University of Pennsylvania
The University Museum
33d and Spruce Sts.
Philadelphia, PA 19104
(215) 898-4065

Contact(s):
Charlotte Conroy and Karen Cadbury, Co-Directors

Educational resource organization
• Coordinates international educational

program in which foreign graduate students visit schools, colleges and community groups; publishes books and audiovisuals describing the program and demonstrating how it can be initiated in any community with a foreign student population

2.038
International Council for Educational Development
680 Fifth Ave.
New York, NY 10019
(212) 582-3970

Contact(s):
James A. Perkins, Chairman

Nonprofit educational organization concerned with educational and public policy relative to higher education and the advancement of education for economic and social development worldwide
• Conducts studies and prepares publications on systems of higher education, access to higher education, higher education for development and foreign languages and international studies
• Publishes a newsletter, a monograph series *Systems of Higher Education* (currently available on Australia, France, West Germany, Iran, Japan, Mexico, the United Kingdom and the U.S.; monographs on Canada, Poland, Sweden and Thailand are out of print, but those countries are treated in *Twelve Systems of Higher Education*, 1978, $8); also publishes *International Dimensions of Private Domestic Institutions* (examines international connections of five New York cultural and educational institutions; $3.50); books should be ordered from Interbook, Inc., 611 Broadway, Room 227, New York, NY 10012

2.039
International Education Assessment Project
777 UN Plaza, Suite 911
New York, NY 10017
(212) 972-9877

Contact(s):
H. Thomas Collins, Ward Morehouse and Judith Torney-Purta, Coordinators

• Studies the impact of elementary and secondary school programs in global and international education; report available

2.040
International Literature and Arts Program
50 East 10th St.
New York, NY 10003
(212) 475-1999

Contact(s):
Bonnie R. Crown, Director

• Conducts workshops and in-service training for teachers designed to expand their ability to introduce students to a broader range of national and cultural arts and literature

2.041
International Theatre Institute of the United States, Inc. (ITI/US)
1860 Broadway, Suite 1510
New York, NY 10023
(212) 245-3950

Contact(s):
Martha W. Coigney, Director

Professional organization affiliated with the UNESCO-sponsored International Theatre Institute, a worldwide organization designed to facilitate the exchange of knowledge and practice in the theater arts
• Maintains library and reference, facilitates research, provides information and answers written and phone inquiries on matters pertaining to the theater around the world (library contains 4,500 volumes, 8,500 plays, a large collection of programs, schedules, newsletters and periodicals on the performing arts in 140 countries); provides consulting

services to American theater professionals on matters pertaining to international theater

• Assists U.S. theater professionals plan trips abroad and offers services and information to foreign theater visitors in the U.S.

• Represents the U.S. at conferences abroad and organizes visits of theater professionals in the U.S. and abroad

• Publishes a newsletter, *Theatre Notes* and *International Directory of Theatre, Dance and Folklore Festivals* (see page 2.137)

2.042
International Women's Tribune Centre
777 United Nations Plaza
New York, NY 10017
(212) 687-8633

Contact(s):
Anne S. Walker, Director
Patricia McLaughlin, Administrative Officer

Educational and international development organization

• Serves as clearinghouse of information on women in development in Third World countries; publishes newsletter *The Tribune* (in English, Spanish and French focusing on projects, resources and international news), a number of resource books on women and development, and other books, manuals and slide tape sets for women

2.043
Las Palomas De Taos
P.O. Box 3400
Taos, NM 87571
(505) 758-9456

Contact(s):
George G. Otero, Director/Founder

Multicultural and global educational training and consulting organization

• Consults with schools and school systems, conducts teacher training and staff development workshops and develops and demonstrates curriculum and training materials aimed at improving knowledge of and skills in dealing with a multicultural, interdependent world; concerned with, among other things, global and multicultural education, ethnic studies, development education and conflict resolution

• Works with general public in weeklong programs on the art and culture of the Southwest emphasizing responsible citizenship in a diverse and changing global environment

2.044
Maryknoll Center for Justice Concerns
50 Dunster Rd.
Chestnut Hill, MA 02167
(617) 232-8050

Contact(s):
Philip E. Pulaski, Co-Director

• Designs college curricula and conducts workshops for adults on Third World development and other current international issues

2.045
National Catholic Educational Association
1077 30th St., NW, Suite 100
Washington, DC 20007
(202) 293-5954

Contact(s):
Sister Loretta Carey, RDC

Resource center for Catholic educators

• Offers consulting, in-service workshops, teaching materials, and assistance in curriculum development for the implementation of school and parish programs in peace and social justice based on the teachings of the Catholic church

2.046
National Council for Geographic Education
Western Illinois University
Macomb, IL 61455
(309) 298-2470

Contact(s):
James W. Vining, Executive Director

Professional educators' association promoting improved teaching of geography
• Provides leadership and assistance in the development of curricula, the training of teachers and the implementation and evaluation of geography instruction, especially at the elementary and secondary levels
• Offers annual scholarship awards to outstanding undergraduate geography students
• Sponsors meetings, conferences and workshops
• Publishes *Journal of Geography*, a newsletter, and a variety of instructional materials

2.047
National Council for the Social Studies
3501 Newark St. NW
Washington, DC 20016
(202) 966-7840

Contact(s):
Deborah J. Drucker, Association Liaison

Professional association of social studies teachers
• Provides advice and assistance to individuals and local councils on matters related to social studies teaching, including world history, global perspectives, and other international subjects
• Publishes social studies teaching handbooks and guides and selected articles from the Council's periodical, *Social Education*, many on international subjects; includes *International Learning and International Education in a Global Age* (see 2.104) and *International Social Studies Directory* (of social studies agencies and organizations in other countries)

2.048
National Council on Foreign Language and International Studies
605 Third Ave., 17th Floor
New York, NY 10158
(212) 490-3520

Contact(s):
Rose Lee Hayden, Executive Director

Nonprofit educational organization established in 1980 to carry on the work of the President's Commission on Foreign Language and International Studies
• Provides information about and assists other national, state and local organizations in promoting language and international studies at all educational levels, in expanding public awareness of international affairs and in developing international studies programs for business and other professionals
• Promotes the study of international education issues and publishes reports on them; prepares directories of language and international studies programs including *Internationalizing Your School: A Handbook and Resource Guide* (see 2.173)

2.049
National Geographic Society Educational Services
Department 84
Washington, DC 20036
(301) 948-5926

• Publishes free annual catalogues of educational materials available to educators which include extensive listings of materials on other countries and cultures, films, videocassettes, books, sound filmstrips, multimedia kits, maps, atlases and globes

2.050
National Information Center for Educational Media
University of Southern California
Research Annex, Suite 301
3716 South Hope St.
Los Angeles, CA 90007
(213) 743-6681

Contact(s):
M. Thomas Risner, Director

Educational resource center
• Compiles information on films, film-strips, videotapes, transparencies and slide sets suitable for educational use; publishes 15 indexes to the various media along with a directory to category and subject matter headings; covers a wide range of international subjects under the following headings: history, foreign cultures, international relations, foreign languages and English as a second language

2.051
National School Boards Association
1055 Thomas Jefferson St. NW, Suite 600
Washington, DC 20007
(202) 337-7666

Contact(s):
H. Barbara Ford, Research and Information
    Services Department

Educational association concerned with improving the effectiveness of school leadership
• Offers a variety of advisory, consulting, training services and publications for school board members and other educational leaders in all areas of educational concern, including global perspectives education
• Publishes *Global Education: Major Reform* (calling on school board members to support global education programs) and *Energy Education: Towards a Global Perspective*, along with the motion picture *Global Connection* which dramatizes world interde-

pendence and demonstrates how to prepare children for the coming "Global Age" (comes with a "Leader Guide")

2.052
Oxfam-America
Community Education and Outreach
115 Broadway
Boston, MA 02116
(617) 247-3304

Contact(s):
Haleh P. Wunder, Director

Development assistance organization
• Produces curriculum and disseminates a wide variety of educational materials on development issues with particular emphasis on development education, food and hunger and human rights; organizes study tours to developing countries and seminars for community organizers; publishes *Facts for Action*, a six-issue per year periodical available by subscription

2.053
Planetary Citizens
Box 1715
New Rochelle, NY 10802
(914) 636-0040

Contact(s):
Donald Keys, President

Nonprofit international educational organization promoting educational and other activities aimed at expanding the global perspective of contemporary society
• Administers worldwide program that registers people as "Planetary Citizens" and serves as secretariat for "Planetary Initiative for the World"
• Sponsors workshops and educational programs for adults and young people, arranges internships for youth in its own global

and educational programs, develops curriculum, and produces audiovisual programs including *Earth, Space and Our Place* (an audiovisual presentation) and the feature film *Earth at Omega*

• Maintains Profile Resource Bank of groups, publications and persons prominently concerned with global problems and/or involved with "Planetary Initiative," disseminates selected materials on globalism and publishes the journal *Planet Earth* (see 2.188), *The Person and the Planet* (a curriculum guide) and several other books

2.054
Population Reference Bureau, Inc.
1337 Connecticut Ave. NW
Washington, DC 20036
(202) 785-4664

Contact(s):
Elaine M. Murphy, Director of Population Education

International agency for the compilation of data on national and world population trends

• Provides information, answers phone inquiries, develops curriculum materials, maintains population film library (rental fee $5 for all films), and conducts pre- and in-service teacher training workshops on population topics; publications include *Population Education: Sources and Resources* (see 2.144), *Food for Thought: A Population Simulation Kit* ($3), *Interchange* (see 2.203) and *Population Bulletin* (discusses major world and national demographic trends; periodic, $3)

2.055
Resource Information Referral Program
Massachusetts Department of Education
Educational Resources and Television
27 Cedar St.
Wellesley, MA 02181
(617) 431-7013 or 727-6395

Contact(s):
Maxine Minkoff, Program Director

• Maintains International Studies/Foreign Language Resource Bank on consultants, materials, programs and resource centers

2.056
Resource Services/Publications Services
Brigham Young University
David M. Kennedy Center for International Studies
130 FOB
Provo, UT 84602
(801) 378-3377

Contact(s):
Stan Taylor, Director, Kennedy Center
V. Lynn Tyler, Resource Services Administrator
Deborah Coon, Manager, Publications Services

• Conducts research, organizes conferences, maintains a materials resource center and otherwise furthers the study of language learning, intercultural communication and international studies

• Provides advice and information to students, practitioners and the scholarly communities on these subjects

• Publishes books and pamphlets on intercultural subjects including the Culturegram Series available for over 80 countries (see 2.191 and individual countries), *Managing Travel Stress, The International Family: Successfully Meeting the Challenge,* and *Coming Home Again: Absorbing Return Shock,* and the Communication Learning Aid Series (see 2.190); also publishes *Intercultural Ready Reference* (a categorization and exemplification of cross-cultural interactions) and *Interaction: An International and Intercultural Synergic Directory* (a very extensive listing of organizations with international or intercultural orientations), two books on IndoChinese refugees, and a series on teaching about Asia, including *Teacher Guide to Resources on Asia* (see 2.149)

2.057
School of Global Education
Livonia Public Schools
33500 West Six Mile Road
Livonia, MI 48152
(313) 261-1250, Ext. 283

Contact(s):
Jonathan Swift, Director

Demonstration alternative public high school-within-a-school which integrates global perspectives and cultural studies with regular high school curriculum
 • Offers information, publishes curriculum materials and can provide training for school personnel (from anywhere in the country) in global education curriculum-building

2.058
Social Science Education Consortium, Inc.
855 Broadway
Boulder, CO 80302
(303) 492-8154

Contact(s):
Kay Kaiser-Cook, Senior Editor

Information resource and service center for social science education
 • Provides consultation and organizes workshops, conferences and training programs for social studies teachers and supervisors in all areas of social studies teaching including global education
 • Maintains resource and demonstration center containing more than 18,000 prints, audiovisuals, games and other teaching materials and publishes an extensive list of books and teaching aids, including a number on global studies; answers questions about resources for any aspect of social studies education
 • Administers the ERIC Clearinghouse for Social Studies/Social Science Education with an extensive collection of materials on global and international education, including the documents on microfiche listed in the ERIC master list *Resources in Education;* develops free reference sheets on specific topics (including the Middle East, Africa, future studies, global problems/international education, cross-cultural and ethnic studies, and world history/world cultures); conducts customized computer searches and sells previously conducted searches (available on global education and world history) at reduced cost; publishes free newsletter

2.059
Social Studies Development Center
513 North Park Ave.
Bloomington, IN 47405
(812) 335-3838

Contact(s):
James M. Becker, Director

Center for the promotion of research, programs and materials development in social studies education, especially oriented toward global studies
 • Develops global education materials (within such projects as the Mid-America Program for Global Perspectives in Education and the Global Studies in Geography Project), analyzes textbooks for the accuracy of their treatment of nations and cultures (Soviet Union and Japan projects), prepares textbooks (*UNESCO Handbook for Teaching Social Studies*), and serves as a resource for Indiana and midwest educators (houses Curriculum Resource Center and serves as headquarters for the Indiana Council for the So-

cial Studies, the Indiana University Coordinator for School Social Studies, the Teacher Associates Program, the Indiana Global Studies Project and the University's African (see 12.019) and East Asian (see 13.045) Outreach Services; publications include A *Global Perspectives Bibliography* ($2)

2.060
Stanford Institute for Intercultural Communication
Box A-D
Stanford, CA 94305
(415) 497-1897

Contact(s):
Clifford Clarke, Director

Summer training center for professionals in education, training, business and other fields
• Provides intensive week-long training workshops during July and August in such subjects as teaching intercultural communication, bilingual education, counseling across cultures, cross-cultural aspects of social work and nursing and developing global perspectives in elementary and secondary education

2.061
Stanford Program on International and Cross-Cultural Studies (SPICE)
Stanford University
Center for Research in International Studies
Room 200, Lou Henry Hoover Bldg.
Stanford, CA 94305
(415) 497-1114

Contact(s):
David L. Grossman, Director

Program of Stanford University designed to facilitate the use of scholarly resources in international studies and education in cooperative endeavors with pre-collegiate educators to improve the international and cross-cul-

tural dimensions of elementary and secondary schools
• Sponsors staff development and in-service training workshops, provides consulting assistance to Northern California educators under five project headings: Africa, China, Japan, Latin America and International Security and Arms Control; program draws on resources of area studies centers at Stanford and the University of California at Berkeley.
• Evaluates existing curriculum materials and advises on the development of new units and programs and provides films, filmstrips and other teaching materials to Bay Area teachers on loan
• Member organization of Bay Area Global Education Program (BAGEP, see 2.012)
• Publishes and disseminates an extensive list of teaching materials consisting of elementary and secondary curriculum units (on social and cultural subjects), simulations and games, slides and other audiovisuals, bibliographies, catalogues of books, periodicals and recommended curriculum materials; approximately 30 units available for sale (catalogue provided upon request)
• Assists in the development of international and cross-cultural projects similar to SPICE at other institutions and conducts in-service programs in other Western states through its Western Regional Program on Japan

2.062
UNESCO Association of the United States of America, Inc.
1418 Lakeside Drive
Oakland, CA 94612
(415) 835-2811

Contact(s):
Dorothy Hackbarth, President

Non-governmental educational organization supporting expanded knowledge of and participation in UNESCO activities

• Provides information about UNESCO, arranges lectures, organizes community, school and college workshops and seminars on UNESCO and helps establish UNESCO clubs

• Publishes newsletter and distributes UNESCO and other UN publications in the U.S.

2.063
United Nations Association of the United States of America
300 East 42d St.
New York, NY 10017
(212) 697-3232

Contact(s):
Peggy Sanford Carlin, Vice President

Association of approximately 200 organizations in the U.S. which seeks to strengthen U.S. capacity to advance the work of the UN and to participate effectively in it

• Sponsors conferences, meetings and model UN educational programs

• Publishes *The Inter Dependent* (see 1.083), an annual Model UN Kit which includes a book providing a substantive review of issues before the current session of the UN General Assembly, a *Guide to Delegate Preparation*, a copy of the UN charter and *Basic Facts About the UN*

• Maintains School Service Program which prepares bibliographies, conducts workshops and distributes materials to teachers covering the UN and world issues addressed by the UN; publications include *Select Bibliography on World Hunger and Development* (see 2.148), *Teaching about the United Nations* ($5), *Films of the United Nations Family* (a catalogue of 16mm films describing over 600 films produced and distributed by the UN system of organizations; $5), *List of Recommended Films* (on UN issues; $1), and *Learning about Global Cooperation and the United Nations System: An Annotated Curriculum Resource Guide* ($1)

2.064
U.S. Committee for *UNICEF*
331 East 38th St.
New York, NY 10016
(212) 686-5522

Contact(s):
Melinda Greenblatt, Chief Librarian

Nonprofit support organization for the United Nations Children's Fund (UNICEF)

• Maintains Information Center on Children's Cultures (see 2.035) which serves as principal contact for educators

• Prepares and distributes instructional materials including books, lesson plans, slide sets, kits, posters, games and puzzles, toys, photosets, records, cassettes, etc. for elementary and secondary schools on UNICEF, the UN, children in other countries, and a variety of world issues (development, peace, education, hunger, the environment, etc.)

2.065
Universities Field Staff International
P.O. Box 150
Hanover, NH 03755
(603) 643-2110

Contact(s):
Manon Spitzer, Associate Director

Nonprofit membership organization which, through researchers resident abroad, collects, analyzes and disseminates current information on world areas and comparative transnational issues to member educational institutions; formerly American Universities Field Staff, Inc.

• Prepares and publishes 40 UFSI Reports annually analyzing political, cultural, economic, technological and social developments in Asia, Africa, Europe and North and South America; designed for use by students, faculty, researchers, business executives, journalists and government officials ($3 per report; full subscription $100 for institutions, $75 for individuals; also available on microfiche at $15 per set and in bound library volumes: 1951 to 1970 only)

• UFSI personnel visit campuses for consultations and teaching assignments, join in obtaining grants and contracts for conferences and collaborative study projects, assist faculty and students studying or doing research abroad, and distribute reports (see below) in multiple copies to libraries and individuals

• Arranges and supervises internships for member institution undergraduates abroad

• Develops documentary films including *Faces of Change* (25 films on current conditions and the effects of modernization in rural communities in five countries: Bolivia, Kenya, Afghanistan, Taiwan and the Soko Islands off the China coast); these films provide the base for *Faces of Culture*, (a national telecourse for collegiate and precollegiate social studies developed by KOCE, Huntington Beach, Calif.

• Conducts faculty and curriculum development seminars for community colleges

• Sponsors Institute of World Affairs, a research and conference center in Salisbury, Connecticut, which conducts a summer program on international issues for advanced students along with seminars and conferences on transnational themes year-round; and the Center for Mediterranean Studies in Rome, Italy, which holds seminars and conferences and provides facilities for cross-disciplinary study of the Mediterranean region

• Publishes books on major political, economic and social issues both within individual countries and transnationally; also publishes books in cooperation with the Indiana University Press (see 11.016)

2.066
World Religions Curriculum Development Center
6425 West 33d St.
St. Louis Park, MN 55426
(612) 925-4300, Ext. 278

Contact(s):
Lee Smith and Wes Bodin, Project Co-Directors

School curriculum development organization

• Develops high school social studies programs about the religious traditions of the U.S. and the world, in particular *Religion in Human Culture* (a six-unit series of printed and audiovisual materials on the Buddhist, Hindu, Islamic, Jewish and Christian traditions along with a component on religious expression; each component consists of a reader, teacher's guide, filmstrip and blackline masters, with supporting information and activities plus other materials)

• Assists schools in adopting and implementing the program through the National Diffusion Network (for which each state has a "State Facilitator") which provides for teacher training and shares costs

2.067
YMCA International Programs
101 North Wacker Drive
Chicago, IL 60606
(312) 977-0031

Contact(s):
Solon B. Cousins, Executive Director

• Conducts student exchange programs (see 3.046), provides International Student Services (see 10.025), and sponsors overseas programs (see 8.026); also offers internships in international program management (see 3.046) and conducts refugee programs

2.068
Zero Population Growth, Inc.
1346 Connecticut Ave. NW
Washington, DC 20036
(202) 785-0100

Contact(s):
Ross Pumfrey, Executive Director

Nonprofit public education organization

• Provides information on population trends and produces and distributes a variety of educational materials including *Global 2000 Countdown Kit* and *Elementary Population*

Activities Kit (each $15; for use in secondary classrooms); catalogue available

• Conducts training workshops in the theory of population dynamics for elementary and secondary school teachers

Outreach, Consulting and Resource Organizations: World Area and Country

2.069
The Africa Fund
198 Broadway
New York, NY 10038
(212) 962-1210

Contact(s):
Jennifer Davis, Executive Secretary

Nonprofit relief and educational organization supporting majority rule in southern African countries; established in 1966

• Conducts research and publishes materials on political and social issues in southern Africa covering South Africa, Namibia, Zimbabwe, Mozambique, Guinea-Bissau and Angola; includes books, posters, pamphlets, information packets and portable photo exhibits

2.070
Africa in the School and Community
Boston University
African Studies Center
270 Bay State Road
Boston, MA 02215
(617) 353-7303 or 3673

Contact(s):
Jo Sullivan, Outreach Coordinator

• Provides advice and materials to pre-college and college teachers; includes slides, books, maps, filmstrips and records on loan; curriculum guides and bibliographies distributed to teachers and librarians; speakers, in-

service workshops and displays also available; publishes newsletter

2.071
African Studies Outreach Services
University of Illinois
African Studies Program
1208 W. California St., #101
Urbana, IL 60801
(217) 333-6335

Contact(s):
Louise Crane, Outreach Coordinator

National resource center for African Studies

• Offers a variety of services to teachers in expanding their ability to teach about Africa; includes in-service workshops and other training programs in the U.S. and abroad; consults with schools on the development of resources, assistance in curriculum development and/or evaluation

• Maintains free lending library of audiovisual materials and publishes curriculum materials including *African Names: People and Places, Curriculum Materials for Teachers* (see 2.165), *African Games of Strategy, Good Tastes in Africa* (cookbook), and *Religions in Africa;* also publishes jointly the newsletter *Update* (see 2.206) with other University of Illinois area studies programs

• Cooperates with University of Illinois Film Center in maintaining an extensive collection of films on Africa; catalogues and guides to their use now in preparation

2.072
Americans for Middle East Understanding, Inc.
Room 771
475 Riverside Drive
New York, NY 10115
(212) 870-2053

Contact(s):
John F. Mahoney, Executive Director

Educational organization providing information about the Middle East and North Africa
   • Maintains information service, sells books, reprints articles, publishes a newsletter and prepares special information packets for teachers and study groups

2.073
Arab World Consultants
2137 Rose St.
Berkeley, CA 94709
(415) 845-6625

Contact(s):
Ahlam Abu-Zayyad, Consultant

   • Conducts teacher workshops, consults on curriculum development, and prepares educational materials on the Arab countries and peoples; materials include *The Arab World; Multi-Media Units for Elementary School Use*, which consists of six units on Arab life and culture composed of cassettes, games and a variety of other materials (available individually at $30–$140 per unit)

2.074
Association of Teachers of Latin American Studies
252-58 63d Ave.
Flushing, NY 11362
(212) 428-1237

Contact(s):
Daniel J. Mugan, President

Association of educators and others designed to expand the capability of American education to portray Latin American life realistically and accurately
   • Prepares instructional materials for teaching about Latin America; materials and other information published in monthly newsletter, *Perspective*
   • Sponsors summer overseas language and/or cultural travel and study programs and tours for teachers; also makes year-round group flight arrangements to and from the major cities of South America

2.075
Center for Latin American Studies Outreach Program
Tulane University
New Orleans, LA 70118
(504) 865-5165

Contact(s):
Richard Greenleaf, Director

   • Conducts workshops for teachers, organizes conferences, maintains a speakers bureau, publishes curriculum materials and helps provide access to Latin American Studies resources at Tulane and in New Orleans
   • Maintains national Latin American Curriculum Resource Center including extensive collection of books and readings, slide collections, filmstrips for classroom use, lesson plans, games and study guides; prepares and distributes free of charge *Catalogue of Lending Library Materials for Teachers* and *A Guide to Hispanic Resources in New Orleans*; publishes *Teaching Modules on Latin America for Grades K–12* (forthcoming)
   • Provides small grants (through the Gulf South Latin American Programming Association) to organizations in the Gulf area to support programs and events designed to expand public awareness of the societies and cultures of Latin America

2.076
Center for Teaching About China
U.S. China People's Friendship Association
110 Maryland Ave., NE
Washington, DC 20002
(202) 544-7010

Contact(s):
Mary Kay Hobbs, Director

Educational project of the U.S.-China Peoples Friendship Association (see 3.043)
- Develops and disseminates teaching materials for introducing China into the curriculum; serves as a consulting and information clearinghouse, conducts in-service workshops, arranges teacher tours to China and handles subscriptions to magazines from China
- Distributes *U.S.-China Review* (bimonthly magazine, $6 per year) and publishes the newsletter *Teaching about China, a Resource Guide and Catalogue of Materials on China* ($2) and approximately 80 topical handouts for students (at minimal cost in quantity)
- Maintains library of slide shows and filmstrips on China

2.077
East Asia Resource Center
University of Washington
Henry S. Jackson School of International
   Studies
DR-05
Seattle, WA 98195
(206) 543-1921

Contact(s):
Mary Hammond Bernson, Director

U.S. Office of Education-funded Outreach Center designed to provide educational materials and activities to colleges, schools and community organizations, especially in the Pacific Northwest

- Offers on free loan basis audiovisual materials, teaching units, teachers manuals, books, periodicals and bibliographies
- Sponsors speakers bureau, arranges conferences, seminars and workshops and advises on the development of East Asian teaching units

2.078
East Asian Curriculum Project
Columbia University
East Asian Institute
International Affairs Bldg.
420 West 118th St.
New York, NY 10027
(212) 280-4278

Contact(s):
Roberta Martin, Director

- Assists schools with in-service training, consults on curriculum development and resource identification and evaluation, and conducts occasional summer workshops on China and Japan
- Publishes comprehensive teaching workbooks on China and Japan (a new edition of the latter is in preparation) and maintains library of teaching materials

2.079
East Asian Outreach Program
Yale University
Council on East Asian Studies
85 Trumbull St.
Box 13A, Yale Station
New Haven, CT 06520
(203) 432-4029

Contact(s):
Constance O'Connell, Director

- Conducts workshops on teaching about China and Japan and an intensive summer seminar on East Asia and maintains a

speakers bureau and an East Asian Resource Center (catalogue, $2) with an extensive collection of audiovisual (including artifact kits) teaching materials on China and Japan available nationally
  • Publishes free newsletter

2.080
Harvard East Asian Program at the Children's Museum
Boston Children's Museum
Museum Wharf
300 Congress St.
Boston, MA 02210
(617) 426-6500

Contact(s):
Leslie Swartz, Outreach Coordinator

Co-sponsored by the Harvard Language and Area Center for East Asian Studies (see 13.054) and the Boston Children's Museum
  • Maintains resources on Japan and China for use by the schools and the general public; includes an authentic two-story Japanese weaver's house, a circulating library of print and audiovisual materials, and learning kits on the Chinese and Japanese cultures; kits, which may be rented (in New England) or purchased, include artifacts, activities, audiovisual aids and reading materials

2.081
Indochina Curriculum Group
11 Garden St.
Cambridge, MA 02138
(617) 354-6583

Contact(s):
Jane Jackson and Sharon Bauer Breakstone, Directors

Educational organization concerned with teaching materials on Indochina and the Vietnam War

  • Publishes materials on Indochina and the Vietnam War, including *The Vietnam Era: A Guide to Teaching Resources* (annotated bibliography for high school teaching, $5)
  • Maintains library; sponsors workshops on request

2.082
Middle East Outreach Council
University of California
405 Hilgard Ave.
Los Angeles, CA 90024
(213) 825-8311

Contact(s):
Jonathan Friedlander, Director

Nonprofit, non-political educational organization of individual members designed to promote the dissemination of educational information and teaching materials
  • Provides information on resource organizations and centers which produce and/or distribute educational materials on the nations of the Middle East and North Africa; publishes *A Resource Guide for Middle Eastern Studies* (see 2.145)

2.083
Middle East Resource Center
University of Washington
318 Thompson (DR-05)
Seattle, WA 98195
(206) 543-7236

Contact(s):
Charlotte F. Albright, Outreach Coordinator

U.S. Department of Education-funded Outreach Center designed to provide educational materials and activities to colleges, schools and community organizations, especially in the Pacific Northwest and nationally
  • Offers on free loan basis audiovisual

materials teaching units, teachers manuals, books, periodicals and bibliographies; publishes *Middle East Film Sampler* (descriptions and rental information on 300 films on the Middle East, 1983, $5)

• Sponsors Speakers Bureau, arranges conferences, seminars and workshops and advises on the development of Middle East teaching units

• Publishes *Middle East Newsletter*

2.084
Outreach Educational Project on South Asia
University of Chicago
South Asia Language and Area Center
Foster Hall
1130 East 59th St.
Chicago, IL 60637
(312) 962-8635

Contact(s):
Susanne Hoeber Rudolph, Director
Joan Erdman, Project Coordinator

Outreach program designed to share the expertise and resources of the University's South Asia Center with educators at all levels and with the wider local, regional and national public

• Develops classroom materials; presents workshops, seminars, film showings and other activities for schools and colleges and the public; maintains a lending library of teaching materials on South Asia, publishes a number of brief guides and commentaries and a newsletter on South Asia for teachers

2.085
School and Community Outreach Program on Asia (SCOPA)
The Ohio State University
University Center for International Studies
308 Dulles Hall
Columbus, OH 43210
(614) 422-9660

Contact(s):
Sara A. Mazak, Coordinator

• Maintains a lending library and speakers bureau, offers consultation on the design of course units, disseminates teaching materials on China and Japan, and publishes *East Asian Quarterly* (a newsletter about East Asian Studies for the Columbus, Ohio, community) and *East Asian Resources in Ohio*

2.086
Southeast Asia Film Library
Audio-Visual Resource Center
8 Research Park
Cornell University
Ithaca, NY 14850
(607) 256-2091

• Contains collection of films on Southeast Asia for classroom use; list sent upon request; films focus primarily on social and cultural themes in Borneo, Burma, Cambodia, Indonesia, the Philippines, Thailand and Vietnam (rental: $10 to cover costs of handling, repairs and postage)

2.087
Southeast Regional Middle East and Islamic Studies Seminar
Old Dominion University
% Center for International Programs
Norfolk, VA 23508-8524
(804) 440-4419

Contact(s):
Jerome B. Bookin-Weiner, Executive
    Secretary

• Conducts seminars, workshops and conferences and maintains film library aimed at expanding Middle East teaching resources and capabilities among pre-college and college faculty

2.088
Texas Program for Educational Resources on Asia (TEXPERA)
University of Texas
Center for Asian Studies
SSB 4.126
Austin, TX 78712
(512) 471-5811

Contact(s):
Louise Flippin, Community Outreach
　Coordinator

• Sponsors teacher in-service training workshops, prepares teaching materials, and organizes group study projects and summer institutes; supports Texas China Council, a community educational organization
• Publishes a newsletter, a *Guide to Asian Studies Resources in Texas*, and various brief bibliographies, reading and source lists, study outlines, and background data sheets on Asia and on individual Asian countries (distributed free)

2.089
Academic Centers which Provide School and Community Outreach Programs and Services
Note: Failure to appear in this list does not mean an institution does not offer outreach services

ARIZONA
University of Arizona
　Department of Oriental Studies (see 13.003)
　Near Eastern Center (see 17.001)
CALIFORNIA
San Diego State University
　Center for Latin American Studies (see 16.011)
Stanford University
　Center for Research in International Studies (see 4.158)
　Stanford Program on International and Cross-Cultural Education (see 2.061)

University of California, Berkeley
　Center for Japanese Studies (see 18.270)
　Center for Slavic and East European Studies (see 14.002)
　Center for South and Southeast Asian Studies (see 13.012)
　Center for Middle Eastern Studies and Department of Near Eastern Studies (see 17.002)
University of California, Los Angeles
　Center for Russian and East European Studies (see 14.003)
　East Asia Studies Center (see 13.017)
　Latin American Center (see 16.014)
　Gustav von Grunebaum Center for Near Eastern Studies (see 17.003)
　Middle East Outreach Council (see 2.082)
　Curriculum Inquiry Center (see 2.024)
University of Southern California
　Center for Public Education in International Affairs (see 2.014)
COLORADO
University of Denver
　Center for Teaching International Relations (see 2.015)
CONNECTICUT
University of Connecticut
　I.N. Thut World Education Center (see 6.088)
　Center for Latin American Studies (see 16.020)
　Center for Slavic and East European Studies (see 14.006)
　Office for International Education and Development (see 4.019)
Yale University
　Russian and East European Studies (see 14.007)
　Latin American Studies National Resource Center (see 16.021)
　East Asian Outreach Program (see 2.079)
DELAWARE
University of Delaware
　International Center (see 4.197)
DISTRICT OF COLUMBIA
Georgetown University
　Center for Contemporary Arab Studies (see 17.011)

Howard University
  African Studies and Research Program
    (see 12.011)
University of the District of Columbia
  International and Multicultural Development Center (see 4.202)
FLORIDA
Florida International University
  Latin American Studies (see 16.025)
University of Florida
  Center for Latin American Studies (see 16.028)
  Center for African Studies (see 12.013)
GEORGIA
Valdosta State College
  International Studies (see 4.207)
HAWAII
University of Hawaii
  Center for Asian and Pacific Studies (see 13.096)
ILLINOIS
Northern Illinois University
  Center for Southeast Asian Studies (see 13.040)
Northwestern University
  Program of African Studies (see 12.015)
University of Chicago
  Center for Middle Eastern Studies (see 17.014)
  Latin American Studies (see 16.033)
  Center for Far Eastern Studies (see 13.042)
  Outreach Educational Project on South Asia (see 2.084)
University of Illinois, Urbana-Champaign
  Russian and East European Center (see 14.011)
  African Studies Program (see 12.018)
  Center for Asian Studies (see 13.044)
  Center for Latin American and Caribbean Studies (see 16.034)
INDIANA
Indiana University, Bloomington
  Inner Asian and Uralic National Resource Center (see 13.046)
  Russian and East European Institute (see 14.014)
  International Programs (see 4.040)

African Studies Program (see 12.019)
  East Asian Studies Center (see 13.045)
St. Joseph's College
  International Studies (see 4.042)
IOWA
University of Iowa
  Asian Studies Program (see 13.048)
KANSAS
Kansas State University
  South Asian Center (see 13.049)
University of Kansas
  Center for East Asian Studies (see 13.050)
KENTUCKY
University of Kentucky
  Patterson School of Diplomacy and International Commerce (see 6.137)
Western Kentucky University
  Center for Latin American Studies (see 16.042)
LOUISIANA
Tulane University
  Center for Latin American Studies Outreach Program (see 2.075)
MAINE
University of Maine, Orono
  Canadian-American Center (see 18.045)
MASSACHUSETTS
Boston University
  Africa in the School and Community (see 2.070)
Brandeis University
  The Philip W. Lown School of Near Eastern and Judaic Studies (see 17.018)
Bridgewater State College
  Canadian Studies Program (see 18.044)
Harvard University
  Soviet and East European Language and Area Center (see 14.020)
  Center for Middle Eastern Studies (see 17.019)
  East Asia Programs (see 13.054)
University of Massachusetts, Amherst
  Soviet and East European Studies Program (see 14.021)
MICHIGAN
Michigan State University
  African Studies Center (see 12.026)
University of Michigan, Ann Arbor

Center for Near Eastern and North African Studies (see 17.023)
South and Southeast Asian Studies (see 13.062)
Center for Chinese Studies (see 18.071)
Center for Japanese Studies (see 18.072)
Wayne State University
Center for Peace and Conflict Studies (see 5.007)
MINNESOTA
University of Minnesota, Twin Cities
Center for Northwest European Languages and Area Studies (see 15.025)
South Asian Center (see 13.066)
Program in Middle Eastern and Islamic Studies (see 17.024)
MISSOURI
University of Missouri, St. Louis
Center for International Studies/Asia Resource Center (see 4.066)
NEW JERSEY
Bergen Community College
Center for International Studies (see 4.070)
Princeton University
Program in East Asian Studies (see 13.070)
Program in Near Eastern Studies (see 17.027)
Seton Hall University
Institute of Far Eastern Studies (see 13.073)
NEW YORK
Adelphi University
Center for International Studies (see 4.078)
Columbia University
Institute on Western Europe (see 15.016)
East Asian Curriculum Project (see 2.078)
School of International and Public Affairs (see 6.151)
Cornell University
Southeast Asia Program (see 13.083)
International Agricultural Program/Center for the Study of World Food Issues (see 6.020)
New York University
Hagop Kevorkian Center for Near Eastern Studies/Princeton-NYU Joint Center for

Near Eastern Studies (see 17.031)
State University of New York, Plattsburgh
Center for the Study of Canada (see 18.047)
NORTH CAROLINA
Duke University
Canadian Studies Center (see 18.049)
Islamic and Arabian Development Studies Program (see 17.034)
Center for International Studies (see 4.095)
University of North Carolina, Charlotte
Center for International Studies (see 4.095)
Wake Forest University
Asian Studies Program (see 13.094)
OHIO
Kent State University
Center for Peace and Change/COPRED (see 5.012)
Oberlin College
East Asian Studies Program (see 13.097)
The Ohio State University
Citizenship Development and Global Education (see 2.016)
Columbus in the World Program (see 2.017)
University Center for International Studies (see 4.107)
School and Community Outreach Program on Asia (see 2.085)
Center for Slavic and East European Studies (see 14.038)
Middle East Program (see 17.036)
Consortium for International Studies Education (see 2.020)
OREGON
Portland State University
Middle East Studies Center (see 17.037)
University of Oregon
Russian and East European Studies Center (see 14.041)
PENNSYLVANIA
University of Pennsylvania
Middle East Studies Center (see 17.039)
South Asia Regional Studies Department (see 13.108)
University of Pittsburgh
Asian Studies Program (see 13.109)

University Center for International Studies (see 4.127)

TEXAS

University of St. Thomas
Center for International Studies (see 4.138)

University of Texas, Austin
Texas Program for Educational Resources on Asia (see 2.088)
Institute for Latin American Studies (see 16.097)
Center for Middle Eastern Studies (see 17.041)

UTAH

Brigham Young University
David M. Kennedy Center for International Studies/Resource Services and Publications Services (see 2.056)

University of Utah
Middle East Language and Area Studies Center (see 17.043)

VERMONT

University of Vermont

Canadian Studies (see 18.051)

VIRGINIA

University of Virginia
East Asian Studies (see 13.119)
Center for South Asian Studies (see 13.120)

WASHINGTON

University of Washington
East Asian Resource Center (see 2.077)
Middle East Resource Center (see 2.083)

Washington State University
Office of International Programs (see 4.243)

Western Washington University
Center for Canadian and Canadian-American Studies (see 18.052)

WISCONSIN

University of Wisconsin, Madison
African Studies Program (see 12.055)
South Asian Area Center (see 13.129)

GUAM

University of Guam
Center for Advancing Intercultural Communication (see 13.131)

International Education: A Select Bibliography

2.090
Advancing International Education
Maxwell C. King and Robert L. Breuder, Editors
Jossey-Bass, Inc., Publishers
433 California St.
San Francisco, CA 94104
1979; paperbound; 127 pages; $8.95

• Design for building international education programs at community colleges including coverage of such areas as language instruction, foreign student resources and the seeking of federal support

2.091
An Attainable Global Perspective
Robert G. Hanvey
Global Perspectives in Education, Inc.
218 East 18th St.
New York, NY 10003

1976; 28 pages; $2

Occasional Paper No. 1
• Defines and outlines in a clear, concise manner a conceptual framework for global perspectives in education; discusses why it is important, why schools should promote it, and how it can be integrated into the curriculum

2.092
The Annals: New Directions in International Education
Sage Publications, Inc.
275 South Beverly Drive
Beverly Hills, CA 90212
1980; Volume 449 of The Annals; 125 pages; hardbound $7.50 (paperbound, $6)

• Brings to bear a wide range of perspectives on the current state of and future prospects for international education

2.093
Approaches to International Education
Earl R. Backman, Editor
Macmillan Publishing Co.
866 Third Ave.
New York, NY 10022
1984; hardbound; 332 pages; $19.95

- Provides 17 case studies on how institutions of higher education have worked to institutionalize their commitment to international education; includes eight state universities, six private four-year colleges and universities and three community colleges

2.094
The Community College and International Education
Seymour Fersh and Edward Fitchen, Editors
International Studies
Brevard Community College
Cocoa, FL 32922
1981; paperbound in binder; 328 pages; $5

- Articles surveying the state of international education in community and junior colleges; covers policy issues, the structure and processes of international education, program implementation, methodologies for selected academic areas and a description of international education at Brevard College, Florida, including examples of curriculum modules in specific classes

2.095
Cross-Cultural Learning
Charles B. Neff, Editor
Jossey-Bass, Inc., Publishers
433 California St.
San Francisco, CA 94104
1981; paperbound; 190 pages; $9.95

- Examines and urges the expanded use

of experiential learning in different or foreign environments; offers case studies, explores the personal dynamics and suggests effective ways of handling admissions, orientation, program design, grading, assessment and language learning

2.096
Curricular Dimensions of Global Education
Pennsylvania Department of Education and Research for Better Schools
444 North Third St.
Philadelphia, PA 19123
1979; hardbound; 236 pages; $24.50

- Discusses the theoretical framework for global education and makes practical suggestions for implementation by teachers in science, mathematics, languages, the arts, health and nutrition, multicultural studies, early childhood education, social studies and environmental studies

2.097
Education and the World View
Change Magazine Press
Transaction Publications
% Rutgers University
New Brunswick, NJ 08903
1981; spiral binding

Published in 7 volumes and a final report
- Comprehensive survey of and commentary on efforts being made to internationalize American undergraduate education
- Volume I, "The Role of the Scholarly Disciplines," discusses intellectual issues involved in expanding global dimensions of the disciplines and examines and makes recommendations relative to international education; 44 pages; $4.95
- Volume II, "The World in the Curriculum," explores methods of internationaliz-

ing the undergraduate curriculum, suggests guidelines for program implementation and provides a list of resource organizations; 272 pages; $6.95

• Volume III, "Handbook of Exemplary International Programs," describes in some detail effective international programs on 62 campuses along with six consortia, 172 pages; $7.95

• Volume IV, "Education and the World View," provides 10 essays by prominent educators and leaders on the impact of contemporary world affairs in undergraduate education; 72 pages; $6.95

• Volume V, "What College Students Know and Believe about Their World," summary of a survey of 3,000 college students to determine the state of their knowledge about world-related matters; describes both methodology and results; 48 pages; $5.95

• Volume VI, "Comprehensive Program Kit," includes Volumes III and IV of the series along with a summary of the survey (Volume V); $14.95

• Volume VII, "What College Students Know About Their World," is a full report on the college student survey; 290 pages; $10.95

• "The Final Task Force Report and Recommendations"; $2

2.098
Education for a World in Change: A Report
David King, James Becker and Larry Condon
Global Perspectives in Education, Inc.
218 East 18th St.
New York, NY 10003
issue #96/97 of *Intercom;* 1980; 61 pages; $5

• A progress report on U.S. global education efforts; includes sections on local initiatives, textbooks, resources and answers to commonly asked questions about global perspectives education

2.099
Expanding the International Dimension of Higher Education
Barbara B. Burn
Jossey-Bass, Inc., Publishers
433 California St.
San Francisco, CA 94104
1980; hardbound; $17.95

• Examines the reasons why international education has been neglected in American education and the consequences thereof and explores possible future directions; covers educational changes, undergraduate international education, foreign language study, student and faculty exchanges, the university in development assistance, advanced training and research, and organizational steps that can be taken

2.100
Geography and International Knowledge
Association of American Geographers
1710 16th St. NW
Washington, DC 20009
1982; booklet; 24 pages; $2.50

• A report which attempts to define the role of geography in improving and expanding the international capabilities of Americans; examines the international content of geography, its contributions to international studies curricula and practical applications in business and public affairs

2.101
Getting Started in Global Education: A Primer for Principals and Teachers
H. Thomas Collins and Sally Banks Zakariya
National Association of Elementary School Principals
1801 North Moore St.
Arlington, VA 22209
1982; booklet; 25 pages; $4 (quantity discounts available)

• Collection of articles addressing the whys, hows and whats of global education relative to the development of programs in elementary and secondary schools

2.102
Global Perspectives Education
Steven L. Lamy, Guest Editor
School of Education
University of Southern California
Phillips Hall
University Park
Los Angeles, CA 90089-0031
quarterly journal; approx. 100 pages; $17.50
  per year; special issue, Volume 8,
  Number 1; $9

This special issue of *Educational Research Quarterly* was co-sponsored by The Immaculate Heart College Center (see 5.023) and the Center for Public Education in International Affairs, University of Southern California (see 2.014)
  • Contains 12 articles by leading specialists in global education discussing major current issues; reviews the field and then covers such areas as teaching, the community, research, the value of cross-cultural experience for the teacher, curriculum, the global perspectives classroom and its school-wide impact and global perspectives consortia

2.103
International and Intercultural Education in Selected State Colleges and Universities
Audrey Ward Gray
American Association of State Colleges and
  Universities (AASCU)
One Dupont Circle, NW, Suite 700
Washington, DC 20036
1977; paperbound; 183 pages; $3.50

U.S. Office of Education-supported study conducted from 1975 to 1977
  • Discusses background of international education in higher education and examines

its development in AASCU member institutions; provides in-depth studies of international education at five institutions (Adams State College, Lock Haven State College, the University of North Carolina at Charlottesville, the University of South Florida, and Ramapo College); and analyzes several major issues in international education, e.g., undergraduate area studies, international and intercultural curriculum approaches and faculty/staffing problems; includes summary, recommendations, appendices and bibliography

2.104
International Learning and International Education in a Global Age
Richard C. Remy, James A. Nathan, James
  M. Becker and Judith V. Torney
National Council for the Social Studies
3501 Newark St. NW
Washington, DC 20016
Bulletin 47; 1975; paperbound; 104 pages;
  $6.95

  • Examines ways to learn about the world, alternative worldviews and designs for world studies programs; includes bibliography and concrete guidelines for classroom implementation

2.105
National Seminar on the Implementation of International Schools: Proceedings
Alan C. Purves, Editor
Curriculum Laboratory
University of Illinois
1210 West Springfield Ave.
Urbana, IL 60801
1981; paperbound; 225 pages; $5

  • Report of a working conference on the proposal made by the President's Commission on Foreign Language and International Studies (now established as the National Council on Foreign Language and International Studies (see 2.048) calling for the creation of 20 model Language and International Studies High Schools around the country; includes discussions of problems of implementation along with reports of workshops covering such subjects as school organization, student selection, curriculum, teacher training, certification and sources of support

2.106
Schooling for a Global Age
James M. Becker, Editor
McGraw-Hill, Inc.
1221 Ave. of the Americas
New York, NY 10020
1979; hardbound; $16.95

• Thorough examination of the need for and imperatives of global education; reviews elementary and secondary programs, curriculum planning and development and resources available for assisting in the development of global education programs; describes exemplary programs and includes an extensive bibliography

2.107
The Tongue-Tied American: Confronting the Foreign Language Crisis
Paul Simon
Continuum Publishing Company
575 Lexington Ave.
New York, NY 10022
1980; hardbound; 224 pages; $12.95

• Examines the results of the studies and reports of the President's Commission on Foreign Language and International Studies; emphasizes the critical need for foreign language competence in business, government and many other phases of American life

2.108
Without a Nickel: The Challenge of Internationalizing the Curriculum and the Campus
Gerald Leinwand
American Association of State Colleges and
    Universities
One Dupont Circle, Suite 700
Washington, DC 20036
1983; paperbound; 55 pages; $4
    (15% discount on orders of 20 or more)

• Reviews and discusses the challenges to and problems in internationalizing a campus, covering policies, the academic program, the international student, faculty exchanges and the general need to mobilize resources; based on a 1983 ASSCU workshop

Sourcebooks and Directories

2.109
Africa From Real to Reel
Steven Ohrn and Rebecca Riley, Compilers
Crossroads Press
African Studies Association
255 Kinsey Hall, UCLA
Los Angeles, CA 90024
1976; paperbound; 144 pages; $15

• Lists and describes approximately 1,300

16mm films on Africa distributed in the U.S. and Canada

2.110
African Outreach
Marylee Crofts, Editor
Crossroads Press
African Studies Association
255 Kinsey Hall, UCLA
Los Angeles, CA 90024

1981; paperbound; 83 pages; $10

• Essays examining various aspects of school and community outreach programs of educational institutions and organizations involved in African Studies, including the less well-known undertakings of educational institutions, individual scholars, the media, religious organizations and the business community

2.111

Americans & World Affairs
Laurel Elmer, Senior Editor
World Without War Council of Northern
　California
1730 Grove St.
Berkeley, CA 94709
1981; paperbound, 210 pages, $6.25

• Lists and provides extensive two-page description of 85 organizations, offices and programs in northern California engaged wholly or partly in World Affairs activities; cross-referenced; also lists with name, address and phone number approximately 500 other organizations including foreign consulates, Bay Area chambers of commerce and trade organizations and a selected listing of religious agencies; preface contains elaborate discussion of a typology of World Affairs organizations and activities; appendix includes extensive discussion of how to use the directory and the resource agencies listed in it to improve world education in elementary and secondary schools

2.112

**An Annotated Bibliography of
Contemporary Middle Eastern and North
African Literature**
Mrs. Nicholas Thacher
Bay Area Global Education Program
World Affairs Council
312 Sutter St.
San Francisco, CA 94108
1983; pamphlet; 33 pages; $2

• Lists and describes anthologies, poetry, novels, plays, short stories and folk tales which are relevant to contemporary issues such as the impact of industrialization and urbanization on traditional societies, the pervasive role of religion, conflicts between the generations, the changing role of women, the search for identity in a changing world, etc.; suitable for high school students and adults; suggests background reading for teachers

2.113

**The Sights and Sounds of the Americas:
Audio Visual Catalogue**
Museum of Modern Art of Latin America
Organization of American States
1889 F St., NW
Washington, DC 20006
paperbound; 18 pages; free

• Lists 35mm color slides and 16mm films, filmstrips and video cassettes on Latin America produced by the OAS Audio-Visual Program and available for sale from the museum; subjects: cultural patterns, geography and scenery, pre-Columbian and contemporary art

2.114

**A Buyer's Guide to Indian Periodicals and
Books for American Schools and Colleges**
Educational Resources Center
New Delhi, India
1976; paperbound; 21 pages; free

Available from Center for International Programs, New York State Education Department, Cultural Education Center, Empire State Plaza, Albany, NY 12230
• Selected list of periodicals, published in India and/or focused on India and South Asia, of interest to educators; includes list of U.S. and Indian book dealers

2.115

Catalog of Resources on International Understanding
Donald W. Myers, Editor
Southwest Educational Development
  Laboratory
211 East 7th St.
Austin, TX 78701
1982; paperbound; 409 pages; $14.50

• Lists and describes materials for teaching global perspectives at all levels; then divides into seven sections covering geographical areas (Africa, Asia, Australia, New Zealand and the South Pacific, Canada, Latin America, the Middle East, the Soviet Union and Eastern Europe) with lists of source materials for each; includes lists of publishers and distributors

2.116

Children's Books on Africa and Their Authors and Supplement to Children's Books on Africa and Their Authors
Nancy J. Schmidt
Holmes & Meier Publishers, Inc.
IUB Bldg.
30 Irving Place
New York, NY 10003
1975; hardbound; 291 pages; $20.50;
  supplement: 1979; 273 pages; hardbound;
  $16

An annotated bibliography in two volumes
• Extensive coverage of books suitable for children's reading; annotations focus on whether the book contributes to an understanding of Africa; indexed

2.117

Children's Books on India: An Annotated Bibliography
Sharada Nayak and Mala Singh
Educational Resources Center
New Delhi, India
1976; paperbound; 97 pages; free

Available from Center for International Programs, New York State Educational Department, Cultural Education Center, Empire State Plaza, Albany, NY 12230
• Annotated bibliography of materials suitable for grades K–8 published between 1961 and 1976; includes Indian literature and books about India published in India and the U.S.

2.118

Children's Fiction about Africa in English
Nancy J. Schmidt
Conch Magazine, Ltd., Publishers
102 Normal Ave. (Symphony Circle)
Buffalo, NY 14213
1981; 256 pages; hardbound, $35;
  paperbound, $17.50

• Reviews the growth of the publishing industry in both Africa and the West; surveys children's fiction about Africa published in Africa and elsewhere; then provides detailed commentary on specific books, arranged by major theme with evaluations designed to aid the teacher and librarian; includes an extensive bibliography of American, European and African children's fiction about Africa

2.119

Children's Literature and Audio-Visual Materials in Africa
Nancy J. Schmidt, Editor
Conch Magazine, Ltd., Publishers
102 Normal Ave. (Symphony Circle)
Buffalo, NY 14213
1977; paperbound; 110 pages; $15

• Reviews of children's books and audiovisual materials about Africa, originally collected for a special edition of *The Conch Review of Books* (see 12.099) in 1976

2.120

The Collegiate Middle East Resource Guide: a Guide for Teaching Middle Eastern Studies in the City of New York and Its Surrounding Area

Middle East Project of the Collegiate School and the Joint Center for Near Eastern Studies of New York University and Princeton University

1982; paperbound; 72 pages; $3

Available from the Hagop Kevorkian Center for Near Eastern Studies, New York University, 50 Washington Square South, New York, NY 10012

• An annotated resource guide for secondary school teachers containing bibliographies organized by subject matter, curriculum guides, and lists of audiovisual materials; includes a list of institutional resources (art galleries, corporate public officers, etc.) in the tri-state metropolitan area of New York that are available to teachers and classroom groups

2.121

Consider Canada

Stanley L. Freeman, Jr.

Canadian/Franco-American Studies Project

University of Maine at Orono

Orono, ME 04473

1981; paperbound; 300 pages; free

• Comprehensive guide to teaching about Canada; discusses Canadian Studies in general, study opportunities for teachers, and the development and planning of Canadian Studies programs and courses; includes large number of specific, concise plans and a resource/sources section with extensive list of U.S. and Canadian programs, institutions and individuals

2.122

Cross-Cultural Learning in K-12 Schools: Foreign Students as Resources

Linda Reed, Project Director

National Association for Foreign Student Affairs

1860 19th St. NW

Washington, DC 20009

1982; paperbound; 104 pages; book, $5; audiovisual presentation, $20

• Examines inexpensive methods and programs to integrate cross-cultural learning into the curriculum; emphasizes ways foreign students can aid in the process but discusses a variety of other educational programs and activities including school-within-a-school, magnet, multilingual/multicultural and peer tutoring programs, intercultural and international communication courses, global education/community discovery projects and international student exchange; describes specific activities for schoolwide and classroom application, recommends evaluation methods and provides an extensive listing with brief descriptions of materials, programs and organizations that offer innovative approaches to cross-cultural education

• Audiovisual presentation demonstrates how foreign students in elementary and secondary schools can be involved as international educational resources

2.123

Directory of Intercultural Education Newsletters

Muriel Wall

Information Consulting Associates

303 West Pleasantview Ave.

Hackensack, NJ 07601

annual; paperbound; 77 pages; $10

• Lists and provides subscription and other data for approximately 160 newsletters of organizations active in international, intercultural and/or domestic multicultural affairs; about half are annotated

2.124
Educational Film Guide for Middle Eastern Studies
Outreach Program
Center for Near Eastern and North African Studies
University of Michigan
144 Lane Hall
Ann Arbor, MI 48109-1290
1980; paperbound; 126 pages; $6

• Comprehensive annotated listing of 600 films on the Middle East; includes suggestions for age group suitability and the names of the distributors from whom the films may be obtained

2.125
Film Resource Guide: Directory for Locating Audio Visuals on Development
CARE
Office of Education
660 First Ave.
New York, NY 10016
1983; 10 pages; mimeographed; $2

• Lists organizational sources of rental films which deal principally with development-related issues; brief annotations indicate resources offered and list important audiovisuals by title

2.126
Films on Africa: An Educator's Guide to 16mm Films
African Studies Program
University of Wisconsin-Madison
1454 Van Hise Hall
1220 Linden Drive
Madison, WI 53706
1979; paperbound; 71 pages

• Descriptive filmography of approximately 325 titles on African subjects (plus about 200 titles from *The Encyclopedia of Cinematographic Films* without descriptions); includes documentary and feature films; gives date, length, color/b.w., an indication of level at which use is recommended, source and rental fee; also provides list of recommended films for approximately 20 specific educational uses

2.127
Films for Korean Studies
Lucius A. Butler and Chaesoon T. Youngs
Center for Korean Studies
University of Hawaii at Manoa
1881 East-West Road
Honolulu, HI 96822
1978; paperbound; 167 pages; $6

• Provides annotated listing of over 300 English-language 16mm films about Korea; indexed; includes list of producers, distributors and other sources of films about Korea

2.128
Filmstrips for Area Studies: A Critical Evaluation on K-12 Learning Materials
Curriculum Inquiry Center
Graduate School of Education
University of California
Los Angeles, CA 90024
1983 paperbound; 140 pages; $3

• Lists and evaluates more than 150 filmstrips for studies of Africa, Asia, the Near East, Russia and East Europe and Latin America; includes an essay on evaluating filmstrip learning materials and an analysis of trends in the field

2.129

Foreign Area Programs at North American Universities: A Directory
California Institute of Public Affairs
P.O. Box 10
Claremont, CA 91711
1979; paperbound; 92 pages; $22.50

• Lists approximately 700 area studies programs and/or research centers in the U.S. and Canada and, for about half of them, gives degrees offered and special interests; cross-indexed by world region and countries of special interest

2.130

Free and Inexpensive Materials on World Affairs
Leonard S. Kenworthy
World Affairs Materials
Box 726
Kennett Square, PA 19348
7th edition; 1983; paperbound; 96 pages; $5, plus 65¢ postage

• Contains extensive list (over 1,600 items) of pamphlets, books, filmstrips, magazines and other resources (such as outline and reference material for the study of various areas and problems of the world) which may be obtained free or for a cost of $2 or less; organized according to grade level, topic, and country or area

2.131

The Future: A Guide to Information Sources
World Future Society
4916 St. Elmo Ave.
Washington, DC 20014
1979; paperbound; 722 pages; $25

• Comprehensive guide to individuals, organizations and publications concerned with issues or actions relative to illuminating or influencing the future or futuristics; includes educational courses and programs, research projects, films, audiotapes, games and simulations and other media (along with sources from which they may be obtained); includes a glossary and geographical and subject indexes

2.132

The Global Yellow Pages
Charles O. Roebuck, Director of
    Publications
Global Perspectives in Education, Inc.
218 East 18th St.
New York, NY 10003
1980; paperbound; 193 pages; $7.50

• Guide to approximately 180 organizations which offer programs, services and/or source materials for international/global education, especially at the elementary and secondary levels; includes address, phone number, name of contact, focus of the organization, services provided, publications and audiovisual materials available, and geographic area served; thoroughly cross-indexed

2.133

Guide to Free-loan Films About Foreign Lands
Serina Press
70 Kennedy St.
Alexandria, VA 22305
1975; $12.95

• Lists and describes over 3,000 16mm. films about 76 countries on a wide range of subjects; includes length, b/w-color; many officially produced by foreign governments

2.134
Guide to Nonprint Materials for Latin American Studies
Martin H. Sable
Blaine Ethridge-Books
13977 Penrod St.
Detroit, MI 48223
hardbound; 152 pages; $16.50

• An annotated bibliography-directory covering most types of nonprint materials for all levels, elementary through graduate school (levels designated), in English and/or Spanish; includes general and specialized information on Latin America in general and on individual nations; three indexes and a directory of firms and institutions are included

2.135
Human Rights: a Topical Bibliography
J. Paul Martin, Editor
Westview Press Inc.
5500 Central Ave.
Boulder, CO 80301
1983; paperbound; 300 pages; $30

Prepared by the Center for the Study of Human Rights, Columbia University
• Lists without annotation over 3,000 publications on human rights under the headings: philosophical and theoretical issues, national and international perspectives, specific rights (civil and political, social and economic, etc.) and teaching human rights; author and subject indexes

2.136
Index to Computer Based Learning
Educational Technology Publications
140 Sylvan Ave.
Englewood Cliffs, NJ 07632
1973; paperbound; 704 pages; $34.95

• Covers instructional programs and techniques for using them in a wide range of areas including the major foreign languages and international aspects of the social sciences

2.137
International Directory of Theatre, Dance and Folklore Festivals
Jennifer Merin with Elizabeth B. Burdick
International Theatre Institute of the United States, Inc.
1860 Broadway, Suite 1510
New York, NY 10023
paperbound; 490 pages; available to nonprofit performing arts companies for $10 from ITI/US

Hardbound edition available to libraries, research centers and commercial enterprises from Greenwood Press, Inc., 88 Post Road West, Westport, CT 06881; $19.95
• Lists events that include any theatrical and/or dance expression including fairs, fiestas, carnivals, ceremonies, celebrations, rituals, theatrical performances, pantomimes, puppets, marionettes and dances, amateur and professional, traditional and modern; gives name, address, phone number and approximate date; listed alphabetically by country, region and city; includes calendar and index by title; titles in English and local language; bibliography

2.138
International Education Programs of the U.S. Government: An Inventory
Helen R. Wiprud, Compiler
U.S. Department of Education
Washington, DC 20202
1980; paperbound; 400 pages; $8.50

Available from the Superintendent of Documents, U.S. Government Printing Office, Washington, DC 20402, or from Information Clearinghouse, Office of International Education Programs, U.S. Department of Education, Washington, DC 20202

• Comprehensive listing of programs sponsored by federal government agencies which are felt by government officials to foster understanding and cooperation between the U.S. and other countries through educational, training and other activities; covers 181 programs funded wholly or partly by the federal government and administered by 28 federal agencies (as of 1979); a large number involve educational exchange and technical training; entries include address, phone number, type and location of program, travel involved, international education functions, beginning date and legislative authority, funding sources and amounts, and statistical information; lists programs in various agencies

2.139
International Education Resources
Pat Kern McIntyre, Editor
U.S. Department of Education
Washington, DC 20202
1980; paperbound; 245 pages

Available from the Superintendent of Documents, U.S. Government Printing Office, Washington, DC 20402, or from Information Clearinghouse, Office of International Education Programs, U.S. Department of Education, Washington, DC 20202

• Lists and annotates published and unpublished research on international education supported by federal government programs (other than the Division of International Education) and other organizations for the period 1956 to 1977; gives source of availability (majority available in microfiche or hard copy through ERIC Document Reproduction Service (see 2.026); contains thorough annotations; lists under the following headings: Teaching and Learning about Other Countries (curriculum and psychological and sociological studies for preschool, secondary

school, college and teacher education); Cross-cultural and Cross-national Aspects of Education; Education Systems of Other Countries; Education and Economic and Social Development of Other Countries; Students from Other Countries Attending U.S. Education Institutions; and Bibliographies and Directories of International Education Resources; indexed by country and world region

2.140
Latin America: Sights and Sounds: A Guide to Motion Pictures and Music for College Courses
Jane Loy, Compiler
Latin American Studies Association
911 West High St., Room 100
Urbana, IL 61801
1975; paperbound; Publication No. 1 of
   Abstracts, $2.50 ($1.50 for members)

• Useful annotated listing of films made in and on Latin America, suitable for use in college and, in many cases, secondary school courses

2.141
Mid-Atlantic Directory to Resources for Asian Study
Archie R. Crouch, Editor
Mid-Atlantic Region Association for Asian
   Studies, Inc.
325 Murray Ave.
Englewood, NJ 07631
1980; paperbound; 144 pages; $4.50

• Lists and describes a wide variety of organizations and institutions which constitute resources for Asian studies in the Mid-Atlantic region; includes offices of foreign governments, educational, commercial and religious organizations, curriculum development services, resource centers, guides and directories to curriculum and audiovisual resources, academic associations, libraries and information services, museums, bookstores and publishers

2.142

The Middle East and North Africa on Film: An Annotated Filmography
Marsha Hamilton McClintock
Garland Publishing, Inc.
136 Madison Ave.
New York, NY 10016
1981; hardbound; 562 pages; $50

• Lists and annotates 8, super 8, 16, and 35mm films and ½-, ¾-, and 2-inch video-tapes on all aspects of Middle East and North Africa Studies; 2,460 entries include English, English-subtitled, or silent films and tapes produced between 1903 and 1980; covers such topics as Israel, religion and the Arab-Israeli conflict

2.143

One Friendship at a Time: Your Guide to International Youth Exchange
Consortium for International Citizen Exchange
3501 Newark St. NW
Washington, DC 20016
1983; paperbound; 61 pages; free

• Discusses President's Youth Exchange Initiative calling for an increase in teen-age (and college-age) exchange activity; provides guidelines for students and families wishing to become involved and describes major organizations which administer youth exchange programs

2.144

Population Education: Sources and Resources
Population Reference Bureau, Inc.
1337 Connecticut Ave. NW
Washington, DC 20036
paperbound; $1 each

• Comprehensive annotated listing of population education materials that includes readings for students and teachers, charts, posters, audiovisual aids and information on low-cost films

2.145

A Resource Guide For Middle Eastern Studies
Charlotte Albright, Ellen-Fairbanks Bodman, Ann Grabhorn, Ruth Matson and Robert Staab, Co-Editors
Middle East Outreach Council
Gustave E. Grunebaum Center for Near Eastern Studies
University of California
405 Hilgard Ave.
Los Angeles, CA 90024
1984; offset, for 3-ring binder; 200 pages; $10

• Chapters include: an outline of how to develop Middle Eastern resources a list and description of resources available from major academic outreach programs, examples of activities sponsored by these programs, a list of Middle Eastern and North African embassies and consulates and an extensive Middle East Film Sampler (also available from the Middle East Resource Center, see 2.083)

2.146

Resource Guide to Teaching Aids in Russian and East European Studies
Outreach Services
Russian and East European Institute
Ballantine Hall 565
Indiana University
Bloomington, IN 47405
1983; paperbound; 46 pages

• Lists and describes audiocassettes, films, filmstrips, videotapes and other audio-visual materials available from the Indiana University Russian and East European Institute (see 14.014) and other programs and of-fices of the University; all entries include date and length, subject classifications and rec-ommended grade levels (also indicates color/ b.w. for films)

2.147
Scholar's Guide to Washington, D.C.: Film and Video Resources in Washington
Bonnie Rowan
Smithsonian Institution Press
Washington, DC 20560
1980; 282 pages; paperbound, $8.95; cloth, $25

• Lists and describes film and video re-sources in Washington in each of the major international studies areas of the world (Af-rica, Asia, Latin America, the Middle East and Russia and Eastern Europe)

2.148
Select Bibliography on World Hunger and Development
United Nations Association of the United States of America, Inc.
300 East 42d St.
New York, NY 10017
1979; paperbound; pages; $.25

• Lists films, learning kits and games, books, manuals and other publications

2.149
Teacher Guide to Resources on Asia
David M. Kennedy Center for International Studies
Brigham Young University
Provo, UT 84602
1983; paperbound; 75 pages; $10

• Lists and describes national organiza-tions, publications and films which constitute

resources for teaching about Asia (special Utah section)

2.150
Teacher's Resource Handbook for African Studies: An Annotated Bibliography of Curriculum Materials Preschool Through Grade Twelve
John N. Hawkins and Jon Maksik
African Studies Center
University of California
Los Angeles, CA 90024
1976; Occasional Paper No. 16; paperbound; 68 pages; $1.50

Published with the assistance of the Curric-ulum Inquiry Center, Graduate School of Education, UCLA (see 2.024)
• Lists, provides technical data and briefly describes books and other print re-sources, audiovisuals and multimedia materi-als for use in teaching about the Near East; grouped by grade level and region

2.151
Teacher's Resource Handbook for Asian Studies: An Annotated Bibliography of Curriculum Materials Preschool Through Grade Twelve
East Asian Studies Center
University of California
Los Angeles, CA 90024
paperbound; $3

Published with the assistance of the Curric-ulum Inquiry Center, Graduate School of Education, UCLA (see 2.024)
• Lists, provides technical data and briefly describes books and other print re-sources, audiovisuals and multimedia materi-als for use in teaching about the Near East; grouped by grade level and region

2.152

Teacher's Resource Handbook for Latin American Studies: An Annotated Bibliography of Curriculum Materials Preschool Through Grade Twelve
John N. Hawkins
Latin American Center
University of California
405 Hilgard Ave.
Los Angeles, CA 90024
1975; paperbound; 220 pages; $2.50

• Describes approximately 14,000 annotated items covering a variety of instructional materials (textbooks, multimedia kits, films, filmstrips, audio cassettes, and transparencies) classified by grade level, format and region

2.153

Teacher's Resource Handbook for Near Eastern Studies: An Annotated Bibliography of Curriculum Materials Preschool Through Grade Twelve
John N. Hawkins and Jon Maksik
Gustave E. von Grunebaum Center for Near Eastern Studies
University of California
Los Angeles, CA 90024
1976; paperbound; 102 pages; $2.50

Published with the assistance of the Curriculum Inquiry Center, Graduate School of Education, UCLA (see 2.024)
• Lists, provides technical data, and briefly describes books and other print resources, audiovisuals and multimedia materials for use in teaching about the Near East; grouped by grade level and region

2.154

Teacher's Resource Handbook for Russian and East European Studies: An Annotated Bibliography of Curriculum Materials Preschool Through Community College
Val D. Rust and Jeff Artz
Center for Russian and East European Studies
University of California
Los Angeles, CA 90024
1981; paperbound; 82 pages; $2.50

Published with the assistance of the Curriculum Inquiry Center, Graduate School of Education, UCLA (see 2.024)
• Lists, provides technical data and briefly describes books and other print resources, audiovisuals and multimedia materials for use in teaching about Russia and Eastern Europe; grouped by grade level and by Soviet Union and the rest of Eastern Europe

2.155

Teacher's Resource Manual on Worldmindedness: An Annotated Bibliography of Curriculum Materials Kindergarten Through Grade Twelve
Ida Urso
Curriculum Inquiry Center
Graduate School of Education
University of California
Los Angeles, CA 90024
1981; spiral binding; Occasional Paper No. 8; 132 pages; $5

• Comprehensive compendium of clearly and succinctly annotated books, films and other audiovisuals in the areas of global education and futuristics, interdependence, general world problems, peace and conflict, and spiritual/emotional issues (called "Farther Reaches of Human Nature"); particular emphasis on peace issues; appendices include a listing of reference books, periodicals, resource centers, opportunities for student participation and an evaluation questionnaire

2.156

Teaching Canada: A Bibliography
William J. McAndrew and Peter J. Elliott
New England-Atlantic Provinces-Quebec
  Center
University of Maine at Orono
Orono, ME 04473
1974; paperbound; 102 pages; free

• Lists books, serials, teaching aids and audiovisual materials with selective annotation for elementary and secondary school study of Canada; includes lists of books in series, books for teachers and school libraries, publishers' addresses and general sources of information on Canada and the U.S.

2.157

U.S. Film Resource Guide
National Film Board of Canada
1251 Ave. of the Americas, 16th Floor
New York, NY 10020
1983; paperbound; 100 pages; $2

• Lists and describes over 500 documentary and educational films produced by the National Film Board of Canada about a wide variety of subjects in Canada, the U.S. and other countries; includes date, length, awards won, educational level and source in the U.S.; free previews available to nonprofit institutions authorized to purchase films

2.158

Washington's Window on the World: A Directory of World Affairs Organizations and Institutions in Washington State
George Weigel, Editor
World Without War Council
1514 Northeast 45th St.
Seattle, WA 98105
1982; paperbound; 224 pages; $8.95

• Lists and provides extensive description of 250 organizations, offices and programs in Washington state engaged wholly or partly in World Affairs activities; includes detailed description of 69 representative organizations and institutions; cross-referenced; also lists foreign consulates, the media, religious agencies, chambers of commerce and trade organizations; preface contains elaborate discussion of a typology of World Affairs organizations and activities; appendix includes extensive discussion of how to use the directory and the resource organizations listed in it to improve world education in elementary and secondary schools

2.159

World Affairs Guides
Leonard S. Kenworthy
Teachers College Press
Columbia University
1234 Amsterdam Ave.
New York, NY 10027
1975; 4 volumes; paperbound; 70–75 pages
  each; $2.90 each

Series of four resource books for pre-college global studies, *Studying China [India, Japan, the U.S.S.R.] in Elementary and Secondary Schools*
• Each volume contains an extensive list of pamphlets, books, filmstrips, magazines and other resources for classroom study; organized according to grade level

2.160

World Hunger
Nicole Ball
ABC Clio, Inc.
Riviera Campus
Box 4397
Santa Barbara, CA 93103
1981; hardbound; 386 pages; $46.50

• Comprehensive bibliography and guide to the study of world hunger; includes 3,286 sources covering books, monographs (individual and series), articles, government documents, conference papers and journals; divided into six major sections: economic development, rural development, constraints in rural development, food, country-specific studies and resources, each prefaced by a critical summary

Manuals and Handbooks

2.161
Africa
Jane Martin, Editor
The Dushkin Publishing Group
Sluice Dock
Guilford, CT 06437
1984; paperbound; 256 pages; $7.95

Part of Global Studies Series which also includes volumes on China (see 2.164) and Latin America (see 2.176)
  • Provides background information on the countries of Africa for K-12 teachers including statistical data and articles on a wide range of subjects

2.162
Asia: Teaching About/Learning From
Seymour Fersh
Teachers College Press
Columbia University
1234 Amsterdam Ave.
New York, NY 10027
1978; paperbound; 180 pages; $8.50

  • Discusses how the study of Asia can meet the special needs of learners at each level of education whether focused on student personal and cultural identification, the processes by which cultures function or the content of cultural studies; stresses the understanding of different perceptions and perspectives and reviews how Asian studies can be used for learning about them; includes specific classroom activities, book and resource lists and deals with the place of Asian-Americans in Asian studies; emphasizes the importance of learning not only about but from Asia, Asians and Asian-Americans

2.163
Beyond Experience
Donald Batchelder and Elizabeth G.
    Warner, Editors
The Experiment in International Living and
    School for International Training
Brattleboro, VT 05301
1977; paperbound; 196 pages; $9

  • Handbook for educators and trainers concerned with the potentials of experiential international and intercultural learning; discusses the nature of cross-cultural interaction and experiential education (including the question of "communicative competence"), with a focus on the preparation of the learner for overseas or cross-cultural learning through experiential exercises and activities usable in a training or educational program; describes experiential training methods including eight simulations or exercises used at the Experiment and the School for International Training and provides guidelines for the assessment of the results

2.164
China
Suzanne Ogden, Editor
The Dushkin Publishing Group
Sluice Dock
Guilford, CT 06437
1984; paperbound; 166 pages; $7.95

Part of Global Studies Series which also includes volumes on Latin America (see 2.176) and Africa (see 2.161)

- Provides background information on China, Taiwan and Hong Kong for K-12 teachers including statistical data and articles on a wide range of subjects

2.165
Curriculum Materials for Teachers
African Studies Program
University of Illinois
1208 W. California St., #101
Urbana, IL 61801
updated annually; spiral binding; 347 pages; $5

- Comprehensive, regularly revised manual and curriculum source for teaching about Africa; contains a number of chapters and articles on resources and methods of using them, along with an extensive and varied collection of curriculum materials under the following headings: general information, materials evaluation and teaching guidelines, government and politics, agriculture and economic development, health and the environment, social institutions, the arts, language and literature, games, film guides, and bibliographies; emphasis on the use of indigenous African materials; grade level indicated

2.166
Education in a World of Rapid Change
John Rye Kinghorn with Karl Clauset, Robert Hanvey, Steve Thompson and John Vaughn
Charles F. Kettering Foundation
5335 Far Hills Ave.
Dayton, OH 45429
1982; four paperbound volumes; free

Consists of four paperbound booklets: *Clinical Workshop for School Improvement* (73 pages), *A Guide to Four Essential Themes—School Improvement* (157 pages), *A Guide to Four Essential Themes—Global Realities* (162 pages) and an *Implementation Guide* (48 pages) for implementing the total program; series is based on a project undertaken by the North Central Association of Colleges and Schools supported by the Charles F. Kettering Foundation

- Presents a design for developing and implementing a global education program in elementary and secondary schools; emphasis is on involvement of entire faculty and staff in step-by-step planning and implementation process; materials are in workbook format calling on both individual and group responses to the issues raised
- *Implementation Guide* helps the reader define "global perspective" and begin to think about the process of introducing it into the school; it also provides a framework for setting objectives and planning strategies
- *Clinical Workshop for School Improvement* is a design, with explicit directions, for a workshop aimed at enabling school personnel to create from a set of "process objectives" an agreed-upon plan for implementing a school global education program
- *Guide to Four Essential Themes—School Improvement* and *Guide to Four Essential Themes—Global Realities* outline, define and discuss the significance of the four basic substantive themes (diversity, inter-dependence, inter-relationships and changing conditions) both in a national and global context, and recommend specific and systematic schoolwide, faculty-wide and classroom activities centered on them

2.167
The Evaluation Handbook for Cross-Cultural Training and Multicultural Education
George Renwick
Intercultural Press, Inc.
Box 768
Yarmouth, ME 04096
1979; paperbound; 66 pages; $4.50

• A practical manual on program evaluation; covers who should do the evaluating, for whom it is done, when it should be done, what should or can be measured, how it is done and how to tabulate, prepare and interpret the findings; contains concrete instructions for using various methods as well as suggestions for their most effective application

2.168

Global Studies: Problems and Promises for Elementary Teachers

Norman V. Overly and Richard D.
  Kimpston, Editors
Association for Supervision and Curriculum
  Development
225 North Washington St.
Alexandria, VA 22314
1976; paperbound; 74 pages; $4.50

• Discusses issues involved in introducing global studies in the elementary school curriculum, suggests a series of "problems and promises" themes (e.g., hunger, pollution, voluntarism, cooperation), recommends steps to take to translate these themes into the design and implementation of teaching strategies and provides bibliography of published resources and films in the area of each theme

2.169

A Guide to Culture in the Classroom

Muriel Saville-Troike
National Clearinghouse for Bilingual
  Education
1500 Wilson Blvd., Suite 802
Rosslyn, VA 22209
paperbound; 70 pages; $4.50

• Analyzes the dynamics of teaching in a cross-cultural classroom and suggests ways teachers can be most effective

2.170

Handbook of Intercultural Training

Dan Landis and Richard W. Brislin, Editors
Pergamon Press
Maxwell House
Fairview Park
Elmsford, NY 10523
1983; hardbound; three volumes; Vol. I, 288
  pages; Vol II, 392 pages; Vol. III, 328
  pages; $40 each

• Comprehensive examination of intercultural (cross-cultural) training; Volume I covers theory and design; Volume II, training methodology and Volume III, area studies (training issues related to selected countries and cultures); Volume III includes a number of articles specifically focused on classroom applications of intercultural training designs and methodologies

2.171

Intercultural Sourcebook: Cross-Cultural Training Methodologies

David S. Hoopes and Paul Ventura, Editors
Intercultural Press, Inc.
Box 768
Yarmouth, ME 04096
1979; paperbound; 188 pages; $7.50

• Guide to techniques and methods used in training programs designed to prepare people for living in and learning from other cultures; provides a description and analysis of each method, plus examples which can be used or adapted for use by trainers and teachers

2.172

Internationalizing the Curriculum and the Campus: Guidelines for AASCU Institutions

Maurice Harari
American Association of State Colleges and
  Universities
One Dupont Circle, Suite 700
Washington, DC 20036

1983; revised edition; paperbound; 60
   pages; $4 (15% discount on orders for 20
   or more)

Reports the findings of a fall 1980 survey of
AASCU campuses regarding their degree of
internationalization

   • Discusses principal options and variations for internationalizing the curriculum, on
the one hand, and the institution as a whole,
on the other; lays out a specific set of guidelines for ASSCU members; appendices include a brief bibliography and a list of possible sources of funding for international
programs

2.173
Internationalizing Your School: A Handbook & Resource Guide for Teachers, Administrators, Parents and School Board Members
Frank H. Rosengren, Marylee Crofts Wiley
   and Davis S. Wiley, Editors
National Council on Foreign Language and
   International Studies
605 Third Ave., 17th Floor
New York, NY 10158
1983; paperbound; 63 pages; $7.50

   • Provides succinct review of the need
for foreign language and international studies
in American education, where and how they
can be initiated and expanded (specifically
what parents, school board members, school
administrators and teachers can do), and areas
here global perspectives can be introduced
into the curriculum (plus strategies for doing
so); then describes and provides references
for a great variety of model innovative programs along with publications and organizations which constitute resources for internationalizing education (including extracurricular
resources)

2.174
Perspectives on Japan: A Guide for Teachers
John C. Cogan and Donald O. Schneider,
   Editors
National Council for the Social Studies
3501 Newark St. NW
Washington, DC 20016
1983; paperbound; 132 pages; $10.25 plus
   $1.50 for postage and handling

   • Offers a rationale for teaching about
Japan, examines dimensions of teaching about
Japan from both the Japanese and the outsider's perspective, and provides activities and
resources for elementary and secondary school
teachers

2.175
Key Ideas and Concepts in Teaching About Latin America
Catherine Cornbleth and Clark C. Gill
Latin American Culture Studies Project
Institute of Latin American Studies
Sid Richardson Hall 1.310
University of Texas at Austin
Austin, TX 78712
1977; paperbound; 41 pages; $2

   • Discusses ideas and concepts which
can be used in teaching about Latin America;
provides framework in which broad general-
izations are examined and major concepts organized for six specific instructional/subject
areas (the physical environment, historical
backgrounds, contemporary society and the
family, contemporary culture, contemporary
economics, contemporary politics, governmental and international relations); also demonstrates how these can be sequenced for use
at different grade levels

2.176
Latin America
Paul Goodwin, Jr., Editor
The Dushkin Publishing Group
Sluice Dock
Guilford, CT 06437
1984; paperbound; 214 pages; $7.95

Part of Global Studies Series which also includes volumes on China (see 2.164) and Africa (see 2.161)
  • Provides background information on the countries of Latin America for K-12 teachers including statistical data and articles on a wide range of subjects

2.177
Latin American Culture Studies:
Information and Materials for Teaching
About Latin America
Edward Glab, Jr., Editor
Institute of Latin American Studies
Sid Richardson Hall 1.310
University of Texas at Austin
Austin, TX 78712
1981; 3rd printing; looseleaf binding; 466
  pages; $9.95

  • Large, comprehensive guide for pre-collegiate teachers of Latin American Studies; includes a rationale for studying about Latin America; articles on ideas, concepts, themes and curriculum development in teaching about Latin America (includes *Key Ideas and Concepts in Teaching About Latin America,* which is also published separately, see 2.175); lesson plans and course outlines for teaching specific topics; games and student activities; arts and crafts activities (including instructions); and an extensive annotated bibliography and resource guide broken down into subject and type categories

2.178
Learning About India: An Annotated
Guide for Nonspecialists
Barbara J. Harrison, Editor
Educational Resources Center
New Delhi, India
1977; paperbound; 349 pages; $3.95

Available from Center for International Programs, New York State Education Department, Empire State Plaza, Cultural Education Center, Albany, NY 12230
  • Includes several essays on teaching about India, then provides extensive bibliography of books and audiovisual materials along with a listing and description of source materials including reference books, bibliographies, periodicals, teaching aids and guides, maps, resource centers and museum collections

2.179
Manual for Multi-Cultural and Ethnic
Studies
Henry Ferguson
Intercultural Press, Inc.
Box 768
Yarmouth, ME 04096
1976; looseleaf; 135 pages; $49

  • A manual designed to assist educators in the development of an inductive cultural learning approach to intercultural education; discusses the philosophical and educational foundations of cultural learning and provides specific guidelines for faculty training, curriculum development and program evaluation; includes 37 lessons for classroom use and practical instructions for developing and publishing one's own teaching materials

2.180
Measures of Global Understanding
Educational Testing Service
Princeton, NJ 08541
1981; specimen set: instrument booklet,
  answer sheet, users' manual for $6.50;
  reusable instrument booklets, 25 per unit,
  $36; answer sheets, 25 per unit, $7.50;
  users' manual will accompany all initial
  orders free; ordered separately, $5

• Collection of test instruments designed to measure knowledge and affective
reactions and self-perception of language
proficiency of college students; provides users'
manual enabling comparison with national
samples of freshmen, seniors and students at
two-year institutions

2.181
**The Middle East: The Image and the
Reality**
Jonathan Friedlander and Mark Newman,
  Editors
Curriculum Inquiry Center
University of California
405 Hilgard Ave.
Los Angeles, CA 90024
1981; paperbound; 150 pages; $8

• Essays by specialists on teaching about
the Middle East; covers strategies for introducing Middle East studies, teaching at elementary, junior high and high school levels,
textbooks, audiovisual resources and other
pertinent subjects including a "Middle East
Content Priority Teaching Guide" suggesting
the essential elements that should be included in units of varying lengths

2.182
The More We Get Together
National Association of Secondary School
  Principals
1904 Association Drive
Reston, VA 22091
1975; 1200-frame filmstrip; $15

• This 18-minute color, sound filmstrip
depicts the experience of a U.S. high school
involved in the exchange of 15 students and
a teacher with a German high school; shows
the impact on the community, the school, the
families and the individual students

2.183
**Moving Toward a Global Perspective:
Social Studies and Second Languages**
Global Perspectives in Education, Inc.
218 East 18th St.
New York, NY 10003
issue #104 of *Intercom;* 1983; 40 pages; $7

• Provides eight lessons as models for
grades 7 to 12 based on three organizing
strategies: global skills, cultural universals and
global concepts

2.184
Studying Australia Today
W. F. Mandel and G. Osborn
Allen and Unwin
9 Winchester Terrace
Winchester, MA 01890
1982; hardbound; 184 pages; $27.50

• Guide to resources for and approaches
to the study of Australia at the undergraduate
level

2.185
**Syllabi and Resources for
Internationalizing Courses in Sociology**
J. Michael Armer and Neal R. Goodman,
  Editors
Teaching Resources Center
American Sociological Association
1722 N St. NW
Washington, DC 20036
1983; paperbound; $10 plus $1.50 postage

• Guide to internationalizing sociology
courses; includes information on teaching aids
and other resources

2.186
Teaching Nonwestern Studies: A
Handbook of Methods and Materials
Center for International Education
University of Massachusetts
Hills House South
Amherst, MA 01003
1972; paperbound; 139 pages

• Slightly out of date but very useful survey; describes approaches to teaching about the non-Western world, provides a number of models for implementing a non-Western Studies Program in a school setting; examines 13 methods (with examples) of teaching non-Western Studies (content analysis, role plays, cultural assimilators, etc.) and offers a descriptive listing of materials and resources; designed particularly for use in high schools but valuable for college instruction as well

2.187
World Problems in the Classroom
Herbert J. Abraham
UNESCO
7 Place de Fontenoy
75700 Paris, France
1973; paperbound; 223 pages; $6.25

Available from UNIPUB, 1180 Ave. of the Americas, New York, NY 10036
• Practical teacher's guide to the study of the UN and of the major world issues with which the UN is concerned: peace, security, disarmament, human rights, social justice, colonialism, development, population, food, environment, health and education; issues are approached within the framework of UN activity and principles

Country Resource Series

2.188
Background Notes: . . .
U.S. Department of State
Washington, DC 20520
regularly updated; paperbound; size ranges
    from 4 to 8 pages; $1 each

Order from Superintendent of Documents, U.S. Government Printing Office, Washington, DC 20402

• Brief factual overview of the land, people, history, government, political conditions, economy and foreign relations, especially vis-a-vis the U.S.; includes travel notes, map, list of government officials and bibliography; one available for almost every country

of the world (see individual countries; see also 1.018 for bound collection)

2.189
Country Study/Area Handbook
for . . . .
Foreign Area Studies
The American University
Washington, DC 20016
published since 1961; updated periodically;
    hardbound; size ranges from 250 to 600
    pages; prices range from $9.50 to $17

Order from Superintendent of Documents, U.S. Government Printing Office, Washington, DC 20402
• Each volume provides broad, substan-

tive review of historical background, social structure (geography, education, religion, living conditions, art, ethnic groups, language and mass communication), political system (government, politics and foreign relations), economic structure (agriculture, industry, commerce and special economic characteristics) and national security; includes extensive bibliography, glossary, index, maps, illustrations and tables of statistics, (approximately 115 countries covered; see individual countries for indication of availability)

2.190
Communication Learning Aids
Series: . . . .
David M. Kennedy Center for International
　Studies Publication Services
Brigham Young University
Box 61 FOB
Provo, UT 84602
8½ x 11 paperbound; 1977 to 1980; approx.
　80 pages; $3 each

• Series of practical guides to effective behavior overseas; provides background on the country, then examines the everyday cultural and social customs that the visitor will encounter and suggests ways to deal with them; uses concrete situations, scenes and incidents as illustrations; includes a general guide, *Intercultural Communicating*, plus guides for Brazil, French-speaking Europe, German-speaking Europe, Hong Kong, Japan, Korea, Latin America, the Philippines, Samoa, Spain and the English-speaking countries other than the U.S.

2.191
Culturegram: . . . .
David M. Kennedy Center for International
　Studies Publications Services
Brigham Young University
Box 61 FOB
Provo, UT 84602
updated periodically; flyer; 4 pages; $.35
　each

• Handy summary for approximately 80 countries of practical information for the traveler; touches on the social customs and the economic, political and historical characteristics of the country useful for the visitor to know (see individual countries for indication of availability)

2.192
Fodor's . . . .
Fodor's Travel Guides
2 Park Ave.
New York, NY 10016
revised annually; paperbound; size ranges
　from 250 to 600 pages; prices range from
　$4.95 to $16.95

• Series of comprehensive guides to individual countries and regions, covering virtually everything the traveler and tourist needs to know to take advantage of visiting a foreign country (see individual countries for indication of availability)

2.193
Historical Dictionary of: . . . .
Scarecrow Press, Inc.
52 Liberty St.
Metuchen, NJ 08840
published since 1972 with new countries
　being added currently; hardbound; size
　ranges from 250 to 450 pages; prices
　range from $11 to $25

• Handy starting point for finding information about the history, people, culture, economy, politics and daily life of a country; items arranged alphabetically in dictionary format (see individual countries for indication of availability)

2.194
Image of . . . .
Organization of American States
Washington, DC 20006
booklet; published in the 1970's; size ranges
　from 16 to 32 pages; $1 each

• Each volume provides a basic illustrated description of the land, history, culture, social and economic conditions and principal cities of one of the members of the Organization of American States; available in English and Spanish (see individual countries for indication of availability)

2.195
Nagel's Encyclopedia-Guide To . . . .
Nagel Publishers
Geneva, Switzerland
publication dates in the 1970's; hardbound;
    size ranges from 200 to 550 pages; prices
    range from $25 to $45

Available from Hippocrene Books, Inc., 171 Madison Ave., New York, NY 10016
• Extensive geographic and social/cultural review, with practical travel and tourist information concentrated in a final chapter (see individual countries for indication of availability)

2.196
. . . .: A Travel Survival Kit
Tony Wheeler
Lonely Planet Publications Pty., Ltd.
P.O. Box 88
South Yarra, Victoria 3141, Australia
published from 1975 to 1983; series
    currently being published and revised;
    size ranges from 140 to 600 pages; prices
    range from $7 to $12

Available in U.S. from Bookpeople, 2940 Seventh St., Berkeley, CA 94710, or from Hippocrene Books, 171 Madison Ave., New York, NY 10016
• Gives basic general information useful to the traveler, then covers the country section by section including information about transportation and accommodations; includes maps and photos (see individual countries for indication of availability)

2.197
Update: . . . .
Alison R. Lanier
Intercultural Press, Inc.
Box 768
Yarmouth, ME 04096
published since 1975; updated periodically;
    8½ x 11, paperbound; size ranges from 70
    to 100 pages; $27.50 each

• Series which provides practical information on relocating to and living in other countries; emphasis on social and cultural differences to be encountered; oriented toward business and professional expatriates but useful to others
• Gives background on country followed by chapters on preparing to leave, what to do on arrival, local business regulations and practices, differences in social customs and cultural patterns, family needs (household, health, children's), automobile and transportation requirements, leisure-time activities; describes major cities and provides a reading list and guide to sources of assistance (see individual countries for indication of availability)

2.198
World Bibliographic Series: . . . .
Robert L. Collison, Editor
ABC-Clio, Inc.
Riviera Campus
2040 Alameda Padre Serra
Box 4397
Santa Barbara, CA 93103
published since 1977 with new countries
    being added currently; size ranges from
    150 to 350 pages; prices range from $25 to
    $50

• Series of books that survey and provide annotated bibliographies of the English-language literature on approximately 30 countries; organized to provide a broad overview of the history and characteristics of the country; items classified under such topics as country and its people, geography, prehistory, population, religion, health and social services, legal system, politics, foreign

relations, media, finance, trade, agriculture, wildlife, etc.; updated periodically (see individual countries for indication of availability)

Periodicals

2.199
Access
Patricia M. Margolf, Editor
Global Perspectives in Education, Inc.
218 East 18th St.
New York, NY 10003
8 issues during academic year; stapled
newsletter; approx. 12 pages; free with
membership in Global Perspectives
Information Network ($18)

• Provides news and information about events important in the global education field (including a calendar); lists and describes new publications in global education and new teaching and other educational resources in such areas as cross-cultural studies, area studies and global issues

2.200
Focus on Asian Studies
Susan L. Rhodes, Editor
The Asia Society, Inc.
725 Park Ave.
New York, NY 10021
published 3 times a year; journal; approx. 64
pages; $5 per year

• Articles, essays, book reviews, curriculum models and teaching resources and a calendar of events aimed at education professionals interested in teaching or learning about Asia

2.201
Global Educator
Robert G. Hanvey
3463 State St.
Santa Barbara, CA 93105
monthly (October through May) newsletter;
4 pages; $8; institutions, $12

• Substantive examination of important issues in and resources for the teaching of global perspectives

2.202
Great Decisions
Nancy L. Hoepli, Editor
Foreign Policy Association
205 Lexington Ave.
New York, NY 10016
annual journal; approx. 96 pages; $6

• Contains impartial analyses of eight major international issues, designed to stimulate the reader to think through the issues and to serve as a basis for foreign policy discussions and debates in community groups and classrooms as well as in more informal settings; each article identifies important points for discussion and provides a list of suggested additional readings; also includes ballots by which readers may express their opinions (ballots are sent to Columbia University where they are tabulated and the results publicized extensively and circulated widely in the foreign policy community); *Great Decisions Teachers Guide* also available

2.203

Interchange
Population Reference Bureau, Inc.
1337 Connecticut Ave. NW
Washington, DC 20036
quarterly newsletter; one-year subscription
　free to educators

• Newsletter for educators; accompanied twice a year by teaching modules or materials which may be purchased separately for $1 each

2.204

Intercom
Global Perspectives in Education, Inc.
218 East 18th St.
New York, NY 10003
three times per year; approx. 40 pages; $18

• Curriculum journal providing in each issue new ideas and materials for teaching global perspectives; many back issues still available

2.205

Intercultural Studies Information Service
Council for Intercultural Studies and
　Programs
777 UN Plaza
New York, NY 10017
monthly during academic year; newsletter;
　wide variation in number of pages; $20
　per year

• Provides information about resources and activities in international studies and global education; normally includes insert materials produced by other organizations and programs

2.206

Update
Published jointly by the African, Asian,
　Latin American and Russian and East
　European Centers
University of Illinois
1208 West California St.
Urbana, IL 61801
quarterly newsletter; approx. 15 pages; free

Newsletter of the Outreach Services of the African, Asian, Latin American and Russian Studies Centers
• Describes generally available resources for teachers in the world areas represented in addition to reporting on activities and resources available locally; valuable aid in keeping current on teaching resources

2.207

World Eagle
World Eagle, Inc.
64 Washburn Ave.
Wellesley, MA 02181
monthly except July and August; magazine;
　32 pages; $24.95 per year

• Supplies comparative and current data suitable for classroom use and adaptable to different courses and levels; includes maps, graphs and tables on such topics as energy, food, population, developing countries, military expenditures, human rights, etc.; some pages suitable for use as duplication masters; duplication given for specified in-school/in-library use

Publishers and Distributors of Instructional Materials

2.208
Alden Films
7820 20th Ave.
Brooklyn, NY 11214
(212) 331-1045

Film rental library
• Rents films on Israel, Judaica and Jewish experience in modern history; catalogue gives length, bw/color, price and full description of each film

2.209
Asterisk Educational Media, Inc.
409 King St. W., Suite 504
Toronto, Ontario
Canada M5V 1K1
(416) 596-1510

Contact(s):
David Springbett and Heather MacAndrew,
 Producers

Film production company
• Specializes in the production of films on international development issues, among them a series entitled *The World's Children*, suitable for classroom use, consisting of 13 films, 11–15 minutes long, for grades 5 to 8; each film focuses on the daily activity in the life of a child in another country; countries included are Australia, Bolivia, Fiji, Hong Kong, Kenya, Nepal, Papua New Guinea, Peru, the Philippines, St. Vincent and Togo

2.210
Center for International Training and Education (CITE)
777 UN Plaza, Suite 9-A
New York, NY 10017
(212) 972-9877

Contact(s):
Leon E. Clark, Director

Educational program of the Council on International and Public Affairs, Inc. (see 0000)
• Publishes books for the study of other countries from the perspectives of the cultures involved; includes *Through Indian Eyes*, *Through Chinese Eyes*, ($5.95 each; lesson plans, $1.50 each) and *Through Middle Eastern Eyes* ($9.95; lesson plans, $2.50)

2.211
Children's Press
1224 West Van Buren St.
Chicago, IL 60607
(312) 666-4200

• Publishes books for elementary and secondary school instruction including country-oriented series *Enchantment of Africa* and *Enchantment of the World*

2.212
Claudia's Caravan
P.O. Box 1582
Alameda, CA 94501
(415) 521-7871

Publisher and distributor of multicultural and multilingual educational materials
• Extensive list of learning materials and activities for elementary students covering a wide range of countries and cultures; includes stories, songs, rhymes, riddles, study prints, coloring books, records, doll cut-outs, games, dances, puppets, folk tales, recipes, card games, books of children's drawings and paintings, craft activities, etc.; also publishes bilingual books in English and Korean, Spanish, Swahili, Hawaiian, Vietnamese, Chinese, Japanese, German, Italian and French

2.213
Constitutional Rights Foundation
1510 Cotner Ave.
West Los Angeles, CA 90025
(213) 473-5091

Contact(s):
Maureen A. Sterling, Project Secretary

Nonprofit law-related education organization designed to promote more effective teaching of the Constitution
• Publishes *International Law in a Global Age,* a curriculum resource for junior/senior high school teachers designed to assist them in introducing perspectives on international law into existing curriculum

2.214
Conch Magazine, LTD., Publishers
102 Normal Ave. (Symphony Circle)
Buffalo, NY 14213
(716) 885-3686

Commercial publisher
• Publishes books and periodicals by Africans about Africa; includes books on politics, social transition, religion and philosophy, language, and science and medicine along with *The Conch* (see 12.098) and *The Conch Review of Books* (see 12.099), *Children's Literature and Audio-Visual Materials in Africa* (see 2.119) and *Children's Fiction About Africa in English* (see 2.118)

2.215
Current Affairs Films
527 Madison Ave.
New York, NY 10022

• Produces and distributes filmstrips on country and area studies and on world issues (hunger, population, East and West Germany)

2.216
The Dushkin Publishing Group
Sluice Dock
Guilford, CT 06437
(203) 453-4351; (800) 243-6532

• Publishes books for school and general audiences including two volumes in an Annual Editions Series *World Politics* and *Comparative Politics* (condensed informational articles), a five-volume Third World Series (providing background information country by country on Africa, South Asia, Latin America, the Middle East and Southeast Asia, $4.95 each), and a Global Studies Series with volumes on China (see 2.164), Latin America (see 2.176), and Africa (see 2.161) for K–12 teachers

2.217
Educational Design, Inc.
47 West 13th St.
New York, NY 10011
(212) 255-7900

Producer of print and audiovisual educational materials
• Offers several series of color-sound filmstrips with each unit composed of both filmstrips and cassettes; includes *Multicultural/Cross-Cultural Program* (consisting of four units: Arts, Music, Sports and Family, which explore the subjects from a practical everyday perspective around the world; 16 filmstrips and 16 cassettes); *Global Concepts: A Cross-Cultural Approach* (examines basic human processes in a comparative framework; 46 filmstrips/cassettes, poster and teacher's manuals); and *Global Cultures and Area Studies* (covers Japan, India and the major world regions including Western Europe and Canada; 49 filmstrips, 28 cassettes and 11 teacher's guides); all units available separately; also produces *Ethnic Studies: Peoples of America* and *Basic Concepts in So-*

cial Studies, interactive filmstrips on 13 basic aspects of society from a global and cross-cultural perspective

2.218
Educational Enrichment
℅ Charles Wieser Associates
Box 538
Department M
El Toro, CA 92630
(714) 581-5022

• Produces and distributes filmstrips on country and regional studies and on international relations

2.219
Encore Visual Education, Inc.
1235 South Victory Blvd.
Burbank, CA 91502
(818) 843-6515

• Produces sound/color filmstrips and cassettes for foreign language study and for cultural studies in English on Latin America, Spain and Portugal, France, Great Britain, Greece, Germany, the Low Countries, Japan, the Soviet Union and Italy; available on 30-day approval basis

2.220
Encyclopedia Britannica Education Corporation
425 North Michigan Ave.
Chicago, IL 60611
(312) 347-7400

• Produces and distributes filmstrips for country and area studies

2.221
Glenhurst Publications
Central Community Center
6300 Walker St.
St. Louis Park, MN 55416
(612) 925-3632

Contact(s):
Susan H. Gross and Marjorie Bingham,
    Producers

• Publishes Women in World Area Studies teaching materials consisting of books and audiovisuals on the status and role of women in other countries and cultures; books cover women in Africa (2 volumes), the Islamic Middle East, traditional and modern China, Israel, India, the U.S.S.R., Latin America, Japan (in preparation), Ancient Greece and Rome and Medieval/Renaissance Europe (each: paper $6.95; hardbound $10.95); sound/filmstrips cover Sub-Saharan Africa, China, India, the Middle East, the U.S.S.R., Ancient Greece and Rome and Medieval/Renaissance Europe (each $29.95)

2.222
Greenhaven Press, Inc.
577 Shoreview Park Road
St. Paul, MN 55112
(612) 482-1582

• Publishes books, including a number in series, on world issues such as revolutions, world problems and the "ism" series (communism, nationalism, etc.)

2.223
Interact
Box 997 G
Lakeside, CA 90025

• Produces and distributes simulations on world issues

2.224
International Film Bureau Inc.
322 South Michigan Ave.
Chicago, IL 60604
(312) 427-4545

• Produces, rents and sells educational films, videocassettes and filmstrips in global education (the Middle East, Europe, Asia, the Americas) and introductory and advanced language learning (Italian, Spanish, French, German and Russian)

2.225
International Film Foundation, Inc.
200 West 72d St.
New York, NY 10023
(212) 580-1111

Contact(s):
Sam Bryan, Executive Director

Nonprofit organization that produces and distributes documentary educational films about world cultures

• Sells approximately 50 films ranging from 2 to 29 minutes in length, examining aspects of many cultures of the world; includes, but is not limited to, films focusing on the following areas: Africa, China, Egypt, Peru, England, Colombia, Brazil, the Middle East, France, Ecuador, Uruguay, Fiji, India, Siberia, Israel, Japan, Italy, Polynesia and the Pacific Islands, New Zealand, Scandinavia, the Soviet Union, Greece and Afghanistan; most produced since 1970

2.226
JACP, Inc.
414 East 3d Ave.
San Mateo, CA 94401
(415) 343-9408

Contact(s):
Florence M. Hongo, President

• Publishes and produces extensive list of books, and elementary and secondary school educational materials on Asia and Asian Americans including stories, folktales, bilingual stories, dolls, filmstrips, movies and videotapes, study prints and posters, games and activities, journals, periodicals and poetry, records, language dictionaries and study materials, cook books and general literature and reference books

2.227
Learning Resources in International Studies
777 UN Plaza, Suite 9A
New York, NY 10017
(212) 972-9877

Contact(s):
Allen Yates, Director

Educational materials distribution network for the Consortium for International Studies in Education (see 2.018), Council for Intercultural Studies and Programs (see 2.023), Council on International and Public Affairs (see 2.022) and the Maxwell School of Syracuse University (see 4.093)

• Distributes books, pamphlets and educational materials, including short study guides and texts on transnational interactions and international political issues, guides to data analysis, bibliographies, resources for teaching Hinduism and Buddhism, simulations and curriculum packages for classroom use, as well as such titles as *The CISP International Studies Funding Book* (see 7.037), *The International Directory for Youth Internships; Self-Instructional Language Programs; Students, Teachers and the Third World in the American College Curriculum; Intercultural Education in the Two-Year College; International/Intercultural Education in the Four-Year College;* and *The Intercultural Traveler: A Teacher's Guide*

2.228
McDougal, Littell & Co.
P.O. Box 1667
Evanston, IL 60204
(312) 967-0900

Commercial publishing house
- Publishes culture studies texts including *World Religions* and the Peoples and Cultures Series which consists of *Learning About Peoples and Cultures,* a cross-cultural learning text for elementary schools by Seymour Fersh, along with country-oriented texts on Africa, China, Japan, the Soviet Union, Latin America, the Mediterranean Rim (Middle East), Southeast Asia and India ($6.60 each) and teacher's manuals ($1.80 each)

2.229
Prentice-Hall, Inc.
Englewood Cliffs, NJ 07632
(201) 767-9520 to 9528
College Accounts: (201) 592-2368

Commercial publishing house
- Publishes textbooks for German, French, Spanish and English as a second language instruction (especially strong in materials for adult education) as well as high school social studies texts including the Inquiry into World Culture Series in which each volume focuses on an important contemporary issue relative to one country or region (covers Brazil, China, India, Kenya, Sweden and the Arab world) and the Idea and Action in World Cultures Series in which a basic aspect of human society or behavior is examined in the context of U.S. and three foreign cultures

2.230
Simile II
Box 910
Del Mar, CA 92014
(714) 755-0272

Producer of simulation games for educational and training purposes

- Produces and distributes elaborate and relatively easy to use simulation games for secondary school, college and adult groups including *Starpower* (experiencing the use and abuse of power), and *Bafá Bafá* (a simulation of cross-cultural experience); also produces elementary school simulations including *Rafá Rafá* (an adaptation of *Bafá);* catalogue includes articles on the theory and use of simulation games

2.231
Social Studies School Service
10,000 Culver Blvd., Department YX
P.O. Box 802
Culver City, CA 90230
(213) 839-2436 (in California)
(800) 421-4246 (from elsewhere in the country)

Contact(s):
Irwin Levin and Sanford Weiner, Co-Owners

Major wholesaler of educational materials
- Serves as distributor for extensive list of books, teaching materials and other educational aids in global, intercultural and multicultural education at the elementary, secondary and college levels; prepares special catalogues: *Global Education* and *Multicultural Education* sent free upon request; most comprehensive single source of international and intercultural education teaching materials

2.232
Social Issues Resources Series, Inc.
P.O. Box 2507
Boca Raton, FL 33432
(305) 994-0079
Toll free: (800) 327-0513 (except Arkansas, Florida and Hawaii)

Publisher of social issues learning materials for secondary school and library use

• Publishes series of volumes on a wide variety of subjects, including one entitled *Third World* ($52); each consists of articles selected from national and international periodicals along with a study guide

• Publishes annual *Watch on World Affairs* containing textbook, teacher's handbook and supplementary information derived from *U.S. News and World Report* ($25)

2.233
Teachers College Press
1234 Amsterdam Ave.
New York, NY 10027
(212) 678-3929

University publishing house

• Publishes *World Affairs Guides* (see 2.159) and other books on world affairs; also publishes books on education in other countries

2.234
United Learning
6633 West Howard St.
Niles, IL 60648
(800) 323-9468
In Illinois, call collect (312) 647-0600

• Produces filmstrips for use in studying world issues and foreign cultures

2.235
United Nations Publications
Sales Section
New York, NY 10017
(212) 754-8303

• Publishes educational materials devel-oped as the result of the work of various UN agencies and projects including *World Concerns and the United Nations: Model Teaching Units for Primary, Secondary and Teacher Education*

2.236
J. Weston Walch Publishers
P.O. Box 658
Portland, ME 04104
(207) 772-2846
orders (800) 341-6094

• Produces and distributes audiovisuals, worktexts and duplicating masters for teaching country and area studies and international relations

2.237
World Bank Educational Materials
World Bank Publications Department
1818 H St. NW
Washington, DC 20433
(202) 477-1234

Contact(s):
James Feather, Director, Publications
    Department

Order from World Bank Publications Sales Unit, Box 37525, Washington, DC 20013

• Publishes instructional materials on world development; includes *Toward a Better World* (a series of multimedia kits for teaching about economic development containing books, pamphlets, filmstrips, teaching guides and case studies of India, Kenya and Mexico) and *The Development Data Book* (which presents statistics in maps, tables, charts, etc., on 125 countries and comes with a teaching guide)

3

Educational Exchange Organizations

Exchange of Persons

3.001
AFS International/Intercultural Programs
313 East 43d St.
New York, NY 10017
(212) 661-4550

Contact(s):
Joe Lurie, Vice President, U.S. Programs
and Operations
Lawrence Bruce, Executive Vice President,
International Programs and Operations

Large international education organization administering educational exchange programs for secondary level students and young professionals; functions through 2,500 local chapters in the U.S. and offices in 63 countries, of which 32 are Third World
• Arranges full-year and short-term exchanges: (1) for foreign high school students to come to the U.S. for a full year to live with a host family and attend high school and in the summer for three weeks of English language training plus a five-week homestay and (2) for American high school students to go abroad for a full year or for a summer, live with a host family or in a group situation and attend a local high school if it is in session; application through local AFS chapters (or call New York (212) 949-4242 for contacts); financial assistance often available through local chapter or New York headquarters; selection competitive; over 8,000 students involved per year
• Administers small eight-week teachers exchange programs with the USSR, Peru, Chile, Thailand and the People's Republic of China as well as other adult exchanges for teachers, youth leaders, volunteers, etc.
• Assists American families in becoming host families for students from abroad

3.002
AISEC-United States, Inc.
14 W. 23rd St.
New York, NY 10010
(212) 206-1888

Contact(s):
Henry H. Wilson, National Committee
Exchange Controller

Student-managed international education organization
• Arranges business and technical internships and employment for students in countries other than their own; internships run from 2 to 18 months; works in 60 countries worldwide; operates through campus-based chapters

3.003
The American Host Foundation
12747 Brookhurst St.
Garden Grove, CA 92640
(714) 537-5711

Contact(s):
Tom and Frances Murphy, Directors

Nonprofit educational exchange organization established in 1962
- Arranges for English-speaking teachers from the noncommunist countries of Europe to stay with American host families for up to two weeks during the summer (the teachers spend four weeks in the U.S. and stay with at least two host families)

3.004
American Institute for Foreign Study Scholarship Foundation
100 Greenwich Ave.
Greenwich, CT 06830
(203) 625-0755

Contact(s):
Paul A. Cook, Executive Director

- Sponsors teen-age exchange programs between the U.S., Europe, Africa and Asia

3.005
American Intercultural Student Exchange, Inc.
7728 Lookout Drive
La Jolla, CA 92037
(714) 459-1356

Contact(s):
Peter S. Wahren, Director

Nonprofit educational organization
- Sponsors teen-age (ages 15–18) exchange programs between the U.S. and other countries

3.006
American Red Cross Youth Services
17th and D Sts. NW
Washington, DC 20006
(202) 737-8300

Contact(s):
Joseph P. Carniglia, Director, International Services

- Invites youth through Red Cross and Red Crescent Societies of various nations to participate in homestays and service-study programs with Red Cross chapters in the U.S.; reciprocal programs arranged for U.S. youths in a number of countries; communications such as albums, artwork, tapes and crafts, prepared by school classes, are also exchanged

3.007
ASSE International, Inc.
228 North Coast Highway
Laguna Beach, CA 92651
(714) 497-6526

Contact(s):
William J. Gustafson, Director

Nonprofit educational organization
- Sponsors teen-age exchange programs between the U.S. and Canada and the Scandinavian countries plus Britain, Germany and Switzerland; summer and year-long programs available

3.008
Association for International Practical Training
(formerly IAESTE/US)
American City Bldg., Suite 217
Columbia, MD 21044
(301) 997-2200

Contact(s):
Robert M. Sprinkle, Executive Director

Educational organization which administers international work experience exchange programs for students and young professionals

• Arranges, as the U.S. affiliate of the International Association for the Exchange of Students for Technical Experience (IAESTE), paid, on-the-job practical training experiences in countries other than their own for college and university students in engineering, architecture, agriculture, mathematics, and the sciences; participants pay travel, insurance, etc.; application deadline for students enrolled at U.S. schools: December 15 annually; application fee: $50 nonrefundable

• Administers smaller programs for young professionals in all fields (except medicine, law and teaching) and special practical training programs for U.S. and foreign organizations

3.009
British American Educational Foundation
351 East 74th St.
New York, NY 10021
(212) 772-3890

Contact(s):
Mrs. Frederick van Pelt Bryan, Executive
   Director

Nonprofit student and teacher exchange organization; established in 1966

• Arranges for American high school students to spend a year at school in the United Kingdom after graduation in the U.S.; total cost, including transportation, vacation travel, etc. is approximately $11,000; some financial aid available; application by early spring of senior year

• Arranges teacher exchange between independent schools in the U.S. and the United Kingdom; application deadline: Dec. 15

3.010
The Carl Duisberg Society, Inc.
425 Park Ave.
New York, NY 10022
(212) 751-5544

Contact(s):
Wolfgang Linz, Executive Director

• Conducts one- to two-year exchange program involving career training in the fields of business, engineering and agriculture for Americans with a knowledge of German and full-time work experience in Germany and for Europeans in the U.S.; also arranges study tours and 1 to 4-week seminars in Germany for schools and other organizations

3.011
Children's International Summer Villages, Inc.
CISV, Inc. USA National Office, Box GG
206 North Main St.
Casstown, OH 45312
(513) 335-4640

All volunteer non-profit exchange organization

• Conducts multinational summer camps, including Village Program for eleven-year-olds (plus junior counselors ages 16–18); a Summer Camp for 17–18 year-olds centered around seminars on cross-cultural communication; also offers an Interchange Program for youths 12–16 which is a two-year family-to-family exchange

3.012
Citizen Exchange Council
18 East 41st St.
New York, NY 10017
(212) 889-7960

Contact(s):
Michael C. Brainerd, President

Nonprofit educational travel organization designed to expand cultural contact between Americans and the people of the USSR
• Sponsors Intercultural Travel Program of tours to the Soviet Union including pre-departure orientation, visits to specially selected Soviet institutions, seminars and lecture-discussions with Soviet educators and students, face-to-face meetings with Soviet counterparts (people in similar occupations or with similar interests) and follow-up evaluations of the experiences; conducts regularly scheduled programs for general participation and special programs arranged for groups with a common interest or professional or special affiliation
• Sponsors hospitality program in the U.S. providing Soviet visitors the opportunity to visit American counterparts in their homes and at their places of work
• Sponsors Soviet/American cultural, educational and professional activities through joint conferences, seminars for Americans and art exchanges; publishes semi-annual newsletter

3.013
Consortium for International Citizen Exchange
3501 Newark St. NW
Washington, DC 20016
(202) 244-2773

Contact(s):
Rosemary Lyon, Director

Consortium of international education exchange organizations
• Assists in promoting the President's International Youth Exchange Initiative

3.014
Council on International Educational Exchange
International Administrative Center
205 East 42nd St.
New York, NY 10017
(212) 661-1414
BRANCHES: Paris, Tokyo

Contact(s):
Colleen Zarich, Deputy Executive Director

Large, nonprofit educational exchange organization with a membership of approximately 160 schools, colleges, universities, academic consortia and other educational organizations (see also 8.010)
• Provides services to secondary schools, including the School Exchange Service (links U.S. schools with schools abroad for the conduct of short-term student and faculty exchange), a Principals Exchange Program (exchange of principals between the U.S., Britain, France and Germany), a teacher exchange program with Britain and a Fellows program sponsored by the Japanese government in which U.S. college graduates serve as consultants and resource persons for Japanese high school English teachers

3.015
Council of International Programs
1030 Euclid Ave.
Cleveland, OH 44115
(216) 861-5478

Contact(s):
Thomas C. Hatcher, Secretary-General

• Conducts exchange programs for young adult professionals (ages 20–45) in education and human services; involves bringing participants to the U.S. from over 80 countries and sending U.S. participants to Sweden, Britain, Turkey, France, Germany and India

3.016
Educational Foundation for Foreign Study
1528 Chapala St.
Santa Barbara, CA 93101
(805) 963-0553
East Coast Office:
235 Greenwich Ave.
Greenwich, CT 06830
(203) 629-2757

Contact(s):
William Harwood, President

Nonprofit educational organization
  • Sponsors teen-age exchange programs between the U.S. and other countries; brings students from Europe, Japan and Mexico for an academic year in America and sends American students to France, Germany, Spain and Sweden for an academic year; ages 16–19

3.017
Educational Resource Development Trust
5455 Wilshire Blvd.
Suite 1406
Los Angeles, CA 90036
(213) 937-6050

Contact(s):
Roger A. Riske, Director

Nonprofit educational organization
  • Sponsors teen-age exchange programs between the U.S. and other countries; also places students in U.S. colleges and universities

3.018
Eisenhower Exchange Fellowships, Inc.
256 South 16th St.
Philadelphia, PA 19102
(215) 546-1738

Contact(s):
Patricia A. Karvounis, Program Director

Exchange program designed to introduce foreign leaders to the U.S.
  • Private organization which brings approximately 25 mature professionals and leaders from other countries to the U.S. each year for three months of travel and observation including professional visits and seminars; covers travel and maintenance costs; applicants must apply in their own countries (not U.S.); country participation by invitation only

3.019
The Experiment in International Living
Kipling Road
Brattleboro, VT 05301
(802) 257-7751

Contact(s):
Charles F. MacCormack, President
Alan Carter, Vice President for International Programs

Large, nonprofit educational exchange organization; also operates the School for International Training (see 4.144)
  • Conducts programs for Americans overseas including the following: (1) Summer Abroad Program: for high school and college students (three- to four-week homestays plus group travel and other activities); (2) New Dimensions Program: semester program for high school students including homestays, enrollment in host country high school and an individual study project; (3) Special Groups Abroad Program: two- to eight-week programs grouping students and adults at many levels and (4) Adult Individual Homestay Program: one- to four-week homestay program for persons over 18
  • Conducts programs for non-Americans in the U.S. including: (1) Individual Ambassador Program: six weeks in a com-

munity, living with two or more families; (2) Incoming Groups Program: three- to four-week homestays for high school, college or professional groups; (3) Individual American Homestay Program: three-week homestays for students or professionals bound for postsecondary U.S. educational institutions or specialized training programs (also available to adults in general who are visiting the U.S. for the first time); and (4) International High School Program: five- to ten-month program for high school students involving homestays and high school experience

3.020
Foundation for International Cooperation
4909 Mohawk Road
Rockford, IL 61107
(815) 397-4599

Contact(s):
John Olsen, President

Exchange organization sponsoring educational travel tours
• Sponsors tours abroad involving programmed cultural learning and experience, including brief homestays, and recruits families and arranges homestays for foreign visitors to this country

3.021
Friendship Force
575 South Omni International
Atlanta, GA 30303
(404) 522-9490

Contact(s):
Wayne Smith, President

Cultural exchange organization
• Organizes two-week group exchanges between matched U.S. and foreign communities

3.022
Future Farmers of America
International Division
Box 15160
5632 Mount Vernon Memorial Highway
Alexandria, VA 22309
(703) 360-3600

Contact(s):
L. H. Gamage, Director

• Sends approximately 200 young farmers (ages 17–24) from the U.S. to European, Pacific and Latin American countries and brings approximately 200 young farmers to the U.S. from these countries for on-farm practical experience and training and for seminars and cultural learning

3.023
Girl Scout International Projects
Girl Scouts in the U.S.A.
830 Third Ave.
New York, NY 10022
(212) 940-7500

Contact(s):
Lucy Dinnes, International Program
  Specialist

• Brings approximately 100 Girl Scouts from other nations to the U.S. and sends the same number of U.S. Girl Scouts abroad each year for 4 to 8 weeks of homestays and participation in Girl Scout activities; provides orientation and program evaluation and assists some of the participants in covering travel costs

3.024
IBERO American Cultural Exchange Program
13920 93rd. Ave. N.E.
Kirkland, WA 98033
(206) 821-1463

Contact(s):
Bonnie P. Mortell, Director

Nonprofit educational organization
    • Sponsors teen-age exchange programs between the U.S. and Spanish-speaking countries emphasizing language learning; U.S. participants are students and teachers of Spanish (high school age to 30 years old) who live in Spanish-speaking homes in Spanish-speaking communities; foreign participants (13–18 years old) serve as teacher assistants and resource persons to Spanish language classes in U.S. junior and senior high schools

3.025
International Christian Youth Exchange (ICYE)
U.S. Committee
134 West 26th St.
New York, NY 10001
(212) 206-7307

Contact(s):
Edwin H. Gragert, Executive Director

Youth exchange program for young people ages 16-24
    • Arranges for American young people to go abroad for a year (from July to July) to live with a family, attend school and/or do community work with college credit (available through the Rockland Community College, Volunteer Service Learning Program, see 4.089); includes 26 countries in Europe, Latin America, Africa and Asia
    • Makes similar arrangements for foreign students in the U.S. and assists American families in becoming host families for foreign youth
    • Publishes newsletter

3.026
International Educational Exchange Liaison Group
11 Dupont Circle NW, Suite 300
Washington, DC 20036
(202) 833-4732

Contact(s):
Norman J. Peterson, Executive Secretary

Association of organizations involved in educational exchange
    • Makes national policy recommendations, monitors legislation and provides information to the general public relative to international educational exchange

3.027
International Student Exchange Program (ISEP)
Georgetown University
1236 36th St. NW
Washington, DC 20057
(202) 625-4737

Contact(s):
Janine M. Farhat, Executive Director
  (Acting)

University-based exchange program open to students from ISEP member institutions
    • Arranges reciprocal exchange among over 120 institutions in 20 countries; participating students pay all expenses (including room and board) at home institution and attend host institution with no money changing hands; students apply to their home institutions

3.028
International Youth Exchange
International Association of Lions Clubs
300 Second St.
Oak Brook, IL 60570
(312) 986-1700

Contact(s):
Roy Schaetzel, Executive Administrator

• Answers inquiries and provides information to individuals and to Lions Clubs on the Lions Club Youth Exchange Program which involves exchanges arranged by Lions Clubs throughout the world; exchanges are open to youths from 15–21 and normally involve a four- to six-week stay with a host family and community; Lions Clubs in some countries also sponsor international camps

3.030
National 4-H Council
7100 Connecticut Ave. NW
Chevy Chase, MD 20815
(301) 656-9000

Contact(s):
Melvin J. Thompson, Coordinator,
   International Relations

Not-for-profit educational organization established in support of the 4-H program of the Cooperative Extension Service of the land-grant universities and the U.S. Department of Agriculture
• Coordinates a variety of international exchange and training programs for 4-H youths and young adults, including cross-cultural educational activities and a host family program in the U.S.

3.031
Ohio International Agricultural Intern Program
The Ohio State University
International Affairs in Agriculture
113 Agricultural Administration Bldg.
2120 Fyffe Road
Columbus, OH 43210
(614) 422-7720

Contact(s):
Michael Chrisman, Program Coordinator

• Internship program for U.S. and European students and non-students interested in agriculture and horticulture; provides long- or short-term on-the-job training on farms or with agribusinesses overseas; optional study period at OSU for Europeans

3.032
Open Door Student Exchange
124 East Merrick Road
Valley Stream, NY 11580
(516) 825-8485

Contact(s):
Howard Bertenthal, Executive Director

High school student exchange program
• Arranges programs for American students to go abroad, live with families and, in most cases, attend school during the summer or a semester; makes similar arrangements for foreign students in the U.S.; programs available to and from Central and South America, Egypt, Greece, Israel, Sweden, Finland and Yugoslavia (other countries to be added); publishes newsletter
• Assists American families in becoming host families for students from abroad

3.033
Operation Crossroads Africa, Inc.
150 Fifth Ave.
New York, NY 10011
(212) 242-8550

Contact(s):
Jerome M. Vogel, Executive Director

Nonprofit education and development assistance organization focused on relationships between and among the nations of Africa, the Caribbean and the U.S.

• Sends U.S. high school students to Caribbean countries to work in community development projects; sends college students to African countries to work in community development, health, agriculture and other projects; administers foreign visitor program bringing approximately 200 African professionals to the U.S. to observe and work in youth and community programs

and offer assistance to the Latin partner in social, educational, economic and technological development) and provides assistance to partnership local agencies in obtaining grants for special programs and projects

• Administers "Partners Appropriate Technology for the Handicapped Program" and "The Inter-American Center for Community Education"

3.034
Pacific American International Student Services
The Icehouse, Suite 506
1075 Battery St.
San Francisco, CA 94111

Contact(s):
John F. Wilhelm, President
Philip R. Johnson, Executive Director

Nonprofit educational organization
• Sponsors Academic Year in the U.S.A. (AYUSA), a teen-age exchange program for students from other countries

3.035
Partners of the Americas
2001 S St. NW
Washington, DC 20009
(202) 332-7332

Contact(s):
Alan A. Rubin, President

Nonprofit education and development assistance organization (also known as National Association of the Partners of the Alliance) promoting expanded contact between U.S. states and Latin American/Caribbean countries; 56 partnerships currently established
• Arranges "partnership relationships" between U.S. states and Latin American countries or regions (relationships promote cultural, professional and technical exchange

3.036
People-to-People-International
2420 Pershing Road, Suite 300
Kansas City, MO 64108
(816) 421-6343

Contact(s):
William C. Menninger, President

Nonprofit cultural exchange organization
• Promotes exchanges between the peoples of the U.S. and other countries through travel abroad, hosting visitors, correspondence exchange chapter programs, the "Meeting the Americans" program, a pen pal program, and other activities; High School Student Ambassador Program sends approximately 1,500 students abroad each summer

3.037
Rotary Youth Exchange Program
1600 Ridge Ave.
Evanston, IL 60201
(312) 328-0100

Contact(s):
Pamela Cohen, Program Coordinator,
　　Community Services and Youth Activities

• Yearly approximately 7000 high school age youth from over 50 countries participate in international exchanges sponsored by Rotary Clubs worldwide; exchanges include both academic year and cultural summer programs

3.038
School Exchange Service
1904 Association Drive
Reston, VA 22091
(703) 860-0200

Contact(s):
Kathleen Driscoll Dunn, Manager

Co-sponsored by the National Association of Secondary School Principals and the Council on International Educational Exchange (see 8.010)
• Sponsors exchanges between U.S. secondary schools and partner schools in the U.K., Canada, Israel, Italy, France, Germany, Japan, Spain, and Venezuela involving 3–4-week reciprocal school/community visits and homestays

3.039
Sister Cities International
1625 Eye St. NW, Suite 424–26
Washington, DC 20006
(202) 293-5504

Contact(s):
Carol Ann Kunz Hardman, Director, SCI National Youth Program

• Promotes exchange and other one-to-one relationships between U.S. and foreign towns and cities; currently there are approximately 725 U.S. cities linked with approximately 1,035 foreign cities in 84 nations around the world
• Advises U.S. member cities on activities and resources for exchanges with their selected sister cities abroad; activities include visits and exchanges of all kinds, organized tours, club and organizational affiliations, exchange of correspondence, school linkages, technical and professional exchanges, youth and student exchanges, exchanges of curricula, amateur radio contact, art and photo exhibits, etc.
• Administers technical assistance pro-

gram under which specialists and technicians may be sent on short-term visits as advisors to developing countries
• Administers national youth program which involves young people in Sister Cities programs, leadership activities and community service
• Publishes handbooks, guides and periodicals which provide guidelines for Sister Cities communities and *Sister Cities by State and Country*, which lists over 700 U.S. cities and their affiliate cities abroad

3.040
Spanish Heritage-Herencia Española
116-53 Queens Blvd.
Forest Hills, NY 11375
(212) 520-1300
BRANCH OFFICES: Camarillo, CA;
Barcelona, Madrid

Contact(s):
M. J. Rodriguez, Director

Nonprofit educational organization
• Sponsors teen-age exchange programs between the U.S. and other countries, Spain in particular; provides teachers of Spanish with information and promotional materials about Spain

3.041
Sweden-California International Academy
24681 Mosquero Lane
Mission Viejo, CA 92691
(714) 770-2010

Contact(s):
Leif R. Montin, Chief Executive Officer

Nonprofit educational organization
• Sponsors teen-age exchange programs between the U.S. and other countries

3.042
United States–South Africa Leader
Exchange Program
1700 17th St. NW, Suite 508
Washington, DC 20009
(202) 232-6720
and
P.O. Box 23053
Johannesburg, 2044
South Africa
(011) 339-6774

Contact(s):
Stephen F. McDonald, Executive Director
Michael Sinclair, Director (South Africa)

Nonprofit, multiracial educational association
privately initiated and funded
• Conducts exchanges of professionals
and a Careers Development Project aimed at
mid-career advancement for black South Africans; arranges team visits and sponsors various symposia

3.043
U.S.–China Peoples Friendship
Association
110 Maryland Ave. NE, Room 111
Washington, DC 20002
(202) 544-7010

Contact(s):
Unita Blackwell, President

Nonprofit educational and international cultural exchange organization
• Promotes the expansion of educational, cultural and person-to-person exchange, including the organizing of study tours, exchange programs and the hosting of visiting Chinese; cooperates with and supports other organizations and runs the Center for Teaching about China (see 2.076)
• Publishes *U.S.–China Review* (see 18.104), and other materials

3.044
U.S. Servas Committee, Inc.
11 John St., Room 406
New York, NY 10038
(212) 267-0252

Nonprofit international cooperative educational program for host families and travelers
• Provides opportunity for persons to visit and stay with host families while traveling abroad and/or to serve as host families at home; families and travelers screened and interviewed; normal visit is two days; host family arrangements available in 83 countries and the majority of the states of the U.S.; small contributions requested from participants

3.045
World Experience
14627 E. Los Robles Ave.
Hacienda Heights, CA 91745
(714) 336-3638

Contact(s):
Bobby J. Fraker, Chief Executive Officer
Marge Archambault, Director

Nonprofit educational organization
• Sponsors teen-age homestay exchange program which brings students from Europe, South America and Asia to the U.S. for periods of a few weeks to a year and sends U.S. students abroad for similar periods

3.046
YMCA International Program Services
236 East 47th St.
New York, NY 10017
(212) 319-0610

Contact(s):

Bonnie Mairs, Camper Exchange, Youth
 Leader Exchanges and International
 Interns
Gwendolyn Bryan, ICCP Abroad
Tom Downing, International Camp
 Counselor Program
Charles Ainsworth, Japan Outbound

• Arranges summer camp counseling
positions for foreign college-age students in
the U.S. (International Camp Counselor Program) and provides placement services for
American college-age (18–25) students wishing to serve as camp counselors abroad (ICCP
Abroad; inquirers should send stamped self-
addressed envelope); sponsors summer
Camper Exchange for groups of campers 15–
17 years old involving camp, host family and
travel experience in another country; arranges short-term exchanges of YMCA youth
leaders and a Japan Outbound program for
U.S. families who have hosted Japanese visitors; also offers internship in international
program management (inquirers should send
stamped self-addressed envelope)

3.047
Youth for Understanding
3501 Newark St. NW
Washington, DC 20016
(202) 966-6808

Contact(s):
Programs Operations

Large educational exchange organization
• Provides international living experiences for approximately 2,000 U.S. high school
students abroad and 5,000 high school age
international students in the U.S. each year;
international students come for either a year
or a six-month program and enroll in a U.S.
high school while living with a host family;
U.S. students may go on full-year or summer
programs abroad; general scholarships available for up to a quarter of the cost of the
program along with special corporate scholarships, a Japanese-U.S. Senate summer
scholarship and a Finnish-U.S. Senate summer scholarship
• Assists American families in becoming
host families for students from abroad

Correspondence Exchange

3.048
League of Friendship, Inc.
P.O. Box 509
Mount Vernon, OH 43050
(614) 392-3166

Contact(s):
Dorothea Snack, Executive Secretary

Pen pal organization
• Provides foreign name and a suggestion sheet on how to compose exchange letters; for persons ages 12–25; inquirers should
send self-addressed stamped envelope; $1
service charge

3.049
Letters Abroad
209 East 56th St.
New York, NY 10022
(212) 752-4290

Contact(s):
Frederick M. Winship, President

Nonprofit educational organization
• Administers correspondence exchange program between the U.S. and other
countries, including matching of correspond-
ents by age, interests and profession, for young
people over 16 and adults

3.050
International Friendship League, Inc.
Pen Pals, Box 106
22 Batterymarch St.
Boston, MA 02109
(617) 523-4273

Contact(s):
Edna R. MacDonough, Executive Secretary

Nonprofit educational organization that sponsors international exchange of correspondence through pen pal program; ages 7–70
  • Provides names of pen pals from over 100 foreign countries who wish to write to an American; contacts for both children and adults available; send stamped, self-addressed envelope for application and brochure

3.051
Student Letter Exchange
910 Fourth St. SE
Austin, MN 55912

Contact(s):
Wayne J. Dankert, General Manager

Pen pal program
  • Arranges foreign and U.S. pen pals for elementary and high school students

3.052
World Pen Pals
1690 Como Ave.
St. Paul, MN 55108
(612) 647-0191

Contact(s):
Loni Fazendin, Secretary

  • Arranges pen pal contacts for individuals or groups; one foreign name per applicant; for persons ages 12–20; inquirers should send large self-addressed stamped envelope; individuals, $2; groups, $1.75 (service charge)

3.053
Worldwide Tapetalk
35 The Gardens, Harrow
Middlesex, England
01 863 0706

Contact(s):
Charles L. Towers, Secretary

System of international interpersonal communication via tapes; fee $10
  • Arranges for exchange of tapes among people around the world; provides contact lists, a guide to message-making, and publishes a magazine

4

International Studies Programs and Offices
Research Centers and Organizations

Degree- or Certificate-Granting Programs and Centers

4.001
International/Intercultural Studies
University of Montevallo
Montevallo, AL 35115
(205) 665-2521

Contact(s):
Charlotte Blackmon, Director

• Offers B.A. (and minor) in International/Intercultural Studies (frequently elected as a dual major) which coordinates varied international education experiences (international course work, overseas travel, study and internships, language study and co-curricular activities)

4.002
Intercultural Communication
Arizona State University
Department of Communication
Tempe, AZ 85287
(602) 965-5095

Contact(s):
Robert S. Goyer, Chair

• Offers B.A., B.S. and M.A. in Communication with specialization in intercultural communication

4.003
Center for International Studies
California State University, Chico
Chico, CA 95926
(916) 895-6880

Contact(s):
Hugh G. Campbell, Director

• Coordinates area studies, critical language training and overseas study; includes a major and minor in Latin American Studies (see 16.004) and minors in African, Middle Eastern and Asian Studies; offers the study of Arabic, Chinese, Hebrew, Japanese, Macedonian Greek, Portuguese, Russian and Swahili under the independent/tutor-assisted Critical Languages Program; provides advisory services to foreign students and to American students and faculty interested in studying, teaching or doing research overseas

4.004
International Center
California State University, Sacramento
6000 J St.
Sacramento, CA 95819
(916) 454-6686

Contact(s):
Preston J. Stegenga, Director

Coordination office for international studies and programs
• Offers two-year M.A. in International Affairs which focuses on the historical, cultural, economic, political and business foun-

dations of contemporary international affairs and which prepares students for careers in foreign service, international business and international education, etc.; includes an area studies component and a student-constructed program of electives, independent study and/or internship in an international organization or agency

    • Sponsors research and advises faculty on overseas research and teaching opportunities, advises students on study abroad and arranges scholarly and public seminars and workshops

    • Advises foreign students and faculty; "Capital Experience" program provides internship and training opportunities in government administration for foreign students and trainees

4.005
International Studies Program
Chapman College
Orange, CA 92666
(714) 633-1346

Contact(s):
Edwin G. Alderson, Director

    • Offers B.A. in International Studies with an emphasis on African, Asian or Latin American Studies

4.006
International Relations Program
The Claremont Colleges/Scripps College
Claremont, CA 91711
(714) 621-8000, Ext. 3255

Contact(s):
James W. Gould, Director

    • Offers B.A. in International Relations emphasizing global interdependence; area studies (Latin America, Western Europe or East Asia) or Peace Research (emphasis on nonviolent practice); overseas study available in France, Germany, Mexico, Japan, the PRC and elsewhere, along with programs at the UN and UNESCO in Geneva and internships in Washington, DC

4.007
Monterey Institute of International Studies
425 Ban Vuren St.
Box 1978
Monterey, CA 93940
(408) 649-3113

Contact(s):
Stephen Garrett, Director, International Policy Studies
Isabelle Armitage, Director, Language and Humanities

Upper division academic institution
    • Offers B.A. and M.A. in International Studies with emphasis on the social sciences, diplomacy, comparative institutions, economics, and regional studies; also offers joint M.A. with Division of Translation and Interpretation in International Studies with specialization in Translation

    • Offers B.A. and M.A. programs in Language Studies including an emphasis on cultural, cross-cultural and intercultural perspectives; languages offered: Chinese, French, German, Japanese, Russian and Spanish

    • Offers joint M.A. in Languages and International Studies as well as M.A.'s in International Education, International Management (see 6.032), International Public Administration (see 6.123) and Translation and Interpretation (see 6.166)

• Three-year B.A./M.A. programs and a four-year B.A. program (with Monterey Peninsula College) available; also offers program in American Language and Culture, an intensive summer language program and a special program of Training in Service Abroad (TAS) for business executives

4.008

Diplomacy and World Affairs
Occidental College
Los Angeles, CA 90041
(213) 259-2769

Contact(s):
William D. Brewer, Chair

• B.A. in Diplomacy and World Affairs with choice of six emphases in political, economic and area studies
• Study year abroad programs available in Britain, France, Germany, Japan and Spain

4.009

Cross Cultural Communication Program
San Francisco State University
Department of Speech and Communication
    Studies
1600 Holloway Ave.
San Francisco, CA 94132
(415) 469-1597

• Offers B.A. and M.A. in Cross Cultural Communication emphasizing communicative behavior between and within different cultures and theoretical perspectives and research methodologies for analyzing the structure and content of cross-cultural communication

4.010

School of International and Intercultural Studies
United States International University
10455 Pomerado Road
San Diego, CA 92131
(714) 271-4300
OTHER CAMPUSES: London, Mexico City, Nairobi

Contact(s):
Wayne Allison, Dean

• Offers B.A. in International Studies and International Relations at San Diego, London and Nairobi campuses, including cultural studies related to each locale

4.011

Institute of International Studies
University of California, Berkeley
215 Moses Hall
Berkeley, CA 94720
.(415) 642-8208

Contact(s):
Carl Rosberg, Director
Neil Smelser, Associate Director
Harry Kreisler, Assistant Director

• Offers undergraduate majors in Political Economy of Industrial Societies and in Development Studies
• Administers Group in Asian Studies (see 13.013)
• Supports and develops faculty research capabilities in international studies and provides administrative support for Visiting Scholar Program, including British Diplomats-in-Residence Program
• Sponsors colloquia, lectures and conferences
• Publishes monographs on foreign policy, international studies, modernization, and population studies

4.013
Council on International and Comparative Studies
University of California at Los Angeles
405 Hilgard Ave.
Los Angeles, CA 90024
(213) 825-4921

Contact(s):
James S. Coleman, Chair

• Coordinates and provides policy guidance on international and area studies programs at UCLA, including African (see 12.003), East Asian (see 13.017), Near Eastern (see 17.003), Latin American (see 16.014) and Russian and East European (see 14.003) studies; oversees international exchange and research and development assistance programs in and with a number of countries including Ghana, Chile, Israel, Yugoslavia, Somalia, Japan, Mexico, Saudi Arabia and the People's Republic of China

4.014
Office of International Programs
University of the Pacific
Bechtel International Center
Stockton, CA 95211
(209) 946-2591

Contact(s):
Cortlandt B. Smith, Director
Len Humphreys, Chair, International Studies

• Offers B.A. in International Studies with a strong emphasis on cross-cultural experience (including a required year of study abroad), and a B.A. in Inter-American Studies (see 16.017)
• Advises faculty and students on study and research abroad, coordinates and arranges overseas study experiences, serves as liaison with the external study abroad agencies and consortia relative to study programs in Europe, Asia, Latin America and Africa

4.015
School of International Relations
University of Southern California
Los Angeles, CA 90089-0043
(213) 743-6278

Contact(s):
Michael G. Fry, Director

Major center for international studies established in 1924
• Offers M.A. and Ph.D. program in five fields of concentration: international politics and diplomacy; defense and strategic studies; international political economy; foreign policy studies and U.S. foreign policy, and regional subsystems with concentrations in East Asia, Latin America, Middle East/North Africa or Soviet Union and the Communist world; Ph.D. in Public Policy and Political Economy (with the Department of Economics and Political Science) and M.A. in International Public Administration (with the School of Public Administration; see 6.127)
• World Affairs Library contains approximately 200,000 volumes on international law, economics, cultural relations and public affairs along with extensive collections of U.S. and foreign government publications and publications from learned societies, the UN and a number of the other principal intergovernmental organizations; receives over 1,500 current journals and has extensive microfiche collection; particularly strong in foreign historical statistics; maintains its own microcomputer and simulation laboratory to facilitate research
• Maintains Center for Public Education in World Affairs (see 2.014)

4.016
Intercultural Program
World College West
Box 3060
San Rafael, CA 94902
(415) 332-6206

Contact(s):
Joyce Bishop, Director

• Requires participation by all students in overseas program, normally in Mexico; focus on global ecology and/or international management and economics; emphasizes cultural studies, cultural immersion and intercultural experience; includes work experience or field project in Mexico or a term working in a Spanish-speaking setting in San Francisco Bay Area and a final term of international and Latin American studies on campus

4.017

Office of International Education
Colorado State University
315 Aylesworth Hall
Fort Collins, CO 80523
(303) 491-5917

Contact(s):
Robert Zimdahl, Director

• Develops special international courses and activities (especially those involving both U.S. and foreign students) and coordinates study abroad programs
• Supervises international and area studies programs, including certificate programs in Asian (see 13.021), Russian and East/Central European (see 14.004), and Latin American Studies
• CSU also maintains an Office of International Training which coordinates international training activities for CSU nondegree training programs for foreign mid-career professionals and which provides cross-cultural training for CSU personnel

4.018

Graduate School of International Studies
University of Denver
Denver, CO 80208
(303) 753-2324

Contact(s):
James H. Mittleman, Dean
E. Thomas Rowe, Associate Dean

• Offers M.A. and Ph.D. programs in International Studies with courses grouped in the following subfields: International Politics, International Economics and Comparative Politics; concentrations offered in the following areas: Global Conflict Analysis, Development Studies, Human Rights, Technology and Policy Analysis, Political Economy and Political Theory and Philosophy; joint degree programs with the Graduate School of Business and Public Management (see 6.037) and with the College of Law (Master of Arts-Juris Doctor); International Studies certificate programs available within the M.A. and/or Ph.D. in Development Studies and Technology and Modernization
• Library contains over 80,000 books and other materials in international relations; program has access to ample media and computer facilities
• Provides a number of fellowships, including special fellowships for minorities
• Maintains linkages with international studies centers in Chile, China (PRC) and West Germany
• Sponsors outreach programs through the Center for Teaching International Relations (see 2.015)
• Publishes Monographs Series on World Affairs (an international and comparative analysis of world issues) and is editorial and publishing headquarters for *Africa Today*

4.019

Office For International Education and Development
University of Connecticut
Wood Hall 301
Storrs, CT 06268
(203) 486-3855

Contact(s):
Rudolf Tökes, Director

• Administers international studies programs including Latin American (see 16.020), Slavic and East European (see 14.006), Middle Eastern (see 17.008) and East Asian (see 13.025) Studies, and an M.A./M.B.A. program in Business Administration and International Studies (see 6.039)

• Administers study abroad programs, provides Fulbright advising, and sponsors outreach and international student exchange activities; develops international studies curriculum and initiates research and instructional support programs; publishes reports and directories on international education at the University, including a descriptive directory of all University international education and research programs

4.020
Concilium on International and Area Studies
Yale University
Box 13A Yale Station
New Haven, CT 06520
(203) 436-3416

• Coordinates international studies at Yale; administers two-year M.A. in International Relations emphasizing history and the social sciences; supervises area studies councils on African Studies (see 12.009), East Asian Studies (see 13.027), Latin American Studies (see 16.021), Russian and East European Studies (see 14.007), Western European Studies (see 15.003) and Southeast Asia Studies (see 13.028) along with committees in Canadian Studies and Middle East Studies and a Southern African Research Program (see 12.010)

4.021
School of Communication
American University
Washington, DC 20016
(202) 686-2058

Contact(s):
Frank J. Jordan, Dean

• Offers B.A. in foreign language and communication media combining courses in communication and the media with advanced foreign language and cultural studies

4.022
School of Advanced International Studies
The Johns Hopkins University
1740 Massachusetts Ave. NW
Washington, DC 20036
(202) 785-6830

• Offers M.A. and Ph.D. in International Studies including functional and regional studies (see 6.133 for full entry)

4.023
Division of International Studies
Brevard Community College
Cocoa Campus
1519 Clearlake Road
Cocoa, FL 32922
(305) 632-1111

Contact(s):
Seymour Fersh, Coordinator of Curriculum Development and Special Projects

• Coordinates four program areas: international studies, foreign languages, English for speakers of other languages, and international student services and provides study abroad advising and programming; plans to introduce new degree emphasis in international studies

4.024
International/Intercultural Education Institute
Broward Community College
North Campus
1000 Coconut Creek Blvd.
Coconut Creek, FL 33066
(305) 973-2206

Contact(s):
William Greene, Director

• Coordinates international education activities at Broward including international studies curriculum, degrees in international studies and international business, overseas study programs (in Spain and other countries), international student services and programs for the expansion of international experience among faculty

4.025
Graduate Program in International Affairs
Florida State University
562 Bellamy Bldg.
Tallahassee, FL 32306-2409
(904) 644-4418

Contact(s):
Richard B. Gray, Director

• Offers M.A. and M.S. in International Affairs with concentration in international development (economic, political or social aspects) and world regional studies (First, Second or Third World)

4.026
Graduate School of International Studies
University of Miami
P.O. Box 248123
Coral Gables, FL 33124
(305) 284-4303

Contact(s):
Robert L. Levine, Acting Interim Dean

• Offers M.A. and Ph.D. in International Affairs including functional and geographic studies (see 6.134 for full description)

4.027
International Studies
University of North Florida
4567 St. John's Bluff Road
Jacksonville, FL 32216
(904) 646-2880

Contact(s):
Thomas M. Leonard, Director

• Offers B.A. in Liberal Studies with international studies concentration; emphasis on cultural and area studies

4.028
Center for International Affairs
University of South Florida
Tampa, FL 33620
(813) 974-2510

Contact(s):
M. T. Orr, Director

• Offers B.A. in International Studies with emphasis on area studies and international relations; provides services and assistance to faculty and students in international research, travel and study
• Study abroad available in Colombia and Venezuela and in other countries through organizations in which USF is a member

4.029
International Studies
University of West Florida
Pensacola, FL 32504
(904) 474-2336

Contact(s):
M. Lal Goel, Director

• B.A. in International Studies with broad social science, humanities and cultural emphasis

4.030
International Studies Program
Morehouse College
Box 139
Atlanta, GA 30314
(404) 681-2800, Ext. 274

Contact(s):
Hamid Taqi, Director

• B.A. in International Studies with political science, economics, history, sociology or language emphasis with sociocultural component in African, Latin American or European area studies

4.031
International Studies Program
Chaminade University of Honolulu
3140 Waialae Ave.
Honolulu, HI 96816
(808) 735-4711

Contact(s):
Robert McKain Smith, Director

• Offers B.A. in International Studies with emphasis on the social sciences

4.032
Institute of International Studies
Bradley University
Peoria, IL 61625
(309) 676-7611

Contact(s):
John R. Howard, Director

• B.A. in International Studies with emphasis on international political relations (with government service and international trade tracks) and comparative civilizations and foreign languages; study abroad encouraged and available in Britain, France, Germany, Spain, Mexico and elsewhere; also offers a

Washington Program, arranges U.S. State Department Internships and conducts a major model UN

4.033
Intercultural Studies
Governors State University
Park Forest South
Chicago, IL 60616
(312) 534-5000

• Offers B.A. and M.A. in Intercultural Studies with a major in African or Hispanic Cultures and an option, at the M.A. level, in Socio-Political Studies; emphasis on Third World perspective, cross-cultural relations and Blacks and Latinos in the Americas

4.034
Culture Studies Program
Roosevelt University
430 South Michigan Ave.
Chicago, IL 60605
(312) 341-3515

• Offers B.A. in Culture Studies emphasizing the study of differences in culture patterns among the world regions, nations and culture groups

4.035
Center for International Studies
University of Chicago
5828 University Ave.
Chicago, IL 60637
(312) 962-8311

Contact(s):
Ralph W. Nicholas, Director

Coordinates program and resource development for international and area studies
• Includes undergraduate program in Russian Civilization, undergraduate and

graduate programs in Near Eastern Languages and Civilizations South Asian Languages and Civilizations and Slavic Languages and Literatures; and interdisciplinary graduate programs in Middle Eastern Studies (see 17.014), Far Eastern Studies (see 13.042), Southern Asian Studies (see 13.043), Balkan and Slavic Studies (see 14.010), African Studies (see 12.017), Latin American Studies (see 16.033) and International Relations; graduate programs in comparative education and in international business also available

4.036
Office of International Programs and Studies

University of Illinois at Urbana-Champaign
707 South Mathews Ave.
3014 Foreign Languages Bldg.
Urbana, IL 61801
(217) 333-6104

Contact(s):
Roger B. Crawford, Director

Coordinating unit for international programs on the University of Illinois campus
• Supervises and promotes international studies and program activities through the following offices: International Faculty and Staff Affairs (for visiting foreign faculty and scholars), Campus Coordinator for Midwest Universities Consortium for International Activities, Office of Overseas Projects and Foreign Visitors (support office for overseas activities and program organization for foreign visitors), Program of Overseas University Collaboration (focused on university managerial problems, especially in developing countries), Office of West European Studies (see 15.007), Office of Women in International Development (promotes research on and concern with the role of women in economic development), and the Study Abroad Office

4.037
International Studies

Earlham College
Richmond, IN 47474
(317) 962-6561

Contact(s):
Lincoln Blake, Coordinator of International Education, Director
Len Holvik, Director of Japanese Studies

• B.A. in International Studies including international relations, cross-cultural and cultural studies with off-campus foreign study required; also offers B.A. in Japanese Studies (see 18.271)
• Earlham study abroad programs available in Japan, England, France, Germany, Austria, Jerusalem, Kenya, Mexico, and Spain, and, through the Great Lakes Colleges Association (see 8.015), in many other countries including China and Colombia

4.038
Program of International Studies

Goshen College
Goshen, IN 46526
(219) 533-3161

Contact(s):
Arlin Hunsberger, Director of International Education

• Requires study-service trimester in developing country, usually in Caribbean or Central America though one program per year is offered in China (PRC); emphasizes cultural studies and cross-cultural learning; includes work in a service project or other field experience

4.039
International Studies

Hanover College
Hanover, IN 47243
(812) 866-2151

Contact(s):
M. Anwarul Haq, Director

• Offers B.A. in International Studies with an emphasis on world areas and a concentration either on intercultural studies or international relations

4.040
International Programs
Indiana University at Bloomington
Bryan Hall, 205
Bloomington, IN 47405
(812) 335-8669

Contact(s):
John V. Lombardi, Dean

• Provides study, research and faculty advising abroad; conducts overseas study and exchange programs; provides community outreach services relative to all world areas (except South Asia); advises foreign students and manages international development projects
• Serves as resource center for Indiana University Area Studies programs and centers (African Studies, see 12.019; West European National Resource Center, see 15.008; Near East Studies Program, see 17.015; East Asian Studies Center, see 13.045; Russian and East European Institute, see 14.014; Inner Asian and Uralic National Resource Center, see 14.013; Latin American Studies, see 16.035; Polish Studies Center, see 18.412; Institute of German Studies, Latin American Music Center, see 16.117; Hungarian Studies, see 18.191 and East Asia Languages & Cultures)

4.041
International Studies
Indiana University/South Bend
South Bend, IN 46615
(219) 237-4455

Contact(s):
Karen Rasmussen, Assistant Dean of Faculties

• B.A. with Certificate in International Studies including the humanities, the social sciences and area studies (Asian, African, East European, Latin American and West European); includes extensive overseas study opportunities

4.042
Program in International Studies
Saint Joseph's College
Box 942
Rensselaer, IN 47978
(219) 866-7111

Contact(s):
J. Phillip Posey, Director

• Offers B.A. with group major in International Studies (two-semester, six-credit non-western component required of all students); provides study and faculty abroad advising, community outreach services and advises foreign students

4.043
International Studies
Saint Mary's College
Notre Dame, IN 46556
(219) 284-4852

Contact(s):
Louis R. Tondreau, Chair

• B.A. in International Studies, including international relations (systems), area studies and the study of values
• Study abroad programs available in Italy and Ireland

4.044
International Relations
Drake University
Department of Political Science
Des Moines, IA 50311
(515) 271-3181

• B.A. in International Relations, including functional and regional studies (Europe, Latin America or Asia)
• Study abroad programs available in Italy, England, France, Germany, Spain, Israel and elsewhere through the Center for International Programs Abroad

4.045
International Studies Program
Graceland College
History Department
Lamoni, IA 50140
(515) 784-5173

Contact(s):
Arthur L. Gardner, Director

• B.A. with emphasis on intercultural communication, cultural studies, politics, economics and with area and disciplinary concentrations

4.046
International Studies
Iowa State University
Ames, IA 50011
(515) 294-5836

Contact(s):
K. H. Friederich, Chair, Advisory
　Committee

• B.A. in International Studies with concentration in either general international studies or area studies (Africa and the Middle East, Latin America, Russia and Eastern Europe, Western Europe); international studies

programs also available in Colleges of Agriculture (see 6.010) and Home Economics (see 6.011)

4.047
World Studies Program
Donnelly College
608 N. 18th St.
Kansas City, KS 66102
(913) 621-6070, Ext. 36

Contact(s):
Martha Ann Linck, Director

• Offers A.A. degrees in International Relations and World Studies-Economics and develops curriculum infusing international studies into the educational experience of all students; coordinates planning with nearby four-year colleges offering B.A.'s in international studies

4.048
International Studies
Kansas State University
Department of Geography
Thompson Hall
Manhattan, KS 66506
(913) 532-6250

Contact(s):
Charles Bussing, Chairman

• B.A. in International Studies including international relations and cultural studies

4.049
International Studies
Wichita State University
Wichita, KS 67208
(316) 689-3085

Contact(s):
John Dreifort, Department of History

• B.A. in International Studies with options in Latin American area studies and combined Latin American studies and international business

4.050
International Studies
Northern Kentucky University
Highland Heights, KY 41076
(502) 572-5323

Contact(s):
Adalberto J. Pinelo, Director

• B.A. in International Studies with options to concentrate in business, the social sciences, Latin American studies, Asian studies or European studies

4.051
International Center
University of Louisville
Louisville, KY 40292
(502) 588-6531

Contact(s):
James A. Van Fleet, Executive Director

• Administers area studies certificate program in Latin American, African, East Asian, Middle Eastern, Soviet/East European and Western European Studies
• Organizes summer study programs in Italy, Spain, England, West Germany and France and advises generally on study abroad
• Administers foreign student and faculty affairs, provides translating services to the business community and publishes a newsletter
• Promotes community-oriented international education through statewide television series on foreign affairs, syndicated radio programming and regularly scheduled public conferences and seminars on trade, finance and foreign policy

4.052
Office of International Programs and Projects
Western Kentucky University
Bowling Green, KY 42101
(502) 745-5333

Contact(s):
John H. Petersen, Director

• Coordinates international studies and programs at Western Kentucky University; includes Center for Latin American Studies (see 16.042), an Asian Studies minor, academic year study programs in France and a number of short-term and summer programs abroad, including field research and practical experience; conducts a number of student and teacher exchanges, advises foreign students, assists students and faculty in applying for Fulbright and other grants for study or research abroad, and maintains cooperative relationships with several Latin American institutions

4.053
International Studies Program
Morgan State University
International Center
Cold Spring Lane and Hillen Road
Baltimore, MD 21239
(301) 444-3205

Contact(s):
Fredric Ritter, Director

• Offers B.A. and M.A. in International Studies with emphasis on general international studies, area studies (African, Asian, European, Middle Eastern or Caribbean and Latin American) or the study of a special aspect of world cultures or international relations; Center provides faculty and study abroad advising

4.054
International Studies
Towson State University
Towson, MD 21204
(301) 321-2955

Contact(s):
David Dent, Coordinator

• B.A. in International Studies with a concentration in a world region or a functional specialization (politics, economics, etc.)

4.055
International Studies
Lesley College
29 Everett St.
Cambridge, MA 02238
(617) 868-9600, Ext. 467

Contact(s):
James Magee, Director

• Offers M.A. in International Studies emphasizing both theory and practice; internship in international or multicultural setting required

4.056
International Studies
Stonehill College
Department of Political Science
North Easton, MA 02356
(617) 238-1081

Contact(s):
Richard Finnegan, Director

• B.A. in International Studies with emphasis on social sciences, area studies (especially Europe or Asia) and study abroad; includes Irish studies minor and semester in Ireland

4.057
International Studies
Hope College
Holland, MI 49423
(616) 392-5111, Ext. 2171

Contact(s):
Neal W. Sobania, Director, Office of
   International Education

• B.A. with composite major in International Studies emphasizing economics, history and political science or history, culture and language; off-campus foreign study strongly encouraged

4.058
International Studies and Programs
Michigan State University
211 Center for International Programs
East Lansing, MI 48824
(517) 355-2352

Contact(s):
Ralph H. Smuckler, Dean

University-wide program and research center
• Administers the African Studies Center (see 12.026), Asian Studies Center (see 13.059), Latin American Studies Center (see 16.050), Western European Studies Program, the Canadian-American Studies Committee, and the Russian and East European Studies Committee (see 14.022)
• Conducts and coordinates study, research and technical assistance programs abroad and develops relationships with foreign institutions
• Administers the Office of International Students and Scholars; provides policy guidance to the Office of Overseas Studies (which advises students on study abroad and conducts some 50 programs in 20 countries); coordinates, with the Institute of International Agriculture (see 6.017), the Center for

Advanced Study of International Development (see 6.142) and the International Library.

• The International Library collects materials in support of the area studies programs, prepares bibliographies of materials held and provides special reference assistance to students, faculty and others

4.059
Center for International Programs
Oakland University
Rochester, MI 48063
(313) 377-2154

Contact(s):
Carlo Coppola, Director

• Offers B.A. in Area Studies with concentrations in African (see 12.027), East Asian (see 13.060), South Asian (see 13.061), Slavic (see 14.024), and Latin American (see 16.051) studies; maintains Area Studies Speakers Bureau, arranges study trips abroad, conducts cross-cultural workshops for international business executives, publishes a newsletter and serves as editorial office for *Six Dynasties Newsletter* (Chinese literary publication), *Journal of South Asian Literature* (articles, essays, poetry and fiction on and by South Asian writers), and *Mir* (articles and essays on Russian history and literature and translations of Russian writers)

4.060
International Education and Programs
Western Michigan University
Kalamazoo, MI 49008
(616) 383-0944

Contact(s):
Norman C. Greenberg, Dean
Charles Houston, Chair, Comparative and
    Cross-Cultural Studies (616) 383-0429

• Offers coordinate B.A. (combined with departmental major) in Comparative/Cross-Cultural Studies emphasizing the comparative study of different cultures and regions particularly in the context of major world issues (population, environment, etc.) and systems (economic, political, etc.)

• Administers the Center for Korean Studies (see 18.309) and coordinates the Canadian Studies Program and bachelor degree programs in African Studies (see 12.029), Asian Studies (see 13.063), European Studies (see 15.013) and Latin American Studies (see 16.052)

• Administers the Foreign Study Service Office which advises students on study and travel abroad and organizes Western Michigan programs in China, Korea, Europe and Latin America

• Administers faculty and student exchange programs and aids in the development and implementation of international research, consulting and technical assistance

4.061
International Center
Macalester College
1600 Grand Ave.
St. Paul, MN 55105
(612) 696-6310

Contact(s):
David B. Sanford, Director
Virginia Schubert, Co-Director,
    International Studies Program

• Offers B.A. in International Studies, advises foreign students, administers American Language and Culture Program, and advises on study abroad

4.062
Intercultural Communication
University of Minnesota
Department of Speech-Communication
317 Folwell Hall
9 Pleasant St. SE
Minneapolis, MN 55455
(612) 373-2617

Contact(s):
William S. Howell, Coordinator

• Offers B.A., M.A. and Ph.D. with emphasis in intercultural communication and an orientation toward the international and the practical dimensions of the subject

4.063
International Relations Program
University of Minnesota
Institute of International Studies
1246 Social Science Bldg.
Minneapolis, MN 55455
(612) 373-2691

Contact(s):
Brian L. Job, Director

• Offers B.A. in International Relations with specialization in one of three curricula: general international relations, international development (with a strong Third World area studies component) or international/intercultural communication

4.064
Office of International Programs
University of Mississippi
University, MS 38677
(601) 232-7404

Contact(s):
Nolan Shepard, Director

• Administers Latin American Studies Program (see 0000), consults with faculty on international education programs in general, provides study abroad, faculty abroad and foreign student advising, and administers study abroad programs in Spain and England; sponsors community programs

4.065
International Studies
Lindenwood College
St. Charles, MO 63301
(314) 946-6912

Contact(s):
Aaron Miller, Coordinator

• B.A. in International Studies emphasizing international, political, economic, and cultural studies and study abroad (in Spain, France, Italy and Greece)

4.066
Center for International Studies
University of Missouri, St. Louis
8001 Natural Bridge Road
St. Louis, MO 63121
(314) 553-5753

Contact(s):
Edwin H. Fedder, Director

• Administers undergraduate certificate programs in International Studies (with a social science emphasis), East Asian Studies, Latin American Studies and European Studies
• Supports and facilitates research by Center Research Associates and other faculty
• Disseminates educational and curriculum materials on Chinese and Japanese culture to elementary and secondary schools through the Asia Resource Center in cooperation with the Continuing Education Extension (which publishes, along with the Missouri Council of the Asia Society, *Missouri Guide to Resources on Asia*)
• Publishes a monograph and occasional papers series

4.067
Office of International Studies
Washington University
Box 1088
St. Louis, MO 63130
(314) 889-6000

Contact(s):
Stanley Spector, Director

• Coordinates international programs in Asian Studies (see 13.068), Latin American Studies (see 16.056), Western European Studies, and International Development (see 6.147) and sponsors research and develops exchange relationships with foreign universities

4.068
Institute for International Studies
University of Nebraska, Lincoln
1034 Oldfather Hall
Lincoln, NE 68588-0320
(402) 472-3076

Contact(s):
Roberto Esquenazi-Mayo, Director

• Offers undergraduate majors in International Affairs, Latin American Studies (see 0000) and Western European Studies and minors in African Studies, Asian Studies and Slavic and East European Studies
• Conducts scholarly exchanges, especially with institutions in the PRC, and sponsors study abroad programs in seven countries

4.069
Office of International Studies and Programs
University of Nebraska, Omaha
238 Arts and Sciences Hall
Omaha, NE 68182
(402) 554-2376

Contact(s):
Thomas E. Gouttierre, Director

• Offers major in International Studies emphasizing a broad understanding of world civilizations, nation states, and the interrelationships of societies and nations; optional specializations in international management and business or a world area, especially Latin American Studies (see 16.058)
• Coordinates international programs including the Center for Afghan Studies (see 18.002), overseas study tours, and student and faculty exchange programs

4.070
Center for International Studies
Bergen Community College
400 Paramus Road
Paramus, NJ 07652
(201) 447-7167

Contact(s):
Lynda Icochea, Director

• Coordinates international education activity on campus; revises and develops curriculum to include international and cross-cultural components; administers International Studies area concentration; develops curriculum for international business concentrations; conducts faculty development programs; organizes short-term study abroad programs (the Dominican Republic, England, France, Italy, Mexico, Spain and Puerto Rico); arranges visits by foreign faculty; publishes a newsletter and conducts extensive extracurricular programs in international business, especially in the areas of trade and import/export issues

4.071
Graduate Institute of International Studies
Fairleigh Dickinson University
Teaneck, NJ 07666
(201) 692-2400

• M.A. in International Studies requiring concentration in both the social sciences and area studies (East Asia, Latin America, the Middle East, the Soviet Union or Eastern Europe)

4.072
International Center
Middlesex County College
Edison, NJ 08818
(201) 548-6000, Ext. 281

Contact(s):
Virgil H. Blanco, Director

• Offers major in International Studies; advises on study and faculty abroad opportunities and administers programs in four countries, including a nursing program in Ireland and a physical education program in Switzerland; advises foreign students

4.073
Council on International and Regional Studies
Princeton University
230 Palmer Hall
Princeton, NJ 08544
(609) 452-4720

Contact(s):
Ezra N. Suleiman, Chair

• Supervises interdepartmental programs on Africa (see 12.032), East Asia (see 13.070), Latin America, Europe, the Near East (see 17.027) and Russia (see 18.515) and cooperates with university research entities including the Center of International Studies (see 4.178) and the Office of Population Research (see 6.018), the Woodrow Wilson School of Public and International Affairs (see 6.149) and the School of Architecture

4.074
International Studies
Ramapo College of New Jersey
505 Ramapo Valley Road
Mahwah, NJ 07430
(201) 825-2800

Contact(s):
Dominick Palazzotto, Director

• Offers B.A. in International Studies covering social change and human development, comparative studies, and problems of humanity; also requires field work (overseas, in an ethnic community, at the UN or with an international organization or business) and either a concentration in Western Europe or international studies (involving study of a historical period, a global problem or a geographical area, e.g., Asia, Africa, Latin America or Europe)

4.075
International Studies
Rutgers University/University College
Robinson Bldg., History Department
Camden, NJ 08100
(609) 445-6108

Contact(s):
Marie G. Wanek, Advisor, History
  Department

• B.A. in International Studies with specialization in area studies (Asian, Latin American or Russian)

4.076
Office of International Programs
Seton Hall University
Student Center
South Orange, NJ 07079
(201) 761-9081

Contact(s):
Patrick J. Kennedy, Coordinator

• Coordinates international programs including Asian Studies (see 13.072), Russian Area Studies (certificate program), Bilingual Education (M.A.) and International Business (M.B.A.)
• Sponsors study abroad program in Mexico

4.077
Office of International Programs and Services
University of New Mexico
1717 Roma NE
Albuquerque, NM 87131
(505) 277-4032

Contact(s):
Gerald M. Slavin, Director

• Coordinates administration of Asian, European, and Russian Studies programs; sponsors international studies seminar; provides advisement to students and faculty interested in studying, teaching or conducting research abroad; conducts overseas summer sessions; administers Intensive English Institute; acts as liaison to community groups interested in international activities; administers student and faculty exchanges abroad; advises foreign students; publishes newsletters and directories

4.078
Center for International Studies
Adelphi University
South Ave.
Garden City, NY 11530
(516) 294-8700, Ext. 7625

Contact(s):
Mordechai Rozanski, Director and Associate Dean for International Studies
James M. Fennelly, Director, Transcultural Studies Program (Ext. 7700)

• Offers B.A. in Global Studies with complementary major in the disciplines or professional studies; emphasis on global issues and the study of a world area
• Administers study abroad programs and advises foreign students; conducts outreach programs for both the general community and the international business community; sponsors training programs and develops global education curriculum for elementary and secondary schools
• Offers M.A. in Transcultural Studies sponsored jointly by the Departments of Anthropology, Philosophy and Religious Studies; emphasis on examination of multicultural nature of world systems and cultural and conceptual issues which transcend the nation-state

4.079
Foreign Area Studies
Barnard College
Columbia University
321A Milbank Hall
New York, NY 10027
(212) 280-5417

Contact(s):
John Meskill, Chair
Gertrude Sakrawa, Co-chair

• B.A. in Foreign Area Studies with country or regional emphasis including Asia (see Oriental Studies, 13.074), Great Britain, Italy, Latin America, Russia or Western Europe

4.080
International Studies Program
City University of New York/City College
Convent Ave. at 138th St.
New York, NY 10031
(212) 690-5466 or 5467

Contact(s):
Sherrie Baver, Director

• Offers B.A. in International Studies emphasizing the social sciences and area studies; credit-bearing internships arranged at the UN and other business and educational organizations engaged in international activities

4.081
Center for International Service
The City University of New York/College of Staten Island
130 Stuyvesant Place, Room 701
Staten Island, NY 10301
(212) 390-7856

Contact(s):
Nan Sussman, Director

• Offers B.A. in International Studies and provides advisory services to foreign students, American students (on study abroad) and American faculty (on overseas research and teaching opportunities); sponsors study abroad in Italy, France and China and administers Intensive English Language Institute

4.082
Center for International Studies
Cornell University
170 Uris Hall
Ithaca, NY 14853
(607) 256-6370

Contact(s):
Davydd J. Greenwood, Director
Mary F. Katzenstein, Associate Director

• Supports international and comparative studies programs including student-developed international studies majors; research and teaching programs include: area studies (China-Japan, see 13.080; Latin America, see 16.067; South Asia, see 13.082; Southeast Asia, see 13.083; Russian and Soviet Studies, see 14.031; and Western Socie-

ties, see 15.017); problem-oriented programs (Peace Studies, see 5.010; International Political Economy; International Population, see 6.022; Participation and Labor-Managed Systems and Rural Development); and professional school programs (International Agriculture, see 6.020; International Business; International and Comparative Labor Relations, see 6.152; International Legal Studies, see 6.113; International Education (with particular emphasis on overseas study and fieldwork), International Nutrition, see 6.021; and International Studies in Planning, see 6.154)
• Coordinates study abroad activities and develops international internships

4.083
International Studies
Elmira College
Elmira, NY 14901
(607) 734-3911

Contact(s):
Teruo Kobayashi, Director
Michael Aung-Thwin, Asian History

• B.A. in International Studies with emphasis on politics, economics, history and area studies (European or Asian)
• Many study abroad programs available in Europe and Asia, including two in Japan and a Japanese internship for business majors
• Offers self-instructional Critical Languages Program in nine major languages

4.084
Friends World College
Plover Lane
Huntington, NY 11743
(516) 549-1102

Contact(s):
Lawrence Weiss, President
Arthur Meyer, Director of Admissions

Non-traditional liberal arts college offering an international program in which students live, study and work in two or more cultures

• Offers self-designed B.A. in most liberal arts disciplines, including area studies (European, Latin American, African, Asian and Middle Eastern); requires residential classroom study in two cultures other than the students' own, combined with language learning and field and/or internship experiences; students may pursue their field studies virtually anywhere in the world that is appropriate

• College maintains academic program centers with resident faculty in Costa Rica, Japan, India, Kenya, Israel, England and the U.S.

4.085
United Nations Graduate Certificate Program/Master of Science in Social Science
Long Island University/The Brooklyn
   Center
University Plaza
Brooklyn, NY 11201
(212) 834-6000, Ext. 3587 or 3598

Contact(s):
Dragos D. Kostich, Director

• Offers, within the Institute for the Study of International Organizations, a Certificate in United Nations Studies with M.S. in Social Science or M.A. in economics, political science, sociology or urban studies; focuses on the study of international organizations, specifically the UN, with particular attention given to operations of UN specialized agencies and the UN Development Programme; includes on-site research/internship at the UN, fortnightly briefing, attendance at sessions, etc.; special emphasis on training in policy-making

• Program also conducted at the Graduate Branch Campus, Dobbs Ferry, and in Manhattan near the UN

4.086
International Studies
Manhattan College
Riverdale, NY 10471
(212) 920-0100

Contact(s):
Edmond C. van den Bossche, Director

• B.A. in International Studies with emphasis on international politics, economics and area studies

4.087
International Studies
Manhattanville College
Purchase, NY 10577
(914) 946-9600

Contact(s):
Kwan Ha Yim, Director

• B.A. in International Studies with concentration in geographic area (East Asia, Latin America, Russia, Western Europe) or functional studies (international politics, economics, management, development and foreign policy); also offers preprofessional Certificate in International Management

4.088
International Studies Program
Mohawk Valley Community College
Room 375, Payne Hall
Utica, NY 13501
(315) 797-9530, Ext. 368

Contact(s):
Rose Danella, Coordinator

• Offers A.A. in International Studies emphasizing global perspectives, language and the social sciences

4.089
International College
Rockland Community College
145 College Road
Suffern, NY 10901
(914) 356-4650, Ext. 506

Contact(s):
Howard A. Berry, Coordinator

• Offers two-year A.A. degree in the humanities with emphasis on international/intercultural studies; includes on-campus study, community-based experience and overseas learning and travel; emphasis may be in world area, global problems, international service, languages (courses available in the commonly taught languages or in the less commonly taught languages through the Self-Study Language Service), ethnic/cultural heritage, or religious studies; overseas study opportunities available worldwide through Study Abroad Office (particularly strong in study programs in Israel); stress on service learning (placement in community service jobs with a strong educational dimension) including a Service-Learning Semester in Britain; establishment of a service-learning consortium in process; Assists in the design and implementation of international/intercultural curriculum units and conducts co-curricular program
• Administers English as a Second Language Institute

4.090
Interpersonal/Intercultural Communication
State University of New York at Albany
Department of Communication
HU355
1400 Washington Ave.
Albany, NY 12222
(518) 457-8470

Contact(s):
Kathleen Kendall, Chair

• Offers M.A. in Interpersonal/Intercultural Communication and a Ph.D. program in Sociology (cooperatively with the Department of Sociology) with a communication specialization and major in interpersonal/intercultural communication; emphasis on research and theory

4.091
Council on International Studies
State University of New York at Buffalo
414 Capen Hall
Amherst Campus
Buffalo, NY 14260
(716) 831-2000

Contact(s):
Edward Dudley, Director

• Supervises a variety of international studies programs

4.092
International Center
State University of New York, College at Oswego
102 Rich Hall
Oswego, NY 13126
(315) 341-2118

Contact(s):
José R. Pérez, Director of International Education
Saisuke Ieno, Foreign Student Advisor

• Offers B.A. in Area Studies with concentrations in Latin America, Middle East-Africa, Russia-Eastern Europe, Asia, and Africa, advises on study abroad and sponsors programs in England, France, Austria, Spain, Jamaica and, through the State University System, in Puerto Rico, Japan and China; advises foreign students

4.093
Foreign and Comparative Studies
Syracuse University
Maxwell School of Citizenship and Public
   Affairs
119 College Place
Syracuse, NY 13210
(315) 423-2552

Contact(s):
John D. Nagel, Director

Graduate, nondegree program established in 1975 to integrate major area studies offerings of the University in an effort to promote increased emphasis on multidisciplinary and comparative approaches to international studies University-wide
   • Specializations available in South Asian (see 13.089), Latin American (see 16.073), and African (see 12.045) Studies; publishes African, Latin American and South Asian Monograph Series; sponsors and supports research abroad, especially in developing countries
   • Syracuse also offers undergraduate degrees in Latin American, Russian and Eastern European (see 0000) and South Asian Studies and a professionally oriented International Relations program with an area studies option

4.094
International Studies
Utica College
Syracuse University
Burrstone Road
Utica, NY 13502
(315) 792-3157 or 3055

Contact(s):
Michael K. Simpson, Director

   • Offers B.A. in International Studies with an emphasis on both social science and cultural studies; includes an optional concentration in International Business (see 6.067)

4.095
Center for International Studies
Duke University
2101 Campus Drive
Durham, NC 27706
(919) 684-2765

Contact(s):
A. Kenneth Pye, Director
Charles Berquist, Chair, Comparative Area
   Studies

   • Coordinates area studies programs including South Asia (see 13.093, Islamic and Arabian Development (see 17.034), Soviet Union and Eastern European (see 14.034), Latin American and Canadian (see 18.049) studies programs; conducts outreach program for public school teachers and college faculty and serves as secretariat for Southern Atlantic States Association for Asian and African Studies; publishes monograph series on international subjects
   • Offers B.A. in Comparative Area Studies emphasizing the comparative, interdisciplinary study of world cultures and regions; study based in either humanities or social sciences with concentration in one world area along with additional courses in international relations, comparative studies or a second geographic area; areas of concentration available: Africa, East Asia, Latin America, the Middle East, Russia and South Asia

4.096
Office of International Programs
University of North Carolina at Chapel Hill
207 Caldwell Hall 009A
Chapel Hill, NC 27514
(919) 962-3094

Contact(s):
Joseph S. Tulchin, Director, International
   Programs
John Florin, Director, International Studies

• Offers B.A. in International Studies with emphasis on the social sciences and either area studies or global issues; coordinates B.A. degree programs in African (see 12.044), Latin American (see 16.074), Middle East (see 14.034), and Russian and East European (see 14.035) Studies; library contains strong collection of international materials, especially those generated by the Institute for Research in Social Science and those dealing with Latin America; administers study abroad programs, advises faculty on Fulbright and other grants and arranges scholarly exchanges; publishes newsletter

4.097

Center for International Studies

University of North Carolina at Charlotte
UNCC Station
Charlotte, NC 28223
(704) 597-2407

Contact(s):
Earl L. Backman, Director

• Offers International Studies concentration which can be combined with virtually every undergraduate liberal arts, professional or preprofessional program; broadly focused on world issues, geographic areas, etc. according to student interest; study abroad encouraged and made available in a number of countries
• Coordinates student exchange and study abroad opportunities for UNCC students
• Coordinates curriculum development and faculty enrichment; advises faculty on research and teaching opportunities abroad
• Advises foreign students and faculty and operates an intensive English language program
• Organizes seminars, workshops and other programs for community organizations
• Publishes newsletter, *International Studies Bulletin*

• Serves as secretariat for National Committee of International Studies and Programs Administrators (see 4.258)

4.098

Intercultural Studies Program

Warren Wilson College
Swannanoa, NC 28778
(704) 298-6008

Contact(s):
Carol Creager, Chair

• Offers B.A. with student-designed major or minor in Intercultural Studies including languages or area studies (Asian or Hispanic) concentration and an emphasis on the development of intercultural awareness; offers overseas study opportunities and the International Development Program, a one-year curriculum of international and development studies culminating in an overseas service experience

4.099

Antioch International

Antioch University
Admissions Office-IMA
Yellow Springs, OH 45387
(513) 767-1031 or 2661

Contact(s):
Paula Spier, Dean

• Offers individualized M.A. program that enables student to construct own course of study in virtually any discipline; emphasis on interdisciplinary, experiential and cross-cultural learning in seminars, workshops, internships and field study in the U.S. and at Antioch Centres in Britain, Germany and elsewhere

4.100
International Studies Program
Ashland College
Department of Social Science
Ashland, OH 44805
(419) 289-4194

Contact(s):
Jae Hyung Chai, Chair

- Offers B.A. in International Studies with broad interdisciplinary focus

4.101
International Studies
Baldwin Wallace College
Berea, OH 44017
(216) 826-2231

Contact(s):
Andrew Talton, Director, International
   Studies Office
Judy Krukty, Advisor, International Studies
   Major

- Offers B.A. in International Studies, advises students and faculty on overseas opportunities and conducts programs abroad

4.102
International Studies Program
Bowling Green State University
Political Science Department
227 Williams Hall
Bowling Green, OH 43403
(419) 372-2921

Contact(s):
William O. Reichert, Chair

- B.A. in International Studies with concentration in area studies (the Middle East, the Soviet Union, Eastern Europe and Western Europe); overseas study strongly recommended (Bowling Green conducts programs in Spain, France and Germany)

4.103
Cultural Area Studies
College of Wooster
Russian Studies Department
Wooster, OH 44691
(216) 263-2000

Contact(s):
Joel L. Wilkinson, Chair

- Offers B.A. in Cultural Area Studies with area concentrations in African, East Asian, Middle Eastern and Islamic, Indian, Russian or Modern Western European Studies; overseas study required; overseas international programs available in approximately 25 countries in all world regions through programs sponsored by Wooster, the Great Lakes Colleges Association (see 8.015) and other organizations

4.104
Academic Programs Abroad
Lake Erie College for Women
Painesville, OH 44077
(216) 352-3361

Contact(s):
Ernest Pick, Director

- Lake Erie requires Academic Term Abroad emphasizing both academic studies and the intercultural experience; programs in Spain, the Netherlands, Israel, Britain, Italy, Mexico and France (open to non-Lake Erie students as well)
- Business students may study at the École de Commerce in France as well as at the University of Tubingen in Germany

4.105
International Studies
Miami University
Langstroth International Center
Oxford, OH 45056
(513) 529-2431

Contact(s):
Howell C. Lloyd, Director

• Offers B.A. in International Studies with emphasis on political and economic relations, area studies, and foreign language; year abroad strongly recommended at Miami University European Center in Luxembourg or other accredited programs. Sponsors summer language study in French, Italian and German and a student exchange in Japan

4.106
Non-Western Studies
Mount Union College
Alliance, OH 44601
(216) 821-5320, Ext. 256

Contact(s):
George L. Montagno, Director

• Offers B.A. in Non-Western Studies with emphasis on South and East Asian cultures

4.107
University Center for International Studies
The Ohio State University
308 Dulles Hall
230 West 17th Ave.
Columbus, OH 43210
(614) 422-9661

Contact(s):
Jan S. Adams, Director

• Offers B.A. in International Studies with specializations in East Asian, Latin American, Middle Eastern or Soviet/East European studies or in more broadly international subjects such as international relations, comparative studies of developing nations, national security studies, etc.; supervises East Asian (see 13.098), Latin American,

Middle Eastern (see 17.036) and Slavic and East European (see 14.033) studies centers and programs; provides study, research and faculty abroad advising; conducts summer overseas programs including language programs in France, Spain and Russia, business programs in France and Japan, and pre-law, architecture and liberal arts programs in Britain; offers community outreach services, especially from the East Asian and Middle Eastern Studies Centers; publishes newsletters and directories (OSU also maintains an International Programs Director in the Office of Academic Affairs, an International Student and Scholar Services Office and an International Affairs in Agriculture Office, and offers Black Studies, B.A. with a strong African component (see 12.047)

4.108
Center for International Studies
Ohio University
Athens, OH 45701
(614) 594-5542

Contact(s):
Felix V. Gagliano, Director

• Offers B.A. in International Studies and M.A. in International Affairs with emphasis on development studies, international administration or area studies; may obtain certificate in African (see 12.048), Latin American (see 16.078) or Southeast Asian (see 13.099) studies

4.109
Center for International Studies
University of Toledo
2801 West Bancroft St.
Toledo, OH 43606
(419) 537-4151/2940

Contact(s):
Abid A. Al-Marayati, Director

• Administers major programs in International Relations, Asian Studies (see 13.101), European Studies (see 15.018), Latin American Studies (see 16.079) and the Middle East and supervises the office of the advisor for study abroad; sponsors conferences and other internationally oriented activities

4.110
Office of International Programs
Oklahoma State University
Center for Global Studies
132 Seretean Center
Stillwater, OK 74078
(405) 624-6535

Contact(s):
William S. Abbott, Director, Office of
   International Programs
Hugh F. Rouk, Director, International
   Education
Azim Nanji, Director, Center for Global
   Studies, College of Liberal Arts

• Administers undergraduate programs in Asian, African, Latin American and Russian Studies and advises students and faculty on overseas opportunities

4.111
International Studies
Mt. Hood Community College
26000 S.E. Stark
Gresham, OR 97030
(503) 667-7305

Contact(s):
Betty J. Pritchett, Dean of Development
   and Special Programs
Mathilda Harris, Coordinator of
   International Education

• Offers two-year program in international studies including an area concentration and global studies

4.112
Intercultural Communication
Portland State University
Department of Communication
Portland, OR 97207
(503) 229-3607

Contact(s):
LaRay Barna, Director

• Offers M.A. in Communication with specialization in intercultural communication

4.113
Office of International Studies
Portland State University
131 Neuberger Hall
Portland, OR 97207
(503) 229-4011

Contact(s):
Charles M. White, Director

• Supervises language and area studies certificate programs including those for Central Europe (see 14.040), Latin America, the Middle East (see 17.037), international business and study abroad; advises students and faculty on overseas opportunities and conducts other international education programs

4.114
International Studies
Reed College
Portland, OR 97202
(503) 771-1112

Contact(s):
Claude Vaucher, Director

• Offers interdisciplinary B.A. in International Studies with broad humanities and social science focus

4.115
International Studies Program
University of Oregon
241 Straub Hall
Eugene, OR 97403-1227
(503) 686-5051

Contact(s):
Clarence E. Thurber, Director

• Offers B.A. and M.A. in International Studies; B.A. focuses on international relations, cultural area and global issues and the M.A. on a non-Western culture, a functional area (trade, foreign policy, etc.) or a world issue, (human rights, development, etc.); cultural areas of emphasis: Asia, Latin America, Russia and Eastern Europe; special interest in Pacific Basin Studies; study abroad opportunities available in a number of countries; publishes *International Studies Newsletter*

4.116
International Studies Program
Willamette University
900 State St.
Salem, OR 97301
(503) 370-6303

Contact(s):
Theodore Shay, Chair

• Offers B.A. in International Studies with three components or foci: global (especially international politics), regional (Western Europe, Eastern Europe, Hispanic, East Asia) and single country/culture

4.117
International Studies
Allegheny College
Meadville, PA 16335
(814) 724-4342

Contact(s):
Jonathan E. Helmreich, Director

• Offers B.A. in International Studies

4.118
International Studies
Dickinson College
Carlisle, PA 17013
(717) 245-1220/1280

Contact(s):
K. Robert Nilsson, Director

• B.A. in International Studies emphasizing international politics and area studies

4.119
Center for International Studies
Indiana University of Pennsylvania
Indiana, PA 15705
(412) 357-2295

Contact(s):
Robert Morris, Director

• Coordinates international studies concentrations in Education (B.A. and M.A. in Social Studies; includes a foreign area specialization), Public Affairs (M.A. in International Service) and Business (M.B.A.); administers study abroad programs in Japan, Hong Kong, Bangladesh and India and advises faculty on overseas opportunities

4.120
International Studies
Juniata College
Huntingdon, PA 16652
(814) 643-4310

Contact(s):
Professors Reed, Kipphan and Vocke,
    Advisors

• Offers B.A. with emphasis on social sciences and study abroad

4.121
International Affairs Program
Lafayette College
Easton, PA 18042
(215) 250-5394 or 253-5390

Contact(s):
Ilan Peleg, Director

• Offers interdepartmental B.A. in International Affairs with emphasis on political science, history, economics, and foreign language; study abroad encouraged

4.122
Foreign Careers Program
Lehigh University
Bethlehem, PA 18015
(215) 861-3141

Contact(s):
Alvin Cohen, Director

• Offers B.A. emphasizing social science analysis, a foreign area concentration (Latin America, Europe, Russia) and either foreign trade or public administration

4.123
International Studies
Lock Haven State College
International Education
Lock Haven, PA 17745
(717) 893-2140

Contact(s):
Jorge J. Mottet, Director

• B.A. in International Studies with emphasis on international political and economic studies and either area studies or international business

4.124
International Studies
Lycoming College
Williamsport, PA 17701
(717) 326-1951

Contact(s):
Robert Larson, Coordinator

• Offers B.A. with emphasis on political and economic relations of the North Atlantic Community

4.125
Educational Linguistics Program
University of Pennsylvania
Graduate School of Education
3700 Walnut St.
Philadelphia, PA 19104
(215) 898-4800

Contact(s):
Nessa Wolfson, Director

• Offers M.S. in Intercultural Communication, a professional program focusing on problems which arise in education, government, industry and other areas as a result of differences in cultural background

4.126
International Relations
University of Pennsylvania
Philadelphia, PA 19104
(215) 898-7654

Contact(s):
C. A. Lee, Chair

• Offers M.A. and Ph.D. in International Relations with study concentrated in functional fields (international relations theory, comparative politics, diplomatic history, foreign and international diplomacy, political and economic development and international business, economics, law and organization) and regional fields (Africa, East Asia, Latin America, the Middle East, South Asia, the Soviet Union and Western Europe)

4.127
Center for International Studies
University of Pittsburgh
Forbes Quadrangle
Pittsburgh, PA 15260
(412) 624-4141

Contact(s):
Burkhart Holzner, Director

• Administers Asian (see 13.109), Latin American (see 16.085), Russian and East European (see 14.043) and West European Studies programs, along with the International and Global Studies Program (which includes the International Security Studies Program, the Institute for Strategic Economics and Industrial Vulnerability and the Regional Structural Change Project), the Contemporary China Program, International Education Studies Program, and the Pennsylvania Ethnic Heritage Center
• Publishes occasional papers and other materials in conjunction with the study programs and produces free bi-annual UCIS International Newsletter
• Conducts school outreach program including in-service workshops, consulting and assistance in curriculum development and the provision of teaching resources

4.128
International Studies
Wilkes College
Political Science Department
Wilkes-Barre, PA 18766
(717) 824-4651, Ext. 265

Contact(s):
Jean Driscoll, Director

• B.A. in International Studies with emphasis on history and the social sciences

4.129
Department of History and International Studies
York College of Pennsylvania
York, PA 17405
(717) 846-7788

Contact(s):
Chin H. Suk, Chairman

• B.A. in International Studies with emphasis on history, the social sciences and intercultural studies (introductory area studies)

4.130
International Studies Program
University of South Carolina
Department of Government and
   International Studies
Columbia, SC 29208
(803) 777-3108

Contact(s):
Gordon B. Smith, Graduate Director

• Offers B.A., M.A. and Ph.D. in International Studies emphasizing international relations theory, foreign policy analysis, national security affairs, and comparative politics/area studies

4.131
Office of International Studies
Memphis State University
Memphis, TN 38152
(901) 454-2813

Contact(s):
James K. Muskelley, Director

• Coordinates teaching, research and

overseas service; supervises academic programs in international business, international relations, African studies (see 12.053), and Latin American studies; and advises on overseas study

4.132
Third World Studies
The University of the South
Department of History
Sewanee, TN 37375
(615) 598-5931, Ext. 322

Contact(s):
Harold J. Goldberg, Chair

• Offers B.A. in Third World Studies with a focus on culture, social, economic, and political development; encompasses most of the nations of Africa, Asia, Latin America and the Middle East

4.133
Global Studies Program
St. Edward's University
3001 South Congress Ave.
Austin, TX 78704
(512) 444-2621

Contact(s):
Don E. Post, Director

• Offers Certificate in Global Studies with emphasis on Third World countries; arranges internships (in Asia, Africa and Latin America) related to career goals of students

4.134
Global Affairs and International Relations Program
St. Mary's University
One Camino Santa Maria
San Antonio, TX 78284
(512) 436-3313

Contact(s):
Gary Gordon, Chair

• Offers M.A. in Global Affairs and International Relations with emphasis on political relationships and a specialization in culture, economics, Inter-American, or European Studies

4.135
International Studies
Southwest Texas State University
Evans Academic Center, Room 313
San Marcos, TX 78666
(512) 245-2143

Contact(s):
Robert Gorman, Director

• B.A. in International Studies with concentration in international relations or area studies (Inter-American, European, Asian, Middle East and African)

4.136
International Studies
Southwestern University
Georgetown, TX 78626
(512) 863-6511

• Offers broadly focused B.A. in International Studies; requires foreign study or comparable intercultural experience

4.137
International and Comparative Studies Program
Trinity University
Department of Foreign Languages
715 Stadium Drive
San Antonio, TX 78284
(512) 736-7531

Contact(s):
Gary L. Chancellor, Chair

• Offers B.A. in International and Comparative Studies with specialization in international affairs, Asian studies, European studies or inter-American studies

4.138
Center for International Studies
University of St. Thomas
3812 Montrose Blvd.
Houston, TX 77006
(713) 522-7911, Ext. 394

Contact(s):
William J. Cunningham, Director

• Offers B.A. in International Studies with emphasis either on cultural studies or professional and management skills; requires internship or study abroad and four years of language study; sponsors supporting activities and conducts seminars on international business for local firms

4.139
International Office
University of Texas at Austin
Drawer A
University Station
Austin, TX 78712
(512) 471-9283

Contact(s):
Joe W. Neal, Director

• Coordinates international programs at the University and collaborates with Institute of Latin American Studies (see 16.097), Center for Middle Eastern Studies (see 17.041), Center for Asian Studies (see 13.113) and the International Studies Program
• Administers international program grants and contracts
• Provides advising on study and research opportunities abroad for students and faculty, advises foreign students, and administers intensive English as a foreign language program
• Coordinative headquarters for the Texas Consortium of International Education and the Texas Association of International Education Administrators

4.140
David M. Kennedy Center for International Studies
Brigham Young University
Provo, UT 84602
(801) 378-3377

Contact(s):
Stanley Turner, Director

• Coordinating center for a variety of programs and services including: Asian Studies (see 13.114), Canadian Studies (see 18.050), European Studies (see 15.021), International Relations (offers B.A. and M.A.), Latin American Studies (see 16.099), and Near Eastern Studies (see 17.042), Publications Services and Resource Services (see 2.056)

4.141
International Programs and Studies
Utah State University
Military Science Bldg. 216
Logan, UT 84321
(801) 750-1106

Contact(s):
E. Boyd Wennergren, Director

• Offers area study certificate programs in East-West Relations and the Causes of War and Conditions for Peace and administers a number of international development and/or technical assistance programs and institutes

4.142
Language Schools
Middlebury College
Middlebury, VT 05753
(802) 388-3711, Ext. 5509

Contact(s):
Edward C. Knox, Director

• Offers B.A. in East Asian Studies (see 13.116) and B.A. with International Major consisting of a major in a non-language/literature discipline, including study of that discipline in a foreign language at one of the Middlebury College Schools Abroad (or the equivalent); schools abroad maintained in Paris, Florence, Madrid, Mainz and Moscow; other study abroad opportunities available; immersion language and culture study programs offered on campus each summer in Arabic, Chinese, French, German, Italian, Japanese, Russian and Spanish

4.143
International Studies Program
Norwich University
Northfield, VT 05663
(802) 485-5011, Ext. 235

Contact(s):
Thomas F. Taylor, Director

• Offers B.A. in International Studies with concentration in history, government, international economics or modern languages

4.144
School for International Training
Kipling Road
Brattleboro, VT 05301
(802) 257-7751

Contact(s):
John Middleton, Director

Accredited senior college and graduate school for international/intercultural education and language studies; founded by the Experiment in International Living (see 3.019) in 1964
• Offers Bachelor of International Studies (2 years, upper division) in World Issues Program which includes two semesters on campus and two semesters of internships in the U.S. and/or abroad, and a Master of Arts in Teaching (languages) providing one year of intensive language study, living with a host family, multidisciplinary course work, field research training, and an independent study project; also offers a 15-week credit-bearing College Semester Abroad Program in approximately 12 countries and an intensive Foreign Language Program
• Offers M.A. in Intercultural Administration (see 6.162), and an International Students of English Program (see 10.033)

4.145
Center for Area and International Studies
University of Vermont
479 Main St.
Burlington, VT 05405
(802) 656-4062

Contact(s):
Thomas H. Geno, Director

• Coordinates undergraduate area studies programs at the University including Canadian Studies (see 18.051), European Studies (see 15.022), Latin American Studies (see 16.100) and Russian and East European Studies (see 14.047); strong selection of courses also available in African and Asian Studies which are not presently offered as a major

4.146
International Studies Program
George Mason University
State University in Northern Virginia
Department of Public Affairs
4400 University Drive
Fairfax, VA 22030
(703) 323-2000

Contact(s):
Harold Gortner, Chair

• Offers B.A. in International Studies

4.147
International Studies Programs
Old Dominion University
Norfolk, VA 23508

Contact(s):
Phillip A. Taylor, Director, International
 Studies, Department of Political Science
 and Geography
 (804) 440-4643
Willard C. Frank, Director, Strategy and
 Policy, Department of History
 (804) 440-3949

• Offers undergraduate certificate program emphasizing world interdependence, global issues, and the developing countries
• Offers M.A. in International Studies with two tracks: International Service and International Resource Management
• Offers graduate Certificate in Strategy and Policy

4.148
International Studies
Virginia Polytechnic Institute and State
 University
Department of Political Science
Blacksburg, VA 24060
(703) 961-6814

Contact(s):
C. L. Taylor, Director

• B.A. emphasizing functional studies (political science and economics), cultural studies (differing cultural patterns) and languages

4.149
International Studies Program
Virginia State University
Box 4002-N
Petersburg, VA 23803
(804) 520-5122

Contact(s):
Stephen K. Ainsworth, Director

• Offers B.A. in International Studies, advises on student and faculty opportunities abroad and administers study programs in the Caribbean and France

4.150
International Affairs Program
Eastern Washington University
Cheney, WA 99004
(509) 359-2363

Contact(s):
Ernst W. Gohlert, Director

• Offers B.A. in International Affairs with emphasis on social science and cultural studies; study/travel abroad strongly recommended

4.151
The Henry M. Jackson School of
International Studies
Thomson Hall DR-05
University of Washington
Seattle, WA 98195
(206) 543-4370

Contact(s):
Kenneth B. Pyle, Director
David J. Cordell, Director of Student
 Services

• Offers B.A. in International Studies (emphasis on world issues and the interaction of politics, economics and culture within the global system), Comparative Religion, Jewish

Studies. B.A. and M.A. in Chinese Studies (see 18.072), Japanese Studies (see 18.274), Korean Studies (see 18.310), Russian and East European Studies (see 14.049) and South Asian Studies (see 13.125), and an M.A. in Middle Eastern Studies (see 17.045); an M.A. in International Studies (emphasis on political, economic and cultural interactions with states and societies around the world) is offered concurrently with graduate degree programs in Business Administration, Forest Resources, Law, Marine Studies, and Public Affairs.

4.152
International Affairs Program
Marshall University
Department of Political Science
Huntington, WV 25701
(304) 696-6636

Contact(s):
Clair W. Matz, Director

• Offers B.A. in International Affairs with a foreign language and social science emphasis

4.153
International Studies
University of Wisconsin-Milwaukee
Milwaukee, WI 53201
(414) 963-4252

Contact(s):
David Garnham, Coordinator

• Offers B.A. with four optional specializations: international relations and American foreign policy, underdeveloped areas, regional studies, and international economics

4.154
International Studies Program
University of Wisconsin at Oshkosh
Polk 114
Oshkosh, WI 54901
(414) 424-1291

Contact(s):
Kenneth J. Grieb, Coordinator

• B.A. in International Studies with broad emphasis on social sciences and humanities, including area studies (Asian, Latin American, European and African)

4.155
International Studies
University of Wisconsin at Whitewater
Department of Political Science
Whitewater, WI 53190
(414) 472-1168

Contact(s):
Robert L. Rothweiler, Director

• B.A. and B.S. in International Studies with emphasis on political, sociological, economic, cultural and foreign language studies

4.156
International Studies
University of Wyoming
Laramie, WY 82071
(307) 766-6484

Contact(s):
Cal Clark, Director

• B.A. and M.A. in International Studies with option to concentrate in a social science discipline, a world area (Africa-Middle East, Asia, Latin America, Soviet Union and Eastern Europe, or Western Europe), international development or ecology

Research Centers

4.157
California Institute of International Studies
766 Santa Ynez
Stanford, CA 94305
(415) 322-2026

Contact(s):
Ronald Hilton, Executive Director

Independent nonprofit research center
   • Conducts research on international affairs with particular emphasis on Soviet foreign policy; publishes monographs and, since 1970, the quarterly *World Affairs Report* (complete text from first issue available on line from DIALOG)

4.158
Center for Research in International Studies
Stanford University
200 Lou Henry Hoover Bldg.
Stanford, CA 94305
(415) 497-4581

Contact(s):
Robert E. Ward, Director

Major university center for development and coordination of international studies and research
   • Develops programs to enhance teaching and research about international subjects, coordinates campus wide language and area studies programs, administers grants for international studies and research, assists in financing research, student fellowships, library development and new faculty appointments; administers Stanford Program in International and Cross-Cultural Education—SPICE (precollege curriculum development, see 2.061); Inter-University Center for Japanese Language Studies, in Tokyo (see 18.277) and Inter-University Center for Chinese Studies, in Taipei (see 18.469)

4.159
Hoover Institution on War, Revolution and Peace
Stanford University
Stanford, CA 94305
(415) 497-1754

Contact(s):
W. Glenn Campbell, Director
John H. Moore, Acting Deputy Director
George Marotta, Public Affairs Coordinator

Archives, library, research institution and press located on Stanford University campus
   • International Studies Program sponsors research by staff and fellows on a wide range of international political, economic and social issues, including such subjects as public policy, African colonialism, post-Mao China, international communism, non-Russian nationalities in the USSR, and the role of education in war, revolution, peace and development; Domestic Studies Program sponsors research on such topics as energy, taxation, health and government regulation
   • Hoover Institution Press (see 11.015) publishes extensive list of books and monographs on the above subjects, including *Yearbook of International Communist Affairs*
   • Houses archives and large collections of materials on Africa, East Asia, Eastern Europe, Latin America, the Middle East, Western Europe and North America; collection consists of approximately 1.5 million volumes, 25,000 periodical titles and files of approximately 6,000 newspapers, including large collections of ephemera and approximately 4,000 collections of personal papers and organizational records; particularly strong in

materials for modern/revolutionary times in Japan, China, Russia, and Eastern, Central and Western Europe; descriptive brochures available for East Asian, Russian and East European, and Central and Western European collections

• Scholars and fellows consult with government and other organizations, and teach and advise on international and domestic affairs

• Sponsors National Fellows Program for Young Scholars (see 7.014)

4.160
Center for International and Strategic Affairs
University of California at Los Angeles
11383 Bunche Hall
Los Angeles, CA 90024
(213) 825-0604 or 6446

Contact(s):
Michael D. Intriligator, Director

• Sponsors and conducts research on international security, strategic policy and doctrine, and the economic and technological aspects of arms control and nuclear proliferation with an emphasis on how they affect Europe, the Middle East and Africa; develops courses and instructional computer simulations; publishes *Working Papers* and *Research Notes* series and a book series "Studies in International and Strategic Affairs"; sponsors conferences and seminars and conducts scholarly exchange programs with institutions in Europe, the Middle East and Africa

4.161
Center for the Study of Comparative Folklore and Mythology
University of California at Los Angeles
Los Angeles, CA 90024
(213) 825-4242

Contact(s):
Patrick K. Ford, Acting Director

• Conducts research on American and comparative folklore, balladry and folk song, comparative classical and Indo-European mythology, and mythologies of other peoples; sponsors conferences, symposia, lectures and seminars; publications include the newsletter, *Folklore and Mythology,* an Annual Report and occasional volumes on selected topics in folklore and mythology

• Maintains reference library of 5,000 volumes on folklore and mythology and a Visual Media Archive of photographic prints, films, video-tapes, color microfiche (including more than 25,000 slides) and a microfilm copy of the Finnish Folklore Archives in Helsinki

4.162
Foreign Area Studies
American University
5010 Wisconsin Ave. NW
Washington, DC 20016
(202) 686-2288

Research program established in 1958 under a contract with the U.S. Department of the Army

• Conducts research for and writes the individual volumes of Country Studies Series (formerly Area Handbook Series) of basic background studies of approximately 110 countries and/or regions of the world (see 2.189)

4.163
The Brookings Institution
1775 Massachusetts Ave. NW
Washington, DC 20036
(202) 797-6000

Contact(s):
James D. Carroll, Director, Advanced Study
  Program

Major research organization for the study of national and international economic and political policies

• Conducts research and arranges seminars and advanced study programs for American business and government executives focusing on business-government relations and on key national and international policy issues

• Publications include extensive list of books on international political, economic and security issues particularly as they relate to U.S. foreign policy

4.164

Center for International Policy
120 Maryland Ave. NE
Washington, DC 20002
(202) 544-4666

Contact(s):
Donald L. Ranard, Director
William Goodfellow, Deputy Director

Project of the Fund for Peace (see 4.179) which studies the impact of U.S. foreign policy on human rights and social and economic conditions in the Third World

• Conducts research, prepares articles and reports, issues press releases on U.S. foreign aid and the activities of the World Bank and other international funding institutions, and proposes ways that human rights and the basic needs of people can be met more effectively in aid grants and loans

• Publishes *International Policy Report* (6–8 reports per year) and *Indochina Issues* (see 13.172)

4.165

Center for Strategic & International Studies
Georgetown University
1800 K St. NW, Suite 400
Washington, DC 20006
(202) 887-0200

Contact(s):
Amos A. Jordan, President

Research center designed to provide U.S. leadership with scholarly perspectives on and a forum for the examination of critical international issues

• Sponsors research, prepares studies and organizes seminars in the following areas: U.S. foreign policy (including "Congressional Outreach," a series of briefings, seminars and study groups aimed at members of the U.S. House and Senate), the Soviet Union, political/military issues, world power, energy, national resources and security, international business, maritime policy, science, technology and arms control, international communications and world regional affairs

• Publishes *The Washington Papers* (see 1.097) and *The Washington Quarterly*

4.166

Institute of Comparative Social and Cultural Studies Inc.
4330 East-West Highway, Suite 900
Washington, DC 20814
(301) 656-7996

Contact(s):
Lorand B. Szalay, Director

• Conducts research on cultural perceptions and other psychocultural issues designed for use in comparative cultural studies and for application in such areas as language training, international education and mental health training

4.167

Woodrow Wilson International Center for Scholars
Smithsonian Institution Bldg.
Washington, DC 20560
(202) 357-2429

Non-profit research center affiliated with the Smithsonian Institution

• Sponsors and provides fellowships for research on international security, Latin America, the Caribbean, inter-American affairs, East Asia, American-Asian relations, and the Soviet Union (within the Kennan Institute for Advanced Russian Studies, see 18.540)

• Publishes the *Wilson Quarterly* and a series of *Scholars Guides* to research facilities and resources in Washington, D.C., for African Studies (see 12.083), Central and East European Studies (see 14.067), Asian Studies (see 13.155), Latin American and Caribbean Studies (see 16.144), and Middle Eastern Studies (see 17.071)

4.168
Center for Strategic and Foreign Policy Studies
5828 South University Ave.
Chicago, IL 60637
(312) 962-8074

Contact(s):
Morton A. Kaplan, Director

Independent research center based at the University of Chicago

• Conducts research on the strategic dimensions of U.S. foreign policy, arms control negotiations and world communism; publishes project reports

4.169
Folklore Institute
Indiana University
504 North Fess St.
Bloomington, IN 47401
(812) 335-8049

Contact(s):
Linda Degh, Director

• Maintains the Archives of Folklore collection, conducts research and teaches folklore classes; publishes *Journal of Folklore, Indiana Folklore,* a monograph series and occasional individual studies; Archives open to visiting scholars

4.170
Center for International Affairs
Harvard University
6 Divinity Ave.
Cambridge, MA 02138
(617) 495-2965

Contact(s):
Samuel P. Huntington, Director
Grant T. Hammond, Executive Officer

• Conducts research and sponsors seminars on U.S. foreign relations, comparative economic, social and political processes, North-South relations, regional studies and contemporary global issues; publishes *Policy Papers Series* and *Harvard Series in International Affairs;* conducts workshops for public leaders and invites 20–25 senior officials from abroad to the Center as Fellows each year; maintains library of approximately 50,000 volumes on international affairs

4.171
Center for International Studies
Massachusetts Institute of Technology
E38-648
Cambridge, MA 02139
(617) 253-3140

Contact(s):
Eugene B. Skolnikoff, Director

• Research center for faculty and graduate students focusing on the international dimension of contemporary issues such as scientific and technological change, arms control, energy, nutrition, environment, communication, development, business, conflict and migration

4.172
World Peace Foundation
Curtis-Saval International Center
22 Batterymarch St.
Boston, MA 02109
(617) 482-3875

Contact(s):
Richard J. Bloomfield, Director and
  Secretary

Nonprofit organization designed to foster public understanding of international relations with a view to furthering the development of policies that will promote a peaceful world
  • Sponsors research in three principal areas: (1) interdependence and the process of change in the international order, (2) international organization and (3) interregional problems
  • Publishes *International Organization* (see 1.086) and arranges for publication of sponsored studies

4.173
Harold Scott Quigley Center of International Studies
University of Minnesota
1246 Social Sciences Bldg.
Minneapolis, MN 55455
(612) 373-2691

Contact(s):
P. Terrence Hopmann, Director

  • Conducts research on full range of international relations issues including foreign policy and political, economic, security, disarmament, world order and communications issues; part of academic program of the Hubert H. Humphrey Institute of Public Affairs (see 6.144); publishes monograph series and maintains library

4.174
The Institute for Advanced Studies of World Religions
2150 Center Ave.
Fort Lee, NJ 07024
(201) 461-8646
and
State University of New York at Stony Brook
Melville Memorial Library
Stony Brook, NY 11794-3383
(516) 246-8362

Contact(s):
C. T. Shen, President
Richard A. Gard, Director of Institute
  Services
Christopher S. George, Director of
  Research

Nonprofit educational foundation designed to encourage and facilitate the study and practice of world religions
  • Collects, analyzes and preserves religious materials; maintains library of 60,000-plus volumes, 280 current and 575 noncurrent periodical titles, 30,000 manuscripts on microfilm in 15 Asian languages and a number of Western languages; active program in locating scarce materials, preserving them, and offering them at cost on microfilm and microfiche; particularly strong in Buddhism, Hinduism and Jainism; library catalogues being developed for Chinese and Tibetan material to be published in book form
  • Provides bibliographic, research, and other informational services; periodically issues special bibliographies under the following titles: *Buddhist Text Information, Buddhist Research Information, Sikh Religious Studies Information,* and *Hindu Text Information* (sample copies available on request)
  • Joins other institutions in projects which facilitate the study of and research into world religions
  • Conducts translation program emphasizing the translation of basic texts and commentaries into Western languages; especially active in translating Tibetan materials

• Promotes and carries out research with emphasis on providing research tools of use to scholars and students, including development of computer software

• Publishes selected religious works, particularly Buddhist and Hindu in the IASWR series

• Sponsors lectures and conferences on religious issues

4.175
Center of International Studies
Princeton University
Corwin Hall
Princeton, NJ 08544
(609) 452-4851

Contact(s):
Cyril E. Black, Director

• Conducts research within the framework of a World Order Studies Program focusing on international politics, foreign policy, security, international organization and modernization with the aim of developing systematic, rigorous, and comprehensive analyses of international issues and U.S. foreign policy

• Publishes the quarterly *World Politics* (see 1.101) and other studies and monographs including the Policy Memorandum Series, Research Monograph Series and Occasional Papers on the World Order Program

4.176
Center for the Study of Human Rights
Columbia University
704 International Affairs Bldg.
420 West 118th St.
New York, NY 10027
(212) 280-2479

Contact(s):
J. Paul Martin, Executive Director
Arthur Danto, Mitchell Ginsberg and Louis
  Henkin, Co-Directors

• Promotes research on and teaching about human rights and the development of curriculum in human rights studies; conducts seminars and an Annual International Symposium on human rights issues; publishes scholarly papers, syllabi for graduate and undergraduate instruction and other materials including Human Rights: A Topical Bibliography (with Westview Press, see 11.034)

4.177
Institute of War and Peace Studies
Columbia University
International Affairs Bldg.
420 West 118th St.
New York, NY 10027
(212) 280-4616

Contact(s):
Warner R. Schilling, Director

• Promotes research and conducts seminars and sponsors publications on peace and security, foreign policy, arms control, international and comparative politics and international institutions; administers Canadian Studies Program, which promotes teaching and research on Canadian subjects

4.178
Research Institute on International Change
Columbia University
International Affairs Bldg.
420 West 118th St.
New York, NY 10027
(212) 280-4638

Contact(s):
Seweryn Bialer, Director

• Promotes research and conducts seminars and sponsors publications on global political changes that affect international relations; includes strong emphasis on the study of communism along with other subjects such as economic development, technology transfer, nationalism, and radicalism, nuclear arms, etc.; publishes semiannual *Global Political Assessment*, a condensed interpretive survey of key events and trends in international affairs

4.179
The Fund for Peace
345 East 46th St.
New York, NY 10017
(212) 661-5900

Contact(s):
James F. Tierney, Executive Director

Nonprofit educational and research organization concerned with world problems that threaten human survival
    • Sponsors research and education projects furthering its aims, including the Center for International Policy (see 4.164), the Institute for the Study of World Politics, the Center for Defense Information (which monitors U.S. defense expenditures), and the Center for National Security Studies (which monitors U.S. national security legislation and practices)

4.180
Center for International Studies
New York University
40 Washington Square South
New York, NY 10012
(212) 598-7644

Contact(s):
Thomas M. Franck, Director

    • Conducts research from legal, economic, political and social perspectives on international political issues, particularly on political change, economic aspects of international relations and the settlement of con-

flicts and disputes; scholars-in-residence program for visiting researchers; publishes books, monographs and reports including the series *Studies in Peaceful Change*

4.181
The Congress on Research in Dance
New York University
Dance and Dance Education Department
35 West 4th St., Room 675
New York, NY 10003
(212) 598-3459

Contact(s):
I. Rouse, Administrative Secretary

Nonprofit educational and research organization designed to encourage scholarly study of the dance from international and interdisciplinary perspectives
    • Provides information and sponsors research, meetings, conferences, workshops, lecture-demonstrations, exhibitions, and concerts
    • Publishes *Dance Research Journal* (see 1.076) and *Dance Research Annual* (reports of major research projects) on such subjects as Asian and Pacific dance, dance research, dance therapy, etc.)

4.182
Center for International and Comparative Programs
Kent State University
124 Bowman Hall
Kent, OH 44242
(216) 672-7980

Contact(s):
Robert W. Clawson, Director
Lawrence S. Kaplan, Director, NATO
    Studies Center

    • Assists in the development of graduate and undergraduate courses in international studies, conducts and promotes the expansion of research on international and comparative subjects among Kent State faculty; organizes exchange programs and workshops on international subjects and administers study abroad programs in Israel, Mexico, Geneva and Italy for undergraduates; includes Lyman L. Lemnitzer Center for NATO Studies; Kent State also sponsors a critical languages program offering programmed (taped) and tutorial instruction in 21 lesser known languages and a Center for the Study of World Musics

• Sponsors conferences on NATO issues, maintains research materials related to NATO and assists students and faculty interested in undertaking NATO studies and/or research

4.183
The Mershon Center
The Ohio State University
199 West 10th Ave.
Columbus, OH 43201
(614) 422-1681

Contact(s):
Charles F. Hermann, Director
Allan Millett, Director, International
  Security and Military Affairs
Chadwick Alger, Director, World Relations
  Program

Social science research and public education center drawing on faculty of Ohio State University

• Conducts research, sponsors public seminars and conferences, holds teacher training workshops, convenes scholarly meetings, makes awards and publishes books, reports, studies, newsletters and instructional materials in six areas: International Security and Military Affairs (arms control, national security, nuclear deterrence, policy, etc.), World Relations (citizen participation in world affairs, the Columbus in the World project (see 2.017), foreign policy behavior, Third

World development, etc.), Citizenship Development and Global Education (see 2.016), Soviet and East European International Behavior (see 14.039), Public Policy (design and evaluation of government programs), and Leadership Development and Public Policy

4.184
Foreign Policy Research Institute
3508 Market St., Science Center
Philadelphia, PA 19104
(215) 382-0685

Contact(s):
Marvin Wachman, President
Nils H. Wessell, Director

Independent research center

• Sponsors research and conferences designed to analyze U.S. foreign and arms control policy and Soviet international strategy; publishes reports and the quarterly *Orbis: Journal of World Affairs*, $15

4.185
Center for Intercultural Studies in
Folklore and Ethnomusicology
University of Texas at Austin
Austin, TX 78712
(512) 471-1288

Contact(s):
Richard Bauman, Director

• Conducts research on folklore and ethnic music with emphasis on Latin American music and folk tales as part of community relationship and on the theory and method of studying folklore; maintains tapes of U.S. and Latin American oral history, reminiscences, folk narrative and folk music

4.186
National Institute for Public Policy
8408 Arlington Blvd., First Floor
Fairfax, VA 22031
(703) 698-0563

Contact(s):
Colin S. Gray, President

Research organization
　• Conducts research on public policy in national/international security, arms control, foreign policy and military strategy; publishes monthly *Information Series* along with other books, monographs and reports

4.187
Center for Intercultural Communication
Marquette University
College of Speech
Milwaukee, WI 53233
(414) 224-7074

Contact(s):
Robert Shuter, Director

Network of cross-cultural researchers in 50 countries
　• Sponsors and promotes research on intercultural communication and links researchers worldwide; publishes reports, monographs and other materials including *International Directory of Intercultural Communication Researchers*, composed of a listing of approximately 550 researchers (with information on the background and scholarly interests of each) and an extensive bibliography of intercultural research

International Program Offices

4.188
Center for International Programs
University of Alabama at Birmingham
University Station
Birmingham, AL 35294
(205) 934-3630

Contact(s):
Blaine A. Brownell, Director

　• Provides study and faculty abroad advising, administers student exchange programs and advises foreign students

4.189
Capstone International Program Center
University of Alabama/Tuscaloosa
P.O. Box 6186
University, AL 35486
(205) 348-5256

Contact(s):
Edward M. Moseley, Director

　• Provides travel grants to faculty to undertake research in Latin America or Southern Europe; sponsors conferences and international business workshops

4.190
Office of Bilingual Education and International Studies
Pima Community College
200 North Stone Ave.
Tucson, AZ 85709
(602) 884-6617

Contact(s):
Henry Oyama, Dean
G. Elizabet Bailey, Director of International Education

　• Conducts faculty training and curriculum/teaching module development to infuse international studies widely into the present liberal arts and vocational curriculum; particular emphasis on international business studies and the provision of training to business personnel involved in international business operations; sponsors study abroad programs in Mexico

4.191
International Education and Exchange
California State University at Fullerton
Fullerton, CA 92634
(714) 773-2300

Contact(s):
Louise G. Lee, Director

• Provides study and faculty abroad advising and advises foreign students

4.192
International Education Center
California State University at Long Beach
1250 Bellflower Blvd.
Long Beach, CA 90840
(213) 498-4106

Contact(s):
Maurice Harari, Director

• Promotes, coordinates and administers all international activities of CSULB, including internationalization of the curriculum, international education linkages with other countries, cooperative programs with the community, foreign student exchanges, study abroad programs, and the American Language Institute (ESL courses); serves as headquarters for the International Community Council of Greater Long Beach (foreign students and faculty services); publishes a quarterly as well as an ad hoc newsletter on international education

4.193
Office of International Education
The Claremont Colleges/Pomona College
Oldenborg Center
Claremont, CA 91711
(714) 621-8154

Contact(s):
J. Patrick Haithcox, Director

• Advises on study and faculty abroad opportunities, sponsors overseas study and exchange programs and offers study/travel abroad services

4.194
Center for International Programs
San Diego State University
San Diego, CA 92182
(619) 265-5423

Contact(s):
William P. Locke, Director

• Administers development assistance and other project grants, advises students on study and travel abroad, and advises and assists faculty on exchanges, research and other projects overseas

4.195
International Student Programs
Sonoma State University
Village 102
1801 East Cotati Ave.
Rohnert Park, CA 94928

Contact(s):
Brian T. Shears, Director

• Provides study abroad advising, conducts student exchange program and manages American Language Institute; offers community outreach services and advises foreign students

4.196
International Programs Office
University of California at Davis
225 Mrak Hall
Davis, CA 95616
(916) 752-7071

Contact(s):
David W. Robinson, Associate Dean,
International Programs

• Supervises International Agricultural Development Program (see 6.005), and administers other training and educational programs overseas

4.197
International Services
University of California at Santa Cruz
240 Central Services
Santa Cruz, CA 95064
(408) 429-2858

Contact(s):
Mary E. McMahon, Coordinator

• Provides foreign student, study abroad and faculty abroad advising and supervises University of California, Santa Cruz-Beijing Language Institute Exchange

4.198
Office of International Education
University of Colorado at Boulder
Campus Box 123
Boulder, CO 80309
(303) 492-7741

Contact(s):
Jean Delaney, Dean

• Advises undergraduate and graduate students on study or research abroad, administers undergraduate overseas programs and graduate exchange relationships with foreign universities and advises foreign students
• Study abroad programs available in England, France, Germany, Sweden, Italy, Spain, Japan, Taiwan, Egypt, Israel, Costa Rica and Mexico

4.199
Center for International Education
University of Denver
2002 South Gaylord Way
Denver, CO 80208
(303) 753-2462

Contact(s):
Karin Millett-Sorensen, Director

• Provides study and faculty abroad advising and advises foreign students

4.200
Center for Area Studies and International Programs
Southern Connecticut State University
Foreign Language Department
501 Crescent St.
New Haven, CT 06515
(203) 397-4450

Contact(s):
Jean-Louis Dumont, Director

• Coordinates area studies minor concentrations, exchanges research and educational materials and pursues affiliations with overseas institutions; advises on study abroad and student exchange

4.201
Office of International Programs
Georgetown University
307 Intercultural Center
Washington, DC 20057
(202) 625-3221

Contact(s):
William W. Cressey, Director

• Advises students and faculty on study and research opportunities abroad; maintains overseas study resource center; advises foreign students

4.202
International and Multicultural Development Center
University of the District of Columbia
4200 Connecticut Ave. NW
Building 39, Suite 202
Washington, DC 20008
(202) 282-7395

Contact(s):
Barbara C. Patterson, Director

• Provides study abroad advising and advises foreign students; conducts intercultural outreach programs, including professional training, seminars, workshops and conferences

4.203
International Center
University of Delaware
Newark, DE 19716
(302) 451-2115

Contact(s):
Dean C. Lomis, Director

• Offers courses on international subjects; advises on study abroad programs; administers Fulbright, Rhodes, and Marshall scholarship programs and a University scholarship exchange with West Germany; advises faculty on overseas opportunities; advises foreign students and faculty; and provides services to community international education and visitor organizations and programs

4.204
International Studies Center
University of Central Florida
Orlando, FL 32816
(305) 275-2608

Contact(s):
Robert L. Bledsoe, Director

• Advises faculty and students on overseas study, research and teaching opportunities and publishes *Global Perspectives* (student research)

4.205
Center for International Studies and Programs
University of Florida
168 Grinter Hall
Gainesville, FL 32611
(904) 392-4904

Contact(s):
Patricia B. Rambo, Assistant to the President for International Studies and Programs

• Conducts summer study abroad programs in 11 countries, advises students and faculty on overseas study and research, and manages technical assistance and other international exchange agreements

4.206
International Studies Center
Emory University
Atlanta, GA 30322
(404) 329-6555

Contact(s):
Kenneth Stein, Director

• Offers supporting assistance to existing departments to augment course offerings and faculty resources and provides co-curricular programs

4.207
International Studies
Valdosta State College
Valdosta, GA 31698
(912) 333-5938

Contact(s):
William M. Gabard, Director

• Develops and coordinates international studies and programs on and off campus; offers minor in international/intercultural studies; advises students and faculty on study and research abroad; conducts seminars and workshops for the community and maintains liaison office with national and regional international education organizations; publishes international studies newsletter for the general community and sponsors model UN program

4.208
Office of International Programs
Illinois State University
140 Stevenson Hall
Normal, IL 61761
(309) 438-5365

Contact(s):
JoAnn McCarthy, Director

• Provides study and faculty abroad advising, conducts overseas programs and advises foreign students

4.209
Office of International and Special Programs
Northern Illinois University
Lowden Hall 203
De Kalb, IL 60115
(815) 753-1988

Contact(s):
Daniel Wit, Dean

• Coordinates international program activities including advising on study abroad, operating study abroad programs (in China (PRC), Denmark, France, Austria, England, Israel, Mexico, Spain and Switzerland), advising on and arranging overseas teaching, research and internship opportunities for graduate students and faculty, assisting and advising foreign faculty and students, and operating or supporting special on-campus programs including an international relations program and the Center for Latino and Latin American Affairs (see 16.032)

4.210
Office of International Education
Southern Illinois University
Carbondale, IL 62901
(618) 536-4451

Contact(s):
Charles Klasek, Director
Jared Dorn, Associate Director,
    International Services (618) 453-5774
Rhonda Vinson, Assistant to the Director for
    International Development

• Administers Vietnamese Studies Center and international technical assistance projects
• International Services Division provides study abroad, faculty abroad and foreign student advising along with a variety of community programs
• Publishes several international bulletins and newsletters

4.211
Office of International Education and Research
Purdue University
26 Agricultural Administration Bldg.
West Lafayette, IN 47907
(317) 494-6876

Contact(s):
D. Woods Thomas, Associate Dean and
    Director
D. Richard Smith, Associate Director
James L. Collom, Associate Director

• Coordinates overseas study, research and scholarly exchange activities; publishes newsletter

4.212
International Educational Services
Iowa State University
E.O. Bldg.
Ames, IA 50011
(515) 294-1120

Contact(s):
Martin Limbird, Director

• Offers study abroad, faculty abroad and foreign student advising, administers American Abroad Information Center and the International Resource Center (from which study kits of artifacts from other cultures are loaned to Iowa schools), conducts community programs (especially a Foreign Student Contact Program for Iowa businesses), and publishes a newsletter which reports on international education activities at and of interest to the university

4.213
Office of International Education & Services
University of Iowa
202 Jefferson Bldg.
Iowa City, IA 52242
(319) 353-6249

Contact(s):
Stephen Arum, Director

• Provides study and faculty abroad advising, advises foreign students and publishes foreign student handbooks, including *Learning with Your Foreign Student* and *Manual for Foreign Teaching Assistants*

4.214
International Program
Wichita State University
Grace Wilkie Hall
Wichita, KS 67208
(316) 689-3730

Contact(s):
Barbara P. Halpin, Director

• Provides study abroad advising and advises foreign students

4.215
Office for International Programs
University of Kentucky
Room 117
Bradley Hall
Lexington, KY 40506
(606) 257-1654

Contact(s):
Willis H. Griffin, Director

• Promotes and conducts international programs and projects on the University campus; counsels students on overseas work, study and research opportunities abroad; administers overseas study and exchange programs (including programs in Germany, Denmark, Spain and Scotland); supervises Peace Corps advising office and the office of the Kentucky-Ecuador Partners of the Americas Program; coordinates curriculum revision, relationships with institutions abroad, and proposals for research and development assistance contracts

4.216
Office of International Programs
Brandeis University
Waltham, MA 02254
(617) 647-2422

Contact(s):
Faire L. Goldstein, Director

• Provides study abroad advising and advises foreign students

4.217
International Education
Bunker Hill Community College
Boston, MA 02129
(617) 241-8600, Ext. 202

Contact(s):
Brenda S. Robinson, Director

• Advises on study and faculty abroad opportunities and administers overseas study, faculty exchanges and technical assistance programs

4.218
Office of International Studies
Cape Cod Community College
West Barnstable, MA 02668
(617) 362-2131, Ext. 455

Contact(s):
David G. Scanlon, Director

• Develops, coordinates and conducts a wide variety of international programs on and off campus; publishes newsletter
• Serves as regional office of the College Consortium for International Studies (see 8.006)

4.219
International Education Programs
Framingham State College
100 State Street
P.O. Box 2000
Framingham, MA 01701
(617) 620-1220, Ext. 269

Contact(s):
Elaine Storella, Director

• Provides study and faculty abroad advising and advises foreign students

4.220
Office of International Affairs
Northeastern University
360 Huntington Ave.
Boston, MA 02115
(617) 437-5570

Contact(s):
Joy W. Viola, Dean

• Coordinates internationally-oriented programs at Northeastern, administers overseas relationships, conducts community programs and advises on international education issues; headquarters for the New England-China Consortium for Educational and Cultural Exchanges

4.221
International Programs Office
University of Massachusetts
239 Whitmore Bldg.
Amherst, MA 01003
(413) 545-0746

Contact(s):
Barbara Burn, Director

• Advises foreign students and faculty; provides study abroad advising and administers study abroad and exchange programs with academic institutions in 14 countries in Europe, South America and the Far East; advises faculty on overseas research and teaching opportunities; organizes conferences and workshops

4.222
Foreign Study Program
Kalamazoo College
Kalamazoo, MI 49007
(616) 383-8470

Contact(s):
Joe K. Fugate, Director

• Provides study abroad advising and conducts overseas programs including a number in Africa (Ghana, Kenya, Liberia, Nigeria, Senegal, Sierra Leone) in cooperation with the Great Lakes Colleges Association (see 8.015)

4.223
Center for Global Service and Education
Augsburg College
731 21st Ave. South
Minneapolis, MN 55454
(612) 330-1159

Contact(s):
Joel Mugge, Director

• Conducts overseas study and travel programs and arranges seminars and conferences focusing on global peace and justice issues; publishes newsletter

4.224
International Studies
St. Olaf College
Northfield, MN 55057
(507) 663-3025

Contact(s):
Sue Clarke, Director

• Administers a wide variety of study abroad programs (in the Far East, the Middle East, England, France, West Germany, Spain, Norway, the USSR, Taiwan and India along with several multicountry programs) and advises foreign students

4.225
Office of International Programs
University of Minnesota
201 Nolte West
315 Pillsbury Drive S.E.
Minneapolis, MN 55455
(612) 373-3793

Contact(s):
Michael F. Metcalf, Acting Director

• Serves as liaison center for international programs and provides coordination in program and policy development; other international programs offices: Extension Classes Office of Study Abroad, Foreign Studies Office, Institute of International Studies, International Student Adviser's Office, Minnesota International Center, World Affairs Center and Center for Global Education, and an International Study and Travel Center (Jon Booth, Director, 44 Coffman Union, 300 Washington Ave., S.E., Minneapolis, MN 55414 (612) 373-0180)

4.226
Center for International Education
The University of Southern Mississippi
Southern Station, Box 5151
Hattiesburg, MS 39406
(601) 266-4344

Contact(s):
William Banks Taylor, Head

• Administrative center for the Office of International Studies (which coordinates and assists in the development of study abroad, including programs in Britain, Italy, Mexico and elsewhere), the English Language Institute, the Office of International Student Admissions and Advisement, and the Institute of Anglo-American Studies (which promotes research on, scholarly exchange with and study of/in Britain)

4.227
Center for International Programs
New Mexico State University
Box 3567
Las Cruces, NM 88003
(505) 646-3199

Contact(s):
Harold R. Matteson, Director

• Coordinates international program activity on campus including foreign/domestic government and institutional contacts, faculty/student exchanges, advisory services to faculty regarding overseas research and teaching opportunities and to U.S. students interested in studying abroad; coordinates international technical assistance programs

4.228
International Programs
State University of New York at Albany
ULB-36
1400 Washington Ave.
Albany, NY 12222
(518) 457-8678

Contact(s):
Alex M. Shane, Director

• Plans and administers study abroad programs (in Denmark, France, Israel and Spain) and academic exchange programs with universities in Brazil, China, England, Japan, the Netherlands, Singapore, the USSR, West Germany and Yugoslavia); advises students and faculty on overseas opportunities and administers academic minor in International Perspectives

4.229
Office of Overseas Academic Programs
State University of New York at Binghamton
Administration Bldg. 141
Binghamton, NY 13901
(607) 798-2336

Contact(s):
Adalberto Lopez, Director

• Sponsors undergraduate study abroad programs in France, Mexico, Austria, Israel and England and graduate and undergraduate programs in Denmark, Peru and Japan
• Advises on study abroad and coordinates faculty and other exchange programs with foreign institutions

4.230
International Education
State University of New York/College at
    Brockport
International Programs Office
Brockport, NY 14420
(716) 395-2119

Contact(s):
John J. Perry, Coordinator

• Provides study and faculty abroad advising and conducts overseas programs

4.231
Office of International Programs
State University of New York at Stony Brook
Stony Brook, NY 11794
(516) 246-7711

Contact(s):
Francis T. Bonner, Dean

• Provides study and faculty abroad advising, conducts overseas programs and advises foreign students

4.232
Center for International Programs
Bowling Green State University
Williams Hall, #16
Bowling Green, OH 43403
(419) 372-2086

Contact(s):
Douglas Daye, Director

• Provides study and faculty abroad advising, conducts overseas programs and advises foreign students

4.233
International Education
Wilmington College
Wilmington, OH 45177
(513) 382-6661, Ext. 296

Contact(s):
Donald R. Liggett, Director

• Coordinates international studies coursework, provides study abroad and faculty abroad advising, conducts overseas programs and advises foreign students

4.234
International Student Services Office
University of Oklahoma, Norman
731 Elm, 213 Hester Hall
Norman, OK 73019
(405) 325-3581

Contact(s):
Millie C. Audas, Assistant Director for
   International Student Programs
Richard Hancock, International Services
   Officer (overseas programs)

• Provides study and faculty abroad advising, conducts overseas study and training programs (major program at Colima, Mexico), and advises foreign students

4.235
Office of International Programs and Studies
Linfield College
Melrose Hall
McMinnville, OR 97128
(503) 472-4121, Ext. 222

Contact(s):
Joseph Navari, Director

• Administers international education programs consisting of an international studies minor, a faculty development program, five-month study abroad programs in Aus-

tria, Costa Rica, France and Japan, and administers an intensive program in English as a second language

4.236
International Programs Office
Lewis and Clark College
LC Box 11
Portland, OR 97219
(503) 244-6161, Ext. 565

Contact(s):
R. Vance Savage, Director

• Provides study abroad and faculty abroad advising and advises foreign students; conducts overseas and off-campus study programs and administers Institute for the Study of American Language and Culture

4.237
Division of International Education
University of Tennessee at Knoxville
205 Alumni Hall
Knoxville, TN 37916
(615) 974-3475

Contact(s):
Nancy McG. McCormack, Associate
   Director
Peter D. Williams, Assistant Director

• Provides information, coordinates exchange visitor programs, advises American faculty and students on fellowship and other opportunities for overseas research and study, advises foreign students, and administers direct reciprocal exchange programs

4.238
Office of International Programs
Texas Southern University
229 Hannah Hall
Houston, TX 77004
(713) 527-7232

Contact(s):

Joseph Jones, Director

• Advises students and faculty on study and research abroad, conducts seminars on international issues and foreign trade; publishes a newsletter and offers minor in International Studies with emphasis on the social sciences, the fine arts and languages

4.239

Office of International Programs and Services

George Mason University
State University in Northern Virginia
4400 University Drive
Fairfax, VA 22030
(703) 323-2001

Contact(s):

France J. Pruitt, Director

• Promotes international studies and programs on campus; coordinates and supervises advising on study abroad for American students and on research and teaching abroad for American faculty; advises foreign students and runs English Language Institute; raises funds for international education and provides seed money for faculty research on international subjects

4.240

Center for International Programs

Old Dominion University
Norfolk, VA 23508
(804) 440-4419

Contact(s):

Jerome Bookin-Weiner, Director

• Responsible for all non-credit programs, community education, faculty development, study and travel abroad, faculty and student exchanges, and inter-institutional agreements

4.241

Office of International Programs

Central Washington University
Barge Hall 308
Ellensburg, WA 98926
(509) 963-3612

Contact(s):

Dieter Romboy, Director

• Administers study abroad programs (West Germany, France, England, Spain, Mexico and the PRC), advises faculty on overseas opportunities and arranges exchange relationships with foreign universities

4.242

International Programs

Pacific Lutheran University
Tacoma, WA 98447
(206) 535-7628

Contact(s):

Ann Kelleher, Director

• Provides on-campus instruction and develops co-curricular activities in global/international studies, advises on study abroad, conducts outreach programs for community college and school faculty, and administers instructional programs for nearby military bases

4.243

Office of International Programs

Washington State University
Bryan Hall 108
Pullman, WA 99164
(509) 335-4508

Contact(s):

V. N. Bhatia, Director

• Provides study and faculty abroad advising, conducts overseas exchange programs, manages community outreach International Education Resources Project, advises foreign students and operates the Intensive American Language Center

4.244
Office of International Studies and Programs
University of Wisconsin Madison
1410 Van Hise Hall
1220 Linden Drive
Madison, WI 53706
(608) 262-2851

Contact(s):
Peter Dorner, Dean

• Promotes and, in some cases, administers international education, research and technical assistance programs and projects at the University; serves as central information source and develops resource guides; administers Fulbright and other faculty and student exchange programs; the University also maintains an Office of Foreign Students and Faculty and a Study Abroad Programs Office

Academic Associations and Agencies Concerned with International Education

4.245
American Association for Applied Linguistics
3520 Prospect St. NW
Washington, DC 20007
(202) 298-7120

Contact(s):
Albert Valdman, Secretary-Treasurer

Professional association of linguistics scholars
• Promotes multidisciplinary approach to language problems and issues and publishes a newsletter

4.246
American Association for the Advancement of Science
Office of International Science
1776 Massachusetts Ave. NW
Washington, DC 20036
(202) 467-5230

Administrative center for AAAS international science programs and activities involving relationships with AAAS affiliates, science organizations in other countries, and UN agencies, focusing on special projects on science

issues of international concern, e.g. arid lands, climate, transfer of science and technology
• Provides the executive secretariat for the Interciencia Association, a federation of scientific organizations whose goal is to promote closer ties among the scientific community of the western hemisphere and the cooperative uses of science and technology to benefit the peoples of the Americas
• Coordinates activities of the AAAS Consortium of Affiliates for International Programs and publishes a news sheet, *Consortium Notes*
• Manages Science, Engineering and Diplomacy Fellows program in cooperation with the U.S. Department of State
• Administers program of exchange with the China Association for Science and Technology
• Organizes workshops and seminars on major international scientific topics
• Occasionally offers small grants to self-sponsored foreign graduate students for attendance at AAAS meetings
• Organizes seminars for foreign science attachés posted at embassies in Washington
• Publishes bi-annual newsletter *Scientific and Engineering Societies in Development* distributed to science societies around the world

4.247
American Association of Community and Junior Colleges
Office of International Services
One Dupont Circle NW, Suite 410
Washington, DC 20036
(202) 293-7050

Contact(s):
James R. Mahoney, Director, Office of
International Services

• Promotes development of international education programs and activities at community colleges through consultation and information services; serves as headquarters for the AACJC International/Intercultural Consortium

4.248
American Council on Education
Division of International Education
11 Dupont Circle NW, Suite 300
Washington, DC 20036
(202) 833-4960

Contact(s):
Cassandra A. Pyle, Vice President, Division of International Education

• Through the 28-member Commission on International Education, identifies issues in international education and explores policy options; helps shape federal policy and coordinate community-wide activities
• Promotes understanding of international education issues and fosters cooperation among campuses and higher education groups
• Organizes task forces and holds special conferences and seminars on issues related to international education
• Serves as contact point for counterpart organizations abroad and foreign institutions of higher education
• Through the Council for International Exchange of Scholars (see 7.007), cooperates in administering the Fulbright Scholar Program

4.249
American Society of Geolinguistics
485 Brooklawn Ave.
Fairfield, CT 06432
(203) 576-4216 (office)
(203) 333-8920 (home)

Contact(s):
Jesse Levitt, Secretary

Professional association concerned with the political, economic and cultural aspects of language distribution and interrelationships
• Sponsors conferences and publishes annual journal *Geolinguistics*

4.250
Comparative and International Education Society
University of Southern California
302 Waite Phillips Hall
University Park
Los Angeles, CA 90007
(213) 741-6162

Contact(s):
William M. Rideout, Jr., Business Manager

Professional association of academics and others concerned with comparative and international education
• Holds conferences and meetings, formulates research projects, and works with international educational agencies on projects of mutual interest
• Publishes a newsletter and the journal *Comparative Education Review*

4.251
Five Colleges, Inc.
Box 740
Amherst, MA 01004
(413) 256-8316

Contact(s):
E. Jefferson Murphy, Coordinator

Cooperative association of academic institutions
   • Promotes cooperative programming, cross-registration and the sharing of resources among members in Asian, Black, African, Slavic, and Latin American Studies, international relations, Italian, French and German language studies, and Interpreter Studies (see 6.168); members are Amherst, Hampshire, Mount Holyoke and Smith Colleges and the University of Massachusetts

4.252
Fulbright Alumni Association
P.O. Box 1042
Bryn Mawr, PA 19010-1042
(215) 645-5038

Contact(s):
Arthur P. Dudden, Executive Director
Eileen A. Ruth, Administrator

Nonprofit association of persons concerned with international educational exchange, the perpetuation of exchange programs and the effective application of cross-cultural learning and insights which stem from the exchange experience
   • Holds meetings and makes recommendations on public policy relative to international educational exchange
   • Publishes a newsletter and *Communications,* an occasional collection of essays

4.253
International Association for Cross-Cultural Psychology
Tilburg University
Department of Psychology
5000 LE Tilburg
The Netherlands

Contact(s):
Y. H. Poortinga, Secretary General

Professional academic association for the advancement of research in comparative human behavior and experience
   • Sponsors conferences, meetings and workshops; publishes *Journal of Cross-Cultural Psychology* (see 1.090), *Cross-Cultural Psychology Bulletin* (quarterly, news of the field plus short theoretical and empirical articles), *Conference Proceedings* and *Directory of Cross-Cultural Research and Researchers* (periodically revised)

4.254
International Council for Traditional Music
Columbia University
Department of Music
New York, NY 10027
(212) 678-0332

Contact(s):
Dieter Christensen, Secretary General

International association of scholars of traditional music (including folk, popular, classical and urban) and dance of all countries
   • Functions of the council include holding conferences, publishing information bulletins and a yearbook, forming study groups, issuing records and films, fostering the development of national and international archives, facilitating the exchange of information and resources and organizing festivals of traditional music

4.255
International Communication Association
P.O. Box 9589
Austin, TX 78766
(512) 454-8299

Contact(s):
Robert L. Cox, Executive Director

Professional academic association

• Sponsors conferences and publishes *Journal of Communication, Human Communication Research, Communication Yearbook* and the *ICA Newsletter;* includes intercultural division concerned with the theory and practice of communication between and among different world cultures

4.256
International Society for Educational, Cultural and Scientific Interchanges
University of Minnesota
717 East River Road
Minneapolis, MN 55455
(612) 373-4094

Contact(s):
Josef A. Mestenhauser, President

Professional association concerned with international academic, scholarly and educational exchange

• Sponsors meetings and conferences, publishes *Bulletin of International Interchange* and serves as a liaison among researchers, practitioners and policy makers in international and intercultural education

4.257
International Studies Association
University of South Carolina
James F. Byrnes International Center
Columbia, SC 29208
(803) 777-2933

Contact(s):
James A. Kuhlman, Executive Director

Professional academic association

• Sponsors meetings and promotes re-

search and the expansion of educational activity in international studies in such areas as military affairs, foreign policy, law, organization, political economy, environment, peace and Soviet-American relations; among affiliated organizations are the Consortium for International Studies Education (see 2.018), the Consortium for Peace Research, Education and Development (see 5.022), and the International Society for Educational, Cultural and Scientific Interchanges (see 4.256)

• Publishes *International Studies Quarterly* (see 1.089), *Notes* (essays on the international studies field) and a newsletter, one issue of which each year is devoted to funding sources for international research and study

4.258
National Committee of International Studies and Program Administrators
University of North Carolina
% Center for International Studies
Charlotte, NC 28223
(704) 597-2407

Contact(s):
Earl L. Backman, Chairman

Professional association in cross-cultural education

• Publishes a newsletter, develops source materials and serves as an information clearinghouse for academics and educators involved in college- and university-based programs of international studies, cross-cultural education and educational exchange

4.259
Society for Intercultural Education, Training and Research (SIETAR)
1414 22d St. NW
Washington, DC 20037
(202) 862-1990

Contact(s):
Diane Zeller, Executive Director

Professional association for academics and practitioners concerned with intercultural communication and cross-cultural human relations
   • Provides information about intercultural educational, training and research activity, conducts professional training programs in intercultural skills and publishes books on intercultural subjects along with the newsletter *Communiqué*

4.260
Southern Atlantic States Association for Asian and African Studies
Center for International Studies
Duke University
Durham, NC 27706
(919) 684-2765

Contact(s):
A. Kenneth Pye, Director

Consortium of 26 Southeastern colleges and universities
   • Sponsors faculty development pro-

grams, including overseas seminars, intensive language training and teaching-oriented workshops; maintains library of educational films and other audiovisual materials and sponsors Asian and African cultural events

4.261
Southern California Consortium on International Studies
University of California
1201 Campbell Hall
405 Hilgard Ave.
Los Angeles, CA 90024
(213) 825-0601

Contact(s):
Carlos M. Haro, Executive Officer

Consortium of approximately 16 colleges and universities
   • Sponsors cooperative overseas study programs, faculty research and development, colloquia, and conferences, particularly in area studies (Canadian, Latin American, East Asian, African and Middle Eastern, and Soviet and Eastern European); maintains area studies film collections (catalogues available for Latin America and Africa)

5
Peace and Conflict Resolution Studies

Academic and Other Training Programs

5.001
Conflict and Peace Studies
University of Colorado
Boulder, CO 80309
(303) 492-8406

Contact(s):
James Frank, Chair

   • Offers a student-designed interdisciplinary B.A. in conflict- and peace-related issues

5.002
Center for Peace Studies
Georgetown University
2 O'Gara St.
Washington, DC 20057
(202) 625-4240

Contact(s):
Rev. Richard T. McSorley, S.J., Director
Pat Cassidy, Assistant to Director

• Offers interdisciplinary B.A. in Peace Studies with emphasis on nuclear issues

5.003
Peace and Conflict Studies
Earlham College
Richmond, IN 47374
(317) 962-6561

Contact(s):
Howard Richards, Director

• Offers action-oriented undergraduate major which includes a required off-campus internship

5.004
Peace Studies Program
Goshen College
Goshen, IN 46526
(219) 533-3161

Contact(s):
J. R. Burkholder, Director

• Offers B.A. with co-major in Peace Studies

5.005
Peace Studies Institute
Manchester College
North Manchester, IN 46962
(219) 982-2141

Contact(s):
Ken Brown, Director

• Offers B.A. or B.S. in Peace Studies with emphasis on cultural analysis

5.006
Peace Studies
Bethel College
N. Newton, KS 67117
(316) 283-2500

Contact(s):
Robert S. Kreider, Director

• Offers B.A. with double major Peace Studies option; emphasis on religious and moral dimensions

5.007
Center for Peace and Conflict Studies
Wayne State University
5229 Cass Ave.
Detroit, MI 48202
(313) 577-3453

Contact(s):
Lillian Genser, Director

University and community center for education about peace and conflict studies
• Offers Co-major in Peace and Conflict Studies in cooperation with history and political science
• Distributes publications and develops materials in the area of peace and conflict studies with a focus on human rights; main-

tains library of publications, curriculum materials, and audiovisual resources on peace and conflict (rents films nationally; filmstrips and slide presentations available in Michigan only)

• Conducts outreach program of training workshops for teachers and maintains clearinghouse for peace education materials K-12

• Serves as headquarters for the Detroit Council for World Affairs

5.008
Peace Studies Program
Seton Hall University
Political Science Department
South Orange, NJ 07079
(201) 762-9000, Ext. 512

Contact(s):
Robert Manley, Director

• Offers Ph.D. in Peace Studies

5.009
Peace and World Order Studies Program
Colgate University
Hamilton, NY 13346
(315) 824-1000

Contact(s):
Carolyn Stephenson, Director

• Offers B.A. in Peace Studies with emphasis on the quest for world community free of war and violence, based on social and economic justice and with a concern for ecological balance

5.010
Peace Studies Program
Cornell University
180 Uris Hall
Ithaca, NY 14853

Contact(s):
Ned Lebow, Director

• Offers graduate M.A. and Ph.D. concentration in Peace Science in the fields of Economics and Regional Science and a minor in other departments (along with the opportunity for postdoctoral research and study); focuses on peace and war, arms control and disarmament and how they affect foreign policy; special Peace Studies fellowships available

5.011
International Peace Academy
777 UN Plaza
New York, NY 10017
(212) 949-8480

Contact(s):
Indar Jit Rikhye, President

International training organization for personnel who work for the UN and other national and international agencies concerned with conflict resolution, mediation, negotiation or peacekeeping

• Conducts training programs in Africa, Asia, Europe, and North and South America on the skills and procedures of conflict management, mediation, negotiation and peacekeeping using simulations and other practical training techniques

• Conducts "action research" on current disputes by arranging off-the-record meetings with parties to the conflict

• Publishes books, a newsletter (*Coping with Conflict*), reports and educational and training materials, including *The Peacekeepers Handbook* (in English and French)

5.012
Peace Studies Institute
Manhattan College
Riverdale, NY 10471
(212) 920-0305

Contact(s):
Joseph J. Fahey, Director

• Offers B.A. in Peace Studies

5.013
Program in Nonviolent Conflict and Change
Syracuse University
249 Physics Bldg.
Syracuse, NY 13210
(315) 423-3870

Contact(s):
Neil Katz, Director

• Offers B.A. in Peace Studies and an interdisciplinary Peace Studies research and training concentration in the Ph.D. interdisciplinary social science program of the Maxwell School of Citizenship and Public Affairs; emphasis on transdisciplinary study of nonviolent means of managing conflicts and bringing about or resisting change

5.014
Center for Peaceful Change
Kent State University
Kent, OH 44242
(216) 672-3143

Contact(s):
Dennis Carey, Director

• Offers B.A. in Peace Studies; headquarters of Consortium on Peace Research, Education and Development (see 5.022)

5.015
Center for Peace Studies
University of Akron
Akron, OH 44325
(216) 375-7008

Contact(s):
Warren F. Kuehl, Director

• Offers Certificate in Peace Studies with emphasis on international/transnational studies; conducts research on peace and human rights issues; serves as clearinghouse on peace studies education and conducts teacher workshops; maintains biographical archives of peace studies researchers; publishes *International Peace Studies Newsletter*

5.016
Peace and Conflict Studies
Juniata College
Huntingdon, PA 16652
(814) 643-4310

Contact(s):
M. Andrew Murray, Director

• Offers B.A. in Peace Studies as applied liberal arts

5.017
Center for Conflict Resolution
George Mason University
State University in Northern Virginia
4400 University Drive
Fairfax, VA 22030
(703) 323-2038

Contact(s):
Bryant Wedge, Director

Center designed to further development of the profession of conflict management
• Offers M.S. in Conflict Management
• Conducts seminars and workshops and disseminates information to increase public awareness of the importance of training in conflict management

5.018
Center for Conflict Resolution
University of Wisconsin at Madison
731 State St.
Madison, WI 53703
(608) 255-0479

Contact(s):
Susan Jarboe, Correspondent

- Provides consultation and training in a broad range of conflict management areas including international conflict resolution; publishes handbooks for group facilitation and consensus decision-making

Service Organizations

5.019
Council for International Understanding
136 East 64th St.
New York, NY 10021

Contact(s):
Moorhead Kennedy, Executive Director

- Fosters a clearer understanding of peacemaking, peace issues and the peace movement through publications, lectures, workshops, and media appearances

5.020
Center for War/Peace Studies
218 East 18th St.
New York, NY 10003
(212) 475-0850

Contact(s):
Richard Hudson, Executive Director

Nonprofit research and educational organization promoting new approaches to achieving a world of peace with justice
- Sponsors the study of world peace issues leading to the development of new ideas

and approaches, with current emphasis on the international decision-making system, arms control/disarmament, the Middle East conflict, and global sharing of ocean, space and Antarctic resources
- Publishes the newsletter *Global Report* and occasional special studies

5.021
The Conference on Peace Research in History
Adelphi University
University College
Garden City, NY 11530
(516) 663-1047

Contact(s):
Michael Lutzker, President
Glen Zeitzer, Secretary-Treasurer

Association of scholars and researchers in history and the social sciences designed to encourage and promote research on peace issues
- Provides information and sponsors meetings and conferences on peace research and compiles lists of research in progress

5.022
Consortium on Peace Research, Education and Development (COPRED)
Kent State University
Center for Peaceful Change
Kent, OH 44242
(216) 672-3143

Contact(s):
William Keeney, Executive Director

Association of individuals and institutions interested in the study of problems of peace, conflict and social justice; especially concerned with action-oriented research as well as classroom and public education
• Advises and recommends contacts for information, consultation and support services for expanding and/or improving peace education programs
• Organizes research and curriculum development projects and sponsors conferences, workshops and symposia on peace studies issues
• Publishes newsletter, *The COPRED Peace Chronicle*, and the journal *Peace and Change* (see 5.035) along with other general and educational materials on peace studies including *Repertoire of Peacemaking Skills* (discusses the peacemaking process and the skills needed for it), *Peace Education Packet* (a collection of material useful in peace education and teaching) *10 Quick Ways to Evaluate Global Education Materials* (free with self-addressed stamped envelope); also available is a set of evaluation tools prepared by other organizations for peace education, $1), *Mini-Directory of Peace Studies Programs* ($.50 postage/handling), and *Creating the Future* (a slide presentation)

5.023
Immaculate Heart College Center
10951 W. Pico Blvd., Suite 2021
Los Angeles, CA 90064
(213) 470-2293

Contact(s):
Margaret Rose-Welch, Outreach
    Coordinator

Nonprofit world issues educational center (successor to Immaculate Heart College)
• Conducts research on world issues, especially peace and conflict (in the Middle East and Northern Ireland), justice and global cooperation, sponsors teacher education workshops and staff development institutes, develops model school projects and graduate degree programs (Professional Studies for a Global Age), and offers public education programs
• Publishes *Global Pages*, a bi-monthly collection of articles, classroom activities, and information on peace, justice and global interdependence for teachers

5.024
The Institute for Peace and Justice
2913 Locust Ave.
St. Louis, MO 63103
(314) 533-4445

Contact(s):
James McGinnis, Executive Officer

Ecumenical educational organization
• Prepares, publishes and disseminates films, books, teaching handbooks and curriculum materials for use by parents and educators in such subjects as peacemaking, justice, arms control, hunger, racism and sexism and economic development, including the two-volume *Educating for Peace and Justice: A Manual for Teachers* (Volume I: National Dimensions; Volume II: Global Dimensions; includes teaching units)

5.025
International Association of Educators for World Peace
P.O. Box 3282
Huntsville, AL 35810
(205) 539-7205 or 859-7429

Contact(s):
Charles Mercieca, Executive Vice President

Association of 17,000 individuals in 58 countries promoting world peace, social progress, and international communication through education and personal contact
• Sponsors meetings, seminars and workshops, including world congresses and regional and national meetings
• Publishes a newsletter and two journals, *Peace Progress* and *Peace Education*

5.026
Peace Research Institute-Dundas
25 Dundana Ave.
Dundas, Ontario
Canada, L9H 4E5
(416) 628-2356

Contact(s):
Alan Newcombe, Hanna Newcombe and
   Ruth Klaassen, Co-directors

• Publishes source materials for peace research including *Peace Research Abstracts Journal* (lists and gives substantive abstracts of books, articles and other research on subjects such as war, military activity, peace, and arms control), a monograph series Peace Research Reviews (topical literature surveys, $3 each) and a periodic compilation of statistics on U.N. roll-call votes

5.027
Peace Science Society
State University of New York at Binghamton
School of Management
Binghamton, NY 13901
(607) 798-4886

Contact(s):
Walter Isard, Executive Secretary

Research organization
• Promotes research on peace and related issues based on scientific analysis and methodologies; publishes semiannual *Conflict Management and Peace Science* along with occasional papers

5.028
World Policy Institute
777 UN Plaza
New York, NY 10017
(212) 490-0010

Contact(s):
Arch Giles, President

Educational organization aimed at defining and bringing into being a "just world order"; concerned with security, disarmament, human rights, peace, technology, environment, ecology, values, culture, hunger and similar issues
• Consults on and assists in the establishment of peace studies and world order courses at colleges and universities
• Sponsors research on alternative international systems with the World Order Models Project
• Offers 6 to 10 teaching fellowships to help establish new world order courses or the development of curriculum materials
• Produces and distributes materials for teaching world order studies; publishes the newsletter *World Policy Forum* (containing a

great deal of practical information for educators), the *World Policy Journal* (see 5.041), *Alternatives: A Journal of World Policy* (see 1.072), and an extensive list of books, pamphlets and working papers on global issues, including *Peace and World Order Studies: A Curriculum Guide* (see 5.037) and *Peace and World Order Systems: Teaching and Research* (see 5.038)

• Conducts curriculum workshops for school and college faculty, organizes seminars for public and private sector leaders and arranges internships and educational programs for youths

5.029
World Without War Council, Inc.
1730 Grove St.
Berkeley, CA 94709
(415) 845-1992
and
175 Fifth Ave.
New York, NY 10010
(212) 674-2085
BRANCHES: Chicago, Eugene, Ore.;
Glenview, Ill.; Portland, Ore.; Seattle

Contact(s):
Robert Pickus, President

Nonprofit educational organization
• Conducts research on foreign policy and peace issues, consults with and/or trains leaders of other organizations in achieving world-without-war aims, and provides in-service training for teachers
• Publishes wide variety of materials on the following subjects: world order, international organizations, violence, non-violence, disarmament, global perspectives and interdependence, development, economic and social issues, and international human rights; includes teaching materials distributed through the Curriculum Resource Center consisting of books, simulations, kits, guides, bibliographies, course units, etc.; maintains World without War Bookstore in Chicago (request lists and place orders for books and curriculum materials from World without War Council/Midwest, 67 East Madison, Suite 1417, Chicago, IL 60603; (312) 236-7459)
• Publishes free quarterly newsletter
• Conducts conferences and seminars, including annual Human Rights Day Conference

Sourcebooks and Periodicals

5.030
Annual of Power and Conflict
Institute for the Study of Conflict
12/12A Golden Square
London W1R 3AF, England
annual; paperbound; 500 pages; $15

• Country-by-country survey of principal problems of strategic conflict, violence, political, social and economic instability and terrorist activity

5.031
Bibliography on World Conflict and Peace: Second Edition
Elsie Boulding, J. Robert Passmore and
    Robert Scott Gassier
Westview Press, Inc.
5500 Central Ave.
Boulder, CO 80301
1979; hardbound; 168 pages; $23

• Relatively up-to-date bibliography for the Peace Studies field

5.032
Conflict Studies
Institute for the Study of Conflict
12/12A Golden Square
London W1R 3AF, England
monthly; £40.00, institutions; £30.00,
    individuals (plus £5 air mail)

Back issues available
    • Series of monographs focused on lo-
cal, regional and transnational military, political, terrorist and communal conflict in each
of the major world regions, with particular
emphasis on the role of the Soviet Union;
includes studies on the nature of conflict

5.033
Creating the Future
Consortium on Peace Research, Education,
    and Development
Stopher Hall
Kent State University
Kent, OH 44242
75 color slides, 20 minutes in length; may
    be rented for $10

    • A slide presentation which examines
the role peace education can play in shaping
a peaceful future; covers basic components of
learning peace and identifies current activities taking place around the country

5.034
The Journal of Conflict Resolution
Bruce M. Russett, Editor
Sage Publications, Inc.
275 South Beverly Drive
Beverly Hills, CA 90212
quarterly journal; approx. 60 pages;
    institutions, $45 per year; individuals,
    $22.50 per year

    • Contains research and theoretical ar-
ticles on questions of peace and human conflict, focusing in particular on nuclear war,
disarmament, social conflicts and conflict
control and resolution; also concerned with
intergroup conflict in general

5.035
**Peace and Change: A Journal of Peace
Research**
Center for Peaceful Change
Kent State University
Kent, OH 44242
3 issues per year; journal; individuals, $15
    per year; institutions, $21 per year

    • Contains scholarly articles and reports
on research in peace studies and on the peace
movement; includes book reviews

5.036
Peace and War: A Guide to Bibliographies
Bernice A. Carroll, Clinton F. Fink and Jane
    E. Mohraz
ABC-Clio, Inc.
Riviera Campus
2040 Alameda Padre Serra
Box 4397
Santa Barbara, CA 93103
1982; hardbound; 325 pages; $42.50

    • Annotated guide to bibliographies of
materials published worldwide from the humanities, social sciences and natural sciences
on peace and war from 1785 to 1981; over
1,300 entries in 34 subject categories

5.037
**Peace and World Order Studies: A
Curriculum Guide**
World Policy Institute
777 UN Plaza
New York, NY 10017
3rd edition, 1981; 4th edition, 1984
    (companion volumes) paperbound; 3rd
    edition, $8; 4th edition, $10

• Contains course syllabi, listings of resources available in the field, essays setting forth the rationale, content and methodology of world order studies, case study articles on major peace programs in North America, and a list of select funding sources for curriculum development seed money

5.038
Peace and World Order Systems: Teaching and Research
Michael A. Washburn and Paul Wehr
Sage Publications, Inc.
275 Beverly Drive
Beverly Hills, CA 90212
1976; paperbound; 255 pages; $6

• Discusses the most effective ways to focus research, develop programs and construct curriculum for world order studies

5.039
To End War: A New Approach to International Conflict
Robert Woito
The Pilgrim Press
132 West 31st St.
New York, NY 10001
1982; 755 pages; hardbound, $25; paperbound, $12.95

Available from World Without War Publications, 421 Wabash Ave., 2d Floor, Chicago, IL 60605
• Comprehensive guide and resource directory, prepared by the World Without War Council—Midwest, to studying and taking action on peace and conflict issues; broken down into two principal sections: "Ideas" and "Actions"; under "Ideas," chapters cover such areas as world politics, military strategy, arms control and other conditions for peace,

the U.S., the Soviet Union and other actors in world politics, major new economic problems that affect world relations, concepts on which the peace movement is based, and the U.S. political context; the author presents both sides of controversial issues discussed; under "Actions," chapters lay out the rationale and specifics of a program of action; each chapter contains an extensive bibliography of general and teaching references; chapters under "Actions" also contain a comprehensive list of organizations that are active in or serve as resources for the peace movement and a list of relevant periodicals

5.040
War Peace Film Guide
John Dowling
World Without War Publications
67 East Madison Ave., Suite 1417
Chicago, IL 60603
1980; paperbound; 188 pages; $5

• Lists and describes 287 films useful in the teaching of war/peace issues; gives full technical details, an indication of suitable educational level and a numerical assessment of the quality of content and production; also includes index of films according to subject area for which each is appropriate, substantive guidelines for effective use of the films in educational programs, lists of other resources (organizations, film distributors, catalogues, periodicals) and a bibliography

5.041
World Policy Journal
Robert C. Johansen, Editor in Chief
World Policy Institute
777 UN Plaza
New York, NY 10017
quarterly journal; $18

• Contains articles providing substantive analyses of peace and world order issues such as defense, disarmament, international politics, revolution, the world economy, etc.

6

International Studies and Research in Professional Education

Agriculture, Health and Human Ecology

6.001
John J. Sparkman Center for International Public Health Education
University of Alabama in Birmingham
University Station
Birmingham, AL 35294
(205) 934-2288

Contact(s):
Juan N. Navia, Director

• Offers M.P.H. in International Health (through Department of International Public Health Sciences) focused on public health problems and issues in developing countries; conducts programs and supports projects in developing countries related to education in public health

6.002
Office of International Agriculture Programs
University of Arizona
College of Agriculture
International Programs
209 Nugent Bldg.
Tucson, AZ 85721
(602) 626-1717

Contact(s):
Michael E. Norvelle, Coordinator

• Offers B.A. in Agriculture with International Agriculture option; emphasis on the social sciences and Asian area studies

6.003
International Agricultural Development Program
California Polytechnic State University
San Luis Obispo, CA 93407
(805) 546-0111

Contact(s):
George Hellyer, Coordinator

• Offers M.S. in International Agricultural Development emphasizing the management and administration of the development process particularly in the areas of policy, marketing, research, extension and small farm economics

6.004
Programs in International Health
Loma Linda University
School of Health
Loma Linda, CA 92350
(714) 824-4902

Contact(s):
P. William Dysinger, Director

• Offers M.S.P.H. (Master of Science in Public Health) and M.P.H. (Master of Public Health) in International Public Health, focusing on the solution to public health problems in foreign countries and the development of cross-cultural health service skills

• Office of International Health Services serves as a resource center for the planning, development and evaluation of approaches to Christian health ministry and outreach to the Third World and conducts public health assistance programs abroad

Contact(s):
James E. C. Walker, Director

• Offers M.S. in Community Health and Ph.D. in Social Sciences and Health Services with an international concentration; maintains Cross-national Study of Health Systems Resource Center; sponsors research and conducts outreach program for organizations in the region; publishes newsletters and bulletins

6.005
International Agricultural Development Program
University of California at Davis
228 Mrak Hall
Davis, CA 95616
(916) 752-0110

Contact(s):
David W. Robinson, Associate Dean

• Offers M.S. in International Agricultural Development combining the study of a specialized agricultural field with an analysis of how technological, social, economic and political forces affect the development process in less developed countries; Davis conducts agricultural development assistance projects in Egypt (Rice Research and Training Program), Mexico, China, Morocco and Nigeria

6.006
Center for International Community Health Studies
University of Connecticut
School of Medicine
Department of Community Medicine
Farmington, CT 06032
(203) 674-2555

6.007
International Studies
Howard University
School of Human Ecology
Washington, DC 20059
(202) 636-7603

Contact(s):
Elizabeth Brabble, Director

• M.S. in Human Ecology in International Studies combining international with ecological studies such as food and nutrition, population studies, environmental studies, consumer affairs and family social sciences

6.008
School of Public Health
University of Hawaii at Manoa
Student Services Office
1960 East-West Road, D208
Honolulu, HI 96822
(808) 948-8267

Contact(s):
Jerrold M. Michael, Dean

• Offers M.P.H., M.S., and Dr.P.H. degrees in Public Health (and Ph.D. degrees in Biostatistics/Epidemiology) with focus on international and cross-cultural aspects of health; offers short-term training in many areas and has cooperative relationships with academic public health institutions in Asia and the Pacific

6.009
International Programs in Agriculture
Purdue University
26 Agricultural Administration Bldg.
West Lafayette, IN 47907
(317) 494-6876

Contact(s):
D. Woods Thomas, Associate Dean and Director
James L. Collom, Associate Director
D. Richard Smith, Associate Director

• Offers B.S. in International Agronomy (focusing on the agronomic aspects of international agricultural development) and in International Agriculture (emphasizing international agricultural studies with either a development, management, technical or production orientation, or a combination thereof)
• Manages international exchange and agricultural development assistance programs of the university

6.010
International Agricultural Programs
Iowa State University
College of Agriculture
115 Curtiss Hall
Ames, IA 50011
(515) 294-4866

Contact(s):
J. T. Scott, Assistant Dean

• Offers B.S.A. with secondary major in International Agriculture with emphasis on practical aspects of international economic, political and technical affairs as they affect agriculture around the world; includes elective summer travel course in agriculture alternating between Europe, Asia and the U.S. in successive years

6.011
International Studies in Home Economics
Iowa State University
128 MacKay Hall
Ames, IA 50011
(515) 294-7244

Contact(s):
Donna Cowan, Assistant Dean for Academic Programs

• Offers B.S. in International Studies in Home Economics (cross-cultural home economics)

6.012
World Food Institute
Iowa State University
E.O. Bldg.
Ames, IA 50011
(515) 294-7699

Contact(s):
Charlotte E. Roderuck, Director

• Supports research on problems, issues and solutions in the area of nutrition, food and food supply, particularly in less developed countries and in the context of international relationships; sponsors foreign scholars; has prepared textbook, *Dimensions of World*

Food Problems and publishes annual report, *World Food Trade and U.S. Agriculture*

6.013
International Development Program
Bethel College
North Newton, KS 67117
(316) 283-2500, Ext. 323

Contact(s):
Paul T. McKay, Director

• Offers B.A. in International Development with concentrations in international agriculture, international health and nutrition or industrial arts; emphasis on rural development with a strong orientation toward peace and justice issues

6.014
Dual Degree Program
Kansas State University
Bluemont Hall
Manhattan, KS 66506
(913) 532-5735

Contact(s):
Dwight Wiebe, Coordinator

• Cooperative B.A./B.S. program of Kansas State University and 16 private colleges in Kansas focusing on the problems of and solutions to world hunger; includes three years of study at one of the private colleges and a year or year and a half at KSU

6.015
School of Public Health and Tropical Medicine
Tulane University
1430 Tulane Ave.
New Orleans, LA 70112
(504) 588-5397

Contact(s):
James E. Banta, Dean

• Offers M.P.H., M.P.H. and T.M. (Master of Public Health and Tropical Medicine), and Doctor of Public Health in International Health with emphasis on preparing students to work in international or Third World public health agencies and systems

6.016
Department of International Health
Johns Hopkins University
School of Hygiene and Public Health
615 North Wolfe St.
Baltimore, MD 21205-2179
(301) 955-3543

Contact(s):
William A. Reinke, Acting Chair

• Offers M.P.H., M.H.S. (Master of Health Sciences) and doctoral programs in International Health covering health planning, nutrition, health care systems, personnel training and supervising, studies of health care systems, economics and epidemiological analysis

6.017
Institute of International Agriculture
Michigan State University
101 Agriculture Hall
East Lansing, MI 48824
(517) 355-0174

Contact(s):
Donald R. Isleib, Director

• Coordinates research on international agricultural issues—food, nutrition, resources, rural development—and serves as international resource for on-campus programs; consults and provides institution-building services

6.018
Office of Population Research
Princeton University
21 Prospect Ave.
Princeton, NJ 08544
(609) 452-5510

Contact(s):
Charles F. Westoff, Director

• Offers instruction at both graduate and undergraduate levels; joint Ph.D. with Economics, Sociology or Statistics Department; special one-year training program for Visiting Scholars; research presently centered on comparative studies of fertility in developing countries and methods of analysis in demography; publishes quarterly bibliographic journal, *Population Index* and maintains library

6.019
International Environmental Studies
Rutgers University/Cook College
Department of Human Ecology
New Brunswick, NJ 08903
(201) 932-9624

Contact(s):
Baruch Boxer, Director

• B.A. or B.S. in International Environmental Studies, emphasizing the study of differences in natural resource availability, the interdependence of nations, strategies for international environmental management, the role of transnational organizations and agencies, and moral and ethical issues; offers five options for concentration: agriculture and food;

earth, oceans, and the atmosphere; human health; international institutions and law; and individually designed programs

6.020
International Agriculture Program
Cornell University
261 Roberts Hall
Ithaca, NY 14853
(607) 256-3037

Contact(s):
Edwin B. Oyer, Director

• Offers B.S. with specialization in International Agriculture; Master of Professional Studies (M.P.S.) in International Agricultural and Rural Development and in International Development; M.S. and Ph.D. in International Food Science/International Nutrition (see 6.021) and International Economics and Development
• The Cornell library for agriculture and human ecology contains over 500,000 volumes and 11,000 serials; world area collections also contain extensive materials on agriculture and development subjects
• The Center for the Study of World Food Issues sponsors research and outreach activities, including serving as a resource and referral center for precollege teachers

6.021
International Nutrition Program
Cornell University
Division of Nutritional Sciences
127 Savage Hall
Ithaca, NY 14850
(607) 256-3041

Contact(s):
Michael C. Latham, Director

• Offers M.S. and Ph.D. in International Nutrition including research, practical training and service to international and Third World agencies

6.022
International Population Program
Cornell University
372 Uris Hall
Ithaca, NY 14853
(607) 256-4924

Contact(s):
J. Mayone Stycos, Director

• Offers M.A. and Ph.D. in Population Studies, emphasizing social and cultural factors

6.023
Center for Demographic Studies
Duke University
2117 Campus Drive
Durham, NC 27706
(919) 684-6126

Contact(s):
George C. Myers, Director

• Conducts research on a variety of demographic subjects, including cross-national studies of population factors that affect economic and social development

6.024
International Agricultural Programs
Texas Tech University
P.O. Box 4620
Lubbock, TX 79409
(806) 742-2218

Contact(s):
I. R. Traylor, Director

• Offers international option in Master of Agriculture degree and an Arid Lands Op-

tion in an interdisciplinary M.A. or M.S.; administers technical assistance, foreign personnel training programs and the International Center for Arid and Semi-Arid Land Studies

6.025
International Agricultural Programs
University of Wisconsin at Madison
240 Agricultural Hall
Madison, WI 53706
(608) 262-1271

Contact(s):
Kenneth H. Shapiro, Associate Dean and Director

• Conducts research on full range of agricultural and rural sociological issues as they affect less developed countries

6.026
The Following Institutions Also Offer Joint Degree Programs in Agriculture, Health and/or Human Ecology and International or Area Studies:
Stanford University (see 16.012, Latin American Studies)

University of California, Los Angeles (see 16.014, Latin American Studies)

Boston University (see 12.023, African Studies)

University of New Mexico (see 16.062, Latin American Studies)

The Ohio State University (see 17.036, Middle East Studies)

University of Pittsburgh (see 13.109, Asian Studies)

University of Texas, Austin (see 16.097 Latin American Studies)

University of Wisconsin, Madison (see 16.104, Ibero-American Studies)

Business

6.027
International Business Studies
University of Alabama at Tuscaloosa
College of Commerce and Business
  Administration
Box J
University, AL 35486
(205) 348-6090

Contact(s):
John S. Hill, Chair

• Offers B.B.A. with concentration in International Marketing Management or International Trade and Finance (or a minor in International Business), M.A. with specialization in International Marketing Management or International Trade and Development and M.B.A. with international business concentration

6.028
American Graduate School of International Management
Thunderbird Campus
Glendale, AZ 85306
(602) 978-7011

Contact(s):
Marshall Geer III, Dean of the Faculty
Robert L. Gulick, Jr., Dean of Admissions
R. Duane Hall, Director of INTERCOM

Graduate educational institution for training students in international business
• Offers Master of International Management completed in three terms; students are required to take courses in three areas; international studies, modern languages and world business; languages offered include Arabic, Chinese, French, German, Japanese, Portuguese, Spanish and English as a second language; program geared to needs of foreign students; internships and cooperative education programs offered; financial aid in the form of loans, scholarships and assistantships available; special overseas programs in Japan, Mexico, England, Egypt and Spain
• Offers research services and in-service training for business executives through INTERCOM (International Counsel for Management); training programs include: (1) Cross-cultural Communication for International Managers (cultural awareness training for executives, country-specific briefings for families on overseas assignment and multicultural organizational development training); (2) International Business Skills (focusing on personnel, accounting, corporate organization, communications, strategic planning, marketing, finance and currency management); (3) Political and Socioeconomic Orientation (for all countries and/or regions); and (4) Key Manager Language and Area Studies Programs (intensive training in all major cultures and languages, including English as a second language; research activities include marketing studies, political analyses and socioeconomic surveys, trade and investment reports, analyses of overseas legal and organizational restrictions and studies of personnel and compensation issues)

6.029
International Management
California Polytechnic State University
Management Department
San Luis Obispo, CA 93407
(805) 546-1301

Contact(s):
Rolf E. Rogers, Chair

• Offers B.S. in Business Administration with concentration in international management

6.030

International Business Center
California State University at Long Beach
School of Business Administration
Long Beach, CA 90846
(213) 498-5760

Contact(s):
Feliksas Palubinskas, Director

• Offers graduate and undergraduate certificates in International Business

6.031

International Management
Golden Gate University
Graduate School of International
    Management
536 Mission St.
San Francisco, CA 94105
(415) 442-7225

Contact(s):
A. Gerlof Homan, Dean

• Offers M.B.A. in International Management with emphasis on finance, import/export operations and intercultural communication and negotiation

6.032

Division of International Management
Monterey Institute of International Studies
425 Van Buren St.
Box 1978
Monterey, CA 93940
(408) 649-3113

Contact(s):
Nathan Dickleyer, Acting Chair

• Offers Masters in International Business Administration requiring the study of a foreign language and culture and of the techniques of international business; emphasis on cross-cultural and group-oriented skills for the international business manager

6.033

Center for World Business
San Francisco State University
School of Business
1600 Holloway Ave.
San Francisco, CA 94132
(415) 469-1180

Contact(s):
Klaus D. Schmidt, Director

• Conducts research on business practices in selected countries and on import-export processes; provides services to California business community

6.034

School of International and Intercultural Studies
United States International University
10455 Pomerado Road
San Diego, CA 92131
(619) 271-4300
OTHER CAMPUSES: London, Mexico City, Nairobi

Contact(s):
Wayne Allison, Dean

• School of Business offers B.A. in Business Administration with international emphasis and M.A. in International Business at all campuses, with San Diego also offering a Ph.D.

6.034

International Business
University of California at Berkeley
School of Business Administration
Berkeley, CA 94720
(415) 642-1424

Contact(s):
Richard H. Holton, Chair

• Offers M.B.A. and Ph.D. in International Business with emphasis on strategic planning, financial management, marketing and applied economics

6.035
International Business and Comparative Management
University of California, Los Angeles
Graduate School of Management
Los Angeles, CA 90024
(213) 825-3045 or 2506

Contact(s):
Hans Schöllhammer, Director

• Offers Ph.D. in International Business and Comparative Management (emphasizing the effect of the international business environment on business finance, management and organization, competence in functional fields, and special skills in international transactions); also offers concurrent M.A./M.B.A. programs jointly with the Latin American and African Studies Centers

6.036
International Business Program
University of Colorado at Boulder
College of Business and Administration
Campus Box 419
Boulder, CO 80309
(303) 492-6155/5131

Contact(s):
Philip R. Cateora, Director

• Offers B.S. in Business with specialization in International Business, emphasizing marketing, transportation and finance

6.037
Graduate School of Business and Public Administration
University of Denver
Business Administration Bldg.
Room 459
Denver, CO 80208
(303) 753-2162

Contact(s):
David Hopkins, Director, MIM Program

• Offers Master of International Management and joint M.B.A. in International Studies with the Graduate School of International Studies (see 4.018)

6.038
International Business
University of Bridgeport
College of Business and Public Management
Bridgeport, CT 06602
(203) 576-4367

Contact(s):
Frank Moriya, Chair

• Offers B.S. and M.B.A. in International Business with an emphasis on marketing

6.039
Business Administration and International Studies
The University of Connecticut
School of Business Administration
Storrs, CT 06268
(203) 486-3137

Contact(s):
John N. Yanouzas, Assistant Dean for
   Graduate Programs (203) 486-2872
Ann Huckenbeck, Assistant Dean for
   Undergraduate Programs (203) 486-2315

• Offers M.B.A./M.A. joint degree in International Studies with concentration in Latin America, Western Europe or the Soviet Union and Eastern Europe with an emphasis on studying international business operations in the context of foreign languages, cultures and politics; elective semester program in English available in the Netherlands for undergraduates and M.B.A. candidates

6.040
International Business
The American University
Kogod College of Business Administration
4400 Massachusetts Ave. NW
Washington, DC 20016
(202) 686-2147

Contact(s):
Michel Struelens, Chair

• Offers B.S., M.A. and M.S. in International Business

6.041
Programs in International Business
George Washington University
School of Government and Business
  Administration
Washington, DC 20052
(202) 676-7373

Contact(s):
Phillip D. Grub, Chair

• Offers B.B.A., M.B.A. and Doctor of Business Administration in International Business with emphasis on financial and marketing management, international banking and technology transfer

6.042
International Business Program
Florida Atlantic University
College of Business and Public
  Administration
Boca Raton, FL 33431
(305) 393-3654

Contact(s):
David M. Georgoff, Chair

• Offers B.B.A. and B.S. in International Business with emphasis on management and marketing

6.043
International Business
Florida International University
College of Business Administration
North Miami, FL 33181
(305) 940-5870

Contact(s):
Kenneth S. Most, Director

• Offers undergraduate co-major in International Business, M.I.B. (Master of International Business) and M.B.A. with certificate in International Business; emphasis on economic theory of international trade and international banking

6.044
Multinational Business Program
Florida State University
College of Business
Tallahassee, FL 32306
(904) 644-1557

Contact(s):
Urban B. Ozanne, Director

• Offers B.S. with Multinational Business as a single or double major

6.045
International Finance and Marketing
University of Miami
School of Business Administration
P.O. Box 248147
Coral Gables, FL 33124
(305) 284-5935

Contact(s):
John M. Dyer, Director

> • Offers major in International Finance and Marketing with emphasis on practical aspects of international business practices and direct contact with multinational companies and international business operations

6.046
Institute of International Business
Georgia State University
College of Business Administration
University Plaza
Atlanta, GA 30303
(404) 658-2723

Contact(s):
James D. Goodnow, Director

> • Offers M.B.A. and Ph.D. in International Business which combines basic disciplines with functional studies and emphasizes managerial problems involved in overseas operations

6.047
International Business Program
University of Georgia
College of Business Administration
Department of Management
Brooks Hall
Athens, GA 30602
(404) 542-1294

Contact(s):
Asterios Kefalas, Director

> • Offers B.A. in International Business

6.048
Pacific Asian Management Institute
University of Hawaii at Manoa
2404 Maile Way
Honolulu, HI 96822
(808) 948-7564 or 8041

Contact(s):
N. H. Paul Chung, Director

> • Offers courses for students in international business during two six-week summer sessions and a Field Study Abroad Program in Asia
> • Offers three-week and six-week executive development programs for middle managers, bankers, government officials and junior business school faculty in international business management, international banking and finance, international marketing management and trans-Pacific management; non-English-speaking countries' participants may take the Business English for Managers Program

6.049
International Economics and Business
Illinois Benedictine College
Department of Economics and Business
5700 College Road
Lisle, IL 60532
(312) 968-7270

Contact(s):
Margarete P. Roth, Chair

> • Offers B.A. in International Economics and Business with emphasis on understanding other cultures and the development of international business skills

6.050
International Business
Roosevelt University
Walter E. Heller College of Business
   Administration
430 South Michigan Ave.
Chicago, IL 60605
(312) 341-3820

Contact(s):
Paul M. Wellen, Director

• Offers M.S.I.B. (Master of Science in International Business) and M.B.A. with concentration in International Business with emphasis on finance, management and marketing

6.051
Institute of Transnational Business
Ball State University
College of Business
Muncie, IN 47306
(317) 285-7893

Contact(s):
Bert C. Faulhaber, Director

• Develops educational programs in international business for Ball State and other institutions of higher learning; consults and conducts international business conferences, seminars and other outreach programs for industry in Indiana and the region; cooperates with the College of Business in offering undergraduate and M.B.A. programs in international business

6.052
International Business Program
Morgan State University
School of Business and Management
Baltimore, MD 21239
(301) 444-3437

Contact(s):
Dinker Raval, Director

• Offers M.B.A. in International Management

6.053
Harvard International Senior Managers Program
Harvard Business School
Boston, MA 02163

• Intensive eight-week course offered once a year by Harvard faculty; using case study method, study focuses on basic management issues as they are reflected in international and multinational corporate operations; subjects include organizational structure, corporate strategy and national interests, cross-national differences in market strategies, product introduction, management of subsidiaries, financing in several currencies and under varying economic pressures, transfer pricing-profit centers, and broad cross-national economic and environmental issues; participants come from throughout the world and must be sponsored by their companies; language of instruction is English

6.054
International Management
Massachusetts Institute of Technology
Sloan School of Management
Cambridge, MA 02139
(617) 253-6688

• Offers M.S. and Ph.D. with concentration in international management; emphasis on management processes, technological transfer and the international business environment

6.055
International Business
Northeastern University
College of Business
214 Hayden Hall
360 Huntington Ave.
Boston, MA 02115
(617) 437-4806

Contact(s):
Ravi Sarathy, Area Coordinator

• Offers B.S. and M.B.A. with concentration in International Business; also conducts workshops for executives

6.056
International Business Administration Program
The University of Michigan, Ann Arbor
Graduate School of Business Administration
1735 Washtenaw Ave.
Ann Arbor, MI 48109
(313) 763-9463

Contact(s):
Bernice Conner, Administrative Officer

• Offers D.B.A. in International Business Administration; also offers Management and Executive Development Programs

6.057
International Business
Mankato State University
P.O. Box 14
Mankato, MN 56001
(507) 389-1600

Contact(s):
Basil J. Janavaras, Director

• Offers B.S. and M.B.A. with concentration in International Business emphasizing marketing, management, finance and foreign

language study; overseas language study encouraged

6.058
International Business
Lindenwood College
St. Charles, MO 63301
(314) 946-6912

Contact(s):
Aaron Miller, Coordinator

• Offers Graduate Certificate Program in International Business, emphasizing planning, risk analysis, communications, finance, management and marketing

6.059
International Business Program
St. Louis University
3674 Lindell Blvd.
St. Louis, MO 63108
(314) 658-3858

Contact(s):
Seung H. Kim, Director

• Offers M.B.A. and Ph.D. in International Business with emphasis on international accounting, international banking, international finance, and international marketing

6.060
International Management
University of New Mexico
Latin American Institute
801 Yale NE
Albuquerque, NM 87131
(505) 277-2961

Contact(s):
Robert Lenberg, Associate Director for
   International Management Programs

• Offers dual degrees in International Management and Latin American Studies (M.B.A. and M.A.; Ph.D. and M.A.)

6.061
International Business Program
Fairleigh Dickinson University
College of Business Administration
Teaneck, NJ 07666
(201) 692-2142

Contact(s):
Alexander Garcia, Director

• Offers B.S. with concentration in International Business and M.B.A. in International Business

6.062
International Business
Middlesex County College
Edison, NJ 08818
(201) 548-6000, Ext. 281

Contact(s):
Virgil H. Blanco, Director

• Offers certificates in International Trade and International Business and conducts special programs for the business community

6.063
Executive Programs
Graduate School of Business
Columbia University
807 Uris Hall
New York, NY 10027
(212) 280-3395

Contact(s):
James Kennelley, Associate Director

Executive program for international managers

• Four-week fall seminar program for executives in established multinational companies in the U.S. and abroad; designed to increase management skills required to develop and implement strategies that work in an international environment; covers organizational behavior, quantitative methods, management accounting, financial management, marketing management, economic policy, international environmental analysis and strategy formation and implementation; conducted at Arden House in Harriman, New York

6.064
International Business
Columbia University
Columbia Business School
101 Uris Hall
New York, NY 10027
(212) 280-3401

Contact(s):
William J. Heffernan

• Offers M.B.A. with concentration in International Business and with broad operational and functional focus

6.065
International Business Administration Program
New York University
School of Business
100 Trinity Place
New York, NY 10006
(212) 285-6204

Contact(s):
Ingo Walter, Chair

• Offers B.S., M.B.A. and Ph.D. in International Business Administration

6.066
Management Dynamics for International Executives
International Management Development
  Department
Syracuse University
105 Roney Lane
Syracuse, NY 13210
(315) 423-3116

Contact(s):
William K. Phipps, Director

Executive development program for international managers
  • Six-week spring and summer management training seminars for foreign and U.S. managers; includes two-week segment, the Management of Multinational Enterprise Operations, which is divided into three sections: (1) Marketing and Financial Management, (2) Policy Formation, Decision-making and Human Resource Planning, and (3) the Cultural Environment of International Business and Political Risk Analysis; conducted at Minnowbrook, Blue Mountain Lake, NY

6.067
International Business
Utica College
Syracuse University
Burrstone Road
Utica, NY 13502
(315) 792-3157 or 3055

Contact(s):
Michael K. Simpson, Director

  • Offers B.B.A. with concentration in International Business emphasizing international trade, management and marketing

6.068
International Business Program
Warren Wilson College
Swannanoa, NC 28778
(704) 298-6008

Contact(s):
Carol Creager, Chair

  • Offers B.A. with major in International Business

6.069
International Management
Baldwin Wallace College
Berea, OH 44017
(216) 826-2231

Contact(s):
Earl Peck, Director

  • Offers M.B.A. in International Management

6.070
Program in International Business
Ohio State University
College of Administration Science
Hagerty Hall
Columbus, OH 43210
(614) 422-5288

Contact(s):
Lee C. Nehrt, Director

  • Offers B.S., B.A. and M.A. in International Business, and M.B.A. and Ph.D. with major in International Business

6.071
International Business
University of Cincinnati
College of Business
Mail Location #20
Cincinnati, OH 45221
(513) 475-4421

Contact(s):
Ruel C. Kahler, Director

  • Offers undergraduate certificate and M.B.A. in International Business

6.072
International Business
University of Toledo
College of Business Administration
Toledo, OH 43606
(419) 537-2093

Contact(s):
James K. Weekly, Director

• Offers B.B.A. and M.B.A. with specialization in International Business and with emphasis on marketing

6.073
International Business Program
Mt. Hood Community College
26000 S.E. Stark
Gresham, OR 97030
(503) 667-7305

Contact(s):
Betty J. Pritchett, Dean of Development
John Dien, Instructor in International
   Business

• Offers two-year program in international business

6.074
International Business
The Pennsylvania State University
College of Business Administration
Department of Business Logistics
509 Business Administration Bldg.
University Park, PA 16802
(814) 865-1866

Contact(s):
John C. Spychalski, Chair (admissions and
   graduate assistantships)
John D. Daniels, Senior Faculty Member
   (314 Carpenter Bldg., (814) 865-1655;
   inquiries on curriculum and research
   activities)

• Offers M.S., M.B.A. and Ph.D. with major in International Business and emphasis on finance, management and multinational enterprises

6.075
International Business Administration
Temple University
School of Business Administration
Philadelphia, PA 19122
(215) 787-8148

Contact(s):
Rajan Chandran, Director

• Offers M.B.A., M.S.B.A. and Ph.D. in International Business Management with emphasis on economics and management

6.076
The Joseph H. Lauder Institute of Management and International Studies
University of Pennsylvania
The Wharton School
3620 Locust Walk, Room 1469
Philadelphia, PA 19104
(215) 898-1215 or 1216

Contact(s):
Jerry Wind, Director

• Offers dual 24-month M.B.A./M.A. in Management and International Studies (jointly with the School of Arts and Sciences) emphasizing internationalized management courses, social science, language study, and area studies (East Asia, Latin America, Western Europe and the U.S.)

6.077
International Economics and Business
Westminster College
Department of Economics and Business
New Wilmington, PA 16172
(412) 946-8761

Contact(s):
Paul E. Frary, Chair

• Offers B.A. in International Economics and Business with equal emphasis on the development of language skills

6.078
Master in International Business Studies
University of South Carolina
College of Business Administration
Columbia, SC 29208
(803) 777-2730

Contact(s):
William R. Folks, Jr., Program Director

• Offers M.I.B.S. (Master of International Business Studies) focusing on the manager of the international enterprise and emphasizing language (German, French, Spanish, Portuguese, Arabic, Japanese and English as a foreign language) and area studies; overseas internship required

6.079
International Management
Baylor University
Hankamer School of Business
Waco, TX 76798
(817) 755-2263

Contact(s):
Joseph A. McKinney, Director

• Offers B.A. with major in International Business and M.I.M. (Master of International Management); emphasis on management and finance

6.080
International Business Program
St. Mary's University
One Camino Santa Maria
San Antonio, TX 78284
(512) 436-3313

Contact(s):
Gary Gordon, Chair

• B.A. in International Business

6.081
Institute for International Business Analysis
University of Houston
University Park
Houston, TX 77004
(713) 749-7605

Contact(s):
Robert R. Miller, Coordinator

• Offers M.B.A. with concentration in International Business and emphasis on international finance; sponsors research on international business issues

6.082
International Business Administration Program
University of Texas, Austin
College of Business Administration &
   Graduate School of Business
Austin, TX 78712
(512) 471-1128

Contact(s):
Robert T. Green, Director

• Offers B.B.A., M.B.A. and Ph.D. in International Business Administration

6.083
International Business
University of Washington
Graduate School of Business Administration
Seattle, WA 98195
(206) 543-8780

Contact(s):
J. Frederick Truitt, Coordinator

• Offers B.A. and M.B.A. with concentration in international business and a tandem M.A.-M.B.A. degree with the School of International Studies (see 4.151) and Ph.D. with International Business major and minor; emphasis on strategic management and the international business environment and special strength in Asia and the Pacific Rim; sponsors Pacific Rim Project designed to increase business faculty knowledge of the Asia-Pacific Rim countries, stimulate research in and on the area, enrich the curriculum, establish student exchanges and provide special training for U.S. and foreign business personnel, including a Pacific Rim Bankers Program

6.084
International Business
University of Wisconsin at Madison
School of Business
1155 Observatory Drive
Madison, WI 53706
(608) 263-1169

Contact(s):
Robert Aubey, Chair

• Offers M.S. in International Business or M.B.A. with major in International Business with emphasis on finance and marketing

6.085
The Following Institutions Also Offer Joint Degree Programs in Business and/or Management and International or Area Studies:

Stanford University (see 13.011, East Asian Studies)

University of Connecticut (see 16.020, Latin American Studies; see 14.006, Slavic and East European Studies)

Northern Illinois University (see 13.040, Southeast Asian Studies)

University of Chicago (see 4.035, International Studies)

Indiana University, Bloomington (see 14.014, Russian and East European Studies)

University of Michigan, Ann Arbor (see 14.024, Russian and East European Studies; see 17.023, Near East and North African Studies)

University of New Mexico (see 16.062, Latin American Studies)

Seton Hall University (see 4.076, International Studies)

Cornell University (see 4.082, International Studies)

Hofstra University (see 13.085, Asian Studies)

Portland State University (see 4.113, International Studies)

Indiana University of Pennsylvania (see 4.119, International Studies)

University of Texas, Austin (see 16.097, Latin American Studies)

University of Texas, El Paso (see 16.098, Inter-American Studies)

University of Washington (see 4.151, International Studies)

University of Wisconsin, Madison (see 16.104, Ibero-American Studies)

Education

6.086
Stanford International Development Education Committee (SIDEC)
Stanford University
School of Education
Stanford, CA 94305
(415) 497-4644

Contact(s):
Hans N. Weiler, Chair

- Offers M.A. and Ph.D. in International Development Education emphasizing the interrelationship between education and economic, political and social change from multidisciplinary and international/cross-cultural perspectives

6.087
Center for Teaching International Relations
University of Denver
Denver, CO 80208
(303) 753-3106

Contact(s):
Ronald Schukar, Director
Steven Clarke, Director of Publications

Graduate center for research and training in global awareness education; established in 1968
- Supervises M.A. program offered by the School of Education in Cooperation with the Graduate School of International Studies (see 4.018)
- Develops and offers courses in teaching cultural awareness, ethnic heritage, comparative studies, communication, and world issues at the elementary and secondary levels
- Consults with schools and school districts on the improvement of global awareness teaching; serves as a National Service Center to assist in the planning and development of global education programs

- Publishes extensive list of and constitutes major resource on global education teaching materials for elementary and secondary levels; emphasis on global awareness, perceptual differences, diversity, ethnic and comparative studies, conflict and other global issues such as food, hunger, energy and population; most publications are in series: global awareness, cultural studies, environmental education, comparative studies and ethnic studies

6.088
The I.N. Thut World Education Center
University of Connecticut
Box U-32, School of Education
Storrs, CT 06268
(203) 486-3321

Contact(s):
Frank A. Stone, Director
Patricia S. Weibust, Associate Director

Nonprofit research and service arm of the University of Connecticut School of Education functioning in four areas: bilingual, multicultural, international and global education (particularly active in the Peoples of Connecticut project involving ethnic groups in Connecticut)
- Prepares and publishes studies of (1) education in other countries (especially the Third World), (2) international development education and (3) international education in the U.S. including catalogues of Asian and Middle Eastern Studies resources in Connecticut
- Develops courses, sponsors conferences, consults with community organizations and provides "World Externs" (educators from abroad) as resource persons; also collects, maintains and distributes materials on international and global education

6.089
International Education Program
The American University
School of Education
4400 Massachusetts Ave. NW
Washington, DC 20016
(202) 686-2186

Contact(s):
Leon E. Clark, Director

• Offers M.A. in International Education with emphasis either on development education overseas or global/multi-cultural education in the U.S.; also covers study of non-formal and adult education, cross-cultural service, curriculum and materials development and comparative education; arranges internships in the U.S. and abroad

6.090
Global Awareness Program
Florida International University
School of Education
Tamiami Campus
Miami, FL 33199
(305) 554-2664

Contact(s):
Jan L. Tucker, Director

• Program of the School of Education designed to infuse Global Studies into educational training through a professional education core program and changes in the social studies curriculum; also provides in-service workshops for teachers and sponsors a wide variety of other public, student, faculty and resource programs

6.091
Global Education Program
University of Georgia
G-4 Aderhold
Athens, GA 30602
(404) 542-3002

Contact(s):
Everett T. Keach, Jr., Director

• Develops programs and activities (including workshops, seminars and the preparation of teaching materials, curriculum and publications) designed to increase international/global experience of faculty and students of the College of Education and to expand global awareness and the teaching of international subjects in the schools

6.092
International Education Program
Illinois State University
College of Education
533 DeGarmo Hall
Normal, IL 61761
(309) 438-5415

Contact(s):
Mario Prada, Coordinator

• Maintains multicultural/global Resource Center and infuses courses with global content to insure that all education students are exposed to global educational experience

6.093
International Education Program
Anderson College
Anderson, IN 46012
(317) 649-9071

Contact(s):
Norman E. Beard, Dean

• Offers B.A. in International Education with emphasis on language and cultural studies and on overseas learning and service experiences

6.094
Comparative Education Center
University of Maryland
College of Education
Department of Education Policy, Planning
   and Administration
College Park, MD 20742
(301) 454-5766

Contact(s):
George A. Male, Director

   • Offers M.A. and Ph.D. programs in
Comparative Education; includes international and cross-cultural as well as comparative studies

6.095
Center for International Education
University of Massachusetts
Hills South
Amherst, MA 01003
(413) 545-0465

Contact(s):
George Urch

   • Offers M.Ed. and Ph.D. in International Education with three areas of concentration: Third World Development
Education, Nonformal Education and Internationalizing American Education; includes
opportunities for study, research and training
abroad; also conducts nondegree training
programs including individually planned study,
workshops, study tours and internships; student body balanced between North Americans and non–North Americans
   • Undertakes development assistance and
other international consulting and training
projects for foreign national, international and
intergovernmental agencies
   • Sponsors research, publishes studies
and curriculum materials (particularly in
nonformal and development education) and
maintains nonformal Education Resource

Center with materials on international education, education and development, nonformal education and innovative program and
teaching materials

6.096
Education and Latin American Studies
University of Massachusetts
School of Education
Room 207
Amherst, MA 01003
(413) 545-0236

Contact(s):
Luis Fuentes, Chair

   • Offers Ed.D. with concentration in
Latin American Studies

6.097
**Institute for International Studies in
Education**
Michigan State University
East Lansing, MI 48824
(517) 355-8332

Contact(s):
Ted Ward, Coordinator

   • Conducts research, develops professional development and study programs for
faculty and students concerned with international education and directs overseas technical assistance programs in education

6.098
Education and East Asian Studies
Seton Hall University
School of Education
South Orange, NJ 07079
(201) 761-9000, Ext. 5119

Contact(s):

Juan Cobarruleios, Director, Bilingual
Program

• Offers M.Ed. and Ed.D. with concentration in East Asian/Bilingual/Bicultural Education in cooperation with the Asian Studies Program

6.099

International Educational Development
Columbia University
Teachers College
525 West 120th St.
New York, NY 10027
(212) 678-3184

Contact(s):

Willard J. Jacobson and William C. Sayres,
Principal Advisors

• M.A., Ed.M. and Ed.D. programs combine educational fields with international education and cross-cultural and area studies, with emphasis on educational development in other countries

6.100

Department of Educational Theory and Practice
The Ohio State University
227 Arps Hall
1945 North High St.
Columbus, OH 43210-1172
(614) 422-5381

Contact(s):

M. Eugene Gilliom, Coordinator of
International Programs

• Conducts broad-based international program to expand global education exposure of faculty and students including the administration of social studies education study tours abroad, the development of courses and curriculum (e.g. the International Content for Teacher Education Project which will produce a series of position papers on the development of a global perspective in undergraduate teacher education), the provision of overseas student teaching opportunities, the establishment of a worldwide network of professional educators for the purpose of research and exchange, and the publication of papers and other materials of global education, including *Perspectives of Global Education: A Sourcebook for Classroom Teachers*

6.101

International and Multicultural Studies
University of Pittsburgh
School of Education
4C01 Forbes Quadrangle
Pittsburgh, PA 15260
(412) 624-1338

Contact(s):

Catherine Cornbleth, Coordinator

• Offers Undergraduate Certificate, M.A. and Ph.D. certificate program (sponsored jointly with the University Center for International Studies, see 4.125) in International and Multicultural Studies which combines cross-cultural study of a theme or issue, ethnic studies or foreign area studies with advanced study in curriculum and instructional development

6.102

International and Development Education Program
University of Pittsburgh
5A01 Forbes Quadrangle
Pittsburgh, PA 15260
(412) 624-5574

Contact(s):

Paul Watson, Director

• Offers M.Ed. or Ph.D. in International and Development Education focusing on how education relates to social and economic change and development in different political and cultural settings around the world, especially in the less developed countries and in the U.S.; includes such areas as educational policy formulation, planning and implementing innovation, nonformal education, transfer of knowledge, comparative and international/multicultural/multiethnic education and language policy

6.103
The Following Institutions Also Offer Joint Degree Programs in Education and International or Area Studies:
Arizona State University (see 13.002, Asian Studies)
Stanford University (see 13.011, East Asian Studies; see 16.012, Latin American Studies)

University of California, Berkeley (see 17.002, Middle East Studies)
University of California, Los Angeles (see 16.014, Latin American Studies)
University of Chicago (see 4.035, International Studies)
Seton Hall University (see 4.076, International Studies)
University of New Mexico (see 16.065, Latin American Studies)
City University of New York, Brooklyn College (see 12.034, African Studies)
City University of New York, Queens College (see 16.065, Latin American Studies)
Cornell University (see 4.082, International Studies)
Bowling Green University (see 13.095, Asian Studies)
Indiana University of Pennsylvania (see 4.119, International Studies)
University of Pennsylvania (see 17.039, Middle East Studies)

Journalism

6.104
International Journalism
Baylor University
Waco, TX 76798
(817) 755-3261

Contact(s):
Loyal N. Gould, Chair

• Offers M.A. in International Journalism emphasizing international news analysis and foreign correspondence; requires foreign internship and speaking knowledge of second language

6.105
The Following Institutions Also Offer Joint Degree Programs in Journalism (Communications) and International or Area Studies:
University of California, Berkeley (see 13.013, Asian Studies)
University of Michigan, Ann Arbor (see 14.024, Russian and East European Studies)
University of Texas, Austin (see 16.097, Latin American Studies)

Law

6.106
School of Law
University of California at Berkeley
Berkeley, CA 94720
(415) 642-1419

Contact(s):
Frank C. Newman, International Law

• Offers J.D., LL.M. and S.J.D. with subject specializations in international economic relations or international human rights

6.107
Georgetown University Law Center
Georgetown University
600 New Jersey Ave. NW
Washington, DC 20001
(202) 624-8357

Contact(s):
John G. Murphy, Jr., Associate Dean
(Graduate Studies)
Allan Goodman and Barry Carter, Co-
Directors, JD/MSFS Program
(202) 624-8038

• Offers LL.M. (International and Comparative Law) and a four-year Juris/Doctor/Master of Science in Foreign Service (JD/MSFS) Program jointly with the School of Foreign Service (see 6.131) which includes advanced work in international studies and international and domestic law; also offers an LL.M. (Common Law Studies) for graduates of foreign law schools (non-common law countries)

6.108
Comparative Law Program
University of Miami
School of Law
P.O. Box 248087
Coral Gables, FL 33124
(305) 284-5402

Contact(s):
Alfred F. Crotti

• Offers J.D. with option to specialize in international law; offers Master of Laws (LL.M.) with specializations in Inter-American Law or International Law; also offers special LL.M. and M.C.L. (Master of Comparative Law) for foreign students

6.109
Graduate School of International Studies
University of Miami
Coral Gables, FL 33124
(305) 284-4303

Contact(s):
George Wise, Director

• Offers M.A., D.A. and Ph.D. in International Affairs with specialization in international law, ocean law and inter-American law and legal institutions (see also 6.134)

6.110
Harvard Law School
Harvard University
Cambridge, MA 02138
(617) 495-3178

Contact(s):
Frederick E. Snyder, Assistant Dean for
International and Comparative Legal
Studies

• Maintains extensive program in International Legal Studies integrated with LL.M. (Master of Law) and S.J.D. (Doctor of Science of Law) programs and geared to both U.S. and foreign students; courses cover international law and organizations, international business law, comparisons of legal systems, legal problems of development and other law subjects; special East Asian Legal Studies Program available focusing on legal systems of East Asia; an International Tax Program offers training in problems of taxation and fiscal administration for students from other countries

6.111
Comparative Law Program
University of Mississippi
University, MS 38677
(601) 232-7361

Contact(s):
Stephen Gorove, Chair

• Offers LL.M. and Master of Comparative Law with concentration in international and comparative law; also offers special program in space law

6.112
Parker School of Foreign and Comparative Law
Columbia University School of Law
435 West 116th St.
Box 62
New York, NY 10027
(212) 280-2693

Contact(s):
Henry P. de Vries, Director

Center within Columbia University School of Law for research and teaching in international, foreign and comparative law
• Offers Certificate of Achievement for law students completing foreign law programs; maintains the following area studies programs: Inter-American Law Center, Center of Japanese Legal Studies, Chinese Legal Studies Program, Middle Eastern Law Center (in development in 1984), African Law Center and Project on European Legal Insti-

tutions; offers Jervey Fellowships in foreign law for law graduates involving a year of foreign law study at Columbia and a year of study overseas at a foreign university or public agency; sponsors summer intensive program in foreign law and publishes reference works on and studies of foreign law and legal systems; offers joint program with the School of International and Public Affairs (see 6.151)

6.113
Cornell Law School
Cornell University
Ithaca, NY 14853
(607) 256-3604

Contact(s):
John J. Barcelo III, Director, International Legal Studies

• Offers J.D. with specialization in International Legal Studies stressing the international aspects of private practice, government service and business, especially international business transactions, public international law and comparative law
• Publishes *Cornell International Law Journal* and sponsors Cornell International Law Society, Cornell Round of the Phillip C. Jessup International Law Moot Court Competition, and a lecture and colloquium series

6.114
American and Islamic Law
University of Pennsylvania
Middle East Center
838 Williams Hall CU
Philadelphia, PA
(215) 243-6335

Contact(s):
Thomas Naff, Director

• Offers joint degree certificate with the Law School in American and Islamic law

6.115
School of Law
University of Washington
JB-20
Seattle, WA 78195

Contact(s):
John O. Haley, Associate Dean for Graduate
Studies (206) 543-5643
Dan F. Henderson, Director, Asian Law
Program (206) 543-4949
William T. Burke, Director, Law and
Marine Affairs (206) 542-2275

• Asian Law Program offers LL.M. in
Asian and Comparative Law focusing on the
laws of China, Japan, Korea and Indonesia;
particular emphasis on legal aspects of investment and trade in the context of U.S.—
Japanese commerce and economic relations;
offers Ph.D. in Asian and Comparative Law
to scholar-lawyers from other countries
• Houses editorial and/or business offices for *Law in Japan, An Annual, The Korean Journal of Comparative Law* and sponsors publication of research on Asian law in
cooperation with the University of Washington Press in an Asian Law Series
• Offers concurrent J.D./M.A. in International Studies and in Chinese, Japanese,
Korean, South Asian, Middle Eastern and
Russian and East European Regional Studies
• Offers LL.M. in Marine Affairs

6.116
The Following Institutions Also Offer Joint Degree Programs in Law and International or Area Studies:
Stanford University (see 16.012, Latin
American Studies; see 13.011, East Asian
Studies)
University of Denver (see 4.018,
International Studies)
Harvard University (see 17.019, Middle
East Studies)
University of Michigan, Ann Arbor (see
14.024, Russian and East European
Studies)
University of Washington (see 4.151,
International Studies)
University of Wisconsin, Madison (see
16.104, Ibero-American Studies)

Library Science

6.118
School of Library and Information Studies
University of California, Berkeley
Berkeley, CA 94720
(415) 642-1464

Contact(s):
Michael K. Buckland, Dean

• Offers M.L.I.S. (Master of Library and
Information Studies), Certificate in Library
and Information Studies (post-Master's) and
Doctor of Philosophy in Librarianship with
specializations in comparative and international studies in librarianship

6.119
The Graduate Library School
The University of Chicago
1100 E. 57th St.
Chicago, IL 60637
(312) 962-8272

Contact(s):
W. Boyd Rayward, Dean

• Offers M.A., Certificate of Advanced
Study and Ph.D. in Library Science with
specialization in International Librarianship;
offers dual degree M.A. programs with the
Department of South Asian Language and

Civilization (see 13.043), the Center for Middle East Studies (see 17.014), the Division of the Social Sciences and the Graduate School of Business

6.120
The Following Institutions Also Offer Joint Degree Programs in Library and Information Science and International or Area Studies:
University of California, Berkeley (see 17.002, Middle East Studies)
University of California, Los Angeles (see 16.014, Latin American Studies)

Public Administration, International Service and Development Studies/Planning

6.121
International Relations
Claremont Graduate School
Claremont, CA 91711
(714) 621-8079

Contact(s):
Lewis W. Snider, Chairman

• Offers one-year Master of Environmental Policy Studies, a two-year Master of International Studies and a Ph.D. in International Relations; emphasizes the analysis of foreign policy and international relations issues and is divided into four subfields of concentration: foreign policy, defense policy, international political economy and international management (includes courses from the M.B.A. program)

6.122
Center for Research in Economic Development
San Diego State University
College Ave.
San Diego, CA 92182
(619) 265-5471

Contact(s):
M. C. Madhaven, Director

• Conducts research on economic development focusing on specific issues in selected countries and regions (e.g., Latin America, Turkey, South Korea, India, Malaysia) with a particular interest in trade relationships

6.123
Division of International Policy Studies
Monterey Institute of International Studies
425 Van Buren St.
Box 1978
Monterey, CA 93940
(408) 649-3113

Contact(s):
Stephen Garrett, Chair

• Offers M.A. in International Public Administration with emphasis on comparative institutions and processes, diplomacy, economics and area studies, including North American Area Studies

6.124
Communication and Development
Stanford University
Department of Communication
Stanford, CA 94305
(415) 497-4621

Contact(s):
Everett Rogers, Director

• Offers M.A. in Communication with a specialization in communication and development

6.125
Department of City and Regional Planning
University of California, Berkeley
Berkeley, CA 94720
(415) 642-3257

Contact(s):
Frederick C. Collignon, Chair

• Offers M.C.P. (Master of City Planning) and Ph.D. in City and Regional Planning with specialization in economic and regional planning and land use and housing, including development planning in Third World countries

6.126
Urban Planning Program
University of California, Los Angeles
Graduate School of Architecture and Urban Planning
Los Angeles, CA 90024
(213) 825-4781

Contact(s):
John Friedmann, Head

• Offers M.A. in Urban Planning including urban and regional studies and rural development with a focus on Third World countries

6.127
International Public Administration
University of Southern California
VKC 322
Los Angeles, CA 90089-0043
(213) 743-6750

Contact(s):
Dean, Public Administration

Professional training program
• Offers two-year M.S. in International Public Administration focused on the management of organizations in foreign or international contexts with an emphasis on government organizations or multinational enterprises in the developing world; second year spent in a management internship in a developing country

6.128
College of Public and International Affairs
The American University
School of Government and Public Administration
Washington, DC 20016
(202) 686-2354

Contact(s):
Coralie Bryant, Co-Director, International Development Programs

• Offers M.A. in International Development and M.S. in Development Management open to U.S. and foreign students

6.129
School of International Service
The American University
College of Public and International Affairs
Washington, DC 20016
(202) 686-2483 (graduate); 2474 (undergraduate)

Contact(s):
William Clinton Olson, Dean
Larman Wilson, Associate Dean (202) 686-2471

• Offers B.A. in International Studies, European Integration, and Language and

Foreign Area Studies, the latter jointly with the Department of Foreign Languages, including Russian Area Studies (see 18.495), Spanish/Latin American Studies (see 16.022) and German/Western European Studies (see 15.005)

• International Studies includes the following fields: international relations, U.S. and comparative foreign policy, regional international systems and area studies, non-Western civilizations, international development, international communication and policy analysis

• European Integration emphasizes business, economics, history and political studies and requires an internship (usually in a U.S. government agency or an international organization) and one period of study and travel in the European Community (the university offers programs in London, Copenhagen and Rome)

• Offers M.A. in International Affairs, International Communication, or International Development and European Integration along with a Ph.D. in International Relations; also the following joint degree offerings: Master of Public Administration in International Affairs (with the College of Public and International Affairs, see 6.128) and a J.D./M.A. in International Law and Organization

• Principal fields of study are international relations, international law and organization, international communication (with emphasis on political/cultural perspectives), U.S. and comparative foreign policy, world human needs, international development, regional international systems (Latin America, Western Europe, the Soviet Union and Eastern Europe, the Middle East, East Asia, Southeast Asia, South Asia and Africa) and comparative cross-national studies

• Arranges cooperative educational employment and graduate internships, including nominations to the Presidential Management Intern Program (two-year appointments in U.S. federal government agencies)

6.130
School of Public and International Affairs
George Washington University
2035 H St. NW
Washington, DC 20052
(202) 676-7050

• Offers B.A. in International Affairs with specialization in international political relations, international economics, international communications or regional studies; M.A. with concentration in political science, history and economics, specialized international fields (law, administration, development, security policy studies, business, education, and science, technology and public affairs) or regional studies, including East Asian, Latin American (see 16.023), Russian and East European, Middle Eastern (see 17.010) and Sino-Soviet Studies (see 13.030)

6.131
Edmund A. Walsh School of Foreign Service
Georgetown University
Washington, DC 20057
(202) 625-4216

Contact(s):
Peter F. Krogh, Dean
Putnam M. Ebinger, Director, BSFS
Allan A. Goodman, Director, MSFS

Professional school of international service
• Offers B.S., M.S. and five-year B.S./M.S. degrees in Foreign Service (B.S.F.S. and M.S.F.S.); undergraduate emphasis on history, diplomacy, politics, foreign language, economics and regional studies; graduate students specialize in a functional field, a policy field or regional studies; regional studies (for which undergraduates may receive a certificate) include Arab Studies, African Studies, Asian Studies and German Studies; certificate available to graduates and undergradu-

ates in International Business Diplomacy and to graduates in Arab/Middle East Studies and German Public and International Affairs

• Offers joint M.S./M.A. programs in Foreign Service and History and Foreign Service and Economics, an M.A. program in Arab Studies through the Center for Contemporary Arab Studies (see 17.011), and a joint J.D./MSFS with the Law Center (see 6.107)

• Sponsors research through the Institute for the Study of Diplomacy (see 6.132) and offers outreach training and educational activities through the Foreign Service Academy and the Program in International Business Diplomacy

• Study abroad encouraged

• In addition to the extensive resources in the Washington area in international affairs, the Georgetown University Library maintains a collection of government documents, books, microfilms and other materials numbering over 1,000,000 items

• Sponsors Fellows Program of study and research for professionals from public and private sectors

• A variety of special scholarships and fellowships are available

6.132
Institute for the Study of Diplomacy
Georgetown University
School of Foreign Service
Washington, DC 20001
(202) 625-6647

Contact(s):
David D. Newsom, Director

• Sponsors research on the practical aspects of the diplomatic process such as reporting, analysis, policy recommendation, negotiation, mediation, conciliation, conference diplomacy, representation and consular affairs and on the relationship between do-

mestic institutions and official diplomacy; conducts meetings and training programs and maintains publishing program

6.133
School of Advanced International Studies
The Johns Hopkins University
1740 Massachusetts Ave. NW
Washington, DC 20036
(202) 785-6830

Contact(s):
George R. Packard, Dean

Graduate division of The Johns Hopkins University; established in 1943 and incorporated into Johns Hopkins in 1950; provides advanced professional education in preparation for careers in international service in government, business, international organizations, teaching and research; offers mid-career training for persons currently working in international fields and conducts scholarly research on problems of U.S. relationships with the governments and institutions of other countries

• Offers M.A. (two years) and Ph.D. in International Studies and a two-year Master of International Public Policy (for U.S. and foreign mid-career candidates); nondegree work also available

• Principal areas of study are international relations, American foreign policy, international politics, international economics, comparative politics and modernization and regional studies (Africa, see 12.012; Asia, see 13.031; Europe, see 15.006; Latin America, see 16.024; the Middle East, see 17.012; and the Soviet Union and American Foreign Policy); language instruction in Arabic, Chinese, French, German, Haitian, Japanese, Portuguese, Russian and Spanish; also maintains Center of Canadian Studies (see 18.043) and Center of Brazilian Studies (see 18.028)

• Offers Work-Study Program integrating formal education with professional experience in international organizations and agencies in the Washington area and "The American Political System and U.S. Foreign Policy," a special course for foreign diplomats assigned to the U.S.

• The Johns Hopkins Foreign Policy Institute conducts research and teaching on current, practical public policy issues in such areas as security, international economics, U.S.-Soviet relations and energy; publishes *SAIS Review* ($8)

• Maintains SAIS branch in Bologna, Italy, providing approximately 110 students (half American/SAIS and half from other countries) instruction in international economics, European studies and international relations; intensive language instruction in Italian and English

• Draws extensively on the international library, research and organizational resources of the Washington, D.C., area

• Offers general fellowships, a number of special fellowships, U.S. government fellowships (including Graduate Professional Opportunities Program fellowships for minority and women students) and research assistantships

6.134
Graduate School of International Studies
University of Miami
Box 248123
Coral Gables, FL 33124
(305) 284-4303

Contact(s):
Robert L. Levine, Acting Interim Dean

• Offers M.A., D.A. and Ph.D. in International Affairs including functional and geographic area specializations; functional specializations available are international relations and foreign policy, strategic studies and national security, international law, ocean law, inter-American law and legal institutions, in-

ternational economics, ideological conflict and political theory, development and developmental processes, urban and regional planning, and international business management (Ph.D. option only); geographic area specializations available: Latin American Studies, the Caribbean and its littoral, Soviet Studies, Middle Eastern Studies, Chinese Studies and East Asian Studies

• Also offers degrees in Inter-American Studies (see 16.029) and Soviet Studies (see 18.500)

6.135
Public Affairs Graduate Programs
Indiana University at Bloomington
School of Public and Environmental Affairs
400 E. Seventh St., Room 327
Bloomington, IN 47405
(812) 332-0211

Contact(s):
Charles R. Wise, Director

• Offers Master of Public Affairs with a concentration in comparative and international affairs; focuses on administration, development and economics with emphasis on area studies, functional studies or on other public administration fields; International Development Internships available through the Agency for International Development

6.136
International Development Institute
400 East 7th St.
Bloomington, IN 47405
(812) 335-8596

Contact(s):
William J. Siffin, Director

Independent research center based at Indiana University

• Conducts research primarily on administrative and organizational aspects of international development; consults and conducts workshops and training programs; publishes books and papers and maintains 4,000-volume library

6.137

Patterson School of Diplomacy and International Commerce
University of Kentucky
Lexington, KY 40506-0027
(606) 257-4666

Contact(s):
Vincent Davis, Director

• Offers professional M.A. degree in Diplomacy and International Commerce with particular focus on the practical dimensions of international economics, business and politics and an orientation toward professional career preparation in international business, foreign affairs, international organizations and other domains of international service (including journalism, the military, agriculture, health care, etc.)
• Sponsors and promotes research, publishes occasional studies on international political issues and maintains guest scholar-in-residence program
• Conducts public outreach programs, particularly the sponsorship of workshops, conferences and symposia for business, schools and community organizations in the region

6.138

World Development Institute
Boston University
270 Bay State Road
Boston, MA 02215

Contact(s):
Paul Streeten, Director

Institute for research on international, global and comparative issues of development

• Coordinates and strengthens the activities of three regional centers of development studies at Boston University and in addition conducts and sponsors research in such fields as comparative studies and the interaction of national and international policies
• African, Asian and Latin American Centers of Devleopment Studies sponsor research on development issues in their respective areas and supervise both foreign and American graduate students working in those areas

6.139

International Development Program
Clark University
Worcester, MA 01610
(617) 793-7201

Contact(s):
Richard Ford, Co-Director
Barbara Thomas, Acting Co-Director

• Offers M.A. in International Development oriented toward resources management, the environment and regional planning, with emphasis on rural development and women and development in the Third World

6.140

Lucius N. Littauer Program in Public Administration
Harvard University
John F. Kennedy School of Government
79 John F. Kennedy St.
Cambridge, MA 02138
(617) 495-1154

Contact(s):
Mary Jane England, Assistant Dean and Director

• Offers nine-month Masters in Public Administration degree program for experienced professionals working in public interest positions; specializations available include International Affairs and Security, International Development, Government and Business, and Environment, Health, Science and Technology

6.141
The Fletcher School of Law and Diplomacy
Tufts University
Medford, MA 02155
(617) 628-7010

Contact(s):
Theodore L. Eliot, Jr., Dean
John P. Roche, Academic Dean

• Offers a one-year (for mid-career applicants) and a two-year M.A. in Law and Diplomacy, and a Ph.D. in Law and Diplomacy; principal divisions: International Law and Organization; Diplomatic History and International Political Relations (including field emphases on Europe, Communist areas, Asia and the Western Hemisphere); International Economic Relations; and Political Institutions and Systems; includes special programs in economic affairs (William L. Clayton Center for International Economic Affairs); Public Diplomacy (Edward R. Murrow Center for Public Diplomacy); Civilization and Foreign Affairs; International Resources Development (including general development studies, energy, resources, the environment and nutrition, food and agriculture); International Security Studies; and International Business Relations
• Participates in student and faculty exchange programs with the Graduate Institute of International Studies in Geneva, Switzerland, and conducts joint degree program with Harvard Law School
• Publishes *The Fletcher Forum: A Journal of Studies in International Affairs* ($9)

6.142
Center for Advanced Study of International Development
Michigan State University
College of Social Science
307 Berkey Hall
East Lansing, MI 48824-1111
(517) 353-5925

Contact(s):
Tom Carroll, Director

• Offers B.A. in a social science discipline with International Development specialization including study of a development sector (agriculture, health, housing, etc.) and a geographic area: Latin America, Africa, Asia or the Middle East; emphasis on the world as a global system and how it affects international relations and national development; overseas field experience or internship strongly encouraged

6.143
Master of Development Administration Program
Western Michigan University
Department of Political Science
Kalamazoo, MI 49008
(616) 383-1886

Contact(s):
Claude S. Phillips, Director

• Offers Master of Development Administration Program for U.S. and foreign students; strength in South Asia and in Nigeria, Turkey and Korea

6.144
Hubert H. Humphrey Institute of Public Affairs
University of Minnesota
909 Social Sciences Bldg.
267 19th Ave. South
Minneapolis, MN 55455
(612) 373-2653

Contact(s):
Dean Abrahamson, Director, M.A. Program
Robert Einsweiler, Director, M.P. Program

• Offers two-year M.A. and M.P. (Master of Planning) in International Development and Foreign Affairs requiring concentrations in two of the following areas: international political relations, political systems, modernization and social change, the environment, development economics, agricultural development, trade and investment, world communication, education, health and human resources, farm systems, rural technology transfer, design and assessment, administration and institutional change and diplomatic practice; internships required of most students

6.145
Minnesota Studies in International Development Program
University of Minnesota
Office of International Programs
201 Nolte West
315 Pillsbury Drive S.E.
Minneapolis, MN 55455
(612) 373-3793

Contact(s):
Tom O'Toole, Director

• Offers B.A. and M.A. in International Development Studies

6.146
International Development
Washington University
Box 1079
St. Louis, MO 63130
(314) 889-6290

Contact(s):
Gerald Gutenschwager, Chair

• B.A. (second major) in International

Development focusing on the world economic system and emphasizing theories and processes, historical, economic and political factors (especially colonialism) and relations with the U.S.

6.147
International Administration
New England College
Henniker, NH 03242
(603) 428-2285

Contact(s):
Montford H. R. Sayce, Director

• Offers B.A. in International Administration with emphasis on international management processes; maintains British campus for overseas study and internship base

6.148
Research Program in Development Studies
Princeton University
Princeton, NJ 08544
(609) 452-6402

Contact(s):
John P. Lewis, Director

• Supports and conducts research on economic development, particularly in the less developed countries, in such areas as policy and planning and investment and income distribution; also undertakes historical studies of economic growth

6.149
Woodrow Wilson School of Public and International Affairs
Princeton University
Princeton, NJ 08544
(609) 452-4800

Contact(s):

Donald E. Stokes, Dean
Ruth Miller, Director of Graduate
    Admissions

• Offers Masters in Public Affairs, a Ph.D. in Public Affairs and a Master in Public Affairs and Urban and Regional Planning; fields of specialization at the M.P.A. level are international relations, development studies, urban affairs and domestic policies and economics and public policy; at the Ph.D. level urban and regional planning and population policy and analysis are added
• Also administers the Center of International Studies (see 4.175) the Office of Population Research (see 6.018) and the Research Program in Development Studies (see 6.148) and participates in the Princeton Center for Energy and Environmental Studies; summer field experience in the U.S. or abroad is part of the program for M.P.A. candidates
• Admits nondegree, mid-career Fellows and has special Parvin Fellows Program to support a limited number of students from developing countries

6.150
Public Administration
University of New Mexico
Latin American Institute
801 Yale NE
Albuquerque, NM 87131
(505) 277-2961

Contact(s):

Jon M. Tolman, Associate Director for
    Academic Programs
Zane Reeves, Director of Public
    Administration
    (505) 277-3312

• Offers dual degrees in Public Administration and Latin American Studies (M.P.A. and M.A.) and Community and Regional Planning and Latin American Studies (M.C.R.P. and M.A.)

6.151
School of International and Public Affairs
Columbia University
420 West 118th St.
New York, NY 10027
(212) 280-3808

Contact(s):

Harvey Picker, Dean

• Offers two-year Masters in International Affairs for general preparation for international careers; includes study of politics, law, foreign policy, economics, statistics and a regional or functional specialization; functional specializations include economic and political development and international business; economy, finance and banking; law and organization; media and communications; political economy, and security policy; regional specializations include Africa (see 12.037), Latin America (see 16.066), East Asia (see 13.077), East Central Europe (see 14.028), the Middle East (see 17.029), Russia (see 18.520), Southern Asia (see 13.079) and Western Europe (see 15.016); a program in Soviet Nationality Problems (see 18.519) is offered in conjunction with the Russian and Middle East programs
• Offers two-year Masters in Public Administration focused on local, state and national government administration
• Offers joint programs with the Graduate School of Business, the Graduate School of Journalism, the School of Law (and the Parker School of Foreign and Comparative Law, (see 6.112), the School of Public Health, and combined programs in international affairs and urban planning and international affairs and public administration
• Overseas study arranged in cooperation with the Graduate Institute of International Studies in Geneva and the Institut d' Études Politique de Paris
• Sponsors several research centers including the Institute of War and Peace Studies (see 4.177), the Research Institute on In-

ternational Change (see 4.178), and the Center for the Study of Human Rights (see 4.176)

• Sponsors International Fellows Program which enables exceptional students to combine professional school with advanced training in international affairs

• Publishes *Journal of International Affairs* (see 1.091). Herbert H. Lehman Library houses over 160,000 books, 1,600 periodicals and 120 foreign newspapers in the international field; collections include the Human Relations Area Files (see 1.112) and the papers of the Bureau of Applied Social Research, Radio Free Europe and the RAND Corporation; University libraries include vast holdings in world areas and international relations; special collections include legislative debates of the French Republic, Russian Duma, German Reichstag, the Indian House of the People, and the British Parliament, materials from the League of Nations, the International Law and Relations Library and the International Library of African Music; extensive other public and private library resources also available in the New York area

• Offers a variety of fellowships, scholarships and awards

• Advises on and arranges overseas study and research opportunities, conducts outreach programs for community organizations and educational institutions and provides services to foreign students

6.152
International and Comparative Labor Relations Program
Cornell University
296 Ives Hall
Ithaca, NY 14850
(607) 256-3447

Contact(s):
John P. Windmuller, Director

• Offers M.A. and Ph.D. in International and Comparative Labor Relations covering both industrialized and less developed countries

6.153
International Development
Cornell University
Center for International Studies
170 Uris Hall
Ithaca, NY 14853
(607) 256-6370

Contact(s):
Norman T. Uphoff, Graduate Faculty Representative

• Offers Master of Professional Studies (International Development) with specialization in an area of concentration (population, planning, nutrition, science and technology or other development policy) supplemented by work in development administration and planning, economics, politics, sociology or international communications

6.154
Program on International Studies in Planning
Cornell University
200 West Sibley Hall
Ithaca, NY 14853
(607) 256-2333

Contact(s):
Porus Olpadwala, Director

Graduate academic program associated with Department of City and Regional Planning and the Center for International Studies (see 4.082) focusing on the practical application of planning theory in urban and rural regional development in developing communities and countries

• Offers M.R.P. and Ph.D. degrees within the Department of City and Regional Planning; includes a Master of Professional Studies (International Development)

• Publishes monographs and dissertations

• Areas of major interest: Caribbean and Latin America, the Middle East, East Africa and South Asia

6.155
International Political Economy and Development
Fordham University
Graduate School of Arts & Sciences
Bronx, NY 10458
(212) 579-2297

Contact(s):
Peter P. Remec, Director

• Offers M.A. in International Political Economy and Development focusing on comparative political analysis, international political economy, international business, trade and finance and economic development

6.156
Nelson A. Rockefeller College of Public Affairs and Policy
State University of New York at Albany
Graduate School of Public Affairs
1400 Washington Ave.
Albany, NY 12222
(518) 455-6127

Contact(s):
David F. Andersen, Dean

• Offers M.P.A. in Comparative and International Administration with emphasis on problems of political and economic development

6.157
International Relations and Public Administration
Syracuse University
Maxwell School of Citizenship and Public Affairs
119 College Place
New York, NY 13210
(315) 423-2552

Contact(s):
Stephen Koff, Director

• Offers M.A. degree in International Relations for students interested in geographic area studies or specific career preparation (public administration, international service, international business, etc.); Ph.D. in International Relations emphasizes the application of quantitative techniques to international and foreign policy problems

• Offers Master of Development Planning (M.R.P.) and an M.P.A. with Development Administration concentration focused on national, regional and urban planning and administration in developing countries

6.158
CROSSCURRENTS International Institute
259 Regency Ridge
Dayton, OH 45459
(513) 434-1909

Contact(s):
William P. Shaw, President

Nonprofit educational and research organization focused on international cooperation; founded as an outgrowth of the work of the International Division of the Charles F. Kettering Foundation

• Conducts research and supporting studies or programs which further understanding of management and governing processes, medical service delivery and the use of appropriate technologies in less developed countries and which offer more effective means of linking policy-makers to social scientists

• Promotes, through conferences, seminars, educational activities and other means, expanded cooperation and communication among people of diverse cultural backgrounds and especially between the U.S. and other countries

6.159
Graduate School of Public and International Affairs
University of Pittsburgh
Pittsburgh, PA 15260
(412) 624-4740

Contact(s):
John Funari, Dean

• Offers Masters in Public and International Affairs with concentration in international affairs or economic and social development (international and domestic) and options to obtain certificates in International Political Economy, International Security Studies or Area Studies (West European Studies; Asian Studies, see 13.109; Latin American Studies, see 16.085; or Russian and East European Studies, see 14.043) or to undertake a dual degree program with the Schools of Law or Social Work; areas of special interest within the program are foreign policy, international organization, international and intercultural transactions, national and international security, development planning, development administration, program and project planning and international development

6.160
International Center for Marine Resource Development
University of Rhode Island
13 Woodward Hall
Kingston, RI 02881
(401) 792-2479

Contact(s):
Jerry Donovan, Dean

• M.A. in Political Science with International Relations specialization and graduate certificate program in International Development Studies

6.161
Foreign Service Program/International Management Program
Baylor University
Waco, TX 76798
(817) 755-3161

Contact(s):
Lyle C. Brown, Director

• Offers B.A. in Foreign Service for government, business, missionary and other areas of international service
• Offers Master of International Management for careers in business and government administration

6.162
Intercultural Administration
School for International Training (SIT)
Kipling Road
Brattleboro, VT 05301
(802) 257-7751

Contact(s):
John Middleton, Director (SIT)

• Offers M.A. in Intercultural Administration in the Program in Intercultural Management (PIM) which includes six months on campus and 12-month internships with an international organization in the U.S. or abroad and focuses on international human service management, intercultural advising and training, and community service management

6.163
Graduate School of Public Affairs
University of Washington
Seattle, WA 98105
(206) 543-4920

Contact(s):
Hubert Locke, Dean

  • Offers joint Master of Public Administration and M.A. in International Studies with School of International Studies (see 4.151)

6.164
The Following Institutions Also Offer Joint Degree Programs in Public Administration, International Service and/or Development Planning and International or Area Studies:

University of California, Los Angeles (see 16.014, Latin American Studies)

George Washington University (see 13.030, Sino-Soviet Studies)

University of Michigan, Ann Arbor (see 14.024, Russian and East European Studies)

University of New Mexico (see 16.062, Latin American Studies)

Indiana University of Pennsylvania (see 4.119, International Studies)

University of Pennsylvania (see 17.039, Middle East Studies Center)

University of Texas, Austin (see 16.098, Latin American Studies)

Old Dominion University (see 4.147, International Studies)

University of Washington (see 4.151, International Studies)

Translation and Interpretation

6.166
Graduate Division of Translation and Interpretation
Monterey Institute of International Studies
425 Van Buren St.
Box 1978
Monterey, CA 93940
(408) 649-3113

Contact(s):
Wilhelm K. Weber, Chair

  • Offers M.A. in Translation, Translation/Interpretation and Conference Interpretation and a joint M.A. with the Division of International Policy Studies (see 6.123); languages offered: French, German, Russian and Spanish

6.167
National Resource Center for Interpretation and Translation
Georgetown University
School of Languages and Linguistics
Washington, DC 20057
(202) 625-4571

Contact(s):
James Alatis, Dean
Margareta Bowen, Head, Division of
    Interpretation and Translation

  • Offers training in interpretation and translation to both graduate and undergraduate students, with emphasis on the development of skills in professional translation and conference interpretation

6.168
Interpreter Studies
University of Massachusetts
Herter Hall
Amherst, MA 01002
(413) 545-2314

Contact(s):
Daniel Martin, Director

• Offers certificate in Interpreter Studies for general language interpretation in French, Spanish, German, Russian, Italian and Portuguese

6.169
Translation Research and Instruction Program
State University of New York at Binghamton
Binghamton, NY 13501
(607) 798-6763

Contact(s):
Marilyn Gaddis Rose, Director

• Offers graduate Certificate combined with a Masters degree in a discipline or professional school (most frequently in comparative literature, the social sciences, business or education); conducts research and publishes occasional papers; particular concern with translation theory and process; part of the National Resource Center for Interpretation and Translation (see 6.167)

Associations and Agencies Concerned with International Studies in the Professions

6.170
Academy of International Business
World Trade Education Center
Cleveland State University
Cleveland, OH 44115
(216) 687-3733

Contact(s):
Ivan R. Vernon, Executive Secretary

Professional association of professors, researchers, writers, managers and executives worldwide concerned with education in international business
• Provides information about international business education and compiles data and holds conferences
• Publishes newsletter, *Journal of International Business Studies, International*
Business Curricula: A Global Survey (see 6.174), and *Internationalizing the Business Curriculum: A Selected and Annotated Bibliography*

6.171
American Assembly of Collegiate Schools of Business
1755 Massachusetts Ave. NW, Suite 320
Washington, DC
(202) 667-9109
HEADQUARTERS: 11500 Olive Street Road
Suite 142
St. Louis, MO 63141
(314) 872-8481

Contact(s):
Robert H. B. Wade, Director, Washington
  Office

Educational association of colleges, universities, corporations and other organizations concerned with promoting and improving higher education in business administration and management

• Conducts surveys of international business education programs, prepares reports to the educational and business communities, and sponsors international conferences and colloquia on management and management education issues

6.172
Association of Professional Schools of International Affairs
Princeton University
Woodrow Wilson School of Public and
    International Affairs
Princeton, NJ 08540

Contact(s):
Donald A. Stokes, Convenor (1984)

Association of nine major academic programs in international and public affairs

• Promotes adherence to high quality training and standards of professionalism in professional schools of international affairs; sponsors cooperative programs which will provide mutual reinforcement to the professional training offered by members

6.173
National Association of State Universities & Land-Grant Colleges
1 Dupont Circle NW
Washington, DC 20036
(202) 293-7120

Contact(s):
James Cowan, Director, Office of
    International Studies and Programs

• Office of International Studies and Programs provides members with information on international education as it is relevant to schools of agriculture; serves as secretariat for the Association of U.S. University Directors of International Agricultural Programs

Sourcebooks and Directories

6.174
International Business Curricula: A Global Survey
Robert Perritt and Gerald W. Perritt
Academy of International Business
World Trade Education Center
Cleveland State University
Cleveland, OH 44115
1980; paperbound; 229 pages; $15

• Survey of instruction in international

business at bachelor, masters and doctoral levels in U.S. and selected foreign universities; indicates for each institution if there is a major, a minor, some courses, and/or a degree or degrees offered in international business and gives number of students who are majors; also provides statistical summaries, a bibliography of international business textbooks, a sampling of standard course outlines and a list of international business faculty and primary teaching areas

7

Grants, Awards and Fellowships for International Studies and Programs

Funding Agencies and Programs

7.001
American Council of Learned Societies
800 Third Ave.
New York, NY 10022
(212) 888-1759

Contact(s):
R. M. Lumiansky, President

Nonprofit educational federation of 43 national scholarly organizations; engages in activities directed toward the advancement of humanistic learning
• Administers grant and fellowship programs for postdoctoral research in the humanities; may be used for research abroad or on international subjects
• Provides grants in Chinese Studies (see 18.073) and Soviet and East European Studies (see 14.055) and administers the International Research and Exchange Board (IREX, see 14.057) and the Universities Service Center in Hong Kong (see 18.190)
• Provides postdoctoral grants-in-aid to support the preparation of a dissertation for publication and to support research in progress by the scholar to meet essential personal expenses
• Offers travel grants to scholars in humanistic disciplines to enable them to participate in conferences outside of North America

7.002
Atlantic Richfield Foundation
515 South Flower St.
Los Angeles, CA 90071
(213) 486-3342

Contact(s):
Walter D. Eichner, Executive Director

Private grant-giving foundation
• Gives grants for continuing support to internationally oriented, nonprofit educational and development assistance organizations; most grants under $50,000; worldwide interests with a slight tilt toward the Middle East

7.003
The Brookings Institution
Research Fellowships in Foreign Policy
    Studies
1775 Massachusetts Ave. NW
Washington, DC 20036
(202) 797-6000

Contact(s):
Richard K. Betts, Coordinator

• Supports pre-dissertation research on the kinds of public policy issues that concern the Brookings Institution

7.004
Carnegie Corporation of New York
437 Madison Ave.
New York, NY 10022
(212) 371-3200

Contact(s):
Sara L. Engelhardt, Secretary

Charitable foundation
• Makes grants primarily to academic and research institutions for projects in specifically defined areas; among them: (1) avoiding nuclear war (including research on new ideas, the development of public education programs, application of social science-based knowledge in the areas of negotiation, decision-making and conflict resolution and projects aimed at producing fundamental changes in U.S.-Soviet relationships); and (2) human resources in developing countries with an emphasis on mothers' and children's health, nutrition, and basic education, especially for women and girls (includes leadership dialogues, technical and scientific cooperation, and assessment of past efforts in human resource development)

7.005
Carthage Foundation
P.O. Box 268
Pittsburgh, PA 15230
(412) 392-2900

Contact(s):
Richard M. Larry, Treasurer

Private grant-giving foundation
• Provides awards to projects that will add to our understanding of public policy questions concerned with national and international issues; no grants to individuals

7.006
Council on Foreign Relations, Inc.
The Harold Pratt House
58 East 68th St.
New York, NY 10021
(212) 737-0400
BRANCH: Washington, DC

Contact(s):
Winston Lord, President

Prestigious membership organization providing a forum for foreign policy study, discussion and debate among academics, business persons, professionals and government leaders
• Provides small number of visiting research-study fellowships in New York and 12-15 International Affairs Fellowships that place young scholars in government positions, principally in Washington, and/or that provide support for research, study and writing projects to public foreign policy professionals

7.007
Council for International Exchange of Scholars (CIES)
American Council on Education
11 Dupont Circle NW, Suite 300
Washington, DC 20036
(202) 833-4950

Contact(s):
Cassandra A. Pyle, Director, CIES

Administers (in cooperation with the U.S. Information Agency and the Board of Foreign Scholarships) the Fulbright program of exchange of American and foreign scholars for university teaching and advanced research
• Provides information and announces awards annually for more than 500 U.S. scholars to lecture or conduct research abroad and 600 foreign scholars to lecture or conduct

research in the U.S.; interested American scholars may register their interests with the CIES and be notified of opportunities; includes fixed-sum grants, travel-only awards, and awards in American Studies for younger scholars; majority of awards to foreign scholars are for travel only; CIES will assist American institutions in locating foreign scholars for temporary assignments

• Administers NATO Research Fellowships in Humanities and Social Sciences which provide substantial postdoctoral or professional fellowships for study and research in any NATO country focused on aspects of the North Atlantic Alliance; research must be intended for publication

• Also administers Indo-American (see 18.205) and Spanish (see 18.440) fellowship programs

7.009

English-Speaking Union of the United States

16 East 69th St.
New York, NY 10021
(212) 879-6800
BRANCHES: 88 cities throughout the country

Contact(s):
John D. Walker, National Director

Individual and corporate membership organization designed to create and maintain cultural ties between and among the English-speaking peoples of the world, involving primarily the U.S. and members of the British Commonwealth

• Gives scholarships and travel grants to U.S. students and educators for visiting Commonwealth countries and to Commonwealth students and educators for visiting the U.S.

7.010

The Ford Foundation

Fellowship Program in Dual Expertise
Office of European and International Affairs
320 East 43rd St.
New York, NY 10017
(212) 573-5000

• Fellowships to graduate students and to postdoctoral candidates for study in either International Security and Arms Control or Soviet-East European Studies in order to equal the competence already achieved in the other

7.011

Ford Foundation International Affairs Grants

320 East 43d St.
New York, NY 10017
(212) 573-5000

Contact(s):
Howard R. Dressner, Secretary

• Offers grants for experimental, demonstration and developmental projects that serve to further the social and economic development of less developed countries; includes such areas as population and area studies, resources, international relations and human rights

7.012

The Fund for the Improvement of Postsecondary Education

7th and D Streets SW
Room 3100
Washington, DC 20202
(202) 245-8091

• Offers grants for programs aimed at solving pressing problems in postsecondary education and expanding future opportunities for learners; a number of grants are awarded annually to international education projects

7.013
The German Marshall Fund of the United States
11 Dupont Circle NW
Washington, DC 20036
(202) 745-3950

Contact(s):
Frank E. Loy, President

Private foundation funded by the Federal Republic of Germany
• Provides expense and stipend grants to U.S. scholars (who have completed their Ph.D.s) for long-term (over three months) full-time research on issues of major political, economic and social significance to industrial societies; must have U.S. and European components (may also have others)

7.014
Hoover Institution on War, Revolution and Peace
National Fellows Program
Stanford University
Stanford, CA 94305
(415) 497-0603

Contact(s):
Dennis Bark, Executive Secretary

Research grant program
• Provides postdoctoral fellowships averaging $15,000 per year for younger scholars in the fields of modern history, sociology, political science, economics and international relations to study and do original unrestricted research at the Hoover Institution (see 4.159)

7.015
Institute of Current World Affairs
Wheelock House
4 West Wheelock St.
Hanover, NH 03755
(603) 643-5548

Contact(s):
Peter Bird Martin, Executive Director

Grant-giving foundation established in 1925
• Awards two-year, full-support overseas travel and research grants; recipients are expected to explore and write reports on a current international issue identified by foundation trustees; write for brochure describing current areas of interest

7.016
Institute for Intercultural Studies
℅ Sloane and Hinshaw
145 East 74th St., Suite 1C
New York, NY 10021
(212) 737-1011

Contact(s):
Ann Brownell Sloane, Administrative
    Associate

• Provides scholarships, fellowships and other assistance to support scholarly research on the customs, behavior, psychology and social organization of the nations and peoples of the world, especially those aspects that affect international and cross-cultural relations

7.017
Institute of International Education
Grants for Graduate Study
809 United Nations Plaza
New York, NY 10017
(212) 883-8497
BRANCHES: Atlanta, Chicago, Denver, Houston, San Francisco, Washington, DC, Bangkok, Harare (Zimbabwe), Hong Kong, Jakarta, Mexico City

Contact(s):
Richard Dye, Vice President, Fellowship and Educational Services

• Administers annual U.S. government Fulbright Grants for graduate study in approximately 50 countries, ITT International Fellowships (similar to Fulbright Grants) in approximately 25 countries and other special fellowship programs in Austria, France, West Germany, Israel, Italy, Switzerland and the UK; grants vary substantially in amount of support, eligibility, fields of study, etc., and are thoroughly described in the free annual IIE publication *Fulbright Grants and Other Grants for Graduate Study Abroad* (see 7.041)

• Administers a variety of other grant programs, including Latin American air travel grants (provided for Latin American students by Pan American Airlines), the Hubert Humphrey North-South Fellowship Program (for mid-career professionals from the developing countries), South African Educational Program (for black South African students), foreign government programs (in Somalia, the Philippines, Korea, Brazil, Taiwan, Central America and the Caribbean), Ford Foundation programs in graduate education and UNESCO Fellowships

7.018
Institute for the Study of World Politics
823 UN Plaza
New York, NY 10017
(212) 661-5900

Contact(s):
Kenneth W. Thompson, Director

• Sponsors Institute Fellowship Program offering approximately 25 fellowships each year for doctoral or postdoctoral research on economic, political and social issues with the aim of expanding knowledge and understanding of international problems and suggesting possible solutions

7.019
The Johnson Foundation
33 East Four Mile Road
Racine, WI 53401
(414) 639-3211

Contact(s):
Henry M. Halsted, Vice President

Private foundation principally engaged in the sponsorship of conferences in cooperation with other organizations and institutions at Frank Lloyd Wright–designed Wingspread near Racine, Wisconsin; facilities for simultaneous interpretation are available

• Plans, holds and shares the cost of small, highly focused conferences of leaders and authorities on topics of national and international interest, including subjects of particular importance to education; produces English- and Spanish-language public affairs radio series (broadcast nationally)

7.020
National Education Association
1201 16th St. NW
Washington, DC 20036
(202) 833-4000

• Provides William G. Carr Scholarship Award of $2,000 each year either to a graduate student or teacher wishing to study educational associations in other countries or to an officer of a professional educational association in the U.S. to improve some phase of organizational work

7.021
National Geographic Society
Committee for Research and Exploration
17th and M Sts. NW
Washington, DC 20036
(202) 857-7439

Contact(s):
Edwin W. Snider, Secretary

• Provides small grants for research anywhere in the world on projects relevant to the field of geography (broadly interpreted); includes virtually all the earth sciences

7.022
National Institutes of Health
International Research and Awards Branch
Fogarty International Center
Bldg. 38A, Room 611
Bethesda, MD 20014
(301) 496-1653

Contact(s):
Chief, International Research and Awards
  Branch

• Offers Senior International Fellowships to mid-career American health scientists at U.S. public or private nonprofit research, clinical, or educational institutions; fellowships enable recipients to go abroad to study, engage in professional activity and share their expertise for three months to a year
• Also administers postdoctoral research fellowships for young medical professionals to undertake work in Sweden (Swedish Medical Research Council fellowships), France (French National Institute of Health and Medical Research fellowships and the NIH-French CNRS Program for Scientific Collaboration), Switzerland (Swiss National Science Foundation fellowship), Ireland (Irish Medical Research Council fellowship), Finland (Academy of Finland fellowship), and Germany (Alexander von Humboldt Foundation fellowship)

7.023
National Science Foundation
Division of International Programs
Washington, DC 20550

• Administers U.S. Government Coop-

erative Science Programs in the following world areas and countries: East Asia (see 13.141), Latin America (see 16.126), Sub-Saharan Africa (see 12.067), Australia (see 18.012), China (see 18.086), Taiwan (see 18.470), South Korea (see 18.313), France (see 18.143), Italy (see 18.258), Japan (see 18.285), New Zealand (see 18.375), and India (see 18.206)
• Also administers:
Special Foreign Currency Program
Osman Shinaishin, Director (202) 357-9402
• Provides grants to pay the costs of science, research and educational programs abroad including international travel; countries involved: Burma, Egypt, Guinea, India and Pakistan
Scientists and Engineers in Economic Development
(202) 632-5798
• Provides grants for scientists and engineers to undertake research and study and to serve as consultants in developing countries
NATO Postdoctoral Fellowships in Science Program
Michael M. Frodyma, Director
• Provides grants for postdoctoral study and/or research in science in NATO countries as well as travel grants for U.S. science graduate students and recent doctorate awardees to attend NATO Advanced Study Institutes

7.024
New York State Education Department
Cultural Education Center
Bureau of Higher and Professional
  Educational Testing
Albany, NY 12230
Attn: Graduate Fellowships
(518) 474-6394

• Offers 30 Herbert H. Lehman Graduate Fellowships in Social Sciences, Public Affairs, or International Affairs to students entering an M.A. or Ph.D. program in the social sciences, public affairs or international affairs at a New York State institution; $4,000 for the first year, $5,000 thereafter (maximum 4 years)

7.025
Newberry Library Fellowship Program
60 West Walton St.
Chicago, IL 60610
(312) 943-9090

Contact(s):
Terry Sullivan, Office of Research and
  Education

• Offers substantial fellowships for scholarly research in residence at the Newberry Library in fields appropriate to the library's collections; these are principally in history and the humanities and include the following international or potentially international areas: history and theory of music, history of cartography, Luso-Brazilian and Mexican history, bibliography and calligraphy

7.026
Princeton University
Center of International Studies
Princeton, NJ 08540
(609) 452-4851

• Offers John Parker Compton fellowships in World Order Studies for predoctoral and postdoctoral research in the areas of advanced technology and international politics, arms policy and the development of international institutions

7.027
The Rockefeller Foundation
1133 Ave. of the Americas
New York, NY 10036
(212) 869-8500

Contact(s):
Simon P. Gourdiner, Secretary

• Offers the following grants:
(1) Approximately 10 substantial one-year International Relations Fellowships to scholars or professionals knowledgeable in their fields for full-time research and analysis of policy alternatives on international issues, in particular (a) the means of reducing threats to international security arising from the intersection of regional conflicts and the competition for security and influence among the major powers and (b) the means to overcome political and institutional obstacles to the sound management of economic relations among countries
(2) Approximately 40 substantial one-year Humanities Fellowships for projects contributing to the analysis and evaluation of contemporary national and international issues and values
(3) Room and board for scholars and artists (and spouses) to reside at the Bellagio Center for the pursuit of creative endeavors in the areas of Foundation interest (arts, humanities, food/hunger, equal opportunity, health, population and international relations)

7.028
The Rotary Foundation of Rotary International
1600 Ridge Ave.
Evanston, IL 60201
(312) 328-0100

Contact(s):
Barbara Brenholts, Scholarship Supervisor

Grant-giving foundation
• Offers five annual international education scholarships for study overseas in countries where there are Rotary Clubs; available to applicants who are citizens of a country where there are Rotary Clubs; schol-

arships awarded in the following five categories: Graduate Scholarships, Undergraduate Scholarships, Vocational Scholarships for persons currently employed in technical fields, Teacher of the Handicapped Scholarships (for teachers of the physically, mentally or educationally handicapped), and Journalism Scholarships (for journalists with two years of experience); awards provide cost of round-trip transportation, educational expenses and room and board, and limited educational travel costs; all but undergraduates may be married; age requirements vary according to scholarship; applications must be made through a Rotary Club and applicants must be sponsored by the Club and District

7.029
Smithsonian Institution
Office of Fellowships and Grants
L'Enfant Plaza, Suite 3300
Washington, DC 20560
(202) 287-3271

Contact(s):
Gretchen Gayle Ellsworth, Director

U.S. government institution concerned with natural sciences, technology, history of art, and cultural and natural history; conducts basic research, engages in transnational cooperative educational research and training programs, publishes studies and other materials, preserves historical artifacts, maintains and circulates exhibits on natural and cultural history, technology, and art history; and participates in the international exchange of scholars and publications
   • Provides pre- and postdoctoral fellowships for periods of six months to one year for study at the Smithsonian in the history of art, the history of science and technology, cultural anthropology, the environmental, biological and earth sciences, and social and cultural history; also makes available ten-

week appointments to graduate students enrolled in a formal graduate program who wish to do research in a Smithsonian discipline
   • Provides grants to institutions for the support of postdoctoral research by established scholars in anthropology, archaeology and related disciplines, systematic and environmental biology, astrophysics and earth sciences and museum programming in countries where Special Foreign Currencies are available

7.030
Social Science Research Council
605 Third Ave.
New York, NY 10158
(212) 557-9500

Nonprofit federation of educational organizations designed to foster and promote social science research
   • Administers awards and research grants to U.S. scholars for research in the following countries and world areas: Asia (see 13.142), Latin America and the Caribbean (see 16.128), Western Europe (see 15.042), the Middle East (see 17.060), Africa (see 12.066), China (see 18.087), Japan (see 18.286) and South Korea (see 18.312)

7.031
United Nations Graduate Student Intern Program
Department of Public Information
Room S-10376
New York, NY 10017
(212) 754-6845

   • Offers four-week study/internship program for approximately 80 graduate students involving briefings from and work assignments with UN officials; no program fee; personal expenses are responsibility of participant

7.032

United States Department of Education
International Education Programs
Washington, DC 20202

International Education Programs is the office responsible for managing U.S. government funding programs in support of international education

Doctoral Dissertation Research Abroad

John Paul, Program Officer (202) 245-2761

• Provides assistance to graduate students to engage in full-time dissertation research abroad in modern foreign language and area studies; emphasis on research in world areas not widely included in American curricula

Group Projects Abroad

Ralph Hines, Program Officer (202) 245-2794

• Provides grants to U.S. educational institutions or nonprofit educational organizations for training, research, advanced foreign language training, curriculum development, and/or instructional materials acquisition in international and intercultural studies; participants may be college faculty, experienced elementary and secondary school teachers, curriculum supervisors and students specializing in foreign language and area studies; includes the following programs: Summer Seminars for Faculty and/or Students, Curriculum Development Teams, Group Research or Study, Summer-Intensive Language Programs and Academic-Year Intensive Language Programs

Faculty Research Abroad

Robert Dennis, Program Officer (202) 245-2761

• Provides awards to key faculty members to maintain expertise, update curricula and improve teaching methods and materials in foreign language and area studies

Foreign Curriculum Consultant

Gwen Lark, Program Officer (202) 245-2794

• Provides services of experts from other countries for an academic year to assist American educational institutions in planning and developing curricula in foreign languages and area studies; priority given to state departments of education, large school systems, smaller four-year colleges with teacher education programs and groups of community colleges

Foreign Language and Area Studies (FLAS) Fellowship

Joe Belmonte, Branch Chief (202) 245-2356

• Offers academic year and summer awards to graduate students in foreign language and area studies via grants to selected U.S. institutions of higher education

International Research and Studies

Richard Scarfo, Branch Chief (202) 245-2761

• Provides grants to institutions of higher education, organizations and individuals to support surveys and studies on instruction in modern foreign language, area and international studies or on effective methods or specialized materials for such instruction

National Resource Centers

Joe Belmonte, Branch Chief (202) 245-2356

• Provides grants to institutions of higher education or consortia thereof to establish, strengthen and/or operate centers focusing on one world region or on general worldwide topics and international studies; world area centers must offer instruction in two or more of that area's principal languages; centers may offer programs at graduate and/or undergraduate levels and must conduct outreach activities for the benefit of state and local educational and community organizations

Special Bilateral Projects

Pat Kern Schaeffer, Branch Chief (202) 245-9700

• Supports short-term institutes, research seminars and exchanges focusing on the study of foreign languages and cultures for scholars, language teachers, curriculum developers, vocational and technical specialists and educational administrators

Teacher Exchange and Seminars Abroad

Pat Kern Schaeffer, Branch Chief (202) 245-9700

• Provides opportunities for elementary and secondary school teachers and, in some cases, college instructors and assistant professors to teach outside the U.S. or to participate in short-term seminars abroad; teaching program usually involves a direct exchange of teachers

Undergraduate International Studies and Foreign Language

Susanna Easton, Program Officer (202) 245-2794

• Awards grants to institutions of higher education and to public and private nonprofit organizations to plan, develop and carry out comprehensive programs to strengthen and improve undergraduate instruction in international studies and foreign languages

Comparative Education

Seymour Rosen, Program Officer (202) 245-9425

• Provides consultative and technical assistance on education systems abroad to U.S. educational institutions, agencies, organizations and individuals and prepares and publishes studies on educational systems of other countries

7.033
United States Information Agency
Educational and Cultural Affairs
301 First St. SW
Washington, DC 20547

Academic Exchange Programs Office

Jean Lashley, Director (202) 485-7409

• Administers Fulbright exchange programs that provide grants to foreign lecturers and professors to teach or undertake research at American colleges and universities

and to U.S. faculty to teach or conduct research at institutions abroad; administered in cooperation with the Council for the International Exchange of Scholars (see 7.007)

• Provides grants to foreign graduate students for study in U.S. colleges and universities and to U.S. graduate students to study in other countries; administered in cooperation with the Board of Foreign Scholarships and the Institute of International Education (see 10.010)

• Provides small educational grants-in-aid to U.S. academic institutions to aid in the development of international linkages and to increase faculty capabilities in teaching about other cultures

• Provides grants for Americans to consult with foreign universities and ministries of education and to conduct workshops and seminars to further the development of educational programs and projects of mutual benefit

Office of Program Coordination and Development

John Mosher, Director (202) 485-2764

• Provides partial support for American academics to speak at or participate in meetings, workshops, seminars, etc., while traveling abroad for other purposes; applications invited

Student Support Services

Joseph Bruns, Acting Chief (202) 485-7434

• Supports and administers programs and activities designed to strengthen overseas advising services and campus and community programs for foreign students and to improve the admission and placement of foreign students into U.S. colleges and universities

Office of Private Sector Programs

Mark Blitz, Director (202) 485-7348

• Responsible for developing and funding cooperative projects with private sector institutions designed to promote a better understanding of the U.S. abroad by means of educational and cultural exchange between Americans and citizens of other nations

Youth Exchange Initiative Office

Donna Oglesby, Director (202) 485-7299

• Administers program of support to private educational exchange organizations designed to expand the number and quality of teenage exchanges between the U.S. and other countries

7.034

U.S. Arms Control and Disarmament Agency
Office of Public Affairs
Washington, DC 20451
(202) 235-9572

• Offers Hubert H. Humphrey Doctoral Fellowships in Arms Control and Disarmament to support unclassified doctoral research on arms control and disarmament

7.035

Woodrow Wilson International Center for Scholars
Smithsonian Institution Bldg.
Washington, DC 20560
(202) 357-2841

Nonprofit research center affiliated with the Smithsonian Institution

• Offers fellowships for international research (see 4.167)

Sourcebooks and Directories

7.036

Annual Register of Grant Support
Marquis Who's Who, Inc.
200 East Ohio St.
Chicago, IL 60611
annual; hardbound; 743 pages; $57.50

• Lists grant support provided by government agencies, public and private foundations, corporations, community trusts, unions and educational and professional associations for scholarships and fellowships, research, educational travel, project development, publications and other purposes; lists approximately 240 international grant programs under International Affairs and Area Studies subdivided into (1) international studies and research abroad, (2) programs for foreign scholars and (3) technical assistance and cooperative research; gives detailed information on grant types, numbers awarded, amounts of funding, eligibility and application procedures

7.037

The CISP International Studies Funding Book
Walter Brown, Robert Leder and Ward Morehouse, Editors
Council for Intercultural Studies and Programs
777 UN Plaza, Suite 9A
New York, NY 10017
1983; looseleaf; 310 pages; $50

• Guide to finding sources of funding for international studies and other international education programs; includes minutes of a number of meetings on the subject (some of it somewhat outdated but useful), an annotated list of books and directories of funding and funding sources, a bibliography of books and articles on how to obtain funding and how to write grant proposals, a list of approximately 150 government and private grant-giving programs and organizations, and profiles of 14 organizations which provide funds and/or in other ways support or offer programs on international education

• Lists by name, address and contact, approximately 140 other organizations involved in international studies or other aspects of international education and lists government and private organizations in 82 other countries that offer sources of support for some form of international study

7.038
Directory of Financial Aid for American Undergraduates Interested in Overseas Study and Travel, 1981–82
Joseph Lurie, Editor
Adelphi University Press
Levermore Hall 201
Garden City, NY 11530
1981; $9

• Provides a listing of sources of financial assistance for undergraduate study abroad

7.039
Directory of Financial Aids for International Activities
Sally Nelson, Editor
Office of International Programs
University of Minnesota
201 Nolte West
315 Pillsbury Drive, SE
Minneapolis, MN 55455
biennial; paperbound; $20

• Provides information on approximately 450 grants, scholarships and fellowships for undergraduate and graduate students, researchers and other academics for travel, study, teaching and research overseas

7.040
Fellowships, Scholarships, and Related Opportunities in International Education
Nancy McG. McCormack, Editor
Division of International Education
University of Tennessee
205 Alumni Hall
Knoxville, TN 37996-0621
biennial; paperbound; $5.95

• Lists approximately 140 graduate student and faculty fellowships and scholarships for study, research and teaching in other countries

7.041
Fulbright Grants and Other Grants for Graduate Study Abroad
Institute of International Education
809 UN Plaza
New York, NY 10017
annual brochure; approx. 60 pages; free

• Comprehensive and detailed listing of all graduate grants and fellowships for overseas study administered by the Institute of International Education (see 10.010); provides statistics on numbers of grants offered and details on eligibility, application procedures, factors affecting selection, the selection process, notification, and other data (including a list of responses to frequent questions), a scholarship and fellowship bibliography and other information about IIE; lists and describes in detail Fulbright Grants, ITT International Fellowships, foreign government grants and other private and government grants in a wide range of fields including the creative and performing arts; lists grants for study in approximately 50 countries each year

7.042
Grant's Register: Postgraduate Awards in the English-Speaking World
Ronald Turner, Editor
St. Martin's Press
175 Fifth Ave.
New York, NY 10010
biennial; hardbound; 775 pages; $26.50

• Lists and gives full information on approximately 2,000 sources of financial aid in English-speaking countries for graduate travel, study and research; many not available to Americans

7.043
A Guide to Scholarships, Fellowships, and Grants: A Selected Bibliography
Institute of International Education
809 UN Plaza
New York, NY 10017
1982; folder; 6 pages; free

• Lists and describes approximately 30 publications that give information on scholarships, fellowships and grants in international education, under the following headings:

general reference, language and area studies, mathematics and the natural sciences, social sciences, humanities, for U.S. nationals, for foreign nationals and for women

7.044
While You're in Washington and New York, Get Me and My College an International Studies Grant: A Guide to Publications That Help the Quest
Walter T. Brown
International Studies Association, Middle Atlantic Region
School of American/International Studies
Ramapo College of New Jersey
Mahwah, NJ 07430
and
Council for Intercultural Studies and Programs
777 UN Plaza
New York, NY 10017
1982; xeroxed materials; 10 pages; free

• Lists and briefly describes publications useful to those developing and/or seeking support for international education programs

8

Study and Educational Travel Abroad

Academic Consortia and Other Study Abroad Organizations

8.001
American Institute for Foreign Study
102 Greenwich Ave.
Greenwich, CT 06830
(203) 869-9090

Contact(s):
Henry C. Kahn, President

• Conducts educational programs in Europe, Africa and Asia for high school and college teachers and students

8.002
Amigos de las Americas
5618 Star Lane
Houston, TX 77057
(800) 231-7796
In Texas: (800) 392-4580

Contact(s):
John Sloan, Acting Executive Director

• Provides for U.S. participants volunteer summer work experiences in Latin America working in human development and health service jobs; includes learning job skills and studying Latin American culture and the Spanish language; for volunteers 16 or older

8.003
Associated Colleges of the Midwest
18 South Michigan Ave.
Chicago, IL 60603
(312) 263-5000

Contact(s):
Elizabeth R. Hayford, Acting President

Educational consortium of 13 private liberal arts colleges in Illinois, Iowa, Minnesota, Wisconsin and Colorado
• Arranges approximately 14 off-campus programs in such areas as cultural studies, environmental studies, arts and sciences and urban studies; includes programs in England, Italy, Yugoslavia, India and Costa Rica

8.004
Brethren Colleges Abroad
Manchester College
Box 184
North Manchester, IN 46962
(219) 982-2141, Ext. 238

Contact(s):
Allen C. Deeter, Administrative
  Coordinator
Helga Walsh

Association of six Brethren Colleges
• Sponsors language and culture study abroad programs at universities in England, France, Germany and Spain

8.005
Center for Arabic Study Abroad
University of Washington
Department of Near Eastern Language and
  Literatures
229B Denny Hall
Seattle, WA 98195
(206) 543-8982

Contact(s):
Farhat J. Ziadeh, Director

Consortium of 18 large universities
• Offers advanced Arabic language study at the American University in Cairo in 2-month (summer) and 12-month (June–May) programs; open to U.S. students in Near Eastern Studies who have two years of Arabic and pass a proficiency exam; fellowships provided covering travel, tuition and maintenance

8.006
College Consortium for International
Studies
Ocean County College
Office of International Education
College Drive
Toms River, NJ 08753
(201) 255-4000, Ext. 273

Contact(s):
William S. Lavundi, Director

Consortium of U.S. colleges and universities
• Organizes approximately 62 overseas academic programs in 25 locations in Denmark, Egypt, England, France, Germany, Ghana, India, Ireland, Israel, Italy, Mexico, Spain and Switzerland; includes short- and long-term programs, structured and independent study programs, and programs involving community service

8.007
Colorado Association for International Education
University of Southern Colorado
% School of Liberal Arts
Pueblo, CO 81001
(303) 549-2835 or 2864

Contact(s):
Alan P. Love, Treasurer
Karin Millett-Sorenson, Chair (University of
    Denver)

Consortium of Colorado colleges and universities
  • Serves as clearinghouse for information about overseas and other international education programs and coordinates statewide activities

8.008
Committee on Institutional Cooperation
990 Grove St.
Evanston, IL 60201
(312) 866-6630

Contact(s):
Frederick H. Jackson, Director

Consortium of large midwestern universities that sponsors joint educational programs
  • Organizes a wide variety of projects, including summer language programs in Mexico and Quebec, Canada, and field study in international agriculture

8.009
The Community Colleges for International Development, Inc.
% Brevard Community College
1519 Clearlake Road
Cocoa, FL 32922
(305) 632-1111, Ext. 304

Contact(s):
James G. Humphrys, Executive Director

Consortium of nine community colleges around the U.S.
  • Sponsors overseas study centers (currently in West Germany), projects for internationalizing the curriculum, student and faculty exchanges in Canada, England and Taiwan, and technical assistance and training programs for educational systems and institutions in other countries

8.010
Council on International Educational Exchange
International Administrative Center
205 East 42nd St.
New York, NY 10017
(212) 661-1414
BRANCHES: Paris, Tokyo

Contact(s):
Colleen Zarich, Deputy Executive Director

  • Large, nonprofit educational exchange organization with a membership of approximately 160 schools, colleges, universities, academic consortia and others
  • Provides consultation and advisory services to institutions involved in educational exchange and serves as an advocacy voice for international educational exchange; conducts conferences and seminars
  • Maintains overseas program and study centers for U.S. academic consortia, including the Cooperative Russian Language Program (Leningrad), Cooperative Study Centers in Rennes, France, and Seville and Cadiz in Spain, the Inter-University Center for Films and Critical Studies (Paris), China Cooperative Language and Study Programs (three sites in the PRC), and the Cooperative International Business and Society Program (Tokyo); offers other college and high school study and work opportunities abroad

• Offers English language programs and services for foreign nationals (see 10.007) and provides educational exchange services to secondary schools (see 3.014)

• Arranges work exchanges for students in the U.S. and six other countries and placements in international work camps for Americans in 12 other countries

• Offers wide range of student travel services for U.S. and foreign nationals through the New York Student Center and Council Travel Services, Inc.; services include: general information, issuance of the International Student Identity Card, low-cost overseas air, land and group travel and arrangements for discount accommodations in the U.S.; special consultative services, discounts and preferences given to members

• Publishes materials on study, work and travel abroad including: *Work, Study and Travel Abroad: The Whole World Handbook* (see 8.045), the *CIEE Student Travel Catalogue* (annual, free, describes CIEE programs and services in detail), and *Wanted Abroad* (free, guide to work opportunities in five European countries); also publishes *Where to Stay USA* (see 10.054) and *Volunteer!: A Comprehensive Guide to Voluntary Service Opportunities in the U.S. and Abroad* (forthcoming)

8.011
Earthwatch
10 Juniper Road, Box 127
Belmont, MA 02178
(617) 489-3030

Contact(s):
Blue Magruder, Director of
   Communications

Nonprofit, volunteer organization
• Offers members of the public (16 or older) the opportunity to join scientific, archaeological and anthropological expeditions as paying research assistants; provides some

scholarship aid for students (16–23); particularly concerned with cross-cultural communication, animal behavior, marine biology, the environment and ethnic studies; publishes *Earthwatch*, a magazine which describes expeditions (3 times per year)

8.012
Education Abroad Program, University of California and Office of International Programs, California State University
400 Golden Shore, Suite 300
Long Beach, CA 90802
(213) 590-5655

Contact(s):
William H. Allaway, Director

• Conducts undergraduate overseas study programs for (and limited to students from) the University of California and the California State University systems

• University of California programs sponsored in Australia, Austria, Brazil, China, Egypt, France, Ghana, West Germany, Hong Kong, Israel, Ireland, Italy, Japan, Kenya, Mexico, Norway, Peru, Sierra Leone, Spain, Sweden, Togo, the United Kingdom and the U.S.S.R.

• California State University programs sponsored in Brazil, Denmark, France, West Germany, Israel, Italy, Japan, Mexico, New Zealand, Peru, Quebec, Spain, Sweden, Taiwan, and the United Kingdom

8.013
Facets USA, Inc.
915 Broadway, Suite 1705
New York, NY 10003
(212) 475-4343

Contact(s):
Ann Cooper, Director

French firm sponsoring educational travel

programs to France; closely connected to the French government

• Sponsors approximately 20 programs for both high school and college students and teachers; includes tours, intensive language instruction, homestays and/or on-campus study for from 10 days to an academic year; will tailor program to needs of school or group

8.014
Florida Collegiate Consortium for International/Intercultural Education
Broward Community College
1000 Coconut Creek Blvd.
Coconut Creek, FL 33066
(305) 973-2206

Contact(s):
William Greene, Executive Director

Consortium of Florida colleges and universities

• Coordinates pooling of resources among members, especially in sharing overseas study programs, promotes faculty development, conducts conferences, develops political support for international education and publishes a newsletter

8.015
The Great Lakes Colleges Association
220 Collingwood, Suite 240
Ann Arbor, MI 48103
(313) 761-4833

Contact(s):
Jon W. Fuller, President

Consortium of 12 colleges in Ohio, Indiana, Illinois and Michigan

• Sponsors and coordinates the conduct of faculty development and off-campus study programs among member institutions; for faculty there are conferences and course-design workshops along with opportunities for

travel and research as overseas program directors; for students there are study programs (most administered by individual colleges as agents of the consortium) in Africa, China, Latin America, India, Yugoslavia, Japan, Scotland and a European Term in Urban Comparative Studies

8.016
Higher Education Consortium for Urban Affairs, Inc.
Hamline University
St. Paul, MN 55104
(612) 646-8831

Contact(s):
Nadinne Cruz, Executive Director

Consortium of 14 colleges and universities in the Upper Midwest

• Offers undergraduate semester programs in Scandinavia and Latin America; focus on social change issues through field study in urban areas

8.017
The Institute of European Studies
700 North Rush St.
Chicago, IL 60611-2573
(312) 944-1750

Contact(s):
Michael S. Steinberg, Senior Program
  Officer and Secretary to the Board

Independent educational organization sponsoring nine undergraduate study programs overseas for American college students; works closely with 41 affiliated colleges and universities

• Operates study programs in Durham and London, England; Paris and Nantes, France; Madrid, Spain; Vienna, Austria; Mexico City, Mexico; and Freiburg, Germany (two programs, one in German Studies and the second focusing on the European Economic Community); courses taught by local faculty in language of country (except the Vienna and Common Market programs which are in English); courses offered within IES centers and host universities; internships available at some locations

• Offers approximately 200 scholarships to needy students accepted for Institute programs, ranging from $250 to $2,500 deducted from Institute program fees

8.018
Institute of International Education
809 United Nations Plaza
New York, NY 10017
(212) 883-8497
BRANCHES: Atlanta, Chicago, Denver, Houston, San Francisco, Washington, DC, Bangkok, Harare (Zimbabwe), Hong Kong, Jakarta, Mexico City

Contact(s):
Richard Dye, Vice President, Fellowships
    and Educational Services

• Administers Fulbright and other grants for graduate study abroad; also serves as information clearinghouse and publishes materials on overseas study in general (see 10.010)

8.019
Institute for Shipboard Education
Box 1527
Orange, CA 92668
(714) 771-6590

Contact(s):
M. A. Griffiths, Executive Director

Educational organization administering the University of Pittsburgh–sponsored educational programs aboard the cruise ship S.S. Universe

• Offers annually two semesters of academic study during around-the-world cruise which docks for three- to seven-day educational visits at 10 foreign ports; provides a wide range of undergraduate courses in business, the humanities and social sciences with emphasis on subjects that relate to the learning possibilities of the voyage

• Offers two- to three-week summer cruises in the western hemisphere with accredited academic programs for students and teachers

8.020
Mid-America State University Association
University of Kansas
127 Strong Hall
Lawrence, KS 66045
(913) 864-3617

Contact(s):
Jerry Hutcheson, Executive Director

Consortium of 11 state universities in Iowa, Kansas, Missouri, Nebraska and Oklahoma
• Sponsors overseas language and study programs for member institutions

8.021
Mobility International USA
P.O. Box 3551
Eugene, OR 97402
(503) 343-1284
or
Mobility International
62 Union St.
London SE1 1TD
England
01-403-5688

Contact(s):
Susan Sygall and April Carney, U.S.
    Representatives
Susannah Beaumont, Information Services
    Officer, England

International organization designed to promote the integration of disabled people into society through international travel and educational exchange

• Sponsors cooperative international programs and exchange activities; London office publishes the newsletter *Mobility International News* and *Europe for the Handicapped Traveler* (guides to specific countries); U.S. office publishes a newsletter and *A Guide to International Workcamps and Educational Exchange for Persons with Disabilities*

8.022
National Registration Center for Study Abroad
823 North 2d St., Lower Lobby
Milwaukee, WI 53203
(414) 278-0631

Contact(s):
Mike Wittig, Director

Commercial study/travel organization
• Provides information about and makes arrangements for participation in study and travel programs conducted by overseas organizations and institutions; publishes directories of these programs for Britain and Ireland ($7.95), Latin America ($4) and Europe ($6.95)

8.023
Northwest International Education Association
Highline Community College 25–5A
Midway, WA 98032-0424
(206) 878-3710, Ext. 248

Contact(s):
Michael Gordon, Coordinator
Mathilda Harris, President
   Graduate School of International Studies,
   University of Denver, Denver, CO 80208
   (303) 753-2324

Consortium of 39 colleges, universities and educational organizations in the Pacific Northwest

• Sponsors wide range of programs aimed at internationalizing the curriculum and expanding international education programs and activities on member campuses; includes faculty development programs and exchanges in the U.S. and abroad, a Global Studies Development Project at college and precollege levels, the coordination of 25 study abroad programs, the publication of manuals and videotape source materials and the development of training programs for students, faculty, business personnel and others

8.024
Resource Services/Publications Services
Brigham Young University
David M. Kennedy Center for International
   Studies
130 FOB
Provo, UT 84602
(801) 378-3377

Contact(s):
Stan Taylor, Director, Kennedy Center
V. Lynn Tyler, Resource Services
   Administrator
Deborah Coon, Manager, Publications
   Services

• Publishes materials on intercultural communication and on traveling and living overseas (see 2.056)

8.025
Scandinavian Seminar
358 North Pleasant St.
Amherst, MA 01002
(413) 549-5836

Contact(s):
William W. Hoffa, Executive Director

• 10-month study program in Denmark, Norway, Sweden or Finland; includes family living experience, language training and attendance at a small folk school

8.026
YMCA Overseas Programs
101 North Wacker Drive
Chicago, IL 60606
(312) 977-0031

Contact(s):

Richard Bertucco, Overseas Personnel
   Programs
William Yates, Overseas Service Corps

• Offers Overseas Personnel Programs involving career work experience at overseas YMCA's for present or prospective YMCA personnel along with opportunities for college graduates to teach conversational English at overseas Y's (Overseas Service Corps)

Intern Abroad Program, YMCA of Metropolitan Washington, 1711 Rhode Island Ave., NW, Washington, DC 20036; contact: Tony Lee

• Offers six- to eight-week internships for college students to work at YMCA's in a developing country; also arranges World Study Tours twice a year

World Ambassadors, State YMCA of Michigan, 301 West Lenawee St., Lansing, MI 48914; contact: Clifford Drury

• Sponsors summer volunteer service projects of five to seven weeks for college students and others to work in youth recreation, community development and similar projects

Manuals, Sourcebooks and Periodicals

8.027
Assessing Study Abroad Programs for Secondary School Students
Helene Z. Loew
Center for Applied Linguistics
3520 Prospect St. NW
Washington, DC 20007
1979; pamphlet; 29 pages; $3.95

Available from Harcourt Brace Jovanovich, Inc., 757 Third Ave., New York, NY 10017

• Surveys the status of study abroad in secondary education and then examines specifics such as information supplied, selection of leaders, academic standards, facilities, evaluation and a number of practical issues like insurance coverage

8.028
Basic Facts on Foreign Study
Institute for International Education
809 UN Plaza
New York, NY 10017
1982; folder; 6 pages; single copies free

• Concise review of factors students need to take into account when considering study abroad; covers such areas as planning, foreign language issues, studying at foreign universities, medical study abroad, undergraduate study abroad, credit, teaching abroad, financial considerations, scholarships, work availability, travel and personal matters; includes list of programs of IIE (see 10.010) and CIEE (see 8.010) and a useful bibliography

8.029

Bibliography on Study, Work, and Travel Abroad

National Association for Foreign Student
  Affairs
1860 19th St. NW
Washington, DC 20009
1982; brochure; 6 pages; free in single
  copies

• Extensive annotated list of books under such headings as Opportunities, Advising, Credit Transfer, Scholarships and Grants, Paid Employment, Work Camps, and General Travel

8.030

Cooperative Listing and Exchange Directory

Association for Innovation in Higher
  Education
P.O. Box 48
Waterville, ME 04901
1983; paperbound; approx. 100 pages; free
  to members of AIHE

• Gives detailed information about Interm (interim/January) programs offered by the members of the Association for Innovation in Higher Education; includes seven programs in Latin America and the Caribbean, 32 in Europe, 11 in the Near East and Africa and three in Japan and China

8.031

Directory of Overseas Summer Jobs

David J. Woodworth, Editor
Writer's Digest Books
9933 Alliance Rd.
Cincinnati, OH 45242
annual; paperbound; $7.95

• Provides listing of hundreds of jobs all over the world and gives work permit and visa information

8.032

International Teaching: Complete Overseas Opportunity Information and Employer Directory

Howard M. Faulkner
P.O. Box 292
Gorham, ME 04038
4th edition, annually updated; paperbound;
  46 pages and supplement; $7.75

• Describes overseas teaching opportunities along with practical matters involved in pursuing them

8.033

Learning Vacations: 1980–81

Gerson G. Eisenberg
Eisenberg Educational Enterprises, Inc.
Petersen's Guides
Box 2123
Princeton, NJ 08540
1982; 4th edition; paperbound; 337 pages;
  $6.95

• Guide to travel programs that have a learning or educational focus; provides extensive list and descriptions of college seminars, art, architectural and archaelogical programs, festivals, educational tours and others

8.034

The New Guide to Study Abroad

John A. Garraty, Lily von Klemperer, and
  Cyril J. H. Taylor, Editors
Harper & Row Publishers, Inc.
10 East 53d St.
New York, NY 10022
annual paperbound; 464 pages; $7.95

• Comprehensive guide to studying abroad; includes chapters on planning, costs, getting the most from the experience and educational systems and practices in the countries receiving the largest numbers of students; briefly describes academic year and summer programs worldwide that are sponsored by foreign and by American institutions, including programs for high school students; also provides information on teaching opportunities abroad and special summer work and travel programs

8.035
Students Abroad: A Guide to Selecting a Foreign Education
National Association for Foreign Student
  Affairs
1860 19th St. NW
Washington, DC 20009
1979; pamphlet; 22 pages; free

• Basic guide to selecting academic programs, work, travel and volunteer service opportunities in other countries

8.036
Study Abroad
The UNESCO Press
7 Place de Fontenoy
75700 Paris, France
1980; paperbound; 1,011 pages; $12.95

Should be ordered from UNIPUB, 345 Park Ave. South, New York, NY 10010 (see 1.133)
• Comprehensive listing of over 200,000 scholarships and/or courses and programs open to foreign students in the countries of the world; in the case of scholarships, indicates nature of award, subjects, where the award is tenable and to whom it is open, duration, value and application date; in the case of courses, briefly describes course, to whom it is open, duration, scholarship offered, fees and application deadline

8.037
Study Abroad Programs: An Evaluation Guide
National Association for Foreign Student
  Affairs
1860 19th St. NW
Washington, DC 20009
1979; booklet; 38 pages; $1

• Provides a set of evaluative criteria for judging the merits of study abroad programs

8.038
Study and Teaching Opportunities Abroad
Pat Kern McIntyre
U.S. Department of Health, Education, and
  Welfare
Washington, DC 20202
1980; pamphlet; 68 pages

Available from Information Clearinghouse, Office of International Education Programs, U.S. Department of Education, Washington, DC 20202
• Lists and describes major public and private organizations involved in sponsoring or providing information about postsecondary work, study, travel and teaching programs abroad and provides extensive annotated list of publications available on the subject; offers guidelines on how to evaluate the programs and identifies federal government sources of financial assistance

8.039
Survival Kit for Overseas Living
Robert Kohls
Intercultural Press Inc.
Box 768
Yarmouth, ME 04096
1979; paperbound; 105 pages, revised
  edition; $5.95

• Guide to effective adaptation to life in a foreign country; discusses cultural differences, attitudes and values, communication problems, culture shock, and other factors which make living abroad a challenge; provides do-it-yourself instructions and suggests concrete steps to take in making the overseas adjustment

8.040
Trans-Cultural Study Guide
Grey Bryan, Ken Darrow, Dan Morrow, and
  Brad Palmquist, Editors
Volunteers in Asia
Box 4543
Stanford, CA 94305
1975; paperbound; 155 pages; $2.50

• Provides directions for the on-site study of another culture through an inquiry method; identifies 12 subject areas (economics, politics, social structure, roles of women and men, religion and beliefs, music and art, food, education, communications, health and welfare, the transcultural experience, and development) and then provides extensive list of basic questions to be asked, explored, or researched; includes guidelines on methods of inquiry

8.041
Transitions
Clayton A. Hubbs, Senior Editor
18 Hulst Road
Amherst, MA 01002
published 4 times per year; magazine;
  approx. 60 pages; $9.50 per year

• Focuses on study, work and educational travel abroad and is addressed to students, teachers and others who travel to learn; reports on study abroad, international educational organizations and programs, low-cost travel (hiking, biking, camping, etc.), overseas educational institutions and systems, employment opportunities, and the student/educational scene in cities and regions where

international educational activity is concentrated; book reviews and bibliographies

8.042
Travel and Learning Abroad
Douglas Grube, Editor
Travel and Learning Abroad
P.O. Box 1122
Brattleboro, VT 05301
bimonthly magazine; approx. 60 pages;
  $9.50 per year

• Publishes articles and information on formal and nonformal opportunities for learning abroad, including information on individual and group travel and features for people from high school age to senior citizens and handicapped travelers

8.043
U.S. College-Sponsored Programs Abroad: Academic Year, the Learning Traveler Series, Volume I
Gail A. Cohen, Editor
Institute of International Education
809 UN Plaza
New York, NY 10017
annual; paperbound; 206 pages; $9.95

• Lists and describes approximately 800 semester and academic-year educational programs abroad sponsored by U.S. colleges and universities and educational consortia, arranged by country of location and cross-indexed by institution; information includes dates, level of instruction, qualifications, subject areas covered, program organization and association with foreign institutions, housing arrangements, language(s) of instruction, cost, work and scholarship availability, travel programs and application date; also provides guidelines on choosing a program, a list of consortia and a bibliography

8.044
Vacation Study Abroad, The Learning Traveler Series, Volume II
Gail A. Cohen, Editor
Institute of International Education
809 UN Plaza
New York, NY 10017
annual; paperbound; 182 pages; $8

• Lists and describes approximately 900 short-term (spring, summer, fall) educational programs abroad for secondary and college students, teachers and others, including a wide variety of special programs in addition to traditional language and culture study; offers guidelines on choosing a program and provides bibliography

8.045
Work, Study, and Travel Abroad: The Whole World Handbook
Marjorie Adoff Cohen
E. P. Dutton Publishing Co., Inc.
2 Park Ave.
New York, NY 10016
1984; paperbound; 338 pages; $6.95

Prepared by and available from Council on International Educational Exchange, 205 East 42d St., New York, NY 10017
• Practical guide for the student or young adult interested in studying, working or traveling unconventionally abroad; provides basic advice and guidance in each of these areas including kinds of programs and jobs available, other sources of information and assistance, and ways to assess and evaluate opportunities; reviews travel options, costs and essentials and then provides the same kind of advice and guidance for each of the world regions, in some cases country by country

Publishers and Distributors of Overseas Study and Travel Materials

8.046
Complete Traveller Bookstore
199 Madison Ave.
New York, NY 10016
(212) 679-4339

Contact(s):
Ed Feeley, Manager

Bookstore specializing in travel and tourist books and materials
• Carries over 2,000 titles; includes language dictionaries, phrasebooks and learning materials along with an extensive collection of maps; one-stop resource for the business, educational or tourist traveler

8.047
Fodor's Travel Guides and David McKay Co., Inc.
2 Park Ave.
New York, NY 10016
(212) 340-9845

Commercial publishing house
• Publishes and distributes travel and language-learning books and materials; includes Fodor's Travel Guides (see 2.192) and Teach Yourself language books (see 9.044)

8.048
Forsyth Travel Library
9154 West 57th St.
P.O. Box 2975
Shawnee Mission, KS 66201-1375
(913) 384-3440

• Major mail order distributor of travel reference publications including books, travel guides, atlases, maps, periodicals, international rail and surface timetables, etc. for all parts of the world and the U.S.; also distributes language learning materials; North American distributor for Thomas Cook Publications

8.049
Hippocrene Books, Inc.
171 Madison Ave.
New York, NY 10016
(212) 685-4371

Commercial publishing house and bookseller
• Publishes and distributes books on travel and language learning, including Nagel Encyclopedia Guides (see 2.195), Lonely Planet Travel Survival Kits (see 2.196), the Editions Today Travel Guide Series, Geographia and Ravenstein maps, carta maps and books, and a variety of other travel and language learning books; runs Complete Traveller Bookstore offering wide selection of travel materials (see 8.046)

8.050
Intercultural Press Inc.
Box 768
Yarmouth, ME 04096
(207) 846-5168

Contact(s):
Margaret D. Pusch, President

• Publishes books on work, study and travel abroad (see 1.114)

8.051
Volunteers in Asia, Inc.
Stanford University
Box 4543
Clubhouse Bldg.
Stanford, CA 94305
(415) 497-3228; 326-7672

Contact(s):
Dwight Clark, Director

Educational exchange program of Stanford University and the University of California at Santa Cruz designed to recruit, train and send students to Asia to teach English
• Publishes materials useful to students and travelers in Asia, including *On-Your-Own Guide to Asia, Staying Healthy in Asia* and *Trans-Cultural Study Guide* (published jointly with the Council on International Educational Exchange)

9

Foreign Language Learning

Professional Associations

9.001
American Association of Teachers of Arabic
SAIS, Johns Hopkins University
1740 Massachusetts Ave., NW
Washington, DC 20036
(202) 785-6237

Contact(s):
Jerry Lampe, Executive Secretary-Treasurer

Professional educational association of college and university teachers, scholars and students of the Arabic language, linguistics and literature
 • Provides information about the study of the Arabic language in the U.S. and sponsors a translation contest for students (Arabic to English)
 • Publishes newsletter and the annual journal *Al'Arabiyya* (see 17.074)

9.002
American Association of Teachers of French
University of Illinois
57 East Armory Ave.
Champaign, IL 61820
(217) 333-2842

Contact(s):
Fred M. Jenkins, National Executive
   Secretary

Professional association of teachers of French
 • Holds meetings, sponsors student contests, awards scholarships for study in France, and arranges teacher and pen pal exchanges

 • Publishes *French Review*, a newsletter and various teaching aids and materials and maintains Pedagogical Aids Bureau

9.003
The American Association of Teachers of German, Inc.
523 Bldg., Suite 201
Route 38
Cherry Hill, NJ 08034
(609) 663-5264

Contact(s):
Robert A. Govier, Executive Director

Professional association of individual teachers of German language, literature and culture at all levels
 • Maintains print and audiovisual teaching materials center (available to members)
 • Publishes teaching materials, *The German Quarterly* (literary criticism, book reviews, etc.), *Die Unterrichtspraxis* (pedagogy and teaching material) and two newsletters
 • Conducts workshops and conferences, organizes travel programs and advises and assists individual members with travel plans
 • Offers annual awards for study in German

9.004
The American Association of Teachers of Italian
French/Italian Department
Indiana University
Bloomington, IN 47401
(812) 335-2508

Contact(s):
Edoardo A. Lebano, Secretary-Treasurer

Association of U.S. and Canadian teachers of Italian language, literature and culture at all levels of instruction
• Conducts annual meeting and contests among high school and college students as well as assisting local chapters in arranging educational events (e.g., Italian week, film programs, fiestas, language days, etc.)
• Publishes a newsletter, a pedagogical journal *Italica* (includes book reviews, special reports and information about the Association) and *The Handbook for Teachers of Italian* ($5)

9.005

The Association of Teachers of Japanese
Cornell University
Department of Modern Languages and
    Linguistics
Ithaca, NY 14853
(518) 256-1000

Contact(s):
E. H. Jorden, President

Professional association of scholars, teachers and students of Japanese language, literature and linguistics; established in 1963
• Promotes professional development of teachers of Japanese, holds conferences and publishes a newsletter and journal

9.006

American Association of Teachers of Slavic and East European Languages
University of Arizona
Modern Languages Bldg., Room 342
Tucson, AZ 85721
(602) 626-2841

Contact(s):
Joe Malik, Jr., Secretary-Treasurer

Professional educational association of teachers, scholars, students and university libraries
• Provides information about the study of Slavic and East European languages and cultures in the U.S., sponsors honor societies and publishes a newsletter and *Slavic and East European Journal* (see 14.073)

9.007

American Association of Teachers of Spanish and Portuguese, Inc.
Mississippi State University
Mississippi State, MS 39762-5720
(601) 232-7442

Contact(s):
James R. Chatham, Executive Director

Professional association of individual teachers of Spanish and Portuguese at all levels
• Provides advice and information on matters related to teaching Spanish and Portuguese and prepares and distributes teaching materials
• Publishes the journal *Hispania* (see 16.149)
• Assists in travel plans, runs job placement bureau for members and maintains a pen pal registry and other services

9.008

The American Council of Teachers of Russian
Russian Center
815 New Gulph Road
Bryn Mawr, PA 19010
(215) 525-6559

Contact(s):
Dan Davidson, Director

• Promotes educational exchange with Russia through the sponsorship of conferences and programs in Russian language, literature and culture at the Pushkin Institute in Moscow; includes an intermediate summer program for undergraduates, a semester program for advanced undergraduates and graduate students, and a ten-month program for graduate students and teachers

• Publishes college and high school Russian language instructional texts

9.009
American Council on the Teaching of Foreign Languages, Inc. (ACTFL, Inc.)
579 Broadway
Hastings-on-Hudson, NY 10706
(914) 478-2011

Contact(s):
C. Edward Scebold, Executive Director

Professional association of teachers of foreign languages established in 1967

• Represents the profession of language teaching, advises members on developments in legislation, public policy and education that affect language education

• Conducts training workshops in conjunction with annual conference

• Maintains a materials center with an extensive collection of books, audiovisuals, and other foreign language teaching aids for sale at discount prices

• Publishes *Foreign Language Annals* (on language teaching methods and materials), an annual bibliography of books and articles on pedagogy in foreign languages, and the *Foreign Language Education Series* (an annual review of the general state of foreign language education)

9.010
Association of Departments of Foreign Languages
62 Fifth Ave.
New York, NY 10011
(212) 741-5592

Contact(s):
Richard I. Brod, Director

Association of academic language departments in two- and four-year colleges; a subsidiary of the Modern Language Association (see 9.014)

• Provides information and assistance to and sponsors programs for foreign language department heads and others concerned with the accreditation of collegiate foreign language programs

• Publishes books and papers on appropriate subjects

9.011
Center for Applied Linguistics
3520 Prospect St. NW
Washington, DC 20007
(202) 298-9292

Contact(s):
G. Richard Tucker, Director

Independent nonprofit organization concerned with the study of language and the application of linguistics to educational, cultural and social concerns; particularly concerned with improvement in the teaching of English as a second language and less commonly taught foreign languages and the study of non-standard varieties of English; organized in five departments: Native and English Language Education, Foreign Language Education, Research, Language and Public Policy and Communication Services (publications are distributed by Harcourt Brace Jovanovich, Inc., 757 Third Ave. New York, NY 10017)

• Sponsors research and conducts surveys on foreign language teaching and publishes and disseminates information on the teaching, learning and real-world use of foreign languages; maintains extensive files of bibliographic and other materials providing access to the study of uncommonly taught languages

• Houses ERIC Clearinghouse on Languages and Linguistics providing computer-based bibliographies and other language education materials; will also conduct searches and prepare special bibliographies on demand

• Provides advice and information to local, state and national educational and government agencies and to international organizations

• Conducts research and publishes materials on English as a second language and on bilingual education (see 10.003)

• Publishes an extensive list of titles covering such areas as bilingual education, ESL and foreign language teaching methods and concepts, classroom activities for language teaching, evaluation and assessment, directories and guides, sociolinguistics, dialects, language handbooks and refugee education materials (including a series of English phrasebooks for speakers of the languages of Indochina); titles include: *Teaching French as a Multicultural Language: The French-Speaking World Outside Europe* ($6.25), *Games and Simulations in the Foreign Language Classroom* ($8.50), *Assessing Study Abroad Programs for Secondary School Students* (see 8.027), *Directory of Foreign Language Service Organizations: 2, A Survey of Materials for the Uncommonly Taught Languages* (languages grouped in 8 separate volumes by world area; see under area studies), and *The Peoples and Cultures of Cambodia, Laos and Vietnam* (describes culture, traditions, behaviors and background of the peoples of Indochina for use in cross-cultural interaction, $6)

9.012
Central States Conference on the Teaching of Foreign Languages
The Ohio State University
Slavic Department
232 Cunz Hall
Columbus, OH 43210
(614) 422-6446

Contact(s):
Gerald L. Ervin, Executive Secretary

Professional association of foreign language teachers

• Promotes foreign language teaching through conferences, awards, and services to language teachers; publishes proceedings of conferences, including *A Global Approach to Foreign Language Education* (available from National Textbook Company, see 9.040)

9.013
Joint National Committee for Languages and Council for Languages and Other International Studies
11 Dupont Circle NW, Suite 210
Washington, DC 20036
(202) 483-7200

Contact(s):
J. David Edwards, Director

Association of professional language organizations for the promotion of foreign language study

• Monitors and provides information on legislative activity; makes recommendations on legislation and keeps legislators and government officers informed of the interests of language educators

• Conducts political action and public awareness workshops and promotes model language education programs

9.014
The Modern Language Association of America
62 Fifth Ave.
New York, NY 10011
(212) 741-7878

Contact(s):
English Showalter, Executive Director

Large professional association of teachers of English and of foreign languages with two major subsidiaries: Association of Departments of Foreign Languages (ADFL, see

9.010) and Association of Departments of English (ADE)

• Holds meetings and conferences, conducts research on the profession, and provides career and job information service

• Publishes the quarterly *PMLA*, a scholarly journal on modern language teaching and research, the *MLA Directory* (names and addresses), the *MLA Program* (for the annual convention) the *MLA Newsletter*, bulletins of ADFL and ADE, *Profession* (an annual anthology of articles on professional and pedagogical subjects) and the *MLA Job Information Lists*, as well as a variety of books on professional aspects of teaching English and the foreign languages, including *Options and Perspectives: a Sourcebook of Innovative Foreign Language Programs in Action, K-12* (descriptions of over 50 innovative programs, $9 plus $1 postage), *A Guide to Professional Organizations for Teachers of Language and Literature* (see 9.027), *MLA Directory of Periodicals* (see 1.048), the *MLA International Bibliography* (see 1.049), and *Options for Undergraduate Foreign Language Programs: Four-year and Two-year Colleges* (see 9.033)

9.015
National Association of Professors of Hebrew
University of Wisconsin at Madison
1346 Van Hise Hall
1220 Linden Drive
Madison, WI 53706
(608) 262-3204

Contact(s):
Albert T. Bilgray, President

Association of professors, students and others

• Promotes research and fosters the study and teaching of Hebrew; publishes a newsletter and *Hebrew Studies Journal*

9.016
National Association of Self-Instructional Language Programs
Temple University
Humanities Bldg., Box 38
Philadelphia, PA 19122
(215) 787-1715

Contact(s):
John B. Means, Executive Director

Association of academic institutions which provide programs of self-instruction in the "critical" (not commonly offered) languages

• Provides information, consults in the development of self-instructional language programs, evaluates and/or supplies instructional and orientation materials and reviews curriculum; engages in funded research in multi-media text development

• Publishes *NASLIP Journal* and other occasional publications

9.017
Northeast Conference on the Teaching of Foreign Languages
Box 623
Middlebury, VT 05753
(802) 388-4017

Contact(s):
James W. Dodge, Secretary-Treasurer

Professional association of foreign language teachers

• Sponsors major annual conference, presents awards for contributions to the foreign language teaching field, disseminates language instructional films, and publishes an annual *Northeast Conference Report* ($7.95) consisting of articles on foreign-language pedagogy

International Language Training Organizations

9.018
Berlitz School of Languages
1101 State Road
Research Park, Bldg. O
Princeton, NJ 08540
(800) 257-9449
BRANCHES: at 65 locations in the U.S. and at 155 locations in 23 other countries

Contact(s):
Service Staff

Large language-training firm
• Offers individual instruction in all languages, emphasizing the development of verbal facility and involving the exclusive use of the target language

9.019
Inlingua
551 Fifth Ave.
New York, NY 10176
(212) 682-8585

Contact(s):
Tom Huarte, President

Large language training organization with 200 schools in 22 countries

• Offers instruction in all spoken languages, including English as a second language, tailored to trainee needs privately or in small groups; uses audiovisual and audiolingual approaches, includes cross-cultural training and offers intensive full-time program for rapid learning; provides proficiency testing and progress reports
• Offers translation and interpreting services

9.020
Linguex International
Box 238
Poncha Springs, CO 81242
(303) 539-6621
BRANCHES: in 6 U.S. and 6 foreign cities

Contact(s):
Raphael Alberola, President

Commercial language training organization
• Offers intensive training in any language using current video disc technology in the classroom with the instructor; also develops computer software

Manuals and Sourcebooks

9.021
Award-Winning Foreign Language Programs
William D. Sims and Sandra B. Hammond
National Textbook Co.
8259 Niles Center Road
Skokie, IL 60077
1982 paperbound; 212 pages; $13

• Describes 50 foreign language programs in U.S. schools which combine success in attracting and retaining students with effectiveness in developing language proficiency

9.022
Bibliography of Audiovisual Instructional Materials for the Teaching of Spanish: Kindergarten through Grade Twelve
Bureau of Compensatory Education
   Evaluation and Research
California State Department of Education
P.O. Box 271
Sacramento, CA 95802
paperbound; 120 pages; $.75

• Lists and describes wide selection of records, tapes, slides, posters, charts, photographs, films and filmstrips

9.023
Bibliography of Instructional Materials for the Teaching of German: Kindergarten through Grade Twelve
ERIC, Dissemination and Improvement of
   Practice Programs
National Institute of Education
Washington, DC 20208
1975; paperbound; 85 pages

• Lists and describes wide selection of records, tapes, slides, posters, charts, photographs, films and filmstrips

9.024
Careers in Foreign Languages: A Handbook
June L. Sherif
Regents Publishing Company, Inc.
2 Park Ave.
New York, NY 10016
1976; paperbound; 240 pages; $3.95

• Describes in detail potential careers for people with competence in a foreign language; includes sources of foreign language materials and information on overseas study and summer camp opportunities, professional associations, etc.

9.025
The Foreign Language Learner: A Guide to Teachers
Mary Finocchiaro and Michael Bonomo
Regents Publishing Co., Inc.
2 Park Ave.
New York, NY 10016
1982; paperbound; 320 pages; $5.95

• Discusses the planning and design of foreign language teaching; includes bibliography of useful books

9.026
A Guide to Language Camps in the United States
Lois Vines
Center for Applied Linguistics
3520 Prospect St. NW
Washington, DC 20007
1980; paperbound; 33 pages; $4.25

Available from Harcourt Brace Jovanovich, Inc., 757 Third Ave., New York, NY 10017
• Lists and describes over 25 camps which offer a foreign language immersion program; includes an annotated bibliography of materials useful in organizing and conducting the programs

9.027
A Guide to Professional Organizations for Teachers of Language and Literature
Joseph Gibaldi and Walter S. Achtert,
   Compilers
Modern Language Association
62 Fifth Ave.
New York, NY 10011
1978; 62 pages; offset from typescript, $5

• Lists 41 organizations serving the profession and briefly describes their programs and activities

9.028
How to Be a More Successful Language Learner
Joan Rubin and Irene Thompson
Heinle & Heinle Publishers, Inc.
286 Congress St.
Boston, MA 02210
1982; paperbound; 110 pages; $8.95

- Discusses the nature of language, communication and language learning and presents a series of 14 strategies by which the learner, alone and in an instructional situation, can make the process easier and more rewarding; recommends learning aids and suggests how best to use them

9.029
Individualized Foreign Language Instruction
Frank M. Grittner and Fred H. La Leike
National Textbook Co.
8259 Niles Center Road
Skokie, IL 60077
1973; paperbound; 111 pages; $6.95

- Describes formula for implementing, equipping, staffing and evaluating a foreign language program which enables students to learn at their own pace

9.030
Language Acquisition Made Practical
E. Thomas Brewster and Elizabeth S.
    Brewster
Lingua House Ministries
135 N. Oakland, Box 114
Pasadena, CA 91101-1790
1976; paperbound; 384 pages; $12

- Extensive, practical guide to learning any language; gives step-by-step suggestions on getting started, answers basic questions about language learning, suggests topics for

beginning learners to focus on, describes best ways to undertake comprehension drills and analyzes differences in sounds and language structure

9.031
New Ways to Learn a Foreign Language
Robert A. Hall, Jr.
Spoken Languages Services, Inc.
P.O. Box 783
Ithaca, NY 14850
1973; paperbound; 188 pages; $6

- Discusses the nature of language, surveys language learning technologies and includes grammatical sketches of eight languages; designed to make the language-learning process less forbidding

9.032
Options and Perspectives: A Sourcebook of Innovative Foreign Language Programs in Action, K-12
William D. Love and Lucille J. Honig
Modern Language Association
62 5th Ave.
New York, NY 10011
1973; paperbound; 361 pages; $7.50

- Describes over 50 programs including those involving immersion, study abroad, mini-courses, summer camps, FLES enrichment institutes, etc.

9.033
Options for Undergraduate Foreign Language Programs: Four-Year and Two-Year Colleges
Renate A. Schulz
Modern Language Association
62 Fifth Ave.
New York, NY 10011
1979; paperbound; 97 pages; $10 plus $1
    postage

• Survey and description of successful undergraduate foreign language programs

9.034
Teaching Culture: Strategies and Techniques
Robert C. Lafayette
Center for Applied Linguistics
Office of Communication and Publications
3520 Prospect St. NW
Washington, DC 20007
1978; paperbound; $3.25

• Examines the question of introducing cultural perspectives into foreign language teaching and discusses the various techniques and resources available to the teacher

9.035
Teaching Culture: Strategies for Foreign Language Educators
H. Ned Seelye
National Textbook Co.
8259 Niles Center Road
Skokie, IL 60076
1974; paperbound; 188 pages; $10

• Practical guide to teaching about culture in the foreign language classroom; discusses the meaning of cross-cultural communication and understanding and deals with the problem of defining "culture"; lays out the goals of cultural instruction, examines methods of teaching, and outlines specific classroom activities
• Selected publishers of self-instructional foreign language materials

Selected Publishers of Self–Instructional Foreign Language Materials

9.036
Barron's Educational Series, Inc.
113 Crossways Park Drive
Woodbury, NY 11797
(516) 921-8750

• Publishes books and cassettes for language study; includes beginning self-instructional materials for French, German, Italian, Japanese and Spanish, specialized verb and idiom guides, conversational courses for travelers, phrasebooks and grammar cards, along with a more limited selection of materials for other languages

9.037
Cortina Institute of Languages
17 Riverside Ave.
Westport, CT 06880
(203) 227-8471

• Publishes language learning materials and courses; courses include records or cassette tapes, a bilingual dictionary, a conversation book, tests (in the form of recordings) and a consultation service; courses available for Italian, German, French and Spanish; also publishes short courses and smaller learning packages of books, records and tapes ("Record Time" course and stereo 8-track cartridge course), cassettes for travelers, a variety of books including a *Vest Pocket* and *Nutshell* series, bilingual dictionaries, readings, and other language learning aids for Japanese, Greek, Russian and Portuguese as well as the four languages above

9.038
Dover Publications, Inc.
31 East 2nd St.
Mineola, NY 11501
(516) 294-7000

Commercial publishing house

• Publishes books and audio courses on language learning; includes booklet series *Say It in. . . .* for 20 languages (see 9.046) and *Listen and Learn* courses on records for 10 languages

9.039
Macmillan Publishing Company, Inc.
866 Third Ave.
New York, NY 10022
(212) 702-2000
or
Customer Service Dept.
Front and Brown Sts.
Riverside, NJ 08370
(609) 461-6500

• Publishes Berlitz foreign language learning materials including basic and comprehensive cassette and/or record courses for French, German, Italian and Spanish (Russian: basic record course only) along with cassette packs (Berlitz for Travellers), records, phrasebooks and/or bilingual pocket dictionaries for these languages plus Arabic, Chinese, Danish, Finnish, Greek, Hebrew, Hungarian, Norwegian, Polish, Portuguese, Russian, Serbo-Croatian, Swahili, Swedish and Turkish

9.040
National Textbook Co.
8259 Niles Center Road
Skokie, IL 60077
(312) 679-4210

Commercial publishing house
• Publishes extensive list of books on foreign language and English as a second language learning and teaching; particularly strong in Spanish, German and English for Spanish speakers; includes readers, workbooks, cassettes, filmstrips, dictionaries, duplicating masters, games and cultural materials; selected materials also available for French, Russian, Vietnamese and Portuguese; publishes professional books for teachers and *Focus on Europe,* a series of individual country guides for students and others going abroad to live, providing historical, social and cultural background; distributes English/foreign dictionaries in most of the languages listed above including *Harrap's French/English Dictionary*

9.041
Spoken Language Services, Inc.
P.O. Box 783
Ithaca, NY 14850
(607) 257-0500

Contact(s):
J. M. Cowan

Producer of self-instructional English and foreign language materials
• Offers Spoken Language Series (self-instructional courses for beginners with cassette tapes keyed to written texts) for 43 of the less commonly taught languages (see 9.047); also publishes other materials related to language learning

Selected Self-Instructional Foreign Language Learning Materials

9.042
Berlitz . . . . For Travellers (Cassettepak)
Macmillan Publishing Co.
866 Third Ave.
New York, NY 10022
published from 1972 to 1981; prices range from $12 to $15

• Conversational lessons on cassette tapes with 32-page script containing pronunciation aids and the text of the dual-language tape (also available on records and eight-track tapes); available for Arabic, French, German, Spanish and other languages (see individual countries for indication of availability)

9.043

Berlitz . . . . For Travellers (Phrasebook)
Macmillan Publishing Co.
866 Third Ave.
New York, NY 10022
published and/or revised 1973 to 1981;
    paperbound; range in price from $3 to $5

• Handy pocket phrasebook; available for Arabic, French, German, Spanish and other languages (see individual countries for indication of availability)

9.044

Teach Yourself . . . .: A Complete Course for Beginners
David McKay Co., Inc.
2 Park Ave.
New York, NY 10016
published from 1950 to 1980; paperbound;
    size ranges from 200 to 300 pages; price
    ranges from $4 to $8

• Series that provides basic materials for beginning language self-instruction; covers pronunciation and grammar and includes exercises, brief readings and vocabulary list; available for Arabic, French, German, Spanish and other languages (see individual country for indication of availability)

9.045

Speak and Read Essential . . .: A Pimsleur Language Program
Paul Pimsleur
Heinle & Heinle Enterprises, Inc.
29 Lexington Rd.
Concord, MA 01742
published from 1971 to 1981; 10–30 units on
    5–15 cassettes plus reading booklet;
    prices range from $150 to $250

• Self-instructional language program based on the graduated-interval recall sys-

tem, designed for learning by use of tapes alone; available for French, German, Spanish, Hebrew and Modern Greek

9.046

Say It In . . . .
Dover Publications, Inc.
31 East 2d St.
Mineola, NY 11501
published from 1960 to 1980; paperbound;
    size ranges from 100 to 300 pages; prices
    range from $1.75 to $3.50

• Quick guide to words and phrases useful to the traveler; available in Arabic, French, German, Spanish and other languages (see individual countries for indication of availability)

9.047

Spoken . . .
Spoken Language Services, Inc.
P.O. Box 783
Ithaca, NY 14850
published from 1973 to 1980; one or more
    books and 6 records or dual-track
    cassettes; price approx. $60; units may be
    purchased separately

• Self-instructional course for beginners with cassettes keyed to the written texts; prepared under the aegis of the American Council of Learned Societies (see 7.001) and the Linguistic Society of America or the Foreign Service Institute (U.S. Department of State); available for Arabic, French, German and Spanish and other languages (see individual countries for indication of availability)

9.048
Vest Pocket . . . .
Joseph Southam Choquette
Institute for Language Study
Montclair, NJ 07042
published between 1960 and 1970;
    paperbound; approx. 120 pages; $1.95
    each

• Each book is both a dictionary and phrasebook for the traveler; in addition to everyday conversational phrases and sentences, it includes a pronunciation guide, a brief explanation of grammar and a bilingual dictionary of over 4,000 words; available for Arabic, French, German, Spanish and other languages (see individual countries for indication of availability)

Importers of Foreign Language Publications

See individual countries for additional listings of importers and distributors of foreign language books

The following companies import and sell books in all languages:

9.049
Barnes & Noble, Inc.
105 Fifth Ave.
New York, NY 10003
(212) 675-5500

9.050
Cambridge Bookstore
1623 Cambridge St.
Cambridge, MA 02138
(617) 354-6220

9.051
European Book Co.
925 Larkin St.
San Francisco, CA 94109
(415) 474-0626

9.052
International Learning Center
1715 Connecticut Ave. NW
Washington, DC 20009
(202) 232-4111

9.053
Kroch's & Brentano's, Inc.
29 South Wabash
Chicago, IL 60603
(312) 263-2681

The following company imports and sells foreign books in French, German and Spanish from France, Germany, Spain and Latin America and accepts special orders for titles not in stock

9.054
Midwest European Publications, Inc.
915 Foster St.
Evanston, IL 60201
(312) 866-6262

The following companies import and sell books in the Arabic language:

9.055
Crescent Imports & Publications
450 South Main St.
P.O. Box 7827
Ann Arbor, MI 48107
(313) 665-3492

9.056
Dar al Kutub wal Nashrat al Islamiyya
94 Albany St.
New Brunswick, NJ 08901
(201) 249-6961

9.057
Kazi Publications
1215 West Belmont Ave.
Chicago, IL 60657
(312) 327-7598

The following companies import and sell books in the French language:

9.058
Europa Bookstore
3229 North Clark
Chicago, IL 60657
(312) 929-1836

9.059
French & Spanish Book Corporation
652 South Olive St.
Los Angeles, CA 90014
(213) 489-7963

9.060
French Institute-Alliance Francaise
Le Bookstore
22 East 60th St.
New York, NY 10022
(212) 355-6100

9.061
Haitian Book Centre
P.O. Box 324
East Elmhurst, NY 11369

9.062
Imported Books
P.O. Box 4414
Dallas, TX 75208
(214) 941-6497

9.063
Modern Language Book & Record Store
3160 O St. NW
Washington, DC 20007
(202) 338-8963

9.064
Schoenhof's Foreign Books, Inc.
1280 Massachusetts Ave.
Cambridge, MA 02138
(617) 547-8855

The following companies import and sell books in the German language:

9.065
Adler's Foreign Books
162 Fifth Ave.
New York, NY 10010
(212) 697-5151

9.066
Europa Bookstore
3229 North Clark
Chicago, IL 60657
(312) 929-1836

9.067
German & International Bookstore
1767 North Vermont Ave.
Los Angeles, CA 90027
(213) 660-0313

9.068
Modern Language Book & Record Store
3160 O St. NW
Washington, DC 20007
(202) 338-8963

9.069
Schoenhof's Foreign Books, Inc.
1280 Massachusetts Ave.
Cambridge, MA 02138
(617) 547-8855

The following companies import and sell books in the Spanish language:

9.070
Downtown Book Center, Inc.
247 SE First St.
Miami, FL 33131
(305) 377-9939

9.071
Europa Bookstore
3229 North Clark
Chicago, IL 60657
(312) 929-1836

9.072
KPB Books
P.O. Box 676
Washington, DC 20044

9.073
Libreria de las Americas
6709 Harrisburg
Houston, TX 77011
(713) 236-9928

9.074
Libreria la Latina Bookstore
2548 Mission St.
San Francisco, CA 94110
(415) 824-0327

9.075
Schoenhof's Foreign Books, Inc.
1280 Massachusetts Ave.
Cambridge, MA 02138
(617) 547-8855

9.076
The Spanish Bookstore
2326 Westwood Blvd.
Los Angeles, CA 90064
(213) 475-0453

10

Foreign Students and Visitors and Resources on English as a Second Language

Resource and Service Organizations

10.001
Aid Participant Training Program
Office of International Training
Agency for International Development
S and T/IT, Room 213
SA 16
Washington, DC 20523
(703) 235-1984

Contact(s):
William T. White, Director

• Large government-to-government program bringing students, trainees and professionals in government, industry and academia to the U.S. for training and/or professional observation; participants nominated and selected through bilateral agreement between the U.S. and the other governments

10.002
America-Mideast Educational & Training Services (AMIDEAST)
1717 Massachusetts Ave. NW
Suite 100
Washington, DC 20036
(202) 797-7900
BRANCHES: Jordan, Lebanon, Egypt, Syria, Morocco, Tunisia, West Bank, Yemen Arab Republic

Contact(s):
Orin D. Parker, President
James McCloud, Director, Information and Development Services

Private, nonprofit organization designed to aid educational exchange relationships between the U.S. and 20 Middle Eastern and North African countries with particular focus on education for development within the region and on assisting U.S. institutions to meet educational needs of students from the region
• Offers in-country educational services to private students from Middle Eastern countries at branch offices or by mail; includes counseling, orientation, credential translation, and information on higher education in the U.S. (test and admission requirements, availability of English-language training, fields of study, etc.); provides full services for government-sponsored students and faculty pursuing educational, vocational, technical and management training programs in the U.S., including planning, placement, counseling, financial administration, supervision and evaluation; services also available to region-wide educational development programs, especially in nonformal, community and occupational skills training areas
• Assists U.S. institutions in developing or expanding capabilities in evaluating and providing orientation and counseling to Middle Eastern/North African students or in organizing other special projects relative to their education
• Arranges visits of educators to or from the region for educational purposes
• Conducts special surveys and studies of education in the Middle East
• Publishes reports on or profiles of major academic institutions and vocational and technical postsecondary institutions in the

region, a quarterly newsletter, *Developments*, which reviews current educational developments in the region, and occasional papers

10.003
Center for Applied Linguistics
3520 Prospect St. NW
Washington, DC 20007
(202) 298-9292

Contact(s):
G. Richard Tucker, Director

Independent nonprofit organization concerned with the study of language and the application of linguistics to educational, cultural and social concerns (see 9.011 for full description)

• Sponsors research, conducts surveys and publishes and disseminates information on the teaching and learning of English as a second language; particularly strong in the teaching, orientation and training of Indochinese refugees; publishes extensive list of books on ESL, bilingual and refugee education

10.004
Center for International Higher Education Documentation
Northeastern University
202 Dodge Library
Boston, MA 02115
(617) 437-2770

Contact(s):
Solveig Turner, Director

• Maintains extensive collection of information on higher education throughout the world with emphasis on national educational systems, organizations in international education and international trends in education; includes the files of the *International Encyclopedia of Higher Education* (see 1.046); holdings are catalogued in Dodge Library and may be borrowed; conducts research on the international equivalency of educational credentials, offers a foreign credentials evaluation service and sponsors training workshops on credential evaluation

10.005
The College Board
Office of International Education
1717 Massachusetts Ave. NW, Suite 704
Washington, DC 20036
(202) 332-1480

Contact(s):
Sanford C. Jameson, Director

The College Board is a nonprofit educational membership organization; the International Education Office is concerned with foreign students and American students overseas seeking information on U.S. institutions of higher education

• Serves as secretariat for the National Liaison Committee on Foreign Student Admissions; the Committee conducts overseas workshops and consultations on U.S. higher education for student advisors overseas; administers a computerized foreign student information clearinghouse designed to assist foreign students in selecting a U.S. college or university to attend; sponsors a National Credentials Evaluation Project which offers consultation and advisory services on foreign student credential evaluation to colleges and universities enrolling fewer than 75 foreign students, and a Foreign Student Recruitment Information Clearinghouse designed to provide information about foreign student recruiting activities (inquiries about these latter two programs should be directed to the National Association for Foreign Student Affairs, see 10.018)

• Provides services to college placement counselors of American secondary students going to schools overseas

• Publishes a number of basic publications in the field including *Entering Higher Education in the United States: A Guide for Students from Other Countries* and *Financial Planning for Study in the United States: A Guide for Students from Other Countries*

• Permanent representative on Policy Council of Test of English as a Foreign Language

10.006
The Colorado Institute for Human Development
Box 875
Crested Butte, CO 81224
(303) 349-5118

Contact(s):
Clay W. Bridgford, Director

Small training organization employing experiential and environmental learning methods

• Conducts intercultural communication workshops for persons of different cultural backgrounds along with summer American Studies programs and adult education tours on western U.S. history and cultures for foreign participants

10.007
Council on International Educational Exchange
International Administrative Center
205 East 42nd St.
New York, NY 10017
(212) 661-1414
BRANCHES: Paris, Tokyo

Contact(s):
Colleen Zarich, Deputy Executive Director

Large, nonprofit educational exchange organization with a membership of approximately 160 schools, colleges, universities, academic consortia and others (see also 8.010)

• Offers English language training in Paris and administers the Test of English as a Foreign Language (TOEFL) in Japan

10.008
Educational Credential Evaluators, Inc.
P.O. Box 17499
Milwaukee, WI 53217
(414) 964-0477

Contact(s):
James S. Frey, Executive Director

Nonprofit agency serving persons who have completed part or all of their education outside of the U.S. or in nontraditional American educational programs

• Provides evaluation reports converting foreign educational achievements into traditional American educational equivalents for educational, employment, professional, and other purposes; charges $35 to $60 per evaluation for foreign educational credentials

• Publishes research on comparative educational systems

• Conducts seminars and workshops on the educational systems of other countries for college and university students, foreign student advisors and other academic personnel and employees of government agencies, professional associations and private organizations

10.009
Foundation for International Services, Inc.
P.O. Box 230278
Portland, OR 97223-0174
(503) 747-4225

Contact(s):
Jack L. Hoover, President

Educational consulting and service organization

• Offers international education services to institutions and organizations including the following: evaluation of foreign educational credentials for U.S. institutions and individuals (and U.S. credentials for foreign institutions); program evaluation; training seminars and workshops on foreign student admissions, credential evaluation and other aspects of international education; orientation of foreign personnel to the U.S.; counseling and placement of foreign students; seminars for overseas counselors of U.S.-bound students; interpreter and translation services (all major languages); and program searches for foreign governments and agencies; services also available to international businesses

10.010
Institute of International Education
809 United Nations Plaza
New York, NY 10017
(212) 883-8248
BRANCHES: Atlanta, Chicago, Denver, Houston, San Francisco, Washington, D.C.; Bangkok, Harare (Zimbabwe), Hong Kong, Jakarta, Mexico City

Contact(s):
Edwin Battle, Director, Communications
   Division

Major nonprofit service organization for post-secondary educational exchange; assists approximately 9,000 exchange students and trainees a year; funded by contributions, government and private grants and contracts, and annual dues of $150–$350 from approximately 600 Educational Associates

• Serves as information clearinghouse on international exchange in post-secondary education, responding to phone and written in-quiries from students, faculty and staff of accredited post-secondary educational institutions (special attention given to those which are IIE Educational Associates), government and business personnel and the general public; provides information and briefings to foreign educators at IIE overseas offices

• Administers U.S. Government-sponsored graduate student (Fulbright) grants and a variety of other government and privately sponsored grant programs for overseas study (see 8.018)

• Places students in English Language and Orientation programs

• Arranges programs for visiting foreign leaders and specialists under U.S. Government and UNESCO support

• Administers exchange programs in the arts, especially in music

• Provides administrative support to personnel in technical cooperative projects in many parts of the world

• Recruits faculty and academic specialists (especially in agriculture) for projects abroad

• Provides purchasing services to foreign educational and research organizations

• Provides professional training and/or consultation services in educational exchange administration

• Publishes wide selection of publications (distributing about 60,000 copies per year) on aspects of international educational exchange, among them: guides to study abroad for U.S. nationals including *Basic Facts on Foreign Study* (see 8.028), *Fulbright and Other Grants for Study Abroad* (see 7.041), *A Guide To Scholarships, Fellowships and Grants* (see 7.043), *U.S. College-Sponsored Programs Abroad: Academic Year* (see 8.043) and *Vacation Study Abroad* (see 8.044); and guides to study in the U.S. for foreign nationals including *English Language and Orientation Programs in the U.S.* (see 10.044), *Practical Guide for Foreign Visitors* (see 10.051), *Open Doors* (see 10.050), and *Study in U.S. Colleges and Universities* (see 10.053)

10.011
Intercultural Communication Consultants, International-USA (ICC, International-USA)
278 Post St., Suite 606
San Francisco, CA 94108
(415) 788-5678

Contact(s):
Mahmood Maghsoudi, Chief Executive Officer and President
G. Vittoria Abbate, Senior Executive Vice-President

Private independent consulting firm
• Offers services to the international educational, business and professional communities including immigration counseling and cross-cultural training programs and seminars; areas of specialization: Europe, Asia and the Middle East

10.012
Inter-Link Associates, Inc.
406 Rosedale Road
Princeton, NJ 08540
(609) 921-0557

Contact(s):
Robert L. Steiner, President

International education and business service and training firm especially oriented toward U.S.-Third World relations
• Offers general consulting on international educational matters and provides selection and/or placement services for foreign students in U.S. postsecondary institutions; includes cultural and educational orientation and assignment to English-language training as determined by appropriate testing; maintains English language training program at Guilford College, Greensboro, North Carolina
• Provides orientation to American faculty and staff for service abroad

• Selects and ships educational materials to organizations and institutions abroad

10.013
International Advisory Services
P.O. Box 583
Mukilteo, WA 98275
(206) 353-8883

Contact(s):
Frederick E. Lockyear, President
Donald A. Azar, Vice President

• Provides comprehensive consultation on the development and expansion of integrated foreign student and English as a second language programs on college campuses, including evaluation of ongoing programs; covers recruitment, orientation, ESL curriculum design, and the training of international education and foreign student program personnel
• Provides foreign student program evaluation and management for organizations and/or groups of students from overseas
• General international training consulting for business and government

10.014
International Consultants Inc. of Delaware
115 Barksdale Professional Center
Newark, DE 19711
(302) 737-8715

Contact(s):
Gary W. Hopkins, President

Consulting firm specializing in international educational procedures
• Offers foreign educational credential evaluation services, counseling and individualized training in English as a second language, and consulting and counseling to educational, business and community agencies

with regard to U.S. government regulations and procedures affecting international exchange, education, employment and travel

10.015
International Visitors Information Service
801 19th St. NW
Washington, DC 20006
(202) 872-8747

Contact(s):
Marianne H. Cruze, Executive Director

Private, nonprofit community organization offering programs and services to international and American visitors in Washington, D.C.; affiliated with Meridian House International
• Offers information and reception assistance to visitors at IVIS Reception/Information Center in Washington, D.C. (Monday to Friday, 9 a.m. to 5 p.m.) and at the IVIS Information Desk in arrivals area at Dulles International Airport (daily noon to 7 p.m.)
• Arranges bilingual guide escorts, professional appointments, social home visits, and information, interpreting and registration assistance at international conferences in the Washington area; requests for these services must be made in advance at the Reception Center
• Multilingual volunteers offer language assistance in over 55 languages seven days a week, 24 hours a day (after 11 p.m. only emergency requests are answered)

10.016
The Latin American Scholarship Program of American Universities
25 Mount Auburn St.
Cambridge, MA 02138
(617) 495-5255

Contact(s):
Lewis A. Taylor, Executive Director

Association of institutions of higher education in the U.S. and Latin America concerned with upgrading the teaching, research, and administrative staffs of universities and other institutions in Latin America and the Caribbean through advanced academic training
• Administers awards made by the U.S. government and other U.S., Latin American and multinational organizations for graduate training, principally at the master's level, and provides such services as selection, evaluation, placement, language training, and academic monitoring

10.017
Meridian House International
1630 Crescent Place NW
Washington, DC 20009
(202) 667-6800 and 332-1025

Contact(s):
Joseph John Jova, President

Nonprofit educational and cultural institution located at historic Washington mansion
• Umbrella administrative organization for international educational exchange programs and organizations, including the Washington International Center (see 10.022), the International Visitor Information Service (see 10.015), the National Council for International Visitors (see 10.019), the Visitor Program Service (develops programs and itineraries for government and privately sponsored international visitors) and The Hospitality and Information Service (provides assistance to diplomats resident in Washington)

10.018
National Association for Foreign Student Affairs
1860 19th St. NW
Washington, DC 20009
(202) 232-1312

Contact(s):

John F. Reichard, Executive Vice President

Georgia Stewart, Director of Information
Services

Professional association for persons involved in international educational exchange including foreign student advisers, teachers of English as a second language, community volunteers, admissions officers and administrators of study abroad programs; institutional and individual membership available

• Offers information and advice on all phases of international student affairs

• Provides in-service consultation and training programs for professionals at member institutions and sponsors national and regional conferences

• Provides small grants to institutions for innovative projects for improving the experience of foreign students in the U.S.

• Publishes the *NAFSA Newsletter* eight times per year plus an extensive list of books, pamphlets and bibliographies of interest to those involved in international educational exchange, including bibliographies for each of the five NAFSA sections: ADSEC (admissions section), ATESL (teachers of English as a second language, see 10.038), CAFSS (foreign student advisers, see 10.040), COMSEC (community volunteers, see 10.039) and SECUSSA (study abroad, see 8.029); among other publications are *Learning Across Cultures: Intercultural Communication and International Educational Exchange, The Administration of Intensive English Language Programs* (see 10.037), *Study Abroad Programs: An Evaluation Guide* (see 8.037), *Cross-cultural Learning in K-12 Schools: Foreign Students as Resources* (see 2.122), *The Foreign Student in Elementary and Secondary Schools: A Guide for Administrators and Pupil Services Personnel* (see 10.046), *Basic Facts on Foreign Study* (see 8.028) and *NAFSA Principles for International Educational Exchange*

• Also publishes a series of books developed with the Committee on Scholarly Communications with the People's Republic of China (see 18.080) on China–U.S. educational relations including *American Study Programs in China* (see 18.089) and *China Bound: A Handbook for American Students, Researchers and Teachers* (see 18.092)

• Maintains large library of films and other audiovisual materials available on loan about international subjects including population, hunger, development and cross-cultural learning

10.019
National Council for International Visitors
Meridian House
1630 Crescent Place NW
Washington, DC 20009
(202) 332-1028

Contact(s):

Alan M. Warne, Executive Director

Association of community-based, non-profit organizations and national programming agencies concerned with providing assistance to visitors to the United States on short-term exchange or training programs

• Provides programs and services designed to encourage effective communication between national agencies that send visitors around the country and local organizations which receive visitors in their communities

10.020
Spoken Language Services, Inc.
P.O. Box 783
Ithaca, NY 14850
(607) 257-0500

Contact(s):

J. M. Cowan

Producer of self-instructional English and foreign language materials

• Offers spoken English as a foreign language materials geared to speakers of specific other languages; consists of self-instructional courses for beginners with cassettes keyed to texts and the texts written in the language of the learner; available for speakers of Burmese, Mandarin Chinese, Greek, Indonesian, Persian, Serbo-Croatian, Korean, Spanish, Thai, Turkish and Vietnamese

10.021
Teachers of English to Speakers of Other Languages
Georgetown University
201 D.C. Transit Bldg.
Washington, DC 20057
(202) 625-4569

Contact(s):
James E. Alatis, Executive Director

Professional educational association
• Promotes research and disseminates information on the teaching of English to speakers of other languages and dialects; sponsors conferences and publishes quarterly journal, newsletter, membership directory and a variety of reference books, bibliographies and other publications on TESOL including *Directory of Teacher Preparation Programs in TESOL and Bilingual Education*, 1981–1984 ($6.50)

10.022
Washington International Center
Meridian House
1630 Crescent Place NW
Washngton, DC 20009
(202) 332-1025

Contact(s):
L. Robert Kohls, Executive Director

Nonprofit educational and cultural organization

• Conducts seminars, conferences and orientation programs for foreign nationals visiting the U.S. under programs sponsored by the U.S. government, foreign governments, international agencies and private educational organizations; programs last from a half-day to two weeks and include those focused on specific area and subject studies as well as those involving general orientation and cross-cultural communication

10.023
World Education Services, Inc.
P.O. Box 745
Old Chelsea Station
New York, NY 10011
(212) 460-5644

Contact(s):
Mariam Assefa Morrissey, Executive
　Director

Nonprofit voluntary agency serving foreign students and American government and private organizations
• Provides educational equivalency evaluations of foreign educational credentials for educational, employment, professional and other purposes; charges $35 to $70 per evaluation
• Publishes research on comparative educational systems

10.024
YMCA International Student Services
236 East 47th St.
New York, NY 10017
(212) 319-0610

Contact(s):
Charles Ainsworth

• Hosts and provides orientation and other program services to foreign students in the U.S. individually and in groups; includes arrival assistance at 18 ports of entry throughout the United States

10.025
American Cultural Exchange
1107 E. 45th, Suite 315A
Seattle, WA 98105
(206) 633-3239
BRANCH: Tacoma

Contact(s):
Burton E. Bard, President

• Offers intensive instruction in English for students entering U.S. colleges; seven-week sessions

English Language Training Organizations with Multiple Centers

10.026
American International Education and Training
5725 Paradise Drive
Corte Madera, CA 94925
(415) 924-7512
BRANCHES: Boston, Redlands (Calif.), Reno and London; representatives in 11 other countries

Contact(s):
Abdelaziz Abbassi, Vice President,
  Academic Affairs/Language Services

English as a second language training organization
• Offers intensive English-language instruction year-round in eight-week sessions at beginning through advanced levels; includes special courses in English for business and economics and English for science and technology; testing, cultural orientation and other services provided
• Also offers short-term summer programs in English conversation and American culture, including homestays (available in Boston, Los Angeles and San Francisco Metropolitan areas)

10.027
American Language Academy
Executive Offices
11426 Rockville Pike
Rockville, MD 20852
(301) 984-3400

PROGRAM LOCATIONS: Ashland, Ore.; Atchison, Kan.; Berkeley, Boston, Cleveland, Philadelphia, Pocatello, Pueblo, Colo.; Tampa, Chicago, Southborough, Mass.

Contact(s):
Director of Program Operations

Educational training organization offering intensive English-language instruction for foreign students at 12 centers in the U.S.
• Offers programs at ten locations for students and professionals entering as undergraduates or graduates in American colleges or universities; ten-week intensive English programs include orientation to the American academic system and to the cultural environment
• Develops computer-assisted instruction software available through the Regents/ALA Company for ESL/EFL and has microcomputers at all locations for computer-assisted instruction as an established feature of the curriculum
• Consults on and develops special English language training programs for companies, agencies and organizations to meet special language and technical training needs
• Publishes *ALA TOEFL Course*, with materials for 30 hours of instruction designed to familiarize students with the skills needed to take the Test of English as a Foreign Language (TOEFL), and the ALA ESP Series, which includes lectures on listening comprehension and materials for teaching the essen-

tials of international trade, management and aviation technology

• Offers intensive English programs at two locations for students at the elementary and secondary levels running from 11 to 16 weeks, including integrated cultural orientation

10.028
Academic Preparation Centers, International Language Institute
5151 Wisconsin Ave. NW
Washington, DC 20016
(202) 362-2505
CENTERS: Elkins, W. Va.; Greensburg; Pa.; Latrobe, Pa.; Washington, D.C.

Contact(s):
Marcel X. Rocca, President

Study and training institute located at four centers on U.S. college campuses for foreign students planning to enter American colleges and universities; division of Transemantics, Inc. of Washington, D.C. (same address)

• Offers intensive training in English as a second language; includes pretechnical English as needed, cultural orientation and study skills training for advanced students

10.029
Bridge International Schools
Linguex International
Box 238
Poncha Springs, CO 81242
(303) 539-6621
BRANCHES: Denver, Orlando

Contact(s):
Raphael Alberola, President

Commercial language training organization

• Offers intensive training in English as a Foreign Language using current video disc technology in the classroom with the instructor; also develops computer software

10.030
ELS Language Centers
5761 Buckingham Parkway
Culver City, CA 90230
(213) 642-0982
BRANCHES: 22 training centers in U.S.; 2 in Japan and one each in England, Korea, Peru, Taiwan and Thailand

Contact(s):
Bill Stevenson, Director of Marketing

Large English as a second language training organization with programs conducted through ELS Language Centers in the U.S. and abroad

• Offers (1) intensive English language programs in four-week sessions, year-round; (2) superintensive programs (nine hours per day); (3) English for Executives; (4) English Study Youth Camps; (5) special programs (homestay, vacation, English for Aviation); and (6) Technical English programs on request

• Provides both undergraduate and graduate placement services to U.S. colleges and universities

• Offers three-week skill-improvement seminars for ESL instructors

10.031
English-Speaking Union of the United States
16 East 69th St.
New York, NY 10021
(212) 879-6800
BRANCHES: 88 in cities throughout the country

Contact(s):
John D. Walker, National Director

Individual and corporate nonprofit membership organization designed to create and maintain cultural ties between and among the English-speaking peoples of the world, involving primarily the U.S. and members of the British Commonwealth

• Sponsors "English-in-Action" program at branches in New York, Chicago, New Haven, Philadelphia, Seattle and Washington, D.C., offering foreign students and trainees regular one-to-one conversation practice in English

10.032
International Center for Language Studies
1346 Connecticut Ave. NW
Washington, DC 20036
(202) 223-3620
BRANCH: Bangor

• Offers four-week intensive instruction in English for students entering U.S. colleges

10.033
International Students of English Program
School for International Training (SIT)
Kipling Road
Brattleboro, VT 05301
(802) 257-7751

Contact(s):
John Middleton, Director (SIT)

• Offers intensive training in English as a second language at Brattleboro, San Rafael, Calif. and Jacksonville, Fla., at beginning, intermediate and advanced levels

10.034
Spring Institute for International Studies
5025 Lowell Blvd.
Denver, CO 80221
(303) 433-6355 or 322-9671
BRANCHES: Greeley and Littleton, Col.

Contact(s):
Robert T. Sample, President

• Offers intensive instruction in English to speakers of other languages; includes cultural studies, a General Educational Development course for the student who has not completed high school, and specialized programs tailored to the needs of specific groups/countries/agencies

10.035
Systran, Inc.
70 West Hubbard St.
Chicago, IL 60610
(321) 312-0707
ENGLISH LANGUAGE CENTERS:
Albuquerque, New Mexico, and Beaumont, Baytown and Pasadena, TX.

International training company
• Runs three U.S. and one Saudi Arabian English for Special Purposes (ESP) and English as a Second Language (ESL/EFL) training centers for foreign students, technicians and vocational trainees; conducts training for foreign nationals in vocational and technical skills; develops language-training curricula, and simplifies technical manuals for use by non-native English speakers

Manuals and Sourcebooks

10.036
Action Guide: Serving the International Visitor
U.S. Travel Service
U.S. Department of Commerce
Washington, DC
1974; paperbound; 78 pages; free

• Provides guidelines and information on resources available to communities which wish to improve their ability to attract foreign visitors to the U.S.; covers public reception centers, emergency services, insurance, hospitality services (hotel, travelers' aid, shopping assistance, home hospitality, etc.), literature in languages other than English, language banks, visitor centers, currency exchange facilities, and includes bibliography and a list of state tourism liaison officers; particular emphasis on assisting the non-English speaker

10.037
The Administration of Intensive English Language Programs
Ralph Pat Barrett
National Association for Foreign Student
    Affairs
1860 19th St. NW
Washington, DC 20009
1982; paperbound; 109 pages; $1

• Guide to the development, organization and implementation of an intensive English as a second language program; extensive list of references and sources of additional information

10.038
ATESL Bibliography
National Association for Foreign Student
    Affairs
1860 19th St. NW
Washington, DC 20009
1982; 2 pages; free in single copies

• Lists 36 books and periodicals of interest to teachers of English as a second language

10.039
COMSEC Bibliography
National Association for Foreign Student
    Affairs
1860 19th St. NW
Washington, DC 20009
1982; 2 pages; free in single copies

• Lists and describes seven books of particular interest to community volunteers

involved in educational exchange and services to foreign students

10.040
CAFSS Bibliography (Council of Advisers to Foreign Students and Scholars)
National Association for Foreign Student
    Affairs
1860 19th St. NW
Washington, DC 20009
1981; photocopied; 5 pages; free in single copies

• Lists 61 publications (with source and occasional annotation) of interest to foreign student advisers under such headings as: Laws and Regulations Affecting Foreign Faculty and Students, Orientation, Counseling and Advising, Financial Aid and Planning, and General Information

10.041
Bibliography of English as a Second Language Materials
National Clearinghouse for Bilingual
    Education
1500 Wilson Blvd., Suite 802
Rosslyn, VA 22209
paperbound; in two volumes; Vol. I, Grades
    K-3: 20 pages, $1.50; Vol. II, Grades
    4-12: 54 pages, $2.75

• Designed for teachers of non-English-speaking students of any language group; contains lists of texts, readers, tests and reference and supplementary materials

10.042
Bring Home the World: A Management Guide for Community Leaders of International Programs
Stephen H. Rhinesmith
AMACOM
P.O. Box 319
Saranac Lake, NY 12983
1975; 126 pages; paperbound; $5.95

• Discusses elements necessary for effective development and administration of non-profit community organizations providing international programming services; includes coverage of general leadership issues, recruiting and motivating volunteers, fundraising and financial management, intercultural communication and adjustment, the significance of value differences, and cross-cultural counseling

10.043
English as a Second Language Bibliography for Adults
National Clearinghouse for Bilingual
   Education
1500 Wilson Blvd., Suite 802
Rosslyn, VA 22209
paperbound; 31 pages; $2.75

• Designed for teachers of non-English-speaking adults who are interested in immediate employment or who are headed for vocational training in English

10.044
English Language and Orientation Programs in the United States
James E. O'Driscoll, Editor, with James J.
   Bauer
Institute of International Education
809 UN Plaza
New York, NY 10017
1984; paperbound; 180 pages; $9

• Lists approximately 900 academic-based and other intensive and non-intensive English language programs for people for whom English is a second language; grouped by state, entries include a brief general description plus information on entrance requirements, orientation activities, schedules, facilities, anticipated clientele, housing availability and fees

10.045
Foreign Student Admissions Bibliography
National Association for Foreign Student
   Affairs
1860 19th St. NW
Washington, DC 20009
1983; brochure; 4 pages; free in single
   copies

• Substantial annotated list of publications, including publications on specific countries, workshop reports and periodicals

10.046
The Foreign Student in Elementary and Secondary Schools: A Guide for Administrators and Pupil Services Personnel
National Association for Foreign Student
   Affairs
1860 19th St. NW
Washington, DC 20009
and
U.S. Department of Education
Washington, DC 20202
1980; paperbound; 90 pages; $2.50

• Guide for K-12 administrators in dealing with foreign students relative to admissions, advising, language problems and government regulations

10.047
Foreign Student's Guide to Study in the United States
David Levin
U.S. Department of Education
Washington, DC 20202
1981; pamphlet; 31 pages; free

Available from Information Clearinghouse, Office of International Education Programs, U.S. Department of Education, Washington, DC 20202

• Identifies sources of information available to the foreign student who wishes to study in the U.S.; includes guidebooks to American higher education covering kinds of institutions and programs and financial matters; also lists organizations involved in foreign student affairs, including those offering general assistance, those assisting students from specific countries or regions, those administering exchange programs and those offering services to students, along with U.S. and other overseas offices and centers which assist foreign students

10.048

Immigration Handbook: Employment of Foreign Nationals

American Council on International
   Personnel, Inc.
515 Madison Ave.
New York, NY 10022
1978; paperbound; 80 pages; $11

• Describes the status of aliens and the kinds of visas available to or required by those entering the U.S. for employment or training in commercial and financial establishments; includes description of special customs and tax regulations; useful to firms and organizations which bring foreign employees to the U.S. for training or work assignments

10.049
Living in the U.S.A.

Alison R. Lanier
Intercultural Press, Inc.
Box 768
Yarmouth, ME 04096
1981; paperbound; 200 pages; $7.50

• Describes American life for the foreigner coming to live or work in the U.S.; discusses social, cultural and workplace customs and gives practical advice and guidelines on how to understand and function effectively in the American environment

10.050
Open Doors: Report on International Educational Exchange

Douglas R. Boyan, Editor
Institute of International Education
809 UN Plaza
New York, NY 10017
annual; paperbound; 200 pages; $22.95

• Statistical survey of foreign students studying in the U.S. and U.S. students studying abroad (in college-sponsored academic-year programs); the extensive information on foreign students in the U.S. includes data on countries of origin, kinds of institutions, areas of study, length of stay, etc. and an analysis of the statistics

10.051
Practical Guide for Foreign Visitors

Barbara Cahn Connotillo
Institute of International Education
809 UN Plaza
New York, NY 10017
1979; paperbound; $3.50

• Handbook for foreign students which describes the U.S. system of higher education and answers questions about admissions, visas, language requirements, cost, orientation, etc.

10.052
Practical Guide to the Teaching of English as a Foreign Language

Robert J. Dixson
Regents Publishing Co., Inc.
2 Park Ave.
New York, NY 10016
1982; paperbound; 128 pages; $50

• Clearly presented instructions for teaching English as a second language including techniques for presenting lessons, stimulating conversation, building vocabulary, etc.

10.053
Study in U.S. Colleges and Universities
Institute of International Education
809 UN Plaza
New York, NY 10017
1983; booklet; 28 pages; single copies free

• Provides information on the U.S. system of higher education, application procedures, entrance examinations, grading and academic credits, accreditation and financial aid; includes bibliography and glossary

10.054
Where to Stay USA
Marjorie A. Cohen
Council on International Educational
    Exchange
205 East 42nd St.
New York, NY 10017
and

Frommer/Pasmentier Publishers
1230 Ave. of the Americas
New York, NY 10020
biennially updated; paperbound; 438 pages;
    $6.25

• Lists and gives costs for over 1,700 places to spend the night in the U.S. for under $25; provides useful background information on each state, on the 15 cities most popular with travelers and on the campus environment of major universities; indicates where discounts are available to holders of Where to Stay USA Discount and International Student Identity cards

11

Publishers and Distributors of Books on World Area Studies

See individual countries for additional area and country studies publishers

11.001
ABC-CLIO, Inc.
Riviera Campus
2040 Alameda Padre Serra
Box 4397
Santa Barbara, CA 93103
(805) 963-4221

• Publishes reference books (especially bibliographies) on international and compar-

ative politics, war/peace studies, library and art reference works and area studies (African, Asian, Eastern European and Latin American); includes *Historical Abstracts* (abstracts current periodical literature on history, see 1.038), *ABC POL SCI* (abstracts current periodical literature on the social sciences, see 1.010), *Information Sources of Political Science* (see 1.040), *The Study of International Relations* (a sourcebook, see 1.060), *Soviet and East European Foreign Policy* (bibliography, see 14.068), *Modern Revolutions and Revolutionists* (a bibliography), *World Hunger* (a bibliography), *Arms Control and Disarmament* (a bibliography), *World Treaty Index* (index referencing 44,500 treaties from Treaty Research Center, University of Washington), *Latin American Political Dictionary* (see 16.141), *The International Relations Dictionary* (see 1.019), *Soviet and East European Political Dictionary* (see 14.069), *Middle East Political Dictionary* (see 17.068), *East European Languages and Literatures* (index to articles in English language journals, see 14.065), *East Central and Southeast Europe* (Library and Archival Resources, see 14.064), *Latin America: Social Science Information Sources*, a number of books in African, Asian and Latin American Studies, and the World Bibliographical Series (see 2.198 and individual countries)

11.002
AMS Press, Inc.
56 East 13th St.
New York, NY 10003
(212) 777-4700

Commercial publisher
• Reprints anthropological ethnographic studies of peoples and cultures of the world; particularly strong in European, Pacific, Southeast Asian and Sub-Saharan African cultures

11.003
Arthur Vanous Co.
616 Kinderkamack Road
River Edge, NJ 07661
(201) 265-7555

Book importer
• Imports and warehouses language dictionaries, texts and cassettes from the Scandinavian countries as well as a number of Eastern European countries (Czechoslovakia, Hungary, Poland and Yugoslavia); will import any Scandinavian book on request

11.004
Biblio Distribution Centre
81 Adams Drive, Box 327
Totowa, NJ 07512
(201) 256-8600

• Importer and distributor of books of foreign (especially European) publishers, including Irish Academic Press (see 18.236)

11.005
Cambridge University Press
American Branch
32 East 57th St.
New York, NY 10022
(212) 688-8888

University publishing house
• Publishes extensive list of books in African, Latin American, South Asian and Chinese studies and on international studies in general

11.006
Columbia University Press
136 South Broadway
Irvington, NY 10533
(914) 591-9111

University publishing house
• Publishes extensive list of books on international affairs and in African and Latin American studies and a particularly large number of books in Asian and Russian/East European studies in such fields as history, literature, politics, philosophy and anthropology

11.007
Cornell University Press
Box 250
124 Roberts Place
Ithaca, NY 14851
(607) 257-7000

• Publishes an extensive list of books on most world areas including particularly large selections in Asian (see 13.184) and African (see 12.115) studies along with strong lists on Russian, Indonesian and Middle Eastern subjects

11.008
Documentary Publications
106 Kenan St.
Chapel Hill, NC 27514
(919) 929-1833

• Publishes books on politics, history and contemporary issues in the Middle East, Africa, Asia, Europe and Latin America (especially Mexico) and on international and diplomatic affairs; includes *Vietnam: An Annotated Bibliography*

11.009
Faber & Faber, Inc.
39 Thompson St.
Winchester, MA 01890
(617) 721-1427

Commercial publishing house
• Publishes "Story of . . . ." Series consisting of basic histories of Canada, Nigeria (see 18.383), Zimbabwe (see 18.604), England, Japan, Australia (see 18.016) and modern Greece (see 18.178)

11.010
Garland Publishing, Inc.
136 Madison Ave.
New York, NY 10016
(212) 686-7492

Commercial publishing house
• Publishes reference books on international affairs and foreign cultures; includes *Middle East and North Africa on Film* (see 2.142), *Western Sahara: A Comprehensive Bibliography* (see 18.361) and bibliographies on Paraguay (see 18.401), Tibet (see 18.103), Guinea-Bissau and Cape Verde (see 18.064)

11.011
G. K. Hall & Company
70 Lincoln St.
Boston, MA 02111
(617) 423-3990

• Publishes extensive lists of books in Latin American (see 16.163), Asian (see 13.186), Middle Eastern (see 17.089) Russian and East European (see 14.077) and African (see 12.117) Studies; includes new country-by-country historical statistics series (presently available for New Zealand, Thailand, Sri Lanka, Cuba, Mali and the Arab World, Turkey and the Balkans)

11.012
Harvard University Press
79 Garden St.
Cambridge, MA 02138
(617) 495-2600

University publishing house
• Publishes extensive list of books in area studies including over 150 on China, 50 on Russia, and significant numbers on Japan and in Asian studies in general, Latin American studies, Middle Eastern studies, and African studies; also a substantial list in comparative and international economics and international politics; includes catalogues of books contained in the Harvard Library world areas collections and audio-visual courses on Japan and China by Edwin O. Reischauer and John K. Fairbanks respectively

11.013
Haskell House Publishers, Ltd.
Box FF, Blythebourne Station
Brooklyn, NY 11219
(212) 435-0500

• Publishes reprints of important studies in West European, Russian and Asian literatures

11.014
Holmes & Meier Publishers, Inc.
IUB Bldg.
30 Irving Place
New York, NY 10003
(212) 254-4100

Large publishing house, which includes Africana Publishing Co.
• Publishes extensive list of publications on international subjects; covers the following countries and world areas: Africa, Australia, the Caribbean, China, India, Latin America, the Middle East and the Soviet Union; books deal with art, culture, development, economics, education, geography, history, Judaica, literature, politics, public administration, sociology, strategic studies and women's studies; major selection of books on Africa including the above categories plus bibliographies, maps, country-by-country surveys and current affairs reference works

11.015
Hoover Institution Press
Stanford University
Stanford, CA 94305
(415) 497-3373
(800) 227-1991

University publishing house
• Publishes books, bibliographies and other reference works on international political affairs covering all world areas with particular emphasis on the world communist movement; titles include annual *Yearbook on International Communist Affairs*, a number of research handbooks and guides, a wide selection of bibliographies on China, the Soviet Union and African history, *Handbook of American Resources for African Studies* (see 12.081) and *Guide to Hungarian Studies* (see 18.196)

11.016
Indiana University Press
10th and Morton Sts.
Bloomington, IN 47401
(812) 337-4203

Large university publishing house
• Publishes books in area studies (Africa, Middle East, Asia, Women's studies, Jewish studies) and international affairs, with strength in Soviet and Eastern European political and economic affairs and art, history, literature and film

11.017
The Johns Hopkins University Press
Baltimore, MD 21218
(301) 338-7875

• Publishes books on international economic and political affairs, history, law, language and country and area studies (Eastern and Western Europe, Latin America and the Middle East); includes *Yemen: Search for a Modern State* (see 18.586), and *Persian Gulf States: A General Survey* (see 17.070) along with economic studies and periodicals prepared by the World Bank and other organizations including *MLN-Modern Language Notes* and *The Human Rights Quarterly*

11.018
Lawrence Hill & Co., Inc.
520 Riverside Ave.
Westport, CT 06880
(203) 226-9392

Commercial publishing house
- Publishes books of literature, biography, and politics with particular focus on the Third World, Africa and Latin America

11.019
Longman Inc.
19 West 44th St.
New York, NY 10036
(212) 764-3950

- Publishes a number of books on international politics, economics and trade and in African and Arab studies

11.020
Ohio University Press
Scott Quadrangle 236-C9S4
Athens, OH 45701-2979
(614) 594-5505

- Publishes research, principally in the social sciences, in African, Latin American and Southeast and Asian Studies and distributes books published by the Gadjah Mada University Press (Indonesia) and the Singapore University Press

11.021
Oxford University Press
200 Madison Ave.
New York, NY 10016
(212) 679-7300

Large academic publishing house
- Publishes extensive lists of books in the following areas: foreign language instructional and reading materials, English/foreign language dictionaries, English as a second language instructional materials (books, tapes, tests, grammars, readers, etc.), international relations, and area studies; emphasis on history, international relations and current affairs in Africa, Asia (especially China, the In-

dian subcontinent and Southeast Asia) and Australasia; includes *African Encyclopedia* (see 12.072), and *Colombo's Canadian References* (see 18.061)

11.022
Pergamon Press, Inc.
Maxwell House
Fairview Park
Elmsford, NY 10523
(914) 592-7700

Large commercial publishing house
- Publishes a number of titles on international and transnational relations, military affairs and national security, cross-cultural psychology, intercultural communication and training, the Soviet Union/Eastern Europe and the Middle East as well as publications produced by the East-West Center Culture Learning Institute (see 13.035); includes an annual *America and the World* series in which well-known analysts examine and review the state of American political and economic relations with the rest of the world; also distributes Haack Wall Maps (in English) for all principal world areas (designed for classroom use)

11.023
Princeton University Press
Princeton, NJ 08540
(609) 452-4900

University publishing house
- Publishes an extensive list of titles on international economics, military affairs, politics and political relations; on the history and politics of Asia, Eastern Europe, Africa, Latin America and the Middle East; and on Asian and African literatures, including an Asian writers in translation series; particular strength in materials on China, India, Japan, and Eastern Europe, especially the Soviet Union (see 18.542)

11.024
Stanford University Press
Stanford, CA 94305
(415) 497-9434

Large university publishing house
• Publishes a long and substantial list of books in area studies covering all areas of the world; major area studies resource

11.025
Three Continents Press
1346 Connecticut Ave. NW, Suite 224
Washington, DC 20036
(202) 457-0288

• Publishes extensive list of books by and about writers from other countries and world areas including the Caribbean (see 16.166), Asia and the Pacific (see 13.193), the Middle East (see 17.092) and Africa (see 12.123)

11.026
Transaction Books
Rutgers University
New Brunswick, NJ 08903
(201) 932-2280

• Publishes extensive list of titles on international economics and politics with selections on military affairs and on Israeli, Asian, Middle Eastern, African and Latin American affairs

11.027
Twayne Publishers
70 Lincoln St.
Boston, MA 02111
(617) 423-3990

• Publishes "World Author Series" of critical analyses of major authors from 40 countries including substantial numbers of Spanish, Russian, Greek, French, Chinese, Danish, Canadian, Dutch, Italian and German authors

11.028
University of Arizona Press
1615 E. Speedway
Tucson, AZ 85719
(602) 621-1441

• Publishes books in Asian studies (in cooperation with the Association for Asian Studies, see 13.136) and on Mexican, American Indian and Mexican-American subjects

11.029
University of California Press
2120 Berkeley Way
Berkeley, CA 94720
(415) 642-4247

• Publishes books in area studies including a very extensive list on Asia (history, literature, culture, social issues and current affairs; especially strong on China, Japan and India), an extensive list on Africa (history, politics, culture and current affairs), an extensive list on Latin America (history, economics, development, politics and literature) and a selection on the Middle East (history, literature and current affairs); also publishes the periodical *Asian Survey* (see 13.166)

11.030
University of Chicago Press
5801 South Ellis Ave.
Chicago, IL 60637
(312) 962-7700

Large university publishing house
• Publishes extensive lists of books in the following areas: Africa, Asia, China, India and Indian literature, Latin America, Mexican history, and the Middle East; particular emphasis on intellectual history and the social sciences

11.031
University of Illinois Press
54 East Gregory Drive
Box 5081, Station A
Champaign, IL 61820
(217) 333-0950

University publishing house
• Publishes a selection of books on Asian and Latin American studies

11.032
University of Texas Press
Box 7819
Austin, TX 78712
(512) 471-7233

• Publishes an extensive list of titles on Latin America (see 16.172) as well as a selection of titles in Middle East Studies

11.033
University of Wisconsin Press
114 North Murray St.
Madison, WI 53715
(608) 262-4928

University publishing house
• Publishes selected list of books in African, Afro-American, Asian and Latin American studies

11.034
Westview Press
5500 Central Ave.
Boulder, CO 80301
(303) 444-3541

Commercial publishing house
• Publishes extensive list of books on current international affairs in the following areas: Africa, Asia (especially on China), the Caribbean, Latin America, Western Europe, Eastern Europe and the Soviet Union, development, international economic and political relationships, international law, military and national security affairs, foreign policy, peace and terrorism; includes titles on major worldwide issues such as energy, food, communications, arms control, environment, futuristics, health, etc., along with a series of basic studies of the nations of the world focusing on current affairs within a historical context, designed for both the student and general reader (see individual countries)

11.035
Yale University Press
92A Yale Station
New Haven, CT 06520
(203) 432-4969

University publishing house
• Publishes extensive lists of books in history and contemporary affairs in the humanities and the social sciences for the following world areas: Africa, Asia and the Pacific (with particular emphasis on China and Japan); includes language instructional materials for Chinese, Japanese, Cambodian, Korean and Cebuano, Latin America, the Middle East and Russia

12

African Area Studies

Area Studies Programs and Research Centers

12.001
African Language and Area Center
Stanford University
Room 200, Lou Henry Hoover Bldg.
Stanford, CA 94305
(415) 497-0295

Contact(s):
William R. Leben, Director
Judith Muchowski, Secretary

Graduate, undergraduate, nondegree area studies program established in 1968; an NDEA center; shares resources with University of California at Berkeley through federally funded Joint Center for African Studies
• Majors/degrees/certificates offered: B.A. in African and Afro-American Studies; departmental M.A. and Ph.D. with African Studies specialization
• Approximate number of faculty teaching area and language courses: 23
• Approximate number of courses available—area: 21; language: 6 (plus courses at University of California at Berkeley)
• Average number of students per year specializing in area: 60 graduate; 150 undergraduate
• Countries covered and areas of emphasis: Sub-Saharan Africa
• Languages offered: Hausa, Swahili and Yoruba with other African languages available on tutorial basis
• Hoover Institution (see 4.159) and Stanford Library contain approximately 55,000 volumes on Africa with supporting materials in professional library; especially strong in colonialism in Africa and African nationalist movements

• Food Research Institute has major long-term research program in African agriculture and food production
• Overseas study programs available in Nigeria, Kenya and Togo
• Extensive outreach program through Stanford Program in Cross-Cultural Education (SPICE, see 2.061)
• Financial assistance includes a number of grants for summer research and study

12.002
Committee on African Studies
University of California at Berkeley
Institute of International Studies
Berkeley, CA 94720

Contact(s):
Carl G. Rosberg, Director (642-8338)
William Banks, Chair, Department of Afro-American Studies (642-7084)

Graduate and undergraduate area studies program; shares resources with Stanford through federally funded Joint Center for African Studies
• Majors/degrees/certificates offered: B.A. in disciplines or in Development Studies and M.A. and Ph.D. in disciplines with specialization in Africa; B.A. in Afro-American Studies
• Approximate number of faculty teaching area and language courses: 25
• Approximate number of courses available—area: 24 (plus courses at Stanford)
• Average number of students per year specializing in area: 50

- Countries covered and areas of emphasis: all countries of Africa and the black nations of the Caribbean
  - Language offered: Arabic

12.003
African Studies Center
University of California at Los Angeles
UCLA Bunche Hall 10244
405 Hilgard Ave.
Los Angeles, CA 90024
(213) 825-3779

Contact(s):
Michael F. Lofchie, Director

Graduate and undergraduate area studies program established in 1959
- Majors/degrees/certificates offered: B.A. with Special Certificate in African Studies; M.A. in discipline with African Area concentration; M.A. with Certificate in Teaching English as a Second Language; Ph.D.'s in social science and humanities disciplines with African Area concentration
- Approximate number of faculty teaching area and language courses: 80
- Approximate number of courses available—area: 166; language: 18
- Average number of students per year specializing in area: 220
- Countries covered and areas of emphasis: countries of the African continent; particularly strong in African arts and culture south of the Sahara
- Languages offered: Hausa, Swahili, Yoruba, Zulu; many other African languages offered on an individual tutorial basis
- University Research Library has a collection of 90,000 books and periodicals and 15,000 maps of Africa while the Center maintains an up-to-date collection of journals and periodicals in its Reading Room, along with a collection of films and other materials; specialized African collections at several of the professional school libraries also available;

International Health Program of the School of Public Health offers courses related to Africa and opportunities for research, field training and overseas service
- Overseas study opportunities available in Kenya, Togo and Sierra Leone through the University of California Education Abroad Program (see 8.012)
- Facilities available to visiting research scholars
- Publishes a number of journals: *African Arts* (see 12.091); *Journal of African Studies* (see 12.102); *Studies in African Linguistics* (see 12.109); *Journal of Legal Pluralism and Contemporary Law; Ufahamu*, a student-edited, interdisciplinary journal of African studies; a newsletter; collections of conference and colloquia papers; and an Occasional Papers series
- Financial assistance includes a Graduate Advancement Program which supports students from groups with historically low participation in graduate work due to economic or social inequities

12.004
Department of Black Studies
University of California at Santa Barbara
3631 South Hall
Santa Barbara, CA 93106
(805) 961-3800, Ext. 47

Contact(s):
Edmond J. Keller, Chair

Undergraduate area studies program established in 1969
- Majors/degrees/certificates offered: B.A. in Black Studies
- Approximate number of courses available—area: 35
- Countries covered and areas of emphasis: Africa and the black populations of the Americas; emphasis on the dispersion of black people and black culture in the Americas, particularly the U.S. and the West In-

dies, and on contemporary social and political issues
• Black Studies collection in University Library
• Overseas study opportunities through the University of California Education Abroad Program (see 8.012)

12.005
African and Middle Eastern Studies
University of Colorado at Boulder
Campus Box 233
Boulder, CO 80309
(303) 492-5122 or 7667

Contact(s):
Gottfried Lang and Ragaei El Mallakh, Co-Chairs

Undergraduate area studies program established in 1967
• Majors/degrees/certificates offered: B.A. in African and Middle Eastern Studies
• Approximate number of faculty teaching area and language courses: 11
• Approximate number of courses available—area: 39; language: 3
• Average number of students per year specializing in area: 9
• Countries covered and areas of emphasis: all countries of Africa and the Middle East; broad emphasis on ancient, medieval and modern history, art, anthropology, religion, economics and politics; includes courses in Black Studies
• Study abroad available through cooperation with other institutions

12.006
African Studies Program
University of Denver
Graduate School of International Studies
Denver, CO 80210
(303) 753-2755

Contact(s):
George W. Shepherd, Director

Graduate area studies program established in 1968
• Majors/degrees/certificates offered: M.A. and Ph.D. with specialization in African Studies
• Approximate number of faculty teaching area and language courses: 10
• Approximate number of courses available—area: 11; language: 4
• Average number of students per year specializing in area: 10–15
• Countries covered and areas of emphasis: all of Africa with emphasis on political economy and international relations
• Languages offered: Swahili and, on demand, Arabic
• Library contains 5,000 volumes on Africa and an extensive collection of periodicals

12.007
African Studies
University of Northern Colorado
History Department
Greeley, CO 80639
(303) 351-2905

Contact(s):
Marshall S. Clough, Director

Graduate and undergraduate area studies program
• Majors/degrees/certificates offered: B.A., M.A. and Doctor of Arts in African Studies
• Approximate number of faculty teaching area and language courses: 8
• Approximate number of courses available—area: 12
• Average number of students per year specializing in area: 35 undergraduate, 10 graduate
• Countries covered and areas of emphasis: all African countries with emphasis on history and politics

12.008
African Studies Committee
Wesleyan University
Middletown, CT 06457
(203) 347-9411

Contact(s):
Jerome Long, Chairman

Undergraduate area studies program
- Majors/degrees/certificates offered: B.A. in African Studies
- Approximate number of faculty teaching area and language courses: 9
- Approximate number of courses available—area: 27; language: 6
- Average number of students per year specializing in area: 15
- Countries covered and areas of emphasis: Sub-Saharan Africa with emphasis on history, politics and the Black Diaspora

12.009
Council on African Studies
Yale University
Box 13A
New Haven, CT 06520
(203) 436-0253

Graduate area studies program
- Majors/degrees/certificates offered: M.A. and Ph.D. through departments
- Approximate number of faculty teaching area and language courses: 22
- Approximate number of courses available—area: 45
- Average number of students per year specializing in area: 15
- Countries covered and areas of emphasis: all countries of Northern, Central and Southern Africa
- Languages offered: Arabic; other African languages offered in Intensive Summer Language Institute
- Africana Library contains approximately 60,000 volumes with additional vol-

umes in other Yale libraries, including full set of Human Relations Area Files (see 1.112)
- Conducts Southern African Research Program (see 12.010) jointly with Wesleyan University

12.010
Southern African Research Program
Yale University
85 Trumbull St.
New Haven, CT 06520
(203) 432-4154

Contact(s):
Leonard M. Thompson, Director (Yale)
Jeffrey Butler, Associate Director (Wesleyan)

Joint research project of Yale and Wesleyan Universities
- Sponsors and promotes research on racial and ethnic conflict in the countries of Southern Africa; conducts colloquia and workshops for visiting postdoctoral fellows and other nearby faculty and researchers

12.011
African Studies and Research Program
Howard University
P.O. Box 231
Washington, DC 20059
(202) 636-7115 or 7116

Contact(s):
Robert J. Cummings, Director
Adwoa Dunn, Coordinator, ASRP Outreach

Graduate area studies program
- Majors/degrees/certificates offered: Ph.D. in African Studies
- Approximate number of courses available—area: 31; language: 25
- Average number of students per year specializing in area: 60
- Languages offered: Twi, Arabic, Swahili, Hausa, Yoruba, Zulu, Tswana, Amharic,

Zezeru, Shona, Kabyle, Fula, Mende, Bassa, Ibo, Lingala, Wolof and Xhosa
- Publishes monographs written by Howard faculty members
- Conducts extensive outreach program of assistance to schools in the area

12.012
African Studies
The Johns Hopkins University
School of Advanced International Studies
1740 Massachusetts Ave. NW
Washington, DC 20036
(202) 785-6200

Graduate area studies program
- Majors/degrees/certificates offered: M.A. and Ph.D. in International Relations with major in African Studies
- Countries covered and areas of emphasis: all countries of Africa with emphasis on contemporary political and economic issues
- Language offered: Arabic; also conducts summer intensive program in Arabic (with Georgetown University)
- Draws on library, organizational and research resources of the Washington area
- Special internships and fellowships available

12.013
Center for African Studies
University of Florida
470 Grinter Hall
Gainesville, FL 32611
(904) 392-2183

Contact(s):
R. Hunt Davis, Jr., Director

Graduate and undergraduate area studies program established in 1964
- Majors/degrees/certificates offered: B.A., M.A. and Ph.D. in discipline with Certificate in African Studies

- Approximate number of faculty teaching area and language courses: 30
- Approximate number of courses available—area: 80; language: 18
- Average number of students per year specializing in area: 5 undergraduate; 20 graduate
- Countries covered and areas of emphasis: the entire African continent; rural development
- Languages offered: Arabic, Shona, Swahili, Yoruba, plus Amharic, ChiNyanja, Ga and Twi on demand, as well as relevant European languages
- 57,000-volume, 500-serial collection of African materials in library
- Conducts school year and summer inservice institutes and workshops for teachers and advises on curriculum development
- Publishes *Irohin* (Outreach newsletter), and edits the *African Studies Review* (journal of the African Studies Association, see 12.063)

12.014
African and Afro-American Studies Program
University of South Florida
Tampa, FL 33620
(813) 974-2427

Contact(s):
F. Ugboaja Ohaegbulam, Director

Undergraduate area studies program
- Majors/degrees/certificates offered: B.A. in African and Afro-American Studies
- Approximate number of faculty teaching area and language courses: 4
- Approximate number of courses available—area: 25
- Average number of students per year specializing in area: 25
- Countries covered and areas of emphasis: Sub-Saharan Africa with emphasis on history, politics and the Black Diaspora

12.015
Program of African Studies
Northwestern University
630 Dartmouth Place
Evanston, IL 60201
(312) 492-7323

Contact(s):
John Paden, Director
Cheryl Johnson, Assistant Director

Graduate and undergraduate area studies program established in 1948
- Majors/degrees/certificates offered: graduate and undergraduate Certificate in African Studies
- Approximate number of faculty teaching area and language courses: 68
- Approximate number of courses available—area: 107; language: 26
- Countries covered and areas of emphasis: all nations of Africa with emphasis on Sub-Saharan Africa
- Languages offered: Krio, Akan/Twi, Amharic, Arabic, Hausa, Pidgin English, Swahili, Yoruba, Portuguese (other languages on request)
- Extensive collection of materials available in the Melville J. Herskovits Library of African Studies
- Extensive program of extracurricular activity focused on Africa

12.016
African, Afro-American and Black Studies
Roosevelt University
430 South Michigan Ave.
Chicago, IL 60605
(312) 341-3817

Contact(s):
S. Miles Woods, Director

Undergraduate area studies program
- Majors/degrees/certificates offered: B.A. in African Studies, Afro-American Studies or Black Studies

- Approximate number of courses available—area: 48; language: 2
- Countries covered and areas of emphasis: Africa south of the Sahara and the black nations and cultures of America; emphasis on black social and political issues
- Language offered: Swahili
- Library contains 10,000-volume Africana collection
- Summer study tours to Africa sponsored occasionally

12.017
Committee on African Studies
University of Chicago
5828 South University Ave.
Chicago, IL 60637
(312) 962-8344

Contact(s):
John Comaroff, Chair

Graduate and undergraduate area studies program established in 1964
- Majors/degrees/certificates offered: B.A. in departments with specialization in African Studies; M.A. in Social Sciences Division with specialization in African Studies
- Approximate number of faculty teaching area and language courses: 15
- Approximate number of courses available—area: 25
- Average number of students per year specializing in area: 20
- Countries covered and areas of emphasis: Sub-Saharan Africa with particular interest in Southern Africa
- Extensive collection of library materials on Africa

12.018
African Studies Program
University of Illinois at Urbana-Champaign
1208 West California, #101
Urbana, IL 61801
(217) 333-6335

Contact(s):
Charles C. Stewart, Director

Graduate and undergraduate area studies program established in 1970
• Majors/degrees/certificates offered: B.A. with concentration in African Studies; M.A. and Ph.D. degrees in disciplines and professional schools with Africa-related emphasis
• Approximate number of faculty teaching area and language courses: 34
• Approximate number of courses available—area: 60; language: 30
• Average number of students per year specializing in area: 40 undergraduate; 50 graduate
• Countries covered and areas of emphasis: the entire African continent
• Languages offered: Swahili, Wolof, Lingala, Arabic, Shona, Hausa, Amharic; tutorial instruction available in Yoruba, Luganda, Mende and several other African languages
• Library contains extensive Africana collection
• Graduate study exchange program with Dakar University, and in Benin and Dar es Salaam; facilitates visiting professorships
• Conducts national school outreach program (see 2.071)

12.019
African Studies Program
Indiana University at Bloomington
Woodburn Hall 221
Bloomington, IN 47405
(812) 335-6825/6734

Contact(s):
Patrick O'Meara, Director
N. Brian Winchester, Assistant Director

Graduate and undergraduate area studies program

• Majors/degrees/certificates offered: Certificate, B.A. and M.A. and Ph.D. in an academic department with specialization in African Studies
• Approximate number of faculty teaching area and language courses: 36 core and 16 affiliated
• Approximate number of courses available—area: 100; language and linguistics: 30 plus
• Countries covered and areas of emphasis: Sub-Saharan Africa
• Core languages offered annually: Arabic, Bambara, Hausa and Swahili; classroom instruction has occasionally been offered in Afrikaans, Dyula, Efik, Ewe, Igbo, Krio, Kru, Lingala, Mende, Susu, Somali, Sonrai, Sotho, Temne, Tswana, Twi, Wolof, Yoruba and Zulu; tutorials have been given in Bamileke, Ijaw, More, Tamacheq, Swazi and West African Pidgin
• Extensive outreach program including teacher in-service workshops, curriculum development, the distribution of films and teaching materials and consulting with libraries and museums
• Publishes several series of monographs and papers, especially in the humanities; also publishes through The Indiana University Press (see 11.016) a number of books and several series: *African Systems of Thought, Traditional African Art, The African Humanities, Change and Development in Africa* and *African Linguistics*

12.020
Africana Studies and Research Center
Purdue University
West Lafayette, IN 47907
(317) 494-5680

Contact(s):
Carol A. Burns

Graduate and undergraduate areas studies program established in 1974

• Majors/degrees/certificates offered: B.A. in Afro-American Studies and departmental M.A. with Afro-American Studies specialization
• Approximate number of faculty teaching area and language courses: 8
• Approximate number of courses available—area: 15
• Countries covered and areas of emphasis: Sub-Saharan Africa with particular interest in West Africa

12.021
Program of African Studies
University of Notre Dame
Department of Government
Notre Dame, IN 46556
(219) 283-7766

Contact(s):
Peter Walshe, Director

Undergraduate area studies program
• Majors/degrees/certificates offered: B.A. with Certificate in African Studies
• Approximate number of faculty teaching area and language courses: 6
• Approximate number of courses available—area: 10
• Average number of students per year specializing in area: 13 undergraduate
• Countries covered and areas of emphasis: countries of Sub-Saharan Africa with emphasis on history and the social sciences
• Library maintains Areas Studies and International Documentation Centers and contains approximately 17,000 volumes on Africa with strength in southern Africa

12.022
Department of African Studies
University of Kansas
104 Lippincott Hall
Lawrence, KS 66045-2107
(913) 864-3054

Contact(s):
Arthur D. Drayton, Chair

Graduate and undergraduate area studies program in Africa and the African diaspora
• Majors/degrees/certificates offered: B.A. and B.G.S. in African Studies (Africa, the Caribbean and Afro-America; Special Studies M.A. and Ph.D. with specialization in African Studies
• Approximate number of faculty teaching area and language courses: 15
• Approximate number of courses available—area: 35; language: 8
• Average number of students per year specializing in area: 6
• Countries covered and areas of emphasis: Sub-Saharan Africa, the Caribbean and the U.S. with emphasis on history and culture
• Languages offered: Arabic and Haitian Creole (Swahili due to be re-introduced)
• Library's African collection contains approximately 35,000 volumes and 200 periodicals, including a number from Africa and the Caribbean

12.023
African Studies Center
Boston University
270 Bay State Road
Boston, MA 02215
(617) 353-3673

Contact(s):
John R. Harris, Director

Graduate and undergraduate area studies program established in 1953
• Majors/degrees/certificates offered: African Studies concentrations in graduate departments of the social sciences; also offers undergraduate minors in African Studies and African literature and a joint Master's degree in economics and public health with The School of Public Health

• Approximate number of faculty teaching area and language courses: 20
• Approximate number of courses available—area: 42; language: 12
• Average number of students per year specializing in area: 10 undergraduate; 20 graduate
• Countries covered and areas of emphasis: all African countries with emphasis on contemporary developmental problems and policy issues and on the following teaching and research areas: development anthropology, health care delivery, economic history, political economy, languages and literature, law and development, rural development, population distribution and migration, urban and regional development, public sector enterprise and African art and curatorship
• Languages offered: Hausa, Swahili, Setswana, Xhosa, Zulu, Mandinka/Bambara and Yoruba; other African languages offered on an individual basis
• African Studies Library contains 80,000 monographs, 800 current and retrospective periodical titles, 125 newspaper titles, 50,000 government documents, 4,000 reels of microfilm, 2,500 pamphlets and a map collection
• Outreach program lends slides, books, films, filmstrips and curriculum guides to educators as well as reproducing and distributing reading lists, background articles and film evaluations; also arranges special institutes, training programs or other outreach activities such as school visits and workshop presentations
• Administers African-American Issues Center which, in cooperation with Harvard and MIT, sponsors conferences, publishes papers and in other ways brings scholarly resources to bear on critical issues in the areas of economic development, constitutionalism and communication
• Organizes international development training programs on behalf of African institutions and maintains ongoing scholarly relations with a number of African universities and research institutions

• Provides research associate status to a limited number of visiting and local scholars
• Publishes extensive list of titles on African affairs, including research studies, working papers, *Catalogue of African Language Materials Available in the African Studies Library* ($5) and *African Newspapers Currently Received by American Libraries* (see 12.073)

12.024
Department of African and Afro-American Studies
Brandeis University
Morton May Hall
Waltham, MA 02154
(617) 647-2771

Contact(s):
Wellington W. Nyangoni, Chair
Yvette Y. Dudley, Administrative Assistant

Undergraduate area studies program established in 1968
• Majors/degrees/certificates offered: B.A. in African and Afro-American Studies
• Approximate number of faculty teaching area and language courses: 10
• Approximate number of courses available—area and language: 36
• Average number of students per year specializing in area: 20
• Countries covered and areas of emphasis: African continent as a whole and the U.S. and Caribbean region with emphasis on cultural, political, economic and social issues that affect all peoples of African origin
• Language offered: Swahili
• Departmental library of 3,300 volumes supplements University library holdings on Africa

12.025
Committee on African Studies
Harvard University
1737 Cambridge St.
Cambridge, MA 02138
(617) 495-5265

Contact(s):
Rita M. Breen, Executive Officer

Committee designed to promote the teaching and study of Africa at Harvard
• Sponsors lectures and seminars and publishes the pamphlet *Harvard University Courses Relating to Sub-Saharan Africa* (free)

12.026
African Studies Center
Michigan State University
100 Center for International Programs
East Lansing, MI 48824
(517) 353-1700

Contact(s):
David Wiley, Director
Marylee Crofts, Outreach Coordinator
Assefa Mehretu, Associate Director

Graduate and undergraduate area studies program established in 1960
• Majors/degrees/certificates offered: B.A. specialization within department major; Graduate Certificate in African Studies within major M.A. and Ph.D. fields; undergraduate certificate in African Studies
• Approximate number of faculty teaching area and language courses: 83 (54 core; 29 consulting)
• Approximate number of courses available—area: 100; language: 75 (21 languages)
• Average number of students per year specializing in area: 75–100
• Countries covered and areas of emphasis: general coverage of all African countries; special emphasis on the Horn of Africa, the countries of the Sahel, Southern Africa, and West Africa
• Languages offered: Akan/Twi, Amharic, Arabic, Hausa, Igbo, Kikuyu, Kpelle, Krio, Lingala, Luganda, Mandingo (Bambara, Maninka, Dyula), Mende, Nyanja, Oromo, Shona, Somali, Swahili, West Africa Pidgin English, Xhosa/Zulu and Yoruba

• Collection of the MSU library includes over 140,000 books and extensive periodical, newspaper, pamphlet and microfilm holdings, along with the Sahel Documentation Center which serves as a repository for Sahelian socioeconomic publications
• Extensive overseas research and study activity in African countries and in collaboration with African universities, including programs or projects in Liberia, Nigeria, the Sudan, Zimbabwe, Malawi, and Ethiopia; includes junior year abroad program
• Offers assistance to other educational institutions and community groups through (1) Educational Resource Center containing teaching materials on Africa available on loan to librarians and teachers K-12; staff consultation also available; and (2) African Media Center and Audio-Visual Collection which prepares guides on Africa-related audiovisual materials including Africa on Film and Videotape, 1960–1982; (3) Michigan Information Network on Africa, for which the Center serves as coordinator; (4) the 4-H African Heritage Program; (5) assistance to Michigan businesses through the International Business Development Program; also publishes Resources for Teaching and Learning about Africa, a series of monographs and curriculum materials for the K-12 classroom
• Publishes newsletter, three journals (*Rural Africana, African Urban Studies, Northeast African Studies* and publications series on Northeast Africa) and books in African studies including a number of source books for researchers

12.027
African Studies Program
Oakland University
Rochester, MI 48063
(313) 377-2154

Contact(s):
Carlo Coppola, Chair
Vincent B. Khapoya, Coordinator

Undergraduate area studies program
• Majors/degrees/certificates offered: B.A. and minor in African Studies
• Approximate number of faculty teaching area and language courses: 9
• Approximate number of courses available—area: 16; language: 10
• Countries covered and areas of emphasis: all countries including North Africa
• Languages offered: French and Spanish
• Study abroad available

12.028
Center for Afro-American and African Studies
University of Michigan at Ann Arbor
1100 South University Ave.
Ann Arbor, MI 48109
(313) 764-5513

Contact(s):
Ali A. Mazrui, Director

Undergraduate area studies program
• Majors/degrees/certificates offered: B.A. in Afro-American and African Studies
• Approximate number of faculty teaching area and language courses: 15
• Approximate number of courses available—area: 16
• Countries covered and areas of emphasis: Sub-Saharan Africa with emphasis on history, culture and politics

12.029
African Studies Program
Western Michigan University
2090 Friedmann
Kalamazoo, MI 49008
(616) 383-0492

Contact(s):
Claude Phillips, Chair

Undergraduate area studies program
• Majors/degrees/certificates offered: coordinate B.A. (combined with departmental major) in African Studies
• Approximate number of courses available—area: 24; language: 4
• Countries covered and areas of emphasis: Sub-Saharan Africa with emphasis on history, culture and contemporary affairs

12.030
African Studies Program
University of Minnesota, Minneapolis
214 Social Science Bldg.
Minneapolis, MN 55455
(612) 373-0143

Contact(s):
Fred T. Smith, Coordinator

Undergraduate area studies program
• Majors/degrees/certificates offered: B.A. in African Studies with options in African Society and Development or in African Arts and Culture
• Approximate number of faculty teaching area and language courses: 16
• Approximate number of courses available—area: 50; language: 12
• Countries covered and areas of emphasis: all countries and areas of Africa
• Languages offered: Swahili, Spanish, Portuguese and Arabic
• Library contains substantial collection of African materials

12.031
Africana Studies Program
Bloomfield College
Bloomfield, NJ 07003
(201) 748-9000

Contact(s):
Austine Okwu, Director

Undergraduate area studies program
- Majors/degrees/certificates offered: B.A. with co-major in Africana Studies
- Approximate number of faculty teaching area and language courses: 3
- Approximate number of courses available—area: 12; language: 2
- Average number of students per year specializing in area: 25
- Countries covered and areas of emphasis: all areas of Africa with emphasis on Sub-Saharan African history and culture and the African-American experience
- Language offered: Swahili
- African study and travel programs available

12.032
Program in African Studies
Princeton University
230 Palmer Hall
Princeton, NJ 08544
(609) 452-4720

Contact(s):
Robert L. Tignor, Director

Undergraduate area studies program
- Majors/degrees/certificates offered: Certificate of Proficiency in African Studies at undergraduate level
- Countries covered and areas of emphasis: all countries of Africa with emphasis on the social sciences
- Languages offered: Arabic, French and Portuguese

12.033
Africana Studies
Rutgers University
New Brunswick, NJ 08903
(201) 932-7820

Contact(s):
S. J. Cookey, Director

Undergraduate area studies program
- Majors/degrees/certificates offered: B.A. in Africana Studies
- Approximate number of faculty teaching area and language courses: 12
- Approximate number of courses available—area: 13; language: 4
- Countries covered and areas of emphasis: Sub-Saharan Africa with emphasis on history and culture and on Pan-Africanism
- Languages offered: Hausa and Swahili

12.034
Africana Studies Department
City University of New York/Brooklyn College
3105 James Hall
Bedford Ave. and Ave. H
Brooklyn, NY 11210
(212) 780-5597

Contact(s):
Milfred C. Fierce, Chair

Undergraduate and graduate area studies program
- Majors/degrees/certificates offered: B.A. in Africana Studies
- Number of faculty teaching area courses: 6
- Approximate number of courses available—area: 35
- Average number of students per year specializing in area: 25
- Countries covered and areas of emphasis: Sub-Saharan Africa and the black countries and peoples of the western hemisphere, with emphasis on history, the arts, literature and the social, political and economic aspects of Pan-Africanism
- Works closely with the Africana Research Institute which promotes research in Africana Studies and on issues of interest to scholars of the black community; sponsors the Martin Luther King, Jr. Distinguished Professorship

• Publishes *Black Prism: Perspectives on the Black Experience*

12.035
Institute for African American Studies
City University of New York/College of
  Staten Island
130 Stuyvesant Place
Staten Island
New York, NY 10301
(212) 390-7990

Contact(s):
Calvin B. Holder, Director

• Conducts interdisciplinary research on aspects of African social, cultural and political history and institutions as well as on Afro-Americans in the U.S.

12.036
Africana Studies Program
City University of New York/Queens College
153-33 61st Road (House 17)
Flushing, NY 11367
(212) 520-7545

Contact(s):
Wentworth Ofuatey-Kodjoe, Director

Undergraduate area studies program established in 1973
• Majors/degrees/certificates offered: B.A. in African Studies; joint major with other departments also available
• Approximate number of faculty teaching area and language courses: 14
• Approximate number of courses available—area: 28; language: 2
• Average number of students per year specializing in area: 23
• Countries covered and areas of emphasis: Sub-Saharan Africa and Afro-American countries and cultures of the western

hemisphere; emphasis on political and social issues and black culture and thought
• Languages offered: Twi, Kiswahili

12.037
Institute of African Studies
Columbia University
1104 International Affairs Bldg.
420 West 118th St.
New York, NY 10027
(212) 280-4633

Contact(s):
Marcia Wright, Director

Graduate area studies program established in 1959
• Majors/degrees/certificates offered: B.A. in Regional Studies (through Columbia College); two-year M.I.A., School of International and Public Affairs, with Certificate in African Studies; M.A. and Ph.D. with Certificate in African Studies
• Approximate number of faculty teaching area and language courses: 18
• Approximate number of courses available—area: 46; language: 4
• Average number of students per year specializing in area: 50
• Countries covered and areas of emphasis: all countries of Africa south of the Sahara, with an emphasis on politics and social and economic development
• Languages offered: Hausa and Swahili, with Arabic, French, German, Portuguese and Spanish available from other departments of the University
• Extensive Africana collections in Columbia University libraries; access available also by researchers to the Schomburg Collection of New York Public Library, Mission Library of Union Theological Seminary, and New York Historical Society; large African art slide collection available in Columbia Department of Art History and Archaeology
• Qualified visiting academics may be attached to the Institute as Visiting Scholars

12.038
Africana Studies and Research Center
Cornell University
310 Triphammer Road
Ithaca, NY 14853
(607) 256-4625

Graduate and undergraduate area studies program
- Majors/degrees/certificates offered: B.A. and M.A. in African and African-American Studies
- Countries covered and areas of emphasis: Sub-Saharan Africa and black countries and cultures of the Americas with emphasis on African and Afro-American history and politics, and on black culture and experience

Contact(s):
Audrey Smedley, Chair

Undergraduate area studies program
- Majors/degrees/certificates offered: B.A. and Certificate in Afro-American and African Studies
- Approximate number of faculty teaching area and language courses: 6
- Approximate number of courses available—area: 23
- Average number of students per year specializing in area: 15
- Countries covered and areas of emphasis: all countries of Africa and black countries of America with emphasis on West Africa and on Afro-America

12.039
Africana Studies
Hofstra University
Hempstead, NY 11550
(515) 560-3532

Contact(s):
Morley Nkosi, Director

Undergraduate area studies program
- Majors/degrees/certificates offered: B.A. in Africana Studies
- Approximate number of courses available—area: 19
- Countries covered and areas of emphasis: emphasis on black African thought and Afro-American experience

12.040
Department of Afro-American and African Studies
State University of New York at Binghamton
Binghamton, NY 13901
(607) 798-2635

12.041
Department of African and Afro-American Studies
State University of New York College at Brockport
Brockport, NY 14420
(716) 395-2211

Contact(s):
Herbert Douglas, Acting Chair

Undergraduate area studies program
- Majors/degrees/certificates offered: B.A. or B.S. in African Studies; optional specialization in African and Caribbean Studies
- Approximate number of faculty teaching area and language courses: 6
- Countries covered and areas of emphasis: Sub-Saharan Africa and the black countries and cultures of the Americas
- Languages offered: Swahili and Twi
- Library contains an Africa/Afro-American collection of approximately 7,000 volumes
- Summer programs available in Ghana and Jamaica

12.042
African Studies Committee
State University of New York at Buffalo
4242 Ridge Lea Road
Amherst, NY 14226
(716) 831-1144

Contact(s):
Phillips Stevens, Jr., Chair
James Pappas, Chair, African/Afro-American
 Studies Department, 202 Spaulding
 Quadrangle, Ellicott Complex (716) 636-
 2082

Undergraduate area studies program
 • Majors/degrees/certificates offered:
B.A. in department with African Studies specialization; B.A. in Black Studies with concentration in African Studies
 • Approximate number of faculty teaching area and language courses: 26
 • Approximate number of courses available—area: 32; language: 2
 • Average number of students per year
specializing in area: 25 graduate; 105 undergraduate
 • Countries covered and areas of emphasis: continental Africa and trans-Atlantic
Connections (Pan-African Area Studies) with
emphasis on anthropology and the social sciences
 • Languages offered: Swahili; on demand: Amharic, Hausa, Igbo, Twi, and Yoruba
 • Library contains approximately 7,000
volumes and 50 periodicals on or from Africa
 • Committee publishes Occasional Papers series; African/Afro-American Studies
Department publishes *Journal of Black Studies*

12.043
Africana Studies
State University of New York at Stony Brook
Stony Brook, NY 11794-4340
(516) 246-4015

Contact(s):
Leslie H. Owens, Chair

Undergraduate area studies program established in 1969
 • Majors/degrees/certificates offered:
B.A. and minor in African Studies
 • Approximate number of faculty teaching area and language courses: 5
 • Approximate number of courses available—area: 27
 • Average number of students per year
specializing in area: 5
 • Countries covered and areas of emphasis: black African nations and cultures
worldwide; emphasis on the diaspora, the
black experience and social and political issues

12.044
African and Afro-American Studies
Curriculum
University of North Carolina at Chapel Hill
401 Alumni Bldg. 004A
Chapel Hill, NC 27514
(919) 966-5496

Contact(s):
Roberta Ann Dunbar, Director, African
 Studies

Undergraduate area studies program
 • Majors/degrees/certificates offered:
B.A. in African Studies
 • Approximate number of faculty teach-
ing area and language courses: 20
 • Approximate number of courses avail-
able—area: 12 African studies; 9 Afro-Amer-
ican
 • Average number of students per year
specializing in area: 10
 • Countries covered and areas of em-
phasis: Sub-Saharan Africa with emphasis on
African and Afro-American history, politics,
and Pan-Africanism
 • Language offered: Arabic

• African library holdings comprise approximately 70,000 volumes, Afro-American over 100,000

12.045
African Studies
Syracuse University
Foreign and Comparative Studies
119 College Place
Syracuse, NY 13210
(315) 423-2552

Contact(s):
John D. Nagel, Director

Graduate undergraduate non-degree area studies program established in 1962
• Majors/degrees/certificates offered: M.A. and Ph.D. with specialization in African Studies through Afro-American Studies and Religion. Departments as well as through a special interdisciplinary program in the humanities and Public Administration (see 6.157); M.A. in Interdisciplinary Linguistics Program through the Development Planning Program; and a graduate Certificate of Competence in African Studies
• Number of faculty teaching area and language courses: 16
• Countries covered and area of emphasis: all areas of Africa
• Tutorial and self-instructional courses available in several African languages through the Institute of Applied Linguistics
• Library contains extensive holdings of books and other materials, including 165 periodicals and 10 newspapers, and many government documents along with a major collection of materials on colonial Kenya (including film copies of virtually the entire collection of records of the British administration in Kenya) and similar, though less extensive, materials for Tanzania, Uganda, Ethiopia, and Malawi (total Africana Microfilm holdings: approximately 4,000 reels)
• Departmental fellowships and assis-

tantships available along with two Shell Fellowships for dissertation research in less developed countries
• Faculty has extensive experience in working in Syracuse development assistance projects in Africa; Research Associate Program offers affiliation for Africanist faculty at nearby institutions
• Summer seminars in East Africa (Kenya, Tanzania, Uganda) available
• Publishes an Africana Series of monographs of several volumes of bibliographies and teaching aids and serves as editorial headquarters for the *African Studies Journal*

12.046
Pan-African and African Studies
Kent State University
Kent, OH 44242

Contact(s):
Edward Crosby, Coordinator, Pan-African Studies (216) 672-7937
Murray Fishel, Coordinator, African Studies (216) 672-2060

• Offers B.A. in Pan-African Studies and B.A. and M.A. with Certificate in African Studies

12.047
African Studies
Ohio State University
Department of Black Studies
486 University Hall
Columbus, OH 43210
(614) 422-3700

Contact(s):
William E. Nelson, Jr., Chair

Graduate and undergraduate area studies program
• Majors/degrees/certificates offered: B.A. and M.A. in African Studies

- Approximate number of faculty teaching area and language courses: 18
- Approximate number of courses available—area: 28; language: 4
- Average number of students per year specializing in area: 26 graduate; 15 undergraduate
- Countries covered and areas of emphasis: Sub-Saharan Africa with emphasis on history and politics and on Pan-Africanism
- Language offered: Swahili
- Library includes holdings of approximately 55,000 volumes on the African in Africa and the Americas
- Affiliation with the University of Ghana

12.048
African Studies Program
Ohio University
Center for International Studies
Athens, OH 45701
(614) 594-5542

Contact(s):
Gifford B. Doxsee, Director

Graduate area studies program established in 1964
- Majors/degrees/certificates offered: M.A. in International Affairs with emphasis on Africa
- Approximate number of courses available—area: 50; language: 12
- Average number of students per year specializing in area: 40 graduate; 10 undergraduate
- Countries covered and areas of emphasis: all countries of Africa with emphasis on Africa south of the Sahara
- Languages offered: Swahili and Arabic

12.049
African Studies Program
Cheney University of Pennsylvania
Cheney, PA 19319
(215) 399-2377

Contact(s):
Arthur C. Willis, Director

Undergraduate area studies program
- Majors/degrees/certificates offered: B.A. in Afro-American Studies
- Approximate number of faculty teaching area and language courses: 6
- Approximate number of courses available—area: 19; language: 2
- Average number of students per year specializing in area: 30
- Countries covered and areas of emphasis: all countries of Africa with emphasis on Sub-Saharan area and the black countries and cultures in the Americas
- Language offered: Swahili
- Library contains a 6,000-volume African and Afro-American collection as well as a collection of African artifacts
- Institute of African Local Government affiliated with the program

12.050
African Studies Program
Slippery Rock State College
107D World Culture Bldg.
Slippery Rock, PA 16057
(412) 794-7310

Graduate and undergraduate area studies program
- Majors/degrees/certificates offered: B.A. and M.A. with specialization in African Studies
- Approximate number of faculty teaching area and language courses: 5
- Approximate number of courses available—area: 9
- Average number of students per year specializing in area: 10 graduate; 10 undergraduate
- Countries covered and areas of emphasis: Sub-Saharan Africa with emphasis on geography and ecology

• Language offered: Swahili (through self-instructional Critical Language Program)

• Conducts East and West Africa summer study programs especially designed for education students

12.051
Department of Pan-African Studies
Temple University
Room 308, Gladfelter
Philadelphia, PA 19122
(215) 787-8491

Contact(s):
Tran Van Dinh, Chair

Undergraduate area studies program
• Majors/degrees/certificates offered: B.A. in Pan-African Studies
• Approximate number of faculty teaching area and language courses: 6
• Approximate number of courses available—area: 19
• Countries covered and areas of emphasis: all Sub-Saharan African countries and black countries and cultures of the western hemisphere; emphasis on the black experience and on the politics of colonialism and independence

12.052
African Studies
University of South Carolina at Columbia
Department of Government and
　International Studies
Columbia, SC 29208
(803) 777-7309

Contact(s):
Mark W. Delancey, Chair

Undergraduate area studies program
• Majors/degrees/certificates offered: B.A. in African Studies
• Approximate number of faculty teaching area and language courses: 15

• Approximate number of courses available—area: 22; language: 10
• Countries covered and areas of emphasis: Sub-Saharan Africa with emphasis on history
• Languages offered: Swahili and Arabic

12.053
African Studies
Memphis State University
Department of Anthropology
Memphis, TN 38152
(901) 454-2618

Contact(s):
Monte R. Kenaston, Director

Undergraduate area studies program
• Majors/degrees/certificates offered: B.A. with Certificate in African Studies
• Approximate number of faculty teaching area and language courses: 4
• Approximate number of courses available—area: 15
• Countries covered and areas of emphasis: all of Africa with emphasis on Sub-Saharan countries and on history and the social sciences
• Library contains approximately 5,000 volumes on Africa, plus 4,000 slides and a substantial map collection

12.054
African and Afro-American Studies and Research Center
University of Texas at Austin
231A Jester Center
Austin, TX 78712
(512) 471-1784

Contact(s):
John Warfield, Director

• Offers area concentration with a strong black American orientation; sponsors and conducts research on Africa and Afro-American subjects; publishes *Research in African Literature* and an Occasional Publications series

12.055
African Studies Program
University of Wisconsin at Madison
1454 Van Hise Hall
1220 Linden Drive
Madison, WI 53706
(608) 262-2380

Contact(s):
Richard Ralston, Director

Graduate and undergraduate area studies program established in 1961
• Majors/degrees/certificates offered: B.A. with concentration in African Studies; B.A. in African Languages and Literatures; departmental M.A. and Ph.D. with Certificate in African Studies; minor field in African Studies
• Approximate number of faculty teaching area and language courses: 35
• Approximate number of courses available—area: 80; language: 51

• Average number of students per year specializing in area: 125
• Countries covered and areas of emphasis: all countries of Africa, including North Africa; emphasis on Sub-Saharan Africa; includes courses on Afro-American subjects; particular strength in linguistics, language, literature and history
• Languages offered: regularly, Arabic, Ancient Egyptian, Hausa, Swahili and Xhosa; occasionally, Fula, Kikuyu, Mende, Wolof, Pedi, Zulu, Southern Sotho, Kamba, Meru, Somali, Krio, Bambara and Luhya
• Library contains extensive Africana collection of over 50,000 books and 600 periodicals and newspapers
• Publishes Occasional Papers series and sponsors the journal *African Economic History; Ba Shiru,* a journal of African languages and literature, is published by the Department of African Languages and Literature
• Conducts extensive outreach program; provides speakers and curriculum advisors to elementary and secondary schools, maintains an Instructional Materials Center of teaching materials and resources; makes available large collection of films on Africa, consults on the acquisition of films and publishes *Films on Africa* (see 2.126), a catalogue for educators

Information and Service Organizations

12.056
Africa Guild
163 West 23rd St.
New York, NY 10011
(212) 242-2388

Contact(s):
Frances Blackwell, Director

Educational and travel organization for people interested in Africa and African culture

• Publishes *African Journal,* a quarterly review focusing on one country in each issue and covering current events, art, culture, handicrafts, books, practical travel information, etc.; a catalogue of African art, handicrafts and gifts for purchase; and a bulletin providing up-to-date information on media and cultural events related to Africa that are scheduled in the U.S.
• Sells books on Africa
• Conducts tours to Africa

12.057
Africa News Service
P.O. Box 3851
Durham, NC 27702
(919) 286-0747

Contact(s):
Charles Ebel, Managing Editor

Nonprofit information and news service focused on current African affairs
• Publishes *Africa News: A Weekly Digest of African Affairs* (see 12.088) provides reprint, photo and research service; prepares newspaper articles and radio news and features; maintains library open to the public

12.058
African-American Institute
833 UN Plaza
New York, NY 10017
(212) 949-5666
and
1320 19th St. NW
Washington, DC 20036
(202) 872-0521

Contact(s):
Donald B. Easum, President
Margaret A. Novicki, Editor, *Africa Report*
Jonathan Weaver, Director, Washington
   Office

Nonprofit educational organization concerned with African development, educational exchanges between the U.S. and Africa and U.S. education about Africa
• Gathers and provides information on African countries and current African affairs and maintains the African Policy Information Center to assist researchers
• Conducts African manpower development program which includes administration of the African Graduate Fellowship Program (AFGRAD), three southern Africa training programs (particularly focused on refugee

students), a program for Portuguese-speaking countries, a Women and African Development Program, and exchange visitor and student counseling programs run from the Washington office
• Publishes *Africa Report* (see 12.089) and *South Africa/Namibia Update* (see 18.365)
• Sponsors conferences, seminars and meetings and conducts Services to Corporations Program which, in addition to holding meetings, arranges contacts between Americans and African visitors with mutual business interests

12.059
African American Museums Association
1538 9th St. NW
Washington, DC 20001
(202) 332-6332

Contact(s):
Joy Ford Austin, Executive Director

Association of individuals and institutions concerned with black museums
• Conducts research, compiles data and provides information on black museums
• Provides training and consulting assistance to African-American museums
• Publishes newsletter on funding and other resources available to black museums

12.060
African Communications Liaison Service, Inc.
1346 Connecticut Ave. N.W., Suite 901
Washington, DC 20036
(202) 223-1392

Information and publications resource on contemporary Africa and U.S.-African relations
• Sponsors information services and publications programs including African Development Information Association, USA (see

12.061) and the African Bibliographic Center (see 12.112)

12.061
African Development Information Association, USA
1346 Connecticut Ave. NW, Suite 909
Washington, DC 20036
(202) 223-1392

Nonprofit membership organization designed to facilitate the flow of information about African development; membership open to individuals and institutions
• Provides information on African development issues
• Publishes bimonthly *Bulletin* with news and analysis of government policy, corporate trends, U.S. donor aid, private investment and individuals active in African development (available to nonmembers for $45 per year); *Dateline Africa,* a quarterly calendar of meetings, conferences and other events focusing on economic development (available to nonmembers for $25 per year or $7 per issue); and occasional special monographs

12.062
African Literature Association
University of Alberta
Comparative Literature Department
Edmonton, Alberta, Canada T6G 2E6
(403) 432-5535

Contact(s):
Stephen Arnold, Secretary-Treasurer

Professional academic association to promote appreciation of African writers and artists
• Conducts meetings and conferences and publishes quarterly *ALA Bulletin* (see 12.097) and *Annual Selected Conference Papers*

12.063
African Studies Association
University of California at Los Angeles
255 Kinsey Hall
Los Angeles, CA 90024
(213) 206-8011

Contact(s):
Donald J. Cosentino, Executive Secretary

Scholarly and professional association serving the Africanist community
• Promotes exchange of ideas and information on Africa and African studies, on library and materials development and on outreach to a broader community of interests and precollege educational levels
• Publishes the scholarly *African Studies Review* (quarterly), *Issues: A Journal of Opinion* (occasional), *ASA News* (quarterly) a quarterly newsletter, *History in Africa* (yearly, $20 plus postage and handling) and conference papers (photocopied); also publishes scholarly and other works through the Crossroads Press (see 12.116)

12.064
Habari News Service
P.O. Box 13096
Washington, DC 20036
(202) 223-1392

Information service on Africa and African-U.S. relations; conducted by African Bibliographic Center (see 12.112) and the Washington Task Force on African Affairs
• Provides free daily telephone news service accessible 24 hours per day seven days a week; call (202) 659-2529; consists of three-minute summary of up-to-date news and public opinion developments relative to Africa, along with information on people, meetings and cultural events; revised nightly (except on weekends)
• Offers Habari Transcript Service including transcripts of daily telephone news

broadcast plus additional background information; available weekly ($250) or quarterly ($100), more for overseas subscribers; transcripts of individual broadcasts $2.50 each

• Prepares and publishes special reports on African affairs

12.065
Munger Africana Library
California Institute of Technology
Pasadena, CA 91125
(213) 356-4469, Ext. 1468

Contact(s):
Susan M. Cave, Librarian

Private library collection; materials not circulated; open to visiting scholars (who should phone in advance); photocopying facilities available

• Covers Sub-Saharan Africa and the offshore islands; includes 21,000 volumes, 878 serials, and extensive collection of clippings, pamphlets, maps, prints, etc.; particular strength in politics (especially of South Africa), history, economics and culture

• Publishes books, bibliographies (especially on South African subjects) and *Munger Africana Library Notes* (commentary on African research, resources, etc.; published five or six times per year)

Sources of Grants and Awards

12.066
Social Science Research Council
International Doctoral Research Fellowships and Postdoctoral Grants for International Research: Africa
605 Third Ave.
New York, NY 10158
(212) 557-9500

• Awards fellowships for doctoral dissertation research in the social sciences and humanities in Africa south of the Sahara; particular attention given to proposals for research in disciplines underrepresented in African studies, such as sociology and economics; students with interdisciplinary training who show genuine competence in the secondary disciplines related to their research are given special consideration

• Awards substantial individual grants of not more than $12,000 to scholars whose competence for research in the social sciences or humanities has been demonstrated

by their previous work and who hold the Ph.D. degree or who have equivalent research experience; applicants must be either citizens or permanent residents of the U.S. or Canada

12.067
National Science Foundation
Sub-Saharan African Program
Division of International Programs
Washington, DC 20550
(202) 357-9550

Contact(s):
Robert Bell, Program Manager

• Provides funding for cooperative scientific endeavors between U.S. and African scientists including cooperative research projects, seminars and workshops and dissertation support

Guides, Sourcebooks and Directories

12.068
The ABC of Modern Africa
Rex F. Manyeto, Editor
African American Trading Co.
4854 Inedale Ave.
Los Angeles, CA 90043
1979; paperbound; 205 pages; $15

• Country-by-country guidebook to 52 African countries; includes for each country brief background on history and people, the political situation, geography and economic condition; provides outline profile with statistics and brief notes for the traveler

12.069
AF-LOG II: African Affairs in Washington, D.C. 1980
African Bibliographic Center
P.O. Box 13096
Washington, DC 20036
1980; paperbound; 130 pages; $7.50

• Directory of academic institutions, nonprofit and profitmaking organizations and government offices located in the nation's capital with an active interest in Africa

12.070
African Book World and Press
Hans M. Zell, Editor
K. G. Saur
Munich, West Germany
1980; hardbound; 244 pages; $85

Distributed by Gale Research Co., Book Tower, Detroit, MI 48226

• Lists and describes country-by-country libraries, booksellers, research institutions, learned societies, professional associations, major periodicals, book clubs, prizes and awards, printers and bookfairs; indexed

12.071
Africa South of the Sahara
Europa Publications, Ltd.
London, England
annual; hardbound; 971 pages; $130

Available from Gale Research Co., Book Tower, Detroit, MI 48226
• Very comprehensive yearbook, survey and compilation of data, statistics and directory-type information
• Covers international organizations active in Africa, including the UN and other political, cultural, educational and economic development organizations
• For each country entry there is an extensive survey of historical and cultural background and then a generous compilation of data, statistics, lists of names and descriptive materials in the following areas: economics, principal characteristics, social structure, government offices and officers, judicial system, media, publishers, financial institutions, trade and industrial entities, transportation, tourism/culture, atomic energy, defense, education and dependencies

12.072
African Encyclopedia
Oxford University Press
200 Madison Ave.
New York, NY 10016
1974; hardbound; 554 pages; $16.95

• Encyclopedia covering a wide range of African and Africa-related subjects

12.073
African Newspapers Currently Received by American Libraries
Daniel A. Britz
African Studies Center
Boston University
10 Lenox St.
Brookline, MA 02146
1979; pamphlet; 15 pages; $3

• Lists 276 newspapers (name only) country-by-country and indicates which of 20 libraries in the U.S. (Library of Congress, Hoover Institution (see 4.157), Munger Africana Library (see 12.065), Boston Public, New York Public and 15 university libraries) receive it

12.074
The African Political Dictionary
Claude Phillips
ABC-Clio, Inc.
Riviera Campus
2040 Alameda Padre Serra
Box 4397
Santa Barbara, CA 93103
1983; 245 pages; hardbound, $30; paperbound, $14.25

• Provides definitions and commentary on the significance of terms, concepts, institutions and events central to the politics and economics of Africa; arranged topically and sequenced parallel to most related texts under such headings as historical perspective, political and cultural ideology, government institutions, political parties, etc.; indexed

12.075
Bibliographies for African Studies, 1970–1975; 1976–1978
Yvette Scheven, Compiler
Crossroads Press
African Studies Association
255 Kinsey Hall, UCLA
Los Angeles, CA 90024
2 volumes, 1978 and 1980; paperbound; 159 and 142 pages; each $20

• Annotated guide to bibliographies in the social sciences and humanities which appear in books, articles, or parts of edited volumes concerning all Sub-Saharan countries; 1970–1975 volume has 993 entries; 1976–1978 volume has 830 entries

12.076
A Bibliography for the Study of African Politics, Volume I and Volume II
Robert Shaw and Richard Sklar, Editors of Volume I
Alan C. Soloman, Compiler of Volume II
Crossroads Press
African Studies Association
255 Kinsey Hall, UCLA
Los Angeles, CA 90024
1978; paperbound; 159 and 193 pages; each $15

• Bibliography for political scientists in the African studies field; the two volumes include over 7,000 entries and cover the literature through 1975

12.077
Current African Directories
I. G. Anderson, Editor
CBD Research Ltd.
154 High St.
Beckenham
Kent BR3 1EA, England
1972; hardbound; 200 pages; $140

Directory incorporates an earlier publication, *African Companies: A Guide to Sources of Information*
• Lists directories published in or relating to all the 55 independent countries and dependent territories of mainland Africa including island states and territories such as Madagascar, Mauritius and Seychelles; includes yearbooks, almanacs, gazetteers, general industrial and commercial directories; telephone, Telex and telegraphic directories; research, library and bibliographic directo-

ries; and regional, specialized and technical directories; provides publisher and bibliographic data, description of content, languages used, frequency, date published, price and size

• Contains two parts, one an alphabetical list of directories by title and the second a country-by-country listing of sources of business information, responsible offices, legal forms required, official gazette, sterling exchange information and an index to directories for each country listed in the first section

12.078

Directory of African & Afro-American Studies in the United States
Mitsue Frey and David Duffy, Editors
Crossroads Press
University of California
255 Kinsey Hall
Los Angeles, CA 90024
1979; hardbound; 320 pages; $30

• Lists and provides substantial information on approximately 600 institutions with significant program offerings in African and Afro-American studies and approximately 300 with lesser offerings

12.079

Global Dimensions of the African Diaspora
Joseph E. Harris, Editor
Howard University Press
2900 Van Ness St. NW
Washington, DC 20008
1982; hardbound; 608 pages; $19.95

• Guide to the study of the dispersal of Africans and African descendants to other parts of the world; in four sections: conceptual framework, assimilation and identity (the process of adaptation), return (immigration back to Africa) and synthesis (which proposes the application of a Pan-African approach to diaspora studies); includes bibliography

12.080

Guide to Federal Archives Relating to Africa
Crossroads Press
African Studies Association
255 Kinsey Hall, UCLA
Los Angeles, CA 90024
1977; hardbound; 556 pages; $75

• Makes accessible by name, place or subject the vast quantity of Africa-related material housed in the National Archives in Washington, D.C.

12.081

Handbook of American Resources for African Studies
Hoover Institution Press
Stanford University
Stanford, CA 94305
1966; hardbound; 218 pages; $9.95

• Guide to the principal library and manuscript collections, church and missionary libraries and archives, art and ethnographic collections, private U.S. collectors and business archives of Africana

12.082

Know Africa
Ralph Uwechue, Editor
Gale Research Co.
Book Tower
Detroit, MI 48226
1981; hardbound; in 3 volumes of 3,290 pages; $250 per set

• *Africa Today* (Volume I) provides detailed information on each of the countries of Africa and extensive data on modern African history; *Makers of Modern Africa* (Volume II) presents biographical sketches of 502 deceased African leaders; *Africa Who's Who* (Volume III) is an up-to-date biographical directory of some 700 contemporary Africans

12.083
Scholar's Guide to Washington, D.C.:
African Studies
Purnima Mehta Bhatt
Smithsonian Institution Press
Washington, DC 20560
1980; 347 pages; paperbound, $9.95,
　　hardbound, $25

Comprehensive listing and description of resources in the Washington area available to researchers and others interested in Africa; divided into two sections: collections (libraries, archives, museums, etc., music and sound, maps, films and data banks) and organizations (research centers and information offices, academic programs, U.S. government agencies, embassies and international organizations, professional associations, exchange and technical assistance organizations, religious organizations and publications/media); available resources described in some detail with clear indication how and from whom to obtain access; appendices include libraries listed by size of holdings, bookstores, housing, transport and other services and a bibliography; indexed by name of resource, personal papers collections, and library subject strength

12.084
Statistics—Africa
Joan M. Harvey, Editor
CBD Research, Ltd.
Beckenham, England
1978; hardbound; 374 pages; $120

Distributed by Gale Research Co., Book Tower, Detroit, MI 48226
　• Provides extensive listing (live and print) of sources of statistical data for each country of Africa; includes central statistical offices and other important statistics collection agencies, principal libraries containing statistics, libraries and information services in other countries that supply statistics on each country, principal bibliographies of statistical compilations and major statistical publications with full address and/or bibliographic information

12.085
Sub-Saharan Africa
W. A. E. Skurnik, Editor
Gale Research Co.
Book Tower
Detroit, MI 48226
1977; hardbound; 130 pages; $40

　• Bibliographic information about works on major African problems and issues; treated in bibliographic essays

12.086
A Survey of Materials for the Study of the Uncommonly Taught Languages: Languages of Sub-Saharan Africa
Dora E. Johnson et al.
Center for Applied Linguistics
3520 Prospect St. NW
Washington, DC 20007
1976; paperbound; 79 pages; $7.95

Exclusively distributed by Harcourt Brace Jovanich, Inc., 757 Third Ave., New York, NY 10017; Attn: Nancy McCloughan
　• One of a series of bibliographies covering all the modern languages except Standard English, German, Italian, Russian and Spanish; designed for use by the adult learner whose native language is English; listed under the headings: teaching materials, readers, grammars and dictionaries; includes books currently in print where feasible, older titles where not; citations appear under the following countries/language groups: Germanic, Ethiopia and Somalia, West Africa, Bantu, Khoisan, Interior Africa and Malayo-Polynesian

Periodicals

12.087
Africa Confidential
Charles Meynell, Editor
Miramoor Publications, Ltd.
5/33 Rutland Gate
London SW7, England
biweekly newsletter; 8 pages; £70 per year

• Each issue provides substantive behind-the-scenes analyses of critical developments and crises in African countries, including North Africa, with a focus on political and economic implications for both Africa and the West

12.088
Africa News: A Weekly Digest of African Affairs
Charles Ebel, Managing Editor
Africa News Service, Inc.
720 Ninth St.
Durham, NC 27702
weekly newsletter; 12 pages; individuals; non-profit institutions, $45; profit institutions, $78

• Provides concise reports on significant current political and economic developments throughout the African continent

12.089
Africa Report
Anthony J. Hughes, Editor
The African-American Institute
833 UN Plaza
New York, NY 10017
bimonthly magazine; approx. 57 pages; individuals, $21; institutions, $28

• Lively articles on current affairs in the countries of Africa with particular focus on social, political and economic issues; includes African Update, a country-by-country update on political developments, and a book review section

12.090
Africa Today
Tilden J. LeMelle and George W. Shepherd, Jr., Editors
Africa Today Associates
% Graduate School of International Studies
University of Denver
Denver, CO 80208
quarterly journal; 80 pages; individuals, $12 per year; institutions, $18 per year

• Includes articles which analyze and interpret African affairs as well as a large number of analytical and critical book reviews of both current and scholarly interest; also surveys coming events in the African Studies community; discusses what other publications and organizations are producing and makes miscellaneous announcements

12.091
African Arts
John F. Povey, Editor
University of California
Los Angeles, CA 90024
quarterly magazine; 92 pages; $20 per year

• Contains articles in high quality format on African art and art exhibitions; extensively illustrated; includes book reviews and listings of events and exhibitions

12.092
African Economic History
Margaret Jean Hay, David Henige, Paul Lovejoy and Marvin P. Miracle, Editors
African Studies Program
University of Wisconsin
1454 Van Hise
1220 Linden Drive
Madison, WI 53706
annual journal; approx. 205 pages; individuals, $8; institutions, $15

• Scholarly articles on African economic history; extensive book review section

12.093
The African Review: A Journal of African Politics and Development and International Affairs
Gelase Mutahaba, Editor
The African Review
Box 35042
Dar Es Salaam, Tanzania
semiannual journal; approx. 130 pages; individuals, $18 per year; institutions $28 per year

• Substantive articles and essays on contemporary African domestic and international economic and political issues; book reviews

12.094
African Studies Review
R. Hunt Davis, Jr., Editor
African Studies Association
University of California
255 Kinsey Hall
405 Hilgard Ave.
Los Angeles, CA 90024
quarterly journal; approx. 100 pages; free with membership; $15–$40 per year

• Contains scholarly articles in African Studies; book reviews

12.095
African Urban Studies
Ruth Simms Hamilton, Editor
African Studies Center
Michigan State University
East Lansing, MI 48824
published 3 times a year; journal; $12 per year, individuals; $18 per year, institutions

• Contains topical and scholarly articles on political, social and economic issues related to African urban development; includes book reviews, announcements and other relevant communications

12.096
Africana Journal
Holmes & Meier Publishers, Inc.
IUB Bldg., 30 Irving Place
New York, NY 10003
quarterly journal; approx. 384 pages; individuals, $28.50 per year; institutions, $55 per year

A bibliographic library journal and review
• Includes bibliographic articles of interest to Africanist researchers, reviews of new books on Africa, and a general bibliography of 300–400 books on Africa published worldwide

12.097
ALA Bulletin
Stephen H. Arnold, Editor
African Literature Association
University of Alberta
Department of Comparative Literature
Edmonton, Alberta, Canada T6G 2E6
quarterly; approx. 40 pages; $25 per year; individuals, $15

• Reports on issues affecting the study of Africa and African literature; includes articles and reviews on African literary subjects

12.098
The Conch
Conch Magazine Ltd., Publishers
102 Normal Ave. (Symphony Circle)
Buffalo, NY 14213
semiannual journal; individuals, $10 per year; institutions, $15 per year

• Sociological journal that examines theories of African cultures and literatures and principles and methods of African poetics, aesthetics and literary criticism

12.099
The Conch Review of Books
Conch Magazine Ltd., Publishers
102 Normal Ave. (Symphony Circle)
Buffalo, NY 14213
quarterly journal; individuals, $10 per year; institutions, $15 per year

• Provides in-depth, timely reviews of significant books and audiovisual materials about Africa

12.100
International Journal of African Historical Studies
African Studies Center
Boston University
270 Bay State Road
Boston, MA 02215
quarterly journal; approx. 190 pages; subscription $50, institutions; $25, individuals

• Scholarly articles on African historical subjects; book reviews

12.101
Journal of African History
David Birmingham, Christopher Fyfe, Robin Law and Andrew Roberts, Editors
Cambridge University Press
32 East 57th St.
New York, NY 10022
quarterly journal; approx. 150 pages; individuals, $39 per year; institutions, $80 per year (individuals must certify that journal is for personal use)

• Scholarly articles and essays on African history; extensive book reviews and notices

12.102
Journal of African Studies
Boniface I. Obichere, Editor
Heldref Publications
4000 Albemarle St. NW, Suite 500
Washington, DC 20016
quarterly journal; approx. 50 pages; 8½ × 11; $40 per year

Sponsored by the African Studies Center of the University of California at Los Angeles
• Contains essays and articles on African history, culture, and political and economic development; includes book reviews

12.103
The Journal of Modern African Studies
David Kimble, Editor
Cambridge University Press
32 East 57th St.
New York, NY 10022
quarterly journal; $99 per year for institutions

Individuals ordering directly from the publishers and who certify that the journal is for their personal use may subscribe at a reduced rate of $44
• Scholarly articles on subjects in African history; includes extensive section of reviews and short notices of books

12.104
Northeast African Studies
Harold G. Marcus, Editor
African Studies Center
Michigan State University
East Lansing, MI 48824
published 3 times a year; journal; approx. 100 pages; $12 per year

• Contains topical and scholarly articles on political, social and economic issues in the Horn of Africa; includes book reviews, announcements and other scholarly communications; covers Ethiopia, Somalia, Eritrea and Sudan

12.105
OAU Echo
Press and Information Division
OAU General Secretariat
Khartoum, Sudan
bimonthly magazine; approx. 32 pages; free

• Publishes documents and reports about the activities of the Organization of African States in promoting African economic development, financial cooperation and mutually beneficial trade relations; in French and English

12.106
Rural Africana
Assefa Mehretu and David Wiley, Editors
African Studies Center
Michigan State University
East Lansing, MI 48824
published 3 times a year; approx. 80 pages; journal; $12 per year

• Contains topical and scholarly articles on political, social and economic issues related to rural African affairs; includes book reviews/analyses of U.S. policy statements, notices and other scholarly communications

12.107
SADEX (Southern Africa Development Information/Documentation Exchange)
African Bibliographic Center
P.O. Box 13096
Washington, DC 20009
bimonthly journal; $30 per year

Available free to selected individuals and institutions specializing in southern African development; supported by the U.S. Agency for International Development and is a part of the Pan-African Documentation and Information System for Social and Economic Development (PADIS); covers Angola, Botswana, Lesotho, Malawi, Mozambique,

Namibia, Swaziland, Tanzania, Zambia and Zimbabwe

• Provides current information on publications, projects and international cooperative efforts related to the development needs and priorities of southern Africa; includes abstracts, information briefs, book reviews, bibliographic listings and identification of forthcoming publications, research in progress, development projects, meetings and conferences

12.108
Southern Africa Magazine
Southern Africa Committee
198 Broadway
New York, NY 10038
10 issues per year; magazine; approx. 33 pages; $10 per year

• Reports and articles on current developments in the southern African countries and their relations with the U.S. from a black liberationist perspective; includes news notes and a listing of recent publications

12.109
Studies in African Linguistics
Russell G. Schuh, Editor
Department of Linguistics and African Studies Center
University of California at Los Angeles
Los Angeles, CA 90024
published 3 times a year; journal; individuals, $12 per year; institutions, $20 per year

• Contains scholarly articles on African languages; includes notes on recent publications

12.110
Transafrica Forum
Transaction Periodicals Consortium
Rutgers University
New Brunswick, NJ 08903
quarterly journal; individuals, $15 per year;
   institutions, $30 per year

• Articles on political, economic and
cultural issues which affect black communities in Africa and the Caribbean

12.111
West Africa
Kaye Whiteman, Editor
West Africa Publishing Co., Ltd.
53 Holborn Viaduct
London EC1A 2FD, England
weekly magazine; approx. 50 pages; $1.25
   per issue

• Surveys current West African political
and economic affairs in newsweekly format;
extensive classified employment ("situations
vacant") section; book reviews

Publishers

12.112
African Bibliographic Center
P.O. Box 13096
Washington, DC 20009
(202) 223-1392

Major information center on current African
affairs; part of the African Communications
Liaison Service, Inc. (see 12.060)
• Provides information on resources about
all phases of contemporary African affairs and
African-U.S. relations
• Publishes the periodicals SADEX
(Southern Africa Development Information/
Documentation Exchange, see 12.107) and
*AMA: Women in African & American
Worlds—An Outlook*, a number of reference
books including *AF-LOG II: African Affairs
in Washington, D.C., 1980–1981* (see 12.069);
Dictionary of Afro-Latin American Civilization (see 16.132); *Who Speaks for Southern
Africa? A Resource Guide to Current Materials for Study & Research* (a guide to recent publications on Southern Africa); *African Refugees: A Guide to Contemporary
Information Sources* (contains a bibliography
and list of organizations), and other bibliographies and reports on current political de-

velopments especially related to U.S. policy
toward Africa
• Runs the Habari News Service (see
12.064)

12.113
African Imprint Library Services
410 W. Falmouth Highway
Box 350
West Falmouth, MA 02574
(617) 540-5378

• Supplies publications from African
countries including commercially published
books, institutional and government reports,
journals and other materials; must request
specific publications (general lists not available)

12.114
Conch Magazine, Ltd., Publishers
102 Normal Ave. (Symphony Circle)
Buffalo, NY 14213
(716) 885-3686

Commercial publisher

• Publishes books and periodicals by Africans about Africa; includes books on politics, social transition, religion and philosophy, language and science and medicine along with *The Conch* (see 12.098), *The Conch Review of Books* (see 12.099), *Children's Literature and Audio-Visual Materials in Africa* (see 2.119) and *Children's Fiction About Africa in English* (see 2.118)

12.115
Cornell University Press
Box 250
124 Roberts Place
Ithaca, NY 14851
(607) 257-7000

• Publishes a list of titles on African social, cultural and political subjects; includes a series Africa in the Modern World which consists of solid, though dated, analyses of specific countries; *Angola* (1979), *Ethiopia* (1971), *Cameroon* (1971), *Guinea* (1977) *Dahomey* (now Benin, 1975) and Malawi (1978)

12.116
Crossroads Press
255 Kinsey Hall
University of California
Los Angeles, CA 90024
(213) 206-8011

Publisher for the African Studies Association (see 0000)
• Publishes extensive list of reference and other materials on Africa and African Studies such as bibliographies, archival series, directories, research and dissertation lists, periodicals and historical studies; includes *Bibliography for the Study of African Politics* (see 12.076), *African Outreach* (see 2.110), *Bibliographies for African Studies* (see 12.075), *Directory of African and Afro-American Studies in the U.S.* (see 12.078), *Guide to Federal Archives Relating to Africa* (see

12.080), *Paperback Books on Africa* and *African Studies Review* (see 12.094)

12.117
G. K. Hall & Company
70 Lincoln St.
Boston, MA 02111
(617) 423-3990

• Publishes extensive list of bibliographies, indexes and other materials in African Studies

12.118
Greenwood Press
Box 5007
88 Post Road West
Westport, CT 06881
(203) 226-3571

Large commercial publisher
• Publishes extensive list of reference and other books on African and Afro-American subjects, including the Special Bibliographic Series of the African Bibliographic Center (see 12.112) covering Ethiopia, Somalia, African ecology, American-Southern African Relations and Afro-Americans and Africa and *Dictionary of Afro-Latin American Civilizations* (see 16.132)

12.119
Howard University Press
2900 Van Ness St. NW
Washington, DC 20008
(202) 686-6696

• Publishes books on African and Afro-American studies; includes *Global Dimensions of the African Diaspora* (see 12.079)

12.120
Interbook, Inc.
611 Broadway, Room 227
New York, NY 10012
(212) 677-9201

Publisher of books of other nonprofit organizations, especially the African American Institute (see 12.058), the African Publications Trust, the Museum of African Art, the International Commission of Jurists and the Center for Inter-American Relations (see 16.110)
  • Publishes wide selection of books on current African affairs and on African arts, along with a number of reports on law, human rights and conflict in other countries or international relations in general, two slide lecture albums on Asian art and a number of studies on international and comparative education for the International Council for Educational Development (see 2.038)

12.121
Northwestern University Press
1735 Benson Ave.
Evanston, IL 60201
(312) 492-5313

University publishing house
  • Publishes selection of titles on Africa and African studies

12.122
Third Press Review
Okpaku Communications Corp.
1995 Broadway
New York, NY 10023
(212) 724-9505
and
P.O. Box 7680
Lagos, Nigeria

Commercial publishing house
  • Publishes contemporary novels, poetry, plays and literary and social commentary by black American and African writers

12.123
Three Continents Press, Inc.
1346 Connecticut Ave. NW, Suite 1131
Washington, DC 20036
(202) 457-0288 or 387-5809

Commercial publishing house
  • Publishes books by and about contemporary African writers and writing along with a few historical, reference and sociological titles

13
Asian and Pacific Area Studies

Area Studies Programs and Research Centers

13.001
Pacific Rim Studies
Alaska Pacific University
4101 University Drive
Anchorage, AK 99508
(907) 561-1266

Contact(s):
Govind Naidu, Coordinator

Undergraduate area studies program
  • Majors/degrees/certificates   offered:
B.A. in Pacific Rim Studies

• Number of courses available—area: 19; language: 11

• Countries covered and areas of emphasis: countries and peoples of the North Pacific Rim; emphasizes Eskimo, Japanese, Chinese and Korean societies as they relate to the U.S.

• Languages offered: Yup'ik, Tlingit, Chinese, Japanese and Russian

• Study abroad available in Japan and Korea

13.002
Center for Asian Studies
Arizona State University
Social Science Bldg., Room 100
Tempe, AZ 85281
(602) 965-7184

Contact(s):
Sheldon W. Simon, Director

Graduate and undergraduate area studies program established in 1966

• Majors/degrees/certificates offered: B.A. with department major and Asian Studies emphasis or B.A. with major or minor in Asian Languages; M.A. and Ph.D. with Asian Studies focus; M.A. in Education with Asian Studies Specialization

• Approximate number of faculty teaching area and language courses: 22

• Approximate number of courses available—area: 35; language: 14

• Average number of students per year specializing in area: 60

• Countries covered and areas of emphasis: countries of East, South and Southeast Asia with emphasis on Japan, China, India and Southeast Asia; particular strength in history and cultural and political studies

• Languages offered: Japanese and Chinese (Mandarin)

• Special collection of Asian materials, especially on China and Japan; Center in-

cludes Reading Room with periodicals and a small collection of books

• Publishes Occasional Papers series

13.003
Department of Oriental Studies
University of Arizona
Tucson, AZ 85721
(602) 626-1264

Contact(s):
William G. Dever, Head
Ruth Patzman, Outreach Coordinator, (602) 626-5463

• Offers B.A., M.A., and Ph.D. in Oriental Studies with specialization in China, Japan, India-Pakistan, the Middle East (in cooperation with the Near East Center, see 17.001), Judaic Studies, general Oriental Studies, Japanese Area Studies (see 18.269) and Chinese Area Studies (see 18.069); includes East Asia Center with active school outreach program

13.004
American University of Oriental Studies
2835 W. Olympic Blvd.
Los Angeles, CA 90006
(213) 487-1235

Contact(s):
Leo M. Pruden, President

Graduate and undergraduate institution established in 1973

• Majors/degrees/certificates offered: B.A. in Asian Studies and Buddhist Ministerial Education; M.A. and Ph.D. programs in Buddhist Studies, Religious Studies, Comparative Religion, East-West Philosophy, East-West Psychology and Asian Studies

• Approximate number of faculty teaching area and language courses: 78

• Approximate number of courses available—area: 320; language: 45

• Average number of part- and full-time students per year: 46

• Countries covered and areas of emphasis: all countries of Asia with emphasis on those where Buddhism is strong

• Languages offered: Chinese, Japanese, Vietnamese, Korean, Sanskrit, Pali, Tibetan, Hindi and Thai

• University library contains 20,000 volumes on Oriental Studies, including extensive collections in Asian philosophy, Buddhist and other religious writings, and literature in Oriental languages

• Students and faculty exchange programs available with colleges and universities in Japan, Taiwan, Hong Kong and India; a year abroad may be arranged at an academic institution or a monastery

13.005

California Institute of Integral Studies
3491 21st St.
San Francisco, CA 94110
(415) 648-1489

Contact(s):
John Broomfield, President

Accredited, degree-granting graduate school (formerly The California Institute for Asian Studies) established in 1968

• Majors/degrees/certificates offered: M.A. in Social and Cultural Anthropology; M.A. and Ph.D. in Psychology (counseling East-West and Clinical); M.A. and Ph.D. in Intercultural Philosophy and Religion

• Approximate number of faculty; 33 (plus visiting faculty and workshop leaders)

• Approximate number of courses available: 160

• Average number of students per year; full-time 117; part-time 97

• Areas of emphasis: cross-cultural studies, the examination of Asian cultures and Eastern philosophies and personal self-integration

13.006

Asian Studies Program
California State University at Fresno
Mathematics Department
Fresno, CA 93740
(209) 294-3026

Contact(s):
Hugo S. Sun, Director

Graduate and undergraduate area studies program established in 1968

• Majors/degrees/certificates offered: B.A. and M.A. minor and special major in cooperation with other departments

• Approximate number of faculty teaching area and language courses: 15

• Approximate number of courses available—area: 5; language: 6

• Average number of students per year specializing in area: 5 graduate; 10 undergraduate

• Countries covered and areas of emphasis: particular emphasis on the Far East

• Languages offered: Chinese and Japanese

13.007

Asian Studies Program
California State University at Long Beach
Long Beach, CA 90840
(213) 498-4141

Contact(s):
Sudershan Chawla, Director

Graduate, undergraduate and nondegree area studies program

• Majors/degrees/certificates offered: B.A. and M.A. in Asian Studies and Certificate in Asian Studies or Japanese Studies

• Approximate number of faculty teaching area and language courses: 20

• Approximate number of courses available—area: 69; language: 12

• Countries covered and areas of em-

phasis: all countries of Asia with emphasis on China, India, Japan and Asian-Americans; strong in cultural studies and philosophy
• Languages offered: Chinese, Japanese, Sanskrit and Pali

13.008
Asian Studies Program
The Claremont Colleges/Pomona College
Pearsons Hall
Claremont, CA 91711
(714) 621-8000, ext. 2920

Contact(s):
Herbert B. Smith, Coordinator

Undergraduate area studies program
• Majors/degrees/certificates offered: B.A. in Asian Studies
• Approximate number of faculty teaching area and language courses: 18
• Approximate number of courses available—area: 38; language: 9
• Average number of students per year specializing in area: 5
• Countries covered and areas of emphasis: all countries of East, Southeast and South Asia; with emphasis on Southeast Asia, particularly Thailand
• Languages offered: Chinese and Japanese; Arabic, Hindu-Urdu, Malay-Indonesian, Sanskrit and Thai offered as needed

13.009
Asian Studies
Occidental College
Los Angeles, CA 90041
(213) 259-2581

Contact(s):
Wellington K. K. Chan, Chair

Undergraduate area studies program
• Majors/degrees/certificates offered: B.A. in major with Asian Studies emphasis

• Countries covered and areas of emphasis: countries of East Asia and India with particular strength in the art, history and culture of Japan
• Language offered: Japanese at all levels
• Study abroad available in Japan
• Limited number of international study abroad fellowships awarded

13.010
Center for Asian Studies
San Diego State University
San Diego, CA 92182-0037
(619) 265-5977

Contact(s):
Paochin Chu, Director

Graduate and undergraduate area studies program established in 1965
• Majors/degrees/certificates offered: B.A. and M.A. in Asian Studies
• Approximate number of faculty teaching area and language courses: 32
• Approximate number of courses available—area: 46; language: 14
• Countries covered and areas of emphasis: all areas of Asia with emphasis on history and the social sciences; particular strength in Japan, China and India
• Languages offered: Chinese and Japanese
• Library contains Asian collection of approximately 10,000 titles with emphasis on East-Asian languages
• Study abroad available in China and Japan

13.011
Center for East Asian Studies
Stanford University
Room 200, Lou Henry Hoover Bldg.
Stanford, CA 94305
(415) 497-3362

Contact(s):
Albert Dien, Director

Graduate and undergraduate area studies program established in 1962
• Majors/degrees/certificates offered: B.A. and M.A. in East Asian Studies; A.M. in East Asian Studies and Secondary School Teaching (with Stanford Teacher Education Program); M.A. in East Asian Studies and J.D. (with Stanford School of Law); Ph.D. specialization in the disciplines and in Schools of Law, Education and Business
• Approximate number of faculty teaching area and language courses: 53
• Approximate number of courses available—area: 123; language: 50
• Average number of students per year specializing in area: 250
• Countries covered and areas of emphasis: China, Japan; strong co-curricular program of colloquia, student-faculty workshops, etc.
• Languages offered: Chinese, Japanese; includes program of Advanced Language Maintenance through structured conversation and the viewing of videotapes
• Extensive collection of primary and secondary source materials in Chinese and Japanese, as well as secondary materials in Western languages at the Hoover Institution and in the University libraries; access to library resources of the University of California at Berkeley is available through the Joint East Asian Center; students may also enroll in courses at Berkeley which are not available at Stanford
• Affiliated with Inter-University Programs for intensive advanced language training in Japan (Tokyo, see 18.277) and Taiwan (Taipei, see 18.469) for graduate and undergraduate students; other overseas study arrangements available, including Volunteers in Asia (see 8.051) which sends students to Asian countries to teach English
• Affiliated with U.S.-China Relations program which promotes scholarly exchange

with the PRC, sponsors research and publishes studies and reports, especially in science and technology in the PRC
• Supports outreach projects on China and Japan of the Stanford Program in Cross-Cultural Education (SPICE, see 2.061)

13.012
Center for South and Southeast Asia Studies
University of California at Berkeley
260 Stephens Hall
Berkeley, CA 94720
(415) 642-3608

Contact(s):
Jyotirindra Das Gupta, Director

• Supports faculty research on all aspects of South and Southeast Asian life and culture and joins in the sponsorship of the degree programs of the Group in Asian Studies (see 13.013); conducts extensive outreach program with schools and community organizations; publishes Occasional Papers series

13.013
Group in Asian Studies
University of California at Berkeley
460 Stevens Hall
Berkeley, CA 94720
(415) 642-0333

Contact(s):
Herbert P. Phillips, Director

Graduate and undergraduate area studies program established in 1946
• Majors/degrees/certificates offered: B.A. in Asian Studies with specialization in China, Japan, Korea, South or Southeast Asia; M.A. degree with specialization in China, Japan and Korea, South Asia and Southeast Asia; Ph.D. in Asian Studies (restricted); joint master's degree program with the School of

Journalism; concurrent programs with the Schools of Law, Business Administration and Education pending

• Approximate number of faculty teaching area and language courses: 85

• Approximate number of courses available—area: 100; language: 50

• Average number of students per year specializing in area: 49

• Countries covered and areas of emphasis: all countries of East Asia, Northeast Asia, South and Southeast Asia (see also 13.012)

• Languages offered: Japanese, Chinese, Altaic, Korean, Indonesian-Malay, Sanskrit, Tamil, Hindi-Urdu, Thai, Tibetan; intensive summer language institute held periodically

• University libraries include East Asiatic Library with 320,000 volumes and 1,800 periodicals; a research library of materials on contemporary China, especially strong in the humanities and social sciences, consisting of 20,000 volumes and 114 periodicals; and the South and Southeast Asia Library of 75,000 volumes and 1,000 periodicals supplemented by a special collection of 1,500 monographs and 90 periodicals

• Overseas study in a year-long program at the Chinese University in Hong Kong is available through the University of California Education Abroad Program (see 8.012); program of graduate studies at Beijing University, PRC, available through Center for Chinese Studies (see 18.070)

• A Joint NDEA East Asian Languages and Area Center provides students and faculty at Stanford and Berkeley access to the resources of both universities

13.014
Institute of East Asian Studies
University of California at Berkeley
460 Stephens Hall
Berkeley, CA 94720
(415) 642-2809

Contact(s):
Robert A. Scalapino, Director

An academically-based research center established in 1978 to provide a focus for East Asian research and interdisciplinary teaching at Berkeley; the Institute brings together major research programs on campus, including the Centers for Chinese (see 18.070), Japanese (see 18.270) and Korean (see 18.307) Studies, the Stanford-Berkeley East Asian National Resource Center, and the Group in Asian Studies (see 0000), emphasizing comparative analysis of the traditional political and social systems and culture of all three countries

• Sponsors and provides financial support for graduate and postdoctoral research on East Asia by Berkeley faculty and graduate students; brings scholars from elsewhere in the U.S. and abroad to do research at Berkeley under the Institute Research Associate Program

• Conducts student-faculty interdisciplinary research colloquia series and sponsors lectures by visiting research scholars

• Publishes three monograph series that cover China, Japan and Korea, with emphasis in history and politics, and a Research Paper and Policy Studies series designed for shorter manuscripts discussing current issues and problems

13.015
East Asian Studies
University of California at Davis
Department of Anthropology
Davis, CA 95616

Contact(s):
D. A. Gibbs, Chair, Curriculum Committee (undergraduate) 916-752-1209
K. C. Liu, Director, Programs for the Study of East Asian Culture (graduate) 916-752-1640

Graduate and undergraduate area studies program established in 1970
- Majors/degrees/certificates offered: B.A. in East Asian Studies; M.A. and Ph.D. with concentration in East Asian culture
- Approximate number of faculty teaching area and language courses: 16
- Approximate number of courses available—area: 50; language: 20
- Average number of students per year specializing in area: 15
- Countries covered and areas of emphasis: China and Japan; emphasis on history and culture
- Languages offered: Chinese and Japanese
- Library contains a 45,000-volume Oriental Languages Research Collection
- University of California Education Abroad Program (see 8.012) offers overseas study opportunities in Japan, China, Hong Kong

13.016
Asian Studies
University of California at Santa Barbara
Santa Barbara, CA 93106
(805) 961-2794

Contact(s):
Robert L. Backus, Chair, Committee on Asian Studies

Graduate and undergraduate area studies program established in 1968
- Majors/degrees/certificates offered: B.A. and M.A. in Asian Studies
- Approximate number of faculty teaching area and language courses: 23
- Approximate number of courses available—area: 60; language: 29
- Average number of students per year specializing in area: 20
- Countries covered and areas of emphasis: all countries of Asia with emphasis on China and Japan and Asian religion and philosophy

- Languages offered: Chinese and Japanese at all levels

13.017
East Asia Studies Center
University of California, Los Angeles
405 Hilgard Ave.
Los Angeles, CA 90024
(213) 825-4321

Contact(s):
Hans Baerwald, Director

Graduate and undergraduate area studies program; part of USC-UCLA Joint NDEA East Asia Studies Center
- Majors/degrees/certificates offered: B.A., M.A. and Ph.D. in East Asian Studies
- Countries covered and areas of emphasis: China, Japan and Korea, with strength in Chinese Studies
- Languages offered: Chinese, Japanese and Korean
- Oriental Library contains major collection of materials in East Asian languages and on East Asia in English and other languages
- Maintains outreach program of assistance to community organizations and schools in the development of resources for East Asian Studies programs
- Conducts faculty and student exchanges, seminars and joint research projects under agreements with five academic and scholarly institutions in China through the UCLA China Exchange Program
- Study abroad opportunities in Japan and South Korea

13.018
Center for South Pacific Studies
University of California at Santa Cruz
Santa Cruz, CA 95064
(408) 429-2191

Contact(s):
Bryan H. Farrell, Director

Undergraduate area studies program
   • Majors/degrees/certificates   offered: B.A. in departments with specialization in South Pacific Studies
   • Countries covered and areas of emphasis: Australia, New Zealand, Malaysia, Indonesia, the Philippines and the smaller Islands of the South Pacific with emphasis on comparative studies among the societies and environments
   • Library contains approximately 12,000 volumes related to the South Pacific
   • Publishes newsletter, monographs and other information

13.019
South and Southeast Asian Studies
University of California at Santa Cruz
Merrill College
Santa Cruz, CA 95064

Contact(s):
Shelly E. Errington, Director

Undergraduate area studies program
   • Majors/degrees/certificates   offered: B.A. in South or Southeast Asia Studies (individual major or specialization within a department)
   • Approximate number of faculty teaching area and language courses: 15
   • Countries covered and areas of emphasis: all countries of South and Southeast Asia with emphasis on the anthropological and ethnomusicalogical study of Indonesia and the history, culture and economics of India
   • Campus maintains a full Indonesian Gamelan ensemble
   • Students may teach English in Southeast Asia through the Volunteers-in-Asia Program (see 8.051), co-sponsored with Stanford University, or study in South or Southeast Asia through the Merrill College Field Program

13.020
East Asian Studies Center
University of Southern California
Von KleinSmid Center 213
University Park
Los Angeles, CA 90089-0044
(213) 743-5080

Contact(s):
Gordon M. Berger, Director

Graduate and undergraduate area studies program established in 1963
   • Majors/degrees/certificates   offered: B.A. in East Asian Studies; Undergraduate Certificate in East Asian Studies; and departmental M.A. and Ph.D. with Graduate Certificate in East Asian Studies
   • Approximate number of faculty teaching area and language courses: 33
   • Average number of courses available—area: 46; language: 55
   • Approximate number of students per year specializing in area: 65
   • Countries covered and areas of emphasis: Japan, China and Korea
   • Languages offered: Cantonese, Mandarin, Japanese and Korean
   • Study abroad available at Waseda University (Tokyo)
   • Headquarters for USC/UCLA Joint East Asian Studies Center

13.021
Asian Studies
Colorado State University
315 Aylesworth Hall
Fort Collins, CO 80523
(303) 491-7201

Contact(s):
William J. Griswold, Director

Undergraduate area studies program
   • Majors/degrees/certificates   offered: B.A. in department with Certificate in Asian Studies

• Approximate number of faculty teaching area and language courses: 16

• Approximate number of courses available—area: 23; language: 4

• Countries covered and areas of emphasis: all areas of Asia including the Middle East, with emphasis on history, culture, philosophy, and literature

• Language offered: Chinese

13.022
Asian Studies Program
University of Colorado
C.B. 331—Ketchum 128
Boulder, CO 80309
(303) 492-8406

Contact(s):
Rodney Taylor, China

Undergraduate area studies program

• Majors/degrees/certificates offered: B.A. in Asian Studies

• Approximate number of courses available—area: 45; language: 20

• Average number of students per year specializing in area: 40

• Countries covered and areas of emphasis: Japan, China, India, Pakistan, Sri Lanka with emphasis on China and Japan; particular strength in art, history, and religion

• Languages offered: Chinese and Japanese

• Special collection of books and materials on Japanese law in Japanese; slide and film collections

• Offers study abroad programs in Taiwan and Kobe, Japan

13.023
East Asian Studies
Central Connecticut State University
Department of History
1615 Stanley St.
New Britain, CT 06050
(203) 827-7447

Contact(s):
Richard A. Williams, Chair, International and Area Studies Committee

Graduate and undergraduate area studies program

• Majors/degrees/certificates offered: B.A. and M.S. available to liberal arts students or in-service teachers

• Approximate number of courses available—area: 22

• Countries covered and areas of emphasis: China, Japan and Korea

13.024
Asian Studies Program
Connecticut College
New London, CT 06320
(203) 447-1911

Contact(s):
Thomas R. H. Havens, Director

Undergraduate area studies program

• Majors/degrees/certificates offered: B.A. in Asian Studies

• Approximate number of courses available—area: 48; language: 14

• Countries covered and areas of emphasis: China, India and Japan

• Languages offered: Chinese and Japanese

• Study abroad available in Taipei, Beijing, and in Kyoto, Japan, through the Associated Kyoto Program

13.025
East Asian Studies Program
University of Connecticut
Wood Hall 208
Storrs, CT 06268
(203) 486-3351

Contact(s):
Herman Mast, Director

• Offers B.A. in East Asian Studies via individualized undergraduate major; offers Chinese, Japanese, Korean and Vietnamese through critical and self-instructional language programs

13.026
East Asian Studies Program
Wesleyan University
Department of Asian Languages and
    Literatures
Middletown, CT 06457
(203) 347-9411

Contact(s):
Anthony H. Chambers and Vera Schwarcz,
    Co-Chairs

Undergraduate area studies program
• Majors/degrees/certificates offered: B.A. in East Asian Studies
• Approximate number of faculty teaching area and language courses: 12
• Approximate number of courses available—area: 32; language: 9
• Average number of students per year specializing in area: 30
• Countries covered and areas of emphasis: China and Japan with emphasis on language, history, art, literature and religion
• Languages offered: Chinese and Japanese
• Overseas study opportunities available in Kyoto, Japan, and at sites in Taiwan or the PRC

13.027
Council on East Asian Studies
Yale University
Box 13A Yale Station
New Haven, CT 06520
(203) 432-4029

Contact(s):
Edwin McClellan, Chair
Stanley Weinstein, Outreach Director

Graduate and undergraduate area studies program
• Majors/degrees/certificates offered: B.A. and M.A. in East Asian Studies, Ph.D. specialization in East Asian Studies (all with emphasis on either Japanese or Chinese language and area studies)
• Approximate number of faculty teaching area and language courses: 41
• Approximate number of courses available—area: 28; language: 25
• Average number of students per year specializing in area: 140
• Countries covered and areas of emphasis: China and Japan
• Languages offered: Chinese and Japanese
• Extensive holdings on China and Japan in English and other Western languages, plus Chinese language (234,000 volumes) and Japanese language (134,000 volumes) holdings and other specialized collections
• Language study programs available at Inter-University Centers in Taiwan (see 18.469) and Japan (Tokyo, see 18.277)
• Yale Outreach Program in East Asian Studies provides Speakers Bureau, Resource Center, and teacher workshops to schools and communities in New England

13.028
Council on Southeast Asia Studies
Yale University
Box 13A Yale Station
New Haven, CT 06520
(203) 436-8897

Contact(s):
James C. Scott, Chair

• Advises on graduate study of Southeast Asia, conducts seminars, promotes research and produces a series of scholarly publications on Southeast Asia; library contains major Southeast Asian collection

13.029
Center for Asian Studies
The American University
School of International Service
Washington, DC 20016
(202) 686-2392 or 2470

Contact(s):
Llewellyn D. Howell, Director

Graduate and undergraduate area studies program established in 1971
• Majors/degrees/certificates offered: M.A. and Ph.D. with major in East and Southeast Asian Studies from School of International Service, several departments and the International Education Program of the School of Education (see 6.089); B.A. and M.A. with Certificate in Asian Studies
• Approximate number of faculty teaching area and language courses: 20
• Approximate number of courses available—area: 35; language: 6
• Average number of students per year specializing in area: graduate, 10; undergraduate, 20
• Countries covered and areas of emphasis: all countries of Asia; particular strength in East and Southeast Asian Studies
• Languages offered: Chinese and Hindi
• Scholarly resources include the Institute of Vaishna Studies (which photographs and makes microfiche copies of endangered Vaishna manuscripts in India)

13.030
Institute for Sino-Soviet Studies
George Washington University
School of Public and International Affairs
Washington, DC 20052
(202) 676-6340

Contact(s):
Gaston J. Sigur, Director

• Coordinates research and graduate programs in Russian-Soviet, East European and East Asian affairs, including an M.A. program in the School of Public and International Affairs and Ph.D. programs offered under the Graduate School of Arts and Sciences which emphasize the Russian, Chinese and Japanese languages with extensive coursework available on East Asian and East European subjects
• Sponsors Soviet faculty research colloquia series
• Maintains specialized research library which has large collection of current Russian and Chinese periodical literature; resources available to visiting faculty

13.031
Asian Studies
The Johns Hopkins University
School of Advanced International Studies
1740 Massachusetts Ave. NW
Washington, DC 20036
(202) 785-6267

Contact(s):
Nathaniel Bowman Thayer, Director

Graduate area studies program established in 1943
• Majors/degrees/certificates offered: M.A. and Ph.D. in International Relations with major in Asian Studies
• Approximate number of faculty teaching area and language courses: 2 full-time plus part-time and visiting faculty
• Approximate number of courses available—area: 16; language: 12
• Average number of students per year specializing in area: M.A. 30; Ph.D. 5
• Countries covered and areas of emphasis: all countries of East, South and Southeast Asia with emphasis on China and Japan (students interested in Japan may include special comparative political studies in the Advanced Industrial Societies Program)
• Languages offered: Chinese and Japanese (3 levels each plus summer program)

• Draws on library, organizational and research resources of the Washington area

• Special internships and fellowships available

13.032
Asian Studies Program
Florida State University
Tallahassee, FL 32306
(904) 644-5832

Contact(s):
Leon Golden, Director

Undergraduate area studies program

• Majors/degrees/certificates offered: B.A. (including business co-major) and M.A. in Asian Studies and Ph.D. in Humanities with concentration in Asian Studies

• Countries covered and areas of emphasis: all countries of Asia with emphasis on China, Japan and India and the arts and humanities

13.033
Asian Studies
University of Florida
402-404 W.W. Little Hall
Gainesville, FL 32611
(904) 392-1581

Contact(s):
Irmgard Johnson, Director

Undergraduate area studies program established in 1973

• Majors/degrees/certificates offered: B.A. and Certificate in Asian Studies

• Approximate number of faculty teaching area and language courses: 15

• Approximate number of courses available—area: 38; language: 9

• Average number of students per year specializing in area: 16 majors; 8 certificate

• Countries covered and areas of emphasis: all of Asia with emphasis on East Asia (China and Japan) and India

• Languages offered: Chinese and Japanese

13.034
The Institute for Polynesian Studies
Brigham Young University
Hawaii Campus
Laie, HI 96762
(808) 293-3665

Contact(s):
Jerry K. Loveland, Director

• Sponsors research on various aspects of Polynesian culture and publishes reports, monographs and a journal, *Pacific Studies*

13.035
East-West Center
1777 East-West Road
Honolulu, HI 96848
(808) 944-7111

Contact(s):
Victor Hoo Li, President

Research, training and education exchange center established by the U.S. government in 1960; supported by the U.S. with assistance from 20 other Asian and Pacific governments

• Undertakes study projects supervised or conducted by staff researchers in the areas of population, natural resources, culture, communication and the environment, especially as they relate to the U.S., the nations of Asia and the Pacific and relationships among them

• Consists of five institutes: the Communication Institute, the Culture Learning Institute, the Environment and Policy Institute, the Population Institute and the Resource Systems Institute

• Offers research, training, residential facilities and financial assistance to U.S., Asian and Pacific Islands visiting fellows and scholars (principally academics in residence for longer periods), University of Hawaii graduate students, doctoral interns, and professional associates (principally nonacademics for shorter periods); participant ratio is one American to two from Asia and the Pacific; awards and grants made primarily within context of one of the institutes, except for the Open Grants program which provides awards and grants to a small number of research fellows to join in interdisciplinary research projects focused on broad global themes, and to students working in a wide variety of disciplines from many different cultures; an Open Grant program supplements formal study with cross-cultural, multidisciplinary learning experiences in seminars, community service, institute projects and field research

• Conducts Pacific Islands Development Program to mount research and education projects aimed at meeting specific needs of Pacific Island countries and cultures

• Publishes (along with the University of Hawaii Press (see 13.195) and Pergamon Press (see 1.124) extensive list of books, monographs, periodicals, articles, educational materials, case studies and audiovisuals; includes publications resulting from the work of each of the Institutes, the Open Grants program and Center-wide publications; includes *East-West Center Programs*, a catalogue describing the types of awards offered by the Center and projects under way in each Institute and giving information on staff and fellows; other publications include a philosophy and culture series, The Chinese Mind, The Japanese Mind and The Indian Mind, and a number of other general books on the history and culture of Japan, China, Korea and India (most published by the University Press of Hawaii) as well as an extensive list on culture learning and cultural and educational interchange

Culture Learning Institute, Gregory Trifonovitch, Acting Director (808) 944-7666

• Conducts and sponsors research, conferences, workshops and training programs in the following areas: culture and the arts, cultural context of health, cultural and interpersonal interaction, and culture and language

• Provides awards to graduate students working simultaneously at the Institute and the University of Hawaii, to research interns for supervised practical training experience in specific Institute projects, to research fellows consisting of established scholars invited to join Institute researchers in specific research endeavors, and to professional associates made up of public officials, scholars and professionals who come to participate in workshops and conferences; in general, awards are made in a ratio of one to an American for each two awarded to a non-American.

• Publishes a general newsletter *EWCLI Report* and *Language Planning Newsletter* (which includes articles on public policy and planning issues worldwide relative to dealing with language diversity), and a number of books; also makes available articles from a series *Topics in Culture Learning* published annually by the Institute from 1973 to 1977 (many of the articles also appear in two volumes *Culture Learning: Concepts, Applications, and Research* and *Research in Culture Learning: Language and Conceptual Studies* published by the University of Hawaii Press

Communication Institute, Jack Lyle, Director (808) 944-7666

• Conducts research on communication policy and the planning needed to develop and implement it; emphasis on impact of media on traditional societies and the role of the media in the assimilation of international migrants; awards scholarships to University of Hawaii graduate students

Population Institute, Lee-Jay Cho, Director
(808) 944-7444

• Conducts research on population issues as they affect the countries and peoples of the Pacific Basin and the development of population policies; provides graduate student and professional training and development programs; publishes monographs and maintains a 12,000-volume library

13.036
Center for Asian and Pacific Studies
University of Hawaii at Manoa
Moore Hall 315
Honolulu, HI 96822
(808) 948-8543

Contact(s):
Stephen Uhalley, Jr., Acting Center
   Director and Director of the Asian
   Studies Program
Cynthia Ning, Outreach Coordinator

• Promotes the expansion of research and study on Asia and the Pacific, develops library and teaching resources, provides research fellowships and sponsors publications; administers Asian, Pacific Islands (see 13.037) and Philippine (see 18.406) Studies programs, and the Center for Korean Studies (see 18.308); sponsors extensive school and community outreach program, including curriculum development and teacher institutes and workshops
• Asian Studies Program offers the B.A. and M.A. in Asian Studies covering China, Japan and the countries of the Pacific Basin; languages offered: Chinese (Mandarin and Cantonese), Japanese and Korean

13.037
Pacific Islands Studies
University of Hawaii, Manoa
Center for Asian and Pacific Studies
215 Moore Hall
Honolulu, HI 96822
(808) 948-8439

Contact(s):
Robert C. Kiste, Director (808) 948-6393

Graduate area studies program established in 1950
• Major/degrees/certificates offered: M.A. in Pacific Island Studies and departmental M.A. or Ph.D. with Certificate in Pacific Islands Studies (undergraduates may earn B.A. in Liberal Studies/Pacific Islands Studies)
• Approximate number of faculty teaching area and language courses: 25
• Approximate number of courses available—area: 30; language: 16
• Average number of students per year specializing in area: 18
• Countries covered and areas of emphasis: smaller islands of the Pacific, especially those of Polynesia, Micronesia and Melanesia
• Languages offered: Hawaiian, Samoan and Tahitian
• Promotes research on Pacific Island Cultures, sponsors conferences and seminars and publishes a newsletter and occasional papers
• Maintains student exchange program with University of the South Pacific, Fiji

13.038
Asian Studies Program
Illinois College
Jacksonville, IL 62650
(217) 245-7126

Contact(s):
Laurence C. Judd, Coordinator and Chair

Undergraduate area studies program
• Majors/degrees/certificates offered: B.A. in International Studies with Asian concentration
• Approximate number of faculty teaching area and language courses: 7
• Approximate number of courses available—area: 15

• Countries covered and areas of emphasis: USSR, the Near East, Iran, Thailand, China, Korea, Japan, Vietnam, Kampuchea, Laos, Malaysia, Singapore, Indonesia, and Burma
• Special holdings on Thailand
• Conducts summer Southeast Asia study tour every three years
• Limited number of partial travel grants

13.039
Asian Studies
Mundelein College
6363 North Sheridan Road
Chicago, IL 60660
(312) 262-8100

Contact(s):
Ann Harrington, Coordinator

Undergraduate area studies program established in 1976
• Majors/degrees/certificates offered: B.A. in Asian Studies
• Approximate number of faculty teaching area and language courses: 11
• Approximate number of courses available—area: 19; language: 12
• Average number of students per year specializing in area: 2
• Countries covered and areas of emphasis: all countries of Asia with emphasis on East Asia and on history, religion, art and literature
• Languages offered: Chinese and Japanese

13.040
Center for Southeast Asian Studies
Northern Illinois University
Zulauf Hall 1015
DeKalb, IL 60115
(815) 753-1771

Contact(s):
Ronald Provencher, Director

Graduate and undergraduate area studies program established in 1963
• Majors/degrees/certificates offered: B.A. with minor in Southeast Asian Studies; M.A. with concentration in Southeast Asian Studies offered in a number of fields; Ph.D. with concentration in Southeast Asian Studies offered in English, political science, economics and psychology; M.S. and M.B.A. with Southeast Asian concentration; M.A. in English-TESOL with Southeast Asian concentration
• Approximate number of faculty teaching area and language courses: 20
• Approximate number of courses available—area: 10; language: 10
• Average number of students per year specializing in area: 60
• Countries covered and areas of emphasis: Thailand, Indonesia, Malaysia, Philippines, Laos, and Burma
• Languages offered: Thai, Indonesian, Lao and Javanese
• Library contains Southest Asian collection of 45,000 volumes in English and Southeast Asian languages, including 1,000 periodicals and 100 newspapers; other collections available in the Chicago area
• Overseas study opportunities available
• Conducts workshops for high school teachers and assists them in curriculum development
• Publishes *Special Reports* and *Occasional Papers* (consisting of scholarly monographs), *Crossroad: An Interdisciplinary Journal of Southeast Asian Studies*, and an annual newsletter

13.041
Asian Studies
Northwestern University
Harris Hall 207A
Evanston, IL 60201
(312) 492-3408

Contact(s):
James E. Sheridan, Chair

Undergraduate area studies program
- Major/degrees/certificates offered: B.A. with major or Certificate in Asian Studies
- Approximate number of faculty teaching area and language courses: 16
- Approximate number of courses available—area: 40; language: 15
- Countries covered and areas of emphasis: all of Asia including the Middle East; particularly strong in Japan, China and India, history and the humanities, and Asian religions, especially Buddhism
- Languages offered: Arabic, Chinese, Hebrew, Japanese and Pali
- Extensive library collection of Asian materials and access to resources of Chicago area (the Art Institute, the Oriental Institute and the Field Museum)
- Overseas study encouraged; opportunities include junior year in one of a number of programs in Asia, a year at Fudan University (Shanghai, China) and application for a Richter International Scholarship permitting independent study and travel abroad

13.042
Center for Far Eastern Studies
University of Chicago
Chicago, IL 60637
(312) 753-1234

- Offers B.A. in East Asian Studies

13.043
South Asia Language and Area Center
University of Chicago
1130 East 59th St.
Chicago, IL 60637
(312) 753-4350

Contact(s):
Edward C. Dimock, Jr., Director

- Offers B.A., M.A. and Ph.D. in South Asian Language and Area Studies

13.044
Center for Asian Studies
University of Illinois at Urbana-Champaign
1208 West California Ave., Room 201
Urbana, IL 61801
(217) 333-4850

Contact(s):
Peter Schran, Director

Graduate and undergraduate area studies program established in 1965
- Majors/degrees/certificates offered: B.A. in Asian Studies (with specialization in language and area studies of a single area; language, literature or cross-cultural studies); M.A. with regional concentrations in East, Southeast, South or West Asia (the Middle East); Ph.D. in departments with Asian specialization
- Approximate number of faculty teaching area and language courses: 61
- Approximate number of courses available—area: 124; language: 80
- Countries covered and areas of emphasis: all countries of Asia including West Asia (the Middle East); particularly strong in the Chinese and Japanese languages and in history and the social sciences; includes East Asian Center
- Languages offered: Arabic, Burmese, Chinese, Hebrew, Hindi/Urdu, Indonesian, Japanese, Korean, Persian, Sanskrit, Thai and Turkish
- Asian library contains 200,000 volumes in Asian languages with additional resources in the Unit for Cinema Studies (films on Asia)
- Operates study year abroad program in Japan (Konan University of Kobe), student and faculty exchange program with Fudan University in Shanghai, Peking University in Beijing (PRC), and Osmania University in Hyderabad, India
- Publishes a series of working papers, *Illinois Papers on Asian Studies*, and a useful school outreach newsletter, *Update* (see 2.206)

13.045
East Asian Studies Center
Indiana University at Bloomington
Goodbody Hall, Room 346
Bloomington, IN 47405
(812) 337-3765

Contact(s):
Philip West, Director
Linda Wojtan, Outreach Coordinator

Graduate and undergraduate area studies program
  • Majors/degrees/certificates offered: B.A., M.A. and Ph.D. in East Asian Studies and M.A. and Ph.D. in Chinese/Japanese Language and Literature; undergraduate Certificate in East Asian Studies
  • Approximate number of faculty teaching area and language courses: 58
  • Approximate number of courses available—area: 75; language: 35
  • Countries covered and areas of emphasis: East Asia with emphasis on China and Japan, especially language and literature
  • Languages offered: Chinese, Japanese, and Korean
  • Sponsors research including current project on ethnicity in China
  • Library contains approximately 110,000 volumes in East Asian Languages, 160,000 volumes on East Asia in other languages along with a variety of current periodicals
  • Conducts extensive outreach program including a newsletter on teaching resources (distributed nationally three times per year with *News and Notes of the Social Sciences),* prepares and distributes handouts to meet teacher needs, sponsors and participates in workshops and conferences and publishes *Free Resources for Teaching about Japan* (1979; revised edition available January, 1985; free)
  • Study abroad offered in Japan and Hong Kong

13.046
Inner Asian and Uralic National Resource Center
Indiana University at Bloomington
Goodbody Hall 101
Bloomington, IN 47405
(812) 335-2398

Contact(s):
Denis Sinor, Director
(812) 335-0954

Academic Area Studies program focusing on the Uralic and Altaic languages and cultures of Eastern Europe and Inner Asia (see 14.012), including those of Mongolia and Tibet

13.047
Research Institute for Inner Asian Studies
Indiana University at Bloomington
Goodbody Hall 344
Bloomington, IN 47405
(812) 335-1605

Contact(s):
Stephen Halkovic, Jr., Director

Research center focusing on portions of China (Sinkiang, Tibet, Inner Mongolia), the Mongolian People's Republic, Afghanistan, Iran and the Turkic-speaking republics of the USSR
  • Conducts and sponsors research, provides research fellowships, and, in cooperation with the Inner Asian and Uralic National Resource Center (see 14.012), offers internships and in-service institutes for college and high school teachers
  • Extensive research resources available in the Institute Library, especially the Antoinette Gordon Collection of Tibetan Art and the Central Asian Archives
  • Publishes *Inner Asia: The Peoples of the Steppe* (teaching techniques and materi-

als for use with readings; for high school students) and other college and high school teaching aids; also responsible for the Indiana University Uralic and Altaic series (monographs), the *Journal of Asian History, Bulletin of the Turkish Studies Association* (see 18.492) and Papers on Contemporary Asia
• Sponsors Mongolian, Turkish, and Turkic Studies programs and co-sponsors long-term research project on ethnicity in China

13.048
Asian Studies Program
University of Iowa
Asian Languages and Literature
314 Gilmore Hall
Iowa City, IA 52242
(319) 353-4262

Contact(s):
W. South Coblin, Acting Chair

Graduate and undergraduate area studies program
• Majors/degrees/certificates   offered: B.A. in Asian Studies and M.A. in Asian Civilization
• Approximate number of faculty teaching area and language courses: 7
• Approximate number of courses available—area: 84; language: 15
• Average number of students per year specializing in area: 40–50
• Countries covered and areas of emphasis: China, Japan and India with emphasis on language and cultural studies
• Languages offered: Mandarin, Japanese and Sanskrit
• Oriental Collection in University library contains 50,000 volumes
• Asian Studies Information Assistance Office provides aid to school, business, and community groups; includes library of audiovisual materials available on loan

13.049
South Asia Center
Kansas State University
Eisenhower Hall, Room 22
Manhattan, KS 66506
(913) 532-5738

Contact(s):
William L. Richter, Director

Graduate and undergraduate area studies program established in 1967
• Majors/degrees/certificates   offered: secondary major in South Asian Studies
• Approximate number of courses available—area: 8–10; language: 4
• Countries covered and areas of emphasis: India, Pakistan, Bangladesh, Afghanistan, Nepal, Bhutan and Sri Lanka (in approximate order of emphasis)
• Languages offered: Urdu and Hindi
• Extensive collection of audiovisual materials in South Asia Media Center available nationwide
• Overseas study opportunities by arrangement with programs at other institutions
• Conducts summer institutes and workshops for college, elementary and secondary school teachers
• Publishes *South Asia Media Catalog* (of materials in the Center) and an offprint series by Center faculty

13.050
Center for East Asian Studies
University of Kansas
105 Lippincott Hall
Lawrence, KS 66045
(913) 864-3849

Contact(s):
Daniel H. Bays, Director

Graduate and undergraduate area studies program

• Majors/degrees/certificates offered: B.A. and M.A. in Chinese Language and Literature, Japanese Language and Literature or East Asian Cultures; Ph.D. in discipline with East Asian emphasis
• Approximate number of courses available—area and language: 50
• Countries covered and areas of emphasis: China, Japan and Korea; emphasis on cultural studies
• Languages offered: Chinese, Japanese and Korean, including intensive summer courses in Chinese and Japanese
• Library contains about 80,000 volumes in East Asian languages plus a large collection on East Asia in Western languages; Spencer Museum on campus contains extensive collection of Chinese and Japanese art; Nelson Gallery in Kansas City also has major collection of Asian art
• Overseas study opportunities available in the PRC, Japan, Korea and Taiwan
• Conducts workshops and other programs for high school teachers and the community
• Publishes a monograph series on East Asian subjects

13.051
Asian Studies Program
Grambling State University
P.O. Box 368
Grambling, LA 71245
(318) 247-6941, Ext. 310

Contact(s):
Yawsoon Sim, Director

Undergraduate area studies program
• Majors/degrees/certificates offered: Certificate in Asian Studies
• Approximate number of faculty teaching area and language courses: 5
• Approximate number of courses available—area: 12

• Average number of students per year specializing in area: 2–5
• Countries covered and areas of emphasis: China and Japan
• Special library collection on Japan

13.052
East Asian Studies
Colby College
Waterville, ME 04901
(207) 873-1131

Contact(s):
Lee Feigon, Director

Undergraduate area studies program established in 1963
• Majors/degrees/certificates offered: B.A. in East Asian Studies
• Approximate number of faculty teaching area and language courses: 7
• Approximate number of courses available—area: 20; language: 10
• Average number of students per year specializing in area: 25
• Countries covered and areas of emphasis: China and Japan
• Languages offered: Chinese and Japanese
• Study abroad opportunities available in Japan, Hong Kong, Taiwan and China (PRC)

13.053
Asian Studies Program
Amherst College
Amherst, MA 01002
(413) 542-2486

Contact(s):
Jerry Dennerline, Chair

• Offers B.A. in Asian Studies with emphasis on Japan, China and South Asia; languages offered: Japanese and Chinese; study abroad available in Japan through Associated Kyoto Program

• Conducts faculty exchange with Doshisha University in Japan

13.054
East Asia Programs
Harvard University
Council on East Asian Studies
1737 Cambridge St.
Cambridge, MA 02138

Contact(s):
Ezra F. Vogel, Chair, Standing Committee on Concentration in East Asian Studies (617) 495-4014; Joseph F. Fletcher, Jr., Chair, Standing Committee on the A.M. in Regional Studies—East Asia (617) 495-2754; and Benjamin I. Schwarz, Chair, Standing Committee on the Ph.D. in History and East Asian Languages (617) 495-4046

• Offers B.A. with concentration in East Asia; M.A. in Regional Studies—East Asia; and Ph.D. in History and East Asian Languages

13.055
Inner Asian and Altaic Studies
Harvard University
1737 Cambridge St.
Cambridge, MA 02138
(617) 495-1000

Contact(s):
Joseph F. Fletcher, Jr., Chair

• Offers M.A. and Ph.D. in Inner Asian and Altaic Studies; languages: Mongolian and Tibetan

13.056
John King Fairbank Center for East Asian Research
Harvard University
1737 Cambridge St.
Cambridge, MA 02138
(617) 495-4946

Contact(s):
Philip A. Kuhn, Director

Harvard University research unit
• Conducts research on the PRC, Korea and Vietnam, with emphasis on Chinese social, economic, political, cultural and historical studies; publishes *Harvard East Asian Series* and *Harvard East Asian Monographs*

13.057
Asian Studies
University of Massachusetts at Amherst
Department of Asian Languages and
　Literatures
14 Thompson Hall
Amherst, MA 01002
(413) 545-0349

Contact(s):
Tomiko Narahara, Advisor

Undergraduate area studies program
• Majors/degrees/certificates offered: B.A. in Japanese Language and Literature and Chinese Language and Literature and Certificate in Asian Studies
• Approximate number of faculty teaching area and language courses: 25
• Approximate number of courses available—area: 13; language: 23 (additional courses available through the Five Colleges Asian Studies Program, see 4.251)
• Countries covered and areas of emphasis: East, Southeast and South Asia with emphasis on Japanese and Chinese languages and literatures

• Languages offered: Japanese and Chinese at all levels
• Study abroad programs in the languages available in China, Japan and Taiwan

13.058
Asian Studies Program
Wheaton College
Norton, MA 02766
(617) 285-7722, Ext. 484

Contact(s):
Vipan Chandra, Coordinator

Undergraduate area studies program established in 1970–71
• Majors/degrees/certificates offered: B.A. in Asian Studies with specialization in the Middle East, South Asia, China or Japan
• Approximate number of faculty teaching area and language courses: 9
• Approximate number of courses available—area: 34; language: 8
• Average number of students per year specializing in area: 3 majors; 4 minors
• Countries covered and areas of emphasis: India, China, Japan and countries of the Middle East
• Languages offered: Chinese and Hebrew
• Study abroad available in Taiwan, China and Japan

13.059
Asian Studies Center
Michigan State University
Center for International Programs, Room 101
East Lansing, MI 48824
(517) 353-1680

Contact(s):
Warren I. Cohen, Director

• Promotes research and study on and in Asia, conducts programs related to Asia and assists in the development and expansion of MSU curriculum in all Asian areas and in most departments and disciplines; directs undergraduate Asian Studies Program in conjunction with departmental majors
• Publishes Occasional Papers series along with *Journal of South Asian Literature* and an Asian Studies newsletter
• Particular emphasis on China and Japan

13.060
East Asian Studies Program
Oakland University
Rochester, MI 48063

Contact(s):
Carlo Coppola, Chair (313) 377-2154
C. Franklin Sayre, Coordinator (313) 377-2060

Undergraduate area studies program established in 1981
• Majors/degrees/certificates offered: B.A. and minor in Chinese or Japanese Studies
• Approximate number of faculty teaching area and language courses: 10
• Approximate number of courses available—area: 29; language: 10
• Average number of students per year specializing in area: 5
• Countries covered and areas of emphasis: China and Japan, with emphasis on history and culture
• Languages offered: Chinese and Japanese
• Sponsors periodic summer study tours to China; study abroad in Japan available at Nanzan University (Nagoya)

13.061
South Asian Studies Program
Oakland University
Rochester, MI 48063
(313) 377-2154

Contact(s):
Carlo Coppola, Chair
Richard P. Tucker, Coordinator

Undergraduate area studies program
- Majors/degrees/certificates offered: B.A. and minor in South Asian Studies
- Approximate number of faculty teaching area and language courses: 7
- Approximate number of courses available—area: 17; language: 8
- Countries covered and areas of emphasis: all countries of South Asia (particularly India, Pakistan and Bangladesh) with emphasis on Indian culture and philosophy
- Languages offered: Hindi and Urdu

13.062
Center for South and Southeast Asian Studies
University of Michigan at Ann Arbor
130 Lane Hall
Ann Arbor, MI 48109
(313) 764-0352

Contact(s):
Karl L. Hutterer, Director, South and
   Southeast Asia

Graduate and undergraduate area studies program established in 1961
- Majors/degrees/certificates offered: B.A. and M.A. in Asian Studies with South and Southeast Asian subfield; dual-degree program M.B.A./M.A. in Asian Studies and Ph.D. in departments with Asian Studies specialization
- Approximate number of faculty teaching area and language courses: 40

- Approximate number of courses available—area: 47; language: 27
- Average number of students per year specializing in area: 100 graduate; 50 undergraduate
- Countries covered and areas of emphasis: all the countries of Southeast Asia plus India, Tibet, Nepal, Pakistan and Sri Lanka
- Languages offered: Burmese, Indonesian, Thai, Tagalog, Old Javanese (Kawi), Sanskrit, Pali, Tamil, Hindi-Urdu, Tibetan, Marathi, and Gujarati
- The Asia Library, South Asia and Southeast Asia Divisions of the Hatcher Graduate Library and other university library resources contain extensive South and Southeast Asia collections including holdings in Thai, Indonesian, Malay, Vietnamese, Hindi and other languages as well as materials on South and Southeast Asia in European languages; strength in such subjects as the Philippines during U.S. colonial period, general humanities and social sciences, family planning, and Hindu, Muslim and Indian law; also extensive materials on Southeast Asia in the Asian Art Archives (including 10,000 photos of architecture and sculpture with particular strength in Thai art) and the Museums of Art and Anthropology
- Publishes extensive list of monographs, reference works and anthologies under three series: Michigan Series in South and Southeast Asian Languages and Linguistics, Michigan Papers on South and Southeast Asia and Special Publications
- Conducts Outreach Program for community and schools through a Resource Center which lends books, curriculum materials and audiovisuals; maintains a regular Speakers Bureau

13.063
Asian Studies Program
Western Michigan University
2090 Friedmann
Kalamazoo, MI 49008
(616) 383-1707

Contact(s):
Alfred Ho, Chair

Undergraduate area studies program
• Majors/degrees/certificates offered: Coordinate B.A. (combined with departmental major) in Asian Studies
• Countries covered and areas of emphasis: all countries of Asia with emphasis on East Asia; focus on cultural, political, social and economic history

13.064
Asian Studies Committee
Carleton College
Northfield, MN 55057
(507) 663-5115

Contact(s):
James F. Fisher, Associate Professor of
Anthropology

Undergraduate area studies program established in 1964
• Majors/degrees/certificates offered: B.A. with major in Asian Studies; major in any other department with a concentration in either South Asian or East Asian Studies
• Approximate number of faculty teaching area and language courses: 12
• Approximate number of courses available—area: 30; language: 7
• Average number of students per year specializing in area: 20
• Countries covered and areas of emphasis: East and South Asia with an emphasis on China, Japan, India, Nepal and Sri Lanka; particular strength in religious studies
• Languages offered: Japanese, Marathi and Chinese (at St. Olaf College)
• Special collection of films and slides on Asian subjects
• Member of Midwest China Center; study abroad available in India, Japan (Tokyo and Kyoto), Hong Kong, Taiwan, the PRC, and Sri Lanka, principally through the Associated Colleges of the Midwest (see 8.003)

13.065
East Asian Studies
University of Minnesota
113 Folwell Hall
9 Pleasant St. S.E.
Minneapolis, MN 55455
(612) 373-2564

Graduate and undergraduate area studies program
• Majors/degrees/certificates offered: B.A., M.A. and Ph.D. in Japanese, Chinese and East Asian Studies
• Countries covered and areas of emphasis: China, Japan, Korea and Vietnam
• Languages offered: Chinese and Japanese
• Language and cultural study abroad available at universities and foreign study centers in Japan, Taiwan, Hong Kong and the PRC
• Library contains approximately 85,000 volumes in Chinese and Japanese languages along with a variety of other holdings on East Asia

13.066
South Asian Center
University of Minnesota
192 Klaeber Court
320 16th Ave. SE
Minneapolis, MN 55455
(612) 373-9834

Contact(s):
Frederick M. Asher, Chair

Graduate and undergraduate area studies program established in 1966
• Majors/degrees/certificates offered: B.A. (with three options: Language and Literature, Civilization, and Contemporary Problems), M.A. and Ph.D. in South Asian Studies
• Approximate number of faculty teaching area and language courses: 15

• Approximate number of courses available—area: 51; language: 39

• Average number of students per year specializing in area: 14 graduate; 7 undergraduate

• Countries covered and areas of emphasis: all countries of South Asia with particular strength in India, Pakistan and Iran

• Languages offered: Bengali, Urdu, Hindi, Sanskrit, Marathi, Persian and Arabic

• Extensive resources available in the Ames Library of South Asia (a large collection which regularly receives books, journals and newspapers from India, Pakistan, Sri Lanka and Nepal through PL 480), the Middle East Library, the private manuscript collection of M.A.R. Barker, the Learning Resources Center, the University Audio-Visual and Slide Library, and the department's own slide and film collection

• Outreach program serves schools and community with cultural events and learning resource assistance

13.067
South Asia Language and Area Center
University of Missouri, Columbia
125 GCB
Columbia, MO 65211
(314) 882-3065

Contact(s):
Bina Gupta, Director

Graduate and undergraduate area studies program established in 1965

• Majors/degrees/certificates offered: B.A. in South Asian Studies or adjunct to another degree; graduate concentration as part of another degree

• Approximate number of faculty teaching area and language courses: 14

• Approximate number of courses available—area: 13; language: 2

• Average number of students per year specializing in area: 1–2 graduate; 3 undergraduate

• Countries covered and areas of emphasis: India, Pakistan, Bangladesh, Sri Lanka and Nepal with special library and faculty resources for Punjabi studies

• Language offered: Hindi

• Invites external faculty to do research in regular and microfilm holdings on Punjab

• Collection of Gandharan sculpture in the Museum of Art and Archeology

13.068
Department of Chinese and Japanese/ Committee on Asian Studies
Washington University
St. Louis, MO 63130
(314) 889-5156

Contact(s):
Robert E. Morrell, Chair, Committee on Asian Studies
Robert E. Hegel, Acting Chair, Department of Chinese and Japanese

Graduate and undergraduate area studies program established in 1956

• Majors/degrees/certificates offered: B.A. and M.A. in Asian Studies, and in Chinese and Japanese; Ph.D. in Chinese and Comparative Literature and Japanese and Comparative Literature

• Approximate number of faculty teaching area and language courses: 21

• Approximate number of courses available—area: 60; language: 12

• Average number of students per year specializing in area: 45

• Countries covered and areas of emphasis: all areas of Asia with particular strength in East Asia

• Languages offered: Chinese and Japanese

• Study abroad available through Washington University program at Waseda University (Waseda, Japan) and other programs in Taiwan, Singapore, Hong Kong and, by individual arrangement, the PRC

13.069
Asian Studies Program
Dartmouth College
Bartlett Hall
Hanover, NH 03755
(603) 646-2861

Contact(s):
Gene R. Garthwaite, Chair

Undergraduate area studies program established in 1974
- Majors/degrees/certificates offered: B.A. in Asian Studies
- Approximate number of faculty teaching area and language courses: 21
- Approximate number of courses available—area: 40; language: 12
- Average number of students per year specializing in area: 15
- Countries covered and areas of emphasis: China, Japan, Southeast Asia, India and South Asia, Western Asia-Middle East
- Language offered: Chinese (Mandarin)
- Special Oriental collection at Baker Library
- Overseas study opportunity at Keio University, Tokyo, and Beijing Normal University, Beijing

13.070
Program in East Asian Studies and the Department of East Asian Studies
Princeton University
211 Jones Hall
Princeton, NJ 08544
(609) 452-4276

Contact(s):
Marion J. Levy, Jr., Director

Graduate and undergraduate area studies program established in 1955
- Majors/degrees/certificates offered: Department of East Asian Studies offers B.A., M.A. (non-terminal), and Ph.D. in Chinese and Japanese language, history and literature; program offers Certificate in East Asian Studies to accompany B.A., M.A. and Ph.D. in the disciplines
- Approximate number of faculty teaching area and language courses: 28
- Approximate number of courses available—area: 58; language: 24
- Average number of students per year specializing in area: 60
- Countries covered and areas of emphasis: China and Japan with particular strength in art, history, literature and Chinese language and civilization
- Languages offered: Chinese and Japanese
- Gest Oriental Library, containing 290,000 volumes, holds major collection of materials on traditional Chinese civilization; large collection of rare books and manuscripts from the Sung (960–1279), Ming (1369–1644) and other periods of Chinese history, as well as more contemporary holdings; Japanese collection strong in early modern and modern Japanese history and literature
- Students use Stanford Interuniversity Language Centers in Taiwan and Tokyo (see 18.277)
- University Art Museum has major collection of Chinese art including paintings, rubbings and bronzes, along with an Oriental art library and an extensive collection of photographs and reproductions
- Exchange relationships for graduate students and faculty with a number of academic institutions; graduates may qualify for teaching fellowships in Hong Kong, Taiwan, Korea and Japan through Princeton-in-Asia
- Conducts conferences and workshops for secondary schools, provides films on loan and runs a speakers bureau
- Publishes newsletter

13.071
Asian Studies Program
Rutgers University
International Center
New Brunswick, NJ 08903
(201) 932-7637

Contact(s):
Peter Li, Director, Committee on Asian
   Studies

Graduate, undergraduate and nondegree area
studies program established in 1969
 • Majors/degrees/certificates offered:
B.A. and M.A. with specialization in Asian
Studies
 • Approximate number of faculty teach-
ing area and language courses: 48
 • Approximate number of courses avail-
able—area: 50; language: 24
 • Average number of students per year
specializing in area: 10
 • Countries covered and areas of em-
phasis: China, Japan, Korea, Bangladesh,
Burma, Cambodia, India, Indonesia, Malay-
sia, Pakistan, Philippines, Sri Lanka, Thai-
land and Vietnam
 • Languages offered: Chinese, Japanese
and Sanskrit
 • Extensive collection of materials in East
Asian Library
 • Conducts exchange programs with Jilin
University in China and Fukui University in
Japan; other study abroad opportunities avail-
able

13.072
Department of Asian Studies
Seton Hall University
South Orange, NJ 07079
(201) 761-9465

Contact(s):
Barry B. Blakeley, Chair

Graduate and undergraduate area studies
program established in 1958

 • Majors/degrees/certificates offered:
B.A. in Asian Studies; M.A. in Chinese, Japanese, or Asian Area Studies; M.A. and Ed.D.
with concentration in East Asian bilingual/
bicultural education (see 6.098)
 • Approximate number of faculty teaching area and language courses: 9
 • Approximate number of courses available—area: 22; language: 12
 • Average number of students per year
specializing in area: 40
 • Countries covered and areas of emphasis: China, Japan, India and Korea, with
particular emphasis on Chinese and Japanese
Studies
 • Languages offered: Chinese and Japanese
 • Special collection of Asian language
materials
 • Faculty and student exchange pro-
grams with Sophia University (Japan) and
Beijing Language Institute and Wuhan Uni-
versity (PRC)
 • Cooperates with Institute of Far Eastern Studies (see 13.073) in the conduct of
Outreach Seminars and workshops and the
sponsorship of research
 • Publishes tapes and texts for Chinese
language instruction (with Yale University
Press, see 11.035)

13.073
Institute of Far Eastern Studies
Seton Hall University
South Orange, NJ 07079
(201) 761-9456

Contact(s):
John Young, Director

 • Conducts research on Asian culture and
philosophy and on the Chinese, Japanese and
Korean languages; compiles dictionaries and
develops textbooks; sponsors conferences and
institutes on the Chinese and Japanese languages; library holds approximately 35,000

volumes on China and Japan; active in the conduct of outreach seminars and other programs

13.074
Oriental Studies
Barnard College
Columbia University
321A Milbank Hall
New York, NY 10027
(212) 280-5417

Contact(s):
John Meskill, Chair

Undergraduate area studies program established in 1960
• Majors/degrees/certificates offered: B.A. in Oriental Studies with specialization in East Asia or the Middle East (including India)
• Approximate number of faculty teaching area and language courses: 50
• Approximate number of courses available—area: 49; language: 75 (in conjunction with Columbia)
• Average number of students per year specializing in area: 20
• Countries covered and areas of emphasis: East and Southeast Asia, India and the Middle East; emphasis on history, literature, religion and philosophy
• Languages offered: Arabic, Armenian, Chinese, Hindi-Urdu, Japanese, Korean, Persian, Sanskrit and Turkish

13.075
East Asian Studies Program
City University of New York/Brooklyn
   College
4239 Boylan Hall
Bedford Ave. and Ave. H
Brooklyn, NY 11210
(212) 780-5451

Contact(s):
Ming-shui Hung, Coordinator

Undergraduate area studies program
• Majors/degrees/certificates offered: B.A. in East Asian Area Studies
• Approximate number of courses available—area: 22; language: 12
• Countries covered and areas of emphasis: China, Japan and Korea, with emphasis on China
• Languages offered: Chinese and Japanese

13.076
Center for the Study of Central Asia
Columbia University
1205 International Affairs Bldg.
420 West 118th St.
New York, NY 10027
(212) 280-2556

Contact(s):
Edward Allworth, Director

• Promotes research and teaching and serves as information resource center on Central Asia covering Afghanistan, Soviet Central Asia (including Kazakhstan) and Xinjiang (Chungking) Autonomous Province of the PRC

13.077
East Asian Institute
Columbia University
914 International Affairs Bldg.
420 West 118th St.
New York, NY 10027
(212) 280-2589

Contact(s):
James W. Morley, Director

Graduate area studies program established in 1949

• Majors/degrees/certificates offered: two-year M.I.A., School of International and Public Affairs, with Certificate in East Asian Studies; M.A. and Ph.D. with Certificate in East Asian Studies

• Approximate number of faculty teaching area and language courses: 42

• Approximate number of courses available—area: 58; language: 25

• Countries covered and areas of emphasis: China, Japan and Korea; strong in the social sciences

• Languages offered: Chinese, Japanese and Korean

• East Asia Library maintains extensive holdings of Asian language materials, including about 220,000 volumes in Chinese, 171,000 in Japanese, 18,000 in Korean, smaller collections in Manchu and Mongol languages, and large numbers in Western languages; archival materials include papers of the Institute of Pacific Relations, the Research Project on Men and Politics in China, the Chinese Oral History Project, the V.K. Wellington Koo collections and materials from the Research Project on Leadership in Communist China

• Publishes books and educational materials on East Asia including scholarly studies, a series on current Japanese foreign and domestic policy and an East Asian Curriculum Project (see 2.078)

13.078
East Asian Studies
Columbia University/Columbia College
912 International Affairs Bldg.
420 West 118th St.
New York, NY 10027
(212) 280-2591/2592

Contact(s):
Carol Gluck, Departmental Representative

Undergraduate area studies program established in 1959

• Majors/degrees/certificates offered: B.A. in East Asian Studies

• Approximate number of faculty teaching area and language courses: 69

• Approximate number of courses available—area: 83; language: 40

• Average number of students per year specializing in area: 80 majors; 60 concentrators

• Countries covered and areas of emphasis: China, Japan and Korea

• Languages offered: Chinese, Japanese and Korean

• East Asia library contains extensive holdings in East Asian and Western languages

• Extensive resources of East Asian Institute (see 13.077), professional schools, Oriental Studies Program (see 13.074) and other offices and organizations on and off campus also available

13.079
Southern Asian Institute
Columbia University
1128 International Affairs Bldg.
420 West 118th St.
New York, NY 10027
(212) 280-4462

Contact(s):
Morton Klass, Director

Graduate area studies program established in 1967

• Majors/degrees/certificates offered: two-year M.I.A., School of International and Public Affairs, with Certificate in Southern Asian Studies; M.A. and Ph.D. with certificate in Southern Asian Studies

• Approximate number of faculty teaching area and language courses: 35

• Approximate number of courses available—area: 119; language: 37

• Average number of students per year specializing in area: 50

• Countries covered and areas of emphasis: India, Pakistan, Bangladesh, Sri Lanka, Nepal and Afghanistan and the countries of Southeast Asia; strong in both the social sciences and the humanities

• Languages offered: Hindi, Urdu, Bengali, Nepali, Sanskrit (including Buddhist Hybrid and Vedic), Pali, Prakit and Tibetan

• Extensive library holdings on South and Southern Asia in the social sciences, business, literature and the arts

13.080
China Japan Program
Cornell University
140 Uris Hall
Ithaca, NY 14853
(607) 256-6222

Contact(s):
T. J. Pempel, Director

Graduate area studies program established in 1960

• Majors/degrees/certificates offered: M.A. and Ph.D. in discipline with China-Japan specialization

• Approximate number of faculty teaching area and language courses: 29

• Approximate number of courses available—area: 111; language: 54

• Average number of students per year specializing in area: 80

• Countries covered and areas of emphasis: China and Japan

• Languages offered: Chinese (Mandarin and Cantonese) and Japanese; includes Full-year Asian Language Concentration (FALCON) involving, intensive, full-time summer and/or academic year study of Japanese or Mandarin Chinese

• Extensive East Asian library collection

• Sponsors research and publishes East

Asia Papers series of research mimeographs (23 volumes currently available)

13.081
Department of Asian Studies Program
Cornell University
388 Rockefeller Hall
Ithaca, NY 14853
(607) 256-5095

Contact(s):
Brett de Bary, Chair
Lucille Broberg, Executive Staff Assistant

Graduate, undergraduate and nondegree area studies program established in 1946

• Majors/degrees/certificates offered: B.A. in Asian Studies; M.A. in Asian Studies (East Asian Studies); M.A./Ph.D. in East Asian Literature; degrees also offered by the China-Japan Program (see 13.080), the South Asia Program (see 13.082) and the Southeast Asia Program (see 13.083)

• Approximate number of faculty teaching area and language courses: 51

• Approximate number of courses available—area: 179; language: 96

• Average number of students per year specializing in area: undergraduate: 33; graduate: 26 (East Asian studies); 9 (East Asian Literature)

• Countries covered and areas of emphasis: all countries of East, Southeast and South Asia

• Languages offered: Chinese, Japanese, Hindi, Sinhalese, Tamil, Telugra, Urdu, Burmese, Cambodian, Cebuano (Bisayan), Indonesian, Javanese, Old Javanese, Tagalog, Thai and Vietnamese; includes Full-year Asian Language Concentrations (FALCON) involving intensive, full-time and/or academic year study of Japanese, Indonesian and/or Mandarin Chinese

• Extensive library holdings in East Asia

• Sponsors research, especially on China

• Overseas languages and cultural study available at several sites in Japan

13.082
South Asia Program
Cornell University
166 Uris Hall
Ithaca, NY 14853
(607) 256-1000

Contact(s):
B. G. MacDougall, Director

Graduate and undergraduate area studies program
 • Majors/degrees/certificates offered: B.A. and M.A. in Asian Studies with a South Asia concentration
 • Approximate number of courses available—area: 20; language: 20
 • Average number of students per year specializing in area: 30
 • Countries covered and areas of emphasis: Bangladesh, India, Nepal, Pakistan and Sri Lanka
 • Languages offered: Hindi, Sinhalese, Tamil, and Urdu
 • Intensive language instruction available in India through The American Institute of Indian Studies (see 18.203)

13.083
Southeast Asia Program
Cornell University
120 Uris Hall
Ithaca, NY 14853
(607) 256-2378

Contact(s):
Stanley J. O'Connor, Jr., Director
Carol J. Compton, Outreach Coordinator

Graduate area studies program established in 1951
 • Majors/degrees/certificates offered: M.A. or Ph.D. with minor in Asian Studies: Southeast Asia or majors in Southeast Asian History or Oriental Art History

 • Approximate number of faculty teaching area and language courses: 20
 • Approximate number of courses available—area: 59; language: 92
 • Average number of students per year specializing in area: 75
 • Countries covered and areas of emphasis: Burma, Brunei, Cambodia, Indonesia, Laos, Malaysia, Philippines, Sarawak, Singapore, Thailand and Vietnam
 • Languages offered: Burmese, Cambodian, Cebuano (Bisayan), Indonesian, Javanese, Old Javanese, Tagalog, Thai and Vietnamese; includes Full-year Language Concentration (FALCON) involving intensive, full-time academic year study of Indonesian (Malay)
 • John M. Echols Southeast Asia Library Collection is largest holding in West; art and art history collection in Herbert Johnson Museum; special materials on Southeast Asian refugee assistance available
 • Advanced Indonesian Abroad in Salatiga, Indonesia, offers intensive summer language study
 • Visiting Fellow status available for scholars wishing to do research using Echols Collection
 • Outreach Program offers resources to schools and community groups including materials available on loan from Southeast Asia Film Library (see 2.086); publishes *Outreach Resources Bulletin* describing resources available
 • Publishes monographs, studies and bibliographies on various Southeast Asian countries, a "Modern Indonesia" series of studies, the semiannual journal *Indonesia*, and print and audiovisual language and cultural teaching materials

13.084
Committee on Asian Studies
Hamilton College
Clinton, NY 13323
(315) 859-7302

Contact(s):
Russell T. Blackwood, Chair

Undergraduate area studies program established in 1968
  • Majors/degrees/certificates offered: B.A. in Asian Studies
  • Approximate number of faculty teaching area and language courses: 10
  • Approximate number of courses available—area: 20; language: 8
  • Average number of students per year specializing in area: 3
  • Countries covered and areas of emphasis: China, Japan, India, Vietnam, Malaysia and Indonesia
  • Languages offered: Chinese, Japanese, Hebrew and Arabic (through self-instructional Program in the Critical Languages)

13.085
Asian Studies Program
Hofstra University
Hempstead, NY 11550
(516) 560-3221

Contact(s):
David Chiu, Director of Asian Studies

Undergraduate area studies program established in 1960
  • Majors/degrees/certificates offered: B.A. in Asian Studies or B.B.A. in Business with Asian Studies minor
  • Approximate number of faculty teaching area and language courses: 9
  • Approximate number of courses available—area: 19; language: 13
  • Average number of students per year specializing in area: 10
  • Countries covered and areas of emphasis: principal focus on China and Japan
  • Languages offered: Chinese and Japanese

  • Hofstra-in-China summer program at East China University, Shanghai, PRC; other opportunities available in Japan or Taiwan

13.086
Institute of Asian Studies
St. John's University
Jamaica, NY 11439
(212) 990-6161

Contact(s):
Chu Djang, Associate Director

Graduate and undergraduate area studies program established in 1962
  • Majors/degrees/certificates offered: B.A. and M.A. in East Asian Studies
  • Approximate number of faculty teaching area and language courses: 10
  • Approximate number of courses available—area: 10; language: 10
  • Average number of students per year specializing in area: 70
  • Countries covered and areas of emphasis: China and Japan
  • Languages offered: Chinese and Japanese
  • Center is housed in its own building with a seminar/reading room, current periodicals, and an exhibition hall
  • Study abroad opportunities in Taiwan, Korea and Japan
  • Publishes a series of papers on Asia in the Modern World, an Asian Translation Series of works by Chinese scholars, and *The American Asian Review,* a quarterly journal

13.087
Asian Studies Committee
State University of New York at Buffalo
Buffalo, NY 14260
(716) 636-2075

Contact(s):
Albert Michaels, Director

Undergraduate area studies program
• Majors/degrees/certificates offered: B.A. in Asian Studies
• Countries covered and areas of emphasis: all countries of Asia with particular emphasis on East Asia and on history, culture and politics
• Publishes the *Journal of Asian Affairs*

13.088
Asian Studies Program
State University of New York
College at New Paltz
New Paltz, NY 12562
(914) 257-2365

Contact(s):
Ronald G. Knapp, Coordinator of Asian
   Studies

Undergraduate area studies program established in 1969
• Majors/degrees/certificates offered: contract major in Asian Studies
• Approximate number of faculty teaching area and language courses: 17
• Approximate number of courses available—area: 35; language: 4
• Average number of students per year specializing in area: 10
• Countries covered and areas of emphasis: China, Japan, India and Southeast Asia
• Languages offered: Chinese and Japanese
• Reciprocal exchange program with Beijing University, People's Republic of China, and programs in China, Japan and Singapore through the State University of New York system

13.089
South Asian Studies
Syracuse University
Foreign and Comparative Studies
119 College Place
Syracuse, NY 13210-2892
(315) 423-2552

Contact(s):
John D. Nagel, Director

Graduate and undergraduate area studies program
• Majors/degrees/certificates offered: B.A. in South Asian Studies; M.A. and Ph.D. with specialization in South Asia through the Religion and most of the Social Sciences departments as well as through a special interdisciplinary program in Public Administration (see 6.157), International Relations (see 4.093) and the Humanities; M.A. in Interdisciplinary Linguistics Program through the Development Planning Program (see 6.157); and a graduate Certificate of Competency from the Foreign and Comparative Studies Program (see 4.093)
• Approximate number of faculty teaching area and language courses: 14
• Countries covered and areas of emphasis: South Asian Sub-continent; particularly strong in social sciences and religion
• Languages offered: Hindi; other South Asian languages available through tutorials and self-instructional courses through the Institute of Applied Linguistics
• South Asian library collection includes over 100,000 books, periodicals and government documents, including materials acquired through the PL 480 Program and microfilm of South Asian materials available through the Center for Research libraries
• Faculty experienced in South Asian development assistance projects; Research Associate Program offers affiliation to Asianist faculty at nearby institutions
• Publishes a South Asian Series of

monographs and a number of bibliographies and monographs
- Two Shell Fellowships for dissertation research in less developed countries available

13.090
Center for Asian Studies/East Asian Language and Area Center
University of Rochester
Rochester, NY 14627
(716) 275-4497

Contact(s):
Robert B. Hall, Jr., Director

Graduate and undergraduate area studies program
- Majors/degrees/certificates offered: B.A. and M.A. in Asian Studies
- Countries covered and areas of emphasis: all countries of Asia with emphasis on East Asia and India
- Sponsors research on Asia

13.091
East Asian Studies
Vassar College
Poughkeepsie, NY 12601
(914) 473-2886

Contact(s):
D. Gillin, Director

Undergraduate area studies program
- Majors/degrees/certificates offered: B.A. in Asian Studies
- Countries covered and areas of emphasis: major countries of East, South and Southeast Asia with particular emphasis on China
- Languages offered: Chinese at all levels and self-instructional Japanese
- Access to additional coursework at State University of New York/College at New Paltz;

study abroad (including intensive Chinese language study) available in Taiwan, Hong Kong and Singapore

13.092
Islamic and Arabian Development Studies Program
Duke University
2114 Campus Drive
Durham, NC 27706
(919) 684-2446

Contact(s):
Ralph Braibanti, Director

Graduate and undergraduate area studies program covering the Islamic countries of the Middle East and Asia (see 17.034)

13.093
Program in Comparative Studies on South Asia
Duke University
Center for International Studies
2101 Campus Drive
Durham, NC 27706
(919) 684-2765

Contact(s):
Joseph Di Bona, Chair
Marion Salinger, Administrative
    Coordinator, Center for International
    Studies

- Offers B.A. (comparative area undergraduate major in South Asian Studies), M.A. and Ph.D. with specialization in South Asian Studies

13.094
Asian Studies Program
Wake Forest University
Box 7547
Winston-Salem, NC 27109
(919) 761-5307

Contact(s):
B. G. Gokhale, Director

Graduate and undergraduate area studies program established in 1960
 • Majors/degrees/certificates offered: B.A. in Asian Studies, M.A. in Asian Studies with a concentration in history
 • Approximate number of faculty teaching area and language courses: 7
 • Approximate number of courses available—area: 19; language: 6
 • Average number of students per year specializing in area: 5 graduate; 60 undergraduate
 • Countries covered and areas of emphasis: India, Pakistan, Nepal, Sri Lanka, Burma, Thailand, Malaysia, Indonesia, Cambodia, Laos, Vietnam, China and Japan with special interest in South Asia
 • Languages offered: Hindi and Chinese
 • Library contains 40,000 books in the Asian area, including a wide selection of periodicals and microfilmed primary source materials; also a large collection of slides and other audiovisuals
 • Conducts special seminars and institutes for high school teachers
 • Publishes volumes in an Asian Studies series from time to time
 • Offers semesters abroad in India, Venice and London

13.095
Asian Studies Program
Bowling Green State University
Bowling Green, OH 43403
(419) 372-2247

Contact(s):
Director, International Programs

Undergraduate area studies program established in 1966
 • Majors/degrees/certificates offered: B.S.

in Asian Studies in Arts and Sciences or Education with major in Asian Studies
 • Approximate number of faculty teaching area and language courses: 14
 • Approximate number of courses available—area: 16
 • Average number of students per year specializing in area: 3–6
 • Countries covered and areas of emphasis: all regions of Asia with particular strength in East Asia; requires in-depth study of Japan, China, India or Korea
 • Languages offered: Chinese (Mandarin) and Japanese
 • Study abroad available in Japan or South Korea

13.096
Asian Studies Program
Kent State University
Department of Political Science
Kent, OH 44242
(216) 672-2060

Contact(s):
Kenneth E. Colton, Coordinator

 • Offers B.A. with Certificate (without language component) or Diploma-Certificate (including language study) in Asian Studies; languages through the self-instructional critical language program: Chinese, Japanese, Hindi and Korean

13.097
East Asian Studies Program
Oberlin College
Oberlin, OH 44074
(216) 775-8313

Contact(s):
Ronald Di Cenzo, Director

Undergraduate area studies program established in 1965

• Majors/degrees/certificates offered: B.A. in East Asian Studies with Japan or China concentration or in Chinese Language and Literature
• Approximate number of faculty teaching area and language courses: 8
• Approximate number of courses available—area: 40; language: 12
• Average number of students per year specializing in area: 45
• Countries covered and areas of emphasis: China and Japan
• Languages offered: Chinese and Japanese
• East Asian Library contains 20,000 books in Chinese and Japanese
• Offers research and teaching opportunities for visiting Asian scholars
• Conducts school outreach program and publishes 9–10 page resource newsletter
• Overseas programs available in Japan (Kyoto and Tokyo), China (Peking University and Nanking University) and Hong Kong (Chinese University)

13.098
East Asian Studies Center
The Ohio State University
University Center for International Studies
308 Dulles Hall
Columbus, OH 43210
(614) 422-9660

Contact(s):
Chung-min Chen, Director
Sara A. Mazak, SCOPA Coordinator

Graduate and undergraduate area studies program established in 1969
• Majors/degrees/certificates offered: B.A. minor and Certificate in Asian Studies; Master of Humanities in East Asian Studies; and M.A. and Ph.D. in disciplines with specialization in East Asian Studies; degrees in History of Asian Art offered through the Department of Art History; Ph.D. in Chinese;

B.A. and M.A. in the Chinese or Japanese languages, and a dual B.A./B.S. degree in Chinese or Japanese and International Business Administration offered through the Department of East Asian Languages
• Approximate number of faculty teaching area and language courses: 35
• Approximate number of courses available—area: 59; language and literature: 120
• Countries covered and areas of emphasis: particular emphasis on history, art, languages and literatures of China and Japan
• Languages offered: Chinese and Japanese
• Sponsors Japanese Business and Outreach Center (providing information on Japan and U.S. businesses) and conducts School and Community Outreach Program on Asia (SCOPA, see 2.085)

13.099
Center for Southeast Asian Studies
Ohio University
56 East Union St.
Athens, OH 45701
(614) 594-6457

Contact(s):
Paul W. van der Veur, Director

Graduate and undergraduate area studies program established in 1966
• Majors/degrees/certificates offered: B.A. or Certificate in Asian studies; M.A. in International Affairs with Southeast Asia concentration
• Approximate number of faculty teaching area and language courses: 32
• Approximate number of courses available—area: 45; language: 8
• Average number of students per year specializing in area: 40
• Countries covered and areas of emphasis: Southeast Asia in general with special interest in Indonesia and Malaysia

• Languages offered: Indonesian/Malay, Javanese, Tagalog and Chinese

• Southeast Asia Collection of books and periodicals includes particularly large collection from Indonesia and Malaysia

• Indonesian Studies Summer Institute includes 10 weeks of language and culture studies

• Tun Abdul Razak Chair in Southeast Asian Studies occupied by Malaysian professor

13.100
Asian Studies Program
University of Cincinnati
Department of Political Science
Cincinnati, OH 45221
(513) 475-3211

Contact(s):
Han-Kyo Kim, Director

Undergraduate area studies program established in 1974

• Majors/degrees/certificates offered: B.A. or Certificate in Asian Studies

• Approximate number of faculty teaching area and language courses: 14

• Approximate number of courses available—area: 16; language: 8

• Average number of students per year specializing in area: majors, 2; certificate, 3

• Countries covered and areas of emphasis: all countries of East, Southeast and South Asia with emphasis on China, India and Japan

• Languages offered: Chinese and Japanese

13.101
Asian Studies Program
University of Toledo
2801 West Bancroft St.
Toledo, OH 43606
(419) 537-2696

Contact(s):
George P. Jan, Adviser

Undergraduate area studies program

• Majors/degrees/certificates offered: B.A. in Asian Studies

• Approximate number of courses available—area: 30

• Average number of students per year specializing in area: 5

• Countries covered and areas of emphasis: China, Japan and Southeast Asia, with emphasis on history and the Social Sciences

• Library contains collection of English-language materials on Asia

• Program conducts study tours to Asia

13.102
East Asian Studies
Wittenburg University
Springfield, OH 45501
(513) 327-7433

Contact(s):
Eugene R. Swanger, Director

Undergraduate area studies program established in 1970

• Majors/degrees/certificates offered: B.A. with major in East Asian Studies

• Approximate number of faculty teaching area and language courses: 7

• Approximate number of courses available—27 courses in languages, history, political science, religion, art and music

• Average number of students per year specializing in area: 48

• Countries covered and areas of emphasis: China and Japan

• Languages offered: Chinese and Japanese

• Library contains 15,000-volume Matsumoto Collection

• Conducts outreach programs for teachers and area business executives

13.103
Asian Studies Program
The University of Oklahoma
Asian Studies Committee
455 West Lindsey, Room 406
Norman, OK 73019
(405) 325-4921/6001

Contact(s):
Sidney D. Brown, Chair

Undergraduate area studies program established in 1955
  • Majors/degrees/certificates offered: B.A. in Asian Studies
  • Approximate number of faculty teaching area and language courses: 5
  • Approximate number of courses available—area: 6; language: 8
  • Average number of students per year specializing in area: 15
  • Countries covered and areas of emphasis: particular emphasis on East Asia, especially China and Japan
  • Languages offered: Chinese and Japanese
  • Sponsors summer seminars in East Asia

13.104
Asian Studies Program and Department of East Asian Languages and Literatures
University of Oregon
Eugene, OR 97403
(503) 686-4005

Contact(s):
Chair, Asian Studies (to be named)
Stephen W. Kohl, Chair, Department of East Asian Languages and Literatures

Graduate and undergraduate area studies program established in 1974
  • Majors/degrees/certificates offered: B.A. in Asian Languages and Asian Studies and M.A. in Asian Studies

  • Approximate number of faculty teaching area and language courses: 22
  • Approximate number of courses available—area: 100; language and literature: 62
  • Average number of students per year specializing in area: 35
  • Countries covered and areas of emphasis: Japan and China; strong emphasis on language and literature
  • Languages offered: Chinese and Japanese
  • Library holds approximately 37,000 volumes in Chinese, Japanese and Korean, 200 periodicals, and an extensive collection on Asia in English
  • Museum of art contains large Oriental collection with strength in China, Japan, Cambodia, Mongolia and Russia
  • Undergraduate study opportunities available in Japan and by special arrangements in Hong Kong, Taiwan and the PRC

13.105
East Asian Studies
Bucknell University
Lewisburg, PA 17837
(717) 524-1450

Contact(s):
James Pusey, Director

Undergraduate area studies program established in 1982
  • Majors/degrees/certificates offered: B.A. in East Asian Studies
  • Approximate number of faculty teaching area and language courses: 4
  • Approximate number of courses available—area: 13; language: 10
  • Average number of students per year specializing in area: 4
  • Countries covered and areas of emphasis: China and Japan
  • Languages offered: Japanese; Chinese offered on tutorial basis (no formal language requirement for Asian studies majors)

• Study abroad available at universities in Kyoto, Nagoya and Tokyo, Japan (primarily for Japanese studies majors, see 18.273)

13.106
East Asian Studies Program
Pennsylvania State University
107 Burrowes Bldg.
University Park, PA 16802
(814) 865-6397

Contact(s):
Parris H. Chang, Director

Undergraduate area studies program established in 1973
• Majors/degrees/certificates   offered: B.A. in East Asian Studies
• Approximate number of faculty teaching area and language courses: 12
• Approximate number of courses available—area: 10; language: 7
• Average number of students per year specializing in area: 30
• Countries covered and areas of emphasis: China, Japan, Korea and Taiwan; particularly strong in history and religious studies
• Languages offered: Chinese and Japanese
• Library contains an ample collection of materials on East Asia, sufficient to support an undergraduate
• Sponsors study abroad program in Taiwan

13.107
East Asian Studies
University of Pennsylvania
Philadelphia, PA 19104
(215) 898-7466

Contact(s):
W. Allyn Rickett, Chair

Graduate and undergraduate area studies program
• Majors/degrees/certificates   offered: B.A., M.A. and Ph.D. in history, history and sociology of science, international relations, Oriental Studies and political science with special qualification in Asian Studies
• Approximate number of faculty teaching area and language courses: 14
• Approximate number of courses available—area: 76; language: 15
• Average number of students per year specializing in area: 20 graduate; 120 undergraduate
• Countries covered and areas of emphasis: East Asia with particular emphasis on China and Japan; strong in history, literature, culture and language
• Languages offered: Chinese, Japanese at all levels, and Korean at beginning and intermediate levels
• Maintains archives of Institute of Medieval Japanese Studies
• Library contains an extensive collection of books on East Asia and in Japanese, Chinese and Korean (all shelved and catalogued together) and maintains Chinese bibliographer; the Derek Bodde East Asian Seminar Room houses reference books and current periodicals in Japanese and Chinese
• Maintains East Asia College House on campus where 80 Asian and American students live in a multicultural living/learning setting
• Overseas study opportunities available in Japan, Taiwan and the PRC (China)

13.108
South Asia Regional Studies Department
University of Pennsylvania
820 Williams Hall
Philadelphia, PA 19104
(215) 898-7475

Contact(s):
Rosane Rocher, Chairman
Robert J. Young, Outreach Coordinator

Graduate and undergraduate area studies program established in 1948

• Majors/degrees/certificates offered: B.A., M.A. and Ph.D. in South Asia Regional Studies

• Approximate number of faculty teaching area and language courses: 25

• Approximate number of courses available—area: 30; language: 20

• Average number of students per year specializing in area: 25 graduate; 10 undergraduate

• Countries covered and areas of emphasis: Afghanistan, Bangladesh, India, Nepal, Pakistan, Sri Lanka and Himalayan border countries

• Languages offered: Hindi, Urdu, Bengali, Marathi, Gujarati, Tamil, Telugu, Kannada, Malayalam, Sanskrit, Pali, Panjabi Persian

• Library's South Asia Collection includes several thousand Indic manuscripts; over 300,000 bound volumes; 2,800 serial publications; 25 newspapers from the area; a photographic archive (maintained cooperatively with the American Institute of Indian Studies (see 18.203) and the Center for Art and Archaeology, Benares, India) of some 45,000 photographs of South Asian architecture, sculpture and other arts; a teaching collection of 10,000 color slides; a South Asian Maps Collection; and several unpublished scholarly collections relating to South Asia; it serves also as repository for materials currently published in the subcontinent

• Outreach program trains, provides curricular assistance and lends films, maps and teaching kits to secondary school teachers; also co-sponsors public lectures, art exhibits, tours to India, etc.

13.109
Asian Studies Program
University of Pittsburgh
Pittsburgh, PA 15260
(412) 624-5566

Contact(s):
L. Keith Brown, Director
Dorothy J. Solinger, Associate Director

Graduate and undergraduate area studies program

• Majors/degrees/certificates offered: M.A. in East Asian Studies and B.A., M.A. and Ph.D. in disciplines with a Certificate in Asian Studies; M.P.I.A. (Master of Public and International Affairs, see 6.159) with Certificate in Asian Studies; joint certificate with Graduate School of Public Health

• Approximate number of faculty teaching area and language courses: 48

• Approximate number of courses available—area: 75; language: 30

• Countries covered and areas of emphasis: all countries of Asia with emphasis on China, Japan and South/Southeast Asia; wide range of disciplines covered, especially on countries of East Asia

• Languages offered: Chinese and Japanese; other Asian languages available through the Uncommonly Taught Languages Program of the University's Language Acquisition Institute

• East Asian Library maintains major research collection including over 110,000 volumes, 2,600 reels of microfilm of Chinese and Japanese materials, and over 1,500 periodicals published in China, Taiwan, Hong Kong, Japan and Korea; particularly strong in both modern and traditional Chinese language materials and vernacular works on modern Japan; also has extensive collection of materials on Asia in Western languages

• Maintains faculty exchange relationships with universities in Japan, Hong Kong, South Korea, Taiwan, the PRC and Hong Kong

• Study abroad available in Japan and Taiwan

• Conducts outreach programs for college, secondary and elementary school teachers and for the business community

13.110
East Asia Language and Area Center
Brown University
Providence, RI 02912
(401) 863-2229

Contact(s):
Lea E. Williams, Director

• Promotes research on and the study of East Asia; particular strength in Chinese Studies; strong East Asian library resources available

13.111
Asian Studies Committee
University of Tennessee
% College of Liberal Arts
Knoxville, TN 37996
(615) 974-5406

Contact(s):
Eric J. Gangloff, Chair

Undergraduate area studies program established in 1970
• Majors/degrees/certificates offered: B.A. with major or minor in Asian Studies; B.A. in Asian Studies with concentration in Middle East studies
• Approximate number of faculty teaching area and language courses: 15
• Approximate number of courses available—area: 57; language: 38
• Average number of students per year specializing in area: 8
• Countries covered and areas of emphasis: the Islamic world, India, China and Japan
• Languages offered: Arabic, Chinese, Hebrew, Japanese, Persian and Sanskrit
• Large collection of films on Islam, China and Japan
• Study abroad opportunities available in Tunisia, Algeria, Japan and the PRC

13.112
East Asian Studies Program
Vanderbilt University
Nashville, TN 37203
(615) 322-2561

Contact(s):
Charles H. Hambrick, Director

Undergraduate area studies program established in 1967
• Majors/degrees/certificates offered: Undergraduate Major in East Asian Studies
• Approximate number of faculty teaching area and language courses: 8
• Approximate number of courses available—area: 23; language: 20
• Countries covered and areas of emphasis: particular emphasis on China and Japan
• Languages offered: Chinese and Japanese

13.113
Center for Asian Studies
University of Texas
SSB 4.126
Austin, TX 78712
(512) 471-5811

Contact(s):
F. Tomasson Jannuzi, Director
Louise Flippin, Community Outreach
  Coordinator

Graduate and undergraduate area studies program established in 1960
• Majors/degrees/certificates offered: B.A. in Asian Studies; graduate degrees in disciplines with Asian Studies focus
• Approximate number of faculty teaching area and language courses: 30
• Approximate number of courses available—area: 65; language: 28
• Average number of students per year specializing in area: 25 undergraduates

• Countries covered and areas of emphasis: principally East and South Asia, especially India, China and Japan

• Languages offered: Hindi-Urdu, Chinese, Japanese, Sanskrit and Dravidian

• Extensive collection of materials on East and South Asia, including Indo-Portuguese collection related to the history of the Portuguese in India

• Provides outreach services through Texas Program for Educational Resources on Asia (TEXPERA, see 2.088)

13.114
Asian Studies
Brigham Young University
134 FOB
Provo, UT 84602
(801) 378-3377

Contact(s):
Larry V. Shumway, Coordinator

• Offers B.A. and M.A. in Asian Studies; particularly strong in East Asia

13.115
East Asian Language and Area Studies Program
University of Utah
Salt Lake City, UT 84112
(801) 581-8060

Contact(s):
Lennox Tierney, Director

Graduate and undergraduate area studies program established in 1971

• Majors/degrees/certificates offered: B.A. and M.A. with Certificate in East Asian Studies

• Approximate number of faculty teaching area and language courses: 8

• Approximate number of courses available—area: 7; language: 7

• Average number of students per year specializing in area: 20

• Countries covered and areas of emphasis: East Asia in general (China, Korea and Japan)

• Languages offered: Chinese and Japanese

• Far Eastern slide library

• Annual summer field trips to China, Korea and Japan

• Student and faculty exchange program with the National Taiwan University

13.116
Program in East Asian Studies
Middlebury College
Sunderland Language Center
Middlebury, VT 05753
(802) 388-3711, Ext. 5520

Contact(s):
Audrey LaRock, Secretary for Chinese
    Department and Oriental Language
    Summer School
John Berninghausen, Chair

Undergraduate area studies program established in 1979

• Majors/degrees/certificates offered: B.A. with major in East Asian Studies

• Approximate number of faculty teaching area and language courses: 10

• Approximate number of courses available—area: 17; language: 8

• Average number of students per year majoring in area: 12; concentrations, 5

• Countries covered and areas of emphasis: China, Japan and Korea with particular strength in Chinese Studies

• Languages offered: Chinese; Chinese and Japanese also offered in nine-week on-campus intensive "total immersion" language and culture study program in the summer

• Study abroad in the Chinese language in Taiwan, the PRC, Hong Kong or Singapore or in the Japanese language in Japan may be arranged

• Languages offered: Japanese and Russian
• Study abroad encouraged
• Offers several special awards and scholarships to Asian Studies students

13.117
Asian Studies Program
James Madison University
Harrisonburg, VA 22802
(703) 433-6168

Contact(s):
Chong-kun Yoon, Chair

Undergraduate area studies program
• Majors/degrees/certificates offered: B.A. minor in Asian Studies
• Countries covered and areas of emphasis: all countries of Asia with particular interest in China, Japan and Korea

13.118
Asian Studies/International Relations
Randolph-Macon Woman's College
Lynchburg, VA 24503
(804) 846-7392

Contact(s):
David F. Anthony, Chair

Undergraduate area studies program established in 1960
• Majors/degrees/certificates offered: B.A. in Asian Civilization or International Relations
• Approximate number of faculty teaching area and language courses: 5
• Approximate number of courses available—area: 12; language: 6
• Average number of students per year specializing in area: 6–10
• Countries covered and areas of emphasis: all of East and South Asia with emphasis on China and Japan

13.119
East Asian Studies Program
University of Virginia
East Asian Language and Area Center
302 Cabel Hall
Charlottesville, VA 22903
(804) 924-7146

Contact(s):
John Israel, Director

Graduate and undergraduate area studies program
• Majors/degrees/certificates offered: B.A. in East Asian Studies and M.A. or Ph.D. in discipline with Certificate in East Asian Studies
• Approximate number of faculty teaching area and language courses: 14
• Countries covered and areas of emphasis: China, Japan and Tibet
• Languages offered: Chinese, Japanese and Tibetan
• Extensive library resources on East Asia available including strong collection of Tibetan materials and 30,000 volumes on traditional China
• Provides school and community outreach programs and services

13.120
Center for South Asian Studies
University of Virginia
Randall Hall
Charlottesville, VA 22903
(804) 924-8815 or 6416

Contact(s):
Richard B. Barnett, Director
Abdulaziz A. Sachedina, Associate Director
Judith Diane Short, Administrator and
   Outreach Coordinator

Graduate and undergraduate area studies program established in 1976
   • Majors/degrees/certificates offered: B.A. in South Asian Studies; departmental M.A. and Ph.D. with specialization in South Asian Studies (including comparative education)
   • Approximate number of faculty teaching area and language courses: 36
   • Approximate number of courses available—area: 100; language: 40
   • Average number of students per year specializing in area: 40 graduate
   • Countries covered and areas of emphasis: Afghanistan, Bangladesh, India, Nepal, Pakistan, Sri Lanka and Tibet; particular interest in Tibet and Buddhism; strong concentration of courses in anthropology, history and religious studies
   • Languages offered: Hindi, Urdu, Tibetan, Pali, Persian, Arabic, Sanskrit and Buddhist Hybrid Sanskrit
   • Library contains extensive South Asian collection with continuing acquisition of monographs, government documents, journals and newspapers from India, Pakistan, Sri Lanka, Tibet, Nepal and Bhutan; particularly strong collection of Tibetan language materials
   • Overseas language study programs available for Hindi (in India) and Urdu (in Pakistan)
   • Maintains a film lending library, participates in faculty exchanges with other institutions, and sponsors weekly public seminars

13.121
East Asian Studies Program
Washington and Lee University
Lexington, VA 24450
(703) 463-9111, Ext 120

Contact(s):
Roger B. Jeans, Director

Undergraduate area studies program established in 1976
   • Majors/degrees/certificates offered: B.A. in East Asian Studies
   • Approximate number of faculty teaching area and language courses: 8
   • Approximate number of courses available—area: 20; language: 10
   • Average number of students per year specializing in area: 5
   • Countries covered and areas of emphasis: China, Japan and Korea; particular strength in Chinese art and culture, Chinese and Japanese Buddhism and modern Chinese history
   • Languages offered: Chinese and Japanese
   • Library contains substantial collection of materials on China and Japan for undergraduate study; university also owns extensive collection of Chinese ceramics and scroll and brush paintings
   • Overseas study available in Japan (religion, language, history and culture), Taiwan (art and language) and Hong Kong (general Chinese studies)

13.122
Asian Studies Program
Central Washington University
Ellensburg, WA 98926
(509) 963-1244

Contact(s):
Daniel B. Ramsdell, Director

Undergraduate area studies program established in 1974
   • Majors/degrees/certificates offered: B.A. in Asian Studies
   • Approximate number of faculty teaching area and language courses: 7

• Approximate number of courses available—area: 21
• Average number of students per year specializing in area: 10–15
• Countries covered and areas of emphasis: East and South Asia with emphasis on China, Japan and India
• Study abroad available in China

13.123
Asian Studies Program
University of Puget Sound
Department of History
Tacoma, WA 98416
(206) 756-3168

Contact(s):
Suzanne W. Barnett, Director

Undergraduate area studies program established in 1973
• Majors/degrees/certificates offered: B.A. in Asian Studies
• Approximate number of faculty teaching area and language courses: 13
• Approximate number of courses available—area: 17; language: 6
• Average number of students per year specializing in area: 30
• Countries covered and areas of emphasis: all countries of East, Southeast and South Asia with emphasis on China, India and Japan and on traditions and change
• Language offered: Japanese
• Sponsors nine-month Pacific Rim/Asia Study-Travel Program every three years

13.124
East Asian Studies
University of Washington
DR-05
Seattle, WA 98195
(206) 543-6148

Contact(s):
Jack L. Dull, Director

• Offers B.A. and M.A. in International Studies with concentrations in Chinese Studies (see 18.072), Japanese Studies (see 18.274) and Korean Studies (see 18.310)

13.125
South Asian Studies
University of Washington
303 Thomson Hall, DR-05
Seattle, WA 98195
(206) 543-4800

Contact(s):
Karl H. Potter, Chair, South Asian Studies

Graduate and undergraduate area studies program
• Majors/degrees/certificates offered: B.A. and M.A. in South Asian Studies or in disciplines with concentration in South Asian studies; Ph.D. with concentration in South Asian Studies
• Approximate number of faculty teaching area and language courses: 20
• Approximate number of courses available—area: 54; language: 35
• Average number of students per year specializing in area: 80
• Countries covered and areas of emphasis: India, Pakistan, Afghanistan, Bangladesh, Sri Lanka, Nepal and Tibet; broad balanced program in the humanities and social sciences; strong in Sanskrit and Tibetan
• Languages offered: Sanskrit, Tamil, Hindi–Urdu, Tibetan and Pali
• Library contains 40,000 volumes in major Indian languages (plus Singhalese) along with 80,000 volumes on South Asia in Western languages; access to the Oriental and Indian Art Collection at the Seattle Art Museum
• Exchange relationship with South Asian program at the University of British Columbia at Vancouver

13.126
Program in East and South Asia
Washington State University
Pullman, WA 99164-4030
(509) 335-3267

Contact(s):
F. W. Blackwell, Director

Undergraduate area studies program established in 1967
- Majors/degrees/certificates offered: B.A. in Asian Studies
- Approximate number of faculty teaching area & language courses: 7
- Approximate number of courses available—area: 27; language: 12
- Countries covered and areas of emphasis: all countries of East and South Asia with emphasis on China, Japan and India
- Languages offered: Hindi, Sanskrit, Chinese and Japanese
- Study abroad available in China, Japan and India

13.127
Center for East Asian Studies
Western Washington University
Bellingham, WA 98225
(206) 676-3041

Contact(s):
Edward H. Kaplan, Director

Undergraduate area studies program established in 1970
- Majors/degrees/certificates offered: B.A. in East Asian Studies
- Approximate number of faculty teaching area and language courses: 8
- Approximate number of courses available—area: 51; language: 20
- Average number of students per year specializing in area: 12–15
- Countries covered and areas of emphasis: China, Japan, Korea and Mongolia

- Languages offered: Chinese, Japanese, Korean and Mongolian
- Library contains approximately 16,000 volumes on the East Asian area, including 4,000 in East Asian languages, 126 serial titles, a collection of U.S. and foreign government documents pertaining to East Asia and an East Asian Reading Room with an extensive collection of audiovisual materials; especially strong in holdings on Mongolia
- Publishes a newsletter, *Studies on East Asia* (works on literature, history and politics) including *Bibliotheca Mongolica* (see 18.355) and *East Asian Research Aids* (new series of catalogs, shelf lists, etc.)
- Maintains faculty exchange relationship with Asia University in Tokyo and annual Mongolian Summer Language Program at Inner Mongolia University which includes undergraduate study opportunities; also maintains Visiting Scholar Program for researchers wishing to use Western Washington East Asian resources

13.128
Center for Southeast Asian Studies
University of Wisconsin at Madison
4115 Helen C. White Hall
Madison, WI 53706
(608) 263-1755

Contact(s):
John Snail, Director
William Albert, Outreach coordinator

Graduate and undergraduate area studies program established in 1973
- Majors/degrees/certificates offered: B.A. in Asian Studies (Southeast Asian concentration); Ph.D. minor in Southeast Asian Studies; Ph.D. minor in Indonesian Language and Literature; nondegree Certificate
- Approximate number of faculty teaching area and language courses: 33
- Approximate number of courses available—area: 46; language: 16

• Average number of students per year specializing in area: 75

• Countries covered and areas of emphasis: Indonesia, Thailand, Brunei, Burma, Laos, Cambodia, Malaysia, Singapore and the Philippines; particular strength in Indonesia, Thailand and the Philippines

• Languages offered: four years of instruction in Indonesian, two years of instruction in Thai, Buddhist canonical languages and occasional Javanese

• Southeast Asia Collection contains 25,000 volumes, 880 serials and seven current newspapers, a large number in Southeast Asian languages; also includes extensive audiovisual materials

• Maintains relationships with several Southeast Asian academic institutions and brings Southeast Asian faculty to Wisconsin to teach and conduct research

• Publishes bibliographies, monographs and studies in Southeast Asian subjects

13.129
Department of South Asian Studies and South Asian Area Center
University of Wisconsin at Madison
1249 Van Hise Hall
Madison, WI 53706
(608) 262-3012

Contact(s):
Velcheru N. Rao, Chair and Director

Graduate and undergraduate area studies program established in 1961

• Majors/degrees/certificates offered: B.A. and M.A. in South Asian Studies; Ph.D. with areas of specialization in South Asian Languages and Literatures, the Religions of South Asia, Buddhist Studies and the disciplines

• Approximate number of faculty teaching area and language courses: 36

• Approximate number of courses available—area: 85; language: 35

• Countries covered and areas of emphasis: India, Pakistan, Bangladesh, Nepal, Bhutan and Sri Lanka; particularly strong in religious and Buddhist studies and in the social sciences; offers program in Nepal studies

• Languages offered: Hindi, Urdu, Teluga, Tamil, Nepali, Sanskrit, Pali, Vedic, Prakrit, Persian, Turkish, Tibetan and Indonesian; Marathi and Bengali offered as needed

• Library collection holds 70,000 volumes in South Asian languages and 50,000 volumes on South Asia in other languages; includes 4,000 periodicals and 25 newspapers; participates in South Asian Microfilm Project; department is headquarters of the International Association of Buddhist Studies

• Art Center contains large collection of Indian miniature paintings

• Overseas study programs available in India (full year) and Nepal (semester)

• Actively encourages visiting scholars and researchers, especially through a program with the Associated Colleges of the Midwest (see 8.003)

• Outreach program of the Center advises elementary and secondary school teachers, conducts teacher workshops and institutes, sponsors community lectures, conferences and symposia, and publishes a community-oriented *News Report;* people outside the University may become associate members of the Center

• Center prepares and publishes language instructional materials and other papers and produces documentary and informational television programs on South Asia

• Wide range of scholarship and fellowship assistance available for on-campus and overseas study

13.130
East Asian Area Studies
University of Wisconsin at Madison
1440 Van Hise Hall
Madison, WI 53706
(608) 262-3643

Contact(s):
Solomon Levine and William Nienhauser, Jr., Co-Chairs

Graduate and undergraduate area studies program established in 1963
• Majors/degrees/certificates offered: B.A. with concentration in East Asian Studies; departmental Ph.D. with concentration or minor in East Asian Studies
• Approximate number of faculty teaching area and language courses: 37
• Approximate number of courses available—area: 88; language: 112
• Average number of students per year specializing in area: 124 graduate; 7 undergraduate
• Countries covered and areas of emphasis: China and Japan
• Languages offered: Chinese and Japanese
• Library contains approximately 150,000 volumes in Chinese and Japanese and 13,000 in Tibetan along with 200 East Asian periodicals; extensive holdings in Western languages, primarily English

13.131
Center for Advancing Intercultural Communication
University of Guam
P.O. Box EK
Agana, GU 96910

Contact(s):
Tom Bruneau, Director

• Conducts research on intercultural communication and education problems; develops curriculum in cultural learning and intercultural relations and offers workshops, seminars and conferences on intercultural communication, especially as they relate to native Chamorros, Micronesian and Filipino cultures, visiting Japanese tourists and other Oriental groups

13.132
Micronesian Area Research Center
University of Guam
MARC/UOG
Mangilao, GU 96913
(671) 734-2921

Contact(s):
Albert L. Williams, Librarian

• Conducts research on the history and cultures of the peoples of the Micronesian Islands; publishes reports and monographs and *The Guam Recorder* (news from the Center); library holds approximately 20,000 volumes on Micronesia and the Pacific Islands and serves as repository for South Pacific Commission documents

Information and Service Organizations

13.133
American Committee for South Asian Art
Amherst College
Department of Fine Arts
Fayerweather Hall
Amherst, MA 01002
(413) 542-2123

Contact(s):
Sara L. Schastok, President

Professional association for advancing the study and awareness of South Asian art
• Develops resources for the study and appreciation of South Asian art including a

color slide collection of South Asian art and architecture, a Microfiche Archive and a slide/cassette study unit on South Asian art for use in schools

• Conducts meetings and symposia and publishes a semiannual newsletter reporting on activities, grants, awards, materials development, academic programs, exhibitions and general activities in the South Asian art field

13.134
American Oriental Society
329 Sterling Memorial Library
Yale Station
New Haven, CT 06520
(203) 436-1040

Contact(s):
Stanley Insler, Treasurer

• Promotes research on Oriental languages, history and civilization; maintains library of periodicals and monographs and offers grants for the study of Chinese art
• Publishes a quarterly journal, a monograph series and occasional essays

13.135
The Asia Society, Inc.
725 Park Ave.
New York, NY 10021
(212) 288-6400
BRANCHES: Houston, Washington, DC

Contact(s):
Robert B. Oxnam, President
Timothy Plummer, Director, Education and
   Communications

Educational organization designed to further knowledge and understanding of Asia in the U.S.

• Provides information and teaching materials, schedules artistic performances and films, maintains art exhibitions at the Asia Society Galleries, organizes conferences, seminars and corporate and media briefings on major political trends and issues; publishes *Asia Society Newsletter, Focus on Asian Studies* (see 2.200); includes a special issue *Vietnam: A Teacher's Guide;* prepares and distributes teaching materials including: "Opening Doors: Contemporary India," "Video Letter from Japan" and guides to films on Asia and China; presents Discover Asia courses and lecture series at New York headquarters; collaborates with broadcasting companies in the production of television and radio presentations; sponsors The China Council of the Asia Society (see 18.077)

13.136
Association for Asian Studies, Inc.
University of Michigan
1 Lane Hall
Ann Arbor, MI 48109
(313) 665-2490

Contact(s):
Carol Jean Johnson, Administrative Officer

Professional association of individuals concerned with Asian Studies

• Provides information on and proposes future directions for Asian Studies
• Publishes the *Asian Studies Newsletter* (see 13.165), several Monograph Series, the *Journal of Asian Studies* (see 13.173), *Bibliography of Asian Studies* (see 13.146), *Directory of Asian Studies Collections in North American Libraries, Focus on Asian Studies* (for teachers) and various other bulletins and newsletters aimed at librarians or specific country specialists
• Conducts national and regional meetings, maintains job placement service and sponsors charter flight to Asia

13.137
Pacific Studies Center
222B View St.
Mountain View, CA 94041
(415) 969-1545

Public interest information center located in Silicon Valley
  • Provides library facilities designed for research in the areas of U.S. foreign and military policy, the political economy of Asia and the Pacific, high technology and its international impact, and peace, arms control and disarmament
  • Conducts file searches by phone or mail request (research fees start at $7.50 per hour)
  • Publishes *Pacific Research* (quarterly, though irregular, journal containing articles on U.S. diplomatic, economic and military

relations with Asia and the Pacific) and the monthly *Global Electronics Information Newsletter*

13.138
The Society for Asian Music
Hagop Kevorkian Center
50 Washington Square South
New York, NY 10012
(212) 598-7944

Contact(s):
Kinza Schuyler, Administrator

Educational association designed to promote appreciation of Asian music and dance
  • Sponsors performances of classical and folk music and dance in New York; publishes *Asian Music*

Sources of Grants and Awards

13.139
The Asia Foundation
550 Kearny St.
San Francisco, CA 94108
(415) 982-4640

Contact(s):
Robert S. Schwantes, Executive Vice
    President

Nonprofit programming and grant-giving philanthropic organization concerned with Asian development
  • Conducts programs and provides grants to individuals and institutions which meet the educational and development needs of Asian countries; includes extensive exchange program which supports conference participation for both Asians and Americans, which brings Asian students, trainees and professionals to the U.S. for study and/or observa-

tion, and which sends American consultants and specialists to Asia
  • Sponsors "Books for Asia" program under which books and periodicals are sent to Asian university and other libraries
  • Publishes newsletter

13.140
East-West Center
1777 East-West Road
Honolulu, HI 96848
(808) 944-7111

Contact(s):
Victor Hooli, President

  • Awards grants for research and training to U.S., Asian and Pacific Islands visiting fellows, scholars, graduate students and professionals (see 13.035)

13.141
National Science Foundation
United States-East Asia Cooperative Science
   Program
Division of International Programs
Washington, DC 20550
(202) 357-9537

Contact(s):
Gordon Hiebert, Program Manager

• Funds programs involving cooperative research, seminars and workshops and short-term visits between the U.S. and five Southeast Asian countries (Indonesia, Malaysia, the Philippines, Singapore and Thailand)

13.142
Social Science Research Council
Fellowships for International Research:
   South and Southeast Asia
605 Third Ave.
New York, NY 10158
(212) 557-9500

• Awards fellowships for dissertation research in the social sciences and humanities, and for the advanced research of students in programs in which the doctoral degree is not usually offered, such as law, architecture, or urban/regional planning; fellowships may be used for research to be carried out in one or more countries in East, Southeast and South Asia, except for India and Pakistan; those who wish to conduct research in India or Pakistan should contact the American Institute of Indian Studies (see 18.203) or the American Institute of Pakistan Studies (see 18.392)
• Awards postdoctoral grants to humanists and social scientists to conduct research on Bangladesh, India, Nepal, Pakistan and Sri Lanka; applicants must be citizens or permanent residents of the U.S. or Canada; does not include support for travel to or research within India and Pakistan since funds are available for those purposes from the American Institute of Indian Studies (see 18.203) and the American Institute of Pakistan Stud-

ies (see 18.392); applications are welcome for research on all aspects of the societies and cultures of historical and contemporary South Asia
• Awards postdoctoral grants to social scientists, humanists, and other professionals to conduct research or analyze previously gathered research materials on Brunei, Burma, Indonesia, Kampuchea, Laos, Malaysia, the Philippines, Thailand, Singapore and Vietnam; proposals are welcome for research on all aspects of the societies and cultures of historical and contemporary Southeast Asia; research may be carried out in Southeast Asia, at major collections of Southeast Asian materials, or at any other appropriate locale
• Awards grants under Indochina Studies Program to researchers, writers, journalists, artists and other professionals and individuals in support of research, writing and the archiving of materials on Cambodia, Laos and Vietnam drawing on the knowledge and experience of refugees from those countries now residing in the United States.

13.143
Taraknath Das Foundation, Inc.
℅ Southern Asian Institute
Columbia University
420 West 118th St.
New York, NY 10027
(212) 280-4462

Contact(s):
Kathryn Linden, Director

Foundation which supports activities related to Indian and Asian studies
• Provides small grants to Indian students studying in the U.S. and to scholars conducting research on India or Asia
• Awards small institutional grants to colleges and universities in the U.S. and abroad in support of international education activities
• Sponsors lectures in New York on Asian and Indian subjects

Guides, Sourcebooks and Directories

13.144

Asia: Reference Works: A Selected Annotated Guide
G. Raymond Nunn, Editor
Mansell Publishing Co.
3 Bloomsbury Place
London WC1A 2QA, England
1980; hardbound; 382 pages; $44

• Lists and describes encyclopedias, handbooks, yearbooks, directories, statistical compilations, bibliographies, atlases and dictionaries for Asia in general, for the regions of Asia and for each country from Japan to Pakistan (does not include Afghanistan, the Middle East or the Pacific)

13.145

Bibliography of Asian Studies
Estrella S. Bryant, Editor
Association for Asian Studies
One Lane Hall
University of Michigan
Ann Arbor, MI 48109
paperbound; 682 pages; $35 per year for
    institutions; nonmembers, $23 per year;
    members, $14 per year

• Comprehensive listing of publications in Western languages on East, South and Southeast Asia in the fields of history, the humanities and social sciences, with selected titles from science and technology when they relate to Asian society and culture; includes monographs, journal articles, commemorative volumes and government documents

13.146

Current Asian & Australasian Directories
I. G. Anderson, Editor
CBD Research, Ltd.
154 High St.
Beckenham
Kent BR3 1EA, England
1978; hardbound; 264 pages; $85

• Lists directories published in or relating to all countries in Asia, Australasia and Oceania, including Turkey and Cyprus, but excluding the Soviet Union; includes yearbooks, almanacs, gazeteers, general industrial and commercial directories; telephone, telex and telegraphic directories; research, library and bibliographic directories; and regional, specialized and technical directories; provides publisher and bibliographic data, description of content, languages used, frequency, date published, price and length

13.147

East Asian Economies
Molly K.S.C. Lee, Editor
Gale Research Co.
Book Tower
Detroit, MI 48226
1979; hardbound; 326 pages; $40

• Bibliographic information about works on the economies of China, Japan, Korea and Taiwan from 1900 to the present

13.148

Far East and Australasia
Europa Publications, Ltd.
London, England
annual hardbound; 912 pages; $140

Available from Gale Research Co., Book Tower, Detroit, MI 48226
• Very comprehensive yearbook, survey and compilation of data, statistics and directory-type information
• Covers international organizations active in the Far East and Australasia, including the UN and other political, cultural, educational and economic development organizations
• For each country entry there is an extensive survey of historical and cultural background and then a generous compilation of

data, statistics, lists of names and descriptive materials in the following areas: economics, principal characteristics, social structure, government offices and officers, judicial system, media, publishers, financial institutions, trade and industrial entities, transportation, tourism/culture, atomic energy, defense, education and dependencies

13.149
Far Eastern Economic Review: Asia Yearbook
Donald Wise, Editor
Far Eastern Economic Review, Ltd.
GPO 160, Hong Kong
annual; 320 pages; hardbound, $11.95;
     paperbound, $8.95

• Surveys region on a country-by-country basis relative to political relationships, food and population, finances, investment, economics, energy, aviation, shipping, trade, foreign aid, refugees and relations with the Middle East
• Lists major political figures and gives both demographic and economic statistics
• Covers 30 countries, entities or regions, Japan to Afghanistan (including Australasia)

13.150
International Directory of Centers for Asian Studies
Asian Research Service
P.O. Box 2232
G.P.O. Hong Kong
1983; paperbound; 140 pages; $30

• Worldwide directory of research centers and institutes concerned with Asian Studies; gives address, personnel, current research projects and titles of selected recent publications

13.151
International Relations of South Asia, 1947–1980
Richard J. Kozicki, Editor
Gale Research Co.
Book Tower
Detroit, MI 48226
1981; hardbound; 166 pages; $40

• Bibliographic information about works on the international relations of eight major South Asian nations

13.152
International Who's Who in Asian Studies
Nelson Leung, Editor
Asian Research Service
P.O. Box 2232
G.P.O., Hong Kong
published periodically; paperbound; approx.
     300 pages each; 3 volumes, $30 each

• Biographical directory with new names listed in separate volumes published serially; each in two parts: (1) biographical information on scholars and (2) a classified authors index to doctoral dissertations

13.153
The Pacific Islands
Douglas Oliver
The University Press of Hawaii
2849 Kolowalu St.
Honolulu, HI 96822
1975; paperbound; 480 pages; $5.95

• A reissue of the 1961 revision of a 1951 classic and readable history of the islands and cultures of the Pacific basin; particularly useful in its review of the dramatic changes that have taken place in the last 50 years; covers geography, economics, ethnology and politics as well as more broadly historical and cultural concerns

13.154
Pacific Islands Year Book
Pacific Publications (Aust.) Pty. Ltd.
29 Alberta St.
Sydney, N.S.W. 2000, Australia
annual; hardbound; 557 pages; $30

Available from International Publications Service, 114 East 32d St., New York, NY 10016
• Provides general and commercial information on the countries and islands of the Pacific (Polynesia, Melanesia, Micronesia and the nontropical islands); covers government offices and officers, economic, cultural and social information and other data; contains much hard-to-find information for this area

13.155
Scholar's Guides to Washington, D.C.:
South Asian Studies, East Asian Studies,
Southeast Asia
Enayetur Rahim
Smithsonian Institution Press
Washington, DC 20560
three separate volumes: *South Asian Studies*, 1982, 438 pages, paperbound, $12.50; hardbound, $29.95; *East Asian Studies*, 1979, 413 pages, paperbound, $9.95; hardbound, $22.50; *Southeast Asian Studies*, 1982, 411 pages, paperbound, $12.50; hardbound, $29.95

Each volume provides a comprehensive listing and description of resources in the Washington area available to researchers and others interested in South, East and Southeast Asia, and is divided into two sections: collections (libraries, archives, museums, etc., music and sound, maps, films, and databanks) and organizations (research centers and information offices, academic programs, U.S. government agencies, embassies and international organizations, professional associations, exchange and technical assistance organizations, religious organizations, and publications/media); resources described in some detail with clear indication how and from whom to obtain access; appendices include lists of libraries (by size of holdings), bookstores, housing, transport and other services, along with a bibliography; indexed by name of resource, personal papers collections, and library subject strength

13.156
South Asian Civilizations: A Selected
Analytical Bibliography
Maureen L. P. Patterson
University of Chicago Press
5801 Ellis Ave.
Chicago, IL 60637
1981; hardbound; 854 pages; $50

• Presents over 28,000 periodical and monograph references on all aspects of Indic and South Asian civilizations

13.157
Southeast Asian Affairs
Heinemann Educational Books, Inc.
4 Front St.
Exeter, NH 03833
annual; hardbound; 362 pages; $32.50

Commissioned by and produced under the auspices of the Institute of Southeast Asian Studies, Singapore
• Yearbook including articles on the region as a whole and on each country providing an overview of current developments and issues

13.158
Statistics—Asia and Australasia
Joan M. Harvey, Editor
CBD Research, Ltd.
Beckenham, England
1974; hardbound; 240 pages; $72

Distributed by Gale Research Co., Book Tower, Detroit, MI 48226

• Provides extensive listing (live and print) of sources of statistical data for each country of Asia and Australasia; includes central statistical offices and other important statistics collection agencies, principal libraries containing statistics, libraries and information services in other countries which supply statistics on each country, principal bibliographies of statistical compilations, and major statistical publications with full address and/or bibliographic information

13.159
A Survey of Materials for the Study of the Uncommonly Taught Languages: Languages of Southeast Asia & the Pacific, South Asia and Eastern Asia
Dora E. Johnson et al.
Center for Applied Linguistics
3520 Prospect St. NW
Washington, DC 20007

1976; paperbound; three separate volumes: Southeast Asia and the Pacific, 59 pages; South Asia, 41 pages; Eastern Asia, 37 pages; each volume $7.95

Exclusively distributed by Harcourt Brace Jovanich, Inc., 757 Third Ave., New York, NY 10017, Attn: Nancy McCloughan

• One of a series of bibliographies covering all the modern languages except Standard English, German, Italian, Russian and Spanish; designed for use by the adult learner whose native language is English; listed under the headings: teaching materials, readers, grammars and dictionaries; includes books currently in print where feasible, older titles where not; citations appear under the following countries/language groups: *Southeast Asia and the Pacific:* Burma (and Yunan), Cambodia, Laos and Thailand, Vietnam, Indonesia and Malaysia, the Philippines, languages of the Pacific and Polynesian; *South Asia:* Indo-Aryan, Dravidian, Munda, Tibeto-Burman and Mon-Khmer; *Eastern Asia:* Chinese, Japanese, Korean, Mongolian and Tibetan

Periodicals

13.160
The Asia Mail
Donna Gays, Managing Editor
Potomac-Asia Communications, Inc.
2d Floor, The Alexandria Gazette Bldg.
717 North St. Asaph St.
Alexandria, VA 22314
monthly tabloid; 30 pages; subscription
    range: $9 to $18

• Presents American perspectives on Asia and the Pacific area; includes well-informed articles and special reports by known writers on current affairs in Asia and on Asian-American relationships and contacts; emphasizes

politics, business and travel; includes classified section and book reviews

13.161
Asia Pacific Community
Hideo Ueno, Editor
Asian Club, Suite 2302
World Trade Center Bldg.
2-4-1, Hamamalsu-cho
Minato-Ku, Tokyo, Japan
quarterly journal; approx. 100 pages; $24
    per year

• Contains general articles and analyses

of contemporary political, economic and international affairs in East Asia and the Pacific Basin

13.162
Asia Research Bulletin

Asia Research (Pte.), Ltd.
P.O. Box 91, Alexandra Post Office
Singapore 9115, Republic of Singapore
monthly; 20 pages; each report $2.90 per
    month; all 5 reports plus political
    supplement $14.50 per month ($3.25 and
    $16.20 airmail)

Bulletin published as five reports and one supplement each month, titled as follows: (1) Plans, Policies and Indicators; (2) Manufacturing and Service Industries; (3) Foreign Aid, Trade and Investment; (4) Commodities and Primary Industries; (5) Energy and Mineral Resources; and (6) Monthly Political Supplement; first five available separately or all together with Political Supplement; designed to be collected and easily used; binder available

    • Reviews significant Asian economic trends and developments in each of the subject areas covered focusing on specific countries, important issues and major sectors of activity; designed for practical use; charts and basic statistics included; front-page index

13.163
Asian Affairs: An American Review

James Hsuing, Stephen Cohen and Donald
    Weatherbee, Editors
Hildref Publications
4000 Albemarle St. NW
Washington, DC 20016
quarterly journal; approx. 80 pages; $40 per
    year

    • Contains substantive but not excessively academic articles on U.S. policy in Asia (Japan to Afghanistan) and on the domestic politics and economies of Asian countries

13.164
Asian Profile

Nelson Leung, Managing Editor
Asian Research Service
P.O. Box 2232
G.P.O., Hong Kong
bimonthly journal; approx. 100 pages; $60
    per year for institutions, $30 per year for
    individuals

    • Contains articles from scholars inside and outside Asia on subjects of current interest to the Asian Studies community; includes book reviews

13.165
Asian Studies Newsletter

Association for Asian Studies, Inc.
1 Lane Hall
University of Michigan
Ann Arbor, MI 48109
published 5 times a year; newsletter;
    approx. 40 pages; $3.50 per year; free to
    members of the Association

    • Reports on news of the Association along with extensive coverage of developments in the field in general, announcements of exhibits, study programs, conferences, publications and resource materials

13.166
Asian Survey

Robert A. Scalapino and Leo E. Rose,
    Editors
University of California Press
Berkeley, CA 94720
monthly journal; approx. 100 pages;
    individuals, $30 per year; institutions, $55
    per year

    • Includes articles on economics, politics and political relationships in East, Southeast and South Asia and between Asian countries and the U.S. and the USSR

13.167
Bulletin of Concerned Asian Scholars
Joe Moore, Editor
Concerned Asian Scholars
Box R
Berthoud, CO 80513
quarterly journal; approx. 70 pages;
    individuals, $20 per year; institutions, $35
    per year

    • Contains articles on contemporary
Asian political, economic and social affairs from
a Marxist perspective

13.168
Contemporary Southeast Asia
Singapore University Press
University of Singapore
Bukit Timah Road
Singapore 10, Singapore
quarterly journal; approx. 100 pages; $12
    per year

    • Contains general articles and com-
mentary on current Southeast Asian economic and political issues

13.169
**East-West Culture Learning Institute
Report**
William Reltz, Editor
East-West Culture Learning Institute
East-West Center
Honolulu, HI 96848
quarterly newsletter; 8 pages; free

    • Provides brief substantive reports on
the subjects of research interest at the Culture Learning Institute (see 13.035) and on
the projects through which they are pursued

13.170
East-West Perspectives
Robert J. Armbruster, Editor
Office of Public Affairs
East-West Center
1777 East-West Rd.
Honolulu, HI 96848
quarterly magazine; approx. 36 pages; $12
    per year

    • Contains short but substantive articles
on subjects of current and general interest to
people concerned with Asian (Pacific)–American affairs; covers culture, society, economics, art and other topics

13.171
Harvard Journal of Asiatic Studies
Harvard-Yenching Institute
2 Divinity Ave.
Cambridge, MA 02138
semiannual journal; approx. 350 pages; $15
    per year

    • Scholarly articles on East Asian Stud-
ies; extensive book reviews

13.172
Indochina Issues
Center for International Policy
120 Maryland Ave. NW
Washington, DC 20002
10 issues per year; newsletter; 8 pages; $9
    per year; $19, foreign air mail

    • Reports on and analyzes political, eco-
nomic and human rights issues in Vietnam,
Laos and Kampuchea, especially in the context of U.S. foreign policy

13.173
The Journal of Asian Studies
Ralph W. Nicholas, Editor
Association for Asian Studies, Inc.
1 Lane Hall
University of Michigan
Ann Arbor, MI 48109
quarterly journal; 200 pages; $40 per year;
    free to members

• Contains substantive articles on subjects of interest to the Asian Studies scholar
along with a large number of book reviews;
includes correspondence section and annual
index

13.174
**Journal of South Asian and Middle
Eastern Studies**
Hafeez Malik, Editor
Pakistan American Foundation
138 Tolentine Hall
Villanova University
Villanova, PA 19085
quarterly journal; approx. 96 pages; $15 per
    year; $18 per year, foreign

• Articles on the modern Islamic and
non-Islamic societies of South Asia, the Middle East and North Africa, with a current
affairs as well as a scholarly orientation

13.175
Journal of Southeast Asian Studies
Yong Mun Cheong, Editor
Singapore University Press
University of Singapore
Bukit Timah Road
Singapore 10, Singapore
semiannual journal; approx. 240 pages; $6
    per copy

• Contains scholarly articles and essays
on Southeast Asian history with some attention to contemporary affairs; extensive book
review section

13.176
Modern Asian Studies
Gordon Johnson, Editor
Cambridge University Press
32 East 57th St.
New York, NY 10022
quarterly journal; approx. 175 pages;
    institutions: $108 per year

Individuals ordering directly from the publishers and who certify that the journal is for
their personal use may subscribe at a reduced rate of $54
• Includes scholarly articles and essays
on aspects of Asian social and political affairs
both contemporary and historical; book reviews

13.177
Philosophy East & West
Eliot Deutsch, Editor
The University Press of Hawaii
2840 Kolowalu St.
Honolulu, HI 96822
quarterly journal; institutions, $18.50;
    individuals, $13.50

• Journal of Asian and comparative
thought and philosophy, including articles
which relate philosophy to the arts, literature, science and social practice of Asian civilizations

13.178
Oceania
P. Lawrence, Editor
Oceania Publications
Mackie Bldg.
University of Sydney
Sydney, N.S.W. 206, Australia
quarterly journal; approx. 80 pages; $26 per
    year

Oceania Publications also publishes a series
of Linguistic Monographs on the languages of

the indigenous peoples of Australia and the larger Pacific Islands

 • Contains scholarly articles on the indigenous peoples of Australia, Melanesia, Micronesia, Indonesia and the Philippines

13.179
Orientations
Pacific Magazines, Ltd.
13th Floor, 200 Lockhart Road
Hong Kong
monthly magazine; approx. 75 pages; $40
  per year

 • Illustrated articles on historic and contemporary Asian (including Near Eastern) art;

includes calendar of current exhibitions and events and book reviews

13.180
Pacific Affairs
H. B. Chamberlain, Editor
University of British Columbia
William Byrd Press
2901 Byrdhill Road
Richmond, VA 23261
quarterly journal; approx. 200 pages; $20
  per year

 • Contains articles on the contemporary social, economic and political affairs of Asia and the Pacific; book reviews

Publishers

13.181
Asia Books
P.O. Box 873
Carbondale, IL 62901

 • Distributes books on Southeast Asian peoples and cultures, especially Vietnam; includes Vietnamese-English dictionaries

13.182
Asian Research Service
G.P.O. Box 2232
Hong Kong
5-733641; 5-731788

Contact(s):
Nelson Leung, Director

International education organization designed to promote research on Asia and arrange contacts among scholars, teachers and students of Asian studies

 • Sponsors major annual international symposium on Asian Studies and publishes the proceedings in five volumes: *China, Japan and Korea, Southeast Asia, South and Southwest Asia* and *Asia and Other Regions* (price range is $10–$40)
 • Publishes monograph series on selected topics in Asian Studies, including military and strategic weapons issues; the *International Who's Who in Asian Studies* (biographical directory along with an index to doctoral dissertations); the *International Directory of Centers for Asian Studies* (see 13.150) and the periodical *Asian Profile* (see 13.164)

13.183
The Cellar Book Shop
18090 Wyoming St.
Detroit, MI 48221
(313) 861-1776

• Distributes books on Southeast Asian and Pacific affairs, especially the Philippines, the Pacific Islands, Australia and New Zealand; includes *An Annotated Bibliography of Philippine Bibliographies: 1965–74* (158 pages; $7.50) and *Thailand: An Annotated Bibliography of Bibliographies* (see 18.479); will send regular flyers announcing new books available from these areas

13.184
Cornell University Press
Box 250
124 Roberts Place
Ithaca, NY 14851
(607) 257-7000

• Publishes an extensive list of titles in Asian Studies primarily in the areas of politics, history, social and economic development and international political and economic relations, particularly on South and Southeast Asia; also includes a number of language volumes (English-Indonesian and Indonesian-English dictionaries and two volumes on Hindi) and a series of solid but slightly out-of-date studies on individual countries (particularly focused on politics): *Malaysia and Singapore* (1978), *Burma* (1977), *Thailand* (1981), *Indonesia* (1972), *Afghanistan* (1971), *Bhutan* (1977), *Nepal* (1970), and *Pakistan* (1970) which are part of two series: Politics and International Relations of Southeast Asia and South Asian Political Systems

13.185
Dharma Publishing
2425 Hillside Ave.
Berkeley, CA 94704
(415) 548-5407

• Publishes extensive list of books on Buddhism for the Western reader

13.186
G. K. Hall & Co.
70 Lincoln St.
Boston, MA 02111
(617) 423-3990

Commercial reference book publisher
• Publishes Asian Studies series of reference books concentrating principally on bibliographies on a wide range of subjects; includes a series on religions (Buddhism, Hinduism, Chinese philosophy); *China: An Annotated Bibliography of Bibliographies* (see 18.091), *Vietnam: A Guide to Reference Sources* (see 18.583) and handbooks of historical statistics for Sri Lanka and Thailand

13.187
Harper & Row, Publishers, Inc.
10 East 53rd St.
New York, NY 10022
(800) 233-4175

• Publishes extensive list of books on Asian subjects particularly in the areas of art, history, current affairs, reference and religion with a particularly strong selection on China and Japan; distributes publications of Kodansha International (see 18.283) and Japan Publications

13.188
Heinemann Educational Books, Inc.
4 Front St.
Exeter, NH 03833
(603) 778-0534

• Publishes extensive list of Asian political, social and economic studies along with fiction and literature; particular strength in Southeast Asia including the annual *Southeast Asian Affairs* (see 13.158)

13.189
International Scholarly School Book Services, Inc.
Box 1632
Beaverton, OR 97075
(503) 292-2602

• Imports and distributes books published in and about Australia and the Pacific Islands; includes *Encyclopaedia of Papua and New Guinea* (see 18.398)

13.190
Paragon Book Reprint Corporation
14 East 38th St.
New York, NY 10016
(212) 532-4920

• Reprints significant works on Asian history and literature, particularly on China and Japan

13.191
South Asia Books
P.O. Box 502
Columbia, MO 65205
(314) 449-1359

• Importer and distributor of books from and about South Asian countries; particularly strong in the culture, history, religion and contemporary social, political and economic affairs of India

13.192
Southeast Asia Resource Center
P.O. Box 4000D
Berkeley, CA 94704
(415) 548-2546

Contact(s):
Martha K. Winnacker, Editor

Resource center on Indochina (Vietnam, Laos and Kampuchea), Thailand, Indonesia and the Philippines; formerly Indochina Resource Center supporting anti-Vietnam War movement

• Publishes *Southeast Asia Chronicle* (bi-monthly) and books and pamphlets on war, peace, human rights, regional politics, Communist Party activity, development, military and technical assistance, and revolution

13.193
Three Continents Press, Inc.
1346 Connecticut Ave. NW, Suite 1131
Washington, DC 20036
(202) 457-0288 or 387-5809

Commercial publishing house
• Publishes books by and about contemporary Asian and Pacific writers and writing, along with a few historical, reference and sociological titles; includes *Asia/Pacific Literatures in English: Bibliographies*

13.194
Charles E. Tuttle Co., Inc.
28 South Main St.
Rutland, VT 05701
(802) 773-8930

Commercial publishing house
• Publishes and distributes a large catalogue of English-language books on East and Southeast Asia and the Pacific with a particularly extensive list on and from Japan, including literature and other materials in Japanese; covers such areas as arts and crafts, sports and games, history, politics, literature, language, culture, customs, religion, philosophy and travel; language materials include dictionaries, grammars, readers, phrase-books, etc. for Chinese, Hawaiian, Indonesian, Malay, Japanese, Korean, Lao, Maori, Tagalog, Thai and Vietnamese (see individual countries/languages)

13.195
University of Hawaii Press
2840 Kolowalu St.
Honolulu, HI 96822
(808) 948-8255

University publishing house
• Publishes extensive list of titles in Asian Studies covering Asia in general, China, Japan, Korea, South Asia and Southeast Asia; particularly strong in Philippine studies and in cultural and cross-cultural studies, development economics, language texts (especially of the Pacific Island languages, including Fijian, Tongan and Tagalog, see country entries), with other titles in history, politics, and economics; includes a variety of dictionaries, bibliographies and sourcebooks and the journals *Korean Studies* (see 18.320), *Asian Perspectives* and *Philosophy East and West*

(see 13.177); also publishes and/or distributes books for the East-West Center, the Korea Development Institute, the University of the Philippines Press, the Polynesian Society, Seoul National University Press, and the Institute for Polynesian Studies

13.196
University of Washington Press
P.O. Box 85569
Seattle, WA 98145
(206) 543-4050

• Publishes extensive selection of books in Asian and Asian American Studies covering current and historical subjects; particularly strong in Chinese art, literature and history

14
East European Area Studies

Area Studies Programs and Research Centers

14.001
Center for Russian and East European Studies
Stanford University
Room 200, Lou Henry Hoover Bldg.
Stanford, CA 94305
(415) 497-3562

Contact(s):
Wayne S. Vucinich, Director

Graduate and undergraduate area studies program established in 1964
• Majors/degrees/certificates offered:

A.M. in Russia and East Europe Studies; also coterminal B.A./M.A. programs in departments of History, Political Science and Slavic Languages and Literatures
• Approximate number of faculty teaching area and language courses: 17
• Approximate number of courses available—area: 17; language and literature: 46
• Average number of students per year specializing in area: 3
• Countries covered and areas of emphasis: particular strength in Russian history and literature and in Soviet and Eastern European politics

• Languages offered: Russian; occasionally Czech or other Slavic languages

• Main campus libraries and the Hoover Institution (see 4.159) contain over 400,000 volumes in the area of Russia/Eastern Europe

• Russian language study available in the Soviet Union

14.002
Center for Slavic and East European Studies
University of California at Berkeley
Berkeley, CA 94720
(415) 642-3230

Contact(s):
Gail W. Lapidus, Chair

Graduate and undergraduate area studies program

• Majors/degrees/certificates offered: Certificate in Russian and East European Studies with B.A., M.A. and Ph.D. in disciplines

• Approximate number of faculty teaching area and language courses: 35

• Approximate number of courses available—area and language: 290

• Average number of students per year specializing in area: 50 graduate; 350 undergraduate

• Countries covered and areas of emphasis: the Soviet Union and the countries of Eastern Europe; strength in the social sciences and philosophy

• Languages offered: Czech, Hungarian, Polish, Romanian, Russian and Serbo-Croatian

• Library contains over 300,000 books and 10,000 serials in Slavic and East European languages along with extensive collections of Western and English language Slavica; graduate library of the Department of Slavic Languages and Literatures houses an additional 10,000 volumes

• Conducts outreach programs for school teachers and the community and a Summer Institute in the Russian Language

• Hosts approximately 70 scholars from Eastern Europe each year; Berkeley faculty and students participate extensively in exchanges with Eastern European institutions

• Overseas study available at Leningrad University

14.003
Center for Russian and East European Studies
University of California at Los Angeles
334 Kinsey Hall
Los Angeles, CA 90024
(213) 825-4060

Contact(s):
Andrzej Korbonski, Director

Graduate and undergraduate area studies program established in 1957

• Majors/degrees/certificates offered: B.A. in language and history departments; M.A. and Ph.D. in language, history and political science departments

• Approximate number of faculty teaching area and language courses: 48

• Approximate number of courses available—area: 114; language: 48

• Average number of students per year specializing in area: 45 B.A., 10 M.A., and 9 Ph.D.

• Countries covered and areas of emphasis: Soviet Union, Hungary, Bulgaria, Finland, Poland, Romania, Czechoslovakia, Albania and Yugoslavia

• Languages offered: Russian, Bulgarian, Czech, Finnish, Hungarian, Lithuanian, Polish, Romanian, Serbo-Croatian and Ukrainian

• Library contains research collections on Eastern Europe and an Eastern European Reading Room; audiovisual teaching materials also available

• Conducts outreach program for community, educational and business organizations

• Overseas study available at Inter-University Center for Postgraduate Studies, Dubrovnik, Yugoslavia

14.004
Russian and East/Central European Studies
Colorado State University
315 Aylesworth
Fort Collins, CO 80523
(303) 491-6854

Contact(s):
Sidney Heitman, Director

Undergraduate area studies program established in 1975

• Majors/degrees/certificates offered: B.A. in department with Certificate in Russian and East/Central European Studies

• Approximate number of faculty teaching area and language courses: 6

• Approximate number of courses available—area: 20; language: 6

• Average number of students per year specializing in area: 12

• Countries covered and areas of emphasis: all countries of Eastern and Central Europe

• Languages offered: Russian and German

14.005
Central and East European Studies
University of Colorado, Boulder
Ketchum Bldg., Room 215
Boulder, CO 80309
(303) 492-6683

Contact(s):
Edward J. Rozek, Chair

• Offers B.A. in Central and East European Studies; languages: German, Russian, Polish and Serbo-Croatian

14.006
Center for Slavic and East European Studies
University of Connecticut
U-149, Wood Hall 333
Storrs, CT 06268
(203) 486-3855

Contact(s):
Samuel F. Orth, Director

Graduate and undergraduate area studies program

• Majors/degrees/certificates offered: B.A. in Slavic and East European Studies; M.A. in International Studies with concentration in Slavic and East European Studies; Ph.D. in departments with specialization in Soviet and East European Studies; dual degree with the School of Business Administration

• Countries covered and areas of emphasis: Europe; particularly strong in Russian/Soviet Studies and the Slavic countries, especially Poland, Bulgaria, Hungary and Yugoslavia

• Languages offered: Russian and Polish; through independent study Critical Languages Program: Ukrainian, Lithuanian, Czech, Serbo-Croatian, Hungarian, Estonian, Armenian, Bulgarian and Romanian

• Sponsors research and maintains exchange relationships with institutions in Yugoslavia, Poland and Hungary

• Summer study abroad available in the U.S.S.R., Poland and Yugoslavia

• Sponsors community outreach program including teacher workshops

• Publishes occasional papers and a number of handbooks

14.007
Russian and East European Studies
Yale University
Box 13A
New Haven, CT 06520
(203) 436-0250

Contact(s):
Paul Bushkovitch

Graduate and undergraduate area studies
program
  • Majors/degrees/certificates offered:
B.A. and two-year M.A. in Russian and East
European Studies; departmental Ph.D. with
concentration in Russian and East European
Studies
  • Approximate number of faculty teach-
ing area and language courses: 34
  • Approximate number of courses avail-
able—area: 36; language: 26
  • Countries covered and areas of em-
phasis: all the nations of the Soviet bloc; strong
in language, literature, history, politics and
economics
  • Languages offered: Bulgarian, Czech,
Hungarian, Polish, Russian, Serbo-Croatian
and Ukrainian (also offered at Yale Summer
Language Institute)
  • Library maintains major Slavic and East
European research collection with approxi-
mately 273,000 volumes in Russian and other
East European languages and 200,000 in
Western languages; contains vast archives and
personal papers in the Russian, Polish and
Czech areas
  • Sponsors Outreach Program of semi-
nars and curriculum development assistance
for elementary and secondary schools

14.008
Institute for Sino-Soviet Studies
George Washington University
School of Public and International Affairs
Washington, DC 20052
(202) 676-6340

Contact(s):
Gaston J. Sigur, Director

  • Research and teaching center on China
and the Soviet bloc (see 13.030)

14.009
**Graduate Program in Slavic and East
European Studies**
Florida State University
562 Bellamy Bldg.
Tallahassee, FL 32306-2049
(904) 644-4418

Contact(s):
Richard B. Gray, Director

  • Offers M.A. in Slavic and East European Studies with emphasis on history and
the social sciences and comparative study of
the U.S., Soviet, and Yugoslav social, economic and political systems; library contains
extensive research collection on Eastern Europe; study abroad encouraged through the
Center for Yugoslav-American Studies, Research and Exchanges (see 18.588)

14.010
Center for Balkan and Slavic Studies
University of Chicago
Chicago, IL 60637
(312) 753-1234

Contact(s):
Eric P. Hamp, Director

  • Promotes study of the cultures of
Southeastern Europe (including the Southern Slavs), the Western Slavs and the nationalities of the western USSR

14.011
Russian and East European Center
University of Illinois at Urbana-Champaign
1208 West California
Urbana, IL 61801
(217) 333-1244

Contact(s):
Ralph T. Fisher, Jr., Director
Marianna Tax Choldin, Research Director
Elizabeth M. Talbot, Outreach Activities

Graduate and undergraduate area studies program established in 1960
• Majors/degrees/certificates offered: B.A. in Russian Language and Area Studies or in East European and Russian Studies; Certificate of Graduate Specialization to accompany M.A. and Ph.D. degrees in the disciplines
• Approximate number of faculty teaching area and language courses: 50
• Approximate number of courses available—area: 122; language: 48
• Average number of students per year specializing in area: 75 undergraduates; 65 graduates
• Countries covered and areas of emphasis: USSR, Bulgaria, Czechoslovakia, Hungary, Poland, Romania and Yugoslavia; particular strength in Russian language and area studies
• Languages offered: Czech, Modern Greek, Polish, Romanian, Russian, Serbo-Croatian and Ukrainian, plus individual instruction in languages too uncommon to be offered regularly, such as Finnish, Magyar, Modern Greek, Turkish and Uzbek
• Slavic and East European Library contains a 410,000-volume collection of materials in East European languages, with the largest number in Russian, followed by Czech, Ukrainian, the Yugoslav languages, Polish, Hungarian, Romanian, Bulgarian, and other Soviet languages (Baltic, Byelorussian, Armenian, Georgian, Azerbaijani, etc.), and 100,000 microtexts and printed works on Russian and Eastern Europe in other languages, including 3,000 current journals and newspapers; maintains Slavic Reference Service (see 14.054) through which it answers questions from researchers at the University and via teletype from other libraries around the U.S. and Canada
• Arranges for students to participate in summer and academic year program in Leningrad
• Conducts Summer Research Laboratory (see 14.012) and Independent Scholars Program for external scholars to pursue research at Illinois; arranges for visiting scholars to become Associates of the Center and to use University facilities at other times; lends audiovisual materials and aids to teachers in Illinois and conducts other outreach activities
• Publishes newsletter, *Update* (see 2.206), a valuable resource for teachers

14.012
Summer Research Laboratory on Russia and Eastern Europe
University of Illinois at Urbana-Champaign
Russian and East European Center
1208 West California Ave.
Urbana, IL 61801
(217) 333-1244

Contact(s):
Marianna Tax Choldin, Research Director

Program of the Russian and East European Center (see 14.011) supported by federal funding
• Offers researchers from the U.S., Canada and other countries the opportunity to use the resources and facilities of the University library, including the Slavic and East European Library Division and the Slavic Reference Service (see 14.054) to pursue their own personal and professional research interests; includes group meetings, mini-conferences, contact with University of Illinois scholars and other assistance from the Center

• Open to faculty, professionally trained researchers and advanced graduate students working on dissertations

• Free housing on campus available for 14 days

14.013
Inner Asian and Uralic National Resource Center
Indiana University at Bloomington
Goodbody Hall 101
Bloomington, IN 47405
(812) 335-2398

Contact(s):
Denis Sinor, Director (812) 335-0954

Graduate and undergraduate area studies program established in 1963; works in conjunction with the Department of Uralic and Altaic Studies

• Majors/degrees/certificates offered: undergraduate Certificate in Inner Asian Studies; graduate Certificate in Hungarian Studies; M.A. and Ph.D. in Uralic and Altaic Studies

• Approximate number of faculty teaching area and language courses: 18

• Approximate number of courses available—area: 53; language: 54

• Average number of students per year specializing in area: 45 graduates

• Countries covered and areas of emphasis: Estonia, Finland, Hungary, Turkey, Turkic-speaking republics of the USSR (Uzbekistan, Azerbaijan, etc.), Mongolia and Tibet

• Languages offered: Estonian, Finnish, Hungarian, Turkish, Uzbek, Azeri, Tatar, Mongol, Tibetan and (irregularly) Tuvin, Kazakh, Chivash, Uighur and other languages of the smaller culture groups

• Extensive resource collection in library of the Research Institute for Inner Asian Studies (see 13.047), including the Antoinette Gordon Collection of Tibetan Art

• Offers scholarships for summer study in Hungary

• Conducts summer institutes on Inner Asian and Hungarian studies and offers internships to college and secondary school teachers

• Publishes *Teaching Aids for the Study of Inner Asia* (for college and secondary school teachers), Indiana University Uralic and Altaic Studies series (140 volumes to date), *Newsletter* of the Permanent International Altaistic Conference, and bulletins, journals, and newsletters of the Mongolia and Tibet Societies

• Conducts in-service institutes on East-West business and economic relationships

14.014
Russian and East European Institute
Indiana University at Bloomington
Ballantine Hall 565
Bloomington, IN 47405
(812) 335-7309

Contact(s):
Alexander Rabinowitch, Director
Richard C. Sutton, Outreach Coordinator

Graduate and undergraduate area studies program established in 1958

• Majors/degrees/certificates offered: undergraduate and graduate Certificates in Russian and East European Studies awarded in conjunction with regular degrees; M.B.A. with Russian and East European emphasis also available

• Approximate number of faculty teaching area and language courses: 60

• Approximate number of courses available—area: 110; language: 85

• Average number of students per year specializing in area: 40 undergraduate; 130 graduate

• Countries covered and areas of emphasis: special Interdisciplinary Program on the Soviet Union and all countries of Eastern

Europe (including Finland, the GDR, Greece and Mongolia), with emphasis on contemporary problems and on East-West economic and political relations; Polish Studies Center (see 18.412) promotes exchanges with and study and research in Poland

• Languages offered: Bulgarian, Czech, Estonian, Finnish, Georgian, Modern Greek, Hungarian, Lithuanian, Polish, Romanian, Russian, Serbo-Croatian, Tartar, Ukrainian and Uzbek; includes intensive Summer Slavic Workshop

• 280,000-volume Slavic Collection, housed at the Institute, includes 68 newspapers and 1,400 serials; University library maintains extensive collection of rare Slavic, especially Russian, books and manuscripts

• Maintains cooperative programs of research and language training with Leningrad and Moscow State Universities in the USSR and Warsaw University in Poland, as well as with universities in Yugoslavia and Hungary; undergraduate study programs in the Soviet Union also available

• Conducts seminars, workshops and conferences for research scholars, college faculty and high school teachers; maintains speakers bureau and audiovisual lending library; distributes information and encourages use of library resources by external researchers

• Publishes newsletter, a monograph series (distributed by the Indiana University Press, see 11.016) and prepares audiovisual materials; includes *Resource Guide to Teaching Aids in Russian and East European Studies* (see 2.146)

14.015
Program of Soviet and East European Studies
University of Notre Dame
G32 Memorial Library
Notre Dame, IN 46556
(219) 239-5051 or 6377

Contact(s):
George A. Brinkley, Director

Graduate and undergraduate area studies program established in 1953

• Majors/degrees/certificates offered: Certificate with departmental B.A., M.A., and Ph.D. degrees

• Approximate number of faculty teaching area and language courses: 9

• Approximate number of courses available—area: 26; language: 10

• Average number of students per year specializing in area: 2 graduate; 10 undergraduate

• Countries covered and areas of emphasis: countries of the Soviet bloc with particular emphasis on the Soviet Union and communism

• Language offered: Russian

• Produces a number of works on historical and political Soviet and Eastern European affairs published by the University of Notre Dame Press

14.016
Russian and East European Studies
Grinnell College
Grinnell, IA 50112
(515) 236-2847

Contact(s):
Daniel Kaiser, Chair

Undergraduate area studies program established in 1976

• Majors/degrees/certificates offered: B.A. in Russian and East European Studies

• Approximate number of faculty teaching area and language courses: 5

• Approximate number of courses available—area: 17; language: 6

• Average number of students per year specializing in area: 5

• Countries covered and areas of em-

phasis: all Soviet bloc countries with principal emphasis on the Soviet Union
- Languages offered: Russian; Serbo-Croatian (by supervised independent study)
- Study abroad available in the USSR and Yugoslavia

14.017
Soviet and East European Studies
University of Kansas
Department of Slavic Languages and
    Literatures
Lawrence, KS 66045
(913) 964-3911

Contact(s):
Stephen J. Parker, Director

Graduate area studies program
- Majors/degrees/certificates offered: M.A. and Graduate Certificate of Proficiency in Soviet and East European Studies
- Approximate number of faculty teaching area and language courses: 31
- Countries covered and areas of emphasis: Soviet Union and the countries of Eastern Europe/Soviet bloc
- Languages offered: Russian, Polish, Serbo-Croatian, Czech, Old Church Slavic and German
- Library contains over 250,000 Slavic publications; includes extensive holdings in non-Slavic languages and 800 current newspapers and periodicals; strong in all aspects of both prerevolutionary and Soviet Russian and Polish history, politics and economics
- Sponsors summer and semester Russian language programs in the Soviet Union and an academic year language and area studies program in Poland

14.018
Center for East Europe, Russia and Asia
Boston College
Chestnut Hill, MA 02167
(617) 969-0100 Ext. 3852

Contact(s):
Thomas J. Blakeley, Director

Graduate and undergraduate area studies program established in 1966
- Majors/degrees/certificates offered: B.A. with concentration; Graduate Certificate
- Approximate number of faculty teaching area and language courses: 16
- Approximate number of courses available—area: 24; language: 18
- Average number of students per year specializing in area: 15
- Countries covered and areas of emphasis: East Europe, Russia and Asia; particularly strong in Soviet politics and philosophy
- Languages offered: Russian, Slavonic, Armenian and Chinese
- Publishes the quarterly *Studies in Soviet Thought* (see 18.552) and *Sovetica* (see 18.551)

14.019
Soviet and East European Program
Boston University
Boston, MA 02215
(617) 353-2642

Contact(s):
R. E. Richardson, Director

Undergraduate area studies program
- Majors/degrees/certificates offered: B.A. in Soviet and East European Studies
- Countries covered and areas of emphasis: all nations of Eastern Europe with emphasis on Soviet social and political thought and Russian culture
- Languages offered: Russian and Polish

14.020
Soviet and East European Language and Area Center

Harvard University
Russian Research Center
1737 Cambridge St.
Cambridge, MA 02138
(617) 495-5851

Contact(s):

Horace G. Lunt, Director
Janet G. Vaillant, Associate Director

Graduate and undergraduate area studies program

• Majors/degrees/certificates offered: B.A. and M.A. in Soviet and Russian Studies; Ph.D. through regular academic departments

• Approximate number of courses available—area: 50

• Countries covered: Soviet Union, Hungary, Bulgaria, Poland, Romania, Czechoslovakia, and East Germany

• Languages offered: Armenian, Turkic, Russian, Serbo-Croatian, Bulgarian, Polish, Ukrainian, Old Church Slavonic, Classical Georgian, Czech, Romanian and Modern Greek; additional languages upon request: Uzbek, Turkmen, Kazakh, Adzerbaidzhani, Tatar (Turkic-related) and Tadjik (Persian-related)

• Harvard University Library has collection of Slavic materials in the U.S. second only to Library of Congress

• Conducts workshops for precollege teachers and provides teaching materials (books, slides, curriculum units) through the Teaching Resource Center

• See also Regional Studies Program: Soviet Union, 18.508

14.021
Soviet and East European Area Studies Program

University of Massachusetts at Amherst
Department of Slavic Languages and
    Literature
Herter Hall
Amherst, MA 01003
(413) 545-2052

Contact(s):

Laszlo Dienes, Director

Undergraduate area studies program established in 1970

• Majors/degrees/certificates offered: B.A. in Soviet and East European Studies

• Approximate number of faculty teaching area and language courses: approximately 30

• Approximate number of courses available—area: 50; language: 24

• Average number of students per year specializing in area: 10

• Countries covered and areas of emphasis: Russia, Poland, Yugoslavia, Romania, Czechoslovakia and Hungary; particular strength in Russian and Polish studies

• Languages offered: Russian and Polish, with Czech, Slovak and Hungarian offered occasionally and on an independent study basis

• Collection of contemporary Russian and dissident writings available in the Center for the Study of New Russian Literature

• Cooperates with Polish Outreach program of the Department of Slavic Languages and Literature

• Publishes annual Occasional Papers series of faculty and student research

14.022
Russian and East European Studies Program
Michigan State University
103 International Center
East Lansing, MI 48824
(517) 355-3277

Contact(s):
William O. McCagg, Jr., Director

Graduate and undergraduate area studies program
- Majors/degrees/certificates offered: undergraduate certificate with concentration in Russian and East European Studies
- Approximate number of faculty teaching area and language courses: 11
- Approximate number of courses available—area: 28; language: 32
- Countries covered and areas of emphasis: all countries of Eastern Europe with emphasis on Russian literature and history
- Languages offered: Russian
- Russian language study in the Soviet Union available

14.023
Slavic Studies Program
Oakland University
Rochester, MI 48063
(313) 377-2154

Contact(s):
Carlo Coppola, Chair
Robert C. Howes, Coordinator

Undergraduate area studies program
- Majors/degrees/certificates offered: B.A. and minor in Slavic Studies
- Approximate number of faculty teaching area and language courses: 5
- Approximate number of courses available—area: 16; language: 10
- Countries covered and areas of emphasis: principally Russia

- Languages offered: Russian and Polish
- Sponsors occasional study tours to the Soviet Union

14.024
Center for Russian and East European Studies
University of Michigan at Ann Arbor
Lane Hall, 204 South State St.
Ann Arbor, MI 48109
(313) 764-0351

Contact(s):
Zvi Gitelman, Director
Ruth Hastie, Outreach Coordinator

Graduate and undergraduate area studies program established in 1961
- Majors/degrees/certificates offered: B.A. and M.A. in Russian and East European Studies; M.A. and Ph.D. with specialization in Russian and East European Studies; joint M.A. programs with the Department of Communication, the School of Business, and the Institute for Public Policy; and a dual M.A. and J.D. degree program with the School of Law
- Approximate number of faculty teaching area and language courses: 39
- Approximate number of courses available—area: 120; language: 65
- Average number of students per year specializing in area: 45
- Countries covered and areas of emphasis: Soviet Union and all Eastern European countries including Turkey; particular strength in Russian and Balkan history and in Slavic languages and literatures
- Languages offered: Russian, Polish, Czech, Hungarian, Serbo-Croatian, Ukrainian, Armenian, Lithuanian and Finnish
- Library holds 175,000 volumes in Russian and the languages of Eastern Europe (including 750 periodicals and 72 newspapers) and many additional in English and Western languages on the area; greatest

strength is in materials in Russian, Polish, Czech and Serbo-Croatian, and in the fields of history, literature, linguistics, economics and politics

• Sponsors outreach activities including a newsletter and seminar programs aimed at teachers

• Center offers use of facilities and affiliate status to external faculty engaged in research on Russia and Eastern Europe

• Publishes "Reprint Series" of journal articles and book chapters on Russian and East European political, economic, literary and sociological subjects

14.025
European Studies Program
Western Michigan University
2090 Friedmann
Kalamazoo, MI 49008
(616) 383-8002

Contact(s):
William Ritchie, Chair

• Area Studies program covering both Eastern and Western Europe (see 15.013)

14.026
Russian and East European Studies Program
St. Louis University
St. Louis, MO 63103
(314) 658-2588

Contact(s):
Louis A. Barth, Director

Undergraduate area studies program established in 1968

• Majors/degrees/certificates offered: Undergraduate Certificate in Russian and East European Studies (in addition to major field)

• Approximate number of faculty teaching area and language courses: 5

• Approximate number of courses available—area: 6; language: 8

• Average number of students per year specializing in area: 10–15

• Countries covered and areas of emphasis: Russia, Slavic nations of Eastern Europe and the Byzantine Empire

• Languages offered: Russian, Polish and Czech

• Library contains good collection of books for undergraduate Russian and East European study

• Sponsors Russian Summer Camp and encourages travel to and study in Russia

• Publishes undergraduate journal *Russkoe Ekho*

14.027
Soviet and East European Area Program
Rutgers University
Slavic and East European Studies
New Brunswick, NJ 08903
(201) 932-7366

Contact(s):
Gerald Pirog, Director

Undergraduate area studies program established in 1975

• Majors/degrees/certificates offered: B.A. or Certificate in Soviet and East European Studies

• Approximate number of faculty teaching area and language courses: 19

• Average number of students per year specializing in area: 6

• Countries covered and areas of emphasis: Soviet Union, Poland, the Ukraine and Yugoslavia with emphasis on Russian and Slavic civilizations

• Languages offered: Russian, Polish, Ukrainian and Serbo-Croatian

• Library maintains Helsinki Library collection on microfiche

14.028
Institute on East Central Europe
Columbia University
1228 International Affairs Bldg.
420 West 118th St.
New York, NY 10027
(212) 280-4008

Contact(s):
Harold B. Segel, Director

Graduate area studies program
 • Majors/degrees/certificates offered: B.A. in Regional Studies (through Columbia College); two-year M.I.A., School of International and Public Affairs, with Certificate in East Central European Studies; M.A. and Ph.D. with Certificate in East Central European Studies
 • Approximate number of faculty teaching area and language courses: 30
 • Approximate number of courses available—area: 67; language: 24
 • Countries covered and areas of emphasis: Finland, the Baltic States, Poland, Czechoslovakia, Hungary, Romania, Yugoslavia, Bulgaria, Albania and Greece; with emphasis on history, literature and linguistics and including Uralic Studies
 • Languages offered: Albanian, Bulgarian, Czech, Estonian, Finnish, Modern Greek, Hungarian, Latvian, Lithuanian, Polish, Romanian, Serbo-Croatian, Yiddish, French, German and Russian
 • Slavic and East European Collection of the University library contains approximately 1.5 million volumes in East European languages with particular strength in history, linguistics, literature, the arts, economics, politics, law, philosophy and library science; includes extensive Hungarian collection, most current Yugoslav and Polish periodicals and a collection of current Polish and Romanian dissident materials; the New York Public Library also has a very extensive Slavic collection

14.029
Subcommittee on Uralic Languages
Columbia University
404 Philosophy Hall
New York, NY 10027
(212) 280-3963

Contact(s):
Robert Austerlitz, Chair

 • Conducts research on the Uralic family of languages and cultures; compiles textbooks and study materials for Hungarian and Finnish; library contains approximately 30,000 volumes on and in the Estonian, Finnish, Hungarian and other Uralic languages

14.030
Russian and Soviet Studies Committee
Cornell University
180 Uris Hall
Ithaca, NY 14853
(607) 256-3311

Contact(s):
Walter M. Pintner, Chair

Graduate and undergraduate area studies program established in 1960
 • Majors/degrees/certificates offered: B.A. with major in Russian and Soviet Studies; M.A. and Ph.D. in discipline with Russian/Soviet specialization
 • Approximate number of faculty teaching area & language courses: 17
 • Approximate number of courses available—area: 10; language: 30
 • Average number of students per year specializing in area: 20 graduate; 20 undergraduate
 • Countries covered and areas of emphasis: USSR/Russia, Poland, Czechoslovakia, and Yugoslavia
 • Languages offered: Russian, Polish, Czech, Serbo-Croatian, Old Church Slavonic and Old Russian

• Approximately 100,000 volumes in library on Russia and the Soviet Union including extensive collection of Russian emigré publications

• Study abroad available in semester programs in Leningrad and Moscow; may also attend School of Slavonic and East European Studies at the University of London

14.031

Russian and East Central European Area Studies
Manhattan College
Bronx, NY 10471
(212) 548-1400

Contact(s):
Wolodymyr Stojko, Director

Undergraduate area studies program established in 1964

• Majors/degrees/certificates offered: B.A. or minor in Russian and East Central European Area Studies

• Approximate number of faculty teaching area and language courses: 9

• Approximate number of courses available—area: 13; language: 4

• Average number of students per year specializing in area: 1–5

• Countries covered and areas of emphasis: Albania, Bulgaria, Czechoslovakia, Hungary, Poland, Romania, Yugoslavia and the USSR with emphasis on history and the social sciences

14.032

Soviet and East European Institute
Niagara University
Niagara, NY 14109
(716) 285-1212

Contact(s):
Richard J. Danilowicz, Director

Graduate area studies program

• Majors/degrees/certificates offered: M.A. in Soviet and East European Studies

• Countries covered and areas of emphasis: all countries of Eastern Europe with special interest in East-West relations, Poland and the Ukraine

14.033

Russian and Eastern European Studies
State University of New York at Binghamton
Binghamton, NY 13901
(607) 798-3075

Contact(s):
Alton Donnelly, Director

Graduate and undergraduate area studies program established in 1966

• Majors/degrees/certificates offered: B.A. with concentration or Certificate in Area Studies; M.A. and Ph.D. in History, Political Science or Economics with a specialization in area studies

• Approximate number of faculty teaching area & language courses: 13

• Approximate number of courses available—area: 13; language: 10

• Average number of students per year specializing in area: 20

• Countries covered and areas of emphasis: Russia/USSR, Czechoslovakia, Poland, Yugoslavia, with particular strength in history, economics and political science

• Language offered: Russian

14.034

Russian and East European Studies
Duke University
Department of Economics
Durham, NC 27706
(919) 684-8111

Contact(s):
Vladimir Treml, Director

Graduate area studies program
- Majors/degrees/certificates offered: M.A. and Ph.D. in Russian and East European Studies offered cooperatively with University of North Carolina (see 14.035)
- Languages offered: Russian and Polish at Duke; Russian, Polish, Czech and Serbo-Croatian at UNC

14.035
Curriculum in Russian and East European Area Studies
University of North Carolina at Chapel Hill
471 Hamilton Hall
Chapel Hill, NC 27514
(919) 962-2184

Contact(s):
Josef Anderle, Director

Undergraduate area studies program established in 1973
- Majors/degrees/certificates offered: B.A. in Russian and East European Area Studies
- Approximate number of faculty teaching area and language courses: 15
- Approximate number of courses available—area: 12; language: 15
- Average number of students per year specializing in area: 20
- Countries covered and areas of emphasis: USSR, Poland, Czechoslovakia and Yugoslavia, with lesser emphasis on Hungary, Romania, and Mongolia
- Languages offered: Albanian, Bulgarian, Czech, Hungarian, Macedonian, Polish, Romanian, Russian, Serbo-Croatian and Turkish
- Large library holdings, developed in cooperation with Duke University
- Shares resources in cooperative program with Duke University

14.036
Institute for Soviet and East European Studies
John Carroll University
University Heights, OH 44118
(216) 491-4320

- Administers concentration in Soviet and East European Studies, gives Teacher Certificate of Competence in World Communism and sponsors conferences on U.S.-Soviet relations and an annual summer in-service teacher training program "Democracy vs. Communism"

14.037
Soviet and East European Studies Program
Kent State University
500 A McGilvrey
Kent, OH 44242
(216) 672-2121

Contact(s):
Jordan Hodgkins, Coordinator

Graduate and undergraduate area studies program
- Majors/degrees/certificates offered: B.A. and M.A. in Soviet and East European Studies
- Approximate number of courses available—area: 25; language: 10 (plus self-instructional critical language offerings)
- Countries covered and areas of emphasis: Soviet Union, Albania, Bulgaria, East Germany, Greece, Hungary, Poland, Romania and Yugoslavia, with emphasis on history and the social sciences
- Languages offered: German, Russian and, through the critical language program, Czech, Estonian, Greek, Hungarian, Latvian, Lithuanian, Polish, Romanian, Serbo-Croatian, Slovak, Slovenian and Ukrainian

14.038
Center for Slavic and East European Studies
Ohio State University
344 Dulles Hall
230 West 17th Ave.
Columbus, Ohio 43210
(614) 422-8770

Contact(s):
Leon I. Twarog, Director

Graduate and undergraduate area studies program established in 1965
 • Majors/degrees/certificates offered: B.A., M.A. and Ph.D. in departments with specialization in Slavic and East European Studies
 • Approximate number of faculty teaching area and language courses: 50
 • Approximate number of courses available—area: 77; language: 125
 • Average number of students per year specializing in area: 80–100
 • Countries covered and areas of emphasis: all countries of Eastern Europe with particular interest in the Soviet Union, Bulgaria, Czechoslovakia and Yugoslavia
 • Languages offered: Russian, Polish, Serbo-Croatian, Bulgarian, Czech, Ukrainian and Hungarian
 • Library contains approximately 200,000 volumes in Slavic languages and on Russia and Eastern Europe and extensive archival collections
 • Overseas research opportunities for graduate students

14.039
Soviet and East European International Behavior
The Ohio State University
The Mershon Center
199 West 10th Ave.
Columbus, OH 43201
(614) 422-1681

Contact(s):
Philip Stewart and Tom Wolf, Directors

Program of The Mershon Center (see 4.183)
 • Conducts research on Soviet national security and on international economic and political policies and publishes books and monographs resulting from the research

14.040
Central European Studies Center
Portland State University
P.O. Box 751
Portland, OR 97207
(503) 229-3916

Contact(s):
Thomas M. Poulsen, Director

Undergraduate area studies program established in 1965
 • Majors/degrees/certificates offered: Certificate in Central European Studies
 • Approximate number of faculty teaching area and language courses: 15
 • Approximate number of courses available—area: 25; language: 8
 • Average number of students per year specializing in area: 20
 • Countries covered and areas of emphasis: East Germany, Poland, Czechoslovakia, Hungary, Romania, Yugoslavia, Bulgaria and Albania; special emphasis on Yugoslavia, Hungary and Romania
 • Languages offered: Serbo-Croatian, Macedonian, Hungarian and (occasionally) Romanian; includes intensive 11-week summer language programs in Hungarian and Serbo-Croatian
 • Summer study program in Yugoslavia and academic year program at the University of Szeged, Hungary
 • Visiting professors occasionally from the University of Skopje, the University of Zagreb and from Romania and Hungary

14.041
Russian and East European Studies Center
University of Oregon
Eugene, OR 97403
(503) 686-3094

Contact(s):
Howard Robertson, Director
Mark Levy, Outreach Coordinator

• Offers undergraduate Certificate in Russian and East European Studies; approximately 20 faculty offer a wide variety of courses; strong in political science, the Russian language and arts and anthropology; languages: Russian, Serbo-Croatian, Polish, Czech, Ukrainian and Old Church Slavonic; language study available in Russia and, during the summer, in Poland, Czechoslovakia, Romania, Bulgaria and Yugoslavia; library has more than 80,000 volumes of Russian language holdings in addition to collections of Serbo-Croatian, Polish, Ukrainian, Czech and Bulgarian materials, and sizable Western language collections; provides school outreach programs

14.042
Slavic and Soviet Language and Area Center
Pennsylvania State University
306 Burrowes
University Park, PA 16802
(814) 865-0436 or 0437

Contact(s):
Vernon V. Aspaturian, Director
Trond Gilbert, Associate Director

Graduate and undergraduate area studies program established in 1956 (Center established in 1965)
• Majors/degrees/certificates offered: Undergraduate Russian Area Certificate; M.A. and Ph.D. with specialization in Slavic and Soviet Studies

• Approximate number of faculty teaching area and language courses: 25
• Approximate number of courses available—area: 48; language: 45
• Average number of students per year specializing in area: 30–50
• Countries covered and areas of emphasis: Soviet Union, Eastern Europe (except Greece); special resource areas: USSR, Romania, Poland and Yugoslavia
• Languages offered: Russian, Polish, Serbo-Croatian, Old Church Slavic and Slovene
• Center maintains a library and reading room stocked with Soviet periodicals
• Conducts special programs in technical and business Russian

14.043
Russian and East European Studies Program
University of Pittsburgh
4E-23 Forbes Quadrangle
Pittsburgh, PA 15260
(412) 624-1215

Contact(s):
Janet G. Chapman, Director

Graduate and undergraduate area studies program established in 1965
• Majors/degrees/certificates offered: B.A. in Slavic Studies with concentration in Russian and East European Studies; M.A. and Ph.D. in departments with Certificate in Russian and East European Studies
• Approximate number of faculty teaching area and language courses: 44
• Approximate number of courses available—area: 60; language: 70 within Slavic Languages and Literatures Department
• Countries covered and areas of emphasis: all countries of Eastern Europe and the Soviet bloc with particular strength in comparative communism
• Languages offered: Polish, Russian,

Serbo-Croatian, Slovak, Old Church Slavonic and Ukrainian
- Library contains over 90,000 volumes in East European languages and 100,000 on the area in other languages; receives 380 periodicals and newspapers; especially strong in Russian, Polish, Yugoslav and Czech materials; also available is the Archive on Political Elites in East Europe (machine readable biographical database on political leaders and parties in six East European countries) and the Social Science Information Utilization Laboratory (computer-based information resource)
- Encourages research, faculty and student colloquia, overseas study and research, and a variety of other activities on campus
- Publishes a Monograph Series in conjunction with the Center for International Studies which also produces *United States Political Science Documents* (see 4.127)

14.044
Russian and East European Studies Committee and Program
University of Tennessee
Knoxville, TN 37996-0470
(615) 974-7157 or 3421

Contact(s):
Donald M. Fiene, Director

Undergraduate area studies program established in 1972
- Majors/degrees/certificates offered: B.A. in Russian and East European Studies with two tracks: political/cultural studies and business/economic studies
- Approximate number of faculty teaching area and language courses: 10
- Approximate number of courses available—area: 45; language: 15
- Average number of students per year specializing in area: 5
- Countries covered and areas of emphasis: primarily Russia, with some attention

to other East European countries, e.g., Yugoslavia and Czechoslovakia
- Languages offered: Russian and occasionally Czech or Serbo-Croatian

14.045
Center for European Studies
Vanderbilt University
Nashville, TN 37235
(615) 322-2528

Contact(s):
M. Donald Hancock, Director

- Offers B.A. in Modern European Studies covering both Eastern and Western Europe (see 15.019)

14.046
Soviet and East European Center
University of Texas at Arlington
Arlington, TX 76019
(817) 273-3161

Contact(s):
Charles T. McDowell, Director

Graduate, undergraduate and nondegree area studies program established in 1968
- Majors/degrees/certificates offered: Certificate or B.A. in Soviet Area Studies
- Approximate number of faculty teaching area and language courses: 10
- Approximate number of courses available—area: 10; language: 20
- Countries covered and areas of emphasis: USSR, Eastern Europe and China (PRC)
- Languages offered: Russian, Czech, Hungarian and Chinese
- Offers annual travel/study programs to the USSR and Eastern Europe as well as individual programs in the PRC
- Offers special translation courses and orientation for persons doing business with the USSR

14.047
Russian and East European Studies
University of Vermont
Center for Area and International Studies
479 Main St.
Burlington, VT 05405
(802) 656-4062

Contact(s):
Kenneth L. Nalibow, Director

Graduate and undergraduate area studies program established in 1963
- Majors/degrees/certificates offered: B.A. in Russian and East European Studies; M.A. Certificate in Russian and East European Studies
- Approximate number of faculty teaching area and language courses: 9
- Approximate number of courses available—area: 12; language: 11
- Average number of students per year specializing in area: 3
- Countries covered and areas of emphasis: Russia and the Soviet bloc countries with particular interest in economics, East-West trade and Soviet religious policy
- Overseas study opportunities available

14.048
Russian and East European Studies
University of Virginia
Charlottesville, VA 22901
(804) 924-3554

Contact(s):
John G. Garrard, Chair

Undergraduate area studies program
- Majors/degrees/certificates offered: B.A. in Russian and East European Studies
- Countries covered and areas of emphasis: Soviet Union with some attention to Eastern Europe; emphasis on history, economics, politics, literature and the Russian language

- Languages offered: Russian along with Bulgarian, Polish, Serbo-Croatian and Ukrainan

14.049
Russian and East European Studies
University of Washington
Jackson School of International Studies
Seattle, WA 98195
(206) 543-4852

Contact(s):
Donald W. Treadgold, Chair

Graduate and undergraduate area studies program established in 1949
- Majors/degrees/certificates offered: B.A. and M.A. in International Studies with specialization in Russian and East European Studies
- Approximate number of faculty teaching area and language courses: 35
- Approximate number of courses available—area and language: 170
- Average number of students per year specializing in area: graduate, 26; undergraduate, 45
- Countries covered and areas of emphasis: Russia and Eastern and Central European countries with emphasis on contemporary political and social issues
- Languages offered: Russian, Serbo-Croatian, Bulgarian, Czech, Polish, Romanian, Hungarian, Old Church Slavic, Turkic languages (Uzbek and others) and Ukrainian

14.050
Russian Area Studies Program
University of Wisconsin at Madison
1446 Van Hise Hall
1220 Linden Drive
Madison, WI 53706
(608) 262-3379

Contact(s):
James Bailey, Chair

Graduate area studies program established in 1959

• Majors/degrees/certificates offered: Ph.D. in discipline with Russian Area Studies concentration

• Approximate number of faculty teaching area and language courses: 17

• Approximate number of courses available—area: 20; language: 22

• Average number of students per year specializing in area: 4

• Countries covered and areas of emphasis: Russia and Eastern Europe

• Languages offered: Russian, Polish, Serbo-Croatian and Czech

• Extensive collection on Eastern Europe in University library

14.051

Russian and East Central European Studies
University of Wisconsin at Stevens Point
Stevens Point, WI 54481
(715) 346-4540

Contact(s):
Robert F. Price, Coordinator

Undergraduate area studies program established in 1969

• Majors/degrees/certificates offered: B.A. major or minor in Russian and East Central European Studies

• Approximate number of faculty teaching area and language courses: 7

• Approximate number of courses available—area: 14; language: 8

• Average number of students per year specializing in area: 6–8

• Countries covered and areas of emphasis: particular emphasis on Russia/Soviet Union and Poland

• Languages offered: Russian; Polish occasionally

• Library has representative collection of most important Russian and Soviet authors

• Study abroad available in Poland, through the University Office of International Programs

• Also conducts annual two-week spring trip to the Soviet Union as part of course "The Soviet Seminar"

Information and Service Organizations

14.052

American Association for the Advancement of Slavic Studies
Stanford University
128 Encina Commons
Stanford, CA 94305
(415) 497-9668

Contact(s):
Dorothy Atkinson, Executive Director

Professional association of scholars in the field of Slavic Studies

• Promotes East European and Soviet Studies, holds conferences and publishes the

Slavic Review (see 14.074), a newsletter, and various other publications including the annual (1966–1980) series: *American Bibliography of Slavic & East European Studies*

14.053

Permanent International Altaistic Conference
Indiana University
Goodbody Hall
Bloomington, IN 47401
(812) 337-2398

Contact(s):
Denis Sinor, Secretary-General

Professional association of scholars in 20 countries with an interest in Altaic and Inner Asian Studies
• Holds an annual meeting, publishes a newsletter and generally promotes Inner Asian Studies worldwide

14.054
Slavic Reference Service
University of Illinois at Urbana-Champaign
225 Library
Urbana, IL 61801
(217) 333-1349 or 1348
TWX (910) 245-0782

Contact(s):
Marianna Tax Choldin, Director

Free, year-round reference service for Slavic, Russian and East European studies
• Answers bibliographic and reference questions in the humanities and social sciences for individuals and institutions; on call between 8 a.m. and 5 p.m. weekdays; questions may be phoned, mailed or teletyped in; items unavailable in North America are normally ordered from European or Soviet libraries and made available on loan

Sources of Grants and Awards

14.055
American Council of Learned Societies
800 Third Ave.
New York, NY 10022
(212) 888-1759

Contact(s):
R. M. Lumiansky, President

Nonprofit educational federation of 43 national scholarly organizations; engages in activities directed toward the advancement of humanistic learning; established in 1919
• Administers grants and fellowship programs for postdoctoral research in the humanities; may be used for research abroad or on international subjects
• Provides grants for problem-oriented and, desirably, comparative research in the social sciences or humanities on East European societies and cultures, including Albania, Bulgaria, Czechoslovakia, the GDR, modern Greece, Hungary, Poland, Romania and Yugoslavia; both small and larger grants

available (other grants in East European and Soviet Studies available from both the Social Science Research Council (see 7.030) and the International Research and Exchange Board (IREX, see 14.057); IREX is administered by ACLS
• Provides postdoctoral grants-in-aid to support the preparation of a dissertation for publication and to support research in progress by the scholar to meet essential personal expenses
• Offers travel grants to scholars in humanistic disciplines to enable them to participate in conferences outside North America

14.056
The Ford Foundation
Fellowship Program in Dual Expertise
Office of European and International Affairs
320 East 43d St.
New York, NY 10017
(212) 573-5000

• Fellowships to graduate students and to postdoctoral candidates for study in either International Security and Arms Control or Soviet-East European Studies in order to equal the competence already achieved in the other

14.057
International Research and Exchanges Board (IREX)
655 Third Ave.
New York, NY 10017
(212) 490-2002

Grant-giving organization created by the American Council of Learned Societies (see 14.055) and the Social Science Research Council (see 7.030) to administer scholarly research and exchange programs with the socialist countries of Eastern Europe and the USSR

• Provides grants, including travel and allowances or stipends to graduate students, young faculty and senior faculty for study and/ or research in the Soviet Union and Eastern European countries, except Albania; in most cases periods of stay run from 2 to 10 months with one Soviet program requiring a semester and preferring a year's duration; another Soviet program involves joint research projects with the Soviet Commission on the Humanities and Social Sciences

• Provides limited number of fellowships to graduate students and post-doctoral researchers in disciplines underrepresented in USSR/Eastern Europe scholarship; also provides fellowships to develop dual area competence for scholars with area expertise and Fellowships for the Study of Nationalities to graduate students for the study of a minority Soviet language needed for research purposes

• Conducts program enabling U.S. teachers of Russian to participate in eight-week summer Russian-language program in Moscow and a one-month program for schol-

ars wishing to study the Bulgarian language in Bulgaria

• Makes available a limited number of travel grants and research grants involving collaboration between U.S. and East European scholars and grants for new exchange activities in the USSR/Eastern European area including Albania and Mongolia

• Pursues special bilateral relationships with Soviet, Hungarian, Polish, and German Democratic Republic Commissions to sponsor conferences and meetings and to develop projects jointly expanding scholarly activity

• Conducts public programs to make accessible to the public the results of the IREX exchanges

14.058
National Academy of Sciences
Exchange Programs with the USSR and
    Eastern Europe
Section on USSR and Eastern Europe
2101 Constitution Ave. NW
Washington, DC 20418
(202) 334-2644

Major scientific professional association

• Provides fellowships in the natural sciences, mathematics, engineering and the precise social and behavioral sciences for postdoctoral research at institutions of the Academy of Sciences in Bulgaria, Czechoslovakia, the G.D.R., Hungary, Poland, Romania, Yugoslavia and the USSR for up to 12 months

14.059
National Council for Soviet and East European Research
1755 Massachusetts Ave., NW, Suite 304
Washington, DC 20036
(202) 387-0168

• Offers contracts for research on Soviet and East European historical, social, economic and political issues; areas of specific interest announced periodically

14.060
National Institutes of Health
International Coordination and Liaison
    Branch
Fogarty International Center
Bldg. 38A, Room 614
Bethesda, MD 20014
(301) 496-4784

Contact(s):
Program Officer

    • Conducts program of health science exchanges between the U.S. and Hungary, Poland, Romania, the USSR and Yugoslavia in support of collaborative activities between and among health scientists in the study of health and biomedical problems

14.061
National Science Foundation
East European Cooperative Science
    Program
Division of International Programs
5225 Wisconsin Ave. NW
Washington, DC 20550
(202) 357-9516

Contact(s):
Deborah L. Wince, Director
Gerson Sher, (Yugoslavia, East Germany
    and Czechoslovakia) (202) 357-7494

    • Funds programs involving cooperative scientific research, seminars and workshops and short-term visits between the U.S. and Romania, Hungary and Bulgaria

14.062
Russian Research Center
Harvard University
1737 Cambridge St.
Cambridge, MA 02138
(617) 495-4037

    • Offers Postdoctoral Research Fellowships for research at Harvard in the humanities and social sciences on subjects related to the Soviet Union and Eastern Europe (see 14.020)

Guides, Sourcebooks and Directories

14.063
Current European Directories
G. P. Henderson, Editor
CBD Research, Ltd.
Beckenham
Kent, England
1981; hardbound; 425 pages; $150

Excludes Great Britain and Ireland (see 18.574) for *Current British Directories*); available from Gale Research Co., Book Tower, Detroit, MI 48226

    • Lists approximately 2,500 directories published in European countries (including Eastern Europe and the Soviet Union but excluding Ireland and the UK); listed by country, though includes a section on international or European-wide directories (many of which are published outside Europe); lists yearbooks, almanacs, general industrial and commercial directories, telephone, telex and telegraphic directories, research, library and bibliographic directories, gazetteers, regional, specialized and technical directories;

provides publisher and bibliographic data, description of content, languages used, frequency, date published, price and length; title translated into English where necessary; indexed by titles and subjects

14.064
East Central and Southeast Europe: A Handbook of Library and Archival Resources in North America
Paul L. Horecky, Chief Editor
David H. Kraus, Associate Editor
ABC-Clio, Inc.
Riviera Campus
2040 Alameda Padre Serra
Box 4397
Santa Barbara, CA 93103
1976; hardbound; 467 pages; $45

• Profiles 43 research libraries, archives and other institutions which have major East-Central and Southeast European collections in the humanities and social sciences; covers Eastern bloc countries, excluding the Soviet Union, along with Yugoslavia and Greece

14.065
East European Languages and Literatures: A Subject and Name Index to Articles in English-Language Journals: 1900–1977
Garth M. Terry
ABC-Clio, Inc.
Riviera Campus
2040 Alameda Padre Serra
Box 4397
Santa Barbara, CA 93103
1978; hardbound; 275 pages; $47.50

• Includes citations of approximately 10,000 articles on the Slavonic and East European languages

14.066
International Relations of Eastern Europe
Robin Alison Remington, Editor
Gale Research Co.
Book Tower
Detroit, MI 48226
1978; hardbound; 273 pages; $44

• Bibliographic information about works on Eastern European countries individually and as a region

14.067
Scholar's Guide to Washington, D.C.: Central and East European Studies
Kenneth J. Dillon
Smithsonian Institution Press
Washington, DC 20560
1980; 329 pages; paperbound, $9.95; hardbound, $25

Comprehensive listing and description of resources in the Washington area available to researchers and others interested in Central and Eastern Europe; divided into two sections: collections (libraries, archives, museums, etc., music and sound, maps, films, and data banks) and organizations (research centers and information offices, academic programs, U.S. government agencies, embassies and international organizations, professional associations, exchange and technical assistance organizations, religious organizations, and publications/media); available resources described in some detail with clear indication how and from whom to obtain access; appendices include libraries listed by size of holdings, bookstores, housing, transport and other services and a bibliography; indexed by name of resource, personal papers collections and library subject strength; covers Central and Eastern Europe and Greece

14.068
Soviet and East European Foreign Policy
Roger E. Kanet
ABC-Clio, Inc.
Riviera Campus
2040 Alameda Padre Serra
Box 4397
Santa Barbara, CA 93103
1974; hardbound; 208 pages; $21.75

• Contains over 3,000 annotated citations of books and articles on the foreign policy of the Soviet Union and East European countries; indexed

14.069
The Soviet and East European Political Dictionary
Barbara P. McCrea, Jack Plano and George
   Klein
ABC-Clio, Inc.
Riviera Campus
2040 Alameda Padre Serra
Box 4397
Santa Barbara, CA 93103
1984; 367 pages; hardbound, $30;
   paperbound, $14.25

• Provides definitions and commentary on the significance of terms, concepts, institutions and events central to the politics and economics of the USSR and East Europe; arranged topically and sequenced parallel to most related texts under such headings as historical perspective, political and cultural ideology, government institutions, political parties, etc.; indexed

14.070
Statistics—Europe
Joan M. Harvey, Editor
CBD Research, Ltd.
Beckenham, England
1981; hardbound; 508 pages; $150

Distributed by Gale Research Co., Book Tower, Detroit, MI 48226
• Provides extensive listing of sources of statistical data for each country of Europe including Turkey and the USSR; includes central statistical office and other important statistics collection agencies, principal libraries containing statistics, libraries and information services in other countries which supply statistics on each country, principal bibliographies of statistical compilations, and major statistical publications with full address and/ or bibliographic information

14.071
A Survey of Materials for the Study of the Uncommonly Taught Languages: Languages of Eastern Europe & The Soviet Union
Dora E. Johnson et al.
Center for Applied Linguistics
3520 Prospect St. NW
Washington, DC 20007
1976; paperbound; 42 pages; $7.95

Exclusively distributed by Harcourt Brace Jovanich, Inc., 757 Third Ave., New York, NY 10017; Attn: Nancy McCloughan
• One of a series of bibliographies covering all the modern languages except Standard English, German, Italian, Russian and Spanish; designed for use by the adult learner whose native language is English; listed under the headings: teaching materials, readers, grammars and dictionaries; includes books currently in print where feasible, older titles where not; citations appear under the following language groups: Eastern Romance, Albanian, West Slavic, South Slavic, East Slavic, Baltic, Armenian, Iranian, Ugric, Balto-Finnic, Eastern Uralic, Central Asian Turkic, Caucasic and Paleo-Siberian

Periodicals

14.072
East European Quarterly
Stephen Fischer-Galati, Editor
East European Quarterly
Boulder, CO 80309
quarterly journal; approx. 130 pages;
    individuals, $10 per year; institutions, $12
    per year

    • Contains scholarly articles and essays
on contemporary Soviet and East European
affairs, book reviews

14.073
Slavic and East European Journal
Howard H. Keller, Editor
American Association of Teachers of Slavic
    and East European Languages, Inc.
University of Arizona, ML-340
Tucson, AZ 85721
quarterly journal; approx. 130 pages;
    libraries and institutions, $20 per year;
    individuals $18 per year

    • Articles on Slavic and East European
languages, literatures, cultures and pedagogy; particularly strong in Russian literature; book reviews

14.074
Slavic Review: American Quarterly of
Soviet and East European Studies
David L. Ransel, Editor
American Association for the Advancement
    of Slavic Studies
128 Encina Commons
Stanford University
Stanford, CA 94305
quarterly journal; 170 pages; free with
    membership ($25–$40 per year)

    • Contains scholarly articles and essays
in Russian and East European studies; extensive book review section; news of the profession

14.075
Soviet Studies
R. A. Clarke, Editor
Longman Group Ltd.
Fourth Ave.
Harlow, Essex CM16 5AA, England
quarterly journal; approx. 160 pages; $52
    per year

    • Contains scholarly articles and essays
on contemporary affairs in the Soviet Union
and the Soviet bloc countries; book reviews

Publishers

14.076
Arthur Vanous Company
Box 650279
Vero Beach, FL 32965

    • Imports and warehouses language dic-
tionaries, texts and cassettes from a number
of East European countries including
Czechoslovakia, Hungary, Poland and Yugoslavia

14.077
G. K. Hall & Co.
70 Lincoln St.
Boston, MA 02111
(617) 423-3990

Commercial reference book publisher
    • Publishes materials on Russian and East
European Studies including the annual library reference work *Bibliographic Guide to*

Soviet and East European Studies (annual, 3 volumes, $350) and *The Russian Empire and The Soviet Union: A Guide to Manuscripts and Archival Materials* (annual, 3 volumes, $350)

14.078
Ragusan Press
2527 San Carlos Ave.
San Carlos, CA 94070
(415) 592-1190

• Publishes and distributes books on the Slavic languages and cultures, and the social and political affairs of Bulgaria and Yugoslavia (including Macedonia); includes language materials, travel guides, social and political studies and bibliographies; includes publications on Slavs in the U.S. (affiliated with the Slavic-American Society)

14.079
Szwede Slavic Books
P.O. Box 1214
Palo Alto, CA 94302-1214
(415) 851-0748

• Imports books in Byelorussian, Bulgarian, Czech, Slovak, Slovenian, Serbian, Croatian, Polish, and Ukranian as well as books about the Slavic countries in western languages; will search

15

West European Area Studies

West European Studies Programs and Research Centers

15.001
European Studies
Claremont Graduate School
Claremont, CA 01711
(714) 621-8000

Contact(s):
Henry Gibbons, Director

Graduate area studies program
• Majors/degrees/certificates offered: M.A. and Ph.D. in European Studies
• Approximate number of faculty teaching area and language courses: 36
• Approximate number of courses available—area: 115
• Countries covered and areas of emphasis: all European countries; emphasis on history, politics, literature and philosophy
• Languages offered: French, German and Spanish

15.002
European Studies Center
San Diego State University
San Diego, CA 92182
(619) 265-5928 or 6586

Contact(s):
Leon Rosenstein, Director

Undergraduate area studies program established in 1970

• Majors/degrees/certificates offered: B.A. in European Studies

• Approximate number of faculty teaching area and language courses: all faculty teaching courses related to Europe

• Approximate number of courses available—area: 193; language: 25

• Average number of students per year specializing in area: 24

• Countries covered and areas of emphasis: Europe in general, especially France, Spain, England, Italy, Germany, Austria, Greece and Portugal; emphasis on contemporary political, social and intellectual history

• Languages offered: French, Italian, German, Russian, Spanish and Portuguese

• Special library of 1,500 books and periodicals supplemental to University library holdings and audiovisual resources, including 18,000 slides and 1,000 records and tapes

• Sponsors overseas summer travel tours to Europe

15.003
Council on West European Studies
Yale University
Box 13A, Yale Station
New Haven, CT 06520
(203) 436-8523

Contact(s):
David R. Cameron, Chair

• Advises on graduate Western European Studies and promotes research on Western Europe; conducts seminars and supports scholarly activity focusing each year on a different topic; sponsors visiting lecturers

15.004
French and West European Area Studies
American University
Department of Language and Foreign
   Studies
Washington, DC 20016
(202) 686-2280

Contact(s):
Anthony Caprio, Chair

Undergraduate area studies program

• Majors/degrees/certificates offered: B.A. in French and West European Studies

• Approximate number of faculty teaching area and language courses: 6

• Approximate number of courses available—area: 6; language: 10

• Average number of students per year specializing in area: 12

• Countries covered and areas of emphasis: combines Western European Studies in School for International Service (see 6.129) with intensive study of the French language

• Language offered: French

• Requires internship or comparable experience

15.005
German and West European Area Studies
American University
Department of Language and Foreign
   Studies
Washington, DC 20016
(202) 686-2280

Contact(s):
Anthony Caprio, Chair

Undergraduate area studies program

• Majors/degrees/certificates offered: B.A. in German and West European Studies

• Approximate number of faculty teaching area and language courses: 4

• Approximate number of courses available—area: 4; language: 7

• Average number of students per year specializing in area: 9

• Countries covered and areas of emphasis: combines Western European Studies in School for International Service (see 6.129) with intensive study of the German language

• Language offered: German

• Requires internship or comparable experience

15.006
European Studies
The Johns Hopkins University
School of Advanced International Studies
1740 Massachusetts Ave. NW
Washington, DC 20036
(202) 785-6200

Graduate area studies program

• Majors/degrees/certificates offered: M.A. and Ph.D. in International Relations with major in European Studies

• Countries covered and areas of emphasis: all countries of Eastern and Western Europe with emphasis on contemporary Western European economic and political issues (may include special comparative political studies in the Advanced Industrial Societies Program)

• Languages offered: French, German, Italian, Portuguese and Russian

• Study abroad opportunities available, especially at SAIS Bologna Center in Italy where students are encouraged to spend a year; Bologna offers instruction in international economics, European Studies, international political affairs and intensive Italian

• Draws on library, organizational and research resources of the Washington area

• Special internships and fellowships available

15.007
Office of West European Studies
University of Illinois at Urbana-Champaign
3027 Foreign Languages Bldg.
707 South Mathews Ave.
Urbana, IL 61801
(217) 333-6663

Contact(s):
Karl H. Schoeps

• Coordinates instruction and serves as a clearinghouse for information on research about modern Europe, with particular emphasis on domestic and foreign policy issues facing advanced industrial societies; offers cognate option in West European Studies with departments

15.008
West European National Resource Center Program in West European Studies
Indiana University at Bloomington
Ballantine Hall 542
Bloomington, IN 47405
(812) 335-3280

Contact(s):
Norman Furniss, Director

Graduate area studies program established in 1966

• Majors/degrees/certificates offered: M.A. in West European Studies; Ph.D. minor; Certificate in West European Studies

• Approximate number of faculty teaching area and language courses: 38 principal, plus many teaching closely related courses and languages

• Approximate number of courses available—area: 30 plus traditional courses and 8–10 special West European Studies courses per semester; language: large number in all languages mentioned below

• Average number of students per year specializing in area: 32 in the social sciences

- Countries covered and areas of emphasis: all European nations holding membership in the European Economic Community, plus Greece, Spain, Portugal, Switzerland, Austria, Iceland, Norway and Sweden; particular interest in Spain, Portugal and Sweden; emphasis on Western Europe since 1945
- Languages offered: all major West European languages, plus Portuguese, Catalan, Dutch, Danish and Finnish
- Program has its own library in addition to holdings of the University library
- Publishes newsletter

15.009
Program of West European Studies
University of Notre Dame
Notre Dame, IN 46556
(219) 239-6623

Contact(s):
Donald Kommers, Director

Graduate and undergraduate area studies program established in 1961
- Majors/degrees/certificates offered: Certificate with departmental B.A. and M.A. degrees
- Approximate number of faculty teaching area and language courses: 44
- Approximate number of courses available—area: 151; language: 63
- Average number of students per year specializing in area: 5
- Countries covered and areas of emphasis: all countries of Western Europe with particular emphasis on history, philosophy and the social sciences
- Languages offered: French, German and Italian

15.010
Western European Studies
Grinnell College
Grinnell, IA 50112
(515) 236-7545

Contact(s):
Sigmund Barber, Chair

Undergraduate area studies program
- Majors/degrees/certificates offered: B.A. in Western European Studies
- Approximate number of courses available—area: 34
- Countries covered and areas of emphasis: Western European countries, with study emphasis on a historical period, a geographic area or a culture
- Languages offered: French, German and Spanish
- Study abroad opportunities available in England, France, Austria, West Germany, Greece, Italy, Norway, Scotland and Spain

15.011
Center for European Studies
Harvard University
5 Bryant St.
Cambridge, MA 02138
(617) 495-4303

Contact(s):
Stanley Hoffman, Chair

- Research center involving U.S. and European scholars designed to promote research and inquiry into issues of common concern to European industrial societies: labor, the role of the state, social movements, urban policies, the crises of industrialization, the effect of domestic culture and politics on international roles, etc.
- Maintains offices for visiting scholars, meeting rooms and a small library of current materials
- Sponsors seminars and study groups

open to the entire student and scholarly community including British, East European, French, German, Greek and Italian study groups, and study groups or seminars on culture and politics, equality and the welfare state, the Jew in modern Europe, labor, the state and capitalism, U.S.-European relations, social theory, women and youth

• Publishes books and monographs including a new series of casebooks Contemporary Problems in European Society and Culture (designed as teaching materials) that support the study of European social, political and cultural issues in a broader contemporary framework

15.012
Center for Western European Studies
University of Michigan at Ann Arbor
5208 Angell Hall
Ann Arbor, MI 48109
(313) 764-4311

Contact(s):
J. Graham Smith, Director

• Supports research, conducts graduate student training and sponsors overseas study programs in Italy, France and Britain

15.013
European Studies Program
Western Michigan University
2090 Friedmann
Kalamazoo, MI 49008
(616) 383-8002

Contact(s):
William Ritchie, Chair

Undergraduate area studies program
• Majors/degrees/certificates offered: Coordinate B.A. (combined with departmental major) in European Studies
• Countries covered and areas of em-

phasis: all countries of Western and Eastern Europe with general focus on European cultures and institutions or on a specific country (Britain, Germany, USSR, etc., or region (Romance Studies, Slavic Studies, etc.)

15.014
Basque Studies Program
University of Nevada
Getchell Library
Reno, NV 89557
(702) 784-4854

Contact(s):
William A. Douglass, Coordinator

• Conducts studies on Basque language, society and culture in Basque Country and in the U.S.; results published in University of Nevada Series on the Basques; publishes newsletter, sponsors study abroad in Basque Country and maintains library collection of more than 16,000 volumes on the Basques

15.015
Center for European Studies
City University of New York/Graduate
   School
33 West 42d St.
New York, NY 10036
(212) 790-4442

Contact(s):
Henry Wasser, Director

• Conducts research on political, cultural and economic issues relative to Western and Central Europe; sponsors seminars, conferences and outreach programs and publishes research studies and bibliographies including *A Selected Bibliography to Western European Films*

15.016
Institute on Western Europe
Columbia University
420 West 118th St., Room 1305A
New York, NY 10027
(212) 280-4618

Contact(s):
Elliot Zupnick, Director

Graduate area studies program established in
1949
• Majors/degrees/certificates offered:
Two-year M.A. in the School of International
and Public Affairs with a Certificate in Western European Studies; M.A. and Ph.D., with
a Certificate in Western European Studies
• Approximate number of faculty teaching area and language courses: 111
• Approximate number of courses avail-
able—area: 112; language: 27
• Average number of students per year
specializing in area: 44
• Countries covered and areas of emphasis: all countries of Western Europe with
faculty research interests particularly in the
EEC (Common Market), the United Kingdom, France and the Mediterranean
• Languages offered: Dutch, Finnish,
French, German, Italian, Portuguese, Span-
ish, Swedish and "French for Diplomats"
• Extensive collections in Columbia
University Library; member of the Research
Libraries Group which provides access to the
libraries of Harvard and Yale and to the re-
search libraries of the New York City Public
Library
• Prepares cassette tapes and curricu-
lum guides for use in secondary education,
including *A Selected Bibliography of Western
European Films: A Study Guide* (Frederick
A. Wasser; $3.75)

15.017
The Western Societies Program
Cornell University
170 Uris Hall
Ithaca, NY 14853
(607) 256-6224

Contact(s):
Steven L. Kaplan, Director

• Promotes research, provides grants and
sponsors lectures on problems of the advanced industrial state with emphasis on cen-
tral-local relations and the transition to modern democratic governments in European
countries; publishes occasional papers on new
avenues of research and new perspectives on
Europe

15.018
European Studies Program
University of Toledo
Toledo, OH 43606
(419) 537-4135

Contact(s):
Jules Gylys, Advisor

Undergraduate area studies program
• Majors/degrees/certificates offered:
B.A. in European Studies
• Countries covered and areas of em-
phasis: Eastern and Western Europe with
emphasis on history and the social sciences

15.019
Center for European Studies
Vanderbilt University
Nashville, TN 37235
(615) 322-2528

Contact(s):
M. Donald Hancock, Director

Undergraduate area studies program established in 1981

- Majors/degrees/certificates offered: B.A. in Modern European Studies (an interdisciplinary major)
- Approximate number of faculty teaching area and language courses: 53
- Approximate number of courses available—area: 71; language: 16
- Average number of students per year specializing in area: 25
- Countries covered and areas of emphasis: Eastern and Western Europe with emphasis on the 20th century
- Languages offered: German, French, Spanish, Portuguese and Russian
- Study abroad encouraged in Vanderbilt programs in France, Germany, Spain and Great Britain

15.020
Center for European Studies
University of Texas at Austin
Student Services Bldg. 4.110
Austin, TX 78712
(512) 471-4626

Contact(s):
Walter Wetzels, Director

- Coordinates B.A. concentration in West or East European Studies within departmental major

15.021
European Studies
Brigham Young University
130 FOB
Provo, UT 84602
(801) 378-3377

- Offers B.A. and M.A. in European Studies

15.022
European Studies
University of Vermont
Center for Area and International Studies
479 Main St.
Burlington, VT 05405
(802) 656-4062

Contact(s):
Susan M. Whitebook, Director

Undergraduate area studies program established in 1972

- Majors/degrees/certificates offered: B.A. in European Studies
- Approximate number of faculty teaching area and language courses: 35
- Approximate number of courses available—area: 80; language: 50
- Average number of students per year specializing in area: 10
- Countries covered and areas of emphasis: Western and Northern Europe and the Mediterranean
- Languages offered: French, German and Spanish
- Overseas study opportunities available

15.023
Western European Area Studies
University of Wisconsin at Madison
818 Van Hise Hall
1220 Linden Drive
Madison, WI 53706
(608) 262-2192

Contact(s):
Charlotte L. Brancaforte, Chair, Steering Committee

Graduate area studies program established in 1968

- Majors/degrees/certificates offered: Departmental M.A. and Ph.D. with Certificate in Western European Area Studies or option B minor for the Ph.D.

- Approximate number of faculty teaching area and language courses: 61
- Approximate number of courses available—area: 134
- Countries covered and areas of emphasis: Western Europe; emphasis on comparative issues in 20th-century Western European affairs

- Languages offered: all Western European languages, including Scandinavian languages
- Overseas study opportunities available in France, Britain, Italy, Spain and West Germany

Programs and Resources for Scandinavian Studies

15.024
Scandinavian Studies
Gustavus Adolphus College
St. Peter, MN 56082
(507) 931-7422

Contact(s):
Roger McKnight and Roland Thorstensson, Co-directors

Undergraduate area studies program established in 1971
- Majors/degrees/certificates offered: B.A. in Scandinavian Studies
- Approximate number of faculty teaching area & language courses: 4
- Approximate number of courses available—area: 12; language: 7
- Average number of students per year specializing in area: 10
- Countries covered and areas of emphasis: Scandinavia with emphasis on Sweden, Denmark and Norway and on Scandinavian immigration to North America
- Language offered: Swedish
- Study abroad can be arranged

15.025
**Center for Northwest European
Language and Area Studies**
University of Minnesota
210 Folwell Hall
9 Pleasant St. SE
Minneapolis, MN 55455

Contact(s):
Michael F. Metcalf, Director

Graduate and undergraduate area studies program established in 1965
- Majors/degrees/certificates offered: B.A., M.A. and Ph.D. in Scandinavian Languages and Literature; B.A., M.A. and Ph.D. with Scandinavian Area Studies as subfield
- Approximate number of faculty teaching area and language courses: 20
- Approximate number of courses available—area: 68; language: 22
- Countries covered and areas of emphasis: Denmark, Finland, Iceland, Norway, and Sweden; particularly strong in art, social sciences, languages and literature; also stresses Scandinavian-American immigrant experience
- Languages offered: Danish, Finnish, Old Norse, Norwegian and Swedish
- 175,000-volume library holdings on Scandinavia, including 200 journals and periodicals; the Alrik Gustafson Strindberg Collection; and Scandinavian Children's Literature Research Collection in original languages and in English translation
- Offers research associate status to visiting scholars and researchers
- Conducts workshops for college and secondary school teachers
- Publishes *The Nordic Bulletin, The Directory of the Conference Group on Nordic Society,* and Occasional Papers series

15.026
German-Scandinavian Studies
Washington University
St. Louis, MO 63130
(314) 889-5000

Contact(s):
Egon Schwarz, Chair

• Area studies program focusing on northwestern Europe (see 18.156)

15.027
Department of Scandinavian Studies
University of Wisconsin at Madison
1220 Linden Drive
Madison, WI 53706
(608) 262-2090

Contact(s):
Harald S. Naess, Chair

Graduate area studies program established in 1949 (Scandinavian Languages Department established in 1875)
• Majors/degrees/certificates offered: M.A. in Scandinavian Studies and departmental Ph.D. with major in Scandinavian Studies
• Approximate number of faculty teaching area and language courses: 11
• Approximate number of courses available—area: 8; language: 16
• Average number of students per year specializing in area: 25
• Countries covered and areas of emphasis: Denmark, Finland, Iceland, Norway and Sweden
• Languages offered: Norwegian, Swedish, Danish, Finnish, and Old Norse-Icelandic
• Provides opportunities for exchange teaching and honorary fellowships to visiting faculty from Scandinavia
• Publishes Pamphlet Series WITS (*Wisconsin Introductions to Scandinavia*)

15.028
The American-Scandinavian Foundation
Exchange Division
127 East 73d St.
New York, NY 10021
(212) 879-9779

Nonprofit educational organization designed to promote educational and cultural exchanges between the U.S. and countries of Scandinavia
• Provides grants ranging from $500 to $7,000 to American graduate students to pursue research or study in Scandinavia in any discipline
• Maintains library of Scandinavian literature in the original languages and in translation; publishes materials on Scandinavian life for Americans; provides grants to Scandinavian students to study in the U.S.

15.029
Society for the Advancement of Scandinavian Studies
University of Illinois at Urbana-Champlain
Department of Germanic Languages
Urbana, IL 61801
(217) 333-7654

Contact(s):
Marianne E. Kalinke, Secretary-Treasurer

• Promotes Scandinavian Studies in the U.S.; publishes newsletter and the quarterly *Scandinavian Studies* (see 15.032)

15.030
Arthur Vanous Co.
Box 650279
Vero Beach, FL 32965

Book importer
• Imports and warehouses language dictionaries, texts and cassettes from the Scandinavian countries; will import any Scandinavian book on request

15.031
University of Minnesota Press
2037 University Ave. SE
Minneapolis, MN 55414
(612) 373-3266

• Publishes books on literature and history of the Scandinavian countries

15.032
Scandinavian Studies
Carol J. Clover, Managing Editor
Society for the Advancement of
    Scandinavian Study
Department of Germanic Languages
707 S. Mathews Ave.
University of Illinois
Urbana, IL 61801
quarterly journal; 127 pages; $30 per year
    for nonmembers

• Contains scholarly articles and essays on Scandinavian history, literature and culture; includes book reviews

Resources on the European Community

15.033
European Community Information Service
2100 M St. NW, Suite 707
Washington, DC 20037
(202) 862-9500

Contact(s):
Barbara Sloan, Head of Public Inquiries

• Answers telephone and written inquiries about the European Community and its policy and developments
• Provides speakers and educational or teaching materials
• Welcomes inquiries from any interested individual or institution
• Provides printed information (including catalogues of publications) about education in the Economic Community and about the Economic Community in general and publishes *Europe* (see 15.037)

15.034
European Communities
J. Bryan Collester, Editor
Gale Research Co.
Book Tower
Detroit, MI 48226
1979; hardbound; 265 pages; $40

• Bibliographic information about works on the European communities, both historical and current

15.035
Research Resources: The European Community
Steven J. Warnecke
Council for European Studies
1509 International Affairs Bldg.
Columbia University
New York, NY 10027
1978; paperbound; 333 pages; $7 plus $1
    postage and handling

• Provides a detailed survey of the structure and organization of the various European Community institutions, the location, contents and availability of archives and libraries, and a selected list of European newspapers, periodicals and news services and university institutes; also contains information on the political institutions, parties and major interest groups of the nine member states, as well as a bibliography of books, articles and documents

15.036
Publications of the European Communities
European Community Information Service
2100 M St. NW, Suite 707
Washington, DC 20037
monthly pamphlet; 60 pages; free

• Lists periodicals and newly published monographs on economic and political affairs issued by members of the European Community

15.037
Europe
Webster Martin, Editor in Chief
Delegation of the European Communities
2100 M St. NW
Washington, DC 20037
bimonthly magazine; approx. 60 pages; $12 per year

• Articles of general interest on business and economic developments in the European Community; includes news briefs, a listing of scholarships and grants, annotations of recent books and a select descriptive list of other European Community publications

Information Sources

15.038
The Council for European Studies
Columbia University
1509 International Affairs Bldg.
New York, NY 10027
(212) 280-4172

Contact(s):
Ioannis Sinanoglou, Executive Secretary

Association of individuals and institutions concerned with Western European Studies
• Sponsors and funds interdisciplinary and cross-national research planning groups, research conferences, and conferences of Europeanists designed to promote long-term collaborative research on contemporary issues and strengthen ties between U.S. and European scholars; grants to groups and/or institutions
• Conducts training workshops for graduate students and administers fellowship program when funds are available

• Publishes the *European Studies Newsletter* and reference works of value to researchers including the handbooks: *Libraries and Archives in France* (see 18.147), *Libraries and Archives in Germany* (see 18.164), *Libraries and Archives in Italy* (see 18.260), *Research Resources: The European Community* (see 15.035) and *Fellowship Guide to Western Europe* (see 15.039)

15.039
Fellowship Guide to Western Europe
Siri Belgum, Editor
Council for European Studies
Columbia University
1509 International Affairs Bldg.
New York, NY 10027
1981; paperbound; 99 pages; $5 plus $1 postage

• Lists and describes 150 sources of financial assistance for travel and graduate and advanced study and research in the countries of Europe outside the Soviet bloc (excludes fellowships restricted to the registered students of the institutions offering them); grouped in the following categories: general, special fellowships for women, fields of study (23 disciplines in the social sciences and humanities), and country; indexed by source of funds

15.040

A Survey of Materials for the Study of the Uncommonly Taught Languages: Languages of Western Europe Pidgins and Creoles (European Based)
Dora E. Johnson et al.
Center for Applied Linguistics
3510 Prospect St. NW
Washington, DC 20007
1976; paperbound; 31 pages; $7.95

Exclusively distributed by Harcourt Brace Jovanich, Inc., 757 Third Ave., New York, NY 10017; Attn: Nancy McCloughan

• One of a series of bibliographies covering all the modern languages except Standard English, German, Italian, Russian and Spanish; designed for use by the adult learner whose native language is English; listed under the headings: teaching materials, readers, grammars and dictionaries; includes books currently in print where feasible, older titles where not; citations appear under the following language groups: Scandinavian, West Germanic, Keltic, Basque, Western European, Uralic, European Based Pidgin and Creole Languages based on French, Portuguese and Spanish

Sources of Grants and Awards

15.041

Social Science Research Council
Fellowships for International Doctoral
    Research: Western Europe
605 Third Ave.
New York, NY 10158
(212) 557-9500

• Awards substantial fellowships for doctoral dissertation research in the social sciences and the humanities in Western Europe; particularly encouraged are applications from disciplines in which relatively less attention has been devoted to Western Europe such as anthropology, economics, social psychology and sociology; program also encourages research on problems of public policy common to Western Europe and North America, particularly urban and regional problems, as well as research on relatively neglected geographical areas of Europe, such as the Low Countries, Portugal, Scandinavia, Spain and Switzerland; applications will also be accepted for research involving both Europe and North America if the comparative nature of the project requires it

• All full time students enrolled in doctoral programs in the U.S. or Canada are eligible; all applicants must expect to spend at least nine months of research in one or more countries of the area

16

Latin American Area Studies

Area Studies Programs and Research Centers

16.001
Latin American Studies Program
University of Alabama
P.O. Box 1974
University, AL 35486
(205) 348-5270

Contact(s):
Lawrence A. Clayton, Director

Graduate and undergraduate area studies program established in 1966
• Majors/degrees/certificates offered: B.A. in Latin American Studies; M.A. in Latin American Studies; M.A. and Ph.D. minor in certain departments
• Approximate number of faculty teaching area and language courses: 16
• Approximate number of courses available—area: 45; language: 18
• Countries covered and areas of emphasis: all countries of Latin America and the Caribbean; particular strength in international economics and business
• Languages offered: Spanish and Portuguese
• Extensive Latin American holdings, including 100 periodicals from Latin America and a 30,000-item collection of Yucatán materials on microfilm
• Sponsors research through Capstone International Program Center (see 4.189)

16.002
Center for Latin American Studies
Arizona State University
Room 213, Social Sciences Bldg.
Tempe, AZ 85287
(602) 965-5127

Contact(s):
Jerry R. Ladman, Director

Graduate and undergraduate area studies program established in 1965
• Majors/degrees/certificates offered: B.A. combined with disciplinary major; specialization with M.A. and Ph.D. departmental degrees
• Approximate number of faculty teaching area and language courses: 65
• Approximate number of courses available—area: 62; language: 26
• Average number of students per year specializing in area: 50
• Countries covered and areas of emphasis: all countries of Latin America and the Caribbean
• Languages offered: Spanish and Portuguese
• Arranges student exchanges with Latin American universities
• Sponsors research and publishes an extensive list of books, monographs and papers, including a number of bibliographies and dictionaries (Latin American authors, government leaders, etc.)

16.003
Latin American Area Center
University of Arizona
Social Sciences 216
Tucson, AZ 85721
(602) 621-1137

Contact(s):
Susan M. Reeds, Assistant Director

Graduate and undergraduate area studies program established in 1965
• Majors/degrees/certificates offered: B.A. and M.A. in Latin American Studies; Ph.D. with minor in Latin American Studies
• Approximate number of faculty teaching area and language courses: 61
• Approximate number of courses available—area: 95; language: 40
• Average number of students per year specializing in area: 25 B.A., 25 M.A.
• Countries covered and areas of emphasis: all Latin American countries; particular emphasis on Mexico, Brazil and Central America
• Languages offered: Spanish and Portuguese
• Library contains over 200,000 volumes on Latin American area
• Intensive language training and Hispanic Studies available at the Guadalajara Summer School in Mexico; study programs also available in Brazil

16.004
Latin America Studies Program
California State University, Chico
Center for International Studies
Chico, CA 95926
(916) 895-6880

Contact(s):
José L. Mas, Coordinator

Undergraduate area studies program established in 1971
• Majors/degrees/certificates offered: B.A. in Latin American Studies
• Approximate number of faculty teaching area and language courses: 20
• Approximate number of courses available—area: 26; language: 9
• Average number of students per year specializing in area: 25
• Countries covered and areas of emphasis: all countries of Latin America; emphasis on the Spanish-speaking countries, particularly Mexico
• Languages offered: Spanish and Portuguese
• Semester study abroad program available in Mexico and summer programs in other Latin American countries

16.005
Latin American Studies
California State University at Fullerton
Fullerton, CA 92634
(714) 773-2594

Contact(s):
William Ketteringham, Coordinator

Undergraduate area studies program established in 1970
• Majors/degrees/certificates offered: B.A. major and minor in Latin American Studies
• Approximate number of faculty teaching area and language courses: 10
• Approximate number of courses available—area: 25; language: 8
• Average number of students per year specializing in area: 15
• Countries covered and areas of emphasis: all of Latin America with particular interest in Brazil and Mexico
• Languages offered: Spanish and Portuguese

16.006
Latin American Studies
California State University at Hayward
Department of Geography
Hayward, CA 94542
(415) 881-3211 or 3388

Contact(s):
John H. Vann, Acting Director

Undergraduate area studies program established in 1967

• Majors/degrees/certificates offered: B.A. in Latin American Studies

• Approximate number of faculty teaching area and language courses: 12

• Approximate number of courses available—area: 36; language: 10

• Average number of students per year specializing in area: 7

• Countries covered and areas of emphasis: Spanish- and Portuguese-speaking Latin America; students emphasize either Hispanic-American or Luso-Brazilian Studies

• Languages offered: Spanish and Portuguese

• Study abroad available through CSUC International Programs (see 8.012)

16.007
Latin American Studies
California State University at Los Angeles
Latin American Studies Center
5151 State University Drive
Los Angeles, CA 90032
(213) 224-2878

Contact(s):
Timothy F. Harding, Director

Graduate and undergraduate area studies program

• Majors/degrees/certificates offered: B.A. and M.A. in Latin American Studies

• Approximate number of courses available—area: 38; language: 10

• Countries covered and areas of emphasis: all countries of Latin America

• Languages offered: Spanish and Portuguese

• Publishes Latin American Bibliography series

16.008
Latin American Studies Program
The Claremont Colleges
Claremont McKenna College
Claremont, CA 91711
(714) 621-8000, Ext. 2770

Contact(s):
Phillip Koldewyn, Coordinator

Undergraduate area studies program; a joint program of the Claremont Colleges: Pomona, Scripps, Claremont Men's, Harvey Mudd, Pitzer and Claremont Graduate School

• Majors/degrees/certificates offered: B.A. in Latin American Studies

• Countries covered and areas of emphasis: all countries of Latin America

16.009
The Institute of Andean Studies
P.O. Box 9307
Berkeley, CA 94709
(415) 525-7816

Contact(s):
John H. Rowe, President
Patricia J. Lyon, Secretary and Treasurer

Nonprofit scientific and educational organization concerned with archaeology of the Andean region of South America; established in 1960

• Holds an annual meeting and publishes annually a journal *Nawpa Pacha* ($10, back issues available) which focuses on the history and archaeology of the Andean region

16.010
Hispanic/Latin American Studies
Occidental College
Los Angeles, CA 90041
(213) 259-2700

Contact(s):
Jane S. Jaquette, Chair

Undergraduate area studies program

• Majors/degrees/certificates offered: B.A. with major in Hispanic/Latin American emphasis

• Countries covered and areas of emphasis: all Spanish-speaking countries of Latin America

- Language offered: Spanish
- Limited number of international study abroad fellowships available

16.011
Center for Latin American Studies
San Diego State University
Social Science Bldg., Room SS-146
San Diego, CA 92182
(619) 265-6685

Contact(s):
Thomas M. Davies, Jr., Director

Graduate and undergraduate area studies program
- Majors/degrees/certificates offered: B.A. major and minor and M.A. in Latin American Studies
- Approximate number of faculty teaching area and language courses: 36
- Approximate number of courses available—area: 83; language: 38
- Average number of students per year specializing in area: 33
- Countries covered and areas of emphasis: all countries of Latin America with particular interest in Mexico, U.S.-Mexican relations, the Andean countries and political, economic and social issues, especially urbanization and modernization
- Languages offered: Spanish and Portuguese
- Library contains over 34,000 volumes, 239 periodicals and several thousand maps of Latin America and is especially strong in Mexico, U.S.-Mexican borderlands, Brazil, the Andes and contemporary urban studies; maintains a Latin American bibliographer
- Center holds extensive collection of Latin American films
- Conducts in-service workshops for elementary and high school teachers
- Study abroad available in Mexico and Peru

16.012
Center for Latin American Studies
Stanford University
582 Alvarado Row
Stanford, CA 94305
(415) 497-4444

Contact(s):
George A. Collier, Director

Graduate and undergraduate area studies program established in 1964
- Majors/degrees/certificates offered: B.A. and M.A. in Latin American Studies; Ph.D. in departments with specialization in Latin America; also available are a joint M.A./J.D. degree with the Law School, a joint degree with the School of Medicine and an M.A. in Teaching Latin American Studies
- Approximate number of faculty teaching area and language courses: 50
- Approximate number of courses available—area: 70; language: 50
- Average number of students per year specializing in area: 100 graduate; 30 undergraduate
- Countries covered and areas of emphasis: covers all countries of Latin America with particular library and teaching strength in the Caribbean, Central America, Brazil, Chile, Colombia, Mexico and Venezuela
- Languages offered: Spanish and Portuguese, plus American Indian languages on an individual basis
- Extensive library resources with special Latin American curator who lectures on Latin American Bibliography; other collections on Latin America available in the Hoover Institution on War, Revolution and Peace (on political, social and economic changes since 1914, especially revolutionary movements, Marxist-Leninist groups, Cuba, socialism and Peronism, see 4.159); the Food Research Institute Library and the Law and Business School libraries
- Co-sponsors SPICE-Latin America Project (see 2.061) (which promotes the development and dissemination of elementary

and secondary teaching materials about Latin America)

• Makes an office available to external post-doctoral research scholar each year and conducts jointly with University of California at Berkeley a short-term summer research grant program for faculty from Northern California and Pacific Northwest institutions, administered under the Stanford-Berkeley National Resource Center for Latin American Studies

• Study abroad available in Peru and Brazil

16.013
Center for Latin American Studies
University of California at Berkeley
2334 Bowditch St.
Berkeley, CA 94720
(415) 642-2088

Contact(s):
David Collier, Chair

Graduate and undergraduate area studies program established in 1958

• Majors/degrees/certificates offered: B.A., M.A. and Ph.D. degrees in Latin American Studies (administered by faculty committees)

• Approximate number of faculty teaching area and language courses: 42

• Approximate number of courses available—area: 30; language: 20

• Average number of students per year specializing in area: 30

• Countries covered and areas of emphasis: all countries of Latin America and the Caribbean; special strength in Mexico and Central America

• Languages offered: Spanish and Portuguese

• Library contains strong collections of materials on Mexico, Central America and Spanish and Mexican influence in the U.S. Southwest

• Undergraduate study through Education Abroad Program (see 8.012) available in Mexico, Lima, and Sao Paulo; graduate study and research available in Costa Rica through the Organization for Tropical Studies (see 16.121)

• Conducts jointly with Stanford University a short-term summer research grant program for faculty from Northern California and Pacific Northwest institutions, administered under the Stanford-Berkeley National Resource Center for Latin American Studies

16.014
Latin American Center
University of California at Los Angeles
405 Hilgard Ave.
Los Angeles, CA 90024
(213) 825-1057

Contact(s):
Ludwig Lauerhass, Executive Director

Graduate, undergraduate and nondegree area studies program established in 1959

• Majors/degrees/certificates offered: B.A. and M.A. in Latin American Area Studies; B.A., M.A., and Ph.D. in disciplines, with Latin American concentration; joint degrees with Schools of Architecture and Urban Planning, Education, Engineering and Applied Science, Law, Library and Information Science, Management and Public Health

• Approximate number of faculty teaching area and language courses: 75

• Approximate number of courses available—area: 115; language: 30

• Average number of students per year specializing in area: 60 graduate; 45 undergraduate

• Countries covered and areas of emphasis: all countries in Latin America and the Caribbean, with particular strengths in Mexico and Brazil

• Languages offered: Spanish, Portuguese, Quechua and Nahuatl

• Strong library holdings of current and retrospective materials; over 150,000 bound volumes, 1,500 periodicals, 25 newspapers, and 8,000 reels of microfilm; Museum of Cultural History contains 10,000 art objects; significant collection of feature and documentary films in Media Library

• Sponsors research, particularly in the social sciences with a focus on economic development

• Member of Southern California Conference on International Studies which makes available Mellon research fellowships

• Study abroad opportunities available in Brazil, Mexico, Peru and Spain through University of California Education Abroad Program (see 8.012)

• Maintains Visiting Scholar Program to bring in specialists in Latin American Studies from Latin America

• Publishes *Hispanic American Periodicals Index* (see 16.137), *Latin American Lore, Statistical Abstract of Latin America* (see 16.145), and a *Teachers Resource Handbook for Latin American Studies* (see 2.152), along with a reference series, several guides to the UCLA Library Latin American Collection, a number of films, and studies on Latin American politics and political statistics, education, literature and folklore, art and iconography, history, theater, cinema and law

16.015
Latin American Studies Program
University of California at Riverside
Library South 2316
Riverside, CA 92521
(714) 787-3864

Contact(s):
William W. Megenney, Director

Undergraduate area studies program
• Majors/degrees/certificates   offered: B.A. in Latin American Studies; may elect joint major in Latin American Studies and Chicano Studies

• Approximate number of courses available—area: 47

• Countries covered and areas of emphasis: all countries of Latin America; particular strength in the social sciences and in Chicano Studies

• Languages offered: Spanish, French and Portuguese

16.016
Latin American Studies Program
Merrill College
University of California at Santa Cruz
Office D
Santa Cruz, CA 95064
(408) 429-4284

Contact(s):
Marta Morello-Frosch, Coordinator

Undergraduate area studies program established in 1972
• Majors/degrees/certificates   offered: B.A. in Latin American Studies

• Approximate number of faculty teaching area and language courses: 21

• Approximate number of courses available—area: 32; language: 18

• Average number of students per year specializing in area: 15–20

• Countries covered and areas of emphasis: covers all of Latin America with particular strength in Mexican Studies

• Language offered: Spanish

• Latin American collection with special bibliographer; there is also a Third World Teaching Resource Center

• Merrill College Field Program arranges individual field study placements for students in Latin American and Spanish-speaking communities in the U.S. and makes available UC Education Abroad Programs (see 8.012) in Peru, Mexico, Brazil and Spain

16.017
Inter-American Studies Program
University of the Pacific/Elbert Covell
  College
Stockton, CA 95204
(209) 946-2578

Contact(s):
Gaylon L. Caldwell, Director

Undergraduate area studies program
   • Majors/degrees/certificates offered:
B.A. in Inter-American Studies and Licen-
ciado (for students from Latin America)
   • Approximate number of faculty teach-
ing area & language courses: 18
   • Approximate number of courses avail-
able—area: 36
   • Average number of students per year
specializing in area: 200
   • Countries covered and areas of em-
phasis: All of Latin America
   • Language offered: Elbert Covell is a
Spanish-speaking college
   • Extensive library collection on Latin
America in Spanish and English
   • Study and internship programs avail-
able in Costa Rica, Mexico and Peru

16.018
Latin American Studies
University of Colorado, Boulder
McKenna 132A
Boulder, CO 80309
(303) 492-0111

Contact(s):
Lillian Fernandez de Robison, Chair

   • Offers B.A. in Latin American Studies

16.019
Center for Latin American Studies
University of Denver
Department of Foreign Languages and
  Literature
Denver, CO 80208
(303) 753-1964

Contact(s):
Oscar U. Somoza, Director

Undergraduate area studies program
   • Majors/degrees/certificates offered:
B.A. in Latin American Studies
   • Approximate number of faculty teach-
ing area and language courses: 12
   • Approximate number of courses avail-
able—area: 16; language: 13
   • Countries covered and areas of em-
phasis: all countries of Latin America, espe-
cially Mexico, with emphasis on history and
Spanish language and literature
   • Language offered: Spanish

16.020
**The Center for Latin American and
Caribbean Studies**
University of Connecticut
U-103
Storrs, CT 06268
(203) 486-4964

Contact(s):
Paul B. Goodwin, Jr., Director
Julia Barstow, Executive Associate

Graduate and undergraduate area studies
program established in 1978
   • Majors/degrees/certificates offered:
B.A. and M.A. in Latin American Studies;
joint M.A./M.B.A. in International Studies
concentrating in Latin American Studies; and
Ph.D. in many fields with concentration in
Latin America
   • Approximate number of faculty teach-
ing area and language courses: 54

• Approximate number of courses available—area: 96; language and literature: 26

• Average number of students per year specializing in area: 75

• Countries covered and areas of emphasis: all of Central and South America plus Caribbean region, with strengths in Argentina, Chile, Mexico and the Caribbean

• Languages offered: Spanish, Portuguese, French, Quechua (Summer Institute)

• Library contains extensive Latin American collection including large holdings in Chilean history and literature and in Caribbean materials and a comprehensive collection of Spanish periodicals; the Institute of Social Inquiry, which encompasses the Roper Public Opinion Research Center, contains an extensive Latin American data base

• Conducts high school outreach program and sponsors a Latin American film series, a lecture series and one major conference per year

• Study abroad in Mexico available through Northeast Consortium; maintains faculty exchange relationship with a Brazilian university

• Maintains, with Yale University, Joint Center for Latin American Studies, with federally funded graduate fellowships

• Publishes newsletter and Occasional Papers series

16.021
Latin American Studies National Resource Center
Yale University
P.O. Box 1881, Yale Station
New Haven, CT 06520
(203) 432-4422

Contact(s):
Colin Bradford, Acting chair
Ann Carter-Drier, Senior Administrative
   Assistant

Graduate and undergraduate area studies program established in 1962

• Majors/degrees/certificates offered: B.A. in Latin American Studies; M.A. and Ph.D. in discipline with Latin American concentration

• Approximate number of faculty teaching area and language courses: 34

• Approximate number of courses available—area: 52; language: 24

• Average number of students per year specializing in area: 110 graduate

• Countries covered and areas of emphasis: Central America, South America and the Caribbean, with particular strength in Brazil, Argentina and Chile; extensive co-curricular program

• Languages offered: Spanish and Portuguese; also offered in the Yale Summer Language Institute

• Latin American library collection of over 250,000 volumes including 3,000 periodicals and serials

• Exchange and scholarly relationships with research centers in Brazil, Mexico, Chile, Argentina, Colombia and Peru; offers Visiting Fellow appointment to externally supported researchers with Ph.D. degrees

• Undergraduate junior year abroad programs available

• Publishes newsletter

• Financial assistance includes mini-grants for summer research/travel for graduate students and National Resource Fellowships for summer language study

16.022
Spanish and Latin American Area Studies
American University
Department of Language and Foreign
   Studies
Washington, DC 20016
(202) 686-2280

Contact(s):
Anthony Caprio, Chair

Undergraduate area studies program
- Majors/degrees/certificates offered: B.A. in Spanish and Latin American Area Studies
- Approximate number of faculty teaching area and language courses: 9
- Approximate number of courses available—area: 6; language: 10
- Average number of students per year specializing in area: 3
- Countries covered and areas of emphasis: combines study in the School for International Service (see 6.129) with Spanish language and literature
- Language offered: Spanish
- Requires internship or comparable experience

16.023
Latin American Studies Program
George Washington University
Quigley's, Room 301
Washington, DC 20052
(202) 676-6187

Contact(s):
Marvin Gordon, Director

Graduate and undergraduate area studies program established in 1960
- Majors/degrees/certificates offered: B.A. and M.A. in Public and International Affairs and Ph.D. in departments with Latin American specialization
- Approximate number of faculty teaching area and language courses: 15
- Approximate number of courses available—area: 52; language: 12
- Average number of students per year specializing in area: 30–40
- Countries covered and areas of emphasis: Latin America in general with particular interest in the Andean area
- Languages offered: Spanish and Portuguese
- Extensive Latin American research resources in libraries and organizations in the Washington area

16.024
Latin American Studies
The Johns Hopkins University
School of Advanced International Studies
1740 Massachusetts Ave. NW
Washington, DC 20036
(202) 785-6830

Contact(s):
Riordan Roett, Director

Graduate area studies program
- Majors/degrees/certificates offered: M.A. and Ph.D. in International Relations with major in Latin American Studies
- Approximate number of faculty teaching area & language courses: 14
- Approximate number of courses available—area: 16, language: six
- Average number of students per year specializing in area: 56
- Countries covered and areas of emphasis: all countries of Latin America with special emphasis on Brazil and on contemporary political and economic issues
- Languages offered: Portuguese and Spanish
- Maintains Center of Brazilian Studies (see 18.028) and conducts an exchange program with the University of Havana, Cuba
- Draws on library, organizational and research resources of the Washington area
- Special internships and fellowships available

16.025
Latin American and Caribbean Center
Florida International University
Tamiami Trail
Miami, FL 33199
(305) 554-2894

Contact(s):

Mark B. Rosenberg, Director

Graduate, undergraduate and nondegree area studies program established in 1974
• Majors/degrees/certificates offered: Certificate in Latin American and Caribbean Studies
• Approximate number of faculty teaching area and language courses: 40
• Approximate number of courses available—area: 62; language: 9
• Average number of students per year specializing in area: 20–25
• Countries covered and areas of emphasis: all countries of South and Central America and the Caribbean with particular strength in the Caribbean and Central American areas
• Languages offered: Spanish (all levels) and Portuguese
• Library contains an extensive Latin American and Caribbean Collection, including approximately 100 films
• Conducts Summer Teacher Training Program and periodic seminars and conferences (occasionally on trade and business) open to the community
• Sponsors summer study abroad programs in Honduras (archaeology) and Mexico (international relations)
• Maintains cooperative research agreement with Universidad de San Pedro Sula, Honduras
• Publishes a newsletter, an Occasional Papers series and the *Caribbean Review*

16.026
Inter-American Studies Program
Florida State University
Tallahassee, FL 32306
(904) 644-6200

Contact(s):
Ernest Rehder, Director

Undergraduate area studies program established in 1962
• Majors/degrees/certificates offered: B.A. in Inter-American Studies
• Approximate number of faculty teaching area and language courses: 10
• Approximate number of courses available—area: 12; language: 6
• Average number of students per year specializing in area: 6
• Countries covered and areas of emphasis: all of Latin America and the Caribbean
• Languages offered: Spanish, French and Portuguese
• Offers summer study program in Costa Rica
• Offers cooperative major with the Business School

16.027
Program in Latin American Studies
Rollins College
Box 2652
Winter Park, FL 32789
(305) 646-2161

Contact(s):
Luis Valdes, Director

Undergraduate area studies program
• Majors/degrees/certificates offered: B.A. in Latin American Studies
• Approximate number of courses available—area: 32; language: 5
• Countries covered and areas of emphasis: all countries of Latin America
• Languages offered: Spanish and Portuguese
• Overseas study encouraged

16.028
Center for Latin American Studies
University of Florida
319 Grinter Hall
Gainesville, FL 32611
(904) 392-0375

Contact(s):
Helen I. Safa, Director
Connie Curtis, Outreach Coordinator

Graduate and undergraduate area studies program established in 1962
- Majors/degrees/certificates offered: M.A. in Latin American Studies; departmental B.S., B.A., M.A. and Ph.D. with Certificate in Latin American Studies
- Approximate number of faculty teaching area and language courses: 57
- Approximate number of courses available—area: 75; language: 40
- Average number of students per year specializing in area: 125
- Countries covered and areas of emphasis: Latin America in general with special emphasis on the Caribbean, the Amazon region, Brazil and Andean South America
- Languages offered: Spanish, Portuguese and Aymara
- Maintains separate collection of Latin American materials with 160,000 volumes, including extensive map collection and a Latin American Serials Documents Project listing holdings of government documents for individual Latin American countries and with special strengths in the Caribbean (West Indies) and Brazil; the Latin American Cartographic Research Laboratory provides map compilation and design services
- Offers overseas summer language study programs in Bogota, Colombia, and Rio de Janeiro, Brazil
- Collaborates in the sponsorship of research and seminar programs with Caribbean universities through membership in the Association of Caribbean Universities and Research Institutes

- Conducts in-service and preservice seminars, workshops and institutes for elementary, secondary and community college teachers
- Publishes a center newsletter, a quarterly newsletter for teachers (*Diálogo*), curriculum monographs and prepares audiovisual materials

16.029
Latin American Studies
University of Miami
Coral Gables, FL 33124
(305) 284-6764 or 4303

Contact(s):
Joaquin Roy, Director

Undergraduate and graduate area studies program established in 1950
- Majors/degrees/certificates offered: B.A. or B.B.A. in Hispanic American Studies; M.A. and Ph.D. in Inter-American Studies offered through the Graduate School of International Studies (see 6.134)
- Approximate number of faculty teaching area and language courses: 25
- Approximate number of courses available—area: 30; language: 60
- Average number of students per year specializing in area: 2–10
- Countries covered and areas of emphasis: all countries in Hispanic America and Brazil; includes focus on Spain and Portugal at undergraduate level and on inter-American relations at graduate level
- Languages offered: Spanish and Portuguese
- Special Latin American collection in University library (particularly strong on Colombia, Cuba and the Caribbean); resources of Miami Latin-American community
- Summer study available at programs in Central America and Spain
- Editorial headquarters for *Journal of Inter-American Studies and World Affairs*

(administered by the Graduate School of International Studies)

16.030
Latin American Studies
Emory University
404-C, Humanities Bldg.
Atlanta, GA 30322
(404) 329-7952

Contact(s):
Ricardo Gutierrez, Director

Undergraduate area studies program
• Majors/degrees/certificates offered: B.A. in Latin American studies
• Approximate number of courses available—area: 10; language: 9
• Countries covered and areas of emphasis: all Latin American and Caribbean countries
• Language offered: Spanish

16.031
Latin American Studies
De Paul University
25 East Jackson St.
Chicago, IL 60604
(312) 321-8000

Contact(s):
Sandra McGee and Rosa Spaulding, Co-Directors

Undergraduate area studies program established in 1976
• Majors/degrees/certificates offered: B.A. and minor in Latin American Studies
• Approximate number of faculty teaching area and language courses: 9
• Approximate number of courses available—area: 56; language: 92 (quarter hours)
• Average number of students per year specializing in area: 8

• Countries covered and areas of emphasis: all countries of Latin America
• Language offered: Spanish
• Access to Chicago's Newberry Library with strong Latin American Collection

16.032
Center for Latino and Latin American Affairs
Northern Illinois University
De Kalb, IL 60115
(815) 753-1986

Contact(s):
Felix M. Padilla, Director

• Coordinates Latino and Latin American Studies, including minor programs; provides student counseling for Latino students, supports research and serves as an information clearinghouse

16.033
Center for Latin American Studies
University of Chicago
1126 East 59th St.
Chicago, IL 60637
(312) 753-2919

Contact(s):
Rene de Costa, Director

Graduate area studies program established in 1977; undergraduate program established in 1984
• Majors/degrees/certificates offered: B.A. and M.A. in Latin American and Caribbean Studies
• Approximate number of faculty teaching area & language courses: 30
• Approximate number of courses available—area: 80; language: 21
• Average number of students per year specializing in area: four-six (M.A.)

• Countries covered and areas of emphasis: all countries of Latin America

• Languages offered: Spanish and Portuguese

• Part of Joint National Resource Center with the University of Illinois; Joint Center publishes a *Directory of Latin Americanists* (in Illinois)

• Conducts community outreach program, including a speakers bureau

• Publishes *Newsletter of Chicago Colloquium on Latin America*

sources available through the Joint Center for Latin American Language and Area Studies (with the University of Chicago) and through the Committee on Institutional Cooperation (see 8.008)

• Summer study program available in Mexico City through the Committee on Institutional Cooperation and in other Latin American countries through the University of Illinois Study Abroad Office

• Special student exchange programs in Brazil and Colombia available

16.034
Center for Latin American and Caribbean Studies
University of Illinois at Urbana-Champaign
1208 West California St., Room 250
Urbana, IL 61801
(217) 333-3182

Contact(s):
Paul Drake, Director

Graduate and undergraduate area studies program established in 1941

• Majors/degrees/certificates offered: B.A. with Latin American and Caribbean field of concentration; M.A. and Ph.D. with Latin American and Caribbean minor

• Approximate number of faculty teaching area and language courses: 46

• Approximate number of courses available—area: 75; language: 50

• Average number of students per year specializing in area: 200

• Countries covered and areas of emphasis: all Latin American and Caribbean countries

• Languages offered: Spanish, Portuguese and Quechua

• University library holds 300,000 volumes on Latin America and the Caribbean, including an extensive map collection; Krannert Art Museum on campus contains a collection of pre-Columbian art; additional re-

16.035
Center for Latin American and Caribbean Studies
Indiana University at Bloomington
520 North Fess St.
Bloomington, IN 47405
(812) 335-9097

Contact(s):
Jack W. Hopkins, Director

Graduate and undergraduate area studies program established in 1963

• Majors/degrees/certificates offered: Ph.D. Area Certificate and outside minor; M.A. degree in Latin American Studies; Undergraduate Certificate or minor in Latin American Studies

• Approximate number of faculty teaching area and language courses: 78

• Approximate number of courses available—area: 39; language: 50 (full range of undergraduate courses also available)

• Average number of students per year specializing in area: 15 M.A. students; 50 Ph.D. area/minor students; 12 undergraduate students

• Countries covered and areas of emphasis: all Central and South American countries with strength in Mexico, Brazil and Venezuela; special resources for the study of (1) vice-royalties of Mexico and Peru and (2) traditional music

• Languages offered: Portuguese, Spanish, Haitian-Creole, Nahuatl, Quechua and Zapotec

• Library contains extensive research holdings including Bernardo Mendel Collection of colonial and early 19th-century Latin American documents; other resources in Archives of Traditional Music, Latin American Music Center, the University Museum and the Data Archive on Latin American Countries in the Political Science Department

• Sponsors research and conducts seminars for teachers and, in Caracas, Venezuela, an Executive Training Program for business executives

• Junior Year Abroad in Lima, Peru; summer study in Mexico City; joint study program in Brazil with Stanford; and access to CIC (see 8.008) program in Mexico

• Publishes Working Paper series including a number of research and resource guides

• A number of special fellowships available, especially to minority group members

16.036
Latin American Area Studies Program
Helen Kellogg Institute for International
   Studies
University of Notre Dame
Notre Dame, IN 46556
(219) 283-7505

Contact(s):
Claude Pomerleau, Director

Undergraduate area studies program
• Majors/degrees/certificates   offered: Certificate with departmental B.A.
• Approximate number of faculty teaching area and language courses: 17
• Approximate number of courses available—area: 69; language: 44
• Countries covered and areas of emphasis: all countries of Latin America; partic-

ular emphasis on history and the social sciences
• Language offered: Spanish
• Advises on study abroad and sponsors program in Mexico
• Kellogg Institute promotes research on Latin American development issues

16.037
Latin American Studies
Grinnell College
Grinnell, IA 50112
(515) 236-7545

Contact(s):
Theda Herz, Chair

Undergraduate area studies program
• Majors/degrees/certificates   offered: B.A. in Latin American Studies
• Approximate number of courses available—area: 15; language: 15
• Countries covered and areas of emphasis: all countries of Latin America
• Language offered: Spanish
• Study abroad opportunities available in Colombia and Costa Rica

16.038
Latin American Studies Program
University of Iowa
405 JB
Iowa City, IA 52242
(319) 353-7440

Contact(s):
Charles Hale, Coordinator

Undergraduate area studies program established in 1978
• Majors/degrees/certificates   offered: Certificate and minor in Latin American Studies
• Approximate number of faculty teaching area and language courses: 12

• Approximate number of courses available—area and language: 35
• Average number of students per year specializing in area: 15
• Countries covered and areas of emphasis: all of Latin America and the Caribbean; strength or special interest in Mexico, Guatemala, Argentina, Belize, Peru, Puerto Rico, Brazil and the English Caribbean islands
• Languages offered: Spanish and Portuguese

16.039
Latin American Studies Program
University of Northern Iowa
Department of History
Cedar Falls, IA 50614
(319) 273-2097

Contact(s):
Robert D. Talbott, Director

Graduate and undergraduate area studies program
• Majors/degrees/certificates offered: B.A. in Latin American Studies and graduate and undergraduate Certificates in Latin American Studies
• Approximate number of courses available—area: 9; language: 11
• Countries covered and areas of emphasis: all countries of Latin America
• Languages offered: Spanish and Portuguese
• Sponsors summer Colombia Interchange Program and graduate and undergraduate exchange programs in Spain

16.040
Center of Latin American Studies
University of Kansas
Lawrence, KS 66045
(913) 864-4213

Contact(s):
Charles L. Stansifer, Director

Graduate and undergraduate area studies program established in 1962
• Majors/degrees/certificates offered: B.A. and M.A. in Latin American Studies; Ph.D. with Certificate in Latin American Studies
• Approximate number of courses available—area: 30; language: 40
• Average number of students per year specializing in area: 38
• Countries covered and areas of emphasis: Latin America in general with special emphasis on Central America and the Caribbean, Brazil and Paraguay
• Languages offered: Spanish, Portuguese Haitian Creole, and Guarani
• Spencer Research Library has strong collection on Brazil, Central America and the Caribbean
• Offers undergraduate study year abroad in Costa Rica
• Faculty and student exchanges with University of Costa Rica, University of Guadalajara, Mexico, and with Catholic and National Universities in Paraguay; cooperates with Kansas-Paraguay Partnerships, a program of community relations
• Sponsors research, especially in the social sciences, focused on Central America
• Publishes a periodical, *Latin American Theater Review,* and several publications containing studies on Latin America based on Kansas Ph.D. dissertations

16.041
Latin American Studies Program
University of Kentucky
Lexington, KY 40506
(606) 257-7036

Contact(s):
Kenneth Coleman, Director

• Offers B.A. in Latin American Studies oriented toward developmental issues, the social sciences, and Spanish language and literature

16.042
Center for Latin American Studies
Western Kentucky University
202 Cravens Graduate Center
Bowling Green, KY 42101
(502) 745-5333

Contact(s):
Kenneth Cann, Director

Undergraduate area studies center established in 1976
• Offers minor in Latin American Studies, conducts extensive on-campus program, maintains Latin American Resource Center, publishes *Intercambio International*, a newsletter containing program information and articles in English and Spanish on subjects of scholarly interest; conducts workshops for teachers, administers exchanges with Latin American universities and sponsors study tours to Latin America

16.043
Center for Latin American Affairs
Louisiana State University
Baton Rouge, LA 70803-4927
(504) 388-5300

Contact(s):
Rodolfo J. Aguilar, Director

Graduate area studies program established in 1964
• Majors/degrees/certificates offered: M.A. in Latin American Studies; departmental Ph.D. with specialization in Latin America

• Approximate number of faculty teaching area and language courses: 22
• Approximate number of courses available—area and language: 39
• Average number of students per year specializing in area: 5
• Countries covered and areas of emphasis: all countries of Latin America
• Languages offered: Spanish and Portuguese

16.044
Center for Latin American Studies
Tulane University
New Orleans, LA 70118
(504) 865-5164

Contact(s):
Richard E. Greenleaf, Director

Graduate and undergraduate area studies program established in 1962
• Majors/degrees/certificates offered: B.A., M.A. and Ph.D. in Latin American Studies; concentrations also available in most disciplines
• Approximate number of faculty teaching area and language courses: 62
• Approximate number of courses available—area: 100; language: 50
• Average number of students per year specializing in area: 70 graduate; 30 undergraduate
• Countries covered and areas of emphasis: all countries of Latin America; special strengths in Mesoamerica, tropical medicine and ecology; major concentrations are Middle American Society, Latin American Politics and Economy, Inter-American Relations, Brazilian Politics and Culture, Latin American Literature and Culture, American Indian Civilizations, Latin American Colonial Societies, Public Health and Tropical Studies, and Business and Economy

• Languages offered: Yucatec, Maya, Nahuatl, Portuguese and Spanish

• Special Latin American Library contains 150,000 volumes with extensive resources on Mexico, Central America and Brazil (including 12,000 volumes of periodicals); also includes extensive collection of early and contemporary maps, especially for Mexico and Central America and of Mayan rubbings; large newspaper collection from 18th, 19th and early 20th centuries; maintains photographic archives of 10,000 art, archaeological, ethnographic and historical photographs; brochure describing the library and its manuscript and photographic collections available on request

• Sponsors extensive outreach program (see 2.075)

• Secretariat of Gulf South Latin American Programming Association which provides grants for the sponsoring of public conferences, lectures, festivals, etc. on Latin America (not on Hispanics in the U.S.)

• Co-sponsors conferences (average 5–6 per year) on international business and operates field program in Spanish and business in Mexico for business executives

• Modest grant program for scholars from the southern U.S. to use Latin American library

• Off-campus study and research available in Costa Rica, Colombia, Guatemala, Mexico (Mexico City and the Yucatan) and Ecuador

• Maintains scholarly relationships with 17 Brazilian universities and one Mexican University

• Publishes newsletter and curriculum aids, especially for studying Native American languages; other publications available through the Middle American Research Institute (see 16.045)

• Mesoamerican Ecology Institute supports faculty and student research on the ecology of Mexico and Central America

• Financial assistance available through FLAS, Shell Foundation, dissertation grants, Tinker Foundation travel grants and ecology grants

16.045
Middle American Research Institute
Tulane University
New Orleans, LA 70118
(504) 865-5110

Contact(s):
E. Wyllys Andrews V, Director

Scholarly research organization

• Conducts and sponsors research on Mexico and Central America and publishes extensive list of books and monographs in the social sciences; particularly strong in the archaeology of Mayan and other pre-Columbian Indian civilizations and on colonial and modern history and anthropology; has extensive research collections from Middle America and elsewhere; maintains small gallery of archaeological and ethnographic material

16.046
Latin American Studies
Hood College
Frederick, MD 21701
(301) 663-3131

Contact(s):
Juana Amelia Hernández, Chair

Undergraduate area studies program

• Majors/degrees/certificates offered: B.A. in Latin American Studies combined with Spanish

• Countries covered and areas of emphasis: all countries of Latin America with particular interest in Mexico and Cuba

• Language offered: Spanish

• Internships with Latin American-oriented organizations are available in the Washington/Virginia area; junior year is spent studying in a Spanish-American country

16.047
Latin American Studies
Brandeis University
Waltham, MA 02254
(617) 647-2878

Contact(s):
Luis Ellicott Yglesias, Chair
Committee on Latin American Studies

Undergraduate area studies program established in 1963
- Majors/degrees/certificates offered: B.A. with major or minor in Latin American Studies
- Approximate number of faculty teaching area and language courses: 14
- Approximate number of courses available—area: 15; language: 8
- Average number of students per year specializing in area: 5
- Countries covered and areas of emphasis: Latin America in general
- Language offered: Spanish
- Summer, semester, or academic year study at Latin American universities encouraged

16.048
Latin American Studies
Smith College
Northampton, MA 01063
(413) 584-2700

Contact(s):
Alice R. Clemente, Chair

Undergraduate area studies program established ca. 1960
- Majors/degrees/certificates offered: B.A. in Latin American Studies
- Approximate number of faculty teaching area and language courses: 15
- Approximate number of courses available—area: 10; language: 38

- Average number of students per year specializing in area: 10
- Countries covered and areas of emphasis: all Latin American and Caribbean countries with emphasis on literature and social sciences and strength in Brazilian Studies
- Languages offered: Portuguese and Spanish
- Overseas study opportunities available in Brazil, Mexico, Peru and Spain

16.049
Latin American Studies Program
University of Massachusetts at Amherst
Machmer Hall
Amherst, MA 01003
(413) 545-2652

Contact(s):
Donald A. Proulx, Chair

Undergraduate area studies program
- Majors/degrees/certificates offered: B.A. with disciplinary major and a Certificate in Latin American Studies; BDIC (B.A. with Individual Concentration) in Latin American studies; M.A., E.Ed. and Ph.D. with concentration in Latin American Studies
- Approximate number of faculty teaching area and language courses: 27
- Approximate number of courses available—area: 27; language: 30
- Average number of students per year specializing in area: 30
- Countries covered and areas of emphasis: all of Latin America, including the Spanish-speaking Caribbean islands
- Languages offered: Spanish and Portuguese
- Library contains large Latin American holdings with extensive acquisitions program in Latin America; includes strong collections related to Argentina, Brazil, Colombia, the Dominican Republic, Mexico and Peru and an easily accessible Browsing Collection on

Latin America; Five College Cooperative Program (see 4.251) provides access to additional coursework, library facilities, and faculty and co-curricular resources
• Internships and study abroad opportunities in Latin America available through the University's International Programs Office
• Publishes Occasional Papers series on Latin American subjects

• Approximate number of faculty teaching area and language courses: 5
• Approximate number of courses available—area: 16; language: 10
• Countries covered and areas of emphasis: all countries of Latin America with emphasis on Mexico
• Languages offered: Spanish and Portuguese
• Periodically sponsors summer study programs in Mexico

16.050
Latin American Studies Center
Michigan State University
East Lansing, MI 48824
(517) 353-1690

Contact(s):
John M. Hunter, Director

• Coordinates and supports Latin American Studies interests on the MSU campus; offers specialization certification for undergraduates, conducts exchange relationship with a Mexican academic institution, promotes research and conducts outreach program for local teachers and community organizations

16.051
Latin American Studies Program
Oakland University
Rochester, MI 48063
(313) 377-2154

Contact(s):
Carlo Coppola, Chair
Kathryn McArdle-Pigott, Coodinator

Undergraduate area studies program
• Majors/degrees/certificates offered: B.A. and minor in Latin American Studies

16.052
Latin American Studies Program
Western Michigan University
2090 Friedmann
Kalamazoo, MI 49008
(616) 383-1735

Contact(s):
David Chaplin, Chair

Undergraduate area studies program established in 1968
• Majors/degrees/certificates offered: coordinate B.A. (combined with departmental major) in Latin American Studies
• Approximate number of faculty teaching area and language courses: 6
• Approximate number of courses available—area: 9; language: 8
• Average number of students per year specializing in area: 2
• Countries covered and areas of emphasis: all countries of Latin America, with emphasis on the social sciences
• Language offered: Spanish
• A variety of overseas study programs are available, including a field seminar in Mexico

16.053
Latin American Studies Program
University of Minnesota
Institute of International Studies
1246 Social Science Bldg.
267 19th Ave. South
Minneapolis, MN 55455
(612) 373-2691

Contact(s):
Hernan Vidal, Chair

Undergraduate area studies program established in 1946
- Majors/degrees/certificates offered: B.A. in Latin American Studies
- Approximate number of faculty teaching area and language courses: 57
- Approximate number of courses available—area: 46; language: 98
- Average number of students per year specializing in area: 12–25
- Countries covered and areas of emphasis: all countries of Latin America and the Caribbean
- Languages offered: Spanish and Portuguese
- Overseas study opportunities available in Mexico, Spain, Costa Rica and Uruguay

16.054
Latin American Studies Program
Saint Louis University
221 North Grand Blvd.
St. Louis, MO 63103
(314) 535-3300

Contact(s):
Henry A. Christopher, Chair

Undergraduate area studies program
- Majors/degrees/certificates offered: B.A. or Certificate in Latin American Studies
- Approximate number of faculty teaching area and language courses: 9

- Approximate number of courses available—area: 17; language: 14
- Average number of students per year specializing in area: 32
- Countries covered and areas of emphasis: all of Latin America; particular interest in development issues
- Languages offered: Spanish and Portuguese

16.055
Latin American Studies
University of Missouri at Columbia
Department of Romance Languages
27 Arts and Sciences Bldg.
Columbia, MO 65211
(314) 882-4874

Contact(s):
Daniel C. Scroggins, Director

Undergraduate area studies program established ca. 1950
- Majors/degrees/certificates offered: B.A. with Latin American Studies concentration
- Approximate number of faculty teaching area and language courses: 14
- Approximate number of courses available—area: 18; language: 12
- Average number of students per year specializing in area: 6
- Countries covered and areas of emphasis: all of Latin America; emphasis on history, the Spanish language and Spanish American literature
- Languages offered: Spanish and Portuguese
- Summer study abroad available in Mexico

16.056
Latin American Studies
Washington University
Box 1077
St. Louis, MO 63130
(314) 889-5145

Contact(s):
John Garganigo, Chair

Graduate and undergraduate area studies program established in 1963
- Majors/degrees/certificates offered: B.A. in Latin American Studies; departmental M.A. and Ph.D. with Latin American Certificate
- Approximate number of faculty teaching area and language courses: 12
- Approximate number of courses available—area: 12; language: 6
- Countries covered and areas of emphasis: all countries of Latin America; particular emphasis on development and modernization
- Languages offered: Portuguese and Spanish
- Overseas study opportunities available in Colombia and Spain

16.057
Latin American Studies Program
University of Nebraska at Lincoln
Institute for International Studies
1034 Oldfather Hall
Lincoln, NE 68588
(402) 472-3076

Contact(s):
Roberto Esquenazi-Mayo, Director, Institute for International Studies
William Sherman, Coordinator, Latin American Studies

Undergraduate area studies program established in 1961

- Majors/degrees/certificates offered: B.A. and minor in Latin American Studies
- Approximate number of courses available—area: 32; language: 20
- Countries covered and areas of emphasis: all countries of Latin America with particular strength in history and literature; special interest in Ecuador, Mexico and Venezuela
- Languages offered: Spanish and Portuguese
- Library contains ample collection of Latin American materials
- Study abroad programs available in Costa Rica and Mexico
- Courses open to students from University of Nebraska at Omaha (see 16.058) who wish to major in Latin American Studies

16.058
Latin American Studies Program
University of Nebraska at Omaha
Office of International Studies and Programs
Omaha, NE 68182
(402) 554-2376

Contact(s):
Norman Luna, Coordinator

Undergraduate area studies program
- Majors/degrees/certificates offered: B.A. major and minor in International Studies with a specialization Latin American Studies majors may take additional courses at University of Nebraska at Lincoln; (see 16.057)
- Approximate number of courses available—area: 32; language: 20
- Countries covered and areas of emphasis: all countries of Latin America, with particular strength in history and literature
- Languages offered: Spanish and Portuguese
- Library contains ample collection of Latin American materials
- Study abroad programs available in Costa Rica and Mexico

16.059
Program in Latin American Studies
Princeton University
240 East Pyne
Princeton, NJ 08544
(609) 452-4756

Contact(s):
Paul E. Sigmund, Director (% Department
of Politics)

Undergraduate area studies program established in 1963
• Majors/degrees/certificates offered: undergraduate Certificate in Latin American Studies
• Approximate number of faculty teaching area and language courses: 10
• Approximate number of courses available—area: 25; language: 13
• Average number of students per year specializing in area: 20
• Countries covered and areas of emphasis: all of Latin America
• Languages offered: Spanish, Portuguese and French

16.060
Latin American Institute
Rutgers University
State University of New Jersey
180 College Ave.
New Brunswick, NJ 08903
(201) 932-7637

Contact(s):
Mark Wasserman, Director

Graduate and undergraduate area studies program established in 1979
• Majors/degrees/certificates offered: B.A. in Latin American Studies or Puerto Rican Studies with a Certificate of emphasis in Ethno-Latin American or Caribbean Studies; departmental M.A. and Ph.D. with Certificate in Latin American Studies

• Approximate number of faculty teaching area and language courses: 50
• Approximate number of courses available—area: 53; language: 18
• Average number of students per year specializing in area: 10
• Countries covered and areas of emphasis: all countries of South and Central America and the Caribbean, with emphasis on developments in the 20th century; strength in language, literature and the social sciences and in Argentine, Mexican, Chilean and Puerto Rican Studies
• Languages offered: Dutch, French, Portuguese (Brazilian) and Spanish
• Library contains extensive collection of Latin American materials with particular strength in 20th-century Argentina, Brazil and Mexico, including a large collection of 20th-century Mexican literary journals
• Junior year abroad available in Mexico City

16.061
Center for Latin American Studies
New Mexico State University
Box 3JBR
Las Cruces, NM 88003
(505) 646-3524

Contact(s):
Louis R. Sadler, Director

Graduate and undergraduate area studies program established in 1979
• Majors/degrees/certificates offered: B.A., M.A. and Ph.D. in Spanish Languages and Literature, Government or History with emphasis on Latin American Studies
• Approximate number of faculty teaching area and language courses: 80
• Approximate number of courses available—area: 90; language: 120
• Average number of students per year specializing in area: 27 graduate; 53 undergraduate

• Countries covered and areas of emphasis: all of Latin America, with special strength in Central America (El Salvador, Panama and Honduras) and Mexico (particularly U.S.-Mexican border relationships and the Mexican Revolution)

• Languages offered: Spanish and Portuguese

• Extensive library collections on Latin America including a Mexican Revolution Archive, the Rio Grande Historical Collection (archival materials on southern New Mexico during the territorial and Mexican Revolution periods) and the Charles and Willoughby Nason Latin American Collection (1,600 items)

• Administers the Joint Border Research Institute (responsible for U.S.-Mexican border-related research activities) and participates in the New Mexico Border Commission (advisory agency to the governor of New Mexico on U.S.-Mexico policy)

16.062
Latin American Institute
University of New Mexico
801 Yale NE
Albuquerque, NM 87131
(505) 277-2961

Contact(s):
Gilbert W. Merkx, Director

Graduate and undergraduate area studies program established in 1941

• Majors/degrees/certificates offered: 27 degree or dual-degree programs including B.A. and M.A. in Latin American Studies, Ph.D. in Ibero-American Studies, Latin American specializations at the Ph.D. level in a number of departments; dual-degree programs at the master's level linking Latin American Studies with Management, Law, Nursing, Public Administration, and Community and Regional Planning; and Latin American emphases for the B.B.A. and

M.B.A. in International Management and the M.A. in Educational Administration

• Approximate number of faculty teaching area and language courses: 138

• Approximate number of courses available—area: 76; language: 123

• Average number of students per year specializing in area: 120 graduates and 45 undergraduates

• Countries covered and areas of emphasis: Latin America as a whole with special strength in Mexico, Ecuador, Argentina, Brazil, Cuba, Panama and the Andean and Caribbean regions

• Languages offered: Spanish, Portuguese and Quechua

• Library contains 220,000-volume Latin American collection with additions of approximately 11,000 volumes per year; includes acquisition of current monographs and other literature from Latin America, Portugal and Spain

• Offers summer study program in Mexico and maintains faculty and student exchange arrangements with universities in Mexico, Argentina, Brazil, Costa Rica and Uruguay

• Publishes *Bulletin* about Institute activities and a Research Paper series; edits the *Latin American Research Review* (see 16.155) and the *Hispanic American Historical Review* (see 16.150)

• Sponsors Teacher-Fellow Program to provide graduate training in Latin American studies for public and private school teachers

16.063
Latin American Area Studies Program
City University of New York/Brooklyn
    College
4239 Boylan Hall
Bedford Ave. and Ave. H
Brooklyn, NY 11210
(212) 780-5451

Contact(s):

Ming-shui Hung, Coordinator

Undergraduate area studies program
• Majors/degrees/certificates offered: B.A. in Latin American Area Studies
• Approximate number of courses available—area: 26; language: 8
• Countries covered and areas of emphasis: all countries of Latin America; includes Puerto Rico and the black countries of the Caribbean

16.064

Inter-American Affairs Program

City University of New York/Hunter College
New York, NY 10021
(212) 570-5027

Contact(s):

Kenneth Paul Erickson, Director

Undergraduate area studies program
• Majors/degrees/certificates offered: B.A. major and minor in Inter-American Affairs
• Approximate number of courses available—area: 48; language: 20
• Countries covered and areas of emphasis: all countries of Latin America and the Caribbean, including English- and French-speaking islands; emphasis on economic, social and political issues; strong in anthropology; includes substantial focus on Puerto Rico and Afro-Caribbean countries
• Languages offered: Portuguese and Spanish
• Field study in Latin America or the Caribbean encouraged

16.065

Latin American Area Studies

City University of New York/Queens College
153-33 61st Road (House 33)
Flushing, NY 11367
(212) 520-7334

Contact(s):

George Priestley, Director

Graduate and undergraduate area studies program established in 1966 (undergraduate); 1970 (graduate)
• Majors/degrees/certificates offered: B.A. in Latin American Area Studies; M.A. and Advanced Certificate (for doctoral candidates) in Latin American Area Studies; also offers joint B.A. in social sciences, education and the Romance languages
• Approximate number of faculty teaching area and language courses: 25
• Approximate number of courses available—area: 12; language: 10
• Average number of students per year specializing in area: 10 graduate; 30 undergraduate
• Countries covered and areas of emphasis: all major countries of Latin America and the Caribbean
• Languages offered: Spanish and Portuguese
• Study abroad available in Mexico, Brazil and Colombia
• Publishes a monthly magazine, *Abigarrada* (for the college community)

16.066

Institute of Latin American and Iberian Studies

Columbia University
833 International Affairs Bldg.
420 West 118th St.
New York, NY 10027
(212) 280-4643

Contact(s):

Lambros Comitas, Director

Graduate area studies program established in 1961
• Majors/degrees/certificates offered: B.A. in Regional Studies (through Columbia College); two-year M.I.A., School of Inter-

national and Public Affairs, with Certificate in Latin American Studies; M.A. and Ph.D. with Certificate in Latin American Studies

• Approximate number of faculty teaching area and language courses: 63

• Approximate number of courses available—area: 46; language: 182

• Countries covered and areas of emphasis: Spain, Portugal and all countries of Latin America and the Caribbean with emphasis on the social sciences and on Spanish language and literature

• Languages offered: Spanish and Portuguese

• Maintains visiting scholar program for scholars from the U.S., Latin America and Europe

• Sponsors Summer Field Training Program in Latin America and the Iberian Peninsula focusing on a social science research project

16.067
Latin American Studies Program
Cornell University
Center for International Studies
190 Uris Hall
Ithaca, NY 14853
(607) 256-3345

Contact(s):
Thomas H. Holloway, Director

• Coordinates and supports teaching and research activities in Latin American Studies at Cornell (faculty includes 32 Latin American specialists); publishes research on Latin America, including an Occasional Papers series and a Dissertation Reprint series; independent majors available in the Colleges of Arts and Sciences and Agriculture and Life Sciences along with a graduate minor program; library contains over 200,000 volumes on Latin America with particularly strong holdings for Brazil and the Andean region

16.068
Center for Latin American and Caribbean Studies
New York University
19 University Place, Room 310
New York, NY 10003
(212) 598-3591

Graduate area studies program
• Majors/degrees/certificates offered: M.A. in Latin American and Caribbean Studies

• Approximate number of faculty teaching area and language courses: 22

• Approximate number of courses available—area: 20; language: 12

• Countries covered and areas of emphasis: all countries of Latin America and the Caribbean including Afro-American cultures, with emphasis on contemporary political, social and economic issues and on relations between the U.S. and Latin America

• Promotes research and maintains a visiting scholar program for researchers on U.S./Latin American issues

• Publishes an Occasional Papers series and *Latin American Population History Newsletter*

16.069
Department of Puerto Rican, Latin American and Caribbean Studies
State University of New York at Albany
1400 Washington, Ave.
Albany, NY 12222
(518) 457-8873

Contact(s):
Edna Acosta-Belén, Chair
James W. Wessman, Associate Chair

Undergraduate area studies program established in 1981
• Majors/degrees/certificates offered:

B.A. with major in Puerto Rican or Latin American Studies
- Approximate number of faculty teaching area and language courses: 22
- Approximate number of courses available—area: 20; language: 10
- Average number of students per year specializing in area: 25
- Countries covered and areas of emphasis: all countries of South and Central America and the Caribbean; special interest in Meso-America, the Caribbean and Puerto Rico
- Languages offered: Spanish and Portuguese
- Study abroad available in Cuernavaca, Mexico, and Puerto Rico for undergraduates

16.070
Latin American and Caribbean Area Studies Program
State University of New York at Binghamton
Binghamton, NY 13901
(607) 798-4868

Contact(s):
Adalberto López, Director

Graduate and undergraduate area studies program established in 1971
- Majors/degrees/certificates offered: B.A. in Latin American and Caribbean Area Studies and undergraduate and graduate certificates
- Approximate number of faculty teaching area and language courses: 13
- Approximate number of courses available—area: 20; language: 10
- Average number of students per year specializing in area: 10
- Countries covered and areas of emphasis: most nations of the area, with emphasis on the Spanish-speaking countries
- Languages offered: Spanish and French
- Maintains a modest Latin American

Cultural Center with books, periodicals and other resource materials on Latin America and the Caribbean; there is also a Latin American Student Union on campus for Latin American and other students, faculty and administrators
- Operates study abroad program in Mexico and Peru and makes others in Colombia, Puerto Rico and Peru accessible
- Publishes newsletter

16.071
Latin American Studies
State University of New York at Buffalo
Council on International Studies
107 Townsend Hall
Buffalo, NY 14214
(716) 636-2075

Contact(s):
Margaret B. Reiling, Campus Coordinator

Graduate area studies program
- Majors/degrees/certificates offered: M.A. in Humanities in Latin American Studies
- Approximate number of faculty teaching area and language courses: 28
- Approximate number of courses available—area: 30; language: 14
- Average number of students per year specializing in area: 5
- Countries covered and areas of emphasis: all of Latin America and the Caribbean; special programs in Puerto Rican and Black (including Caribbean countries) Studies
- Languages offered: Spanish, Portuguese and Quechua; other languages available through Critical Language Center
- Maintains set of Human Relations Area Files (see 1.112) and Latin American resources in FAUL (Five Associated University Libraries)

• Publishes newsletter and a Special Studies series on Latin America

16.072
Latin American Studies Program
State University of New York at Plattsburgh
Plattsburgh, NY 12901
(518) 564-2086/2112

Contact(s):
Stuart F. Voss, Coordinator

Undergraduate area studies program
• Majors/degrees/certificates offered: B.A. in Latin American Studies
• Approximate number of faculty teaching area & language courses: 10
• Approximate number of courses available—area: 24; language: 12
• Average number of students per year specializing in area: 16
• Countries covered and areas of emphasis: all countries of Latin America with strength in history and the social sciences
• Languages offered: Spanish and Portuguese
• Study abroad strongly encouraged in SUNY programs in Brazil, Colombia, the Dominican Republic, Mexico and Puerto Rico

16.073
Latin American Studies
Syracuse University
Foreign and Comparative Studies
119 College Place
Syracuse, NY 13210-2392
(315) 423-2552

Contact(s):
John D. Nagel, Director

Graduate and undergraduate area studies program
• Majors/degrees/certificates offered: B.A. in Latin American Studies; M.A. and

Ph.D. with specialization in Latin America through the Religion and most of the Social Sciences departments as well as through a special interdisciplinary program in Public Administration (see 6.157), International Relations (see 4.093) and the Humanities; M.A. in Interdisciplinary Linguistics Program through the Development Planning Program (see 6.157); and a graduate Certificate of Competency from the Foreign and Comparative Studies Program (see 4.093)
• Library has substantial Latin American holdings; maintains collection of publications of the Organization of American States (see 16.127), subscribes to the Latin American Microform Project and holds personal papers of several prominent Latin American scholars
• Publishes a Latin American Series of monographs
• Financial assistance includes two Shell Fellowships for dissertation research in less developed countries

16.074
Institute of Latin American Studies
University of North Carolina at Chapel Hill
315 Hamilton Hall 070A
Chapel Hill, NC 27514
(919) 962-3041

Contact(s):
Enrique A. Balogra, Director

Graduate and undergraduate area studies program established in 1940
• Majors/degrees/certificates offered: B.A. in Latin American Studies; M.A. Certificate in Latin American Studies (degree must be from a department)
• Approximate number of faculty teaching area and language courses: 20
• Approximate number of courses available—area: 36; language: 17
• Average number of students per year specializing in area: 25 undergraduate

Countries covered and areas of emphasis: Central and South America; especially Mexico, Cuba and the Southern cone
• Languages offered: Spanish and Portuguese
• Latin American Bibliographical Center of the Davis Library contains extensive collection of Latin American resources and is especially strong in holdings related to Venezuela, Argentina, Chile, Paraguay, Uruguay and Cuba; also contains the Latin American Public Events Data Bank
• Study abroad available in Spain, Venezuela and other Latin American countries

16.075
Latin American Studies
University of North Carolina at Greensboro
Department of Geography
Greensboro, NC 27412
(919) 379-5489

Contact(s):
Craig Lanier Dozier, Chair

Undergraduate area studies program
• Majors/degrees/certificates offered: B.A. in Latin American Studies
• Approximate number of faculty teaching area and language courses: 13
• Approximate number of courses available—area: 23; language: 5
• Countries covered and areas of emphasis: all of Latin America
• Language offered: Spanish
• Summer study available in Mexico and Colombia

16.076
Latin American Studies
Bowling Green State University
Department of History
202 Williams Hall
Bowling Green, OH 43403
(419) 372-2805

Contact(s):
Jack Thomas, Director

Undergraduate area studies program
• Majors/degrees/certificates offered: B.A. in Latin American Studies; special program for students in social studies education
• Countries covered and areas of emphasis: all countries of Latin America with strength in the social sciences and emphasis on Mexico and Mexican-American relations
• Languages offered: Portuguese and Spanish
• Summer and year-long study abroad programs available in Mexico; student teaching assignments available in Brazil and Colombia

16.077
Latin American Studies Program
Kent State University
119B Bowman Hall
Kent, OH 44242
(216) 672-2444

Contact(s):
Doris Turner, Director

Undergraduate area studies program established in 1969
• Majors/degrees/certificates offered: B.A. with dual degree in Latin American Studies and a discipline
• Approximate number of faculty teaching area and language courses: seven
• Approximate number of courses available—area: 12; language: eight
• Countries covered and areas of emphasis: all Latin American countries with special interest in Brazil and Mexico
• Languages offered: Spanish and Portuguese

16.078
Latin American Studies Program
Ohio University
Center for International Studies
Athens, OH 45701
(614) 594-5542

Contact(s):
Michael Grow, Director

Graduate and undergraduate area studies program established in 1970
• Majors/degrees/certificates offered: B.A. and M.A. in International Affairs with concentration in Latin American Studies
• Approximate number of faculty teaching area and language courses: 21
• Approximate number of courses available—area: 25; language: 10
• Average number of students per year specializing in area: 8 graduate; 6 undergraduate
• Countries covered and areas of emphasis: all Latin American countries, with particular interest in Nicaragua, Peru, Belize and Mexico
• Languages offered: Spanish and, occasionally, Portuguese
• Good collection of library materials
• Provides outreach program to assist elementary and secondary school teachers
• Provides field work in Belize and language study opportunities in Mexico for undergraduates
• Publishes a series of papers in Latin American Studies

16.079
Latin American Studies Program
University of Toledo
Toledo, OH 43606
(419) 537-2696

Undergraduate area studies program
• Majors/degrees/certificates offered: B.A. in Latin American Studies

• Countries covered and areas of emphasis: all countries of Latin America with emphasis on history and the social sciences
• Language offered: Spanish

16.080
Latin American Studies Program
University of Oklahoma at Norman
Department of Political Science
455 West Lindsey St., Room 205
Norman, OK 73019
(405) 325-2061

Contact(s):
Richard D. Baker, Professor of Political Science

Graduate and undergraduate area studies program
• Majors/degrees/certificates offered: B.A. and M.A. in Latin American Studies
• Countries covered and areas of emphasis: all countries of Latin America and the Caribbean area
• Language offered: Spanish

16.081
Latin American Studies
Allegheny College
Meadville, PA 16335
(814) 724-4345

Contact(s):
Giles Wayland-Smith, Director

Offers B.A. with specialization in Latin American Studies

16.082
Latin American Studies
Pennsylvania State University
604 Liberal Arts Tower
University Park, PA 16802
(814) 865-1367

Contact(s):
Charles D. Ameringer, Director

Undergraduate area studies program established in 1956
- Majors/degrees/certificates offered: B.A. major or minor in Latin American Studies
- Approximate number of courses available—area: 26; language: 12
- Countries covered and areas of emphasis: all countries of Latin America
- Languages offered: Spanish and Portuguese

16.083
Latin American Studies Program
St. Joseph's University
Philadelphia, PA 19131
(215) 879-7563

Contact(s):
Charles Shreiner, Director

Undergraduate area studies program established in 1960
- Majors/degrees/certificates offered: B.A. in major with Certificate in Latin American Studies
- Approximate number of faculty teaching area and language courses: 13
- Approximate number of courses available—area: 9; language: 14
- Average number of students per year specializing in area: 40
- Countries covered and areas of emphasis: all of Latin America
- Languages offered: Spanish and, occasionally, Portuguese
- Semester or year abroad offered in Mexico City

16.084
Inter American Studies Center
Temple University
Philadelphia, PA 19122
(215) 787-7527

Contact(s):
Clement G. Motten, Director

Graduate and undergraduate area studies program established in 1978
- Majors/degrees/certificates offered: B.A. and M.A. with specialization in Inter-American Studies
- Approximate number of faculty teaching area and language courses: 7
- Approximate number of courses available—area: 5; language: 10
- Average number of students per year specializing in area: 10
- Countries covered and areas of emphasis: all countries of Latin America with particular interest in Brazil and Colombia
- Languages offered: Portuguese and Spanish, including semester-long Spanish language/Latin American Studies immersion program for undergraduates

16.085
Center for Latin American Studies
University of Pittsburgh
4E04 Forbes Quadrangle
Pittsburgh, PA 15260
(412) 624-5563

Contact(s):
Carmelo Mesa-Lago, Director

Graduate and undergraduate area studies program established in 1964
- Majors/degrees/certificates offered: graduate and undergraduate Certificate in Latin American Studies and undergraduate related concentration in Latin American Studies
- Approximate number of faculty teaching area and language courses: 50
- Approximate number of courses available—area: 166; language: 66

- Countries covered and areas of emphasis: all countries generally identified as composing Latin America with extensive resources on Bolivia, Cuba, Ecuador, Peru, Mexico, Guatemala, Brazil and Venezuela; special interest in social security in Latin America
- Languages offered: Spanish and Portuguese at all levels; Quechua, Aymara, Yucatec Maya and Maya Quiche are taught by the Language Acquisition Institute utilizing tapes and tutor/informants for the language offered
- Library holds 172,000 books and 4,200 periodicals on Latin America, with very large Bolivian and Cuban collections; audiovisual center has wide range of documentaries and feature films on Latin America
- Has scholarly exchange agreements with 20 institutions in 10 Latin American countries
- Offers summer research fellowships to external faculty to provide access to university library resources
- Conducts seven-week research seminar in Latin America for undergraduates; awards summer research grants to University of Pittsburgh faculty for research in Latin America
- Publishes the journal *Cuban Studies* (see 18.116); *CLASicos*, a general newsletter; the Latin American Monograph and Document Series which includes *A Guide to Cuban Cinema; Cuba in Africa; Latin American Music Materials Available at the University of Pittsburgh and the Carnegie Library of Pittsburgh* (limited supply available free); and the Latin American Reprint Series; also contributes to the University's Latin American series of books published by the University of Pittsburgh Press (Pitt Latin American series)
- Average number of students per year specializing in area: 80 graduate; 50 undergraduate

16.086
Latin American Studies Program
Brown University
Box 1906
Providence, RI 02912
(401) 863-2569

Contact(s):
José Amor y Vázquez, Director

Undergraduate area studies program
- Majors/degrees/certificates offered: B.A. in Latin American Studies
- Approximate number of courses available—area: 29; language: 12
- Countries covered and areas of emphasis: all countries of Latin America
- Languages offered: Portuguese and Spanish
- Study abroad in junior year encouraged

16.087
Program in Latin American Studies
Providence College
Providence, RI 02918
(401) 865-2629

Contact(s):
Robert H. Trudeau, Director

Undergraduate area studies program established in 1972
- Majors/degrees/certificates offered: B.A. in Latin American Studies
- Approximate number of faculty teaching area and language courses: 9
- Approximate number of courses available—area: 26; language: 10
- Average number of students per year specializing in area: 5
- Countries covered and areas of emphasis: all countries of Latin America
- Languages offered: Spanish and Portuguese
- Study abroad encouraged

16.088
Latin American Studies
Rhode Island College
600 Mount Pleasant Ave.
Providence, RI 02908
(401) 274-4900

Contact(s):
Eileen Maynard, Director

Undergraduate area studies program established in 1974
• Majors/degrees/certificates offered: B.A. in Latin American Studies
• Approximate number of faculty teaching area and language courses: 9
• Approximate number of courses available—area: 14; language: 9
• Average number of students per year specializing in area: 3–7
• Countries covered and areas of emphasis: all countries of Latin America and the Caribbean with emphasis on the social sciences and the process of cultural change
• Languages offered: Spanish and Portuguese

16.089
Latin American Studies
University of Rhode Island
Department of Languages
Independence Hall
Kingston, RI 02881
(401) 792-5911

Contact(s):
Thomas Morin, Chair, Latin American Studies Committee

Undergraduate area studies program
• Majors/degrees/certificates offered: B.A. in Latin American Studies
• Approximate number of courses available—area: 14; language: 16
• Countries covered and areas of emphasis: all Latin American countries

• Languages offered: Portuguese and Spanish

16.090
Latin American Studies
University of South Carolina at Columbia
Columbia, SC 29208
(803) 777-2575

Contact(s):
Nestor A. Morena, Chair

Undergraduate area studies program
• Majors/degrees/certificates offered: B.A. in Latin American Studies
• Countries covered and areas of emphasis: all of Latin America with special interest in Mexico and Colombia
• Language offered: Spanish

16.091
Latin American Area Studies Program
South Dakota State University
Brookings, SD 57007-0494
(605) 688-5101

Contact(s):
Merritt W. Bates, Director

Undergraduate area studies program established in 1972
• Majors/degrees/certificates offered: B.A. with a coordinated program in Latin American Studies and a minor in Spanish
• Approximate number of courses available—area: 5; language: 7
• Countries covered and areas of emphasis: Spanish countries of Latin America
• Language offered: Spanish

16.092
Latin American Studies
University of Tennessee
Knoxville, TN 37916
(615) 974-2311

Contact(s):
Michael Handelsman, Chair

Undergraduate area studies program established in 1970
- Majors/degrees/certificates offered: B.A. in Latin American Studies
- Approximate number of faculty teaching area and language courses: 20
- Approximate number of courses available—area: 22; language: 15
- Average number of students per year specializing in area: 25
- Countries covered and areas of emphasis: all countries of Latin America with particular interest in Mexico
- Languages offered: Spanish and Portuguese
- Study abroad available

16.093
Center for Latin American and Iberian Studies
Vanderbilt University
Nashville, TN 37235
(615) 322-2561

Contact(s):
Enrique Pupo-Walker, Director

Graduate and undergraduate area studies program
- Majors/degrees/certificates offered: departmental B.A. with concentration in Latin American Studies; M.A. in Latin American Studies; departmental Ph.D. with Certificate or minor in Latin American Studies
- Approximate number of faculty teaching area and language courses: 20
- Countries covered and areas of em-

phasis: all Latin American countries; particular interest in Brazil, Colombia, Peru, Mexico and Venezuela
- Languages offered: Spanish, Portuguese and Nahuatl

16.094
Latin American Studies
Baylor University
Waco, TX 76798
(817) 755-3711, Ext. 6009

Contact(s):
Joseph F. Velez, Director

Graduate and undergraduate area studies program established in 1968
- Majors/degrees/certificates offered: B.A. major and M.A. and Ph.D. minor in Latin American Studies
- Approximate number of faculty teaching area and language courses: 14
- Approximate number of courses available—area: 15; language: 14
- Average number of students per year specializing in area: 20
- Countries covered and areas of emphasis: all Latin American countries
- Languages offered: Spanish and Portuguese

16.095
Latin American Studies
St. Mary's University
1 Camino Santa Maria
San Antonio, TX 78284
(512) 436-3608

Contact(s):
Josephine Schulte, Coordinator

Undergraduate area studies program established in 1972

• Majors/degrees/certificates offered: B.A. with specialization in Latin American Studies

• Approximate number of faculty teaching area and language courses: 7

• Approximate number of courses available—area: 17; language: 6

• Average number of students per year specializing in area: 3

• Countries covered and areas of emphasis: all of Latin America; particular interest in Mexico and the Spanish borderlands

• Language offered: Spanish

• Overseas study encouraged

16.096
Ibero American Studies
Southern Methodist University
Dallas, TX 75275
(214) 692-3143

Contact(s):
Conchita H. Winn, Director

Graduate and undergraduate area studies program

• Majors/degrees/certificates offered: B.A. and M.A. in Ibero-American Civilization

• Approximate number of faculty teaching area and language courses: 15

• Approximate number of courses available—area: 25; language: 15

• Average number of students per year specializing in area: 24

• Countries covered and areas of emphasis: all countries of Latin America, Spain and Portugal; strong in Mexican Studies

• Language offered: Spanish

• Extensive collection of library materials including a 90,000-volume collection on Mexico and the Andean countries, the Bridwell Collection relating to church and pastoral activities and a collection of 5,000 slides of Ibero-American countries

16.097
Institute of Latin American Studies
University of Texas at Austin
Sid Richardson Hall—Unit I
Austin, TX 78712
(512) 471-5551

Contact(s):
William Glade, Director

Graduate and undergraduate area studies program established in 1915

• Majors/degrees/certificates offered: B.A., M.A. and Ph.D. in Latin American Studies; special concentrations available in Mexican, Brazilian, and public sector studies, joint Master's degrees in International Business, Community and Regional Planning, Public Health, Communications, and Public Affairs

• Approximate number of faculty teaching area and language courses: 69

• Approximate number of courses available—area: 200; language: 48

• Average number of students per year specializing in area: 40 undergraduate; 120 graduate

• Countries covered and areas of emphasis: Latin America in general, especially Mexico, Peru and Brazil

• Languages offered: Spanish and Portuguese

• Library contains Benson Latin American Collection of 400,000 books plus extensive periodical, manuscript, map, photograph and microfilm holdings

• Study abroad in Brazil, Peru and Mexico

• Special study and research fellowships available to Mexican students and faculty

• Publishes extensive list of materials principally in the areas of history, politics, and social and economic development; includes two series: *Latin American Monographs*, available from the University of Texas Press (see 16.172) and *Latin American Studies*, available from Greenwood Press (51 Riverside Ave., Westport, CT 06880) which contain approximately 70 studies on historical and contemporary subjects, a 12-volume *Guide and Bibliographies* series, which includes a variety of miscellaneous studies, lectures and some materials in English and Spanish (available in part from the Institute and in part from the University of Texas Press), and an off-print series of approximately 100 articles (available from the Institute); also publishes and makes available from the Institute offices a series of curriculum units for undergraduate college courses, including two teaching guides, *Latin American Culture Studies: Information and Materials for Teaching About Latin America* (see 2.177) and *Key Ideas and Concepts in Teaching About Latin America* (see 2.175), and *A Latin American Filmography* (130 pages; $5)

16.098
Center for Inter-American and Border Studies
University of Texas at El Paso
Miners Hall 209
El Paso, TX 79968
(915) 747-5196

Contact(s):
Oscar J. Martinez, Acting Director

Undergraduate area studies program established in 1946
- Majors/degrees/certificates offered: B.A. in Latin American Studies; also offers business, economics, humanities, behavioral science and Spanish/linguistics options
- Approximate number of faculty teaching area and language courses: 30
- Approximate number of courses available—area: 18; language: 8
- Average number of students per year specializing in area: 20

- Countries covered and areas of emphasis: all major countries of Central and South America and the Caribbean
- Languages offered: Spanish and Portuguese
- General collection of Latin American materials with special Mexican and Southwest border and Chicano collections
- Oral History Institute focuses on Latin American/Mexican subjects
- Publishes newsletter, books and monographs

16.099
Latin American Studies
Brigham Young University
130 FOB
Provo, UT 84602
(801) 378-3377

Contact(s):
Berkley A. Spencer, Coordinator

Graduate and undergraduate area studies program
- Majors/degrees/certificates offered: B.A. and M.A. in Latin American Studies or joint M.A. with a department (undergraduates required to co-emphasize a practical or career-oriented study field
- Approximate number of courses available—area: 54; language: 20
- Average number of students per year specializing in area: 30 undergraduate; five graduate
- Countries covered and areas of emphasis: all countries of Latin America
- Languages offered: Portuguese, Spanish and, by tutorial on demand, Aymara, Cakchiquel, Guarani, Kekchi, Mam Quiche and Quechua
- Extensive study abroad opportunities available and participation is strongly encouraged

16.100
Latin American Studies Program
University of Vermont
Center for Area and International Studies
479 Main St.
Burlington, VT 05405
(802) 656-4062

Contact(s):
Daniel W. Gade, Director

Undergraduate area studies program
• Majors/degrees/certificates offered:
B.A. in Latin American Studies
• Approximate number of courses available—area: 7; language: 8
• Average number of students per year specializing in area: 5
• Countries covered and areas of emphasis: all of Latin America
• Language offered: Spanish
• Students encouraged to participate in semester and academic year programs in Latin America available through other institutions and agencies

16.101
Latin American Studies
Randolph Macon Woman's College
Lynchburg, VA 24503
(804) 846-7392

Contact(s):
Ernest A. Duff and Charlotte Stern, Chairs

Undergraduate area studies program
• Majors/degrees/certificates offered:
B.A. in Latin American Studies
• Approximate number of faculty teaching area and language courses: 6
• Approximate number of courses available—area: 8; language: 7
• Countries covered and areas of emphasis: all countries of Latin America
• Language offered: Spanish

16.102
Latin American Area Studies
Ripon College
300 Seward St., Box 248
Ripon, WI 54971
(414) 748-8135

Contact(s):
Alexander C. Hooker, Jr., Director

Undergraduate area studies program established in 1965
• Majors/degrees/certificates offered:
B.A. in Latin American Studies
• Approximate number of courses available—area: 11; language: 7
• Average number of students per year specializing in area: 2
• Countries covered and areas of emphasis: Latin America in general; special emphasis on Costa Rica and Mexico
• Language offered: Spanish
• Students encouraged to participate in Associated Colleges of the Midwest (see 8.003) Central American Field Studies Program in Costa Rica

16.103
Latin American Studies
University of Wisconsin at Eau Claire
Hibbard Humanities Hall, Room 368
Eau Claire, WI 54701
(715) 836-4215

Contact(s):
Antonio Lazcano, Director

Undergraduate area studies program established in 1964
• Majors/degrees/certificates offered:
B.A. in Latin American Studies
• Approximate number of faculty teaching area and language courses: 8
• Approximate number of courses available—area: 17; language: 7

• Average number of students per year specializing in area: 12

• Countries covered and areas of emphasis: all areas of Latin America with emphasis on the Spanish-speaking countries, particularly Mexico

• Language offered: Spanish

• One summer of study in a Latin American University required; summer and academic year programs offered at the Monterey Institute of Technology and Higher Studies (Monterey, Mexico)

16.104
Ibero-American Studies Program
University of Wisconsin at Madison
1470 Van Hise Hall
2220 Linden Drive
Madison, WI 53706
(608) 262-2811

Contact(s):
Thomas E. Skidmore, Director

Graduate and undergraduate area studies program established in 1930

• Majors/degrees/certificates offered: B.A. and M.A. in Ibero-American Studies (interdisciplinary), B.S. in Ibero-American Studies/Education; Ph.D. minor concentration; also conducts cooperative degree programs with the School of Engineering and cooperative programs with the Schools of Law, Business and Medicine

• Approximate number of faculty teaching area and language courses: 60

• Approximate number of courses available—area: 75; language: 50

• Average number of students per year specializing in area: 100 graduate; 50 undergraduate

• Countries covered and areas of emphasis: Latin America, the Caribbean, Spain and Portugal, with special faculty expertise and library resources in the Andean area, Brazil and Mexico

• Languages offered: Spanish, Portuguese and Quechua

• Major research collection in Memorial Library including extensive library resources on Latin American and Iberian language and literature with special strength in Argentina, Brazil, Chile, Mexico and Peru; fulltime bibliographer; headquarters of Seminar on the Acquisition of Latin American Library Materials; also major research collection in Land Tenure Center Library with materials on agrarian reform, agriculture and rural development and land tenure

• Extensive extracurricular program including colloquia in Spanish

• Offers Tinker Visiting Professorship, Nave Visiting Scholar and Artist Program and a program of grants for use of library collections for scholars from institutions with limited resources

• Study abroad opportunities in Madrid, Spain; Sao Paulo, Brazil; and Mexico City, Mexico; summer program through CIC (see 8.008)

• Numerous relationships and joint research/training programs with overseas institutions including grants for Madison faculty to do research abroad

• Publishes *Luso-Brazilian Review*, biannual scholarly journal on the Portuguese-speaking world (see 18.035) and *Wisconsin Latin Americanist*, a newsletter

16.105
Center for Latin America
University of Wisconsin at Milwaukee
Milwaukee, WI 53201
(414) 963-4401

Contact(s):
Donald R. Shea, Director
Virginia Gibbs, Director, Latin American
  Resource Center

Graduate and undergraduate area studies program

• Majors/degrees/certificates offered: B.A. and B.S. with specialization in Latin American Studies; M.A./M.S. and Ph.D. in departments with concentration in Latin American Studies

• Approximate number of faculty teaching area and language courses: 50

• Approximate number of courses available—area: 100; language: 40

• Countries covered and areas of emphasis: all countries of Latin America; particular interest in development issues and architecture and urban planning

• Languages offered: Spanish and Portuguese

• Maintains Latin American Resource Center which provides services to entire Wisconsin State University system

• Secretariat for North Central Council of Latin Americanists

• Publishes several series of essays, papers and special studies and the newsletter of the North Central Council

• Semester study program in Mexico

16.106
Latin American Studies Program
University of Wisconsin at Stevens Point
Stevens Point, WI 54481
(715) 346-2147

Contact(s):
Robert J. Knowlton, Coordinator

Undergraduate area studies program established in 1966

• Majors/degrees/certificates offered: B.A. and B.S. with major or minor in Latin American Studies

• Approximate number of faculty teaching area and language courses: nine

• Approximate number of courses available—area: 10; language: 11

• Average number of students per year specializing in area: two

• Countries covered and areas of em-

phasis: Latin America in general and modern Mexican history

• Languages offered: Spanish; Portuguese if requested

• Draws on resources of other institutions in Wisconsin University system

16.107
Institute of Caribbean Studies
University of Puerto Rico
Box BM, University Station
Rio Piedras, PR 00931
(809) 764-0000

Contact(s):
Gordon K. Lewis, Director

• Sponsors and conducts comparative research on virtually all aspects of life and culture in the societies of the Caribbean; publishes the quarterly *Caribbean Studies* and *Caribbean Monthly Bulletin*

16.108
Caribbean Research Institute
College of the Virgin Islands
St. Thomas
U.S. Virgin Islands 00801
(809) 774-9200

Contact(s):
Norwell Harrigan, Director

Government-funded institute which conducts research on Caribbean natural resources and on social issues, especially "microstate studies"

• Sponsors conferences and meetings

• Publishes reports, studies and monographs and sponsors the publication of *Microstate Studies*

Information and Service Organizations

16.109
Association of Caribbean Universities and Research Institutes
P.O. Box 11532
Caparra Heights Station
San Juan, Puerto Rico 00922

Contact(s):
Thomas Mathews, Secretary General

Association of institutions designed to promote Caribbean social, educational and technical development through a sharing of resources
• Conducts programs advancing educational development in Caribbean countries; includes Caribbean, African, Asian and other international studies

16.110
Americas Society Center for Inter-American Relations
680 Park Ave.
New York, NY 10021
(212) 249-8950

Contact(s):
Edna Phillips, Director, Public Information

Nonprofit center designed to broaden public awareness and appreciation in the U.S. of the cultural heritage of Latin America, the Caribbean, and Canada and to expand understanding of contemporary issues confronting the western hemisphere
• Sponsors cultural and public affairs programs and projects through study groups, the media, cultural performances, literary translations, concerts and exhibits
• Publishes visual arts catalogues, a public affairs series and the journal *Review* (see 16.157)

16.111
Caribbean Studies Association
University of Puerto Rico
P.O. Box 22875
Rio Piedras, PR 00931

Contact(s):
John Zebrowski, Secretary-Treasurer

Professional association of scholars interested in the Caribbean area
• Sponsors an annual conference and publishes a quarterly newsletter

16.112
Conference of Latin Americanist Geographers
Department of Geography
Ball State University
Muncie, IN 47306
(317) 285-6382

Contact(s):
Tom L. Martinson, Executive Secretary

Professional association
• Provides information on and maintains liaison with other organizations that sponsor and support the professional interests of its members
• Holds meetings and publishes a newsletter, Proceedings, Yearbook and Occasional Papers, including a membership directory and a cartographic guide and bibliography of theses and dissertations based on geographical research in Latin America (1909–78), and videotaped sessions of the organization's 1980 conference

16.113
Council on Hemispheric Affairs
1900 L St. NW, Room 201
Washington, DC 20036
(202) 775-0216

Contact(s):
Larry Birns, Director

Educational research and information organization concerned with inter-American relations and U.S. policy toward the other nations of the western hemisphere
• Researches current issues in inter-American affairs, especially focused on human rights violations, U.S. policy initiatives and legislation and regional matters; provides information, maintains a speakers bureau and issues press releases
• Publishes a newsletter, *Washington Report on the Hemisphere*
• Offers internships to graduate and undergraduate students

16.114
Hispanic Institute
Columbia University
612 West 116th St.
New York, NY 10027
(212) 280-4940

Contact(s):
Susana Redondo de Feldman, Director

• Sponsors cultural activities related to the culture and civilization of the Spanish- and Portuguese-speaking countries; promotes research, maintains an archive of materials on literature and culture and publishes *Revista Hispánica Moderna*

16.115
Inter-American Music Council
17th St. and Constitution Ave. NW
Washington, DC 20006
(202) 789-3158

Contact(s):
Efrain Paesky, Secretary General

Nonprofit cultural organization

• Promotes contact among musicians and facilitates the exchange of information about music in the Americas; assists scholars, educators, musicians and others in pursuing research on music in the Americas and in making contacts with musicians

16.116
International Institute of Iberoamerican Literature
University of Pittsburgh
1312 C.L.
Pittsburgh, PA 15260
(412) 624-3359

Contact(s):
Alfredo A. Roggiano, Director

Association of scholars concerned with Latin American literature
• Sponsors conferences and publishes the quarterly *Revista Iberoamericana* and other learned works and textbooks

16.117
Latin American Music Center
Indiana University
Bloomington, IN 47405
(812) 337-2991

Contact(s):
Juan A. Orrego-Salas, Director

Unit of the Indiana University School of Music designed to promote research on and the performance of Latin American music, both composed and folk, including new scores
• Collects and maintains library of scores, books, records, tapes, ethnomusicological documents and other materials and makes them available to all interested parties; publishes catalogue of materials and advises inquirers on how to obtain them
• Fosters the establishment of scholarships and research grants to graduate stu-

dents, teachers, and scholars and the funding of research teams wishing to do field studies in Latin America

    • Sponsors exchanges of scores, and recordings and materials as well as performers, arts and scholars between the U.S. and Latin America

    • Publishes studies and other materials on Latin American music and welcomes manuscript submissions

16.118
Latin American Studies Association
University of Texas
Sid Richardson Hall, Unit 1
Austin, TX 78731
(512) 471-6237

Contact(s):
Richard N. Sinkin, Executive Director
Jana Greenlief, Associate Director

Professional academic association

    • Promotes the study of Latin America through more effective education, teaching, training and research; serves as headquarters for the Consortium of Latin American Studies Programs; conducts meetings and publishes books, periodicals, teaching materials and reference works including *The Latin American Research Review* (see 16.155), the LASA Forum, *Latin America; Sights and Sounds: A Guide to Motion Pictures and Music for College Courses, Data Banks and Archives for Social Science Research on Latin America* (see 16.131), *Directory of Latin American Studies Programs and Faculty in the U.S.* (see 16.133), *Latin America: An Acquisitions Guide for Colleges and Public Libraries* ($10), and guides to obtaining financial aid, studying in Latin America, planning cross-cultural lessons, conducting simulations and other teaching aids

16.119
North American Congress on Latin America
151 West 19th St., 9th Floor
New York, NY 10011
(212) 989-8890

Nonprofit research organization

    • Conducts research and publishes materials on current Latin American affairs with particular emphasis on politics, economics and U.S. involvement in Latin American countries

    • Publishes books and *Report on the Americas* (see 16.156)

16.120
Organization of American States
17th St. and Constitution Ave. NW
Washington, DC 20006
(202) 789-3760

Contact(s):
Thomas L. Welch, Director, Columbus
    Memorial Library (202) 789-6037

    • Provides information and fosters research on Latin American nations; promotes cultural exchange and artistic performances; maintains Museum of Modern Latin American Art and the Inter-American Statistical Institute (in Washington) and the Pan-American Institute of Geography and History and the Inter-American Indian Institute (in Mexico City); the Inter-American Council for Education, Science and Culture has general responsibility for the promotion of educational, scientific and cultural cooperation and exchange

    • Columbus Memorial Library contains over 500,000 monographs and documents of the OAS and other organizations and over 200,000 periodicals; *Guide to the Columbus Memorial Library* available free upon request

    • Publishes *Americas* (see 16.147), *Inter-American Review of Bibliography* (see

16.151) and a large number of other books, pamphlets, reports, periodicals, etc. (subscription to all OAS publications available at $80 per year

16.121
Organization for Tropical Studies
P.O. Box DM
Duke Station
Durham, NC 27706
(919) 684-5774

Contact(s):
Donald E. Stone, Director

Consortium of 23 U.S. and four Costa Rican institutions of higher learning
  • Promotes biological research and offers field-oriented biology courses in Costa Rica for U.S. and Latin graduate students

16.122
Pan American Institute of Geography and History
Ex-Arzobispado No. 29
Mexico 18, D.F.
2775888

Contact(s):
Jose A. Saenz, Secretary General

Specialized agency of the Organization of American States (see 16.120) to promote the study of geography, cartography, anthropology, geophysics and history of the western hemisphere

  • Conducts studies and prepares research guides on American cartography/geography, history and geophysics
  • Publishes journals in Spanish and an extensive list of books in Spanish and English, including research guides in English to Colombia (see 18.110), Honduras (see 18.184), Costa Rica (see 18.113), Guatemala (see 18.184) and Peru, and in Spanish to Colombia, Nicaragua, Honduras, Costa Rica, El Salvador, Panama, Guatemala and Chile

16.123
Washington Office on Latin America
110 Maryland Ave. NE
Washington, DC 20002
(202) 544-8045

Contact(s):
Joseph T. Eldridge, Director

Nonprofit information center sponsored principally by church groups concerned with human rights in Latin America
  • Conducts research, provides information, sponsors meetings and responds to individual requests for information on conditions in Latin America and on U.S. policy, particularly where human rights issues are involved; maintains liaison with and among other organizations, government agencies and institutions
  • Publishes bimonthly newsletter, *Latin America Update*, analyzing U.S. government activities that affect Latin America, and issues news releases

Sources of Grants and Awards

16.124
Doherty Fellowship Committee
Princeton University
240 East Pyne
Princeton, NJ 08540
(212) 732-1040

Private grant-giving foundation
• Offers one-year fellowships to U.S. citizens for advanced graduate and postdoctoral study in social studies in Spanish- and Portuguese-speaking republics of Latin America; not normally awarded to students under 40 with prior experience in Latin America; grant range: $6,000–$8,000

16.125
Inter-American Foundation
Fellowship Programs
1515 Wilson Blvd.
Rosslyn, VA 22209
(703) 841-3864

Contact(s):
Elizabeth Veatch, Coordinator

• Offers approximately 20 doctoral fellowships to candidates who have completed all work for doctorate except dissertation grants to undertake research on indigenous rural social and economic development programs in Latin American and Caribbean countries from an interdisciplinary perspective; must speak language of the country; approximately $550 per month (varies according to country)
• Offers approximately 20 masters fellowships to support 3–6 months of research in Latin American and Caribbean countries by candidates for M.A. degrees in Latin American Studies; approximately $500 per month

16.126
United States Latin American Cooperative Science Program Division of International Programs
National Science Foundation
Division of International Programs
Washington, DC 20550
(202) 357-9558

Contact(s):
Eduardo Feller, Program Manager (Brazil, Argentina and Mexico)
Christine French, Program Manager (all other countries)

• Funds programs involving cooperative research, seminars and workshops and short-term visits between the U.S. and Brazil, Argentina, Mexico and other Latin American countries

16.127
Organization of American States
17th St. and Constitution Ave. N.W.
Washington, DC 20006
(202) 789-3902

Contact(s):
J. C. Torchia-Estrada, Director, Department of Fellowships and Training

• Awards OAS Regular Training Program-Fellowships for research or advanced study and training in subjects which foster the social, cultural, scientific and/or economic development of member states of the OAS; covers travel, registration and maintenance

16.128
Social Science Research Council
Grants for International Research: Latin
  America and the Caribbean
605 Third Ave.
New York, NY 10158
(212) 557-9500

• Awards substantial grants to social scientists and humanists from any country for
research related to cultural, economic, political, social or scientific development in Latin
America or the Caribbean area; research proposals on any topic are eligible for support,
although proposals in disciplines from which
few applications have been received in the
past will be especially welcome, e.g., demography and population studies, economics
and social psychology; program also seeks to
promote research on geographical areas that
have received limited research attention, such
as Cuba, other Caribbean countries and Central America

• Research proposals relevant to more
than one area or country in Latin America or
the Caribbean or involving a Latin American
and a non-Latin American country are welcome; Latin American scholars may present
proposals for research in their own country
or abroad, as appropriate

• Awards substantial grants jointly to two
scholars of approximately equal scholarly maturity in the social sciences or the humanities
who wish to collaborate on a research project
dealing with Latin American or Caribbean
history, cultures, societies and institutions; one
of the collaborators must be working in, and

be a citizen of, a Latin American or Caribbean country; the other collaborator must be
working in another country within or outside
Latin America and the Caribbean

• Awards substantial fellowships for doctoral dissertation research in the social sciences and the humanities; program particularly seeks to encourage research in disciplines
from which few applications have been received in the past, such as art history, demography and population studies, drama,
economics and literature; similarly, proposals
for research on geographical areas that have
received limited research attention, such as
Cuba, other Caribbean countries and Central
America, are particularly welcome; consideration will be given to comparative projects
involving Latin America or the Caribbean and
other areas of the world

16.129
The Tinker Foundation, Inc.
645 Madison Ave.
New York, NY 10022
(212) 421-6858

Charitable foundation

• Provides, under the Tinker Postdoctoral Fellowship Program, one-year awards
covering travel and stipend to scholars (who
must have completed their doctoral studies
between 3 and 10 years before application) in
the fields of Ibero or Latin American Studies
to pursue research in the social sciences, marine sciences or international relations

Guides, Sourcebooks and Directories

16.130
The Complete Caribbeana 1900–1975: A Bibliographic Guide to the Scholarly Literature
Lambros Comitas
Kraus International Publications
Route 100
Millwood, NY 10546
1977; hardbound; 4 volumes; $240

• Contains citations of over 17,000 books, monographs, journal articles, conference proceedings, masters and doctoral theses, reports and pamphlets published in the 20th century; covers Suriname, French Guiana, Guyana, Belize, Bermuda, the Bahamas and most islands of the Antillean archipelago; citations of material in foreign languages include an English translation of the title; author index and geographical index

16.131
Data Banks and Archives for Social Science Research on Latin America
William Tyler, Editor
Latin American Studies Association
Sid Richardson Hall, Unit 1
University of Texas
Austin, TX 78731
1976; paperbound; Publication No. 5 of
   Abstracts; $7; $3.50 for members

• Identifies and describes major collections of Latin American materials of value to the social science teacher

16.132
Dictionary of Afro-Latin American Civilization
Benjamin Nunez
African Bibliographic Center
P.O. Box 13096
Washington, DC 20009
and

Greenwood Press
88 Post Road West
Westport, CT 06881
hardbound; 608 pages; $45

• Reference guide to the African tradition in the western hemisphere, identifying approximately 4,700 terms, phrases, historical and political events and people significant in the life and culture of blacks in Latin America

16.133
Directory of Latin American Studies Programs and Faculty in the United States
Margo L. Smith, Compiler
Consortium of Latin American Studies
   Programs
Box 13362
University Station
Gainesville, FL 32604
1975; paperbound; 282 pages; $18.50

• Lists and provides details (including names and interests of full- and part-time faculty) on 67 Latin American Studies programs in U.S. colleges and universities; in separate sections lists institutions by disciplinary specialty of the faculty and lists institutes sponsoring field studies; also provides an alphabetical list of Latin American faculty and a list of non-responding institutions

16.134
Global Dimensions of the African Diaspora
Joseph E. Harris, Editor
Howard University Press
2900 Van Ness St. NW
Washington, DC 20008
1982; hardbound; 608 pages; $19.95

• Guide to the study of the dispersal of Africans and African descendants to other parts of the world; in four sections: conceptual framework, assimilation and identity (the process of adaptation), return (immigration back to Africa) and synthesis (which proposes the application of a Pan-African approach to diaspora studies); includes bibliography

16.135
Guide to Nonprint Materials for Latin American Studies
Martin H. Sable
Blaine Ethridge-Books
13977 Penrod St.
Detroit, MI 48223
hardbound; 152 pages; $16.50

• An annotated bibliography-directory covering most types of nonprint materials for all levels, elementary through graduate school (levels designated), in English and/or Spanish; includes general and specialized information on Latin America in general and on individual nations; three indexes and a directory of firms and institutions are included

16.136
A Guide to Reviews of Books From and About Hispanic America/Guia a las Reseñas de Libros de y sobre Hispanoamérica
Antonio Matos, Editor
Blaine Ethridge-Books
13977 Penrod St.
Detroit, MI 48223
annual; hardbound; approx. 1,700 pages;
   prices vary from $45–$110

• Indexes reviews in about 580 North and South American and European publications in the social sciences and humanities; summaries are 25–100 words long in language of original review; covers over 3,000 books each issue

16.137
Hispanic American Periodicals Index
Barbara G. Cox, Editor
Latin American Center
University of California
405 Hilgard Ave.
Los Angeles, CA 90024
annual; hardbound; 608 pages; $75

• Provides author and subject indexing of the contents of 238 scholarly journals in the humanities and social sciences published in Spanish-speaking America, Brazil, Europe, the U.S. and the Caribbean

16.138
Informational and Technical Publications of the General Secretariat of the OAS
Organization of American States
Washington, DC 20006
annual subscription in English; $80

• Subscriber receives all the publications of the OAS including books, pamphlets, reports, directories, periodicals and other materials published by the OAS during the year; publications cover economics, law, statistics, education, social sciences, literature, art, folklore and other areas of general information

16.139
Latin America: An Introduction
Jan Knippers Black, Editor
Westview Press
5500 Central Ave.
Boulder, CO 80301
1984; 450 pages; hardbound, $30;
   paperbound, $14.50

• Introduction for the novice and the student to what is most interesting about Latin America; conveys the unifying aspects of Latin American culture and society, together with the distinct characteristics of major subgroups and regions

16.140

Latin America: International Relations
John J. Finan and John Child, Editors
Gale Research Co.
Book Tower
Detroit, MI 48226
1981; hardbound; 236 pages; $40

• Bibliographic information about works on Latin America as a whole and on individual nations

16.141

The Latin American Political Dictionary
Ernest E. Rossi and Jack C. Plano
ABC-Clio, Inc.
Riviera Campus
2040 Alameda Padre Serra
Box 4397
Santa Barbara, CA 93103
1980; 261 pages; hardbound, $26;
    paperbound, $13.50

• Provides definitions and commentary on the significance of terms, concepts, institutions and events central to the politics and economics of Latin America; arranged topically and sequenced parallel to most related texts under such headings as historical perspective, political and cultural ideology, government institutions, political parties, etc.; indexed

16.142

Latin American Studies Directory
Martin H. Sable
Blaine Ethridge Books
13977 Penrod St.
Detroit, MI 48223
1981; hardbound; 124 pages; $16.50

• Lists without description 474 institutions worldwide offering course work in Latin American Studies (317 in the U.S.); lists and describes 100 research centers, 105 profes-

sional associations, 15 international, U.S. and intergovernmental agencies worldwide all of which are concerned with Latin American Studies or inter-American affairs; also lists and describes fellowships and grants, libraries, information centers and databanks, and lists without description book publishers and periodical subscription agents along with a select list of U.S. specialists on Latin America (3 from each of 15 disciplines)

16.143

The Newer Caribbean: Decolonization, Democracy and Development
Paget Henry and Carl Stone
Institute for the Study of Human Issues
3401 Market St.
Philadelphia, PA 19104
1983; 350 pages; hardbound, $30;
    paperbound, $12.95

Inter-American Politics Series, Volume IV
• Up-to-date review of the development of the smaller nations of the Caribbean, especially those which have become independent in recent years

16.144

Scholar's Guide to Washington, D.C.: Latin American and Caribbean Studies
Michael Grow
Smithsonian Institution Press
Washington, DC 20560
1978; 346 pages; paperbound, $9.95;
    hardbound, $25

Comprehensive listing and description of resources in the Washington area available to researchers and others interested in Latin America and the Caribbean; divided into two sections: collections (libraries, archives, museums, etc., music and sound, maps, films, and data banks) and organizations (research centers and information offices, academic programs, U.S. government agencies, embassies and international organizations, professional associations, exchange and technical assistance organizations, religious organizations, and publications/media); available resources described in some detail with clear indication how and from whom to obtain access; appendices include libraries listed by size of holdings, bookstores, housing, transport and other services and a bibliography; indexed by name of resource, personal papers collections, and library subject strength

16.145
Statistical Abstract of Latin America
James W. Wilkie and Peter Reich, Editors
Latin American Center
University of California at Los Angeles
405 Hilgard Ave.
Los Angeles, CA 90024
annual; approx. 400 pages; $25,
    paperbound; $32.50, hardbound

• Statistical data derived from many different sources designed to aid in the study of specific topics and in the comparative analysis of 20 Latin American countries, the U.S. and the rest of the world

16.146
A Survey of Materials for the Study of the Uncommonly Taught Languages: Languages of North, Central & South America
Dora E. Johnson et al.
Center for Applied Linguistics
3520 Prospect St. NW
Washington, DC 20007
1976; paperbound; 51 pages; $7.95

Exclusively distributed by Harcourt Brace Jovanovich, Inc., 757 Third Ave., New York, NY 10017; Attn: Nancy McCloughan
• One of a series of bibliographies covering all the modern languages except Standard English, German, Italian, Russian and Spanish; designed for use by the adult learner whose native language is English; listed under the headings: teaching materials, readers, grammars and dictionaries; includes books currently in print where feasible, older titles where not; citations appear under the following language groups: Arctic, Macro-Algonquian, Macro-Siouan, Na-Dene, Hokan, Oto-Manguean, Penutian, Mayan, Keres, Tarascan, Andean Equatorial, Macro-Chibchan, Macro Ge-Pano-Carib and Witoto

Periodicals

16.147
Americas
Organization of American States
Washington, DC 20006
bi-monthly magazine; $15 per year

• Articles on social, cultural, economic and other aspects of the member nations of the OAS (see 16.120)

16.148
Caribbean Quarterly
R. M. Nettleford, Editor
Department of Extra-Mural Studies
University of the West Indies
Mona, Kingston 7, Jamaica
quarterly journal; approx. 100 pages; $22
    per year

• Contains scholarly research and commentary on contemporary political affairs in the countries of the Caribbean; book reviews

16.149
Hispania
Theodore A. Sackett, Editor
American Association of Teachers of Spanish
  and Portuguese, Inc.
University of Mississippi
University, MS 38677
5 issues per year; journal; approx. 150
  pages; $15 per year; free to members

• Combines scholarly essays with practical articles and reports on the teaching of Spanish and Portuguese; gives news of the profession

16.150
The Hispanic American Historical Review
John J. Johnson, Managing Editor
Duke University Press
P.O. Box 6697, College Station
Durham, NC 27708
quarterly journal; approx. 200 pages;
  individuals, $15; institutions, $30;
  registered students, $9

• Scholarly articles on Latin American historical subjects; large book review section

16.151
Inter-American Review of Bibliography
Organization of American States
Washington, DC 20006
quarterly journal; approx. 40 pages; $8 per
  year

• Covers book reviews, research in progress, recent articles, recent doctoral dissertations, recent publications of the U.S. Congress, and OAS publications in the social sciences and humanities in the area of Latin America and the Caribbean

16.152
Journal of Interamerican Studies
John P. Harrison, Editor
Graduate School of International Studies
University of Miami
Miami, FL 33124
quarterly journal; 120 pages; individuals,
  $22 per year; institutions, $48 per year

Available from Sage Publications, 275 South Beverly Drive, Beverly Hills, CA 90212
• Contains scholarly articles and papers on political and economic issues in and among the countries of the Western Hemisphere; book reviews

16.153
Journal of Latin American Studies
Harold Blakemore and Alan Angell, Co-
  editors
Cambridge University Press
32 East 57th St.
New York, NY 10022
semi-annual journal; 222 pages; institutions
  $68 per year plus postage

Individuals ordering directly from the publishers and who certify that the journal is for their personal use may subscribe at a reduced rate of $34
• Includes scholarly articles and essays on aspects of Latin American social and political affairs both contemporary and historical; includes extensive section of reviews and shorter notices of books

16.154
Latin American Literary Review
Yvette Espinosa Miller, Editor in chief
Department of Modern Languages
Carnegie-Mellon University
Baker Hall
Pittsburgh, PA 15213
biannual journal; 110 pages; $13 per year

• Articles on Latin American literature, reviews of literary works and texts of contemporary poems, essays, stories and dramatic writing in English

16.155
Latin American Research Review
Gilbert W. Merkx, Editor
Latin American Institute
801 Yale N.E.
University of New Mexico
Albuquerque, NM 87131
3 issues per year; journal; approx. 275
    pages; institutions, $30; individuals, $15;
    students, $12

Microfilm copies available from University Microfilms, 300 North Zeeb Road, Ann Arbor, MI 48106
    • Scholarly articles on subjects of interest to Latin Americanists; book review essays

16.156
Report on the Americas
North American Congress on Latin America
151 West 19th St., 9th Floor
New York, NY 10011
bimonthly magazine; individuals, $15;
    institutions, $29

    • Examines current affairs in Latin American countries stressing nationalism, revolution and U.S. involvement; each issue focuses on a single country and/or a single theme

16.157
Review
Rosario Santos, Managing Editor
Center for Inter-American Relations, Inc.
680 Park Ave.
New York, NY 10021

published 2 times per year; journal; approx.
    88 pages; individuals, $12 per year;
    institutions, $20 per year

    • Articles on Latin American poets, writers and their works along with fiction and poetry in translation; book reviews

16.158
Revista/Review
Inter American University Press
G.P.O. Box 3255
San Juan, Puerto Rico 00936
quarterly journal; approx. 158 pages; $26
    per year, institutions; $18 per year,
    individuals

    • Articles in Spanish or English on Puerto Rican, Caribbean and Latin American affairs in the areas of politics, history, literature, linguistics and the social sciences; includes poetry, fiction and book reviews

16.159
Studies in Latin American Popular Culture
Harold E. Hinds and Charles M. Tatum,
    Editors
Department of Foreign Languages
Box 3L
New Mexico State University
Las Cruces, NM 88003
annual journal; individuals, $15; institutions,
    $25

    • Articles examine theoretical and practical aspects of popular culture (sports, cartoons, films, television, etc.) in Latin American countries; book review essays

Publishers

16.160
Blaine Ethridge—Books
13977 Penrod
Detroit, MI 48223

Publisher of books on Latin America, ethnicity and bilingualism
• Publishes books on Latin American history and literature, along with a number of reference books including *The Latin American Studies Directory* (see 16.142), and *Guide to Nonprint Materials for Latin American Studies* (see 16.135), and the periodical *A Guide to Reviews of Books from and About Hispanic America* (see 16.136)

16.161
Caribbean Imprint Library Services
410 W. Falmouth Highway
Box 350
West Falmouth, MA 02574
(617) 540-5378

• Supplies publications from Caribbean and Central American countries including commercially published books, institutional and government reports, journals and other materials; must request specific publications (general lists not available)

16.162
Ecumenical Program for Interamerican Communication and Action (EPICA)
1470 Irving St. NW
Washington, DC 20010
(202) 332-0292

• Publishes books and reports, principally on the countries of Central America and the Caribbean, focused on revolutionary and reform movements and the involvement of the U.S. in the area

16.163
G. K. Hall & Co.
70 Lincoln St.
Boston, MA 02111
(617) 423-3990

Commercial reference book publisher
• Publishes Latin American Studies series of reference books including a large project indexing collective biographies (currently available for Central America and the Caribbean, Mexico and the Andean countries) and a wide variety of bibliographies on literary and historical subjects; includes *Venezuelan History: A Comprehensive Working Bibliography* (see 18.582), *Cuba: A Handbook of Historical Statistics* and the library reference work *Bibliographic Guide to Latin American Studies* (annual, 3 volumes, $350)

16.164
Inter American University Press
G.P.O. Box 3255
San Juan, Puerto Rico 00936
(809) 754-8415 or 8370

Small educational publishing house
• Publishes books in Spanish or English on Puerto Rican, Caribbean and Latin American affairs in the areas of politics, history, literature, linguistics and the social sciences, including *Revista/Review* (see 16.158)

16.165
Kraus International Publications
Route 100
Millwood, NY 10546
(914) 762-2200

• Publishes extensive list of reference works, bibliographies and Monograph series in the social sciences and the humanities; includes *The Complete Haitiana: A Bibliographic Guide* (see 18.188), *The Complete Caribbeana: A Bibliographic Guide* (see 18.130) and *Cuba, 1953–1978: A Bibliographic Guide to the Literature* (forthcoming)

16.166
Three Continents Press, Inc.
1346 Connecticut Ave. NW, Suite 224
Washington, DC 20036
(202) 457-0288 or 387-5809

Commercial publishing house
  • Publishes books by and about contemporary Caribbean writers and writing along with a few historical, reference and sociological titles; includes *Caribbean Writers: A Bio-Bibliographical-Critical Encyclopedia* and *Bibliography of the Literature of Guyana* (covering 24 categories and including a short history of the country)

16.167
The University of Alabama Press
P.O. Box 2877
University, AL 35486
(205) 348-5180

Large university publishing house
  • Publishes a number of titles on Latin American history

16.168
University Presses of Florida
15 NW 15th St.
Gainesville, FL 32603
(904) 392-1351

Central agency for scholarly publishing of the State of Florida's university system
  • Publishes extensive list of books on Latin America including a monograph series on historical, political and socioeconomic is-

sues, a handbook series of articles on Latin American studies with the humanities and social sciences covered in separate volumes, a number of publications on Caribbean affairs (with the Caribbean Research Institute, see 16.108), the periodical *Microstate Studies*, and a collection of teaching units and materials *Cross-Cultural Models of Teaching: Latin American Examples*

16.169
University of New Mexico Press
Albuquerque, NM 87131
(505) 277-2346

  • Publishes extensive list of titles on Latin America

16.170
University of Oklahoma Press
1005 Asp Ave.
Norman, OK 73019
(405) 325-5111

Large university publishing house
  • Publishes books on Latin American history with particular strength on the Indians of North and South America

16.171
University of Pittsburgh Press
127 N. Bellefield Ave.
Pittsburgh, PA 15260
(412) 624-4110

  • Publishes the Pitt Latin American Series consisting of books focused on political developments in individual countries and in Latin America as a whole and on political relationships between Latin America and the U.S.; particularly strong in analyses of contemporary Cuba

16.172
University of Texas Press
Box 7819
Austin, TX 78712
(512) 471-7233

• Publishes an extensive list of titles on Latin American history, politics and development, particularly in cooperation with the University of Texas (Austin) Institute of Latin American Studies; also a selection of titles in Middle East Studies

17

Middle East Area Studies

Area Studies Programs and Research Centers

17.001
Near Eastern Center
University of Arizona
Department of Oriental Studies
Tucson, AZ 85721
(602) 621-5456

Contact(s):
Ludwig W. Adamec, Director
Sheila Scoville, Outreach Coordinator

Graduate and undergraduate area studies program established in 1975

• Majors/degrees/certificates offered: B.A. and M.A. in Oriental Studies—Middle East or departmental degrees with concentration in Middle East Studies; Ph.D. in Middle East Studies

• Approximate number of faculty teaching area and language courses: 30

• Approximate number of courses available—area: 55; language: 22

• Average number of students per year specializing in area: 10

• Countries covered and areas of em-

phasis: Islamic North Africa, the Fertile Crescent and Arabia, Turkey, Iran, Afghanistan, and those portions of the Indian subcontinent which are, or have been historically, under Muslim influence

• Languages offered: Arabic, Hebrew, Persian, Hindi-Urdu and Akkadian; access to intensive summer language programs at other institutions available

• Oriental Studies Library Collection includes 50,000 volumes in English, 20,000 in Arabic, 1,500 in Persian, 1,000 in Turkish, 8,200 in Urdu, and 4,500 in Hebrew; includes periodicals, maps, microfilms, monographs and various nonbook media; additional resources available through the Arid Lands Research Center

• Exchange programs and overseas study opportunities also available

• Outreach program includes summer workshops for teachers, the provision of reference and teaching materials and other activities

• Publishes Center newsletter

17.002
Center for Middle Eastern Studies and the Department of Near Eastern Studies
University of California at Berkeley
215 Moses Hall
Berkeley, CA 94720
(415) 642-8208

Contact(s):

Dan I. Slobin, Director, Center for Middle Eastern Studies
Laurence O. Michalak, Coordinator

Graduate and undergraduate area studies program established in 1894; Middle East Center established in 1962
• Majors/degrees/certificates offered: B.A., M.A. and Ph.D. in Near Eastern Studies and in departments with a Near Eastern Studies specialization; M.A. in Teaching Arabic or Hebrew and M.A. in Librarianship and Near Eastern Studies
• Approximate number of faculty teaching area and language courses: 42
• Approximate number of courses available—area: 65; language: 79
• Average number of students per year specializing in area: 110 graduate; 65 undergraduate
• Countries covered and areas of emphasis: Arab world, Turkey, Iran and Israel
• Languages offered: Arabic, Persian, Turkish, Akkadian, Sumerian, Hittite, Egyptian, classical Hebrew, Persian (classical), Iranian, Aramaic, Syriac and Ugaritic
• Libraries contain over 60,000 volumes and 380 periodicals plus an extensive collection on the Middle East in English and slide and audiovisual materials
• Overseas study and research available in Israel, Egypt and Turkey
• Postdoctoral awards and research associate appointments available to external scholars
• Affiliated with a number of Middle East study and research institutes

17.003
Gustave E. Von Grunebaum Center for Near Eastern Studies
University of California at Los Angeles
405 Hilgard Ave., RBH 10286
Los Angeles, CA 90024
(213) 825-1455

Contact(s):

Georges Sabagh, Acting Director
Jonathan Friedlander, Outreach Coordinator

Graduate and undergraduate non-degree area studies program established in 1957
• Majors/degrees/certificates offered: B.A. in Near Eastern Studies; M.A. and Ph.D. in Islamic Studies
• Approximate number of faculty teaching area and language courses: 52
• Approximate number of courses available—area and language: 488
• Countries covered and areas of emphasis: countries of the Middle East and North Africa where Islam predominates and the principal languages are Arabic, Persian and Turkish
• Languages offered: Amharic, Arabic, Armenian, Avestan, Bashkir, Berber, Chagatay, Hebrew, Turkish, Old Persian, Ottoman, Pahlavi, Persian, Uighur, Uzbek and Vedic
• Library contains over 200,000 volumes in the languages of the area including a rare manuscripts collection (Arabic, Armenian, Persian, Turkish) of some 8,500 volumes; the Museum of Cultural History includes an extensive collection of Near Eastern archaeological and ethnographical materials
• Serves as resource center for Los Angeles County School District in disseminating teaching materials, videotapes and teaching modules; publishes outreach materials
• Maintains Visiting Scholar Program
• Publishes Studies in Near Eastern Culture and Society series, conference proceedings, teaching materials and a newsletter

17.004
Interdisciplinary Major in Middle East Studies
University of California at Santa Cruz
Department of History, Merrill College
Santa Cruz, CA 95064
(408) 429-2287

Contact(s):
Edmund Burke III, Director

Undergraduate area studies program
 • Majors/degrees/certificates offered: B.A. in Social Sciences with major in Africa and the Middle East
 • Approximate number of faculty teaching area & language courses: 10
 • Approximate number of courses available—area: 13; language: 6
 • Countries covered and areas of emphasis: all countries of the Middle East and North Africa; emphasis on the social sciences
 • Language offered: Hebrew

17.005
African and Middle Eastern Studies
University of Colorado at Boulder
Campus Box 233
Boulder, CO 80309
(303) 492-5122 or 7667

Contact(s):
Gottfried Lang and Ragaei El Mallakh, Co-chairs

Undergraduate area studies program (see 12.005)

17.006
Duncan Black Macdonald Center for the Study of Islam and Christian-Muslim Relationships
Hartford Seminary
77 Sherman St.
Hartford, CT 06105
(203) 232-4451

Contact(s):
Willem A. Bijefeld, Director

 • Center for study, research and public education in Christian-Muslim relations; administers M.A. in Islamic Studies (see 17.007), maintains library collection on Islam and publishes *The Muslim World* (see 17.087)
 • Works jointly with the Task Force on Christian-Muslim Relations of the National Council of Churches in the U.S.A. to sponsor conferences and lectures; publishes a newsletter and otherwise stimulates Christian concern with Muslim-Christian relations

17.007
Islamic Studies
Hartford Seminary
Duncan Black Macdonald Center
77 Sherman St.
Hartford, CT 06105
(203) 232-4451

Contact(s):
Byron L. Haines, Director of Degree
 Programs

Graduate area studies program established in 1973
 • Majors/degrees/certificates offered: M.A. in Religious Studies with concentration in Islamics
 • Approximate number of faculty teaching area and language courses: 5
 • Approximate number of courses available—area: 16; language: 2
 • Average number of students per year specializing in area: 4
 • Countries covered and areas of emphasis: focuses on Islam, Islamic society and interfaith relationships, especially between Christians and Muslims
 • Language offered: Arabic
 • Maintains library of approximately 40,000 volumes on Arabic and Islamic Studies, including many in Arabic

- Close cooperative relationship with Trinity and St. Joseph Colleges

17.008
Program for Middle East Language and Area Studies
The University of Connecticut
307 Wood Hall, Box U-207
Storrs, CT 06268
(203) 486-3855, 3861

Contact(s):
Ramon Knauerhase, Director

Graduate, undergraduate and nondegree area studies program
- Majors/degrees/certificates offered: B.A. and M.A. in Middle East Language and Area Studies
- Approximate number of faculty teaching area and language courses: 15
- Approximate number of courses available—area: 35; language: 16
- Countries covered and areas of emphasis: all countries of the Middle East; students may pursue humanities, social sciences or business administration tracks
- Languages offered: Arabic, Hebrew, and independent study programs in Farsi, Turkish and Armenian
- Draws on resources of Duncan Black Macdonald Center for Study of Islam and Christian-Muslim Relations, Hartford Seminary (see 17.006)

17.009
Jewish Studies
The American University
Washington, DC 20016
(202) 686-2410

Contact(s):
Benjamin M. Kahn, Director

Undergraduate area studies program

- Majors/degrees/certificates offered: B.A. in Jewish Studies
- Approximate number of faculty teaching area & language courses: 21
- Approximate number of courses available—area: 21; language: 4
- Average number of students per year specializing in area: 13
- Countries covered and areas of emphasis: history of the Jews in the U.S., Europe and the Middle East, including Israel
- Language offered: Hebrew

17.010
Middle East Studies Program
George Washington University
School of Public and International Affairs
Washington, DC 20052
(202) 676-6240

Contact(s):
Bernard Reich, Director

Graduate and undergraduate area studies program established in 1979
- Majors/degrees/certificates offered: B.A. and M.A. in Middle East Studies
- Approximate number of faculty teaching area and language courses: 15
- Approximate number of courses available—area: 45; language: 20
- Average number of students per year specializing in area: 15
- Countries covered and areas of emphasis: all countries of the Middle East and North Africa with emphasis on the social sciences
- Languages offered: Hebrew and Yiddish; Arabic, Persian and Turkish available through Washington Consortium of Universities and the Middle East Institute (see 17.055)
- Summer study program in the Middle East takes place partly in Cairo and partly in Jerusalem

17.011
Center for Contemporary Arab Studies
Georgetown University
School of Foreign Service
Washington, DC 20057
(202) 625-3128

Contact(s):
Michael C. Hudson, Director

Graduate and undergraduate area studies program established in 1975
 • Majors/degrees/certificates offered: undergraduate and graduate Certificates and M.A. in Arab Studies
 • Approximate number of faculty teaching area and language courses: 31
 • Approximate number of courses available—area: 58; language: 32
 • Average number of students per year specializing in area: 40
 • Countries covered and areas of emphasis: Arab countries of North Africa and the Middle East; emphasis on social sciences and international relations
 • Language offered: Arabic
 • Library contains extensive collection of books, monographs and periodicals on Arabic subjects in Arabic and Western languages
 • Sponsors research and publishes books and studies on Arab-related issues and conducts public affairs program
 • Maintains Community Resource Center which provides materials and services to community organizations and schools
 • Arranges overseas study, travel and internship experiences

17.012
Middle East Studies
The Johns Hopkins University
School of Advanced International Studies
1740 Massachusetts Ave. NW
Washington, DC 20036
(202) 785-6200

Graduate area studies program
 • Majors/degrees/certificates offered: M.A. and Ph.D. in International Relations with major in Middle East Studies
 • Countries covered and areas of emphasis: all countries of the Middle East and the Arab World with emphasis on contemporary economic and political issues in the area bounded by Egypt, Turkey, Iran and the Arabian Peninsula
 • Language offered: Arabic
 • Draws on library, organizational and research resources of the Washington area
 • Special internships and fellowships available

17.013
Asian Studies
Northwestern University
Harris Hall 207A
Evanston, IL 60201
(312) 492-3408

Contact(s):
James E. Sheridan, Chair

 • Undergraduate area studies program in Asian and Middle Eastern Studies (see 13.041)

17.014
Center for Middle Eastern Studies
University of Chicago
5848 South University
Chicago, IL 60637
(312) 962-8297

Contact(s):
Richard L. Chambers, Director
Warren Schulz, Outreach Coordinator

Graduate and undergraduate area studies program established in 1965
 • Majors/degrees/certificates offered:

M.A. in Middle Eastern Studies; B.A., M.A., and Ph.D. in disciplines with concentration in Middle Eastern Studies

- Approximate number of faculty teaching area and language courses: 47
- Approximate number of courses available—area: 216; language: 246
- Average number of students per year specializing in area: 38
- Countries covered and areas of emphasis: the Arab world, Afghanistan, Pakistan, Iran, Turkey and Muslim Central Asia; includes fields of concentration in contemporary Middle Eastern Studies, Arabic Studies, Middle Eastern History, Hebrew Studies, Islamic Studies, Persian Studies, Islamic Art and Architecture and Turkish Studies; particular strength in the study of the ancient Middle East
- Languages offered: Akkadian, Arabic, Aramaic, Egyptian, Hebrew, Hittite, Persian, Sumerian, Turkish and Urdu; co-curricular programs conducted in Arabic, Hebrew, Persian and Turkish
- 250,000-volume Middle East Library Collection, including 115,000 in Middle Eastern languages (Arabic, Hebrew, Persian, Turkish and Urdu) and European languages as well as extensive collections for the study of the ancient Middle East and 1,000 serials; 5,000 volumes added annually; Museum of the Oriental Institute consists of five galleries housing collections of antiquities (70,000 items) from Egypt, Nubia, Palestine, Syria, Anatolia, Assyria, Babylonia, Sumer and Ancient Persia
- Overseas language study available through Center for Arabic Study Abroad (see 8.005)
- "Visiting Scholar" and "Research Associate" status available to external faculty and researchers
- Publishes research works on the Middle East in conjunction with the University of Chicago Press (see 11.030)
- Fellowships and assistantships available, including a limited number specifically for work toward the M.A. in Middle Eastern Studies

17.015
Near East Studies Program
Indiana University at Bloomington
Department of Near Eastern Languages and Cultures
216 Goodbody Hall
Bloomington, IN 47405
(812) 335-4323

Contact(s):
Victor Danner, Chair

- Offers Ph.D. with emphasis on Near East in history, political science and Uralic and Altaic Studies

17.016
Research Institute for Inner Asian Studies
Indiana University at Bloomington
Goodbody Hall 101
Bloomington, IN 47405
(812) 335-1605

Contact(s):
Stephen Halkovic, Jr., Director

- Research center focusing on the countries of inner Asia including Afghanistan, Iran and Turkey (see 13.047)

17.017
Middle East Civilization
University of Kentucky
Lexington, KY 40506
(606) 257-3761

Contact(s):
Paul G. Forand, Director

Undergraduate area studies program established in 1973

• Majors/degrees/certificates offered: B.A. in Middle East Civilization

• Approximate number of faculty teaching area and language courses: 4

• Approximate number of courses available—area: 38; language: 5

• Average number of students per year specializing in area: 3

• Countries covered and areas of emphasis: all countries of the Near East and North Africa with emphasis on Islam, Judaism and history (ancient, medieval and modern)

• Languages offered: Arabic and Hebrew

17.018
The Philip W. Lown School of Near Eastern and Judaic Studies
Brandeis University
Department of Near Eastern and Judaic Studies
Waltham, MA 02254
(617) 647-2647

Contact(s):
Marvin Fox, Director

Graduate area studies program
• Majors/degrees/certificates offered: M.A. and Ph.D. in Near Eastern and Judaic Studies

• Approximate number of faculty teaching area and language courses: 21

• Approximate number of courses available—area and language: 143

• Countries covered and areas of emphasis: emphasis on Biblical studies, ancient history, Hebrew/Jewish literature and thought and modern Jewish and Middle Eastern Studies

• Languages offered: Arabic, Aramaic, Hebrew, Akkadian, Egyptian, Coptic, Ugaritic and other ancient Near Eastern languages

• Library contains approximately 100,000 volumes of Hebraica and Judaica in several languages; especially strong in biblical studies, rabbinica, modern Jewish history, Jewish and Islamic philosophy, Hebrew and Yiddish literature; includes large number of periodicals in Hebrew, Yiddish and other languages

17.019
Center for Middle Eastern Studies
Harvard University
1737 Cambridge St.
Cambridge, MA 02138
(617) 495-4055

Contact(s):
Nadav Safran, Director

Graduate area studies program established in 1955
• Majors/degrees/certificates offered: M.A. in Regional Studies—the Middle East; joint Ph.D. with Departments of Anthropology, Economics, Fine Arts and History; joint degree with the Harvard Law School

• Approximate number of faculty teaching area and language courses: 52

• Approximate number of courses available—area: 46; language: 77

• Average number of students per year specializing in area: 17 graduate; 46 undergraduate

• Countries covered and areas of emphasis: all countries of the Middle East

• Languages offered: Arabic, Hebrew, Persian, Turkish, Akkadian, Aramaic, Armenian, Kurdish, Sumerian and Urdu

• Middle Eastern and Judaica divisions of the Harvard library contain over 300,000 volumes, with the Middle Eastern language collection increasing at the rate of approximately 5,000 volumes per year

• Conducts joint seminars and programs with other Harvard schools and sponsors a Faculty Associates Program for Middle Eastern specialists teaching in New England colleges; conducts outreach program for precollegiate schools and the community at large and maintains a Teaching Resource Center which houses a multimedia lending library; publishes a monthly newsletter, conducts workshops and offers consulting services

• Promotes research and supports a number of Research Associates

• Publishes a Monograph Series and edits the Middle Eastern Studies Series of the Harvard University Press (see 11.012)

• Opportunities for overseas study and research available through a number of international research institutes

17.020

The Aga Khan Program for Islamic Architecture at Harvard University and the Massachusetts Institute of Technology
Massachusetts Institute of Technology
Room 10-390
Cambridge, MA 02139
(617) 253-1400

Contact(s):
Oleg Grabar, Director at Harvard
William L. Porter, Director at MIT

• Provides instructional, research and scholarship resources to Harvard and MIT to promote teaching and research in Islamic art and architecture; conducts summer seminar and maintains Aga Khan Documentation Center at the two institutions

17.021

Asian Studies Program
Wheaton College
Norton, MA 02766
(617) 285-7722, Ext. 484

Contact(s):
Vipan Chandra, Coordinator

• Undergraduate area studies program in Asian and Middle Eastern Studies (see 13.058)

17.022

Middle East Studies Committee
Michigan State University
306 Linton Hall
East Lansing, MI 48824
(517) 355-8332

Contact(s):
Alford T. Welch, Department of Religious Studies

Graduate and undergraduate area studies program established in 1975

• Majors/degrees/certificates offered: B.A., B.S., M.A. and Ph.D. in Middle East Studies or in discipline with specialization in Middle East Studies

• Approximate number of faculty teaching area and language courses: 10

• Approximate number of courses available—area: 15; language: 12

• Countries covered and areas of emphasis: all countries of the Middle East and North Africa with emphasis on history, culture and religion

• Languages offered: Amharic, Arabic, Hebrew and Swahili

• Study abroad available and encouraged

17.023

Center for Near Eastern and North African Studies
University of Michigan at Ann Arbor
144 Lane Hall
Ann Arbor, MI 48109-1290
(313) 764-0350

Contact(s):
Ernest N. McCarus, Director
Elizabeth Barlow, Outreach Coordinator

Graduate and undergraduate area studies program established in 1961

• Majors/degrees/certificates offered: B.A. and M.A. in Modern Near Eastern and

North African Studies; B.A., M.A. and Ph.D. in a department with specialization in Near Eastern and North African Studies; joint M.A./ M.B.A. program with the School of Business Administration also available

• Approximate number of faculty teaching area and language courses: 32

• Approximate number of courses available—area: 143; language: 88

• Average number of students per year specializing in area: 51 graduate; 65 undergraduate

• Countries covered and areas of emphasis: all countries of the Near East and North Africa from Iran to Morocco including Turkey and the Gulf

• Languages offered: Modern Standard Arabic, Moroccan Arabic, Egyptian Colloquial Arabic, Syrian Arabic, Berber, Persian, Hebrew, Turkish and Kurdish

• Library contains approximately 192,000 volumes in the field of Near Eastern Studies with about 107,000 in Arabic, Hebrew, Persian and Turkish; specialized Near Eastern collection also available in the Law Library (especially Islamic law), the Business Library, the Center for Research in Economic Development and the Music Library; undergraduate library contains a special collection of literature in translation and audiovisual materials

• University museum contains important collections of Near Eastern and Egyptian materials

• Conducts extensive co-curricular program on campus and outreach program for undergraduate and precollege faculty including a Faculty Enrichment Program enabling teachers in the region to spend up to a week studying and doing research at the university; also develops and publishes curriculum materials

• Publishes newsletter, colloquial Arabic texts and teaching guides and materials including *Educational Film Guide for Middle Eastern Studies* (see 2.124), *Annotated Bibliography on the Modern History of the Near East, Politics and International Relations in the Middle East: An Annotated Bibliography,* and *An Annotated Bibliography of Ethnography of the Middle East and North Africa* ($6), along with nine teaching modules on various contemporary and historical subjects in Middle Eastern affairs

17.024
Program in Middle Eastern and Islamic Studies
University of Minnesota
Department of Middle Eastern and South
     Asian Studies
Minneapolis, MN 55455
(612) 373-9834 or 5724

Contact(s):
Caesar E. Farah, Director

Undergraduate area studies program established in 1965

• Majors/degrees/certificates offered: B.A. in Arabic, Middle Eastern or Islamic Studies; M.A. in Arabic/Islamic Studies

• Approximate number of faculty teaching area and language courses: 9

• Approximate number of courses available—area: 26; language: 10

• Average number of students per year specializing in area: 30–50

• Countries covered and areas of emphasis: the Middle East and North Africa and other Arab-speaking and/or Islamic countries/areas; emphasis on Arabic language and Arab and Islamic history and culture

• Languages offered: Arabic, Persian and, occasionally, Turkish

• Study abroad available in Tunisia

• Headquarters for the Upper Midwest Middle East Outreach Consortium (covering Minnesota, Western Wisconsin, Northern Iowa, and the Eastern Dakotas); offers wide range of school and community outreach programs and services

17.025
Middle East Studies Program
Southwest Missouri State University
Hill Hall 202-A
Springfield, MO 65802
(417) 836-5927

Contact(s):
David L. Heinlein, Chair, Middle East
Studies Committee

Graduate and undergraduate area studies
program established in 1981
• Majors/degrees/certificates offered:
B.A., B.S. and M.A. in Middle East Studies
• Approximate number of faculty teaching area and language courses: 20
• Approximate number of courses available—area: 24; language: 8
• Average number of students per year specializing in area: 20
• Countries covered and areas of emphasis: all countries of the Middle East and Islam (including North Africa)
• Languages offered: Arabic and Hebrew; on demand: Coptic, Aramaic, Ugaritic, Hittite and Sumerian
• Overseas archaeological and sociological expeditions available
• Exchange affiliation with a university in Saudi Arabia

17.026
Danciger Judaic Studies Program
University of Missouri at Kansas City
5200 Rockhill Road
Kansas City, MO 64110
(816) 276-1633, 1631

Contact(s):
Joseph P. Schultz, Director

Graduate and undergraduate area studies
program established in 1973
• Majors/degrees/certificates offered:
B.A. in Judaic Studies and M.A. in History with a concentration in Judaic Studies
• Approximate number of faculty teaching area and language courses: 6
• Approximate number of courses available—area: 19; language: 4
• Average number of students per year specializing in area: 8
• Areas of emphasis: historical and contemporary Jewish experience
• Language offered: Hebrew
• Provides adult education courses and seminars for the community
• Special fellowships available to Judaic Studies majors

17.027
Program in Near Eastern Studies
Princeton University
110 Jones Hall
Princeton, NJ 08544
(609) 452-4272

Contact(s):
L. Carl Brown, Director

Graduate and undergraduate area studies
program established in 1947
• Majors/degrees/certificates offered:
B.A., M.A. and Ph.D. in Near Eastern Studies or as concentration with degrees in anthropology, history, politics, or sociology; also given by the Woodrow Wilson School of Public and International Affairs (see 6.149)
• Approximate number of faculty teaching area and language courses: 26
• Approximate number of courses available—area: 60; language: 30
• Average number of students per year specializing in area: 40 graduate; 20 undergraduate
• Countries covered and areas of emphasis: all countries in the Near East and North Africa, with emphasis at the undergraduate level on the Ottoman legacy, the Arab World, Hebrew Studies, North Africa

and Iran and, at the graduate level, on the Ancient Near East or Islamic Studies; strong historical orientation

- Languages offered: Arabic, Hebrew, Persian, Turkish, Aramaic and Syriac
- Extensive manuscript collections in Near Eastern languages and books in both Near Eastern and European languages on Islam and the Muslim Near East and North Africa
- Visiting Fellow program makes Princeton resources available to scholars for research and study
- Publishes *Princeton Near East Papers* (approximately 31 in print), focused mainly on economic and political issues; also promotes research and the publication of *Princeton Studies on the Near East*, mainly on historical subjects (published by various presses)
- Offers school outreach services via the Princeton/NYU Joint Center for Near Eastern Studies headquartered at the NYU Hagop Kevorkian Center for Near Eastern Studies (see 17.031)

17.028
Middle East and North Africa Area Studies Program
City University of New York/Brooklyn
  College
4239 Boylan Hall
Bedford Ave. and Ave. H
Brooklyn, NY 11210
(212) 780-5451

Contact(s):
Ming-shui Hung, Coordinator

Undergraduate area studies program
- Majors/degrees/certificates offered: B.A. in Middle East and North Africa Area Studies
- Approximate number of courses available—area: 21; language: 5
- Countries covered and areas of em-

phasis: all countries of the Middle East and North Africa
- Languages offered: Arabic and Hebrew

17.029
Middle East Institute
Columbia University
1114 International Affairs Bldg.
420 West 118th St.
New York, NY 10027
(212) 280-2584

Contact(s):
Jacob C. Hurewitz, Director

Graduate area studies program established in 1954
- Majors/degrees/certificates offered: two-year M.I.A., School of International and Public Affairs (see 6.151), with Certificate in Middle Eastern Studies; M.A. and Ph.D. with Certificate in Middle Eastern Studies
- Approximate number of faculty teaching area and language courses: 33
- Approximate number of courses available—area: 93; language: 43
- Countries covered and areas of emphasis: Middle East and North Africa from Afghanistan to Morocco; requires subregional specialization in the Arab states, Armenia, Israel, Iran or Turkey and Central Asia; particularly strong in history, language, literature and Islamic Studies
- Languages offered: Armenian, Arabic, Persian, Hebrew, Turkish and Uzbek
- Library holdings in Middle East languages exceed 100,000 volumes, including substantial rare books collections in Hebrew, Arabic and Persian; maintains subscriptions to selected Middle Eastern newspapers and periodicals

17.030
Near Eastern Studies
Cornell University
Ithaca, NY 14853
(607) 256-6275

Contact(s):
Urbain DeWinter, Chair
D. S. Powers, Director of Undergraduate
  Studies

Graduate and undergraduate area studies program established in 1965
  • Majors/degrees/certificates offered: B.A., M.A. and Ph.D. in Near Eastern Studies
  • Approximate number of faculty teaching area and language courses: 8
  • Approximate number of courses available—area: 54; language: 18
  • Average number of students per year specializing in area: 9
  • Countries covered and areas of emphasis: all countries of the Near East with emphasis on Arabic language and literature and Jewish Studies, including biblical and Hebrew history and literature, and ancient history
  • Languages offered: Akkadian, Arabic, Aramaic, Turkish, Ugaritic, Hebrew and Yiddish
  • Junior year study in the Near East available

17.031
Hagop Kevorkian Center for Near Eastern Studies
New York University
50 Washington Square South
New York, NY 10012
(212) 598-2697

Contact(s):
Farhad Kazemi, Director

Graduate area studies program established in 1966
  • Majors/degrees/certificates offered: M.A. with concentration in the modern Near East; M.B.A. with Certificate in Near Eastern Studies; Ph.D. jointly in Near Eastern Studies and history, anthropology or political science; M.A. in Near Eastern Studies with concentration in Museum Studies
  • Approximate number of faculty teaching area and language courses: 25
  • Approximate number of courses available—area and language: 75
  • Average number of students per year specializing in area: 40
  • Countries covered and areas of emphasis: North African and Middle Eastern Arab and Islamic countries from Morocco to Afghanistan including Israel; broad-based academic coverage and extensive program of co-curricular activities
  • Languages offered: Arabic, Hebrew, Persian, Turkish and Ancient Semitic languages (Akkadian, Aramaic and Ugaritic)
  • Housed in its own building, the Center contains a library of 20,000 books and periodicals supplementing the University library collection; NYU's Grey Art Gallery, the nearby Metropolitan Museum and other art museums and institutes offer extensive opportunities to study Near Eastern art
  • Cooperative program with Princeton (see below) provides for exchanges of students and faculty and access to library resources
  • Offers summer language programs in Persian and Turkish; additional intensive summer language programs available at other institutions through a consortium in Near Eastern Studies and at the Arabic Program in Tunisia
  • Serves as headquarters for Princeton/ NYU Joint Center for Near Eastern Studies which, among other things, provides school outreach programs and services including a series of teacher "primers" on Middle Eastern subjects and *The Collegiate Middle East*

Resource Guide (see 2.120); conducts summer seminar for New York high school teachers

• Publishes *Studies in Near Eastern Civilization*, a series of original works designed to examine neglected areas of Near Eastern culture, the Kevorkian Series in Near Eastern Art and Civilization, an Occasional Papers series, and the *Center Newsletter* (devoted principally to identifying educational resources for teachers and others)

17.032
Program in Southwest Asian–North African Studies
State University of New York at Binghamton
Binghamton, NY 13901
(607) 798-4738

Contact(s):
Don Peretz, Chair, SWANA Executive
   Committee

Graduate and undergraduate area studies program established in 1966

• Majors/degrees/certificates offered: B.A., M.A. and Ph.D. with Certificates in Southwest Asian (Middle East) and North African Studies

• Approximate number of faculty teaching area and language courses: 18

• Approximate number of courses available—area: 25; language: 15

• Average number of students per year specializing in area: 10–12 graduate; 20–25 undergraduate

• Countries covered and areas of emphasis: Middle East and North Africa, Israel, Iran, Turkey, and Islamic countries of Sub-Saharan Africa

• Languages offered: Arabic, Hebrew, and Persian

• Special Middle East collection with 85,000 volumes, including many in Arabic, Hebrew, Persian and Turkish, and an extensive selection of periodicals and journals

• Junior year abroad programs at Haifa University, Israel

• Faculty exchange with Haifa University

• Assistantships and limited number of dissertation fieldwork fellowships

17.033
Middle East Studies Committee, Council on International Studies
State University of New York at Buffalo
Department of Sociology
Spaulding Quad
Buffalo, NY 14261
(716) 636-3075

Contact(s):
Russell A. Stone, Committee Chair

Graduate and undergraduate area studies program

• Majors/degrees/certificates offered: independently designed majors, B.A., M.A. or M.S. in Middle East Studies

• Approximate number of faculty teaching area and language courses: 6

• Approximate number of courses available—area: 26; language: 14

• Countries covered and areas of emphasis: Near East and North Africa with emphasis on comparative socio-political structures, Islam, and Judaic Studies

• Languages offered: Arabic and Hebrew and, through self-instructional methods, Turkish and Persian

• Study abroad encouraged

17.034
Islamic and Arabian Development Studies Program
Duke University
2114 Campus Drive
Durham, NC 27706
(919) 684-2446

Contact(s):
Ralph Braibanti, Director

Graduate and undergraduate area studies program established in 1977
• Majors/degrees/certificates offered: B.A. in Comparative Area Studies and Ph.D. in departments with Islamic and Arabian Development Studies specialization
• Approximate number of faculty teaching area and language courses: 9
• Approximate number of courses available—area: 15; language: 6
• Average number of students per year specializing in area: 30
• Countries covered and areas of emphasis: all countries of the Islamic world as well as countries with substantial Islamic minorities, e.g. the Philippines, the Soviet Union, India, China, etc.; emphasis on contemporary problems of development
• Languages offered: Arabic, Persian and Urdu-Hindi
• Conducts training program for college teachers and an outreach program which sends lecturers to liberal arts colleges in the southeast U.S.
• Study abroad available at the American University in Cairo

17.035
Middle East and Islamic Studies Program
University of North Carolina at Chapel Hill
544 Hamilton Hall
Chapel Hill, NC 27514
(919) 962-2115

Contact(s):
Herbert L. Bodman, Jr., Director

Graduate and undergraduate area studies program
• Majors/degrees/certificates offered: B.A., M.A. and Ph.D. in discipline with Middle East and Islamic Studies

• Approximate number of faculty teaching area and language courses: 6
• Approximate number of courses available—area: 14; language: 12
• Countries covered and areas of emphasis: Middle East and North Africa with emphasis on Islamic history and civilization; includes Islamic areas of Sub-Saharan Africa
• Languages offered: Arabic, colloquial Egyptian, Hebrew, Akkadian, Hausa and Swahili

17.036
Middle East Studies Program
Ohio State University
308 Dulles Hall
230 West 17th Ave.
Columbus, OH 43210
(614) 422-3980

Contact(s):
Stephen Dale, Director

Undergraduate area studies program
• Majors/degrees/certificates offered: B.A. undergraduate Certificate and graduate concentration; B.A. in International Agriculture with emphasis in Middle East Studies
• Approximate number of faculty teaching area and language courses: 26
• Countries covered and areas of emphasis: all countries of the Middle East and North Africa with emphasis on languages, history and culture
• Languages offered: Arabic, Hebrew, Persian and Turkish
• Library contains approximately 45,000 volumes in Arabic, Hebrew, Persian and Turkish, along with 30,000 titles in English and other European languages on the Middle East; it also subscribes to 580 periodicals and newspapers in these languages; extensive reference collection
• Conducts school and community outreach program

• Overseas study and research encouraged

17.037
Middle East Studies Certificate Program
Portland State University
P.O. Box 751
Portland, OR 97207
(503) 229-3609
Charles M. White, Director, International
   Studies

Graduate and undergraduate area studies program established in 1961
• Majors/degrees/certificates offered: B.A., M.A. and Ph.D. in departments with specialization in Middle East Studies; Certificate in Middle East Studies
• Approximate number of faculty teaching area and language courses: 13
• Approximate number of courses available—area: 19; language: 24
• Countries covered and areas of emphasis: Middle East and North Africa with emphasis on history and the social sciences
• Languages offered: Arabic, Hebrew and Persian
• Conducts outreach programs for schools and community organizations and co-sponsors a summer school offering area courses and intensive study of Middle Eastern languages, including a number that are seldom taught
• Study abroad opportunities available and participation encouraged

17.038
Department of Modern Jewish History and Middle Eastern Studies
Dropsie College for Hebrew and Cognate
   Learning
Philadelphia, PA 17013
(215) 229-0110

Graduate area studies program
• Majors/degrees/certificates offered: M.A. in Judaic Studies and M.A. and Ph.D. in Modern Jewish History and Middle Eastern Studies
• Approximate number of courses available—area: 34; language: 23
• Areas of emphasis: Jews worldwide and in Israel
• Languages offered: Hebrew, Arabic and Persian
• Library contains over 150,000 books and periodicals in Jewish, biblical and Near Eastern Studies, including special collections on Palestine, the Muslim Middle East, Hebrew literature and Sumerology; over 300 foreign journals and periodicals received regularly; extensive microfilm collections from the Soviet Union, Poland, Hungary and the Vatican Hebrew Collection
• Publishes *Jewish Quarterly Review*

17.039
Middle East Center
University of Pennsylvania
838 Williams Hall CU
Philadelphia, PA 19104
(215) 243-6335

Contact(s):
Ahmet Evin, Director

Graduate and undergraduate area studies program established in 1965
• Majors/degrees/certificates offered: B.A., M.A. and Ph.D. in department with specialization in Mid-East Studies coordinated by Center; also conducts joint degree programs with graduate professional schools of business, education, fine arts (city and regional planning), and law (including Program in Law, Islamic Law and Middle East Studies)
• Approximate number of faculty teaching area and language courses: 75

• Approximate number of courses available—area: 130; language: 30

• Countries covered and areas of emphasis: all countries of the Middle East and North Africa; includes specialization in Iranian Studies (see 18.224) and a strong Jewish Studies program

• Languages offered: Arabic, Turkish, Persian, Hebrew; Akkadian, Armenian, Aramaic, Coptic, Egyptian (Middle, Late, Old), Hittite, Old and Middle Iranian, Sumerian, Syriac, Ugaritic, Avestan, and Old Persian

• Library contains over 180,000 volumes on the Middle East and Middle Eastern languages

• Promotes research in the Middle East, participates in principal overseas Middle Eastern research institutes and maintains cooperative educational and scholarly relations with academic institutes in Egypt, Israel, Jordan, Saudi Arabia, Syria and Turkey; includes conducting seminars, conferences, etc., student, faculty and publications exchanges, training programs and other activities

• Conducts outreach and joint programs with nearby institutions including a museum program, teacher training and curriculum development, public information activities and the provision of data, workshops, translation and other services to business

• Publishes *Edebiyat*, papers on Islamic history and a series of country data papers on each of the countries of the Middle East

17.040
Asian Studies Committee
University of Tennessee
% College of Liberal Arts
Knoxville, TN 37996
(615) 974-5406

Contact(s):
Eric J. Gangloff, Chair

• Offers B.A. in Asian Studies with concentration in Middle East Studies (see 13.111)

17.041
Center for Middle Eastern Studies
University of Texas at Austin
Austin, TX 78712
(512) 471-3881

Contact(s):
M. A. Jazayery, Director

Graduate and undergraduate area studies program established in 1960

• Majors/degrees/certificates offered: B.A., M.A. and Ph.D. in departments with specialization in Middle Eastern Studies

• Approximate number of faculty teaching area and language courses: 29

• Approximate number of courses available—area: 70; language: 22

• Average number of students per year specializing in area: 60–75

• Countries covered and areas of emphasis: Middle East and North Africa with broad offerings in most disciplines, including modern as well as archaeological studies; also courses in such specialized areas as architecture, curriculum development, and international business

• Languages offered: Arabic (including Cairo and other colloquial forms), Hebrew (including Biblical and Modern Israeli), Turkish and Persian; computer-assisted instruction in Arabic available

• Library contains extensive Middle East collection with approximately 45,000 volumes in Persian and Arabic and 400 periodicals

• Maintains Middle East Resource Center which houses teaching materials and assists schools and community organizations; headquarters for the Texas Association for Middle Eastern Scholars

• Publishes a series of books focusing

mainly on the modern Middle East (19th and 20th centuries)

17.042
Near Eastern Studies Program
Brigham Young University
Provo, UT 84602
(801) 378-3377/6338

Contact(s):
David C. Montgomery, Coordinator

Undergraduate area studies program
• Majors/degrees/certificates offered: B.A. in Near Eastern Studies; M.A. in Ancient Near Eastern Studies
• Approximate number of faculty teaching area & language courses: 18
• Approximate number of courses available—area: 23; language: 20
• Average number of students per year specializing in area: 30 graduate and undergraduate
• Countries covered and areas of emphasis: from Egypt to India and Soviet Turkistan to the Arabian Peninsula with an emphasis on history, languages and Christian religious studies; covers ancient, medieval and modern Near East
• Languages offered: Arabic, Hebrew, Aramaic, Ugaritic and Akkadian
• Six-month study abroad program available in Jerusalem

17.043
Middle East Center
University of Utah
Salt Lake City, UT 84112
(801) 581-6181

Contact(s):
Khosrow Mostofi, Director
Robert Staab, Outreach Coordinator

Graduate and undergraduate area studies program established in 1960
• Majors/degrees/certificates offered: B.A. in languages (Arabic, Hebrew, Persian and Turkish), M.A. and Ph.D. in Middle East Studies or in discipline with Certificate in Middle East Studies
• Approximate number of faculty teaching area and language courses: 35
• Approximate number of courses available—area: 80; language: 90
• Average number of students per year specializing in area: 30 undergraduate; 60 graduate
• Countries covered and areas of emphasis: Middle East and North African countries; strength in Iranian Studies
• Languages offered: Arabic, Greek, Hebrew, Persian and Turkish; rare Middle East languages on demand (Egyptian, Coptic, Akkadian, Aramaic, Ugaritic, Hittite, Old Turkic, Middle Turkic and Middle Mongolian)
• 100,000-volume library collection of works, periodicals, manuscripts and microfilms in Arabic, Hebrew, Persian, Turkish and major western languages; includes collection of Islamic manuscripts and rare documents
• Conducts intensive summer language programs both on campus and abroad (as part of the Consortium of Western Universities) and offers undergraduate study abroad opportunities through the Center for Arabic Study Abroad (see 8.005); exchange relationships with University of Tunis in Tunisia and the University of Alexandria in Egypt; arranges field study and research abroad for graduate students
• Conducts research, operates archaeological projects, provides development assistance, and participates in faculty exchange and Visiting Scholar programs in a number of Middle Eastern countries
• Advises and conducts workshops and arranges overseas projects for school teachers and students; maintains lending resource library

- Publishes research monographs and a newsletter
- Fellowships available for study at the University of Tunis and for the overseas summer intensive language programs

17.044
Middle East Studies Program
University of Virginia
Department of Oriental Languages
Cabell Hall
Charlottesville, VA 22903
(804) 924-7917

Contact(s):
Mohammad R. Ghanoonparvar, Chair

Graduate and undergraduate area studies program established in 1981
- Majors/degrees/certificates offered: B.A., M.A. and Ph.D. in department with specialization in Middle East Studies
- Approximate number of faculty teaching area and language courses: 16
- Approximate number of courses available—area: 29; language: 26
- Average number of students per year specializing in area: 100
- Countries covered and areas of emphasis: Middle East and North Africa, with emphasis on history and politics, especially of the Persian Gulf area, and religious studies (which includes a study program in the Muslim Shi'ite sect)
- Languages offered: Arabic, Hebrew, Persian and Urdu; Turkish by special arrangement
- Library contains extensive holdings on the Middle East and in Middle Eastern languages, particularly Arabic, Hebrew and Urdu, and a large collection of serials and monographs in Western languages

17.045
Middle East Center
University of Washington
318 Thompson Hall (DR-05)
Seattle, WA 98195
(206) 543-7236

Contact(s):
Jere L. Bachrach, Director
Charlotte Albright, Outreach Coordinator

Graduate and undergraduate area studies program established in 1975
- Majors/degrees/certificates offered: B.A. and M.A. in Near Eastern Languages and Civilizations and M.A. in International Studies with a specialization in Middle East Studies
- Approximate number of faculty teaching area and language courses: 30
- Approximate number of courses available—area: 50; language: 75
- Countries covered and areas of emphasis: Afghanistan, Iran, Iraq, Turkey, Lebanon, Syria, Israel, Jordan, Egypt, Libya, Tunisia, Algeria and Morocco
- Languages offered: Persian, Arabic, Turkish, Hebrew, Uzbek, Turkic and Altaic
- Study abroad made available through the Center for Arabic Studies Abroad (see 8.005)
- Outreach activities through Middle East Resource Center (see 2.083)
- Publishes *Middle East Newsletter*

17.046
Middle East Studies Program
University of Wisconsin at Madison
4121 Humanities Building
Madison, WI 53706
(608) 263-1825

Contact(s):
Kemal H. Karpat, Chair

Graduate and undergraduate area studies program established in 1971
- Majors/degrees/certificates offered: B.A., M.A. and Ph.D. in History, Hebrew and Semitic Studies, South Asian Studies and in other departments with a Middle East concentration
- Approximate number of faculty teaching area and language courses: 18
- Approximate number of courses available—area: 58; language: 44
- Average number of students per year specializing in area: 20
- Countries covered and areas of emphasis: all countries of the Middle East and North Africa
- Languages offered: Arabic, Turkish, Ottoman Turkish, Persian, Hebrew, Hindi-Urdu, Urdu, Aramaic, Syriac and Ugaritic
- Overseas programs in Israel available through Department of Hebrew and Semitic Studies
- Sponsors publication of the *International Journal of Turkish Studies*

17.047
Middle Eastern and North African Studies
University of Wisconsin at Milwaukee
Department of History
Milwaukee, WI 53201
(414) 963-4361 or 5206

Contact(s):
Abbas H. Hamdani, Chair

Undergraduate area studies program established in 1975
- Majors/degrees/certificates offered: departmental B.A. with certificate in Middle Eastern and North African Studies
- Approximate number of faculty teaching area and language courses: 14
- Approximate number of courses available—area: 44; language: 15
- Average number of students per year specializing in area: 10
- Countries covered and areas of emphasis: all countries of the Middle East and North Africa, with emphasis on history, Jewish civilization, the Bible and Islam
- Languages offered: Hebrew, Arabic and Aramaic

Information and Service Organizations

17.048
American-Arab Affairs Council
1730 N St., NW, Suite 411
Washington, DC 20036
(202) 296-6767

Contact(s):
George Amel Naifeh, President

Cultural relations organization
- Provides information and organizes programs and projects on Arab and Islamic culture; publishes the journal *American-Arab Affairs* and a series of special reports

17.049
American Institute of Islamic Studies
P.O. Box 10398
Denver, CO 80210
(303) 936-0108

Contact(s):
Charles Geddes, Director

Research and service organization in Islamic studies
- Promotes and supports the preparation of scholarly studies, research and teaching materials

• Sponsors meetings, exhibitions and other public presentations

• Maintains Muslim Bibliographic Center with an extensive collection of library and bibliographic materials

• Publishes comprehensive bibliographies, guides, and directories for Islamic studies

17.050

Armenian Film Foundation
580 East Thousand Oaks Blvd., Suite 101
Thousand Oaks, CA 91360
(805) 495-0717

Contact(s):
J. Michael Hagopian, Chair

Educational and cultural organization

• Produces and distributes films on subjects related to Armenian culture; assists in the establishment of Armenian film libraries and maintains a film archive; conducts film festivals; awards film scholarships, film grants and internships

17.051

Association of Arab-American University Graduates, Inc.
556 Trapelo Road
Belmont, MA 02178
(617) 484-5483

Contact(s):
Faith Zeadey, Director

Cultural and educational association designed to promote understanding between the American and Arab peoples, established in 1967; membership open to non-Arabs

• Provides information, advice and speakers on Arab-American affairs and educational activities relative thereto

• Publishes the *Arab Studies Quarterly* (see 17.076); an extensive list of books, pamphlets and monographs on Arab-Americans, contemporary Arab affairs and Arab-U.S. relations; *The Arab World: A Handbook* (country-by-country overview of Arab countries and the Palestinians); three bibliographies (The *Arab-Israeli Conflict, Women in the Arab World* and *Education of the Palestinians*) and several films on Palestine and the Palestinians; particular emphasis on the Arab-Israeli conflict and the Palestine issue

17.052

The Association of Muslim Social Scientists
P.O. Box 38
Plainfield, IN 46168
(317) 839-8157

Contact(s):
Talat Sultan, President

Small nonprofit educational association of Muslim scholars and academics established in 1972

• Promotes research and scientific inquiry on current issues in the social sciences and humanities from an Islamic perspective

17.053

Center for Arabic Study Abroad
University of Washington
Department of Near Eastern Languages and
  Literature
229B Denny Hall
Seattle, WA 98195
(206) 543-8982

Contact(s):
Farhat J. Ziadeh, Director

Consortium of 18 large universities

• Offers advanced Arabic language study at the American University in Cairo in 2-month (summer) and 12-month (June–May) programs; open to U.S. students in Near Eastern Studies who have two years of Arabic and pass a proficiency exam; fellowships provided covering travel, tuition and maintenance

17.054
Institute for Palestine Studies
Box 19449
Washington, DC 20036
(202) 745-0868

Contact(s):
Mohamed Rabie, Executive Director

Nonprofit research organization
• Sponsors and conducts research on the Palestinians and the Palestine problem; maintains library, archives and resources; gives awards and publishes the *Journal of Palestine Studies* (see 17.080) and other relevant reports, reprints, monographs and documents

17.055
The Middle East Institute
1761 N St. NW
Washington, DC 20036
(202) 785-1141

Contact(s):
Steven R. Dorr, Director of Programs and Secretary

Nonprofit cultural and educational organization concerned with Middle Eastern affairs
• Provides information and answers telephone, written, and personal inquiries on the Middle East and serves as clearinghouse for information on women in the Middle East; maintains library of 15,000 volumes and 400 periodicals, principally in Western languages, though there is a 1,500-volume collection of major works in Arabic; sponsors public meetings, conferences, symposia, lectures and cultural events
• Offers courses in Arabic, Hebrew, Farsi,

and Turkish, as well as in Middle East culture and international political issues
• Publishes a newsletter reporting on activities in Middle East Studies, *The Middle East Journal* (see 17.086) and other books and materials on contemporary Middle Eastern issues

17.056
Middle East Resource Center
1322 18th St. NW
Washington, DC 20036
(202) 822-8462

Contact(s):
Janice Murphy, Coordinator

Information resource organization on the Arab-Israeli conflict and the status of the Palestinians
• Provides information to public officials and others, arranges meetings between U.S. policymakers and Palestinian, Israeli and American leaders concerned with the Palestine question, holds news conferences and issues press releases
• Publishes newsletter, *Palestine/Israel Bulletin*

17.057
Middle East Studies Association
University of Arizona
Department of Oriental Studies
Tucson, AZ 85721
(602) 621-5850

Contact(s):
Michael E. Bonine, Executive Secretary

Professional education association designed to promote high standards of scholarship and instruction relative to the Middle East
• Promotes the study and evaluation of research and educational materials on the Middle East

• Administers travel/lecture grants for scholars from the Middle East

• Publishes a quarterly *Bulletin*, the quarterly *International Journal of Middle East Studies* (see 17.078) and reports resulting from its materials evaluation

• Holds an annual conference

17.058

National Association of Arab Americans
1825 Connecticut Ave. NW, Suite 211
Washington, DC 20009
(202) 797-7757

Contact(s):
Ronald W. Cathell, Communications
   Director

Association of Americans of Arab ancestry designed to represent Arab-American views on U.S. relations with the Arab world

• Provides information and conducts seminars on the Middle East for academics and educators; publishes newsletters on U.S.-Middle East political and economic relations and is undertaking a demographic survey of Arab Americans

17.059

National Association for Armenian Studies and Research
175 Mt. Auburn St.
Cambridge, MA 02138
(617) 876-7630

Contact(s):
Manoog S. Young, Board Chairman

Educational and cultural organization

• Promotes the study of Armenian language, culture and history through support of academic programs at U.S. universities, the offering of research grants and fellowships, and support for publications and conferences and scholar-in-residence programs

• Maintains Armenian information center and a research and reference library and will respond to inquiries about Armenian Studies

• Makes English-language books on Armenia available through the Armenian Book Clearinghouse and publishes books through the American Heritage Press; also publishes a newsletter and *Journal of Armenian Studies*

• Sponsors conferences, exhibits and other forms of public education

Sources of Grants and Awards

17.060

Social Science Research Council
Fellowships for International Research: Near
   and Middle East
605 Third Ave.
New York, NY 10158
(212) 557-9500

• Awards substantial fellowships for doctoral dissertation research in the social sciences or the humanities for the area including North Africa, the Middle East, Turkey, Iran and Afghanistan; research projects must

be concerned with the time period since the beginning of Islam; all full time students enrolled in doctoral programs in the U.S. or Canada and citizens and permanent residents of the U.S. and Canada enrolled as full time students in doctoral programs abroad are eligible to apply; award recipients must expect to spend at least nine months of research in one or more countries of the area

• Awards substantial grants to citizens and permanent residents of the U.S. or Canada whose competence for research in the area has been demonstrated by their previous work and who intend to make continuing contributions to the field; preference will be given to scholars without access to other major research support and to projects or regions on which insufficient research has been done; the area is defined to include North Africa, the Middle East, Turkey, Iran and Afghanistan; research projects must be concerned with the period since the beginning of Islam

17.061
Society for Armenian Studies
Six Divinity Ave., Room 103
Cambridge, MA 02138

Contact(s):
Kevork B. Bardakjian, Chair

Scholarly association
  • Promotes research on Armenian history and culture and sponsors conferences; publishes an annual bibliography of Armenian Studies and *Journal of the Society for Armenian Studies*

Guides, Sourcebooks and Directories

17.063
Book World Directory of the Arab Countries, Turkey, and Iran
Anthony Rudkin and Irene Butcher, Editors
Gale Research Co.
Book Tower
Detroit, MI 48226
1981; hardbound; 143 pages; $98

  • Lists and describes (country by country) periodicals, libraries, booksellers and commercial and institutional publishers in 20 Middle Eastern nations

17.064
A Concise History of the Middle East
Arthur Goldschmidt, Jr.
Westview Press
5500 Central Ave.
Boulder, CO 80301
1983; revised edition; 450 pages;
  hardbound, $30; paperbound, $11.95

  • Readable, up-to-date basic text

17.065
Graduate and Undergraduate Programs and Courses in Middle East Studies in the United States, Canada, and Abroad
Karen Segar, Editor
Middle East Studies Association of North
  America, Inc.
Department of Oriental Studies
University of Arizona
Tucson, AZ 85721
1982; paperbound; 193 pages; $10

  • Lists and provides substantial information on 210 institutions in the U.S. and abroad which have degree programs or offer courses in Middle East Studies; appendices list institutions by state (U.S.), province (Canada), and country (other overseas institutions) and by faculty and staff alphabetically

17.066
International and Regional Politics in the Middle East and North Africa
Ann Schulz, Editor
Gale Research Co.
Book Tower
Detroit, MI 48226
1977; hardbound; $40

• Bibliographic information about works on the colonial experience, Arab state politics, foreign policies of Middle Eastern States and related subjects

17.067
Middle East and North Africa
Europa Publications, Ltd.
London, England
annual; hardbound; 985 pages; $105

Available from Gale Research Co., Book Tower, Detroit, MI 48226
• Very comprehensive yearbook, survey and compilation of data, statistics and directory-type information
• Covers international organizations active in the Middle East and North Africa, including the UN and other political, cultural, educational and economic development organizations
• For each country entry there is an extensive survey of historical and cultural background and then a generous compilation of data, statistics, lists of names and descriptive materials in the following areas: economics, principal characteristics, social structure, government offices and officers, judicial system, media, publishers, financial institutions, trade and industrial entities, transportation, tourism, atomic energy, defense, and education

17.068
The Middle East Political Dictionary
Lawrence Ziring
ABC-Clio, Inc.
Riviera Campus
2040 Alameda Padre Serra
Box 4397
Santa Barbara, CA 93103
1984; 452 pages; hardbound, $37.50;
  paperbound, $15

• Provides definitions and commentary on the significance of terms, concepts, institutions and events central to the politics and economics of the Middle East; arranged topically and sequenced parallel to most related texts under such headings as historical perspective, political and cultural ideology, government institutions, political parties, etc.; indexed

17.069
Oman and Southeastern Arabia: A Bibliographic Survey
Michael Owen Shannon
G. K. Hall & Co.
70 Lincoln St.
Boston, MA 02111
1978; hardbound; 165 pages; $21

• Surveys all Western literature on Oman and Southeastern Arabia from prehistory through the late 1970s; entries on over 1,000 books, articles and reports covering politics and society, geology, geography, maritime affairs, international law and government; selected annotations

17.070
The Persian Gulf States: A General Survey
Alvin J. Cottrell, General Editor
The Johns Hopkins University Press
Baltimore, MD 21218
1981; hardbound; 695 pages; $37.50

• Comprehensive reference book on the Persian Gulf area covering history, economic development, religions, language, literature, art and social structure; includes appendices providing extensive geographic, economic, natural resources and other data; indexed

17.071
Scholars' Guide to Washington, D.C.:
Middle Eastern Studies
Steven R. Dorr
Smithsonian Institution Press
Washington, DC 20560
1982; 564 pages; paperbound, $15;
    hardbound, $29.95

• Comprehensive listing and description of resources in the Washington area available to researchers and others interested in the Middle East; divided into two sections: collections (libraries, archives, museums, etc., music and sound, maps, films, and data banks) and organizations (research centers and information offices, academic programs, U.S. government agencies, embassies and international organizations, professional associations, exchange and technical assistance organizations, religious organizations, and publications/media); available resources described in some detail with clear indication of how and from whom to obtain access; appendices include libraries listed by size of holdings, bookstores, housing, transport and other services and a bibliography; indexed by name of resource, personal papers collections, and library subject strength; covers Egypt, the Sudan, the Arab states of the Middle East, Iran, Israel, Turkey and Cyprus

17.072
The Study of the Middle East: Research and Scholarship in the Humanities and Social Sciences
Leonard Binder, Editor
John Wiley & Sons, Inc.
605 Third Ave.
New York, NY 10016
1976; hardbound; 648 pages; $43.50

• Discusses the processes and reviews the state of research and scholarship on the Middle East in 11 chapters, each by a different scholar; covers religion, history, art, linguistics and the other humanities and social science disciplines

17.073
A Survey of Materials for the Study of the Uncommonly Taught Languages: Languages of the Middle East & North Africa
Dora E. Johnson et al.
Center for Applied Linguistics
3520 Prospect St. NW
Washington, DC 20007
1976; paperbound; 42 pages; $7.95

Exclusively distributed by Harcourt Brace Jovanovich, Inc., 757 Third Ave., New York, NY 10017; Attn: Nancy McCloughan
• One of a series of bibliographies covering all the modern languages except Standard English, German, Italian, Russian and Spanish; designed for use by the adult learner whose native language is English; listed under the headings: teaching materials, readers, grammars and dictionaries; includes books currently in print where feasible, older titles where not; citations appear under the following language groups: Turkic, Iranian, Semitic and Berber

Periodicals

17.074
Al-'Arabiyya
Issa J. Boullata, Editor
American Association of Teachers of Arabic
University of Chicago, Oriental Institute
1155 East 58th St.
Chicago, IL 60637
semiannual journal; approx. 160 pages;
     individuals, $10 per year ($3 for students);
     institutions, $15 per year

• Articles on Arabic language and linguistics and on the literatures of Arabic-
speaking countries; book reviews

17.075
Arab Book World
Inter-Crescent Publishing Co., Inc.
P.O. Box 31413
Dallas, TX 75231
quarterly newsletter; approx. 12 pages; $48
     per year

• Reviews books published in the U.S.
and other countries on the Arab World; especially designed for librarians

17.076
Arab Studies Quarterly
Association of Arab-American University
     Graduates
556 Trapelo Road
Belmont, MA 02178
quarterly journal; approx. 60 pages;
     individuals, $16 per year; institutions, $35
     per year

• Critical articles on Arab society, politics, economy and history from Arab perspectives

17.077
Aramco World Magazine
Paul F. Hoye, Editor
Aramco
1345 Ave. of the Americas
New York, NY 10019
bimonthly magazine; 32 pages

Distributed without charge to a limited number of readers with an interest in Aramco,
the oil industry, or the history, culture, geography and economy of the Middle East
• Attractively illustrated articles on cultural, social and economic aspects of life in
Arab Islamic countries

17.078
International Journal of Middle East Studies
Afaf Lutfi Al-Sayyid-Marsot, Editor
Middle East Studies Association of North
     America, Inc. and Cambridge University
     Press
32 East 57th St.
New York, NY 10022
quarterly journal; 128 pages; $75 per year
     plus postage

Members of the Middle East Studies Association of North America, Inc. (see 17.057) receive the journal free; membership fee, $45
• Includes scholarly articles and essays
on aspects of Middle Eastern social, political
and cultural affairs both contemporary and
historical; book reviews

17.079
Jewish Social Studies
Toby B. Gittelle, Editor
Conference on Jewish Social Studies
2112 Broadway
New York, NY 10023
quarterly journal; approx. 90 pages; $30 per
    year

    • Contains articles and essays on contemporary and historical aspects of Jewish life worldwide

17.080
Journal of Palestine Studies
Institute for Palestine Studies
Box 19449
Washington, DC 20036
quarterly journal; approx. 240 pages; $24
    per year

    • Contains articles, reports, and commentary on historical and contemporary Palestine with emphasis on current Palestinian affairs and the Arab-Israeli conflict from a Palestinian perspective

17.081
Journal of South Asian and Middle Eastern Studies
Hafeez Malik, Editor
Pakistan American Foundation
138 Tolentine Hall
Villanova University
Villanova, PA 19085
quarterly journal; approx. 96 pages; $15 per
    year; $18 per year, foreign

    • Articles on the modern Islamic and non-Islamic societies of South Asia, the Middle East and North Africa with a current affairs as well as a scholarly orientation

17.082
Merip Reports
Joe Stork, Editor
Middle East Research and Information
    Project, Inc.
Box 43445
Washington, DC 20010
9 times a year; magazine; individuals, $18
    per year; institutions, $30 per year

    • Contains substantive articles on political, economic and social developments in the Middle East and in U.S.-Middle East relationships from Third World perspective; book and film reviews

17.083
The Middle East
Nadia Hijab, Editor in chief
IC Publications Ltd.
P.O. Box 261
Carlton House
69 Great Queen St.
London WC2B 5BN
England
monthly magazine; 98 pages; $60 per year

Available from IC Publications Ltd., 122 East 42d St., Room 1121, New York, NY 10017
    • Magazine in a newsweekly format; includes current news reporting and in-depth analyses of Middle Eastern political and economic affairs, especially as they relate to Western countries

17.084
The Middle East Annual: Issues and Events
David H. Partington, Editor
G. K. Hall & Co.
70 Lincoln St.
Boston, MA 02111
annual since 1981; hardbound; 250–275
    pages; $47

• Reviews recent history and surveys current developments in the Middle East and discusses their significance relative to U.S. interests; each volume includes an annotated bibliography of monograph and serial literature published during the year plus a day-by-day chronicle of events and issues

17.085
Middle East International
Michael Wall, Editor
Middle East International
21 Collingham Rd.
London SW5 0N0, England
bimonthly magazine; approx. 25 pages; $120 per year ($60 for six months)

Available from Box 53365, Temple Heights Station, Washington, DC 20005
• Contains reports and analyses of current events in the Middle East with particular emphasis on the Arab-Israeli conflict

17.086
The Middle East Journal
Richard B. Parker, Editor
Middle East Institute
1761 N St. NW
Washington, DC 20036
quarterly journal; 200 pages; $19 per year

• Includes analytical and interpretive articles on the Middle East/North African region and large numbers of critical and analyt-ical book reviews of current and scholarly interest; contains chronologies of recent Middle Eastern events, bibliographies and other information of interest to the Middle East Studies community; takes advertising

17.087
Muslim World
Willem A. Bijefeld, Wadi' Z. Haddad and
    Yvonne Y. Haddad, Editors
Duncan Black Macdonald Center
Hartford Seminary
77 Sherman St.
Hartford, CT 06105
quarterly journal; individuals, $12;
    institutions, $15

• Scholarly articles and essays on Islam in Muslim countries worldwide and on Christian-Muslim relationships; notes, book reviews and surveys of periodicals

17.088
Orientations
Pacific Magazines, Ltd.
13th Floor, 200 Lockhart Rd.
Hong Kong
monthly magazine; approx. 75 pages; $40 per year

• Illustrated articles on historic and contemporary Asian (including Near Eastern) art; includes calendar of current exhibitions and events and book reviews

Publishers

17.089
G. K. Hall & Co.
70 Lincoln St.
Boston, MA 02111
(617) 423-3990

Commercial reference book publisher
• Publishes a Middle East Studies series of reference books; includes *Oman and Southeastern Arabia: A Bibliographic Survey* (see 17.069), *Index Libycus: A Cumulative*

Index to Bibliography of Libya, 1915–1975 (see 18.333), *Arabic Materials in English Translation*, the journal *The Middle East Annual* (see 17.084), and *The Contemporary Middle East, 1948–1973: A Selected Bibliography*

17.090
International Book Centre
P.O. Box 295
Troy, MI 48099
(313) 879-8436

Publisher and distributor of books on Arabic subjects; sole U.S. distributor of books of the Librairie du Liban (Lebanese publisher)
• Extensive list of books on Arab and Middle Eastern history and culture, including books on Islamic Studies, fiction, audiovisual materials, language reference books and learning materials, teaching aids, children's stories and classical Western literature translated into Arabic

17.091
Syracuse University Press
1600 Jamesville Ave.
Syracuse, NY 13210
(315) 423-2596

University publishing house
• Publishes books on the Middle East under series title Contemporary Issues in the Middle East and distributes publications (on Middle Eastern subjects) of the American University in Beirut (AUB), Lebanon, and the Shiloah Center for Middle Eastern and African Studies (Tel-Aviv University), including *A Selected and Annotated Bibliography of Economic Literature in the Arab Countries of the Middle East, 1938–1965*, two volumes

17.092
Three Continents Press, Inc.
1346 Connecticut Ave. NW, Suite 224
Washington, DC 20036
(202) 457-0288 or 387-5809

Commercial publishing house
• Publishes books by and about contemporary Middle Eastern writers and writing along with a few historical, reference and sociological titles; includes *A Bibliography of the Architecture, Arts and Crafts of Islam*

18
Academic Programs and Selected Resources for Country Studies

Afghanistan

Organizations

18.001
Afghanistan Studies Association
University of Nebraska
Center for Afghan Studies
A & S Hall 238
Omaha, NE 68182
(402) 554-2376

Contact(s):
Thomas E. Gouttierre, Secretary of Executive Committee

Scholarly association
• Promotes research and teaching on Afghanistan; maintains library and list of scholars working in Afghanistan Studies; publishes newsletter

18.002
Center for Afghanistan Studies
University of Nebraska/Omaha
A & S Hall 238
Omaha, NE 68182
(402) 554-2376

Contact(s):
Thomas E. Gouttierre, Director

• Conducts research and develops teaching materials for Afghanistan history and civilization

Publications

18.003
Afghanistan: Key to a Continent
John C. Griffiths
Westview Press
5500 Central Ave.
Boulder, CO 80301
1980; hardbound; 200 pages; $23.50

• Concise introduction both for the student and the general reader to contemporary Afghanistan; examines the history, geography, politics, international relations, economic development, culture and social aspects of the country; also explores the forces that have shaped modern Afghanistan and discusses the Soviet invasion and what the future might hold

18.004
Annotated Bibliography of Afghanistan
Jamil M. Hanifi, Editor
Human Relations Area Files Press
2015 Yale Station
New Haven, CT 06520
1982; paperbound; 545 pages; $45

- Revision and update of an earlier bibliography by Donald N. Wilber

18.005
A Bibliography of Afghanistan
K. S. McLachlan and W. Whittaker
Westview Press
5500 Central Ave.
Boulder, CO 80301
1983; hardbound; 626 pages; $45

- Working bibliography for social scien-

tists and historians covering the history, geography, anthropology and sociology of Afghanistan

18.006
Revolutionary Afghanistan
Beverly Male
St. Martin's Press
175 Fifth Ave.
New York, NY 10010
1982; hardbound; 226 pages; $27.50

- Review of developments in Afghanistan since the communist government came to power

The following are standard resources available on Afghanistan
INFORMATION SOURCES
- *Background Notes:* (see 2.188)
- *Country Study/Area Handbook.* . . . (see 2.189)
- *Historical Dictionary of.* . . . (see 2.193)

Albania

Publications

18.008
Albania and the Albanians
Ramadan Marmullaku; translated by Margot and Bosko Milosavljevic
ShoeString Press
995 Sherman Ave.
Box 4327
Hamden, CT 06514
1975; hardbound; 178 pages; $17.50

- Discusses historical background of

contemporary Albania and predominant characteristics of Albanian culture and society

The following are standard resources available on Albania
INFORMATION SOURCES
- *Background Notes:* (see 2.188)
- *Country Study/Area Handbook.* . . . (see 2.189)

Algeria

The following are standard resources available on Algeria

INFORMATION SOURCES
- *Background Notes:* (see 2.188)
- *Country Study/Area Handbook. . . .* (see 2.189)
- *Historical Dictionary of. . . .* (see 2.193)
- *World Bibliographical Series. . . .* (see 2.198)

TRAVELER RESOURCES
- *Nagel's Encyclopedia-Guide to. . . .* (see 2.195)

LANGUAGE LEARNING RESOURCES
For the "International" Languages (Arabic, French, German and Spanish) see listings under Chapter IX *Foreign Language Teaching and Learning*

Angola

Publications

18.009
Angola: Five Centuries of Conflict
Lawrence Henderson
Cornell University Press
124 Roberts Place
Ithaca, NY 14850
1979; hardbound; 256 pages; $19.50

- Examines the historical and contem-

porary forces which are shaping current conditions in Angola

The following are standard resources available on Angola

INFORMATION SOURCES
- *Background Notes:* (see 2.188)
- *Country Study/Area Handbook. . . .* (see 2.189)
- *Historical Dictionary of. . . .* (see 2.193)

Argentina

Organizations

18.010
Embassy of the Argentine Republic
1600 New Hampshire Ave. NW
Washington, DC 20009
(202) 387-0705

- Answers telephone and written inquiries about Argentina regarding educational matters
- Recommends films and audiovisual materials

- Welcomes inquiries from any interested individual or institution
- Provides printed information about Argentina

The following are standard resources available on Argentina

INFORMATION SOURCES
- *Background Notes:* (see 2.188)
- *Country Study/Area Handbook.* . . . (see 2.189)
- *Historical Dictionary of.* . . . (see 2.193)
- *Image of.* . . . (see 2.194)

TRAVELER RESOURCES
- *Culturegram:* (see 2.191)

LANGUAGE LEARNING RESOURCES

For the "International" Languages (Arabic, French, German and Spanish) see listings under Chapter IX *Foreign Language Teaching and Learning*

Fulbright Grants and ITT Fellowships for graduate study in Argentina normally available (see 7.041)

Australia

Organizations

18.011
Australian Information Service
Information Office
Embassy of Australia
1601 Massachusetts Ave. NW
Washington, DC 20036-2273
(202) 797-3000
or
Consulates General: New York, San
   Francisco

Contact(s):
Information Counselor

- Offers extensive information about Australia, including *Australia Handbook* (see 18.013), a series of fact sheets on specific aspects of Australian social, economic and cultural life, a series of reference papers providing a more detailed description of major

sectors such as foreign policy, education and minerals, and a bi-weekly *Australia News* and *Business News from Australia*

18.012
National Science Foundation
United States-Australia Cooperative Science
   Program
Division of International Programs
Washington, DC 20550
(202) 357-9558

Contact(s):
Alan Milsap, Program Manager

- Funds programs involving cooperative research, seminars and workshops and short-term visits between the U.S. and Australia

Publications

18.013
Australia Handbook
Australian Information Service
P.O. Box 12 Canberra
Australia 2600
1979; paperbound; 157 pages; free

Available from Information Office, Embassy of Australia, 1601 Massachusetts Ave. NW, Washington, DC 20036
 • Attractive description of Australian life covering the government, economy, industry, trade, minerals, education, culture, etc.; includes maps, measurement conversions and economic and financial statistics

18.014
Australian Outlook
Ian Clark, Editor
Australian Institute of International Affairs
Box E181, QVT, P.O., Canberra
ACT 2600, Australia
quarterly journal; approx. 60 pages; $25 per
    year

 • Contains substantive articles on Australian international, political and economic affairs

18.015
Interact: Australia/U.S.
George Renwick
Intercultural Press, Inc.
Box 768
Yarmouth, ME 04096
1981; paperbound; 60 pages; $10

 • Analyzes how Americans and Australians do things differently and how these differences affect working relationships between them; covers such subjects as communication styles, family relationships, sex roles, and attitudes toward work, achievement, authority, decision-making, negotiations, cooperation and competition

18.016
The Story of Australia
A.G.L. Shaw
Faber and Faber, Inc.
39 Thompson St.
Winchester, MA 01890
1983; 5th ed., paperbound; 336 pages; $6.95

 • Thorough basic survey of Australian history and society up to the present time; index; suggestions for further reading

The following are standard resources available on Australia
INFORMATION SOURCES
 • *Background Notes:* (see 2.188)
 • *Country Study/Area Handbook.* . . . (see 2.189)
TRAVELER RESOURCES
 • *Culturegram:* (see 2.191)
 • *Fodor's Guide to.* . . . (see 2.192)
 • . . . . .: *A Travel Survival Kit* (see 2.196)
Fulbright Grants and ITT Fellowships for graduate study in Australia normally available (see 7.041)

Austria

Organizations

18.017
Austrian Press and Information Service
31 East 69th St.
New York, NY 10021
(212) 535-4120

• Provides a wide variety of informational literature about Austria including *Austria: Facts and Figures* and surveys of the Austrian economy, political system, labor code, social security, etc.
• Publishes monthly magazine *Austrian Information* with news from and articles on Austria (subscription free)
• Gives specific information on Austria or advises how to find it

18.018
Austrian Institute
11 East 52nd St.
New York, NY 10022
(212) 759-5165

Contact(s):
Peter Marboe, Director

Austrian government agency for cultural affairs under the direction of the Austrian Federal Ministry of Foreign Affairs
• Advises and provides information on any Austria-related subject
• Publishes and distributes free printed material on Austria and offers audiovisual materials about Austria to schools and universities free of charge
• Houses reference library on Austrian history, arts, music and literature
• Provides nine-month grants for teachers and students with good command of the language to pursue study and research in German (age: 20–35)

Publications

18.019
Austria: Facts and Figures
Austrian Federal Chancellery
Federal Press Service
A-1014 Vienna
Ballhausplatz 2, Austria
1979; paperbound; 238 pages

Available to institutions with a substantive interest in Austria from the Austrian Press and Information Service, 31 East 69th St., New York, NY 10021, the Austrian Embassy (2343

Massachusetts Ave. NW, Washington, D.C. 20008), and Austrian Consulates General in Chicago and Los Angeles
• Thorough, illustrated description of basic aspects of Austrian life and society with ample factual data; covers history, government and politics, the economy, social services, sporting scene, education, science and research, culture and the media

The following are standard resources available on Austria

INFORMATION SOURCES
- *Background Notes:* (see 2.188)
- *Country Study/Area Handbook.* . . . (see 2.189)

TRAVELER RESOURCES
- *Culturegram:* (see 2.191)
- *Fodor's Guide to.* . . . (see 2.192)
- *Nagel's Encyclopedia Guide to.* . . . *(see 2.195)*

LANGUAGE LEARNING RESOURCES
For the "International" Languages (Arabic, French, German and Spanish) see listings under Chapter IX *Foreign Language Teaching and Learning*
Fulbright Grants and ITT Fellowships for graduate study in Austria normally available along with several Austrian government grants (see 7.041)

Bahamas

18.020
Embassy of the Commonwealth of the Bahamas
600 New Hampshire Ave. NW, Suite 865
Washington, DC 20037
(202) 338-3940
CONSULATE GENERAL: Miami

- Answers telephone and written inquiries about the Bahamas regarding educational matters
- Recommends educational and teaching materials
- Welcomes inquiries from individuals and educational institutions

- Provides printed information about the Bahamas in general
- Recommends these other sources of information: the Bahamas Consulate, 767 Third Ave., 9th Floor, New York 10017, the Consulate General, and the Bahamas Tourist Office, 30 Rockefeller Plaza, New York, NY 10020

The following are standard resources available on the Bahamas:
INFORMATION SOURCES
- *Background Notes* (see 2.188)

Bangladesh

The following are standard resources available on Bangladesh
INFORMATION SOURCES
- *Background Notes:* (see 2.188)

- *Country Study/Area Handbook.* . . . (see 2.189)
- *World Bibliographical Series.* . . . (see 2.198)

Barbados

The following are standard resources available on Barbados

INFORMATION SOURCES
- *Background Notes:* (see 2.188)
- *Image of. . . .* (see 2.194)

Belgium

Organizations

18.021
Belgian American Educational
Foundation, Inc.
195 Church St.
New Haven, CT 06510
(203) 777-5765

Contact(s):
Emile L. Boulpaep, President

Nonprofit educational organization
- Provides generous fellowships for advanced graduate study for 6–10 months at a Belgian university in any discipline

18.022
Consulate General of Belgium
50 Rockefeller Plaza
New York, NY 10020
(212) 586-5110

- Answers telephone and written inquiries about Belgium including educational matters
- Provides audiovisual materials

- Provides printed information about education in Belgium and about Belgium in general
- Recommends these other sources of information: Belgian National Tourist Office, 745 Fifth Ave., New York, NY 10151

The following are standard resources available on Belgium
INFORMATION SOURCES
- *Background Notes:* (see 2.188)
- *Country Study/Area Handbook. . . .* (see 2.189)
TRAVELER RESOURCES
- *Culturegram:* (see 2.191)
- *Update:* (see 2.197)
- *Kummerly & Frey Map of. . . .* (see 1.127)
LANGUAGE LEARNING RESOURCES
For the "International" Languages (Arabic, French, German and Spanish) see listings under Chapter IX *Foreign Language Teaching and Learning*
Fulbright Grants and ITT Fellowships for graduate study in Belgium normally available (see 7.041)

Belize

Publications

The following are standard resources available on Belize
INFORMATION SOURCES
- *Background Notes:* (see 2.188)

- *World Bibliographical Series.* . . . (see 2.198)

TRAVELER RESOURCES
- *Fodor's Guide to.* . . . (see 2.192)

Benin

Organizations

18.023
Embassy of the People's Republic of Benin
2737 Cathedral Ave. NW
Washington, DC 20008
(202) 232-6656

- Provides mimeographed information on

Benin, the government, history and aspects of the country, including travel and tourism

The following are standard resources available on Benin
INFORMATION SOURCES
- *Background Notes:* (see 2.188)
- *Historical Dictionary of.* . . . (see 2.193)

Bhutan

Publications

18.024
The Politics of Bhutan
Leo E. Rose
Cornell University Press
124 Roberts Place
Ithaca, NY 14850
1977; hardbound; 305 pages; $25

- Analysis of the contemporary political situation in Bhutan and the country's relationship to India

The following are standard resources available on Bhutan

INFORMATION SOURCES
- *Background Notes:* (see 2.188)

- *Country Study/Area Handbook.* . . . (see 2.189)

Bolivia

The following are standard resources available on Bolivia

INFORMATION SOURCES
- *Background Notes:* (see 2.188)
- *Country Study/Area Handbook.* . . . (see 2.189)
- *Historical Dictionary of.* . . (see 2.193)
- *Image of.* . . . (see 2.194)

TRAVELER RESOURCES
- *Culturegram:* (see 2.191)
- *Nagel's Encyclopedia Guide to.* . . . (see 2.195)

LANGUAGE LEARNING RESOURCES
For the "International" Languages (Arabic, French, German and Spanish) see listings under Chapter IX *Foreign Language Teaching and Learning*

Botswana

Organizations

18.025
Embassy of the Republic of Botswana
4301 Connecticut Ave. NW, Suite 404
Washington, DC 20008
(202) 244-4990

- Answers phone and written inquiries about Botswana
- Distributes carefully prepared travel and tourist literature, including tourist maps and the magazine *Botswana* (see 18.026)

Publications

18.026
Botswana
Lesiba Mamashela, Editor
Botswana Department of Information and
  Broadcasting
Private Bag 0600
Gaborone, Botswana
semiannual magazine; 69 pages; P2.00 (or
  equivalent in foreign currency)

Available from the Embassy of Botswana, 4301 Connecticut Ave. NW, Washington, DC 20008, or from the Botswana Mission to the UN, 866 Second Ave., New York, NY 10017
- Attractively presented articles on the life, culture and economy of Botswana

18.027
Botswana: An African Growth Economy
Penelope Hartland-Thunberg
Westview Press, Inc.
5500 Central Ave.
Boulder, CO 80301
1978; hardbound; 151 pages; $23.50

- Examines current affairs in Botswana

with particular attention to economic development

The following are standard resources available on Botswana
INFORMATION SOURCES
- *Background Notes:* (see 2.188)
- *Historical Dictionary of. . . .* (see 2.193)

Brazil

Area Study and Research Programs

18.028
Center of Brazilian Studies
The Johns Hopkins University
School of Advanced International Studies
1740 Massachusetts Ave. NW
Washington, DC 20036
(202) 785-6832

Contact(s):
Riordan Roett, Director
Ray Kennedy, Program Associate

Graduate area studies program established in 1977
- Majors/degrees/certificates offered: part of the SAIS program in Latin American Studies (see 16.024)
- Develops and offers courses on Brazilian topics, conducts public conferences and seminars, and offers internships in Brazil for U.S. students
- Publishes Occasional Papers series, conference reports, and other materials including *Infobrazil* (see 18.034)

Organizations

18.029
Embassy of Brazil
3006 Massachusetts Ave. NW
Washington, DC 20008
(202) 797-0100
CONSULATES GENERAL: Chicago, Los Angeles, New Orleans, New York

- Answers telephone and written inquiries about Brazil including educational matters

- Provides audiovisual and educational or teaching materials and recommends performers and exhibits
- Welcomes inquiries from any interested individual or institution
- Provides printed information on Brazil in general and on education in Brazil
- Offers Brazilian Government Scholarship for graduate study in Brazil involving short-term research, 10-month internships and work toward an M.A. or Ph.D. at a Brazilian institution; includes travel and a stipend

18.030
Vanderbilt University Press
2505 (Rear) West End Ave.
Nashville, TN 37203
(615) 322-3585

University publishing house
• Publishes a number of books on contemporary Brazil, including two on the grammar of Brazilian Portuguese

Publications

18.031
The Brasilians
Edilberto Mendes, Editor
Brazilian Promotion Center
37 West 46th St.
New York, NY 10036
monthly tabloid newspaper; 24 pages; $.50

• News (about Brazil and Brazilians in the U.S.) of interest both to Brazilians and to Americans concerned with Brazil; covers general and political news, business, travel and tourism, culture and fashion; includes book reviews; also published in Portuguese (but quite different in content)

18.032
Historical Dictionary of Brazil
Robert M. Levine
Scarecrow Press, Inc.
52 Liberty St.
Metuchen, NJ 08840
1979; hardbound; 309 pages; $14.50

• Handy starting point for finding information about the history, people, culture, economy, politics and daily life of Brazil; items arranged alphabetically in dictionary format

18.033
A History of Brazil
E. Bradford Burns
Columbia University Press
136 South Broadway
Irvington, NY 10533
1980; 500 pages; hardbound, $35; paperbound, $12.50

• Covers all major aspects of Brazilian society including contemporary economic developments

18.034
Infobrazil
Center of Brazilian Studies
School of Advanced International Studies
The Johns Hopkins University
1740 Massachusetts Ave. NW
Washington, DC 20036
5 issues per year; newsletter; 8 pages; $25
　per year

• Reports on current Brazilian political, economic and business affairs

18.035
Luso-Brazilian Review
Mary L. Daniel and Thomas E. Skidmore,
　Editors
Ibero-American Studies
1470 Van Hise Hall
University of Wisconsin
Madison, WI 53706
semiannual journal; approx. 180 pages;
　libraries and institutions, $30 per year;
　individuals, $15

• Scholarly articles in Portuguese and English on Brazilian society, politics, economics and culture; book reviews

The following companies import and sell books in the Portuguese language:

18.036
Imported Books
P.O. Box 4414
Dallas, TX 75208
(214) 941-6497

18.037
Universal Bookstore
5458 North Fifth St.
Philadelphia, PA 19120
(215) 549-2897

The following are standard resources available on Brazil
INFORMATION SOURCES
- *Background Notes:* (see 2.188)
- *Country Study/Area Handbook. . . .* (see 2.189)

- *Historical Dictionary of. . . .* (see 2.193)
- *Image of. . . .* (see 2.194)
TRAVELER RESOURCES
- *Communication Learning Aids:* (see 2.190)
- *Culturegram:* (see 2.191)
- *Update:* (see 2.197)
- *Fodor's Guide to. . . .* (see 2.192)
- *Nagel's Encyclopedia Guide to. . . .* (see 2.195)
LANGUAGE LEARNING RESOURCES
- *Berlitz. . . . for Travelers* ("Portuguese" Cassettepak, see 9.042)
- *. . . .: Complete Course for Beginners* (see 9.044)
- *Say It in:* (see 9.046)
- *Spoken. . . .* (see 9.047)
- *Berlitz. . . . for Travelers* (Phrasebook, see 9.043)
Fulbright Grants and ITT Fellowships for graduate study in Brazil normally available (see 7.041)

Bulgaria

The following are standard resources available on Bulgaria
INFORMATION SOURCES
- *Background Notes:* (see 2.188)
- *Country Study/Area Handbook. . . .* (see 2.189)

TRAVELER RESOURCES
- *Culturegram:* (see 2.191)
- *Nagel's Encyclopedia Guide to. . . .* (see 2.195)
LANGUAGE LEARNING RESOURCES
- *Spoken. . . .* (see 9.047)

Burma

Publications

18.038
Burma: A Selected and Annotated
Bibliography
Frank N. Trager
Human Relations Area Files Press
2015 Yale Station
New Haven, CT 06520
1973; hardbound; 368 pages; $25

• Carefully compiled and annotated bibliography

18.039
Burma: A Socialist Nation of
Southeast Asia
David I. Steinberg
Westview Press
5500 Central Ave.
Boulder, CO 80301
1982; hardbound; 144 pages; $18.50

• Concise introduction both for the student and the general reader to contemporary Burma; examines the history, geography, politics, international relations, economic development, culture and social aspects of the country; also explores the way the military government has attempted to create national unity through political, economic and cultural mobilization

The following are standard resources available on Burma
INFORMATION SOURCES
• *Background Notes:* (see 2.188)
• *Country Study/Area Handbook. . . .* (see 2.189)
• *Historical Dictionary of. . . .* (see 2.193)
TRAVELER RESOURCES
• *. . . . : A Travel Survival Kit* (see 2.196)
LANGUAGE LEARNING RESOURCES
• *Spoken. . . .* (see 9.047)

Burundi

The following are standard resources available on Burundi
INFORMATION SOURCES
• *Background Notes:* (see 2.188)
• *Country Study/Area Handbook. . . .* (see 2.189)

• *Historical Dictionary of. . . .* (see 2.193)

Fulbright Grants for study in Burundi normally available (see 7.041)

Cameroon

Organizations

18.040
Cultural Service, Embassy of the Republic of Cameroon
2349 Massachusetts Ave. NW
Washington, DC 20008
(202) 265-8790

• Answers telephone and written inquiries about Cameroon, including travel/tourist and educational matters
• Welcomes inquiries from all interested individuals and organizations
• Provides printed information about Cameroon, including a series of substantive guidebooks (in French and English) on each of the provinces and major cities, a newsletter, and maps when available

Publications

18.041
An African Experiment in Nation Building: The Bilingual Cameroon Republic Since Reunification
Ndiva Kofele-Kale, Editor
Westview Press, Inc.
5500 Central Ave.
Boulder, CO 80301
1980; hardbound; 396 pages; $33.50

• Examines forces shaping contemporary Cameroon

18.042
A Bibliography of Cameroon
Mark and Virginia DeLancey, Editors
Holmes & Meier Publishers, Inc.
IUB Bldg.
30 Irving Place
New York, NY 10003
1975; hardbound; 673 pages; $27.50

• Bibliography of use to Africanists in general as well as to researchers on the Cameroon; indexed

The following are standard resources available on Cameroon
INFORMATION SOURCES
• *Background Notes:* (see 2.188)
• *Country Study/Area Handbook.* . . . (see 2.189)
• *Historical Dictionary of.* . . . (see 2.193)

For the "International" Languages (Arabic, French, German and Spanish) see listings under Chapter IX *Foreign Language Teaching and Learning*
Fulbright Grants for study in Cameroon normally available (see 7.041)

Canada

Area Study and Research Programs

18.043
Center of Canadian Studies
The Johns Hopkins University
School of Advanced International Studies
1740 Massachusetts Ave. NW
Washington, DC 20036
(202) 785-6292

Contact(s):
Charles F. Doran, Director

Graduate area studies program established in 1969
• Majors/degrees/certificates offered: M.A. and Ph.D. in International Relations with major in Canadian Studies
• Approximate number of faculty teaching area and language courses: 2 full-time plus part-time and visiting faculty, including many from Canada
• Approximate number of courses available—area: 9
• Average number of students per year specializing in area: 20
• Areas of emphasis: contemporary economic and political issues (may include special comparative political studies in the Advanced Industrial Societies Program)
• Language offered: French (administered by Language Department of the School; proficiency in oral and written French required for degree)
• Study in Canada available at Université Laval (Quebec) and Carleton University (Ottawa); biennial winter field trip to Ottawa and Quebec City
• Draws on library, organizational and research resources of the Washington area
• Special internships and fellowships available

18.044
Canadian Studies Program
Bridgewater State College
Bridgewater, MA 02324
(617) 697-1200, Ext. 2288

Contact(s):
John F. Myers, Chair, Canadian Studies Council

Undergraduate area studies program established in 1973
• Majors/degrees/certificates offered: B.A. in English, French or history with Canadian Studies emphasis
• Approximate number of faculty teaching area and language courses: 15
• Approximate number of courses available—area: 17; language: 3
• Average number of students per year specializing in area: 5
• Language offered: French
• Library contains 2,500 titles, more than 60 periodicals and 3 daily Canadian newspapers
• Occasionally conducts summer institute for teachers and consults with public schools on curriculum development

18.045
Canadian-American Center
University of Maine
Canada House
154 College Ave.
Orono, ME 04469
(207) 581-4222

Contact(s):
Ronald D. Tallman, Director
Victor A. Konrad, Associate Director

Graduate and undergraduate area studies program established in 1968

• Majors/degrees/certificates offered: B.A. major and M.A. and Ph.D. concentrations

• Approximate number of faculty teaching area and language courses: 33

• Approximate number of courses available—area: 44; language: 40

• Average number of students per year specializing in area: 53

• Areas of emphasis: Quebec and Atlantic provinces

• Language offered: French (Quebec Studies courses taught in French)

• Extensive Canadiana Collection, including films and other audiovisuals

• "Canada Year" study program arranged at different universities across Canada

• Faculty exchange programs with a number of Canadian universities

• Conducts workshops for secondary schools and holds seminars for American journalists

• Publishes *Teaching Canada, A Bibliography* (see 2.156) and *Consider Canada, A Handbook for Teachers,* (see 2.121)

18.046
Canadian Studies Program
St. Lawrence University
Canton, NY 13617
(315) 379-6555

Contact(s):
Allen P. Splete, Director

• Offers M.A. in Canadian Studies

18.047
The Center for the Study of Canada
State University of New York at Plattsburgh
133 Court St.
Plattsburgh, NY 12901
(518) 564-2086

Contact(s):
Richard Beach, Director
Jeanne Kissner, Associate Director

Undergraduate and nondegree area studies program established in 1975

• Majors/degrees/certificates offered: B.A. and minor in Canadian Studies

• Approximate number of faculty teaching area and language courses: 30

• Approximate number of courses available—area: 50; language: 25

• Average number of students per year specializing in area: 75+

• Areas of emphasis: Canada/U.S. relations

• Language offered: French

• College library contains a special Canadian section

• Offers academic year or semester study programs at McGill University (Montreal), Université Laval (Quebec city) and Carlton University (Ottawa) and six-week French language immersion programs at three Quebec universities

• Sponsors summer Canadian Studies Workshop and four-week French-Canadian Institute for Language and Culture (two weeks on campus two weeks in Quebec) for high school teachers; offers one-week summer seminar in Quebec for university faculty; develops Canadian Studies curriculum materials including *Canadian Studies: A Syllabus* ($2), *Canadian Studies Teaching Strategies and Resources Guide for Use at the Secondary Level* ($5), *Canadian Studies Syllabus and Resource Guide for Elementary and Intermediate Level Teachers* ($5), and *Teaching Canada: A Newsletter for Teachers* (three times per year, free); also sponsors programs on Canadian-U.S. business relations

• Approximately ten $300 scholarships available each semester (5–10 in the summer); sponsors annual Canadian Studies essay contest with substantial prizes for high school students

18.048
Canadian Studies Program
University of Rochester
Harkness Hall
Rochester, NY 14627
(716) 275-5466 or 4291

Contact(s):
Peter Regenstreif, Coordinator

Graduate area studies program established in 1954
- Majors/degrees/certificates offered: Ph.D. in Political Science with concentration in Canadian Studies
- Approximate number of faculty teaching area and language courses: 3
- Approximate number of courses available—area: 3
- Average number of students per year specializing in area: 5
- Area of emphasis: Canadian-U.S. relations and Canadian politics
- Maintains 30-year survey research data file on Canadian politics
- Financial assistance available for travel to and research in Canada

18.049
Canadian Studies Center
Duke University
2101 Campus Drive
Durham, NC 27706
(919) 684-2765

Contact(s):
Richard H. Leach, Director
Marion C. Salinger, Admin Coordinator

Graduate and undergraduate area studies program established in 1973
- Majors/degrees/certificates offered: B.A. with minor or second major in Canadian Studies
- Approximate number of faculty teaching area and language courses: 26

- Approximate number of courses available—area: 58; language: 3
- Average number of students per year specializing in area: 24
- Language offered: French
- Library holdings include Lionel Stevenson Collection of Canadian Literature and Canadian materials in the University's British Commonwealth Collection
- Student study opportunities and faculty exchange and research projects at Laval, McGill, Alberta, Lethbridge, and Calgary universities in Canada
- Conducts workshops on Canada for school teachers and prepares and distributes teaching materials and guides; also sponsors programs of assistance for other colleges and their faculty
- Publishes minitexts on Canada for the public schools and Occasional Papers
- Fellowships available to graduate students including support for research on Canada

18.050
Canadian Studies
Brigham Young University
David M. Kennedy Center for International Studies
Provo, UT 84602
(801) 378-3377

Contact(s):
Earl H. Fry, Coordinator

- Offers B.A. in Canadian Studies

18.051
Canadian Studies
University of Vermont
114 Old Mill Bldg.
Burlington, VT 05405
(802) 656-3062

Contact(s):
E. J. Miles, Director

Undergraduate area studies program established in 1963
- Majors/degrees/certificates offered: B.A. and minor in Canadian Studies
- Approximate number of faculty teaching area and language courses: 25
- Approximate number of courses available—area: 37; language: 14
- Average number of students per year specializing in area: 12
- Areas of emphasis: Canada as a whole; Canada-U.S. relations; Quebec Studies
- Language offered: French
- Offers summer, tuition-free, credit-granting, introductory and advanced seminar-workshops for teachers

18.052
Center for Canadian and Canadian-American Studies
Western Washington University
Bellingham, WA 98225
(206) 676-3728

Contact(s):
Robert L. Monahan, Director

Undergraduate area studies program established in 1970
- Majors/degrees/certificates offered: B.A. in Canadian Studies
- Approximate number of faculty teaching area and language courses: 30
- Approximate number of courses available—area: 23; language: 40
- Average number of students per year specializing in area: 15
- Language offered: French
- Special Canadian collection libraries serve as repositories for Canadian government documents and all topographical maps issued by the Canadian Department of Mines and Resources; nearby access to Canadian cities and universities
- Develops and publishes curriculum units on studying Canada for secondary school use

Organizations

18.053
Association for Canadian Studies in the United States
1776 Massachusetts Ave. NW, Suite 225
Washington, DC 20036
(202) 822-8688

Contact(s):
Ellen R. Babby, Executive Officer

Professional educational association of individuals and institutions
- Promotes Canadian Studies in the U.S. and serves as clearinghouse for information about Canadian Studies; sponsors conferences and meetings and publishes a triannual journal, *The American Review of Canadian Studies,* and a biannual newsletter, *Canadian Studies Update* (also furnishes a list of institutions active in teaching about Canada)

18.054
Center for Inter-American Relations
680 Park Ave.
New York, NY 10021
(212) 249-8950

Contact(s):
Edna Phillips, Director, Public Information

- Nonprofit center designed to broaden public awareness and appreciation in the U.S. of the cultural heritage of Latin America, the Caribbean, and Canada (see also 16.110)

18.055
Embassy of Canada,
Public Affairs Division
1771 N St. NW
Washington, DC 20036
(202) 785-1400

CONSULATES GENERAL: Atlanta, Boston, Buffalo, Chicago, Cleveland, Dallas, Detroit, Los Angeles, Minneapolis, New Orleans, New York, Philadelphia, San Francisco, Seattle

• Answers telephone and written inquiries about Canada, including travel/tourist and educational matters
• Welcomes inquiries from libraries and museums, U.S. government agencies, travel and tourist agencies and cultural organizations
• Provides printed information about travel, education and Canada in general
• Recommends Consulates General as first point of contact

18.056
Statistics Canada
R. H. Coats Bldg.
Holand Ave.
Ottawa, Ontario K1A 0T6, Canada
(613) 995-7406

Major repository for statistical information about Canada
• Central data base for the whole range of statistics on the economic and social activities of the Canadian people; classified in eight categories: (1) general; (2) primary industries;

(3) manufacturing, transportation, communication and utilities; (4) commerce, construction, finance and prices; (5) employment, unemployment and labor income; (6) education and culture; (7) health and welfare; and (8) census; available in print, microfiche or online machine-readable formats; machine-readable data accessible through Canadian Socio-economic Information Management System (CANSIM) with data grouped under the following subject headings: system of national accounts, prices and price indexes; labor, manufacturing and primary industries; capital and finance; construction, merchandising and services; external trade, transportation, agriculture and food; population estimates and projections; and health and welfare; catalog of publications available

18.057
The William H. Donner Foundation, Inc.
630 Fifth Ave., Room 2452
New York, NY 10020
(212) 765-1695

Charitable foundation
• Provides financial support to key U.S. academic institutions committed to Canadian studies for teaching, research, doctoral and postdoctoral study, particularly to encourage research on U.S.-Canadian bilateral policy issues

Publications

18.058
Canada Handbook
Margaret Smith, Editor
Statistics Canada
Information Division
Ottawa, Canada K1A OS9
annual; paperbound; 345 pages; $7.20

• Thorough, illustrated description of life and society in Canada with emphasis on current developments in social, cultural and

economic affairs including ample factual data

18.059
Canadian Almanac & Directory
Susan Walters, Editor
Copp Clark Publishing
517 Wellington St. West
Toronto, Ontario M5V 1G1, Canada
annual; hardbound; 960 pages; $28.50;
    available from Beekman Publishers, Inc.,
    53 Park Place, New York, NY 10007

• Extensive compilation of data and information about Canada including such things as lists of banks, lawyers, trade associations, chambers of commerce, consular offices, magazines and newspapers, stock exchanges, transportation and shipping organizations, etc., along with statistics, social and cultural data and a complete directory of municipal, provincial and federal governments

18.060
The Canadian Historical Review
David Bercuson and J. C. Granatstein, Editors
University of Toronto Press
5201 Dufferin St.
Downsview, Ontario M3H 5T8 Canada
quarterly journal; approx. 200 pages;
    individuals, $19 per year; institutions, $30 per year

• Contains scholarly articles and essays on aspects of Canadian history; extensive book review section; notes and comments

18.061
Colombo's Canadian References
John Robert Colombo
Oxford University Press
200 Madison Ave.
New York, NY 10016
1976; hardbound; 584 pages; $35

• General reference book on Canada covering arts, entertainment, business, transportation, government, politics, sports, places, people and events; 6,000 entries

18.062
Economic History of Canada
Trevor J. O. Dick, Editor
Gale Research Co.
Book Tower
Detroit, MI 48226
1978; hardbound; 174 pages; $40

• Bibliographic information about works on Canadian economics past and present

18.063
Journal of Canadian Studies/Revue D'Etudes Canadiennes
John Wadland, Editor
Trent University
Box 4800
Peterborough, Ontario K9J 7B8, Canada
quarterly journal; approx. 150 pages;
    individuals, $12 per year; institutions, $25 per year

• Contains scholarly articles and essays on all aspects of Canadian Studies; book reviews; news of the field

The following are standard resources available on Canada
INFORMATION SOURCES
    • *Background Notes:* (see 2.188)
    • *Image of.* . . . (see 2.194)
TRAVELER RESOURCES
    • *Culturegram:* (see 2.191)
    • *Fodor's Guide to.* . . . (see 2.192)
    • *Nagel's Encyclopedia Guide to.* . . . (see 2.195)
    • . . . . . *: A Travel Survival Kit* (see 2.196)

Cape Verde

Publications

18.064
Guinea-Bissau and Cape Verde: A
Comprehensive Bibliography
Joseph M. McCarthy
Garland Publishing, Inc.
136 Madison Avenue, 2d Floor
New York, NY 10016
1977; hardbound; 180 pages; $21

- Useful research and study tool

18.065
The People of the Cape Verde Islands:
Exploitation and Emigration
Antonio Carreira
ShoeString Press, Inc.
995 Sherman Ave.
P.O. Box 4327
Hamden, CT 06514
1982; hardbound; 224 pages; $21.50

- Review of history of Cape Verde Islands, the impact of colonization and emigration, and an examination of contemporary conditions

The following are standard resources available on Cape Verde
INFORMATION SOURCES
- *Background Notes:* (see 2.188)
- *Historical Dictionary of. . . .* (see 2.193)

Central African Republic

The following are standard resources available on Central African Republic
INFORMATION SOURCES
- *Background Notes:* (see 2.188)
- *Historical Dictionary of. . . .* (see 2.193)

Chad

The following are standard resources available on Chad
INFORMATION SOURCES
- *Background Notes:* (see 2.188)
- *Country Study/Area Handbook. . . .* (see 2.189)
- *Historical Dictionary of. . . .* (see 2.193)

For the "International" Languages (Arabic, French, German and Spanish) see listings under Chapter IX *Foreign Language Teaching and Learning*

Chile

Organizations

18.066
Cultural Department, Embassy of Chile
1732 Massachusetts Ave. NW
Washington, DC 20036
(202) 785-1746 or 785-3151

• Provides printed materials on Chile including *Chilean Cultural Panorama* and *Chile* (a tourist booklet)

Publications

18.067
Chile
National Tourist Board
SERNATUR
P.O. Box 14082
Santiago, Chile
1981; booklet; 63 pages; free

Available from the Embassy of Chile, 1732 Massachusetts Ave. NW, Washington, DC 20036
• Attractive booklet providing illustrated descriptions of Chile's major cities and tourist attractions along with traveler information

18.068
Chile: The Legacy of Hispanic Capitalism
Brian Loveman
Oxford University Press
200 Madison Ave.
New York, NY 10016
1979; 442 pages; hardbound, $22.50; paperbound, $8.95

• Broad examination of Chilean history and contemporary conditions in Chile, emphasizing the tension between the Hispanic tradition and contemporary (principally external) factors which have affected Chilean development

The following are standard resources available on Chile
INFORMATION SOURCES
  • *Background Notes:* (see 2.188)
  • *Country Study/Area Handbook. . . .* (see 2.189)
  • *Historical Dictionary of. . . .* (see 2.193)
  • *Image of. . . .* (see 2.194)
TRAVELER RESOURCES
  • *Culturegram:* (see 2.191)
LANGUAGE LEARNING RESOURCES
For the "International" Languages (Arabic, French, German and Spanish) see listings under Chapter IX *Foreign Language Teaching and Learning*
Fulbright Grants and ITT Fellowships for graduate study in Chile normally available (see 7.041)

China

Area Study and Research Programs

18.069
Chinese Area Studies
University of Arizona
Tucson, AZ 85721
(602) 621-7505

Contact(s):
Robert M. Gimello, Director

Graduate, undergraduate and nondegree area studies program
- Majors/degrees/certificates offered: M.A. and Ph.D. in Chinese Area Studies
- Approximate number of courses available—area and language: 56
- Areas of emphasis: history, language and literature
- Language offered: Chinese at all levels

on China by Berkeley faculty and graduate students; brings scholars from elsewhere in the U.S. and abroad to do research at Berkeley under the Center Research Associate Program and Postdoctoral Fellowship Program
- Conducts student-faculty interdisciplinary research colloquium series and regional seminars for faculty from other institutions
- Extensive library holdings of modern Asian materials
- Conducts exchange program in contemporary Chinese Studies with Stanford and the University of London
- Publishes China Research Monographs on modern political and social issues in China

18.070
Center for Chinese Studies
University of California at Berkeley
12 Barrows Hall
Berkeley, CA 94720
(415) 642-5618

Contact(s):
Joyce K. Kallgren, Chair

Academically-based research center established in 1958; one of three East Asian Research Centers at Berkeley within the Institute of East Asian Studies (see 13.014); for Korean Center, (see 18.307); for Japanese Center, (see 18.270); emphasizes the comparative analysis of the political and social systems and culture of China since 1949
- Sponsors and provides financial support for graduate and postdoctoral research

18.071
Center for Chinese Studies
University of Michigan at Ann Arbor
104 Lane Hall
Ann Arbor, MI 48109
(313) 764-6308

Contact(s):
Albert Feuerwerker, Director

Graduate area studies program established in 1961
- Majors/degrees/certificates offered: M.A. in Asian Studies with specialization in Chinese Studies and departmental Ph.D. with specialization in Chinese Studies
- Approximate number of faculty teaching area and language courses: 27
- Approximate number of courses available—area: 70; language: 30

• Average number of students per year specializing in area: 100

• Countries covered and areas of emphasis: China, past and present, including the PRC, Taiwan, etc.

• Languages offered: Classical Chinese, Modern Mandarin and Cantonese

• University's Asia Library has extensive collection of Chinese language materials; particularly strong in 19th- and 20th-century documents, including extensive collection on the Cultural Revolution and materials from the contemporary Chinese Institute and the Union Research Institute

• Asian Art Archives includes extensive photographic record of paintings and decorative art collections of the Chinese National Palace Museum and other collections

• Publishes several series: *Michigan Papers in Chinese Studies; Science, Medicine and Technology in East Asia* and *Michigan Abstracts of Chinese and Japanese Works on Chinese History;* principal emphasis on history, politics, economics and literature

• Conducts school outreach programs, including an annual Instructors' Summer Institute

18.072
Chinese Regional Studies
University of Washington
Henry S. Jackson School of International
   Studies
Seattle, WA 98195
(206) 543-6148

Contact(s):
Jack L. Dull, Chair

• Offers B.A. and M.A. in International Studies with specialization in Chinese Studies

Organizations

18.073
American Council of Learned Societies
228 East 45th St.
New York, NY 10017
(212) 697-1505

Contact(s):
John William Ward, President

Nonprofit educational federation of 43 national scholarly organizations; engages in activities directed toward the advancement of humanistic learning; established in 1919

• Administers grants and fellowship programs for postdoctoral research in the humanities; may be used for research abroad or on international subjects

• Provides grants for research in Chinese Studies including postdoctoral grants for research in the U.S. or abroad on Chinese Studies and Mellon Program in Chinese Studies (jointly sponsored with the Social Science Research Council); provides postdoctoral research and study fellowships, language training fellowships (abroad), summer intensive language training grants and travel grants to enable U.S. and Canadian scholars to attend scholarly research conferences in the PRC (and Chinese to attend conferences in the U.S.); grants in Mellon program aimed principally at younger scholars

• Provides postdoctoral grants-in-aid to support the preparation of a dissertation for publication and to support research in progress by the scholar to meet essential personal expenses

• Offers travel grants to scholars in humanistic disciplines to enable them to participate in conferences outside North America

• Administers Universities Service Center in Hong Kong (see 18.190)

18.074
American Association for Chinese Studies
St. John's University
Sun Yat Sen Hall
Jamaica, NY 11439
(212) 969-8000

Contact(s):
Tien-yi, President

Professional association of scholars teaching
Chinese languages or cultural studies
• Promotes research, compiles statistics
and publishes a newsletter, monographs and
teaching materials (including a catalogue of
audiovisual materials for Chinese Studies)

18.075
**Center for United States-China Arts
Exchange**
Columbia University
423 West 118th St., #1E
New York, NY 10027
(212) 280-4648

Contact(s):
Chou Wen-chung, Director

• Facilitates exchanges of specialists and
materials in the literary, performing and visual arts between the U.S. and the PRC and
maintains a collection of Chinese musical
scores

18.076
China Books & Periodicals, Inc.
2929 24th St.
San Francisco, CA 94110
(415) 282-2994
BRANCHES: Chicago, New York

Distributor of books and periodicals on China
and Chinese language and culture
• Sells periodicals and adult and children's books on Chinese life, literature, culture, politics, art and a wide range of contemporary issues; includes travel guidebooks,
phrasebooks and other language learning
materials

18.077
The China Council of the Asia Society
725 Park Ave.
New York, NY 10021
(212) 288-6400

Contact(s):
Robert B. Oxnam, Director

Program of the Asia Society designed to expand public understanding of contemporary
China and Sino-American relations
• Offers briefings, seminars and consultations to and prepares materials for the press
and broadcast media on aspects of current
Chinese national and international affairs and
on Sino-American relations
• Advises and assists regional/local China
Councils and other organizations in program
and resource development; includes occasional modest financial support
• Sponsors the preparation and publication of books, articles, pamphlets, films, etc.
on contemporary and traditional Chinese Affairs; includes *Communicating with China*
(available from Intercultural Press, see 1.114)

18.078
China Publications Service
P.O. Box 49614
Chicago, IL 60649

Contact(s):
Qian Xiaowei, Representative

• Imports publications from China, including books, periodicals, and microforms
along with originals and reproductions of
Chinese art work

18.079

Chinese Language Teachers Association
Seton Hall University
Institute of Far Eastern Studies
South Orange, NJ 07079
(201) 761-9447

Contact(s):
John Young, Secretary-Treasurer

• Promotes the study of the Chinese language at all levels; publishes a newsletter, a journal and an annual directory

18.080

Committee on Scholarly Communication with the People's Republic of China
2101 Constitution Ave. NW
Washington, DC 20418
(202) 334-2718

Contact(s):
Kyna Rubin, Staff Associate

Scholarly and educational organization sponsored by the American Council of Learned Societies (see 18.073), the National Academy of Sciences and the Social Science Research Council (see 18.087); conducts research, study and lecture exchange programs with the PRC
• Sponsors National Program for Advanced Study and Research in China which provides opportunities for senior and junior researchers and graduate students to pursue research in the PRC (selected in the U.S. by national competition)
• Sponsors lecture exchange program involving exchange of lecturers (individuals invited by receiving side; sending country pays travel, receiving country pays in-country costs)
• Administers U.S. side of bilateral symposia taking place in the U.S. and China (selects U.S. delegation and pays international travel; pays U.S. expenses for Chinese delegation); also provides information and names and addresses of contacts for U.S.

government-sponsored bilateral research and educational agreements with China
• Maintains Information Services Center with materials on contemporary developments in Chinese science and education and the U.S.-PRC exchange activities
• Publishes quarterly newsletter *China Exchange News* (see 18.094); from 1980–82 co-published with the National Association for Foreign Student Affairs, a number of pamphlets on education in China, educational exchange program activities in and between the U.S. and the PRC, and guides for students, researchers and teachers coming to the U.S. or going to the PRC; (these publications emerged from the now inoperative US-China Education Clearinghouse and are available from the National Association for Foreign Student Affairs, see 10.018)

18.081

The Free Press
806 Third Ave.
New York, NY 10022
(212) 935-2000

• Publishes a strong selection of books in Chinese Studies including *Mao's China* ($8.95)

18.082

The Tibet Society, Inc.
P.O. Box 1968
Bloomington, IN 47402
(812) 337-4339

Contact(s):
Thubten J. Norbu, Executive Director

Professional academic association dedicated to the study and preservation of Tibetan culture
• Publishes *The Journal of the Tibet Society* (research articles, commentary and reviews of books on Tibetan civilization), *The*

Tibet Society Newsletter and occasional papers

  • Provides aid to Tibetan refugees and assistance to groups seeking to preserve Tibetan civilization including contributions to the Tibetan Library and Archive in Dharamsala

18.083
Inter-University Center for Chinese Studies in Taipei
Stanford University
Center for Research in International Studies
Room 200, Lou Henry Hoover Bldg.
Stanford, CA 94305
(415) 497-4581

Contact(s):
Lyman P. Van Slyke, Executive Secretary
James Dew, Field Director (Taipei)

  • Offers intensive instruction in the Chinese language (see 18.469)

18.084
M. E. Sharpe, Inc.
80 Business Park Drive
Armonk, NY 10504
(914) 273-1800

  • Publishes books on contemporary Chinese culture and politics

18.085
National Committee on United States-China Relations
777 United Nations Plaza
New York, NY 10164
(212) 922-1385

Contact(s):
Arthur H. Rosen, President

  • Promotes exchanges between the U.S.

and China in education, culture, governmental administration and management; consults with and supports organizations involved in exchanges, and prepares and disseminates briefing kits on China; publishes newsletter and annual report

18.086
National Science Foundation
United States-People's Republic of China
  Cooperative Science Program
Division of International Programs
Washington, DC 20550
(202) 357-7393

Contact(s):
Pierre Perrolle, Program Manager

  • Funds programs involving cooperative research and seminars and workshops

18.087
Social Science Research Council
China Program
605 Third Ave.
New York, NY 10158
(212) 557-9500

  • Awards substantial grants to citizens or permanent residents of the U.S. and Canada for postdoctoral research in all humanistic and social science disciplines on post-Imperial China; research may be pursued in the U.S. or abroad; Mongolia and overseas Chinese in Asia are also acceptable topics

18.088
The Yale-China Association
905A Yale Station
New Haven, CT 06520
(203) 436-4422

Contact(s):
John Bryan Starr, Executive Director

Cultural and educational organization associated with Yale University

• Sponsors educational and cultural programs between Yale and Hong Kong and the PRC; Yale Bachelor's program provides Yale graduates as English teachers to New Asia College/Chinese University of Hong Kong, Hunan Medical College and Huazhong Teachers College in the PRC; Medical Exchange Program facilitates exchanges between Yale School of Medicine and Hunan Medical College; co-sponsors Chinese University of Hong Kong International Asian Studies Program (open to all North American students); sponsors tours to the PRC and cooperates with other organizations in community outreach programs

Publications

18.089
American Study Programs in China: An Interim Report Card
Peggy Blumenthal
Committee on Scholarly Communication
    with the People's Republic of China
National Academy of Sciences
2101 Constitution Ave. NW
Washington, DC 20418
and
National Association for Foreign Student
    Affairs
1860 19th St. NW
Washington, DC 20009
1981; paperbound; 51 pages; available
    through ERIC

Order from the National Association for Foreign Student Affairs

• Examines the problems and issues related to the undertaking of academic study in the PRC, including attitudes, availability and validity of information, access, distribution and characteristics of students, program models (including summer language programs), curriculum, language learning, research problems, living in China and student supervision

18.090
Beijing Review
Guo Ji, International Editor
The Beijing Review
Beijing, China
weekly magazine; 31 pages; $13.50 per year

Available in the U.S. from China Books and Periodicals, Inc., 2929 24th St., San Francisco, CA 94110

• Newsweekly reporting on current political and economic developments in China and expressing Chinese viewpoints on domestic and international issues

18.091
China: An Annotated Bibliography of Bibliographies
Tsuen-Hsuin Tsuen
G. K. Hall & Co.
70 Lincoln St.
Boston, MA 02111
1978; hardbound; 604 pages; $49

• Covers separate works, bibliographies in periodicals and serials, bibliographic essays, surveys of literature on specific periods or fields, and listings of bibliographies in monographs; approximately 2,500 entries

18.092
China Bound: A Handbook for American Students, Researchers and Teachers
Karen Turner Gottschang
Committee on Scholarly Communication
    with the People's Republic of China
National Academy of Sciences
2101 Constitution Ave. NW
Washington, DC 20418
and

National Association for Foreign Student
Affairs
1860 19th St. NW
Washington, DC 20009
1981; paperbound; 143 pages; available
through ERIC

Order from the National Association for Foreign Student Affairs
• Covers practical and educational concerns of U.S. students and scholars going to
China; includes sections on preparing to leave,
what to take (for both personal and student
or professional use), settling in, study and
research, teaching matters, services available, and departure; 13 appendices with
practical information

18.093
China Directory
Takashi Tamaki, Editor
annual; hardbound; 657 pages; $85

Available from International Publications Service, 114 East 32d St., New York, NY 10016;
and Radiopress, Inc., Fuji Television Bldg., 7
Ichigaya Kawadacho, Shinju, Tokyo 162,
Japan
• Provides current information on Communist Party and government organizations
(national, local and overseas), economic commissions and foreign trade bodies, scientific
and trade institutes, universities and other
organizations; includes addresses, names of
officials and positions held; also contains
"Who's Who" and "Gazetteer" sections

18.094
China Exchange News
Pierre Perrolle, Editor
Committee on Scholarly Communication
    with the People's Republic of China
National Academy of Sciences
2101 Constitution Ave. NW
Washington, DC 20418
bimonthly newsletter; 23 pages; free

• Reports on developments and significant events in scholarly and educational exchange between the U.S. and the PRC; includes identification of individual exchanges,
reviews of new books, a bibliography of recent writings on China and China-U.S. relations of interest to the scholarly community

18.095
The China Phone Book & Address
Directory
The China Phone Book Co., Ltd.
GPO Box 11581
Hong Kong
annual; paperbound; 192 pages; $25

• Directory in the form of a phone book,
covering over 60 cities in China; serves as a
guide to trade and commerce, to scientific,
educational and cultural organizations, travel
and leisure activities and the foreign community
• For the larger cities it includes Chinese
government foreign trade corporations and
other foreign trade organizations and bureaus, industries, transportation and shipping offices, banks and financial institutions,
academies, educational institutes and societies, publications and media, travel facilities,
cultural organizations, national and local government offices, foreign affairs organizations,
shops, services and leisure activities, and the
foreign community, especially in Peking; bilingual listings (with Pinyin spelling) include
names, addresses, phone and Telex numbers;
takes advertising

18.096
China Quarterly: An International
Journal for the Study of China
Brian Hook, Editor
Contemporary China Institute
School of Oriental and African Studies
Malet Street
London WC1E 7HP
England
quarterly journal; approx. 220 pages; £30
    per year

• Contains articles and essays particularly focused on contemporary China, including Taiwan, Hong Kong and overseas Chinese

18.097
China Reconstructs: North American Edition
China Reconstructs
Wai Wen Bldg.
Beijing (37) China
monthly magazine; approx. 70 pages; $8 per year

Available from China Books and Periodicals, 2929 24th St., San Francisco, CA 94110
• Contains articles, photos and reports on contemporary life and culture in China and on Canada/U.S.-PRC cultural relations

18.098
China Traveler's Phrasebook
China Books & Periodicals, Inc.
2929 24th St.
San Francisco, CA 94110
1980; paperbound; 192 pages; $5.95

• 2,000 words and phrases listed by categories covering day-to-day contingencies; includes introduction to the Chinese language; English phrases translated into Chinese characters, Pinyin (romanized Chinese) and phonetic Mandarin pronunciation

18.099
Chinese/English Phrase Book for Travelers/and Cassette
John S. Montanaro
John Wiley & Sons, Inc.
605 Third Ave.
New York, NY 10016
1981; paperbound; 304 pages; book, $8.95; cassette, $9.95

• Covers 2,000 of the phrases and words most commonly used and needed by travelers; arranged by situation (greetings, when you arrive, at the bank, etc.) with Pinyin romanization and supplementary phonetic spellings; includes list of guidebooks on the PRC, tips for the tourist and other useful information

18.100
Modern China: International Quarterly of History and Social Science
Philip C. C. Huang, Editor
Sage Publications Inc.
275 South Beverly Drive
Beverly Hills, CA 90210
quarterly journal; approx. 120 pages; individuals, $22 per year; institutions, $50 per year

• Contains scholarly articles, essays and commentary on modern Chinese life and society; book reviews

18.101
The People's Republic of China: A Handbook
Harold C. Hinton, Editor
Westview Press
5500 Central Ave.
Boulder, CO 80301
1979; hardbound; 443 pages; $36.50

• Practical review of basic aspects of Chinese society covering geography, population, history, politics, agriculture, economics and development, science and technology, social affairs, education and culture, security and foreign relations

18.102
The Pinyin Chinese-English Dictionary
Wu Jingrong, Editor in chief
Beijing Foreign Language Institute
Beijing, China
1979; hardbound; 300 pages; $61.50

Available from John Wiley & Sons, Inc., 605 Third Ave., New York, NY 10016

• Contains 6,000 single-character entries, 50,000 compound character entries and over 70,000 words and phrases all with Pinyin romanization; entries arranged according to Chinese phonetic alphabet; includes indexes and appendices on aspects of Chinese phonetics and special lists of countries, regions, weights and measures, etc.

18.103
Traditional Tibet: A Selected and Annotated Bibliography of European-Language Materials on the Pre-Communist Period
Gay D. Henderson
Garland Publishing, Inc.
136 Madison Ave.
New York, NY 10016
1982; hardbound; 200 pages; $24

• Covers the humanities, social sciences and the natural sciences

18.104
U.S.-China Review
Robert J. Mendel, Editor
U.S.-China People's Friendship Association
110 Maryland Ave. NW
Washington, DC 20002
bimonthly magazine; approx. 30 pages;
    individuals, $12 per year; institutions, $14
    per year

• Reports on exchanges, cultural events and other matters of interest to persons concerned with current U.S.-China relations; book reviews

The following companies import and sell books in the Chinese language:

18.105
China Cultural Center
970 North Broadway, Suite 210
Los Angeles, CA 90012
(213) 489-3827

18.106
Eastwind Books & Arts, Inc.
1435-A Stockton Street
San Francisco, CA 94133
(415) 781-3331

The following are standard resources available on China
INFORMATION SOURCES
• *Background Notes:* (see 2.188)
• *Country Study/Area Handbook.* . . .
  (see 2.189)
TRAVELER RESOURCES
• *Bartholomew Map of.* . . . (see 1.109)
• *Culturegram:* (see 2.191)
• *Fodor's Guide to.* . . . (see 2.192)
• *Nagel's Encyclopedia Guide to.* . . .
  (see 2.195)
LANGUAGE LEARNING RESOURCES
• *Berlitz.* . . . *for Travelers* (Cassette-pak see 9.042)
• . . . . : *Complete Course for Beginners*
  (see 9.044) "Mandarin Chinese,"
  "Cantonese"
• *Say It in:* (see 9.046)
• *Spoken.* . . . (see 9.047) "Amoy Hokkien," "Cantonese," "Mandarin Chinese"
• *Berlitz.* . . . for Travelers (phrasebook see 9.043)

Colombia

Organizations

18.107
Colombia Information Service
140 East 57th St.
New York, NY 10022
(212) 421-8270

Government information office
• Distributes printed information about Colombia

18.108
Embassy of Colombia
2118 Leroy Place NW
Washington, DC 20008
(202) 387-8338

CONSULATES GENERAL: Houston, Jacksonville, New York, San Francisco, San Juan, Puerto Rico

• Answers telephone and written inquiries about Colombia, including travel/tourist and educational matters
• Welcomes inquiries from any interested individual or institution
• Provides printed information about travel and education in Colombia and on Colombia in general
• Recommends these other sources of information: Colombia Information Service (see 18.107) and the Colombian Government Tourist Office, 140 East 57th St., New York, NY 10022

Publications

18.109
Colombia: Portrait of Unity and Diversity
Harvey F. Kline
Westview Press
5500 Central Ave.
Boulder, CO 80301
1983; hardbound; 144 pages; $18

• Concise introduction both for the student and the general reader to contemporary Colombia; examines the history, geography, politics, international relations, economic development, culture and social aspects of the country; also discusses the heterogeneity of the Colombian people and the country's special political history and constructs a Colombian "model" of Latin American development

18.110
Research Guide to Colombia
Tom L. Martinson
Pan American Institute of Geography and History,
Ex-Arzobispado No. 29
Mexico 18, D.F.
1975; paperbound; 59 pages; $8

• Provides basic guidelines and bibliography for pursuing research on Colombia

The following are standard resources available on Colombia
INFORMATION SOURCES
• *Background Notes:* (see 2.188)
• *Country Study/Area Handbook.* . . . (see 2.189)

- *Historical Dictionary of. . . .* (see 2.193)
- *Image of. . . .* (see 2.194)

TRAVELER RESOURCES
- *Culturegram:* (see 2.191)

LANGUAGE LEARNING RESOURCES

For the "International" Languages (Arabic, French, German and Spanish) see listings under Chapter IX *Foreign Language Teaching and Learning*

Fulbright Grants for study in Colombia normally available (see 7.041)

Comoros

Publications

18.111
The Comoro Islands
Malyn Newitt
Westview Press
5500 Central Ave.
Boulder, CO 80301
1984; hardbound; 135 pages; $17.50

- Concise introduction both for the student and the general reader to contemporary Comoros; examines the history, geography, politics, international relations, economic development, culture and social aspects of the country; also discusses links between the Islands and Africa and France and explores current problems, especially agricultural development and overpopulation

The following are standard resources available on Comoros
INFORMATION SOURCES
- *Background Notes:* (see 2.188)

Congo

The following are standard resources available on Congo
INFORMATION SOURCES
- *Background Notes:* (see 2.188)

- *Country Study/Area Handbook. . . .* (see 2.189)
- *Historical Dictionary of. . . .* (see 2.193)

Costa Rica

Publications

18.112
The Costa Ricans
Richard Biesanz
Prentice-Hall, Inc.
Englewood Cliffs, NJ 07632

1982; paperbound; 304 pages; $15.95
- Thorough review of the history of Costa Rica and of the forces that have shaped contemporary economic, social and political conditions

18.113
Research Guide to Costa Rica
Pan American Institute of Geography and
   History
Ex-Arzobispado No. 29
Mexico 18, D.F.
1977; paperbound; 138 pages; $8

   • Provides basic guidelines and bibliography for pursuing research on Costa Rica

The following are standard resources available on Costa Rica

INFORMATION SOURCES
   • *Background Notes:* (see 2.188)
   • *Country Study/Area Handbook. . . .* (see 2.189)
   • *Historical Dictionary of. . . .* (see 2.193)
   • *Image of. . . .* (see 2.194)
TRAVELER RESOURCES
   • *Culturegram:* (see 2.191)
LANGUAGE LEARNING RESOURCES
For the "International" Languages (Arabic, French, German and Spanish) see listings under Chapter IX *Foreign Language Teaching and Learning*

Cuba

Organizations

18.114
Cuban American National Foundation
1000 Thomas Jefferson St., NW, Suite 601
Washington, DC 20007
(202) 265-2822

Contact(s):
Frank Calzón, Executive Director

Nonprofit organization designed to gather and disseminate information about Cuba and the Cuban people
   • Provides information and maintains clearinghouse on information about Cuba and about the current policies of the Cuban government
   • Maintains speakers bureau and publishes books and other materials on contemporary issues

Publications

18.115
Cuban Communism
Irving Louis Horowitz, Editor
Transaction Books
Rutgers University
New Brunswick, NJ 08903
1984 (fifth edition); paperbound; 804 pages;
   $19.95

   • Analyzes all aspects of present-day Cuban economic, social, political and military affairs

18.116
Cuban Studies
Carmelo Mesa-Lago, Editor
Center for Latin American Studies
University of Pittsburgh
Pittsburgh, PA 15260
biannual journal; approx. 150 pages;
   individuals, $10; institutions, $20

   • Articles, essays and analyses of aspects of contemporary Cuban affairs; includes a large number of book reviews, a classified bibliography and a listing of current research

The following are standard resources available on Cuba
INFORMATION SOURCES
- *Background Notes:* (see 2.188)
- *Country Study/Area Handbook. . . .* (see 2.189)

- *Historical Dictionary of. . . .* (see 2.193)

LANGUAGE LEARNING RESOURCES
For the "International" Languages (Arabic, French, German and Spanish) see listings under Chapter IX *Foreign Language Teaching and Learning*

Cyprus

The following are standard resources available on Cyprus
INFORMATION SOURCES
- *Background Notes:* (see 2.188)

- *Country Study/Area Handbook. . . .* (see 2.189)

LANGUAGE LEARNING RESOURCES
(see under Greece and Turkey)

Czechoslovakia

Organizations

18.117
Embassy of the Czechoslovak Socialist Republic
3900 Linnean Ave. NW
Washington, DC 20008-3897
(202) 363-6315

- Answers telephone and written inquiries about Czechoslovakia regarding educational matters

- Welcomes inquiries from U.S. government agencies and from individuals
- Provides printed information about Czechoslovakia
- Recommends these other sources of information: the Czechoslovak Travel Bureau, 10 East 40th St., Suite 1902, New York, NY 10016, and Czechoslovak Airlines, 545 Fifth Ave., New York, NY 10017

Publications

18.118
Twentieth-Century Czechoslovakia: The Meanings of Its History
Josef Korbel
Columbia University Press
136 South Broadway
Irvington, NY 10533

1977; hardbound; 346 pages; $14

- Examines major themes of modern Czechoslovak history

The following companies import and sell books in the Czech language:

18.119
FAM Book Service
69 Fifth Ave.
New York, NY 10003
(212) 255-8348

18.120
Four Continent Book Corp.
149 Fifth Ave.
New York, NY 10010
(212) 533-0250

The following are standard resources available on Czechoslovakia
INFORMATION SOURCES
- *Background Notes:* (see 2.188)
- *Country Study/Area Handbook. . . .* (see 2.189)
TRAVELER RESOURCES
- *Culturegram:* (see 2.191)
- *Nagel's Encyclopedia Guide to. . . .* (see 2.195)
LANGUAGE LEARNING RESOURCES
- *. . . .: Complete Course for Beginners* (see 9.044)
- *Say It in:* (see 9.046)

Denmark

Organizations

18.121
Danish Information Office
Consulate General
280 Park Ave.
New York, NY 10017
(212) 697-5101
OTHER CONSULATES GENERAL: Chicago, Hollywood

- Answers telephone and written inquiries about Denmark regarding educational matters
- Provides a list of films on Denmark including Greenland and the Faroe Islands available from the Consulates General
- Welcomes inquiries from educational institutions, libraries/museums, U.S. government agencies, cultural organizations and individuals
- Provides printed information about education in Denmark and on Denmark in general
- Recommends these other sources of information: Danish Tourist Board, 75 Rockefeller Plaza, New York, NY 10019

The following are standard resources available on Denmark

INFORMATION SOURCES
- *Background Notes:* (see 2.188)
TRAVELER RESOURCES
- *Culturegram:* (see 2.191)
- *Kummerly & Frey Map of. . . .* (see 1.127)
- *Nagel's Encyclopedia Guide to. . . .* (see 2.195)
LANGUAGE LEARNING RESOURCES
- *Berlitz. . . . for Travelers* (Cassette-pak, see 9.042)
- *. . . . .: Complete Course for Beginners* (see 9.044)
- *Say It in:* (see 9.046)
- *Spoken. . . .* (see 9.047)
- *Berlitz. . . . for Travelers* (Phrasebook, see 9.043)

Fulbright Grants and ITT Fellowships for graduate study in Denmark normally available (see 7.041)

Djibouti

18.122
Djibouti: Pawn of the Horn of Africa
Robert Tholomier
Scarecrow Press, Inc.
52 Liberty St.
Metuchen, NJ 08840
1981; 177 pages; hardbound; $10

• Examination of the history and current state of the society, culture, economy
and politics of Djibouti; written by a French
engineer long a resident there

The following are standard resources avail-
able on Djibouti
INFORMATION SOURCES
• *Background Notes:* (see 2.188)

Dominican Republic

Publications

18.123
The Dominican Republic: A Caribbean Crucible
Howard J. Wiarda and Michael J. Kryzanek
Westview Press
5500 Central Ave.
Boulder, CO 80301
1981; 128 pages; hardbound, $21.50;
  paperbound; $9.50

• Concise introduction both for the student and the general reader to the contemporary Dominican Republic; examines the
history, geography, politics, international relations, economic development, culture and
social aspects of the country; also explores
the efforts at national social, economic and
political development that have occurred since
the assassination of Trujillo in 1964

The following are standard resources avail-
able on the Dominican Republic
INFORMATION SOURCES
• *Background Notes:* (see 2.188)
• *Country Study/Area Handbook. . . .*
  (see 2.189)
• *Image of. . . .* (see 2.194)
LANGUAGE LEARNING RESOURCES
For the "International" Languages (Arabic,
  French, German and Spanish) see listings
  under Chapter IX *Foreign Language
  Teaching and Learning*

Ecuador

Organizations

18.124
Embassy of Ecuador
2535 15th St. NW
Washington, DC 20009
(202) 234-7200
CONSULATES GENERAL: Los Angeles, Miami, New Orleans, New York, San Francisco

• Answers telephone and written inquiries about Ecuador, including educational matters
• Provides speakers on occasion
• Welcomes inquiries from any interested individual or institution
• Provides printed information about Ecuador in general (pamphlets and brochures)
• Recommends these other sources of information: Ecuatoriana Airlines, 1650 L St. NW, Washington, DC 20036

The following are standard resources available on Ecuador

INFORMATION SOURCES
• *Background Notes:* (see 2.188)
• *Country Study/Area Handbook....* (see 2.189)
• *Historical Dictionary of....* (see 2.193)
• *Image of....* (see 2.194)
TRAVELER RESOURCES
• *Culturegram:* (see 2.191)
LANGUAGE LEARNING RESOURCES
For the "International" Languages (Arabic, French, German and Spanish) see listings under Chapter IX *Foreign Language Teaching and Learning*

Fulbright Grants for study in Ecuador normally available (see 7.041)

Egypt

Organizations

18.125
American Research Center in Egypt, Inc.
Columbia University
1117 International Affairs Bldg.
New York, NY 10027
(212) 280-2045
and
Second Floor at 2, Midan Qasr el-Doubara
  in Garden City
Cairo, Egypt
33052 or 28239

Center for research on all phases of Egyptian civilization from ancient times to the present

• Awards approximately 30 scholarships annually to advanced graduate students and post-doctoral scholars for research in Egyptology, the humanities, the social sciences, art history, Islamic studies, archaeology and related disciplines; conducts archaeological excavations and surveys; researches, edits and translates manuscripts; publishes a newsletter and *The Journal of the American Research Center in Egypt*

18.126
Cultural and Educational Bureau
Embassy of Egypt
2200 Kalorama Road NW
Washington, DC 20008
(202) 265-6400
CONSULATES GENERAL: Chicago, Houston, New York, San Francisco, Washington, DC

• Answers written inquiries about Egypt, including educational matters

• Provides audiovisual materials and recommends speakers, performers and exhibits (when they are available in the U.S.)
• Welcomes inquiries from any interested individual or institution
• Provides printed information about education in Egypt and about Egyptian culture
• Recommends these other sources of information: Consulates General, Press & Information Office and the Egyptian Government Tourist Office, 630 Fifth Ave., New York, NY 10111

Publications

18.127
An Introduction to Egyptian Arabic
Ernest T. Abdel-Massih
Center for Near Eastern and North African
    Studies
University of Michigan
144 Lane Hall
Ann Arbor, MI 48109-1290
1981; paperbound; 405 pages; $12

Some drills available on tape from Michigan Media Resource Center, Tape Duplication Service, University of Michigan, 400 South Fourth St., Ann Arbor, MI 48109

• Course text which discusses phonology and provides basic reading and conversation lessons, grammatical notes, drills, word lists, stories and English-Arabic (Egyptian) and Arabic-English lexicon

The following are standard resources available on Egypt
INFORMATION SOURCES
• *Background Notes:* (see 2.188)
• *Country Study/Area Handbook.* . . . (see 2.189)
• *Historical Dictionary of.* . . . (see 2.193)
TRAVELER RESOURCES
• *Culturegram:* (see 2.191)
• *Update:* (see 2.197)
• *Kummerly & Frey Map of.* . . . (see 2.123)
• *Fodor's Guide to.* . . . (see 2.192)
• *Nagel's Encyclopedia Guide to.* . . . (see 2.195)
For the "International" Languages (Arabic, French, German and Spanish) see listings under Chapter IX *Foreign Language and Learning*
ITT Fellowships for graduate study in Egypt normally available (see 7.041)

El Salvador

The following are standard resources available on El Salvador
INFORMATION SOURCES
- *Background Notes:* (see 2.188)
- *Country Study/Area Handbook. . . .* (see 2.189)
- *Historical Dictionary of. . . .* (see 2.193)

- *Image of. . . .* (see 2.194)
TRAVELER RESOURCES
- *Culturegram:* (see 2.191)
For the "International" Languages (Arabic, French, German and Spanish) see listings under Chapter IX *Foreign Language Teaching and Learning*

Ethiopia

Publications

18.128
Concise Amharic Dictionary
Wolfe Leslau
California University Press
2120 Berkeley Way
Berkeley, CA 94720
1976; hardbound; 2 volumes; $69.50

- Includes English-Amharic and Amharic-English sections

18.129
Greater Ethiopia: The Evolution of a Multiethnic Society
Donald N. Levine
University of Chicago Press
5801 Ellis Ave.
Chicago, IL 60637
1977; 170 pages; paperbound, $3.95;
  hardcover, $16

- Study of historical and contemporary Ethiopia

The following are standard resources available on Ethiopia
INFORMATION SOURCES
- *Background Notes:* (see 2.188)
- *Country Study/Area Handbook. . . .* (see 2.189)
- *Historical Dictionary of. . . .* (see 2.193)

Fiji

Publications

18.130
Colour, Culture & Conflict: A Study of Pluralism in Fiji
Alexander E. Mamak
Pergamon Press, Inc.
Maxwell House
Fairview Park
Elmsford, NY 10523
1979; paperbound; $15.50

• Study of the forces in Fijian society that shaped its recent history

18.131
Fiji Focus
Ministry of Information
Suva, Fiji
bimonthly magazine; 16 pages; free

Available from the Fiji Mission to the United Nations, One UN Plaza, New York, NY 10017
• Reports on current social, political and economic news from Fiji

18.132
Fiji Handbook and Travel Guide
John Carter, Editor
Pacific Publications
New Zealand
1980; paperbound; 304 pages; $13.95

Available from Books Australia, 15601 SW 83d St., Miami, FL 33157

• Thorough guide to Fiji for the traveler; provides a great deal of information about the culture and society as well as traveler information

18.133
Fiji Today
Ministry of Information
Suva, Fiji
1982; booklet; 32 pages; free

Available from the Fiji Mission to the United Nations, One UN Plaza, New York, NY 10017
• Provides basic information about social, political and economic aspects of life in Fiji

18.134
Spoken Fijian
Albert J. Schutz and Rusiate T. Komaitai
University of Hawaii Press
2840 Kolowalu St.
Honolulu, HI 96822
1971; paperbound; 204 pages; $10

• A thorough language-learning text and guide

The following are standard resources available on Fiji
INFORMATION SOURCES
• *Background Notes:* (see 2.188)

Finland

Organizations

18.135

Embassy of Finland
3216 New Mexico Ave. NW
Washington, DC 20016
(202) 363-2430
CONSULATES GENERAL: New York, Los
Angeles

- Answers telephone and written inquiries about Finland, including travel/tourist and educational matters
- Provides or recommends speakers, performers and exhibits
- Welcomes inquiries from any interested individual or institution
- Provides printed information about education and travel in Finland and on Finland in general
- Recommends these other sources of information: Films of the Nations (provides films on Finland) and the Finland National Tourist Office, 75 Rockefeller Plaza, New York, NY 10019

18.136

League of Finnish-American Societies
151 West 51st St., Suite 200
New York, NY 10019
(212) 582-3649
or
Mechelininkatu 10
00100 Helsinki 10
Finland
90-440 711

Nonprofit organization promoting cultural and educational exchanges between the U.S. and Finland
- Provides information about Finland and advises on travel to, education in, and study of Finland; includes services of FinAm Travel Agency and access to inexpensive group flights; cooperates with other organizations in the support of exchange programs
- Arranges scholarships and traineeships for Finns in the U.S. and, through the Finnish-American Cultural Institute in Finland, disseminates knowledge about the U.S. among Finns and offers English-language instruction

The following are standard resources available on Finland
INFORMATION SOURCES
- *Background Notes:* (see 2.188)
- *Country Study/Area Handbook.* . . . (see 2.189)
- *World Bibliographical Series.* . . . (see 2.198)
TRAVELER RESOURCES
- *Culturegram:* (see 2.191)
- *Kummerly & Frey Map of.* . . . (see 1.127)
- *Nagel's Encyclopedia Guide to.* . . . (see 2.195)
LANGUAGE LEARNING RESOURCES
- *Berlitz.* . . . *for Travelers* (Cassette-pak, see 9.042)
- . . . . .: *Complete Course for Beginners* (see 9.044)
- *Spoken.* . . . (see 9.047)
- *Berlitz.* . . . *for Travelers* (Phrase-book, see 9.043)

Fulbright Grants and ITT Fellowships for graduate study in Finland normally available along with several Finnish government grants (see 7.041)

France

Organizations

18.137
Alliance Française-French Institute
22 East 60th St.
New York, NY 10022
(212) 355-6100

Contact(s):
Jean Vallier, Executive Director

Nonprofit organization designed to encourage the study of French language and culture in the U.S.

• Offers French language instruction at beginning, intermediate and advanced levels in 7- or 14-week sessions; regular classes include 8 to 12 students and small group classes, 3 to 5 students; special audiovisual and audiolingual (for beginners) and filmed (for intermediate and advanced students) instruction; private lessons are also available; winter and summer terms

• Offers graduate scholarships in all areas of study for U.S. students in France and French students in the U.S.; $3,000 per year; age: 20–30; U.S. students inquire at the Institute of International Education (see 10.010)

• Sponsors cultural events, films, lectures, recitals and drama; runs an exhibition gallery, a library and a bookstore; and offers instruction in French cooking

18.138
Conference Group on French Politics and Society
Center for European Studies
Harvard University
5 Bryant St.
Cambridge, MA 02138
(617) 495-4303

Contact(s):
George Ross, Newsletter Editor

Association of scholars

• Furthers the study of contemporary French political and social issues through conferences and the award of a biennial prize for the best doctoral dissertation in the field; publishes newsletter

18.139
Embassy of France
2535 Belmont Road NW
Washington, DC 20008
(202) 234-0990
CONSULATES GENERAL: Boston, Beverly Hills, Chicago, Detroit, Houston, New Orleans, New York, San Francisco, Washington, DC, Hato Rey, Puerto Rico

• All inquiries on education, camps, employment and French culture are referred to the French Cultural Services of the French Embassy (see 18.140) serving your state

• All inquiries on political, economic, social, trade matters and tourism are referred to the Press and Information Division of the French Embassy (see 18.141) serving your state

• All inquiries concerning student visas are handled by the Consulates General

18.140
Embassy of France, French Cultural Services
972 Fifth Ave.
New York, NY 10021
(212) 570-4400

BRANCHES: Boston, Beverly Hills, Chicago, Houston, New Orleans, New York, Washington, DC

• Offers extensive educational, cultural and information services and will send materials describing them fully

• Provides exhibits, audiovisual aids (through FACSEA, see 18.144) and educational or teaching materials

• Welcomes requests from institutions, organizations or individuals

• Provides printed information, including teaching materials and packages on French art, culture and language and a large number of brochures and information sheets on educational opportunities in France; also provides quarterly magazine *France Education* (free, in French) reviewing current trends in French education

18.141
Embassy of France, Press and Information Service
972 Fifth Ave.
New York, NY 10021
(212) 570-4400

• Provides general information on political, economic and social subjects; information also provided by the Press Attaché of the Consulates General and the French Cultural Services (see 18.140)

18.142
Institute for American Universities
Scholarships & Teaching Fellowships
27 Place de l'Université
13625 Aix-en-Provence, France

• Offers small partial tuition grant ($200–$400) to study at the Institute and a small fellowship ($1,500) to lecture there

18.143
National Science Foundation
United States-France Cooperative Science Program
Division of International Programs
Washington, DC 20550
(202) 357-7554

Contact(s):
Kenneth G. Hancock, Senior Program Manager

• Funds programs involving cooperative research, seminars and workshops and short-term visits between the U.S. and France

18.144
Society for French American Cultural Services and Educational Aid (FACSEA)
972 Fifth Ave.
New York, NY 10021
(212) 570-4400

Contact(s):
Anne Marie Morotte, Executive Director

• Maintains fee-based lending library of materials for the teaching of French language and civilization, including films, videocassettes, slides and TV series; publishes newsletter and a film catalogue

18.145
United Chapters of Phi Beta Kappa
1811 Q St. NW
Washington, DC 20009
(202) 265-3808

• Offers $7000 non-renewable Mary Isabel Sibley Fellowship for advanced study in Greek language, literature, history or archaeology (odd-numbered years) or French language or literature (even-numbered years); candidates must be unmarried women between 25 and 35 years of age and hold a Ph.D. or have completed all requirements except the dissertation; application deadline: January 15 of award year

Publications

18.146
The French Review
Stirling Haig, Editor in Chief
American Association of Teachers of French
57 East Armory
Champaign, IL 61820
published 6 times a year (October through
　　May); paperbound; approx. 314 pages; $21
　　per year

　　• Articles on French literature and language and on the teaching of French; large number of book reivews

18.147
Libraries and Archives in France: A Research Handbook
Erwin K. Welsch
Council for European Studies
1509 International Affairs Bldg.
Columbia University
New York, NY 10027
1979; paperbound; 147 pages; $6 (members
　　$4.50), plus $1 postage

Part of Research Series which includes *The European Community* (see 15.035), *Libraries and Archives in Italy: A Research Handbook* (see 18.260) and *Libraries and Archives in Germany: A Research Handbook* (see 18.164)
　　• Provides detailed information on important research, library and archival resources in France covering Paris and each department; entries include information on holdings, printed and manuscript guides and catalogs, as well as such practical information as hours and annual closings; many descriptions add notes on research aids and how to use the collections most effectively
　　• Includes lengthy bibliography of books and articles on archival and library holdings; appendices cover archival classification and provide guidelines on how to locate manuscripts in French libraries; descriptions based

on information supplied by scholars who have used the libraries

18.148
Modern France: Mind, Politics and Society, 1870–1970
Barnett Singer
University of Washington Press
Box 85569
Seattle, WA 98105
1981; hardbound; 240 pages; $17.95

　　• Basic analysis of contemporary France and the social, economic and political issues facing it

18.149
Passport to France
André Fertey
EMC Publishing
300 York Ave.
St. Paul, MN 55101
1978; 5 filmstrips, 5 open reel tapes or
　　cassettes, and Teacher's Guide with
　　student activities on blackline originals;
　　$128

　　• Multimedia program in English and French designed as a beginning language-learning mini-course for students and travelers who are going to France

The following are standard resources available on France
INFORMATION SOURCES
　　• *Background Notes:* (see 2.188)
　　• *Country Study/Area Handbook.* . . . (see 2.189)
　　• *Historical Dictionary of.* . . . (see 2.193) French Antilles
　　• *World Bibliographical Series.* . . . (see 2.198)
TRAVELER RESOURCES

- *Communication Learning Aids:* (see 2.190)
- *Culturegram:* (see 2.191)
- *Update:* (see 2.197)
- *Kummerly & Frey Map of. . . .* (see 1.127)
- *Fodor's Guide to. . . .* (see 2.192)

LANGUAGE LEARNING RESOURCES

For the "International" Languages (Arabic, French, German and Spanish) see listings under Chapter IX *Foreign Language Teaching and Learning*

Fulbright Grants and ITT Fellowships for graduate study in France normally available along with several French government fellowships, approximately 40 teaching assistantships in English, approximately 10 Alliance Francaise Scholarships and 3 Annette Kade Fellowships in the creative and performing arts (see 7.041)

Gabon

The following are standard resources available on Gabon

INFORMATION SOURCES

- *Background Notes:* (see 2.188)
- *Historical Dictionary of. . . .* (see 2.193)

LANGUAGE LEARNING RESOURCES

For the "International" Languages (Arabic, French, German and Spanish) see listings under Chapter IX *Foreign Language Teaching and Learning*

The Gambia

Publications

18.150
A General Bibliography of The Gambia, Up to 31 December 1977
S. David P. Gamble
G. K. Hall & Co.
70 Lincoln St.
Boston, MA 02111
1979; hardbound; 283 pages; $45

- Comprehensive bibliography of more

than 2,500 books and periodical references to the history, economy, political development and cultural life of The Gambia

The following are standard resources available on The Gambia

INFORMATION SOURCES

- *Background Notes:* (see 2.188)
- *Historical Dictionary of. . . .* (see 2.193)

German Democratic Republic (GDR)

Organizations

18.151
Embassy of the German Democratic Republic
1717 Massachusetts Ave. NW
Washington, DC 20036
(202) 232-3134

• Provides a variety of publications de-scribing life in the GDR and GDR policies from a Marxist perspective; includes *The German Democratic Republic Illustrated, GDR: Facts and Figures, Introducing the GDR* (see 18.154), *Geographic Manual* (see 18.152) and a series of 20 booklets under the general title *First-hand Information* ("What Is Life Like in the GDR?," "Youth," "Law and Justice," etc.

Publications

18.152
Geographic Manual: German Democratic Republic
Government of the German Democratic Republic, DDR
8012 Dresden, Julian-Grimau-Allee
German Democratic Republic
1978; 15-page booklet and 7 maps; free

Available from the German Democratic Republic Embassy, 1717 Massachusetts Ave., Washington, DC 20036
• Booklet and series of maps describing and depicting the GDR from the following perspectives: (1) physical and political geography, (2) transportation and communications, (3) the counties of the GDR, (4) industry, (5) agriculture, food and related industries, (6) cultural and educational institutions, and (7) recreation

18.153
The German Democratic Republic
Henry Krisch
Westview Press
5500 Central Ave.
Boulder, CO 80301
1982; hardbound; 128 pages; $16.50

• Concise introduction both for the student and the general reader to the contemporary German Democratic Republic; examines the history, geography, politics, international relations, economic development, culture and social aspects of the country; also explores the significance of East Germany within the Soviet Alliance system in relation to its common heritage with West Germany

18.154
Introducing the GDR
Panorama DDR
1054 Berlin
Wilhelm Pieck Strasse 49
German Democratic Republic
1978; paperbound; 336 pages; free

Available from the Embassy of the German Democratic Republic, 1717 Massachusetts Ave., Washington, DC 20036
• Provides some useful factual data and a large number of photographs, along with a description of the GDR from a Marxist perspective

18.155
Libraries and Archives in Germany:
A Research Handbook
Erwin K. Welsch
Council for European Studies
1509 International Affairs Bldg.
Columbia University
New York, NY 10027
1975; paperbound; 275 pages; $6, plus $1
   postage and handling

Part of Research Resources Series which includes *The European Community* (see 15.035), *Libraries and Archives in France: A Research Handbook* (see 18.147) and *Libraries and Archives in Italy: A Research Handbook* (see 18.260)
• Includes libraries and archives in both the German Federal Republic and the German Democratic Republic and an introductory essay on problems of research in both parts of Germany; covers archives and libraries in 33 cities in West Germany and national, university, regional, special and institute libraries and archives in East Germany; each collection is described and procedures for use are indicated

The following are standard resources available on the German Democratic Republic
INFORMATION SOURCES
• *Background Notes:* (see 2.188)
• *Country Study/Area Handbook.* . . . (see 2.189)
TRAVELER RESOURCES
• *Communication Learning Aids:* (see 2.190)
• *Kummerly & Frey Map of.* . . . (see 1.127)
• *Nagel's Encyclopedia Guide to.* . . . (see 2.195)
LANGUAGE LEARNING RESOURCES
For the "International" Languages (Arabic, French, German and Spanish) see listings under Chapter IX *Foreign Language Teaching and Learning*

Germany, Federal Republic of

Area Study and Research Programs

18.156
German-Scandinavian Studies
Washington University
St. Louis, MO 63130
(314) 889-5000

Contact(s):
Egon Schwarz, Chair

Graduate area studies program
• Majors/degrees/certificates   offered:

M.A. in German-Scandinavian Area Studies
• Approximate number of faculty teaching area & language courses: 9
• Approximate number of courses available—area and language: 42
• Countries covered and areas of emphasis: East Germany, West Germany, Denmark, Norway, and Sweden; particular emphasis on German history and literature
• Languages offered: German or Scandinavian language prerequisite to admission

Organizations

18.157
American Council on Germany
680 Fifth Ave.
New York, NY 10019
(212) 541-7878

Contact(s):
David Klein, Executive Director

Nonprofit policy-oriented organization designed to improve communication, understanding, and exchange between the U.S. and the Federal Republic of Germany; established in 1952
• Sponsors conferences and workshops for U.S. and German leaders, specialists, young professionals and other concerned groups and institutions
• Offers fellowships under the John J. McCloy Fund to young German and American professionals for travel and study in the U.S. or Germany; includes persons in urban affairs, labor, journalism, art, and farm management
• Arranges exchanges of journalists and political leaders

18.158
Conference Group on German Politics—Directory of Current Research
David Conradt, Research Coordinator
Conference Group on German Politics
1267 Delaware Ave. SW
Washington, DC 20024
biennial; hardbound; approx. 250 pages; $5

• Provides information on researchers and on research projects related to East and West German politics over a five-year period

18.159
Embassy of the Federal Republic of Germany
4645 Reservoir Road NW
Washington, DC 20007
(202) 298-4000

• All requests are referred to the appropriate offices, such as the German National Tourist Office, 747 Third Ave., 33d Floor, New York, NY 10017; exhibitions and smaller guest-performances, Goethe House, (see 18.162); and general questions, requests for material or speakers, German Information Center (see 18.161)

18.160
German Academic Exchange Service
535 Fifth Ave., Suite 1107
New York, NY 10017
(212) 599-0464

Contact(s):
Arnold Ebel, Director

• Offers grants to Americans to meet a variety of research and study needs in West Germany, including short- and long-term, pre- and post-doctoral research and study/visit grants, summer intensive German language study (including two for persons not teaching or majoring in German), and grants for participation in summer German Studies seminars (including one in English); except as noted a good working knowledge of German is expected in most cases; also offers traineeships in agriculture, law and other areas, and program and financial assistance for study tour groups organized by U.S. academic institutions

18.161
German Information Center
410 Park Ave.
New York, NY 10022
(212) 888-9840

Contact(s):
Inge Godenschweger .

Government information center
• Answers phone or written inquiries about Germany and about sources of information on all aspects of German life
• Sponsors lecture tours by German professionals
• Distributes *Facts About Germany* (see 18.163), a series of summary brochures about many facets of German life, newsletters reporting on current German political, cultural and social affairs, and other publications of interest to the educator or student
• Houses reference library and research archives open to the public and a large selection of German-language newspapers and periodicals

18.162
Goethe House New York—German Cultural Center
1014 Fifth Ave.
New York, NY 10028
(212) 744-8310
BRANCHES: Ann Arbor, Atlanta, Boston, Chicago, Houston, Los Angeles, San Francisco, Seattle, St. Louis

Contact(s):
Christoph Wecker, Director

Center for promoting German language study abroad and cultural cooperation; sponsored by West German government
• Provides information on current German cultural affairs; sponsors workshops and seminars on teaching German language and culture for German departments in high schools and colleges; maintains a service center for teachers of German providing information on currently available teaching materials and instructional techniques and offers audiovisual teaching aids on loan; publishes newsletter for German-language teachers
• Conducts cultural and scientific programs in cooperation with American institutions and maintains library of 12,000 books and 100 periodicals (in German and English, including eight leading German newspapers) and a collection of recordings; most materials available on interlibrary loan
• Sponsors German American Partnership Program of four- to six-week school exchanges between a total of 120 schools in the U.S. and West Germany

Publications

18.163
Facts About Germany
Heinz Dieter Bulka and Susanne Lücking, Editors
Bertelsmann Lexikothek Verlag
Gütersloh
Federal Republic of Germany
1984; paperbound; 416 pages; free

Available from the German Information Center, 410 Park Ave., New York, NY 10022

• Thorough description of West Germany, its people and its society; covers history, geography, economy, government, social services and culture; includes a variety of statistics and fact lists

18.164
Libraries and Archives in Germany: A Research Handbook
Erwin K. Welsch
Council for European Studies
1509 International Affairs Bldg.
Columbia University
New York, NY 10027
c.1975; paperbound; 275 pages; $6, plus $1 postage and handling

Part of Research Resources Series which includes *The European Community* (see 15.035), *Libraries and Archives in France: A Research Handbook* (see 18.147) and *Libraries and Archives in Italy: A Research Handbook* (see 18.260)
  • Includes libraries and archives in both the German Federal Republic and the German Democratic Republic and an introductory essay on problems of research in both parts of Germany; covers archives and libraries in 33 cities in West Germany and national, university, regional, special and institute libraries and archives in East Germany; each collection is described and procedures for use are indicated

18.165
Passport to Germany
Wolfgang Kraft
EMC Publishing
300 York Ave.
St. Paul, MN 55101
1978; 5 filmstrips, 5 open reel tapes or cassettes, and Teacher's Guide with Student activities on blackline originals; $128

  • Multimedia program in English and German designed as a beginning language-learning mini-course for students and travelers who are going to Germany

The following are standard resources available on the Federal Republic of Germany

INFORMATION SOURCES
  • *Background Notes:* (see 2.188)
  • *Country Study/Area Handbook. . . .* (see 2.189)

TRAVELER RESOURCES
  • *Communication Learning Aids:* (see 2.190)
  • *Culturegram:* (see 2.191)
  • *Update:* (see 2.197)
  • *Kummerly & Frey Map of. . . .* (see 1.127)
  • *Fodor's Guide to. . . .* (see 2.192)
  • *Nagel's Encyclopedia Guide to. . . .* (see 2.195)

LANGUAGE LEARNING RESOURCES
For the "International" Languages (Arabic, French, German and Spanish) see listings under Chapter IX *Foreign Language Teaching and Learning*
Fulbright Grants and ITT Fellowships for graduate study in West Germany normally available; 50 German Academic Exchange Service Grants 20 teaching assistantships in English, several Quadrillo Grants in specialized areas of study and an Annette Kade Fellowship in the performing arts (see 7.041)

Ghana

Organizations

18.166
Information Section, Embassy of Ghana
2460 16th St. NW
Washington, DC 20009
(202) 462-0761
CONSULATE GENERAL: New York

• Answers telephone and written inquiries about Ghana, including travel/tourist and educational matters

• Provides speakers, exhibits, and audiovisual materials
• Welcomes inquiries from any interested institution
• Provides printed information about travel in Ghana and on Ghana in general, including posters, a large tourist map, *Facts About Ghana* (a press release) and the monthly newsletter *Ghana News* (see 18.168)
• Recommends this other source of information: Consulate General

Publications

18.167
Ghana: Evolution & Change in the 19th & 20th Centuries
Longman, Inc.
19 West 44th St.
New York, NY 10036
1979; paperbound; 120 pages; $5.50

• Review of Ghanaian history and the forces that have shaped contemporary Ghana

18.168
Ghana News
Information Section
Embassy of Ghana
2460 16th St. NW
Washington, DC 20009
monthly newsletter; 11 pages; free

• Lively newsletter reporting on current political and economic developments in Ghana

18.169
Ghana Year Book
Ghana Graphic Corp.
P.O.B. 742
Accra, Ghana
annual; hardbound; 216 pages; $87

• Provides information on social, political, geographic and economic aspects of Ghana and on government organizations and activities; identifies persons in leadership positions

The following are standard resources available on Ghana
INFORMATION SOURCES
  • *Background Notes:* (see 2.188)
  • *Country Study/Area Handbook. . . .* (see 2.189)

Greece

Area Study and Research Programs

18.170
Greek Studies Program
Regis College
Weston, MA 02193
(617) 893-1820

Contact(s):
A. L. Macrakis, Director

Undergraduate area studies program established in 1972
• Majors/degrees/certificates offered: Certificate of Greek Studies or B.A. with individually designed major in Greek Studies
• Approximate number of faculty teaching area and language courses: 4
• Approximate number of courses available—area: 8–12; language: 2–6
• Average number of students per year specializing in area: 5
• Countries covered and areas of emphasis: Greece (ancient and modern) with some attention to the Balkans and the Eastern Mediterranean
• Languages offered: ancient and modern Greek

• Library holds a substantial collection of ancient Greek, Byzantine, and especially modern Greek books and audiovisual materials
• Offers a full year, semester or six months (including summer) in Greece at College Year in Athens, Study in Greece, or Aegean Institute programs

18.171
Center For Neo-Hellenic Studies
1010 West 22d St.
Austin, TX 78705
(512) 477-5526

Contact(s):
E. G. Arnakis, Acting Director

• Conducts research on modern (13th–20th century) Greek history and culture with particular interest in Greek literature; offers prizes for work in these areas; publishes bulletin *Neo-Hellenika*

Organizations

18.172
American Hellenic Institute, Inc.
1730 K St. NW, Suite 903
Washington, DC 20006
(800) 424-9607 or (202) 785-8430

Contact(s):
Georgia Alexander-Delyannis, Executive
  Director

Public policy organization designed to promote trade relationships between the U.S. and Greece and Cyprus and to mobilize support for the reunification of Cyprus
• Provides information on commercial and public-policy issues relative to U.S.-Greek relations and maintains information center with collection of books, bibliographies, reports, etc. of relevance to U.S.-Greek trade and political relations; publishes American-Hellenic *Who's Who in Business and the Professions* (Americans of Greek descent) and other materials

18.173
Modern Greek Studies Association
Box 1826
New Haven, CT 06508
(203) 397-4189

Contact(s):
John O. Iatrides, Executive Director

Nonprofit educational association designed to promote the study of modern Greece
- Answers questions and provides information about Greek Studies, organizes conferences and symposia, sponsors studies and publishes *Journal of Modern Greek Studies* (semi-annual), the *MGSA Bulletin* (semi-annual) and *Modern Greek Society: A Newsletter* (a social science bibliographic guide)

18.174
Press and Information Office, Embassy of Greece
2211 Massachusetts Ave. NW
Washington, DC 20008
(202) 332-2727
CONSULATES GENERAL: Chicago, New York, San Francisco
CONSULATES: Atlanta, Boston, New Orleans

- Answers telephone and written inquiries about Greece, including travel/tourist and educational matters
- Provides or recommends speakers, films and other audiovisual materials
- Welcomes inquiries from any interested individual or institution
- Provides printed information about education and travel in Greece and on Greece in general, including the booklet *Facts About Greece*
- Recommends these other sources of information: Consulates General and Greek Tourist Organization, Olympic Tower, 645 Fifth Ave., New York, NY 10022

18.175
United Chapters of Phi Beta Kappa
1811 Q St. NW
Washington, DC 20009

- Offers Mary Isabel Sibley Fellowship to unmarried women scholars between 25 and 35 years old who hold the doctorate (or have completed all requirements but the dissertation); awarded in Greek language, literature, history or archaeology in odd-numbered years and in French language or literature in even-numbered years

Publications

18.176
Greece: The Week in Review
Press & Information Office
Embassy of Greece
2211 Massachusetts Ave. NW
Washington, DC 20008
weekly bulletin; 4 pages; free

- Newsletter reporting on current political, social economic, and cultural affairs in Greece

18.177
Greece: A Portrait
Research and Publicity Center Kede, Ltd.
10 Amerikis St.
Athens, Greece
1979; paperbound; 191 pages; free

Available from Office of Press and Information, Embassy of Greece, 2211 Massachusetts Ave. NW, Washington, DC 20008
- Comprehensive introduction to Greece

filled with practical data for the business executive, educator and traveler; includes lists of government agencies, political party headquarters, Greek embassies, Greek and foreign banks, trade, cultural and social organizations, Greek tourist offices abroad, museums, galleries and libraries, church headquarters, universities, educational and research organizations, communications organizations, news agencies and newspapers (Greek and foreign) and radio and TV stations

18.178
Modern Greece: A Short History
C. M. Woodhouse
Faber and Faber, Inc.
39 Thompson St.
Winchester, MA 01890
1977; paperbound; 336 pages; $7.95

• Thorough basic survey of Greek history and society up to the present time

18.179
Speak and Read Essential (Modern) Greek: A Pimsleur Language Program
Paul Pimsler
Heinle & Heinle Enterprises, Inc.
29 Lexington Rd.
Concord, MA 01742
1971; 20 units on 10 cassettes and reading booklet, in vinyl album; $249.95

• Self-instructional language program based principally on the graduated-interval recall system designed for learning by use of tapes alone

The following company imports and sells books in the Greek language:

18.180
Bibliophilos-European Publications Service
83 Trowbridge St.
Cambridge, MA 02138
(617) 876-1746

The following are standard resources available on Greece
INFORMATION SOURCES
  • *Background Notes:* (see 2.188)
  • *Country Study/Area Handbook. . . .* (see 2.189)
  • *World Bibliographical Series. . . .* (see 2.198)
TRAVELER RESOURCES
  • *Culturegram:* (see 2.191)
  • *Fodor's Guide to. . . .* (see 2.192)
  • *Nagel's Encyclopedia Guide to. . . .* (see 2.195)
LANGUAGE LEARNING RESOURCES
  • *Berlitz. . . . for Travelers* (Cassette-pak, see 9.042)
  • *. . . .: Complete Course for Beginners* (see 9.044)
  • *Say It in:* (see 9.046)
  • *Spoken. . . .* (see 9.047)
  • *Vest Pocket. . . .* (see 9.048)
  • *Berlitz. . . . for Travelers* (Phrasebook, see 9.043)
Fulbright Grants and ITT Fellowships for graduate study in Greece normally available (see 7.041)

Grenada

Publications

18.181
Grenada News
Permanent Mission of Grenada to the
   Organization of American States
1424 16th St. NW
Washington, DC 20036
monthly; 16 pages; free

- Provides information on political and
economic developments in Grenada and on
the policies of the government

The following are standard resources available on Grenada
INFORMATION SOURCES
- *Background Notes:* (see 2.188)
- *Image of. . . .* (see 2.194)

Guatemala

Organizations

18.182
Embassy of Guatemala
2220 R St. NW
Washington, DC 20008
(202) 745-4952

- Answers telephone and written inquiries about Guatemala, including travel/
tourist and educational matters
- Provides audiovisual materials
- Welcomes inquiries from any interested individual or organization
- Provides printed information about education and travel to and in Guatemala, including a large tourist map

Publications

18.183
Guatemala Guide
Paul Glassman
Passport Press
Box 596
Moscow, VT 05662
1977; paperbound; 345 pages; $15

- Discusses Guatemalan history and culture and then provides thorough guidebook information for the traveler

18.184
Research Guide to Guatemala
Pan American Institute of Geography and
   History
Ex-Arzobispado No. 29
Mexico 18, D.F.
1978; paperbound; 157 pages; $8

In English and Spanish
- Provides basic guidelines and bibliography for pursuing research on Guatemala

The following are standard resources available on Guatemala

INFORMATION SOURCES
- *Background Notes:* (see 2.188)
- *Country Study/Area Handbook.* . . . (see 2.189)
- *Historical Dictionary of.* . . . (see 2.193)
- *World Bibliographical Series.* . . . (see 2.198)

- *Image of.* . . . (see 2.194)

TRAVELER RESOURCES
- *Culturegram:* (see 2.191)

LANGUAGE LEARNING RESOURCES
For the "International" Languages (Arabic, French, German and Spanish) see listings under Chapter IX *Foreign Language Teaching and Learning*

Guinea

The following are standard resources available on Guinea

INFORMATION SOURCES
- *Background Notes:* (see 2.188)
- *Country Study/Area Handbook.* . . . (see 2.189)
- *Historical Dictionary of.* . . . (see 2.193)

LANGUAGE LEARNING RESOURCES
For the "International" Languages (Arabic, French, German and Spanish) see listings under Chapter IX *Foreign Language Teaching and Learning*

Guinea-Bissau

Publications

18.185
Guinea-Bissau and Cape Verde: A Comprehensive Bibliography
Joseph M. McCarthy
Garland Publishing, Inc.
136 Madison Ave., 2d Floor
New York, NY 10016
1977; hardbound; 180 pages; $21

- Useful research and study tool

The following are standard resources available on Guinea-Bissau

INFORMATION SOURCES
- *Background Notes:* (see 2.188)
- *Historical Dictionary of.* . . . (see 2.193)

Guyana

Organizations

18.186
Embassy of the Republic of Guyana
2490 Tracy Place NW
Washington, DC 20008
(202) 265-6900
CONSULATES GENERAL: East Chicago, IN,
Los Angeles, New York, Panama City, FL,
Waco, TX, Washington, DC

• Answers telephone inquiries about
Guyana, including travel/tourist and educational matters
• Provides speakers and audiovisual materials

• Welcomes inquiries from any interested individual or institution
• Provides printed information about education and travel in Guyana and Guyana in general
• Recommends these other sources of information: Consulates General

The following are standard resources available on Guyana
INFORMATION SOURCES
• *Background Notes:* (see 2.188)
• *Country Study/Area Handbook.* . . . (see 2.189)

Haiti

Organizations

18.187
Embassy of Haiti
2311 Massachusetts Ave. NW
Washington, DC 20008
(202) 332-4090
CONSULATES GENERAL: Chicago, Miami,
New York, San Juan, Puerto Rico
• Answers telephone and written inquiries about Haiti, including travel/tourist and educational matters

• Provides speakers
• Welcomes inquiries from travel/tourist organizations and individuals
• Provides printed information about travel in Haiti and on Haiti in general
• Recommends this other source of information: Haiti Government Tourist Bureau, 30 Rockefeller Plaza, New York, NY 10112

Publications

18.188
The Complete Haitiana: A Bibliographic Guide to the Scholarly Literature, 1900–1980
Michel Laguerre
Kraus International Publications
Route 100
Millwood, NY 10546

1982; hardbound; 2 volumes; $270

• Encompasses the humanities and the social sciences; covers books, monographs, dissertations, journal and magazine articles, major newspaper articles, government documents, pamphlets, documents of international organizations and feasibility studies;

contains approximately 10,000 entries in various languages, including Haitian Creole, with each entry accompanied by an English translation; author and subject indexes

The following are standard resources available on Haiti
INFORMATION SOURCES
  • *Background Notes:* (see 2.188)
  • *Country Study/Area Handbook.* . . . (see 2.189)

  • *Historical Dictionary of.* . . . (see 2.193)
  • *Image of.* . . . (see 2.194)

LANGUAGE LEARNING RESOURCES
For the "International" Languages (Arabic, French, German and Spanish) see listings under Chapter IX *Foreign Language Teaching and Learning*

Honduras

Publications

18.189
Research Guide to Honduras
Pan American Institute of Geography and
  History
Ex-Arzobispado No. 29
Mexico 18, D.F.
1977; paperbound; 45 pages; $5

  • Provides basic guidelines and bibliography for pursuing research on Honduras

The following are standard resources available on Honduras

INFORMATION SOURCES
  • *Background Notes:* (see 2.188)
  • *Country Study/Area Handbook.* . . . (see 2.189)
  • *Historical Dictionary of.* . . . (see 2.193)
  • *Image of.* . . . (see 2.194)
  • *Culturegram:* (see 2.191)
LANGUAGE LEARNING RESOURCES
For the "International" Languages (Arabic, French, German and Spanish) see listings under Chapter IX *Foreign Language Teaching and Learning*

Hong Kong

Organizations

18.190
Universities Service Centre, Hong Kong
% American Council of Learned Societies
228 E. 45th St.
New York, NY 10017
(212) 697-1505
and

155 Argyle St.
Kowloon
Hong Kong

Contact(s):
John Dolfin, Director, Hong Kong (phone
  K7110261)

Center designed to facilitate predoctoral field research on topics dealing with modern Chinese affairs; users should contact the Hong Kong Centre directly

- Provides orientation, library facilities and administrative assistance to researchers

Publications

The following are standard resources available on Hong Kong
INFORMATION SOURCES
- *Background Notes:* (see 2.188)
TRAVELER RESOURCES
- *Communication Learning Aids:* (see 2.190)

- *Culturegram:* (see 2.191)
- *Update;* (see 2.197)
LANGUAGE LEARNING RESOURCES
- *. . . .: Complete Course for Beginners* (see 9.044) "Cantonese"
- *Spoken. . . .* (see 9.047) "Cantonese"

Hungary

Area Study and Research Programs

18.191
Hungarian Studies
Indiana University at Bloomington
Goodbody Hall 101
Bloomington, IN 47405
(812) 335-2398

Contact(s):
Denis Sinor, Director

- Offers Graduate Certificate in Hungarian Studies under Inner Asian and Uralic National Resource Center (see 14.013)

Organizations

18.192
American Hungarian Educators Association
707 Snider Lane
Silver Spring, MD 20904
(301) 426-6323

Contact(s):
Enikö Molnár Basa, Executive Director

Educational organization for the promotion of Hungarian Studies

- Provides information on Hungarian Studies and answers inquiries about educational resources from scholars, teachers and schools; conducts and supports research; publishes newsletter and directory

18.193
American Hungarian Library and Historical Society
215 East 82d St.
New York, NY 10028
(212) 744-5298

Contact(s):
Paul E. Vesenyi, President

Cultural organization designed to collect materials on the literature, history and politics of Hungary
• Arranges lectures and answers inquiries relative to the study of Hungarian literature, history and politics
• Maintains library of materials, but access currently restricted because of limited financial resources

18.194
Embassy of the Hungarian People's Republic
3910 Shoemaker St. NW
Washington, DC 20008
(202) 362-6730
CONSULATE GENERAL: New York

• Answers telephone and written inquiries about Hungary, including travel/tourist and educational matters
• Welcomes inquiries from any interested institution or individual
• Provides printed information about travel, education and general interest subjects; includes extensive collection of booklets, pamphlets and newsletters on Hungary in general, on individual cities and on Hungarian life, economy and culture; among them:

Hungarian Digest (see 18.197), *A Short History of Musical Life in Hungary, Women in Hungary, A Brief History of Hungary* and several newsletters covering current political, social and economic affairs (all, except *Hungarian Digest,* are free)
• Recommends this other source of information: Hungarian Travel Bureau IBUSZ, 630 Fifth Ave., New York, NY 10111

18.195
Hungarian Cultural Foundation
P.O. Box 364
Stone Mountain, GA 30086
(404) 377-2600

Contact(s):
Joseph M. Ertavy-Barath, President

Nonprofit educational organization established in 1966 to promote increased knowledge of Hungarian culture in the U.S.
• Publishes monographs and other materials on Hungarian culture, history and civilization, including the translation of Hungarian authors; sponsors lectures, exhibitions, etc.
• Maintains 6,000-volume library and archival collections
• Occasionally provides grants or scholarships for the study of Hungary; provides internships for students of Hungarian language and literature

Publications

18.196
Guide to Hungarian Studies
Elemer Bako
Hoover Institution Press
Stanford University
Stanford, CA 94305
1973; hardbound; 1,218 pages in 2 volumes;
    $45 per set

• An extensive bibliography of diversified material for English-speaking students of Hungary

18.197
Hungarian Digest
Tibor Zador, Editor
Lapkiado Publishing House
H-1073 Budapest
Lenin krt. 9-11, Hungary
bimonthly magazine; 128 pages; $6 per year

Available from Center of Hungarian Literature, 4418 16th Ave., Brooklyn, NY 11004
• English-language *Readers Digest*-like magazine with articles on Hungarian life and

culture, covering such areas as politics, economics, music, sciences, sports, literature and current social affairs

18.198
Hungary: A Nation of Contradictions
Ivan Volgyes
Westview Press
5500 Central Ave.
Boulder, CO 80301
1981; hardbound; 128 pages; $17.50

• Concise introduction both for the student and the general reader to contemporary Hungary; examines the history, geography, politics, international relations, economic development, culture and social aspects of the country; includes a particularly thorough analysis of Hungary under communism

The following companies import and sell books in the Hungarian language:

18.199
FAM Book Service
69 Fifth Ave.
New York, NY 10003
(212) 255-8348

18.200
Hungarian Books & Records
11802 Buckeye Road
Cleveland, OH 44120
(216) 991-3737

18.201
Kerekes Brothers, Inc.
177 East 87th St.
New York, NY 10028
(212) 289-2020

The following are standard resources available on Hungary
INFORMATION SOURCES
• *Background Notes:* (see 2.188)
• *Country Study/Area Handbook.* . . . (see 2.189)
• *World Bibliographical Series.* . . . (see 2.198)
TRAVELER RESOURCES
• *Culturegram:* (see 2.191)
• *Kummerly & Frey Map of.* . . . (see 1.127)
• *Nagel's Encyclopedia Guide to.* . . . (see 2.195)
LANGUAGE LEARNING RESOURCES
• *Berlitz.* . . . *for Travelers* (Phrasebook, see 9.043)
• *Spoken.* . . . (see 9.047)

Iceland

Publications

18.202
Iceland: The First New Society
Richard F. Tomasson
University of Minnesota Press
2037 University Ave. SE
Minneapolis, MN 55414
1980; hardbound; 240 pages; $17.50

• Thorough review of the history, society and culture of Iceland

The following are standard resources available on Iceland
INFORMATION SOURCES
• *Background Notes:* (see 2.188)

TRAVELER RESOURCES
- *Culturegram:* (see 2.191)
- *Nagel's Encyclopedia Guide to. . . .* (see 2.195)

LANGUAGE LEARNING RESOURCES
- *. . . .: Complete Course for Beginners* (see 9.044)

Fulbright Grants for study in Iceland normally available along with an Icelandic government grant in Icelandic Studies (see 7.041)

India

Organizations

18.203
American Institute of Indian Studies
University of Chicago
Foster Hall
1130 East 59th St.
Chicago, IL 60637

Contact(s):
Edward L. Dimock, Jr., President

Educational organization for the promotion of research on and in India
- Offers grants to faculty (both India specialists and others), to librarians and to doctoral students for research in India; conducts language and training program in India and supports the translation of Indian texts into English
- Maintains cooperative photographic archives with the University of Pennsylvania South Asia Regional Studies Department (see 13.108)

18.204
Embassy of India
Education Wing
2107 Massachusetts Ave. NW
Washington, DC 20008
(202) 265-5050
CONSULATES GENERAL: Chicago, New York, San Francisco

- Answers telephone and written inquiries about India regarding educational matters
- Recommends speakers, performers, exhibits, films, audiovisuals and other educational materials
- Welcomes inquiries from any interested individual or institution
- Provides printed information about education in India as well as about India in general
- Recommends these other sources of information: Consulates General and Government of India Tourist Office, 30 Rockefeller Plaza, N. Mezzanine, New York, NY 10020

18.205
Indo American Fellowship Program of Advanced Research/Professional Development in India
Council for International Exchange of
    Scholars (CIES)
11 Dupont Circle NW, Suite 300
Washington, DC 20036
(202) 833-4985

Contact(s):
Lydia Z. Gomez, Program Officer

- A program administered by the Council for International Exchange of Scholars (see 7.007) which annually provides approximately 20-25 short- and long-term grants (including monthly stipends, travel and allowances) for established academics or professionals with little or no experience in India to undertake research in India which helps open new channels of communication between academic and professional groups in India and the U.S.; may be in any discipline or field; application deadline: June 15

18.206
National Science Foundation
United States-India Cooperative Science
    Program
Division of International Programs
Washington, DC 20550
(202) 357-9550

Contact(s):
Osman Shinaishin, Senior Program
    Manager

    • Funds programs involving research and

short-term visits between the U.S. and India

18.207
Taraknath Das Foundation, Inc.
Columbia University
℅ Southern Asian Institute
420 West 118th St.
New York, NY 10027
(212) 280-4462

Contact(s):
Kathryn Linden, Director

Foundation which supports activities related to Indian and Asian studies
    • Provides small grants to scholars conducting research on India or Asia and to Indian students studying in the U.S.
    • Awards small institutional grants to colleges and universities in the U.S. and abroad in support of international education activities
    • Sponsors lectures in New York on Asian and Indian subjects

Publications

18.208
India News
Information Service
Embassy of India
2107 Massachusetts Ave. NW
Washington, DC 20008
weekly tabloid; 8 pages; $5 per year

    • Reports in brief on Indian political, economic, social, educational and cultural activities of interest to the American reader; book reviews

18.209
Indian & Foreign Review
H. B. Mathur, Chief Editor
Government of India
Patiala House
New Delhi 110001, India
biweekly tabloid; 28 pages; $9 per year

Microform editions of the Review are available from University Microfilms, 300 North Zeeb, Ann Arbor, MI 48106
    • Contains articles on Indian life and

culture and on aspects of India's relations with other countries as well as commentary on current developments in Indian international affairs; book reviews

18.210
The Times of India Directory and Yearbook, Including Who's Who
International Publications Service
114 East 32d St.
New York, NY 10016
annual; paperbound; approx. 950 pages; $45

    • Survey of the year's developments in most areas of Indian life

18.211
Your India Trip: An Orientation Guide
Educational Resources Center
D-53 Defence Colony
New Delhi-110024, India
1980; paperbound; 46 pages; free

Available from Center for International Programs, New York State Education Department, Cultural Education Center, Empire State Plaza, Albany, NY 12230
    • Useful guide for the student, scholar or other visitor to India; covers basic traveler and tourist information on such things as what to bring, health, food, social customs, etc., along with a description of salient features of Indian culture

    The following companies import and sell books in the Hindi language:

18.212
Annapurna Publications
P.O. Box 465
Santa Rosa, CA 95402
(707) 523-1726

18.213
Tec-Books, Ltd.
39-41 William
Plattsburgh, NY 12901
(518) 561-0005

The following are standard resources available on India
INFORMATION SOURCES
    • *Background Notes:* (see 2.188)
    • *Country Study/Area Handbook.* . . . (see 2.189)
    • *Historical Dictionary of.* . . . (see 2.193)
    • *World Bibliographical Series.* . . . (see 2.198)
TRAVELER RESOURCES
    • *Culturegram:* (see 2.191)
    • *Fodor's Guide to.* . . . (see 2.192)
    • *Nagel's Encyclopedia Guide to.* . . . (see 2.195)
    • *. . . .: A Travel Survival Kit* (see 2.196)
LANGUAGE LEARNING RESOURCES
    • *. . . .: Complete Course for Beginners* (see 9.044) "Punjabi"
    • *Say It in:* (see 9.046) "Hindi"
    • *Spoken.* . . . (see 9.047) "Hindustani," "Telugu"
Fulbright Grants for study in India normally available (see 7.041)

Indonesia

Area Study and Research Programs

18.214
Cornell Modern Indonesia Project
Cornell University
102 West Ave.
Ithaca, NY 14850
(607) 256-4359

Contact(s):
George McT. Kahin, Director
• Conducts research on contemporary Indonesian political and social development, history, culture and foreign affairs; publishes semiannual *Indonesia*

Organizations

18.215
Embassy of Indonesia
Information Division
2020 Massachusetts Ave. NW
Washington, DC 20036
(202) 293-1745

• Answers telephone and written inquiries about Indonesia including travel/tourist and educational matters

• Welcomes inquiries from interested institutions and individuals
• Provides free printed information, including a monthly magazine *Focus on Indonesia* (see 18.217), a periodic newsletter *Indonesia: News and Views* (emphasizing current political and economic news with occasional travel notes) and various pamphlets covering such subjects as history, dance, cooking, etc.

Publications

18.216
Emerging Indonesia
Donald Wilhelm
Barnes and Noble Books
81 Adams Drive
Box 327
Totowa, NJ 07511
1980; hardbound; 192 pages; $26.50

• Examines current dvelopments in Indonesia in historical context

18.217
Focus on Indonesia
Information Division
Embassy of Indonesia
2020 Massachusetts Ave. NW
Washington, DC 20036
quarterly magazine; approx. 32 pages; free

• Contains articles covering aspects of current political, economic and social affairs in Indonesia

18.219
A History of Modern Indonesia
M. C. Ricklefs
Indiana University Press
10th and Morton Sts.
Bloomington, IN 47405
1981; hardbound; 352 pages; $22.50

- Describes the growth of Indonesia as an independent modern nation

18.220
Indonesia: A Bibliography of Bibliographies
J. B. N. Tairas
Oleander Press
210 Fifth Ave.
New York, NY 10010
1975; paperbound; 95 pages; $15

- Useful research and study tool

18.221
Indonesian Language Course
John U. Wolff
The Language Laboratory
Department of Modern Languages
Morrill Hall
Cornell University
Ithaca, New York 14853
see below for prices

- Books composing complete course in the Indonesian language suitable for self-instruction; include:

Beginning Indonesian, 1977–78, 1,124 pages, $12.50 each (Part I and II)

Beginning Indonesian Through Self-Instruction, 1984, 1,000 pages, price to be announced

Indonesian Readings, 1978, 480 pages, $12.50

Indonesian Conversation, 1978, 297 pages, $12.50

Formal Indonesian, 1980, 460 pages, $12.50

(All five books available as a set at $55 per set)

Cassette tape recordings for these Indonesian books are available as follows:

71 cassettes, *Beginning Indonesian*, Part I, $194.40; Part II, $189

20 cassettes, *Indonesian Conversations*, $108

30 cassettes, *Beginning Indonesian Through Self-Instruction*, $162

18.222
Javanese-English Dictionary
Elinore C. Horne
Yale University Press
302 Temple St.
New Haven, CT 06520
1974; hardbound; 728 pages; $55

- Useful dictionary for those learning to read Javanese

The following are standard resources available on Indonesia

INFORMATION SOURCES
- *Background Notes:* (see 2.188)
- *Country Study/Area Handbook.* . . . (see 2.189)

TRAVELER RESOURCES
- *Culturegram:* (see 2.191)
- *Update:* (see 2.197)

LANGUAGE LEARNING RESOURCES
- . . . .*: Complete Course for Beginners* (see 9.044)

Iran

Area Study and Research Programs

18.223
American Institute of Iranian Studies
University of Pennsylvania
325 University Museum
Philadelphia, PA 19104
(215) 898-7427 or 7466

Contact(s):
William L. Hanaway, Jr., President

Educational organization for the promotion of research on and in Iran
• Promotes research on Iran and facilitates research in Iran for American scholars when conditions permit
• Publishes newsletter and a directory of research in progress

18.224
Iranian Studies
University of Pennsylvania
325 University Museum
Philadelphia, PA 19104
(215) 898-5207

Contact(s):
Brian Spooner, Coordinator

• Offers graduate specialization in Iranian Studies under the auspices of the Middle East Center (see 17.039) and within a number of departments of the humanities and social sciences

Organizations

18.225
Society for Iranian Studies
% Center for Middle Eastern Studies
Harvard University
1737 Cambridge St.
Cambridge, MA 02138
(617) 495-4055

Contact(s):
Habib Lajevardi, Executive Secretary

Association of scholars and students
• Promotes scholarship on Iran, holds meetings and publishes the quarterly journal *Iranian Studies* and a newsletter

Publications

18.226
Bibliographical Guide to Iran
L. P. Elwell-Sutton, Editor
Littlefield, Adams & Co.
81 Adams Drive
Box 327
Totowa, NJ 07511
1983; hardbound; 300 pages; $35

• Comprehensive listing of the most significant books and articles in the field of Iranian studies with chapters on history, religion, philosophy, science, geography, language, art and the social sciences; epilogue lists important reference works on the Iranian revolution and surveys of general bibliographical material

18.227
Iranian Studies
Ervand Abrahamian Farhad Kazeni, Editor
Hagop Kevorkian Center for Near Eastern
   Studies
New York University
50 Washington Square South
New York, NY 10012
quarterly journal; approx. 120 pages;
   individuals, $25 per year; institutions, $30
   per year

• Scholarly articles and essays on Iranian history with some attention to current affairs; book reviews and bibliographies

The following are standard resources available on Iran
INFORMATION SOURCES
• *Background Notes:* (see 2.188)
• *Country Study/Area Handbook. . . .*
   (see 2.189)
TRAVELER RESOURCES
• *Bartholomew Map of. . . .* (see 1.109)
• *Culturegram:* (see 2.191)
• *Nagel's Encyclopedia Guide to. . . .*
   (see 2.195)
LANGUAGE LEARNING RESOURCES
"Persian"
• *. . . .: Complete Course for Beginners*
   (see 9.044)
• *Spoken. . . .* (see 9.047)

Iraq

Organizations

18.228
Iraqi Interests Section
℅ Embassy of India
Cultural Office
1801 P St. NW
Washington, DC 20036
(202) 797-2700

• Answers telephone and written inquiries about education in Iraq

• Provides or recommends speakers
• Welcomes inquiries from educational institutions, U.S. government agencies, cultural organizations and individuals
• Provides printed information about Iraq in general, particularly the illustrated book *Revolution and Development in Iraq* (description of contemporary political, social and economic conditions in Iraq, profusely illustrated with color photos, charts and graphs)

Publications

18.229
Iraq: The Contemporary State
Tim Niblock, Editor
St. Martin's Press
175 Fifth Ave.
New York, NY 10010

1982; hardbound; 322 pages; $27.50

• Basic review of contemporary political, social and economic conditions in Iraq

18.230
The Modern History of Iraq
Phebe Marr
Westview Press
5500 Central Ave.
Boulder, CO 80301
1984; hardbound; 275 pages; $25

• Concise introduction both for the student and the general reader to contemporary Iraq; examines the history, geography, politics, international relations, economic development, culture and social aspects of the country; also explores the changing social and economic structure of Iraq and its distinctive character as an Arab state in transition

The following are standard resources available on Iraq

INFORMATION SOURCES
     • *Background Notes:* (see 2.188)
     • *Country Study/Area Handbook.* . . . (see 2.189)
TRAVELER RESOURCES
     • *Bartholomew Map of.* . . . (see 1.109)
LANGUAGE LEARNING RESOURCES

For the "International" Languages (Arabic, French, German and Spanish) see listings under Chapter IX *Foreign Language Teaching and Learning*

Ireland

Area Study and Research Programs

18.231
Irish Studies Program
University of Massachusetts, Amherst
Amherst, MA 01003
(413) 545-0929

Contact(s):
Maria Tymoczko, Department of `
    Comparative Literature

Undergraduate area studies program; includes resources of the other members of the Five College Consortium (see 4.251)
     • Majors/degrees/certificates offered: B.A. in Irish Studies
     • Approximate number of faculty teaching area & language courses: 21 (plus 13 at other members of the Five College Consortium)
     • Approximate number of courses available language and area: 18 (plus 13 at other members of the Five College Consortium)

     • Languages offered: Middle Welsh and Old Irish
     • Library contains substantial Irish Studies resources including Alspach Yeats Collection
     • Study abroad opportunities in Cork and Dublin

18.232
Irish Studies
City University of New York/Queens College
Irish Studies House 35, 61st Road
Flushing, NY 11367
(212) 520-7146

Contact(s):
Kevin Sullivan, Director

Undergraduate area studies program established in 1974
     • Majors/degrees/certificates offered:

interdisciplinary B.A. in Irish Studies (English and History)

   • Approximate number of faculty teaching area & language courses: 6

   • Approximate number of courses available—language and area: 14

   • Average number of students per year specializing in area: 50–60

   • Areas of emphasis: language, literature and history

   • Language offered: Irish

   • Maintains substantial library collection of Irish Studies and Irish language materials

Organizations

18.233
American Committee for Irish Studies
Hofstra University
244 Student Center
Hempstead, NY 11550
(516) 560-6600

Contact(s):
Maureen Murphy, Secretary

Professional academic association of institutions and individuals in the U.S., Canada and Ireland

   • Holds conferences, issues reports on current research, and publishes a newsletter, a reprint series and *A Guide to Irish Studies in the U.S.* (see 18.241)

18.234
Embassy of Ireland
2234 Massachusetts Ave. NW
Washington, DC 20008
(202) 462-3939
CONSULATES GENERAL: Boston, Chicago, New York, San Francisco

   • Answers telephone and written inquiries about Ireland regarding educational matters

   • Recommends speakers, performers, exhibits, films/audio-visuals and educational materials

   • Welcomes inquiries from any interested individual or institution

   • Provides printed information about Ireland in general and about education, in particular a guide to higher education

   • Recommends these other sources of information: Consulates General; Irish International Airlines, 122 E. 42nd St., New York, NY 10017; Irish Tourist Board, 590 Fifth Ave., New York, NY 10022; and CIE Tours International, 590 Fifth Ave., New York, NY 10036

18.235
Irish Books and Media
683 Osceola Ave.
St. Paul, MN 55105
(612) 647-5678

Contact(s):
Eóin McKiernan, President

Book distributor

   • Distributor of books by Irish authors and about Ireland; includes *Books Ireland* (see 18.238)

18.236
Irish Academic Press
Kill Lane, Blackrock, Co.
Dublin, Ireland 850922

Distributed by Biblio Distribution Centre, 81 Adams Drive, Box 227, Totowa, NJ 07512

   • Publishes extensive list of books in Irish Studies

18.237
Irish American Cultural Institute
683 Osceola Ave.
St. Paul, MN 55105
(612) 647-5678

Contact(s):
Eóin McKiernan, President

Nonprofit educational organization designed to promote greater knowledge of Ireland in the U.S.

• Sponsors lectures and artistic activities, especially tours of Irish artists, craftsmen and scholars in the U.S., and contributes money to the arts in Ireland; gives grants to authors of books written in Irish or on Irish-American life and to lecturers who deal with subjects of Irish interest

• Disseminates information about Irish life and literature of particular interest to Irish-Americans; includes *Eire-Ireland: A Journal of Irish Studies* (see 18.240); affiliated with Irish Books and Media (see 18.235)

Publications

18.238
Books Ireland
Irish Books and Media
683 Osceola Ave.
St. Paul, MN 55105
10 issues per year; $14 per year surface
   mail; $25 per year air mail

• Reviews books by Irish writers and of Irish interest; other articles cover news of the literary and publishing worlds

18.239
Current British Directories
I. G. Anderson, Editor
CBD Research, Ltd.
154 High St.
Beckenham, Kent, BR3 1EA, England
1979; hardbound; 384 pages; $105

• Lists approximately 2,900 directories published in or relating to Great Britain and Ireland, including a selection published in or relating to the Commonwealth and to South Africa, Pakistan and Bangladesh; includes yearbooks, almanacs, gazetteers, general industrial and commercial directories; telephone, telex and telegraphic directories; research, library and bibliographic directories, and regional, specialized and technical directories; provides publisher and bibliographic data, description of content, languages used, frequency, date published, price and size

• Arranged by region and towns in Britain and Ireland and by Britain, Ireland and the Commonwealth countries as a whole; includes subject index

18.240
Éire-Ireland: A Journal of Irish Studies
Eóin McKiernan, Editor
Irish American Cultural Institute
683 Osceola Ave
St. Paul, MN 55105
quarterly journal; approx. 160 pages; $10
   per year to libraries (only)

Free to members of the Irish American Cultural Institute (see 18.237) who contribute $25 or more

• Scholarly articles principally on Irish culture, writing and writers; book reviews

18.241
A Guide to Irish Studies
American Committee for Irish Studies
Hofstra University
Hempstead, NY 11550
1982; pamphlet; 59 pages; free with
   membership ($6)

• Lists colleges and universities which offer courses in Irish literature and history and the Irish language, including course titles, faculty and selected program descriptions

18.242
Ireland & the Irish
Karl S. Bottigheimer
Columbia University Press
562 West 113th St.
New York, NY 10025
1982; 256 pages; $19.95, hardbound;
   paperbound, $10.95

• Up-to-date study of Ireland and what makes the Irish tick

18.243
Ireland: A Nation in the Currents of Change
Richard B. Finnegan
Westview Press
5500 Central Ave.
Boulder, CO 80301
1983; hardbound; 185 pages; $18.50

• Concise introduction both for the student and the general reader to contemporary Ireland; examines the history, geography, politics, international relations, economic development, culture and social aspects of the country; also explores the rapid social and economic transformation of contemporary Ireland and the tensions produced by the conflict in Northern Ireland

The following companies import and sell books in the Gaelic language:

18.244
Facsimile Bookshop, Inc.
16 West 55th St.
New York, NY 10019
(212) 581-2672

18.245
Irish American Center
2123 Market St.
San Francisco, CA
(415) 621-2200

The following are standard resources available on Ireland
INFORMATION SOURCES
   • *Background Notes:* (see 2.188)
TRAVELER RESOURCES
   • *Culturegram:* (see 2.191)
   • *Fodor's Guide to. . . .* (see 2.192)
   • *Nagel's Encyclopedia Guide to. . . .* (see 2.195)
LANGUAGE LEARNING RESOURCES
   • *. . . .: Complete Course for Beginners* (see 9.044)
ITT Fellowships for graduate study in Ireland normally available (see 7.041)

Israel

Organizations

18.246
Embassy of Israel
Information Department
3514 International Drive NW
Washington, DC 20008
(202) 364-5000
INFORMATION DEPARTMENTS IN
CONSULATES GENERAL: Atlanta, Boston,
Chicago, Houston, Los Angeles, New York,
Philadelphia, San Francisco

• Provides extensive materials on Israel
under the following headings: Israel (general), Jerusalem, Foreign Policy, the Arab-Israeli Conflict, as well as the book *Facts about Israel* (see 18.249); list of movies on these subjects available upon request

18.247
United States-Israel Binational Science Foundation
2 Alharizi St.
Jerusalem 91076, Israel
(02) 667314

Contact(s):
Zeev Rotem, Executive Director

Binational center for the promotion of cooperative science research
• Offers grants submitted through universities and nonprofit research organizations supporting projects in the health, natural and selected social sciences involving close collaboration between U.S. and Israeli scientists on research to be performed essentially in Israel

18.248
World Zionist Organization—American Section, Inc.
Haym Greenberg Hebrew College
Department of Education and Culture
515 Park Ave.
New York, NY 10022
(212) 752-0600, Ext. 372

Contact(s):
Asher Quell

• Offers 50 partial scholarships to undergraduate or graduate students to spend a semester or year in Jerusalem, Israel, studying Judaism, the Hebrew language, and/or historic and contemporary Israel

Publications

18.249
Facts About Israel
Hanan Sher, Moshe Aumann, Edna Marks,
   Channa Palti, Gayle Waxman, Editors
Information Division
Ministry of Foreign Affairs
Jerusalem, Israel
1979; paperbound; 243 pages; free

Available from the Information Department, Embassy of Israel, 3514 International Drive NW, Washington, DC 20008, or from the Consulates General in Chicago, Houston, Philadelphia, San Francisco and Los Angeles
• Surveys major aspects of Israeli life and history including geography, ancient and modern history, foreign policy, population,

government, education, culture, economics, tourism and American Jewish organizations

18.250
Israel Now: Portrait of a Troubled Land
Lawrence Meyer
Delacorte Press
245 East 47th St.
New York, NY 10017
1982; hardbound; 404 pages; $16.95

• Analysis of the current state of Israel and social, political and economic problems

18.251
Israel Scene
Helen Davis, Editor
World Zionist Organization
515 Park Ave.
New York, NY 10022
monthly magazine; approx. 30 pages; $12 per year

• Contains short articles and commentary on current social, cultural and political affairs in Israel from Zionist perspective

18.252
Israel Yearbook
Israel Yearbook Publications Ltd.
21 Hashron St.
P.O.B. 1199
Tel Aviv, Israel
annual; paperbound; 388 pages; $8

• Provides wide range of social, cultural, economic and political information on Israel

18.253
Speak and Read Essential Hebrew: A Pimsleur Language Program
Paul Pimsleur
Heinle & Heinle Enterprises, Inc.
29 Lexington Rd.
Concord, MA 01742
1982; 25-unit cassette program and reading booklet, in vinyl album; $229.95

• Self-instructional language program based principally on the graduated-interval recall system designed for learning by use of tapes alone

The following companies import and sell books in the Hebrew language:

18.254
J. Roth-Bookseller
9427 West Pico Blvd.
Los Angeles, CA 90035
(213) 557-1848

18.255
Shaller's Hebrew Book Store
2555 Amsterdam Ave.
New York, NY 10033
(212) 928-2140

The following are standard resources available on Israel
INFORMATION SOURCES
 • *Background Notes:* (see 2.188)
 • *Country Study/Area Handbook.* . . . (see 2.189)
TRAVELER RESOURCES
 • *Culturegram:* (see 2.191)
 • *Fodor's Guide to.* . . . (see 2.192)
 • *Nagel's Encyclopedia Guide to.* . . . (see 2.195)
LANGUAGE LEARNING RESOURCES
"Hebrew"

- *Berlitz. . . . for Travelers* (Phrase-book, see 9.043)
- *. . . .: Complete Course for Beginners* (see 9.044)
- *Say It in:* (see 9.046)
- *Spoken. . . .* (see 9.047)

Fulbright Grants and ITT Fellowships for graduate study in Israel normally available along with several Israeli government grants in Judaic/Jewish studies and Weizmann Institute Grants in the natural sciences (see 7.041)

Italy

Organizations

18.256
Conference Group on Italian Politics
University of Nebraska
Department of Political Science
Lincoln, NE 68588
(402) 472-2346

Contact(s):
Raphael Zariski, Executive Secretary-Treasurer

Association of academics, government people and interested individuals
- Promotes the study of and research on contemporary Italian political issues

18.257
Italian Cultural Institute
686 Park Ave.
New York, NY 10021
(212) 879-4242

Contact(s):
Director

- Answers telephone and written in-quiries about Italy, including educational matters
- Provides or recommends exhibits and films
- Welcomes inquiries from any interested individual or institution
- Recommends this other source of information: Italian Government Travel Office, 630 Fifth Ave., New York, NY 10111

18.258
National Science Foundation
United States-Italy Cooperative Science Program
Division of International Programs
Washington, DC 20550
(202) 357-7554

Contact(s):
Henryk M. Uznanski, Program Manager

- Funds programs involving cooperative research, seminars and workshops, long-term research visits and postdoctoral fellowships for American scientists

Publications

18.259
A Handbook for Teachers of Italian
Anthony Mollica, Editor
American Association of Teachers of Italian
4 Oakmont Rd.
Welland, Ontario L3C 4X9, Canada
paperbound; $5 (including postage)

• Collection of articles offering practical guidelines and identification of resources on aspects of both language instruction in general and Italian language instruction specifically; covers such areas as preparation for teaching, where to earn a degree, teaching methodologies, resource materials, etc.

18.260
Libraries and Archives in Italy: A Research Handbook
Rudolf J. Lewanski and Richard C.
   Lewanski, Editors
Council for European Studies
1509 International Affairs Bldg.
Columbia University
New York, NY 10027
1980; paperbound; 101 pages; $6 plus $1
   postage and handling (members $4.50)

Part of Research Resources Series which includes *The European Community* (see 15.035), *Libraries and Archives in France: A Research Handbook* (see 18.147) and *Libraries and Archives in Germany: A Research Handbook* (see 18.164)
• Gives details of the collections available in the major and minor state and local archives and libraries in Italy divided into the following sections: Subject Collections, Major Archives and Libraries (by city), Local Administration Archives, Notaries Public Archives, and Library-related Services; includes bibliography of national and local guides to libraries, U.S. literature on Italian libraries, and catalogs and Union Catalogs, Italian dictionaries and a guide to archival and library terminology; also provides a general introduction and a guide to obtaining permission to use the materials

The following companies import and sell books in the Italian language:

18.261
Cavalli Italian Bookstore
1441 Stockton St.
San Francisco, CA 94133
(415) 421-4219

18.262
Rizzoli International Bookstore
712 Fifth Ave.
New York, NY 10019
(212) 397-3700

18.263
Schoenhof's Foreign Books, Inc.
1280 Massachusetts Ave.
Cambridge, MA 02138
(617) 547-8855

The following are standard resources available on Italy

INFORMATION SOURCES
• *Background Notes:* (see 2.188)
• *Country Study/Area Handbook.* . . . (see 2.189)
• *World Bibliographical Series.* . . . (see 2.198)

TRAVELER RESOURCES
• *Culturegram:* (see 2.191)
• *Fodor's Guide to.* . . . (see 2.192)

LANGUAGE LEARNING RESOURCES
- *Berlitz. . . . for Travelers* (Cassette-pak, see 9.042)
- *. . . .: Complete Course for Beginners* (see 9.044)
- *Say It in:* (see 9.046)
- *Spoken. . . .* (see 9.047)
- *Vest Pocket. . . .* (see 9.048)

- *Berlitz. . . . for Travelers* (Phrasebook, see 9.043)

Fulbright Grants and ITT Fellowships for graduate study in Italy normally available, along with two Lusk Memorial Fellowships in the creative and performing arts (see 7.041)

Ivory Coast

Organizations

18.264
Embassy of the Republic of Ivory Coast
2424 Massachusetts Ave. NW
Washington, DC 20008
(202) 483-2400

- Will provide mimeographed materials on historical, political and economic aspects of Ivory Coast, along with travel information

Publications

18.265
Ivory Coast Today
Jean Hureau
J. A. Editions
France
1980; hardbound; 240 pages; $14.95

Available from Hippocrene Books, Inc., 171 Madison Ave., New York, NY 10016
- Travel guide to, description of and report on contemporary Ivory Coast; illustrations

The following are standard resources available on Ivory Coast
INFORMATION SOURCES
- *Background Notes:* (see 2.188)
- *Country Study/Area Handbook. . . .* (see 2.189)

LANGUAGE LEARNING RESOURCES
For the "International" Languages (Arabic, French, German and Spanish) see listings under Chapter IX *Foreign Language Teaching and Learning*
Fulbright Grants for study in Ivory Coast normally available (see 7.041)

Jamaica

Organizations

18.266
Embassy of Jamaica
1850 K St. NW, Suite 355
Washington, DC 20006
(202) 452-0660
CONSULATES: Miami, New York

• Answers telephone and written inquiries about Jamaica, including travel/tourist and educational matters
• Provides audiovisual materials and educational or teaching aids and recommends speakers
• Welcomes inquiries from any interested individual or institution
• Provides printed information about education and travel in Jamaica and on Jamaica in general, including a road map and a number of guides for the traveler
• Recommends these other sources of information: Jamaica Tourist Board, 866 Second Ave., 10th Floor, 2 Hammarskjold Plaza, New York, NY 10017

Publications

18.267
Jamaica: An Island Microcosm
Barry Floyd
St. Martin's Press, Inc.
175 Fifth Ave.
New York, NY 10010
1979; hardbound; $14.50

• Fast-paced examination of contemporary Jamaican society and the forces that have shaped it

18.268
Jamaica Journal
Olive Senior, Editor
Institute of Jamaica
12-16 East St.
Kingston, Jamaica

quarterly journal; approx. 70 pages; $20 per year

• Contains illustrated articles on Jamaican cultural, scientific and historical subjects; book and art reviews

The following are standard resources available on Jamaica
INFORMATION SOURCES
• *Background Notes:* (see 2.188)
• *Country Study/Area Handbook. . . .* (see 2.189)
• *Image of. . . .* (see 2.194)

Japan

Area Study and Research Programs

18.269
Japan Area Studies
University of Arizona
Department of Oriental Studies
Tucson, AZ 85721
(602) 626-1264

Contact(s):
Don C. Bailey, Director

Graduate area studies program
- Majors/degrees/certificates offered: M.A. and Ph.D. in Japanese Area Studies (with a separate track for M.A. candidates not taking language instruction)
- Approximate number of faculty teaching area and language courses: 5
- Language offered: Japanese at all levels
- Oriental Studies Collection in the library contains approximately 18,000 volumes in Japanese

18.270
Center for Japanese Studies
University of California at Berkeley
361 Stephens Hall
Berkeley, CA 94720
(415) 642-3156

Contact(s):
Irwin Scheiner, Chair

Academically based research center established in 1958; one of three East Asian research centers at Berkeley within the Institute of East Asian Studies (see 18.014; for Chinese Center, see 18.070; for Korean Center, see 18.307); emphasizes the comparative analysis of the traditional political and social system and culture of Japan

- Sponsors and provides financial support for graduate and postdoctoral research on Japan by Berkeley faculty and graduate students; brings scholars from elsewhere in the U.S. and abroad to do research at Berkeley under the Center Research Associate Program
- Conducts student-faculty interdisciplinary research colloquium series and regional seminars for faculty from other institutions
- Publishes series of papers through the University of California Press focusing on various aspects of ancient and modern Japan, as well as a Monograph Series through the Institute of East Asian Studies

18.271
Japanese Studies
Earlham College
Richmond, IN 47374
(317) 962-6561

Contact(s):
Len Holvik, Director

- Offers B.A. in Japanese Studies; study in Japan encouraged

18.272
Center for Japanese Studies
University of Michigan at Ann Arbor
104 Lane Hall
Ann Arbor, MI 48109
(313) 764-6307

Contact(s):
John C. Campbell, Director
Lori Sobson, Student Services Assistant (outreach)

Graduate area studies program established in 1947

• Majors/degrees/certificates offered: M.A. in Asian Studies with specialization in Japanese Studies; departmental Ph.D. with specialization in Japanese Studies

• Approximate number of faculty teaching area and language courses: 16

• Approximate number of courses available—area: 60; language: 25

• Average number of students per year specializing in area: 15

• Language offered: Japanese (classical and modern)

• University Asia Library contains extensive collection of materials in Japanese and Western languages including over 150,000 printed volumes and 5,500 reels of microfilm; particularly strong in legislation (proceedings of the Japanese Diet), local history, education, economics, the era of Allied occupation and drama; holds several donated private collections

• Far Eastern Art Archives includes approximately 10,000 photographs of Japanese painting, sculpture and decorative arts and the Museum of Art and Anthropology contains Japanese and Far Eastern materials

• Publishes monographs in Japanese Studies, with emphasis on language and literature, and a number of bibliographic publications including *Bibliography of Reference Works for Japanese Studies* (see 18.290)

• Prepares and lends curriculum and audiovisual materials and offers in-service training to teachers in the region

• Conducts school outreach programs

18.273
Japanese Studies
Bucknell University
Lewisburg, PA 17837
(717) 524-1450

Contact(s):
David Lu, Director

Undergraduate area studies program established in 1965

• Majors/degrees/certificates offered: B.A. in Japanese Studies

• Approximate number of faculty teaching area and language courses: 7

• Approximate number of courses available—area: 11; language: 10

• Average number of students per year specializing in area: 7

• Language offered: Japanese

• Study abroad available at universities in Kyoto, Nagoya and Tokyo, Japan; member of the Associated Kyoto Program with Doshisha University, Japan

18.274
Japanese Studies
University of Washington
School of International Studies
Seattle, WA 98195
(208) 543-6148

Contact(s):
Kozo Yamamura, Chair

• Offers B.A. and M.A. in International Studies with specialization in Japanese Studies and publishes *Journal of Japanese Studies* (see 18.295)

Organizations

18.275
Information & Culture Center, Embassy of Japan
917 19th St. NW
Washington, DC 20006
(202) 234-2266

CONSULATES GENERAL: Anchorage, Atlanta, Boston, Chicago, Honolulu, Houston, Kansas City, Los Angeles, New Orleans, New York, Portland, Ore., San Francisco, Seattle

• Answers telephone and written inquiries about Japan regarding educational matters

• Recommends speakers and films and offers audiovisual materials on loan

• Welcomes inquiries from any interested individual or institution

• Provides printed information about Japan and education in Japan

• Recommends these other sources of information: Consulates General

18.276
Harvard Yenching Library Travel Grants
Harvard University
Harvard-Yenching Library
2 Divinity Ave.
Cambridge, MA 02138
(617) 495-3327

Contact(s):
Eugene W. Wu, Head

• Provides grants of up to $200 each to scholars outside of Boston to enable them to conduct research in the Library's Japanese collection

18.277
Inter-University Center for Japanese Studies in Tokyo
Stanford University
Center for Research in International Studies
Room 200, Lou Henry Hoover Bldg.
Stanford, CA 94305
(415) 497-4581

Contact(s):
Peter Duus, Executive Secretary
Delmer Brown, Field Director (Tokyo)

Cooperative program of eleven major academic institutions in the U.S. and Canada administered by Stanford

• Provides intensive year-long, audiolingual instruction in Japanese for graduate and undergraduate students with emphasis on preparing the student to conduct research in the language

18.278
Japan Economic Institute
1000 Connecticut Avenue NW
Washington, DC 20036
(202) 296-5633

Contact(s):
Robert Angel, President

Works under contract to the Japanese government to provide information to American government, media and academic circles on the Japanese economy and Japan-U.S. economic relations

• Publishes weekly reports on political and economic situation in Japan and the U.S. relative to Japan-U.S. economic relations; aimed at business, government and academic subscribers; $40 per year

• Publishes bimonthly newsletter summarizing information from the weekly reports (free; persons in responsible positions will be added to the mailing list on request)

• Publishes *Yearbook* reviewing the previous year: includes graphs, chronologies, statistical charts and a discussion of Japanese and American economic activity vis-a-vis each other as well as in relation to the world economy; aimed at noneconomists ($6)

18.279
The Japan Foundation
Watergate Office Bldg., Suite 570
600 New Hampshire Ave. NW
Washington, DC 20037
(202) 965-4313

Contact(s):
Osuke Watanabe, Director

Japanese government grant-giving organization

• Provides short- and long-term Professional Fellowships to academics, writers and other professionals (including translators, librarians and museum personnel) who are already knowledgeable about Japan and who wish to pursue research in Japan or upgrade their professional competence

• Provides Dissertation Fellowships for 4 to 14 months to doctoral candidates in the humanities and social sciences for research in Japan; particular emphasis on social sciences

• Donates Japanese books, journals and newspapers on microfilm to colleges and other institutions and provides small grants to assist publishers in covering printing costs of works on Japan in the humanities and social sciences in languages other than Japanese

• Provides partial support to academic institutions for inviting scholars or artists-in-residence from Japan to lecture or teach in the area of Japanese Studies; for the establishment of new teaching positions in Japan-related areas; for research, principally in the U.S., on Japan-related subjects; for conferences, workshops and seminars; and for groups of students and teachers to travel to Japan for intensive language training or cultural study; also provides up to $10,000 for summer programs in Japanese studies for faculty, students and school teachers

18.280
Japan Institute for Social and Economic Affairs
Office for JISEA Fellowships
1333 Gough St., Suite 6F
San Francisco, CA 94109
(415) 922-5600

• Offers once a year all-expenses-paid travel fellowships to elementary and secondary social studies educators from the U.S. and Canada for a study/observation tour to Japan; selection based on quality of applicant's proposals for curriculum development upon return from Japan

18.281
Japan Society
333 East 47th St.
New York, NY 10017
(212) 832-1155

Contact(s):
David MacEachron, President

Promotes cultural relations between Japan and the U.S.

• Offers courses for Americans in the Japanese language and for Japanese in the English language

• Serves as clearinghouse for information about films on Japan available in the U.S. and rents out its own collection of 35mm feature films (in Japanese with English subtitles) and smaller assortment of 16mm films on Japan

• Conducts two to three tours to Japan of two to three weeks' duration each year for members

• Sponsors lectures, films, symposia and conferences in New York

• Offers information and advice and can identify best information sources on cultural and educational questions about Japan

• Publishes newsletter for members, including information about major Japan-oriented events around the country

• Serves as Secretariat for Associated Japan-America societies of the United States

18.282
Japan-United States Friendship Commission
1875 Connecticut Ave. NW
Washington, DC 20009
(202) 673-5295

Contact(s):
Richard A. Ericson, Jr., Executive Director

Administers U.S. government trust fund to support educational and cultural relations between Japan and the U.S.

- Gives grants to institutions to support activities in the following categories:

(1) Japanese Studies in American graduate schools of law, business, journalism and architecture/urban planning (to support graduate fellowships, new faculty positions and research)

(2) The development of major library collections of Japanese books

(3) Elementary, secondary and teacher education programs

(4) American Studies in Japan (including support to select Japanese universities for research materials and library acquisitions, grants for new faculty positions, grants to selected organizations for support of individual research by Japanese scholars and grants to institutions for special projects)

(5) Exchange programs in the arts (including exchange of creative artists, exchange of artistic and cultural performances and support for the study and performance of traditional Japanese theater and music in the U.S.)

- (6) Exchange of cultural exhibitions and support for American museums with Japanese collections

(7) Production of educational TV films

(8) Translations from Japanese to English through Japanese Translation Center, Tokyo

(9) Counterpart exchanges of leaders between institutions in government, education, politics, the media, economics and public affairs

(10) Public affairs programming about Japan by regional and national organizations in the U.S.

- Also gives grants for collaborative research on policy issues important to contemporary Japan-U.S. relations

18.283
Kodansha International/USA, Ltd.
10 East 53d St.
New York, NY 10022
(212) 207-7050

- Publishes books on Japan and/or by Japanese and distributes publications of Japan Publications Books; includes extensive list of titles on arts, crafts and other aspects of Japanese culture and society (ceramics, poetry and sculpture, literature, floral art and the martial arts) and Japanese language texts including the *Kodansha English–Japanese Dictionary* and the *Kodansha Japanese–English Dictionary* ($22.50 each)

18.284
National Endowment for the Arts
2401 E St. NW
Washington, DC 20506
(202) 634-6380

Contact(s):
Kathleen Bannon, International Programs Officer

- Awards five fellowships to Americans in the creative and performing arts for the pursuit of artistic study and activities in Japan; Japanese artists come to the U.S. under reciprocal arrangements

18.285
National Science Foundation
United States-Japan Cooperative Science Program
Division of International Programs
Washington, DC 20550
(202) 357-9537

Contact(s):
Charles Wallace, Program Manager

- Funds programs involving cooperative research, seminars and workshops and short-term visits between the U.S. and Japan

18.286
Social Science Research Council
Postdoctoral Grants for International
    Research: Japan
605 Third Ave.
New York, NY 10158
(212) 557-9500

• Awards substantial grants to citizens or permanent residents of the U.S. or Canada for research in the social sciences and humanities relating to Japan, to be conducted in North America or abroad; deadline for applications, December 1

18.287
Charles E. Tuttle Co., Inc.
285 South Main St.
Rutland, VT 05701
(802) 773-8930

Commercial publishing house
• Publishes and distributes a large catalogue of English-language books on East and Southeast Asia and the Pacific with a particularly extensive list on and from Japan, including literature and other materials in Japanese; covers such areas as arts and crafts, sports and games, history, politics, literature, language, culture, customs, religion, philosophy and travel; language materials include dictionaries, grammars, readers, phrasebooks, etc. for Chinese, Hawaiian, Indonesian, Malay, Japanese, Korean, Lao, Maori, Tagalog, Thai and Vietnamese (see individual countries/languages)

18.288
U.S.-Japan Cross Culture Center
Suite 305
244 South San Pedro St.
Los Angeles, CA 90012
(213) 617-2039

Contact(s):
Peter Y. Yamauchi, Executive Director

• Facilitates cultural exchange between Japan and the U.S., assists U.S. students, teachers and travelers going to Japan (includes providing information about teaching English in Japan), offers instruction in Japanese, and distributes extensive list of Japanese language teaching and reference materials

18.289
U.S.-Japan Culture Center
2139 Wisconsin Ave. NW
Washington, DC 20007
(202) 333-6760
and
% International Education Center
21 Yotsuya 1-chome, Shinjuku-ku
Tokyo 160, Japan
359-9621

Contact(s):
Mikio Kanda, Director

Research and educational center on Japanese culture and Japan-U.S. relations
• Maintains research library of recent Japanese and English publications
• Answers inquiries and provides information and assistance in finding source materials on matters relating to Japan and Japan-U.S. relations
• Sponsors conferences, lectures, seminars, and essay contests, and conducts Japanese language classes
• Promotes exchange programs and arranges internships at the Center for Japanese and American university students
• Publishes a monthly newsletter

Publications

18.290
Bibliography of Reference Works for Japanese Studies
Naomi Fukuda, Editor
Center for Japanese Studies
University of Michigan
108 Lane Hall
Ann Arbor, MI 48109
1979; 210 pages; paperbound, $6;
    (hardbound edition also available)

• Annotated bibliography of books and periodicals, principally in Japanese, held in the Asia Library of the University of Michigan as of December 1977; titles listed in Japanese and translated into English; annotations in English; covers following subject areas: general reference works, philosophy and religion, fine arts, language, literature, history, biography, geography, social sciences, political science, economics, sociology and ethnology

18.291
Interact: Japan/U.S.
John C. Condon
Intercultural Press, Inc.
Box 768
Yarmouth, ME 04096
1982; paperbound; 75 pages; $7.50

• Analyzes differences between American and Japanese cultural practices and how these differences affect working relationships between them; covers such subjects as communication styles, family relationships, sex roles and attitudes toward work, achievement, authority, decision-making, negotiations, cooperation and competition

18.292
Japan English Books in Print: 1980–81
Intercontinental Marketing Corp.
IPO Box 5056
Tokyo 100-31, Japan
1980; paperbound; 276 pages; $60 (new edition due 1984)

• Lists approximately 15,000 titles published in Japan in the English language; includes substantial numbers under business, cultural and educational subjects, language and linguistics, travel, tourism, and many others; cross-referenced by publisher (with publisher's address)

18.293
Japan English Magazine Directory
Intercontinental Marketing Corp.
IPO Box 5956
Tokyo 100-31, Japan
1981; 184 pages; paperbound; $60

• Comprehensive directory of approximately 1,700 periodicals published in Japan and Hong Kong in the English language giving basic subscription data and the names and addresses of the approximately 1,300 publishers involved; cross-referenced by subject category; for example, business, banking, finance, trade, economics, education, Asian Studies, science, technology and travel/tourism

18.294
Japan: Profile of a Postindustrial Power
Ardath W. Burks
Westview Press
5500 Central Ave.
Boulder, CO 80301
1983; revised and updated edition; 260 pages; hardbound, $27.50; paperbound, $10.50

• Concise introduction both for the student and the general reader to contemporary Japan; examines the history, geography, politics, international relations, economic development, culture and social aspects of the country; also explores in depth current developments in culture, life-style, national identity and the rapid pace of technical modernization

18.295
The Journal of Japanese Studies
Kenneth B. Pyle, Editor
The Society for Japanese Studies
Thomson Hall, DR-05
University of Washington
Seattle, WA 98195
semiannual journal; approx. 210 pages;
  individuals, $15; institutions, $20;
  students, $10

• Articles and essays on Japan and Japanese studies covering most areas of the humanities and social sciences

The following companies import and sell books in the Japanese language:

18.296
Kinokuniya Bookstores of America
1581 Webster St.
San Francisco, CA 94115
(415) 567-7625

18.297
Naropa Institute Bookstore
2011 10th St.
Boulder, CO 80302
(303) 449-6219

18.298
Nippon Book Co.
364 East First St.
Los Angeles, CA 90012
(213) 624-2089

18.299
Tokyo Sales Corp. Bookstore
521 Fifth Ave.
New York, NY 10036
(212) 840-9455

The following are standard resources available on Japan
INFORMATION SOURCES
  • *Background Notes:* (see 2.188)
  • *Country Study/Area Handbook.* . . .
    (see 2.189)
TRAVELER RESOURCES
  • *Bartholomew Map of.* . . . (see 1.109)
  • *Communication Learning Aids:* (see 2.190)
  • *Culturegram:* (see 2.191)
  • *Update:* (see 2.197)
  • *Fodor's Guide to.* . . . (see 2.192)
  • *Nagel's Encyclopedia Guide to.* . . .
    (see 2.195)
  • *. . . . .: A Travel Survival Kit* (see 2.196)
LANGUAGE LEARNING RESOURCES
  • *Berlitz.* . . . *for Travelers* (Cassette-pak, see 9.042)
  • *. . . . .: Complete Course for Beginners* (see 9.044)
  • *Say It in:* (see 9.046)
  • *Spoken.* . . . (see 9.047)
  • *Vest Pocket.* . . . (see 9.048)
  • *Berlitz.* . . . *for Travelers* (phrasebook, see 9.043)
Fulbright Grants for study in Japan normally available (see 7.041)

Jordan

Organizations

18.300
Jordan Information Bureau
1701 K St. NW
Washington, DC 20006
(202) 659-3322

Official information office of the Jordan Government

• Provides general information about Jordan and publishes and distributes a variety of publications, a quarterly magazine of general cultural and tourist interest, *Jordan* (see 18.302), and audiovisual material of general interest

Publications

18.301
An Insight and Guide to Jordan
Christine Osborne
Longman, Inc.
19 West 44th St.
New York, NY 10036
1982; hardbound; 218 pages; $13.95

• Travel guide to Jordan which also describes the culture and history of the country

18.302
Jordan
Peter Gubser
Westview Press
5500 Central Ave.
Boulder, CO 80301
1982; 128 pages; hardbound, $16.50;
   paperbound, $10.95

• Concise introduction both for the student and the general reader to contemporary Jordan; examines the history, geography, politics, international relations, economic development, culture and social aspects of the country; also discusses the forces which have buffeted Jordan and the efforts that have been made to establish a diversified economy, a stable social system and a political approach

based on relationships with the Arab states rather than Britain or the U.S.

18.303
Jordan
Jordan Information Bureau
1701 K St. NW
Washington, DC 20006
quarterly magazine; 33 pages; free

• Articles survey both current and historical Jordan, covering culture, history, business, economic development, education, travel and other aspects of the country

The following are standard resources available on Jordan
INFORMATION SOURCES
   • *Background Notes:* (see 2.188)
   • *Country Study/Area Handbook.* . . .
      (see 2.189)
TRAVELER RESOURCES
   • *Bartholomew Map of.* . . . (see 1.109)
   • *Fodor's Guide to.* . . . (see 2.192)
LANGUAGE LEARNING RESOURCES
For the "International" Languages (Arabic, French, German and Spanish) see listings under Chapter IX *Foreign Language Teaching and Learning*

Kampuchea

Publications

18.304
English-Khmer Dictionary
Franklin Huffman
Yale University Press
302 Temple St.
New Haven, CT 06520
1978; hardbound; 690 pages; $40

• Useful dictionary for those learning to speak or write Khmer

18.305
A History of Cambodia
David P. Chandler
Westview Press
5500 Central Ave.
Boulder, CO 80301
1983; hardbound; 225 pages; $25

• Concise introduction both for the student and the general reader to contemporary Cambodia; examines the history, geography, politics, international relations, economic development, culture and social aspects of the country; also explores how patterns of Cambodian thinking and social and political styles provide a framework for understanding the country and its people today

The following are standard resources available on Kampuchea
INFORMATION SOURCES
• *Background Notes:* (see 2.188)
• *Country Study/Area Handbook.* . . . (see 2.189)

Kenya

Publications

18.306
Modern Kenya
Guy Arnold
Longman, Inc.
19 West 44th St.
New York, NY 10036
1981; paperbound; 156 pages; $8.95

• Analysis of contemporary Kenya and the forces that have shaped it

The following are standard resources available on Kenya

INFORMATION SOURCES
• *Background Notes:* (see 2.188)
• *Country Study/Area Handbook.* . . . (see 2.189)
• *Historical Dictionary of.* . . . (see 2.193)
• *World Bibliographical Series.* . . . (see 2.198)

TRAVELER RESOURCES
• *Culturegram:* (see 2.191)
LANGUAGE LEARNING RESOURCES
"Swahili"

- *Berlitz. . . . for Travelers* (phrasebook, see 9.043)
- *. . . .: Complete Course for Beginners* (see 9.044)
- *Say It in:* (see 9.046)

- *Spoken. . . .* (see 9.047)

Fulbright Grants and ITT Fellowships for graduate study in Kenya normally available (see 7.041)

Korea (North and South)

Area Study and Research Programs

18.307
Center for Korean Studies
University of California at Berkeley
460 Stephens Hall
Berkeley, CA 94720
(415) 642-5618

Contact(s):
John C. Jamieson, Chair

Academically based research center, formerly part of the Center for Japanese and Korean Studies, established in 1979 under the Institute of East Asian Studies (see 13.014; for Chinese Center, see 18.070; for Japanese Center, see 18.270); emphasizes the comparative analysis of the traditional political and social system and culture of Korea

- Sponsors and provides financial support for graduate and postdoctoral research on Korea by Berkeley faculty and graduate students; brings scholars from elsewhere in the U.S. and abroad to do research at Berkeley under the Center Research Associate Program
- Conducts student-faculty interdisciplinary research colloquium series and regional seminars for faculty from other institutions
- Extensive library holdings of modern Asian materials
- Publishes a series of papers through the University of California Press focusing on

various aspects of ancient and modern Korea, as well as a Monograph Series through the Institute of East Asian Studies

18.308
Center for Korean Studies
University of Hawaii
1881 East-West Road
Honolulu, HI 96822
(808) 948-7041

Contact(s):
Dae-Sook Suh, Director

Research and coordination center for Korean studies at the University

- Assists in development of courses; recommends research policies and evaluates proposals; recommends policies on publications and supervises the editing and publishing of pamphlets, books and articles on Korea; serves as liaison with the Korean community in Hawaii and the national and international scholarly community interested in Korean studies; conducts conferences and maintains a collection of books, journals, documents and audiovisual materials on Korea
- Publishes the journal *Korean Studies* (see 18.320), research aids, Occasional Papers and a Colloquium Papers Series; titles include *Films for Korean Studies, Japanese Sources on Korea in Hawaii* (a bibliographic

guide to Japanese sources on Korea in the Asia Collection at the University of Hawaii library, 150,000 entries, $8) and *Studies on Korea: A Scholar's Guide* (see 18.322)

18.309
Center for Korean Studies
Western Michigan University
2090 Friedmann
Kalamazoo, MI 49008
(616) 383-1678

Contact(s):
Andrew Nahm, Director

     • Promotes research on Korean culture, government and politics; conducts conferences and workshops; administers a professor exchange program with a Korean university, and publishes articles and monographs on Korean culture

18.310
Korean Studies
University of Washington
School of International Studies
Seattle, WA 98105
(206) 543-4947

Contact(s):
James B. Palais, Chair

     • Offers B.A. and M.A. in International Studies with specialization in Korean Studies and publishes *Journal of Korean Studies* and an Occasional Papers series

Organizations

18.311
Embassy of Korea (South)
Information Office
1414 22d St. NW, Suite 101
Washington, DC 20037
(202) 296-4256/57

Contact(s):
Chang-Rim Ku, Counselor (Culture and
     Information)

     • Answers questions and provides information about Korea, including traveler and tourist materials; includes *Facts about Korea* (see 18.315) and *New Pearl of the Orient: Korea* (a visitor guidebook, see 18.321)

18.312
Social Science Research Council
Postdoctoral Grants for International
     Research: Korea
605 Third Ave.
New York, NY 10158
(212) 557-9500

     • Awards substantial grants to citizens or permanent residents of the U.S. or Canada for research on North or South Korea to be undertaken in North America or abroad; deadline for applications, December 1

18.313
National Science Foundation
United States-Republic of Korea
     Cooperative Science Program
Division of International Programs
Washington, DC 20550
(202) 357-9537

Contact(s):
Gerald Edwards, Program Manager

     • Funds programs involving cooperative research and short- and long-term visits between the U.S. and South Korea

18.314
The University of Hawaii Press
2840 Kolowalu St.
Honolulu, HI 96822
(808) 948-8255

• Offers extensive list of books on Korea, publishes *Korean Studies* (see 18.320), and distributes publications of the Korea Development Institute

Publications

18.315
Facts About Korea
Korean Overseas Information Service
Ministry of Culture & Information
Seoul, South Korea
1977; paperbound; 192 pages; free

Available from the Information Office, Embassy of South Korea, 2370 Massachusetts Ave. NW, Washington, DC 20008
• Covers basic aspects of Korean life including history, government, politics, economics, education, communications and the media, customs, the arts, religion and tourism; includes map

18.316
An Introductory Course in Korean
Fred Lukoff
University of Washington Press
P.O. Box 85569
Seattle, WA 98145
1983; paperbound; 518 pages; $20

• Basic preparation for learning to read Korean; designed to help students to read material related to their academic studies; Korean orthography is used (romanization of forms occasionally given)

18.317
Korea: An Analytical Guide to Bibliographies
Hesung Chun Koh and Joan Steffens, Editors

Human Relations Area Files Press
2015 Yale Station
New Haven, CT 06520
1971; hardbound; 352 pages; $25

• Lists and discusses bibliographies on Korea

18.318
Korean Annual
(Identity of publisher not available); annual; hardbound, 650 pages; $30

May be ordered from International Publications Service, 114 East 32d St., New York, NY 10016
• Provides almanac-type information on all aspects of South Korean society covering politics, government, the economy, finance, trade, culture, education, etc.

18.319
A Korean-English Dictionary
Samuel E. Martin, Yang Ha Lee and Sung-un Chang
Yale University Press
302 Temple St.
New Haven, CT 06520
1967; hardbound; 1,902 pages; $95

• Useful dictionary for those learning to read Korean

18.320
Korean Studies
Peter H. Lee, Managing Editor
University of Hawaii Press
2840 Kolowalu St.
Honolulu, HI 96822
annual; paperbound; approx. 147 pages;
   $13.50 (volumes 2 and 3 $9.50 each)

Publication of the Center for Korean Studies
   • Scholarly articles on Korean culture and history; book reviews

18.321
New Pearl of the Orient: Korea
Korea National Tourism Corp.
198-1, Kwanhoon-dong, Chongno-ku
Seoul, Korea
paperbound; 1979; 120 pages; free

Available from Korea National Tourism Corp., Room 628, Korea Center Bldg., 460 Park Ave., New York, NY 10022
   • Attractively produced booklet giving extensive information of interest to the traveler and tourist, including country data, what to see, entertainment, accommodations, and a miscellany of other information

18.322
Studies on Korea: A Scholar's Guide
Han-Kyo Kim, Editor
Center for Korean Studies
University of Hawaii at Manoa
1881 East-West Road
Honolulu, HI 96822
1980; hardbound; 438 pages; $25

   • Consists of 16 chapters; the first provides a general bibliography, the next 13 are devoted to individual social sciences and humanities disciplines, the 15th covers North

Korean Studies and the 16th covers Russian language materials on Korea; each chapter is written by a specialist in the particular area and includes an introductory essay followed by an annotated bibliography

The following companies import and sell books in the Korean language:

18.323
Cheng & Tsui Co.
25-31 West St.
Boston, MA 02111
(617) 426-6074

18.324
Jeong Eum SA Imports, Inc.
3030 West Olympic Blvd., Suite 111
Los Angeles, CA 90006
(213) 387-4082

The following are standard resources available on South Korea
INFORMATION SOURCES
   • *Background Notes:* (pamphlets available for North Korea and South Korea, see 2.188)
   • *Country Study/Area Handbook. . . .* (volumes available for North Korea and South Korea, see 2.189)
TRAVELER RESOURCES
   • *Communication Learning Aids:* (South and North Korea, see 2.190)
   • *Culturegram:* (South Korea, see 2.191)
   • *Update:* (South Korea, see 2.197)
   • *Fodor's Guide to. . . . (see 2.192)*
   • *. . . . .: A Travel Survival Kit* (South Korea, see 2.201)
LANGUAGE LEARNING RESOURCES
   • *Spoken. . . .* (see 9.047)
Fulbright Grants for study in South Korea normally available (see 7.041)

Kuwait

Organizations

18.325
Embassy of Kuwait
Cultural Division
4340 Connecticut Ave. NW, Fifth Floor
Washington, DC 20008
(202) 244-4709

• Answers questions and offers information about Kuwait, including a pamphlet, *A View of Kuwait*, which provides information of both general and tourist interest

Publications

18.326
The Kuwaiti Digest
Haidar Ahmad, Editor
Kuwait Oil Co., Ltd.
Ahmadi 22, Kuwait
quarterly magazine; free

• General review of life in Kuwait, including commercial and economic affairs

18.327
Kuwait: Social Change in Historical Perspective
Jacqueline S. Ismael
Syracuse University Press
1600 Jamesville Ave.
Syracuse, NY 13210
1982; hardbound; 214 pages; $22

• Examines both "pre-oil" and "post-oil" Kuwait in an analysis of the forces that have shaped Kuwaiti society and transformed it into a Muslim capitalist society

The following are standard resources available on Kuwait
INFORMATION SOURCES
• *Background Notes:* (see 2.188)
TRAVELER RESOURCES
• *Update:* (see 2.197)

LANGUAGE LEARNING RESOURCES
For the "International" Languages (Arabic, French, German and Spanish) see listings under Chapter IX *Foreign Language Teaching and Learning*

Laos

Publications

18.328
Contemporary Laos
Martin Stuart Fox, Editor
St. Martin's Press
175 Fifth Ave.
New York, NY 10010
1982; hardbound; 367 pages; $27.50

• Review of social, political and economic developments in Laos since 1975

18.329
History of Laos
M. Jumsai
Paragon Book Reprint Corp.
14 East 38th St.
New York, NY 10016
1971; hardbound; 190 pages; $12.50; second
   revised edition

• Review of Laotian history and the forces that have shaped contemporary Laos

The following are standard resources available on Laos
INFORMATION SOURCES
   • *Background Notes:* (see 2.188)
   • *Country Study/Area Handbook....* (see 2.189)
LANGUAGE LEARNING RESOURCES
   • *Spoken....* (see 9.047)

Lebanon

Publications

18.330
The Republic of Lebanon: A Nation in Jeopardy
David C. Gordon
Westview Press
5500 Central Ave.
Boulder, CO 80301
1983; 175 pages; hardbound, $22.50;
   paperbound, $11.95

• Concise introduction both for the student and the general reader to contemporary Lebanon; examines the history, geography, politics, international relations, economic development, culture and social aspects of the country; also explores the reasons for the recent disintegration of Lebanon as a viable society

The following are standard resources available on Lebanon
INFORMATION SOURCES
   • *Background Notes:* (see 2.188)
   • *Country Study/Area Handbook....* (see 2.189)
   • *World Bibliographical Series....* (see 2.198)

TRAVELER RESOURCES
- *Bartholomew Map of. . . .* (see 1.127)
- *Culturegram:* (see 2.191)

LANGUAGE LEARNING RESOURCES
For the "International" Languages (Arabic, French, German and Spanish) see listings under Chapter IX *Foreign Language Teaching and Learning*

Lesotho

Organizations

18.331
Embassy of Lesotho
Caravel Bldg., Suite 300
1601 Connecticut Ave. NW
Washington, DC 20009
(202) 462-4190

- Answers questions and provides booklets on Lesotho primarily oriented toward the traveler and tourist

The following are standard resources available on Lesotho

INFORMATION SOURCES
- *Background Notes:* (see 2.188)
- *Historical Dictionary of. . . .* (see 2.193)
- *World Bibliographical Series. . . .* (see 2.198)

TRAVELER RESOURCES
- *Culturegram:* (see 2.191)
Fulbright Grants for study in Lesotho normally available (see 7.041)

Liberia

Publications

18.332
Liberia & Sierra Leone
C. Claphan
Cambridge University Press
32 East 57th St.
New York, NY 10022
1976; hardbound; 160 pages; $24.95
- Reviews the history and contemporary affairs of Liberia and Sierra Leone

The following are standard resources available on Liberia

INFORMATION SOURCES
- *Background Notes:* (see 2.188)
- *Country Study/Area Handbook. . . .* (see 2.189)

Libya

Publications

18.333
Index Libycus: A Cumulative Index to Bibliography of Libya, 1915–1975
Hans Schlüter
G. K. Hall & Co.
70 Lincoln St.
Boston, MA 02111
1981; hardbound; 275 pages; $25

• Covers 11,000 titles published both in Libya and elsewhere including monographs and periodical articles about Libya, special reports, conference proceedings, symposia and selected earlier writings; references from most Western-language publications, particularly those in English, French, Italian and German

18.334
Libya
John Wright
The Johns Hopkins University Press
Baltimore, MD 21218
1983; hardbound; 288 pages; $25

• Comprehensive and up-to-date review of Libyan history and society with approximately half of the book devoted to cur-

rent conditions under the Socialist People's Libyan Arab Jamahiriyah

18.335
Libya Since Independence
J. A. Allan, Editor
St. Martin's Press
175 Fifth Ave.
New York, NY 10010
1982; hardbound; 187 pages; $22.50

• Review of economic and social development of Libya in modern times

The following are standard resources available on Libya
INFORMATION SOURCES
• *Background Notes:* (see 2.188)
• *Country Study/Area Handbook. . . .* (see 2.189)
• *Historical Dictionary of. . . .* (see 2.193)
LANGUAGE LEARNING RESOURCES
For the "International" Languages (Arabic, French, German and Spanish) see listings under Chapter IX *Foreign Language Teaching and Learning*

Luxembourg

Organizations

18.336
Embassy of Luxembourg
2200 Massachusetts Ave. NW
Washington, DC 20008
(202) 265-4171

- Answers telephone and written inquiries about Luxembourg
- For additional information recommends the Luxembourg National Office of Tourism, 801 2nd Ave., 13th floor, New York, NY 10017

Publications

The following are standard resources available on Luxembourg
INFORMATION SOURCES
- *Background Notes:* (see 2.188)
- *World Bibliographical Series. . . .* (see 2.198)
TRAVELER RESOURCES
- *Culturegram:* (see 2.191)
- *Fodor's Guide to. . . .* (see 2.192)

LANGUAGE LEARNING RESOURCES
For the "International" Languages (Arabic, French, German and Spanish) see listings under Chapter IX *Foreign Language Teaching and Learning*
Fulbright Grants and ITT Fellowships for graduate study in Luxembourg normally available (see 7.041)

Madagascar

Publications

18.338
Madagascar Today
Sennen Andriamirado
J. A. Editions
France
1979; hardbound; 240 pages; $14.95

Available from Hippocrene Books, Inc., 171 Madison Ave., New York, NY 10016

- Travel guide to, a description of and a report on contemporary Madagascar

The following are standard resources available on Madagascar
INFORMATION SOURCES
- *Background Notes:* (see 2.188)
- *Country Study/Area Handbook. . . .* (see 2.189)

Malawi

The following are standard resources available on Malawi

INFORMATION SOURCES
- *Background Notes:* (see 2.188)
- *Country Study/Area Handbook.* . . . (see 2.189)

- *Historical Dictionary of.* . . . (see 2.193)
- *World Bibliographical Series.* . . . (see 2.198)

Malaysia

Organizations

18.339
Embassy of Malaysia
Information Office
2401 Massachusetts Ave. NW
Washington, DC 20008
(202) 328-2700

- Provides information on Malaysian social, cultural, economic and political life, including *Malaysian Digest* (see 18.341), *Malaysian Panorama* (see 18.343), *Malaysia in Brief* (see 18.342) and information on Malaysian development

Publications

18.340
Malaysia and Singapore: The Building of New States
Stanley S. Bedlington
Cornell University Press
124 Roberts Place
Ithaca, NY 14850
1978; 304 pages; hardbound, $19.50; paperbound, $6.95

- Analysis of the emergence of Malaysia and Singapore as modern independent states

18.341
Malaysian Digest
External Information Division
Ministry of Foreign Affairs
Jalan Wisma Putra
Kuala Lumpur, Malaysia
biweekly newspaper; 8 pages; free

Available from the Embassy of Malaysia, 2401 Massachusetts Ave. NW, Washington, DC 20008
- Tabloid-style newspaper covering current Malaysian political, cultural and economic affairs

18.342
Malaysia in Brief
External Information Division
Ministry of Foreign Affairs
Kuala Lumpur, Malaysia
paperbound; 272 pages; free

Available from the Embassy of Malaysia, 2401 Massachusetts Ave. NW, Washington, DC 20008
 • Provides information on the country, people, history, government, the economy and economic development, business and finance, social services, communications and the media, culture, tourist attractions and travel regulations and formalities

18.343
Malaysian Panorama
External Information Division
Ministry of Foreign Affairs
Jalan Wisma Putra
Kuala Lumpur, Malaysia
quarterly magazine; 24 pages; free

Available from the Embassy of Malaysia, 2401 Massachusetts Ave. NW, Washington, DC 20008
 • Glossy magazine depicting Malaysian economic, social and cultural life

The following are standard resources available on Malaysia

INFORMATION SOURCES
 • *Background Notes:* (see 2.188)
 • *Country Study/Area Handbook.* . . . (see 2.189)
 • *World Bibliographical Series.* . . . (see 2.198)

TRAVELER RESOURCES
 • *Culturegram:* (see 2.191)

LANGUAGE LEARNING RESOURCES
 • *. . . .: Complete Course for Beginners* (see 9.044)
 • *Spoken.* . . . (see 9.047)

Maldives

Publications

18.344
People of the Maldive Islands
Clarence Maloney
Orient Longman
Hong Kong
1981; paperbound; 456 pages; $27.95

Available from South Asia Books, Box 502, Columbia, MO 65205

 • Reviews the history, society and culture of the Maldive people

The following are standard resources available on Maldives
INFORMATION SOURCES
 • *Background Notes:* (see 2.188)

Mali

The following are standard resources available on Mali
INFORMATION SOURCES
- *Background Notes:* (see 2.188)
- *Historical Dictionary of. . . .* (see 2.193)

Malta

Publications

18.345
Malta
Thornton Cox
Hippocrene Books, Inc.
171 Madison Ave.
New York, NY 10016
1982; laminated paper binding; 120 pages;
$6.95

- Guide to Malta including general data for the traveler, suggested sightseeing itineraries and cultural and historical background

18.346
The Malta Yearbook
De La Salle Brothers Publications
St. Benild School
Church St.
Sliema, Malta
annual; paperbound; 416 pages; $10

- Provides extensive information on the Maltese Islands covering the economy, trade, government, tourism, and social, cultural and political affairs; includes review of year past

The following are standard resources available on Malta
INFORMATION SOURCES
- *Background Notes:* (see 2.188)
TRAVELER RESOURCES
- *Nagel's Encyclopedia Guide to. . . .* (see 2.195)
- *. . . . .: A Travel Survival Kit* (see 2.196)

Mauritania

The following are standard resources available on Mauritania
INFORMATION SOURCES
  * *Background Notes:* (see 2.188)
  * *Country Study/Area Handbook. . . .* (see 2.189)

  * *Historical Dictionary of. . . .* (see 2.193)
Fulbright Grants for study in Mauritania normally available (see 7.041)

Mauritius

Organizations

18.348
Embassy of Mauritius
4302 Connecticut Ave. NW
Washington, DC 20008
(202) 244-1491
CONSULATE: Encino, Cal.

  * Answers telephone and written inquiries about Mauritius, regarding educational matters
  * Provides printed information about travel to and in Mauritius

  * Recommends these other sources of information: Mauritius Tourist Information Services, 2 West 45th St., #803, New York, NY 10036

The following are standard resources available on Mauritius
INFORMATION SOURCES
  * *Background Notes:* (see 2.188)
  * *Historical Dictionary of. . . .* (see 2.193)
Fulbright Grants for study in Mauritius normally available (see 7.041)

Mexico

Organizations

18.350
Embassy of Mexico
2829 16th St. NW
Washington, DC 20009
(202) 265-5112

CONSULATES GENERAL: Albuquerque, Chicago, Dallas, Los Angeles, Miami, New Orleans, Nogales, Ariz., Sacramento, San Bernadino, San Francisco, Seattle

• Answers telephone and written inquiries about Mexico including educational matters

• Welcomes inquiries from any interested individual or institution

• Provides printed information about education in Mexico and about Mexico in general

• Offers Abraham Lincoln-Benito Juarez Scholarship providing one- to two-year scholarships to graduate students for study in Mexico

• Recommends these other sources of information: Consulates General and the Mexican National Tourist Council, 405 Park Ave., New York, NY 10022

Publications

18.351
Interact: Mexico/U.S.
John C. Condon
Intercultural Press, Inc.
Box 768
Yarmouth, ME 04096
1981; paperbound; 60 pages; $10

• Analyzes how Americans and Mexicans do things differently and how these differences affect working relationships between them; covers such subjects as communication styles, family relationships, sex roles and attitudes toward work, achievement, authority, decision-making, negotiations, cooperation and competition

18.352
Mexico
Daniel Levy and Gabriel Szekely
Westview Press
5500 Central Ave.
Boulder, CO 80301
1982; 300 pages; hardbound, $27.50;
   paperbound, $12.95

• Concise introduction both for the student and the general reader to contemporary Mexico; examines the history, geography, politics, international relations, economic development, culture and social aspects of the country; also explores in particular the unique characteristics of the Mexican political system and what might be in store for the future

18.353
Passport to Mexico
Robert Brett
EMC Publishing
300 York Ave.
St. Paul, MN 55101
1978; 5 filmstrips, 5 open reel tapes or
   cassettes, and Teacher's Guide with
   Student Activities on blackline originals;
   $128

• Multimedia program in English and Spanish designed as a beginning language-learning mini-course for students and travelers who are going to Mexico

The following are standard resources available on Mexico

INFORMATION SOURCES

• *Background Notes:* (see 2.188)
• *Country Study/Area Handbook.* . . . (see 2.189)
• *Historical Dictionary of.* . . . (see 2.193)
• *Image of.* . . . (see 2.194)

TRAVELER RESOURCES

• *Culturegram:* (see 2.191)
• *Update:* (see 2.197)
• *Nagel's Encyclopedia Guide to.* . . . (see 2.198)
• *. . . . .: A Travel Survival Kit* (see 2.196)

LANGUAGE LEARNING RESOURCES
For the "International" Languages (Arabic, French, German and Spanish) see listings under Chapter IX *Foreign Language Teaching and Learning*

Fulbright Grants for study in Mexico normally available (see 7.041)

Mongolia

Organizations

18.354
The Mongolia Society, Inc.
P.O. Drawer 606
Bloomington, IN 47402
(812) 335-1566

Contact(s):
John G. Hangin, Vice President and
    Executive Director

Professional academic association designed to promote the study of Mongolian history, language and culture

- Publishes *Mongolian Studies* (see 18.358) and Occasional and Special Papers Series on aspects of Mongolian history, culture and language, including *Contemporary Mongolia* (V.A. Maslennikov, $2) and *The Pre-Revolutionary Culture of Outer Mongolia* (George A. Cheney, $4)
- Orders and imports books, periodicals, prints, slide transparencies and records from Mongolia, including both current and past publications
- Provides small supplementary grants for research on or study of Mongolia; preference to graduate students in Oriental Studies in the U.S.

Publications

18.355
Bibliotheca Mongolica, Part I: Works in English, French, and German
Henry G. Schwarz, Editor
Center for East Asian Studies
Western Washington University
Bellingham, WA 98225
1978; hardbound; 355 pages; $20

- Guide to literature on Mongolia

18.356
A Concise English-Mongolian Dictionary
John G. Hangin
Research Center for the Language Sciences
516 E. Sixth St.
Indiana University
Bloomington, IN 47405
1970; paperbound; 300 pages; $10

Volume 89 of the Uralic and Altaic Series

• Contains approximately 10,000 English words with equivalents in modern spoken Mongolian

18.357
Mongolia's Culture & Society
Sechin Jagched and Paul Hyer
Westview Press, Inc.
5500 Central Ave.
Boulder, CO 80301
1979; hardbound; 461 pages; $37.50

• Full description and analysis of traditional nomadic Mongolian culture and society and the impact of modernization and revolutionary political and social change upon it

18.358
Mongolian Studies: Journal of the Mongolia Society
Larry W. Moses, Editor
The Mongolia Society, Inc.
P.O. Drawer 606
Bloomington, IN 47402
annual journal; approx. 125 pages; $15

• Scholarly articles on Mongolian history and culture; book reviews

The following are standard resources available on Mongolia
INFORMATION SOURCES
• *Background Notes:* (see 2.188)
• *Country Study/Area Handbook. . . .* (see 2.189)
TRAVELER RESOURCES
• *Culturegram:* (see 2.191)

Morocco

Organizations

18.359
Embassy of Morocco
1601 21st St. NW
Washington, DC 20009
(202) 462-7979
• Answers telephone and written inquiries about Morocco, including educational matters

• Welcomes inquiries from any interested individual or institution
• Provides printed information about education in Morocco and on Morocco in general, including background information on the country and its history and brochures of principal cities

Publications

18.360
An Introduction to Moroccan Arabic
Ernest T. Abdel-Massih
Center for Near Eastern and North African Studies

University of Michigan
144 Lane Hall
Ann Arbor, MI 48109-1290
1982; paperbound; 460 pages; $9

Some drills are available on tape from Michigan Media Resource Center, Tape Duplication Service, University of Michigan, 400 South 4th St., Ann Arbor, MI 48109

• Course text which discusses phonology and provides basic reading and conversation lessons, grammatical notes, drills, word lists, stories and English-Arabic (Moroccan) and Arabic-English lexicon

18.361
Western Sahara: A Comprehensive Bibliography
Lynn F. Sipe
Garland Publishing, Inc.
136 Madison Ave.
New York, NY 10016
1984; hardbound; 448 pages; $54

• Identifies all significant primary and secondary publications in Western European languages, from early 19th-century European contacts to the present; covers magazine, journal and newspaper articles, government documents, monographs, dissertations, maps and newsletters; selectively annotated; 6,600 entries; indexed

The following are standard resources available on Morocco
INFORMATION SOURCES
• *Background Notes:* (see 2.188)
• *Country Study/Area Handbook.* . . . (see 2.189)
• *Historical Dictionary of.* . . . (see 2.193) "Morocco," "Western Sahara"
TRAVELER RESOURCES
• *Nagel's Encyclopedia Guide to.* . . . (see 2.195)
LANGUAGE LEARNING RESOURCES
For the "International" Languages (Arabic, French, German and Spanish) see listings under Chapter IX *Foreign Language Teaching and Learning*

Mozambique

Publications

18.362
Mozambique: From Colonialism to Revolution, 1900–1982
Allen Isaacman and Barbara Isaacman
Westview Press
5500 Central Ave.
Boulder, CO 80301
1983; 160 pages; hardbound, $25; paperbound, $11.95

• Concise introduction both for the student and the general reader to contemporary Mozambique; examines the history, geography, politics, international relations, economic development, culture and social aspects of the country; profiles Mozambique in the context of its poverty, resistance to colonialism and the need for economic development

18.363
Mozambique: A History
Thomas H. Henriksen
Rowman & Littlefield, Inc.
81 Adams Drive
Box 327
Totowa, NJ 07511
1979; hardbound; 276 pages; $25.75

Review of history, society and culture of Mozambique

The following are standard resources available on Mozambique

INFORMATION SOURCES
- *Background Notes:* (see 2.188)
- *Country Study/Area Handbook.* . . . (see 2.189)

Namibia

Publications

18.364
Namibia: Political and Economic Prospects
Robert I. Rotberg, Editor
Lexington Books
D. C. Heath and Co.
125 Spring St.
Lexington, MA 02173
1982; hardbound; 144 pages; $20

- Series of essays reviews the economic, political and social forces at work in and on Namibia relative to its current and future status

18.365
South Africa/Namibia Update
African-American Institute
833 UN Plaza
New York, NY 10017
published 15 times per year; newsletter; 4 pages; free
- Provides detailed information on political and economic events in South Africa and Namibia with particular attention to areas such as trade union activity and black politics that the daily press does not cover in depth
The following are standard resources available on Namibia
INFORMATION SOURCES
- *Background Notes:* (see 2.188)

Nauru

Publications

18.366
The Nauruans
Solange Petit
Macduff Press
660 Market St., Suite 204
San Francisco, CA 94104
1981; hardbound; 315 pages; $22.80, plus $1.50 postage

- An anthropological study of traditional Nauruan culture; useful background to contemporary Nauru

The following are standard resources available on Nauru
INFORMATION SOURCES
- *Background Notes:* (see 2.188)

Nepal

Organizations

18.367
Embassy of Nepal
2131 Leroy Place NW
Washington, DC 20008
(202) 667-4550

• Answers questions and provides tourist and travel information on Nepal, including the booklet *Nepal*

Publications

18.368
Nepal: Profile of a Himalayan Kingdom
Leo E. Rose and John T. Scholz
Westview Press
5500 Central Ave.
Boulder, CO 80301
1980; hardbound; 144 pages; $18.50

• Concise introduction both for the student and the general reader to contemporary Nepal; examines the history, geography, politics, international relations, economic development, culture and social aspects of the country; also discusses the impact of ethnic diversity and the problems raised by rapid population growth

The following are standard resources available on Nepal

INFORMATION SOURCES
• *Background Notes:* (see 2.188)
• *Country Study/Area Handbook.* . . . (see 2.189)
• *Historical Dictionary of.* . . . (see 2.193)
TRAVELER RESOURCES
• *Fodor's Guide to.* . . .(see 2.192)
• *Nagel's Encyclopedia Guide to.* . . . (see 2.195)
• . . . .: *A Travel Survival Kit* (see 2.196)

Netherlands

Organizations

18.369
Embassy of the Netherlands
4200 Linnean Ave. NW
Washington, DC 20008
(202) 244-5300
CONSULATES GENERAL: Chicago, Houston, Los Angeles, New York, San Francisco

• Answers telephone and written inquiries about the Netherlands including travel/tourist and educational matters
• Provides or recommends films and audiovisual materials as well as educational materials

- Welcomes inquiries from any interested individual or institution
- Provides wide selection of printed information about education, travel and the country in general

- Recommends these other sources of information: Netherlands National Tourist Office, 576 Fifth Ave., New York, NY 10036 and Netherlands Consulates General

Publications

18.370
The Netherlands: An Historical and Cultural Survey, 1795–1977
Gerald Newton
Westview Press, Inc.
5500 Central Ave.
Boulder, CO 80301
1977; hardbound; 300 pages; $36.50

- Broad-ranging review of the history of the modern Netherlands

18.371
A Short History of the Netherlands Antilles and Surinam
Cornelius C. Goslinga
Martinus Nijhoff, Netherlands; 1978;
    paperbound; 215 pages; $20

Available from Kluwer Boston, Inc., 190 Old Derby St., Hingham, MA 02043
- Review of history, society and culture of the Netherlands Antilles and Surinam

The following companies import and sell books in the Dutch language:

18.372
W. S. Heinman—Imported Books
225 West 57th St.
P.O. Box 926
New York, NY 10019
(212) 757-7628

18.373
Sky Books International, Inc.
48 East 50th St.
New York, NY 10022
(212) 688-5086

The following are standard resources available on the Netherlands
INFORMATION SOURCES
- *Background Notes:* (see 2.188)
TRAVELER RESOURCES
- *Culturegram:* (see 2.191)
- *Kummerly & Frey Map of.* . . . (see 1.127)
- *Fodor's Guide to.* . . . (see 2.192)
LANGUAGE LEARNING RESOURCES
- *Berlitz.* . . . *for Travelers* (cassette-pak, see 9.042)
- . . . .: *Complete Course for Beginners* (see 9.044)
- *Say It in:* (see 9.046)
- *Spoken.* . . . (see 9.047)
- *Berlitz.* . . . *for Travelers* (phrase-book, see 9.043)

Fulbright Grants and ITT Fellowships for graduate study in the Netherlands normally available (see 7.041)

New Zealand

Organizations

18.374
Information Office, Embassy of New Zealand
37 Observatory Circle NW
Washington, DC 20008
(202) 328-4800
BRANCH OFFICES: Los Angeles, New York, and San Francisco

• Provides travel and tourist brochures and maps, including *New Zealand: Information for Tourists* and the pamphlet *About New Zealand* which describes in words and photos the history, government, people, foreign relations, trade and economic conditions, tourism, and social and cultural affairs of New Zealand

18.375
National Science Foundation
United States-New Zealand Cooperative
  Science Program
Division of International Programs
Washington, DC 20550
(202) 357-9558

Contact(s):
Alan Milsap, Program Manager

• Funds programs involving cooperative research and short-term visits between the U.S. and New Zealand

Publications

The following are standard resources available on New Zealand

INFORMATION SOURCES
• *Background Notes:* (see 2.188)
• *World Bibliographical Series.* . . . (see 2.198)

TRAVELER RESOURCES
• *Bartholomew Map of.* . . . (see 1.109)
• *Culturegram:* (see 2.191)
• *Fodor's Guide to.* . . . (see 2.192)
• *. . . .: A Travel Survival Kit* (see 2.196)
Fulbright Grants for study in New Zealand normally available (see 7.041)

Nicaragua

Publications

18.376
Nicaragua: The Land of Sandino
Thomas W. Walker
Westview Press, Inc.
5500 Central Ave.
Boulder, CO 80301
1981; 137 pages; hardbound, $23;
   paperbound, $10.95

• Concise introduction both for the student and the general reader to contemporary Nicaragua; examines the history, geography, politics, international relations, economic development, culture and social aspects of the country; also provides an extensive historical analysis of the forces that have shaped Nicaragua (domestic exploitation, foreign interventions, etc.) up through the overthrow of Somoza and the establishment of the Sandinista social revolutionary system

The following are standard resources available on Nicaragua
INFORMATION SOURCES
• *Background Notes:* (see 2.188)
• *Country Study/Area Handbook.* . . . (see 2.189)
• *Historical Dictionary of.* . . . (see 2.193)
• *Image of.* . . . (see 2.194)
TRAVELER RESOURCES
• *Culturegram:* (see 2.191)
LANGUAGE LEARNING RESOURCES
For the "International" Languages (Arabic, French, German and Spanish) see listings under Chapter IX *Foreign Language Teaching and Learning*

Niger

Organizations

18.377
Embassy of The Republic of Niger
2204 R St. NW
Washington, DC 20008
(202) 483-4224

• Answers telephone and written inquiries about Niger, including travel/tourist and educational matters
• Welcomes inquiries from any interested individual or institution
• Provides printed information about Niger, including a substantial mimeographed pamphlet of general information

Publications

18.378
Introductory Hausa
Charles H. Kraft and Marguerite Kraft
California University Press
2120 Berkeley Way
Berkeley, CA 94720
1973; hardbound; $27.50
    • A thorough language-learning text and linguistic guide

The following are standard resources available on Niger

INFORMATION SOURCES
    • *Background Notes:* (see 2.188)
    • *Historical Dictionary of. . . .* (see 2.193)
LANGUAGE LEARNING RESOURCES
"Hausa"
    • *. . . .: Complete Course for Beginners* (see 9.044)
    • *Spoken. . . .* (see 9.047)
Fulbright grants for study in Niger normally available (see 7.041)

Nigeria

Organizations

18.379
Embassy of Nigeria
Information Service Center
Embassy of Nigeria Annex
2215 M St. NW
Washington, DC 20037
(202) 822-1680/1681
CONSULATES GENERAL: Atlanta, New York, San Francisco

    • Answers telephone and written inquiries about Nigeria regarding educational matters
    • Recommends speakers, exhibits, films, and audiovisual materials
    • Welcomes inquiries from any interested individual or institution
    • Provides printed information about Nigeria and about education in Nigeria
    • Recommends these other sources of information: Consulates General

Publications

18.380
The Federal Republic of Nigeria at a Glance
Third Press International
1995 Broadway
New York, NY 10023
For the Federal Ministry of Information, Lagos, Nigeria; free

Available from the Embassy of Nigeria, 2201 M St. NW, Washington, DC 20037
    • Large fold-out map (on one side) and information sheet (on the other) providing data for the traveler and tourist

18.381
Introductory Hausa
Charles H. Kraft and Marguerite Kraft
California University Press
2120 Berkeley Way
Berkeley, CA 94720
1973; hardbound; $27.50

• A thorough language-learning text and
linguistic guide

18.382
Nigeria Handbook
Information Division
Federal Ministry of Information
Lagos, Nigeria
annual; paperbound; 402 pages, free

Also available from Third Press International,
1995 Broadway, New York, NY 10023
• Thorough description of Nigeria, its
people and its society; covers history, geography, economy, government, social services
and culture; includes a variety of fact lists

18.383
The Story of Nigeria
Michael Crowder
Faber & Faber, Inc.
39 Thompson St.
Winchester, MA 01890
1978; hardbound, $17.95; paperbound,
    $9.95; 432 pages; fourth edition

• Thorough review of history, society and
culture of Nigeria

The following are standard resources avail-
able on Nigeria
INFORMATION SOURCES
• *Background Notes:* (see 2.188)
• *Country Study/Area Handbook.* . . .
    (see 2.189)
TRAVELER RESOURCES
• *Culturegram:* (see 2.191)
• *Update:* (see 2.197)
LANGUAGE LEARNING RESOURCES
• . . . .: *Complete Course for Beginners*
    (see 9.044) "Hausa", "Yoruba"
• *Spoken.* . . . (see 9.047) "Hausa,"
    "Yoruba"
Fulbright grants for study in Nigeria nor-
    mally available (see 7.041)

Norway

Area Study and Research Programs

18.384
Scandinavian Studies
Luther College
Decorah, IA 52101
(319) 387-1287

Contact(s):
Kathleen Stokker, Director

• Offers B.A. in Scandinavian Studies
which focuses primarily on Norway, the Norwegian language and literature, and Norwegian immigration to the U.S.

Organizations

18.385
The Norwegian Information Service in the United States
825 Third Ave.
New York, NY 10022
(212) 421-7333
BRANCHES: Information also from
Consulates General in: New York, Chicago,
Los Angeles, Minneapolis, and San
Francisco

• Answers written and phone inquiries
about Norway in general
• Provides information, prepares news
releases, identifies films, publishes a newsletter and lends recordings, slides and photos; publications include *What You Should Know About Norway* and a variety of other booklets, brochures and fact sheets

18.386
University of Oslo International Summer School
North American Admissions Office
% St. Olaf College
Northfield, MN 55057
(507) 663-3269

Contact(s):
Kjetil Flatin, Director (in Norway)
Jo Ann Kleber, Administrator (in U.S.)

Six-week summer school program in Norway
offering courses in Norwegian language, society and culture, including graduate and undergraduate courses; two years of college required
• Offers scholarships of varying amounts, usually approximately one-half of the fee; available for graduates and upperclass undergraduates

Publications

18.387
Mini-Facts About Norway, 1979–80
Arne Enderud, Editor
The Press & Cultural Relations Department
The Royal Ministry of Foreign Affairs
Olso, Norway
annual; paperbound; 48 pages; free

bor market, migration, indexes, education, culture, development assistance, transportation, communication, defense, the media, holidays and foreign service

Available from the Norwegian Information Service, 825 Third Ave., New York, NY 10022
• Handy, pocket-sized booklet packed with statistical information on geography, climate, counties, towns, political parties, elections, government, balance of payments, fiscal budget, industries, agriculture, fishing, hunting, shipping, tourism, foreign trade, la-

18.388
Norwegian-English Dictionary
University of Wisconsin Press
114 North Murray St.
Madison, WI 53715
1965; paperbound; 504 pages; $17.50

• A pronouncing and translating dictionary of modern Norwegian with a historical and grammatical introduction

18.389
**University Studies in Norway: A Guide-
Book for Foreign Students**
Guro Nordahl-Olsen, Editor
Norwegian Information Service
825 Third Ave.
New York, NY 10022
1975; booklet; 64 pages; free

• Provides general information for foreign students interested in studying in both
short- and long-term programs at Norwegian
institutes; describes programs and requirements at universities, including brief descriptions of research institutes in Oslo, Bergen,
Trondheim and Tromsø

The following are standard resources avail-
able on Norway
INFORMATION SOURCES
    • *Background Notes:* (see 2.188)
TRAVELER RESOURCES
    • *Culturegram:* (see 2.191)
    • *Update:* (see 2.197)
LANGUAGE LEARNING RESOURCES
    • *Berlitz. . . . for Travelers* (cassette-
      pak, see 9.042)
    • *. . . . : Complete Course for Beginners*
      (see 9.044)
    • *Say It in:* (see 9.046)
    • *Spoken. . . .* (see 9.047)
    • *Berlitz. . . . for Travelers* (phrase-
      book, see 9.043)
Fulbright Grants and ITT Fellowships for
graduate study in Norway normally avail-
able (see 7.041)

Oman

Publications

18.390
Oman: The Reborn Land
F. A. Clements
Longman, Inc.
19 West 44th St.
New York, NY 10036
1980; hardbound; 181 pages; $27

• Analysis of contemporary Oman society and the forces that have shaped it

18.391
**Oman and Southeastern Arabia: A
Bibliographic Survey**
Michael Owen Shannon
G. K. Hall & Co.
70 Lincoln St.
Boston, MA 02111
1978; hardbound; 165 pages; $22

• Surveys all Western literature on Oman
and Southeastern Arabia from prehistory
through the late 1970s; entries on over 1,000
books, articles and reports covering politics
and society, geology, geography, maritime affairs, international law and government; selectively annotated

The following are standard resources avail-
able on Oman
INFORMATION SOURCES
    • *Background Notes:* (see 2.188)
    • *World Bibliographical Series. . . .* (see
      2.198)
LANGUAGE LEARNING RESOURCES
For the "International" Languages (Arabic,
    French, German and Spanish) see listings
    under Chapter IX *Foreign Language
    Teaching and Learning*

Pakistan

Organizations

18.392
American Institute of Pakistan Studies
Villanova University
138 Tolentine Hall
Villanova, PA 19085
(215) 645-4738 or 4791
Academic research organization

• Offers fellowships to scholars and advanced graduate students for travel and research in Pakistan in the following categories: predoctoral research, postdoctoral research, library service, and professional development; includes all fields of the humanities and social sciences

18.393
Embassy of Pakistan
Information Division
2315 Massachusetts Ave. NW
Washington, DC 20008
(202) 939-6200

• Provides information and publications including a series of pamphlets *Facts About Pakistan* (on travel, postage stamps, festivals, coins, customs, handicrafts, cuisine, folk tales, etc.), brochures with maps on individual cities, *Pakistan* (a general brochure for the tourist), and the newsletter *Pakistan Affairs*
• Lends educational and documentary films on Pakistan

Publications

18.394
Pakistan Horizon
Naveed Ahmad, Acting Editor
Pakistan Institute of International Affairs
Aiwan-e-Sadar Road
Karachi-1, Pakistan
quarterly journal; approx. 170 pages; $20
    per year

• Contains substantive articles, essays and commentary on current national and international political issues from the Pakistani perspective; book reviews

18.395
Pakistan: A Nation in the Making
Shavid Javed Burki
Westview Press, Inc.
5500 Central Ave.
Boulder, CO 80301
1983; hardbound; 128 pages; $16

• Concise introduction both for the student and the general reader to contemporary Pakistan; examines the history, geography, politics, international relations, economic development, culture and social aspects of the country; also traces and attempts to explain the events leading to Pakistani nationhood and the economic and political turbulence that has characterized the country in recent decades

The following are standard resources available on Pakistan
INFORMATION SOURCES
• *Background Notes:* (see 2.188)
• *Country Study/Area Handbook. . . .* (see 2.189)
• *World Bibliographical Series. . . .* (see 2.198)

TRAVELER RESOURCES
- *Culturegram:* (see 2.191)
- . . . .: *A Travel Survival Kit* (see 2.197)

LANGUAGE LEARNING RESOURCES
- . . . .: *Complete Course for Beginners* (see 9.044) "Urdu"
- *Spoken.* . . . (see 9.047) "Urdu," "Hindustani"

Panama

Publications

18.396
Focus On Panama
Ken Jones, Managing Editor
Promociones Turisticas de Panama y El
   Caribe, S.A.
Apartado 7656
Panama 5, R d. P.
semiannual; paperbound; 110 pages; free

Available from the Embassy of Panama, 2862
McGill Terrace NW, Washington, DC 20008,
and from the Panama Government Tourist
Bureaus in New York and San Francisco
   • Offers information, advertisements and
articles of interest to travelers, tourists and
vacationers; covers entertainment, culture,
hotels, services, restaurants, museums, etc.
and focuses on specific towns and cities; includes maps; in English and Spanish

The following are standard resources avail-
able on Panama
INFORMATION SOURCES
- *Background Notes:* (see 2.188)
- *Country Study/Area Handbook.* . . . (see 2.189)
- *Historical Dictionary of.* . . . (see 2.193)
- *World Bibliographical Series.* . . . (see 2.203)
- *Image of.* . . . (see 2.194)

TRAVELER RESOURCES
- *Culturegram:* (see 2.191)

LANGUAGE LEARNING RESOURCES
For the "International" Languages (Arabic,
   French, German and Spanish) see listings
   under Chapter IX *Foreign Language
   Teaching and Learning*
Fulbright Grants for study in Panama nor-
   mally available (see 7.041)

Papua New Guinea

Organizations

18.397
Embassy of Papua New Guinea
1140 19th St. NW, Suite 503
Washington, DC 20036
(202) 659-0856

- Answers telephone and written inquiries about Papua New Guinea, including
travel/tourist matters
- Provides printed information about
travel to and in Papua New Guinea as well as

information about Papua New Guinea in general, including an attractively produced periodical, *Papua New Guinea Foreign Affairs Review*

Publications

18.398
Encyclopaedia of Papua and New Guinea
Peter Ryan
Melbourne University Press
Victoria, Australia 3053
In association with the University of Papua New Guinea; 1972; hardbound; 3 volumes; 1,340 pages; $55

Available from the International Scholarly Book Services, Inc., Box 1632, Beaverton, OR 97075
   • Comprehensive work of reference covering every discipline and branch of knowledge relating to Papua New Guinea (and West Irian)

18.399
Papua New Guinea
University of Hawaii Press
2840 Kolowalu St.
Honolulu, HI 96822
1976; hardbound; 68 pages; $9.95

   • An introductory series of essays on aspects of Papuan life, culture, history, government and economy

18.400
Papua New Guinea Handbook and Travel Guide
Stuart Inder
Pacific Publications
Australia
1980; paperbound; 280 pages; $13.95

Available from Books Australia, 15601 SW 83d St., Miami, FL 33157
   • Guide to Papua New Guinea for the traveler

The following are standard resources available on Papua New Guinea
INFORMATION SOURCES
   • *Background Notes:* (see 2.188)
TRAVELER RESOURCES
   • . . . .: *A Travel Survival Kit* (see 2.196)

Paraguay

Publications

18.401
Paraguay: A Bibliography
David L. Jones
Garland Publishing, Inc.
136 Madison Ave.
New York, NY 10016
1979; hardbound; 499 pages; $52

   • Useful research and study tool
The following are standard resources available on Paraguay
INFORMATION SOURCES
   • *Background Notes:* (see 2.188)
   • *Country Study/Area Handbook. . . .* (see 2.189)

- *Historical Dictionary of...* (see 2.193)
- *Image of...* (see 2.194)

TRAVELER RESOURCES
- *Culturegram:* (see 2.191)

LANGUAGE LEARNING RESOURCES
For the "International" Languages (Arabic, French, German and Spanish) see listings under Chapter IX *Foreign Language Teaching and Learning*

Peru

Organizations

18.402
Embassy of Peru
1700 Massachusetts Ave. NW
Washington, DC 20036
(202) 833-9860

Contact(s):
Alfonso Espinosa, Cultural Minister-
   Counselor

- Provides tourist brochures and maps on Peru in general and on specific cities and regions; publishes *Peru News*, covering social, political and economic developments and subjects of tourist interest

Publications

18.403
Guide to Cartographic and Natural Resources Information of Peru
Pan American Institute of Geography and
   History
Ex-Arzobispado No. 29
Mexico 18, D.F.
1979; paperbound; 99 pages; $8

- Provides basic guidelines and bibliography for pursuing research on Peru

18.404
Peru: A Cultural History
Henry F. Dobyns and Paul L. Doughty
Oxford University Press
200 Madison Ave.
New York, NY 10016
1976; 442 pages; hardbound, $22.50;
   paperbound, $9.95

- Charts the rise of modern Peru and explores extensively the cultural traditions which provided the framework for its evolution

18.405
Peru: A Short History
David P. Werlich
Southern Illinois University Press
Box 3697
Carbondale, IL 62901
1978; hardbound; 447 pages; $24.95

- Thorough review of Peruvian history and the forces that have shaped modern Peru

The following are standard resources available on Peru
INFORMATION SOURCES
- *Background Notes:* (see 2.188)

- *Country Study/Area Handbook.* . . . (see 2.189)
- *Image of.* . . . (see 2.194)

TRAVELER RESOURCES
- *Culturegram:* (see 2.191)
- *Nagel's Encyclopedia Guide to.* . . . (see 2.195)

LANGUAGE LEARNING RESOURCES
For the "International" Languages (Arabic, French, German and Spanish) see listings under Chapter IX *Foreign Language Teaching and Learning*
Fulbright grants for study in Peru normally available (see 7.041)

Philippines

Area Study and Research Programs

18.406
Philippines Studies Program
University of Hawaii at Manoa
Center for Asian and Pacific Studies
210 Moore Hall
Honolulu, HI 96822
(808) 948-6393/6394

Contact(s):
Belinda A. Aquino, Director

Undergraduate area studies program established in 1975
- Majors/degrees/certificates offered: B.A. with major in Philippine Studies; M.A.

in Southeast Asian Studies with concentration in Philippine Studies
- Approximate number of faculty teaching area and language courses: 15
- Approximate number of courses available—area: 15; language: 11
- Average number of students per year specializing in area: 15–20
- Languages offered: Ilokano and Tagalog (four levels each)
- Asia Collection of the university library maintains substantial holdings in Philippine studies materials
- Publishes Occasional Papers series and conducts lecture series on the Philippines

Organizations

18.407
Embassy of the Philippines
Information Office
1617 Massachusetts Ave. NW
Washington, DC 20036
(202) 483-1414
CONSULATES GENERAL: Chicago, Honolulu, Houston, Los Angeles, New Orleans, New York, San Francisco, Seattle

- Answers telephone and written inquiries about the Philippines regarding educational matters
- Recommends speakers and films and audiovisual materials
- Welcomes inquiries from educational institutions, libraries/museums, U.S. government agencies, cultural organizations and individuals

• Provides printed information about travel and education in the Philippines and on the Philippines in general

• Recommends other sources of information: Consulates General

Publications

18.408
Philippine Studies
Ateneo de Manila University
Box 154
Manila 2801, Philippines
quarterly journal; $12 per year; single copy, $3

• Contains articles, reviews, notes and commentary on Filipino history, culture and contemporary affairs

18.409
The Philippines: A Singular and a Plural Place
David Joel Steinberg
Westview Press, Inc.
5500 Central Ave.
Boulder, CO 80301
1982; 135 pages; hardbound, $18.50; paperbound, $10.95

• Concise introduction both for the student and the general reader to the contemporary Philippines; examines the history, geography, politics, international relations, economic development, culture and social aspects of the country; also explores conflicting social, linguistic, cultural and ethnic forces that both unite and divide the Filipinos

18.410
Tagalog for Beginners
T. V. Ramos and V. de Guzman
University of Hawaii Press
2840 Kolowalu St.
Honolulu, HI 96822
1971; paperbound; 875 pages; $14

• Thorough language-learning text and linguistic guide

18.411
Tagalog Language Guide
Superintendent of Documents
U.S. Government Printing Office
Washington, DC 20402
1973; paperbound; 86 pages; $4.25 (Stock Number: S/N 008-020-00535-5)

• Phrasebook for the visitor; provides directions on pronunciation (with phonetic spellings), useful words and phrases and instructional exercises; prepared originally for U.S. military personnel, but useful to others

The following are standard resources available on the Philippines

INFORMATION SOURCES
• *Background Notes:* (see 2.188)
• *Country Study/Area Handbook. . . .* (see 2.189)
TRAVELER RESOURCES
• *Communication Learning Aids:* (see 2.190)
• *Culturegram:* (see 2.191)
• *Nagel's Encyclopedia-Guide to. . . .* (see 2.195)
• *. . . . : A Travel Survival Kit* (see 2.196)

Fulbright Grants for study in the Philippines normally available (see 7.041)

Poland

Area Study and Research Programs

18.412
Polish Studies Center
Indiana University at Bloomington
Goodbody Hall 319/320
Bloomington, IN 47405
(812) 335-8119

Contact(s):
Mary Ellen Solt, Director

Study center established by an agreement with the Polish government under which an American Studies Center was also created at Warsaw University in Poland in 1976; U.S. Center designed to stimulate interest in Polish Studies at Indiana University and to promote research and study in the areas of language, history and the social sciences; part of the Russian and East European Institute (see 14.014)

• Conducts research, administers faculty and student exchanges, publishes newsletter and sponsors other campus and community activities

Organizations

18.413
Jozef Pilsudski Institute of America for Research in the Modern History of Poland, Inc.
381 Park Ave. South
New York, NY 10016
(212) 683-4342

Contact(s):
Yanina Kulikowska, Secretary of Board

• Sponsors research on the history of modern Poland and maintains extensive archives of research material

18.414
Polish Institute of Arts and Sciences in America
59 East 66th St.
New York, NY 10021
(212) 988-4338

Contact(s):
Feliks Gross, Executive Director

• Promotes and conducts research on all aspects of Polish culture; sponsors conferences, lectures and other programs; maintains library and archives on Poland and publishes *Polish Review*

Publications

18.415
The Poles
Steven Stewart
Macmillan, Inc.
866 Third Ave.
New York, NY 10022
1982; hardbound; 320 pages; $15.95

• Broad-ranging discussion of the people, culture and society of Poland

The following companies import and sell books in the Polish language:

18.416
FAM Book Service
69 Fifth Ave.
New York, NY 10003
(212) 255-8348

18.417
Four Continent Book Corp.
149 Fifth Ave.
New York, NY 10010
(212) 533-0250

18.418
Polish Book Store
5347 Chene St.
Detroit, MI 48211
(313) 921-2479

The following are standard resources available on Poland
INFORMATION SOURCES
- *Background Notes:* (see 2.188)
- *Country Study/Area Handbook. . . .* (see 2.189)
- *World Bibliographical Series. . . .* (see 2.198)

TRAVELER RESOURCES
- *Culturegram:* (see 2.191)
- *Nagel's Encyclopedia-Guide to. . . .* (see 2.195)

LANGUAGE LEARNING RESOURCES
- *Berlitz. . . . for Travelers* (phrasebook, see 9.043)
- *. . . .: Complete Course for Beginners* (see 9.044)
- *Say It in:* (see 9.046)
- *Spoken. . . .* (see 9.047)

Fulbright Grants for study in Poland normally available along with a number of Polish government grants (see 7.041)

Portugal

Organizations

18.419
Embassy of Portugal
2125 Kalorama Road NW
Washington, DC 20008
(202) 265-1643

- Answers telephone and written inquiries about Portugal, including educational matters
- Provides educational or teaching materials
- Welcomes inquiries from any interested individual or institution
- Provides printed information about education in Portugal and on Portugal in general

18.420
Luso-American Education Foundation
P.O. Box 1768
Oakland, CA 94604
(415) 452-4465

Contact(s):
Scholarship Program Director

Grant-giving educational foundation
- Provides scholarships to California students who are enrolled in Portuguese classes in a four-year college or who are of Portuguese descent; also gives grants to students and teachers of Portuguese for study in Portugal or for other comparable purposes

• Supports conferences and various other activities in California that promote a wider knowledge of the Portuguese language and culture in the U.S.

• Publishes newsletter

Publications

18.421
Contemporary Portugal
Allen & Unwin
9 Winchester Terrace
Winchester, MA 01890
1979; hardbound; 230 pages; $28.50

• Thorough analysis of the forces that have shaped contemporary Portugal from historical, social, economic and political perspectives

18.422
A Portuguese-English Dictionary
James L. Taylor
Stanford University Press
Stanford, CA 94305
1970; hardbound; 662 pages; $25

• Useful dictionary for learning to read Portuguese

The following companies import and sell books in the Portuguese language:

18.423
Imported Books
P.O. Box 4414
Dallas, TX 75208
(214) 941-6497

18.424
Universal Bookstore
5458 North 5th St.
Philadelphia, PA 19120
(215) 549-2897

The following are standard resources available on Portugal

INFORMATION SOURCES
• *Background Notes:* (see 2.188)
• *Country Study/Area Handbook.* . . . (see 2.189)

TRAVELER RESOURCES
• *Bartholomew Map of.* . . . (see 1.127)
• *Culturegram:* (see 2.191)
• *Fodor's Guide to.* . . . (see 2.192)
• *Nagel's Encyclopedia Guide to.* . . . (see 2.195)

LANGUAGE LEARNING RESOURCES
• . . . .: *Complete Course for Beginners* (see 9.044)
• *Say It in:* (see 9.046)
• *Spoken.* . . . (see 9.047)
• *Berlitz.* . . . *for Travelers* (phrasebook, see 9.043)
Fulbright Grants for study in Portugal normally available (see 7.041)

Qatar

Organizations

18.425
Embassy of Qatar
Office of the Cultural Attaché
600 New Hampshire Ave. NW, Suite 1180
Washington, DC 20037
(202) 338-0111
or

Ministry of Information
Box 1836
Doha-Qatar
Arabian Gulf

• Provides printed materials on Qatar including general information and a large road map

Publications

18.426
The Creation of Qatar
Rosemarie Said Zahlan
Barnes & Noble Books
81 Adams Drive
Totowa, NJ 07512
1979; hardbound; 155 pages; $24.50

• Review of the history and formation of the contemporary state of Qatar

The following are standard resources available on Qatar
INFORMATION SOURCES
• *Background Notes:* (see 2.188)
TRAVELER RESOURCES
• *Update:* (see 2.197)
LANGUAGE LEARNING RESOURCES
For the "International" Languages (Arabic, French, German and Spanish) see listings under Chapter IX *Foreign Language Teaching and Learning*

Romania

Publications

18.427
Romania: A Developing Socialist State
Lawrence S. Graham
Westview Press, Inc.
5500 Central Ave.
Boulder, CO 80301
1981; hardbound; 140 pages; $18

• Concise introduction both for the stu-

dent and the general reader to contemporary Romania; examines the history, geography, politics, international relations, economic development, culture and social aspects of the country; also gives particular attention to Romanian nationalism and contemporary political and socioeconomic development

18.428
The following are standard resources available on Romania
INFORMATION SOURCES
- *Background Notes:* (see 2.188)
- *Country Study/Area Handbook. . . .* (see 2.189)
TRAVELER RESOURCES
- *Culturegram:* (see 2.191)

- *Nagel's Encyclopedia Guide to. . . .* (see 2.195)
LANGUAGE LEARNING RESOURCES
- *. . . .: Complete Course for Beginners* (see 9.044)
- *Spoken. . . .* (see 9.047)
Fulbright Grants for study in Romania normally available along with a number of Romanian government grants (see 7.041)

Rwanda

The following are standard resources available on Rwanda
INFORMATION SOURCES
- *Background Notes:* (see 2.188)
- *Country Study/Area Handbook. . . .* (see 2.189)

Samoa, Western

Organizations

18.430
Embassy of Western Samoa
℅ Permanent Mission of Samoa to the UN
820 2nd Ave., Suite 800
New York, NY 10017
(212) 599-6196

- Answers telephone and written in-

quiries about Western Samoa, including travel/tourist and educational matters
- Welcomes inquiries from travel/tourist agencies and organizations and individuals
- Provides printed information about travel to and in Western Samoa

Publications

18.431
Islands of Samoa: Reference Map of Tutuila, Manu'a, 'Upolu, and Savai'i
James A. Bier
University of Hawaii Press
2840 Kolowalu St.
Honolulu, HI 96822
1980; $2.95

• Comprehensive reference and travel map of both American and Western Samoa

18.432
Samoa: Yesterday, Today and Tomorrow
Napaleone A. Tuiteleleapaga
Todd & Honeywell, Inc.
10 Cuttermill Road
Great Neck, NY 11021
1980; paperbound; 160 pages; $9.95

• Overview of the nature of Samoan society, its history and current status

18.433
The Samoans: A Selected Bibliography
Ramsay Leung Hay Shu
Pacific/Asian American Mental Health
 Research Center
1001 West Van Buren St.
Chicago, IL 60607
1981; pamphlet; 33 pages; $2

• Unannotated bibliography containing approximately 280 citations on the Samoan people, including published literature, theses and dissertations, government publications, etc.

The following are standard resources available on Western Samoa
INFORMATION SOURCES
 • *Background Notes:* (see 2.188)
TRAVELER RESOURCES
 • *Communication Learning Aids:* (see 2.190)
 • *Culturegram:* (see 2.191)

Saudi Arabia

Publications

18.434
The American in Saudi Arabia
Eve Lee
Intercultural Press, Inc.
Box 768
Yarmouth, ME 04096
1980; paperbound; 117 pages; $8.50

• Guide for people going to live or work in Saudi Arabia; concentrates on differences in behavior and social structure between Saudi

and American societies; includes series of descriptive incidents helpful to individuals or in cross-cultural training programs

18.435
The Kingdom of Saudi Arabia
Norman Anderson and George Rentz
Merrimack Book Service
99 Main St.
Salem, NH 03079
1983; hardbound; 256 pages; $60

- Up-to-date review of Saudi Arabia past and present

The following are standard resources available on Saudi Arabia

INFORMATION SOURCES
- *Background Notes:* (see 2.188)
- *Country Study/Area Handbook. . . .* (see 2.189)
- *World Bibliographical Series. . . .* (see 2.198)

TRAVELER RESOURCES
- *Culturegram:* (see 2.191)
- *Update:* (see 2.197)

LANGUAGE LEARNING RESOURCES

For the "International" Languages (Arabic, French, German and Spanish) see listings under Chapter IX *Foreign Language Teaching and Learning*

Senegal

Publications

18.436
Senegal
Sheldon Gellar
Westview Press, Inc.
5500 Central Ave.
Boulder, CO 80301
1982; hardbound; 128 pages; $16.50

- Concise introduction both for the student and the general reader to contemporary Senegal; examines the history, geography, politics, international relations, economic development, culture and social aspects of the country; also explores the forces that have shaped modern Senegal and the efforts of the government to establish political democracy and pursue economic and social development

The following are standard resources available on Senegal

INFORMATION SOURCES
- *Background Notes:* (see 2.188)
- *Country Study/Area Handbook. . . .* (see 2.189)
- *Historical Dictionary of. . . .* (see 2.193)

LANGUAGE LEARNING RESOURCES

For the "International" Languages (Arabic, French, German and Spanish) see listings under Chapter IX *Foreign Language Teaching and Learning*

Fulbright Grants for study in Senegal normally available (see 7.041)

Seychelles

Publications

18.437
The Seychelles: Unquiet Islands
Marcas Franda
Westview Press, Inc.
5500 Central Ave.
Boulder, CO 80301
1982; hardbound; 128 pages; $18

• Concise introduction both for the student and the general reader to Seychelles; examines the history, geography, politics, international relations, economic develop-ment, culture and social aspects of the country; also focuses on environment, social and racial relations, economic development and internal and external politics to explain the change and turbulence in the recent history of Seychelles

The following are standard resources available on Seychelles
INFORMATION SOURCES
• *Background Notes:* (see 2.188)

Sierra Leone

Publications

18.438
A Bibliography of Sierra Leone 1925–1967
Geoffrey J. Williams, Editor
Holmes & Meier Publishers, Inc.
IUB Bldg.
30 Irving Place
New York, NY 10003
1971; hardbound; 216 pages; $25

• Comprehensive coverage of books and important papers; includes over 3,100 entries

18.439
Liberia & Sierra Leone
C. Claphan
Cambridge University Press
32 East 57th St.
New York, NY 10022
1976; hardbound; 160 pages; $24.95

• Reviews the history and contemporary affairs of Liberia and Sierra Leone

The following are standard resources available on Sierra Leone
INFORMATION SOURCES
• *Background Notes:* (see 2.188)
• *Country Study/Area Handbook.* . . . (see 2.189)
• *Historical Dictionary of.* . . . (see 2.193)
Fulbright Grants for study in Sierra Leone normally available (see 7.041)

Singapore

The following are standard resources available on Singapore

INFORMATION SOURCES
- *Background Notes:* (see 2.188)
- *Country Study/Area Handbook. . . .* (see 2.189)

TRAVELER RESOURCES
- *Culturegram:* (see 2.191)
- *Update:* (see 2.197)

LANGUAGE LEARNING RESOURCES
- *Berlitz. . . . for Travelers* (cassette-pak, see 9.042) "Chinese"
- *. . . .: Complete Course for Beginners* (see 9.044) "Mandarin Chinese"
- *Spoken. . . .* (see 9.047) "Mandarin Chinese"
- *Vest Pocket. . . .* (see 9.048) "Chinese"
- *Berlitz. . . . for Travelers* (phrase-book, see 9.043) "Chinese"

Somalia

The following are standard resources available on Somalia

INFORMATION SOURCES
- *Background Notes:* (see 2.188)
- *Country Study/Area Handbook. . . .* (see 2.189)
- *Historical Dictionary of. . . .* (see 2.198)

South Africa

Organizations

18.440
Embassy of South Africa
Information Office
3051 Massachusetts Ave. NW
Washington, DC 20008
(202) 232-4400
CONSULATES GENERAL: Beverly Hills, Chicago, Houston, New York

- Answers telephone and written inquiries about South Africa, including educational matters
- Provides or recommends speakers, exhibits, films and audiovisual materials and educational or teaching materials
- Welcomes inquiries from all interested individuals and institutions

• Provides printed information about South Africa in general as well as information on travel and education, including the booklet *This is South Africa* (see 18.443) and an extensive series of 8-page "Backgrounders" covering virtually every aspect of the society, economy and culture

• Recommends these other sources of information: Consulates General, South Africa Tourist Corporation and South African Airways

Publications

18.441
South Africa/Namibia Update
African-American Institute
833 UN Plaza
New York, NY 10017
published 15 times per year; newsletter; 4
    pages; free

• Provides detailed information on political and economic events in South Africa and Namibia with particular attention to areas such as trade union activity and black politics that the daily press does not cover in depth

18.442
South Africa: Official Yearbook of the Republic of South Africa
Chris Van Reusburg Publications
Box 25272
2048 Ferreerasdrop
Johannesburg, South Africa
annual; hardbound; 1011 pages; inquire for
    price

• Very extensive coverage of current political, economic, social and foreign affairs in South Africa, compiled by the Department of Foreign Affairs and Information

18.443
This Is South Africa
Information Office
Government of South Africa
Private Bag X152
Pretoria, South Africa
1980; paperbound; 116 pages; free

• Pocket-sized guide to general aspects of South African society; covers government, economy, trade, agriculture, education, culture, tourism and other subjects

The following are standard resources available on South Africa
INFORMATION SOURCES
    • *Background Notes:* (see 2.188)
    • *Country Study/Area Handbook.* . . .
        (see 2.189)
    • *Historical Dictionary of.* . . . (see
        2.193)
World Bibliographical Series. . . . (see 2.198)
TRAVELER RESOURCES
    • *Culturegram:* (see 2.191)

Spain

Organizations

18.444
Council for International Exchange of Scholars
Postdoctoral Research Grants in Spain
11 Dupont Circle NW
Washington, DC 20036
(202) 833-4967

- Offers fellowships for research in the social sciences, humanities, law and education, for scholars with a demonstrated professional interest in Spanish studies

18.445
Hispanic Institute
Columbia University
612 West 116th St.
New York, NY 10027
(212) 280-4940

Contact(s):
Susana Redondo de Feldman, Director

- Sponsors cultural activities related to the culture and civilization of the Spanish- and Portuguese-speaking countries; promotes research, maintains an archive of materials on literature and culture and publishes *Revists Hispánica Moderna*

18.446
Information Department, Embassy of Spain
785 National Press Bldg.
1346 F St. NW
Washington, DC 20004
(202) 347-6777
CONSULATE GENERAL: Washington, DC

- Answers telephone and written inquiries about Spain in general including travel/tourist and educational matters
- Provides films (list available)
- Welcomes inquiries from all sources
- Provides printed information about Spain in general
- Recommends these other sources of information: the Consulate General and the Spanish National Tourist Office, 665 Fifth Ave., New York, NY 10022

18.447
Tinker Foundation, Inc.
645 Madison Ave.
New York, NY 10022
(212) 421-6858

Charitable foundation
- Provides fellowship covering travel and stipend to scholars in the fields of Iberian or Latin American studies to pursue research in the social sciences, marine sciences or international relations

18.448
University of Nevada Press
Reno, NV 89557
(702) 784-6573

Small university publishing house
- Publishes a series of titles on the Basques, covering such areas as the culture, daily life, nationalist activities and Basques in the U.S.

Publications

18.449
Hispania
Donald W. Bleznick, Editor
American Association of Teachers of Spanish
　　and Portuguese, Inc.
Holy Cross College
Worcester, MA 01610
5 issues per year; journal; approx. 150
　　pages; $15 per year; free to members

• Combines scholarly essays with practical articles and reports on the teaching of Spanish and Portuguese and gives news of the profession

18.450
Passport to Spain
León Narváez
EMC Publishing
300 York Ave.
St. Paul, MN 55101
1978; 5 filmstrips, 5 open reel tapes or
　　cassettes, and Teacher's Guide with
　　Student activities on blackline originals;
　　$128

• Multimedia program in English and Spanish designed as a beginning language-learning mini-course for students and travelers who are going to Spain

The following are standard resources available on Spain
INFORMATION SOURCES
　　• *Background Notes:* (see 2.188)
　　• *Country Study/Area Handbook.* . . .
　　　　(see 2.189)
TRAVELER RESOURCES
　　• *Bartholomew Map of.* . . . (see 1.109)
　　• *Communication Learning Aids:* (see
　　　　2.190)
　　• *Culturegram:* (see 2.191)
　　• *Fodor's Guide to.* . . . (see 2.192)
　　• *Nagel's Encyclopedia Guide to.* . . .
　　　　(see 2.195)
LANGUAGE LEARNING RESOURCES
For the "International" Languages (Arabic, French, German and Spanish) see listings under Chapter IX *Foreign Language Teaching and Learning*
Fulbright Grants and ITT Fellowships for graduate study in Spain normally available along with a number of Spanish government grants (see 7.041)

Sri Lanka

Organizations

18.451
**Embassy of the Democratic Socialist
Republic of Sri Lanka**
2148 Wyoming Ave. NW
Washington, DC 20008
(202) 483-4025

• Answers telephone and written inquiries about Sri Lanka, including travel/tourist and educational matters
• Recommends speakers, performers, exhibits and audiovisual materials
• Welcomes inquiries from educational

institutions, museums, and cultural organizations

• Provides printed information about education and on Sri Lanka in general, including a substantive fact sheet

• Recommends this other source of information: Sri Lanka Tourist Board, 609 Fifth Ave., Suite 308, New York, NY 10017

Publications

18.452
Modern Sri Lanka: A Society in Transition
Tissa Fernando & Robert N. Kearney
Syracuse University
Foreign & Comparative Studies Program
119 College Place
Syracuse, NY 13210
1979; paperbound; 297 pages; $9

• Analysis of contemporary Sri Lankan society and the economic, political and social forces that are bringing about rapid change

The following are standard resources available on Sri Lanka
INFORMATION SOURCES
• *Background Notes:* (see 2.188)
• *Country Study/Area Handbook. . . .* (see 2.189)
• *World Bibliographical Series. . . .* (see 2.198)
TRAVELER RESOURCES
• *Culturegram:* (see 2.191)
• *Nagel's Encyclopedia Guide to. . . .* (see 2.195)
• *. . . . .: A Travel Survival Kit* (see 2.196)
• *Spoken. . . .* (see 9.047) "Sinhalele"

Sudan

Organizations

18.454
Embassy of Sudan
Information Office
2210 Massachusetts Ave. NW
Washington, DC 20008
(202) 338-8565

• Answers telephone and written inquiries about Sudan including travel/tourist and educational matters

• Provides or recommends speakers, exhibits and educational or teaching materials

• Welcomes inquiries from any interested individual or institution

• Provides printed information about travel, education and Sudan in general, including *Sudan: The Country and Its Market*

Publications

18.455
The History of the Sudan From the
Coming of Islam to the Present Day
P. M. Holt and M. W. Daly
Westview Press, Inc.
5500 Central Ave.
Boulder, CO 80301
1980; hardbound; 296 pages; $32.50

   • Substantive overview of Sudanese history with emphasis on those elements that have shaped the modern Sudanese nation

18.456
Sudanow
Mohamed Osman Abu Sag, Editor in Chief
Ministry of Culture and Information
P.O. Box 2651
7 Sharia Gamhouria
Khartoum, Sudan
monthly magazine; 66 pages; £23 surface
   mail, £31 airmail

   • Commentary in newsweekly format on current social, political and economic affairs in Sudan; covers business, education and tourism

The following are standard resources available on Sudan
INFORMATION SOURCES
   • *Background Notes:* (see 2.188)
   • *Country Study/Area Handbook.* . . . (see 2.189)
   • *Historical Dictionary of.* . . . (see 2.193)

Suriname

Publications

18.457
A Short History of the Netherlands
Antilles and Suriname
Cornelius C. Goslinga
Martinus Nijhoff
Netherlands
1978; paperbound; 215 pages; $20

Available from Kluwer Boston, Inc., 190 Old Derby Street, Hingham, MA 02043

   • Review of history, society and culture of the Netherlands Antilles and Surinam

The following are standard resources available on Suriname
INFORMATION SOURCES
   • *Background Notes:* (see 2.188)
   • *Image of.* . . . (see 2.189)
LANGUAGE LEARNING RESOURCES
(See Netherlands)

Swaziland

The following are standard resources available on Swaziland
INFORMATION SOURCES
- *Background Notes:* (see 2.188)
- *Historical Dictionary of.* . . . (see 2.193)
- *World Bibliographical Series.* . . . (see 2.198)

Sweden

Organizations

18.458
The American Swedish Historical Foundation and Museum
1900 Pattison Ave.
Philadelphia, PA 19145
(215) 389-1776

Contact(s):
Lynn C. Malmgren, Director

Historical museum
- Maintains collection related to historical and cultural aspects of Sweden and of the Swedes in America; mounts temporary exhibits supporting contemporary cultural exchange with all Nordic nations

18.459
Embassy of Sweden
600 New Hampshire Ave. NW, Suite 1200
Washington, DC 20037
(202) 298-3500
CONSULATES GENERAL: Chicago, Los Angeles, Minneapolis, New York

- Answers telephone and written inquiries about Sweden, including educational matters
- Welcomes inquiries from any interested individual or institution
- Provides printed information about education in Sweden and on Sweden in general
- Recommends these other sources of information: Swedish Information Service (see 18.460) and Swedish National Tourist Office, 75 Rockefeller Plaza, New York, NY 10019

18.460
Swedish Information Service
825 Third Ave.
New York, NY 10022
(212) 751-5900
Office of the Swedish Ministry for Foreign Affairs
- Maintains extensive library of books, periodicals, reference works and other materials on Sweden for use by researchers, the

media and educators; includes a selection of 16mm films

    • Conducts seminars for Swedish and American professionals on current issues and arranges cultural events

    • Provides resources for teaching and research about Sweden in U.S. colleges and universities, brings guest lecturers from Sweden and administers a modest program of grants and scholarships; includes assistance in making contacts and identifying resources in Sweden and limited funds for opinion-makers to visit Sweden

18.461
Texas Swedish Cultural Foundation, Inc.
2234 Inwood Drive
Houston, TX 77019
(713) 522-7154

Contact(s):
Gudrun Merrill

Swedish government organization
    • Provides $2,500 scholarship to Texas resident to use in covering any costs in pursuing graduate study in Sweden; application deadline April 15

Publications

18.462
Documentation of Sweden
Documentation Section
The Swedish Institute
Box 7434
S-103 91 Stockholm, Sweden
1979; booklet; 35 pages; free

Available from the Embassy of Sweden, Suite 1200, 600 New Hampshire Ave. NW, Washington, DC 20037
    • A list of fact sheets, pamphlets, booklets and other informally published materials in English on Sweden and Swedish conditions, covering such areas as libraries, culture and communication, education, the arts, social sciences and the law, technology, industry and transportation, economics and finance, and natural science and medicine; published materials are produced by the Swedish government, universities, and trade, cultural and research organizations in Sweden; addresses for sources provided

18.463
Swedes as Others See Them
Jean Phillips-Martinsson
Studentlitteratur, Box 1719
2210 Lund, Sweden
1981; paperbound; 123 pages; $15

Available from Intercultural Press, Inc., Box 768, Yarmouth, ME 04096
    • A guide to the predominant cultural characteristics of Swedes as they are perceived by foreigners; written for Swedes but valuable to anyone going to Sweden or wishing to understand the Swedes better

The following are standard resources available on Sweden
INFORMATION SOURCES
    • *Background Notes:* (see 2.188)
TRAVELER RESOURCES
    • *Culturegram:* (see 2.191)
    • *Nagel's Encyclopedia-Guide to. . . .* (see 2.195)
LANGUAGE LEARNING RESOURCES
    • *Berlitz. . . . for Travelers* (cassette-pak, see 9.042)
    • *. . . .: Complete Course for Beginners* (see 9.044)
    • *Say It in:* (see 9.046)
    • *Spoken. . . .* (see 9.047)
    • *Berlitz. . . . for Travelers* (phrase-book, see 9.043)
Fulbright Grants and ITT Fellowships for graduate study in Sweden normally available (see 7.041)

Switzerland

Organizations

18.464
Embassy of Switzerland
2900 Cathedral Ave. NW
Washington, DC 20008-3499
(202) 745-7900
CONSULATES GENERAL: Chicago, Los
Angeles, New Orleans, New York, San
Francisco

• Answers telephone and written inquiries about Switzerland including travel/tourist and educational matters
• Recommends speakers, performers, exhibits and audiovisual materials
• Welcomes inquiries from any interested individual or institution
• Provides printed information about education and travel in Switzerland and on Switzerland in general
• Recommends these other sources of information: Swiss National Tourist Office, The Swiss Center, 608 Fifth Ave., New York, NY 10020

18.465
Swiss-American Historical Society
University of Illinois at Urbana-Champaign
German Department
3072 Foreign Languages Bldg.
707 South Mathews
Urbana, IL 61801
(217) 367-2674

Contact(s):
Marianne Burkhard, President

Educational organization designed to expand knowledge of Switzerland, Swiss Americans and Swiss-U.S. relations; includes members in Canada, the U.S. and Switzerland.
• Holds annual meeting and publishes newsletter and reprints of scholarly papers and books

Publications

The following are standard resources available on Switzerland
INFORMATION SOURCES
• *Background Notes:* (see 2.188)
TRAVELER RESOURCES
• *Culturegram:* (see 2.191)
• *Fodor's Guide to. . . .* (see 2.192)
LANGUAGE LEARNING RESOURCES
For the "International" Languages (Arabic, French, German and Spanish) see listings under Chapter IX *Foreign Language Teaching and Learning*
ITT Fellowships for graduate study in Switzerland normally available, along with a number of Swiss university and Swiss government grants (see 7.041)

Syria

Organizations

18.466
Embassy of the Syrian Arab Republic
2215 Wyoming Ave. NW
Washington, DC 20008
(202) 232-6313

• Provides printed information on Syrian life and culture

Publications

18.467
Syria Today
Jean Hureau
J. A. Editions
France
1979; hardbound; 256 pages; $14.95

Available from Hippocrene Books, Inc., 171 Madison Ave., New York, NY 10016
• Travel guide to, description of and a report on contemporary Syria; illustrated

The following are standard resources available on Syria

INFORMATION SOURCES
• *Background Notes:* (see 2.188)
• *Country Study/Area Handbook.* . . . (see 2.189)
TRAVELER RESOURCES
• *Bartholomew Map of.* . . . (see 1.109)
LANGUAGE LEARNING RESOURCES
For the "International" Languages (Arabic, French, German and Spanish) see listings under Chapter IX *Foreign Language Teaching and Learning*
Fulbright Grants for study in Syria normally available along with a number of Syrian government grants (see 7.041)

Taiwan

Organizations

18.468
Coordination Council for North American Affairs (CCNAA)
Cultural Division
4301 Connecticut Ave. NW, Suite 131
Washington, DC 20008
(202) 686-1638

Contact(s):
Bertrand S. Y. Mao, Director

Office of the Republic of China (Taiwan)
• Offers Ministry of Education scholarship for study in Taiwan

18.469
Inter-University Center for Chinese Studies in Taipei
Stanford University
Center for Research in International Studies
Room 200, Lou Henry Hoover Bldg.
Stanford, CA 94305
(415) 497-4581

Contact(s):
Lyman P. Van Slyke, Executive Secretary
James Dew, Field Director (Taipei)

Cooperative program of eleven major academic institutions in the U.S. and Canada administered by Stanford
• Provides intensive year-long, audio-lingual instruction in Chinese for graduate and undergraduate students with emphasis on preparing the student to conduct research in the language

18.470
National Science Foundation
United States-Taiwan Cooperative Science
    Program
Division of International Programs
Washington, DC 20550
(202) 357-9537

Contact(s):
Gordon Hiebert, Program Manager

• Funds programs involving cooperative research, seminars and workshops and short-term visits between the U.S. and Taiwan

Publications

18.471
Contemporary Republic of Taiwan
Praeger Publishers
521 Fifth Ave.
New York, NY 10017
1981; hardbound; 540 pages; $33.95

• Analysis of contemporary Taiwan society and the forces that are shaping it

18.472
Echo Publishing Co.
Linda Wu, Editor
5-2 Pa Teh Road
Section 4, Lane 72, Alley 16
Taipei, Taiwan

• Books on social and cultural aspects of life in Taiwan with an emphasis on the traditional in Chinese society

The following are standard resources available on Taiwan
INFORMATION SOURCES
• *Background Notes:* (see 2.188)
• *Country Study/Area Handbook. . .*
    (see 2.189)
TRAVELER RESOURCES
• *Culturegram:* (see 2.191)
• *Update: (see 2.197)*
• *. . . .: A Travel Survival Kit* (see 2.196)
LANGUAGE LEARNING RESOURCES
• *. . . .: Complete Course for Beginners*
    (see 9.044) "Taiwanese"
• *Spoken. . . .* (see 9.047) "Amoy Hokkien," "Taiwanese"
ITT Fellowships for graduate study in Taiwan normally available (see 7.041)

Tanzania

Publications

18.473
The Long Transition: Building Socialism in Tanzania
Idrian Resnik
Monthly Review Press
62 W. 14th St.
New York, NY 10011
1982; hardbound; 416 pages; $18.50

• Analysis of Tanzanian society and its social, economic and political policies

18.474
Tanzania: An African Experiment
Rodger Yeager
Westview Press, Inc.
5500 Central Ave.
Boulder, CO 80301
1982; 136 pages; hardbound, $22.50; paperbound, $10.95

• Concise introduction both for the student and the general reader to contemporary Tanzania; examines the history, geography, politics, international relations, economic development, culture and social aspects of the country; also explores the reasons why there is such passionate disagreement over whether Tanzanian social and economic development has been a great success or a massive failure

The following are standard resources available on Tanzania
INFORMATION SOURCES
• *Background Notes:* (see 2.188)
• *Country Study/Area Handbook.* . . . (see 2.189)
• *Historical Dictionary of.* . . . (see 2.193)
LANGUAGE LEARNING RESOURCES
"Swahili"
• *Berlitz.* . . . *for Travelers* (phrasebook, see 9.043)
• . . . .: *Complete Course for Beginners* (see 9.044)
• *Say It in:* (see 9.046)
• *Spoken.* . . . (see 9.047)
Fulbright Grants for study in Tanzania normally available (see 7.041)

Thailand

Organizations

18.475
Embassy of Thailand
2300 Kalorama Road NW
Washington, DC 20008
(202) 667-1446

• Answers inquiries and provides information about Thailand to educators and educational organizations, tourists, mass media and general public

Publications

18.476
A.U.A. Language Center Thai Course
J. Marvin Brown
A.U.A. Language Center
179 Rajadamri Road
Bangkok 5, Thailand

Institutions requiring a set of master cassettes should order directly from the publisher. Cassette tapes for individual student use can be ordered from The Language Laboratory, Department of Modern Languages, Morrill Hall, Cornell University, Ithaca, NY 14853; cassettes are sold in sets only
     • Complete course in the Thai language suitable for self-instruction; includes printed materials: *Books* 1, 2 and 3 ($4.50 each); supplementary tapes and drills for these books, $2; *Small Talk* (Dialogue Book A, $5); *Getting Help* (Dialogue Book B, $5); *Thai Reading* ($5); *Thai Writing* ($5)
     • Cassette tapes of the printed materials are sold in sets only: 8 cassettes each for *Books* 1, 2 and 3 ($43.20 per set); 3 cassettes for *Small Talk* (Dialogue Book A, $16.20 per set); 4 cassettes for *Getting Help* (Dialogue Book B, $2.60 per set)

18.477
Interact: Thailand/U.S.
John Paul Fieg
Intercultural Press, Inc.
Box 768
Yarmouth, ME 04096
paperbound; 1981; 60 pages; $10

     • Analyzes how Americans and Thais do things differently and how these differences affect working relationships between them; covers such subjects as communication styles, family relationships, sex roles, and attitudes toward work, achievement, authority, decision-making, negotiations, cooperation and competition

18.478
Thai-English Student's Dictionary
Mary R. Haas
Stanford University Press
Stanford, CA 94305
1964; hardbound; 638 pages; $20

     • Useful dictionary for learning to read Thai

18.479
Thailand: An Annotated Bibliography of Bibliographies
Donn V. Hart
Center for Southeast Asian Studies
Northern Illinois University
De Kalb, IL 60115
1974; 159 pages; paperbound; $7.50

Available from The Cellar Book Shop, 18090 Wyoming St., Detroit, MI 48221
     • Thorough, indexed guide to bibliographies on Thailand

18.480
Thailand: Society and Politics
John L. S. Girling
Cornell University Press
124 Roberts Place
Ithaca, NY 14850
1981; hardbound; 320 pages; $24.50

     • Analysis of contemporary social and political conditions in Thailand

The following are standard resources available on Thailand

INFORMATION SOURCES
     • *Background Notes:* (see 2.188)
     • *Country Study/Area Handbook.* . . . (see 2.189)
     • TRAVELER RESOURCES
     • *Communication Learning Aids:* (see 2.190)

- *Culturegram:* (see 2.191)
- *Nagel's Encyclopedia Guide to. . . .* (see 2.195)

- . . . . .: *A Travel Survival Kit* (see 2.196)

LANGUAGE LEARNING RESOURCES
- *Spoken. . . .* (see 9.047)

Togo

18.481
The following are standard resources available on Togo
INFORMATION SOURCES
- *Background Notes:* (see 2.188)
- *Historical Dictionary of. . . .* (see 2.193)

LANGUAGE LEARNING RESOURCES
For the "International" Languages (Arabic, French, German and Spanish) see listings under Chapter IX *Foreign Language Teaching and Learning*
Fulbright Grants for study in Togo normally available (see 7.041)

Tonga

Organizations

18.482
The Tonga Visitors Bureau
P.O. Box 37
Nuku' alofa
Kingdom of Tonga

- Provides tourist brochures and information on Tongan crafts and culture

Publications

18.483
Intensive Course in Tongan

Eric B. Shumway
University of Hawaii Press
2849 Kolowalu St.
Honolulu, HI 96822
1971; paperbound; 671 pages; $15

- A thorough language-learning text and linguistic guide
The following are standard resources available on Tonga
INFORMATION SOURCES
- *Background Notes:* (see 2.188)
TRAVELER RESOURCES
- *Culturegram:* (see 2.191)

Trinidad and Tobago

Publications

18.484
Tobago
David L. Niddrie
Methuen, Inc.
733 Third Ave.
New York, NY 10017
1981; paperbound; $8.50

• Insightful discussion of Tobagoan society and its people

The following are standard resources available on Trinidad and Tobago
INFORMATION SOURCES
• *Background Notes:* (see 2.188)
• *Country Study/Area Handbook.* . . . (see 2.189)
• *Image of.* . . . (see 2.194)

Tunisia

Organizations

18.485
Embassy of Tunisia
2408 Massachusetts Ave. NW
Washington, DC 20008
(202) 234-6644
CONSULATE GENERAL: San Francisco

• Answers telephone and written inquiries about Tunisia regarding educational matters

• Recommends films and audiovisual materials
• Welcomes inquiries from any interested individual or institution
• Provides printed information about Tunisia in general
• Recommends these other sources of information: Consulate General

Publications

18.486
Tunisia Today
Jean Hureau
J. A. Editions
France
1979; 256 pages; $14.95

Available from Hippocrene Books, Inc., 171 Madison Ave., New York, NY 10016
• Travel guide to, description of and a report on contemporary Tunisia; illustrated
The following are standard resources available on Tunisia

INFORMATION SOURCES
- *Background Notes:* (see 2.188)
- *Country Study/Area Handbook.* . . . (see 2.189)

TRAVELER RESOURCES
- *Kummerly & Frey Map of.* . . . (see 1.127)

LANGUAGE LEARNING RESOURCES
For the "International" Languages (Arabic, French, German and Spanish) see listings under Chapter IX *Foreign Language Teaching and Learning*

Turkey

Organizations

18.487
American Research Institute in Turkey
% The University Museum
33d and Spruce St.
Philadelphia, PA 19104
(215) 898-4781

Contact(s):
Cecil L. Striker, President

Research institute sponsored by a consortium of colleges and universities in the U.S. and Canada; maintains research offices in Istanbul and Ankara, Turkey
- Sponsors and supports research and study in Turkey on historical and contemporary aspects of Turkish society and culture; offers fellowships for travel and maintenance for scholars and advanced graduate students
- Offers Summer Fellowships for Intensive Advanced Turkish language study, open to U.S. citizens or permanent residents with a minimum of 2 years college level study of the Turkish language
- Publishes selected reports and studies prepared by the Institute Fellows along with a newsletter

18.488
The American Turkish Society, Inc.
850 3rd Ave.
New York, NY 10022
(212) 319-2452

Contact(s):
Executive Secretary

Nonprofit association of persons concerned with commercial and cultural relations between the U.S. and Turkey
- Provides information, answers inquiries, and sponsors lectures and symposia on aspects of Turkish history, culture, the arts and contemporary Turkish and American-Turkish community affairs
- Publishes newsletter reporting on Turkish and American-Turkish community affairs

18.489
Embassy of the Republic of Turkey
Office of the Press Counselor
2010 Massachusetts Ave. NW
Washington, DC 20036
(202) 462-8411
CONSULATES GENERAL: Chicago, Los Angeles, New York

- Answers written inquiries about Turkey, including travel/tourist and educational matters
- Provides or recommends exhibits and audiovisual materials
- Welcomes inquiries from any interested individual or institution
- Provides printed information about

travel in Turkey and on Turkey in general, including a variety of attractively produced general information brochures and pamphlets, information on major cities and a large road map

• Recommends this other source of information: Turkish Tourist Office, 821 UN Plaza, New York, NY 10017

18.490
Institute of Turkish Studies
2010 Massachusetts Ave. NW
Washington, DC 20036
(202) 296-4502

Contact(s):
Heath W. Lowry, Director

• Promotes the growth of Turkish Studies at U.S. colleges and universities particularly through the awarding of grants for pub-

lications, library acquisitions, faculty positions, scholarships, conferences and lectures, and other similar educational activities

18.491
Turkish American Association
1472 Broadway
New York, NY 10036
(212) 354-0737

Contact(s):
Inci Fenik, Secretary

Educational organization concerned with relations between Turkey and Turkish Americans

• Provides information, organizes festivals, arranges lectures, sponsors tours to Turkey and produces radio and TV programs

Publications

18.492
Bulletin of the Turkish Studies Association
Gustav Bayerle, Editor
Department of Uralic and Altaic Studies
Indiana University
Bloomington, IN 47405
biannual newsletter; approx. 48 pages; free with $10 membership fee ($25 to institutions)

• Reports on research and activities among scholars in Turkish Studies (the Turkish Studies Association meets with the Middle East Studies Association and has no central office)

The following are standard resources available on Turkey
INFORMATION SOURCES
• *Background Notes:* (see 2.188)

• *Country Study/Area Handbook.* . . . (see 2.189)
• *World Bibliographical Series.* . . . (see 2.198)
TRAVELER RESOURCES
• *Kummerly & Frey Map of.* . . . (see 1.127)
• *Fodor's Guide to.* . . . (see 2.192)
• *Nagel's Encyclopedia Guide to.* . . . (see 2.195)
• . . . .: *A Travel Survival Kit* (see 2.196)
LANGUAGE LEARNING RESOURCES
• . . . .: *Complete Course for Beginners* (see 9.044)
• *Say It in:* (see 9.046)
Fulbright Grants for study in Turkey normally available along with a number of Turkish government grants (see 7.041)

Uganda

Organizations

18.493
Embassy of the Republic of Uganda
5909 16th St. NW
Washington, DC 20011
(202) 726-7100

• Answers telephone and written inquiries about Uganda, including travel/tour-
ist and educational matters
• Provides speakers and audiovisual materials
• Welcomes inquiries from any interested individual or organization

• Provides printed information about
travel in Uganda and about Uganda in general
• Recommends this other source of information: Permanent Mission of the Republic of Uganda to the UN

The following are standard resources avail-
able on Uganda
INFORMATION SOURCES
• *Background Notes:* (see 2.188)
• *Country Study/Area Handbook.* . . .
(see 2.189)
• *World Bibliographical Series.* . . . (see
2.198)

Union of Soviet Socialist Republics

Area Study and Research Programs

18.494
Soviet Studies
Occidental College
Los Angeles, CA 90041
(213) 259-2731

Contact(s):
Lawrence Caldwell, Chair

Undergraduate area studies program established in 1968
• Majors/degrees/certificates offered:
B.A. and major in Diplomacy and World Affairs or Political Science with Soviet Studies
emphasis
• Approximate number of faculty teaching area and language courses: 2

• Approximate number of courses available—area: 6; language: 4
• Average number of students per year
specializing in area: 5–6
• Language offered: Russian
• Study opportunities in the USSR
available

18.495
Russian/USSR Area Studies
American University
Department of Language and Foreign
Studies
Washington, DC 20016
(202) 686-2280

Contact(s):
Anthony Caprio, Chair

Undergraduate area studies program
• Majors/degrees/certificates offered: B.A. in Russian/USSR Area Studies
• Approximate number of faculty teaching area and language courses: 7
• Approximate number of courses available—area: 9; language: 9
• Average number of students per year specializing in area: 7
• Combines study in the School for International Service with Russian language and literature
• Language offered: Russian
• Requires internship or comparable experience

18.496
Russian Area Studies Program
566 Intercultural Center
Georgetown University
Washington, DC 20057
(202) 625-4676

Contact(s):
Gerald Mara, Director

Graduate area studies program
• Majors/degrees/certificates offered: M. A. in Russian Studies
• Approximate number of courses available—area: 60; language: 20
• Countries covered and areas of emphasis: USSR with some courses related to the Soviet bloc countries
• Language offered: Russian literature and linguistics
• Special library collection at Georgetown; wide range of library resources available in Washington area; also contacts with government and nongovernment individuals and organizations that specialize in Russian and East European affairs

18.497
Soviet Studies
The Johns Hopkins University
School of Advanced International Studies
1740 Massachusetts Ave. NW
Washington, DC 20036
(202) 785-6200

Graduate area studies program
• Majors/degrees/certificates offered: M.A. and Ph.D. in International Relations with major in Soviet Studies
• Areas of emphasis: Contemporary economic and political issues (may include special comparative political studies in the Advanced Industrial Societies Program)
• Draws on library, organizational and research resources of the Washington area
• Special internships and fellowships available

18.498
Russian Area Studies
Eckerd College
St. Petersburg, FL 33733
(813) 867-1166

Contact(s):
William H. Parsons, Director

Undergraduate area studies program established in 1969
• Majors/degrees/certificates offered: B.A. in Russian Studies
• Approximate number of faculty teaching area and language courses: 3
• Approximate number of courses available—area: 6; language: 6
• Average number of students per year specializing in area: 10
• Language offered: Russian
• Occasionally organizes a winter term study tour to the USSR

18.499
Russian Studies
Stetson University
DeLand, FL 32720
(904) 734-4121

Contact(s):
Paul D. Steeves, Director

Undergraduate area studies program established in 1962
- Majors/degrees/certificates offered: B. A. in Russian Studies
- Approximate number of faculty teaching area and language courses: 5
- Approximate number of courses available—area: 14; language: 2
- Average number of students per year specializing in area: 2
- Language offered: Russian
- Arranges study-travel programs in the Soviet Union

18.500
Soviet Studies
University of Miami
Center for Advanced International Studies
Coral Gables, FL 33124
(305) 284-4303

Contact(s):
Carl G. Jacobsen, Director

- Offers M.A. in Soviet Studies and D.A. (Doctor of Arts) and Ph.D. in International Affairs with specialization in Soviet Studies

18.501
Russian Area Studies
University of Hawaii at Manoa
Department of European Languages and
   Literature
Moore Hall 470
Honolulu, HI 96822
(808) 948-8975

Undergraduate area studies program
- Majors/degrees/certificates offered: Certificate in Russian Area Studies
- Approximate number of faculty teaching area and language courses: 16
- Approximate number of courses available—area: 12; language: 11
- Average number of students per year specializing in area: 10
- Language offered: Russian

18.502
Russian Studies
Illinois State University
Department of Foreign Languages
Stevenson 412
Normal, IL 61761
(309) 438-3604

Contact(s):
Jean M. Alexander, Chair

Undergraduate area studies program established in 1976
- Majors/degrees/certificates offered: B.A. in Russian Studies (also available as a double major)
- Approximate number of faculty teaching area and language courses: 5
- Approximate number of courses available—area: 16; language: 6
- Average number of students per year specializing in area: 15
- Areas of emphasis: history and politics
- Language offered: Russian
- Study tour to the Soviet Union arranged every other year

18.503
Research Institute for Inner Asian Studies
Indiana University at Bloomington
Goodbody Hall 101
Bloomington, IN 47405
(812) 335-1605

Contact(s):
Stephen Halkovic, Jr., Director

• Research center focusing on the countries of inner Asia including the Turkic-speaking republics of the USSR

18.504
Russian Area Studies Program
University of Kentucky
Lexington, KY 40506
(606) 257-3761

Contact(s):
Gerald Janecek, Director

• Offers B.A. in Russian Area Studies oriented toward the social sciences and Russian language and literature

18.505
Russian Area Studies Program
Louisiana State University
Baton Rouge, LA 70803
(504) 388-4471

Contact(s):
Thomas C. Owen, Director

Undergraduate area studies program established in 1969
• Majors/degrees/certificates offered: B.A. in Russian Area Studies
• Approximate number of faculty teaching area and language courses: 7
• Approximate number of courses available—area: 15; language: 19
• Average number of students per year specializing in area: 3–6
• Countries covered and areas of emphasis: Soviet Union and Eastern Europe
• Language offered: Russian

18.506
Program of Soviet Studies
University of Maine at Presque Isle
Presque Isle, ME 04769
(207) 764-0311

Contact(s):
David W. Folts, Director

Undergraduate area studies program established in 1972
• Majors/degrees/certificates offered: B.A. with Certificate in Soviet Studies
• Approximate number of faculty teaching area and language courses: 4
• Approximate number of courses available—area: 12; language 6
• Average number of students per year specializing in area: 4–7
• Language offered: Russian
• Sponsors summer study trips to the Soviet Union

18.507
Russian Area Studies Program
University of Maryland
College Park, MD 20742
(301) 454-2843

Contact(s):
John R. Lampe, Director

Undergraduate area studies program
• Majors/degrees/certificates offered: B.A. in Russian Studies
• Language offered: Russian

18.508
Regional Studies Program: Soviet Union
Harvard University
1737 Cambridge St.
Cambridge, MA 02138
(617) 495-4037

Contact(s):

Adam B. Ulam, Gurney Professor of
   History and Political Science
Christine Balm, Administrative Coordinator
Lubomyr Hajda, Academic Coordinator

Graduate area studies program established in
1948
   • Majors/degrees/certificates   offered:
M.A. in Regional Studies: Soviet Union
   • Approximate number of faculty teaching area and language courses: 30 (excluding
language)
   • Approximate number of courses available—area: 40; language: 17 (in Slavic lan-
guages)
   • Average number of students per year
specializing in area: 20
   • Countries covered and areas of emphasis: Soviet Union, including individual
Soviet republics/nationalities, Eastern Europe and China; particular emphasis on Soviet nationality problems; stresses independent, guided study and research
   • Languages offered: Russian, Polish,
Ukrainian, etc.
   • Harvard University library has the
largest collection of Slavic materials in the
U.S.
   • Courses at MIT and Tufts available
through cross-registration (figures above do
not include MIT and Tufts offerings)
   • Affiliated with Russian Research Center (see 18.509) and Soviet and East European Language and Area Center (see 14.020)

18.509
Russian Research Center
Harvard University
1737 Cambridge St.
Cambridge, MA 02138
(617) 495-4037

Contact(s):
Adam B. Ulam, Director

Major research center with a staff of 9 and 75
affiliated scholars
   • Promotes (and offers postdoctoral fellowships for) research at Harvard in Soviet
and East European studies; provides facilities
at Harvard for scholars, researchers, advanced graduate students, lawyers, diplomats, journalists and others from the U.S.
and abroad
Sponsors Russian Research Center series
published by the Harvard University Press
(see 11.012), publishes the historical journal
Kritika and *RRC Newsletter* covering financial and economic issues
   • Administers the Harvard Soviet Union
Program which offers an M.A. in Regional
Studies (see 18.508)
   • Conducts the Corporate Sponsor Program, an annual series of conferences on U.S.-
USSR relations for scholars and U.S. government officials

18.510
Russian Area Studies
Associated Colleges of the Twin Cities
214 Aquinas Hall
2115 Summit Ave.
St. Paul, MN 55105

Contact(s):
Norma Noonan, Augsburg (612-330-1198)
C. R. Moyer, Hamline (612-641-6570)
P. Weisensel, Macalester, (612-647-6570)
J. Cunningham, St. Catherine (612-690-
   6545)
C. W. Chrislock, St. Thomas (612-647-5668)

Undergraduate area studies program con-
ducted jointly by five colleges (Augsburg,
Hamline, Macalester, St. Catherine and St.
Thomas)
   • Majors/degrees/certificates   offered:
B.A. in Russian Area Studies
   • Approximate number of courses avail-
able—area: 27; language: 5
   • Areas of emphasis: history, literature
and the social sciences

18.511
Russian Studies
St. Olaf College
Northfield, MN 55057
(507) 663-2222
and
Carleton College
Northfield, MN 55057
(507) 663-4000

Contact(s):
Robert Nichols, Director (St. Olaf College)
Joe Shephard, Director (Carleton College)

Undergraduate area studies program established in 1972
• Majors/degrees/certificates offered: B.A. in Russian Studies
• Approximate number of faculty teaching area & language courses: 10
• Approximate number of courses available—area: 13; language: 6
• Average number of students per year specializing in area: 7–8 (both colleges combined)
• Sponsors in alternate years a one-month interim program in the USSR

18.512
Russian Area Studies
University of Missouri at Columbia
451 General Classroom Bldg.
Columbia, MO 65211
(314) 882-3368

Contact(s):
James M. Curtis, Director

Undergraduate area studies program established in 1958
• Majors/degrees/certificates offered: B.A. with interdisciplinary area specialization in Russian and Soviet Studies
• Approximate number of courses available—area: 20; language: 9

• Average number of students per year specializing in area: 12
• Language offered: Russian

18.513
Russian Area Studies
Dartmouth College
Hanover, NH 03755
(603) 646-1110

Contact(s):
Barry P. Scherr, Chair

Undergraduate area studies program established in 1967
• Majors/degrees/certificates offered: B.A. in Russian Area Studies
• Approximate number of faculty teaching area and language courses: 13
• Approximate number of courses available—area: 15; language: 14
• Average number of students per year specializing in area: 15
• Language offered: Russian
• Library contains ample collection of Russian materials for undergraduate study
• Sponsors summer eight-week foreign study program at the University of Leningrad with visits to other Soviet cities

18.514
Russian Area Studies
Drew University
College of Liberal Arts
Madison, NJ 07940
(201) 377-3000

Contact(s):
Lois E. Beekey, Director

Undergraduate area studies program established in 1975
• Majors/degrees/certificates offered: B.A. in Russian Area Studies
• Approximate number of faculty teaching area & language courses: 5

• Approximate number of courses available—area: 15; language: 11
• Average number of students per year specializing in area: 3–4
• Credit given for study in the Soviet Union in Moscow and Leningrad programs sponsored by other institutions

18.515
Program in Russian Studies
Princeton University
Department of History
Princeton, NJ 08544
(609) 452-3063

Contact(s):
Richard Wortman, Director

• Coordinates Master's Program in Russian Studies and interdisciplinary concentrations in Russian Studies for (1) students working on doctorates in economics, history, politics, sociology and comparative literature and (2) undergraduates in the same departments plus Slavic Languages and Literatures and (3) for M.P.A. candidates in the Woodrow Wilson School; (see 16.149); designed to assure mastery of the language and a broad grounding in Russian and Soviet society

18.516
Russian Area Studies Program
Seton Hall University
South Orange, NJ 07079
(201) 761-5088

Contact(s):
William L. Mathes, Director

Undergraduate area studies program established in 1968
• Majors/degrees/certificates offered: B.A. in Russian Area Studies and Certificate in Russian Area Studies

18.517
Russian Area Studies Graduate Program
City University of New York/Hunter College
Box 522
695 Park Ave.
New York, NY 10021
(212) 772-5502 or 5499 (messages: 772-5500)

Contact(s):
Gregory J. Massell, Director

Graduate area studies program
• Majors/degrees/certificates offered: M.A. in Russian Area Studies; M.A. in conjunction with advanced professional study in Teacher Education
• Approximate number of faculty teaching area and language courses: 16
• Approximate number of courses available—area: 25; language: 15
• Average number of students per year specializing in area: 25
• Countries covered and areas of emphasis: contemporary Soviet affairs; some focus on the Soviet bloc countries
• Languages offered: Russian, Polish and Ukrainian
• Library contains approximately 30,000 volumes on Russia in Russian and other languages; resources of Slavonic Division of the New York Public Library also available

18.518
Center for the Study of Central Asia
Columbia University
1205 International Affairs Bldg.
420 West 118th St.
New York, NY 10027
(212) 280-2556

Contact(s):
Edward Allworth, Director

• Promotes research and teaching and serves as information resource center on Central Asia covering Afghanistan, Soviet

Central Asia (including Kazakhstan) and Xinjiang (Chungking) Autonomous Province of the PRC

18.519
Program on Soviet Nationality Problems
Columbia University
1205 International Affairs Bldg.
420 West 118th St.
New York, NY 10027
(212) 280-2556

Contact(s):
Edward Allworth, Director

• Offers seminars and conducts research on Soviet nationality issues which may be recognized as a concentration in the Graduate School of International and Public Affairs (see 6.151), the Harriman Institute, the Middle East Institute (see 17.029) or any of several University social science and humanities departments; particular focus on the Asian areas of the USSR as well as the Baltic region, Trans-Caucasus and Slavic areas of the Soviet West; maintains a special collection of recent publications in the local languages of Soviet Central Asia, Trans-Caucasus, Tatarstan and the Ukraine; promotes research on and produces studies of Soviet nationality problems

18.520
Russian Institute
Columbia University
1214 International Affairs Bldg.
420 West 118th St.
New York, NY 10027
(212) 280-4623

Contact(s):
Marshall Shulman, Director

Graduate area studies program
• Majors/degrees/certificates offered: two-year M.I.A., School of International and Public Affairs (see 6.151), with Certificate in Russian Studies; M.A. and Ph.D. with Certificate in Russian Studies
• Approximate number of faculty teaching area and language courses: 50
• Approximate number of courses available—area: 45; language: 29
• Countries covered and areas of emphasis: Russia and contiguous states in Central Asia and Eastern Europe, with emphasis on the social sciences, language and literature
• Languages offered: Russian and Old Church Slavic
• Library contains vast collection of Russian language materials and maintains policy of acquiring all significant books and journals published in the Russian language in the social and political sciences, literature, law, philosophy and several other fields; extensive holdings in history, linguistics and folklore; Oral History Collection includes taped reminisences of Nikita Khrushchev; archival materials from czarist era are held in the Bakhmeteff Archive of Russian and East European History and Culture

18.521
Soviet Studies
Fordham University
Political Science Department
Bronx, NY 10458
(212) 579-2304 or 2297

Contact(s):
Richard M. Mills, Director

Undergraduate area studies program established in 1950
• Majors/degrees/certificates offered: B.A. in Soviet Studies
• Approximate number of faculty teaching area & language courses: 9
• Approximate number of courses available—area: 30; language: 5

• Average number of students per year specializing in area: 10
• Areas of emphasis: Soviet Union with emphasis on contemporary affairs
• Language offered: Russian
• Summer study abroad opportunity in Leningrad

18.522
Russian Studies
Syracuse University
Maxwell School of Citizenship and Public
　Affairs
119 College Place
Syracuse, NY 13210
(315) 423-2552

Contact(s):
John D. Nagel, Director

• Offers B.A. with major in Russian Studies

18.523
Russian Studies
Wells College
Aurora, NY 13026
(315) 364-3011

Contact(s):
Vahan Barooshian, Director

Undergraduate area studies program established in 1965
• Majors/degrees/certificates　offered: B.A. in Russian Studies
• Approximate number of faculty teaching area and language courses: 2
• Approximate number of courses available—area: 10; language: 10
• Average number of students per year specializing in area: 2
• Areas of emphasis: Russian literature and history
• Language offered: Russian at all levels

• Offers a semester or summer program in Moscow each year

18.524
Russian Studies
University of North Carolina at Greensboro
Greensboro, NC 27412
(919) 379-5709

Contact(s):
David MacKenzie, Chair

Undergraduate area studies program
• Majors/degrees/certificates　offered: B.A. in Russian Studies
• Approximate number of faculty teaching area and language courses: 5
• Approximate number of courses available—area: 20; language: 6
• Language offered: Russian

18.525
Soviet Studies
University of Oklahoma at Norman
Department of History
455 West Lindsey, Room 406
Norman, OK 73019

Contact(s):
V. Stanley Vardys, Director

Graduate area studies program
• Majors/degrees/certificates　offered: M.A. in Soviet Studies
• Language offered: Russian

18.526
Russian Area Studies
Juniata College
Department of Russian
Huntingdon, PA 16652
(814) 643-4310

Contact(s):
George T. Dolnikowski, Director

Undergraduate area studies program established in 1973
- Majors/degrees/certificates offered: B.A. in Russian Area Studies
- Approximate number of faculty teaching area and language courses: 2
- Approximate number of courses available—area: 7; language: 5
- Average number of students per year specializing in area: 4–5
- Areas of emphasis: language and literature
- Language offered: Russian
- Summer and semester study programs in the USSR available

18.527
Russian and Soviet Area Studies Program
Dickinson College
Carlisle, PA 17013
(717) 245-1274

Contact(s):
Helen Segall, Director

Undergraduate area studies program established in 1969
- Majors/degrees/certificates offered: B.A. in Russian and Soviet Area Studies
- Approximate number of faculty teaching area and language courses: 11
- Approximate number of courses available—area: 19; language: 10
- Average number of students per year specializing in area: 14
- Areas of emphasis: providing a historical and cultural perspective on current Soviet affairs
- Languages offered: Russian and Polish (on an independent study basis)
- Language study in Russia available

18.528
Russian Studies
Muhlenberg College
Allentown, PA 18104

Contact(s):
Arvids Ziedonis, Jr., Director

Undergraduate area studies program
- Majors/degrees/certificates offered: B.A. in Russian Studies; also may be part of double major
- Approximate number of faculty teaching area and language courses: 7
- Approximate number of courses available—area: 15; language: 6
- Areas of emphasis: language, literature and the social sciences
- Language offered: Russian
- Sponsors summer study tour in the USSR

18.529
Russian Area Studies Program
West Chester State College
Foreign Language Department
West Chester, PA 19380
(215) 436-2585

Contact(s):
Dusan P. Glumac, Coordinator

Undergraduate area studies program established in 1968
- Majors/degrees/certificates offered: B.A. in Russian Area Studies
- Approximate number of faculty teaching area and language courses: 2
- Approximate number of courses available—area: 6; language: 10
- Average number of students per year specializing in area: 10
- Countries covered and areas of emphasis: USSR and Yugoslavia
- Languages offered: Russian, Serbo-Croatian and Old Church Slavic
- Library contains over 10,000 volumes in Russian

18.530
Slavic Language and Area Center
Vanderbilt University
Nashville, TN 37235
(615) 322-2561

Contact(s):
Richard N. Porter, Acting Director

Graduate and undergraduate area studies program
  • Majors/degrees/certificates offered: B.A. in Russian and Area Studies; departmental M.A. and Ph.D. with concentration in Slavic Languages and Area Studies
  • Approximate number of faculty teaching area and language courses: 9
  • Approximate number of courses available—area: 44; language: 22
  • Languages offered: Russian and, on demand, Polish, Serbo-Croatian and Old Church Slavonic

18.531
Russian Studies
University of Houston
432 CO
Houston, TX 77004
(713) 749-4881

Contact(s):
Joseph L. Nogee, Chair

Undergraduate area studies program established in 1975
  • Majors/degrees/certificates offered: B.A. in Russian Studies
  • Approximate number of faculty teaching area and language courses: 6
  • Approximate number of courses available—area: 8; language: 8
  • Average number of students per year specializing in area: 12
  • Language offered: Russian

18.532
Russian Studies
Hollins College
Hollins College, VA 24020
(703) 362-6401

Contact(s):
John Atwell, Chair

Undergraduate area studies program
  • Approximate number of faculty teaching area and language courses: 2
  • Areas of emphasis: Russian history and literature
  • Language offered: Russian
  • Study and travel programs in the Soviet Union available

18.533
Russian Studies
Randolph-Macon Woman's College
Lynchburg, VA 24503
(804) 846-7392

Contact(s):
Margot K. Frank, Chair

Undergraduate area studies program established in 1955
  • Majors/degrees/certificates offered: B.A. in Russian Studies
  • Approximate number of faculty teaching area and language courses: 3
  • Approximate number of courses available—area: 9; language: 9
  • Average number of students per year specializing in area: 3–4
  • Language offered: Russian
  • Offers semester abroad in Leningrad and Moscow

18.534
Russian Area Studies Program
University of Richmond
Richmond, VA 23173
(804) 285-6335

Contact(s):
Joseph C. Troncale, Coordinator

Undergraduate area studies program established in 1970
• Majors/degrees/certificates offered: B.A. in Russian Area Studies
• Approximate number of faculty teaching area & language courses: 6

• Approximate number of courses available—area and language: 18
• Average number of students per year specializing in area: 3–4
• Areas of emphasis: history, literature and culture
• Sponsors spring trip to the Soviet Union

Organizations

18.535
Association for the Advancement of Baltic Studies, Inc.
231 Miller Road
Mahwah, NJ 07430
(202) 529-2887

Contact(s):
Jánis Gaigulis, Executive Director

Association of scholars concerned with the study of the Baltic States: Latvia, Lithuania and Estonia
• Provides information and promotes research on Baltic Studies; conducts meetings and conferences in various countries
• Publishes a quarterly newsletter, the *Journal of Baltic Studies* (see 18.546), and a number of other books and conference reports

18.536
Corinth Films, Inc.
410 East 62nd St.
New York, NY 10021
(212) 421-4770

• Rents and distributes films produced in the Soviet Union; catalogue (*The Soviet Cinema*) available listing films made from 1917 to the present

18.537
Embassy of the Union of Soviet Socialist Republics
Office of Information Counselor
1706 18th St. NW
Washington, DC 20009
(202) 232-0039

• Answers written inquiries about the USSR
• Provides speakers on Soviet foreign and domestic policy and educational or teaching materials
• Welcomes inquiries from educational institutions, libraries/museums, U.S. government agencies, cultural organizations and individuals
• Provides printed information about the USSR, including a series *The Soviet Union Today and Tomorrow* covering a number of the Soviet Republics and many aspects of Soviet life and economy, along with many that promote Soviet ideology; distributes *Soviet Life*, photo journal on Soviet life and culture ($8.35)

18.538
Estonian Learned Society in America
Estonian House
243 East 34th St.
New York, NY 10016
(212) 684-0336

Contact(s):
Tönu Parming, Secretary

Professional academic society designed to advance the study of Estonian and Baltic culture
　• Sponsors and funds research and publications, provides travel grants and facilitates publications exchange among universities and learned societies around the world

18.539
Forum for U.S.-Soviet Dialogue
22 Hemlock Hill
Amherst, NH 03031
(603) 673-8639

Contact(s):
James J. O'Rourke, Chair

Cultural and educational exchange organization
　• Sponsors annual conferences for American and Soviet citizens to exchange ideas with the aim of promoting mutual understanding; delegates are mostly young professionals and others interested in the Soviet Union with preference given to those 21–40 years of age

18.540
Kennan Institute for Advanced Russian Studies
Woodrow Wilson International Center for
　Scholars
Smithsonian Institution Bldg.
Washington, DC 20560
(202) 357-2415

　• Fellowships available to scholars and qualified professionals for research in the humanities and social sciences on Russia/U.S.S.R. while in residence at the Institute

18.541
Lithuanian American Council, Inc.
2606 West 63d St.
Chicago, IL 60629
(312) 778-6900/6901

Contact(s):
Kazys Sidlauskas, President

Association of persons interested in the heritage of Lithuania
　• Provides information on Lithuania and the Baltic states, including the recommendation of lecturers

18.542
Princeton University Press
Princeton, NJ 08540
(609) 452-4900

University publishing house
　• Publishes extensive list of titles on Soviet politics and international relations, history, and literature; includes compilations of information in archives and manuscript repositories in the USSR, specifically in Moscow, Leningrad, Estonia, Latvia and Belorussia, and *Soviet Foreign Relations and World Communism: A Selected Annotated Bibliography of 7,000 Books in 30 Languages* (1965, $60)

18.543
Shevchenko Scientific Society, Inc.
63 Fourth Ave.
New York, NY 10003
(212) 254-5130 or 5239

Ukrainian arts and science academy
　• Offers grants to support the study of the Ukraine in the social science and humanities disciplines; conducts research in Ukrainian history, literature, language, etc.; publishes the serial *Shevchenko Scientific Society Memoirs*

18.544
Ukrainian Research Foundation, Inc.
6931 South Yosemite St.
Englewood, CO 80110
(303) 770-1220

Contact(s):
Bohdan S. Wynar, President

Nonprofit research organization concerned with promoting and facilitating scholarly research on the Ukraine and on the Ukranian heritage in the U.S.
• Maintains library and Reference and Information Center which answers questions and provides information on request to the media, organizations and individuals
• Publishes scholarly works on the Ukraine, including *Documents of Ukrainian History*

Publications

18.545
Baltica in Microform
Association for the Advancement of Baltic
   Studies
231 Miller Rd.
Mahwah, NJ 07430
1981; 36 pages; xerox in binder; $5

Inquiries concerning this guide and requests for interim updates are available from the compiler, Valdis J. Zeps, Department of Linguistics, 1168 Van Hise Hall, University of Wisconsin, Madison, WI 53711
• Guide to Baltic titles available in microfilm or microfiche format; lists 960 titles of publications and over 40 microfilm publishers and/or public repositories

18.546
Journal of Baltic Studies
Toivo U. Raun, Editor
Association for the Advancement of Baltic
   Studies
231 Miller Road
Mahwah, NJ 07430
quarterly journal; $27.50; $12.50 for full-
   time students

• Scholarly articles on literature and history of the Baltic States; includes book reviews and news and notes of the field

18.547
Organizations Involved in Soviet-American Relations
The Forum Institute
1225 15th St. NW
Washington, DC 20005
1983; paperbound; 250 pages; $5

• Directory of approximately 180 organizations which constitute possible resources on the Soviet Union and Soviet-U.S. relations (130 are described in detail, including publications and resources produced)

18.548
Russia
Igor Birman and Valery Chalidze
Chalidze Publications
505 Eighth Ave.
New York, NY 10018
quarterly magazine; 40 pages; $20
   (institutions, $28)

• Articles focusing on everyday life and culture and on political and economic policies in the USSR

18.549
Russian Review
The Russian Review, Inc.
1737 Cambridge St.
Cambridge, MA 02138
quarterly journal; approx. 130 pages;
   individuals, $16 per year; institutions, $22
   per year

   • Contains scholarly articles and essays
on Russia past and present; extensive book
review section

18.550
Scholar's Guide to Washington, D.C.:
Russian/Soviet Studies
Steven A. Grant
Smithsonian Institution Press
Washington, DC 20560
1983; 403 pages; hardbound, $29.95;
   paperbound, $12.50

Comprehensive listing and description of resources in the Washington area available to
researchers and others interested in Russia
and the Soviet Union; divided into two sections: collections (libraries, archives, museums, etc., music and sound, maps, films,
and data banks) and organizations (research
centers and information offices, academic
programs, U.S. government agencies, embassies and international organizations,
professional associations, exchange and technical assistance organizations, religious organizations, and publications/media); available
resources described in some detail with clear
indication how and from whom to obtain access; appendices include libraries listed by
size of holdings, bookstores, housing, transport and other services and a bibliography;
indexed by name of resource, personal papers collections and library subject strength

18.551
Sovietica
D. Reidel Publishing Co.
160 Old Derby St.
Hingham, MA 02043
published since 1947; hardbound; over 40
   volumes; each 200–300 pages; price range
   $20–50

Publications and monographs of the Institute
of East European Studies at the University of
Fribourg, Switzerland, the Center for East
Europe, Russia and Asia at Boston College,
and the Seminar for Political Theory and Philosophy at the University of Munich, Germany
   • Series of books on the origins, development, influence and philosophical significance of Marxism-Leninism; covers related
philosophies and theories, neo-Marxism and
contemporary applications; includes subjects
such as Soviet philosophy, Marxism and religion, Communist ideology, Marxist ethical
theory, Russian and American comparative
philosophy, etc.

18.552
Studies in Soviet Thought
Thomas J. Blakeley, Guido Kung, and
   Nikolaus Lobkowicz, Editors
Center for East Europe, Russia and Asia
Boston College
quarterly journal; approx. 120 pages; $22.50
   per year

Available from D. Reidel Publishing Co., 160
Old Derby St., Hingham, MA 02043
   • Research papers, reports, commentary, critical reviews and essays on Soviet
philosophy; emphasis on contemporary Soviet thought with some coverage of pre-
Revolutionary developments; includes bibliography of recent Soviet philosophical publications taken from the major Russian philo-
sophic journals

The following company imports and sells books in the Ukrainian language:

18.553
Arka Co.
48 East 7th St.
New York, NY 10003
(212) 473-3550

The following companies import and sell books in the Latvian language:

18.554
Robert Krukliti's Latvian Bookstore
P.O. Box 1594
East Lansing, MI 48823
(517) 332-1206

18.555
Latvian Bookshop
27 Miller Place
Hempstead, NY 11550
(516) 483-1739

The following companies import and sell books in the Lithuanian language:

18.556
Draugas, Lithuanian Daily Friend
4545 West 63d St.
Chicago, IL 60629
(312) 585-9500

18.557
Spauda Bookstore
33 Congress Ave.
Waterbury, CT 06708
(203) 756-5173

The following companies import and sell books in the Russian language:

18.558
Four Continent Book Corp.
149 Fifth Ave.
New York, NY 10010
(212) 533-0250

18.559
Victor Kamkin Bookstore
2320 Westwood Blvd.
Los Angeles, CA 90064
(213) 474-4034

18.560
Schoenhof's Foreign Books, Inc.
1280 Massachusetts Ave.
Cambridge, MA 02138
(617) 547-8855

The following are standard resources available on the USSR

INFORMATION SOURCES
- *Background Notes:* (see 2.188)
- *Country Study/Area Handbook. . . .* (see 2.189)
- *World Bibliographical Series. . . .* (see 2.198)

TRAVELER RESOURCES
- *Culturegram:* (see 2.191)
- *Fodor's Guide to. . . .* (see 2.192)
- *Nagel's Encyclopedia Guide to. . . .* (see 2.195)

LANGUAGE LEARNING RESOURCES
- *Berlitz. . . . for Travelers* (cassette-pak, see 9.042)
- *. . . .: Complete Course for Beginners* (see 9.044)
- *Spoken. . . .* (see 9.047)
- *Vest Pocket. . . .* (see 9.048)
- *Berlitz. . . . for Travelers* (phrase-book, see 9.043)

United Arab Emirates

Organizations

18.561
Embassy of the United Arab Emirates
Cultural Division
1010 Wisconsin Ave. NW, Suite 505
Washington, DC 20007
(202) 342-1111

• Answers telephone and written inquiries about the United Arab Emirates including travel/tourist and educational matters
• Welcomes inquiries from any interested individual or institution
• Provides printed information about
education in the United Arab Emirates and
on the United Arab Emirates in general

Publications

18.562
The United Arab Emirates: Unity in Fragmentation
Ali Mohammed Khalifa
Westview Press, Inc.
5500 Central Ave.
Boulder, CO 80301
1979; hardbound; 235 pages; $30

• Discusses the background of the formation of the United Arab Emirates and as-
sesses the results

The following are standard resources avail-
able on the United Arab Emirates
INFORMATION SOURCES
• *Background Notes:* (see 2.188)
TRAVELER RESOURCES
• *Update:* (see 2.197)
LANGUAGE LEARNING RESOURCES
For the "International" Languages (Arabic,
French, German and Spanish) see listings
under Chapter IX *Foreign Language
Teaching and Learning*

United Kingdom

Area Study and Research Programs

18.563
British Studies Program
Yale University
Yale Center for British Art
1080 Chapel St., Rooms 3–4
New Haven, CT 06520
(203) 432-4594

Contact(s):
Alan Liu, Director
• Offers B.A. in British Studies involving broad interdisciplinary offerings with an
emphasis on intellectual and art history; study
also available at the Paul Mellon Center for
Studies in British Art in London

18.564
Institute of Scottish Studies
Old Dominion University
Norfolk, VA 23508-9510
(804) 440-3179

Contact(s):
Charles Haws, Director

• Promotes the study of Scotland through community seminars, genealogical research, study programs in Scotland, courses on Scotland, the study of Gaelic and the publication of *Scotia: American/Canadian Journal of Scottish Studies*

Organizations

18.565
British Embassy
3100 Massachusetts Ave. NW
Washington, DC 20008
(202) 462-1340
CONSULATES GENERAL: Atlanta, Boston, Chicago, Cleveland, Houston, Los Angeles, New York, San Francisco, Washington, DC

• All general information inquiries are forwarded to the British Information Service and to the British Tourist Authority, 680 Fifth Ave., New York, NY 10019
Accepts inquiries about Marshall Aid Commemoration Scholarships (see 18.567)

18.566
British Information Service
845 Third Ave.
New York, NY 10022
(212) 752-8400

Contact(s):
Elizabeth Zackheim, Reference Section

• Answers telephone and written inquiries about the United Kingdom, including travel/tourist and educational matters
• Welcomes inquiries from any interested individual or institution
• Provides printed information about education and travel in the United Kingdom and about the United Kingdom in general,

including a series of substantive pamphlets on major aspects of British social, political and economic life along with general cultural information and a brochure *Study in Britain*
• Recommends these other sources of information: British Tourist Authority, 680 Fifth Ave., New York, NY 10019

18.567
Marshall Aid Commemoration Scholarships
British Embassy
3100 Massachusetts Ave. NW
Washington, DC 20008
(202) 462-1340
or
British Information Services
845 3rd Ave.
New York, NY 10022
CONSULATES GENERAL: Atlanta, Boston, Chicago, San Francisco

• Offers up to 30 substantial scholarships per year to U.S. citizens under 26 years of age who have undergraduate degrees from U.S. institutions to study for a degree at a British university for a period of at least two years; application should be made to the British Embassy, to Consulates General, or to the British Information Services

18.568
The North American Conference on British Studies
George Washington University
Department of History
Washington, DC 20052

Contact(s):
Lois G. Schwoerer, Executive Secretary

Association of individuals interested in British Studies, particularly history, literature, art and politics
   • Promotes the study of British civilization through conferences, prizes for articles, books and monographs, and publications, including the semiannual *Journal of British Studies* (see 18.575), *Albion* (see 18.573), and the *British Studies Intelligencer*

18.569
St. Andrew's Society of the State of New York
281 Park Ave. South
New York, NY 10010
(212) 473-6912

Contact(s):
Fergus McLarty, Executive Secretary

   • Offers several scholarships to Americans of Scottish descent for one year of graduate study at any Scottish university; must be residents of Pennsylvania, New York, New Jersey or New England and recommended by an institution of higher learning (one per institution); application deadline January 30

18.570
Society of Inter-Celtic Arts and Culture
96 Marguerite Ave.
Waltham, MA 02154
(617) 899-2204

Contact(s):
Kevin Dixon Gilligan, Executive Director

Educational organization concerned with the cultures of the Celtic societies of Ireland, Scotland, Wales, Cornwall, the Isle of Man and Brittany
   • Provides information and answers inquiries on Celtic civilization and culture, fosters cultural exchange and cooperative endeavors among Celtic groups worldwide and sponsors cultural activities
   • Publishes *Keltica*, a 100-page annual journal covering all aspects of Celtic culture, history and current affairs

18.571
The Rhodes Scholarships
Office of the American Secretary
The Rhodes Scholarship Trust
Pomona College
Claremont, CA 91711
(714) 621-8138

Contact(s):
David Alexander, American Secretary

   • Offers 32 substantial two-year scholarships to Americans of outstanding academic achievement to study at Oxford University after completing B.A. in the U.S.; renewable for a third year; age 18–24

18.572
Winston Churchill Foundation of the United States
P.O. Box 1240, Gracie Station
New York, NY 10028
(212) 879-3480

Contact(s):
Harold Epstein, Executive Director

   • Offers, under the Churchill Foundation Scholarships Program, approximately 10 substantial scholarships for one to three years of study at Cambridge University to U.S. cit-

izens with a bachelor's degree from one of 35 participating institutions; age 19–26

Publications

18.573
Albion
Michael J. Moore, Editor
Appalachian State University
Department of History
Boone, NC 28608
quarterly journal; approx. 150 pages; $30 per year for institutions, $10 for individuals

Albion is affiliated with the North American Conference on British Studies, Department of History, S.U.N.Y. Amherst Campus, Buffalo, NY 14261; available free to members (fee, $20 per year)
   • Scholarly articles primarily on British historical subjects; includes large number of book reviews

18.574
Current British Directories
I. G. Anderson, Editor
CBD Research, Ltd.
154 High St.
Beckenham
Kent, BR 3 1EA, England
1979; hardbound; 384 pages; $105

   • Lists approximately 2,900 directories published in or relating to Great Britain and Ireland, including a selection published in or relating to the Commonwealth and to South Africa, Pakistan and Bangladesh; includes yearbooks, almanacs and gazetteers; general industrial and commercial directories; telephone, telex and telegraphic directories; research, library and bibliographic directories, and regional, specialized and technical directories; provides publisher and bibliographic

data, description of content, languages used, frequency, date published, price and size
   • Arranged by region and towns in Britain and Ireland and by Britain, Ireland and the Commonwealth countries as a whole; includes subject index

18.575
The Journal of British Studies
Bentley Brinkerhoff Gilbert, Editor
The Conference on British Studies
University of Illinois at Chicago Circle
Department of History
Box 4348
Chicago, IL 60680
semiannual journal; 124 pages; $12 per year

   • Scholarly articles primarily on British historical subjects

18.576
Nor'wester
The Northwester Co., Ltd.
P.O. Box 243
Grand Cayman
Cayman Islands, British West Indies
monthly; magazine; 80 pages; $30 per year

   • News magazine covering general current affairs in the Cayman Islands

18.577
Whitaker's Almanack
J. Whitaker & Sons, Ltd.
12 Dyott St.
London, England
WC1 A1DF
annual; hardbound; 1,220 pages; $46

Distributed by Gale Research Co., Book Tower, Detroit, MI 48226

- Worldwide almanac of current events and information; particularly extensive in its coverage of Great Britain

The following are standard resources available on the United Kingdom
INFORMATION SOURCES
- *Background Notes:* (see 2.188)

TRAVELER RESOURCES
- *Culturegram:* (see 2.191)
- *Update:* (see 2.197)
- *Fodor's Guide to. . . .* (see 2.192)

Fulbright Grants and ITT Fellowships for graduate study in the United Kingdom normally available along with a Lusk Memorial Fellowship in the creative and performing arts (see 7.041)

Upper Volta

The following are standard resources available on Upper Volta
18.578
INFORMATION SOURCES
- *Background Notes:* (see 2.188)

- *Historical Dictionary of. . . .* (see 2.193)

Fulbright Grants for study in Upper Volta normally available (see 7.041)

Uruguay

The following are standard resources available on Uruguay
INFORMATION SOURCES
- *Background Notes:* (see 2.188)
- *Country Study/Area Handbook. . . .* (see 2.189)
- *Historical Dictionary of. . . .* (see 2.193)

TRAVELER RESOURCES
- *Culturegram:* (see 2.191)

LANGUAGE LEARNING RESOURCES
For the "International" Languages (Arabic, French, German and Spanish) see listings under Chapter IX *Foreign Language Teaching and Learning*
Fulbright Grants for study in Uruguay normally available (see 7.041)

Venezuela

Organizations

18.579
Embassy of Venezuela
Information and Culture Service
2437 California St. NW
Washington, DC 20008
(202) 797-3856
CONSULATES GENERAL: Baltimore, Boston, Chicago, Houston, Los Angeles, Miami, New Orleans, New York, Philadelphia, San Francisco, San Juan, P.R.

- Answers telephone and written inquiries about Venezuela regarding educational matters

- Recommends speakers, performers, exhibits, films/audiovisuals, and educational or teaching materials
- Welcomes inquiries from any interested individual or institution
- Provides printed information about Venezuela in general and about education in Venezuela
- Recommends these other sources of information: Consulates General and the Venezuelan Government Office, 450 Park Ave., New York, NY 10022

Publications

18.580
Traveling in Venezuela
John Wilcox
Hippocrene Books, Inc.
171 Madison Ave.
New York, NY 10016
1979; paperbound; 115 pages; $12

- Useful guide to Venezuela for the visitor

18.581
Venezuela: The Search for Order, The Dream of Progress
John V. Lombardi
Oxford University Press, Inc.
200 Madison Ave.
New York, NY 10016
1982; 368 pages; hardbound, $25; paperbound, $7.95

- Insightful analysis of contemporary Venezuelan society

18.582
Venezuelan History: A Comprehensive Working Bibliography
John V. Lombardi, German Carrera Damas and Roberta E. Adams
G. K. Hall & Co.
70 Lincoln St.
Boston, MA 02111
1977; hardbound; 530 pages; $25

- Covers politics and political history, economics, social history, intellectual and artistic history, and natural history; approximately 4,000 entries

The following are standard resources available on Venezuela

INFORMATION SOURCES

- *Background Notes:* (see 2.188)
- *Country Study/Area Handbook. . . .* (see 2.189)
- *Historical Dictionary of. . . .* (see 2.193)
- *Image of. . . .* (see 2.194)

TRAVELER RESOURCES
- *Culturegram:* (see 2.191)
- *Update:* (see 2.197)

LANGUAGE LEARNING RESOURCES
For the "International" Languages (Arabic, French, German and Spanish) see listings under Chapter IX *Foreign Language Teaching and Learning*

Vietnam

Publications

18.583
Vietnam: A Guide to Reference Sources
Michael Cotter
G. K. Hall & Co.
70 Lincoln St.
Boston, MA 02111
1978; hardbound; 604 pages; $54

- Provides reference sources in the humanities, sciences, and social sciences from the 17th century through 1976 including many publications in French and romanized Vietnamese

18.584
Vietnam: A Nation in Revolution
William J. Duiker
Westview Press, Inc.
5500 Central Ave.
Boulder, CO 80301
1983; 171 pages; hardbound, $18.50; paperbound, $10.95

- Concise introduction both for the student and the general reader to contemporary Vietnam; examines the history, geography, politics, international relations, economic development, culture and social aspects of the country; also explores how a generation of conflict has affected Vietnam and produced the problems with which the communist regime is currently wrestling

The following are standard resources available on Vietnam
INFORMATION SOURCES
- *Background Notes:* (see 2.188)
- *Country Study/Area Handbook. . . .* (see 2.189)

LANGUAGE LEARNING RESOURCES
- *Spoken. . . .* (see 9.047)

Yemen, North (Yemen Arab Republic)

Area Study and Research Programs

18.585
American Institute for Yemeni Studies
Northern Illinois University
DeKalb, IL 60115
(815) 753-1901, Ext. 265

Contact(s):
Manfred Wenner, President
Lealan Swanson, Resident Director (in
Sana'a, Yemen)

Consortium of academic institutions to promote research in and on Yemen
- Maintains library and research facilities in Sana'a (capital of the Yemen Arab Republic), as well as a residence for visiting scholars; promotes, assists, and supervises research projects in various disciplines for individual and institutional members; provides support and assistance for members in obtaining necessary permits and government support for research
- Aids in the placement of Yemeni students and scholars in U.S. institutions
- Offers a $6,000 fellowship each year to either an American or a Yemeni graduate student undertaking research on some aspect of Yemen
- Publishes newsletter on scholarly activities and contemporary affairs related to Yemen and the practical Yemen Guide Series including *Introduction to Yemen for Researchers, Scholars and Visitors* ($4) and *Libraries and Scholarly Resources in the Yemen Arab Republic* ($5)

Publications

18.586
Yemen: The Search for a Modern State
J. E. Peterson
The Johns Hopkins University Press
Baltimore, MD 21218
1982; 224 pages; hardbound; $22.50

- Studies political and social change and development in contemporary North Yemen, focusing on the conflict between tradition and modernization

The following are standard resources available on North Yemen
INFORMATION SOURCES
- *Background Notes:* (see 2.188)
- *Country Study/Area Handbook....* (see 2.189)
LANGUAGE LEARNING RESOURCES
For the "International" Languages (Arabic, French, German and Spanish) see listings under Chapter IX *Foreign Language Teaching and Learning*

Yemen, South (People's Democratic Republic of Yemen)

Publications

18.587
South Yemen: A Marxist Republic in Arabia
Robert W. Stookey
Westview Press, Inc.
5500 Central Ave.
Boulder, CO 80301
1982; hardbound; 128 pages; $17.50

• Concise introduction both for the student and the general reader to contemporary South Yemen; examines the history, geography, politics, international relations, economic development, culture and social aspects of the country; also discusses the forces that caused the dramatic growth of South Ye-

men, brought about the undermining of traditional life, and led to a doctrinaire Marxist regime

The following are standard resources available on South Yemen
INFORMATION SOURCES
• *Background Notes:* (see 2.188)
• *Country Study/Area Handbook.* . . . (see 2.189)
LANGUAGE LEARNING RESOURCES
For the "International" Languages (Arabic, French, German and Spanish) see listings under Chapter IX *Foreign Language Teaching and Learning*

Yugoslavia

Area Study and Research Programs

18.588
Center for Yugoslav-American Studies, Research, and Exchanges
Florida State University
930 West Park Ave.
Tallahassee, FL 32306
(904) 644-5465

Contact(s):
George Macesich, Director

Graduate and undergraduate area studies program established in 1961

• Majors/degrees/certificates offered: B.A. in Slavic and East European Studies; graduate Certificate in Comparative Policy (Yugoslav-American) Studies
• Approximate number of faculty teaching area and language courses: 10–12
• Approximate number of courses available—area: 16
• Average number of students per year specializing in area: 25
• Special library holdings in Serbo-Croatian

• Seminar in Yugoslavia during summer term

• Stress is placed on faculty and student exchanges with several universities in Yugoslavia, focusing on the comparative study of economic policy issues based on research in Yugoslavia and the U.S.

• Publishes summaries of research seminars

• Limited number of stipends available to qualified American and Yugoslav students

Organizations

18.589
The Croatian Academy of America
P.O. Box 1767
Grand Central Station
New York, NY 10017

Contact(s):
Maria K. Tuskan, Executive Secretary

Association of scholars and others concerned with expanding knowledge in America of Croatian history, literature and culture
• Sponsors conferences and publishes *Journal of Croatian Studies* (see 18.596)

18.590
Embassy of Yugoslavia
2410 California St. NW
Washington, DC 20008
(202) 462-6566
CONSULATES GENERAL: Chicago, Cleveland, Pittsburgh, New York, San Francisco, Washington, DC

• All requests for information are referred to the Yugoslav Press & Cultural Center (see 18.592) or to the Yugoslav National Tourist Office, 630 Fifth Ave., New York, NY 10020

18.591
Society for Slovene Studies
Columbia University
1232 International Affairs Bldg.
New York, NY 10027
(212) 280-4002

Contact(s):
Rado L. Lencek, President

Professional association of scholars interested in Slovene Studies
• Organizes conferences and meetings and publishes a newsletter and *Slovene Studies: Journal of the Society for Slovene Studies*

18.592
Yugoslav Press & Cultural Center
767 Third Ave., 18th Floor
New York, NY 10017
(212) 838-2306

• Answers telephone and written inquiries about Yugoslavia
• Provides or recommends speakers, exhibits, films and audiovisual materials and educational or teaching materials
• Welcomes inquiries from any interested individual and institution
• Provides printed information about Yugoslavia and education in Yugoslavia
• Recommends this other source of information: Yugoslav National Tourist Office, 630 Fifth Ave., New York, NY 10020

Publications

18.593
Facts About Yugoslavia
Nebojša Tomašević, Editor in Chief
Federal Secretariat for Information
Belgrade, Yugoslavia
1979; paperbound; 108 pages; free

Available from Yugoslav Embassy Information
Office, 2410 California St. NW, Washington,
DC 20008
    • Provides brief background informa-
tion on history, people, culture and economy
of Yugoslavia, with separate sections for each
of the provinces (Socialist Republics)

18.594
**A Guide & Bibliography to Research on
Yugoslavia in the United States and
Canada**
Adam S. Eterovich
Ragusan Press
2527 San Carlos Ave.
San Carlos, CA 94070
1978; paperbound; 200 pages; $10

    • Useful research and study tool

18.595
**A Guide to Yugoslav Libraries and
Archives**
Paul L. Horecky, Chief Editor
Joint Committee on Eastern Europe
   Publication Series
American Association for the Advancement
   of Slavic Studies
Stanford University, History Dept.
Stanford, CA 94305
1975; paperbound; 108 pages

    • Provides data on major archival and
library collections in Yugoslavia; gives address, director, hours and describes collections; lists publications of the library and books
and articles about it; lists approximately 75
libraries and archives broken down by region

18.596
Journal of Croatian Studies
Jerome Jareb and Karlo Mirth, Managing
   Editors
Croatian Academy of America
P.O. Box 1767
Grand Central Station
New York, NY 10017
annual; paperbound; 150–200 pages; $12

    • Articles and essays on Croatian his-
tory, literature, fine arts and music, sociology
and economics plus translations from Croatian literature (poetry, short stories) and book
reviews

18.597
**New English-Croatian and Croatian-
English Dictionary**
F. A. Bogadek
Macmillan Publishing Co.
866 Third Ave.
New York, NY 10022
1982; paperbound; 1,121 pages; $25.95

    • Useful bilingual dictionary for reading
or speaking Croatian

18.598
Review of International Affairs
Velimir Popavić, Editor
Jugoslovenska Stuarnost
Nemanjina 34
Beograd, Yugoslavia
bimonthly journal; approx. 30 pages; $18
   per year

• Contains articles on international political and economic issues, particularly as they affect Yugoslavia

18.599
Twentieth-Century Yugoslavia
Fred Singleton
Columbia University Press
136 South Broadway
Irvington, NY 10533
1976; 346 pages; hardbound, $24;
   paperbound, $11

• Comprehensive survey of Yugoslavia; gives particularly thorough coverage to economic, political and social developments since World War II

18.600
Yugoslavia Today
George Orr
J. A. Editions
France
1979; hardbound; 264 pages; $14.95

Available from Hippocrene Books, Inc., 171 Madison Ave., New York, NY 10016
• Travel guide, a description of and a report on contemporary Yugoslavia; illustrated

18.601
The Yugoslavs
Dusko Doder
Random House, Inc.
201 East 50th St.,
New York, NY 10022
1978; hardbound; 175 pages; $10
• Reviews the history of the Yugoslav people and Yugoslav society and culture

The following are standard resources available on Yugoslavia
INFORMATION SOURCES
• *Background Notes:* (see 2.188)
• *Country Study/Area Handbook.* . . . (see 2.189)
• *Historical Dictionary of.* . . . (see 2.193)
TRAVELER RESOURCES
• *Culturegram:* (see 2.191)
• *Kummerly & Frey Map of.* . . . (see 1.127)
• *Fodor's Guide to.* . . . (see 2.192)
• *Nagel's Encyclopedia Guide to.* . . . (see 2.195)
LANGUAGE LEARNING RESOURCES
"Serbo-Croatian"
• *Berlitz.* . . . *for Travelers* (phrasebook, see 9.043)
• . . . .: *Complete Course for Beginners* (see 9.044)
• *Spoken.* . . . (see 9.047)
Fulbright Grants for study in Yugoslavia normally available (see 7.041)

Zaire

Publications

18.602
Zaire Today
J. A. Editions
France
1979; hardbound; 264 pages; $14.95

Available from Hippocrene Books, Inc., 171 Madison Ave., New York, NY 10016
• Travel guide to, a description of and a report on contemporary Zaire; illustrated

The following are standard resources available on Zaire

INFORMATION SOURCES
- *Background Notes:* (see 2.188)
- *Country Study/Area Handbook. . . .* (see 2.189)

LANGUAGE LEARNING RESOURCES
For the "International" Languages (Arabic, French, German and Spanish) see listings under Chapter IX *Foreign Language Teaching and Learning*
Fulbright Grants for study in Zaire normally available (see 7.041)

Zambia

The following are standard resources available on Zambia
INFORMATION SOURCES
- *Background Notes:* (see 2.188)
- *Country Study/Area Handbook. . . .* (see 2.189)
- *Historical Dictionary of. . . .* (see 2.193)

Zimbabwe

Organizations

18.603
Embassy of the Republic of Zimbabwe
2852 McGill Terrace NW
Washington, DC 20008
(202) 332-7100

- Answers phone and written inquiries about Zimbabwe including general and tourist information
- Provides general and tourist brochures, maps and other printed materials on Zimbabwe, including *Independent Zimbabwe* (an occasional periodical reporting current events) and *Zimbabwe in Brief*

Publications

18.604
The Struggle for Zimbabwe
David Martin and Phyllis Johnson
Faber & Faber, Inc.
39 Thompson St.
Winchester, MA 01890
1976; hardbound; 374 pages; $25

• Thorough review of the history of Southern Rhodesia and how it was transformed into Zimbabwe

The following are standard resources available on Zimbabwe
INFORMATION SOURCES
  • *Background Notes:* (see 2.188)
  • *Historical Dictionary of. . . .* (see 2.193)
  • *World Bibliographical Series. . . .* (see 2.198)
TRAVELER RESOURCES
  • *Culturegram:* (see 2.191)

Index of Organizations

Index of Publications

Topical Index

Central Asian studies. *See* Asian
studies, Central
Central European studies. *See* East
European studies
Chad. *See* Table of contents
Chamorros studies, 13.131
Children's cultures, 2.035
Chile, 18.066–18.068
teacher exchange programs, 3.001
Chilean studies, 16.020, 16.021
China, People's Republic of,
18.069–18.106
audiovisuals, 2.076, 2.079, 2.225
bibliographies, 11.015
books, 1.110, 1.126, 1.136,
11.001–11.035 *passim*
educational exchange, 3.001,
3.043, 4.220, 10.018, 13.011
teaching materials, 2.076, 2.078,
2.080, 2.085, 2.159, 2.164, 2.228,
4.065
China, Republic of. *See* Taiwan
China, women in, 2.221
Chinese. *See also* Cantonese;
Mandarin, instruction in,
13.001–13.132 *passim*,
18.069–18.072, 18.469
Chinese, language learning
resources. *See* China; Hong Kong;
Singapore; Taiwan
Chinese and international business
studies, 13.098
Chinese art, 13.050, 13.069, 13.121,
13.134
Chinese language, book importers,
18.105–18.106
Chinese law, university program,
6.112, 6.115
Chinese studies, 13.001–13.132
passim, 18.069–18.072. *See also*
Asian studies; Sino-Soviet studies
research centers, 4.127, 4.159
ChiNyanja, instruction in, 12.013
Chivash, instruction in, 14.013
Christian-Muslim relations, research
center, 17.006
Club of Rome, 1.008
Colombia, 2.225, 18.107–18.110
Commerce, international, university
program, 6.137
Common law studies, university
program, 6.107
Common Market. *See* European
Community
Commonwealth countries, travel
grants, 7.009
Communication, development,
6.124
Communication and East
European/Russian studies, 14.022

Communication studies,
international, 4.021, 4.165, 4.255,
6.129, 13.035
Communism. *See also* Marxism;
East European and Russian area
studies; Russian studies; Soviet
studies
Afghanistan, 18.006
books, 1.111, 11.015
comparative, 14.041
Cuban, 18.115
Latin American, 16.012
research center, 4.159, 4.167, 4.178
Soviet, 18.551
study of, 14.015, 14.036
Community colleges consortium,
4.247
Community foreign visitor host
organizations. *See* Foreign
students
Community health studies,
international. *See* Agriculture
international studies
Community outreach programs,
college/university, 4.188–4.244
passim
Community service,
college/university program, 6.162
Comoros, 18.111
Comparative communism, 14.041
Comparative cultures, research
center, 4.166
Comparative development studies,
4.107
Comparative education, 4.250, 6.094
Comparative educational systems.
See Foreign students
Comparative law. *See* Law,
international
Comparative management. *See*
Business administration,
international
Comparative religion, 4.151
Comparative studies. *See*
International studies
Conflict management. *See* Peace
studies
Conflict resolution. *See* Peace
studies
Congo. *See* Table of contents
Consular offices, foreign, 1.035
Coptic, instruction in, 17.018,
17.025, 17.039, 17.043
Correspondence exchange,
3.048–3.053
Costa Rica, 18.112–18.113
Country and area studies, books,
11.001–11.035
Credential evaluation, foreign. *See*
Foreign students and visitors

Croatian language learning
resources. *See* Yugoslavia
Croatian studies, 18.589, 18.596
Cross-cultural orientation. *See*
Cross-cultural training
Cross-cultural psychology, 11.022
Cross-cultural relations, research
grants, 7.016
Cross-cultural studies. *See*
International studies
Cross-cultural training, 2.023, 2.036,
2.060, 4.259
books, 1.114, 1.124, 2.163, 2.170,
2.171, 2.179, 4.017, 4.259
evaluation, 2.167
Cross-cultural training for
managers, 6.028
Cuba, 18.114–18.116
Cuban studies, publications, 11.011,
16.085, 16.166
Cultural area studies. *See*
International studies
Cultural exchange, organizational
directory, 1.043
U.S.-China, 18.080
Culture learning, 13.035, 13.169
Curriculum. *See also* Software
curriculum; specific topics,
internationalizing, 2.172
Curriculum development grants,
7.032
Cyprus, 18.172. *See also* Table of
contents
Czech, book importers,
18.119–18.120
instruction in, 14.001–14.041
passim
Czechoslovakia, 18.117–18.120

Dance, 1.076 4.181, 13.138
Dance festivals, 2.137
Danish, instruction in, 15.008,
15.025, 15.027
Danish language resources. *See*
Denmark
Demographic research, 6.023
Denmark, 11.027, 18.121
Development, audiovisuals, 2.209,
2.124, 2.237, 10.018
Development, books, 1.136, 11.034
research centers, 4.159, 4.178,
6.122, 6.135, 6.148, 6.158
research grants, 7.004, 7.011
teaching materials, 2.237
women in, 2.042
Development, international
agricultural. *See* Agriculture-
international studies
Development, education,
college/university programs,
6.086, 6.088, 6.089, 6.095, 6.102

558713

Matthew Helmke

with Andrew Hudson
and Paul Hudson

Ubuntu

UNLEASHED

2012 Edition
Covering 11.10 and 12.04

 800 East 96th Street, Indianapolis, Indiana 46240 USA

Ubuntu Unleashed 2012 Edition: Covering Ubuntu 11.10 and 12.04

ISBN-13: 978-0-672-33578-5
ISBN-10: 0-672-33578-6

Library of Congress Cataloging-in-Publication Data:

Helmke, Matthew.
  Ubuntu unleashed / Matthew Helmke. — 2012 ed.
     p. cm.
  "Covering 11.10 and 12.04."
  ISBN-13: 978-0-672-33578-5 (pbk. : alk. paper)
  ISBN-10: 0-672-33578-6 (pbk. : alk. paper)
  1. Ubuntu (Electronic resource) 2. Linux. 3. Operating systems (Computers) I. Title.
  QA76.76.O63U36 2012
  005.4'32—dc23

                              2011041953

Printed in the United States of America

First Printing: January 2012

Trademarks

Warning and Disclaimer

Bulk Sales

Pearson offers excellent discounts on this book when ordered in quantity for bulk purchases or special sales. For more information, please contact:

U.S. Corporate and Government Sales
1-800-382-3419
corpsales@pearsontechgroup.com

For sales outside of the U.S., please contact:

International Sales
+1-317-581-3793
international@pearsontechgroup.com

Editor-in Chief
Mark Taub

Executive Editor
Debra Williams Cauley

Senior Development Editor
Chris Zahn

Managing Editor
Kristy Hart

Project Editor
Andrew Beaster

Copy Editor
Keith Cline

Indexer
Christine Karpeles

Proofreader
Water Crest Publishing

Technical Editors
Kris Healy
Dustin Kirkland
John Wregglesworth

Publishing Coordinator
Kim Boedigheimer

Multimedia Developer
Dan Scherf

Interior Designer
Gary Adair

Cover Designer
Gary Adair

Compositor
Nonie Ratcliff

Contents at a Glance

Table of Contents

About the Authors

Matthew Helmke is an active member of the Ubuntu community. He served from 2006 to 2011 on the Ubuntu Forum Council, providing leadership and oversight of the Ubuntu Forums (www.ubuntuforums.org), and spent two years on the Ubuntu regional membership approval board for Europe, the Middle East, and Africa. He has written about Ubuntu for several magazines and websites, is a lead author of *The Official Ubuntu Book*, and coauthored *The VMware Cookbook*. He works for The iPlant Collaborative (www.iplantcollaborative.org), which is funded by the National Science Foundation and is building the world's first cyberinfrastructure for the biological sciences. Matthew first used Unix in 1987 while studying LISP on a Vax at the university. He has run a business using only free and open source software, has consulted, and has recently completed a master's degree in Information Resources and Library Science from the University of Arizona. You can find out more about Matthew at matthewhelmke.com or drop him a line with errata or suggestions at matthew@matthewhelmke.com.

Andrew Hudson is a freelance journalist who specializes in writing about Linux. He has significant experience in Red Hat and Debian-based Linux distributions and deployments and can often be found sitting at his keyboard tweaking various settings and config files just for the hell of it. He lives in Wiltshire, which is a county of England, along with his wife, Bernice, and their son, John. Andrew does not like Emacs. He can be reached at andy.hudson@gmail.com.

Paul Hudson is a recognized expert in open-source technologies. He is also a professional developer and full-time journalist for *Future Publishing*. His articles have appeared in *MacFormat*, *PC Answers*, *PC Format*, *PC Plus*, and *Linux Format*. Paul is passionate about free software in all its forms and uses a mix of Linux and BSD to power his desktops and servers. Paul likes Emacs. Paul can be contacted through http://hudzilla.org.

Dedication

To Heather, Saralyn, Sedona, and Philip—the most amazing family
a guy could hope for, to my grandfather for always believing in me
and teaching me to believe in myself, and to my friends in the
Ubuntu, developer, sysadmin, and DevOps communities.

—Matthew Helmke

Acknowledgments

I am solely responsible for this edition of *Ubuntu Unleashed* but freely acknowledge that I am standing on the shoulders of giants. I want to express my gratitude to Andrew and Paul Hudson for the solid foundation that past editions of the book (up to *Ubuntu Unleashed 2008*) provided to this update. Thanks to Ryan Troy for helping with the 2010 edition. Thank you to the many people who helped with technical edits and both formal and informal advice, especially Andrew Lenards, John Wregglesworth, Kris Healy, Dustin Kirkland, and several developers who wanted to remain anonymous. A huge debt of gratitude is owed to the Ubuntu community, Canonical, and Mark Shuttleworth for inviting me to participate in the community, including my role in the forums, a turn on the EMEA membership board, and two Ubuntu Developer Summits. Thanks to the Ubuntu All Stars for the chance to jam with you on guitar. Thank you to the entire Ubuntu community for your labor of love to create this wonderful operating system. Finally, thanks to my colleagues at Pearson, especially Debra Williams Cauley, for the trust placed in me and the opportunity to collaborate on projects like this one.

—Matthew Helmke

For additional information about the various GNU software licenses, browse to www.gnu.org/. For a definition of open-source and licensing guidelines, along with links to the terms of nearly three dozen open-source licenses, browse to www.opensource.org/.

Who This Book Is For

There are several groups who this book is for, but in this section, two broad audiences are discussed.

Those Wanting to Become Intermediate or Advanced Users

Ubuntu Unleashed is intended for intermediate and advanced users, or those who wish to become one. Our goal is to give you a nudge in the right direction, to help you enter the higher stages by exposing you to as many different tools and ideas as possible; we want to give you some thoughts and methods to consider, and spur you on to seek out more. Although the contents are aimed at intermediate to advanced users, new users who pay attention will benefit from the advice, tips, tricks, traps, and techniques presented in each chapter. Pointers to more detailed or related information are also provided at the end of each chapter.

If you are new to Linux, you might need to learn some new computer skills, such as how to research your computer's hardware, how to partition a hard drive, and (occasionally) how to use a command line. This book helps you learn these skills and shows you how to learn more about your computer, Linux, and the software included with Ubuntu. Most important, it will help you overcome your fear of the system by learning more about what it is and how it works.

We would like to take a moment to introduce a concept called *"The Three Levels of Listening"* from Alistair Cockburn's *Agile Software Development*, published by Addison Wesley. These levels describe how a person learns and masters a technique. We all start at the first stage and progress from there. Few reach the last stage, but those who do are incredibly effective and efficient. People aiming for this stage are the very ones for whom we intend this book:

- ▶ **Following**—The stage where the learner looks for one very detailed process that works and sticks to it to accomplish a task.

- ▶ **Detaching**—The stage where the learner feels comfortable with one method and begins to learn other ways to accomplish the same task.

- ▶ **Fluent**—The stage where the learner has experience with or understanding of many methods and doesn't think of any of them in particular while doing a task.

A myriad of books focus on the first set of users. This is not one of them. It is our goal in *Ubuntu Unleashed* to write just enough to be sufficient to get you from where you are to where you want or need to be. This is not a book for newcomers who want or need every step outlined in detail, although we do that occasionally. This is a book for people who want help learning about what can be done and a way to get started doing it. The internet is an amazing reference tool, so this is not a comprehensive reference book. This book is a tool to help you see the landscape; to learn enough about what you seek to get you started in the right direction with a quality foundational understanding.

Sysadmins, Programmers, and DevOps

Systems administrators, or Sysadmins, are the people who keep servers and networks up and running. Their role is sometimes called *operations*. They deal with software installation and configuration, security, and do all the amazing things behind the scenes that let others use these systems for their work. They are often given less respect than they deserve, but the pay is good and it is a ton of fun to wield the ultimate power over a computer system. It is also a great responsibility and these amazing guys and gals work hard to make sure they do their jobs well, striving for incredible system uptime and availability. Ubuntu is an excellent operating system for servers and networks and much of the knowledge needed to get started in this role can be found in this book.

Programmers are the people who write software. They are sometimes called *developers*. Programmers work with others to create the applications that run on top of those systems. Ubuntu is a great platform for writing and testing software. This is true whether you are doing web application development or writing software for desktop or server systems. It also makes a great platform for learning new programming languages and trying out new ideas. This book can help you get started.

DevOps is a portmanteau of *developer* and *operations*. It signifies a blending of the two roles above. The information technology (IT) world is changing and roles are becoming less clear cut and isolated from one another. In the past, it was common to witness battles between programmers excited about new technology and sysadmins in love with stability. DevOps realizes that neither goal is healthy in isolation, but that seeking a balance between the two can yield great results by removing the barriers to communication and understanding that sometimes causes conflict within a team. Because of the rise of cloud computing and virtualization, which are also covered in this book, and more agile forms of development, DevOps is a useful perspective that enables people working in IT to do an even better job of serving their ultimate clients: end users. This book is a great foundation for those wanting to learn knowledge that will help with both roles, hopefully presented in a way that balances them nicely.

What This Book Contains

Ubuntu Unleashed is organized into six parts, described below. A disc containing the entire distribution is included so that you have everything you need to get started:

▶ Part I, "Installation and Configuration," takes you through installing Ubuntu on your computer in the place of any other operating system you may be running, such as Windows.

▶ Part II, "Desktop Ubuntu," is aimed at users who want to use Ubuntu on desktop systems.

▶ Part III, "System Administration," covers both elementary and sophisticated details of setting up a system for specific tasks and maintaining that system.

▶ Part IV, "Ubuntu as a Server," gives you the information you need to start building your own file, web, and other servers for use in your home or office.

▶ Part V, "Programming Linux," provides a great introduction to how you can extend Ubuntu capabilities even further using the development tools supplied with it.

▶ Part VI, "Appendices," are references that give you scope to explore in even more depth some of the topics covered in this book, as well as historical context to Ubuntu and installation resources.

Conventions Used in This Book

It is impossible to cover every option of every command included in Ubuntu. Besides, with the rise of the internet and high-speed connections, reference materials are far less valuable than they used to be since most of these details are only a quick Google search away. Instead, we focus on teaching you how to find information you need while giving a quality overview worthy of the intermediate or advanced user. Sometimes this book offers tables of various options, commands, and keystrokes to help condense, organize, and present information about a variety of subjects.

To help you better understand code listing examples and sample command lines, several formatting techniques are used to show input and ownership. For example, if the command or code listing example shows typed input, the input is formatted in boldface after the sample command prompt, as follows:

```
matthew@seymour:~$ ls
```

If typed input is required, as in response to a prompt, the sample typed input also is in boldface, like so:

```
Delete files? [Y/n] y
```

You start by researching and documenting your hardware. This information will prove helpful later on during the installation.

Researching Your Hardware Specifications

At the absolute minimum, you should know the basics of your system, such as how much RAM you have installed and what type of mouse, keyboard, and monitor you have. Knowing the storage capacity and type of hard drive you have is important because it helps you plan how you will divide it up for Ubuntu and troubleshoot if problems occur. A small detail, such as whether your mouse uses the USB or PS/2 interface, will ensure proper pointer configuration—something that should happen without any problem, but you will be glad you knew in case something does go wrong. The more information you have, the better prepared you will be for any problems.

You can make an inventory or at least a quick list of some basic features of your system. Again, the items you most want to know include the amount of installed memory, the size of your hard drive, the type of mouse, the capabilities of the display monitor (such as maximum resolution), and the number of installed network interfaces (if any).

DVD Installation Jump Start

To install Ubuntu Desktop from the disc included with this book, you must have at least a 1GHz Pentium 4 CPU, 5GB of hard drive space, and 512MB RAM. A monitor with a display resolution of at least 1024 x 768 is strongly recommended. Internet access is not required, but is very helpful and also recommended.

Installation Options

Ubuntu is made available in three main forms: the Desktop CD, the Server install CD, and the Alternate install CD. (We are not including derivative distributions like Kubuntu or Lubuntu in this list.) For most people, the Desktop CD is what you want; the alternate is mainly used for upgrading existing Ubuntu users to the latest version, as well as allowing installation on either low-powered systems or in places where fine-tuned, custom requirements exist. The Server install CD can get a LAMP server up and running in about 20 minutes (Linux, Apache, MySQL, and PHP), but as you learn in this book, all these components are available to the Ubuntu default distribution. You can find a list of the currently available ISO images in a couple of places. An ISO image contains the entire contents of a CD or DVD in a single file that can be used as if it were a CD or DVD and which can be burned to a physical CD or DVD if desired. The easy place that will be best for most people is www.ubuntu.com/download, which includes a nice graphical menu system and links to easy-to-read information and detailed instructions. Those with more specific requirements, like a desire to use one of the official alternate Ubuntu versions like Kubuntu or Lubuntu, can find what they need by navigating the menus at cdimage.ubuntu.com.

Official Ubuntu Flavors

Ubuntu has 12 official variants, called *flavors*, as follows:

- ▶ Ubuntu
- ▶ Ubuntu Server
- ▶ Ubuntu Cloud
- ▶ Ubuntu Netboot
- ▶ Ubuntu Core
- ▶ Kubuntu Desktop
- ▶ Kubuntu Mobile
- ▶ Xubuntu Desktop
- ▶ EdUbuntu
- ▶ Mythbuntu
- ▶ Ubuntu Studio
- ▶ Lubuntu

Almost everything in this book applies to any of these flavors. The exceptions include GUI-specific content, such as Unity-specific descriptions, and content referring to programs not installed by default, such as many of the server and programming options.

To install using the DVD included with this book, ignore the next couple of paragraphs and then keep reading this chapter.

To install using a CD or DVD that you create, download the ISO image you need from either source above. You need to download a program to enable you to burn this image to physical media. For Windows, try either InfraRecorder (http://infrarecorder.org) or ISO Recorder (http://isorecorder.alexfeinman.com/isorecorder.htm) and follow the instructions given by the authors. For Mac OS X, you can use Apple's Disk Utility, which is installed by default. For Ubuntu, right-click on the icon for an ISO image and select Write to Disc. Once the CD or DVD is created, use it as you follow the installation instructions in this section.

You can also install using a USB thumb drive (use one that holds at least 2GB). Download the ISO image you need from either source above. You need to download a program that enables you to use this image to create a bootable USB drive. For Windows, try Universal USB Installer (www.pendrivelinux.com/universal-usb-installer-easy-as-1-2-3/) or ISO Recorder (http://isorecorder.alexfeinman.com/isorecorder.htm) and follow the instructions given by the authors. For Ubuntu, use the installed Startup Disk Creator program available from the System, Administration menu (for Ubuntu versions 10.10 or older) or by searching in the Dash (Ubuntu versions 11.04 or newer). It is not recommended to use a bootable USB drive to install on Apple Mac hardware. Once the ISO is written to the USB drive, use it as you follow the installation instructions in this section.

Planning Partition Strategies

Partitioning is a topic that can make novice Linux users nervous. Coming from a Microsoft world, where you might be used to having just one hard drive, it can seem a bit strange to use an operating system that makes partitioning a hard drive possible or even preferable and common.

Depending on your needs, you can opt to have a single large partition to contain everything, which is the official recommendation of the Ubuntu community and developers. You may prefer to segment your installation across several partitions if you have advanced knowledge and specific needs.

If you are installing Ubuntu in a corporate or business environment, the needs of the business should be a primary concern. Be careful to ensure that you build in an adequate upgrade path that allows you to extend the life of the system and add any additional storage or memory.

Knowing how software is placed on your hard drive for Linux involves knowing how Ubuntu organizes its file system. This knowledge will help you make the most out of hard drive space. In some instances, such as when you're planning to have user directories mounted via NFS or other means, this information can help head off data loss, increase security, and accommodate future needs. Create a great system, and you'll be the hero of information services. The Linux file system is covered along with commands to manipulate files and directories in Chapter 10, "Command-Line Quickstart."

To plan the best partitioning scheme, research and know the answers to these questions:

▶ How much disk space does your system require?

▶ Do you expect your disk space needs to grow significantly in the future?

▶ Will the system boot only Ubuntu, or do you need a dual-boot system?

▶ How much data requires backup, and what backup system will work best? (See Chapter 16, "Backing Up," for more information about backing up your system.)

The Boot Loader

During installation, Ubuntu automatically installs *GRUB2 (Grand Unified Boot Loader)* to the *Master Boot Record (MBR)* of your hard drive. Handily enough, it also detects any other operating systems, such as Windows, and adds entries in GRUB2 as appropriate. If you have a specific requirement not to install GRUB2 to the MBR, you need to install using the Alternate disc, which will allow you to specify the install location for GRUB2.

NOTE

Dual Boot Not Recommended, But You Can Try It If You Want

If you are attempting to create a dual-boot system using both Windows and Ubuntu, where multiple operating systems exist on the hard drive and the user selects which one to use at boot time, you should install Windows first because it will overwrite the

MBR and ignore any other operating systems on the disk. Ubuntu also overwrites the MBR, but does so in a way that creates a boot menu that includes all operating systems it detects on the disk. Dual booting works, but in the past few years, some options have arisen that are better for most people.

If you decide you must dual boot, make sure you have your Windows recovery media available and that you either already have enough free space on your hard drive or know how to shrink the existing Windows partition and create a new partition on the hard drive for Ubuntu. No support or instructions for doing this are given in this book.

You should consider using Wubi instead of dual booting. See the "Wubi: The Easy Installer for Windows" section later in this chapter. This book recommends this option or the next one.

You can also use virtualization. See Chapter 32, "Virtualization on Ubuntu," for more information.

Installing from CD or DVD or USB Drive

The BIOS of most PCs support booting directly from a CD, DVD, or USB drive and enable you to set a specific order of devices (such as floppy, hard drive, CD-ROM, or USB) to search for bootable software. Turn on your PC and set its BIOS if required (usually accessed by pressing a Function or the Del key after powering on); then insert your Ubuntu install media and boot to install Ubuntu.

Step-by-Step Installation

This section provides a basic step-by-step installation of Ubuntu from the install DVD included with this book, but these instructions also work with media you create yourself using an ISO image you downloaded and wrote to a disk or USB drive using the instructions provided earlier; just replace mentions of DVD with your install medium. The install process itself is fairly straightforward, and you should not encounter any real problems.

WARNING

Back Up First

If you have anything at all on your computer that you want to save, back it up first. Installing an operating system has become easier to do, but it is still a major change. Your entire hard drive will be erased and new information written to it. This is expected when installing Ubuntu to the entire hard drive, but can even happen due to user error or gremlins (unexplained problems) when attempting a dual boot installation. Back up anything you want to preserve. Save data and files to an external hard drive or other medium. You can even back up your entire operating system and current installation using something like Clonezilla (http://clonezilla.org). Whatever you do, go in with the perspective that everything currently on the computer will disappear. If this is okay, continue.

It is useful and recommended to have your computer connected to the Internet as you proceed so that you can download updates while installing.

Installing

To get started, insert the DVD into your drive and reboot your computer. The initial screen offers a variety of languages for you to use during installation (see Figure 1.1) and two options. Try Ubuntu boots and runs Ubuntu from the DVD without making any changes to your system so that when you remove the DVD and reboot, everything will be as it was before. Install Ubuntu installs Ubuntu instead of your current operating system, or alongside it (for dual booting). Select Install Ubuntu to begin.

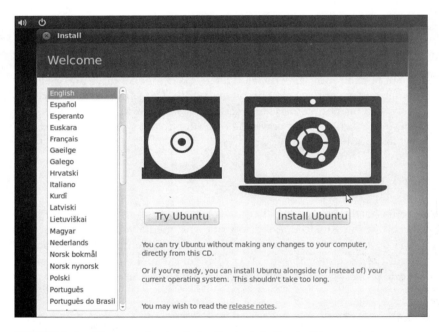

FIGURE 1.1   Choose a language for the installation in this opening screen.

Figure 1.2 shows the Preparing to Install Ubuntu screen. If you select the two check boxes at the bottom, Ubuntu downloads extra software, such as multimedia codecs and any software updates that have been released since the disk was created, and includes them in the installation. Doing so is recommended.

If other operating systems are found on your system, you are given the option to install Ubuntu alongside them or to erase them and use the whole disk for Ubuntu. See the dual-boot note and backup warning earlier in this chapter before continuing.

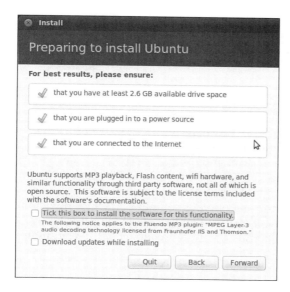

FIGURE 1.2   Before proceeding, double-check that your system meets the requirements shown.

Next, you have the option to either erase and use the entire hard disk for your installation (recommended for people who are new to Linux and are nervous about partitioning a hard drive) or specifying partitions manually, which is not as difficult as it sounds, as shown in Figure 1.3.

FIGURE 1.3   What do you want to do with your hard drive?

Because this is a book for people who want a deeper understanding of their system, we show a simple partitioning scheme here and give some reasons for our choices.

Your needs may vary, so we give some principles to consider so that you may adjust our recommendations to your situation.

Many users will benefit from three simple partitions, shown in Figure 1.4. Here we have a swap partition, a root partition (denoted by /), and a home partition where data for each user on the system will be stored. The swap partition was previously used for those times when there was not enough memory for running processes, so the Linux kernel could move stored information from RAM to the hard drive and use that swap space as extra RAM. This is slow, but sometimes it is quite useful. These days, desktop systems come with more memory, and the swap space is used mainly for storing information during suspend and hibernate, which can be used instead of turning off your computer. Having /home on a separate partition can be a good idea because it enables you to install a different Linux distribution or a different release of Ubuntu on your / partition while retaining your user data (neither of which are covered in this book).

FIGURE 1.4   A simple, but useful, partitioning scheme.

NOTE

Suspend saves your current system state to RAM and then turns off power to most of the system, but maintains just enough power use to keep that state saved in RAM. When you restart your system, it comes back quickly and to the same state it was in. Hibernate saves your current system state to the hard disk. These days, it is just as fast to boot from scratch as it is to hibernate and restore, so there isn't much point in using it.

If you choose to manually partition instead of using the entire disk, we recommend a / partition of at least 3GB, a swap partition that is about 1.5 to 2 times the size of your installed RAM, and then using the rest of the disk for /home. More complex systems, such as servers, may find more complex partitioning schemes useful, especially when multiple hard drives are available. Read Chapter 10 for a quick discussion of the parts of the Linux file system to get an idea of parts of the file system that could benefit from residing on their own (or even multiple!) partitions or disks.

After you have made your partitioning selections, installation continues by asking about your current location; it helps you select the most appropriate keyboard layout for your system based on that location and the most common language used there, and asks you to enter your name, a username that you will use to login to the system, and a password. You can even choose to encrypt your /home folder during the process.

A Quick Aside on Passwords

When you create your password, be sure to remember what you entered. If you forget it, you cannot use your new system because you will not be able to log on to it.

When setting a password, the common advice is to make sure that it has a mixture of letters and numbers to make it more secure. For instance, a good example of a historically recommended style of password is T1a5c0p. Although this might seem like garbage at first glance, the easy way to remember it is by remembering the phrase This Is A Good Choice Of Password, shortened to Tiagcop, and finally substituting some of the letters with similar-looking numbers.

There are some reasons why this might not be the best recommendation anymore, because computer systems are much faster than they used to be. It is a true statement that the longer a password is, the harder it is to break. For this reason, the newest recommendation is to use a passphrase consisting of at least four words, perhaps something like *green monkeys chortle often*. There is no doubt that a password the length of four common words combined together would be harder to break than the T1a5c0p example. From that perspective, it seems like a no-brainer. On the other hand, a longer password that does not use any words found in a dictionary would be even better, but the problem here is that these passwords, and even the T1a5c0p example, can be hard to remember and may end up being written down on a sticky note next to the computer, perhaps even stuck to the monitor. That is worse, especially if you use good security and create a different password for every website and computer system that requires one.

One solution is to choose a really good password for your system, one that you will remember, like the four-words example or a long passphrase like PeanutButterandJelly$andwiches, and then create one more good password to use with a password manager program like KeyPassX (available in the Ubuntu software repositories; see Chapter 9, "Managing Software," for details on how to find and install it), which can generate long, completely random passwords for you and keep them in a list that can only be viewed by accessing your system and then accessing the program, both of which will use good passwords. Let's get back to the installation.

While you are answering the questions asked by the installer, the Ubuntu install has already begun to copy files to your hard drive. Performing these tasks in parallel makes the process even faster than it used to be. Now that all necessary information has been input, you are shown a series of information screens while the installation is completed. These are filled with interesting content about Ubuntu and are worth reading while you wait.

When the process is complete, you are prompted to restart the computer. Do so, and remove the install media when it is ejected. Then log in when the reboot is complete. That's it.

In previous editions of this book, this chapter was longer and described a process that was sometimes confusing and fraught with peril. The Ubuntu developers deserve high praise for making this so incredibly easy and fast. The Linux kernel supports more hardware than ever, and the Ubuntu kernel gurus (who make the decisions about what hardware modules to enable, among other things) do a great job so that most hardware works out of the box.

If you do run into trouble, go to ubuntuforums.org as a great first resource, give a list of your hardware (you did make that list we suggested, right?) and any error messages you have received, and you should either find someone who can help you or get some direction to another source of assistance.

First Update

It used to be that the first thing that you needed to do with your new system was update it to the latest package versions. You do this mainly to ensure that you have the latest security updates available. Remember that first installation step where we recommended checking the box to have software updates downloaded during the installation process? That means these updates were acquired during the installation and that your system should be up-to-the-minute current.

If you want to double-check that you have all the current versions of software and security updates installed, see Chapter 9 for assistance.

Wubi: The Easy Installer for Windows

Also included on the Ubuntu CD is Wubi, which allows you to install an Ubuntu system within Windows. In effect, Wubi creates a large file to hold all the Ubuntu information and provides a way, using the Windows bootloader, to boot into Ubuntu without having to do any partitioning at all. What's more, it's almost as fast as the real thing and much faster than a Live CD. To get started with Wubi, you need to insert the Ubuntu disc into your CD drive while Windows is booted. You'll see a screen similar to Figure 1.5.

Click the option to Install inside Windows to be taken to the next screen; there you can choose some basic configuration options using the drop-down menus, as shown in Figure 1.6.

Wubi creates an image file on your hard drive and modifies the Windows bootloader to allow you to boot into Ubuntu or Windows. Don't worry, though; your hard disk hasn't actually been modified, but a rather large file has been created to hold Ubuntu. When you restart your system, you'll see the Ubuntu option, so press the down-arrow key and press Enter to begin booting into your new Ubuntu system.

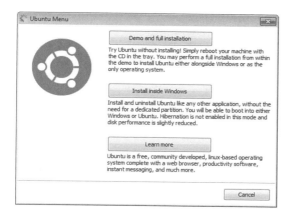

FIGURE 1.5   The auto-start menu gives you a gateway to Ubuntu. Click Install inside Windows to start the Wubi installation.

FIGURE 1.6   You can select some configuration options before you start the installation.

The first time you start up a Wubi Ubuntu installation, it does some post-installation configuration before loading the Unity desktop. You now have a fully functional Ubuntu system.

If you decide that you want to do a regular installation, you'll need to remove Ubuntu and Wubi. Fortunately, as part of the Wubi installation, an entry is added to the Add/Remove Programs tool in Windows, allowing you to quickly and easily remove Wubi and the associated Ubuntu installation. Just remember to first back up any files that you want to keep.

Shutting Down

At some point, you are going to want to shut down your computer. As with most things in Linux, there are different ways to do it. You can use the power icon located in the upper-right corner of your screen and its drop-down menu, as shown in Figure 1.7. From there, you can also choose to hibernate (saves a copy of the running state to disk and shuts down) or suspend (saves the current running state to memory).

FIGURE 1.7   You have several options in the power icon menu.

If you are working at the command line, you can immediately shut down your system by using the shutdown command like this:

```
$ sudo shutdown -h now
```

You can also use the shutdown command to restart your computer, as follows:

```
$ sudo shutdown -r now
```

For new users, installing Ubuntu is the beginning of a new and highly rewarding journey on the path to learning Linux. For Ubuntu system administrators, the task ahead is to fine-tune the installation and to customize the server or user environment.

References

▶ **www.ubuntu.com**—The place to start when looking for news, information, and documentation about installing, configuring, and using Ubuntu.

▶ **www.ubuntu.com/desktop/get-ubuntu/download**—This page has specific information and links for downloading, burning, and installing the current release of the Ubuntu Desktop edition. There are comparable links available from the main page for Ubuntu Netbook and Server editions and other projects.

▶ **www.nwc.com/columnists/1101colron.html**—How to use Intel's Pre-execution Environment (PXE) protocol to remote boot workstations.

▶ **www.gnu.org/software/grub/**—Home page for the GRUB boot loader.

CHAPTER 2

Post-Installation Configuration

Now that the primary task of installing Ubuntu has been completed, you can begin to customize your new operating system.

In this chapter, we look at getting up and running with Ubuntu. A tour around the desktop is the goal of Chapter 3, "Working with Unity." These two chapters should be read together. In this chapter, you learn how to do some basic administration tasks. By the end of this chapter, you should feel comfortable enough to move on through the rest of the book.

Troubleshooting Post-Installation Configuration Problems

A lot of work has gone into Ubuntu to make it as versatile as possible, but sometimes you may come across a piece of hardware that Ubuntu is not sure about. Knowing what to do in these situations is important, especially when you are working with Ubuntu for the first time.

Because Ubuntu (and Linux in general) is built on a resilient UNIX foundation, it is much more stable than some operating systems. However, even though things might seem to be working fine, Ubuntu could have a problem that might not affect the appearance of the system. In this section, you learn how to examine some of Ubuntu's built-in error logs to help you discover or diagnose unseen problems.

Ubuntu has a command that responds with detailed messages that are output directly by the operating system:

the dmesg command. This command is commonly used with the grep command to filter output. The dmesg command takes its output directly from the /var/log/messages file, so you can choose to either run dmesg or to read the file directly by typing less /var/log/messages. The output is fairly detailed, so be prepared for an initial shock when you see how much information is generated. You might find it easier to generate a file with the dmesg output by using the following command:

```
matthew@seymour:~$ dmesg > dmesg.txt
```

This takes the output from the dmesg command and stores it in a new text file called dmesg.txt. You can then browse it at your leisure using your choice of text editor, such as vi or emacs. You can even use the less command, like so:

```
matthew@seymour:~$ less dmesg.txt
```

The messages are generated by the kernel, by other software run by /etc/init.d, and by Ubuntu's runlevel scripts. You might find what appear to be errors at first glance, but some errors are not really problems (for example, if a piece of hardware is configured but not present on your system).

Thanks to Google, troubleshooting is no longer the slow process it used to be. You can copy and paste error messages into Google's search bar to bring up a whole selection of results similar to the problem you face. Remember, Google is your friend, especially www.google.com/linux, which provides a specialized search engine for Linux. You can also try http://marc.info, which browses newsgroup and mailing list archives. Either way, you are likely to come across people who have had the same problem as you.

It is important to work on finding and testing only one solution to one problem at a time; otherwise, you might end up getting no work done whatsoever. You should also get into the habit of making backup copies of all files that you modify, just in case you make a bad situation worse. Use the copy (cp) command like this:

```
matthew@seymour:~$ cp file file.backup20101010
```

You should not use a .bak extension on your backup file because this could get overwritten by another automatic process and leave you frustrated when you try to restore the original file. I like to use backupYYYYMMDD, as in the preceding code where I used the release date for Ubuntu 10.10: 2010(year)10(month)10(day).

If something breaks as a result of your changing the original file, you can always copy the original back into place using the command like this:

```
matthew@seymour:~$ cp file.backup20101010 file
```

(Something as simple as this can really save you, especially when you are under pressure because you've changed something you shouldn't have changed on a production system. It is better not to make sweeping changes on a production system.)

The sudo Command

You will find as you work through this book that Ubuntu relies on the sudo command while working at the command line. This command is used in front of other commands to tell Ubuntu that you want to run the specified command with super user powers. This sounds really special, and it actually is. When you work using the sudo command, you can make wide-ranging changes to your system that impact the way it runs. Be extra careful when running any command prefixed with sudo, however; a wrong option or incorrect command can have devastating consequences.

The use of sudo is straightforward. All you have to do is enter it like this:

```
matthew@seymour:~$ sudo command commandoptions
```

Just replace the word *command* with the command that you want to run, along with any options. For example, the following command opens your xorg.conf file in vi and enables you to make any changes as the super user before being able to save it:

```
matthew@seymour:~$ sudo vi /etc/X11/xorg.conf
```

Whenever you execute a command using sudo, you are prompted for your password. This is the same password that you use to log in to Ubuntu, so it is important that you remember it.

Sometimes, however, you may want to work with a classic root prompt instead of having to type sudo in front of every command (perhaps if you have to work with lots of commands at the command line that require super user access, for example). sudo enables you to do this by using the sudo -i command. Again, you are prompted for your password, which you should enter, after which Ubuntu gives you the standard root prompt, as follows:

```
matthew@seymour:~#
```

From here, you can execute any command without having to keep entering sudo.

Finding Programs and Files

In the past, Ubuntu used a system of menus to guide users searching for programs. Use the Dash to find these programs. Access the Dash by clicking the Ubuntu logo at the upper left of the screen. This brings up the menu shown in Figure 2.1. Start typing in the Search box to find specific programs or documents on your system. The icons in the row along the bottom of the Dash provide categories of things that will be listed or to narrow searches. The house icon brings you to the main Dash screen, as shown here. The second icon shows installed applications and lists others available for installation. Click the arrow next to See more results to view all installed software. The third icon shows documents. The fourth icon shows media. The Dash is covered in more detail in Chapter 3.

FIGURE 2.1   The Dash is the place to find programs and files.

Software Update

This topic is covered in greater detail in Chapter 9, "Managing Software," but it is worthy of a quick mention now so that from the start you can benefit from any available security and bug fixes. The easiest way to check for updates is Update Manager, which is really a GUI wrapper for the command apt-get. Open Update Manager from the Dash by typing **update manager** to search for it. When the window opens, click Check and enter your password. Update Manager then checks the Ubuntu software repositories to determine whether any updates are available. When it detects that new versions of installed software are available, they appear in the window. Each one has a check box that you can uncheck if you don't want to install a particular software update. Then click Install Updates to complete the process (see Figure 2.2). Software repositories are discussed later in this chapter.

Another way of updating your system is to use the command line. This is vital on servers that do not have a GUI installed, and it is sometimes quicker than using Update Manager on a desktop computer. I like to use the command line to manage all the computers on my home network because I can use Secure Shell (SSH) to connect to each from a terminal and perform updates from another room in the house, and anyone using that computer is left undisturbed. You learn how to connect like this later in the book; I just want to whet your appetite for now.

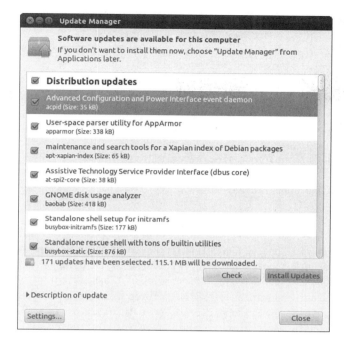

FIGURE 2.2   Update Manager showing available software updates.

To use the command line, go to the Applications, Accessories menu and select Terminal. This is the command line (commonly referred to as the *terminal*) and is one of the most powerful features of Linux. It is covered in more detail in Chapter 10, "Command-Line Quickstart," and Chapter 11, "Command-Line Master Class," so we do not delve too deeply here.

You are greeted with a prompt similar to the one here:

```
matthew@seymour:~$
```

A blinking cursor also displays. Ubuntu is awaiting your first command. Here we want to issue the following command:

```
matthew@seymour:~$ sudo apt-get update
```

This command tells the package management utility apt-get to check the Ubuntu repositories and look for any updates to your installed software. In a matter of seconds, Ubuntu completes all of this, and your screen should look something like this:

```
matthew@seymour:~$ sudo apt-get update
[sudo] password for matt:
Hit http://security.ubuntu.com oneiriconeiric-security Release.gpg
Ign http://security.ubuntu.com/ubuntu/ oneiriconeiric-security/main Translation-en
Hit http://us.archive.ubuntu.com oneiriconeiric Release.gpg
```

```
Ign http://us.archive.ubuntu.com/ubuntu/ oneiriconeiric/main Translation-en
Ign http://us.archive.ubuntu.com/ubuntu/ oneiriconeiric/main Translation-en_US
Ign http://security.ubuntu.com/ubuntu/ oneiriconeiric-security/main Translation-en_US
Ign http://security.ubuntu.com/ubuntu/ oneiriconeiric-security/multiverse
➥Translation-en
Ign http://security.ubuntu.com/ubuntu/ oneiriconeiric-security/multiverse
➥Translation-en_US
Ign http://security.ubuntu.com/ubuntu/ oneiriconeiric-security/restricted
➥Translation-en
Ign http://security.ubuntu.com/ubuntu/ oneiriconeiric-security/restricted
➥Translation-en_US
Ign http://security.ubuntu.com/ubuntu/ oneiriconeiric-security/universe
➥Translation-en
Ign http://security.ubuntu.com/ubuntu/ oneiriconeiric-security/universe
➥Translation-en_US
Ign http://us.archive.ubuntu.com/ubuntu/ oneiriconeiric/multiverse Translation-en
Ign http://us.archive.ubuntu.com/ubuntu/ oneiriconeiric/multiverse Translation-en_US
Ign http://us.archive.ubuntu.com/ubuntu/ oneiriconeiric/restricted Translation-en
Ign http://us.archive.ubuntu.com/ubuntu/ oneiriconeiric/restricted Translation-en_US
Ign http://us.archive.ubuntu.com/ubuntu/ oneiriconeiric/universe Translation-en
Ign http://us.archive.ubuntu.com/ubuntu/ oneiriconeiric/universe Translation-en_US
Hit http://us.archive.ubuntu.com oneiriconeiric-updates Release.gpg
Hit http://security.ubuntu.com oneiriconeiric-security Release
Ign http://us.archive.ubuntu.com/ubuntu/ oneiriconeiric-updates/main Translation-en
Ign http://us.archive.ubuntu.com/ubuntu/ oneiriconeiric-updates/main
➥Translation-en_US
Ign http://us.archive.ubuntu.com/ubuntu/ oneiriconeiric-updates/multiverse
➥Translation-en
Ign http://us.archive.ubuntu.com/ubuntu/ oneiriconeiric-updates/multiverse
➥Translation-en_US
Ign http://us.archive.ubuntu.com/ubuntu/ oneiriconeiric-updates/restricted
➥Translation-en
Ign http://us.archive.ubuntu.com/ubuntu/ oneiric-updates/restricted Translation-en_US
Ign http://us.archive.ubuntu.com/ubuntu/ oneiric-updates/universe Translation-en
Ign http://us.archive.ubuntu.com/ubuntu/ oneiric-updates/universe Translation-en_US
Hit http://security.ubuntu.com oneiric-security/main Sources
Hit http://us.archive.ubuntu.com oneiric Release
Hit http://us.archive.ubuntu.com oneiric-updates Release
Hit http://security.ubuntu.com oneiric-security/restricted Sources
Hit http://security.ubuntu.com oneiric-security/universe Sources
Hit http://security.ubuntu.com oneiric-security/multiverse Sources
Hit http://security.ubuntu.com oneiric-security/main i386 Packages
Hit http://security.ubuntu.com oneiric-security/restricted i386 Packages
Hit http://us.archive.ubuntu.com oneiric/main Sources
Hit http://security.ubuntu.com oneiric-security/universe i386 Packages
Hit http://security.ubuntu.com oneiric-security/multiverse i386 Packages
```

```
Hit http://us.archive.ubuntu.com oneiric/restricted Sources
Hit http://us.archive.ubuntu.com oneiric/universe Sources
Hit http://us.archive.ubuntu.com oneiric/multiverse Sources
Hit http://us.archive.ubuntu.com oneiric/main i386 Packages
Hit http://us.archive.ubuntu.com oneiric/restricted i386 Packages
Hit http://us.archive.ubuntu.com oneiric/universe i386 Packages
Hit http://us.archive.ubuntu.com oneiric/multiverse i386 Packages
Hit http://us.archive.ubuntu.com oneiric-updates/main Sources
Hit http://us.archive.ubuntu.com oneiric-updates/restricted Sources
Hit http://us.archive.ubuntu.com oneiric-updates/universe Sources
Hit http://us.archive.ubuntu.com oneiric-updates/multiverse Sources
Hit http://us.archive.ubuntu.com oneiric-updates/main i386 Packages
Hit http://us.archive.ubuntu.com oneiric-updates/restricted i386 Packages
Hit http://us.archive.ubuntu.com oneiric-updates/universe i386 Packages
Hit http://us.archive.ubuntu.com oneiric-updates/multiverse i386 Packages
Reading package lists... Done
matthew@seymour:~$
```

Upgrade your software by entering the following:

```
matthew@seymour:~$ apt-get dist-upgrade
```

Because you have already checked for updates, Ubuntu automatically knows to download and install only the packages it needs. The dist-upgrade option works intelligently to ensure that any dependencies that are needed can be satisfied and will be installed, even if major changes are needed. You can also use the option upgrade. It isn't as smart as dist-upgrade, but may be a better choice on a production server because upgrade will not make major changes to software installations, but only those necessary for security and simple package updates. This allows the systems administrator more flexibility to keep up-to-date with security but keep running setups otherwise unchanged.

Command Line apt-get Alternatives

Ubuntu has an alternative to apt-get called aptitude. It works in pretty much the same way as apt-get with the exception that aptitude also includes any recommended packages on top of the requested packages when installing or upgrading. You use aptitude mostly the same as you use apt-get; for instance, you could issue the command aptitude update and it would update the repository information. To upgrade, the options are aptitude safe-upgrade and aptitude full-upgrade. You can also issue the command aptitude without any options, which brings up a text-based package manager that you can use to select packages.

Configuring Software Repositories

Ubuntu uses software repositories to get information about available software that can be installed on your system. Ubuntu is based on a much older Linux distribution called

Debian. Debian has access to tens of thousands of different packages, which means that Ubuntu has access to these packages, too. The Debian packages are made available in Ubuntu's Universe repository. A set of volunteers called *Masters of the Universe (MOTUs)* are well trained and follow strict guidelines to package software and make even more packages available to Ubuntu users in Universe. The Universe repository is filled with optional and often useful or fun software and is enabled by default, along with other official repositories containing software necessary for Ubuntu to be installed and run in all its various official forms, security updates, and software updates.

You can adjust which repositories are enabled using the Software Sources GUI tool, available in Update Manager by clicking Settings. On the first tab (Ubuntu Software), you have five options to choose from. The default settings are shown in Figure 2.3. It is entirely up to you which options you check, but make sure that as a minimum, the first check box is checked to allow you access to Canonical-supported Open Source software, which includes all the packages necessary for a basic Ubuntu installation and a few more that are commonly used. The more boxes you check, the wider your selection of software. It's also a good idea to make sure that the Proprietary Drivers for Devices box is checked so that you can benefit from drivers that may enhance your system's performance.

FIGURE 2.3   You can find or add other options under the Updates and Other Software tabs.

Open Source Versus Proprietary

You may hear some arguments about using proprietary drivers or other software in Ubuntu. Some people feel that it goes against what *open source* stands for because the program code that is used for the drivers or software cannot be viewed and modified by the wider community but only by the original developers or company that owns it. There is also a strong argument that says users should have to undergo the least amount of work for a fully functional system.

Ubuntu takes a middle-of-the-road stance on this and leaves it up to the user to decide. Open-source software is installed by default, but options are given to allow pro-prietary software to be installed easily.

After you are happy with your selections, switch to the Updates tab to configure Ubuntu's behavior when updates are available (see Figure 2.4). By default, both the important secu-rity updates and recommended updates are checked to ensure that you have the latest bug fixes and patches. You can also choose to receive proposed updates and *backports* (software that is released for a newer version of Ubuntu but reprogrammed to be compatible with the current release), but we recommend this only if you are happy to carry out testing for the community, because any updated software from these repositories can adversely affect your system.

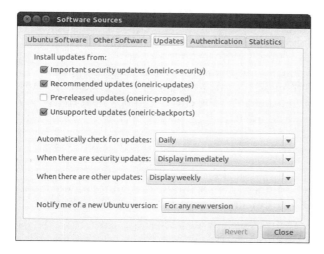

FIGURE 2.4   In the Updates tab of Software Sources, configure which updates you want and how you want them to be handled.

Ubuntu also allows you to configure how often it checks for updates and how they are installed. By default, Ubuntu checks daily for updates and, if any are available, notifies you. However, you can change the frequency and the actions Ubuntu carries out when it finds available updates. We recommend keeping the notification-only option because this allows you to see what updates are available prior to them being installed. If you want to save time, choose Download All Updates in the Background to configure Ubuntu to silently download the updates before giving you the option to install them.

> **CAUTION**
>
> We don't recommend selecting the option that automatically installs security updates. It's important that you have the option of choosing to install updates because there is always the chance that an update may cause problems. The last thing you want is for your system to suddenly stop working because an update was installed that has broken something without your knowledge.

Part of the magic of Ubuntu is the ease in which you can upgrade from major version to major version, such as moving from 11.04 to 11.10. Some Ubuntu releases are called LTS, for *Long Term Support*, and are intended for those who do not want to upgrade their operating system as often. It is possible to do this. By ensuring that the release upgrade option is set to Long Term Supported releases only, you'll be prompted to upgrade your version of Ubuntu only to what will be the next LTS version, which is scheduled to be 12.04, to be released in April 2012.

The Other Software tab lets you add other repositories. It comes by default with everything you need to connect to and use Canonical's partner repository, with nonfree (usually in the licensing sense, but occasionally for payment) software from companies that have an agreement with Canonical to make it easily available to interested users. This repository is disabled by default and you must enable it by checking a box next to its entry in the Other Software tab if you want to use it.

System Settings

To configure system settings, search the Dash for System Settings. This brings up the menu in Figure 2.5 from which you may make adjustments as desired. A couple of the options are described here.

Installing Additional Drivers

Ubuntu is extremely good at detecting and configuring graphics cards. You can check whether you have a video card or some other piece of hardware that could benefit from using a proprietary driver with the Additional Drivers manager. When you open it, it scans your system, and then you can choose to enable or disable any proprietary drivers found, depending on your personal preference. (See the "Open-Source Versus Proprietary" note earlier in this chapter.)

You can find the Additional Drivers manager in the System Settings menu. The window is shown in Figure 2.6.

If you elect to use a listed proprietary driver, Ubuntu first confirms that you are happy to proceed and then automatically downloads and installs the driver. This may require you to log out and back in again for the driver to take effect.

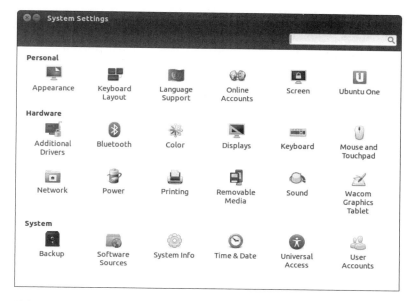

FIGURE 2.5   Adjust your system settings.

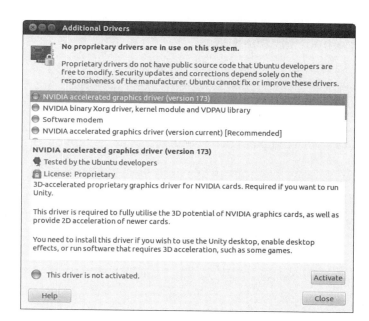

FIGURE 2.6   Toggle the usage of proprietary and other drivers with a simple point-and-click interface.

For the most part, Ubuntu detects and configures the majority of graphics cards from the start, and even if it has problems, it attempts to give you a display of some sort. This feature is known as *BulletProofX*, and it gives you access to tools that may help you fix your problem by trying different combinations of graphics cards and monitors.

Detecting and Configuring a Printer

Setting up a printer in Linux used to be so difficult that previous editions of this book included an entire chapter filled with command-line magic and scary-looking configuration files. This is no longer the case most of the time. Ubuntu includes drivers for many printers, and it is usually easier to install and use a printer in Ubuntu than in other operating systems. This is not an absolute rule, though. Some printer manufacturers do not write and release drivers for Linux, and for some printers, no open source driver exists. It is still a good idea to spend some time on the Internet searching for printers that are well known to work with Linux before buying. One great resource is the Open Printing database from The Linux Foundation, at www.openprinting.org/printers.

If you choose wisely, all you need to do is plug your printer into the computer and turn it on. In many cases, Ubuntu finds the printer and adds the driver automatically. Within a couple of minutes, you should be able to use it. You can find Printing in the System Settings menu and use it to see all installed and configured printers and change their settings. From here, you can choose to enable printer sharing on a network, set options for default print quality, print a test page, and more.

Configuring Power Management in Ubuntu

Using the Power option in the System Settings menu, you can control how Ubuntu will handle power-saving features in specific situations (see Figure 2.7). You can have the display dim the backlight to use less power when on battery, put the display to sleep after a certain amount of inactivity, spin down your hard disks (kind of like turning them off, but not completely; this just makes them stop moving until a request is made from them, saving power in the interim), and set your computer to suspend, hibernate, or turn off when the battery reaches a certain level.

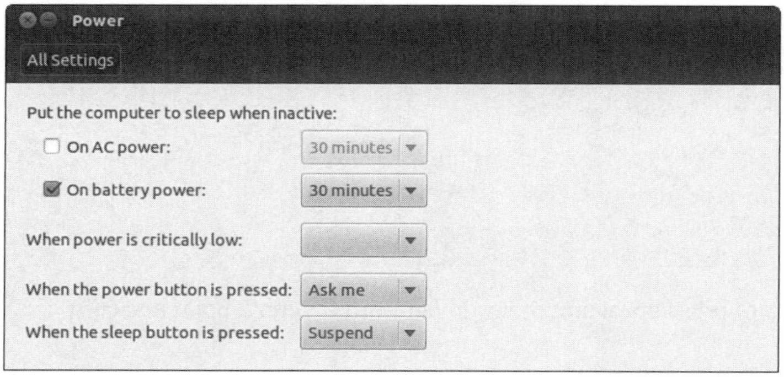

FIGURE 2.7   Configure specific power-related actions with Power Management Preferences.

Ubuntu provides good support for suspend and hibernate. *Suspend* means that your computer writes its current state to memory and goes into a low-power mode, whereas *Hibernate* writes the current state of the system to disk and powers off the computer. Either way, your computer will start much faster the next time you use it.

Setting the Date and Time

Linux provides a system date and time; your computer hardware provides a hardware clock-based time. In many cases, it is possible for the two times to drift apart. Linux system time is based on the number of seconds elapsed since January 1, 1970. Your computer's hardware time depends on the type of clock chips installed on your PC's motherboard, and many motherboard chipsets are notoriously subject to drift.

Keeping accurate time is important on a single workstation, but it is critically important in a network environment. Backups, scheduled downtimes, and other networkwide actions need to be accurately coordinated.

The Ubuntu installer sets the date and time during the installation process when it asks for your location. If you move or just want to change the settings (for example, to have your computer automatically synchronize its clock with official time servers on the Internet), you can do so.

Changing the Time and Date

Ubuntu's graphical tool is the simplest way to set your system date and time and the most obvious for a desktop user. The client is called Time & Date in the System Settings menu.

To make any changes to this tool, you need to unlock it by clicking the Unlock button. Only a user who has administrator privileges may use this tool, and you must enter your password to authenticate. After you've done this, you can change any of the options.

Manually set the date and time in the GUI (see Figure 2.8), or have your computer obtain updated date and time information via the Internet by selecting Automatically from the Internet. The Clock tab includes settings to adjust what is displayed at the upper right of your desktop screen.

Using the date Command

Use the date command to display or set your Linux system time. This command requires you to use a specific sequence of numbers to represent the desired date and time. To see your Linux system's idea of the current date and time, use the date command like this:

```
matthew@seymour:~$ date
Sat Sep  4 10:20:51 MST 2010
```

To adjust your system's time (for example, to September 4, 2010 at 10:33 a.m.), use a command line with the month, day, hour, minute, and year, like so:

```
matthew@seymour:~$ sudo date 090410332010
Sat Sep  4 10:33:00 MST 2010
```

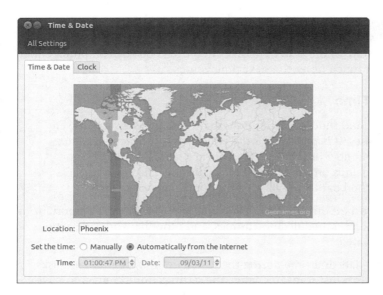

FIGURE 2.8   Set your system date and time with this GUI.

Using the hwclock Command

Use the hwclock command to display or set your Linux system time, display or set your PC's hardware clock, or to synchronize the system and hardware times. To see your hardware date and time, use hwclock with its --show option, like so:

```
matthew@seymour:~$ sudo hwclock --show
Sat 04 Sep 2010 05:25:17 PM MST  -0.806770 seconds
```

Use hwclock with its —set and —date options to manually set the hardware clock, as follows:

```
matthew@seymour:~$ sudo hwclock --set --date "09/04/10 10:33:00"
matthew@seymour:~$ hwclock --show
Sat 04 Sep 2010 10:33:09 AM MST  -0.904668 seconds
```

In these examples, the hardware clock has been set using hwclock, which is then used again to verify the new hardware date and time. You can also use hwclock to set the Linux system date and time using your hardware clock's values with the Linux system date and time.

For example, to set the system time from your PC's hardware clock, use the --hctosys option, like so:

```
matthew@seymour:~$ sudo hwclock --hctosys
```

To set your hardware clock using the system time, use the --sytohc option, like so:

```
matthew@seymour:~$ sudo hwclock --systohc
```

Configuring Wireless Networks

Wireless networking used to be a bear to configure for Linux, requiring a lot of complicated steps to connect to a wireless network. That has become a much easier task, and Ubuntu includes a great utility called Network Manager that makes connecting to and managing wireless networks extremely easy.

When you log in to Ubuntu, the Network Manager applet appears in the top panel (see Figure 2.9). This applet handles and monitors network connections.

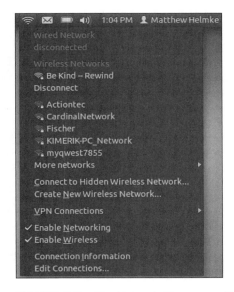

FIGURE 2.9   The Network Manager notification applet, shown here already connected to a wireless network.

Click the applet icon in the toolbar to connect to a wireless network. If your wireless access point broadcasts its *service set identifier (SSID)*, it should appear in the list under wireless networks. Click the desired network, and Network Manager detects what encryption (if any) is in use and asks you for the passkey. Enter this and Network Manager starts the wireless connection. The passkey is then stored in the default keyring, a secure area that is unique to your login. From now on, whenever you log in to Ubuntu and are in range of this network, Network Manager will start the connection automatically.

If for some reason your wireless network does not appear (you might have your SSID hidden), you must use the Connect to Other Wireless Network option, in which you enter the network name, wireless security type, and when needed, the password for the connection.

Network Manager can handle WEP and WPA Personal encryption. You are advised to use WPA encryption because it is the stronger of the two. WEP encryption is easily broken.

Network Manager can also connect to Cisco VPN connections, using the vpnc software. Install this from the Ubuntu repositories (see Chapter 9), and you will be able to specify connection settings as appropriate, or if you have access to a predefined configuration (PCF file), you can import it directly into Network Manager.

References

In lieu of reference material for this chapter, you are instead directed to read Chapter 3.

CHAPTER 3

Working with Unity

IN THIS CHAPTER

▶ Foundations and the X Server

▶ Using Unity, a Primer

▶ Power Shortcuts

▶ References

Imagine a world of black screens with white text, or for those of you who remember, dark green screens with light green text. That used to be the primary interface for users to access computers. Computing has moved on significantly and has adopted the *graphical user interface (GUI)*, as standard on most desktop and workstation platforms. Not only that, but GUIs have gradually changed and evolved over time. This chapter starts with low-level information about what lies underneath the GUI and builds up to a description of the Unity desktop and how to use it.

Foundations and the X Server

Ubuntu uses the X Window System, the graphical networking interface found on many Linux distributions that provides the foundation for a wide range of graphical tools and window managers. More commonly known as just X, it can also be referred to as X11R7 and X11 (as found on Mac OS X). Coming from the world-renowned Massachusetts Institute of Technology, X has gone through several versions, each of which has extended and enhanced the technology. The open-source implementation is managed by the X.Org foundation, whose board includes several key figures from the open-source world.

The best way to think about how X works is to see it as a client/server system. The X server provides services to programs that have been developed to make the most of the graphical and networking capabilities that are available under the server and in the supported libraries. X.Org provides versions for many platforms, including Linux and Mac OS X. Originally implemented as XFree86, X.Org was forked when a row broke out over certain restrictions that were going to be included in the XFree86 license. Taking a snapshot of code that was licensed under the previous version of the license, X.Org drove forward with its own implementation based on the code. Almost in unison, most Linux distributions turned away from XFree86 and switched their development and efforts to X.Org.

A desktop environment for X provides one or more window managers and a suite of clients that conform to a standard graphical interface based on a common set of software libraries. When they are used to develop associated clients, these libraries provide graphical consistency for the client windows, menus, buttons, and other onscreen components, along with some common keyboard controls and client dialogs. In this chapter, you learn how to work with GNOME and learn something about the version of X that is included with Ubuntu. If you want to learn more about some of the other desktop environments that are available to use with Ubuntu, including KDE and Xfce, take a look at Chapter 7, "Other Ubuntu Desktops."

The Ubuntu Family

When people talk about Ubuntu, they generally mean the standard distribution, which uses the GNOME window manager. However, a number of derivatives of Ubuntu use other window managers, and they are freely available for you to download and use. For instance, Kubuntu uses the KDE window manager, whereas Xubuntu uses Xfce. Despite their visual differences, all three rely on the same core system. It is easy for you to add that window manager to your existing system by using one of the *-desktop meta-packages. These packages are designed to install all the base applications that are linked to that version of Ubuntu, so installing the kubuntu-desktop package automatically installs all the software needed for Kubuntu while retaining your existing desktop environment.

Basic X Concepts

The underlying engine of X11 is the X protocol, which provides a system of managing displays on local and remote desktops. The protocol uses a client/server model that allows an abstraction of the drawing of client windows and other decorations locally and over a network. An X server draws client windows, dialog boxes, and buttons that are specific to the local hardware and in response to client requests. The client, however, does not have to be specific to the local hardware. This means that system administrators can set up a network with a large server and clients and enable users to view and use those clients on workstations with totally different CPUs and graphics displays.

Because X offers users a form of distributed processing, Ubuntu can be used as a very cheap desktop platform for clients that connect to a powerful X server. The more powerful the X server, the larger the number of X-based clients that can be accommodated. This functionality can breathe new life into older hardware, pushing most of the graphical processing on to the server. A fast network is a must if you intend to run many X clients because X can become bandwidth hungry.

NOTE

A great way to demonstrate the capability of X to handle remote clients is Edubuntu's use of LTSP, covered in Chapter 31, "Linux Terminal Server Project (LTSP)." It is designed to set up a main server and a set of dumb terminals that display programs that are being run on the server.

X is hugely popular in the UNIX and Linux world for a variety of reasons. That it supports nearly every hardware graphics system is a strong point. This and strong multiplatform programming standards give it a solid foundation of developers committed to X. Another key benefit of X is its networking capability, which plays a central point in administration of many desktops and can also assist in the deployment of a thin-client computing environment. Being able to launch applications on remote desktops and also standardize installations highlight the versatility of this powerful application.

More recent versions of X have also included support for shaped windows (that is, nonrectangular), graphical login managers (also known as *display managers*), and compressed fonts. Each release of X brings more features designed to enhance the user experience, including being able to customize how X client applications appear, right down to buttons and windows. Most office and home environments run Linux and X on their local machines. The more-enlightened companies and users harness the power of the networking features of X, enabling thin-client environments and allowing the use of customized desktops designed specifically for that company. Having applications launch from a single location makes the lives of system administrators a lot easier because they have to work on only one machine, rather than several.

Using X

X.Org (www.x.org) is the X server that is used with Ubuntu. The base distribution consists of many packages, including the server, support and development libraries, fonts, various clients, and documentation. An additional 1,000 or more X clients, fonts, and documentation are also available in the Ubuntu repositories.

The /usr directory and its subdirectories contain the majority of the Xorg software. Some important subdirectories are as follows:

- ▶ **/usr/bin**—This is the location of the X server and various X clients. (Note that not all X clients require active X sessions.)

- ▶ **/usr/include**—This is the path to the files necessary for developing X clients and graphics such as icons.

- ▶ **/usr/lib**—This directory contains required software libraries to support the X server and clients.

- ▶ **/usr/lib/X11**—This directory contains fonts, default client resources, system resources, documentation, and other files that are used during X sessions and for various X clients. You will also find a symbolic link to this directory, named X11, under the /usr/lib directory.

▶ **/usr/lib/modules**—This path to drivers and the X server modules used by the X server enables use of various graphics cards.

The main components required for an active local X session are installed on your system if you choose to use a graphical desktop. These components are the X server, miscellaneous fonts, a *terminal client* (that is, a program that provides access to a shell prompt), and a client known as a *window manager*. Window managers administer onscreen displays, including overlapping and tiling windows, command buttons, title bars, and other onscreen decorations and features.

Elements of the `xorg.conf` File

Traditionally, the most important file for Xorg has been the `xorg.conf` configuration file. This file contained configuration information that was vital for X to function correctly and was usually created during the installation of Ubuntu.

BulletProofX

Ubuntu now comes with a useful feature called BulletProofX. In short, it is designed to work no matter what may happen. So, in the event of some cataclysmic event that destroys your main X system, you will still have some graphical way of getting yourself back into a fully functional X-based system.

Modern versions of Xorg do not create an `xorg.conf` file by default. Instead, various files ending in `*.conf` reside in the `/usr/share/X11/xorg.conf.d` directory and are automatically loaded by X at boot, prior to reading any `xorg.conf`. These files can each contain one or more sections in the same format used by `xorg.conf`. Users can create the file and continue making custom configurations in `/etc/xorg.conf` as has been traditionally done, but the file is not created by default. What is included in the previously mentioned individual files should not be changed, but you may override those settings by creating your own `xorg.conf` file.

NOTE

We refer to using an `xorg.conf` file from here on, but keep the preceding information in mind to prevent confusion.

Let's take a look at the potential contents of `xorg.conf` so that you can get an idea of what X is looking for. The components, or sections, of the `xorg.conf` file specify the X session or *server layout*, along with pathnames for files that are used by the server, any options relating directly to the server, any optional support modules needed, information relating to the mouse and keyboard attached to the system, the graphics card installed, the monitor in use, and the resolution and color depth that Ubuntu uses. These are the essential components:

- ▶ **ServerLayout**—Defines the display, defines one or more screen layouts, and names input devices.

- ▶ **Files**—Defines the location of colors, fonts, or port number of the font server.

- ▶ **Module**—Tells the X server what graphics display support code modules to load.

- ▶ **InputDevice**—Defines the input devices, such as the keyboard and mouse; multiple devices can be used.

- ▶ **Monitor**—Defines the capabilities of any attached display; multiple monitors can be used.

- ▶ **Device**—Defines one or more graphics cards and specifies what optional features (if any) to enable or disable.

- ▶ **Screen**—Defines one or more resolutions, color depths, perhaps a default color depth, and other settings.

The following sections provide short descriptions of these elements; the xorg.conf man page contains full documentation of all the options and other keywords you can use to customize your desktop settings.

The ServerLayout Section

As noted previously, the ServerLayout section of the xorg.conf file defines the display and screen layouts, and it names the input devices. A typical ServerLayout section from an automatically configured xorg.conf file might look like this:

```
Section "ServerLayout"
        Identifier       "single head configuration"
        Screen        0  "Screen0" 0 0
        InputDevice      "Mouse0" "CorePointer"
        InputDevice      "Keyboard0" "CoreKeyboard"
        InputDevice      "DevInputMice" "AlwaysCore"
EndSection
```

In this example, a single display is used (the numbers designate the position of a screen), and two default input devices, Mouse0 and Keyboard0, are used for the session.

The Files Section

The Files section of the xorg.conf file might look like this:

```
Section "Files"
    RgbPath       "/usr/lib/X11/rgb"
    FontPath   "unix/:7100"
EndSection
```

This section lists available session colors (by name, in the text file rgb.txt) and the port number to the X font server. The font server, xfs, is started at boot and does not require an active X session. If a font server is not used, the FontPath entry could instead list each font directory under the /usr/lib/X11/fonts directory, as in this example:

```
FontPath "/usr/lib/X11/fonts/100dpi"
FontPath "/usr/lib/X11/fonts/misc"
FontPath "/usr/lib/X11/fonts/75dpi"
FontPath "/usr/lib/X11/fonts/type1"
FontPath "/usr/lib/X11/fonts/Speedo"
...
```

These directories contain the default compressed fonts that are available for use during the X session. The font server is configured by using the file named config under the /etc/X11/fs directory. This file contains a listing, or catalog, of fonts for use by the font server. By adding an alternate-server entry in this file and restarting the font server, you can specify remote font servers for use during X sessions. This can help centralize font support and reduce local storage requirements (even though only 25MB is required for the almost 5,000 fonts installed with Ubuntu and X).

The Module Section

The Module section of the xorg.conf file specifies loadable modules or drivers to load for the X session. This section might look like this:

```
Section "Module"
        Load    "dbe"
        Load    "extmod"
        Load    "fbdevhw"
        Load "glx"
        Load "record"
        Load    "freetype"
        Load    "type1"
        Load    "dri"

EndSection
```

These modules can range from special video card support to font rasterizers. The modules are located in subdirectories under the /usr/lib/modules directory.

The InputDevice Section

The InputDevice section configures a specific device, such as a keyboard or mouse, as in this example:

```
Section "InputDevice"
        Identifier    "Keyboard0"
        Driver        "kbd"
```

```
        Option   "XkbModel"      "pc105"
        Option   "XkbLayout"     "us"
EndSection
Section "InputDevice"
        Identifier  "Mouse0"
        Driver      "mouse"
        Option      "Protocol" "IMPS/2"
        Option      "Device" "/dev/input/mice"
        Option      "ZAxisMapping" "4 5"
        Option      "Emulate3Buttons" "yes"
EndSection
```

You can configure multiple devices, and multiple InputDevice sections might exist. The preceding example specifies a basic keyboard and a two-button PS/2 mouse (actually, a Dell touchpad pointer). An InputDevice section that specifies use of a USB device could be used at the same time (to enable mousing with PS/2 and USB pointers) and might look like this:

```
Section "InputDevice"
        Identifier  "Mouse0"
        Driver      "mouse"
        Option      "Device" "/dev/input/mice"
        Option      "Protocol" "IMPS/2"
        Option      "Emulate3Buttons" "off"
        Option      "ZAxisMapping" "4 5"
EndSection
```

The Monitor Section

The Monitor section configures the designated display device as declared in the ServerLayout section, as shown in this example:

```
Section "Monitor"
        Identifier   "Monitor0"
        VendorName   "Monitor Vendor"
        ModelName    "Monitor Model"
        DisplaySize  300     220
        HorizSync    31.5-48.5
        VertRefresh 50-70
        Option "dpms"
EndSection
```

Note that the X server automatically determines the best video timings according to the horizontal and vertical sync and refresh values in this section. If required, old-style mode-line entries (used by distributions and servers prior to XFree86 4.0) might still be used. If the monitor is automatically detected when you configure X (see the "Configuring X" section, later in this chapter), its definition and capabilities are inserted in your xorg.conf file from the MonitorsDB database. This database contains more than 600 monitors and is located in the /usr/share/hwdata directory.

The Device Section

The Device section provides details about the video graphics chipset used by the computer, as in this example:

```
Section "Device"
        Identifier        "Intel Corporation Mobile 945GM/GMS,\943/940GML Express
Integrated Graphics Controller"
        Driver            "intel"
        BusID             "PCI:0:2:0"
EndSection
```

This example identifies an installed video card as using an integrated Intel 945 graphics chipset. The Driver entry tells the Xorg server to load the intel kernel module. Different chipsets have different options. For example, here's the entry for a NeoMagic video chipset:

```
Section "Device"
        Identifier     "NeoMagic (laptop/notebook)"
        Driver         "neomagic"
        VendorName     "NeoMagic (laptop/notebook)"
        BoardName       "NeoMagic (laptop/notebook)"
    Option      "externDisp"
    Option      "internDisp"
EndSection
```

In this example, the Device section specifies the driver for the graphics card (neomagic_drv.o) and enables two chipset options (externDisp and internDisp) to allow display on the laptop's LCD screen and an attached monitor.

The Xorg server supports hundreds of different video chipsets. If you configure X11 but subsequently change the installed video card, you need to edit the existing Device section or generate a new xorg.conf file, using one of the X configuration tools discussed in this chapter, to reflect the new card's capabilities. You can find details about options for some chipsets in a companion man page. You should look at these sources for hints about optimizations and troubleshooting.

The Screen Section

The Screen section ties together the information from the previous sections (using the Screen0, Device, and Monitor Identifier entries). It can also specify one or more color depths and resolutions for the session. Here's an example:

```
Section "Screen"
        Identifier "Screen0"
        Device     "Videocard0"
        Monitor    "Monitor0"
        DefaultDepth    24
        SubSection "Display"
                Viewport   0 0
```

```
        Depth      16
        Modes      "1024x768" "800x600" "640x480"
  EndSubSection
```

```
EndSection
```

In this example, a color depth of thousands of colors and a resolution of 1024768 is the default, with optional resolutions of 800 x 600 and 64 x 480. Multiple `Display` subsection entries with different color depths and resolutions (with settings such as Depth 24 for millions of colors) can be used if supported by the graphics card and monitor combination. You can also use a `DefaultDepth` entry (which is 24, or thousands of colors, in the example), along with a specific color depth to standardize display depths in installations.

You can also specify a desktop resolution larger than that supported by the hardware in your monitor or notebook display. This setting is known as a *virtual* resolution in the `Display` subsection. This allows, for example, an 800 x 600 display to pan (that is, slide around inside) a virtual window of 1024 x 768.

NOTE

If your monitor and graphics card support multiple resolutions and the settings are properly configured, you can use the key combination of Ctrl+Alt+(Keypad)+ or Ctrl+Alt+(Keypad)- to change resolutions on-the-fly during your X session.

Starting X

You can start X sessions in a variety of ways. The Ubuntu installer sets up the system to have Linux boot directly to an X session using a display manager called *LightDM*, for Light(weight) Display Manager. This is an X client that provides a graphical login. After you log in, you use a local session (running on your computer) or, if the system is configured to do so, an X session running on a remote computer on the network.

Logging in via a display manager requires you to enter a username and password. You can also start X sessions from the command line. The following sections describe these two methods.

NOTE

If you have used the Server install, your system boots to a text login. See Chapter 10, "Command-Line Quickstart," for more information about what to do here.

Using a Display Manager

An X display manager presents a graphical login that requires a username and password to be entered before access is granted to the X desktop. It also allows you to choose a different desktop for your X session. Whether an X display manager is presented after you boot

Linux is controlled by a *runlevel*—a system state entry in /etc/event.d/. The following runlevels as handled by Ubuntu are as follows:

- ▶ 0—Halt (Do *not* set initdefault to this.)
- ▶ 1—Multiuser text mode
- ▶ 2—X graphical multiuser mode
- ▶ 6—Reboot (Do *not* set initdefault to this.)

You may see mention of runlevels 3 through 5; these can be ignored because they are treated the same as runlevel 2 in Ubuntu. Historically, Ubuntu used the /etc/inittab file to handle runlevels, but with Upstart, this file no longer exists. (See Chapter 14, "The Boot Process," for information about Upstart.) Instead, there are several files under the /etc/events.d/ directory, including an individual file for each of the virtual consoles (accessible by pressing Ctrl+Alt+F1 to F7). However, you can still create an inittab file, if you want to override any defaults held by Ubuntu. Make sure you create the inittab file as root and include at least one line similar to the following:

```
id:1:initdefault:
```

This forces your system to start up in text mode.

Changing Window Managers

Ubuntu makes it fairly painless to switch to another window manager or desktop environment. By *desktop environment,* we refer to not only the window manager but also the suite of related applications, such as productivity or configuration tools.

First, you need to ensure that you have the relevant desktop environment installed on your system; the easiest way to do this is by installing the relevant *-desktop package (as described earlier in the sidebar "The Ubuntu Family") You can do this by installing the package kubuntu-desktop, for example (in the case of a KDE desktop); just search for "desktop" and look for Xubuntu or Kubuntu, and so on. After the download and installation is complete (you might want to grab a coffee while you wait because these packages include a ton of dependencies and take some time to download, install, and configure), you are all set to change environments.

Next, you need to log out of Ubuntu. When you return to the login page, select your name as usual and then select the session named for the desktop you want to use. Chapter 7 provides a brief introduction to some of the desktop environments other than Unity that are available from the Ubuntu repositories.

Using Unity, a Primer

Unity is a fresh take on the GUI. It has been created with the assistance of user interface professionals and graphic designers and aims toward elegance, beauty, and efficiency while providing obvious ways to perform tasks. Unity is a long-term project being created in steps that coincide with Ubuntu's six-month release schedule. Each new Ubuntu release benefits from new features and extended functionality. Unity is new, but it is already growing in popularity and is considered to be at the forefront of GUI development, not just for Linux, but for human-computer interaction in general. This section gives a tour of the basic features and use and then moves into more specific details that are likely to thrill power users.

Mark Shuttleworth on Unity

"Our goal with Unity is unprecedented ease of use, visual style, and performance on the Linux desktop."

—from a blog post on August 16, 2011; www.markshuttleworth.com/archives/717

The Desktop

When you boot your computer and log in to a Unity session, you are greeted by the desktop you see in Figure 3.1. This screen is made up of many parts, each of which is described in this chapter.

FIGURE 3.1   The default look of Ubuntu Unity.

The Launcher

To the left of the screen is a vertical bar. This is the Launcher (see Figure 3.2). Icons in the Launcher represent programs that are either running or which have been set to be listed in the Launcher at all times. Click an icon to open a program. Right-click an icon for additional options, including an option to keep an item in the Launcher at all times.

FIGURE 3.2   The Launcher as it looks by default.

A special icon in the Launcher is the Workspace Switcher. It is near the bottom of the main set of icons and looks like a rectangle divided into four. Click this icon to show all workspaces. Double-click one of the workspaces when they appear on the screen to switch to it.

Workspaces

Workspaces are kind of like extra screens. Unity has four workspaces by default. You can open an application on one workspace, and then keep it open there while switching to another workspace where you can open something else. Then, switching back and forth is as easy as pressing a couple of keys. The four workspaces are arranged in a 2 x 2 square. To switch between them, use Ctrl+Alt and an arrow key.

The Dash

Click the Ubuntu logo icon at the top of the Launcher to open the Dash (see Figure 3.3). The Dash is the primary way to find programs and files in Unity. At the bottom of the Dash is a row of icons. These represent *lenses*, which are different ways to focus your searching with the Dash.

FIGURE 3.3   The Dash helps you find programs and files.

The default Dash lens is represented by a house icon. This lens gives a set of shortcuts to often-used features. At the top is a Search box that searches your computer for programs, files, and directories that match any search terms input and then categorizes the results according to type (see Figure 3.4).

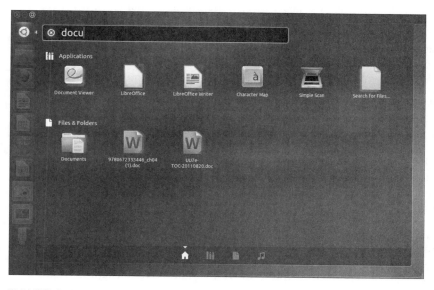

FIGURE 3.4   Sorted results in the main Dash lens.

The applications Dash lens is represented by a ruler-pencil-pen icon. This lens will list and search installed applications and also applications that are available from the Ubuntu Software Center (see Chapter 9, "Managing Software"), as in Figure 3.5. You can click to view more results and perform a visual search if you do not know the name of a program.

FIGURE 3.5   Exploring applications in the Dash.

The files and folders Dash lens is represented by a sheet of paper icon. You can search by entering a term in the Search box or visually by clicking through what is shown here, as in Figure 3.6.

Other Dash lenses may appear depending on your configuration. Possibilities include, but are not limited to, a Music lens for audio files and a Gwibber lens for interactive media such as Twitter and Facebook updates. More are likely to arrive as Unity matures.

In any Dash lens in which it appears, you can click Filter results to view predefined ways to filter what is shown. Figure 3.7 shows a list of available filters for the applications lens.

The Panel

The panel is the bar across the top of the screen. When a program is being used, it will house various menus and buttons. (Some of these appear only when you hover your mouse over the panel; so if you can't find the File menu or close button, point at the panel with your mouse, and it is likely to appear.) The right side of the panel has a series of useful indicators. The Networking indicator was discussed in Chapter 2, "Post-Installation Configuration," because it is often needed right away to connect a computer to the Internet. Other indicators:

▶ Help manage your mail and social applications like chat (envelope icon).

▶ Show your batter status and provide quick access to power settings.

▶ Provide volume and playback controls for the Banshee media player.

▶ Give quick access to the clock and calendar.

▶ Show active users and sessions.

▶ Give convenient access to commonly used system administration options and the logout menu.

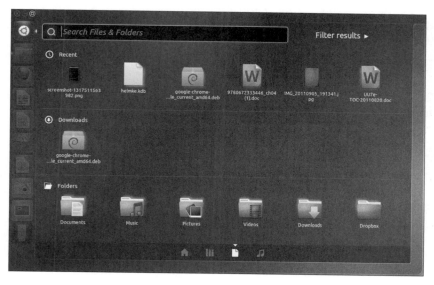

FIGURE 3.6   Exploring applications in the Dash.

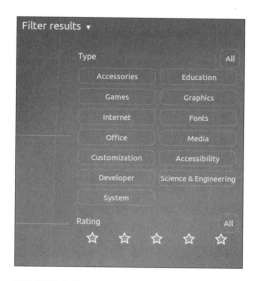

FIGURE 3.7   Filtering applications in the Dash.

Customizing and Configuring Unity

Everyone likes to customize. Unity is quite new, and as a result, not everything is customizable (yet). All existing options for customization and system settings are available in the System Settings menu.

System Settings

Search for "system settings" in the Dash. Click the System Settings icon to open the menu. The menu includes entries that allow you to change your desktop appearance, set up online accounts, configure additional languages for the system to use for colors, keyboards, displays, and much more (see Figure 3.8).

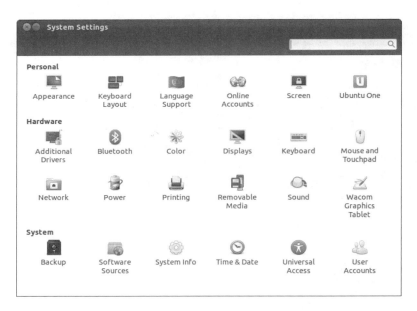

FIGURE 3.8   The System Settings menu.

Other Settings

Many other GUI-related settings can be configured or adjusted by installing a package from the Ubuntu repositories called the CompizConfig Settings Manager (see Chapter 9). The documentation for these settings is not always clear, so go slowly.

Power Shortcuts

Often, power users want to avoid using the mouse. They don't want to take their hands off of the keyboard unless absolutely necessary because doing so slows them down. Here are some of the more useful keyboard shortcuts that readers of this book are likely to appreciate, many of which can be configured or adjusted by installing a package from the Ubuntu repositories called the CompizConfig Settings Manager (see Chapter 9):

- ▶ Use the Special key (that is, the Windows key) to open the Dash. Click Esc to close the Dash without selecting anything in it.

- ▶ Use the middle mouse button to click on an icon in the Launcher to open more than one instance of the same program. On a laptop, you can do this by clicking both right and left buttons simultaneously.

- ▶ Holding Alt+Tab brings up a menu of icons showing open programs so that you may switch between them quickly. Hold Alt and press Tab repeatedly to move from one program to the next until you reach the one you desire. Shift+Alt+Tab scrolls through them in reverse order. This and the next shortcut work together as a powerful combination when the application you want has multiple windows or instances.

- ▶ Switching from Alt+Tab to Alt+` (on an English keyboard; for other keyboards, read on) modifies the Alt+Tab menu so that it shows miniature images of open program windows when there are multiple instances of the same program. Hold Alt and press ` repeatedly to scroll through and select a specific instance. If you begin this while the desktop focus is on an instance of a program that has multiple instances open, you automatically begin with this set of open instances to select from among them. (On an English keyboard, ` is the key just above the Tab key. For other language keyboards, it is the whatever key in this same location, regardless of the character represented on the key itself.)

- ▶ Icons in the Launcher indicate when multiple instances of a program are open or when a program has multiple windows. Click twice on an icon in the Launcher that shows multiple arrows next to it, and all of its windows will be displayed for you to select the one you desire.

- ▶ Click PrtSc (Print Screen) to take a screenshot of the current workspace.

- ▶ Use Special + T to open the trash can.

- ▶ Click Ctrl+Alt+*arrow-key* to move up, down, right, and left from workspace to workspace.

References

- ▶ **www.gnome.org/**—The launch point for more information about GNOME, links to new clients, and GNOME development projects.

- ▶ **www.x.org/**—Curators of the X Window System.

- ▶ **www.x.org/Downloads_mirror.html**—Want to download the source to the latest revision of X? Start at this list of mirror sites.

- ▶ **www.xfree86.org/**—Home of The XFree86 Project, Inc., which provided a graphical interface for Linux for nearly 10 years.

▶ **https://wiki.ubuntu.com/X**—The place to get started when learning about X and Ubuntu.

▶ **https://wiki.ubuntu.com/X/Config**—Great information about configuring X on Ubuntu.

▶ **http://www.freedesktop.org/wiki/Software/LightDM**—LightDM, a new window manager.

▶ **http://castrojo.tumblr.com/post/4795149014/the-power-users-guide-to-unity**—From Jorge Castro, a leader in the Ubuntu community, this is a great guide to moving beyond the basics. Because Unity is still maturing, some info here may be out-of-date, but at the time of this writing, it is the best resource outside of this book.

CHAPTER 4

On the Internet

The Internet is everywhere. From cell phones to offices, from game consoles to iPads, we are surrounded by multiple access routes to online information and communication. Ubuntu is no outsider when it comes to accessing information through the Internet; it comes equipped with all the tools you need to connect to other people across the globe.

In this chapter, we look at some of the popular Internet applications that are available with Ubuntu. You'll find out about Firefox and the new option, Google Chrome. We also investigate some of the email clients available. Other topics include RSS feed readers, instant messaging (through IRC and other networks), and reading newsgroups.

A Brief Introduction to the Internet

The Internet itself was first brought to life by the U.S. Department of Defense in 1969. It was called ARPANET after the Department of Defense's Advanced Research Projects Agency. Designed to build a network that would withstand major catastrophe (this was the peak of the Cold War), it soon grew to encompass more and more networks to build the Internet. Then, in 1991, Tim Berners-Lee of CERN developed the idea of the World Wide Web, including *Hypertext Transfer Protocol (HTTP)* and *Hypertext Markup Language (HTML)*. This gave us what we now know to be the Internet.

Getting Started with Firefox

One of the most popular web browsers, and in fact the default web browser in Ubuntu, is Mozilla Firefox (see Figure 4.1). Built on a solid code base that is derived from the Mozilla suite, Firefox offers an open source and more secure alternative to surfing the Internet using Internet Explorer, regardless of your operating system.

FIGURE 4.1   Mozilla Firefox—rediscover the Web. Firefox enables you to add on numerous extensions, further enhancing your experience.

In Ubuntu, you can find Firefox in the menu at Applications, Internet. An even simpler way to start Firefox is to click the small Firefox icon in the top panel next to the System menu. Either way, Firefox opens.

Beyond the basic program are a wealth of plug-ins and extensions that can increase the capabilities of Firefox beyond simple web browsing. Plug-ins such as Shockwave, Flash, and Java are available for installation instantly, offered to you when first needed, as are multimedia codecs for viewing video content. Extensions provide useful additions to the browsing experience. For example, ForecastFox is an extension that gives you your local weather conditions, and Bandwidth Tester is a tool that calculates your current bandwidth. As Firefox grows, there will be more and more extensions and plug-ins that you can use to enhance your browsing pleasure.

You can find and obtain these plug-ins and extensions easily because Mozilla developers have created a site dedicated to helping you get more from Firefox. You don't have to search to find the site as there is a link in the Firefox menu at Tools, Add-ons, Get Add-ons that takes you directly to it. Particular favorites are the Adblock Plus and the StumbleUpon plug-ins. Adblock Plus enables you to nuke all those annoying banners and animations that take up so much bandwidth while you are browsing. StumbleUpon is a neat plug-in that takes you to web pages based on your preferences. Be warned, though, that StumbleUpon can be quite addictive, and you will end up wasting away many hours clicking the stumble button.

4

Flash

You can easily enable Flash in your browser by installing the `flashplugin-installer` package or better yet, you can deal with the whole issue of codecs and functionality for your entire operating system right off by installing `ubuntu-restricted-extras`. Either way, Ubuntu downloads the official package from Adobe and installs it on your system. A browser restart is required before you try to access any Flash-enabled content.

To make things even easier, if you have not yet installed this package and visit a web page that requires flash, a pop-up window appears with information and a link to help you install it easily.

Another plug-in that we make a lot of use of is Xmarks. If, like us, you work across multiple computers and operating systems, you will no doubt have had to re-create bookmarks at every different computer and try to keep them the same. Xmarks makes this whole process much easier by allowing you to synchronize your bookmarks to multiple browsers (for example, Firefox and Google Chrome) running on different operating systems (Windows, Mac OS X, or Linux).

Checking Out Google Chrome and Chromium

Anyone who has been paying attention to tech news over the past year has heard about the explosive appearance of Google Chrome (see Figure 4.2). This new browser is fast, secure, expandable with extensions, and the hottest new toy on geek desktops. It is based on WebKit and other technologies, and it downloads and renders quickly while being standards compliant. You can learn more about the easy installation of Google Chrome at www.google.com/chrome?platform=linux.

FIGURE 4.2   Google Chrome running in Ubuntu.

Chrome is not a completely open source, but the main foundational parts are made available as Google Chromium, shown in Figure 4.3, which has most of the functionality of Chrome, but it is missing the Google branding, automatic updates, and is used as the test and development foundation for Chrome releases. As a point of interest, chromium is the metal from which chrome is made, hence the names.

You can learn more about Chromium at http://code.google.com/chromium/. It used to be necessary to install Chromium from the Google website or from the Personal Package Archive of the Google Chromium developers. Now, you may simply install chromium-browser from the Ubuntu repositories.

Choosing an Email Client

Back in the earlier days of UNIX, there were various text-based email clients such as elm and pine (Pine Is Not Elm). Although they looked basic, they allowed the average user to interact with email, both for composing and reading correspondence, and had some sophisticated and useful features that might not have been expected. Still, when computing became mainstream, there was a realization that people wanted friendly *graphical user interfaces (GUIs)*. Soon there came a flood of email clients, some of them even cross-platform and compatible among Linux, Windows, and Mac OS X, and even traditional UNIX.

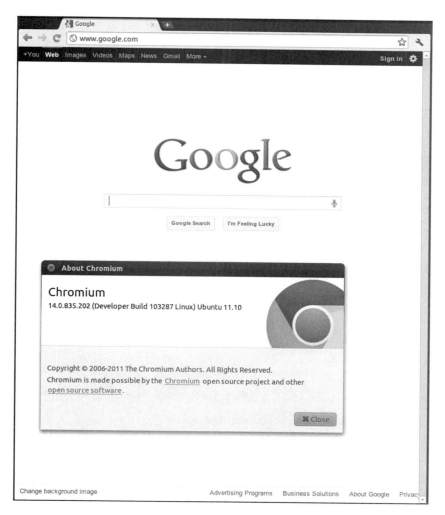

FIGURE 4.3   Chromium is the source from which Chrome is made, and it works very well.

Evolution

Up until Ubuntu 11.10, Evolution was the standard email client in Ubuntu, although to call it simply an email client is to sincerely underrate its usefulness as an application. Not only does it handle email, but it can also look after contacts and calendars and help you manage your tasks (see Figure 4.4).

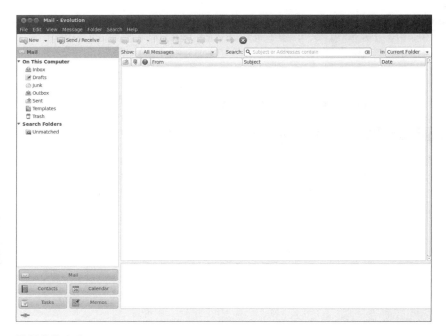

FIGURE 4.4   With Evolution, you can handle all your email and contacts, as well as make appointments and track tasks.

You need to have the following information to successfully configure Evolution (or any email client):

▶ Your email address

▶ Your incoming email server name and type (that is, pop.email.com, POP, and IMAP)

▶ Your username and password for the incoming mail server

▶ Your outgoing mail server name (that is, smtp.email.com)

As many people are moving to web-based mail options like Google's Gmail or Yahoo! Mail, email programs have started to decline in popularity. One thing that sets Evolution apart is that you can still use it for the other features and disable the email portion of the program by selecting "none" as your mail transfer agent instead of POP, IMAP, and so on. In addition, Evolution can interact with an existing web calendar program if it uses one of the common formats, such as CalDAV. This allows you to use your calendar remotely as you are used to, but also permits the Ubuntu desktop to have access to your events and embed them into your desktop panel (which it does by default using Evolution).

Mozilla Thunderbird

Mozilla Thunderbird (see Figure 4.5) is the sister program to Firefox and, starting with Ubuntu 11.10, is the default email application in Ubuntu. Whereas Firefox is designed to browse the Web, Thunderbird's specialty is communication. It can handle email, network news (see later in this chapter), and RSS feeds.

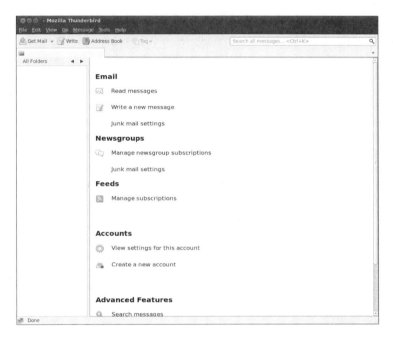

FIGURE 4.5   The natural companion to Firefox, Mozilla's lightweight email client, Thunderbird, can be found in use all over the world.

As with Firefox, there are many plug-ins and extensions to enhance your email. You can also use Thunderbird for Usenet news reading.

Other Mail Clients

The mail clients that we've covered are only a few of those available. Claws is very popular because it offers spell check while typing and is well suited for use in large network environments in which network overhead and RAM usage are important considerations. Mutt is an older text-based email program that is still beloved by sysadmins for its configurability and feature set, including the easy use of GPG keys for signing email. Alpine is another text-based program based on the classic Pine, with a few upgrades. Kmail is commonly used by lovers of the KDE desktop that is commonly run as a part of many Linux-based operating systems. All of these and more are available for installation from the Ubuntu software repositories.

RSS Readers

RSS is one of the protocols of Web 2.0, the current generation of Internet content. RSS has really taken off, thanks to adoption by a large number of websites and portals.

The key advantage of RSS is that you can quickly read news from your choice of websites at a time that suits you and from one location, meaning you don't have to go to each site to view their content. Some services offer just the articles' headlines, whereas others offer full articles for you to view. RSS feeds can be accessed in various ways, even through your web browser!

Firefox

Firefox implements RSS feeds as what it calls Live Bookmarks (shown in Figure 4.6), which are essentially bookmarks with subbookmarks, each linking to a new page from your chosen website. Some people like to have several news sites grouped together in a folder called News in the Firefox toolbar, because this allows them to quickly browse through a collection of sites and pick out articles of interest.

FIGURE 4.6   Live Bookmarks for Firefox, making all your news fixes just a mouse click away.

Liferea

Of course, not everyone wants to read RSS feeds with the browser. The main problem with reading RSS feeds with Firefox is that you get to see only the headline, rather than any actual text. This is where a dedicated RSS reader comes in handy, and Liferea is one of the best (see Figure 4.7).

It is not installed by default, but Liferea is available from the repositories under the name liferea. After it is installed, you can find it in the menu at Applications, Internet, Liferea.

By default, Liferea offers a number of RSS feeds, including Planet Debian, Groklaw, and Slashdot. Adding a new feed is straightforward. You select New Subscription under the Feeds menu and paste the URL of the RSS feed into the box. Liferea then retrieves all the current items available through that field and displays the feed name on the left side for you to select and start reading.

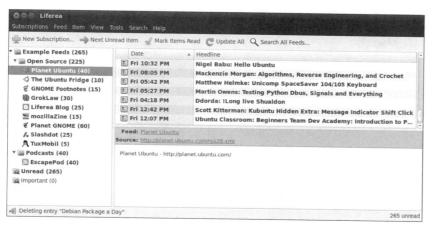

FIGURE 4.7   Read your daily news feeds with Liferea, a fantastic and easy-to-use RSS feed reader.

Instant Messaging and Video Conferencing with Empathy

Instant messaging is one of the biggest ways for people to interact over the Web. AOL was the primary force behind this, especially in America, but other networks and systems soon entered the market, providing users with a wealth of choice.

No longer just a consumer tool, instant messaging is now a part of the corporate world, with many companies deploying internal instant messaging software for collaboration.

Empathy is the default messaging program in Ubuntu; it can be found in the menu at Applications, Internet, Empathy and is shown in Figure 4.8. It supports text, voice, and video chat as well as file transfers using common protocols like Google Talk, AIM, and more. All you have to do is know your account information with a specific service and enter it in to Empathy—and the rest is easy.

You can learn more about Empathy at https://help.ubuntu.com/community/Empathy.

Internet Relay Chat

As documented in RFC 2812 and RFC 2813, the *Internet Relay Chat (IRC)* protocol is used for text conferencing. Like mail and news, IRC uses a client/server model. Although it is rare for an individual to set up and run an IRC server, it can be done. Most people use public IRC servers and access them with IRC clients. IRC is also the favorite and most common form of quick communication among developers in the Ubuntu community, so if that interests you, you will certainly want to learn to use this tool.

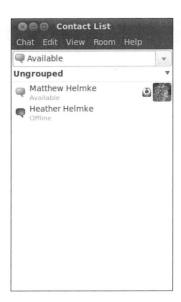

FIGURE 4.8   Empathy is easy to set up and use for great collaboration.

Ubuntu provides a number of graphical IRC clients in the repositories, including XChat, Pidgin, and Quassel. You can even use Empathy, although other products are better suited for this specific task. Ubuntu also makes the console clients epic and irssi available in the repositories for those who eschew X and a graphical interface. Don't laugh—there are actually many who do this, and not just server admins, especially because they can be run on a remote server and accessed over *Secure Shell (SSH)* using Byobu or Screen, allowing them to be left running 24/7 on that remote server. For more about Byobu and Screen, see Chapter 11, "Command-Line Master Class." If you don't already have a favorite IRC client, you should try them all.

XChat is a very popular IRC client, and the most common recommendation for IRC newcomers using Ubuntu, so we use it as an example. After you install the program, the documentation for XChat is available in /usr/share/docs/xchat. It is a good idea to read that before you begin because they include an introduction and cover some of the basics of IRC.

The XChat application enables you to assign yourself up to three nicknames. You can also specify your real name and your username. Because many people choose not to use their real names in IRC chat, you are free to enter any names you desire in any of the spaces provided. You can select multiple nicknames; you might be banned from an IRC channel under one name, and you could then rejoin using another. If this seems slightly juvenile to you, you are beginning to get an idea of the type of behavior on many IRC channels (but not the ones where serious developer and Ubuntu community interactions take place).

When you open the main XChat screen, a list of IRC servers appears, as shown in Figure 4.9. After you choose a server by double-clicking it, you can view a list of channels available on that server by choosing Window, Channel List. The XChat Channel List window appears. In that window, you can choose to join channels featuring topics that interest you. To join a channel, you double-click it. Ubuntu uses irc.freenode.net for the server and the primary support channel is #ubuntu.

FIGURE 4.9   The main XChat screen presents a list of available public servers from which to select.

The Wild Side of IRC

Do not be surprised at the number of lewd topics and the use of crude language on public IRC servers. For a humorous look at the topic of IRC cursing, see www.irc.org/fun_docs/nocuss.html. This site also offers some tips for maintaining IRC etiquette, which is essential if you do not want to be the object of any of that profanity. Here are some of the most important IRC etiquette rules:

▶ Do not use colored text, all-capitalized text, blinking text, or "bells" (beeps caused by sending ^G to a terminal).

▶ Show respect for others.

▶ Ignore people who act inappropriately.

After you select a channel, you can join in the conversation, which appears as onscreen text. The messages scroll down the screen as new messages appear. For an example, see Figure 4.10. You can continue learning about IRC at https://help.ubuntu.com/community/InternetRelayChat.

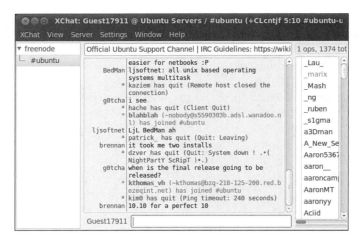

FIGURE 4.10   Join in an online chatroom about your favorite distro, with XChat.

TIP

You can establish your own IRC server, even though Ubuntu does not provide one. Setting up a server is not a task for anyone who is not well versed in Linux or IRC.

A popular server is IRCd, which you can obtain from ftp://ftp.irc.org/irc/server/. Before you download IRCd, look at the README file to determine what files you need to download, and read the information at www.irchelp.org/irchelp/ircd/.

Usenet Newsgroups

The concept of newsgroups revolutionized the way information was exchanged between people across a network. The Usenet network news system created a method for people to electronically communicate with large groups of people with similar interests. As you will see, many of the concepts of Usenet news are embodied in other forms of collaborative communication.

Usenet newsgroups act as a form of public bulletin board system. Any user can subscribe to individual newsgroups and send (or post) messages (called articles) to the newsgroup so that all the other subscribers of the newsgroup can read them. Some newsgroups include an administrator, who must approve each message before it is posted. These are called *moderated newsgroups*. Other newsgroups are open, allowing any subscribed member to post a message. When an article is posted to the newsgroup, it is transferred to all the other hosts in the news network.

Usenet newsgroups are divided into a hierarchy to make it easier to find individual newsgroups. The hierarchy levels are based on topics, such as computers, science, recreation, and social issues. Each newsgroup is named as a subset of the higher-level topic. For example, the newsgroup comp relates to all computer topics. The newsgroup comp.laptops relates to laptop computer issues. Often the hierarchy goes several layers deep. For example, the newsgroup comp.databases.oracle.server relates to Oracle server database issues.

NOTE

The format of newsgroup articles follows the strict guidelines defined in the Internet standards document *Request for Comments (RFC)* 1036. Each article must contain two distinct parts: header lines and a message body.

The header lines identify information about when and by whom the article was posted. The body of the message should contain only standard ASCII text characters. No binary characters or files should be posted within news articles. To get around this restriction, binary files are converted to text data, through the use of either the standard UNIX uuencode program or the newer *Multipurpose Internet Mail Extensions (MIME)* protocol. The resulting text file is then posted to the newsgroup. Newsgroup readers can then decode the posted text file back into its original binary form.

A collection of articles posted in response to a common topic is called a thread. A thread can contain many articles as users post messages in response to other posted messages. Some newsreader programs allow users to track articles based on the threads to which they belong. This helps simplify the organization of articles in the newsgroup.

TIP

The free news server, news.gmane.org, makes the Red Hat and Ubuntu mail lists available via newsgroups. The beta list is available as gmane.linux. redhat.rhl.beta. It is a handy way to read threaded discussions, and some prefer it to using the Ubuntu mail list archives.

The protocol used to transfer newsgroup articles from one host to another is *Network News Transfer Protocol (NNTP)*, defined in RFC 975. (You can search RFCs at ftp://metalab.unc. edu/pub/docs/rfc/; look at the file rfc-index.txt.) NNTP was designed as a simple client/server protocol that enables two hosts to exchange newsgroup articles in an efficient manner.

Whether or not your Ubuntu machine is set up as a news server, you can use a newsreader program to read newsgroup articles. The newsreader programs require just a connection to a news server. It does not matter whether the news server is on the same machine or is a remote news server on the other side of the world.

Several programs are available to connect to news servers to read and post articles in newsgroups. If you are interested in Usenet, you might want to check out a program from the Ubuntu repositories called Pan. Pan is a graphical newsreader client that can download and display all the newsgroups available on a server and display posted news articles.

However, Usenet is an old system that predates the creation of the World Wide Web. It was the place to be in the early days and the source of many great memories, but today is little better than a ghost town with wind-blown tumbleweeds, spam, and illegal exchanges of pirated content. Most Internet service providers used to run free Usenet servers, and connecting was easy and common, but most of the free ones are gone now and traffic has dwindled. Feel free to experiment or try to relive the glory days, but Usenet is, alas, well past its prime.

Ubuntu One Cloud Storage

Anyone who has installed Ubuntu has access to a free online cloud storage application called Ubuntu One. The service is built in to the Ubuntu desktop, and the best place to begin is from the menu at System, Preferences, Ubuntu One. By signing up, you will receive 2GB of space to use to store anything you would like and make it available to multiple computers with access from Ubuntu desktops (with plans to expand to other Linux distributions and even other operating systems in the future) as well as via a web interface. If that isn't enough space, larger accounts are available for a fee, which in turn helps support future Ubuntu development. An Ubuntu One account is also needed to purchase music from the Ubuntu One Music Store, covered in Chapter 6, "Multimedia Applications."

References

- ▶ **www.novell.com/products/desktop/features/evolution.html**—The home of Evolution, the standard email client for Ubuntu.

- ▶ **www.mozilla.com/**—The home page for Mozilla Firefox, Thunderbird, and the Mozilla Suite.

- ▶ **www.spreadfirefox.com/**—The Firefox advocacy home page is useful for converting those Internet Explorer types.

- ▶ **https://one.ubuntu.com/**—The website for Ubuntu One.

- ▶ **http://en.wikipedia.org/wiki/Usenet**—For a history of Usenet.

# CHAPTER 5

Productivity Applications

Many businesses have already found a way to benefit from free and open-source software, such as office productivity suites like OpenOffice.org. These have the cost benefits of not having to pay license fees or support costs. However, more applications beyond these are available in Ubuntu. In this chapter, we explore some of them.

NOTE

It's important to understand that even though free and open-source software does very well most of the time, especially with less-complex documents, it is not 100 percent compatible with Microsoft Office. Why is this? Microsoft is notoriously secretive about its proprietary file formats, and the only way that free and open-source alternatives could ensure compatibility would be to reverse-engineer each file format, an exercise akin to taking apart a telephone to see how it works. This reverse-engineering is difficult to do in a legal way and is rarely perfect. However, many manage to maintain a very high standard of importing and exporting, so you should not experience too many problems except with documents of great complexity. As an example, this book was written using LibreOffice, whereas the post-production at the publisher uses Microsoft tools.

The biggest compatibility issue between Microsoft Office and others like LibreOffice is that Microsoft's *Visual Basic for Applications (VBA)* and scripts produced using it do not transfer. If you use VBA scripts, you need to find another way to perform the functions for which they were written.

A *productivity suite* is defined as two or more applications bundled together and used for creating documents, presentations, spreadsheets, and databases. Other applications that may be included in the bundle are email clients, calculators/formula editors, illustration or drawing software, and more. Commonly, they are all tied together by a default look and feel, which makes sticking to one particular suite much easier. Because Ubuntu uses LibreOffice as its standard office suite (see Figure 5.1), we introduce you to that first. We also take a brief look at some of the other Linux-based productivity applications.

FIGURE 5.1   The LibreOffice suite provided by Ubuntu is simple to configure and use.

Productivity for the Typical User

For the majority of users of productivity suites, LibreOffice should fulfill most, if not all, of your requirements. However, the first hurdle is not whether it can do what you require of it, but rather whether it can successfully import and export to proprietary Microsoft formats at a standard that is acceptable to your needs. Most of the time, LibreOffice should import and export with minimal hassle, perhaps getting a bit stuck with some of the more esoteric Microsoft Office formatting. Given that most users do not go much beyond tabs, columns, and tables, this level of compatibility should suffice.

However, you are strongly advised to round up a selection of documents and spread-sheets that seem the most likely to be difficult for the import/export filter and test them thoroughly (of course, keeping a backup of the originals). There is nothing worse for a system administrator who has deployed a new productivity suite than to suddenly get users complaining that they cannot read their files. This would quickly destroy any benefits gained from the other useful functions within LibreOffice, and could even mark the return of proprietary formats and expensive office suites.

On the positive side, LibreOffice supports a huge array of file formats and can export to nearly 70 types of documents. Such a variety of file formats means that you should be able to successfully use LibreOffice in nearly any environment, including formats no longer used by currently produced and maintained software, so it may be able to open some old files and documents you had once given up for lost.

Introducing LibreOffice

LibreOffice contains a number of productivity applications for use in creating text docu-ments, preparing spreadsheets, organizing presentations, managing projects, and so on. The following components of the LibreOffice package are included with Ubuntu:

- ▶ **Writer**—This word processing program enables you to compose, format, and orga-nize text documents. If you are accustomed to using Microsoft Word, the functional-ity of LibreOffice Writer will be familiar to you.

- ▶ **Calc**—This spreadsheet program enables you to manipulate numbers in a spread-sheet format. Support for all but the most esoteric Microsoft Excel functions means that trading spreadsheets with Excel users should be successful. Calc offers some limited compatibility with Excel macros, but those macros generally have to be rewritten.

- ▶ **Impress**—This presentation program is similar to Microsoft PowerPoint and enables you to create slideshow presentations that include graphs, diagrams, and other graphics. Impress also works well with most PowerPoint files.

NOTE

The following five applications are not included by default with Ubuntu, but are quite useful. All but Dia are a part of the LibreOffice project and add features to the suite that are not used as often as those Ubuntu installs by default. You must install them from the Ubuntu repositories if you want or require their functionality.

- ▶ **Math**—This math formula editor enables you to write mathematical formulas with a number of math fonts and symbols for inclusion in a word processing document. Such symbols are highly specialized and not easily included in the basic functional-ity of a word processor. This is of interest primarily to math and science writers, but Math can be useful to anyone who needs to include a complex formula in text.

- **Base**—This is a fully functional database application.

- **Draw**—This graphics application allows you to create images for inclusion in the documents produced with LibreOffice. It saves files only in LibreOffice format, but it can import most common image formats.

- **Dia**—This technical drawing editor from the GNOME Office suite enables you to create measured drawings, such as those used by architects and engineers. Its functionality is similar to that of Microsoft Visio.

- **Planner**—You can use this project management application for project planning, scheduling, and tracking; this application is similar to, but not compatible with, Microsoft Project. Once installed, you will find it under the name Project Management.

A Brief History of LibreOffice

The OpenOffice.org office suite is based on a commercial suite called StarOffice. Originally developed by a German company, StarOffice was purchased by Sun Microsystems in the United States. One of the biggest complaints about the old StarOffice was that all the component applications were integrated under a StarOffice "desktop" that looked very much like a Microsoft Windows desktop, including a Start button and menus. This meant that to edit a simple document, unneeded applications had to be loaded, making the office suite slow to load, slow to run, and quite demanding on system resources.

After the purchase of StarOffice, Sun Microsystems released a large part of the StarOffice code under the GNU Public License, and development began on what has become OpenOffice.org, which is freely available under the GPL. Sun also continued development on StarOffice. The significant differences between the free and commercial versions of the software are that StarOffice provides more fonts and even more import/export file filters than OpenOffice.org (these filters cannot be provided in the GPL version because of licensing restrictions), and StarOffice provides its own relational database, Software AGs Adabas D database.

Sun was bought by Oracle. Oracle recently suffered from a major disagreement with the developer community surrounding OpenOffice.org, and the developers left to form The Document Foundation, hoping that Oracle would eventually join. Because the code for OpenOffice.org was licensed using a free software license, The Document Foundation created a fork, or a new version of the same software, using what they intended as a temporary name, LibreOffice. The hope was merely to change how the project was governed, from being led by one company to being led by a community with many companies and individuals participating. Oracle chose not to join The Document Foundation and instead relicensed the OpenOffice.org code for all future versions, which they may do as the owners of that code, and gave the code to the Apache Software Foundation, who is licensing it under the less-restrictive Apache license that allows open-source code to be used in proprietary products. To make things more interesting, IBM is using this Apache-licensed version of OpenOffice.org as the foundation for its own free-as-in-cost office suite based on it called Lotus Symphony, which also has some proprietary additions.

As the saga continues, the ultimate winner may be the end user, as this effectively creates three competing office suites. For now, LibreOffice has the most developers, the strongest community, and the most mature software with the most rapid addition of new or improved features.

Other Office Suites for Ubuntu

As mentioned earlier, LibreOffice is the default application suite for Ubuntu. However, as is common in the open-source world, there are plenty of alternatives should you find that LibreOffice does not meet your specific requirements. These include the popular GNOME Office and also KOffice, the default KDE productivity suite. You are more likely to hear more about LibreOffice, especially as more and more people realize that it is generally compatible with Microsoft Office file formats. Interestingly, the state of Massachusetts not long ago elected to standardize on two file formats for use in government: the Adobe Acrobat PDF format and the OASIS OpenDocument format, both of which are supported natively in LibreOffice.

5

> **NOTE**
>
> The decision by the state of Massachusetts to standardize on PDF and OpenDocument has huge ramifications for the open-source world. It is the first time that OpenDocument, an open standard, has been specified in this way. It means that anyone who wants to do business with the state government must use OpenDocument-based file formats, and not the proprietary formats in use by Microsoft. Unfortunately for Microsoft, it does not have support for OpenDocument in any of its applications, making them useless to anyone wanting to work with the state government. This is despite Microsoft being a founding member of OASIS, who developed and ratified the OpenDocument standard.

Working with GNOME Office

The other office suite available for GNOME is GNOME Office, which is a collection of individual applications. Unlike LibreOffice, GNOME Office does not have a coherent suite of applications, meaning that you have to get used to using a word processor that offers no integration with a spreadsheet and cannot work directly with a presentation package. However, if you need only one or two components, it is worthwhile investigating GNOME Office.

The GTK Widget Set

Open-source developers are always trying to make it easier for people to build applications and help in development. To this end, there are a number of widgets or toolkits that other developers can use to rapidly create and deploy GUI applications. These widgets control things such as drop-down lists, Save As dialogs, window buttons, and general look and feel. Unfortunately, whereas Windows and Apple developers have to worry about only one set of widgets each, Linux has a plethora of different widgets, including GTK+, QT, and Motif. What is worse is that these widgets are incompatible with one another, making it difficult to easily move a finished application from one widget set to another.

GTK is an acronym for *GIMP Tool Kit*. GIMP, the *GNU Image Manipulation Program*, is a graphics application very similar to Adobe Photoshop. By using the GTK-based jargon, we save ourselves several hundred words of typing and help move along our discussion of GNOME Office. You might also see similar references to QT and Motif, as well as other widget sets, in these chapters.

Here are some of the primary components of the GNOME Office suite that are available in Ubuntu:

▶ **AbiWord**—This word processing program enables you to compose, format, and organize text documents and has some compatibility with the Microsoft Word file format. It uses plug-ins (programs that add functionality such as language translation) to enhance its functionality.

▶ **Gnumeric**—This spreadsheet program enables you to manipulate numbers in a spreadsheet format. Support for all but the most esoteric Microsoft Excel functions means that users should have little trouble trading spreadsheets with Excel users.

▶ **GIMP**—This graphics application allows you to create images for general use. It can import and export all common graphic file formats. GIMP is similar to Adobe's Photoshop application and is described in Chapter 6, "Multimedia Applications."

▶ **Evolution**—Evolution is a mail client with an interface similar to Microsoft Outlook, providing email, scheduling, and calendaring. It is described in Chapter 4, "On the Internet."

The loose association of applications known as GNOME Office includes several additional applications that duplicate the functionality of applications already provided by Ubuntu. Those extra GNOME applications are not included in a default installation of Ubuntu to eliminate redundancy. They are all available from the GNOME Office website, at www.gnome.org/gnome-office/, and in the Ubuntu software repositories.

Working with KOffice

The KDE office suite KOffice was developed to provide tight integration with the KDE desktop. Integration enables objects in one application to be inserted in other applications via drag and drop, and all the applications can communicate with each other, so a change in an object is instantly communicated to other applications. The application integration provided by KDE is a significant enhancement to productivity. (Some GNOME desktop applications share a similar communication facility with each other.) If you use the KDE desktop instead of the default GNOME desktop, you can enjoy the benefits of this integration, along with the Konqueror web and file browser.

The word processor for KOffice is KWord. KWord is a frames-based word processor, meaning that document pages can be formatted in framesets that hold text, graphics, and objects in enclosed areas. Framesets can be used to format text on a page that includes text and images within columns that the text needs to flow around, making KWord an excellent choice for creating documents other than standard business letters, such as newsletters and brochures.

KWord and other components of KOffice are still under development and lack all the polished features of LibreOffice and AbiWord. However, it does have the capability to work with the OpenDocument format found in LibreOffice, as well as limited compatibility with Microsoft file formats.

The KOffice KSpread client is a functional spreadsheet program that offers graphing capabilities along with all the other standard spreadsheet functionality.

KDE includes other productivity options in KOffice. These include an address book, time tracker, calculator, notepad, and scheduler. One popular application is Kontact, which provides daily, weekly, work week, and monthly views of tasks, to-do lists, and scheduled appointments with background alarms.

Other Useful Productivity Software

The office suites already discussed in this chapter are ideal for typical office-focused file interactions: creating basic documents, spreadsheets, and so on. However, some of us have more complex or precise needs. This section covers some of the options available to help you be productive in those instances.

Working with PDF

Reading a PDF in Ubuntu is simple. The functionality is available by default, thanks to an installed program called Evince. Open a PDF, and Evince will open and let you read it. Sometimes filling out forms is less straightforward, as the form may have been created using functionality only available from Adobe. You can install Adobe Reader from the Ubuntu Software Center from the Canonical Partners section. Adobe Reader should work with any PDF form created using Adobe software, whether it was created on Windows, Mac OS X, or Linux.

On occasion, you find that you have a PDF file that you want to edit. That is a little more complex, but not as difficult as it used to be. There are two good methods to get you started: install an extension to LibreOffice, or use a program created just for editing PDF files.

To install the LibreOffice extension, you must download PDF Import from www.libreof-fice.org/features/extensions/ and install using the instructions on that site. It should be able to import and allow you to edit and save PDF files. This option is easier to use than the next option.

If you prefer to use a different program altogether, install PDF Editor (pdfedit) from the Ubuntu Software Center. On the surface, this option seems simple enough, but it has great power that is not immediately obvious. Advanced users can learn to use pdfedit in scripts to make sweeping changes quickly. Of course, as with most powerful tools, it comes with the cost of complexity and learning how to use it.

Working with XML and DocBook

Like its ancestor SGML and cousin HTML, XML is a markup language. It is designed for use in a plain-text document. Tags surround specific sections of the text to denote how that section is to be displayed. Listing 5.1 contains a very short example.

LISTING 5.1   Sample XML Excerpt

```
<?xml version="1.0"?>
<xml-stylesheet type="text/css" href="book.css"?>
<book>
<title>Ubuntu Unleashed 2012</title>
<edition>7</edition>
<chapter>
        <number>1</number>
        <title>Installing Ubuntu</title>
        <text>
                <paragraph><dropcap>N</dropcap>ot that long ago,the mere mention...
                ...</paragraph>
        ...
        </text>
</chapter>
...
</book>
```

This could easily be written using a simple text editor like the one installed by default, Gedit (called Text Editor in the Dash and the listings in the Ubuntu Software Center). However, doing it that way would be tedious for most people. A better option is to use an editor expressly designed and intended for dealing with XML files. Because DocBook is an open-source standard form of XML that has been designed explicitly for use with, docu-mentation, many editors that can work with one will work with both. If you only need to do something quick, one of these should be suitable. Start with Gedit, which is installed by default. If it is not suitable, look in the Ubuntu Software Center for other options like the ones discussed next.

If you intend to write a lot or just complicated documentation in only the DocBook format, the most common recommendation for Ubuntu is a program called Publican. Publican is not just an editor; it is also a publication system for DocBook. It tests your XML to ensure it is in a valid DocBook form so that your output conforms to publication standards. It automates output into multiple formats such as HTML and PDF, and it allows complete control for custom skinning and formatting. You can install Publican from the Ubuntu Software Center.

A more powerful option is XML Copy Editor. It is designed for editing most markup languages, including XML, DocBook, DITA, and more. It also features schema validation, syntax highlighting, tag completion, and spell checking. This is the most useful option for the professional documentation specialist. You can install XML Copy Editor from the Ubuntu Software Repositories, and their website has a version available for use on Windows. See http://xml-copy-editor.sourceforge.net for more information.

Working with LaTeX

LaTeX was created for and is widely used in academia. It is a WYGIWYW document markup language created for the TeX typesetting system. Multiple editors are available for use with LaTeX, and they are likely to be found for just about every operating system in existence.

NOTE

WYSIWYG is an acronym for "what you see is what you get" that has often been used to describe word processors and document creation systems that use a graphical interface. Unfortunately, anyone who has created documents with these programs, including the ones we promoted earlier in this chapter like LibreOffice, knows that what you see on the screen is not always what appears in the printed version on paper. There are no promises about how things will or will not look on the screen while using a LaTeX editor for your TeX document, but the format promises that the ultimate output will be exactly what you ask for.

A couple of the more popular LaTeX editors available from the Ubuntu Software Center are discussed in this section. You can also create and edit using any text editor, including Gedit.

Texmaker not only has a version in the Ubuntu Software Center, but also offers versions for Windows and Mac OS X from www.xm1math.net/texmaker/. It is free, easy to use, and mature. The program has been around for a while, it is stable, has many useful features, and is rather popular in the TeX world.

LyX follows suit with both a version in the Ubuntu Software Center and versions available for Windows and Mac OS X from their website at www.lyx.org. The main appeal for LyX users is its graphical interface, which makes it an interesting bridge from WYSIWYG to LaTeX. It also has many plug-ins available to expand functionality.

Kile was written and designed for use with KDE. As such, it blends in well to Kubuntu, but will run well on a standard Ubuntu installation. It also has a Windows version available; see http://kile.sourceforge.net for details.

Productivity Applications Written for Microsoft Windows

Microsoft Windows is fundamentally different from Linux, yet you can install and run some Microsoft Windows applications in Linux by using an application named Wine. Wine enables you to use Microsoft Windows and DOS programs on UNIX-based systems. Wine includes a program loader that you can use to execute a Windows binary, along with a DLL library that implements Windows command calls, translating them to the equivalent UNIX and X11 command calls. Because of frequent updates to the Wine code base, Wine is not included with Ubuntu. Download a current version of Wine from www. winehq.org/. To see whether your favorite application is supported by Wine, you can look at the Wine application database at http://appdb.winehq.org/appbrowse.php.

Other solutions, primarily CrossOver Office from CodeWeavers, enable use of Microsoft productivity applications. If you are after a closer-to-painless way of running not only Microsoft Office, but also Apple iTunes and other software, you should investigate CodeWeavers. CrossOver Office is one of the simplest programs you can use to get Windows-based programs to work. Check out www.codeweavers.com to download a trial version of the latest software.

References

- ▶ www.libreoffice.org—The home page for the LibreOffice suite.

- ▶ www.documentfoundation.org—The home page for The Document Foundation.

- ▶ www.openoffice.org—The home page for the OpenOffice.org office suite.

- ▶ http://incubator.apache.org/openofficeorg—The home page for the Apache Software Foundation's incubator project for OpenOffice.org.

- ▶ www.oracle.com/us/products/applications/open-office/index.html—The home page for Oracle Open Office, a paid version of the office suite with proprietary upgrades.

- ▶ www.gnome.org/gnome-office/—The GNOME Office site.

- ▶ www.koffice.org/—The home page for the KOffice suite.

- ▶ http://pdfedit.cz/en/index.html—The home page for PDF Edit.

- ▶ www.codeweavers.com/—The home page for CrossOver Office from CodeWeavers that allows you to run some Windows programs under Linux.

# CHAPTER 6

Multimedia Applications

The twenty-first century has become the century of the digital lifestyle, with millions of computer users around the world embracing new technologies, such as digital cameras, MP3 players, and other assorted multimedia gadgets. Whereas 10 years ago you might have had a small collection of WAV files scattered about your Windows installation, today you are more likely to have hundreds, if not thousands, of MP3 files scattered across various computers. Along with video clips, animations, and other graphics, the demand for organizing and maintaining these vast libraries is driving development of applications. Popular proprietary applications such as iTunes and Google's Picasa are coveted by Linux users, but open-source applications are appearing that provide real alternatives, and for some people, these are the final reasons they need to move to Linux full time.

This chapter provides an overview of some of the basic multimedia tools included with Ubuntu. In this chapter, you learn how to create your own CDs, watch TV, rip audio CDs into the open-source Ogg audio format for playback, as well as manage your media library. You also learn about how Ubuntu handles graphics and pictures and more.

Sound and Music

Linux had a reputation of lacking good support for sound and multimedia applications in general. However, great strides have been made in recent years to correct this, and support is now a lot better than it used to be. (It might make you smile to know that Microsoft no longer supports the Microsoft Sound Card, but Linux users still enjoy support for it, no doubt just to annoy the folks in

Redmond.) UNIX, however, has always had good multimedia support, as David Taylor, UNIX author and guru, points out:

> The original graphics work for computers was done by Evans and Sutherland on UNIX systems. The innovations at MIT's Media Lab were done on UNIX workstations. In 1985, we at HP Labs were creating sophisticated multimedia immersive work environments on UNIX workstations, so maybe UNIX is more multimedia than suggested. Limitations in Linux support doesn't mean UNIX had the same limitations. I think it was more a matter of logistics, with hundreds of sound cards and thousands of different possible PC configurations.

That last sentence sums it up quite well. UNIX had a limited range of hardware to support; Linux has hundreds of sound cards. Sound card device driver support has been long lacking from manufacturers, and there is still no single standard for the sound subsystem in Linux.

In this section, you learn about sound cards, sound file formats, and the sound applications provided with Ubuntu.

Sound Cards

Ubuntu supports a wide variety of sound hardware and software. Two models of sound card drivers compete for prominence in today's market:

▶ ALSA, the *Advanced Linux Sound Architecture*, which is entirely open source

▶ OSS, the *Open Sound System*, which offers free and commercial drivers

Ubuntu uses ALSA because ALSA is the sound architecture for the 2.6 series, and now the 3.0 series of kernels. OSS may still be found here and there, but it is no longer in widespread use and should be considered deprecated.

ALSA supports a long list of sound cards. You can review the list at www.alsa-project.org/main/index.php/Main_Page if you are interested, but Ubuntu detects most sound cards during the original installation and should detect any new additions to the system during boot. To configure the sound card at any other time, use the sound preferences graphical tool found in the menu at System, Preferences, Sound.

In addition, Ubuntu uses an additional layer of software called *PulseAudio*. PulseAudio is a sound server and acts as a mediator between the various multimedia programs that have sound output and the ALSA kernel drivers. Over the years, there have been many different sound servers used in Linux, each with different strengths, usability issues, and levels of documentation. These various sound servers have often been forced to run side by side on the same computer, causing all sorts of confusion and issues. PulseAudio aims to replace all of them and work as a single handler to accept output from applications that use the APIs for any of the major sound servers already in use, such as ESD, OSS, GStreamer, and aRts, and route the various output streams together through one handler. This gives several advantages, including the ability to control the output volume of various programs individually.

PulseAudio is still quite young, and its full potential has not yet been realized; however, it has matured over the last several releases and is better and more powerful than ever in 11.10. Although there were stability issues and complaints in the first release that included PulseAudio, those don't seem to be a problem anymore except in unusual hardware combinations and special cases and more and more features have been implemented. For more information about PulseAudio, see www.pulseaudio.org/.

Adjusting Volume

Ubuntu offers a handy utility that you can use to control the volumes for various outputs from your computer. For a simple master volume control, just click the speaker icon in the top-right corner of the screen and move the slider left or right, as shown in Figure 6.1.

FIGURE 6.1   Control the master volume level with the volume slider.

Alternatively, you can control all the output volumes for the system to make sure that you have set everything to your taste, as shown in Figure 6.2. To access the volume control, left-click the speaker icon and select Sound Preferences.

Sound Formats

A number of formats exist for storing sound recordings. Some of these formats are associated with specific technologies, and others are used strictly for proprietary reasons. Ubuntu supports several of the most popular sound formats, including the following:

▶ **RAW (.raw)**—More properly known as *headerless format*, audio files using this format contain an amorphous variety of specific settings and encodings. All other sound files contain a short section of code at the beginning—a header—that identifies the format type.

▶ **MP3 (.mp3)**—A popular, but commercially licensed, format for the digital encoding used by many Linux and Windows applications. MP3 is not supported by any software included with Ubuntu by default, but may be easily installed later. In fact, the first time you try to play an MP3 file, Ubuntu asks whether you want to install the codec needed and walks you through the whole, simple process.

▶ **WAV (.wav)**—The popular uncompressed Windows audio-visual sound format. It is often used as an intermediate file format when encoding audio.

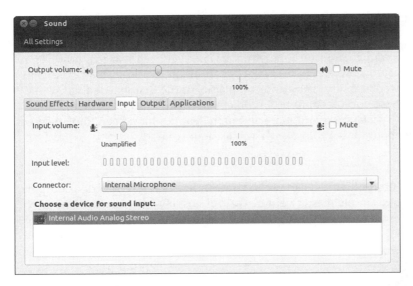

FIGURE 6.2   Use the volume control to manage volume settings for all your sound output devices.

▶ **Ogg-Vorbis** (`.ogg`)—Ubuntu's preferred audio encoding format. You enjoy better compression and audio playback, and freedom from lawsuits when you use this open-source encoding format for your audio files.

▶ **FLAC** (`.flac`)—This is a lossless format popular with audiophiles. The name stands for *Free Lossless Audio Format* and it is a compressed format, like MP3, but does not suffer from any loss of quality.

NOTE

Because of patent and licensing issues, Ubuntu does not by default support the MPEG, MPEG2, and MPEG3 (MP3) file formats. Although we cannot offer any legal advice, it appears that individuals using MP3 software are okay; it is just that Ubuntu cannot distribute the code because of how the code is licensed.

You can also enable the MP3 codec within Ubuntu by downloading a plug-in for GStreamer, the GNOME audio system. You do this by installing the `gstreamer0.10-plugins-ugly` package, which enables the MP3 codec in all the GNOME applications. Even better, there is a package called `ubuntu-restricted-extras` that you can install that enables all the major formats you are ever likely to encounter. The package can be found in the repositories, and as mentioned earlier in the chapter, Ubuntu also recommends specific packages as needed when you attempt to use a file type that does not currently have an installed codec package. It really is that easy to deal with multimedia formats in Ubuntu.

Ubuntu even includes software in the repositories (such as the sox command used to convert between sound formats) so that you can more easily listen to audio files provided in a wide variety of formats, such as AU (from NeXT and Sun), AIFF (from Apple and SGI), IFF (originally from Commodore's Amiga), RA (from Real Audio), and VOC (from Creative Labs).

> **TIP**
>
> For an introduction to audio formats, check out the list of audio file formats at www.file-info.com/filetypes/audio, with links to detailed information for each.

Ubuntu also offers several utilities for converting sound files from one format to another. Conversion utilities come in handy when you want to use a sound in a format not accepted by your current application of choice. The easiest one to use is also the easiest to install. Install the soundconverter package and then look for the application in the menu at Applications, Sound & Video, Sound Converter. It has a clear graphical interface and easy-to-understand configuration options.

Listening to Music

If you're anything like we are, you might be a huge music fan. One of the downsides of having a fairly large music collection is the physical problem of having to store so many CDs. Wouldn't it be great if you could pack them all away somewhere, yet still have access to all the music when you want it? Some manufacturers experimented with rather bulky jukeboxes that stored 250 CDs at once. The main downside with that was that finding a particular piece of music could take hours, having to cycle through each CD in the hope that it would match your mood.

Fortunately for you and me, Ubuntu is fantastic at working with CDs, even allowing you to rip all your CD collection into a vast searchable music library, letting you quickly create playlists, and enabling you to create your own customized CDs. Getting started couldn't be easier, mainly because Ubuntu comes preconfigured with everything you need to get started.

Rhythmbox

Rhythmbox is a useful application that plays CDs if you insert an audio CD into your computer. It also attempts to obtain information about the CD from the Internet. If it's successful, you see the name of the CD appear in Rhythmbox.

When you're ready to play your CD, just click the name of the CD under the Devices section and click the Play button. You can also define whether the CD should just repeat itself until stopped or whether you want to shuffle the music (randomize the playlist).

Of course, just listening to your CDs doesn't really change anything; Rhythmbox acts just like a regular CD player, allowing you to listen to specific tracks and define how you want to listen to your music by using playlists or sorting it by artists. The real fun starts when you click the Copy to Library button on your toolbar. Rhythmbox then starts to extract, or rip, the audio from your CD and store it within the `Music` directory that is found under your `/home` directory.

Depending on the speed of your optical drive and the power of your computer, the ripping process can take up to 15 minutes to complete a full CD. As it goes along, Rhythmbox automatically adds the files to your media library, which you can access by clicking the Music button on the left side of the Rhythmbox screen, as you can see in Figure 6.3.

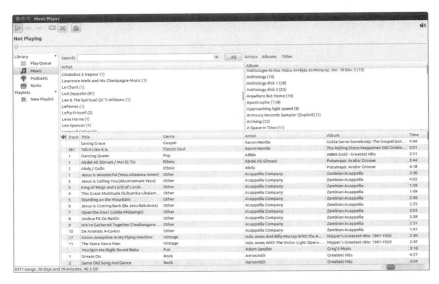

FIGURE 6.3   Rhythmbox displays a list of the music you have available.

Within the Rhythmbox interface, you can easily browse through the list of artist names or album titles, which affects the track listing that appears at the bottom of the screen. The numbers after each artist and album tell you how many tracks are assigned to that specific entry, giving you a heads up before you click them. Double-clicking any entry automatically starts the music playing. So, for example, double-clicking an artist's name causes the music tracks associated with that artist to start playing. When a track starts to play, Rhythmbox automatically attempts to retrieve the CD artwork, which it then displays in the lower-left corner of the screen.

There's a lot more that you can do with Rhythmbox, including download and listen to podcasts. A good place to start is the Ubuntu UK podcast at http://podcast.ubuntu-uk.org/. All you have to do is click an RSS link for the feed on that page, copy the link URL, and go to Rhythmbox. There, press Ctrl+P, or go to Music, New Podcast Feed, paste the link into the field, and click the Add button. Rhythmbox then contacts the server and attempts to download the most recent episodes of your chosen podcast.

Rhythmbox used to be installed by default in Ubuntu and is still available in the Ubuntu Software Center, but has been eclipsed by Banshee. Banshee is now installed by default and is discussed next.

Banshee

Banshee is another music application that can handle ripping and playing back music, download cover art, sync with portable players, and can even play video (see Figure 6.4). It has a similar look and feel to Rhythmbox, but is more actively maintained.

FIGURE 6.4   Banshee gives you a neat interface to browse through your music collection.

Getting Music into Ubuntu with Sound Juicer

A handy utility that is included with Ubuntu is Sound Juicer, found under Applications, Sound & Video as the Audio CD Extractor. Sound Juicer automatically detects when you install a CD and attempt to retrieve the track details from the Internet. From there, it rips the CD tracks into Ogg files for storage on your file system. You can see Sound Juicer in action in Figure 6.5.

Buying Music in the Ubuntu One Music Store

Chapter 4, "On the Internet," mentioned Ubuntu One cloud storage. If you sign up for a free account, not only do you have the ability to store files on Ubuntu-run servers in the cloud, but you also gain access to the Ubuntu One Music Store. The store is available right inside Rhythmbox Music Player (and at the time of this writing, plans were in place to add it to Banshee also). In Rhythmbox, simply click the Ubuntu One link in the window on the left of the screen to get started (see Figure 6.6).

FIGURE 6.5   Create your own digital music collection with Sound Juicer.

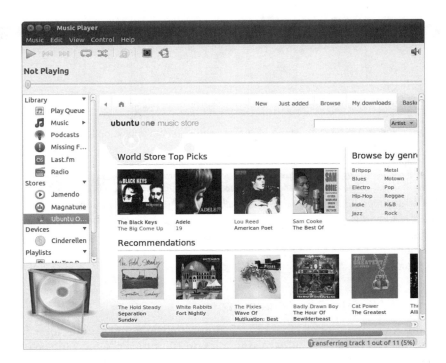

FIGURE 6.6   Ubuntu One Music Store.

Graphics Manipulation

Over a short period of time, digital cameras and digital imagery have become extremely popular, to the point where some traditional film camera manufacturers are switching solely to digital. This meteoric rise has led to an increase in the number of applications that can handle digital imagery. Linux, thanks to its rapid pace of development, is now highly regarded as a multimedia platform for editing digital images.

By default, Ubuntu installs the useful Shotwell Photo Manager in Applications, Graphics, Shotwell Photo Manager (see Figure 6.7). This application is similar to other photo managers, such as iPhoto, and includes simple tools that are adequate for many users, such as red-eye reduction, cropping, color adjustment, and the ability to interact with online photo hosts, such as Facebook, Flickr, and Picasa.

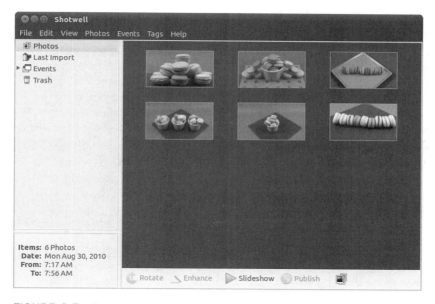

FIGURE 6.7   For most people, the simple tools in Shotwell Photo Manager are sufficient.

The rest of this section discusses GIMP, a powerful graphics manipulation tool that intermediate and advanced users are likely to enjoy. You also learn about graphic file formats supported by Ubuntu and some tools you can use to convert them if the application you want to use requires a different format.

The GNU Image Manipulation Program

One of the best graphics clients available is GIMP. GIMP is a free, GPL-licensed image editor with sophisticated capabilities that can import and export more than 30 different graphics formats, including files created with Adobe Photoshop. It is often compared with

Photoshop, and GIMP represents one of the first significant successes of GNU Projects. Many images in Linux were prepared with GIMP.

GIMP is not installed by default, but after you install it from the repositories, you can find it in the menu at Applications, Graphics, GIMP Image Editor.

You see an installation dialog box when GIMP is started for the first time, and then a series of dialog boxes that display information regarding the creation and contents of a local GIMP directory. This directory can contain personal settings, preferences, external application resource files, temporary files, and symbolic links to external software tools used by the editor.

What Does Photoshop Have that GIMP Does Not?

Although GIMP is powerful, it does lack two features Adobe Photoshop offers that are important to some graphics professionals.

The first of these is the capability to generate color separations for commercial press printers (CMYK, for the colors cyan, magenta, yellow, and key [or black]). GIMP uses RGB (red, green, and blue), which is great for video display, but not so great for printing presses. The second feature GIMP lacks is the use of Pantone colors (a patented color specification) to ensure accurate color matching. These deficiencies might not last long. A CMYK plug-in is in the works (an early version is available from http://cue.yellowmagic.info/softwares/separate-plus/index.html), and the Pantone issues are likely to be addressed in the near future, as well.

If these features are unimportant to you, GIMP is an excellent tool. If you must use Adobe Photoshop, you might want to explore using Wine or Codeweavers; there have been consistent reports of success running Photoshop on Linux with these tools. Bear in mind, though, that both Ubuntu and Photoshop release regularly, so check www.winehq.org/ and www.codeweavers.com/ for the current info before assuming it will work.

After the initial configuration has finished, GIMP's main windows and toolboxes appear (see Figure 6.8). GIMP's main window contains tools used for selecting, drawing, moving, view enlarging or reducing, airbrushing, painting, smudging, copying, filling, and selecting color.

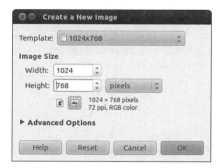

FIGURE 6.8   Right-click an image window to access GIMP's cascading menus.

Using Scanners in Ubuntu

With the rise of digital photography, there has been an equal decline in the need for image scanners. However, there are still times that you want to use a scanner, and Ubuntu makes it easy with a program installed by default in the menu at Applications, Graphics, Simple Scan. Simple Scan is designed to do one thing: scan photos or documents easily (see Figure 6.9). It has few settings or options, but does all the things most people would want or need.

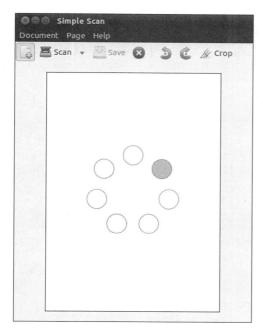

FIGURE 6.9   Simple Scan makes scanning easy.

You can also use many types of image scanners with GIMP, which is likely to be the choice of people who like to tinker with settings and options or who need greater flexibility than is offered by Simple Scan. If it wasn't installed when you installed GIMP, install the xsane package. Then, when you scan from GIMP, you will have an abundance of settings and options that you can use. You can also use XSane by itself, finding it in the menu at Applications, Graphics, XSane Image Scanner.

Working with Graphics Formats

Image file formats are developed to serve a specific technical purpose (lossless compression, for example, where the file size is reduced without sacrificing image quality) or to meet a need for a proprietary format for competitive reasons. Many file formats are covered by one or more patents. For example, the GIF format had fallen into disfavor with the open-source crowd because the patent holder waited awhile before deciding to enforce his patent rights rather than being upfront with requests for patent royalties.

If you want to view or manipulate an image, you need to identify the file format to choose the proper tool for working with the image. The file's extension is your first indicator of the file's format. The graphics image formats supported by the applications included with Ubuntu include the following:

- ▶ **BMP (.bmp)**—Bitmapped graphics, commonly used in Microsoft Windows
- ▶ **GIF (.gif)**—CompuServe Graphics Interchange Format
- ▶ **JPG (.jpg)**—Joint Photographic Experts Group
- ▶ **PCX (.pcx)**—IBM Paintbrush
- ▶ **PNG (.png)**—Portable Network Graphics
- ▶ **SVG (.svg)**—Scalable Vector Graphics
- ▶ **TIF (.tif)**—Tagged Image File format

You can find an extensive list of image file extensions in the man page for ImageMagick, an excellent application included with Ubuntu, which you learn more about in upcoming sections of this chapter.

TIP

Ubuntu includes dozens of graphics conversion programs in its software repositories that are accessible through the command line and from a *graphical user interface (GUI)*, and there are few, if any, graphics file formats that cannot be manipulated when using Linux. These programs can be called in Perl scripts, shell scripts, or command-line pipes to support many types of complex format-conversion and image-manipulation tasks. See the man pages for the ppm, pbm, pnm, and pgm families of commands. Also see the man page for the convert command, which is part of a suite of extremely capable programs included with the ImageMagick suite.

Sometimes, a file you want to manipulate in some way is in a format that cannot be used by either your graphics application or the final application. The solution is to convert the image file—sometimes through several formats. The convert utility from ImageMagick is useful, as is the netpbm family of utilities. If it is not already installed, ImageMagick can be installed easily from the Ubuntu repositories; the netpbm tools are always installed by default. Convert is super simple to use from the command line. Here is an example:

```
matthew@seymour:~$ convert image.gif image.png
```

The convert utility converts between image formats recognized by ImageMagick. Color depth and size also can be manipulated during the conversion process. You can use ImageMagick to append images, surround them with borders, add labels, rotate and shade them, and perform other manipulations well suited to scripting. Other commands associated with ImageMagick include display, animate, identify, and import. The application supports more than 130 different image formats (all listed in the man page for ImageMagick).

The netpbm tools are installed by default because they compose the underpinnings of graphics format manipulation. The man page for each image format lists related conversion utilities; the number of those utilities gives you some indication of the way that format is used and shows how one is built on another:

▶ The man page for ppm, the *portable pixmap* file format, lists 47 conversion utilities related to ppm. This makes sense because ppm, or *portable pixmap*, is considered the lowest common denominator for color image files. It is therefore often used as an intermediate format.

▶ The man page for pgm, the *portable graymap* file format, lists 22 conversion utilities. This makes sense because pgm is the lowest common denominator for grayscale image files.

▶ The man page for pnm, the *portable anymap* file format, lists 31 conversion utilities related to it. However, there is no format associated with PNM because it operates in concert with ppm, pgm, and pbm.

▶ An examination of the man page for pbm, the *portable bitmap* file format, reveals no conversion utilities. It's a monochrome format and serves as the foundation of the other related formats.

▶ The easiest way to resize or rotate image files is to install the nautilus-image-converter package from the repositories. This lets you right-click an image when you are viewing files in the File Browser (for example, from Places, Pictures) and choose menu options to resize or rotate one or multiple images without opening another program.

Capturing Screen Images

You can use graphics-manipulation tools to capture images that are displayed on your computer screen. Although this technique was used for the production of this book, it has broader uses; there is truth to the cliché that a picture is worth a thousand words. Sometimes it is easier to show an example than it is to describe it.

A captured screen image (also called a screen grab or a screenshot) can be used to illustrate an error in the display of an application (a font problem, for example) or an error dialog that is too complex to copy down by hand. You might just want to share an image of your beautifully crafted custom desktop configuration with your friends or illustrate your written documents.

When using the default GNOME desktop, you can take advantage of the built-in screen-shot mechanism (gnome-panel-screenshot). You can use this tool by pressing the Print

Screen key. (Alt+Print Screen takes a screenshot of only the window that has focus on a desktop.) Captured images are saved in PNG format. You can also find the tool in the Dash with a search for "take screenshot."

Using Digital Cameras with Ubuntu

Most digital cameras used with Ubuntu fall into one of two categories: webcams (small, low-resolution cameras connected to the computer's interface) or handheld digital cameras that record image data on disks or memory cards for downloading and viewing on a PC. Ubuntu supports both types. Other types of cameras, such as surveillance cameras that connect directly to a network via wired or wireless connections, need no special support (other than a network connection and viewing software) to be used with a Linux computer.

Ubuntu supports hundreds of different digital cameras, from early parallel-port (CPiA chipset based) cameras to today's USB-based cameras. You can even use Intel's QX3 USB microscope with Ubuntu. The following sections describe some of the more commonly used types of still camera hardware and software supported by Ubuntu.

Handheld Digital Cameras

Because of the good development carried out in the Linux world, you can plug almost any digital camera in to your computer through a USB interface and Ubuntu automatically recognizes the camera as a USB mass storage device. You can even set Ubuntu to recognize when a camera is plugged in so that it automatically imports your photographs for you.

Using Shotwell Photo Manager

Ubuntu comes by default with a pretty good photo manager called Shotwell Photo Manager that includes simple adjustment tools (see Figure 6.10). You can import your photos into Shotwell, assign tags to them, sort and arrange them, and even upload them to your favorite Internet photo-hosting sites, such as Facebook, Flickr, and Picasa.

Burning CDs and DVDs in Ubuntu

Linux is generally distributed via the Internet as disc images called ISOs that are ready to be written to CDs or DVDs. Therefore, learning how to burn discs is essential if you have to download and install a Linux distribution. You can use CDs and DVDs to do the following:

▶ Record and store multimedia data, such as backup files, graphics images, and music.

▶ Rip audio tracks from music CDs (*ripping* refers to extracting music tracks from a music CD) and compile your own music CDs for your personal use.

Although USB storage devices such as thumb drives are making CDs and DVDs almost as rare as floppy disks, they aren't quite gone, and many people still find them useful. As long as that remains true, we want to make sure this information is available.

FIGURE 6.10   Browse your photo collection and correct minor problems with Shotwell Photo Manager.

Creating CDs and DVDs with Brasero

Although adequate for quick burns and use in shell scripting, the command-line technique for burning CDs and DVDs is an awkward choice for many people (but we still cover doing so later in this chapter, because others find it useful and desirable). Fortunately, Ubuntu provides several graphical clients; the most useful is Brasero.

Brasero is an easy-to-use graphical CD and DVD burning application that is installed by default. You can find it in the menu at Applications, Sound & Video, Brasero Disc Burner.

Brasero takes a project-based approach to disc burning, opening up with a wizard from which you can select from four different tasks that you'll commonly want to do. Figure 6.11 shows the opening screen. Brasero also remembers previous "projects," allowing you to quickly create several copies of a disc, which is ideal if you're planning to pass on copies of Ubuntu to your friends and family.

Burning a data CD or DVD is as easy as selecting the option in the opening screen and dragging and dropping the files you want to include from the directory tree on the left to the drop area on the right. If you insert a blank CD or DVD in your writer, Brasero keeps an eye on the disc size, and tells you when you reach or exceed the limits. It also creates ISO files, which are disc images that contain everything that would exist on the medium if you burned a real CD or DVD in one file that can be mounted by computer file systems, which is useful if you want to create multiple copies of the same disc or if you want to share a disc image, perhaps using a USB thumb drive or over the Internet.

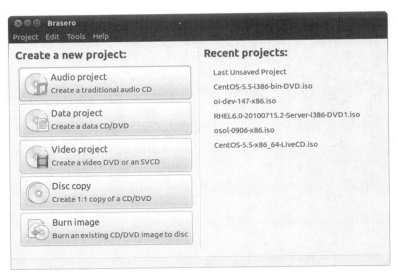

FIGURE 6.11   Brasero gives you an intuitive way to create data and audio CDs and DVDs.

Finally, click the Burn button, input a label for the disc, and Brasero starts creating your new CD or DVD or image file. How long it takes to create a CD or DVD depends on the amount of data you are writing and the speed of your drive.

Creating CDs from the Command Line

In Linux, creating a CD at the command line is a two-step process. You first create the ISO9660-formatted image, and you then burn or write the image onto the CD. The ISO9660 is the default file system for CD-ROMs.

Use the `mkisofs` command to create the ISO image. The `mkisofs` command has many options (see the man page for a full listing), but use the following for quick burns:

```
matthew@seymour:~$ mkisofs -r -v -J -l -o /tmp/our_special_cd.iso /source_directory
```

The options used in this example are as follows:

▶ `-r`—Sets the permission of the files to more useful values. `UID` and `GID` (individual and group user ID requirements) are set to `0`, all files are globally readable and searchable, and all files are set as executable (for Windows systems).

▶ `-v`—Displays verbose messages (rather than terse messages) so that you can see what is occurring during the process; these messages can help you resolve problems if they occur.

▶ `-J`—Uses the Joliet extensions to ISO9660 so that your Windows-using buddies can more easily read the CD. The Joliet (for Windows), Rock Ridge (for UNIX), and HSF (for Mac) extensions to the ISO9660 standard are used to accommodate long filenames rather than the eight-character DOS filenames that the ISO9660 standard supports.

▶ **-1**—Allows 31-character filenames; DOS does not like it, but everyone else does.

▶ **-o**—Defines the directory where the image will be written (that is, the output) and its name. The /tmp directory is convenient for this purpose, but the image could go anywhere you have write permissions.

▶ **/source_directory**—Indicates the path to the source directory; that is, the directory containing the files you want to include. There are ways to append additional paths and exclude directories (and files) under the specified path; it is all explained in the man page, if you need that level of complexity. The simple solution is to construct a new directory tree and populate it with the files you want to copy, and then make the image using that directory as the source.

Many more options are available, including options to make the CD bootable.

After you have created the ISO image, you can write it to the CD with the cdrecord command:

```
matthew@seymour:~$ cdrecord -eject -v speed=12 dev=0,0,0 /tmp/our_special_cd.iso
```

The options used in this example are as follows:

▶ **-eject**—Ejects the CD when the write operation is finished.

▶ **-v**—Displays verbose messages.

▶ **speed=**—Sets the speed; the rate depends on the individual drive's capabilities. If the drive or the recordable medium is poor, you can use lower speeds to get a good burn.

▶ **dev=**—Specifies the device number of the CD writer.

NOTE

You can also use the blank = option with the cdrecord command to erase CD-RW disks. The cdrecord command has fewer options than mkisofs does, but it offers the -multi option, which enables you to make multisession CDs. A multisession CD enables you to write a data track, quit, and then add more data to the CD later. A single-session CD can be written to only once; any leftover CD capacity is wasted. Read about other options in the cdrecord man page.

Current capacity for CD media is 700MB of data or 80 minutes of music. (There are 800MB/90-minute CDs, but they are rare.) Some CDs can be overburned; that is, recorded to a capacity in excess of the standard. The cdrecord command and some graphical programs are capable of overburning if your CD-RW drive supports it. You can learn more about overburning CDs at www.cdmediaworld.com/hardware/cdrom/cd_oversize.shtml/.

Creating DVDs from the Command Line

There are several competing formats for DVD, as follows:

- ▶ DVD+R
- ▶ DVD-R
- ▶ DVD+RW
- ▶ DVD-RW

Differences in the + and – formats have mostly to do with how the data is modulated onto the DVD itself, with the + format having an edge in buffer underrun recovery. How this is achieved impacts the playability of the newly created DVD on any DVD player. The DVD+ format also has some advantages in recording on scratched or dirty media. Most drives support the DVD+ format. As with any technology, your mileage may vary.

We focus on the DVD+RW drives because most drives support that standard. The software supplied with Ubuntu has support for writing to DVD-R/W (rewritable) media, as well. It will be useful for you to review the DVD+RW/+R/-R[W] for Linux HOWTO at http://fy.chalmers.se/~appro/linux/DVD+RW/ before you attempt to use dvd+rw-tools, which you need to install to enable DVD creation (also known as *mastering*) and the cdrtools package. You can ignore the discussion in the HOWTO about kernel patches and compiling the tools.

> **TIP**
>
> The 4.7GB size of DVD media is measured as 1000 megabytes per gigabyte, instead of the more traditionally used, but not entirely accurate, 1024 megabytes per gigabyte (more appropriately written GiB), so do not be surprised when the actual formatted capacity, about 4.4GB, is less than you anticipated. A good explanation of the difference and the need for the correction is available at http://en.wikipedia.org/wiki/Gibibyte. Most hard drive manufacturers have also made the switch. dvd+rw-tools does not allow you to exceed the capacity of the disk.

You need to have the dvd+rw-tools package installed (as well as the cdrtools package). The dvd+rw-tools package contains the growisofs application (which acts as a front end to mkisofs) and the DVD formatting utility.

You can use DVD media to record data in two ways. The first way is much the same as that used to record CDs in a session, and the second way is to record the data as a true file system using packet writing.

Session Writing

To record data in a session, you use a two-phase process:

1. Format the disk with dvd+rw-format /dev/scd0 (only necessary the first time you use a disk, where /dev/scd0 is the device name for your drive).

2. Write your data to the disk with growisofs -Z /dev/scd0 -R -J /your_files.

The growisofs command simply streams the data to the disk. For subsequent sessions, use the -M argument rather than -Z. The -Z argument is used only for the initial session recording; if you use the -Z argument on an already-used disk, it erases the existing files.

CAUTION

Some DVDs come preformatted; formatting them again when you use them for the first time can make the DVD useless. Always be sure to carefully read the packaging your DVD comes in to ensure that you are not about to create another coaster.

TIP

Writing a first session of at least 1GB helps maintain compatibility of your recorded data with other optical drives. DVD players calibrate themselves by attempting to read from specific locations on the disk; you need data there for the drive to read it and calibrate itself.

Also, because of limitations to the ISO9660 file system in Linux, do not start new sessions of a multisession DVD that would create a directory past the 4GB boundary. If you do so, it causes the offsets used to point to the files to "wrap around" and point to the wrong files.

Packet Writing

Packet writing treats the CD or DVD disk like a hard drive in which you create a file system (like ext3) and format the disk and then write to it randomly as you would to a conventional hard drive. This method, although commonly available on Windows-based computers, was long considered experimental for Linux and was never used much anyway because USB thumb drives became common before the use of CD or DVD-RWs had the opportunity. We do not cover this in detail here, but a quick overview is appropriate.

TIP

DVD+RW media are capable of only about 1,000 writes, so it is very useful to mount them with the noatime option to eliminate any writing to update their inodes or simply mount them read-only when it's not necessary to write to them.

It is possible to pipe data to the growisofs command:

```
matthew@seymour:~$ sudo your_application | growisofs -Z /dev/scd0=/dev/fd/0
```

It is also possible to burn from an existing image (or file, named pipe, or device):

```
matthew@seymour:~$ sudo growisofs -Z /dev/scd0=image
```

The dvd+rw-tools documentation, found at /usr/share/doc/dvd+rw-tools/index.html, is required reading before your first use of the program. We also suggest that you experiment with DVD-RW (rewritable) media first, because if you make mistakes, you can still reuse the disk, instead of creating several new coasters for your coffee mug.

Viewing Video

You can use Ubuntu tools and applications to view movies and other video presentations on your PC. This section presents some TV and motion picture video software tools included with the Ubuntu distribution you received with this book.

TV and Video Hardware

To watch TV and video content on your PC, you must install a supported TV card or have a video/TV combo card installed. You can find a current list of TV and video cards supported in Linux at www.exploits.org/v4l/.

Freely available Linux support for TV display from video cards that have a TV-out jack is improved over a couple of years ago, but still rather poor. That support must come from the X driver, not from a video device that Video4Linux supports with a device driver. Some of the combo TV-tuner/video display cards have support, including the Matrox Marvel, the Matrox Rainbow Runner G-Series, and the RivaTV cards. Many other combo cards lack support, although an independent developer might have hacked something together to support his own card. Your best course of action is to perform a thorough Internet search with Google.

Many of the TV-only PCI cards are supported. In Linux, however, they are supported by the video chipset they use, and not by the name some manufacturer has slapped on a generic board. (The same board is typically sold by different manufacturers under different names.) The most common chipset is the Brooktree Bt*** series of chips; they are supported by the bttv device driver.

If you have a supported card in your computer, it should be detected during installation. If you add it later, the hardware-detection utility should detect it and configure it. It is possible to try to configure it by hand, but because the Ubuntu kernel czars try to compile every hardware option available as a module and make it available, doing so isn't likely to be of much use. Even so, this is what you would do.

First, to determine what chipset your card has, use the lspci command to list the PCI device information, find the TV card listing, and look for the chipset that the card uses. For example, the lspci output for one computer shows the following.

```
matthew@seymour:~$ lspci
00:00.0 Host bridge: Advanced Micro Devices [AMD] AMD-760 [IGD4-1P] System
➥Controller (rev 13)
00:01.0 PCI bridge: Advanced Micro Devices [AMD] AMD-760 [IGD4-1P] AGP Bridge
00:07.0 ISA bridge: VIA Technologies, Inc. VT82C686 [Apollo Super South] (rev 40)
```

```
00:07.1 IDE interface: VIA Technologies, Inc. VT82C586B PIPC Bus Master IDE (rev 06)
00:07.2 USB Controller: VIA Technologies, Inc. USB (rev 1a)
00:07.3 USB Controller: VIA Technologies, Inc. USB (rev 1a)
00:07.4 SMBus: VIA Technologies, Inc. VT82C686 [Apollo Super ACPI] (rev 40)
00:09.0 Multimedia audio controller: Ensoniq 5880 AudioPCI (rev 02)
00:0b.0 Multimedia video controller: Brooktree Corporation Bt878 Video Capture
➥(rev 02)
00:0b.1 Multimedia controller: Brooktree Corporation Bt878 Audio Capture (rev 02)
00:0d.0 Ethernet controller: Realtek Semiconductor Co., Ltd. RTL-8029(AS)
00:0f.0 FireWire (IEEE 1394): Texas Instruments TSB12LV23 IEEE-1394 Controller
00:11.0 Network controller: Standard Microsystems Corp [SMC] SMC2602W EZConnect
01:05.0 VGA compatible controller: nVidia Corporation NV15 [GeForce2 Ti] (rev a4)
```

Here, the lines listing the multimedia video controller and multimedia controller say that this TV board uses a Brooktree Bt878 Video Capture chip and a Brooktree Bt878 Audio Capture chip. This card uses the Bt878 chipset. Your results will be different, depending on what card and chipset your computer has. This card happened to be an ATI All-in-Wonder VE (also known as ATI TV-Wonder). (The VE means *Value Edition*; hence, there is no TV-out connector and no radio chip on the card; what a value!)

Then you figure out what module is needed, probably using Google to search for "Bt878 linux" or "Bt878 Ubuntu," and start reading documentation. You want to look for official pages first rather than blog posts. Finally, you need to enter some information into /etc/modules.conf. This file does not exist anymore in a default Ubuntu installation but may be created as needed and will be read at boot time. Then, you would calculate the module and kernel dependencies with sudo depmod -a and sudo modprobe *module name* to load the module. Again, this is not necessary in Ubuntu because the people doing kernel configuration create a module for everything that exists, so if it is available to them, they will make it available to you with no extra work on your part, and the system scans to see what should be loaded at boot and pulls in what is needed then.

Video Formats

Ubuntu recognizes a variety of video formats. The formats created by the MPEG group, Apple, and Microsoft dominate, however. At the heart of video formats are the *codecs*—the encoders and decoders of the video and audio information. These codecs are typically proprietary, but free codecs do exist. Here is a list of the most common video formats and their associated file extensions, although many more exist:

▶ AVI (.avi)—The Windows audio visual format

▶ FLV (.flv)—Used in Adobe Flash, supports H.264 and others

▶ MPEG (.mpeg)—The MPEG video format; also known as .mpg

▶ MOV (.mov)—Another QuickTime video format

▶ OGV/OGG (.ogv/.ogg)—The Ogg Theora freely licensed video format

▶ **QT (`.qt`)**—The QuickTime video format from Apple

▶ **WEBM (`.webm`)**—Google's royalty-free container for audio and video (such as in VP8 format) designed for HTML5

Viewing Video in Linux

Out of the box, Ubuntu does not support any of the proprietary video codecs due to licensing restrictions. However, this functionality can be acquired if you install the `ubuntu-restricted-extras` package from the Ubuntu software repositories. You can learn more about this at https://help.ubuntu.com/community/RestrictedFormats.

You can watch video files and video DVDs with Totem Movie Player (see Figure 6.12), which is installed by default and may be found in the menu at Applications, Sound & Video, Movie Player. This may also be used with several other file formats and for both video and audio and is especially well suited for almost anything you are likely to want to use after the `ubuntu-restricted-extras` package is installed.

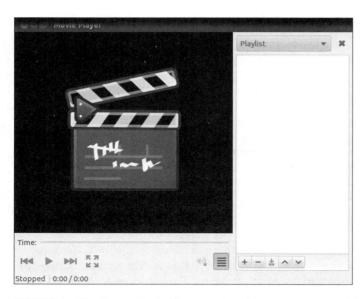

FIGURE 6.12   Totem Movie Player works with most common video and audio formats.

Adobe Flash

The Adobe Flash plug-in for the Firefox browser is a commercial multimedia application that isn't provided with Ubuntu out of the box, but many people find it useful. Adobe Flash enables you to view Flash content at websites that support it. The easiest way of getting hold of the official version of Flash is to install the `ubuntu-restricted-extras` package. After you've done this, any flash animations will play quite happily within any Firefox-based browsers.

Another interesting video viewer application is VLC, which is available in the software repositories and also for other operating systems like Windows and Mac OS X (see Figure 6.13). VLC uses its own set of audio and video codecs and supports a wider range of video formats than any other media player we have encountered. If VLC can't play it, it probably can't be played.

FIGURE 6.13   VLC is a powerful and capable media player.

Personal Video Recorders

The best reason to attach a television antenna to your computer, however, is to use the video card and the computer as a personal video recorder.

The commercial personal video recorder, TiVo, started a new trend by using Linux running on a PowerPC processor to record television programming with a variety of customizations. You can turn your computer into a personal digital video recorder with Myth TV from www.mythtv.org/, a Linux-based digital video recorder software project, made even easier for Ubuntu users by the Mythbuntu project at www.mythbuntu.org/. Everything you need is available in the Ubuntu repositories and may be installed and configured easily, thanks to the people involved in these projects.

Video Editing

You can now create and edit video in Ubuntu using PiTiVi (see Figure 6.14). It is not installed by default, but a quick search for "PiTiVi Video Editor" in the Ubuntu Software Center will get you started. You may import any video clip in any format that is supported by GStreamer, the main multimedia framework used in Ubuntu. This should include the files created by your digital camera, which should mount in Ubuntu as a storage device, making the transfer of the files from the camera to your computer quick and easy. PiTiVi lets you move scenes around, cut things, add your own soundtrack, and more.

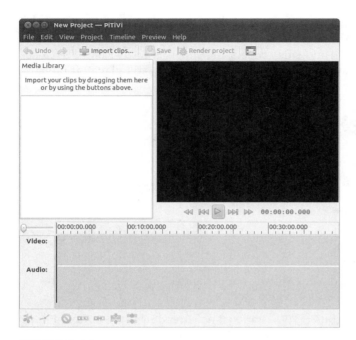

FIGURE 6.14   PiTiVi Video Editor.

References

▶ **www.videolan.org/**—A VideoLAN project with good documentation.

▶ **http://fy.chalmers.se/~appro/linux/DVD+RW/**—The DVD+RW/+R/-R[W] for Linux, a HOWTO for creating DVDs under Linux.

▶ **www.gimp.org**—Home page of The GIMP (*GNU Image Manipulation Program*).

▶ **http://f-spot.org**—Home page of the F-Spot project.

▶ **www.sane-project.org**—Home page of the SANE (*Scanner Access Now Easy*) project.

▶ **www.imagemagick.org**—Home page for ImageMagick.

▶ **http://gimp.net/tutorials/**—Official tutorials for The GIMP.

# CHAPTER 7

Other Ubuntu Desktops

When you install Ubuntu, by default you use the Unity desktop, discussed in Chapter 3, "Working With Unity." The Unity desktop has specific strengths that appeal to many users. However, some of us have unique requirements or just like to tinker. This chapter discusses some of the alternatives to Unity, their strengths and weaknesses, and how to install them. This is not a complete listing of all the options available, but rather a brief survey of some of the more popular options to consider helping you get your feet wet in the realm of Linux desktop software.

Unity Is Not the Only Option

When you install Ubuntu, you also install the Unity desktop. However, this is neither your only option nor are you limited to only one desktop installed at a time. Each of the desktops we discuss in this chapter may be installed alongside Unity in standard Ubuntu, and you will be allowed to choose which one to use each time you log in and which one to use by default. This makes testing a new option less risky because switching back to what you already know is simple.

Desktop Environment

A desktop environment is a *graphical user interface (GUI)* for computers, specifically an interface that uses the idea of a physical office desk as a metaphor to make interacting with the computer simple to comprehend. As in a real-world office, a computer desktop environment will use files to contain documents that contain information that is necessary for office tasks to be done. Computer systems take the metaphor further by adding applications, programs that allow users to create, manipulate, and delete those documents as needed, much as might be done in the real world, but with greater efficiency and often with greater power.

A computer desktop includes a windowing system, another metaphoric way to deal with information that makes conceptualizing the complexity occurring behind the scenes in the digital realm easier. Files, folders (or directories), and applications open in a graphic display that may be moved around the user's desktop just as paper documents and file folders may be moved to different locations on a physical desktop for convenience and efficiency. This windowing system includes the graphical bits (called *widgets*) needed to draw the windows on the screen and all the program code needed to perform the actions desired behind the scenes while displaying those actions using the pretty metaphor. For example, moving a document from one folder to another on a desktop involves little more than a mouse click followed by a drag and drop. Behind the scenes, the desktop environment is listening to the window manager's instructions to move a file from one directory to another and then telling the window manager to draw the event on the screen as it is accomplished.

The Ubuntu software repositories include all the popular desktop environments available for Linux and make installing and trying them out easy to do. It is also possible for an adventurous person to find other desktop environments that will work on Ubuntu and download and install them. We don't cover that process here.

It is also possible to use one desktop environment while substituting a different window manager into that environment instead of using the one that comes with the desktop environment by default. For example, the standard GNOME window manager is called Metacity. It is stable and works quite well. However, Ubuntu uses a different window manager called Compiz if the installation process detects the presence of video hardware capable of taking advantage of the extra flashy features it provides (otherwise, the installer configures Ubuntu to use Metacity). To make matters more interesting, you can replace either of those with other window managers such as Enlightenment (see Figure 7.1), which does things in a unique and interesting manner.

In this chapter, we focus on complete desktop environments using the default window manager. In addition, because this is an Ubuntu-focused book, we focus on Ubuntu-refined versions of environments such as KDE and Xfce rather than their default versions, although the default versions are also available in the Ubuntu repositories if you want to seek them out.

KDE and Kubuntu

The KDE project began back in 1996 with the goal of creating a quality desktop environment for the Linux desktop that was free, worked well, and which was well integrated, meaning that programs and interfaces would have a consistent look and feel where all the parts fit together seamlessly, rather than looking like a jumbled compilation of a bunch of assorted bits.

FIGURE 7.1   Enlightenment is a unique and interesting desktop environment option.

The project has always been focused on end users rather than creating a simple GUI for the systems administrator. This is an important point, because from the beginning, the intent has been to make any computer user comfortable and able to do what they want to do without necessarily requiring a full grasp of what is happening behind the scenes. This focus continues today and is shared by other desktop environments, notably GNOME, which was started in 1997 by people once involved in the KDE project who left after a dispute over software licensing.

The cause of that dispute no longer exists as the licenses today are equivalently free, but the projects diverged a bit in their focus: GNOME seeks a desktop of zenlike simplicity with simple and elegant defaults and use, while KDE pursues more flash and configuration options. Honestly, they are each great desktop environments that are well-integrated with a high degree of professionalism and quality and are easily the top two in the Linux world—try them both and see which you prefer.

Kubuntu is a project that started in the Ubuntu community very early on with the simple goal of allowing users to install and use KDE in Ubuntu. To make this even easier for people who already know they prefer KDE over GNOME, you can download an install disk for Kubuntu, which is Ubuntu minus GNOME plus KDE plus a few Kubuntu-specific enhancements. You may also install Kubuntu in standard Ubuntu and alongside GNOME by installing the kubuntu-desktop package from the Ubuntu software repositories.

Kubuntu (see Figure 7.2) uses a different set of default programs for most tasks: web browsing, email, and so on. Most were written specifically for the KDE desktop environment, making KDE one of the most closely integrated and consistent Linux desktops available.

FIGURE 7.2   The Kubuntu desktop.

Xfce and Xubuntu

Xfce is a lighter desktop environment that requires less memory and processing power than either GNOME or KDE and is therefore often suggested for use on older machines. It does not deserve to be relegated to that role because it also works great on current hardware and is often a quality choice for a different reason. Xfce has been developed using the traditional UNIX philosophy of software: do one thing, do it well, and play well with others.

Each part of the Xfce desktop environment is modular, you may add or remove bits at will, substitute other programs that perform the same function, and everything created by or included in Xfce is expected to work according to simple standards that allow other programs to interact with it easily.

On one hand, this sometimes means that people look at Xfce and think it isn't as seamlessly integrated and smooth as the two main desktop environments. On the other hand, it means that if you prefer the GNOME file manager (Nautilus) over the one included with Xfce (Thunar), then just install Nautilus and use it, either side by side with Thunar or remove Thunar completely. This is a huge part of what makes Xfce so lightweight that it has very few dependency requirements and is highly flexible.

Originally, Xubuntu (see Figure 7.3) was designed to create a lighter-weight version of Ubuntu that would run well on older hardware because of the lighter code dependencies of Xfce. Over time, some people discovered that they liked the desktop environment for other reasons, and the older hardware use case became less of a focus. It was the modularity of Xfce combined with a smoothness of operation that won people over, and the distribution began to take some of the favored bits from Ubuntu's customized version of GNOME and added them to Xfce to replace some of its defaults. What we have today is a nice amalgamation of Ubuntu GNOME bits, Xfce bits, and a few other things not included by default in either.

FIGURE 7.3   The Xubuntu desktop.

Xubuntu still uses less memory and fewer CPU cycles than a standard Ubuntu or Kubuntu install; however, thinking of it only in those terms doesn't do it justice. To install Xubuntu with the Xfce desktop environment, install the `xubuntu-desktop` package.

LXDE and Lubuntu

The previously discussed desktop environments are all officially recognized derivatives of Ubuntu, acknowledged by the developer community and well represented within it. This section discusses a project that is hoping to achieve that same status, but which is still quite new and experimental: Lubuntu. Lubuntu is based on LXDE.

LXDE is an extremely fast desktop environment that uses less memory and fewer CPU cycles than any of the others discussed. It is being developed specifically with lower-powered computers such as netbooks in mind, but that isn't the sole use case. For example, Knoppix, which is a Linux distribution that runs from a live, bootable CD or DVD, now uses LXDE. Knoppix is a longtime favorite of sysadmins for emergency repairs of unbootable systems and for its portability. It recently switched from KDE to LXDE to benefit from this lightness because running an operating system from a CD or DVD is generally much slower than when it is installed on a hard drive.

As the focus in Xubuntu turned from speed and lightness to enjoying the flexibility of Xfce, a gap was created. Users and developers interested in less-expensive hardware, such as mobile Internet devices and ARM or MIPS processor-based computers, wanted to find a way to run a distribution of Linux that shared the community of Ubuntu, a beautiful and useful desktop, and that did not get bogged down on slower machines. LXDE is quite new and its development philosophy fits quite well with the hopes and dreams of these users, so it seems to be a perfect fit.

The Lubuntu (see Figure 7.4) distribution is still very new and is not yet recommended for use as a primary desktop. The developers are working within the Ubuntu community and making consistent progress, and if you are inclined, they are also appealing for interested people to join the development team and help out. You may install `lubuntu-desktop` from the Ubuntu repositories to check out the current progress. Who knows? Maybe you will discover it is already both stable and useful enough for your needs. Even if it isn't ready, it may excite or interest you so much that you decide to jump in and help out.

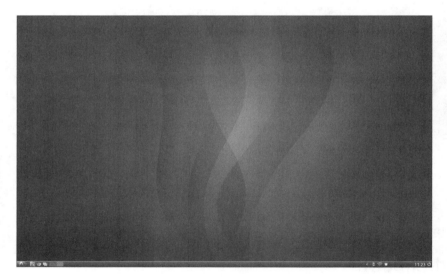

FIGURE 7.4   The Lubuntu desktop is quite attractive.

GNOME

Starting with Ubuntu 4.10, the default desktop for Ubuntu has been based on GNOME. Until recently, it was close to a standard GNOME desktop with only a few customizations. Once development began on GNOME 3, the desktop took a turn that did not suit the needs or desires of Ubuntu quite as well. This was when development began on Unity, as described in Chapter 3.

GNOME 3 is available in Ubuntu for those who prefer it over Unity. As development and support are ending for the classic GNOME 2 environment, it is no longer recommended and will not be available much longer (perhaps not even in the Ubuntu repositories for 11.10).

GNOME 3 is somewhat similar to Unity in that both are trying to push the Linux desktop into new territory. They both discard older metaphors and require a bit of adjusting for the user. The goal of GNOME 3 is to create an elegant desktop that is easy to use, uncluttered, and consistent (see Figure 7.5). If you want to try GNOME 3, install `gnome-shell` from the Ubuntu software repositories. Most of the programs are the same as are used in Unity, which is based on GNOME 3, but with a different user interface.

FIGURE 7.5   The GNOME 3 desktop.

References

- **http://blogs.gnome.org/metacity/2007/12/23/start-reading-here/**—Metacity does not have an official home page, as this post on the official Metacity blog explains.

- **www.compiz.org/**—The official site of Compiz.

- **www.enlightenment.org/**—The official site of Enlightenment.

- **www.kde.org/**—The official site for the KDE desktop.

- **www.kubuntu.org/**—The official Kubuntu site.

- **www.xfce.org/**—The official site for the Xfce desktop.

- **www.xubuntu.org/**—The official Xubuntu site.

- **www.lxde.org/**—The official site for the LXDE desktop.

- **http://lubuntu.net/**—The official Lubuntu site.

- **www.gnome.org/**—The official site for the GNOME desktop.

▶ **www.knoppix.net/**—The site for the live CD/DVD Linux distribution, Knoppix.

▶ **http://xwinman.org/**—A nice discussion of many of the different window managers and desktop environments available for Linux and UNIX systems. Much of the discussion on this site is dated, but the links are generally valid and useful, and the site gives a good overview of the many options available.

▶ **http://en.wikipedia.org/wiki/Desktop_environment**—A detailed definition of a desktop environment, how they work, why they exist, and so on.

▶ **http://en.wikipedia.org/wiki/Comparison_of_X_Window_System_desktop_ environments**—An amazing list of available desktop environments complete with a comparison of features.

CHAPTER 8

Games

Playing games is a fun part of computing. For some of us, games are a big part of the appeal of any operating system, at least for uses beyond the business or corporate environment. From the humble card games that entertain millions during their coffee breaks, to the heavily involved first-person shooters that involve players dotted around the globe, Linux offers a quality gaming platform that may surprise you.

In this chapter, we explore some of the common games available for you to download and install easily in Ubuntu.

Ubuntu Gaming

A small number of games come installed by default with standard desktop Ubuntu, mostly simple things to divert your attention for a few minutes between tasks—games such as solitaire or sudoku (see Figure 8.1). These are easy to try out and learn, and you may find them enjoyable.

Most of us who enjoy games will want to find something more. Thankfully, games for Linux do not stop there—several popular games have native Linux support. We discuss a small number of our favorites here.

Emulators

In addition, emulators enable you to play classic games, such as the LucasArts ScummVM games like Secret of Monkey Island, natively under Linux. There are emulators for DOS, NES, SNES, and many more. If you are interested in them, do a search online for Dgen/SDL, DosBox, xtrs, FCEUltra,

GnGeo, SDLMama, ScummVM, and Stella. The documentation for emulators is hit or miss, but if you are lucky, you may be able to play your favorite old games for consoles or operating systems that no longer exist or which current OS versions do not support.

FIGURE 8.1   The default games as listed in the dash under Applications, Games.

Installing Proprietary Video Drivers

A major gripe of Linux users has been the difficulty involved in getting modern 3D graphics cards to work. Thankfully, both AMD (owner of the now-defunct ATI brand) and Nvidia support Linux, albeit by using closed-source drivers. This means that Ubuntu does not ship with native 3D drivers activated for either graphics card, but they are easily installed, often during or just after the operating system is installed. These drivers are needed for most of the more visually spectacular games.

Both Nvidia and AMD produce proprietary drivers, meaning that the source code is not open or available for outside developers to read or modify. Because of this, it is hard for some Linux distros to include them as part of their standard installation. The Ubuntu community has taken a pragmatic approach of including both Nvidia and AMD drivers within the main Ubuntu distro, but disabled by default. That way, anyone who has Nvidia or AMD hardware and wants to do so can activate those drivers to take advantage of their features.

> **NOTE**
>
> If you think that proprietary drivers are the only way on Linux, we should mention that there is a lot of development going into providing totally free and open-source drivers for slightly older graphics cards. Ubuntu automatically selects the best "free" driver for your system and allows you to switch the proprietary driver should you want to. Although the open-source drivers provide 3D acceleration, this support doesn't always extend to a full feature set or to the more recent graphics cards.

It's easy to activate the proprietary driver, if you need to, from the Dash search for "additional drivers."

Installing a different hardware driver requires super user privileges, so a confirmation check is run to determine whether you are permitted and then you are asked for your password. After the Hardware Drivers dialog window has opened, read the descriptions and look for the recommended entry for your hardware, highlight it, and click Activate at the lower right. Ubuntu confirms that you want to use the proprietary driver and, if you agree, automatically downloads and configures the relevant driver. If you want to revert to the open driver, do the same thing, but select the activated driver and click Remove at the lower right, as shown in Figure 8.2, in the same place where the earlier Activate button was.

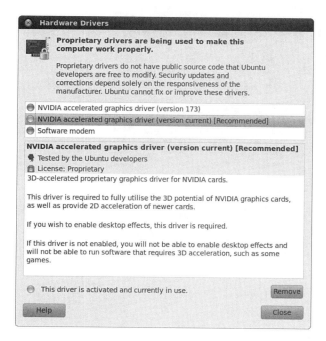

FIGURE 8.2   Use the Additional Drivers manager to activate or deactivate the appropriate proprietary graphics driver for your graphics card.

Installing Games in Ubuntu

In this section, you learn how to install some of the more popular games for Ubuntu, all of which may be easily installed using Ubuntu Software Center, along with hundreds more listed under Games. Alongside the usual shoot-'em-up games, you'll also find one or two strategy-focused titles.

Warsow

Warsow is a free and fast-paced *first-person shooter (FPS)* game that is available on Windows, Mac OS X, and Linux. Members of the Ubuntu community have packaged the game and make it available directly and easily for Ubuntu users from the software repositories. The game involves quick movements, grabbing power-ups and weapons before your enemies do, and trying to plant a bomb and steal your enemy's flag without anyone seeing you. You can jump, dash, dodge, and even wall jump your way throughout the colorful 3D environment. Figure 8.3 shows a game just getting started, with lots of weapons, platforms and ramps, and power-ups in sight.

FIGURE 8.3   Warsow is one of the newest and fastest FPS games available.

Scorched 3D

Scorched 3D is based on an old DOS game called Scorched Earth. The object and game play are similar: There are multiple players, and you enter targeting details to try to destroy the other players using a variety of missile-like weapons. You earn points for each win and can buy new weapons at the end of each round. This time around, there is an amazing array of weapons available, and the game play is completely in stunning 3D, as shown in Figure 8.4.

FIGURE 8.4   Scorched 3D in action.

Scorched 3D is based on turns. Each player shoots once, and then all other players take a shot before the first player shoots again. The game allows you to have more than 20 players at the same time, including both human and computer-controlled players. You may play a local game, over a LAN, or even over the Internet. Scorched 3D also runs on Windows, Mac OS X and Linux, so you may play with your friends regardless of what platform their computer uses.

Frozen Bubble

Frozen Bubble is an amusing little game with sharp graphics, nice music, and easy game play. You may play alone or against another player. The goal is to use your colored marbles to knock down the ones above you within a certain amount of time. You have to hit at least two at a time that are the same color as the one you shoot for anything to fall; otherwise, your shot joins the menagerie above and brings your demise somewhat more quickly, as illustrated in Figure 8.5. There is a lot more to Frozen Bubble, but even with the details, it is easy enough for a child to play and interesting enough to hold the interest of most adults.

FIGURE 8.5   Move left or right to aim, press up to fire.

SuperTux

Many of us grew up in the era when game play was more important than graphics. Even so, we still liked flashy and pretty-looking games. SuperTux is a throwback to the Mario era. It is a 2D side scroller in which you jump, run, and occasionally shoot something if you have the appropriate power-up. This time, your hero is Tux, the Linux penguin. More than 25 levels are available, as is a level editor for you to create your own. If you enjoy running, jumping, hitting your head to get money, and jumping on your enemies, this game is for you. Figure 8.6 gives you the basic look and feel.

Battle for Wesnoth

One of the most popular games currently available for Linux is Battle for Wesnoth (see Figure 8.7), a strategy game featuring both single and multiplayer options. Based in a fantasy land, you are responsible for building armies to wage war against your foes who are attacking you. Game play may be based on scenarios, such as in single-player mode where some scenarios are preinstalled and others may be easily downloaded, or based on trying to better your friends at a LAN party or online.

Battle for Wesnoth also comes with a map editor that lets you create your own scenarios. An active community shares their work and welcomes new contributions. You can find more information about Battle for Wesnoth at http://wesnoth.org/.

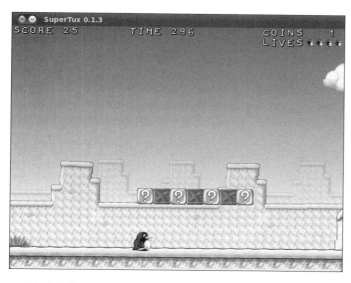

FIGURE 8.6   Although the look and feel of this game takes me back to my childhood, it is far from dull or boring.

FIGURE 8.7   Flex your strategic brain by playing Battle for Wesnoth, a rich and full land of fantasy of adventure.

Frets on Fire

Frets on Fire is similar to games like Guitar Hero (see Figure 8.8). Players try to keep up with a song and "play" it correctly. It supports songs from Guitar Hero I and II and, unlike these proprietary games, is expandable by the community, as well, with more songs available for download from the Internet. The game is completely open source and has content-compatible versions for Linux, Windows, and Mac OS X.

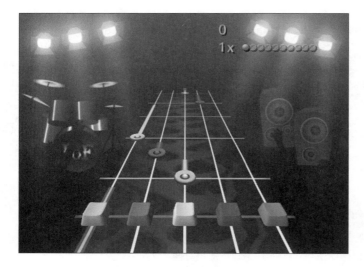

FIGURE 8.8   Frets on Fire offers flashy graphics and familiar game play.

Games for Kids

Kids, both young and old, are not left out. Check out game packages such as gCompris, Childsplay, and TuxPaint to get started. Some of these are educational, some teach computer skills such as using a mouse or a keyboard, and others are just for amusement. Many developers are also parents who have placed a high priority on making quality software for their children to enjoy on their favorite platform. You can search for children's games in the Ubuntu Software Center and find lots of great things to try.

Commercial Games

Something new in the past year or so is that Canonical has made a way for commercial software companies to make their products available for installation in Ubuntu via the Ubuntu Software Center. This includes games. A special section of the Ubuntu Software Center labeled For Purchase has been created. Look here for some new and flashy options from commercial vendors. Payment is required and the details are taken care of within the Ubuntu Software Center.

Playing Windows Games

Ubuntu is primarily aimed at desktop computer users who want a system that is stable, powerful, and easy to use. It is not primarily a gaming platform. In fact, compared to Windows, there are not nearly as many games available or being developed (although the number is growing and has improved). This doesn't mean hard-core gamers need to feel left out, though. There are two projects that exist to help game lovers play most Windows-based games on Linux.

A project called Wine uses application interfaces to make Windows programs believe they are running on a Windows platform and not a Linux platform. Bear in mind that Wine stands for *Wine is not an emulator*, so do not start thinking of it as such—the community can get quite touchy about it!

Wine is a compatibility layer (not an emulator) that aims to make Windows software believe it is running on Windows even when it is running on Linux. Although the open-source, free software project won't run everything, it does run a very large number of Windows programs, including many games.

Cedega is a fork of the Wine project that adds some proprietary touches and a focus on games and, for a fee, allows you to download and use their compatibility layer.

Crossover Games is another commercial option, and is available in the Ubuntu Software Center under For Purchase.

> **TIP**
>
> The keys to successful gaming in Linux are to always read the documentation thoroughly, always investigate the Internet resources thoroughly, and always understand your system. Installing games is a great way to learn about your system because the reward of success is so much fun.

References

- ▶ www.linuxgames.com/—A good source of up-to-date information about the state of Linux gaming.

- ▶ www.warsow.net/—The official site of Warsow.

- ▶ www.scorched3d.co.uk/—The official site of Scorched 3D.

- ▶ www.frozen-bubble.org/—The official site of Frozen Bubble.

- ▶ http://supertux.lethargik.org/—The official site of SuperTux.

- ▶ http://wesnoth.org/—The official site of Battle for Wesnoth.

- ▶ http://gcompris.net/—The official site of gCompris.

- ▶ http://fretsonfire.sourceforge.net—The official site of Frets on Fire.

- ▶ **http://childsplay.sourceforge.net/index.php**—The official site of Childsplay.

- ▶ **www.tuxpaint.org/**—The official site of TuxPaint.

- ▶ **www.nvnews.net/vbulletin/forumdisplay.php?f=14**—The Official Nvidia Linux driver support forum.

- ▶ **www.nvidia.com/object/unix.html**—Home page for the Nvidia Unix/Linux drivers.

- ▶ **http://support.amd.com/us/gpudownload/Pages/index.aspx**—Home page for the ATI Linux drivers, including drivers for Linux.

- ▶ **https://help.ubuntu.com/community/Wine**—Ubuntu community documentation for Wine.

- ▶ **www.winehq.org/**—The official site of Wine, which includes good information about software that is known to work with the current version in an application database subsite at http://appdb.winehq.org/.

- ▶ **https://help.ubuntu.com/community/Cedega**—Ubuntu community documentation for Cedega.

- ▶ **www.transgaming.com/**—The official TransGaming Technologies website provides details of games that are directly supported under Cedega.

12/29/2019

Items checked out at Tredyffrin Library to:

p1649782x

Ubuntu unleashed / Matthew

Barcode 3 1379 02379 5967

Due **01-19-20**

Visit Tredyffrin Public Library at
www.tredyffrinlibraries.org

# CHAPTER 9

Managing Software

In this chapter, we look at the options you have to manage your software in Ubuntu. If you are used to a Windows environment where you are reliant on visiting different vendor websites to download updates, you are in for a pleasant surprise. Updating a full Ubuntu installation, including all the application software, is as simple as running the Update Manager program. You will discover just how easy it is to install and even remove various software packages.

Ubuntu provides a variety of tools for system resource management. The following sections introduce the graphical software management tools that you will use for most of your software management. This chapter also covers monitoring and managing memory and disk storage on your system.

Ubuntu Software Center

The Ubuntu Software Center is a graphical utility for package management in Ubuntu. You will find it in the Applications menu as Ubuntu Software Center; it is named `software-center`. The Ubuntu Software Center enables you to easily select and install a large array of applications by using the intuitive built-in search and easy one-click installation. When you open the program, you see the Package Browsing screen, as shown in Figure 9.1.

Along the left side of the screen, you have three menu options: Get Software, Installed Software, and History. At the top is a search bar that you can use to search for packages. When you click the Get Software link, you are presented with options to explore software Provided by Ubuntu or software For Purchase. Clicking the Installed Software link presents you with a list of all the installed applications on your Ubuntu desktop.

FIGURE 9.1   The initial Ubuntu Software Center screen enables you to browse through packages sorted by groups.

Installing new software via Ubuntu Software Center is as simple as finding it in the package list, double-clicking, and clicking the Install button. When you do so, you may be asked for your password; then the application is downloaded and installed. You can remove an application by finding it in Ubuntu Software Center and clicking the Remove button.

Use the Search box at the top to search for a specific application in the list. Note that this searches within the current category; so if you are in the Games category and search for "office," you will get no results. The best place to search is within the Get Free Software category, to make sure you search all areas.

Using Synaptic for Software Management

The Add/Remove Applications dialog works just fine for adding applications, but if you need to install something very specific—such as a library—or if you want to reconfigure your installation system, you need to use Synaptic (see Figure 9.2). You can install Synaptic using the Ubuntu Software Center described earlier; it is not installed by default.

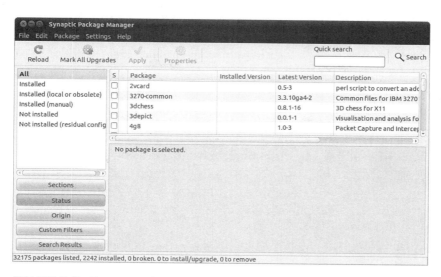

FIGURE 9.2   For more advanced software management in a GUI, Synaptic is the preferred tool.

At first glance, Synaptic looks a little like the Add/Remove Applications window. Along the left are software categories (although this time, there are more of them), along the top right are the package selections for that category, and on the bottom right is the Package Information window that shows information about the currently selected package. To install or remove software, click the check box to the left of its name, and you'll see a menu that offers the following options:

▶ **Unmark**—If you have marked this package for installation, upgrade, or one of the other options, this removes that mark.

▶ **Mark for Installation**—Add this package to the list that will be installed.

▶ **Mark for Re-installation**—If you have some software already installed, but for some reason it's not working, this reinstalls it from scratch.

▶ **Mark for Upgrade**—If the software has updates available, this will download and install them.

▶ **Mark for Removal**—This deletes the selected package from your system, but leaves its configuration files intact, so that if you ever reinstall it, you do not have to reconfigure it.

▶ **Mark for Complete Removal**—This deletes the selected package from your system, but also removes any configuration files, purging everything from the system.

After you have made your changes, click the Apply button to have Synaptic download, install, upgrade, and uninstall as necessary. If you close the program without clicking Apply, your changes will be lost.

Beneath the categories on the left side of the screen, you will see four buttons: Sections, Status, Search, and Custom, with Sections selected. These customize the left list: Sections is the Categories view, Status lets you view packages that are installed or upgradable, Search stores results of your searches, and Custom has some esoteric groupings that are useful only to advanced users.

You can press Ctrl+F at any time to search for a particular package. By default, it is set to search by package name. You may change the Look In box setting to Description and Name. As mentioned already, your search terms are saved under the Search view (the button on the bottom left), and you can click from that list to re-search on that term.

As well as providing the method of installing and removing software, Synaptic provides the means to configure the servers you want to use for finding packages. In fact, this is where you can make one of the most important changes to your Ubuntu system: You can open it up to the Ubuntu Universe and Multiverse.

Ubuntu is based on the Debian distribution, which has more than 15,000 software packages available for installation. Ubuntu uses only a small subset of that number, but makes it easy for you to enable the others. When you use Synaptic, you see small orange Ubuntu logos next to every package; this identifies them as being officially supported by the Canonical supported Ubuntu developers. The other packages do not have this logo, but they are still supported by the wider Ubuntu community of developers.

To enable the Universe and Multiverse repositories, go to Settings, Repositories. This list shows all the servers you have configured for software installation and updates, and includes the Universe and Multiverse repositories. When you find them, check them, and then click Close.

Synaptic shows a message box warning you that the repository listings have changed and that you need to click the Reload button (near the top left of the Synaptic window) to have it refresh the package lists. Go ahead and do that, and you should see a lot more software appear for your selection. However, notice that only a small number have the official Ubuntu "seal" attached, which means you need to be a bit more careful when installing software.

NOTE

Much of the software discussed in this book is available only through the Universe repository. Therefore, we highly recommend enabling it to get full use out of this book and your Ubuntu installation.

Staying Up-to-Date

Although you can manage your software updates through Synaptic, Ubuntu provides a dedicated tool in the form of Update Manager (launched through System, Administration, Update Manager, and shown in Figure 9.3). This tool is designed to be simple to use: When you run it, Update Manager automatically downloads the list of updates available and checks them all in the list it shows. If the update list was downloaded automatically not too long ago, you can force Ubuntu to refresh the list of available updates by clicking the Check button. Otherwise, all you need to do is click Install Updates and your system will be brought up-to-date. If you want a little more information about the updates, click Show Details at the bottom to see what has changed in the update.

FIGURE 9.3   If you need to update your software to apply bug fixes and security upgrades, use Update Manager.

Ubuntu automatically checks for updates periodically and notifies you when critical updates are available. However, there's no harm running Update Manager yourself every so often, just to make sure; it's better to be safe than sorry.

Working on the Command Line

With so much software available for installation, it is no surprise that Debian-based distros have many ways to manage software installation. At their root, however, they all use Debian's world-renowned *Advanced Package Tool (APT)*. A person posting on Slashdot.com once said, "Welcome to Slashdot. If you can't think of anything original, just say how much APT rocks and you'll fit right in." You see, even though many other distros have tried to equal the power of APT, nothing else even comes close.

Why is APT so cool? Well, it was the first system to properly handle dependencies in software. Other distros, such as Red Hat, used RPM files that had dependencies. For example, an RPM for Gimp would have a dependency on Gtk, the graphical toolkit on which Gimp is based. As a result, if you tried to install your Gimp RPM without having the Gtk RPM, your install would fail. So, you grab the Gtk RPM and try again. Aha: Gtk has a dependency on three other things that you need to download. And those three other things have dependencies on 20 other things. And so on, and so on, usually until you can't find a working RPM for one of the dependencies, and you give up.

APT, on the other hand, was designed to automatically find and download dependencies for your packages. So, if you want to install Gimp, it downloads Gimp's package and any other software it needs to work. No more hunting around by hand, no more worrying about finding the right version, and certainly no more need to compile things by hand. APT also handles installation resuming, which means that if you lose your Internet connection part-way through an upgrade (or your battery runs out, or you have to quit, or whatever), APT picks up where it left off the next time you rerun it.

Day-to-Day Usage

To enable you to search for packages both quickly and thoroughly, APT uses a local cache of the available packages. Try running this command:

```
matthew@seymour:~$ sudo apt-get update
```

The apt-get update command instructs APT to contact all the servers it is configured to use and download the latest list of file updates. If your lists are outdated, it takes a minute or two for APT to download the updates. Otherwise, this command executes it in a couple of seconds.

After the latest package information has been downloaded, you are returned to the command line. You can now ask APT to automatically download any software that has been updated, using this command:

```
matthew@seymour:~$ sudo apt-get upgrade
```

If you have a lot of software installed on your machine, there is a greater chance of things being updated. APT scans your software and compares it to the latest package information from the servers and produces a report something like this:

```
matthew@seymour:~$ sudo apt-get upgrade
Reading package lists... Done
Building dependency tree
Reading state information... Done
The following packages will be upgraded:
  cabextract google-chrome-beta icedtea6-plugin language-pack-en
  language-pack-en-base language-pack-gnome-en language-pack-gnome-en-base
  libfreetype6 libfreetype6-dev libsmbclient libwbclient0 openjdk-6-jre
  openjdk-6-jre-headless openjdk-6-jre-lib samba-common samba-common-bin
  smbclient upstart winbind xserver-common xserver-xorg-core
21 upgraded, 0 newly installed, 0 to remove and 0 not upgraded.
```

```
Need to get 84.8MB of archives.
After this operation, 623kB of additional disk space will be used.
Do you want to continue [Y/n]?
```

Each part of that report tells us something important. Starting at the top, the line "the following packages will be upgraded" gives us the exact list of packages for which updates are available. If you're installing new software or removing software, you'll see lists titled "The following packages will be installed" and "The following packages will be removed." A summary at the end shows a total of 21 packages that APT will upgrade, with 0 new packages, 0 to remove, and 0 not upgraded. Because this is an upgrade rather than an installation of new software, all those new packages take up only 623KB of additional space. Although we have an 84.8MB download, the packages are overwriting existing files.

It's important to understand that a basic apt-get upgrade never removes software or adds new software. As a result, it is safe to use to keep your system fully patched, because it should never break things. However, occasionally you will see the "0 not upgraded" status change, which means some things cannot be upgraded. This happens when some software must be installed or removed to satisfy the dependencies of the updated package, which, as previously mentioned, apt-get upgrade will never do.

In this situation, you need to use apt-get dist-upgrade, so named because it's designed to allow users to upgrade from one version of Debian/Ubuntu to a newer version—an upgrade that inevitably involves changing just about everything on the system, removing obsolete software, and installing the latest features. This is one of the most-loved features of Debian because it allows you to move from version to version without having to download and install new CDs. Keeping regular upgrades and distro upgrades separate is very useful for making sure that security updates and simple bug fixes don't change software configurations that you may be counting on, especially on a machine that needs to be consistently available and working, such as a server.

Whereas apt-get upgrade and apt-get dist-upgrade are there for upgrading packages, apt-get install is responsible for adding new software. For example, if you want to install the MySQL database server, you run this:

```
matthew@seymour:~$ sudo apt-get install mysql-server
```

Internally, APT would query "mysql-server" against its list of software and find that it matches the mysql-server-5.0 package. It would then find which dependencies it needs that you don't already have installed and give you a report like this one:

```
matthew@seymour:~$ sudo apt-get install mysql-server
Reading package lists... Done
Building dependency tree... Done
The following extra packages will be installed:
  libdbd-mysql-perl libdbi-perl libnet-daemon-perl libplrpc-perl
  mysql-client-5.0 mysql-server-5.0
Suggested packages:
  dbishell libcompress-zlib-perl
```

```
Recommended packages:
  mailx
The following NEW packages will be installed
  libdbd-mysql-perl libdbi-perl libnet-daemon-perl libplrpc-perl
  mysql-client-5.0 mysql-server mysql-server-5.0
0 upgraded, 7 newly installed, 0 to remove and 11 not upgraded.
Need to get 28.5MB of archives.
After unpacking 65.8MB of additional disk space will be used.
Do you want to continue [Y/n]?
```

This time, you can see that APT has picked up and selected all the dependencies required to install MySQL Server 5.0, but it has also listed one recommended package and two suggested packages that it has not selected for installation. The "recommended" package is just that: The person who made the MySQL package (or its dependencies) thinks it would be a smart idea for you to also have the mailx package. If you want to add it, press N to terminate apt-get and rerun it like this:

matthew@seymour:~$ **sudo apt-get install mysql-server mailx**

The "suggested" packages are merely a lower form of recommendation. They don't add any crucial features to the software you selected for install, but it's possible that you might need them for certain smaller things.

> **NOTE**
>
> APT maintains a package cache where it stores DEB files it has downloaded and installed. This usually lives in /var/cache/apt/archives and can sometimes take up many hundreds of megabytes on your computer. You can have APT clean out the package cache by running apt-get clean, which deletes all the cached DEB files. Alternatively, you can run apt-get autoclean, which deletes cached DEB files that are beyond a certain age, thereby keeping newer packages.

If you try running apt-get install with packages you already have installed, APT considers your command to be apt-get update and looks to see whether new versions are available for download.

The last day-to-day package operation is removing things you no longer want. This is done through the apt-get remove command, as follows:

matthew@seymour:~$ **sudo apt-get remove firefox**

Removing packages can be dangerous, because APT also removes any software that relies on the packages you selected. For example, if you were to run apt-get remove libgtk2.0-0 (the main graphical toolkit for Ubuntu), you would probably find that APT insists on removing more than a hundred other things. The moral of the story is this: When you remove software, read the APT report carefully before pressing Y to continue with the uninstall.

A straight `apt-get remove` leaves behind the configuration files of your program so that if you ever reinstall it, you do not also need to reconfigure it. If you want the configuration files removed as well as the program files, run this command instead:

matthew@seymour:~$ **sudo apt-get remove --purge firefox**

That performs a full uninstall.

NOTE

You can see a more extensive list of `apt-get` parameters by running `apt-get` without any parameters. The cryptic line at the bottom, "This APT has Super Cow Powers," is made even more cryptic if you run the command `apt-get moo`.

Finding Software

With so many packages available, it can be hard to find the exact thing you need using command-line APT. The general search tool is called `apt-cache` and is used like this:

matthew@seymour:~$ **apt-cache search kde**

Depending on which repositories you have enabled, that tool returns about a thousand packages. Many of those results will not even have KDE in the package name, but will be matched because the description contains the word *KDE*.

You can filter through this information in several ways. First, you can instruct `apt-cache` to search only in the package names, not in their descriptions. This is done with the –n parameter, like this:

matthew@seymour:~$ **apt-cache -n search kde**

Now the search has gone down from more than 1,000 packages to a few hundred.

Another way to limit search results is to use some basic regular expressions, such as ^, meaning "start," and $, meaning "end." For example, you might want to search for programs that are part of the main KDE suite and not libraries (usually named something like `libkde`), additional bits (such as `xmms-kde`), and things that are actually nothing to do with KDE yet still match our search (like `tkdesk`). This can be done by searching for packages that have a name starting with `kde`, as follows:

matthew@seymour:~$ **apt-cache -n search ^kde**

Perhaps the easiest way to find packages is to combine `apt-cache` with `grep`, to search within search results. For example, if you want to find all games-related packages for KDE, you could run this search:

matthew@seymour:~$ **apt-cache search games | grep kde**

When you've found the package you want to install, run it through apt-get install as per usual. If you first want a little more information about that package, you can use apt-cache showpkg, like this:

matthew@seymour:~$ **apt-cache showpkg mysql-server-5.0**

This shows information on "reverse depends" (which packages require, recommend, or suggest mysql-server-5.0), "dependencies" (which packages are required, recommended, or suggested to install mysql-server-5.0), and "provides" (which functions this package gives you). The "provides" list is quite powerful because it allows different packages to provide a given resource. For example, a MySQL database-based program requires MySQL to be installed, but isn't fussy whether you install MySQL 4.1 or MySQL 5.0. In this situation, the Debian packages for MySQL 4.1 and MySQL 5.0 will both have "mysql-server-4.1" in the provides list, meaning that they offer the functionality provided by MySQL 4.1. Therefore, you can install either version to satisfy the MySQL-based application.

Compiling Software from Source

Compiling applications from source is not that difficult. There are two ways to do this: You can use the source code available in the Ubuntu repositories, or you can use source code provided by upstream developers (most useful for those projects that are not available in the Ubuntu repositories). For either method, you will need to install the package build-essential to ensure that you have the tools you need for compilation. You may also need to install automake and checkinstall, which are build tools.

Compiling from a Tarball

Most source code that is not in the Ubuntu repositories is available as compressed source *tarballs*—that is, tar files that have been compressed using gzip or bzip. The compressed files typically uncompress into a directory containing several files. It is always a good idea to compile source code as a regular user to limit any damage that broken or malicious code might inflict, so create a directory named source in your home directory.

From wherever you downloaded the source tarball, uncompress it into the ~/source directory using the -C option to tar:

matthew@seymour:~$ **tar zxvf packagename.tgz -C ~/source**

matthew@seymour:~$ **tar zxvf packagename.tar.gz -C ~/source**

matthew@seymour:~$ **tar jxvf packagename.bz -C ~/source**

matthew@seymour:~$ **tar jxvf packagename.tar.bz2 -C ~/source**

If you are not certain what file compression method was used, use the `file` command to figure it out:

matthew@seymour:~$ **file packagename**

Now, change directories to ~/source/packagename and look for a file named README, INSTALL, or a similar name. Print out the file if necessary because it contains specific instructions on how to compile and install the software. Typically, the procedure to compile source code is as follows:

matthew@seymour:~/source/packagename$ **./configure**

This runs a script to check whether all dependencies are met and the build environment is correct. If you are missing dependencies, the configure script normally tells you exactly which ones it needs. If you have the Universe and Multiverse repositories enabled in Synaptic, chances are you will find the missing software (usually libraries) in there.

When your configure script succeeds, run the following to compile the software:

matthew@seymour:~/source/packagename$ **make**

And finally, run the following:

matthew@seymour:~/source/packagename$ **sudo make install**

If the compile fails, check the error messages for the reason and run the following before you start again:

matthew@seymour:~/source/packagename$ **make clean**

You can also run the following to remove the software if you do not like it:

matthew@seymour:~/source/packagename$ **sudo make uninstall**

Compiling from Source from the Ubuntu Repositories

A person might sometimes want to recompile a package, even though a binary package is available in the Ubuntu repositories. For example, a program may have been compiled into a binary with a specific feature disabled that you would like to use. Here is how you can do this. We will call the software package we want to compile *foo*.

First, get the source from the Ubuntu repositories:

matthew@seymour:~$ apt-get source foo

Install the build dependencies for the package:

matthew@seymour:~$ sudo apt-get build-dep foo

Change to the directory for the source code (may include the version number):

matthew@seymour:~$ cd foo-4.5.2

Make whatever changes you want to make to the package or to the compilation flags. You can do this using ./configure and make, or sometimes by making manual changes to a configuration file. Each package has the potential to do this differently, so you will need to see that program's documentation. Try looking for a README file in the source code to get started.

Next, create a new debian/changelog entry. After you enter this command, you need to enter a message that tells why a new version was made, perhaps something like *Matthew's flight of fancy with extra sauce.*

NOTE

Ubuntu package numbering follows a specific pattern. To help yourself later, you should stick to this pattern. Using the foo numbers shown here, a typical Ubuntu package that was inherited from Debian with no changes would then be 4.5.2-1. A package inherited from Debian, but changed for Ubuntu would be 4.5.2-1ubuntu1 (and then ubuntu2 for a second version, and so on). A package that did not have a version in Debian but which was created for Ubuntu would be 4.5.2-0ubuntu1 (and ubuntu2 and so on).

---

matthew@seymour:~$ dch -i

Build the source package. This creates all the files necessary for uploading a package:

matthew@seymour:~$ debuild -S

Finally, you are left with a foo-4.5.2-1ubuntu1custom.deb package (using whatever version number or suffix you created earlier) that you can install, and later uninstall as well, using your package manager. In some instances, multiple DEB files may be created, in which case you would replace the individual package name in the following example with *.deb:

matthew@seymour:~$ sudo dpkg -Oi foo-4.5.2-1ubuntu1custom.deb

Server/Configuration Management

This section provides a quick introduction to some tools that may be useful, especially for people who manage large numbers of servers. The tools here are designed for system administrators and developers, people who are responsible for keeping more than one or two servers up and running, managing their configurations, and so on. Systems have grown to the point that managing each one individually is becoming unwieldy at times and so tools have been created that decrease some of the stress and complexity by reducing the job to managing the software that in turn manages all of the servers. Okay, any system administrator or developer will tell you that this is a bit of an oversimplification, but it is close.

Puppet

Puppet is a configuration management tool written in Ruby. It is designed to make it easier to deploy servers and scale applications across a network and does so using a custom declarative language. It has been around longer than Chef and is both more widely known and more commonly used. However, both are highly regarded.

Chef

Chef is a configuration management tool, also written in Ruby. It uses a services-oriented architecture to help automate tasks. For Chef, you write recipes that describe how you want your server or a specific server software to be configured, such as an HTTP server or database server. The recipes describe each resource, such as services that should be running or packages that should be installed, and the state in which each should be found. It then makes sure that configuration is maintained or updated across all servers being managed.

Juju

Juju is Ubuntu's entry into this field. It is new and not yet considered stable or ready for anything but testing. Hopefully, by 12.04, however, it will be set to go. Juju is designed to do the same things as Chef and Puppet, but more as well. Juju is covered in Chapter 33, "Ubuntu in the Cloud."

Landscape

Landscape is an enterprise-focused systems management and monitoring tool that is available from Canonical. It is a part of the Ubuntu Advantage program (www.canonical.com/enterprise-services/ubuntu-advantage), which is a paid service. Landscape can be run as a hosted service from Canonical's Ubuntu Advantage or can be installed locally. It can monitor both local servers as well as cloud servers, such as are discussed in Chapter 33.

dotdee

If you run Linux-based systems, you will find a series of directories that end with a .d and which store configuration files. These are sometimes called .d or "dot dee" directories. If you look in /etc, you will find many (such as apparmor.d and pam.d). Opening these directories reveals a large number of configuration files and perhaps other directories containing even more. In Ubuntu or other Debian-based systems, it is a violation of etiquette (and Debian policy) for any software package to be allowed to directly change the configuration files of another package. This can be problematic if you want to use system configuration management software.

dotdee solves this problem by allowing you to take any flat file in your filesystem and replace it with a symlink pointing to a file that is generated from a .d-style directory. It then saves the original file and then updates the generated file automatically and dynamically any time any file in the original .d directory is added, deleted, or modified. This way, the Debian policy and general etiquette standards are met, but configurations can be modified as needed by an external program.

dotdee works its magic using `inotify` to dynamically and instantly update the master file. The master file can be built three different ways: using flat files, which are concatenated; using diff/patch files, which are applied in a quiltlike manner; and using executables, which process `stdin` and dump to `stdout`. This flexibility should make any system administrator or developer guru happy.

At the time of this writing, dotdee has been added to the Ubuntu software repositories, and it looks as if it will be used by Juju and the Ubuntu Orchestra Project, a tool for deploying large numbers of Ubuntu servers in a short amount of time and which is covered in Chapter 33.

References

- ▶ **www.debian.org/doc/manuals/project-history/ch-detailed.en.html**—History of the Debian Linux package system.

- ▶ **www.nongnu.org/synaptic/**—The home of the Synaptic package manager.

- ▶ **www.ubuntu.com/usn**—The official list of Ubuntu security notices.

- ▶ **www.opscode.com/chef/**—The official website for Chef.

- ▶ **www.puppetlabs.com**—The official website for Puppet.

- ▶ **juju.ubuntu.com**—The official website for Ubuntu's Juju.

- ▶ **http://help.ubuntu.com/11.10/serverguide/C/index.html**—The official Ubuntu server guide.

# CHAPTER 10

Command-Line Quickstart

The Linux command line is one of the most powerful tools available for computer system administration and maintenance. The command line is also known as the terminal, shell, the console, the command prompt, and the *command-line interface (CLI)*. For the purposes of this chapter and the next, these terms are interchangeable, although fine-grained differences do exist between them.

The command line is an efficient way to perform complex tasks accurately and much more easily than it would seem at a first glance. Knowledge of the commands available to you and also how to string them together will make using Ubuntu even easier for many tasks. Many of the commands were created by the GNU Project as free software analogs to previously existing proprietary UNIX commands. If you are interested, you can learn more about the GNU Project at www.gnu.org/gnu/thegnuproject.html.

This chapter looks at some of the basic commands that you need to know to be productive at the command line. You will find out how to get to the command line and learn some of the commands used to navigate the file system and perform basic operations with files, directories, and users. This chapter does not give comprehensive coverage of all the commands discussed, but only enough to get you started. Chapter 11, "Command-Line Master Class," advances the subject further while expanding on some of the commands from this chapter. The skills you learn in this chapter will help you get started using the command line with confidence.

What Is the Command Line?

If you spend any amount of time with experienced Linux users, you will hear them mention the command line. Some, especially those who have begun their journey in the Linux world using distributions, like Ubuntu, that make it easy to complete many tasks using a *graphical user interface (GUI)*, may speak with trepidation about the mysteries of the text interface. Others will either praise its power or comment about doing something via the command line as if it is the most natural and obvious way to complete a task.

It is not necessary for you to embrace either extreme. You may develop an affinity for the command line when performing some tasks and prefer the GUI for others. This is where most users end up today. Some may say that you will never need to access the command line because Ubuntu offers a slew of graphical tools that enable you to configure most things on your system. Although the premise may be true most of the time, there are some good reasons to acquire a fundamental level of comfort with the command line that you should consider before embracing that view.

Sometimes things go wrong, and you may not have the luxury of a graphical interface to work with. In these situations, a fundamental understanding of the command line and its uses can be a real lifesaver. Also, some tasks end up being far easier and faster to accomplish from the command line. More important, though, you will be able to make your way around a command-line-based system, which you will encounter if you ever work with a Linux server because most Linux servers have no GUI and all administration is done using a command-line interface.

> **NOTE**
>
> Don't be tempted to skip over this chapter as irrelevant. You should take the time to work through the chapter and ensure that you are comfortable with the command line before moving on. Doing so will benefit you greatly for years to come.

Initially, some may be tempted to think of the command line as the product of some sort of black and arcane art, and in some ways, it can appear to be extremely difficult and complicated to use. However, with a little perseverance, by the end of this chapter, you will start to feel comfortable using the command line and you'll be ready to move on to Chapter 11.

This chapter introduces you to commands that enable you to perform the following:

- ▶ **Routine tasks**—Logging in and out, changing passwords, and listing and navigating file directories.

- ▶ **Basic file management**—Creating files and folders, copying or moving them around the file system, and renaming and deleting them.

- ▶ **Basic system management**—Shutting down or rebooting, changing file permissions, and reading man pages, which are entries for commands included as files already on your computer in a standardized manual format

The information in this chapter is valuable for individual users or system administrators who are new to Linux and are learning to use the command line for the first time.

TIP

Those of you who have used a computer for many years will probably have come into contact with MS-DOS, in which case being presented with a black screen will fill you with a sense of nostalgia. Don't get too comfy; the command line in Linux is different from (and actually more powerful than) its distant MS-DOS cousin. Even cooler is that whereas MS-DOS skills are transferable only to other MS-DOS environments, the skills that you learn at the Linux command line can be transferred easily to other UNIX and UNIX-like operating systems, such as Solaris, OpenBSD, FreeBSD, and even Mac OS X, which provides access to the terminal.

Accessing the Command Line

You can quickly access the terminal using the desktop menu option Terminal. This opens gnome-terminal, from which you can access the terminal while remaining in a GUI environment. This time, the terminal appears as white text on an aubergine (dark purple) background. This is the most common method for accessing the terminal for most desktop users.

NOTE

Finding and running programs, such as Terminal, from a GUI is covered in Chapter 3, "Working with Unity," as is logging it to a Linux system using a graphical interface. This chapter focuses on text-based logins and the use of Linux.

The second most common way for graphical desktop users to access the command line is to press the key combination Ctrl+Alt+F1, after which Ubuntu switches to a black screen and a login prompt like this:

```
Ubuntu 11.10 oneric seymour tty1
seymour login:
```

TIP

This is tty1, one of six virtual consoles that Ubuntu provides. After you have accessed a virtual console, you can use the Ctrl+Alt + any of F1 through F6 to switch to a different console, tty1 through tty6. If you want to get back to the graphical interface, press Ctrl+Alt+F7. You can also switch between consoles by holding the Alt key and pressing either the left or the right cursor key to move down or up a console, such as tty1 to tty2.

Regardless of which way you access the terminal, using the virtual tty consoles accessible at Ctrl+Alt+F1-6 or via the windowed version atop your GUI desktop, you will find the rest of the usage details that we cover work the same. As you continue to learn and experiment beyond the contents of this book, you may start to discover some subtle differences between the two and develop a preference. For our purposes, either method works quite well.

There are many other ways to access and use the command line. You could use a traditional console with a monitor, keyboard, and mouse attached to the PC, but which boots into a command-line interface instead of a GUI. You can also connect to your system through a wired or wireless network using the `telnet` or `ssh` commands, as covered in Chapter 18, "Remote Access with SSH and Telnet."

With that, let's begin.

Text-Based Console Login

However you connect to a command-line interface, you start with a prompt similar to this one:

```
Ubuntu 11.10 oneric seymour tty1
seymour login:
```

Your prompt might vary, depending on the version of Ubuntu you are using and the method you are using to connect. In any event, at this prompt, type in your username and press Enter. When you are prompted for your password, type it in and press Enter.

> **NOTE**
>
> Your password is not echoed back to you, which is a good idea. Why is it a good idea? Well, people are prevented from looking over your shoulder and seeing your screen input. It is not difficult to guess that a five-letter password might correspond to the user's spouse's first name.

At the login prompt, type your username and press the Enter key. You are asked for your password, which you type. Note that Ubuntu does not show any characters while you are typing in your password. This is a good thing because it prevents any shoulder surfers from seeing what you've typed or the length of the password.

Pressing the Enter key drops you to a shell prompt, signified by the dollar sign:

```
matthew@seymour:~$
```

This particular prompt tells me that I am logged in as the user `matthew` on the system `seymour` and I am currently in my home directory; Linux uses the tilde (~) as shorthand for the home directory, which would usually be something like /home/matthew.

Navigating through the system at the command line can get confusing at times, especially when a directory name occurs in several places. Fortunately, Linux includes a simple command that tells you exactly where you are in the file system. It's easy to remember because the command is just an abbreviation of present working directory, so type pwd at any point to get the full path of your location. For example, typing pwd after following these instructions shows /home/yourusername, meaning that you are currently in your home directory.

Using the pwd command can save you a lot of frustration when you have changed your directory half a dozen times and have lost track.

Logging Out

Use the `exit` or `logout` command or Ctrl+D to exit your session. You are then returned to the login prompt. If you use virtual consoles, remember to exit each console before leaving your PC. (Otherwise, someone could easily sit down and use your account.)

Logging In and Out from a Remote Computer

Although you can happily log in on your computer, an act known as a *local* login, you can also log in to your computer via a network connection from a remote computer. Linux-based operating systems provide a number of remote access commands you can use to log in to other computers on your *local area network (LAN), wide area network (WAN),* or the Internet. Note that you must have an account on the remote computer *and* the remote computer must be configured to support remote logins; otherwise, you won't be able to log in.

See Chapter 17, "Networking," to see how to set up network interfaces with Linux to support remote network logins and Chapter 18 to see how to start remote access services (such as sshd).

The best and most secure way to log in to a remote Linux computer is to use ssh, the Secure Shell client. Your login and session are encrypted while you work on the remote computer. The ssh client features many command-line options, but can be simply used with the name or IP address of the remote computer, as follows:

```
matthew@seymour:~$ ssh 192.168.0.41
The authenticity of host '192.168.0.41 (192.168.0.41)' can't be established.
RSA key fingerprint is e1:db:6c:da:3f:fc:56:1b:52:f9:94:e0:d1:1d:31:50.
Are you sure you want to continue connecting (yes/no)?
```

yes

The first time you connect with a remote computer using ssh, Linux displays the remote computer's encrypted identity key and asks you to verify the connection. After you type yes and press Enter, you are warned that the remote computer's identity (key) has been entered in a file named known_hosts under the .ssh directory in your home directory. You are also prompted to enter your password:

```
Warning: Permanently added '192.168.0.41' (RSA) \
to the list of known hosts.
matthew@192.168.0.41's password:
matthew@babbage~$
```

After entering your password, you can work on the remote computer, which you can confirm by noticing the changed prompt that now uses the name of the remote computer on which you are working. Again, because you are using ssh, everything you enter on the keyboard in communication with the remote computer is encrypted. When you log out, you return to the shell on your computer:

```
matthew@babbage~$ logout
matthew@seymour:~$
```

User Accounts

A good place to start is with the concept of user-based security. For the most part, only two types of people will access the system as users. (Although there will be other accounts that run programs and processes, here we are talking about accounts that represent human beings rather than something like an account created for a web server process.) Most people have a regular user account. These users can change anything that is specific to their account, such as the wallpaper on the desktop, their personal preferences, and the configuration for a program when it is run by them using their account. Note that the emphasis is on anything that is *specific to their account*. This type of user cannot make systemwide changes that could affect other users.

To make systemwide changes, you need to use super-user privileges, such as can be done using the account you created when you started Ubuntu for the first time (see Chapter 1, "Installing Ubuntu"). With super-user privileges, you have access to the entire system and can carry out any task, even destructive ones. To help prevent this from happening, this user does not run with these powers enabled at all times, but instead spends most of the time as a regular user.

To use super-user privileges from the command line, you need to preface the command you want to execute with another command, sudo, followed by a space and the command you want to run. As a mnemonic device, some think of this as "super user do." When you press Enter (after typing the remaining command), you are prompted for your password, which you should type in followed by the Enter key. As usual on any UNIX-based system, the password does not appear on the screen while you are typing it as a security measure, in case someone is watching over your shoulder. Ubuntu then carries out the command, but with super-user privileges.

An example of the destructive nature of working as the super user can be found in the age-old example, `sudo rm -rf /`, which erases everything on your hard drive. If you enter a command using `sudo` as a regular user who does not have an account with super-user privileges, an error message appears and nothing happens because the command will not run. We recommend that you don't try this particular command as a test, though. If you enter this command using an account with super-user privileges, you will soon find yourself starting over with a fresh installation and hoping you have a current backup of all of your data. You need to be especially careful when using your super-user privileges; otherwise, you may do irreparable damage to your system.

However, the ability to work as the super user is fundamental to a healthy Linux system and should not be feared, but rather respected, even while used only with focused attention. Without this ability, you could not install new software, edit system configuration files, or do a large number of important administration tasks. By the way, you have already been performing operations with super-user privileges from the GUI if you have ever been asked to enter your password to complete a specific task, such as installing software updates. The difference is that most graphical interfaces limit the options that users have and make it a little more difficult to do some of the big, disruptive tasks, even the ones that are incredibly useful.

Ubuntu works slightly differently from many other Linux distributions. If you study some other Linux distros, especially older or more traditional ones, you will hear about a specific user account called root, which is a super-user account. In those distros, instead of typing in `sudo` before a command while using a regular user account with super-user privileges, you log in to the root account and simply issue the command without entering a password (at least by default; in almost all cases, `sudo` can be installed and configured in these distros). In those cases, you can tell when you are using the root account at the command line because you will see a pound sign (#) in the command-line prompt in the place of the dollar sign ($).

For example: `matthew@seymour:~#` versus the usual `matthew@seymour:~$`

In Ubuntu, the root account is disabled by default because forcing regular users with super-user privileges to type a specific command every time they want to execute a command as a super user should have the benefit of making them carefully consider what they are doing when they use that power. It is easy to forget to log out of a root account, and entering a powerful command while logged in to root can be catastrophic. However, if you are more experienced and comfortable with the more traditional method of using super-user privileges and want to enable the root account, you can use the command `sudo passwd`. When prompted, enter your user password to confirm that your user account has super-user privileges. You are then asked for a new UNIX password, which will be the password for the root account, so make sure and remember it. You are also prompted to repeat the password, in case you've made any mistakes. After you've typed it in and pressed Enter, the root account is active. You'll find out how to switch to root later on.

10

An alternative way of getting a root prompt, without having to enable the root account, is to issue the command sudo -i. After entering your password, you will find yourself at a root prompt (#). Do what you need to do and when you are finished, type exit, and press Enter to return to your usual prompt. You can learn more about sudo and root from an Ubuntu perspective at https://help.ubuntu.com/community/RootSudo.

Understanding the Linux File System Hierarchy

Linux has inherited from UNIX a well-planned hierarchy for organizing where things may be found. It isn't perfect, but it is generally logical and mostly consistent, although distributions do tend to make some modifications that force some thinking and adaptation when moving between, say, Fedora, Slackware, and Ubuntu. Table 10.1 shows some of the top-level directories that are part of a standard Linux distro.

TABLE 10.1   Basic Linux Directories

Name	Description
/	The root directory
/bin	Essential commands
/boot	Boot loader files, Linux kernel
/dev	Device files
/etc	System configuration files
/home	User home directories
/lib	Shared libraries, kernel modules
/lost+found	Directory for recovered files (if found after a file system check)
/media	Mount point for removable media, such as DVDs and floppy disks
/mnt	Usual mount point for local, remote file systems
/opt	Add-on software packages
/proc	Kernel information, process control
/root	Super user (root) home
/sbin	System commands (mostly root only)
/srv	Holds information relating to services that run on your system
/sys	Real-time information on devices used by the kernel
/tmp	Temporary files
/usr	Software not essential for system operation, such as applications
/var	Variable data (such as logs); spooled files

Knowing these directories can help you find files when you need them. This knowledge can even help you partition hard drives when you install new systems by letting you choose to put certain directories on their own distinct partition, which can be useful for things like isolating directories from one another, such as a server security case like putting a directory like /boot that doesn't change often on its own partition and making it read-only and unchangeable without specific operations being done by a super user during a maintenance cycle. Desktop users probably won't need to think about that, but the directory tree is still quite useful to know when you want to find the configuration file for a specific program and set some program options systemwide to affect all users.

Some of the important directories in Table 10.1, such as those containing user and root commands or system configuration files, are discussed in the following sections. You may use and edit files under these directories when you use Ubuntu.

Essential Commands in /bin and /sbin

The /bin directory contains essential commands used by the system for running and booting the system. In general, only the root operator uses the commands in the /sbin directory. The software in both locations is essential to the system; they make the system what it is, and if they are changed or removed, it could cause instability or a complete system failure. Often, the commands in these two directories are *statically* linked, which means that the commands do not depend on software libraries residing under the /lib or /usr/lib directories. Nearly all the other applications on your system are *dynamically* linked, meaning that they require the use of external software libraries (also known as *shared* libraries) to run. This is a feature for both sets of software.

The commands in /bin and /sbin are kept stable to maintain foundational system integrity and do not need to be updated often, if at all. For the security of the system, these commands are kept in a separate location and isolated where changes are more difficult and where it will be more obvious to the system administrator if unauthorized changes are attempted or made.

Application software changes more frequently, and applications often use the same functions that other pieces of application software use. This was the genesis of shared libraries. When a security update is needed for something that is used by more than one program, it has to be updated in only one location, a specific software library. This enables easy and quick security updates that will affect several pieces of non-system-essential software at the same time by updating one shared library, contained in one file on the computer.

Configuration Files in /etc

System configuration files and directories reside under the /etc directory. Some major software packages, such as Apache, OpenSSH, and xinetd, have their own subdirectories in /etc filled with configuration files. Others like crontab or fstab use one file. Examples of system-related configuration files in /etc include the following:

▶ **fstab**—The file system table is a text file listing each hard drive, CD-ROM, floppy, or other storage device attached to your PC. The table indexes each device's partition information with a place in your Linux file system (directory layout) and lists other options for each device when used with Linux (see Chapter 21, "Kernel and Module Management"). Nearly all entries in fstab can be manipulated by root using the mount command.

▶ **modprobe.d/**—This folder holds all the instructions to load kernel modules that are required as part of the system startup.

▶ **passwd**—The list of users for the system, including special-purpose nonhuman users like syslog and CouchDB, along with user account information.

▶ **sudoers**—A list of users or user groups with super user access.

User Directories: /home

The most important data on a non-server Linux system often resides in the user's directories, found under the /home directory. User directories are named by default according to account usernames, so on a computer where I have an account named matthew, my home directory would generally be found in /home/matthew. This can be changed, and doing so is covered for the curious in Chapter 11.

Segregating the system and user data can be helpful in preventing data loss and making the process of backing up easier. For example, having user data reside on a separate file system or mounted from a remote computer on the network might help shield users from data loss in the event of a system hardware failure. For a laptop or desktop computer at home, you might place /home on a separate partition from the rest of the file system, so that if the operating system is upgraded, damaged, or reinstalled, /home would be more likely to survive the event intact.

Using the Contents of the /proc Directory to Interact with the Kernel

The content of the /proc directory is created from memory and exists only while Linux is running. This directory contains special files that either extract information from or send information to the kernel. Many Linux utilities extract information from dynamically created directories and files under this directory, also known as a *virtual file system*. For example, the free command obtains its information from a file named meminfo:

```
matthew@seymour:~$ free
```

	total	used	free	shared	buffers	cached
Mem:	4055680	2725684	1329996	0	188996	1551464
-/+ buffers/cache:		985224	3070456			
Swap:	8787512	0	8787512			

This information constantly changes as the system is used. You can get the same information by using the cat command to see the contents of the meminfo file:

```
matthew@seymour:~$ cat /proc/meminfo
MemTotal:              4055680 KB
MemFree:               1329692 KB
Buffers:                189208 KB
Cached:                1551488 KB
SwapCached:                  0 KB
Active:                1222172 KB
Inactive:              1192244 KB
Active(anon):           684092 KB
Inactive(anon):             16 KB
Active(file):           538080 KB
Inactive(file):        1192228 KB
Unevictable:                48 KB
Mlocked:                    48 KB
SwapTotal:             8787512 KB
SwapFree:              8787512 KB
Dirty:                     136 KB
Writeback:                   0 KB
AnonPages:              673760 KB
Mapped:                 202308 KB
Shmem:                   10396 KB
Slab:                   129248 KB
SReclaimable:           107356 KB
SUnreclaim:              21892 KB
KernelStack:              2592 KB
PageTables:              30108 KB
NFS_Unstable:                0 KB
Bounce:                      0 KB
WritebackTmp:                0 KB
CommitLimit:          10815352 KB
Committed_AS:          1553172 KB
VmallocTotal:        34359738367 KB
VmallocUsed:            342300 KB
VmallocChunk:        34359387644 KB
HardwareCorrupted:           0 KB
HugePages_Total:             0
HugePages_Free:              0
HugePages_Rsvd:              0
HugePages_Surp:              0
Hugepagesize:             2048 KB
DirectMap4k:             38912 KB
DirectMap2M:           4153344 KB
```

The /proc directory can also be used to dynamically alter the behavior of a running Linux kernel by "echoing" numerical values to specific files under the /proc/sys directory. For example, to "turn on" kernel protection against one type of denial-of-service (DoS) attack known as *SYN flooding*, use the echo command to send the number 1 to the following /proc path:

```
matthew@seymour:~$ $ sudo echo 1 >/proc/sys/net/ipv4/tcp_syncookies
```

Other ways to use the /proc directory include the following:

▶ Getting CPU information, such as the family, type, and speed from /proc/cpuinfo.

▶ Viewing important networking information under /proc/net, such as active interfaces information under /proc/net/dev, routing information in /proc/net/route, and network statistics in /proc/net/netstat.

▶ Retrieving file system information.

▶ Reporting media mount point information via USB; for example, the Linux kernel reports what device to use to access files (such as /dev/sda) if a USB camera or hard drive is detected on the system. You can use the dmesg command to see this information.

▶ Getting the kernel version in /proc/version, performance information such as uptime in /proc/uptime, or other statistics such as CPU load, swap file usage, and processes in /proc/stat.

Working with Shared Data in the /usr Directory

The /usr directory contains software applications, libraries, and other types of shared data for use by anyone on the system. Many Linux system administrators give /usr its own partition. A number of subdirectories under /usr contain manual pages (/usr/share/man), software package shared files (/usr/share/*name_of_package*, such as /usr/share/emacs), additional application or software package documentation (/usr/share/doc), and an entire subdirectory tree of locally built and installed software, /usr/local.

Temporary File Storage in the /tmp Directory

As its name implies, the /tmp directory is used for temporary file storage; as you use Linux, various programs create files in this directory.

Accessing Variable Data Files in the /var Directory

The /var directory contains subdirectories used by various system services for spooling and logging. Many of these variable data files, such as print spooler queues, are temporary, whereas others, such as system and kernel logs, are renamed and rotated in use. Incoming email is usually directed to files under /var/spool/mail.

Linux also uses /var for other important system services. These include the topmost *File Transfer Protocol (FTP)* directory under /var/ftp (see Chapter 25, "Remote File Serving with FTP"), and the Apache web server's initial home page directory for the system, /var/www/html. (See Chapter 23, "Apache Web Server Management," for more information about using Apache.)

> **NOTE**
>
> There is a recent trend to move data that is served from `/var/www` and `/var/ftp` to `/srv`, but this is not universal.

Navigating the Linux File System

In the Linux file system, as with its predecessor UNIX, everything is a file: data files, binary files, executable programs, even input, and output devices. These files are placed in a series of directories that act like file folders. A directory is nothing more than a special type of file that contains a list of other files/directories. These files and directories are used to create a hierarchical structure that enables logical placement of specific types of files. Later in this chapter, we discuss the standard hierarchy of the Linux file system. First, you learn how to navigate and interact with the file system.

> **NOTE**
>
> A directory with contents is called a *parent* and its contents are called *children*, as in "`/home/matthew/Documents` is a child directory of `/home/matthew`, its parent."

Listing the Contents of a Directory with `ls`

The `ls` command lists the contents of the current directory. It is commonly used by itself, but a number of options (also known as switches) are available for `ls` and give you more information. If you have just logged in as described earlier, this command lists the files and directories in your user's home directory:

```
matthew@seymour:~$ ls
Documents      Music       file.txt  Pictures  Music
```

> **NOTE**
>
> All directory listings in this chapter are abbreviated to save space.

By itself, the `ls` command shows just a list of names. Some are files, some are directories. This is useful if I know what I am looking for but cannot remember the exact name. However, using `ls` in this matter has some limitations. First, it does not show hidden files. Hidden files use filenames that start with a period (.) as the first character. They are often used for configuration of specific programs and are not accessed frequently. For this reason, they are not included in a basic directory listing. You can see all the hidden files by adding a switch to the command like this:

```
matthew@seymour:~$ ls -a
.                  .bash_logout     Documents     Music
..                 .bashrc          file.txt      Pictures
.bash_history      .config          .local        .profile
```

There is still more information available about each item in a directory. To include details such as the file/directory permissions, owner and group (all of which are discussed later in this chapter), as well as the size, and the date and time it was last modified, enter the following:

```
matthew@seymour:~$ ls -al
total 608
drwxr-xr-x 38 matthew matthew   4096 2011-06-04 08:20 .
drwxr-xr-x  3 root    root      4096 2011-05-16 16:48 ..
-rw-------  1 matthew matthew    421 2011-06-04 10:27 .bash_history
-rw-r--r--  1 matthew matthew    220 2011-05-16 16:48 .bash_logout
-rw-r--r--  1 matthew matthew   3353 2011-05-16 16:48 .bashrc
drwxr-xr-x 13 matthew matthew   4096 2011-05-21 10:42 .config
drwxr-xr-x  2 matthew matthew   4096 2011-05-16 17:07 Documents
-rw-r--r--  1 matthew matthew    335 2011-05-16 16:48 file.txt
drwxr-xr-x  3 matthew matthew   4096 2011-05-16 17:07 .local
drwxr-xr-x  2 matthew matthew   4096 2011-05-16 17:07 Music
drwxr-xr-x  3 matthew matthew   4096 2011-05-16 18:07 Pictures
-rw-r--r--  1 matthew matthew    675 2011-05-16 16:48 .profile
```

The listing (abbreviated here) is now given with one item per line, but with multiple columns. The listing starts with the number of items in the directory. (Both files and subdirectories are included; remember that the listing here is abbreviated.) Then, the details are as shown in Figure 10.1.

FIGURE 10.1   Decoding the output of a detailed directory listing.

These details are discussed more completely later in the chapter in the "Working with Permissions" section.

Another useful switch is this:

```
matthew@seymour:~$ ls -R
```

This command scans and lists all the contents of the subdirectories of the current directory. This is likely to be a lot of information, so you may want to redirect the output to a text file so that you can browse through it at your leisure by using the following:

```
matthew@seymour:~$ ls -laR > listing.txt
```

The previous command sends the output of `ls -laR` to a file called `listing.txt` and demonstrates part of the power of the Linux command line. At the command line, you can use files as inputs to commands, or you can generate files as outputs as shown. For more information about redirects and combining commands, see Chapter 11. In the meantime, note that you can read the contents of that text file using the command `less listing.txt`, which lets you read the file bit by bit using the arrow keys to navigate in the file (or Enter to move to the next line), the spacebar to move to the next page, and q to exit when done.

Changing Directories with `cd`

Use the `cd` command to move within the file system from one directory to another. It may help you remember this command to think of it meaning "change directory." The most basic usage of `cd` is this:

```
matthew@seymour:~$ cd somedir
```

That looks in the current directory for the `somedir` subdirectory, then moves you into it. You can also specify an exact location for a directory, like this:

```
matthew@seymour:~$ cd /home/matthew/stuff/somedir
```

The `cd` command can also be used with several shortcuts. For example, to quickly move up to the *parent* directory, the one above the one you are currently in, use the `cd` command like this:

```
matthew@seymour:~$ cd ..
```

To return to your home directory from anywhere in the Linux file system, use the `cd` command like this:

```
matthew@seymour:~$ cd
```

You can also use the `$HOME` shell environment variable to accomplish the same thing. Environment variables are discussed in greater detail in Chapter 11. Type this command and press Enter to return to your home directory:

```
matthew@seymour:~$ cd $HOME
```

You can accomplish the same thing by using the tilde (~) like this:

```
matthew@seymour:~$ cd ~
```

Finding Your Current Directory with `pwd`

Use `pwd` to remind you where you are within the file system.

Working with Permissions

Under Linux (and UNIX), everything in the file system, including directories and devices, is a file. And every file on your system has an accompanying set of permissions based on ownership. These permissions provide data security by giving specific permission settings to every single item denoting who may read, write, or execute the file. These permissions are set individually for the file's owner, for members of the group the file belongs to, and for all others on the system.

You can examine the default permissions for a file you create by using the umask command, which lists default permissions using the number system explained next, or by using the touch command and then the ls command's long-format listing like this:

```
matthew@seymour:~$ touch file
matthew@seymour:~$ ls -l file
-rw-r--r-- 1 matthew matthew 0 2010-06-30 13:06 file
```

In this example, the touch command is used to quickly create a file. The ls command then reports on the file, displaying the following (from left to right):

▶ **The type of file created**—Common indicators of the type of file are in the leading letter in the output. A blank (which is represented by a dash, as in the preceding example) designates a plain file, d designates a directory, c designates a character device (such as /dev/ttyS0), and b is used for a block device (such as /dev/sda).

▶ **Permissions**—Read, write, and execute permissions for the owner, group, and all others on the system. (You learn more about these permissions later in this section.)

▶ **Number of links to the file**—The number 1 designates that there is only one file, whereas any other number indicates that there might be one or more hard-linked files. Links are created with the ln command. A hard-linked file is an exact copy of the file, but it might be located elsewhere on the system. Symbolic links of directories can also be created, but only the root operator can create a hard link of a directory.

▶ **The owner**—The account that owns the file; this is originally the file creator, but you can change this designation using the chown command.

▶ **The group**—The group of users allowed to access the file; this is originally the file creator's main group, but you can change this designation using the chgrp command.

▶ **File size and creation/modification date**—The last two elements indicate the size of the file in bytes and the date the file was created or last modified.

Assigning Permissions

Under Linux, permissions are grouped by owner, group, and others, with read, write, and execute permission assigned to each, as follows:

```
Owner    Group    Others
rwx      rwx      rxw
```

Permissions can be indicated by mnemonic or octal characters. Mnemonic characters are listed here:

- ▶ r indicates permission for an owner, member of the owner's group, or others to open and read the file.

- ▶ w indicates permission for an owner, member of the owner's group, or others to open and write to the file.

- ▶ x indicates permission for an owner, member of the owner's group, or others to execute the file (or read a directory).

In the previous example for the file named file, the owner, matthew, has read and write permission. Any member of the group named matthew may only read the file. All other users may only read the file. Also note that default permissions for files created by the root operator (while using sudo or a root account) will differ because of umask settings assigned by the shell.

Many users prefer to use numeric codes, based on octal (base 8) values, to represent permissions. Here's what these values mean:

- ▶ 4 indicates read permission.

- ▶ 2 indicates write permission.

- ▶ 1 indicates execute permission.

In octal notation, the previous example file has a permission setting of 664 (read + write or 4 + 2, read + write or 4 + 2, read-only or 4). Although you can use either form of permissions notation, octal is easy to use quickly after you visualize and understand how permissions are numbered.

NOTE

In Linux, you can create groups to assign a number of users access to common directories and files, based on permissions. You might assign everyone in accounting to a group named accounting and allow that group access to accounts payable files while disallowing access by other departments. Defined groups are maintained by the root operator, but you can use the newgrp command to temporarily join other groups to access files (as long as the root operator has added you to the other groups). You can also allow or deny other groups' access to your files by modifying the group permissions of your files.

10

Directory Permissions

Directories are also files under Linux. For example, again use the `ls` command to show permissions like this:

```
matthew@seymour:~$ mkdir directory
matthew@seymour:~$ ls -ld directory
drwxr-xr-x  2 matthew  matthew  4096 2010-06-30 13:23 directory
```

In this example, the `mkdir` command is used to create a directory. The `ls` command, and its `-ld` option, is used to show the permissions and other information about the directory (not its contents). Here you can see that the directory has permission values of 755 (read + write + execute or 4 + 2 + 1, read + execute or 4 + 1, and read + execute or 4 + 1).

This shows that the owner can read and write to the directory and, because of execute permission, also list the directory's contents. Group members and all other users can list only the directory contents. Note that directories require execute permission for anyone to be able to view their contents.

You should also notice that the `ls` command's output shows a leading d in the permissions field. This letter specifies that this file is a directory; normal files have a blank field in its place. Other files, such as those specifying a block or character device, have a different letter.

For example, if you examine the device file for a Linux serial port, you will see the following:

```
matthew@seymour:~$ ls -l /dev/ttyS0
crw-rw---- 1 root dialout 4, 64 2010-06-30 08:13 /dev/ttyS0
```

Here, /dev/ttyS0 is a character device (such as a serial communications port and designated by a c) owned by root and available to anyone in the `dialout` group. The device has permissions of 660 (read + write, read + write, no permission).

On the other hand, if you examine the device file for an IDE hard drive, you see this:

```
matthew@seymour:~$ ls -l /dev/sda
brw-rw-- -- 1 root disk 8, 0 2010-06-30 08:13 /dev/sda
```

In this example, b designates a block device (a device that transfers and caches data in blocks) with similar permissions. Other device entries you will run across on your Linux system include symbolic links, designated by s.

Altering File Permissions with `chmod`

You can use the `chmod` command to alter a file's permissions. This command uses various forms of command syntax, including octal or a mnemonic form (such as u, g, o, or a and rwx, and so on) to specify a desired change. The `chmod` command can be used to add, remove, or modify file or directory permissions to protect, hide, or open up access to a file by other users (except for the root account or a user with super-user permission and using sudo, either of which can access any file or directory on a Linux system).

The mnemonic forms of chmod's options are (when used with a plus character, +, to add, or a minus sign, -, to remove):

▶ **u**—Adds or removes user (owner) read, write, or execute permission.

▶ **g**—Adds or removes group read, write, or execute permission.

▶ **o**—Adds or removes read, write, or execute permission for others not in a file's group.

▶ **a**—Adds or removes read, write, or execute permission for all users.

▶ **r**—Adds or removes read permission.

▶ **w**—Adds or removes write permission.

▶ **x**—Adds or removes execution permission.

For example, if you create a file, such as a readme.txt, the file has the following default permissions (set by the umask setting in /etc/bashrc):

```
-rw-r--r-- 1 matthew matthew 0 2010-06-30 13:33 readme.txt
```

As you can see, you can read and write the file. Anyone else can only read the file (and only if it is outside your home directory, which will have read, write, and execute permission set only for you, the owner). You can remove all write permission for anyone by using chmod, the minus sign (-), and aw, as follows:

```
matthew@seymour:~$ chmod a-w readme.txt
matthew@seymour:~$ ls -l readme.txt
-r--r--r-- 1 matthew matthew 0 2010-06-30 13:33 readme.txt
```

Now, no one can write to the file (except you, if the file is in your /home or /tmp directory because of directory permissions). To restore read and write permission for only you as the owner, use the plus sign (+) and the u and rw options like so:

```
matthew@seymour:~$ chmod u+rw readme.txt
matthew@seymour:~$ ls -l readme.txt
-rw-r--r-- 1 matthew matthew 0 2010-06-30 13:33 readme.txt
```

You can also use the octal form of the chmod command (for example, to modify a file's permissions so that only you, the owner, can read and write a file). Use the chmod command and a file permission of 600, like this:

```
matthew@seymour:~$ chmod 600 readme.txt
matthew@seymour:~$ ls -l readme.txt
-rw------- 1 matthew matthew 0 2010-06-30 13:33 readme.txt
```

If you take away execution permission for a directory, files might be hidden inside and may not be listed or accessed by anyone else (except the root operator, of course, who has access to any file on your system). By using various combinations of permission settings, you can quickly and easily set up a more secure environment, even as a normal user in your /home directory.

10

File Permissions with `chgrp`

You can use the `chgrp` command to change the group to which a file belongs:

matthew@seymour:~$ **chgrp wheel filename**

Changing File Permissions with `chown`

You can use the `chown` command to change the owner of a file:

matthew@seymour:~$ **chown matthew filename**

You can also use the `chown` command to change the group of a file at the same time:

matthew@seymour:~$ **chown matthew:wheel filename**

Understanding Set User ID and Set Group ID Permissions

Two more types of permission are "set user ID," known as *suid*, and "set group ID," or *sgid*. These settings, when used in a program, enable any user running that program to have program owner or group owner permissions for that program. These settings enable the program to be run effectively by anyone, without requiring that each user's permissions be altered to include specific permissions for that program.

One commonly used program with suid permissions is the `passwd` command:

matthew@seymour:~$ **ls -l /usr/bin/passwd**

-rwsr-xr-x 1 root root 42856 2010-01-26 10:09 /usr/bin/passwd

This setting allows normal users to execute the command (as root) to make changes to a root-only-accessible file /etc/passwd.

You also can assign similar permission with the `chfn` command. This command allows users to update or change `finger` information in /etc/passwd. You accomplish this permission modification by using a leading 4 (or the mnemonic s) in front of the three octal values.

> **NOTE**
>
> Other files that might have suid or guid permissions include at, rcp, rlogin, rsh, chage, chsh, ssh, crontab, sudo, sendmail, ping, mount, and several UNIX-to-UNIX Copy (UUCP) utilities. Many programs (such as games) might also have this type of permission to access a sound device.

Files or programs that have suid or guid permissions can sometimes present security holes because they bypass normal permissions. This problem is compounded if the permission extends to an executable binary (a command) with an inherent security flaw because it could lead to any system user or intruder gaining root access. In past exploits, this typically happened when a user fed a vulnerable command with unexpected input (such as a long pathname or option); the command would fail, and the user would be presented a root prompt. Although Linux developers are constantly on the lookout for poor programming practices, new exploits are found all the time, and can crop up unexpectedly, especially in newer software packages that haven't had the benefit of peer developer review.

Savvy Linux system administrators keep the number of suid or guid files present on a system to a minimum. The `find` command can be used to display all such files on your system:

```
matthew@seymour:~$ sudo find / -type f -perm /6000 -exec ls -l {} \;
```

> **NOTE**
>
> The `find` command is quite helpful and can be used for many purposes, such as before or during backup operations.

Note that the programs do not necessarily have to be removed from your system. If your users really do not need to use the program, you can remove the programs execute permission for anyone. You have to decide, as the root operator, whether your users are allowed, for example, to mount and unmount CD-ROMs or other media on your system. Although Linux-based operating systems can be set up to accommodate ease of use and convenience, allowing programs such as mount to be suid might not be the best security policy. Other candidates for suid permission change could include the chsh, at, or chage commands.

Working with Files

Managing files in your home directory involves using one or more easily remembered commands.

Creating a File with `touch`

To create an empty file called filename within your current directory, use the following command:

```
matthew@seymour:~$ touch filename
```

To edit this file, you must use a text editor. Several are discussed in Chapter 11. However, it is sometimes useful to create an empty file as this creates an access record because of the time and date information that is connected to the file. You can also use touch to update this information, called a timestamp, without otherwise accessing or modifying a file.

You can create a file in a different location by changing what is after `touch`. To create a new file in `/home/matthew/randomdirectory`, if I am already in my home directory, I can use the following:

```
matthew@seymour:~$ touch randomdirectory/newfile
```

Or from anywhere using an absolute path, I use this:

```
matthew@seymour:~$ touch /home/matthew/randomdirectory/newfile
```

Or from anywhere using a path shortcut, I use the following command:

```
matthew@seymour:~$ touch ~/randomdirectory/newfile
```

Creating a Directory with `mkdir`

To create an empty directory called newdirectory within your current directory, use this command:

```
matthew@seymour:~$ mkdir newdirectory
```

You can create a directory in a different location by changing what is after `mkdir`. To create a new directory in `/home/matthew/music`, if I am already in my `/home` directory, I can use the following:

```
matthew@seymour:~$ mkdir music/newdirectory
```

Or from anywhere using an absolute path, I can use this:

```
matthew@seymour:~$ mkdir /home/matthew/music/newdirectory
```

Or from anywhere using a path shortcut, I can use the following command:

```
matthew@seymour:~$ mkdir ~/music/newdirectory
```

The `-p` option is valuable. It allows you to create a directory and its parent directories at the same time, if they do not already exist. This can be a real time saver. If the parent directories exist, the command works normally. For example, suppose I make a new directory with two layers of subdirectories. In this example, music and newdirectory already exist, but subdir1 and subdir2 are to be created:

```
matthew@seymour:~$ mkdir -p ~/music/newdirectory/subdir1/subdir2
```

Deleting a Directory with `rmdir`

To delete an empty directory named directoryname, use the following command:

```
matthew@seymour:~$ rmdir directoryname
```

You can remove a directory in a different location by changing what is after `rmdir`. To remove a directory in /home/matthew/music, if I am already in my /home directory, I can use the following:

```
matthew@seymour:~$ rmdir music/directoryname
```

Or from anywhere using an absolute path, I can use this:

```
matthew@seymour:~$ rmdir /home/matthew/music/directoryname
```

Or from anywhere using a path shortcut, I can use the following command:

```
matthew@seymour:~$ rmdir ~/music/directoryname
```

The directory must be empty to be removed using `rmdir`. However, there is a way to remove a directory with its contents using `rm`.

WARNING

You cannot easily recover anything that has been deleted using `rmdir` or `rm`, so proceed carefully. Be absolutely certain you will never need what you are about to delete before you do so. Only a professional data recovery service is likely to be able to recover the files, and even then at great expense.

Deleting a File or Directory with `rm`

To delete a file named filename, use this command:

```
matthew@seymour:~$ rm filename
```

You can remove a directory in a different location by changing what is after `rm`. To remove a directory in /home/matthew/randomdirectory, if I am already in my /home directory, I can use the following:

```
matthew@seymour:~$ rm randomdirectory/filename
```

Or from anywhere using an absolute path, I can use this:

```
matthew@seymour:~$ rm /home/matthew/randomdirectory/filename
```

Or from anywhere using a path shortcut, I can use the following command:

```
matthew@seymour:~$ rm ~/randomdirectory/filename
```

If you try to use `rm` to remove an empty directory, you will receive an error message: `rm: cannot remove `random/': Is a directory`. In this case, you must use `rmdir`. However, you can remove a directory and its contents using `rm`.

WARNING

Here Be Dragons

Be sure that all the contents of a directory are known and unwanted if you choose to delete them. There is no way to recover them later. Also, be careful that you don't have extra spaces, mistype the name of the directory, or use sudo to delete something that you shouldn't be deleting. Linux gives you great power, and it will let you use that power without questioning you about it; that's the human's job.

To delete a directory and all its contents, use the `-R` recursive switch. This switch works with many commands, not only `rm`:

matthew@seymour:~$ **rm -R /home/matthew/randomdirectory/**

Everything in `randomdirectory` as well as in the directory itself will be deleted.

Moving or Renaming a File with mv

In Linux land, moving and renaming a file are the same thing. It doesn't matter whether you are moving the directory to another or from one filename to another filename in the same directory, there is only one command to remember. To move a file named `filename` from ~/documents to ~/archive, use this command:

matthew@seymour:~$ **mv documents/filename archive**

Notice that the filename is not included in the destination. The destination here must be an existing directory. If it is not, the file is renamed to the term used. Some examples will make this clear.

To rename a file that is in my current directory, I could use the following:

matthew@seymour:~$ **mv oldfilename newfilename**

To rename a file as I move it from ~/documents to ~/archive, I could use this:

matthew@seymour:~$ **mv documents/oldfilename archive/newfilename**

Or from anywhere using an absolute path, I could use the following command:

matthew@seymour:~$ **mv /home/matthew/documents/oldfilename**
/home/matthew/archive/newfilename

Or from anywhere using a path shortcut, I could use this:

matthew@seymour:~$ **rm ~/documents/oldfilename ~/archive/newfilename**

Copying a File with `cp`

Copying works similarly to moving, but retains the original in the original location. To copy a file named `filename` from `~/documents` to `~/archive`, use this command:

```
matthew@seymour:~$ cp documents/filename archive
```

Notice that the filename is not included in the destination. The destination here must be an existing directory. If it is not, the file is renamed to the term used. Some examples will make this clear.

To copy a file that is in my current directory, I could use the following, and it will work exactly the same as `mv`, except that both files will exist afterward:

```
matthew@seymour:~$ cp oldfilename newfilename
```

To rename a file as I copy it from `~/documents` to `~/archive`, I could use this:

```
matthew@seymour:~$  cp documents/oldfilename archive/newfilename
```

Or from anywhere using an absolute path, I could use the following command:

```
matthew@seymour:~$ cp /home/matthew/documents/oldfilename
/home/matthew/archive/newfilename
```

Or from anywhere using a path shortcut, I can use this:

```
matthew@seymour:~$ cp ~/documents/oldfilename ~/archive/newfilename
```

Displaying the Contents of a File with `cat`

To view the contents of a text file named `filename` on your screen, use this command:

```
matthew@seymour:~$ cat filename
```

Notice that the text is displayed on your screen but that you cannot edit or work with the text in any way. This command is convenient when you want to know the contents of a file but don't need to make any changes. Text editors for the terminal are covered in Chapter 11. This command works best with short files because the contents of longer files will scroll off of the screen too quickly to be read.

Displaying the Contents of a File with `less`

When you need to view the contents of a longer text file from the command line, you can use `less`. This produces a paged output, meaning that output stops each time your screen is full. You can then use your up- and down-arrow keys and page-up and page-down keys to scroll through the contents of the file. Then, use q to quit and return to the command line:

```
matthew@seymour:~$ less filename
```

There was a program that did give paged output in the early days of UNIX called more. It was the first paged output program but did not include the ability to scroll up and down. less was written to add that capability and was named as a bit of hacker humor, because "less is more." You can also use more, but today it is merely an alias for less.

Using Wildcards and Regular Expressions

Each of these commands can be used with pattern-matching strings known as *wildcards* or *regular expressions*. For example, to delete all files in the current directory beginning with the letters abc, you can use an expression beginning with the first three letters of the desired filenames. An asterisk (*) is then appended to match all these files. Use a command line with the rm command like this:

```
matthew@seymour:~$ rm abc*
```

Linux shells recognize many types of file naming wildcards, but this is different from the capabilities of Linux commands supporting the use of more complex expressions. You learn more about using wildcards in Chapter 11, "Command-Line Master Class," and in Chapter 13, "Automating Tasks and Shell Scripting."

> **NOTE**
>
> You can also learn more about using expressions by reading the grep manual pages (man grep), but because both man and grep are covered in Chapter 11, consider this mention as included only to whet your appetite.

Working as Root

The root, or super user account, is a special account and user on UNIX and Linux systems. Super-user permissions are required in part because of the restrictive file permissions assigned to important system configuration files. You must have root permission to edit these files or to access or modify certain devices (such as hard drives). When logged in as root, you have total control over your system, which can be dangerous.

When you work in root, you can destroy a running system with a simple invocation of the rm command, like this:

```
matthew@seymour:~$ sudo rm -rf /
```

This command line not only deletes files and directories, but also could wipe out file systems on other partitions and even remote computers. This alone is reason enough to take precautions when using root access.

The only time you should run Linux as the super user is when you are configuring the file system, for example, or to repair or maintain the system. Logging in and using Linux as the root operator isn't a good idea because it defeats the entire concept of file permissions.

Knowing how to run commands as the super user (root) without logging in as root can help avoid serious missteps when configuring your system. In Ubuntu, you can use sudo to allow you to execute single commands as root and then quickly return to normal user status. For example, if you would like to edit your system's file system table (a simple text file that describes local or remote storage devices, their type, and location), you can use sudo like this:

```
matthew@seymour:~$ sudo nano -w /etc/fstab
Password:
```

After you press Enter, you are prompted for a password that gives you access to root. This extra step can also help you "think before you leap" into the command. Enter the root password, and you are then editing /etc/fstab, using the nano editor with line wrapping disabled (thanks to the -w).

CAUTION

Before editing any important system or software service configuration file, make a backup copy. Then make sure to launch your text editor with line wrapping disabled. If you edit a configuration file without disabling line wrapping, you could insert spurious carriage returns and line feeds into its contents, causing the configured service to fail when restarting. By convention, nearly all configuration files are formatted for 80-character text width, but this is not always the case. By default, the vi and emacs editors don't use line wrap.

Creating Users

When a Linux system administrator creates a user, an entry in /etc/passwd for the user is created. The system also creates a directory, labeled with the user's username, in the /home directory. For example, if you create a user named heather, the user's home directory is /home/heather.

NOTE

In this chapter, you learn how to manage users from the command line. See Chapter 12, "Managing Users," for more information on user administration, including doing so using graphical administration utilities.

Use the useradd command, along with a user's name, to quickly create a user:

```
matthew@seymour:~$ sudo useradd heather
```

10

After creating the user, you must also create the user's initial password with the passwd command:

matthew@seymour:~$ **sudo passwd heather**

Changing password for user heather.
New password:
Retype new password:
passwd: all authentication tokens updated successfully.

Enter the new password twice. If you do not create an initial password for a new user, the user cannot log in.

You can view useradd's default new user settings by using the command and its -D option, like this:

matthew@seymour:~$ useradd -D
GROUP=100
HOME=/home
INACTIVE=-1
EXPIRE=
SHELL=/bin/sh
SKEL=/etc/skel
CREATE_MAIL_SPOOL=no

These options display the default group ID, home directory, account and password policy (active forever with no password expiration), the default shell, and the directory containing defaults for the shell.

The useradd command has many command-line options. The command can be used to set policies and dates for the new user's password, assign a login shell, assign group membership, and other aspects of a user's account. See man useradd for more info.

Deleting Users

Use the userdel command to delete users from your system. This command removes a user's entry in the system's /etc/passwd file. You should also use the command's -r option to remove all the user's files and directories (such as the user's mail spool file under /var/spool/mail):

matthew@seymour:~$ **sudo userdel -r andrew**

If you do not use the -r option, you have to manually delete the user's directory under /home, along with the user's /var/spool/mail queue.

Shutting Down the System

Use the shutdown command to shut down your system. The shutdown command has a number of different command-line options (such as shutting down at a predetermined time), but the fastest way to cleanly shut down Linux is to use the -h or halt option, followed by the word now or the numeral zero (0), like this:

matthew@seymour:~$ **sudo shutdown -h now**

or

matthew@seymour:~$ **sudo shutdown -h 0**

To incorporate a timed shutdown and a pertinent message to all active users, use shutdown's time and message options, as follows:

matthew@seymour:~$ **sudo shutdown -h 18:30 "System is going down for maintenance this evening at 6:30 p.m. Please make sure you have saved your work and logged out by then or you may lose data."**

This example shuts down your system and provides a warning to all active users 15 minutes before the shutdown (or reboot). Shutting down a running server can be considered drastic, especially if there are active users or exchanges of important data occurring (such as a backup in progress). One good approach is to warn users ahead of time. This can be done by editing the system *Message of the Day (MOTD)* motd file, which displays a message to users when they login using the command-line interface, as is common on multi-user systems.

It used to be that to create a custom MOTD, you only had to use a text editor and change the contents of /etc/motd. However, this has changed in Ubuntu as the developers have added a way to automatically and regularly update some useful information contained in MOTD using cron. To modify how the MOTD is updated, you should install update-motd and read the man page.

You can also make downtimes part of a regular schedule, perhaps to coincide with security audits, software updates, or hardware maintenance.

You should shut down Ubuntu for only a few very specific reasons:

► You are not using the computer, no other users are logged in or expected to need or use the system (such as your personal desktop or laptop computer), and you want to conserve electrical power.

► You need to perform system maintenance that requires any or all system services to be stopped.

► You want to replace integral hardware.

10

TIP

Do not shut down your computer if you suspect that intruders have infiltrated your system; instead, disconnect the machine from any or all networks and make a backup copy of your hard drives. You might want to also keep the machine running to examine the contents of memory and to examine system logs. Exceptions to this are when the system contains only trivial data files and nonessential services, such as a personal computer that is only used to run a web browser, and when you have no intention of trying to track down what an intruder may have changed, either to repair the damage or to try to catch them using computer forensics, but rather plan to merely wipe everything clean and rebuild or reinstall the system from scratch.

Rebooting the System

You should also use the shutdown command to reboot your system. The fastest way to cleanly reboot Linux is to use the -r option, and the word now or the numeral zero (0):

```
matthew@seymour:~$ sudo shutdown -r now
```

or

```
matthew@seymour:~$ sudo shutdown -r 0
```

Both rebooting and shutting down can have dire consequences if performed at the wrong time (such as during backups or critical file transfers, which arouses the ire of your system's users). However, Linux-based operating systems are designed to properly stop active system services in an orderly fashion. Other commands you can use to shut down and reboot Linux are the halt and reboot commands, but the shutdown command is more flexible.

Reading Documentation

Although you learn the basics of using Ubuntu in this book, you need time and practice to master and troubleshoot more complex aspects of the Linux operating system and your distribution. As with any operating system, you can expect to encounter some problems or perplexing questions as you continue to work with Linux. The first place to turn for help with these issues is the documentation included with your system; if you cannot find the information you need there, check Ubuntu's website.

Using apropos

Linux, like UNIX, is a self-documenting system, with man pages accessible through the man command. Linux offers many other helpful commands for accessing its documentation. You can use the apropos command (for example, with a keyword such as partition) to find commands related to partitioning, like this:

```
matthew@seymour:~$ apropos partition
addpart      (8)    - Simple wrapper around the "add partition" ioctl
all-swaps    (7)    - Event signaling that all swap partitions have been ac...
cfdisk       (8)    - Curses/slang based disk partition table manipulator fo...
delpart      (8)    - Simple wrapper around the "del partition" ioctl
fdisk        (8)    - Partition table manipulator for Linux
gparted      (8)    - Gnome partition editor for manipulating disk partitions.
Mpartition   (1)    - Partition an MSDOS hard disk
Partprobe    (8)    - Inform the OS of partition table changes
Partx        (8)    - Telling the kernel about presence and numbering of on-...
Pvcreate     (8)    - Initialize a disk or partition for use by LVM
Pvresize     (8)    - Resize a disk or partition in use by LVM2
Sfdisk       (8)    - Partition table manipulator for Linux
```

To find a command and its documentation, you can use the whereis command. For example, if you are looking for the fdisk command, you can do this:

```
$ whereis fdisk
fdisk: /sbin/fdisk /usr/share/man/man8/fdisk.8.gz
```

Using Man Pages

To learn more about a command or program, use the man command followed by the name of the command. Man pages are stored in places like /usr/share/man and /usr/local/share/man, but you don't need to know that. To read a man page, such as the one for the rm command, use the man command like this:

```
matthew@seymour:~$ man rm
```

After you press Enter, the less command (a Linux command known as a *pager*) displays the man page. The less command is a text browser you can use to scroll forward and backward (even sideways) through the document to learn more about the command. Type the letter h to get help, use the forward slash (/) to enter a search string, or press q to quit.

> **NOTE**
>
> Nearly all the hundreds of commands included with Linux each have a man page; however, some do not or may only have simple pages. You may also use the info command to read more detailed information about some commands or as a replacement for others. For example, to learn even more about info (which has a rather extensive manual page), use the info command, like this:
>
> $ info info
>
> Use the arrow keys to navigate through the document and press q to quit reading.

The following programs and built-in shell commands are commonly used when working at the command line. These commands are organized by category to help you understand the command's purpose. If you need to find full information for using the command, you can find that information under the command's man page.

▶ **Managing users and groups**—chage, chfn, chsh, edquota, gpasswd, groupadd, groupdel, groupmod, groups, mkpasswd, newgrp, newusers, passwd, umask, useradd, userdel, usermod

▶ **Managing files and file systems**—cat, cd, chattr, chmod, chown, compress, cp, dd, fdisk, find, gzip, ln, mkdir, mksfs, mount, mv, rm, rmdir, rpm, sort, swapon, swapoff, tar, touch, umount, uncompress, uniq, unzip, zip

▶ **Managing running programs**—bg, fg, kill, killall, nice, ps, pstree, renice, top, watch

▶ **Getting information**—apropos, cal, cat, cmp, date, diff, df, dir, dmesg, du, env, file, free, grep, head, info, last, less, locate, ls, lsattr, man, more, pinfo, ps, pwd, stat, strings, tac, tail, top, uname, uptime, vdir, vmstat, w, wc, whatis, whereis, which, who, whoami

▶ **Console text editors**—ed, jed, joe, mcedit, nano, red, sed, vim

▶ **Console Internet and network commands**—bing, elm, ftp, host, hostname, ifconfig, links, lynx, mail, mutt, ncftp, netconfig, netstat, pine, ping, pump, rdate, route, scp, sftp, ssh, tcpdump, traceroute, whois, wire-test

References

▶ **https://help.ubuntu.com/community/UsingTheTerminal**—The Ubuntu community help page for using the terminal.

▶ **https://help.ubuntu.com/community/LinuxFilesystemTreeOverview**—The Ubuntu community help page for and overview of the Linux file system tree.

▶ **https://help.ubuntu.com/community/RootSudo**—An Ubuntu community page explaining sudo, the philosophy behind using it by default, and how to use it.

# CHAPTER 11

Command-Line Master Class

Some Linux users like to focus on the graphical environments that are available—they rush to tell new users that the command line isn't vital when using Linux. Although there are some amazing *graphical user interface (GUI)* desktops and this statement is mostly true, avoiding the command line limits your options and makes some tasks more difficult. The command-line interface is where the greatest power and flexibility are found, and those who actively avoid learning how to use it are also actively limiting their abilities and options. You learned the basics earlier in Chapter 10, "Command-Line Quickstart." In this chapter, we dig in deeper.

It is with some trepidation that this chapter retains its classic title "Command-Line Master Class." Entire books have been published covering the depth and breadth of the command line. To believe that two short chapters will make any reader a true master is foolish. Our greatest hope is to give enough information to enable any reader to perform all basic and vital tasks from the command line while inspiring readers to go on a quest to discover all the beauty and grandeur that we do not have space to cover here. Please keep this in mind as we continue.

In his book *The Art of Unix Programming*, Eric Raymond wrote a short story that perfectly illustrates the power of the command line versus the GUI. It's reprinted here with permission, for your reading pleasure:

> One evening, Master Foo and Nubi attended a gathering of programmers who had met to learn from each other. One of the programmers asked Nubi to what school he

and his master belonged. Upon being told they were followers of the Great Way of Unix, the programmer grew scornful.

"The command-line tools of Unix are crude and backward," he scoffed.

"Modern, properly designed operating systems do everything through a graphical user interface."

Master Foo said nothing, but pointed at the moon. A nearby dog began to bark at the master's hand.

"I don't understand you!" said the programmer.

Master Foo remained silent, and pointed at an image of the Buddha. Then he pointed at a window. "What are you trying to tell me?" asked the programmer.

Master Foo pointed at the programmer's head. Then he pointed at a rock.

"Why can't you make yourself clear?" demanded the programmer.

Master Foo frowned thoughtfully, tapped the programmer twice on the nose, and dropped him in a nearby trash can.

As the programmer was attempting to extricate himself from the garbage, the dog wandered over and piddled on him.

At that moment, the programmer achieved enlightenment.

Whimsical as the story is, it does illustrate that there are some things that the GUI just does not do well. Enter the command line: It is a powerful and flexible operating environment and—if you practice—can actually be quite fun, too!

In this chapter, you learn how to master the command line so that you can perform common tasks through it and can also link commands together to create new command groups. We also look at the three most popular Linux text editors: vim, emacs, and nano.

Why Use the Command Line?

Moving from the GUI to the command line is a conscious choice for most people, although it is increasingly rare that it is an absolute choice accompanied by a complete abandoning of GUIs.

Reasons for using the command line include the following:

▶ You want to chain two or more commands together.

▶ You want to use a command or parameter available only on the shell.

▶ You are working on a text-only system.

▶ You have used it for a long time and feel comfortable there.

Chaining two or more commands together, or *piping*, is what gives the shell its real power. Hundreds of commands are available, and by combining them in different ways you get tons of new options. Some of the shell commands are available through the GUI, but these commands usually have only a small subset of their parameters available, which limits what you can do with them.

Working from a text-only system is useful both for working locally with a broken GUI and for connecting to a remote, text-only system. If your Linux server is experiencing problems, the last thing you want to do is load it down with a GUI connection; working in text mode is faster and more efficient.

Many people use the shell simply because it is familiar to them. Some people even use the shell to start GUI applications just because it saves them taking their hands off the keyboard for a moment. This is not a bad thing; it provides fluency and ease with the system and is a perfectly valid way of working. Working from the command line is faster. The mouse is slow, and taking your fingers away from the keyboard makes your work even slower. Anyone looking to achieve the zen-like power user state hinted at by Eric Raymond will understand this after making the effort to learn.

Using Basic Commands

It is impossible to know how many commands the average command-line citizen uses, but if we had to guess, we would place it at about 25. Some of these were introduced in Chapter 10, but are covered here with greater depth. Others will be new to the reader. Still others are only mentioned in this list to give the reader ideas for further study. Here are some commands that every command-line user will want to learn:

- ▶ **cat**—Prints the contents of a file.
- ▶ **cd**—Changes directories.
- ▶ **chmod**—Changes file access permissions.
- ▶ **cp**—Copies files.
- ▶ **du**—Prints disk usage.
- ▶ **emacs**—Edits text files.
- ▶ **find**—Finds files by searching.
- ▶ **gcc**—Compiles C/C++/Fortran programs.
- ▶ **grep**—Searches for a string in input.
- ▶ **less**—Filter for paging through output.
- ▶ **ln**—Creates links between files.
- ▶ **locate**—Finds files from an index.
- ▶ **ls**—Lists files in the current directory.
- ▶ **make**—Compiles and installs programs.
- ▶ **man**—Displays manual pages for reading.

▶ **mkdir**—Makes directories.

▶ **mv**—Moves files.

▶ **ps**—Lists processes.

▶ **rm**—Deletes files and directories.

▶ **ssh**—Connects to other machines using a secure shell connection.

▶ **tail**—Prints the last lines of a file.

▶ **top**—Prints resource usage.

▶ **vim**—Edits text files.

▶ **which**—Prints the location of a command.

▶ **xargs**—Executes commands from its input.

Many other commands also are available to you that get used fairly often—cut, diff, gzip, history, ping, su, tar, uptime, who, and so on—but if you can understand the 25 listed here, you have sufficient skill to concoct your own command combinations.

Note that we say *understand* the commands, not know all their possible parameters and usages. This is because several of the commands, although commonly used, are used only in any complex manner by people with specific needs. gcc and make are good examples of this: Unless you plan to become a programmer, you need not worry about these beyond just typing make and make install now and then. If you want to learn more about these two, see Chapter 39, "C/C++ Programming Tools for Ubuntu."

Similarly, both emacs and vim are text editors that have a text-based interface all of their own, and are covered later in this chapter, and SSH is covered in detail in Chapter 18, "Remote Access with SSH and Telnet."

What remains is 20 commands, each of which has many parameters to customize what it actually does. Again, we can eliminate much of this because many of the parameters are esoteric and rarely used, and, the few times in your Linux life that you need them, you can just read the manual page.

We go over these commands one by one, explaining the most common ways to use them. There is one exception: The xargs command requires you to understand how to join commands together, which we cover at that point in the chapter.

Printing the Contents of a File with cat

Many of Ubuntu's shell commands manipulate text strings, so if you want to be able to feed them the contents of files, you need to be able to output those files as text. Enter the cat command, which prints the contents of any files you pass to it.

Its most basic use is like this:

```
matthew@seymour:~$ cat myfile.txt
```

That prints the contents of `myfile.txt`. For this usage, there are two extra parameters that are often used: `-n` numbers the lines in the output, and `-s` ("squeeze") prints a maximum of one blank line at a time. That is, if your file has 1 line of text, 10 blank lines, 1 line of text, 10 blank lines, and so on, `-s` shows the first line of text, a single blank line, the next line of text, a single blank line, and so forth. When you combine `-s` and `-n`, cat numbers only the lines that are printed—the 10 blank lines shown as one will count as 1 line for numbering.

This command prints information about your CPU, stripping out multiple blank lines and numbering the output:

```
matthew@seymour:~$ cat -sn /proc/cpuinfo
```

You can also use cat to print the contents of several files at once, like this:

```
matthew@seymour:~$ cat -s myfile.txt myotherfile.txt
```

In that command, cat merges `myfile.txt` and `myotherfile.txt` on the output, stripping out multiple blank lines. The important thing is that cat does not distinguish between the files in the output; there are no filenames printed, and no extra breaks between the 2. This allows you to treat the 2 as 1 or, by adding more files to the command line, to treat 20 files as 1.

Changing Directories with cd

Changing directories is surely something that has no options, right? Not so. cd is actually more flexible than most people realize. Unlike most of the other commands here, cd is not a command in itself—it is built into bash (or whichever shell interpreter you are using), but it is still used like a command.

The most basic usage of cd is this:

```
matthew@seymour:~$ cd somedir
```

That looks in the current directory for the somedir subdirectory, and then moves you into it. You can also specify an exact location for a directory, like this:

```
matthew@seymour:~$ cd /home/matthew/stuff/somedir
```

The first part of cd's magic lies in the characters (- and ~, a dash and a tilde). The first means "switch to my previous directory," and the second means "switch to my home directory." This conversation with cd shows this in action:

```
matthew@seymour:~$  cd /usr/local
matthew@seymour/usr/local$  cd bin
matthew@seymour/usr/local/bin$  cd -
/usr/local
matthew@seymour/usr/local$ cd ~
matthew@seymour:~$
```

In the first line, we change to /usr/local and get no output from the command. In the second line, we change to bin, which is a subdirectory of /usr/local. Next, cd - is used to change back to the previous directory. This time bash prints the name of the previous directory so we know where we are. Finally, cd ~ is used to change back to our /home directory, although if you want to save an extra few keystrokes, just typing cd by itself is equivalent to cd ~.

The second part of cd's magic is its capability to look for directories in predefined locations. When you specify an absolute path to a directory (that is, one starting with a /), cd always switches to that exact location. However, if you specify a relative subdirectory—for example, cd subdir—you can tell cd where you would like that to be relative to. This is accomplished with the CDPATH environment variable. If this variable is not set, cd always uses the current directory as the base; however, you can set it to any number of other directories.

This next example shows a test of this. It starts in /home/matthew/empty, an empty directory, and the lines are numbered for later reference:

```
1 matthew@seymour:~/empty$ pwd
2 /home/matthew/empty
3 matthew@seymour:~/empty$ ls
4 matthew@seymour:~/empty$ mkdir local
5 matthew@seymour:~/empty$ ls
6 local
7 matthew@seymour:~/empty$ cd local
8 matthew@seymour:~/empty/local$ cd ..
9 matthew@seymour:~/empty$ export CDPATH=/usr
10 matthew@seymour:~/empty$ cd local
11 /usr/local
12 matthew/usr/local$ cd -
13 /home/matthew/empty
14 matthew@seymour:~/empty$ export CDPATH=.:/usr
15 matthew@seymour:~/empty$ cd local
16 /home/matthew/empty/local
17 matthew@seymour:~/empty/local$
```

Lines 1–3 show that we are in /home/matthew/empty and that it is indeed empty; ls had no output. Lines 4–6 show the local subdirectory being made, so that /home/matthew/empty/local exists. Lines 7 and 8 show you can cd into /home/matthew/empty/local and back out again.

In line 9, CDPATH is set to /usr. This was chosen because Ubuntu has the directory /usr/local, which means our current directory (/home/matthew/empty) and our CDPATH directory (/usr) both have a local subdirectory. In line 10, while in the /home/matthew/empty directory, we use cd local. This time, bash switches us to /usr/local and even prints the new directory to ensure we know what it has done.

Lines 12 and 13 move us back to the previous directory, /home/matthew/empty. In line 14, CDPATH is set to be .:/usr. The : is the directory separator, so this means bash should look first in the current directory, ., and then in the /usr directory. In line 15, cd local is issued again, this time moving to /home/matthew/empty/local. Note that bash has still printed the new directory; it does that whenever it looks up a directory in CDPATH.

Changing File Access Permissions with chmod

Your use of chmod can be greatly extended through one simple parameter: -c. This instructs chmod to print a list of all the changes it made as part of its operation, which means we can capture the output and use it for other purposes. For example:

```
matthew@seymour:~$ chmod -c 600 *
mode of '1.txt' changed to 0600 (rw-------)
mode of '2.txt' changed to 0600 (rw-------)
mode of '3.txt' changed to 0600 (rw-------)
matthew@seymour:~$ chmod -c 600 *
matthew@seymour:~$
```

There the chmod command is issued with -c, and you can see it has output the result of the operation: Three files were changed to rw------- (read and write by user only). However, when the command is issued again, no output is returned. This is because -c prints only the changes that it made. Files that already match the permissions you are setting are left unchanged and therefore are not printed.

There are two other parameters of interest: --reference and -R. The first allows you to specify a file to use as a template for permissions rather than specifying permissions yourself. For example, if you want all files in the current directory to have the same permissions as the file /home/matthew/myfile.txt, you use this:

```
chmod --reference /home/matthew/myfile.txt *
```

You can use -R to enable recursive operation, which means you can use it to chmod a directory and it will change the permissions of that directory as well as all files and subdirectories under that directory. You could use chmod -R 600 /home to change every file and directory under /home to become read/write to their owner.

Copying Files with cp

Like mv, which is covered later, cp is a command that is easily used and mastered. However, two marvelous parameters rarely see much use (which is a shame) despite their power. These are --parents and -u. The first copies the full path of the file into the new directory; the second copies only if the source file is newer than the destination.

Using --parents requires a little explanation, so here is an example. You have a file, /home/matthew/desktop/documents/work/notes.txt, and want to copy it to your /home/matthew/backup folder. You could do a normal cp, but that would give you

/home/matthew/backup/notes.txt, so how would you know where that came from later? If you use --parents, the file is copied to /home/matthew/backup/desktop/documents/work/notes.txt.

The -u parameter is perfect for synchronizing two directories because it allows you to run a command like cp -Ru myfiles myotherfiles and have cp recopy only files that have changed. The -R parameter means recursive and allows you to copy directory contents.

Printing Disk Usage with du

The du command prints the size of each file and directory that is inside the current directory. Its most basic usage is as easy as it gets:

matthew@seymour:~$ **du**

That outputs a long list of directories and how much space their files take up. You can modify that with the -a parameter, which instructs du to print the size of individual files as well as directories. Another useful parameter is -h, which makes du use human-readable sizes like 18M (18MB) rather than 17532 (the same number in bytes, unrounded). The final useful basic option is -c, which prints the total size of files.

So, using du, we can get a printout of the size of each file in our /home directory, in human-readable format, and with a summary at the end, like this:

matthew@seymour:~$ **du -ahc /home/matthew**

Two advanced parameters deal with filenames you want excluded from your count. The first is --exclude, which allows you to specify a pattern that should be used to exclude files. This pattern is a standard shell file-matching pattern as opposed to a regular expression, which means you can use ? to match a single character or * to match zero or many characters. You can specify multiple —exclude parameters to exclude several patterns. For example:

matthew@seymour:~$ **du --exclude="*.xml" --exclude="*.xsl"**

However, typing numerous --exclude parameters repeatedly is a waste of time, so you can use -X to specify a file that has the list of patterns you want excluded. The file should look like this:

```
*.xml
*.xsl
```

That is, each pattern you want excluded should be on a line by itself. If that file were called xml_exclude.txt, we could use it in place of the previous example, like this:

matthew@seymour:~$ **du -X xml_exclude.txt**

You can make your exclusion file as long as you need, or you can just specify multiple -X parameters.

Running du in a directory where several files are hard-linked to the same inode counts the size of the file only once. If you want to count each hard link separately for some reason, use the `-l` parameter (lowercase *L*).

Finding Files by Searching with `find`

The `find` command is one of the darkest and least understood areas of Linux, but it is also one of the most powerful. Admittedly, the `find` command does not help itself by using X-style parameters. The UNIX standard is `-c`, `-s`, and so on, whereas the GNU standard is `--dosomething`, `--mooby`, and so forth. X-style parameters merge the two by having words preceded by only one dash.

However, the biggest problem with `find` is that it has more options than most people can remember; it truly is capable of doing most things you could want. The most basic usage is this:

```
matthew@seymour:~$ find -name "*.txt"
```

That searches the current directory and all subdirectories for files that end in `.txt`. The previous search finds files ending in `.txt` but not `.TXT`, `.Txt`, or other case variations. To search without case sensitivity, use `-iname` rather than `-name`. You can optionally specify where the search should start before the `-name` parameter, like this:

```
matthew@seymour:~$ find /home -name "*.txt"
```

Another useful test is `-size`, which lets you specify how big the files should be to match. You can specify your size in kilobytes and optionally use + or - to specify greater than or less than. For example:

```
matthew@seymour:~$ find /home -name "*.txt" -size 100k
matthew@seymour:~$ find /home -name "*.txt" -size +100k
matthew@seymour:~$ find /home -name "*.txt" -size -100k
```

The first brings up files of exactly 100KB, the second only files larger than 100KB, and the last only files under 100KB.

Moving on, the `-user` option enables you to specify the user who owns the files you are looking for. So, to search for all files in `/home` that end with `.txt`, that are under 100KB, and that are owned by user `matthew`, you use this:

```
matthew@seymour:~$ find /home -name "*.txt" -size -100k -user matthew
```

You can flip any of the conditions by specifying `-not` before them. For example, you can add a `-not` before `-user matthew` to find matching files owned by everyone but `matthew`:

```
matthew@seymour:~$ find /home -name "*.txt" -size -100k -not -user matthew
```

You can add as many -not parameters as you need, even using -not -not to cancel each other out. (Yes, that is pointless.) Keep in mind, though, that -not -size -100k is essentially equivalent to -size +100k, with the exception that the former will match files of exactly 100KB, whereas the latter will not.

You can use -perm to specify which permissions a file should have for it to be matched. This is tricky, so read carefully. The permissions are specified in the same way as with the chmod command: u for user, g for group, o for others, r for read, w for write, and x for execute. However, before you give the permissions, you need to specify either a plus, a minus, or a blank space. If you specify neither a plus nor a minus, the files must exactly match the mode you give. If you specify -, the files must match all the modes you specify. If you specify +, the files must match any of the modes you specify. Confused yet?

The confusion can be cleared up with some examples. This next command finds all files that have permission o=r (readable for other users). Notice that if you remove the -name parameter, it is equivalent to * because all filenames are matched:

```
matthew@seymour:~$ find /home -perm -o=r
```

Any files that have o=r set are returned from that query. Those files also might have u=rw and other permissions, but as long as they have o=r, they will match. This next query matches all files that have o=rw set:

```
matthew@seymour:~$ find /home -perm -o=rw
```

However, that query does not match files that are o=r or o=w. To be matched, a file must be readable and writeable by other users. If you want to match readable or writeable (or both), you need to use +, like this:

```
matthew@seymour:~$ find /home -perm +o=rw
```

Similarly, this next query matches only files that are readable by user, group, and others:

```
matthew@seymour:~$ find /home -perm -ugo=r
```

Whereas this query matches files as long as they are readable by the user, or by the group, or by others, or by any combination of the three:

```
matthew@seymour:~$ find /home -perm +ugo=r
```

If you use neither + or -, you are specifying the exact permissions to search for. For example, the next query searches for files that are readable by user, group, and others but not writeable or executable by anyone:

```
matthew@seymour:~$ find /home -perm ugo=r
```

You can be as specific as you need to be with the permissions. For example, this query finds all files that are readable for the user, group, and others and writeable by the user:

```
matthew@seymour:~$ find /home -perm ugo=r,u=w
```

To find files that are not readable by others, use the `-not` condition, like this:

```
matthew@seymour:~$ find /home -not -perm +o=r
```

Now, on to the most advanced aspect of the find command: the `-exec` parameter. This enables you to execute an external program each time a match is made, passing in the name of the matched file wherever you want it. This has very specific syntax: Your command and its parameters should follow immediately after `-exec`, terminated by `\;`. You can insert the filename match at any point using `{}` (an opening and a closing brace side by side).

So, you can match all text files on the entire system (that is, searching recursively from `/` rather than from `/home` as in our previous examples) over 10KB, owned by `matthew`, that are not readable by other users, and then use `chmod` to enable reading, like this:

```
matthew@seymour:~$ find / -name "*.txt" -size +10k -user matthew -not -perm
+o=r -exec chmod o+r {} \;
```

When you type your own `-exec` parameters, be sure to include a space before `\;`. Otherwise, you might see an error such as `missing argument to '-exec'`.

Do you see now why some people think the `find` command is scary? Many people learn just enough about `find` to be able to use it in a very basic way, but hopefully you will see how much it can do if you give it chance.

Searches for a String in Input with `grep`

The `grep` command, like `find`, is an incredibly powerful search tool in the right hands. Unlike `find`, though, `grep` processes any text, whether in files, or just in standard input.

The basic usage of `grep` is this:

```
matthew@seymour:~$ grep "some text" *
```

That searches all files in the current directory (but not subdirectories) for the string `some text` and prints matching lines along with the name of the file. To enable recursive searching in subdirectories, use the `-r` parameter, as follows:

```
matthew@seymour:~$ grep -r "some text" *
```

Each time a string is matched within a file, the filename and the match are printed. If a file contains multiple matches, each of the matches is printed. You can alter this behavior with the `-l` parameter (lowercase *L*), which forces `grep` to print the name of each file that contains at least one match, without printing the matching text. If a file contains more than one match, it is still printed only once. Alternatively, the `-c` parameter prints each filename that was searched and includes the number of matches at the end, even if there were no matches.

You have a lot of control when specifying the pattern to search for. You can, as we did previously, specify a simple string like `some text`, or you can invert that search by specifying the `-v` parameter. For example, this returns all the lines of the file `myfile.txt` that do not contain the word *hello*:

```
matthew@seymour:~$ grep -v "hello" myfile.txt
```

You can also use regular expressions for your search term. For example, you can search `myfile.txt` for all references to *cat*, *sat*, or *mat* with this command:

```
matthew@seymour:~$ grep "[cms]at" myfile.txt
```

Adding the `-i` parameter to that removes case sensitivity, matching *Cat*, *CAT*, *MaT*, and so on:

```
matthew@seymour:~$ grep -i [cms]at myfile.txt
```

The output can also be controlled to some extent with the `-n` and `--color` parameters. The first tells `grep` to print the line number for each match, which is where it appears in the source file. The —color parameter tells `grep` to color the search terms in the output, which helps them stand out when among all the other text on the line. You choose which color you want using the `GREP_COLOR` environment variable: export `GREP_COLOR=36` gives you cyan, and export `GREP_COLOR=32` gives you lime green.

This next example uses these two parameters to number and color all matches to the previous command:

```
matthew@seymour:~$ grep -in --color [cms]at myfile.txt
```

Later you learn how important `grep` is for piping with other commands.

Paging Through Output with `less`

The `less` command enables you to view large amounts of text in a more convenient way than the `cat` command. For example, your `/etc/passwd` file is probably more than a screen long, so if you run `cat /etc/passwd`, you are not able to see what the lines at the top were. Using `less /etc/passwd` enables you to use the cursor keys to scroll up and down the output freely. Type q to quit and return to the shell.

On the surface, `less` sounds like an easy command; however, it has the infamy of being one of the few Linux commands that have a parameter for every letter of the alphabet. That is, `-a` does something, `-b` does something else, `-c`, `-d`, `-e` ... `-x`, `-y`, `-z`, they all do things, with some letters even differentiating between upper- and lowercase. Furthermore, these parameters are only used when invoking `less`. After you are viewing your text, even more commands are available. Make no mistake—`less` is a complex beast to master.

Input to `less` can be divided into two categories: what you type before running `less` and what you type while running it. The former category is easy, so we start there.

We have already discussed how many parameters `less` can take, but they can be distilled down to three that are very useful: `-M`, `-N`, and `+`. Adding `-M` (this is different from `-m`) enables verbose prompting in `less`. Instead of just printing a colon and a flashing cursor, `less` prints the filename, the line numbers being shown, the total number of lines, and the percentage of how far you are through the file. Adding `-N` (again, this is different from `-n`) enables line numbering.

The last option, `+`, allows you to pass a command to `less` for it to execute as it starts. To use this, you first need to know the commands available to you in `less`, which means we need to move to the second category of `less` input: what you type while `less` is running.

The basic navigation keys are the up, down, left, and right cursors; Home and End (for navigating to the start and end of a file); and Page Up and Page Down. Beyond that, the most common command is `/`, which initiates a text search. You type what you want to search for and press Enter to have `less` find the `first` match and highlight all subsequent matches. Type `/` again and press Enter to have `less` jump to the next match. The inverse of that is `?`, which searches backward for text. Type `?`, enter a search string, and press Enter to go to the first previous match of that string, or just use `?` and press Enter to go to the next match preceding the current position. You can use `/` and `?` interchangeably by searching for something with `/` and then using `?` to go backward in the same search.

Searching with `/` and `?` is commonly used with the `+` command-line parameter from earlier, which passes `less` a command for execution after the file has loaded. For example, you can tell `less` to load a file and place the cursor at the first match for the search *hello*, like this:

```
matthew@seymour:~$ less +/hello myfile.txt
```

Or, to place the cursor at the last match for the search *hello*:

```
matthew@seymour:~$ less +?hello myfile.txt
```

Beyond the cursor keys, the controls primarily involve typing a number and then pressing a key. For example, to go to line 50, you type `50g`, or to go to the 75 percent point of the file, you type `75p`. You can also place invisible mark points through the file by pressing `m` and then typing a single letter. Later, while in the same `less` session, you can press `'` (a single quote) and then type the letter, and it will move you back to the same position. You can set up to 52 marks, named a–z and A–Z.

One clever feature of `less` is that you can, at any time, press `v` to have your file opened inside your text editor. This defaults to `vim`, but you can change that by setting the `EDITOR` environment variable to something else.

If you have made it this far, you can already use `less` better than most users. You can, at this point, justifiably skip to the next section and consider yourself proficient with `less`. However, if you want to be a `less` guru, there are two more things to learn: how to view multiple files simultaneously and how to run shell commands.

Like most other file-based commands in Linux, `less` can take several files as its parameters. For example:

matthew@seymour:~$ **less -MN 1.txt 2.txt 3.txt**

That loads all three files into `less`, starting at `1.txt`. When viewing several files, `less` usually tells you which file you are in, as well as numbering them: `1.txt (file 1 of 3)` should be at the bottom of the screen. However, certain things will make that go away, so you should use `-M` anyway.

You can navigate between files by typing a colon and then pressing n to go to the next file or press p to go to the previous file; these are referred to from now on as :n and :p. You can open another file for viewing by typing :e and providing a filename. This can be any file you have permission to read, including files outside the local directory. Use Tab to complete filenames. Files you open in this way are inserted one place after your current position, so if you are viewing file 1 of 4 and open a new file, the new file is numbered 2 of 5 and is opened for viewing right away. To close a file and remove it from the list, use :d.

Viewing multiple files simultaneously has implications for searching. By default, `less` searches within only one file, but it is easy to search within all files. When you type / or ? to search, follow it with a *. You should see `EOF-ignore` followed by a search prompt. You can now type a search and it will search in the current file; if nothing is found, it looks in subsequent files until it finds a match. Repeating searches is done by pressing Esc and then either n or N. The lowercase option repeats the search forward across files, and the uppercase repeats it backward.

The last thing you need to know is that you can get to a shell from `less` and execute commands. The simplest way to do this is just to type ! and press Enter. This launches a shell and leaves you free to type all the commands you want, as per normal. Type `exit` to return to `less`. You can also type specific commands by entering them after the exclamation mark, using the special character % for the current filename. For example, `du -h %` prints the size of the current file. Finally, you can use !! to repeat the previous command.

Creating Links Between Files with `ln`

Linux allows you to create links between files that look and work like normal files for the most part. Moreover, it allows you to make two types of links, known as hard links and *symbolic links (symlinks)*. The difference between the two is crucial, although it might not be obvious at first.

Each filename on your system points to what is known as an inode, which is the absolute location of a file. Linux allows you to point more than one filename to a given inode, and the result is a hard link—two filenames pointing to the same file. Each of these files shares the same contents and attributes. So, if you edit one, the other changes because they are both the same file.

On the other hand, a symlink—sometimes called a soft link—is a redirect to the real file. When a program tries to read from a symlink, it automatically is redirected to what the symlink is pointing at. The fact that symlinks are really just dumb pointers has two advantages: You can link to something that does not exist (and create it later if you want), and you can link to directories.

Both types of links have their uses. Creating a hard link is a great way to back up a file on the same disk. For example, if you delete the file in one location, it still exists untouched in the other location. Symlinks are popular because they allow a file to appear to be in a different location; you could store your website in /var/www/live and an under-construction holding page in /var/www/construction. Then you could have Apache point to a symlink /var/www/html that is redirected to either the live or construction directory, depending on what you need.

TIP

The shred command overwrites a file's contents with random data, allowing for safe deletion. Because this directly affects a file's contents, rather than just a filename, this means that all filenames hard linked to an inode are affected.

Both types of link are created using the ln command. By default, it creates hard links, but you can create symlinks by passing it the -s parameter. The syntax is ln [-s] *something somewhere*, for example:

matthew@seymour:~$ **ln -s myfile.txt mylink**

That creates the symlink mylink that points to myfile.txt. You don't see it here, but the file I created is 341 bytes. This is important later. Remove the -s to create a hard link. You can verify that your link has been created by running ls -l. Your symlink should look something like this:

lrwxrwxrwx 1 matthew matthew   5 Feb 19 12:39 mylink -> myfile.txt

Note how the file properties start with l (lowercase *L*) for link and how ls -l also prints where the link is going. Symlinks are always very small in size; the previous link is 5 bytes. If you created a hard link, it should look like this:

-rw-rw-r   2 matthew matthew   341 Feb 19 12:39 mylink

This time the file has normal attributes, but the second number is 2 rather than 1. That number is how many hard links point to this file, which is why it is 2 now. The file size is also the same as that of the previous filename because it is the file, as opposed to just being a pointer.

Symlinks are used extensively in Linux. Programs that have been superseded, such as sh, now point to their replacements (in this case, bash), and library versioning is accomplished through symlinks. For example, applications that link against zlib load /usr/lib/libz.so. Internally, however, that is just a symlink that points to the actual zlib library: /usr/lib/libz.so.1.2.1.2. This enables multiple versions of libraries to be installed without application developers needing to worry about these specific details.

Finding Files from an Index with `locate`

When you use the `find` command, it searches recursively through each directory each time you request a file. This is slow, as you can imagine. Fortunately, Ubuntu ships with a `cron` job that creates an index of all the files on your system every night. Searching this index is extremely fast, which means that if the file you are looking for has been around since the last index, this is the preferable way of searching.

To look for a file in your index, use the command `locate` followed by the names of the files you want to find, like this:

```
matthew@seymour:~$ locate myfile.txt
```

On a relatively modern computer (1.5GHz or higher), `locate` should be able to return all the matching files in under a second. The trade-off for this speed is lack of flexibility. You can search for matching filenames, but, unlike `find`, you cannot search for sizes, owners, access permissions, or other attributes. The one thing you can change is case sensitivity; use the `-i` parameter to do a search that is not case sensitive.

Although Ubuntu rebuilds the filename index nightly, you can force a rebuild whenever you want by running the command `updatedb` with `sudo`. This usually takes a few minutes, but when it's done, the new database is immediately available.

Listing Files in the Current Directory with `ls`

The `ls` command, like `ln`, is one of those you expect to be very straightforward. It lists files, but how many options can it possibly have? In true Linux style, the answer is many, although again you need only know a few to wield great power!

The basic usage is simply `ls`, which lists the files and directories in the current location. You can filter that using normal wildcards, so all these are valid:

```
matthew@seymour:~$ ls *
matthew@seymour:~$ ls *.txt
matthew@seymour:~$ ls my*ls *.txt *.xml
```

Any directories that match these filters are recursed into one level. That is, if you run `ls my*` and you have the files `myfile1.txt` and `myfile2.txt` and a directory `mystuff`, the matching files are printed first. Then `ls` prints the contents of the `mystuff` directory.

The most popular parameters for customizing the output of `ls` are as follows:

▶ **-a**—Includes hidden files.

▶ **-h**—Uses human-readable sizes.

- ▶ **-1**—(Lowercase *L*) Enables long listing.

- ▶ **-r**—Reverse order.

- ▶ **-R**—Recursively lists directories.

- ▶ **-s**—Shows sizes.

- ▶ **--sort**—Sorts the listing.

All files that start with a period are hidden in Linux, so that includes the .gnome directory in your /home directory, as well as .bash_history and the . and .. implicit directories that signify the current directory and the parent. By default, ls does not show these files, but if you run ls -a, they are shown. You can also use ls -A to show all the hidden files except . and ...

The -h parameter needs to be combined with the -s parameter, like this:

matthew@seymour:~$ **ls -sh *.txt**

That outputs the size of each matching file in a human-readable format, such as 108KB or 4.5MB.

Using the -l parameter enables much more information about your files. Instead of just providing the names of the files, you get output like this:

```
drwxrwxr-x 24 matthew matthew  4096 Dec 24 21:33 arch
-rw-r--r--  1 matthew matthew 18691 Dec 24 21:34 COPYING
-rw-r--r--  1 matthew matthew 88167 Dec 24 21:35 CREDITS
drwxrwxr-x  2 matthew matthew  4096 Dec 24 21:35 crypto
```

That shows four matches and prints a lot of information about each of them. The first row shows the arch directory; you can tell it is a directory because its file attributes starts with a d. The rwxrwxr-x following that shows the access permissions, and this has special meanings because it is a directory. Read access for a directory allows users to see the directory contents, write access allows you to create files and subdirectories, and execute access allows you to cd into the directory. If a user has execute access but not read access, the user can cd into the directory but not list files.

Moving on, the next number on the line is 24, which also has a special meaning for directories: It is the number of subdirectories (including . and ..). After that is matthew matthew, which is the name of the user owner and the group owner for the directory. Next is the size and modification time, and finally the directory name itself.

The next line shows the file COPYING, and most of the numbers have the same meaning, with the exception of the 1 immediately after the access permissions. For directories, this is the number of subdirectories, but for files this is the number of hard links to this file. A 1 in this column means this is the only filename pointing to this inode, so if you delete it, it is gone.

Ubuntu comes configured with a shortcut command for `ls -l`: `ll`.

The `--sort` parameter allows you to reorder the output from the default alphabetic sorting. You can sort by various things, although the most popular are extension (alphabetically), size (largest first), and time (newest first). To flip the sorting (making size sort by smallest first), use the `-r` parameter also. So, this command lists all `.ogg` files, sorted smallest to largest:

`matthew@seymour:~$` **`ls --sort size -r *.ogg`**

Finally, the `-R` parameter recurses through subdirectories. For example, typing `ls /etc` lists all the files and subdirectories in `/etc`, but `ls -R /etc` lists all the files in and subdirectories in `/etc`, all the files and subdirectories in `/etc/acpi`, all the files and subdirectories in `/etc/acpi/actions`, and so on until every subdirectory has been listed.

Reading Manual Pages with `man`

Time for a much-needed mental break: The `man` command is easy to use. Most people use only the topic argument, like this: `man gcc`. However, two other commands work closely with `man` that are very useful: `whatis` and `apropos`.

The `whatis` command returns a one-line description of another command, which is the same text you get at the top of that command's man page. For example:

`matthew@seymour:~$`   **`whatis ls`**
`ls     (1) - list directory contents`

The output there explains what `ls` does but also provides the man page section number for the command so you can query it further.

The `apropos` command takes a search string as its parameter and returns all man pages that match the search. For example, `apropos mixer` returns this list:

`alsamixer (1) - soundcard mixer for ALSA soundcard driver`
`mixer (1) - command-line mixer for ALSA soundcard driver`
`aumix (1) - adjust audio mixer`

So, use `apropos` to help you find commands and use `whatis` to tell you what a command does.

One neat trick is that many of the tips and tricks we learned for `less` also work when viewing man pages (for example, using / and ? to search). This is one of the beautiful things about UNIX systems: Gaining knowledge in one area often benefits you in other areas.

You can use a number of other commands to search the file system, including the following:

▶ **`whereis command`**—Returns the location of the command (for example, `/bin`, `/sbin`, or `/usr/bin/command`) and its man page, which is an entry for the command included as a file already on your computer in a standardized manual format.

▶ **`whatis command`**—Returns a one-line synopsis from the command's man page.

► **locate file**—Returns locations of all matching files; an extremely fast method of searching your system because locate searches a database containing an index of all files on your system. However, this database (which is several megabytes in size and named mlocate.db, under the /var/lib/mlocate directory) is built daily at 6:25 a.m. by default, and does not contain pathnames to files created during the workday or in the evening. If you do not keep your machine on constantly, you can run the updatedb command with super user privileges to manually start the building of the database. More advanced users can change the time the database is updated by changing a cron job that calls the command. There is a script in /etc/cron.daily called mlocate that does this as part of the daily maintenance for the database. You would need to either remove that script from /etc/cron.daily and put it the root crontab or change when the daily tasks are run. If you don't know how to do this right now, you can come back after you have read and understand Chapter 13, "Automating Tasks and Shell Scripting," and its discussion of cron, and the preceding description will be clear.

► **type name**—Returns how a name would be interpreted if used as a command. This generally shows options or the location of the binary that will be used. For example, type ls returns ls is aliased to 'ls –color=auto'.

Making Directories with `mkdir`

Making directories is as easy as it sounds, although there is one parameter you should be aware of: -p. If you are in /home/matthew and you want to create the directory /home/matthew/audio/sound, you get an error like this:

```
mkdir: cannot create directory 'audio/sound': No such file or directory
```

At first glance, this seems wrong; mkdir cannot create the directory because it does not exist. What it actually means is that it cannot create the directory sound because the directory audio does not exist. This is where the -p parameter comes in: If you try to make a directory within another directory that does not exist, like the previous, -p creates the parent directories, too. So:

```
matthew@seymour:~$ mkdir -p audio/sound
```

That first creates the audio directory and then creates the sound directory inside it.

Moving Files with `mv`

This command is one of the easiest around. There are two helpful parameters to mv: -f, which overwrites files without asking; and -u, which moves the source file only if it is newer than the destination file. That's it.

Listing Processes with ps

This is the third and last "command that should be simple, but isn't" that is discussed here. The ps command lists processes and gives you an extraordinary amount of control over its operation.

The first thing to know is that ps is typically used with what are known as BSD-style parameters. Back in the section "Finding Files by Searching with find," we discussed UNIX-style, GNU-style, and X-style parameters (-c, --dosomething, and -dosomething, respectively), but BSD-style parameters are different because they use single letters without a dash.

So, the default use of ps lists all processes that you are running that are attached to the terminal. However, you can ask it to list all your processes attached to any terminal (or indeed no terminal) by adding the x parameter: ps x. You can ask it to list all processes for all users with the a parameter or combine that with x to list all processes for all users, attached to a terminal or otherwise: ps ax.

However, both of these are timid compared with the almighty u option, which enables user-oriented output. In practice, that makes a huge difference because you get important fields like the username of the owner, how much CPU time and RAM are being used, when the process was started, and more. This outputs a lot of information, so you might want to try adding the f parameter, which creates a process forest by using ASCII art to connect parent commands with their children. You can combine all the options so far with this command: ps faux. (Yes, with a little imagination, you spell words with the parameters.)

You can control the order in which the data is returned by using the --sort parameter. This takes either a + or a - (although the + is default) followed by the field you want to sort by: command, %cpu, pid, and user are all popular options. If you use the minus sign, the results are reversed. This next command lists all processes, ordered by CPU usage descending:

matthew@seymour:~$ **ps aux --sort=-%cpu**

There are many other parameters for ps, including a huge amount of options for compatibility with other UNIXes. If you have the time to read the man page, give it a try.

Deleting Files and Directories with rm

The rm command has only one parameter of interest: --preserve-root. By now, you should know that issuing rm -rf / with sudo will destroy your Linux installation because -r means recursive and -f means force (do not prompt for confirmation before deleting). It is possible for a clumsy person to issue this command by accident—not by typing the command on purpose, but by putting a space in the wrong place. For example:

matthew@seymour:~$ **rm -rf /home/matthew**

That command deletes the /home directory of the user matthew. This is not an uncommon command; after you have removed a user and backed up the user's data, you will probably want to issue something similar. However, if you add an accidental space between the / and the *h* in *home*, you get this:

matthew@seymour:~$ **rm -rf / home/matthew**

This time, the command means "delete everything recursively from / and then delete home/matthew"—quite a different result! You can stop this from happening by using the --preserve-root parameter, which stops you from catastrophe with this message:

```
rm: it is dangerous to operate recursively on '/'
rm: use --no-preserve-root to override this failsafe.
```

However, no one wants to keep typing --preserve-root each time when running rm, so you could add this line to the .bashrc file in your /home directory:

```
alias rm='rm --preserve-root'
```

That alias automatically adds --preserve-root to all calls to rm in future bash sessions. Ubuntu (and Debian, and perhaps other distributions now) have done this by default, not by adding an alias in bashrc, but by making --preserve-root the default for the command.

Printing the Last Lines of a File with `tail`

If you want to watch a log file as it is written to, or want to monitor a user's actions as they are occurring, you need to be able to track log files as they change. In these situations, you need the tail command, which prints the last few lines of a file and updates as new lines are added. This command tells tail to print the last few lines of /var/log/httpd/access_log, the Apache hit log:

matthew@seymour:~$ **tail /var/log/httpd/access_log**

To get tail to remain running and update as the file changes, add the -f parameter (follow):

matthew@seymour:~$ **tail -f /var/log/httpd/access_log**

You can tie the lifespan of a tail follow to the existence of a process by specifying the --pid parameter. When you do this, tail continues to follow the file you asked for until it sees that the process identified by *process ID (PID)* is no longer running, at which point it stops tailing.

If you specify multiple files on the command line, tail follows both, printing file headers whenever the input source changes. Press Ctrl+C to terminate tail when in follow mode.

Printing Resource Usage with `top`

The `top` command is unusual in this list because the few parameters it takes are rarely, if ever, used. Instead, it has a number of commands you can use while it is running to customize the information it shows you. To get the most from these instructions, open two terminal windows. In the first, run the program `yes` and leave it running; in the second, run `top`.

The default sort order in `top` shows the most CPU-intensive tasks first. The first command there should be the `yes` process you just launched from the other terminal, but there should be many others also. First, we want to filter out all the other users and focus on the user running `yes`. To do this, press u and enter the username you used when you ran `yes`. When you press Enter, `top` filters out processes not being run by that user.

The next step is to kill the PID of the `yes` command, so you need to understand what each of the important fields means:

- ▶ **PID**—The process ID
- ▶ **User**—The owner of the process
- ▶ **PR**—Priority
- ▶ **NI**—Niceness
- ▶ **Virt**—Virtual image size in kilobytes
- ▶ **Res**—Resident size in kilobytes
- ▶ **Shr**—Shared memory size in kilobytes
- ▶ **S**—Status
- ▶ **%CPU**—CPU usage
- ▶ **%Mem**—Memory usage
- ▶ **Time+**—CPU time
- ▶ **Command**—The command being run

Several of them are unimportant unless you have a specific problem. The ones we are interested in are PID, User, Niceness, %CPU, %MEM, Time+, and Command. The Niceness of a process is how much time the CPU allocates to it compared to everything else on the system: 19 is the lowest, and –19 is the highest.

With the columns explained, you should be able to find the PID of the errant `yes` command launched earlier; it is usually the first number below PID. Now type k, enter that PID, and press Enter. You are prompted for a signal number (the manner in which you want the process killed), with 15 provided as the default. Signal 15 (also known as SIGTERM, for terminate) is a polite way of asking a process to shut down, and all processes that are not wildly out of control should respond to it. Give `top` a few seconds to update itself, and hopefully the `yes` command should be gone. If not, you need to be more forceful: Type k again, enter the PID, and press Enter. When prompted for a signal to send, enter 9 and press Enter to send SIGKILL, or "terminate whether you like it or not."

You can choose the fields to display by pressing f. A new screen appears that lists all possible fields, along with the letter you need to press to toggle their visibility. Selected fields are marked with an asterisk and have their letter, as follows:

```
* A: PID       = Process Id
```

If you press the a key, the screen changes to this:

```
a: PID         = Process Id
```

When you have made your selections, press Enter to return to the normal top view with your normal column selection.

You can also press F to select the field you want to use for sorting. This works in the same way as the field selection screen, except that you can select only one field at a time. Again, press Enter to get back to top after you have made your selection, and it will be updated with the new sorting.

If you press B, text bolding is enabled. By default, this bolds some of the header bar as well as any programs that are currently running (as opposed to sleeping), but if you press x, you can also enable bolding of the sorted column. You can use y to toggle bolding of running processes.

The last command to try is r, which allows you to renice—or adjust the nice value—of a process. You need to enter the PID of the process, press Enter, and enter a new nice value. Keep in mind that 19 is the lowest and –20 is the highest; anything less than 0 is considered "high" and should be used sparingly.

Printing the Location of a Command with which

The purpose of which is to tell you the exact command that would be executed if you typed it. For example, which mkdir returns /bin/mkdir, telling you that running the command mkdir runs /bin/mkdir.

Redirecting Output and Input

Sometimes, the output of a command is too long to view on one screen. At other times, there may be an advantage to preserving the output as a file, perhaps to be edited later. You can't do that using cat or less, at least not using them as we have described so far. Good news: It is possible using redirection.

Commands take their input and give their output in a standard place. This is called standard input and standard output. By default, this is configured as the output of a keyboard for standard input, because it comes in to the computer from the keyboard, and the screen for standard output, because the computer displays the results of a command to the user using that screen. Standard input and standard output can be redirected.

To redirect output, the command line uses >. Sometimes people read this as "in to." Here is an example:

```
matthew@seymour:~$ cat /proc/cpuinfo > file.txt
```

We know the first part of this line will read the information about the CPU from the file /proc/cpuinfo. Usually this would print it to the screen, but here the output is redirected into a file called file.txt, created in my /home directory, because that is the directory in which I issued the command. I can now read, edit, or use this file in any way I like.

WARNING

Be aware that you can overwrite the contents of a file using a redirect in this manner, so be certain that the destination file you name either does not exist or that its current contents do not need to be preserved.

What if we want to take the contents of an existing file and use that data as an input to a command? It is as simple as reversing the symbol from > to <:

```
matthew@seymour:~$ cat < file.txt
```

This takes the contents of file.txt and display them on the screen. At first glance, that does not seem useful because the command is doing the same thing it usually does, it is printing the contents of a file to the screen. Perhaps a different example would be helpful.

Ubuntu uses a software packaging system called apt, which is discussed in Chapter 9, "Managing Software." Using a command from the apt stable, dpkg, we can quickly list all software that has been installed using apt on a system and record that info into a file using a redirect:

```
matthew@seymour:~$ sudo dpkg --get-selections > pkg.list
```

This creates a text file named pkg.list that contains the list we want. You can open it with a text editor to confirm this. Now, we can use this file as input to dpkg, perhaps on another system on which we want the exact same software to be installed:

```
matthew@seymour:~$ sudo dpkg --set-selections < pkg.list
```

This tells dpkg to mark for installation any of the items in the list that are not already installed on the second system. One more quick command and these will be installed (included here for completeness of the example, even though it has nothing to do with redirection...): sudo apt-get -u dselect-upgrade.

Earlier in the chapter, we gave an example of using cat to display several files simultaneously. This example can be modified slightly to redirect the output into a file, thereby making a new file that includes the contents of the previous two using the order in which they are listed:

```
matthew@seymour:~$ cat myfile.txt myotherfile.txt > combinedfile.txt
```

Add the power of redirection to the information in this next section and you will finally begin to understand the potential and the power that a command-line-savvy user has, and why so many who learn the command line absolutely love it.

Combining Commands

So far, we have been using commands only individually, and for the large part, that is what you do in practice. However, some of the real power of these commands lies in the capability to join them together to get exactly what you want. There are some extra little commands that we have not looked at that are often used as glue because they do one very simple thing that enables a more complex process to work.

All the commands we have looked at have printed their information to the screen, but this is often flexible. There are two ways to control where output should go: piping and output redirection. A pipe is a connector between one command's output and another's input. Instead of sending its output to your terminal, using a pipe sends that output directly to another command as input. Output redirection works in a similar way to pipes but is usually used for files. We will look at pipes first and then output redirection.

Two of the commands we have looked at so far are ps and grep: the process lister and the string matcher. We can combine the two to find out which users are playing Nethack right now:

```
matthew@seymour:~$ ps aux | grep nethack
```

That creates a list of all the processes running right now and sends that list to the grep command, which filters out all lines that do not contain the word nethack. Ubuntu allows you to pipe as many commands as you can sanely string together. For example, we could add in the wc command, which counts the numbers of lines, words, and characters in its input, to count precisely how many times Nethack is being run:

```
matthew@seymour:~$ ps aux | grep nethack | wc -l
```

The -l parameter (lowercase L) to wc prints only the line count.

Using pipes in this way is often preferable to using the -exec parameter to find, simply because many people consider find to be a black art and so anything that uses it less frequently is better. This is where the xargs command comes in: It converts output from one command into arguments for another.

For a good example, consider this mammoth find command from earlier:

```
matthew@seymour:~$ find / -name "*.txt" -size +10k -user matthew -not -perm
+o=r -exec chmod o+r {} \;
```

That searches every directory from / onward for files matching *.txt that are greater than 10KB, are owned by user matthew, and do not have read permission for others. Then it executes chmod on each of the files. It is a complex command, and people who are not familiar with the workings of find might have problems understanding it. So, what we can do is break it up into two—a call to find and a call to xargs. The most conversion would look like this:

```
matthew@seymour:~$ find / -name "*.txt" -size +10k -user matthew -not -perm
 +o=r | xargs chmod o+r
```

That has eliminated the confusing {} \; from the end of the command, but it does the same thing, and faster, too. The speed difference between the two is because using -exec with find causes it to execute chmod once for each file. However, chmod accepts many files at a time and, because we are using the same parameter each time, we should take advantage of that. The second command, using xargs, is called once with all the output from find, and so saves many command calls. The xargs command automatically places the input at the end of the line, so the previous command might look something like this:

```
matthew@seymour:~$ xargs chmod o+r file1.txt file2.txt file3.txt
```

Not every command accepts multiple files, though, and if you specify the -l parameter, xargs executes its command once for each line in its input. If you want to check what it is doing, use the -p parameter to have xargs prompt you before executing each command.

For even more control, the -i parameter allows you to specify exactly where the matching lines should be placed in your command. This is important if you need the lines to appear before the end of the command or need it to appear more than once. Either way, using the -i parameter also enables the -l parameter so each line is sent to the command individually. This next command finds all files in /home/matthew that are larger than 10,000KB in size (10MB) and copies them to /home/matthew/archive:

```
matthew@seymour:~$ find /home/matthew -size +10000k | xargs -i cp {}
./home/matthew/archive
```

Using find with xargs is a unique case. All too often, people use pipes when parameters would do the job just as well. For example, these two commands are identical:

```
matthew@seymour:~$ ps aux --sort=-%cpu | grep -v 'whoami'
matthew@seymour:~$ ps -N ux --sort=-%cpu
```

The former prints all users and processes and then pipes that to grep, which in turn filters out all lines that contain the output from the program whoami (our username). So, line one prints all processes being run by other users, sorted by CPU use. Line two does not specify the a parameter to ps, which makes it list only our parameters. It then uses the -N parameter to flip that, which means it is everyone but us, without the need for grep.

The reason people use the former is often just simplicity: Many people know only a handful of parameters to each command, so they can string together two commands simply rather than write one command properly. Unless the command is to be run regularly, this is not a problem. Indeed, the first line would be better because it does not drive people to the manual to find out what ps -N does.

Using Environment Variables

A number of in-memory variables are assigned and loaded by default when you log in. These variables are known as *environment variables* and can be used by various commands to get information about your environment, such as the type of system you are running, your /home directory, and the shell in use. Environment variables are used to help tailor the computing environment of your system and include helpful specifications and setup, such as default locations of executable files and software libraries. If you begin writing shell scripts, you might use environment variables in your scripts. Until then, you need to be aware only of what environment variables are and do.

The following list includes a number of environment variables, along with descriptions of how the shell uses them:

▶ **PWD**—Provides the full path to your current working directory, used by the pwd command, such as /home/matthew/Documents.

▶ **USER**—Declares the user's name, such as matthew.

▶ **LANG**—Sets the default language, such as English.

▶ **SHELL**—Declares the name and location of the current shell, such as /bin/bash.

▶ **PATH**—Sets the default locations of executable files, such as /bin, /usr/bin, and so on.

▶ **TERM**—Sets the type of terminal in use, such as vt100, which can be important when using screen-oriented programs, such as text editors.

You can print the current value of any environment variable using echo $VARIABLENAME, like this:

```
matthew@seymour:~$ echo $USER
matthew
matthew@seymour:~$
```

> **NOTE**
>
> Each shell can have its own feature set and language syntax, as well as a unique set of default environment variables.

You can use the env or printenv command to display all environment variables, as follows:

```
matthew@seymour:~$ env
ORBIT_SOCKETDIR=/tmp/orbit-matthew
SSH_AGENT_PID=1729
TERM=xterm
SHELL=/bin/bash
WINDOWID=71303173
GNOME_KEYRING_CONTROL=/tmp/keyring-qTEFTw
GTK_MODULES=canberra-gtk-module
USER=matt
hew
SSH_AUTH_SOCK=/tmp/keyring-qTEFTw/ssh
DEFAULTS_PATH=/usr/share/gconf/gnome.default.path
SESSION_MANAGER=local/seymour:/tmp/.ICE-unix/1695
USERNAME=matthew
XDG_CONFIG_DIRS=/etc/xdg/xdg-gnome:/etc/xdg
DESKTOP_SESSION=gnome
PATH=/usr/local/sbin:/usr/local/bin:/usr/sbin:/usr/bin:/sbin:/bin:/usr/games
PWD=/home/matthew
hew
GDM_KEYBOARD_LAYOUT=us
LANG=en_US.utf8
GNOME_KEYRING_PID=1677
MANDATORY_PATH=/usr/share/gconf/gnome.mandatory.path
GDM_LANG=en_US.utf8
GDMSESSION=gnome
HISTCONTROL=ignoreboth
SPEECHD_PORT=7560
SHLVL=1
HOME=/home/matt
hew
LOGNAME=matt
hew
LESSOPEN=| /usr/bin/lesspipe %s
DISPLAY=:0.0
LESSCLOSE=/usr/bin/lesspipe %s %s
XAUTHORITY=/var/run/gdm/auth-for-matthew-PzcGqF/database
COLORTERM=gnome-terminal
OLDPWD=/var/lib/mlocate
_=/usr/bin/env
```

This abbreviated list shows some of the common variables. These variables are set by configuration or *resource* files contained in the /etc, /etc/skel or in the user's /home directory. You can find default settings for bash, for example, in /etc/profile and

/etc/bashrc as well as .bashrc or .bash_profile files in your /home directory. Read the man page for bash for details about using these configuration files.

One of the most important environment variables is $PATH, which defines the location of executable files. For example, if, as a regular user, you try to use a command that is not located in your $PATH (such as the imaginary command command), you will see something like this:

```
matthew@seymour:~$ command
-bash: command: command not found
```

If the command that you're trying to execute exists in the Ubuntu software repositories, but is not yet installed on your system, Ubuntu responds with the correct command to install the command:

```
matthew@seymour:~$ command

The program 'command' is currently not installed. You can install it by typing:

sudo apt-get install command
```

However, you might know that command is definitely installed on your system, and you can verify this by using the whereis command, like this:

```
matthew@seymour:~$ whereis command
command: /sbin/command
```

You can also run the command by typing its full pathname or complete directory specification, as follows:

```
matthew@seymour:~$ /sbin/command
```

As you can see in this example, the command command is indeed installed. What happened is that by default, the /sbin directory is not in your $PATH. One of the reasons for this is that commands under the /sbin directory are normally intended to be run only by root. You can add /sbin to your $PATH by editing the file .bash_profile in your /home directory (if you use the bash shell by default, like most Linux users). Look for the following line:

```
PATH=$PATH:$HOME/bin
```

You can then edit this file, perhaps using one of the text editors discussed later in this chapter, to add the /sbin directory, like so:

```
PATH=$PATH:/sbin:$HOME/bin
```

Save the file. The next time you log in, the /sbin directory is in your $PATH. One way to use this change right away is to read in the new settings in .bash_profile by using the bash shell's source command, as follows:

```
matthew@seymour:~$ source .bash_profile
```

You can now run commands located in the /sbin directory without the need to explicitly type the full pathname.

Some Linux commands also use environment variables to acquire configuration information (such as a communications program looking for a variable such as BAUD_RATE, which might denote a default modem speed).

To experiment with the environment variables, you can modify the PS1 variable to manipulate the appearance of your shell prompt. If you are working with bash, you can use its built-in export command to change the shell prompt. For example, if your default shell prompt looks like this:

```
matthew@seymour:~$
```

You can change its appearance by using the PS1 variable like this:

```
$ PS1='$OSTYPE r00lz ->'
```

After you press Enter, you see the following:

```
linux-gnu r00lz ->
```

NOTES

See the bash man page for other variables you can use for prompt settings.

Using Common Text Editors

Linux distributions include a number of applications known as *text editors* that you can use to create text files or edit system configuration files. Text editors are similar to word processing programs, but generally have fewer features, work only with text files, and might or might not support spell checking or formatting. Text editors range in features and ease of use and are found on nearly every Linux distribution. The number of editors installed on your system depends on what software packages you've installed on the system.

The more popular console-based text editors include the following:

▶ **emacs**—The comprehensive GNU emacs editing environment, which is much more than an editor; see the section "Working with emacs," later in this chapter.

▶ **nano**—A simple text editor similar to the classic pico text editor that was included with the once-common pine email program.

▶ **vim**—An improved, compatible version of the vi text editor (which we call vi in the rest of this chapter because it has a symbolic link named vi and a symbolically linked manual page).

Note that not all text editors are *screen oriented*, meaning designed for use from a terminal. Some of the text editors are designed to run from a graphical desktop and which provide a graphical interface with menu bars, buttons, scrollbars, and so on, are as follows:

▶ **gedit**—A GUI text editor for GNOME, which is installed by default with Ubuntu.

▶ **kate**—A simple KDE text editor.

▶ **kedit**—Another simple KDE text editor.

A good reason to learn how to use a text-based editor, such as vi or nano, is that system maintenance and recovery operations almost never take place during GUI sessions, negating the use of a GUI editor. Many larger, more complex and capable editors do not work when Linux is booted to its single-user or maintenance mode. If anything does go wrong with your system and you can't log into the GUI, knowledge and experience of using both the command line and text editors will turn out to be very important. Make a point of opening some of the editors and playing around with them; you never know, you might just thank me someday.

Another reason to learn how to use a text-based editor under the Linux console mode is so that you can edit text files through remote shell sessions, because many servers will not host graphical desktops.

NOTE

Before you take the time to get familiar with a nonstandard text editor, consider this. All three of the editors we include here are readily available and common. Two of them, nano and vi, are almost universally installed. If you spend your time learning a nonstandard editor, you will find yourself having to install it on every system or fighting against the software that is already there instead of using your time productively. Feel free to use any text editor you prefer, but we strongly recommend that you make sure you have at least a basic working knowledge of these standard editors so that you can walk up to any system and start working when necessary.

Working with nano

This one is listed first as it has the easiest learning curve. It is neither the most powerful nor the most guru approved, but nano is a respectable text editor that can be run from the command line and is often perfect for quick tasks such as editing configuration files.

Learning how to use nano is quick and easy. You might need to edit files on a Linux system with a minimal install, or a remote server without a more extensive offering of installed text editors. Chances are nearly 100 percent that nano will be available.

You can start an editing session by using the nano command like this:

matthew@seymour:~$ **nano file.txt**

When you first start editing, you will see the text on the screen with a title bar across the top and a list of simple commands across the bottom. The editor is simple enough that you can use it without any instruction. Here are the basic commands, just so you can compare them with other listed editors (^ is the Control key):

- ▸ **Cursor movement**—Arrow keys (left, down, up, and right), Page Up and Page Down keys, or ^y and ^v page up and down

- ▸ **Add characters**—Type at the cursor location

- ▸ **Delete character**—Backspace or Delete

- ▸ **Exit**—^x (prompts to ask whether to save changes)

- ▸ **Get Help**—^g

> **NOTE**
>
> nano really is that easy to use, but that does not mean that it cannot be used by power users. Take a little time and read the contents of Help to discover some of the more interesting and powerful capabilities of this editor.

Working with vi

The one editor found on nearly every UNIX and Linux system is the vi editor, originally written by Bill Joy. This simple-to-use but incredibly capable editor features a somewhat cryptic command set, but you can put it to use with only a few commands. Although many experienced UNIX and Linux users use vi extensively during computing sessions, many users who do only quick and simple editing might not need all its power and may prefer an easier-to-use text editor such as nano. Diehard GNU fans and programmers often use emacs for pretty much everything.

However, learning how to use vi is a good idea. You might need to edit files on a Linux system with a minimal install or on a remote server without a more extensive offering of installed text editors. Chances are nearly 100 percent that vi will be available.

You can start an editing session by using the vi command like this:

matthew@seymour:~$ **vi file.txt**

The vi command works by using an insert (or editing) mode and a viewing (or command) mode.

When you first start editing, you are in the viewing mode. You can use your arrow or other navigation keys (as shown later) to scroll through the text. To start editing, press the i key to insert text or the a key to append text. When you're finished, use the Esc key to toggle out of the insert or append modes and into the viewing (or command) mode. To enter a command, type a colon (:), followed by the command, such as w to write the file, and press Enter.

Although vi supports many complex editing operations and numerous commands, you can accomplish work by using a few basic commands. These basic vi commands are as follows:

- ▶ **Cursor movement**—h, j, k, l (left, down, up, and right)

- ▶ **Delete character**—x

- ▶ **Delete line**—dd

- ▶ **Mode toggle**—Esc, Insert (or i)

- ▶ **Quit**—:q

- ▶ **Quit without saving**—:q!

- ▶ **Run a shell command**—:sh (use 'exit' to return)

- ▶ **Save file**—:w

- ▶ **Text search**—/

> **NOTE**
>
> Use the vimtutor command to quickly learn how to use vi's keyboard commands. The tutorial takes less than 30 minutes, and it teaches new users how to start or stop the editor, navigate files, insert and delete text, and perform search, replace, and insert operations.

Working with emacs

Richard M. Stallman's GNU emacs editor, like vi, is included with Ubuntu and nearly every other Linux distribution. Unlike other UNIX and Linux text editors, emacs is much more than a simple text editor. It is an editing environment and can be used to compile and build programs and act as an electronic diary, appointment book, and calendar. Use it to compose and send email, read Usenet news, and even play games. The reason for this capability is that emacs contains a built-in language interpreter that uses the Elisp (emacs LISP) programming language. emacs is not installed in Ubuntu by default. To use emacs, the package you need to install is called emacs. See Chapter 9, "Managing Software."

You can start an emacs editing session like this:

```
matthew@seymour:~$ emacs file.txt
```

TIP

If you start emacs when using X11, the editor launches in its own floating window. To force emacs to display inside a terminal window instead of its own window (which can be useful if the window is a login at a remote computer), use the -nw command-line option like this: emacs -nw file.txt.

The emacs editor uses an extensive set of keystroke and named commands, but you can work with it by using a basic command subset. Many of these basic commands require you to hold down the Ctrl key, or to first press a *meta* key (generally mapped to the Alt key). Table 11.1 lists the basic commands.

TABLE 11.1   **emacs** Editing Commands

Action	Command
Abort	Ctrl+g
Cursor left	Ctrl+b
Cursor down	Ctrl+n
Cursor right	Ctrl+f
Cursor up	Ctrl+p
Delete character	Ctrl+d
Delete line	Ctrl+k
Go to start of line	Ctrl+a
Go to end of line	Ctrl+e
Help	Ctrl+h
Quit	Ctrl+x, Ctrl+c
Save As	Ctrl+x, Ctrl+w
Save file	Ctrl+x, Ctrl+s
Search backward	Ctrl+r
Search forward	Ctrl+s
Start tutorial	Ctrl+h, t
Undo	Ctrl+x, u

One of the best reasons to learn how to use emacs is that you can use nearly all the same keystrokes to edit commands on the bash shell command line, although it is possible to change the default to use vi keybindings. Another reason is that like vi, emacs is universally available for installation on nearly every UNIX and Linux system, including Apple's Mac OS X.

Working with Compressed Files

Another file management operation is compression and decompression of files, or the creation, listing, and expansion of file and directory archives. Linux distributions usually include several compression utilities you can use to create, compress, expand, or list the contents of compressed files and archives. These commands include the following:

- ▶ **bunzip2**—Expands a compressed file.

- ▶ **bzip2**—Compresses or expands files and directories.

- ▶ **gunzip**—Expands a compressed file.

- ▶ **gzip**—Compresses or expands files and directories.

- ▶ **tar**—Creates, expands, or lists the contents of compressed or uncompressed file or directory archives known as *tape archives* or *tarballs*.

Most of these commands are easy to use. However, the tar command, which is the most commonly used of the bunch, has a somewhat complex set of command-line options and syntax. This flexibility and power are part of its popularity; you can quickly learn to use tar by remembering a few of the simple command-line options. For example, to create a compressed archive of a directory, use tar's czf options, like this:

matthew@seymour:~$ **tar czf compressedfilename.tgz directoryname**

The result is a compressed archive (a file ending in .tgz) of the specified directory (and all files and directories under it). Add the letter v to the preceding options to view the list of files added during compression and archiving while the archive is being created. To list the contents of the compressed archive, substitute the c option with the letter t, like this:

matthew@seymour:~$ **tar tzf archive**

However, if many files are in the archive, a better invocation (to easily read or scroll through the output) is this:

matthew@seymour:~$ **tar tzf archive | less**

To expand the contents of a compressed archive, use tar's zxf options, as follows:

matthew@seymour:~$ **tar zxf archive**

The tar utility decompresses the specified archive and extracts the contents in the current directory.

Using Multiple Terminals with byobu

Many Linux veterans have enjoyed and use the screen command. Screen was designed to enable you to use one terminal to control several terminal sessions easily. Although screen has been a welcome and useful tool, a better one has appeared called byobu; it is an enhanced version of screen. *Byobu* is a Japanese term for decorative, multipanel vertically folding screens that are often used as room dividers.

Picture this scene: You connect to a server via *Secure Shell (SSH)* and are working at the remote shell. You need to open another shell window so you can have the two running side by side; perhaps you want the output from top in one window while typing in another. What do you do? Most people would open another SSH connection, but that is both wasteful and unnecessary. Like screen, byobu is a terminal multiplexer, which is a fancy term for a program that lets you run multiple terminals inside one terminal.

The best way to learn byobu is to try it yourself. So, open a console, type byobu, and then press Enter. Your display will blink momentarily and then be replaced with a new console with new information in a panel at the bottom. Now, let's do something with that terminal. Run top and leave it running for the time being. Press F2. Your prompt clears again, leaving you able to type. Run the uptime command.

Pop quiz: What happened to the old terminal running top? It is still running, of course. You can type F3 to return to it. Type F4 to go back to your uptime terminal. While you are viewing other terminals, the commands in the other terminals carry on running as normal so you can multitask. Here are some of the basic commands in byobu:

- ▶ **F2**—Create a new window.
- ▶ **F3**—Go to the previous window.
- ▶ **F4**—Go to the next window.
- ▶ **F9**—Open the Byobu menu for help and configuration.

To close a terminal within byobu, simply log out of it normally using exit or Ctrl+d. When you exit the last terminal session that is open in byobu, the program closes as well and drops you to the regular terminal session you used to start byobu.

However, there are two alternatives to quitting a byobu session: locking and disconnecting. The first, activated with F12, locks access to your screen data until you enter your system password.

The second is the most powerful feature of screen and also works beautifully in byobu: You can exit it and do other things for a while and then reconnect later; both screen and byobu pick up where you left off. For example, you could be typing at your desk, detach from a session and go home, reconnect, and carry on as if nothing had changed. What's more, all the programs you ran from screen or byobu carry on running even while screen or byobu is disconnected. It even automatically disconnects for you if someone closes your terminal window while it is in a locked state (with Ctrl+a+x).

To disconnect, press F6. You are returned to the prompt from which you launched `screen` or `byobu` and can carry on working, close the terminal you had opened, or even log out completely. When you want to reconnect, run the command `screen -r` or `byobu -r`. You can, in the meantime, just run `screen` or `byobu` and start a new session without resuming the previous one, but that is not wise if you value your sanity. You can disconnect and reconnect the same session as many times you want, which potentially means you need never lose your session again.

Although this has been a mere taste of what `byobu`/`screen` can do, hopefully you can see how useful it can be. Check the man pages for each to learn more.

References

- ▶ **www.gnu.org/**—The website of the GNU project, it contains manuals and downloads for lots of command-line software.

- ▶ **http://oreilly.com/linux/command-directory/**—A wide selection of Linux commands and explanations of what they do take from O'Reilly's excellent book *Linux in a Nutshell*, which is a dictionary of Linux commands.

- ▶ **www.tuxfiles.org/linuxhelp/cli.html**—Several short command-line tutorials.

- ▶ **www.linuxcommand.org/**—Describes itself as "your one-stop command-line shop!" It contains a wealth of useful information about the console.

- ▶ Understanding the way UNIX works at the nuts and bolts level can be both challenging and rewarding, and there are several good books that will help guide you on your way. Perhaps the best is *The Art of UNIX Programming* by Eric Raymond (Addison-Wesley, ISBN: 0-13-142901-9), which focuses on the philosophy behind UNIX and manages to mix in much about the command line.

- ▶ **www.vim.org/**—Home page for the `vim` (`vi` clone) editor included with Linux distributions. Check here for updates, bug fixes, and news about this editor.

- ▶ **www.gnu.org/software/emacs/emacs.html**—Home page for the FSF's GNU `emacs` editing environment; you can find additional documentation and links to the source code for the latest version here.

- ▶ **www.nano-editor.org/**—Home page for the GNU `nano` editor environment.

- ▶ O'Reilly's *The UNIX CD Bookshelf* (ISBN: 0-596-00392-7) contains seven highly respected books in one, although it retails for more than $120 as a result. However, it is incomparable in its depth and breadth of coverage.

Managing Users

System administrators would have a boring, but much easier, life without users. In reality, it's impossible to have a system with absolutely no users, so it is important that you learn how to effectively manage and administer your users as they work with your system. Whether you are creating a single user account or modifying a group that holds hundreds of user accounts, the fundamentals of user administration are the same.

User management and administration includes allocating and managing /home directories, putting in place good password policies, and applying an effective security policy that includes things such as disk quotas and file and directory access permissions. We look at all these areas within this chapter and some of the different types of users that you are likely to find on a typical Linux system.

User Accounts

You normally find three types of users on Linux systems: the super user, the day-to-day user, and the system user. Each type is essential to the smooth running of your system. Learning the differences between the three is essential if you are to work efficiently and safely within your Linux environment.

All users who access your system must have accounts on the system. Ubuntu uses the /etc/passwd file to store information on the user accounts that are present on the system. All users, regardless of their type, have a one-line entry in this file that contains their username (typically used for logging in to the system), an encrypted field for the password (which contains an *X* to denote that a password is present), a user ID (commonly referred to as the UID), and a group ID (commonly referred to as the GID). The last two fields show the location of the /home directory (usually /home/username) and the default shell for the user (/bin/bash is the default for new users). There is also a field called GECOS that uses a comma-delimited list to record information about the account or the user; most often when this is used, it will record the user's full name and contact information.

NOTE

Although the Password field contains an *X*, this doesn't mean that what you read here is the actual password. All passwords are stored in /etc/shadow in an encrypted format for safekeeping. Ubuntu automatically refers to this file whenever a password is required.

In keeping with long-standing tradition in UNIX-style operating systems, Ubuntu make use of the well-established UNIX file ownership and permission system. To start with, everything in these systems is treated as a file, and all files (which can include directories and devices) can be assigned one or more of read, write, and execute permissions. These three "flags" can also be assigned as desired to each of three categories: the owner of the file, a member of a group, or anyone else on the system. The security for a file is drawn from these permissions and from file ownership. As the system administrator (also commonly referred to as the *super user*), it is your responsibility to manage these settings effectively and ensure that the users have proper UIDs and GIDs. Perhaps most important, the system administrator can lock away sensitive files from users who should not have access to them through these file permissions.

The Super User/Root User

No matter how many system administrators there are for a system, there can only be one super user account. The super user account, more commonly referred to as the *root user*, has total and complete control over all aspects of the system. They can access any part of the file system; read, change, or delete any file, grant and revoke access to files and directories; and can carry out any operation on the system, including destroying it if they so wish. The root user is unique in that it has a UID of 0 and GID of 0.

In other words, the root user has supreme power over your system. With this in mind, it's important that you do not work as root all the time, because you may inadvertently cause serious damage to your system, perhaps even making it totally unusable. Instead, rely on root only when you need to make specific changes to your system that require root privileges. As soon as you've finished your work, you can switch back to your normal user account to carry on working.

In Ubuntu, you execute a command with root, or super user, privileges using the sudo command, like this:

```
matthew@seymour:~$ sudo apt-get update
```

You are then prompted for your password, which will not show on the screen as you enter it. After typing in your password, press Enter. Ubuntu then carries out the command (in this case, updating information about available software) as if you were running it as root.

The Root User

If you've used other Linux distros, you might be a little puzzled by the use of the sudo command, because not all distros use it. In short, Ubuntu allows the first user on the system access to full root privileges using the sudo command. It also disables the root account so that no one can actually log in with the username root.

In other Linux distros, you change to the root user by issuing the command su -nd and then entering the root password when prompted. This lands you at the root prompt, which is shown as a pound sign (#). From here, you can execute any command you want. To get to a root prompt in Ubuntu, you need to execute the command sudo -i which, after you enter your password, will give you the prompt so familiar to other Linux distros. When you've finished working as root, just type exit and hit Enter to get back to a normal user prompt ($).

A regular user is someone who logs on to the system to use it for nonadministrative tasks, such as word processing or email. These users do not need to make system-wide changes or manage other users. However, they might want to be able to change settings specific to their account (for instance, a desktop background). Depending on how much control the system administrator (the root or super user) likes to wield, regular users might not even be able to do that.

The super user grants privileges to regular users using file and directory permissions (as covered in Chapter 10, "Command-Line Quickstart"). For example, if the super user does not want you to change your settings in ~/.profile (the ~ is a shell shortcut representing your /home directory), root can alter the permissions so that you may read from, but not write to, that file.

CAUTION

Because of the potential for making a catastrophic error as the super user, always use your system as a regular user and only use your super user powers temporarily to do specific administration tasks. This is easier to remember in Ubuntu where the use of sudo is default and the root account is initially disabled. If you work on a multiuser system, consider this advice an absolute rule; if root were to delete the wrong file or kill the wrong process, the results could be disastrous for the system (and likely the business that owns and operates it). On your home system, you can do as you please. Running as root makes many things easier, but much less safe, and we still do not recommend doing so. In any setting, however, the risks of running as root are significant and we cannot stress how important it is to be careful when working as root.

The third type of user is the system user. The system user is not a person, but rather an administrative account that the system uses during day-to-day running of various services.

For example, the system user named www-data owns the Apache web server and all the associated files. Only that user and root can have access to these files; no one else can access or make changes to these files. System users do not have a home directory or password, nor do they permit access to the system through a login prompt.

You will find a list of all the users on a system in the /etc/passwd file.

User IDs and Group IDs

A computer is, by its very nature, a number-oriented machine. It identifies users and groups by numbers known as the *user ID (UID)* and *group ID (GID)*. The alphabetic names display on your screen just for ease of use.

As previously mentioned, the root user is UID 0. Numbers from 1 through 499 and number 65,534 are the system, sometimes called logical or pseudo-users. Regular users have UIDs beginning with 1,000; Ubuntu assigns them sequentially beginning with this number.

With only a few exceptions, the GID is the same as the UID.

Ubuntu creates a private GID for every UID of 1,000 and greater. The system administrator can add other users to a GID or create a totally new group and add users to it. Unlike Windows NT and some UNIX variants, a group cannot be a member of another group in Ubuntu (or any Linux distribution).

File Permissions

As you learned in Chapter 4, "On the Internet," there are three types of permissions: read, write, and execute (r, w, x). For any file or directory, permissions are assigned to three categories: user, group, and other. In this section, we focus on group permissions. Before we do, we want to highlight three commands used to change the group, user, or access permissions of a file or directory:

▶ **chgrp**—Changes the group ownership of a file or directory.

▶ **chown**—Changes the owner of a file or directory.

▶ **chmod**—Changes the access permissions of a file or directory.

These commands can be used to reproduce organizational structures and permissions in the real world in your Ubuntu system (see the next section, "Managing Groups"). For example, a human resources department can share health-benefit memos to all company employees by making the files readable (but not writable) by anyone in an accessible directory. Programmers in the company's research and development section, although able to access each other's source code files, would not have read or write access to HR payscales or personnel files (and certainly would not want HR or marketing poking around R&D).

These commands are used to easily manage group and file ownerships and permissions from the command line. It is essential that you know these commands because there are times when you are likely to have only a command-line interface to work with, such as when a well-meaning but fat-fingered system administrator set incorrect permissions on

X11 rendering the system incapable of working with a graphical interface. (No, we won't tell that story, but if you press them, most systems administrators have similar tales of woe.)

User Stereotypes

As is the case in many professions, exaggerated stereotypes have emerged for users and system administrators. Many stereotypes contain elements of truth mixed with generous amounts of hyperbole and humor and serve to assist us in understanding the characteristics of and differences in the stereotyped subjects. The stereotypes of the *luser* and the *BOFH* (not-so-nice terms for users and administrators, respectively) serve as cautionary tales describing what behavior is acceptable and unacceptable in the computing community.

Understanding these stereotypes allows you to better define the appropriate and inappropriate roles of system administrators, users, and others. You can find a description of each on Wikipedia at: http://en.wikipedia.org/wiki/BOFH and http://en.wikipedia.org/wiki/Luser.

Managing Groups

Groups can make managing users a lot easier. Instead of having to assign individual permissions to every user, you can use groups to grant or revoke permissions to a large number of users quickly and easily. Setting group permissions allows you to set up workspaces for collaborative working and to control what devices can be used, such as external drives or DVD writers. This approach also represents a secure method of limiting access to system resources to only those users who need them. As an example, the system administrator could put the users matthew, ryan, heather, holly, debra, and mark in a new group named unleashed. Those users could each create files intended for their group work and chgrp those files to unleashed.

Now, everyone in the unleashed group—but no one else except root—can work with those files. The system administrator would probably create a directory owned by that group so that its members could have an easily accessed place to store those files. The system administrator could also add other users such as sonya and nicole to the group and remove existing users when their part of the work is done. The system administrator could make the user matthew the group administrator so that matthew could decide how group membership should be changed. You could also put restrictions on the DVD writer so that only matthew could burn DVDs, thus protecting sensitive material from falling into the wrong hands.

Group Listing

Different UNIX operating systems implement the group concept in various ways. Ubuntu uses a scheme called *UPG (user private group)* where, by default, all users are assigned to a group with their own name. (The user's username and group name are identical.) All the groups on a system are listed in /etc/group file.

Here is an example of a portion of the /etc/group file:

```
matthew@seymour:~$ cat /etc/group
root:x:0:
daemon:x:1:
bin:x:2:
sys:x:3:
adm:x:4:matthew
tty:x:5:
disk:x:6:
mail:x:8:
news:x:9:
fax:x:21:matthew
voice:x:22:
cdrom:x:24:matthew
floppy:x:25:matthew
tape:x:26:matthew
www-data:x:33:
crontab:x:107:
ssh:x:109:
admin:x:115:matthew
saned:x:116:
gdm:x:119:
matthew:x:1000:
ntp:x:122:
```

In this example, you see a number of groups, mostly for services (mail, news, and so on) and devices (floppy, disk, and so on). As previously mentioned, the system services groups allow those services to have ownership and control of their files. For example, adding postfix to the mail group, as shown previously, enables the postfix application to access mail's files in the manner that mail would decide for group access to its file. Adding a regular user to a device's group permits the regular user to use the device with permissions granted by the group owner. Adding user matthew to the group cdrom, for example, allows matthew to use the optical drive device. You learn how to add and remove users from groups in the next section.

Group Management Tools

Ubuntu provides several command-line tools for managing groups, but also provides graphical tools for doing so. Most experienced system administrators prefer the command-line tools because they are quick and easy to use, are always available even when there is no graphic user interface, and because they can be included in scripts she may write if the system administrator wants to write a quick program to perform a repetitive task.

Here are the most commonly used group management command-line tools:

- **groupadd**—This command creates and adds a new group.

- **groupdel**—This command removes an existing group.

- **groupmod**—This command creates a group name or GIDs but doesn't add or delete members from a group.

- **gpasswd**—This command creates a group password. Every group can have a group password and an administrator. Use the -A argument to assign a user as group administrator.

- **useradd -G**—The -G argument adds a user to a group during the initial user creation. (More arguments are used to create a user.)

- **usermod -G**—This command allows you to add a user to a group so long as the user is not logged in at the time.

- **grpck**—This command checks the /etc/group file for typos.

Let's say there is a DVD-RW device (/dev/scd0) on our computer that the system administrator wants a regular user named ryan to have permission to access. This is the process to grant ryan that access:

1. Add a new group with the groupadd command:

   matthew@seymour:~$ **sudo groupadd dvdrw**

2. Change the group ownership of the device to the new group with the chgrp command:

   matthew@seymour:~$ **sudo chgrp dvdrw /dev/scd0**

3. Add the approved user to the group with the usermod command:

   matthew@seymour:~$ **sudo usermod -G dvdrw ryan**

4. Make user ryan the group administrator with the gpasswd command so that he can add new users to the group:

   matthew@seymour:~$ **sudo gpasswd -A ryan**

Now ryan has permission to use the DVD-RW drive, as would anyone else added to the group by either the super user or ryan because he is now also a group administrator and can add users to the group.

The system administrator can also use the graphical interface that Ubuntu provides, as shown in Figure 12.1. It is accessed from the menu at System, Administration, Users and Groups.

FIGURE 12.1   Use Manage Groups to assign users to groups.

Note that the full set of group commands and options are not available from the graphical interface. This limits the usefulness of the GUI to a subset of the most frequently used commands. You learn more about using the Ubuntu User Manager GUI in the next section of this chapter.

Managing Users

Users must be created, assigned a UID, provided a /home directory, provided an initial set of files for their home directory, and assigned to groups so that they can use the system resources securely and efficiently. The system administrator in some situations might want or need to not only restrict a user's access to specific files and folders, but also the amount of disk space an account may use.

User Management Tools

As with groups, Ubuntu provides several command-line tools for managing users, but also provides graphical tools for doing so. Most experienced system administrators prefer the command-line tools because they are quick and easy to use, are always available even when there is no GUI, and because they can be included in scripts she may write if the system administrator wants to write a quick program to perform a repetitive task. Here are the most common commands to manage users:

- ▶ **useradd**—This command adds a new user account to the system. Its options permit the system administrator to specify the user's /home directory and initial group or to create the user with the default /home directory and group assignments (based on the new account's username).

- ▶ **useradd -D**—This command sets the system defaults for creating the user's /home directory, account expiration date, default group, and command shell. See the specific options in the useradd man page. Used without any arguments, it displays the defaults for the system. The default set of files for a user are found in /etc/skel.

NOTE

The set of files initially used to populate a new user's home directory are kept in /etc/skel. This is convenient for the system administrator because any special files, links, or directories that need to be universally applied can be placed in /etc/skel and will be duplicated automatically with appropriate permissions for each new user:

```
matthew@seymour:~$ ls -la /etc/skel
total 32
drwxr-xr-x   2 root root  4096 2010-04-25 12:14 .
drwxr-xr-x 154 root root 12288 2010-07-01 16:30 ..
-rw-r--r--   1 root root   220 2009-09-13 22:08 .bash_logout
-rw-r--r--   1 root root  3103 2010-04-18 19:15 .bashrc
-rw-r--r--   1 root root   179 2010-03-26 05:31 examples.desktop
-rw-r--r--   1 root root   675 2009-09-13 22:08 .profile
```

Each line provides the file permissions, the number of files housed under that file or directory name, the file owner, the file group, the file size, the creation date, and the filename.

As you can see, root owns every file here. The useradd command copies everything in /etc/skel to the new home directory and resets file ownership and permissions to the new user.

Certain user files might exist that the system administrator doesn't want the user to change; the permissions for those files in /home/username can be reset so that the user can read them but can't write to them.

▶ **userdel**—This command completely removes a user's account (thereby eliminating that user's home directory and all files it contains).

▶ **passwd**—This command updates the "authentication tokens" used by the password management system.

TIP

To lock a user out of his account, use the following command:

```
matthew@seymour:~$ sudo passwd -l username
```

This prepends an ! (exclamation point, also called a bang) to the user's encrypted password; the command to reverse the process uses the -u option.

▶ **usermod**—This command changes several user attributes. The most commonly used arguments are -s to change the shell and -u to change the UID. No changes can be made while the user is logged in or running a process.

▶ **chsh**—This command changes the user's default shell. For Ubuntu, the default shell is /bin/bash, known as the Bash, or Bourne Again Shell.

Adding New Users

The command-line approach to adding a user is quite simple and can be accomplished on a single line. In the following example, the system administrator uses the useradd command to add the new user heather. The command adduser (a variant found on some UNIX systems) is a symbolic link to useradd, so both commands work the same. In this example, we use the -p option to set the password the user requested; we use the -s to set her special shell (in place of the default bash shell), and the -u option to specify her UID. (If we create a user with the default settings, we do not need to use these options.) All we want to do can be accomplished on one line:

```
matthew@seymour:~$ sudo useradd heather -p c00kieZ4ME -s /bin/zsh -u 1042
```

The system administrator can also use the graphical interface that Ubuntu provides. You find this in the menu at System, Administration, Users and Groups. Here, the system administrator is adding a new user to the system where user heather uses the bash command shell.

We used the following steps to add the same account as shown in the preceding command, but using the graphical User Manager interface:

1. Launch the Ubuntu User Manager graphical interface from the menu at System, Administration, Users and Groups.

2. Click the Add User button to bring up the Add User dialog window (refer back to Figure 12.1).

3. Fill in the form with the new user's name and desired username (see Figure 12.2).

4. Assign a good password (see Figure 12.3).

5. Highlight the new user in the list and click Advanced Settings (see Figure 12.4).

6. You may change User Privilege settings here as you like, and then click the Advanced tab (see Figure 12.5).

7. Open the drop-down Shell menu to select the desired shell (see Figure 12.6).

8. Either use the arrows to the right of the User ID box to adjust the UID up or down, or assign a number greater than 1000 by entering it directly in the box. The system will prevent you from assigning a number already in use by another user account (see Figure 12.7).

9. Click OK to save the settings.

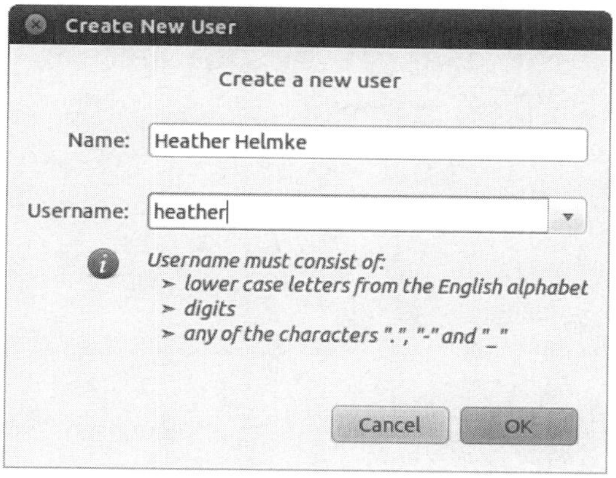

FIGURE 12.2   Adding a new user is simple. The GUI provides a set of options for user management spread over several screens, as shown here.

FIGURE 12.3   Change user password.

Note that the user is being manually assigned the UID of 1042 because that is her UID on another machine that will be connected to this machine. Systems keep track of users by UID numbers and not by names. Even though the accounts would have the same user-names, the two machines would not recognize heather as the same user if two different UIDs were assigned.

FIGURE 12.4   Look for the Advanced Settings button.

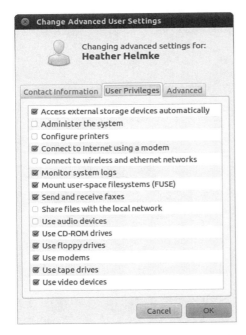

FIGURE 12.5   Change Advanced User Settings, User Privileges.

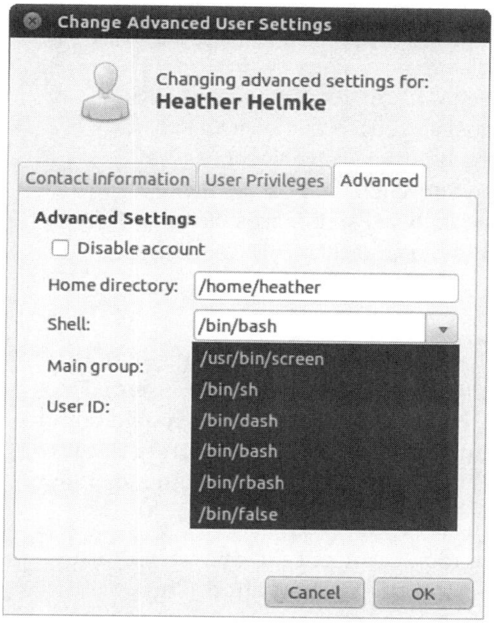

FIGURE 12.6   Change Advanced User Settings, Advanced, Shell.

FIGURE 12.7   Change Advanced User Settings, Advanced, UID.

> **NOTE**
>
> A Linux username can be any alphanumeric combination that does not begin with a special character reserved for shell script use. (See Chapter 13, "Automating Tasks and Shell Scripting," for disallowed characters, mostly <space> and punctuation characters.) Usernames are often the user's first name plus the first initial of her last name or the first initial of the user's first name and his entire last name. These are common practices on larger systems with many users because it makes life simpler for the system administrator, but neither is a rule nor a requirement.

Monitoring User Activity on the System

Monitoring user activity is part of the system administrator's duties and an essential task in tracking how system resources are being used. The w command tells the system administrator who is logged in, where he is logged in, and what he is doing. No one can hide from the super user. The w command can be followed by a specific user's name to show only that user.

The ac command provides information about the total connect time of a user measured in hours. It accesses the /var/log/wtmp file for the source of its information. The ac command proves most useful in shell scripts to generate reports on operating system usage for management review. Note that to use the ac command, you must install the acct package from the Ubuntu repositories.

> **TIP**
>
> Interestingly, a phenomenon known as *time warp* can occur where an entry in the wtmp files jumps back into the past and ac shows unusual amounts of time accounted for users. Although this can be attributed to some innocuous factors having to do with the system clock, it is worthy of investigation by the system administrator because it can also be the result of a security breach.

The last command searches through the /var/log/wtmp file and lists all the users logged in and out since that file was first created. The user reboot exists so that you might know who has logged in since the last reboot. A companion to last is the command lastb, which shows all failed, or bad, logins. It is useful for determining whether a legitimate user is having trouble or a hacker is attempting access.

> **NOTE**
>
> The accounting system on your computer keeps track of usage user statistics and is kept in the current /var/log/wtmp file. That file is managed by the init and login processes. If you want to explore the depths of the accounting system, use the GNU info system: info accounting.

Managing Passwords

Passwords are an integral part of Linux security, and they are the most visible part to the user. In this section, you learn how to establish a minimal password policy for your system, where the passwords are stored, and how to manage passwords for your users.

System Password Policy

An effective password policy is a fundamental part of a good system administration plan. The policy should cover the following:

- ▶ Allowed and forbidden passwords

- ▶ Frequency of mandated password changes

- ▶ Retrieval or replacement of lost or forgotten passwords

- ▶ Password handling by users

The Password File

The password file is `/etc/passwd`, and it is the database file for all users on the system. The format of each line is as follows:

```
username:password:uid:gid:gecos:homedir:shell
```

The fields are self-explanatory except for the `gecos` field. This field is for miscellaneous information about the user, such as the user's full name, office location, office and home phone numbers, and possibly a brief text message. For security and privacy reasons, this field is little used today, but the system administrator should be aware of its existence because the `gecos` field is used by traditional UNIX programs such as `finger` and `mail`. For that reason, it is commonly referred to as the *finger information field*. The data in this field will be comma delimited; the `gecos` field can be changed with the `chfn` (change `finger`) command.

Note that a colon separates all fields in the `/etc/passwd` file. If no information is available for a field, that field is empty, but all the colons remain.

If an asterisk appears in the password field, that user will not be permitted to log on. Why does this feature exist? So that a user can be easily disabled and (possibly) reinstated later without having to be created all over again. The traditional UNIX way of accomplishing this task is for the system administrator to manually edit this field. Ubuntu provides a more elegant method with the `passwd -l` command mentioned earlier in this chapter.

Several services run as pseudo-users, usually with root permissions. These are the system, or logical, users mentioned previously. You would not want these accounts available for general login for security reasons, so they are assigned `/sbin/nologin` or `/bin/false` as their shell, which prohibits any logins from these accounts.

A list of /etc/passwd reveals the following (abridged for brevity):

```
matthew@seymour:~$ cat /etc/passwd
root:x:0:0:root:/root:/bin/bash
bin:x:2:2:bin:/bin:/bin/sh
sys:x:3:3:sys:/dev:/bin/sh
games:x:5:60:games:/usr/games:/bin/sh
man:x:6:12:man:/var/cache/man:/bin/sh
mail:x:8:8:mail:/var/mail:/bin/sh
news:x:9:9:news:/var/spool/news:/bin/sh
uucp:x:10:10:uucp:/var/spool/uucp:/bin/sh
www-data:x:33:33:www-data:/var/www:/bin/sh
gnats:x:41:41:Gnats Bug-Reporting System (admin):/var/lib/gnats:/bin/sh
nobody:x:65534:65534:nobody:/nonexistent:/bin/sh
messagebus:x:102:106::/var/run/dbus:/bin/false
avahi:x:105:111:Avahi mDNS daemon,,,:/var/run/avahi-daemon:/bin/false
couchdb:x:106:113:CouchDB Administrator,,,:/var/lib/couchdb:/bin/bash
haldaemon:x:107:114:Hardware abstraction layer,,,:/var/run/hald:/bin/false
kernoops:x:109:65534:Kernel Oops Tracking Daemon,,,:/:/bin/false
gdm:x:112:119:Gnome Display Manager:/var/lib/gdm:/bin/false
matthew:x:1000:1000:Matthew Helmke,,,,:/home/matthew:/bin/bash
sshd:x:114:65534::/var/run/sshd:/usr/sbin/nologin
ntp:x:115:122::/home/ntp:/bin/false
pulse:x:111:117:PulseAudio daemon,,,:/var/run/pulse:/bin/false
```

Note that none of the password fields show a password, but rather contain an *X*. This is because they are shadow passwords, a useful security enhancement to Linux.

Shadow Passwords

It is considered a security risk to keep passwords in /etc/passwd because anyone with read access could run a cracking program on the file and obtain the passwords with little trouble. To avoid this risk, *shadow passwords* are used so that only an *X* appears in the password field of /etc/passwd; the real passwords are kept in /etc/shadow, a file that can only be read by the system administrator (and *PAM*, the *Pluggable Authentication Modules* authentication manager; see the "PAM Explained" sidebar for an explanation of PAM).

Special versions of the traditional password and login programs must be used to enable shadow passwords. Shadow passwords are automatically enabled during installation of Ubuntu.

Let's examine an abbreviated listing of the shadow companion to /etc/passwd, the /etc/shadow file:

```
matthew@seymour:~$ sudo cat /etc/shadow
root:!:14547:0:99999:7:::
daemon:*:14544:0:99999:7:::
bin:*:14544:0:99999:7:::
```

```
sys:*:14544:0:99999:7:::
games:*:14544:0:99999:7:::
man:*:14544:0:99999:7:::
mail:*:14544:0:99999:7:::
www-data:*:14544:0:99999:7:::
irc:*:14544:0:99999:7:::
nobody:*:14544:0:99999:7:::
libuuid:!:14544:0:99999:7:::
syslog:*:14544:0:99999:7:::
messagebus:*:14544:0:99999:7:::
kernoops:*:14544:0:99999:7:::
gdm:*:14544:0:99999:7:::
matthew:$6$wtML.mV4$.I5WeTp9tgGkIjJM4uLR5p6TVUqPrSvJ0N2W/t//0jVBrWQrOySEEDvXsA/sKSEl
QsfmNmfPJYxVrjZ21/Ir70:14564:0:99999:7:::
sshd:*:14547:0:99999:7:::
ntp:*:14548:0:99999:7:::
usbmux:*:14724:0:99999:7:::
pulse:*:14725:0:99999:7:::
```

The fields are separated by colons and are, in order:

- ▶ The user's login name.

- ▶ The encrypted password for the user.

- ▶ The day of which the last password change occurred, measured in the number of days since January 1, 1970. This date is known in UNIX circles as the *epoch*. Just so you know, the billionth second since the epoch occurred was in September 2001; that was the UNIX version of Y2K—as with the real Y2K, nothing much happened.

- ▶ The number of days before the password can be changed (prevents changing a password and then changing it back to the old password right away—a dangerous security practice).

- ▶ The number of days after which the password must be changed. This can be set to force the change of a newly issued password known to the system administrator.

- ▶ The number of days before the password expiration that the user is warned it will expire.

- ▶ The number of days after the password expires that the account is disabled (for security).

- ▶ Similar to the password change date, although this is the number of days since January 1, 1970 that the account has been disabled.

- ▶ The final field is a "reserved" field and is not currently allocated for any use.

Note that password expiration dates and warnings are disabled by default in Ubuntu. These features are not often used on home systems and usually not even used for small offices. It is the system administrator's responsibility to establish and enforce password expiration policies if they are to exist.

The permissions on the /etc/shadow file should be set so that it is not writable or readable by regular users: The permissions should be 600.

PAM Explained

Pluggable Authentication Modules (PAM) is a system of libraries that handle the tasks of authentication on your computer. It uses four management groups: account management, authentication management, password management, and session management. This allows the system administrator to choose how individual applications will authenticate users. Ubuntu has preinstalled and preconfigured all the necessary PAM files for you.

The configuration files in Ubuntu are found in /etc/pam.d. These files are named for the service they control, and the format is as follows:

```
type control module-path module-arguments
```

The type field is the management group that the rule corresponds to. The control field tells PAM what to do if authentication fails. The final two items deal with the PAM module used and any arguments it needs. Programs that use PAM typically come packaged with appropriate entries for the /etc/pam.d directory. To achieve greater security, the system administrator can modify the default entries. Misconfiguration can have unpredictable results, so back up the configuration files before you modify them. The defaults provided by Ubuntu are adequate for home and small office users.

An example of a PAM configuration file with the formatted entries as described previously is shown next. Here are the contents of /etc/pam.d/gdm:

```
#%PAM-1.0
auth    requisite    pam_nologin.so
auth    required     pam_env.so readenv=1
auth    required     pam_env.so readenv=1 envfile=/etc/default/locale
auth    sufficient    pam_succeed_if.so user ingroup nopasswdlogin
@include common-auth
auth    optional     pam_gnome_keyring.so
@include common-account
session [success=ok ignore=ignore module_unknown=ignore default=bad]
pam_selinux.so open
session required     pam_limits.so
@include common-session
session [success=ok ignore=ignore module_unknown=ignore default=bad]
pam_selinux.so close
session optional     pam_gnome_keyring.so auto_start
@include common-password
```

Amusingly, even the PAM documents state that you do not really need (or want) to know a lot about PAM to use it effectively.

You will likely need only the PAM system administrator's guide. You can find it at www. kernel.org/pub/linux/libs/pam/Linux-PAM-html/Linux-PAM_SAG.html.

Managing Password Security for Users

Selecting appropriate user passwords is always an exercise in trade-offs. A password such as *password* (do not laugh—it has been used too often in the real world and with devastating consequences) is just too easy to guess by an intruder. So are simple words or number combinations (the numbers from a street address or date of birth, for example). You would be surprised how many people use easily guessed passwords such as 123456, iloveyou, Qwerty, or abc123.

In contrast, a password such as 2a56u'"F($84u&#^Hiu44Ik%$([#EJD is sure to present great difficulty to an intruder (or an auditor). However, that password is so difficult to remember that it would be likely that the password owner would write that password down on a sticky note attached to his monitor.

The system administrator has control, with settings in the /etc/shadow file, over how often the password must be changed. The settings can be changed by the super user using a text editor, or the chage command. (See the shadow and chage man pages for details.)

Changing Passwords in a Batch

On a large system, there might be times when a large number of users and their passwords need some attention. The super user can change passwords in a batch by using the chpasswd command, which accepts input as a name/password pair per line in the following form:

```
matthew@seymour:~$ sudo chpasswd username:password
```

Passwords can be changed *en masse* by redirecting a list of name and password pairs to the command. An appropriate shell script can be constructed with the information gleaned from Chapter 11, "Command-Line Master Class."

However, Ubuntu also provides the newusers command to add users in a batch from a text file. This command also allows a user to be added to a group, and a new directory can be added for the user, too.

Granting System Administrator Privileges to Regular Users

On occasion, it may be necessary for regular users to run a command as if they were the root user. They usually do not need these powers, but a user might on a special occasion— for example, to temporarily access certain devices or run a command for testing purposes.

There are two ways to run commands with root privileges. The first way is useful if you are the owner of both the super user account (an enabled root account) and a regular user; the second way is useful if you are not a regular user but are not privileged to access all super user functions. (This might happen on a large, multiuser network with senior and junior administrators as well as regular users.) Let's look at each.

Temporarily Changing User Identity with the su Command

This first scenario requires the existence of a root account, which is not enabled by default on Ubuntu systems and is not generally recommended in the Ubuntu community. However, there are times when it makes sense. Discussing that is beyond the scope of this chapter, but for the sake of argument, for the scenario and details in this section assume we are operating in one of those special cases and that a root account has been enabled.

What if you have access to an enabled root account as a super user, but are logged on as a regular user because you are performing nonadministrative tasks, and you find you need to do something that only the super user can do? The su command is available for this purpose.

> **NOTE**
>
> A popular misconception is that the su command is short for *super user*—it really just means *substitute user*. An important but often overlooked distinction is that between su and su -. In the former instance, you become that user but keep your own environmental variables (such as paths). In the latter, you inherit the environment of that user. This is most noticeable when you use su to become the super user, root. Without appending the -, you do not inherit the path variable that includes /bin or /sbin, so you must always enter the full path to those commands when you just su to root.
>
> Don't forget that on a standard Ubuntu system, the first created user is classed as root, while the true root account is disabled. To enable the root account, you enter the command sudo passwd at the command line and enter your password and a new root password. After this has been completed, you can su to root. We suggest you read this before doing so to ensure that you understand the reason the root account is not enabled by default: https://help.ubuntu.com/community/RootSudo.

Because almost all Linux file system security revolves around file permissions, it can be useful to occasionally become a different user with permission to access files belonging to other users or groups or to access special files (such as the communications port /dev/ttyS0 when using a modem or the sound device /dev/audio when playing a game). You can use the su command to temporarily switch to another user identity, and then switch back.

The su command spawns a new shell, changing both the UID and GID of the existing user and automatically changes the environmental variables associated with that user, known as *inheriting the environment*. For more information about environment variables, see Chapter 4.

The syntax for the `su` command is as follows:

```
matthew@seymour:~$ su option username arguments
```

The man page for `su` gives more details, but some highlights of the `su` command are here:

```
-c, --command COMMAND
      pass a single COMMAND to the shell with -c
```

```
-m, --preserve-environment
      do not reset environment variables
```

```
-l   a full login simulation for the substituted user,
      the same as specifying the dash alone
```

You can invoke the `su` command in different ways that yield diverse results. By using `su` alone, you can become root, but you keep your regular user environment. This can be verified by using the `printenv` command before and after the change. Note that the working directory (you can execute `pwd` as a command line to print the current working directory) has not changed. By executing the following, you become root and inherit root's environment:

```
matthew@seymour:~$ su -
```

By executing the following, you become that user and inherit the super user's environment—a pretty handy tool. (Remember: Inheriting the environment comes from using the dash in the command; omit that, and you keep your "old" environment.) To become another user, specify a different user's name on the command line:

```
matthew@seymour:~$ su - other_user
```

When leaving an identity to return to your usual user identity, use the `exit` command. For example, while logged on as a regular user

```
matthew@seymour:~$ su - root
```

the system prompts for a password:

```
Password:
```

When the password is entered correctly, the root user's prompt appears:

```
root~#
```

To return to the regular user's identity, just type the following:

```
root~# exit
```

This takes you to the regular user's prompt:

```
matthew@seymour:~$
```

If you need to allow other users access to certain commands with root privileges, you must give them the password for the root account (often referred to as the root password) so that they can use su; that definitely is not a secure solution. The next section describes a more flexible and secure method of allowing normal users to perform selected root tasks and the preferred method for sharing and using super-user privileges in Ubuntu.

Granting Root Privileges on Occasion: The sudo Command

It is often necessary to delegate some of the authority that root wields on a system. For a large system, this makes sense because no single individual will always be available to perform super user functions. The problem is that UNIX permissions come with an all-or-nothing authority. Enter sudo, an application that permits the assignment of one, several, or all the root-only system commands.

> **NOTE**
>
> As mentioned earlier, the sudo command is pervasive in Ubuntu because it is used by default. If you want to get to a root shell, thereby removing the need to type sudo for every command, just enter sudo -i to get the root prompt. To return to a normal user prompt, enter exit and press Return. Again, this is a bit dangerous because if you are not paying attention and forget to exit root, you could cause severe damage to the system. It is usually better to choose one method or the other and use it consistently, and the Ubuntu community consistently uses and recommends using sudo for each command, even if it gets tedious, because it is a good reminder to think about what you are doing.

After it is configured, using sudo is simple. An authorized user merely precedes a super user authority-needed command with sudo, like this:

```
matthew@seymour:~$ sudo command
```

When the command is entered, sudo checks the /etc/sudoers file to see whether the user is authorized to wield super-user privileges; if so, sudo use is authorized for a specific length of time. The user is then prompted for her password (to preserve accountability and provide some measure of security), and then the command is run as if root had issued it. During the time allotted, which is 15 minutes by default in Ubuntu, sudo can be used again once or multiple times without a password. If an unauthorized user attempts to execute a sudo command, a record of the unauthorized attempt is kept in the system log and a mail message is sent to the super user.

Three man pages are associated with sudo: sudo, sudoers, and visudo. The first covers the command itself, the second the format of the /etc/sudoers file, and the third the use of the special editor for /etc/sudoers. You should use the special editing command because it checks the file for parse errors and locks the file to prevent others from editing it at the same time. The visudo command uses the vi editor, so you might need a quick review of the vi editing commands found in Chapter 11, in the section "Working with vi." You begin the editing by executing the visudo command with this:

```
matthew@seymour:~$ sudo visudo
```

The default /etc/sudoers file looks like this:

```
# /etc/sudoers
#
# This file MUST be edited with the 'sudo' command as root.
#
# See the man page for details on how to write a sudoers file.
#
Defaults        env_reset

# Host alias specification

# User alias specification

# Cmnd alias specification

# User privilege specification
root     ALL=(ALL) ALL

# Uncomment to allow members of group sudo to not need a password
# (Note that later entries override this, so you might need to move
# it further down)
# %sudo ALL=NOPASSWD: ALL

# Members of the admin group may gain root privileges
%admin ALL=(ALL) ALL
```

The basic format of a sudoers line in the file is as follows:

```
user host_computer=command
```

The user can be an individual user or a group. (A % in front identifies a name as a group.) The host_computer is normally ALL for all hosts on the network and localhost for the local machine, but the host computer can referenced as a subnet or any specific host. The command in the sudoers line can be ALL, a list of specific commands, or a restriction on specific commands (formed by prepending a ! to the command). A number of options are available for use with the sudoers line, and aliases can be used to simplify the assignment of privileges. Again, the sudoers man page gives the details, but here are a few examples:

If we add the line

```
%wheel          ALL=(ALL)          NOPASSWD: ALL
```

any user we add to the wheel group can execute any command without a password.

Suppose that we want to give a user john permission across the network to be able to add users with the graphical interface. We would add the following line:

```
john ALL=/users-admin
```

Or perhaps we would grant permission only on her local computer:

```
john 192.168.1.87=/usr/bin/users-admin
```

If we want to give the editor group systemwide permission with no password required to delete files, we use the following:

```
%editors ALL=NOPASSWD: /bin/rm
```

If we want to give every user permission with no password required to mount the CD drive on the localhost, we do so as follows:

```
ALL localhost=NOPASSWD:/sbin/mount /dev/scd0 /mnt/cdrom /sbin/umount /mnt/cdrom
```

It is also possible to use wildcards in the construction of the sudoers file. Aliases can be used, too, to make it easier to define users and groups. The man page for sudoers contains some examples, and www.komar.org/pres/sudo/toc.html provides illustrative notes and comments about sudo use at a large company. The sudo home page at www.sudo.ws/ is also a useful resource for additional explanations and examples.

The following command presents users with a list of the commands they are entitled to use:

```
matthew@seymour:~$ sudo -l
```

Adding Extra sudo Users

As mentioned earlier, by default Ubuntu grants the first created user full root access through the sudo command. If you need to add this capability for other users, you can do this easily by adding each user to the admin group or by using the User Manager tool to allow them to administer the System, which can be found in the User Privileges tab when you edit the properties for a user.

Disk Quotas

On large systems with many users, you often need to control the amount of disk space a user can use. Disk quotas are designed specifically for this purpose. Quotas, managed per partition, can be set for both individual users and for groups; quotas for the group need not be as large as the aggregate quotas for the individuals in the groups.

When files are created, both a user and a group own them; ownership of the files is always part of the metadata about the files. This makes quotas based on both users and groups easy to manage.

> **NOTE**
>
> Disk quota management is not really useful or needed on a home system and rarely, if ever, on a small office system. It is unlikely you will see or implement this in either circumstance.

To manage disk quotas, you must have the `quota` and `quotatool` packages installed on your system. Quota management with Ubuntu is not enabled by default and has traditionally been enabled and configured manually by system administrators. System administrators use the family of quota commands, such as `quotacheck` to initialize the quota database files, `edquota` to set and edit user quotas, `setquota` to configure disk quotas, and `quotaon` or `quotaoff` to control the service. (Other utilities include `warnquota` for automatically sending mail to users over their disk space usage limit.)

Implementing Quotas

Quotas are not enabled by default, even if the quota software package is installed on your Ubuntu system. When quotas are installed and enabled, you can see which partitions have either user quotas, group quotas, or both by looking at the fourth field in the `/etc/fstab` file. For example, one line in `/etc/fstab` shows that quotas are enabled for the `/home` partition:

```
/dev/hda5     /home     ext3        defaults,usrquota,grpquota 1 1
```

The root of the partition with quotas enabled will have the files `quota.user` or `quota.group` in them (or both files, if both types of quotas are enabled), and the files will contain the actual quotas. The permissions of these files should be `600` so that users cannot read or write to them. (Otherwise, users would change them to allow ample space for their music files and Internet art collections.) To initialize disk quotas, the partitions must be remounted. This is easily accomplished with the following:

```
matthew@seymour:~$ sudo mount -o ro,remount partition_to_be_remounted mount_point
```

The underlying console tools (complete with man pages) are as follows:

- ▶ **quotaon, quotaoff**—Toggles quotas on a partition.
- ▶ **repquota**—A summary status report on users and groups.

▶ **quotacheck**—Updates the status of quotas (compares new and old tables of disk usage); run after `fsck`.

▶ **edquota**—A basic quota management command.

Manually Configuring Quotas

Manual configuration of quotas involves changing entries in your system's file system table, `/etc/fstab`, to add the `usrquota` mount option to the desired portion of your file system. As an example in a simple file system, quota management can be enabled like this:

```
LABEL=/            /              ext3    defaults,usrquota      1 1
```

Group-level quotas can also be enabled by using the `grpquota` option. As the root operator, you must then create a file (using our example of creating user quotas) named `quota.user` in the designated portion of the file system, like so:

```
matthew@seymour:~$ sudo touch /quota.user
```

You should then turn on the use of quotas using the `quotaon` command:

```
matthew@seymour:~$ sudo quotaon -av
```

You can then edit user quotas with the `edquota` command to set hard and soft limits on file system use. The default system editor (`vi` unless you change your `EDITOR` environment variable) is launched when editing a user's quota.

Any user can find out what their quotas are with the following:

```
matthew@seymour:~$ quota -v
```

> **NOTE**
>
> Ubuntu does not support any graphical tools that enable you to configure disk quotas. A Quota mini-HOWTO is maintained at www.tldp.org/HOWTO/Quota.html.

Related Ubuntu Commands

You use these commands to manage user accounts in Ubuntu:

▶ **ac**—A user account-statistics command.

▶ **change**—Sets or modifies user password expiration policies.

▶ **chfn**—Creates or modifies user finger information in `/etc/passwd`.

▶ **chgrp**—Modifies group memberships.

▶ **chmod**—Changes file permissions.

▶ **chown**—Changes file ownerships.

▶ **chpasswd**—Batch command to modify user passwords.

▶ **chsh**—Modifies a user's shell.

▶ **groups**—Displays existing group memberships.

▶ **logname**—Displays a user's login name.

▶ **newusers**—Batches user management command.

▶ **passwd**—Creates or modifies user passwords.

▶ **su**—Executes shell or command as another user.

▶ **sudo**—Manages selected user execution permissions.

▶ **useradd**—Creates, modifies, or manages users.

▶ **usermod**—Edits a user's login profile.

12

References

▶ **http://tldp.org/HOWTO/User-Authentication-HOWTO/**—The User-Authentication HOWTO describes how user and group information is stored and used for authentication.

▶ **http://tldp.org/HOWTO/Shadow-Password-HOWTO.html**—The Shadow-Password HOWTO delves into the murky depths of shadow passwords and even discusses why you might not want to use them.

▶ **http://tldp.org/HOWTO/Security-HOWTO/**—A must-read HOWTO, the Security HOWTO is a good overview of security issues. Especially applicable to this chapter are sections on creating accounts, file permissions, and password security.

▶ **http://tldp.org/LDP/sag/html/index.html**—A general guide, the Linux System Administrator's Security Guide has interesting sections on limiting and monitoring users.

▶ **www.kernel.org/pub/linux/libs/pam/index.html**—The Pluggable Authentication Modules suite contains complex and highly useful applications that provide additional security and logging for passwords. PAM is installed by default in Ubuntu. It isn't necessary to understand the intricacies of PAM to use it effectively.

# CHAPTER 13

Automating Tasks and Shell Scripting

In this chapter, we cover ways to automate tasks on your system using task schedulers. This chapter is also an introduction to the basics of creating *shell scripts*, or executable text files written to conform to shell syntax. Shell scripts run like any other command under Linux and can contain complex logic or a simple series of Linux command-line instructions. You can also run other shell scripts from within a shell program. The features and functions for several Linux shells are discussed in this chapter after a short introduction to working from the shell command line. You learn how to write and execute a simple shell program using bash, one of the most popular Linux shells and the default shell in Ubuntu and most other distributions.

Scheduling Tasks

There are three ways to schedule commands in Ubuntu, all of which work in different ways. The first is the at command, which specifies a command to run at a specific time and date relative to today. The second is the batch command, which is actually a script that redirects you to the at command with some extra options set so your command runs when the system is quiet. The last option is the cron daemon, which is the Linux way of executing tasks at a given time.

Using at and batch to Schedule Tasks for Later

If there is a time-intensive task you want to run, but you do not want to do it while you are still logged in, you can tell

Ubuntu to run it later with the at command. To use at, you need to tell it the time at which you want to run and then press Enter. You will then see a new prompt that starts with at>, and everything you type there until you press Ctrl+D will be the commands you want at to run.

When the designated time arrives, at performs each action individually and in order, which means later commands can rely on the results of earlier commands. In this next example, run at just after 5 p.m., at is used to download and extract the latest Linux kernel at a time when the network should be quiet:

```
matthew@seymour:~$ at now + 7 hours
at> wget http://www.kernel.org/pub/linux/kernel/v3.0/linux-3.0.tar.bz2
at> tar xvfjp linux-3.0.tar.bz2
at> <EOT>
job 2 at 2011-07-08 20:01
```

Specifying now + 7 hours as the time does what you would expect: at was run at 8 p.m., so the command will run just after 3 a.m.

If you have a more complex job, you can use the -f parameter to have at read its commands from a file, like this:

```
echo wget http://www.kernel.org/pub/linux/kernel/v3.0/linux-3.00.tar.bz2\;
tar xvfjp linux-3.0.tar.bz2 > myjob.job
at -f myjob.job tomorrow
```

As you can see, at is flexible about the time format it takes; you can specify it in three ways:

▶ Using the now parameter, you can specify how many minutes, hours, days, or weeks relative to the current time. For example, now + 4 weeks runs the command 1 month from today.

▶ You can also specify several special times, including tomorrow, midnight, noon, or teatime (4 p.m.). If you do not specify a time with tomorrow, your job is set for precisely 24 hours from the current time.

▶ You can specify an exact date and time using HH:MM MM/DD/YY format (for example, 16:40 22/12/12 for 4:40 p.m. on the 22nd of December 2012).

When your job is submitted, at reports the job number, date, and time that the job will be executed; the queue identifier; plus the job owner (you). It also captures all your environment variables and stores them along with the job so that, when your job runs, it can restore the variables, preserving your execution environment.

The job number and job queue identifier are both important. When you schedule a job using at, it is placed into queue "a" by default, which means it runs at your specified time and takes up a normal amount of resources.

There is an alternative command, batch, which is really just a shell script that calls at with a few extra options. These options (-q b -m now, if you were interested) set at to run on queue b (-q b), mailing the user on completion (-m), and running immediately (now). The queue part is what is important: Jobs scheduled on queue b will only be executed when system load falls below 0.8—that is, when the system is not running at full load. Furthermore, it runs with a lower niceness, meaning a queue jobs usually have a niceness of 2, whereas b queue jobs have a niceness of 4.

Because batch always specifies now as its time, you need not specify your own time; it will simply run as soon as the system is quiet. Having a default niceness of 4 means that batched commands get less system resources than a queue job's (at's default) and less system resources than most other programs. You can optionally specify other queues using at. Queue c runs at niceness 6, queue d runs at niceness 8, and so on. However, it is important to note that the system load is only checked before the command is run. If the load is lower than 0.8, your batch job will be run. If the system load subsequently rises beyond 0.8, your batch job will continue to run, albeit in the background, thanks to its niceness value.

When you submit a job for execution, you are also returned a job number. If you forget this or just want to see a list of other jobs you have scheduled to run later, use the atq command with no parameters. If you run this as a normal user, it prints only your jobs; running it as a super user will print everyone's jobs. The output is in the same format as when you submit a job, so you get the ID number, execution time, queue ID, and owner of each job.

If you want to delete a job, use the atrm command followed by the ID number of the job you want to delete. This next example shows atq and atrm being used to list jobs and delete one:

```
matthew@seymour:~$ atq
14      2012-01-20 23:33 a matthew
16      2012-02-03 22:34 a matthew
17      2012-01-25 22:34 a matthew
15      2012-01-22 04:34 a matthew
18      2012-01-22 01:35 b matthew
matthew@seymour:~$ atrm 16
matthew@seymour:~$ atq
14      2012-01-20 23:33 a matthew
17      2012-01-25 22:34 a matthew
15      2012-01-22 04:34 a matthew
18      2012-01-22 01:35 b matthew
```

In that example, job 16 is deleted using atrm, and so it does not show up in the second call to atq.

The default configuration for at and batch is to allow everyone to use it, which is not always the desired behavior. Access is controlled through two files: /etc/at.allow and /etc/at.deny. By default, at.deny exists but is empty, which allows everyone to use at and batch. You can enter usernames into at.deny, one per line, to stop those users scheduling jobs.

Alternatively, you can use the at.allow file; this does not exist by default. If you have a blank at.allow file, no one except root is allowed to schedule jobs. As with at.deny, you can add usernames to at.allow one per line, and those users will be able to schedule jobs. You should use either at.deny or at.allow: When someone tries to run at or batch, Ubuntu checks for her username in at.allow. If it is in there, or if at.allow does not exist, Ubuntu checks for her username in at.deny. If her username is in at.deny or at.deny does not exist, she is not allowed to schedule jobs.

Using cron to Run Jobs Repeatedly

The at and batch commands work well if you just want to execute a single task at a later date, but they are less useful if you want to run a task frequently. Instead, the cron daemon exists for running tasks repeatedly based on system (and user) requests. The cron daemon has a similar permissions system to at: Users listed in the cron.deny file are not allowed to use cron, and users listed in the cron.allow file are. An empty cron.deny file—the default—means everyone can set jobs. An empty cron.allow file means that no one (except root) can set jobs.

There are two types of jobs: system jobs and user jobs. Only root can edit *system* jobs, whereas any user whose name appears in cron.allow or does not appear in cron.deny can run *user* jobs. System jobs are controlled through the /etc/crontab file, which by default looks like this:

```
SHELL=/bin/sh
PATH=/usr/local/sbin:/usr/local/bin:/sbin:/bin:/usr/sbin:/usr/bin

# m h dom mon dow user    command
17 *    * * *    root    cd / && run-parts --report /etc/cron.hourly
25 6    * * *    root    test -x /usr/sbin/anacron || ( cd / && run-parts --report
➥/etc/cron.daily )
47 6    * * 7    root    test -x /usr/sbin/anacron || ( cd / && run-parts --report
➥/etc/cron.weekly )
52 6    1 * *    root    test -x /usr/sbin/anacron || ( cd / && run-parts --report
➥/etc/cron.monthly )
```

The first two lines specify which shell should be used to execute the job (defaults to the shell of the user who owns the crontab file, usually /bin/bash), and the search path for executables that will be used. It's important that you avoid using environment variables in this path statement, because they may not be set when the job runs.

The next line starts with a pound sign (#) and so is treated as a comment and ignored. The next four lines are the important parts: They are the jobs themselves.

Each job is specified in seven fields that define the time to run, owner, and command. The first five commands specify the execution time in quite a quirky order: minute (0–59), hour (0–23), day of the month (1–31), month of the year (1–12), and day of the week (0–7). For day of the week, both 0 and 7 are Sunday, which means that 1 is Monday, 3 is

Wednesday, and so on. If you want to specify "all values" (that is, every minute, every hour, every day, and so on), use an asterisk, `*`.

The next field specifies the username of the owner of the job. When a job is executed, it uses the username specified here. The last field is the command to execute.

So, the first job runs at minute 17, every hour of every day of every month and executes the command `run-parts /etc/cron.hourly`. The `run-parts` command is a simple script that runs all programs inside a given directory (in this case, `/etc/cron.hourly`). So, in this case, the job will execute at 00:17 (17 minutes past midnight), 01:17, 02:17, 03:17, and so on, and will use all the programs listed in the `cron.hourly` directory.

The next job runs at minute 25 and hour 6 of every day of every month, running `run-parts /etc/cron.daily`. Because of the hour limitation, this script runs only once per day, at 6:25 a.m. Note that it uses minute 25 rather than minute 17 so that daily jobs do not clash with hourly jobs. You should be able to guess what the next two jobs do, simply by looking at the commands they run.

Inside each of those four directories (`cron.hourly`, `cron.daily`, `cron.weekly`, and `cron.monthly`) are a collection of shell scripts that will be run by `run-parts`. For example, in `cron.daily` you will have scripts like `logrotate`, which handles backing up of log files, and `makewhatis`, which updates the `whatis` database. You can add other system tasks to these directories if you want to, but be careful to ensure that your scripts are correct.

> **CAUTION**
>
> The `cron` daemon reads all the system `crontab` files and all user `crontab` files once a minute (on the minute; that is, at 6:00:00, 6:01:00, and so on) to check for changes. However, any new jobs it finds will not be executed until at least 1 minute has passed.
>
> For example, if it is 6:01:49 (that is, 49 seconds past 1 minute past 6 a.m.) and you set a `cron` job to run at 6:02, it will not execute. At 6:02, the `cron` daemon will reread its configuration files and see the new job, but it will not be able to execute it. If you set the job to run at 6:02 a.m. every day, it will be executed the following morning and every subsequent morning.
>
> This same situation exists when deleting jobs. If it is 6:01:49 and you have a job scheduled to run at 6:02, deleting it will make no difference: `cron` will run it before it rereads the `crontab` files for changes. However, after it has reread the `crontab` file and noticed the job is no longer there, it will not be executed in subsequent days.

There are alternative ways of specifying dates. For example, you can use sets of dates and times by using hyphens or commas, such as hours 9–15 would execute at 9, 10, 11, 12, 13, 14, and 15 (from 9 a.m. to 3 p.m.), whereas 9, 11, 13, 15 would miss out at the even hours. Note that it is important you do not put spaces into these sets because the `cron` daemon interprets them as the next field. You can define a step value with a slash (/) to show time division: `*/4` for hours means "every 4 hours all day," and `0-12/3` means "every 3 hours from midnight to noon." You can also specify day and month names rather than numbers, using three-character abbreviations: Sun, Mon, Tue, Fri, Sat for days, or Jan, Feb, Mar, Oct, Nov, Dec for months.

As well as system jobs, there are user jobs for those users who have the correct permissions. User jobs are stored in the /var/spool/cron directory, with each user having his own file named after his username (for instance, /var/spool/cron/philip or /var/spool/cron/root). The contents of these files contain the jobs the user wants to run and take roughly the same format as the /etc/crontab file, with the exception that the owner of the job should not be specified because it will always be the same as the filename.

To edit your own crontab file, type crontab –e. This brings up a text editor (vim by default, but you can set the EDITOR environment variable to change that) where you can enter your entries. The format of this file is a little different from the format for the main crontab because this time there is no need to specify the owner of the job—it is always you.

So, this time each line is made up of six fields: minute (0–59), hour (0–23), day of the month (1–31), month of the year (1–12), day of the week (0–7), and then the command to run. If you are using vim and are new to it, press i to enter insert mode to edit your text; then press Esc to exit insert mode. To save and quit, type a colon followed by wq and press Enter.

When programming, we tend to use a sandbox subdirectory in our home directory where we keep all sorts of temporary files that we were just playing around with. We can use a personal job to empty that directory every morning at 6 a.m. so that we get a fresh start each morning. Here is how that would look in our crontab file:

```
0 6 * * * rm -rf /home/matthew/sandbox/*
```

If you are not allowed to schedule jobs, you will be stopped from editing your crontab file.

After your jobs are placed, you can use the command crontab -l to list your jobs. This just prints the contents of your crontab file, so its output will be the same as the line you just entered.

If you want to remove just one job, the easiest thing to do is type crontab -e to edit your crontab file in vim; then, after having moved the cursor to the job you want to delete, type dd (two *d*'s) to delete that line. If you want to delete all your jobs, you can use crontab -r to delete your crontab file.

Basic Shell Control

Ubuntu includes a rich assortment of capable, flexible, and powerful shells. Each shell is different but has numerous built-in commands and configurable command-line prompts and might include features such as command-line history, the ability to recall and use a previous command line, and command-line editing. As an example, the bash shell is so powerful that it is possible to write a minimal web server entirely in bash's language using 114 lines of script. (See the link at the end of this chapter.)

Although there are many shells to choose from, most people stick with the default, bash. This is because bash does everything most people need to do, and more. Only change your shell if you really need to.

Table 13.1 lists each shell, along with its description and location, in your Ubuntu file system.

TABLE 13.1   Shells with Ubuntu

Name	Description	Location
bash	The Bourne Again SHell	/bin/bash
ksh	The Korn shell	/bin/ksh, /usr/bin/ksh
pdksh	A symbolic link to ksh	/usr/bin/pdksh
rsh	The restricted shell (for network operation)	/usr/bin/rsh
sh	A symbolic link to bash	/bin/sh
tcsh	A csh-compatible shell	/bin/tcsh
zsh	A compatible csh, ksh, and sh shell	/bin/zsh

Learning More About Your Shell

All the shells listed in Table 13.1 have accompanying man pages, along with other documentation under the /usr/share/doc directory. Some of the documentation can be quite lengthy, but it is generally much better to have too much documentation than too little. The bash shell includes more than 100 pages in its manual, and the zsh shell documentation is so extensive that it includes the zshall meta man page (use man zshall to read this overview).

The Shell Command Line

Having a basic understanding of the capabilities of the shell command line can help you write better shell scripts. If, after you have finished reading this short introduction, you want to learn more about the command line, check out Chapter 11, "Command-Line Master Class." You can use the shell command line to perform a number of different tasks, including the following:

▶ Searching files or directories with programs using pattern matching or expressions. These commands include the GNU gawk (linked as awk) and the grep family of commands, including egrep and fgrep.

▶ Getting data from and sending data to a file or command, known as *input* and *output redirection*.

▶ Feeding or filtering a program's output to another command (called using *pipes*).

A shell can also have built-in *job-control* commands to launch the command line as a background process, suspend a running program, selectively retrieve or kill running or suspended programs, and perform other types of process control.

Multiple commands can be run on a single command line using a semicolon to separate commands:

```
matthew@seymour:~$ w ; free ; df
 18:14:13 up  4:35,  2 users,  load average: 0.97, 0.99, 1.04
 USER     TTY       FROM             LOGIN@   IDLE   JCPU   PCPU WHAT
 matthew   tty7      :0               13:39   4:35m 24:34   0.32s gnome-session
 matthew   pts/0     :0.0             17:24   0.00s  1.19s  4.98s gnome-terminal
           total      used      free    shared   buffers    cached
 Mem:    4055692   1801104   2254588        0    134096    757532
 -/+ buffers/cache:    909476   3146216
 Swap:   8787512         0   8787512
 Filesystem     1K-blocks      Used Available Use% Mounted on
 /dev/sda1       14421344   6509276   7179508  48% /
 none             2020136       336   2019800   1% /dev
 none             2027844      3004   2024840   1% /dev/shm
 none             2027844       224   2027620   1% /var/run
 none             2027844         0   2027844   0% /var/lock
 none             2027844         0   2027844   0% /lib/init/rw
 /dev/sda6      284593052 144336704 125799860  54% /home
```

This example displays the output of the w, free, and df commands. Long shell command lines can be extended inside shell scripts or at the command line by using the backslash character (\), as follows:

```
matthew@seymour:~$ echo "this is a long \
> command line and" ; echo "shows that multiple commands \
> may be strung out."
this is a long command line and
shows that multiple commands may be strung out.
```

The first three lines of this example are a single command line. In that single line are two instances of the echo command. Note that when you use the backslash as a line-continuation character, it must be the last character on the command line (or in your shell script, as you will see later on in this chapter).

Using the basic features of the shell command line is easy, but mastering use of all features can be difficult. Entire books have been devoted to using shells, writing shell scripts, and using pattern-matching expressions. The following sections provide an overview of some features of the shell command line relating to writing scripts.

Grokking grep

If you plan to develop shell scripts to expand the capabilities of pattern-matching com-
mands such as grep, you will benefit from learning more about using expressions.
One of the definitive guides to using the pattern-matching capabilities of UNIX and
Linux commands is *Mastering Regular Expressions* by Jeffrey E. F. Freidl (O'Reilly),
ISBN: 0-596-52812-4.

Shell Pattern-Matching Support

The shell command line allows you to use strings of specially constructed character
patterns for wildcard matches. This is a different simpler capability than that supported by
GNU utilities such as grep, which can use more complex patterns, known as *expressions,* to
search through files or directories or to filter data input to or out of commands.

The shell's pattern strings can be simple or complex, but even using a small subset of the
available characters in simple wildcards can yield constructive results at the command
line. Common characters used for shell pattern matching include the following:

> ► *—Matches any character. For example, to find all files in the current directory
> ending in .txt, you could use this:
>
>   matthew@seymour:~$ **ls *.txt**

> ► ?—Matches a single character. For example, to find all files in the current directory
> ending in the extension .d?c (where ? could be 0–9, a–z, or A–Z), you could use the
> following:
>
>   matthew@seymour:~$ **ls *.d?c**

> ► **[xxx]** or **[x-x]**—Matches a range of characters. For example, to list all files in a
> directory with names containing numbers, you could use this:
>
>   matthew@seymour:~$ **ls *[0-9]***

> ► **\x**—Matches or escapes a character such as ? or a tab character. For example, to
> create a file with a name containing question mark, you could use the following:
>
>   matthew@seymour:~$ **touch foo\?**

Note that the shell might not interpret some characters or regular expressions in the same
manner as a Linux command, and mixing wildcards and regular expressions in shell
scripts can lead to problems unless you're careful. For example, finding patterns in text is
best left to regular expressions used with commands such as grep; simple wildcards should
be used for filtering or matching filenames on the command line. And although both
Linux command expressions and shell scripts can recognize the backslash as an escape
character in patterns, the dollar sign ($) will have two wildly different meanings (single-
character pattern matching in expressions and variable assignment in scripts).

13

> **CAUTION**
>
> Make sure you read your command carefully when using wildcards; an all-too-common error is to type something like `rm -rf * .txt` with a space between the * and the `.txt`. By the time you wonder why the command is taking so long, Bash will already have deleted most of your files. The problem is that it will treat the * and the `.txt` separately. * will match everything, so Bash will delete all your files.

Redirecting Input and Output

You can create, overwrite, and append data to files at the command line, using a process called *input* and *output redirec*tion. The shell recognizes several special characters for this process, such as >, <, or >>.

In this example, the output of the `ls` command is redirected to create a file named `textfiles.listing`:

```
matthew@seymour:~$ ls *.txt >textfiles.listing
```

Use output redirection with care because it is possible to overwrite existing files. For example, specifying a different directory but using the same output filename will overwrite the existing `textfiles.listing`:

```
matthew@seymour:~$ ls /usr/share/doc/mutt-1.4/*.txt >textfiles.listing
```

Fortunately, most shells are smart enough to recognize when you might do something foolish. Here, the bash shell warns that the command is attempting to redirect output to a directory:

```
matthew@seymour:~$ mkdir foo
matthew@seymour:~$ ls >foo
bash: foo: Is a directory
```

Output can be appended to a file without overwriting existing content by using the append operator, >>. In this example, the directory listing will be appended to the end of `textfiles.listing` instead of overwriting its contents:

```
matthew@seymour:~$ ls /usr/share/doc/mutt-1.4/*.txt >>textfiles.listing
```

You can use *input redirection* to feed data into a command by using the < like this:

```
matthew@seymour:~$ cat < textfiles.listing
```

You can use the shell *here* operator, <<, to specify the end of input on the shell command line:

```
matthew@seymour:~$ cat >simple_script <<DONE
> echo ""this is a simple script""
> DONE
matthew@seymour:~$ cat simple_script
echo ""this is a simple script""
```

In this example, the shell feeds the cat command you are typing (input) until the pattern DONE is recognized. The output file simple_script is then saved and its contents verified. This same technique can be used in scripts to create content based on the output of various commands and define an end-of-input or delimiter.

Piping Data

Many Linux commands can be used in concert in a single, connected command line to transform data from one form to another. Stringing Linux commands together in this fashion is known as using or creating *pipes*. Pipes are created on the command line with the bar operator (|). For example, a pipe can be used to perform a complex task from a single command line like this:

```
matthew@seymour:~$ find /d2 -name '*.txt' -print | xargs cat | \
tr ' ' '\n' | sort | uniq >output.txt
```

This example takes the output of the find command to feed the cat command (via xargs) the name of all text files in the /d2 directory. The content of all matching files is then fed through the tr command to change each space in the data stream into a carriage return. The stream of words is then sorted, and identical adjacent lines are removed using the uniq command. The output, a raw list of words, is then saved in the file named output.txt.

Background Processing

The shell allows you to start a command and then launch it into the background as a process by using an ampersand (&) at the end of a command line. This technique is often used at the command line of an X terminal window to start a client and return to the command line. For example, to launch another terminal window using the xterm client, you can use the following:

```
matthew@seymour:~$ xterm &
[3] 1437
```

The numbers echoed back show a number (3 in this example), which is a *job* number, or reference number for a shell process, and a *process ID* number, or PID (1437 in this example). The xterm window session can be killed by using the shell's built-in kill command, along with the job number like this:

```
matthew@seymour:~$ kill %3
```

Or the process can be killed by using the kill command, along with the PID, as follows:

```
matthew@seymour:~$ kill 1437
```

Background processing can be used in shell scripts to start commands that take a long time, such as backups:

matthew@seymour:~$ **tar -czf** /**backup**/**home.tgz** /**home &**

Writing and Executing a Shell Script

Why should you write and use shell scripts? Shell scripts can save you time and typing, especially if you routinely use the same command lines multiple times every day. Although you could also use the history function (press the Up or Down keys while using bash or use the history command), a shell script can add flexibility with command-line argument substitution and built-in help.

Although a shell script won't execute faster than a program written in a computer language such as C, a shell program can be smaller in size than a compiled program. The shell program does not require any additional library support other than the shell or, if used, existing commands installed on your system. The process of creating and testing shell scripts is also generally simpler and faster than the development process for equivalent C language commands.

> **NOTE**
>
> Hundreds of commands included with Ubuntu are actually shell scripts, and many other good shell script examples are available over the Internet—a quick search will yield numerous links to online tutorials and scripting guides from fellow Linux users and developers. For example, the startx command, used to start an X Window session from the text console, is a shell script used every day by most users. To learn more about shell scripting with bash, see the "Advanced Bash-Scripting Guide," listed in the "Reference" section at the end of this chapter. You'll also find *Sams Teach Yourself Shell Programming in 24 Hours* to be a helpful guide to learning more about using the shell to build your own commands.

When you are learning to write and execute your first shell scripts, start with scripts for simple but useful tasks. Begin with short examples, and then expand the scripts as you build on your experience and knowledge. Make liberal use of comments (lines preceded with a pound sign, #) to document each section of your script. Include an author statement and overview of the script as additional help, along with a creation date or version number. Write shell scripts using a text editor such as vi because it does not automatically wrap lines of text. Line wrapping can break script syntax and cause problems. If you use the nano editor, include its -w flag to disable line wrap.

In this section, you learn how to write a simple shell script to set up a number of *aliases* (command synonyms) whenever you log on. Instead of typing all the aliases every time you log on, you can put them in a file by using a text editor, such as vi, and then execute the file. Normally these changes are saved in systemwide shell configuration files under the /etc directory to make the changes active for all users or in your .bashrc, .cshrc (if you use tcsh), or .bash_profile files in your home directory.

Here is what is contained in myenv, a sample shell script created for this purpose (for bash):

```
#!/bin/sh
alias ll='ls -L'
alias ldir='ls -aF'
alias copy='cp'
```

This simple script creates command *aliases*, or convenient shorthand forms of commands, for the ls and cp commands. The ll alias provides a long directory listing: The ldir alias is the ls command, but prints indicators (for directories or executable files) in listings. The copy alias is the same as the cp command. You can experiment and add your own options or create aliases of other commands with options you frequently use.

You can execute myenv in a variety of ways under Linux. As shown in this example, you can make myenv executable by using the chmod command and then execute it as you would any other native Linux command:

```
matthew@seymour:~$ chmod +x myenv
```

This line turns on the executable permission of myenv, which can be checked with the ls command and its -l option like this:

```
matthew@seymour:~$ ls -l myenv
-rwxr-xr-x   1 matthew matthew  0 2010-07-08 18:19 myenv
```

Running the New Shell Program

You can run your new shell program in several ways. Each method produces the same results, which is a testament to the flexibility of using the shell with Linux. One way to run your shell program is to execute the file myenv from the command line as if it were a Linux command:

```
matthew@seymour:~$ ./myenv
```

A second way to execute myenv under a particular shell, such as pdksh, is as follows:

```
matthew@seymour:~$ pdksh myenv
```

This invokes a new pdksh shell and passes the filename myenv as a parameter to execute the file. A third way requires you to create a directory named bin in your home directory and to then copy the new shell program into this directory. You can then run the program without the need to specify a specific location or to use a shell. You do so like this:

```
matthew@seymour:~$ mkdir bin
matthew@seymour:~$ mv myenv bin
matthew@seymour:~$ myenv
```

This works because Ubuntu is set up by default to include the executable path $HOME/bin in your shell's environment. You can view this environment variable, named PATH, by piping the output of the env command through fgrep like so:

```
matthew@seymour:~$ env | fgrep PATH
/usr/kerberos/bin:/usr/local/bin:/bin:/usr/bin: \
/usr/X11R6/bin:/sbin:/home/matthew/bin
```

As you can see, the user (matthew in this example) can use the new bin directory to hold executable files. Another way to bring up an environment variable is to use the echo command along with the variable name (in this case, $PATH):

```
matthew@seymour:~$ echo $PATH
/usr/kerberos/bin:/usr/local/bin:/usr/bin:/bin:/usr/X11R6/bin:/home/bball/bin
```

> **CAUTION**
>
> Never put . in your $PATH to execute files or a command in the current directory—this presents a serious security risk, especially for the root operator, and even more so if . is first in your $PATH search order. Trojan scripts placed by crackers in directories such as /tmp can be used for malicious purposes, and will be executed immediately if the current working directory is part of your $PATH.

Storing Shell Scripts for Systemwide Access

After you execute the command myenv, you should be able to use ldir from the command line to get a list of files under the current directory and ll to get a list of files with attributes displayed. However, the best way to use the new commands in myenv is to put them into your shell's login or profile file. For Ubuntu, and nearly all Linux users, the default shell is bash, so you can make these commands available for everyone on your system by putting them in the /etc/bashrc file. Systemwide aliases for tcsh are contained in files with the extension .csh under the /etc/profile.d directory. The pdksh shell can use these command aliases, as well.

> **NOTE**
>
> To use a shell other than bash after logging in, use the chsh command from the command line or the system-config-users client during an X session. You'll be asked for your password (or the root password if using system-config-users) and the location and name of the new shell (see Table 13.1). The new shell will become your default shell, but only if its name is in the list of acceptable system shells in /etc/shells.

Interpreting Shell Scripts Through Specific Shells

The majority of shell scripts use a *shebang line* (#!) at the beginning to control the type of shell used to run the script; this bang line calls for an sh-incantation of bash:

```
#!/bin/sh
```

A shebang line (it is short for "sharp" and "bang," two names for # and !) tells the Linux kernel that a specific command (a shell, or in the case of other scripts, perhaps awk or Perl) is to be used to interpret the contents of the file. Using a shebang line is common practice for all shell scripting. For example, if you write a shell script using bash, but want the script to execute as if run by the Bourne shell, sh, the first line of your script will contain #!/bin/sh, which is a link to the bash shell. Running bash as sh causes bash to act as a Bourne shell. This is the reason for the symbolic link sh, which points to bash.

The Shebang Line

The shebang line is a magic number, as defined in /usr/share/magic—a text database of magic numbers for the Linux file command. Magic numbers are used by many different Linux commands to quickly identify a type of file, and the database format is documented in the section five manual page named magic (read by using man 5 magic). For example, magic numbers can be used by the Linux file command to display the identity of a script (no matter what filename is used) as a shell script using a specific shell or other interpreter such as awk or Perl.

You might also find different or new environment variables available to your scripts by using different shells. For example, if you launch csh from the bash command line, you will find several new variables or variables with slightly different definitions, such as the following:

```
matthew@seymour:~$ env
...
VENDOR=intel
MACHTYPE=i386
HOSTTYPE=i386-linux
HOST=thinkpad.home.org
On the other hand, bash might provide these variables or variables of the same name
with a slightly different definition, such as
$ env
...
HOSTTYPE=i386
HOSTNAME=thinkpad.home.org
```

Although the behavior of a shebang line is not defined by POSIX, variations of its use can prove to be helpful when you are writing shell scripts. For example, as described in the wish man page, you can use a shell to help execute programs called within a shell script without needing to hard code pathnames of programs. The `wish` command is a windowing *Tool Control Language* (`tcl`) interpreter that can be used to write graphical clients. Avoiding the use of specific pathnames to programs increases shell script portability because not every UNIX or Linux system has programs in the same location.

For example, if you want to use the `wish` command, your first inclination might be to write this:

```
#!/usr/local/bin/wish
```

Although this will work on many other operating systems, the script will fail under Linux because `wish` is located under the `/usr/bin` directory. However, if you write the command line this way

```
#!/bin/sh
exec wish "$@"
```

you can use the `wish` command (as a binary or a shell script itself).

Using Variables in Shell Scripts

When writing shell scripts for Linux, you work with three types of variables:

▶ **Environment variables**—Part of the system environment, you can use them in your shell program. New variables can be defined, and some of them, such as `PATH`, can also be modified within a shell program.

▶ **Built-in variables**—Variables such as options used on the command (interpreted by the shell as a *positional argument*) are provided by Linux. Unlike environment variables, you cannot modify them.

▶ **User variables**—Variables defined within a script when you write a shell script. You can use and modify them at will within the shell script but are not available to be used outside of the script.

A major difference between shell programming and other programming languages is that in shell programming, variables are not *typed*—that is, you do not have to specify whether a variable is a number or a string, and so on.

Assigning a Value to a Variable

Suppose that you want to use a variable called `lcount` to count the number of iterations in a loop within a shell program. You can declare and initialize this variable as follows:

Command	Environment
`lcount=0`	**pdksh and bash**
`set lcount=0`	`tcsh`

> **NOTE**
>
> Under pdksh and bash, you must ensure that the equal sign (=) does not have spaces before and after it.

To store a string in a variable, you can use the following:

Command	Environment
myname=Sedona	pdksh and bash
set myname=Sedona	tcsh

Use the preceding variable form if the string doesn't have embedded spaces. If a string has embedded spaces, you can do the assignment as follows:

Command	Environment
myname="Saralyn"	pdksh and bash
set myname="Saralyn"	tcsh

Accessing Variable Values

You can access the value of a variable by prefixing the variable name with a dollar sign ($). That is, if the variable name is var, you can access the variable by using $var.

If you want to assign the value of var to the variable lcount, you can do so as follows:

Command	Environment
lcount=$var	pdksh and bash
set	tcsh
lcount=$var	

Positional Parameters

It is possible to pass options from the command line or from another shell script to your shell program.

These options are supplied to the shell program by Linux as *positional parameters*, which have special names provided by the system. The first parameter is stored in a variable called 1 (number 1) and can be accessed by using $1 within the program. The second parameter is stored in a variable called 2 and can be accessed by using $2 within the program, and so on. One or more of the higher-numbered positional parameters can be omitted while you're invoking a shell program.

Understanding how to use these positional parameters and how to access and use variables retrieved from the command line is necessary when developing more advanced shell programs.

A Simple Example of a Positional Parameter

For example, if a shell program `mypgm` expects two parameters—such as a first name and a last name—you can invoke the shell program with only one parameter, the first name. However, you cannot invoke it with only the second parameter, the last name.

Here is a shell program called `mypgm1`, which takes only one parameter (a name) and displays it on the screen:

```
#!/bin/sh
#Name display program
if [ $# -eq 0 ]
then
    echo "Name not provided"
else
    echo "Your name is "$1
fi
```

If you execute `mypgm1`, as follows

```
matthew@seymour:~$ bash mypgm1
```

you get the following output:

```
Name not provided
```

However, if you execute `mypgm1`, as follows

```
matthew@seymour:~$ bash   mypgm1 Heather
```

you get the this output:

```
Your name is Heather
```

The shell program `mypgm1` also illustrates another aspect of shell programming: the built-in variables provided to the shell by the Linux kernel. In `mypgm1`, the built-in variable `$#` provides the number of positional parameters passed to the shell program. You learn more about working with built-in variables in the next major section of this chapter.

Using Positional Parameters to Access and Retrieve Variables from the Command Line

Using positional parameters in scripts can be helpful if you need to use command lines with piped commands requiring complex arguments. Shell programs containing positional parameters can be even more convenient if the commands are infrequently used. For example, if you use your Ubuntu system with an attached voice modem as an answering machine, you can write a script to issue a command that retrieves and plays the voice messages. The following lines convert a saved sound file (in .rmd or voice-phone format) and pipe the result to your system's audio device:

```
#!/bin/sh
# play voice message in /var/spool/voice/incoming
rmdtopvf /var/spool/voice/incoming/$1 | pvfspeed -s 8000 | \
pvftobasic >/dev/audio
```

A voice message can then easily be played back using this script (perhaps named pmm):

```
matthew@seymour:~$ pmm name_of_message
```

Shell scripts that contain positional parameters are often used for automating routine and mundane jobs, such as system log report generation, file system checks, user resource accounting, printer use accounting, and other system, network, or security administration tasks.

Using a Simple Script to Automate Tasks

You could use a simple script, for example, to examine your system log for certain keywords. If the script is run via your system's scheduling table, /etc/crontab, it can help automate security monitoring. By combining the output capabilities of existing Linux commands with the language facilities of the shell, you can quickly build a useful script to perform a task normally requiring a number of command lines. For example, you can create a short script, named greplog, like this:

```
#!/bin/sh
#    name:  greplog
#     use:  mail grep of designated log using keyword
# version:  v.01 08aug02
#
#  author: bb
#
# usage: greplog [keyword] [logpathname]
#
#  bugs: does not check for correct number of arguments

# build report name using keyword search and date
log_report=/tmp/$1.logreport.`date '+%m%d%y'`

# build report header with system type, hostname, date and time
echo "=============================================================" \
     >$log_report
echo "            S Y S T E M   M O N I T O R   L O G" >>$log_report
echo uname -a >>$log_report
echo "Log report for" `hostname -f` "on" `date '+%c'`      >>$log_report
echo "=============================================================" \
     >>$log_report ; echo "" >>$log_report
```

```
# record log search start
echo "Search for->" $1 "starting" `date '+%r'` >>$log_report
echo "" >>$log_report

# get and save grep results of keyword ($1) from logfile ($2)
grep -i $1 $2 >>$log_report

# build report footer with time
echo "" >>$log_report
echo "End of" $log_report at `date '+%r'` >>$log_report

# mail report to root
mail -s "Log Analysis for $1" root <$log_report

# clean up and remove report
rm $log_report
exit 0
```

In this example, the script creates the variable $log_report, which will be the filename of
the temporary report. The keyword ($1) and first argument on the command line is used
as part of the filename, along with the current date (with perhaps a better approach to use
$$ instead of the date, which will append the script's PID as a file extension). Next, the
report header containing some formatted text, the output of the uname command, and the
hostname and date is added to the report. The start of the search is then recorded, and
any matches of the keyword in the log are added to the report. A footer containing the
name of the report and the time is then added. The report is mailed to root with the
search term as the subject of the message, and the temporary file is deleted.

You can test the script by running it manually and feeding it a keyword and a pathname
to the system log, /var/log/messages, like this:

matthew@seymour:~# **greplog FAILED /var/log/messages**

Note that your system should be running the syslogd daemon. If any login failures have
occurred on your system, the root operator might get an email message that looks like this:

```
Date: Thu, 23 Oct 2003 16:23:24 -0400
From: root <root@stinkpad.home.org>
To: root@stinkpad.home.org
Subject: FAILED


===============================================================
            S Y S T E M   M O N I T O R   L O G
Linux stinky 2.4.22-1.2088.nptl #1 Thu Oct 9 20:21:24 EDT 2003 i686 i686 i386
+GNU/Linux
Log report for stinkpad.home.org on Thu 23 Oct 2003 04:23:24 PM EDT
===============================================================
```

```
Search for-> FAILED starting 04:23:24 PM

Oct 23 16:23:04 stinkpad login[1769]: FAILED LOGIN 3 FROM (null) FOR bball,
+Authentication failure

End of /tmp/FAILED.logreport.102303 at 04:23:24 PM
```

To further automate the process, you can include command lines using the script in another script to generate a series of searches and reports.

Built-In Variables

Built-in variables are special variables provided to shell by Linux that can be used to make decisions within a shell program. You cannot modify the values of these variables within the shell program.

Some of these variables are as follows:

- ▶ **$#**—Number of positional parameters passed to the shell program.
- ▶ **$?**—Completion code of the last command or shell program executed within the shell program (returned value).
- ▶ **$0**—The name of the shell program.
- ▶ **$***—A single string of all arguments passed at the time of invocation of the shell program.

To show these built-in variables in use, here is a sample program called mypgm2:

```
#!/bin/sh
#my test program
echo "Number of parameters is $#"
echo "Program name is $0"
echo "Parameters as a single string is $*"
```

If you execute mypgm2 from the command line in pdksh and bash as follows:

```
matthew@seymour:~$ bash mypgm2 Sanjiv Guha
```

you get the following result:

```
Number of parameters is 2
Program name is mypgm2
Parameters as a single string is Sanjiv Guha
```

Special Characters

Some characters have special meaning to Linux shells; these characters represent commands, denote specific use for surrounding text, or provide search parameters. Special characters provide a sort of shorthand by incorporating these rather complex meanings into a simple character. Some special characters are shown in Table 13.2.

TABLE 13.2   Special Shell Characters

Character	Explanation
$	Indicates the beginning of a shell variable name
|	Pipes standard output to next command
#	Starts a comment
&	Executes a process in the background
?	Matches one character
*	Matches one or more characters
>	Output redirection operator
<	Input redirection operator
`	Command substitution (the backquote or backtick—the key above the Tab key on most keyboards)
>>	Output redirection operator (to append to a file)
<<	Wait until following end-of-input string (HERE operator)
[ ]	Range of characters
[a-z]	All characters a through z
[a,z] or [az]	Characters a or z
Space	Delimiter between two words

Special characters are very useful to you when you're creating shell scripts, but if you inadvertently use a special character as part of variable names or strings, your program will behave incorrectly. As you learn in later parts of this section, you can use one of the special characters in a string if you precede it with an *escape character* (\, or backslash) to indicate that it isn't being used as a special character and shouldn't be treated as such by the program.

A few special characters deserve special note. They are the double quotes ("), the single quotes ('), the backslash (\), and the backtick (`)—all discussed in the following sections.

Using Double Quotes to Resolve Variables in Strings with Embedded Spaces

If a string contains embedded spaces, you can enclose the string in double quotes (") so that the shell interprets the whole string as one entity instead of more than one.

For example, if you assigned the value of abc def (abc followed by one space, followed by def) to a variable called x in a shell program as follows, you would get an error because the shell would try to execute def as a separate command:

Command	Environment
x=abc def	pdksh and bash
set x = adb def	Tcsh

The shell executes the string as a single command if you surround the string in double quotes as follows:

Command	Environment
x="abc def"	pdksh and bash
set x="abc def"	Tcsh

The double quotes resolve all variables within the string. Here is an example for pdksh and bash:

```
var="test string"
newvar="Value of var is $var"
echo $newvar
```

Here is the same example for tcsh:

```
set var="test string"
set newvar="Value of var is $var"
echo $newvar
```

If you execute a shell program containing the preceding three lines, you get the following result:

```
Value of var is test string
```

Using Single Quotes to Maintain Unexpanded Variables

You can surround a string with single quotes (') to stop the shell from expanding variables and interpreting special characters. When used for the latter purpose, the single quote is an *escape character*, similar to the backslash, which you learn about in the next section.

Here, you learn how to use the single quote to avoid expanding a variable in a shell script. An unexpanded variable maintains its original form in the output.

In the following examples, the double quotes in the preceding examples have been changed to single quotes:

```
pdksh and bash:
var='test string'
newvar='Value of var is $var'
echo $newvar
tcsh:
set var = 'test string'
set newvar = 'Value of var is $var'
echo $newvar
```

If you execute a shell program containing these three lines, you get the following result:

```
Value of var is $var
```

As you can see, the variable var maintains its original format in the results, rather than having been expanded.

Using the Backslash as an Escape Character

As you learned earlier, the backslash (\) serves as an escape character that stops the shell from interpreting the succeeding character as a special character. Say that you want to assign a value of $test to a variable called var. If you use the following command, the shell reads the special character $ and interprets $test as the value of the variable test. No value has been assigned to test; a null value is stored in var as follows:

Command	Environment
var=$test	pdksh and bash
set var=$test	Tcsh

Unfortunately, this assignment may work for bash and pdksh, but it returns an error of "undefined variable" if you use it with tcsh. Use the following commands to correctly store $test in var:

Command	Environment
var=\$test	pdksh and bash
set var = \$test	Tcsh

The backslash before the dollar sign (\$) signals the shell to interpret the $ as any other ordinary character and *not to associate any sp*ecial meaning to it. You could also use single quotes (') around the $test variable to get the same result.

Using the Backtick to Replace a String with Output

You can use the backtick (`` ` ``) character to signal the shell to replace a string with its output when executed. This is called command substitution. This special character can be used in shell programs when you want the result of the execution of a command to be stored in a variable. For example, if you want to count the number of lines in a file called `test.txt` in the current directory and store the result in a variable called `var`, you can use the following command:

Command	Environment
var=`wc -l test.txt`	pdksh and bash
set var = `wc -l test.txt`	tcsh

Comparison of Expressions in `pdksh` and `bash`

Comparing values or evaluating the differences between similar bits of data—such as file information, character strings, or numbers—is a task known as *comparison of expressions*. Comparison of expressions is an integral part of using logic in shell programs to accomplish tasks. The way the logical comparison of two operators (numeric or string) is done varies slightly in different shells. In `pdksh` and `bash`, a command called `test` can be used to achieve comparisons of expressions. In `tcsh`, you can write an expression to accomplish the same thing.

This section covers comparison operations using the `pdksh` or `bash` shells. Later in the chapter, you learn how to compare expressions in the `tcsh` shell.

The `pdksh` and `bash` shell syntax provide a command named `test` to compare strings, numbers, and files. The syntax of the `test` command is as follows:

```
test expression
or
[ expression ]
```

Both forms of the `test` commands are processed the same way by `pdksh` and `bash`. The `test` commands support the following types of comparisons:

▶ String comparison

▶ Numeric comparison

▶ File operators

▶ Logical operators

String Comparison

The following operators can be used to compare two string expressions:

▶ `=`—To compare whether two strings are equal.

▶ `!=`—To compare whether two strings are not equal.

▶ **-n**—To evaluate whether the string length is greater than zero.

▶ **-z**—To evaluate whether the string length is equal to zero.

Next are some examples using these operators when comparing two strings, `string1` and `string2`, in a shell program called `compare1`:

```
#!/bin/sh
string1="abc"
string2="abd"
if [ $string1 = $string2 ]; then
   echo "string1 equal to string2"
else
   echo "string1 not equal to string2"
fi

if [ $string2 != string1 ]; then
   echo "string2 not equal to string1"
else
   echo "string2 equal to string2"
fi

if [ $string1 ]; then
   echo "string1 is not empty"
else
   echo "string1 is empty"
fi

if [ -n $string2 ]; then
   echo "string2 has a length greater than zero
else
   echo "string2 has length equal to zero"
fi

if [ -z $string1 ]; then
   echo "string1 has a length equal to zero"
else
  echo "string1 has a length greater than zero"
fi
If you execute compare1, you get the following result:
string1 not equal to string2
string2 not equal to string1
string1 is not empty
string2 has a length greater than zero
string1 has a length greater than zero
```

If two strings are not equal in size, the system pads out the shorter string with trailing spaces for comparison. That is, if the value of string1 is "abc" and that of string2 is "ab", string2 is padded with a trailing space for comparison purposes; it will have a value of "ab " (with a space after the letters).

Number Comparison

The following operators can be used to compare two numbers:

- ▶ **-eq**—To compare whether two numbers are equal.

- ▶ **-ge**—To compare whether one number is greater than or equal to the other number.

- ▶ **-le**—To compare whether one number is less than or equal to the other number.

- ▶ **-ne**—To compare whether two numbers are not equal.

- ▶ **-gt**—To compare whether one number is greater than the other number.

- ▶ **-lt**—To compare whether one number is less than the other number.

The following shell program compares three numbers—number1, number2, and number3:

```
#!/bin/sh
number1=5
number2=10
number3=5

if [ $number1 -eq $number3 ]; then
    echo "number1 is equal to number3"
else
    echo "number1 is not equal to number3"
fi

if [ $number1 -ne $number2 ]; then
    echo "number1 is not equal to number2"
else
    echo "number1 is equal to number2"
fi

if [ $number1 -gt $number2 ]; then
    echo "number1 is greater than number2"
else
    echo "number1 is not greater than number2"
fi

if [ $number1 -ge $number3 ]; then
    echo "number1 is greater than or equal to number3"
else
    echo "number1 is not greater than or equal to number3"
```

```
fi

if [ $number1 -lt $number2 ]; then
    echo "number1 is less than number2"
else
    echo "number1 is not less than number2"
fi

if [ $number1 -le $number3 ]; then
    echo "number1 is less than or equal to number3"
else
    echo "number1 is not less than or equal to number3"
fi
```

When you execute the shell program, you get the following results:

```
number1 is equal to number3
number1 is not equal to number2
number1 is not greater than number2
number1 is greater than or equal to number3
number1 is less than number2
number1 is less than or equal to number3
```

File Operators

The following operators can be used as file comparison operators:

- ▶ **-d**—To ascertain whether a file is a directory.

- ▶ **-f**—To ascertain whether a file is a regular file.

- ▶ **-r**—To ascertain whether read permission is set for a file.

- ▶ **-s**—To ascertain whether a file exists and has a length greater than zero.

- ▶ **-w**—To ascertain whether write permission is set for a file.

- ▶ **-x**—To ascertain whether execute permission is set for a file.

Assume that a shell program called compare3 is in a directory with a file called file1 and a subdirectory dir1 under the current directory. Assume that file1 has a permission of r-x (read and execute permission) and dir1 has a permission of rwx (read, write, and execute permission). The code for the shell program would look like this:

```
#!/bin/sh
if [ -d $dir1 ]; then
    echo "dir1 is a directory"
else
    echo "dir1 is not a directory"
fi
```

```
if [ -f $dir1 ]; then
   echo "dir1 is a regular file"
else
   echo "dir1 is not a regular file"
fi

if [ -r $file1 ]; then
   echo "file1 has read permission"
else
   echo "file1 does not have read permission"
fi

if [ -w $file1 ]; then
   echo "file1 has write permission"
else
   echo "file1 does not have write permission"
fi

if [ -x $dir1 ]; then
   echo "dir1 has execute permission"
else
   echo "dir1 does not have execute permission"
fi
```

If you execute the shell program, you get the following results:

```
dir1 is a directory
file1 is a regular file
file1 has read permission
file1 does not have write permission
dir1 has execute permission
```

Logical Operators

Logical operators are used to compare expressions using Boolean logic, which compares values using characters representing NOT, AND, and OR:

- ▶ **!**—To negate a logical expression.

- ▶ **-a**—To logically AND two logical expressions.

- ▶ **-o**—To logically OR two logical expressions.

This example named `logic` uses the file and directory mentioned in the previous compare3 example:

```
#!/bin/sh
if [ -x file1 -a -x dir1 ]; then
   echo file1 and dir1 are executable
```

```
else
    echo at least one of file1 or dir1 are not executable
fi

if [ -w file1 -o -w dir1 ]; then
    echo file1 or dir1 are writable
else
    echo neither file1 or dir1 are executable
fi

if [ ! -w file1 ]; then
    echo file1 is not writable
else
    echo file1 is writable
fi
If you execute logic, it will yield the following result:
file1 and dir1 are executable
file1 or dir1 are writable
file1 is not writable
```

Comparing Expressions with `tcsh`

As stated earlier, the method for comparing expressions in `tcsh` is different from the method used under `pdksh` and `bash`. The comparison of expression demonstrated in this section uses the syntax necessary for the `tcsh` shell environment.

String Comparison

The following operators can be used to compare two string expressions:

▶ ==—To compare whether two strings are equal.

▶ !=—To compare whether two strings are not equal.

The following examples compare two strings, `string1` and `string2`, in the shell program `compare1`:

```
#!/bin/tcsh
set string1 = "abc"
set string2 = "abd"

if (string1 == string2)   then
    echo "string1 equal to string2"
else
    echo "string1 not equal to string2"
endif
```

```
if  (string2 != string1)  then
   echo "string2 not equal to string1"
else
   echo "string2 equal to string1"
endif
```

If you execute compare1, you get the following results:

```
string1 not equal to string2
string2 not equal to string1
```

Number Comparison

These operators can be used to compare two numbers:

► >=—To compare whether one number is greater than or equal to the other number.

► <=—To compare whether one number is less than or equal to the other number.

► >—To compare whether one number is greater than the other number.

► <—To compare whether one number is less than the other number.

The next examples compare two numbers, number1 and number2, in a shell program called compare2:

```
#!/bin/tcsh
set number1=5
set number2=10
set number3=5

if  (number1 > number2)  then
   echo "number1 is greater than number2"
else
   echo "number1 is not greater than number2"
endif

if  (number1 >= number3) then
   echo "number1 is greater than or equal to number3"
else
   echo "number1 is not greater than or equal to number3"
endif

if  (number1 < number2)  then
   echo "number1 is less than number2"
else
   echo "number1 is not less than number2"
endif
```

```
if  (number1 <= number3) then
   echo "number1 is less than or equal to number3"
else
   echo "number1 is not less than or equal to number3"
endif
```

When executing the shell program `compare2`, you get the following results:

```
number1 is not greater than number2
number1 is greater than or equal to number3
number1 is less than number2
number1 is less than or equal to number3
```

File Operators

These operators can be used as file comparison operators:

- ▶ **-d**—To ascertain whether a file is a directory.

- ▶ **-e**—To ascertain whether a file exists.

- ▶ **-f**—To ascertain whether a file is a regular file.

- ▶ **-o**—To ascertain whether a user is the owner of a file.

- ▶ **-r**—To ascertain whether read permission is set for a file.

- ▶ **-w**—To ascertain whether write permission is set for a file.

- ▶ **-x**—To ascertain whether execute permission is set for a file.

- ▶ **-z**—To ascertain whether the file size is zero.

The following examples are based on a shell program called `compare3`, which is in a directory with a file called `file1` and a subdirectory `dir1` under the current directory. Assume that `file1` has a permission of `r-x` (read and execute permission) and `dir1` has a permission of `rwx` (read, write, and execute permission).

The following is the code for the `compare3` shell program:

```
#!/bin/tcsh
if  (-d dir1) then
   echo "dir1 is a directory"
else
   echo "dir1 is not a directory"
endif

if (-f dir1)  then
   echo "file1 is a regular file"
```

```
else
   echo "file1 is not a regular file"
endif

if (-r file1) then
   echo "file1 has read permission"
else
   echo "file1 does not have read permission"
endif

if (-w file1) then
   echo "file1 has write permission"
else
   echo "file1 does not have write permission"
endif

if (-x dir1) then
   echo "dir1 has execute permission"
else
   echo "dir1 does not have execute permission"
endif

if (-z file1) then
   echo "file1 has zero length"
else
   echo "file1 has greater than zero length"
endif
```

If you execute the file compare3, you get the following results:

```
dir1 is a directory
file1 is a regular file
file1 has read permission
file1 does not have write permission
dir1 has execute permission
file1 has greater than zero length
```

Logical Operators

Logical operators are used with conditional statements. These operators are used to negate a logical expression or to perform logical ANDs and ORs:

- ▶ !—To negate a logical expression.

- ▶ &&—To logically AND two logical expressions.

- ▶ ||—To logically OR two logical expressions.

This example named logic uses the file and directory mentioned in the previous compare3 example:

```
#!/bin/tcsh
if ( -x file1 && -x dir1 ) then
    echo file1 and dir1 are executable
else
    echo at least one of file1 or dir1 are not executable
endif

if ( -w file1 || -w dir1 ) then
    echo file1 or dir1 are writable
else
    echo neither file1 or dir1 are executable
endif

if ( ! -w file1 ) then
    echo file1 is not writable
else
    echo file1 is writable
endif
```

If you execute logic, it will yield the following result:

```
file1 and dir1 are executable
file1 or dir1 are writable
file1 is not writable
```

The for Statement

The for statement is used to execute a set of commands once each time a specified condition is true. The for statement has a number of formats. The first format used by pdksh and bash is as follows:

```
for curvar in list
do
    statements
done
```

This form should be used if you want to execute statements once for each value in list. For each iteration, the current value of the list is assigned to vcurvar. list can be a variable containing a number of items or a list of values separated by spaces. The second format is as follows:

```
for curvar
do
    statements
done
```

In this form, the `statements` are executed once for each of the positional parameters passed to the shell program. For each iteration, the current value of the positional parameter is assigned to the variable `curvar`.

This form can also be written as follows:

```
for curvar in $
do
    statements
done
```

Remember that `$@` gives you a list of positional parameters passed to the shell program, quoted in a manner consistent with the way the user originally invoked the command.

Under `tcsh`, the `for` statement is called `foreach`. The format is as follows:

```
foreach curvar (list)
    statements
end
```

In this form, `statements` are executed once for each value in `list`, and, for each iteration, the current value of `list` is assigned to `curvar`.

Suppose that you want to create a backup version of each file in a directory to a subdirectory called `backup`. You can do the following in `pdksh` and `bash`:

```
#!/bin/sh
for filename in *
do
    cp $filename backup/$filename
    if [ $? -ne 0 ]; then
        echo "copy for $filename failed"
    fi
done
```

In the preceding example, a backup copy of each file is created. If the copy fails, a message is generated.

The same example in `tcsh` is as follows:

```
#!/bin/tcsh
foreach filename (`/bin/ls`)
    cp $filename backup/$filename
```

```
    if ($? != 0) then
        echo "copy for $filename failed"
    endif
end
```

The while Statement

The while statement can be used to execute a series of commands while a specified condition is true. The loop terminates as soon as the specified condition evaluates to false. It is possible that the loop will not execute at all if the specified condition initially evaluates to false. You should be careful with the while command because the loop will never terminate if the specified condition never evaluates to false.

Endless Loops Have Their Place in Shell Programs

Endless loops can sometimes be useful. For example, you can easily construct a simple command that constantly monitors the 802.11b link quality of a network interface by using a few lines of script:

```
#!/bin/sh
while :
 do
   /sbin/iwconfig eth0 |  grep Link | tr '\n' '\r'
 Done
```

The script outputs the search, and then the tr command formats the output. The result is a simple animation of a constantly updated single line of information:

```
Link Quality:92/92 Signal level:-11 dBm Noise level:-102 dBm
```

This technique can also be used to create a graphical monitoring client for X that outputs traffic information and activity about a network interface:

```
#!/bin/sh
xterm -geometry 75x2 -e \
bash -c \
 "while :; do \
     /sbin/ifconfig eth0 | \
     grep 'TX bytes' | \
      tr '\n' '\r' ; \
 done"
```

The simple example uses a bash command-line script (enabled by -c) to execute a command line repeatedly. The command line pipes the output of the ifconfig command through grep, which searches ifconfig's output and then pipes a line containing the string "TX bytes" to the tr command. The tr command then removes the carriage return at the end of the line to display the information inside an /xterm X11 terminal window, automatically sized by the -geometry option:

```
RX bytes:4117594780 (3926.8 Mb)  TX bytes:452230967 (431.2 Mb)
```

Endless loops can be so useful that Linux includes a command that will repeatedly execute a given command line. For example, you can get a quick report about a system's hardware health by using the sensors command. But instead of using a shell script to loop the output endlessly, you can use the `watch` command to repeat the information and provide simple animation:

```
$ watch "sensors -f | cut -c 1-20"
```

In `pdksh` and `bash`, the following format is used for the `while` flow control construct:

```
while expression
do
    statements
done
In tcsh, the following format is used:
while (expression)
    Statements
End
```

If you want to add the first five even numbers, you can use the following shell program in `pdksh` and `bash`:

```
#!/bin/bash
loopcount=0
result=0
while [ $loopcount -lt 5 ]
do
    loopcount=`expr $loopcount + 1`
    increment=`expr $loopcount \* 2`
    result=`expr $result + $increment`
done


echo "result is $result"
```

In `tcsh`, this program can be written as follows:

```
#!/bin/tcsh
set loopcount = 0
set result = 0
while ($loopcount < 5)
    set loopcount = `expr $loopcount + 1`
    set increment = `expr $loopcount \* 2`
    set result = `expr $result + $increment`

end

echo "result is $result"
```

The `until` Statement

The `until` statement can be used to execute a series of commands until a specified condition is true.

The loop terminates as soon as the specified condition evaluates to true.

In `pdksh` and `bash`, the following format is used:

```
until expression
do
     statements
done
```

As you can see, the format of the `until` statement is similar to that of the `while` statement, but the logic is different: In a `while` loop, you execute until an expression is false, but in an `until` loop, you loop until the expression is true. An important part of this difference is that `while` is executed zero or more times (potentially not executed at all), but `until` is repeated one or more times, meaning it will be executed at least once.

If you want to add the first five even numbers, you can use the following shell program in `pdksh` and `bash`:

```
#!/bin/bash
loopcount=0
result=0
until [ $loopcount -ge 5 ]
do
    loopcount=`expr $loopcount + 1`
    increment=`expr $loopcount \* 2`
    result=`expr $result + $increment`
done

echo "result is $result"
```

The example here is identical to the example for the `while` statement, except that the condition being tested is just the opposite of the condition specified in the `while` statement.

The `tcsh` shell does not support the `until` statement.

The `repeat` Statement (`tcsh`)

The `repeat` statement is used to execute only one command a fixed number of times.

If you want to print a hyphen (-) 80 times with one hyphen per line on the screen, you can use the following command:

```
repeat  80 echo '-'
```

The `select` Statement (pdksh)

The `select` statement is used to generate a menu list if you are writing a shell program that expects input from the user online. The format of the `select` statement is as follows:

```
select  item in itemlist
do
    Statements
Done
```

`itemlist` is optional. If it isn't provided, the system iterates through the `item` entries one at a time. If `itemlist` is provided, however, the system iterates for each entry in `itemlist` and the current value of `itemlist` is assigned to `item` for each iteration, which then can be used as part of the statements being executed.

If you want to write a menu that gives the user a choice of picking a `Continue` or a `Finish`, you can write the following shell program:

```
#!/bin/ksh
select  item in Continue Finish
do
   if [ $item = "Finish" ]; then
      break
   fi
done
```

When the `select` command is executed, the system displays a menu with numeric choices to the user—in this case, 1 for `Continue` and 2 for `Finish`. If the user chooses 1, the variable `item` contains a value of `Continue`; if the user chooses 2, the variable `item` contains a value of `Finish`. When the user chooses 2, the `if` statement is executed and the loop terminates.

The `shift` Statement

The `shift` statement is used to process the positional parameters, one at a time, from left to right. As you'll remember, the positional parameters are identified as $1, $2, $3, and so on. The effect of the `shift` command is that each positional parameter is moved one position to the left and the current $1 parameter is lost.

The `shift` statement is useful when you are writing shell programs in which a user can pass various options. Depending on the specified option, the parameters that follow can mean different things or might not be there at all.

The format of the `shift` command is as follows:

```
shift  number
```

The parameter `number` is the number of places to be shifted and is optional. If not specified, the default is 1; that is, the parameters are shifted one position to the left. If specified, the parameters are shifted `number` positions to the left.

The `if` Statement

The `if` statement evaluates a logical expression to make a decision. An `if` condition has the following format in `pdksh` and `bash`:

```
if [ expression ]; then
    Statements
elif [ expression ]; then
    Statements
else
    Statements
fi
```

The `if` conditions can be nested. That is, an `if` condition can contain another `if` condition within it. It isn't necessary for an `if` condition to have an `elif` or `else` part. The else part is executed if none of the expressions that are specified in the `if` statement and are optional if subsequent `elif` statements are true. The word `fi` is used to indicate the end of the `if` statements, which is very useful if you have nested `if` conditions. In such a case, you should be able to match `fi` to `if` to ensure that all `if` statements are properly coded.

In the following example for `bash` or `pdksh`, a variable `var` can have either of two values: Yes or No. Any other value is invalid. This can be coded as follows:

```
if [ $var = "Yes" ]; then
    echo "Value is Yes"
elif [ $var = "No" ]; then
    echo "Value is No"
else
    echo "Invalid value"
fi
```

In `tcsh`, the `if` statement has two forms. The first form, similar to the one for `pdksh` and `bash`, is as follows:

```
if (expression) then
    Statements
else if (expression) then
    Statements
Else
    Statements
endif
```

Using the example of the variable `var` having only two values, Yes and No, here is how it is coded with `tcsh`:

```
if ($var == "Yes") then
    echo "Value is Yes"
else if ($var == "No" ) then
```

```
    echo "Value is No"
else
    echo "Invalid value"
endif
```

The second form of the `if` condition for `tcsh` is as follows:

```
if (expression) command
```

In this format, only a single command can be executed if the expression evaluates to true.

The case Statement

The `case` statement is used to execute statements depending on a discrete value or a range of values matching the specified variable. In most cases, you can use a `case` statement instead of an `if` statement if you have a large number of conditions.

The format of a `case` statement for `pdksh` and `bash` is as follows:

```
case str in
    str1 | str2)
        Statements;;
    str3|str4)
        Statements;;
    *)
        Statements;;
esac
```

You can specify a number of discrete values—such as `str1`, `str2`, and so on—for each condition, or you can specify a value with a wildcard. The last condition should be an asterisk (`*`) and is executed if none of the other conditions are met. For each of the specified conditions, all the associated statements until the double semicolon (`;;`) are executed.

You can write a script that will echo the name of the month if you provide the month number as a parameter. If you provide a number that isn't between 1 and 12, you get an error message. The script is as follows:

```
#!/bin/sh

case $1 in
    01 | 1) echo "Month is January";;
    02 | 2) echo "Month is February";;
    03 | 3) echo "Month is March";;
    04 | 4) echo "Month is April";;
    05 | 5) echo "Month is May";;
    06 | 6) echo "Month is June";;
    07 | 7) echo "Month is July";;
```

```
08 | 8) echo "Month is August";;
09 | 9) echo "Month is September";;
10) echo "Month is October";;
11) echo "Month is November";;
12) echo "Month is December";;
*) echo "Invalid parameter";;
esac
```

You need to end the statements under each condition with a double semicolon (;;). If you do not, the statements under the next condition are also executed.

The format for a case statement for tcsh is as follows:

```
switch (str)
    case str1|str2:
        Statements
        breaksw
    case str3|str4:
        Statements
        breaksw
    default:
        Statements
        breaksw
endsw
```

You can specify a number of discrete values—such as str1, str2, and so on—for each condition, or you can specify a value with a wildcard. The last condition should be default and is executed if none of the other conditions are met. For each of the specified conditions, all the associated statements until breaksw are executed.

The example that echoes the month when a number is given, shown earlier for pdksh and bash, can be written in tcsh as follows:

```
#!/bin/tcsh

set month = 5
switch ( $month )
    case 1: echo "Month is January" ;   breaksw
    case 2: echo "Month is February" ;   breaksw
    case 3: echo "Month is March" ;   breaksw
    case 4: echo "Month is April" ;   breaksw
    case 5: echo "Month is May" ;  breaksw
    case 6: echo "Month is June" ;   breaksw
    case 7: echo "Month is July" ;   breaksw
    case 8: echo "Month is August"  ;   breaksw
    case 9: echo "Month is September" ;   breaksw
```

```
    case 10: echo "Month is October"  ;   breaksw
    case 11: echo "Month is November"  ;   breaksw
    case 12: echo "Month is December"  ;   breaksw
    default: echo "Oops! Month is Octember!"  ;   breaksw
endsw
```

You need to end the statements under each condition with breaksw. If you do not, the statements under the next condition are also executed.

The break and exit Statements

You should be aware of two other statements: the break statement and the exit statement.

The break statement can be used to terminate an iteration loop, such as a for, until, or repeat command.

exit statements can be used to exit a shell program. You can optionally use a number after exit. If the current shell program has been called by another shell program, the calling program can check for the code (the $? or $status variable, depending on shell) and make a decision accordingly.

Using Functions in Shell Scripts

As with other programming languages, shell programs also support functions. A function is a piece of a shell program that performs a particular process; you can reuse the same function multiple times within the shell program. Functions help eliminate the need for duplicating code as you write shell programs.

The following is the format of a function in pdksh and bash:

```
func(){
   Statements
}
```

You can call a function as follows:

```
func param1 param2 param3
```

The parameters param1, param2, and so on are optional. You can also pass the parameters as a single string—for example, $@. A function can parse the parameters as if they were positional parameters passed to a shell program from the command line as command-line arguments, but instead use values passed inside the script. For example, the following script uses a function named Displaymonth() that displays the name of the month or an error message if you pass a month number out of the range 1 to 12. This example works with pdksh and bash:

13

```
#!/bin/sh
Displaymonth() {
   case $1 in
      01 | 1) echo "Month is January";;
      02 | 2) echo "Month is February";;
      03 | 3) echo "Month is March";;
      04 | 4) echo "Month is April";;
      05 | 5) echo "Month is May";;
      06 | 6) echo "Month is June";;
      07 | 7) echo "Month is July";;
      08 | 8) echo "Month is August";;
      09 | 9) echo "Month is September";;
      10) echo "Month is October";;
      11) echo "Month is November";;
      12) echo "Month is December";;
      *) echo "Invalid parameter";;
   esac
}
Displaymonth 8
```

The preceding program displays the following output:

```
Month is August
```

References

- ▶ **www.gnu.org/software/bash/bash.html**—The bash home page at the GNU Software Project.

- ▶ **www.tldp.org/LDP/abs/html/**—Mendel Cooper's "Advanced Bash-Scripting Guide."

- ▶ **www.freeos.com/guides/lsst/**—Linux shell scripting tutorial.

- ▶ **http://kornshell.com/**—The Korn Shell website.

- ▶ **http://web.cs.mun.ca/~michael/pdksh/**—The pdksh home page.

- ▶ **www.tcsh.org/**—Find out more about tcsh here.

- ▶ **www.zsh.org/**—Examine zsh in more detail here.

CHAPTER 14

The Boot Process

In this chapter, you learn about making tasks into services that run as your system starts, and making them into services you can start and stop by hand. You also learn about the entire boot process.

After you turn on the power switch, the boot process begins with the computer executing code stored in a chip called the *BIOS*; this process occurs no matter what operating system you have installed. The Linux boot process begins when the code known as the *boot loader* starts loading the Linux kernel and ends only when the login prompt appears.

As a system administrator, you will use the skills you learn in this chapter to control your system's services and manage runlevels on your computer. Understanding the management of the system services and states is essential to understanding how Linux works (especially in a multi-user environment) and will help untangle the mysteries of a few of your Ubuntu system's configuration files. Furthermore, a good knowledge of the cron daemon that handles task scheduling is essential for administrators at all skill levels, so you will want to combine this knowledge with that in Chapter 13, "Automating Tasks and Shell Scripting."

Running Services at Boot

Although most people consider a computer to be either on or off, in Ubuntu and Linux in general, there are a number of states in between. Known as *runlevels*, they define what system services are started upon boot. These services are simply applications running in the background that provide some needed function to your system, such as getting information from your mouse and sending it to the display; or a service could monitor the partitions to see whether they have enough free space left on them. Services are typically loaded and run (also referred to as being started) during the boot process, in the same way as Microsoft Windows services are. Internally, Ubuntu uses a system known as Upstart instead of the classic and venerable SysVinit, but Upstart has a special backward-compatibility layer that can use runlevels in the way that Linux veterans are accustomed to doing for services not otherwise handled by Upstart. There is more on Upstart later in this chapter.

You can manage nearly every aspect of your computer and how it behaves after booting via configuring and ordering boot scripts and by using various system administration utilities included with Ubuntu. In this chapter, you learn how to work with these boot scripts and system administration utilities. This chapter also offers advice for troubleshooting and fixing problems that might arise with software configuration or the introduction or removal of various types of hardware from your system.

Beginning the Boot Loading Process

Although the actual boot loading mechanism for Linux varies on different hardware platforms (such as the SPARC, Alpha, or PowerPC systems), Intel-based PCs running Ubuntu most often use the same mechanism throughout product lines. This process is accomplished through a basic input/output system, or BIOS. The BIOS is an application stored in a chip on the motherboard that initializes the hardware on the motherboard (and often the hardware that's attached to the motherboard). The BIOS gets the system ready to load and run the software that we recognize as the operating system.

As a last step, the BIOS code looks for a special program known as the boot loader or boot code. The instructions in this little bit of code tell the BIOS where the Linux kernel is located, how it should be loaded into memory, and how it should be started.

If all goes well, the BIOS looks for a bootable volume such as a floppy disk, CD-ROM, hard drive, RAM disk, USB drive, or other media. The bootable volume contains a special hexadecimal value written to the volume by the boot loader application (such as Ubuntu's default GRUB2 since Ubuntu 9.10 or GRUB in older releases, or even LILO, which some older distributions used, although LILO has never been shipped by default by Ubuntu) when the boot loader code was first installed in the system's drives. The BIOS searches volumes in the order established by the BIOS settings (for example, USB first, followed by a DVD-ROM, and then a hard drive) and then boots from the first bootable volume it finds. Modern BIOSs allow considerable flexibility in choosing the device used for booting the system.

NOTE

If the BIOS detects a hardware problem, the boot process fails, and the BIOS generates a few beeps from the system speaker. These "beep codes" indicate the nature of the problem the BIOS has encountered. The codes vary among manufacturers, and the diagnosis of problems occurring during this phase of the boot process is beyond the scope of this book and does not involve Linux. If you encounter a problem, consult the motherboard manual or contact the manufacturer of the motherboard.

Next, the BIOS looks on the bootable volume for boot code in the partition boot sector also known as the *Master Boot Record (MBR)* of the first hard disk. The MBR contains the boot loader code and the partition table—think of it like an index for a book, plus a few comments on how to start reading the book. If the BIOS finds a boot loader, it loads the boot loader code into memory. At that point, the BIOSs job is completed, and it passes control of the system to the boot loader.

The boot loader locates the Linux kernel on the disk and loads it into memory. After that task is completed, the boot loader passes control of the system to the Linux kernel. You can see how one process builds on another in an approach that enables many different operating systems to work with the same hardware.

NOTE

Linux is very flexible and can be booted from multiple images on a CD-ROM, over a network using PXE (pronounced "pixie") or NetBoot, or on a headless server with the console display sent over a serial or network connection. Work is even underway to create a special Linux BIOS at www.coreboot.org/ that will expedite the boot process because Linux does not need many of the services offered by the typical BIOS.

This kind of flexibility enables Linux to be used in a variety of ways, such as remote servers or diskless workstations, which are not generally seen in personal home use.

Loading the Linux Kernel

In a general sense, the kernel manages the system resources. As the user, you do not often interact with the kernel, but instead you interact with the applications that you are using. Linux refers to each application as a process, and the kernel assigns each process a number called a *process ID (PID)*. Traditionally, the Linux kernel loads and runs a process named init, which is also known as the "ancestor of all processes" because it starts every subsequent process. Ubuntu has replaced init with Upstart, which is being written by Ubuntu developers and made available for any distribution to use, but we will walk through the traditional method first because Upstart allows for backward compatibility for those services it is not yet configured to handle. We discuss Upstart shortly.

14

This next step of the boot process traditionally begins with a message that the Linux kernel is loading, and a series of messages that are printed to the screen, giving you the status of each command. A failure should display an error message. The quiet option may be passed to the kernel at boot time to suppress many of these messages. Ubuntu does not display these messages by default, but instead uses a boot process created by the Fedora/Red Hat developers called Plymouth that is fast and incorporates a beautiful boot screen.

If the boot process were halted at this point, the system would just sit idle and the screen would be blank. To make the system useful for users, we need to start the system services. Those services are some of the applications that allow us to interact with the system.

System Services and Runlevels

The init command traditionally boots a Linux system to a specific system state, commonly referred to as its *runlevel*.

Runlevels determine which of the many available system services are started, as well as in which order they start. A special runlevel is used to stop the system, and a special runlevel is used for system maintenance. As you will see, there are other runlevels for special purposes.

You traditionally use runlevels to manage the system services running on a Linux computer. All these special files and scripts are set up during installation but you can change and control them manually.

Runlevel Definitions

The runlevels are defined in a traditional Linux system in /etc/init.d. Some distributions use the traditional /etc/inittab file to manage boot services. Ubuntu has not used this for several years since Upstart has been created and is used in the boot process, so by default, the file does not exist. However, if you have used one in the past and want to create one in Ubuntu, it will be read and honored. Because it is not standard in Ubuntu, we do not cover /etc/inittab.

Each runlevel tells the init command what services to start or stop. Although runlevels might all have custom definitions, Ubuntu has adopted some standards for runlevels:

- ▶ **Runlevel 0**—Known as "halt," this runlevel is used to shut down the system.

- ▶ **Runlevel 1**—This is a special runlevel, defined as "single," which boots Ubuntu to a root access shell prompt where only the root user may log in. It has networking, X, and multi-user access turned off. This is the maintenance or rescue mode. It allows the system administrator to perform work on the system, make backups, or repair configuration or other files.

- ▶ **Runlevel 2**—This is the default runlevel for Ubuntu.

- ▶ **Runlevels 3–5**—These runlevels aren't used in Ubuntu but are often used in other Linux distributions.

- ▶ **Runlevel 6**—This runlevel is used to reboot the system.

Runlevel 1 (also known as single-user mode or maintenance mode) is most commonly used to repair file systems and change the root password on a system when the password has been forgotten. Trespassers with physical access to the machine can also use runlevel 1 to access your system.

> **CAUTION**
>
> Never forget that uncontrolled physical access is a virtual guarantee of access to your data by an intruder.

Booting into the Default Runlevel

Ubuntu boots into runlevel 2 by default, which means it starts the system as normal and leaves you inside the X Window System looking at the graphical login prompt. It knows what runlevel 2 needs to load by looking in the rc*.d directories in /etc. Ubuntu contains directories for rc0.d through to rc5.d and rcS.d.

Assuming that the value is 1, the rc script then executes all the scripts under the /etc/rc.1 directory and then launches the graphical login.

If Ubuntu is booted to runlevel 1, for example, scripts beginning with the letter *K* followed by scripts beginning with the letter *S* under the /etc/rc1.d directory are then executed:

```
matthew@seymour:~$ ls /etc/rc1.d/
K10jackd          K20rsync            K20vboxdrv    K80cups      S70pppd-dns
K15pulseaudio     K20saned            K20winbind    README       S90single
K20acpi-support   K20saslauthd        K74bluetooth  S30killprocs
K20kerneloops     K20speech-dispatcher K77ntp       S70dns-clean
```

These scripts, as with all scripts in the rc*.d directories, are actually symbolic links to system service scripts that reside in the /etc/init.d directory.

The rc1.d links are prefaced with a letter and number, such as K15 or S10. The *K* or *S* in these prefixes indicate whether a particular service should be killed (K) or started (S) and pass a value of stop or start to the appropriate /etc/init.d script. The number in the prefix executes the specific /etc/init.d script in a particular order. The symlinks have numbers to delineate the order in which they are started. Nothing is sacred about a specific number, but some services need to be running before others are started. You would not want your Ubuntu system to attempt, for example, to mount a remote *Network File System (NFS)* volume without first starting networking and NFS services.

Understanding init Scripts and the Final Stage of Initialization

Each /etc/init.d script, or init script, contains logic that determines what to do when receiving a start or stop value. The logic might be a simple switch statement for execution, as in this example:

```
case "$1" in
  start)
        start
        ;;
  stop)
        stop
        ;;
  restart)
        restart
        ;;
  reload)
        reload
        ;;
  status)
        rhstatus
        ;;
  condrestart)
        [ -f /var/lock/subsys/smb ] && restart || :
        ;;
  *)
        echo $"Usage: $0 {start|stop|restart|status|condrestart}"
        exit 1
esac
```

Although the scripts can be used to customize the way that the system runs from power-on, absent the replacement of the kernel, this script approach also means that the system does not have to be halted in total to start, stop, upgrade, or install new services.

Note that not all scripts use this approach, and that other messages might be passed to the service script, such as restart, reload, or status. Also, not all scripts respond to the same set of messages (with the exception of start and stop, which they all have to accept by convention) because each service might require special commands.

After all the system scripts have been run, your system is configured and all the necessary system services have been started. If you are using a runlevel other than 5, the final act of the init process is to launch the user shell—bash, tcsh, zsh, or any of the many command shells available. The shell launches, and you see a login prompt on the screen.

Controlling Services at Boot with Administrative Tools

You can configure what services run at startup from the Dash with a search for Startup Applications (shown in Figure 14.1). Here Ubuntu lists all the services that you can have automatically start at boot time. They are usually all enabled by default, but you can uncheck the ones you don't want and click OK. It is not recommended that you disable services randomly "to make things go faster." Some services might be vital for the continuing operation of your computer, such as the graphical login manager and the system communication bus.

FIGURE 14.1   You can enable and disable Ubuntu's boot services by toggling the check boxes in the Services dialog.

Changing Runlevels

After making changes to system services and runlevels, you can use the `telinit` command to change runlevels on-the-fly on a running Ubuntu system. Changing runlevels this way allows system administrators to alter selected parts of a running system to make changes to the services or to put changes into effect that have already been made (such as reassignment of network addresses for a networking interface).

For example, a system administrator can quickly change the system to maintenance or single-user mode by using the `telinit` command with its S option, like this:

```
matthew@seymour:~$ sudo telinit S
```

The `telinit` command uses the init command to change runlevels and shut down currently running services.

After booting to single-user mode, you can then return to multi-user mode, like this:

```
matthew@seymour:~$ sudo telinit 2
```

TIP

Linux is full of shortcuts: If you exit the single-user shell by typing `exit` at the prompt, you go back to the default runlevel without worrying about using `telinit`.

Troubleshooting Runlevel Problems

Reordering or changing system services during a particular runlevel is rarely necessary when using Ubuntu unless some disaster occurs. But system administrators should have a basic understanding of how Linux boots and how services are controlled in order to perform troubleshooting or to diagnose problems. By using additional utilities such as the `dmesg | less` command to read kernel output after booting or by examining system logging with `cat /var/log/messages | less`, it is possible to gain a bit more detail about what is going on when faced with troublesome drivers or service failure.

To better understand how to troubleshoot service problems in Ubuntu, look at the diagnosis and resolution of a typical service-related issue.

In this example, X will not start: You don't see a desktop displayed, nor does the computer seem to respond to keyboard input. The X server might either be hung in a loop, repeatedly failing, or might exit to a shell prompt with or without an error message.

The X server only attempts to restart itself in runlevel 2, so to determine whether the X server is hung in a loop, try switching to runlevel 1.

TIP

If you are working on a multi-user system and might inadvertently interrupt the work of other users, first ask them to save their current work, and then change to a safer runlevel, such as single-user mode.

Change to runlevel 1 by running the command `telinit 1`. Changing this switch to runlevel 1 will stop the X server from attempting to restart itself.

Now you can easily examine the error and attempt to fix it.

First, try to start the X server "naked" (without also launching the window manager). If you are successful, you will get a gray screen with a large X in the middle. If so, kill X with the Ctrl+Alt+Backspace key combination, and look at your window manager configuration. (This configuration varies according to which window manager you have chosen.)

Let's assume that X won't run "naked." If we look at the log file for Xorg (it's clearly identified in the `/var/log` directory), we'll pay attention to any line that begins with (EE), the special error code. We can also examine the error log file, `.xsessions-error`, in our home directory if such a file exists.

If we find an error line, the cause of the error might or might not be apparent to us. The nice thing about the Linux community is that it is very unlikely that you are the first person to experience that error. Enter the error message (or better, a unique part of it) into www.google.com/linux and discover what others have had to say about the problem. You might need to adjust your search to yield usable results, but that level of detail is beyond the scope of this chapter. Make adjustments and retest as before until you achieve success.

Fix the X configuration and start X with startx. Repeat as necessary.

> **CAUTION**
>
> Before making any changes to any configuration file, always make a backup copy of the original, unmodified file. Our practice is to append the extension .original to the copy because that is a unique and unambiguous identifier.
>
> If you need to restore the original configuration file, do not rename it, but copy it back to its original name.

Starting and Stopping Services Manually

If you change a configuration file for a system service, it is usually necessary to stop and restart the service to make it read the new configuration. If you are reconfiguring the X server, it is often convenient to change from runlevel 2 to runlevel 1 to make testing easier and then switch back to runlevel 2 to reenable the graphical login. If a service is improperly configured, it is easier to stop and restart it until you have it configured correctly than it is to reboot the entire machine.

The traditional way to manage a service (as root) is to call the service's /etc/init.d name on the command line with an appropriate keyword, such as start, status, or stop. For example, to start the Apache web server, call the /etc/init.d/apache2 script like this:

```
sudo /etc/init.d/apache2 start
Starting apache 2.2 web server                           [  OK  ]
```

The script executes the proper programs and reports the status of them. Stopping services is equally easy, using the stop keyword.

Using Upstart

Upstart was originally developed for Ubuntu. It is currently in use by a growing number of distributions including Fedora (9 and later), Nokia's Maemo platform, and Google's Chrome OS. Upstart is an event-based replacement for the /sbin/init daemon and System-V init system. It handles starting of tasks and services during boot and stops them during shutdown. It also supervises them while the system is running and is intended to become a way to have tasks and services start or stop automatically based on specific events that happen rather than having to call a script manually to start or stop them. This is a big change and a big deal because it will make the overall system much more flexible, configurable, and responsive to conditions.

Basically, in Upstart, tasks and services are started and stopped by events. Events are generated as other tasks and services are started and stopped and may be received from any other process on the system. Services may be respawned if they die unexpectedly and communication with the init daemon occurs over D-Bus. Planned features that have not yet been implemented include the ability for events to be created at timed intervals or at scheduled times or as files or directories are changed and the creation of user services that users can start and stop themselves. This means that eventually Upstart jobs could even replace the venerable cron and do things previously impossible on any UNIX or Linux version.

For now, Upstart is being used for boot and shutdown, and not all services have Upstart jobs written. Those that exist reside as expected in /etc/init and are easily accessible in the same basic manner as init jobs. If an Upstart job exists and you try to manage it using the traditional method, you get a message like this:

```
matthew@seymour:~$ sudo /etc/init.d/ufw stop
```

Instead of invoking init scripts through /etc/init.d, use the service(8) utility (for example, service ufw stop). Because the script you are attempting to invoke has been converted to an Upstart job, you may also use the stop(8) utility (for example, stop ufw).

In this case, to start or stop Ubuntu's *Uncomplicated Firewall (UFW)*, you just enter sudo start ufw or sudo stop ufw. Simple.

Upstart is still quite new and in heavy development. Not much documentation exists, and this is on purpose. Processes and features are not yet set in stone, so while the foundation is being extended, the development team felt it best to keep the details a bit muddy to keep information that is changing quickly from propagating and requiring a ton of work or making it impossible to fix or replace incorrect or changed information later in the public knowledgebase. If you want to learn more about Upstart, start with http://upstart. ubuntu.com/. More details are expected to be released as development continues, but if you are the impatient type who loves to play with the latest shiny toy and aren't afraid of getting your hands dirty, then with some digging, you should be able to find what you want or need using the website and the examples already installed on your computer.

References

▶ **http://usr/src/linux/init/main.c**—The best place to learn about how Linux boots. Fascinating reading, really. Get it from the source. You need to have the kernel source installed to read this.

▶ **https://help.ubuntu.com/community/Grub2**—Ubuntu community documentation for GRUB2.

▶ **www.ibm.com/developerworks/linux/library/l-grub2/index.html**—An IBM guide for migrating to GRUB2. The still yet-to-be-completed manual can be found at www. gnu.org/software/grub/manual/.

# CHAPTER 15

System-Monitoring Tools

To keep your system in optimum shape, you need to be able to monitor it closely. This is imperative in a corporate environment where uptime is vital and any system failures and downtime can be quite expensive. Whether it is checking processes for errant daemons, or keeping a close eye on CPU and memory usage, Ubuntu provides a wealth of utilities designed to give you as little or as much feedback as you want. This chapter looks at some of the basic monitoring tools, along with some tactics designed to keep your system up longer. Some of the monitoring tools cover network connectivity, memory, and hard drive usage, and in this chapter, you learn how to manipulate active system processes using a mixture of graphical and command-line tools.

Console-Based Monitoring

Those familiar with UNIX system administration already know the ps, or process display, command commonly found on most flavors of UNIX. Because of the close relationship between Linux and UNIX, it also includes this command, which enables you to see the current processes running on the system and who owns them and how resource-hungry they are.

Although the Linux kernel has its own distinct architecture and memory management, it also benefits from enhanced use of the /proc file system, the virtual file system found on many UNIX flavors. Through the /proc file system, you can communicate directly with the kernel to get a deep view of what is currently happening. Developers tend to use the /proc file system as a way of extracting information from the kernel and for their programs to manipulate that information into human-readable formats. A full discussion of the /proc file system is beyond the scope of this book. To get a better idea of what it contains, you can take a look at http://en.tldp.org/LDP/Linux-Filesystem-Hierarchy/html/proc.html for an excellent and in-depth guide.

Processes can also be controlled at the command line, which is important because you might sometimes have only a command-line interface. Whenever an application or command is launched, either from the command line or a clicked icon, the process that comes from the kernel is assigned an identification number called a *process ID (PID)*. This number is shown in the shell if the program is launched via the command line:

```
matthew@seymour:~$ gedit &
[1] 9649
```

In this example, gedit has been launched in the background, and the (bash) shell reported a shell job number ([1] in this case). A job number or job control is a shell-specific feature that allows a different form of process control, such as sending or suspending programs to the background and retrieving background jobs to the foreground. (See your shell's man pages for more information if you are not using bash.)

The second number displayed (9649 in this example) represents the PID. You can get a quick list of your processes by using the ps command, like this:

```
matthew@seymour:~$ ps
  PID TTY          TIME CMD

 9595 pts/0    00:00:00 bash

 9656 pts/0    00:00:00 gedit

 9657 pts/0    00:00:00 ps
```

As you can see, the output includes the PID along with other information such as the name of the running program. As with any UNIX command, many options are available; the proc man page has a full list. One useful option is -e, which lists all processes running on the system. Another is aux, which provides a more detailed list of all the processes. You should also know that ps works not by polling memory, but through the interrogation of the Linux /proc or process file system.

The /proc directory contains many files, some of which include constantly updated hardware information (such as battery power levels and so on). Linux administrators often pipe the output of ps through grep to display information about a specific program, like this:

```
matthew@seymour:~$ ps aux | grep bash
matthew      9656  0.0  0.1  21660  4460 pts/0    Ss   11:39   0:00 bash
```

This example returns the owner (the user who launched the program) and the PID, along with other information such as the percentage of CPU and memory usage, size of the command (code, data, and stack), time (or date) the command was launched, and name of the command. Processes can also be queried by PID as follows:

```
matthew@seymour:~$ ps 9656
   PID TTY       STAT   TIME COMMAND
  9656 pts/0      S     0:00 gedit
```

You can use the PID to stop a running process by using the shell's built-in `kill` command. This command asks the kernel to stop a running process and reclaim system memory. For example, to stop gedit in the example, use the `kill` command like this:

```
matthew@seymour:~$ kill 9656
```

After you press Enter, and then press Enter again, the shell reports the following:

```
[1]+  Terminated              gedit
```

Note that users can kill only their own processes, but root can kill them all. Controlling any other running process requires root permission, which should be used judiciously (especially when forcing a kill by using the -9 option); by inadvertently killing the wrong process through a typo in the command, you could bring down an active system.

Using the `kill` Command to Control Processes

The `kill` command is a basic UNIX system command. You can communicate with a running process by entering a command into its interface, such as when you type into a text editor. But some processes (usually system processes rather than application processes) run without such an interface, and you need a way to communicate with them as well, so we use a system of signals. The `kill` system accomplishes that by sending a signal to a process, and you can use it to communicate with any process. The general format of the `kill` command is as follows:

```
matthew@seymour:~$ kill option PID
```

Note that if you are using `kill` on a process you do not own, you need to have super user privileges and preface the `kill` command with `sudo`.

A number of signal options can be sent as words or numbers, but most are of interest only to programmers. One of the most common is the one we used previously to kill `gedit`:

```
matthew@seymour:~$ kill PID
```

This tells the process with PID to stop; you supply the actual PID. However, without a signal option, there is no guarantee that a process will be killed because programs can catch, block, or ignore some terminate signals (and this is a good thing, done by design).

```
matthew@seymour:~$ kill -9 PID
```

This includes a signal for `kill` that cannot be caught (9 is the number of the `SIGKILL` signal); you can use this combination when the plain `kill` shown previously does not work. Be careful, though. Using this does not allow a process to shut down gracefully, and shutting down gracefully is usually preferred because it closes things out that the process may have been using and ensures that things such as logs are written before the process disappears.

```
matthew@seymour:~$ kill -1 PID
```

This is the signal to "hang up"—stop—and then clean up all associated processes as well (1 is the number of the `SIGHUP` signal).

As you become proficient at process control and job control, you will learn the utility of a number of `kill` options. You can find a full list of signal options in the `kill` man page.

Using Priority Scheduling and Control

No process can make use of the system's resources (CPU, memory, disk access, and so on) as it pleases. After all, the kernel's primary function is to manage the system resources equitably. It does this by assigning a priority to each process so that some processes get better access to system resources and some processes might have to wait longer until their turn arrives. Priority scheduling can be an important tool in managing a system supporting critical applications or in a situation in which CPU and RAM usage must be reserved or allocated for a specific task. Two useful applications included with Ubuntu include the `nice` and `renice` commands. (`nice` is part of the GNU `Coreutils` package, and `renice` is inherited from BSD UNIX.)

The `nice` command is used with its `-n` option, along with an argument in the range of -20 to 19, in order from highest to lowest priority (the lower the number, the higher the priority). For example, to run the Conky client with a low priority, use the `nice` command like this (more on Conky later in this chapter):

```
matthew@seymour:~$ nice -n 12 conky &
```

The `nice` command is typically used for disk- or CPU-intensive tasks that might be obtrusive or cause system slowdown. The `renice` command can be used to reset the priority of running processes or control the priority and scheduling of all processes owned by a user. Regular users can only numerically increase process priorities (that is, make tasks less important) with this command, but a user with super user privileges can use `sudo` to access the full nice range of scheduling (-20 to 19).

System administrators can also use the `time` command to get an idea of how much time and what proportion of a system's resources are required for a task, such as a shell script. (Here, `time` is used to measure the duration of elapsed time; the command that deals with civil and sidereal time is the date command.) This command is used with the name of another command (or script) as an argument like this:

```
matthew@seymour:~$ sudo time -p find / -name conky
/home/matthew/conky
/etc/conky
/usr/lib/conky

/usr/bin/conky
real 30.19
user 1.09
sys 2.77
```

Output of the command displays the time from start to finish, along with the user and system time required. Other factors you can query include memory, CPU usage, and file system *input/output (I/O)* statistics. See the time command's man page for more details.

Nearly all graphical process-monitoring tools include some form of process control or management. Many of the early tools ported to Linux were clones of legacy UNIX utilities. One familiar monitoring (and control) program is top. Based on the ps command, the top command provides a text-based display of constantly updated console-based output showing the most CPU-intensive processes currently running. It can be started like this:

```
matthew@seymour:~$ top
```

After you press Enter, you see a display, as shown in Figure 15.1. The top command has a few interactive commands: Pressing h displays the help screen; pressing k prompts you to enter the PID of a process to kill; pressing n prompts you to enter the PID of a process to change its nice value. The top man page describes other commands and includes a detailed description of what all the columns of information that top can display actually represent; have a look at top's well-written man page.

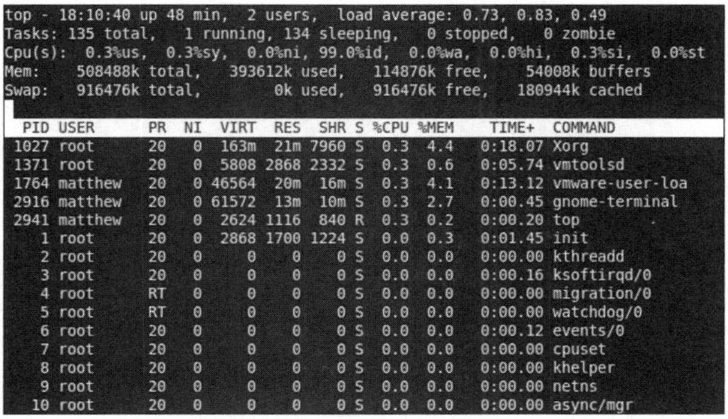

```
top - 18:10:40 up 48 min,  2 users,  load average: 0.73, 0.83, 0.49
Tasks: 135 total,   1 running, 134 sleeping,   0 stopped,   0 zombie
Cpu(s):  0.3%us,  0.3%sy,  0.0%ni, 99.0%id,  0.0%wa,  0.0%hi,  0.3%si,  0.0%st
Mem:    508488k total,   393612k used,   114876k free,    54008k buffers
Swap:   916476k total,        0k used,   916476k free,   180944k cached

  PID USER      PR  NI  VIRT  RES  SHR S %CPU %MEM    TIME+  COMMAND
 1027 root      20   0  163m  21m 7960 S  0.3  4.4  0:18.07 Xorg
 1371 root      20   0  5808 2868 2332 S  0.3  0.6  0:05.74 vmtoolsd
 1764 matthew   20   0 46564  20m  16m S  0.3  4.1  0:13.12 vmware-user-loa
 2916 matthew   20   0 61572  13m  10m S  0.3  2.7  0:00.45 gnome-terminal
 2941 matthew   20   0  2624 1116  840 R  0.3  0.2  0:00.20 top
    1 root      20   0  2868 1700 1224 S  0.0  0.3  0:01.45 init
    2 root      20   0     0    0    0 S  0.0  0.0  0:00.00 kthreadd
    3 root      20   0     0    0    0 S  0.0  0.0  0:00.16 ksoftirqd/0
    4 root      RT   0     0    0    0 S  0.0  0.0  0:00.00 migration/0
    5 root      RT   0     0    0    0 S  0.0  0.0  0:00.00 watchdog/0
    6 root      20   0     0    0    0 S  0.0  0.0  0:00.12 events/0
    7 root      20   0     0    0    0 S  0.0  0.0  0:00.00 cpuset
    8 root      20   0     0    0    0 S  0.0  0.0  0:00.00 khelper
    9 root      20   0     0    0    0 S  0.0  0.0  0:00.00 netns
   10 root      20   0     0    0    0 S  0.0  0.0  0:00.00 async/mgr
```

FIGURE 15.1 The top command can be used to monitor and control processes.

The `top` command displays quite a bit of information about your system. Processes can be sorted by PID, age, CPU or memory usage, time, or user. This command also provides process management, and system administrators can use its k and r keypress commands to kill and reschedule running tasks, respectively.

The `top` command uses a fair amount of memory, so you want to be judicious in its use and not leave it running all the time. When you've finished with it, simply press q to quit `top`.

Displaying Free and Used Memory with `free`

Although `top` includes some memory information, the free utility displays the amount of free and used memory in the system in kilobytes. (The `-m` switch displays in megabytes.) On one system, the output looks like this:

```
matthew@seymour:~$ free
              total       used       free     shared    buffers     cached
Mem:        4055680    3327764     727916          0     280944    2097568
-/+ buffers/cache:      949252    3106428
Swap:       8787512          0    8787512
```

This output describes a machine with 4GB of RAM memory and a swap partition of 8GB. Note that none of the swap is being used and that the machine is not heavily loaded. Linux is very good at memory management and "grabs" all the memory it can in anticipation of future work.

TIP

A useful trick is to employ the watch command; it repeatedly reruns a command every two seconds by default. If you use

```
matthew@seymour:~$  watch free
```

you can see the output of the free command updated every two seconds. Use Ctrl+C to quit.

Another useful system-monitoring tool is `vmstat` *(virtual memory statistics)*. This command reports on processes, memory, I/O, and CPU, typically providing an average since the last reboot; or you can make it report usage for a current period by telling it the time interval in seconds and the number of iterations you desire, like this:

```
matthew@seymour:~$ vmstat 5 10
```

This runs `vmstat` every five seconds for 10 iterations.

Use the `uptime` command to see how long it has been since the last reboot and to get an idea of what the load average has been; higher numbers mean higher loads.

Disk Space

Along with system load, it is important to keep an eye on the amount of free hard drive space that your computer has remaining.

It is easy to do this, mainly by using the df command, as follows:

```
matthew@seymour:~$ df
```

Just using the command alone returns this output:

```
Filesystem          1K-blocks        Used Available Use% Mounted on
/dev/sda1           14421344      6584528   7104256  49% /
none                 2020124          348   2019776   1% /dev
none                 2027840         2456   2025384   1% /dev/shm
none                 2027840          220   2027620   1% /var/run
none                 2027840            0   2027840   0% /var/lock
none                 2027840            0   2027840   0% /lib/init/rw

/dev/sda6          284593052    147323812 122812752  55% /home
```

Here you can see each drive as mounted on your system, as well as the used space, the available space, the percentage of the total usage of the disk, and finally where it is mounted on your system.

Unless you are good at doing math in your head, you might find it difficult to work out exactly what the figures mean in megabytes and gigabytes, so it is recommended that you use the -h switch to make the output human readable, like this:

```
matthew@seymour:~$ df -h
Filesystem          Size  Used Avail Use% Mounted on
/dev/sda1            14G  6.3G  6.8G  49% /
none                2.0G  348K  2.0G   1% /dev
none                2.0G  2.4M  2.0G   1% /dev/shm
none                2.0G  220K  2.0G   1% /var/run
none                2.0G     0  2.0G   0% /var/lock
none                2.0G     0  2.0G   0% /lib/init/rw

/dev/sda6           272G  141G  118G  55% /home
```

Disk Quotas

Disk quotas are a way to restrict the usage of disk space either by user or by groups. Although rarely—if ever—used on a local or standalone workstation, quotas are definitely a way of life at the enterprise level of computing. Usage limits on disk space not only conserve resources, but also provide a measure of operational safety by limiting the amount of disk space any user can consume.

Disk quotas are more fully covered in Chapter 12, "Managing Users."

15

Graphical Process and System Management Tools

The GNOME and KDE desktop environments offer a rich set of network and system-monitoring tools. Graphical interface elements, such as menus and buttons, and graphical output, including metering and real-time load charts, make these tools easy to use. These clients, which require an active X session and (in some cases) root permission, are included with Ubuntu.

If you view the graphical tools locally while they are being run on a server, you must have X properly installed and configured on your local machine. Although some tools can be used to remotely monitor systems or locally mounted remote file systems, you have to properly configure pertinent X11 environment variables, such as $DISPLAY, to use the software or use the ssh client's -X option when connecting to the remote host.

System Monitor

The first place to look in the standard Ubuntu desktop for a graphical monitoring tool is in the menu at System, Administration, System Monitor. This tool is informative, easy to use and understand, and very useful. It has tabs for information about your system configuration, running processes, available resources, and local file systems (see Figures 15.2 to 15.5).

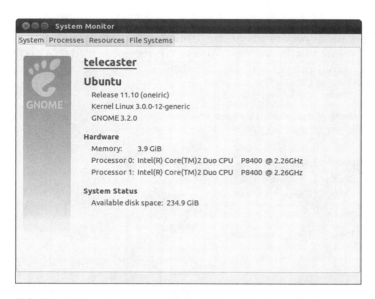

FIGURE 15.2   The System tab in System Monitor.

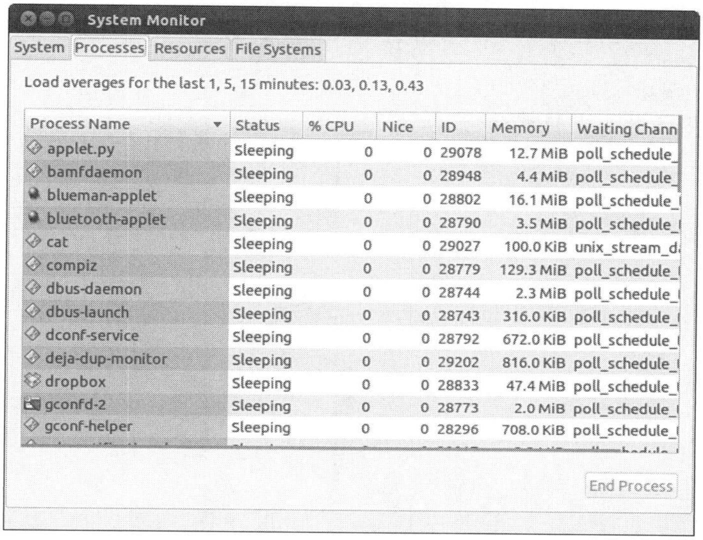

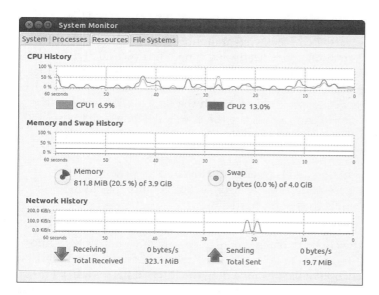

FIGURE 15.3   The Processes tab in System Monitor.

15

FIGURE 15.4   The Resources tab in System Monitor.

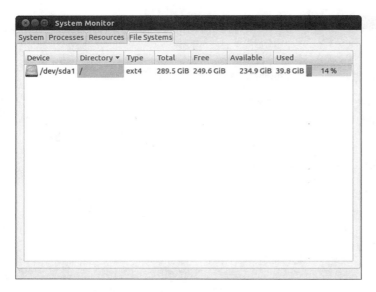

FIGURE 15.5   The File Systems tab in System Monitor.

Conky

Conky is a highly configurable, rather complex system monitor that is light on system resources and can give you information about nearly anything. The downside is that you need to learn how to configure it. Simply installing Conky from the software repositories only gets you started. However, for those of us who want specific information displayed on our desktop at all times, it is invaluable and well worth the time it takes to figure it out. We give an example here, but to truly appreciate the power, flexibility, and possibilities of Conky, visit http://conkyhardcore.com/ and this long-running thread on the Ubuntu Forums http://ubuntuforums.org/showthread.php?t=281865.

Conky uses text files for configuration and is often started using a short script. The example shown in Figure 15.6 is from Matthew's personal configuration on his desktop and is intended as a simple example to get you started.

In this example, Conky gives information about the kernel, the operating system, the hostname of the system, and the current time and date. It continually updates with information on load averages, CPU usage and temperature, battery status, and RAM and disk usage. In addition, it shows networking details, including the internal network IP address and the IP address assigned to the outside-facing router the network uses to connect to the wider world and current inbound and outbound network connections. (The IP address is assigned by the ISP, and it changes, so if you try to attack Matthew's home network using it, you will find that the IP address is being used by someone else now.) That is a lot of information in a small space. This setup is not as pretty as some you will see at the previous links, nearly all of which have their setup details made freely available by the person who wrote the configurations.

FIGURE 15.6   Conky can be configured to give up-to-the-moment information about anything.

In this example, Matthew is using two files to run Conky. The first is called conkyrc and is a text file that includes the configuration details for what you see in Figure 15.6:

```
# Use Xft?
use_xft yes
# Xft font when Xft is enabled
xftfont Ubuntu:size=9
# gap is the number of pixels from the starting point under alignment
#minimum_size 10 10
gap_x 13
gap_y 45
# Text alignment, other possible values are commented#alignment top_left
alignment top_right
#alignment bottom_left
#alignment bottom_right
# Add spaces to keep things from moving about?  This only affects certain objects.
```

```
use_spacer right
# Subtract file system buffers from used memory?
no_buffers yes
# Use double buffering (reduces flicker, may not work for everyone)
double_buffer yes
# Allows icons to appear, window to be moved, and transparency
own_window yes
own_window_type override
own_window_transparent yes
#own_window_hints undecorated,below,skip_taskbar
# set to yes if you want Conky to be forked in the background
background yes
# Update interval in seconds
update_interval 1
cpu_avg_samples 1
net_avg_samples 1
# -- start display config -
TEXT
${alignc}${color #EA6B36}$sysname kernel $kernel
${alignc}${color #EA6B36}${exec cat /etc/issue.net} on $machine host $nodename
${color #EA6B36}Time:${color #E7E7E7}    $time
${color #EA6B36}Load average:${color #E7E7E7}    $loadavg
${color #EA6B36}Current CPU usage:${color #E7E7E7}  ${color #EA6B36}CPU0:${color
#E7E7E7} ${cpu cpu0}% ${color #EA6B36}CPU1:${color #E7E7E7} ${cpu cpu1}% ${color
#EA6B36}CPU2:${color #E7E7E7} ${cpu cpu2}% ${color #EA6B36}CPU3:${color #E7E7E7}
${cpu cpu3}%

  ${color #EA6B36}CPU4:${color #E7E7E7}  ${cpu cpu4}% ${color #EA6B36}CPU5:${color
#E7E7E7} ${cpu cpu5}% ${color #EA6B36}CPU6:${color #E7E7E7} ${cpu cpu6}% ${color
#EA6B36}CPU7:${color #E7E7E7} ${cpu cpu7}%${color #EA6B36}Updates: ${color
#E7E7E7}${execi 3600 /usr/lib/update-notifier/apt_check.py --human-readable | grep
updated}

${color #EA6B36}Security: ${color #E7E7E7}${execi 3600 /usr/lib/update-
notifier/apt_check.py --human-readable | grep security}
${color #EA6B36}Status:${color #E7E7E7}    ${battery BAT0}
${color #EA6B36}CPU usage            ${alignr}PID    CPU%    MEM%
${color #E7E7E7} ${top name 1}${alignr}${top pid 1}    ${top cpu 1}    ${top mem 1}
${color #E7E7E7} ${top name 2}${alignr}${top pid 2}    ${top cpu 2}    ${top mem 2}
${color #E7E7E7} ${top name 3}${alignr}${top pid 3}    ${top cpu 3}    ${top mem 3}
${color #EA6B36}Mem usage
${color #E7E7E7} ${top_mem name 1}${alignr}${top_mem pid 1}    ${top_mem cpu 1}
${top_mem mem 1}
${color #E7E7E7} ${top_mem name 2}${alignr}${top_mem pid 2}    ${top_mem cpu 2}
${top_mem mem 2}
${color #E7E7E7} ${top_mem name 3}${alignr}${top_mem pid 3}    ${top_mem cpu 3}
```

```
${top_mem mem 3}
${color #EA6B36}RAM Usage:${color #E7E7E7} $mem/$memmax - $memperc% $membar
${color #EA6B36}Swap Usage:${color #E7E7E7} $swap/$swapmax - $swapperc% ${swapbar}
${color #EA6B36}Processes:${color #E7E7E7} $processes  ${color
#EA6B36}Running:${color #E7E7E7} $running_processes ${color #EA6B36}
${color #EA6B36}Hard disks:
  / ${color #E7E7E7}${fs_used /}/${fs_size /} ${fs_bar /}
  ${color #EA6B36}/TheLair ${color #E7E7E7}${fs_used /media/TheLair}/${fs_size
/media/TheLair} ${fs_bar /media/TheLair}
${color #EA6B36}Wireless Networking:
  ${color #EA6B36}ESSID: ${color #E7E7E7}${wireless_essid wlan0}  ${color
#EA6B36}AP: ${color #E7E7E7}${wireless_ap wlan0}
 ${color #EA6B36}${exec iwconfig wlan0 | grep "Frequency" | cut -c 24-44}
  ${color #EA6B36}Mode: ${color #E7E7E7}${wireless_mode wlan0}  ${color
#EA6B36}Bitrate: ${color #E7E7E7}${wireless_bitrate wlan0}
  ${color #EA6B36}Local IP ${color #E7E7E7}${addr wlan0}  ${color #EA6B36}Link
Quality: ${color #E7E7E7}${wireless_link_qual_perc wlan0}
  ${color #EA6B36}total download: ${color #E7E7E7}${totaldown wlan0}
  ${color #EA6B36}total upload: ${color #E7E7E7}${totalup wlan0}
  ${color #EA6B36}download speed: ${color #E7E7E7}${downspeed wlan0}${color #E7E7E7}
${color #EA6B36} upload speed: ${color #E7E7E7}${upspeed wlan0}
  ${color #E7E7E7}${downspeedgraph wlan0 15,150 ff0000 0000ff} $alignr${color
#E7E7E7}${upspeedgraph wlan0 15,150 0000ff ff0000}
${color #EA6B36}Wired Networking:
  ${color #EA6B36}Local IP ${color #E7E7E7}${addr eth0} ${color #EA6B36}
  ${color #EA6B36}total download: ${color #E7E7E7}${totaldown eth0}
  ${color #EA6B36}total upload: ${color #E7E7E7}${totalup eth0}


  ${color #EA6B36}download speed: ${color #E7E7E7}${downspeed eth0}${color #E7E7E7}
${color #EA6B36} upload speed: ${color #E7E7E7}${upspeed eth0}
  ${color #E7E7E7}${downspeedgraph eth0 15,150 ff0000 0000ff} $alignr${color
#E7E7E7}${upspeedgraph eth0 15,150 0000ff ff0000}
${color #EA6B36}Public IP ${color #E7E7E7}${execi 5 curl 'http://***a-website-that-
returns-your-ip-address-see below***'}
${color #EA6B36}Port(s) / Connections:
${color #EA6B36}Inbound: ${color #E7E7E7}${tcp_portmon 1 32767 count}  ${color
#EA6B36}Outbound: ${color #E7E7E7}${tcp_portmon 32768 61000 count}  ${color
#EA6B36}Total: ${color #E7E7E7}${tcp_portmon 1 65535 count}
${color #EA6B36}Outbound Connection ${alignr} Remote Service/Port${color #E7E7E7}
 ${tcp_portmon 1 65535 rhost 0} ${alignr} ${tcp_portmon 1 65535 rservice 0}
 ${tcp_portmon 1 65535 rhost 1} ${alignr} ${tcp_portmon 1 65535 rservice 1}
 ${tcp_portmon 1 65535 rhost 2} ${alignr} ${tcp_portmon 1 65535 rservice 2}
 ${tcp_portmon 1 65535 rhost 3} ${alignr} ${tcp_portmon 1 65535 rservice 3}
 ${tcp_portmon 1 65535 rhost 4} ${alignr} ${tcp_portmon 1 65535 rservice 4}
 ${tcp_portmon 1 65535 rhost 5} ${alignr} ${tcp_portmon 1 65535 rservice 5}
```

15

Most of these details are clear, but one is particularly interesting. There are commercial and other sites that, if you visit them, will return your IP address. This is easily accomplished in several ways. Matthew chose to put the following PHP in a file named `myip.php` on a server he owns and he calls it directly. Doing so can help you not to feel guilty about constantly hitting someone else's server for this information.

```
<?
 $remote = $_SERVER["REMOTE_ADDR"];
   echo $remote;
 ?>
```

Finally, although you can run Conky from the command line at any time after it is set up, to make it more convenient, many people choose to keep their config files in their /home directory somewhere and then write a script with the custom location. If you add a pause to the beginning of the script, you can add the script to Startup Applications (search in the Dash to find it) and have it come up after all your other desktop processes are up and running. Here is a simple example:

```
#!/bin/bash
sleep 45 &&
exec conky -d -c ~/conky/conkyrc &
# sleep 50 &&
# exec conky -d -c ~/conky/conkyrc_weather &
exit
```

Save it in /home/username/conky along with all your Conky config files, make it executable, and then have the startup applications process call it at boot. Notice that this way, you can also run more than one instance of Conky at a time, perhaps having your regular instance in the upper right of the screen and a weather instance or something else in a different location. The possibilities are vast.

Other

Graphical system- and process-monitoring tools that come with Ubuntu include the following:

▶ **vncviewer**—AT&T's open-source remote session manager (part of the Xvnc package), which can be used to view and run a remote desktop session locally. This software (discussed in more detail in Chapter 18, "Remote Access with SSH and Telnet") requires an active, background, X session on the remote computer.

▶ **gnome-nettool**—A GNOME-developed tool that enables system administrators to carry out a wide range of diagnostics on network interfaces, including port scanning and route tracing.

▶ **ethereal**—This graphical network protocol analyzer can be used to save or display packet data in real time and has intelligent filtering to recognize data signatures or patterns from a variety of hardware and data captures from third-party data-capture programs, including compressed files. Some protocols include AppleTalk, *Andrew File System (AFS)*, AOL's Instant Messenger, various Cisco protocols, and many more.

KDE Process- and System-Monitoring Tools

KDE provides several process- and system-monitoring clients. Integrate the KDE graphical clients into the desktop taskbar by right-clicking the taskbar and following the menus.

These KDE monitoring clients include the following:

▶ **kdf**—A graphical interface to your system's file system table that displays free disk space and enables you to mount and unmount file systems with a pointing device.

▶ **ksysguard**—Another panel applet that provides CPU load and memory use information in animated graphs.

Enterprise Server Monitoring

Servers used in enterprise situations require extreme uptime. It is beyond the scope of this book to discuss topics such as redundancy, failsafe and failover safeguards, and so on. However, there are a couple of tools we wanted to mention to help an enterprise sysadmin get started.

Landscape

Canonical, the company that finances much of the Ubuntu development, has a monitoring service incorporated into its systems administration tool, Landscape. Landscape has a special dashboard that gives monitoring information and creates an interface for managing multiple Ubuntu systems easily including Ubuntu Enterprise Cloud and Amazon EC2 installations. For more information, see www.canonical.com/enterprise-services/landscape.

Other

A number of top-quality monitoring tools are available. We have touched on only one of the more basic options. For more information about other enterprise server monitoring options, such as Zenoss and Nagios, take a look at https://help.ubuntu.com/community/Servers#Monitoring.

References

▶ **http://and.sourceforge.net/**—Home page of the *auto nice daemon (AND)*, which can be used to prioritize and reschedule processes automatically.

▶ **http://sourceforge.net/projects/schedutils/**—Home page for various projects offering scheduling utilities for real-time scheduling.

▶ **www.ethereal.com/**—Home page for the `ethereal` client.

▶ **https://help.ubuntu.com/community/VNC**—Setting up *Virtual Network Computing (VNC)* remote desktop software on Ubuntu.

CHAPTER 16

Backing Up

This chapter examines the practice of safeguarding data by creating backup copies, restoring that same data if necessary, and recovering data in case of a catastrophic hardware or software failure. The chapter gives you a full understanding of the reasons for sound backup practices. You can use the information here to make intelligent choices about which strategies are best for you. The chapter also shows you how to perform some types of data recovery and system restoration on your own and advises on when to seek professional assistance.

Choosing a Backup Strategy

Backups are always trade-offs. Any backup consumes time, money, and effort on an ongoing basis; backups must be monitored, validated, indexed, and stored, and new media continuously purchased. Sound expensive? The cost of not having backups is the loss of your critical data. Re-creating the data from scratch costs time and money, and if the cost of doing it all again is greater than the cost associated with backing up, you should be performing backups. At their most basic, backups are nothing more than insurance against financial loss for you or your business.

Your first step in formulating and learning to use an effective backup strategy is to choose the strategy that is right for you. First, you must understand some of the most common (and not so common) causes of data loss so that you are better able to understand the threats your system faces. Then, you need to assess your own system, how it is used and by whom, your available hardware and software resources, and your budget constraints. The following sections look at each of these issues in detail and provide some backup system examples and discuss their use.

Why Data Loss Occurs

Files disappear for any number of reasons: They can be lost because the hardware fails and causes data loss; your attention might wander and you accidentally delete or overwrite a file. Some data loss occurs as a result of natural disasters, and other circumstances beyond your control. A tornado, flood, or earthquake could strike, the water pipes could burst, or the building could catch on fire. Your data, as well as the hardware, would likely be destroyed in such a disaster. A disgruntled employee might destroy files or hardware in an attempt at retribution. And any equipment might fail, and it all will fail at some time—most likely when it is extremely important for it not to fail.

A Case in Point

A recent Harris poll of Fortune 500 executives found that roughly two-thirds of them had problems with their backups and disaster recovery plans. How about you?

Data can also be lost because of malfunctions that corrupt the data as it attempts to write to the disk. Other applications, utilities, and drivers might be poorly written, buggy (the phrase most often heard today is "still beta quality"), or might suffer some corruption and fail to correctly write that all-important data you have just created. If that happened, the contents of your data file would be indecipherable garbage of no use to anyone.

All these accidents and disasters offer important reasons for having a good backup strategy; however, the most frequent cause of data loss is human error. Who among us has not overwritten a new file with an older version or unintentionally deleted a needed file? This applies not only to data files, but also to configuration files and binaries. While perusing the mail lists, Usenet newsgroup postings, or online forums, stories about deleting entire directories such as /home, /usr, or /lib seem all too common. On a stable server that is not frequently modified or updated, you can choose to mount /usr read-only to prevent writing over or deleting anything in it. Incorrectly changing a configuration file and not saving the original in case it has to be restored (which happens more often than not because the person reconfigured it incorrectly) is another common error.

TIP

To make a backup of a configuration file you are about to edit, use the cp command:

    matthew@seymour:~$ cp filename filename.original

And to restore it, use the following:

    matthew@seymour:~$ cp filename.original filename

Never edit or move the *.original file, or the original copy will be lost. You can change the file's mode to be unwriteable; then if you try to delete it, you are prevented from doing so and receive a warning.

Proper backups can help you recover from these problems with a minimum of hassle, but you have to put in the effort to keep backups current, verify they are intact, and practice restoring the data in different disaster scenarios.

Assessing Your Backup Needs and Resources

By now you have realized that some kind of plan is needed to safeguard your data, and, like most people, you are overwhelmed by the prospect. Entire books, as well as countless articles and whitepapers, have been written on the subject of backing up and restoring data. What makes the topic so complex is that each solution is truly individual.

Yet, the proper approach to making the decision is very straightforward. You start the process by asking the following:

- ▶ What data must be safeguarded?
- ▶ How often does the data change?

The answers to these two questions determine how important the data is, determine the volume of the data, and determine the frequency of the backups. This in turn determines the backup medium. Only then can the software be selected to accommodate all these considerations. (You learn about choosing backup software, hardware, and media later in this chapter.)

Available resources are another important consideration when selecting a backup strategy. Backups require time, money, and personnel. Begin your planning activities by determining what limitations you face for all these resources. Then, construct your plan to fit those limitations, or be prepared to justify the need for more resources with a careful assessment of both backup needs and costs.

> **TIP**
>
> If you are not willing or capable of assessing your backup needs and choosing a backup solution, legions of consultants, hardware vendors, and software vendors would love to assist you. The best way to choose one in your area is to ask other UNIX and Linux system administrators (located through user groups, discussion groups, or mail lists) who are willing to share their experiences and make recommendations. If you cannot get a referral, ask the consultant for references and check them out.

Many people also fail to consider the element of time when formulating their plan. Some backup devices are faster than others, and some recovery methods are faster than others. You need to consider that when making choices.

To formulate your backup plan, you need to determine the frequency of backups. The necessary frequency of backups should be determined by how quickly the important data on your system changes. On a home system, most files never change, a few change daily, and some change weekly. No elaborate strategy needs to be created to deal with that. A

16

good strategy for home use is to back up (to any kind of removable media) critical data frequently and back up configuration and other files weekly.

At the enterprise level on a larger system with multiple users, a different approach is called for. Some critical data is changing constantly, and it could be expensive to re-create; this typically involves elaborate and expensive solutions. Most of us exist somewhere in between these extremes. Assess your system and its use to determine where you fall in this spectrum.

Backup schemes and hardware can be elaborate or simple, but they all require a workable plan and faithful follow-through. Even the best backup plan is useless if the process is not carried out, data is not verified, and data restoration is not practiced on a regular basis. Whatever backup scheme you choose, be sure to incorporate in it these three principles:

▶ **Have a plan**—Design a plan that is right for your needs and have equipment appropriate to the task. This involves assessing all the factors that affect the data you are backing up. We delve into more detail later in the chapter.

▶ **Follow the plan**—Faithfully complete each part of your backup strategy, and then verify the data stored in the backups. Backups with corrupt data are of no use to anyone. Even backup operations can go wrong.

▶ **Practice your skills**—Practice restoring data from your backup systems from time to time, so when disaster strikes, you are ready (and able) to benefit from the strength of your backup plan. (For restoring data, see the section "Using Backup Software.") Keep in mind that it is entirely possible that the flaws in your backup plan will become apparent only when you try restoring.

Sound Practices

You have to create your own best backup plan, but here are some building blocks that go into the foundation of any sound backup program:

▶ Maintain more than one copy of critical data.

▶ Label the backups.

▶ Store the backups in a climate-controlled and secure area.

▶ Use secure, offsite storage of critical data. Many companies choose bank vaults for their offsite storage, and this is highly recommended.

▶ Establish a backup policy that makes sense and can be followed religiously. Try to back up your data when the system is consistent (that is, no data is being written), which is usually overnight.

▶ Keep track of who has access to your backup media, and keep the total number of people as low as possible. If you can, allow only trusted personnel near your backups.

▶ Routinely verify backups and practice restoring data from them.

▶ Routinely inspect backup media for defects and regularly replace them (after destroying the data on them if it is sensitive).

Evaluating Backup Strategies

Now that you are convinced you need backups, you need a strategy. It is difficult to be specific about an ideal strategy because each user or administrator's strategy will be highly individualized, but here are a few general examples:

▶ **Home user**—At home, the user has the Ubuntu installation DVD that takes less than an hour to reinstall, so the time issue is not a major concern. The home user will want to back up any configuration files that have altered, keep an archive of any files that have been downloaded, and keep an archive of any data files created while using any applications. Unless the home user has a special project in which constant backups are useful, a weekly backup is probably adequate. The home user will likely use a DVD-RW, external hard drive, or other removable media for backups.

▶ **Small office**—Many small offices tend to use the same strategy as the home user, but are more likely to back up critical data daily and use manually changed tape drives. If they have a tape drive with adequate storage, they will likely have a full system backup, as well, because restoring from the tape is quicker than reinstalling from the CDs. They also might be using a CD-RW or DVD writers for backups. Although they will use scripts to automate backups, most of it is probably done by hand.

▶ **Small enterprise**—Here is where backups begin to require higher-end equipment such as autoloading tape drives with fully automated backups. Commercial backup software usually makes an introduction at this level, but a skillful system administrator on a budget can use one of the basic applications discussed in this chapter. Backups are highly structured and supervised by a dedicated system administrator.

▶ **Large enterprise**—These are the most likely setting for the use of expensive, proprietary, highly automated backup solutions. At this level, data means money, lost data means lost money, and delays in restoring data means money lost as well. These system administrators know that backups are necessary insurance and plan accordingly.

Does all this mean that enterprise-level backups are better than those done by a home user? Not at all. The "little guy" with Ubuntu can do just as well as the enterprise operation at the expense of investing more time in the process. By examining the higher-end strategies, we can apply useful concepts across the board.

16

NOTE

If you are a new system administrator, you might be inheriting an existing backup strategy. Take some time to examine it and see if it meets the current needs of the organization. Think about what backup protection your organization really needs, and determine if the current strategy meets that need. If it does not, change the strategy. Consider whether the current policy is being practiced by the users, and, if not, why it is not.

Backup Levels

UNIX uses the concept of backup levels as a shorthand way of referring to how much data is backed up in relation to a previous backup. It works this way:

A level 0 backup is a full backup. The next backup level is 1.

Backups at the other numbered levels will back up everything that has changed since the last backup at that level or a numerically higher level. (The dump command, for example, offers 10 different backup levels.) For example, a level 3 followed by a level 4 generates an incremental backup from the full backup, and a level 4 followed by a level 3 generates a differential backup between the two.

The following sections examine a few of the many strategies in use today. Many strategies are based on these sample schemes; one of them can serve as a foundation for the strategy you construct for your own system.

Simple Strategy

If you need to back up just a few configuration files and some small data files, copy them to a USB stick, engage the write-protect tab, and keep it someplace safe. If you need just a bit more backup storage capacity, you can copy the important files to a CD-RW disk (up to 700MB in size), or a DVD-RW disk (up to 8GB for data). Many users have switched to using an external hard drive for backups because they are becoming less and less expensive and hold a great amount of data.

In addition to configuration and data files, you should archive each user's /home directory and their entire /etc directory. Between the two, that backup would contain most of the important files for a small system. Then, you can easily restore this data from the backup media device you have chosen, after a complete reinstall of Ubuntu, if necessary.

Experts used to say that if you have more data than can fit on a floppy disk, you really need a formal backup strategy. Because a floppy disk only held a little over 1MB (and is now incredibly obsolete), perhaps we should change that to "if you have more data than can fit on a cheap USB stick." In any case, some formal backup strategies are discussed in the following sections. We use a tape media backup as an example for convenience because they have been incredibly popular and standard in the past and are still quite common, even as people move to new options such as portable hard drives and cloud storage.

Full Backup on a Periodic Basis

This backup strategy involves a backup of the complete file system on a weekly, bi-weekly, or other periodic basis. The frequency of the backup depends on the amount of data being backed up, the frequency of changes to the data, and the cost of losing those changes.

This backup strategy is not complicated to perform, and it can be accomplished with the swappable disk drives discussed later in the chapter. If you are connected to a network, it is possible to mirror the data on another machine (preferably offsite); the rsync tool is particularly well suited to this task. Recognize that this does not address the need for archives of the recent state of files; it only presents a snapshot of the system at the time the update is done.

Full Backups with Incremental Backups

This scheme involves performing a full backup of the entire system once a week, along with a daily incremental backup of only those files that have changed in the previous day, and it begins to resemble what a system administrator of a medium to large system traditionally uses.

This backup scheme can be advanced in two ways. In one way, each incremental backup can be made with reference to the original full backup. In other words, a level 0 backup is followed by a series of level 1 backups. The benefit of this backup scheme is that a restoration requires only two tapes (the full backup and the most recent incremental backup). But because it references the full backup, each incremental backup might be large (and grow ever larger) on a heavily used system.

Alternatively, each incremental backup could reference the previous incremental backup. This is a level 0 backup followed by a level 1, followed by a level 2, and so on. Incremental backups are quicker (less data each time), but require every tape to restore a full system. Again, it is a classic trade-off decision.

Modern commercial backup applications such as Amanda or BRU assist in organizing the process of managing complex backup schedules and tracking backup media. Doing it yourself using the classic dump or employing shell scripts to run tar requires that system administrators handle all the organization themselves. For this reason, complex backup situations are typically handled with commercial software and specialized hardware that are packaged, sold, and supported by vendors.

Mirroring Data or RAID Arrays

Given adequate (and often expensive) hardware resources, you can always mirror the data somewhere else, essentially maintaining a real-time copy of your data on hand. This is often a cheap, workable solution if no large amounts of data are involved. The use of *redundant array of independent disks (RAID)* arrays (in some of their incarnations) provides for a recovery if a disk fails.

Note that RAID arrays and mirroring systems just as happily write corrupt data as valid data. Moreover, if a file is deleted, a RAID array will not save it. RAID arrays are best suited for protecting the current state of a running system, not for backup needs.

Making the Choice

Only you can decide what is best for your situation. After reading about the backup options in this book, put together some sample backup plans; run through a few likely scenarios and assess the effectiveness of your choice.

In addition to all the other information you have learned about backup strategies, here are a couple of good rules of thumb to remember when making your choice:

- ▶ If the backup strategy and policy is too complicated (and this holds true for most security issues), it will eventually be disregarded and fall into disuse.

- ▶ The best scheme is often a combination of strategies; use what works.

Choosing Backup Hardware and Media

Any device that can store data can be used to back it up, but that is like saying that anything with wheels can take you on a cross-country trip. Trying to fit 10GB worth of data on a big stack of CD-RWs is an exercise in frustration, and using an expensive automated tape device to save a single copy of an email is a waste of resources.

Many people use what hardware they already have for their backup operations. Many consumer-grade workstations have a DVD-RW drive, but they usually do not have the abundant free disk space necessary for performing and storing multiple full backups.

In this section, you learn about some of the most common backup hardware available and how to evaluate its appropriateness for your backup needs. With large storage devices becoming increasingly affordable (2TB hard drives can now be had for around $100), decisions about backup hardware for the small business and home users have become more interesting.

Removable Storage Media

Choosing the right media isn't as easy as it used to be back when floppy drives were the only choice. Today, most machines have DVD-ROM drives that can read but not write DVDs, which rules them out for backup purposes. Instead, USB hard drives and solid-state "pen" drives have taken over the niche previously held by floppy drives. You can get a 4GB drive for under $10, and you can even get capacities up to 128GB for good prices if you shop around. Both USB hard drives and solid-state drives are highly portable. Support for these drives under Ubuntu is very good, and the storage space is rising while prices are continuing to fall. A 1TB USB external hard drive costs about $50. The biggest benefits of USB drives are data transfer speed and portability.

CD-RW and DVD+RW/-RW Drives

Compared to floppy drives and some removable drives, CD-RW drives and their cousins, DVD+RW/-RW drives, can store large amounts of data and are useful for a home or small business. CD writers and media that were once very expensive are at commodity prices today, although automated CD changing machines, necessary for automatically backing up large amounts of data, are still quite costly. A benefit of CD and DVD storage over tape devices is that the archived uncompressed file system can be mounted and its files accessed randomly just like a hard drive (you do this when you create a data CD, see Chapter 6, "Multimedia Applications"), making the recovery of individual files easier.

Each CD-RW disk can hold 650MB to 700MB of data (the media comes in both capacities at roughly the same cost); larger chunks of data can be split to fit on multiple disks. Some backup programs support this method of storage. After they are burned and verified, the shelf life for the media is at least a decade or longer.

DVD+RW/-RW is similar to CD-RW, but it is more expensive and can store up to 8GB of uncompressed data per disk.

Honestly, though, these are an old technology, and although they haven't completely died off, the use of either CDs or DVDs for backup has dropped off considerably. It won't be long before they become almost as rare as floppy disks and drives.

Network Storage

For network backup storage, remote arrays of hard drives provide one solution to data storage. With the declining cost of mass storage devices and the increasing need for larger storage space, network storage (*NAS* or *network-attached storage*) is available and supported in Linux. These are cabinets full of hard drives and their associated controlling circuitry, as well as special software to manage all of it. These NAS systems are connected to the network and act as a huge (and expensive) mass storage device.

More modest and simple network storage can be done on a remote desktop-style machine that has adequate storage space (up to eight 1TB drives is a lot of storage space, easily accomplished with off-the-shelf parts), but then that machine (and the local system administrator) has to deal with all the problems of backing up, preserving, and restoring its own data, doesn't it? Several hardware vendors offer such products in varying sizes.

Tape Drive Backup

Tape drives have been used in the computer industry from the beginning. Tape drive storage has been so prevalent in the industry that the `tar` command (the most commonly used command for archiving) is derived from the words *tape archive*. Capacities and durability of tapes vary from type to type and range from a few gigabytes to hundreds of gigabytes with commensurate increases in cost for the equipment and media. Autoloading tape-drive systems can accommodate archives that exceed the capacity of the file systems.

16

> **TIP**
>
> Older tape equipment is often available in the used equipment market and might be useful for smaller operations that have outgrown more limited backup device options.

Tape equipment is well supported in Linux and, when properly maintained, is extremely reliable. The tapes themselves are inexpensive, given their storage capacity and the ability to reuse them. Be aware, however, that tapes do deteriorate over time and, being mechanical, tape drives can and will fail.

> **CAUTION**
>
> Neglecting to clean, align, and maintain tape drives puts your data at risk. The tapes themselves are also susceptible to mechanical wear and degradation. Hardware maintenance is part of a good backup policy. Do not ever forget that it is a question of when—not if—hardware will fail.

Cloud Storage

Services such as Amazon's AWS and S3 or Canonical's Ubuntu One offer a way to create and store backups offsite. Larger companies may create their own offsite, online storage options as well. In each of these and similar cases, data is copied and stored remotely on a file server set aside specifically for that purpose. The data backups may be scheduled with great flexibility and according to the plans and desires of the customer. These are generally more expensive options than the average home user may need, but not always as shown by Ubuntu One's offer of up to 2GB of free storage that is easily kept in sync with your Ubuntu desktop with an option to increase the space for a fee.

Cloud storage is a backup solution that is recent and growing in popularity, but it is also a technology that is changing rapidly. To learn more about the options mentioned here, take a look at https://one.ubuntu.com/ and http://aws.amazon.com/s3/. Although these are not the only services of the kind available, they offer a good introduction to the concept. If you like to roll your own, you definitely want to take a look at Ubuntu Enterprise Cloud at www.ubuntu.com/cloud.

Using Backup Software

Because there are thousands of unique situations requiring as many unique backup solutions, it comes as no surprise that Linux offers many backup tools. Along with command-line tools such as tar and dd, Ubuntu also provides a graphical archiving tool for desktop installations called *Déjà Dup* that is quite powerful. Another excellent, but complicated alternative is the Amanda backup application—a sophisticated backup application that works well over network connections and can be configured to automatically back up all the computers on your network. Amanda works with drives as well as tapes.

> **NOTE**
>
> The software in a backup system must support the hardware, and this relationship can determine which hardware or software choices you make. Many system administrators choose particular backup software not because they prefer it to other options, but because it supports the hardware they own.
>
> The price seems right for free backup tools, but consider the software's ease of use and automation when assessing costs. If you must spend several hours implementing, debugging, documenting, and otherwise dealing with overly elaborate automation scripts, the real costs go up.

tar: The Most Basic Backup Tool

The tar tool, the bewhiskered old man of archiving utilities, is installed by default. It is an excellent tool for saving entire directories full of files. For example, here is the command used to back up the /etc directory:

```
matthew@seymour:~$ sudo tar cvf etc.tar /etc
```

Here, the options use `tar` to create an archive, be verbose in the message output, and use the filename `etc.tar` as the archive name for the contents of the directory `/etc`.

Alternatively, if the output of `tar` is sent to the standard output and redirected to a file, the command appears as follows:

```
matthew@seymour:~$ sudo tar cv /etc > etc.tar
```

The result is the same.

All files in the `/etc` directory will be saved to a file named `etc.tar`. With an impressive array of options (see the man page), `tar` is quite flexible and powerful in combination with shell scripts. With the `-z` option, it can even create and restore `gzip` compressed archives, and the `-j` option works with `bzipped` files.

Creating Full and Incremental Backups with `tar`

If you want to create a full backup, the following creates a `bzip2` compressed tarball (the j option) of the entire system:

```
matthew@seymour:~$ sudo tar cjvf fullbackup.tar.bz2 /
```

To perform an incremental backup, you must locate all the files that have been changed since the last backup. For simplicity, assume that you do incremental backups on a daily basis. To locate the files, use the `find` command:

```
matthew@seymour:~$ sudo find / -newer name_of_last_backup_file ! -a -type f -print
```

When run alone, `find` generates a list of files systemwide and prints it to the screen. The `!` `-a` `-type` eliminates everything but regular files from the list; otherwise, the entire directory is sent to `tar` even if the contents were not all changed.

Pipe the output of our `find` command to `tar` as follows:

```
matthew@seymour:~$ sudo find / -newer name_of_last_backup_file ! -type d -print |\
 tar czT - backup_file_name_or_device_name
```

Here, the T - option gets the filenames from a buffer (where the - is the shorthand name for the buffer).

NOTE

The `tar` command can back up to a raw device (one with no file system) and to a formatted partition. For example,

```
matthew@seymour:~$ sudo tar cvzf /dev/hdd  /boot  /etc /home
```

backs up those directories to device `/dev/hdd` (not `/dev/hda1`, but to the unformatted device itself).

The `tar` command can also back up over multiple floppy disks:

```
matthew@seymour:~$ sudo tar czvMf /dev/fd0 /home
```

This backs up the contents of /home and spreads the file out over multiple floppies, prompting you with this message:

```
Prepare volume #2 for '/dev/fd0' and hit return:
```

Restoring Files from an Archive with `tar`

The xp option in `tar` restores the files from a backup and preserves the file attributes, as well, and `tar` creates any subdirectories it needs. Be careful when using this option because the backups might have been created with either relative or absolute paths. You should use the tvf option with `tar` to list the files in the archive before extracting them so that you know where they will be placed.

For example, to restore a `tar` archive compressed with bzip2, use the following:

```
matthew@seymour:~$ sudo tar xjvf ubuntutest.tar.bz2
```

To list the contents of a tar archive compressed with bzip2, use this:

```
matthew@seymour:~$ sudo tar tjvf ubuntutest.tar.bz2
tar: Record size = 8 blocks

drwxr-xr-x matthew/matthew          0 2010-07-08 14:58 other/

-rwxr-xr-x matthew/matthew       1856 2010-04-29 14:37 other/matthew helmke public.asc

-rwxr-xr-x matthew/matthew        170 2010-05-28 18:11 backup.sh

-rwxr-xr-x matthew/matthew       1593 2009-10-11 10:38 backup method
```

Note that because the pathnames do not start with a backslash, they are relative pathnames and will install in your current working directory. If they were absolute pathnames, they would install exactly where the paths state.

The GNOME File Roller

The GNOME desktop file archiving graphical application File Roller (file-roller) will view, extract, and create archive files using `tar`, gzip, bzip, compress, zip, rar, lha, and several other compression formats. Note that File Roller is only a front end to the command-line utilities that actually provide these compression formats; if they are not installed, File Roller cannot use that format.

CAUTION

File Roller will not complain if you select a compression format that is not supported by installed software until after you attempt to create the archive. So, install any needed compression utilities first.

File Roller is well-integrated with the GNOME desktop environment to provide convenient drag-and-drop functionality with the Nautilus file manager. To create a new archive, select Archive, New to open the New Archive dialog box, and navigate to the directory where you want the archive to be kept. Type your archive's name in the Selection: /root text box at the bottom of the New Archive dialog box. Use the Archive type drop-down menu to select a compression method. Now, drag the files that you want to be included from Nautilus into the empty space of the File Roller window, and the animated icons will show that files are being included in the new archive. When you have finished, a list of files appears in the previously blank File Roller window. To save the archive, select Archive, Close. Opening an archive is as easy as using the Archive, Open dialog to select the appropriate archive file. You can learn more at https://help.ubuntu.com/community/File%20Roller.

Ubuntu also offer the KDE ark and kdat GUI tools for backups; they are installed only if you select the KDE desktop during installation, but you can search through Synaptic to find them. Archiving has traditionally been a function of the system administrator and not seen as a task for the individual user, so no elaborate GUI was believed necessary. Backing up has also been seen as a script driven, automated task in which a GUI is not as useful. Although that's true for system administrators, home users usually want something a little more attractive and easier to use, and that's the gap ark was created to fill.

The KDE ark Archiving Tool

You launch ark by launching it from the command line. It is integrated with the KDE desktop (such as File Roller is with GNOME), so it might be a better choice if you use KDE. This application provides a graphical interface for viewing, creating, adding to, and extracting from archived files. Several configuration options are available with ark to ensure its compatibility with Microsoft Windows. You can drag and drop from the KDE desktop or Konqueror file browser to add or extract files, or you can use the ark menus.

As long as the associated command-line programs are installed, ark can work with tar, gzip, bzip2, zip, and lha files (the last four being compression methods used to save space by compaction of the archived files).

Existing archives are opened after launching the application itself. You can add files and directories to the archive or delete them from the archive. After opening the archive, you can extract all of its contents or individual files. You can also perform searches using patterns (all *.jpg files, for example) to select files.

Choosing New from the File menu creates new archives. You then type the name of the archive, providing the appropriate extension (.tar, .gz, and so on), and then proceed to add files and directories as you desire.

Déjà Dup

Déjà Dup is a simple backup tool with a useful GUI. It supports local, remote, or cloud backups. It can encrypt and compress your data for secure and fast transfers and more. Search the Dash to find Déjà Dup (see Figure 16.1).

FIGURE 16.1   The Déjà Dup icon is easy to find in the Dash.

Start with Déjà Dup Backup Preferences. This menu item brings up a configuration wizard that lets you set where the backup will be stored, what will be backed, a schedule for automatic backups, and more. The following screenshots tell the story (see Figures 16.2, 16.3, and 16.4).

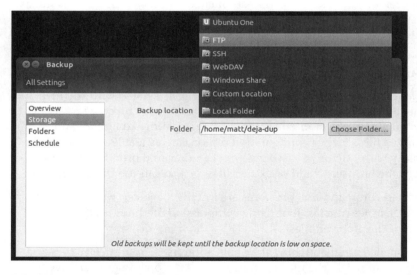

FIGURE 16.2   Storage options include cloud storage, local, via FTP or SSH, and more.

Click Close when you are done with configuration. When you are ready to run Déjà Dup at a later time, click the same icon in the Dash. This brings up the same interface showing the Overview tab. Click Restore to restore from a previous backup. Click Back Up Now to back up using the settings enabled earlier (see Figure 16.5).

FIGURE 16.3   Set the files and folders you want to back up or exclude.

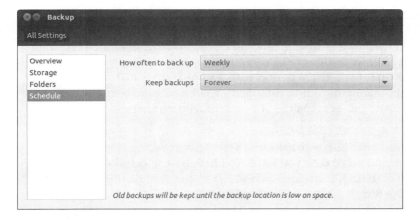

FIGURE 16.4   Set a schedule for automatic backups.

Back In Time

Back In Time is a viable alternative to Déjà Dup for many users. It is easily available from the Ubuntu Software Center, stable, has a clear and easy to understand interface, and is actually little more than a GUI front end for well-established tools.

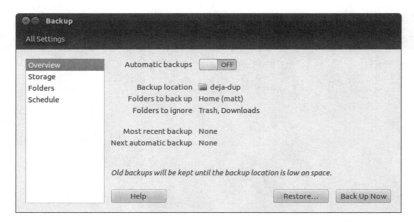

FIGURE 16.5   Backing up and restoring is easy from the Déjà Dup Overview.

Back In Time uses rsync, diff, and cp to monitor, create, and manipulate files, and it uses cron to schedule when it will run. Using these command-line tools is described later in this chapter. Back In Time is little more than a well-designed GUI front end designed for GNOME that also works well with Ubuntu's Unity interface. Back In Time also offers a separate package in the Ubuntu Software Center with a front end for KDE, if that is your preference. If you use the standard Ubuntu interface, install a package from the Ubuntu Software Center called nautilus-actions to get context menu access to some of the backup features.

The first time you run Back In Time, a snapshot of your drive is taken. This takes a long time, depending on the amount of data you have. You designate which files and directories to back up and where to back them up. Then set when to schedule the backup. The program takes care of the rest.

To restore, select the most recent snapshot from the list at the left of the screen (see Figure 16.6). Then browse through the list of directories and files at the right until you find the file that interests you. You may right-click the file to view a pop-up menu, from which you may open a file, copy a file to a desired location, or view the various snapshots of a file and compare them to determine which you might want to restore.

Back In Time keeps multiple logs of actions and activities, file changes and versions, and is a useful tool. It does have one main weakness: For the moment, it remains unable to schedule backups to be made over a network. If you are backing up to a second hard drive or if you always have a network drive mounted on your system, this is not an issue. However, if you want to back up to cloud storage or via ssh, this tool may not suit your needs.

You can find the official documentation for Back In Time at http://backintime.le-web.org.

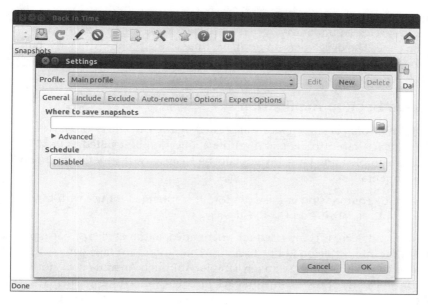

FIGURE 16.6   Back In Time makes finding and restoring files easy.

Unison

Unison is a file-synchronization tool that works on multiple platforms, including Linux, other flavors of UNIX such as Solaris and Mac OS X, and Windows. Once set up, it synchronizes files in both directions and across platforms. If changes are made on both ends, files are updated in both directions. When file conflicts arise, such as when the same file was modified on each system, the user is prompted to decide what to do. Unison can connect across a network using many protocols, including ssh. It can connect with and synchronize many systems at the same time and even to the cloud.

Unison was a project developed at the University of Pennsylvania as a research project among several academics. It is no longer under active development as a research project, but it does appear to continue to be maintained with bug fixes and very occasional feature additions. The original developers claim to still be using it daily, so it is not completely abandoned.

Unison is powerful and configurable. The foundation is based on rsync, but with some additions that enable functionality that is generally only available from a version control system. See Chapter 34, "Opportunistic Development," for an introduction to these, as well as a brief mention later in this chapter in the context of backing up configuration files.

Even though the project is no longer the primary focus of any of the developers, many people still Unison, and it still gets press, as in a recent *Linux Journal* article. For that reason, it gets a mention in this chapter and may be worthy of your time and effort if you are interested. Unison is released under the free GPL license, so you might decide you want to dig in to the code. The developers do not have time to maintain it regularly, but welcome patches and contributions. If this sounds like a project that interests you, see www.cis.upenn.edu/~bcpierce/unison/.

Using the Amanda Backup Application

Amanda is a powerful network backup application created by the University of Maryland at College Park. Amanda is a robust backup and restore application best suited to unattended backups with an autoloading tape drive of adequate capacity. It benefits from good user support and documentation.

Amanda's features include compression and encryption. It is intended for use with high-capacity tape drives, floptical, CD-R, and CD-RW devices.

Amanda uses GNU `tar` and `dump`; it is intended for unattended, automated tape backups, and is not well suited for interactive or ad hoc backups. The support for tape devices in Amanda is robust, and file restoration is relatively simple. Although Amanda does not support older Macintosh clients, it uses Samba to back up Microsoft Windows clients, as well as any UNIX client that can use GNU tools (which includes Mac OS X). Because Amanda runs on top of standard GNU tools, file restoration can be made using those tools on a recovery disk even if the Amanda server is not available. File compression can be done on either the client or server, thus lightening the computational load on less-powerful machines that need backed up.

CAUTION

Amanda does not support dump images larger than a single tape and requires a new tape for each run. If you forget to change a tape, Amanda continues to attempt backups until you insert a new tape, but those backups will not capture the data as you intended them to. Do not use too small a tape or forget to change a tape; otherwise, you will not be happy with the results.

There is no GUI for Amanda. Configuration is done in the time-honored UNIX tradition of editing text configuration files located in /etc/amanda. The default installation in Ubuntu includes a sample `cron` file because it is expected that you will be using `cron` to run Amanda regularly. The client utilities are installed with the package `amanda-client`; the Amanda server is called `amanda-server`. Install both. As far as backup schemes are concerned, Amanda calculates an optimal scheme on-the-fly and schedules it accordingly. It can be forced to adhere to a traditional scheme, but other tools are possibly better suited for that job.

The man page for Amanda (the client is `amdump`) is well written and useful, explaining both the configuration of Amanda and detailing the several programs that actually make up Amanda. The configuration files found in /etc/amanda are well commented; they provide a number of examples to assist you in configuration.

The program's home page is www.amanda.org. There you can find information about subscribing to the mail list and links to Amanda-related projects and a FAQ.

Alternative Backup Software

Commercial and other freeware backup products do exist; BRU and Veritas are good examples of effective commercial backup products. Here are some useful free software backup tools that are not installed with Ubuntu:

▶ **flexbackup**—This backup tool is a large file of Perl scripts that makes dump and restore easier to use. flexbackup's command syntax can be found by using the command with the -help argument. It also can use afio, cpio, and tar to create and restore archives locally or over a network using rsh or ssh if security is a concern. Its home page is www.edwinh.org/flexbackup/. Note that it has not received any updates or changes in a very long time.

▶ **afio**—This tool creates cpio formatted archives, but handles input data corruption better than cpio (which does not handle data input corruption very well at all). It supports multivolume archives during interactive operation and can make compressed archives. If you feel the need to use cpio, you might want to check out afio at http://freshmeat.net/projects/afio/.

Many other alternative backup tools exist, but covering all of them is beyond the scope of this book. Two good places to look for free backup software are Freshmeat (www.freshmeat.net) and Google (www.google.com/linux).

Copying Files

Often, when you have only a few files that you need to protect from loss or corruption, it might make better sense to simply copy the individual files to another storage medium rather than to create an archive of them. You can use the tar, cp, rsync, or even the cpio commands to do this, as well as a handy file management tool known as mc. Using tar is the traditional choice because older versions of cp did not handle symbolic links and permissions well at times, causing those attributes (characteristics of the file) to be lost; tar handled those file attributes in a better manner. cp has been improved to fix those problems, but tar is still more widely used. rsync has recently been added to Ubuntu and is an excellent choice for mirroring sets of files, especially when done over a network.

To illustrate how to use file copying as a backup technique, the examples here show how to copy (not archive) a directory tree. This tree includes symbolic links and files that have special file permissions we need to keep intact.

Copying Files Using `tar`

One choice for copying files into another location is to use the tar command; you just create a tar file that is piped to tar to be uncompressed in the new location. To accomplish this, first change to the source directory. Then, the entire command resembles this:

```
matthew@seymour:~$ tar -cvf files | (cd target_directory ; tar -xpf)
```

In this command, *files* are the filenames you want to include; use * to include the entire current directory.

Here is how this command works: You have already changed to the source directory and executed tar with the cvf arguments that tell tar to do the following:

▶ c—Create an archive.

▶ v—Verbose; lists the files processed so we can see that it is working.

▶ f—The filename of the archive will be what follows. (In this case, it is -.)

The following tar commands can be useful for creating file copies for backup purposes:

▶ l—Stay in the local file system (so that you do not include remote volumes).

▶ atime-preserve—Do not change access times on files, even though you are accessing them now (to preserve the old access information for archival purposes).

The contents of the tar file (held for us temporarily in the buffer, which is named -) are then piped to the second expression, which extracts the files to the target directory. In shell programming (refer to Chapter 13, "Automating Tasks and Shell Scripting"), enclosing an expression in parentheses causes it to operate in a subshell and be executed first.

First, we change to the target directory, and then:

▶ x—Extract files from a tar archive.

▶ p—Preserve permissions.

▶ f—The filename will be -, the temporary buffer that holds the files archived with tar.

Compressing, Encrypting, and Sending tar Streams

The file copy techniques using the tar command in the previous section can also be used to quickly and securely copy a directory structure across a LAN or the Internet (using the ssh command). One way to make use of these techniques is to use the following command line to first compress the contents of a designated directory, and then decompress the compressed and encrypted archive stream into a designated directory on a remote host:

```
matthew@seymour:~$ tar -cvzf data_folder | ssh remote_host '( cd ~/mybackup_dir;
tar -xvzf )'
```

The tar command is used to create, list, and compress the files in the directory named data_folder. The output is piped through the ssh (Secure Shell) command and sent to the remote computer named remote_host. On the remote computer, the stream is then extracted and saved in the directory named /mybackup_dir. You are prompted for a password to send the stream.

Copying Files Using cp

To copy files, we could use the cp command. The general format of the command when used for simple copying is as follows:

```
matthew@seymour:~$ cp -a source_directory target_directory
```

The -a argument is the same as giving -dpR, which would be as follows:

▶ **-d**—Preserves symbolic links (by not dereferencing them) and copies the files that they point to instead of copying the links.

▶ **-p**—Preserves all file attributes if possible. (File ownership might interfere.)

▶ **-R**—Copies directories recursively.

The cp command can also be used to quickly replicate directories and retain permissions by using the -avR command-line options. Using these options preserves file and directory permissions, gives verbose output, and recursively copies and re-creates subdirectories. A log of the backup can also be created during the backup by redirecting the standard output like this:

```
matthew@seymour:~$ sudo cp -avR directory_to_backup destination_vol_or_dir 1 >
/root/backup_log.txt
```

or

```
matthew@seymour:~$ sudo cp -avR ubuntu /test2 1 > /root/backup_log.txt
```

This example makes an exact copy of the directory named /ubuntu on the volume named /test2 and saves a backup report named backup_log.txt under /root.

Copying Files Using mc

The Midnight Commander (available in the Universe repository, under the package mc; see Chapter 9, "Managing Software," for how to enable the Universe and Multiverse repositories) is a command-line file manager that is useful for copying, moving, and archiving files and directories. The Midnight Commander has a look and feel similar to the Norton Commander of DOS fame. By executing mc at a shell prompt, a dual-pane view of the files is displayed. It contains drop-down menu choices and function keys to manipulate files. It also uses its own virtual file system, enabling it to mount FTP directories and display the contents of tar files, gzip tar files (.tar.gz or .tgz), bzip files, DEB files, and RPM files, as well as extract individual files from them. As if that is not enough, mc contains a File Undelete virtual file system for ext2/3 partitions. By using cd to "change directories" to an FTP server's URL, you can transfer files using FTP. The default font chosen for Ubuntu makes the display of mc ugly when used in a tty console (as opposed to an xterm), but does not affect its performance.

In the interface, pressing the F9 key drops down the menu, and pressing F1 displays the Help file. A "feature" in the default GNOME terminal intercepts the F10 key used to exit

16

mc, so use F9 instead to access the menu item to quit, or just click the menu bar at the bottom with your mouse. The configuration files are well documented, and it would appear easy to extend the functionality of mc for your system if you understand shell scripting and regular expressions. It is an excellent choice for file management on servers not running X.

Using rsync

An old favorite for backing up is rsync. One big reason for this is because rsync enables you to copy those files that have changed only since the last backup. So although the initial backup may take a long time, subsequent backups are much faster. It is also highly configurable and can be used with removable media such as USB hard drives or over a network. Here is one way to use rsync.

First, create an empty file and call it backup.sh:

matthew@seymour:~$ **sudo touch backup.sh**

Then, using your favorite text editor, enter the following command into the file and save it:

```
sudo rsync --force --ignore-errors --delete --delete-excluded --exclude-
from=/home/matthew-exclude.txt --backup --backup-dir=`date +%Y-%m-%d` -av /
/media/externaldrive/backup/seymour
```

Make the file executable:

matthew@seymour:~$ **sudo chmod +x backup.sh**

This command uses several options with rsync and puts them in a script that is quick and easy to remember and run. The script can be run at the command line using sudo sh ./backup.sh or as an automated cron job.

Here is a rundown of what is going on in the command. Basically, rsync is told to copy all new and changed files (what to back up) and delete from any existing backup any files that have been deleted on the source (and back them up in a special directory, just to be safe). It is told where to place the backup copy, and is given details on how to deal with specific issues in the process. Read the rsync man page for more options and to customize to your needs.

Following are the options used here:

▶ **--force**—Forces deletion of directories in the target location that are deleted in the source, even if the directories in the destination are not empty.

▶ **--ignore-errors**—Tells --delete to go ahead and delete files even when there are I/O errors.

▶ **--delete**—Deletes extraneous files from destination directories.

▶ **--delete-excluded**—Also deletes excluded files from destination directories.

▶ **--exclude-from=/home/matt-exclude.txt**—Prevents backing up files or directories listed in this file. (It is a simple list with each excluded directory on its own line.)

▶ **--backup**—Creates backups of files before deleting them from a currently existing backup.

▶ **--backup-dir=`date +%Y-%m-%d`**—Creates a backup directory for the previously mentioned files that looks like this: 2010-07-08.

▶ **-av**—Tells rsync to use archive mode and verbose mode.

▶ **/**—Denotes the directory to back up. In this case, it is the root directory of the source, so everything in the file system is being backed up. You could put /home here to backup all user directories, or make a nice list of directories to exclude in the file system.

▶ **/media/externaldrive/backup/seymour**—Sets the destination for the backup as the /backup/seymour directory on an external hard drive mounted at /mount/externaldrive.

To restore from this backup to the same original location, you reverse some of the details and may omit others. Something like this works nicely:

```
matthew@seymour:~$ sudo rsync --force --ignore-errors --delete --delete-excluded
/media/externaldrive/backup/seymour /
```

Version Control for Configuration Files

For safety and ease of recovery when configuration files are corrupted or incorrectly edited, the use of a version control system is recommended. In fact, this is considered an industry best practice. Many top-quality version control systems are available, such as Git, Subversion, Mercurial, and Bazaar. If you already have a favorite, perhaps one that you use for code projects, you can do what we describe in this section using that version control system. The suggestions here are to get people thinking about the idea of using version control for configuration files and to introduce a few well-used and documented options for those who are unfamiliar with version control. First, some background.

Version control systems are designed to make it easy to revert changes made to a file, even after the file has been saved. This is done a little bit differently by each system, but the basic idea is that not only is the current version of the file saved, but each and every version that existed previously is also saved. Some version control systems do this by saving the entire file every time. Some use metadata to describe just the differences between each version. In any case, it is possible to roll back to a previous version of the file, to restore a file to a state before changes were made. Developers who write software are well aware of the power and benefit to being able to do this quickly and easily; it is no longer required that the file editor remember the technical details of where, what, or even how a file has been edited. When a problem occurs, the file is simply restored to its previous state. The version control system is also able to inform the user where and how each file has changed at each save.

Using a version control system for configuration files means that every time a configuration is changed, those changes are recorded and tracked. This enables easy discovery of intruders (if a configuration has been changed by an unauthorized person trying to reset, say, the settings for Apache so that the intruder can allow a rogue web service or site to run on your server), easy recovery from errors and glitches, and easy discovery of new features or settings that have been enabled or included in the configuration by software upgrades.

Many older and well-known tools do this task, such as changetrack, which is quite a good example. All of them seek to make the job of tracking changes to configuration files easier and faster, but with the advances in version control systems, most provide very little extra benefit. Instead of suggesting any of these tools, you are probably better off learning a modern and good version control system. One exception is worth a bit of discussion because of its ability to work with your software package manager, which saves you the task of remembering to commit changes to your version control system each time the package manager runs. This exception is etckeeeeper.

etckeeper takes all of your /etc directory and stores the configuration files from it in a version control system repository. The program can be configured by editing the etckeeper.conf file to store data in a Git, Mercurial, Bazaar, or Subversion repository. In addition, etckeeper connects automatically to the APT package management tool used by Ubuntu and automatically commits changes made to /etc and the files in it during normal software package upgrades. Other package managers, such as Yum, can also be tracked when using other Linux distributions like Fedora. It even tracks file metadata that is often not easily tracked by version control systems, like the permissions in /etc/shadow.

> **WARNING**
>
> Using any version control system to track files that contain sensitive data such as passwords can be a security risk. Tracked files and the version control system itself should be treated with the same level of care as the sensitive data itself.

By default, etckeeper uses Git. On Ubuntu, this is changed to Bazaar (bzr) because it is the version control system used by Ubuntu developers. Because this is configurable, we mention just the steps here and leave it to you to adapt them for your particular favorite version control system.

First, edit /etc/etckeeper/etckeeper.conf to use your desired settings, such as the version control system to use, the system package manager being used, and whether to have changes automatically committed daily.

Once etckeeper is installed from the Ubuntu repositories, it must be initiated from the command line:

```
matthew@seymour:~$ etckeeper init
```

If you are only going to use etckeeper to track changes made to /etc when software updates are made using APT, you do not need to do anything else. If you edit files by hand, make sure you use your version control system's commands to commit those changes or use the following:

matthew@seymour:~$ **etckeeper commit "Changed prompt style"**

The message in quotes should reflect the change just made. This makes reading logs and finding exact changes much easier later.

Recovering or reverting file changes is then done using your version control system directly. Suppose, for example, that you have made a change in /etc/bash.bashrc, the file that sets the defaults for your bash shell. You read somewhere how to change the prompt and did not like the result. However, because the changes are being tracked, you can roll it back to the previous version. Because bzr is the default for etckeeper in Ubuntu, here is how you do that with bzr. First, check the log to find the commit number for the previous change:

matthew@seymour:~$ **bzr log /etc/bash.bashrc**
- -
revno: 2
committer: matthew <matthew@seymour>
branch nick: seymour etc repository
timestamp: Tue 2011-07-16 11:08:22 -0700
message:
  Changed /etc/bash.bashrc
- -
revno: 1
committer: matthew <matthew@seymour>
branch nick: seymour etc repository
timestamp: Tue 2011-07-16 11:00:16 -0700
message:
  Changed /etc/bash.bashrc
- -

I know the change was made in the most recent revision, denoted revno 2 (for revision number two), so I now revert back to that version:

matthew@seymour:~$ **bzr revert -revision 2 /etc/bash.bashrc**

Today it is common for programmers, systems administrators, and developer types to back up their dotfiles using version control. Dotfiles are the configuration files and directories in a user's /home directory, all of which begin with a dot, like .bashrc. These are not necessarily backed up by all software, and because they are often customized by highly technical people to suit their desires, backing them up is a good idea. Version control systems are commonly used. A new program for Ubuntu called *dotdee* performs this task for a different type of configuration file or directory that ends with .d and is stored in /etc. You can find more information about dotdee in Chapter 9.

System Rescue

There will come a time when you need to engage in system rescue efforts. This need arises when the system will not even start Linux so that you can recover any files. This problem is most frequently associated with the boot loader program or partition table, but it could be that critical system files have been inadvertently deleted or corrupted. If you have been making backups properly, these kinds of system failures are easily, though not quickly, recoverable through a full restore. Still, valuable current data might not have been backed up since the last scheduled backup, and the backup archives are found to be corrupt, incomplete, or missing. A full restore also takes time you might not have. If the problem causing the system failure is simply a damaged boot loader, a damaged partition table, a missing library, or misconfiguration, a quick fix can get the system up and running and the data can then be easily retrieved.

In this section, you learn a couple of quick things to try to restore a broken boot loader or recover your data when your system fails to boot.

The Ubuntu Rescue Disc

The Ubuntu installation DVD works quite well as a live DVD. To use it, insert the disc and reboot the computer, booting from the DVD just as you did when you installed Ubuntu originally and ran it from the DVD.

Restoring the GRUB2 Boot Loader

The easiest way to restore a broken system's GRUB2 files is simply to replace them. This will work with Ubuntu 9.10 or later only and only if the system uses GRUB2 (which it will if it was originally installed using 9.10 or later, but might not if Ubuntu was originally installed using an older Ubuntu release and upgraded as GRUB2 is not automatically installed during release upgrades).

To get started, boot using the live DVD and open a terminal from the menu at Applications, Accessories, Terminal. Then determine which of the hard drive's partitions holds the Ubuntu installation, which you can discover using the following:

```
matthew@seymour:~$ sudo fdisk -l
```

Unless you customized your installation, in which case you probably already know your partitioning scheme and the location of your Ubuntu installation, the partition will probably be on a drive called sda on the first partition, which you can mount now using this:

```
matthew@seymour:~$ sudo mount /dev/sda1 /mnt
```

This mounts the drive in the current file system (running from the live DVD) at /mnt, where it will be accessible to you for reading and modifying as needed. Next, you reinstall GRUB2 on this device:

```
matthew@seymour:~$ sudo grub-install -root-directory=/mnt/ /dev/sda
```

At this point, reboot (using your hard drive and not the live DVD), and all should be well. After the reboot is complete, enter the following:

```
matthew@seymour:~$ sudo update-grub
```

This refreshes the GRUB2 menu and completes the restoration. You can find a lot of great information about GRUB2 at https://help.ubuntu.com/community/Grub2.

Saving Files from a Nonbooting Hard Drive

If restoring the GRUB2 boot loader fails and you still cannot boot from the hard drive, try to use the live DVD to recover your data. Boot and mount the hard drive as shown previously, and then attach an external storage device such as a USB thumb drive or an external hard drive. Then, copy the files you want to save from the mounted drive to the external drive.

If you cannot mount the drive at all, your options become more limited and possibly more expensive. It is likely that either the hardware has failed or the files system has become badly corrupted. In either case, recovery is either impossible or more difficult and best left to experts if the data is important to you. But, the good news is that you have been making regular backups, right? So, you probably only lost a day or maybe a week of work and can buy a new drive, install it, and start from scratch, putting the data from your backup on your new Ubuntu installation on the new hardware.

Every experienced system administrator has had this happen, because no hardware is infallible. We expect occasional hardware failures, and that's why we have good backup and recovery schemes in place for data. There are two types of system administrators: those who lose data when this happens and those who have good schemes in place. Be forewarned and be wise.

If you did not have a backup, which happens to most system administrators only once in their lives (because they learn from the mistake), immediately stop messing with the hard drive. Your best bet to recover the data will be very expensive, but you should look for a company that specializes in the task and pay them to do it. If your data is not worth the expense for recovery and you want to try to recover it yourself, you can try, but this is not a task for the faint of heart, and more often than not, the data is simply lost. Again, the moral of the story is back up regularly, check your backups to be sure they are valid, and repeat. Practice restoring from backups before you need to do it, perhaps with a test system that is not vital and will not hurt anything if you make a mistake.

16

References

▶ **https://help.ubuntu.com/community/BackupYourSystem**—An excellent place to start for learning and examining backup methods in Ubuntu.

▶ **www.tldp.org/**—The Linux Documentation Project offers several useful HOWTO documents that discuss backups and disk recovery.

▶ **http://book.git-scm.com/**—The Git Community Book.

▶ **http://svnbook.red-bean.com/**—The Version Control with Subversion book.

CHAPTER 17

Networking

One of the benefits of open-source technology in general and Linux is particular is that it can be used effortlessly across several networking environments and the Internet. With strong support for the standard Internet protocol TCP/IP, Linux can talk to all the UNIX flavors, including Mac OS X, Windows (with the help of Samba), NetWare (IPX), and even older protocols such as DECNET and Banyan Vines. Many organizations use Linux as an Internet gateway, allowing many different clients to access the Internet through Linux, as well as communicate via email and instant messaging. Most important is its built-in support for IPv6, which should start to see a significant uptake very soon. It's safe to say that whatever networking protocol you'll come across, Linux will be able to work with it in some way.

This chapter covers network and Internet connectivity, as most networks invariably end up connected to the Internet in some shape or form. You learn about how to get the basics right, including configuration and management of network cards (*NICs*) and other network services with Ubuntu. You also find out how to manage network services from the command line—again an important lesson in case you are ever confined to a command prompt. We also look at connectivity options, both for inbound and outbound network traffic and the importance of *Point-to-Point Protocol (PPP)*.

We focus on the use of text interfaces and manual configurations in this chapter. We also include an overview of basic graphical network management in Ubuntu, which is becoming more and more popular. The *graphical user interface (GUI)* option has become much more stable, useful, and easy to comprehend, to the point that this will be the way most desktop users now inter-act with networking. However, this is a book for power users who want to learn about the guts of their system, so let's roll up our sleeves and prepare to get our hands dirty.

Laying the Foundation: The `localhost` Interface

The first thing that needs to be in place before you can successfully connect to a network or even to the Internet is a `localhost` interface, sometimes called a *loopback interface*, but more commonly referenced as `lo`. The TCP/IP protocol (see the section "Networking with TCP/IP" later on in this chapter) uses this interface to assign an IP address to your computer and is needed for Ubuntu to establish a PPP interface.

Checking for the Availability of the Loopback Interface

You should not normally have to manually create a loopback interface because Ubuntu creates one automatically for you during installation. To check that one is set up, you can use the `ifconfig` command, which lists all networking interfaces available, including the `lo` interface if it exists, like this:

```
matthew@seymour:~$ ifconfig

lo        Link encap:Local Loopback
          inet addr:127.0.0.1  Mask:255.0.0.0
          inet6 addr: ::1/128 Scope:Host
          UP LOOPBACK RUNNING  MTU:16436  Metric:1
          RX packets:270 errors:0 dropped:0 overruns:0 frame:0
          TX packets:270 errors:0 dropped:0 overruns:0 carrier:0
          collisions:0 txqueuelen:0
          RX bytes:20748 (20.7 KB)  TX bytes:20748 (20.7 KB)
```

What you see in this example is evidence that the loopback interface is present and active. The `inet addr` is the IP number assigned to the `localhost`, typically `127.0.0.1` along with the broadcast mask of `255.0.0.0` and that there has been little activity on this interface (`RX` = receive and `TX` = transmit). If your output does not look like the one shown previ-ously, you must hand-configure the `localhost` interface after you finish the rest of this section. You can also see the IPv6 address that is assigned to `lo`, which is `::1/128`, referred to as the `inet6 addr`.

Configuring the Loopback Interface Manually

The `localhost` interface's IP address is specified in a text configuration file that is used by Ubuntu to keep record of various network-wide IP addresses. The file is called `/etc/hosts` and usually exists on a system, even if it is empty. The file is used by the Linux kernel and other networking tools to enable them to access local IP addresses and hostnames. If you have not configured any other networking interfaces, you may find that the file looks something like this:

```
127.0.0.1    localhost
127.0.1.1    seymour
```

```
# The following lines are desirable for IPv6 capable hosts
```

```
::1     localhost ip6-localhost ip6-loopback
```

```
fe00::0 ip6-localnet
```

```
ff00::0 ip6-mcastprefix
```

```
ff02::1 ip6-allnodes
```

```
ff02::2 ip6-allrouters
```

```
ff02::3 ip6-allhosts127.0.0.1       localhost
```

The first line defines the special `localhost` interface and assigns it an IP address of `127.0.0.1`. You might hear or read about terms such as `localhost`, *loopback*, and *dummy interface*; all these terms refer to the use of the IP address `127.0.0.1`. The term *loopback interface* is used to describe how to Linux networking drivers, it looks as though the machine is talking to a network that consists of only one machine; the kernel sends network traffic to and from itself on the same computer. This is sometimes referred to as a *dummy interface* because the interface doesn't really exist; it is not a real address as far as the outside world is concerned; it exists only for the local machine, to trick the kernel into thinking that it and any network aware programs running that require a network interface to operate have one available without them actually being aware that the connection is a connection to the same machine. It is a dummy, not in the sense of stupid or silent, but in the sense that it is a mockup or substitute for something real.

Each networked Ubuntu machine on a LAN will use this same IP address for its `localhost`. If for some reason you discover that an Ubuntu computer does not have this interface, perhaps because some well-meaning person deleted it without understanding it was needed, you can edit the `/etc/hosts` file to add the `localhost` entry as you saw previously, and then use the `ifconfig` and `route` commands using your sudo permissions to create the interface like this:

```
matthew@seymour:~$ sudo /sbin/ifconfig lo 127.0.0.1
matthew@seymour:~$ sudo /sbin/route add 127.0.0.1 lo
```

These commands create the `localhost` interface in memory (all interfaces, such as `eth0` or `ppp0`, are created in memory when using Linux), and then add the IP address `127.0.0.1` to an internal (in-memory) table so that the Linux kernel's networking code can keep track of routes to different addresses.

Use the ifconfig command as shown previously to test the interface.

You should now be able to use the ping command to check that the interface is responding properly like this (using either localhost or its IP address):

```
matthew@seymour:~$ ping -c 3 localhost
PING localhost (127.0.0.1) 56(84) bytes of data.

64 bytes from localhost (127.0.0.1): icmp_seq=1 ttl=64 time=0.154 ms

64 bytes from localhost (127.0.0.1): icmp_seq=2 ttl=64 time=0.159 ms

64 bytes from localhost (127.0.0.1): icmp_seq=3 ttl=64 time=0.153 ms


--- localhost ping statistics ---

3 packets transmitted, 3 received, 0% packet loss, time 1998ms

rtt min/avg/max/mdev = 0.153/0.155/0.159/0.010 ms
```

The -c option is used to set the number of pings, and the command, if successful (as it was here), returns information regarding the round-trip speed of sending a test packet to the specified host.

The second line in the /etc/hosts file uses the actual hostname of the computer and assigns it to a similar private IP address that is unique to that computer. In the earlier code example, you can see that 127.0.1.1 is assigned to seymour, which is the computer on which that hosts file resides.

The remaining lines are used for IPv6 and can be ignored with the exception of the line that begins ::1. This is used to define the localhost connection for IPv6, which you can text with the ping6 command at the terminal, as follows:

```
matthew@seymour:~$ ping6 -c 3 ::1

PING ::1(::1) 56 data bytes

64 bytes from ::1: icmp_seq=1 ttl=64 time=0.102 ms

64 bytes from ::1: icmp_seq=2 ttl=64 time=0.140 ms
```

```
64 bytes from ::1: icmp_seq=3 ttl=64 time=0.140 ms

--- ::1 ping statistics ---

3 packets transmitted, 3 received, 0% packet loss, time 1998ms

rtt min/avg/max/mdev = 0.102/0.127/0.140/0.020 ms
```

Networking with TCP/IP

The basic building block for any network based on UNIX hosts is the *Transport Control Protocol/Internet Protocol (TCP/IP)* suite, which includes three protocols, even though only two get to be in the abbreviation. The suite consists of the *Internet Protocol (IP)*, *Transport Control Protocol (TCP)*, and *Universal Datagram Protocol (UDP)*. IP is the base protocol. The TCP/IP suite is *packet* based, which means that data is broken into little chunks on the transmit end for transmission to the receiving end. Breaking data up into manageable packets allows for faster and more accurate transfers. In TCP/IP, all data travels via IP packets, which is why addresses are referred to as IP addresses. It is the lowest level of the suite.

TCP is also a connection-based protocol. Before data is transmitted between two machines, a connection is established between them. When a connection is made, a stream of data is sent to the IP to be broken into the packets that are then transmitted. At the receiving end, the packets are put back in order and sent to the proper application port. TCP/IP forms the basis of the Internet; without it the Internet would be a very different place indeed, if it even existed. In contrast, UDP is a connectionless protocol. Applications using this protocol just choose their destination and start sending. UDP is normally used for small amounts of data or on fast and reliable networks. If you are interested in the internals of TCP/IP, see the "References" section at the end of this chapter for places to look for more information.

17

Ubuntu and Networking

Chances are that your network card was configured during the installation of Ubuntu. You can use the `ifconfig` command or Ubuntu's graphical network configuration tools to edit your system's network device information or to add or remove network devices on your system. Hundreds of networking commands and utilities are included with Ubuntu—far too many to cover in this chapter and more than enough for coverage in two or three volumes.

Nearly all Ethernet cards can be used with Linux, along with many PCMCIA wired and wireless network cards. The great news is that many USB wireless networking devices also work just fine with Linux, and more are supported with each new version of the Linux kernel. You can check the Linux USB Project at www.linux-usb.org/ for the latest developments or to verify support for your device.

After reading this chapter, you might want to learn more about other graphical network clients for use with Linux. The GNOME ethereal client (more at www.ethereal.com/), for example, can be used to monitor all traffic on your LAN or specific types of traffic. Another client, Nmap, can be used to scan a specific host for open ports and other running services (more at http://nmap.org/).

TCP/IP Addressing

To understand networking with Linux, you need to know the basics of TCP/IP addressing. Internet IP addresses (also known as *public* IP addresses) are different from those used internally on a *local area network* (LAN). Internet IP addresses are assigned (for the United States and some other hosts) by the American Registry for Internet Numbers, available at www.arin.net/. Entities that need an Internet address apply to this agency to be assigned an address. The agency assigns *Internet service providers (ISPs)* one or more blocks of IP addresses, which the ISPs can then assign to their subscribers.

You will quickly recognize the current form of TCP/IP addressing, known as *IP version 4 (IPv4)*. In this method, a TCP/IP address is expressed of a series of four decimal numbers: a 32-bit value expressed in a format known as dotted-decimal format, such as 192.168.0.1. Each set of numbers is known as an *octet* (eight 1s and 0s, such as 10000000 to represent 128) and ranges from 0 to 255.

The first octet usually determines what *class* the network belongs to. There are three classes of networks:

▶ **Class A**—Consists of networks with the first octet ranging from 1 to 126. There are only 126 Class A networks, each composed of up to 16,777,214 hosts. (If you are doing the math, there are potentially 16,777,216 addresses, but no host portion of an address can be all 0s or 255s.) The 10. network is reserved for local network use, and the 127. network is reserved for the loopback address of 127.0.0.1. Loopback addressing is used by TCP/IP to enable Linux network-related client and server programs to communicate on the same host. This address does not appear and is not accessible on your LAN.

> **NOTE**
>
> Notice that 0 is not included in Class A. The 0 address is used for network-to-network broadcasts. Also, note that there are two other classes of networks, Classes D and E. Class D networks are reserved for multicast addresses and not for use by network hosts. Class E addresses are deemed experimental, and thus are not open for public addressing.

▶ **Class B**—Consists of networks defined by the first two octets, with the first ranging from 128 to 191. The 128. network is also reserved for local network use. There are 16,382 Class B networks, each with 65,534 possible hosts.

▶ **Class C**—Consists of a network defined by the first three octets, with the first ranging from 192 to 223. The 192. network is another that is reserved for local network use. There are a possible 2,097,150 Class C networks of up to 254 hosts each.

No host portion of an IP address can be all 0s or 255s. These addresses are reserved for broadcast addresses. IP addresses with all 0s in the host portion are reserved for network-to-network broadcast addresses. IP addresses with all 255s in the host portion are reserved for local network broadcasts. Broadcast messages are not typically seen by users.

These classes are the standard, but a *netmask* also determines what class your network is in. The netmask determines what part of an IP address represents the network and what part represents the host. Common netmasks for the different classes are as follows:

▶ **Class A**—255.0.0.0

▶ **Class B**—255.255.0.0

▶ **Class C**—255.255.255.0

Because of the allocation of IP addresses for Internet hosts, it is now impossible to get a Class A network. It is also nearly impossible to get a Class B network (all the addresses have been given out, but some companies are said to be willing to sell theirs), and Class C network availability is dropping rapidly with the continued growth of Internet use worldwide.

Limits of Current IP Addressing

The current IPv4 address scheme is based on 32-bit numbering and limits the number of available IP addresses to about 4.1 billion. Many companies and organizations (particularly in the United States) were assigned very large blocks of IP addresses in the early stages of the growth of the Internet, which has left a shortage of "open" addresses. Even with careful allocation of Internet-connected host IP addresses and the use of *Network Address Translation (NAT)* to provide communication to and from machines behind an Internet-connected computer, the Internet might run out of available addresses.

To solve this problem, a newer scheme named *IP version 6 (IPv6)* is being implemented. It uses a much larger addressing solution that is based on 128-bit addresses, with enough room to include much more information about a specific host or device, such as *global positioning server (GPS)* or serial numbering. Although the specific details about the entire contents of the an IPv6 address have yet to be finalized, all Internet-related organizations appear to agree that something must be done to provide more addresses.

You can get a good overview of the differences between IPv4 and IPv6 policies regarding IP address assignments, and the registration process of obtaining IP addresses at www.arin.net/knowledge/v4-v6.html and www.arin.net/resources/request.html.

Ubuntu supports the use of IPv6 and includes a number of networking tools conforming to IPv6 addressing.

Migration to IPv6 is slow in coming, however, because the majority of computer operating systems, software, hardware, firmware, and users are still in the IPv4 mindset. Supporting IPv6 requires rewriting many networking utilities, portions of operating systems currently in use, and firmware in routing and firewall hardware.

Using IP Masquerading in Ubuntu

Three blocks of IP addresses are reserved for use on internal networks and hosts not directly connected to the Internet. The address ranges are from 10.0.0.0 to 10.255.255.255, or 1 Class A network; from 172.16.0.0 to 172.31.255.255, or 16 Class B networks; and from 192.168.0.0 to 192.168.255.255, or 256 Class C networks. Use these IP addresses when building a LAN for your business or home. Which class you choose can depend on the number of hosts on your network.

Internet access for your internal network can be provided by a PC running Ubuntu or a router. The host or device is connected to the Internet and is used as an Internet gateway to forward information to and from your LAN. The host should also be used as a firewall to protect your network from malicious data and users while functioning as an Internet gateway.

A PC used in this fashion typically has at least two network interfaces. One is connected to the Internet and the other connected to the computers on the LAN (via a hub or switch). Some broadband devices also incorporate four or more switching network interfaces. Data is then passed between the LAN and the Internet using NAT, sometimes known in Linux circles as *IP masquerading*.

NOTE

Do not rely on a single point of protection for your LAN, especially if you use wireless networking, provide dial-in services, or allow mobile (laptop or PDA) users internal or external access to your network. Companies, institutions, and individuals relying on a "moat mentality" have often discovered to their dismay that such an approach to security is easily breached. Make sure that your network operation is accompanied by a security policy that stresses multiple levels of secure access, with protection built into every server and workstation—something easily accomplished when using Linux.

Ports

Most servers on your network have more than one task. For example, web servers often have to serve both standard and secure pages. You might also be running an FTP server on the same host. For this reason, applications are provided *ports* to use to make "direct" connections for specific software services. These ports help TCP/IP distinguish services so that data can get to the correct application. If you check the file /etc/services, you will see the common ports and their usage. For example, for FTP, HTTP, and POP3 (email retrieval server), you will see the following:

```
ftp        21/tcp
http       80/tcp       http      # WorldWideWeb HTTP
pop3       110/tcp      pop-3     # POP version 3
```

The ports defined in /etc/services in this example are 21 for FTP, 80 for HTTP, and 110 for POP3. Some other common port assignments are 25 for *Simple Mail Transport Protocol (SMTP)* and 22 for *Secure Shell (SSH)* remote login. Note that these ports are not set in stone, and you can set up your server to respond to different ports. For example, although port 22 is listed in /etc/services as a common default for SSH, the sshd server can be configured to listen on a different port by editing its configuration file /etc/ssh/sshd_config. The default setting (commented out with a pound sign, #) looks like this:

```
#Port 22
```

Edit the entry to use a different port, making sure to select an unused port number, as follows:

```
Port 2224
```

Save your changes, and then restart the sshd server. (See Chapter 13, "Automating Tasks and Shell Scipting," to see how to restart a service.) Remote users must now access the host through port 2224, which can be done using ssh's -p (port) option, like this:

```
$ ssh -p 2224 remote_host_name_or_IP
```

Network Organization

Properly organizing your network addressing process grows more difficult as the size of your network grows. Setting up network addressing for a Class C network with fewer than 254 devices is simple. Setting up addressing for a large, worldwide company with a Class A network and many different users can be extremely complex. If your company has fewer than 254 *hosts* (meaning any device that requires an IP address, including computers, printers, routers, switches, and other devices) and all your workgroups can share information, a single Class C network will be sufficient.

Subnetting

Within Class A and B networks, there can be separate networks called *subnets*. Subnets are considered part of the host portion of an address for network class definitions. For example, in the 128. Class B network, you can have one computer with an address of 128.10.10.10 and another with an address of 128.10.200.20; these computers are on the same network (128.10.), but they have different subnets (128.10.10. and 128.10.200.). Because of this, communication between the two computers requires either a router or a switch. Subnets can be helpful for separating workgroups within your company.

Often subnets can be used to separate workgroups that have no real need to interact with or to shield from other groups' information passing among members of a specific workgroup. For example, if your company is large enough to have its own HR department and payroll section, you could put those departments' hosts on their own subnet and use your router configuration to limit the hosts that can connect to this subnet. This configuration prevents networked workers who are not members of the designated departments from being able to view some of the confidential information the HR and payroll personnel work with.

Subnet use also enables your network to grow beyond 254 hosts and share IP addresses. With proper routing configuration, users might not even know they are on a different subnet from their co-workers. Another common use for subnetting is with networks that cover a wide geographic area. It is not practical for a company with offices in Chicago and London to have both offices on the same subnet, so using a separate subnet for each office is the best solution.

Subnet Masks

Subnet masks are used by TCP/IP to show which part of an IP address is the network portion and which part is the host. Subnet masks are usually referred to as *netmasks*. For a pure Class A network, the netmask is 255.0.0.0; for a Class B network, the netmask is 255.255.0.0; and for a Class C network, the netmask is 255.255.255.0. Netmasks can also be used to deviate from the standard classes.

By using customized netmasks, you can subnet your network to fit your needs. For example, your network has a single Class C address. You have a need to subnet your network. Although this is not possible with a normal Class C subnet mask, you can change the mask to break your network into subnets. By changing the last octet to a number greater than zero, you can break the network into as many subnets as you need.

For more information on how to create customized subnet masks, see Day 6, "The Art of Subnet Masking," in *Sams Teach Yourself TCP/IP Network Administration in 21 Days*. That chapter goes into great detail on how to create custom netmasks and explains how to create an addressing cheat sheet for hosts on each subnet. The Linux Network Administrator's Guide also has good information about how to create subnets at www.tldp.org/LDP/nag2/index.html.

Broadcast, Unicast, and Multicast Addressing

Information can get to systems through three types of addresses: unicast, multicast, and broadcast. Each type of address is used according to the purpose of the information being sent, as explained here:

▶ **Unicast**—Sends information to one specific host. Unicast addresses are used for Telnet, FTP, SSH, or any other information that needs to be shared in a one-to-one exchange of information. Although it is possible that any host on the subnet/network can see the information being passed, only one host is the intended recipient and will take action on the information being received.

▶ **Multicasting**—Broadcasts information to groups of computers sharing an application, such as a video conferencing client or online gaming application. All the machines participating in the conference or game require the same information at precisely the same time to be effective.

▶ **Broadcasting**—Transmits information to all the hosts on a network or subnet. *Dynamic Host Configuration Protocol (DHCP)* uses broadcast messages when the DHCP client looks for a DHCP server to get its network settings, and *Reverse Address Resolution Protocol (RARP)* uses broadcast messages for hardware address to IP address resolution. Broadcast messages use .255 in all the host octets of the network IP address. (10.2.255.255 will broadcast to every host in your Class B network.)

Hardware Devices for Networking

As stated at the beginning of this chapter, networking is one of the strong points of the Linux operating system. This section covers the classes of devices used for basic networking. Note that this section talks about hardware devices, and not Linux networking devices, which are discussed in the section "Using Network Configuration Tools."

Network Interface Cards

A computer must have a *network interface card (NIC)* to connect to a network. Currently, there are several topologies (ways of connecting computers) for network connections. These topologies range from the old and mostly outdated 10BASE-2 to the much newer and popular wireless Wi-Fi or 802.11 networking.

Each NIC has a unique address (the hardware address, known as *Media Access Control [MAC]*), which identifies that NIC. This address is six pairs of hexadecimal bits separated by colons (:). A MAC address looks similar to this: 00:60:08:8F:5A:D9. The hardware address is used by DHCP (see the section "Dynamic Host Configuration Protocol," later in this chapter) to identify a specific host. It is also used by the *Address Resolution Protocol (ARP)* and *Reverse Address Resolution Protocol (RARP)* to map hosts to IP addresses.

This section covers some of the different types of NIC used to connect to your network.

Token Ring

Token Ring networking was developed by IBM. As the name implies, the network is set up in a ring. A single "token" is passed from host to host, indicating the receiving host's permission to transmit data.

Token Ring has a maximum transfer rate of 16Mbps (16 million bits per second). Unlike 10BASE-2 and 10BASE-5, Token Ring uses what is called *unshielded twisted pair (UTP)* cable. This cable looks a lot like the cable that connects your phone to the wall. Almost all Token Ring NICs are recognized by Linux.

10BASE-T

10BASE-T was the standard for a long time. A large number of networks still use it. 10BASE-T also uses UTP cable. Instead of being configured in a ring, 10BASE-T mostly uses a star architecture. In this architecture, the hosts all connect to a central location (usually a hub, which you learn about later in the "Hubs and Switches" section). All the data is sent to all hosts, but only the destination host takes action on individual packets. 10BASE-T has a transfer rate of 10Mbps.

10BASE-T has a maximum segment length of 100 meters (about 325 feet). There are many manufacturers of 10BASE-T NICs, and most are recognized by Ubuntu.

100BASE-T

100BASE-T was popular around the turn of the millennium, keeping the same ease of administration as 10BASE-T while increasing the speed by a factor of 10. For most networks, the step from 10BASE-T to 100BASE-T is as simple as replacing NICs and hubs. Most 100BASE-T NICs and hubs can also handle 10BASE-T and can automatically detect which is in use. This allows for a gradual network upgrade and usually does not require rewiring your whole network. Nearly every known 100BASE-T NIC and most generic NICs are compatible with Linux. 100BASE-T requires Category 5 UTP cabling.

1000BASE-T

1000BASE-T—usually referred to as *Gigabit Ethernet*—is the accepted standard in enterprise networking, with most NICs being detected and configured correctly by Ubuntu. Like 100BASE-T NICs, gigabit NICs automatically downgrade if they are plugged in to a slower network. Also like 100BASE-T, gigabit NICs require Category 5 UTP cabling; however, many institutions are now deploying Category 6 cables because they have much longer range and so are often worth the extra cost. You will find that most newer computers are sold with gigabit NICs.

Fiber Optic and Gigabit Ethernet

Fiber optic is more commonly used in newer and high-end installations because the cost of upgrading can be prohibitive for older sites.

Fiber optics were originally used on *fiber distributed data interface (FDDI)* networks, similar to token ring in structure except that there are two rings (one primary, the other secondary). The primary ring is used exclusively, and the secondary sits idle until there is a break in the primary ring. That is when the secondary ring takes over, keeping the network alive. FDDI has a speed of 100Mbps and has a maximum ring length of 100 kilometers (62 miles). FDDI uses several tokens at the same time that, along with the faster speed of fiber optics, account for the drastic increase in network speed.

As stated, switching to a fiber-optic network can be very costly. To make the upgrade, the whole network has to be rewired, and all NICs must be replaced at the same time. Most FDDI NICs are recognized by Linux.

Fiber-related gigabit that uses fiber-optics is termed *1000BASE-X*, whereas 1000BASE-T Gigabit Ethernet uses twisted-pair cabling (see the "Unshielded Twisted Pair" section, later in this chapter).

Wireless Network Interfaces

Wireless networking, as the name states, works without network cables and is an extremely popular option, particularly for those whose spouses do not like wires trailing everywhere. Upgrading is as easy as replacing network cards and equipment, such as routers and switches. Wireless networking equipment can also work along with the traditional wired networking using existing equipment.

It might not be practical to upgrade a desktop or large server to wireless just yet if the wiring is already in place. Wireless networking is still generally slower than a traditional wired network. However, this situation is changing with wider adoption of newer protocols, such as 802.11n (alongside the older 802.11b and the still current and common 802.11g), along with the introduction of more compliant and inexpensive wireless NICs. Some 802.11g NICs work at up to 108Mbps, which appears faster than 100BASE-T wired networking on the surface. However, in practice, it is a great deal slower: Unless your networking environment has paper-thin walls, you can usually halve the reported speed of Wi-Fi network devices, so 108Mbps works about to be about half the speed of 100BASE-T. The newer 802.11n promises to be up to seven times faster than 802.11g, but adoption of and standardization within implementations of 802.11n is going slowly.

With each new Linux kernel release, more and more wireless NICs are compatible. That said, it is usually better to get brand-name wireless NICs because you have a better chance of compatibility. Wireless networking is discussed more later in this chapter.

Network Cable

Currently, three types of network cable are available: coaxial, UTP, and fiber. Coaxial cable (rarely used today) looks a lot like the coaxial cable used to connect your television to the cable jack or antenna. UTP looks a lot like the cable that runs from your phone to the wall jack (the jacks are a bit wider). Fiber cable looks sort of like the RCA cables used on your stereo or like the cable used on your electrical appliances in your house (two separate segments connected together). The following sections discuss UTP and fiber network cable in more detail.

Unshielded Twisted Pair

UTP uses color-coded pairs of thin copper wire to transmit data. The six categories of UTP each serve a different purpose:

- **Category 1 (Cat1)**—Used for voice transmissions, such as your phone. Only one pair is used per line (one wire to transmit and one to receive). An RJ-11 plug is used to connect the cable to your phone and the wall.

- **Category 2 (Cat2)**—Used in early Token Ring networks. Has a transmission rate of 4Mbps and has the slowest data transfer rate. An RJ-11 plug is also used for cable connections.

- **Category 3 (Cat3)**—Used for 10BASE-T networks. It has a transmission rate of 10Mbps. Three pairs of cables are used to send and receive signals. RJ-11 or RJ-45 plugs can be used for Cat3 cables, usually deferring to the smaller RJ-11. RJ-45 plugs are similar in design to RJ-11, but are larger to handle up to four pairs of wire and are used more commonly on Cat5 cables.

▶ **Category 4 (Cat4)**—Used in modern Token Ring networks. It has a transmission rate of 16Mbps and is less and less common because companies are switching to better alternatives. RJ-45 plugs are used for cable connections.

▶ **Category 5 (Cat5)**—The fastest of the UTP categories with a transmission rate of up to 1000Mbps. It is used in both 100BASE-T and 1000BASE-T networks and uses four pairs of wire. Cat5 cable came out just as 10BASE-T networks were becoming popular and isn't much more expensive than Cat3 cable. As a result, most 10BASE-T networks use Cat5 UTP rather than Cat3. Cat5 cable uses RJ-45 plugs.

▶ **Category 6 (Cat6)**—Also rated at 1000Mbps, this cable is available in two forms: stranded for short runs (25-meter runs, about 80 feet) and solid for up to 100-meter runs (about 325 feet), but which should not be flexed.

Fiber-Optic Cable

Fiber-optic cable (fiber) is usually orange or red in color. The transmission rate is 100Mbps and has a maximum length of 100 kilometers (62 miles). Fiber uses a two-pronged plug to connect to devices. Fiber provides a couple of advantages because it uses light rather than electricity to transmit its signal: It is free from the possibility of electromagnetic interference, and it is also more difficult to tap into and eavesdrop.

Hubs and Switches

Hubs and switches are used to connect several hosts together on a star architecture network. They can have any number of connections; the common sizes are 4, 8, 16, 24, and 48 connections (ports); each port has a light that comes on when a network connection is made (link light). Their use enables you to expand your network easily; you can just add new hubs or switches when you need to add new connections. Each unit can connect to the other hubs or switches on the network, typically, through a port on the hub or switch called an *uplink* port. This enables two hubs or switches, connected by their uplink ports, to act as one hub or switch. Having a central location where all the hosts on your network can connect allows for easier troubleshooting of problems. If one host goes down, none of the other hosts are affected (depending on the purpose of the downed host). Because hubs and switches are not directly involved with the Linux operating system, compatibility is not an issue.

If you are constructing a small to midsize network, it is important to consider whether you intend to use either hubs or switches. Hubs and switches are visually the same in that they have rows of network ports. However, under the hood, the difference is quite important. Data is sent as packets of information across the network; with a hub the data is transmitted simultaneously to all the network ports, irrespective of which port the destination computer is attached to.

Switches, however, are more intelligent because they can direct packets of information to the correct network port that leads to the destination computer. They do this by "learning" the MAC addresses of each computer that is attached to them. In short, using switches minimizes excess packets being sent across the network, thus increasing network bandwidth available. In a small network with a handful of computers, the use of hubs might be perfectly acceptable, and you will find that hubs are generally cheaper than switches. However, for larger networks of 15 computers or more, you should consider implementing a switched network.

TIP

Troubleshooting network connections can be a challenge, especially on large networks. If a user complains that he has lost his network connection, the hub or switch is a good place to start. If the link light for the user's port is lit, chances are the problem is with the user's network configuration. If the link light is not on, the host's NIC is bad, the cable is not inserted properly, or the cable has gone bad for some reason.

Routers and Bridges

Routers and bridges are used to connect different networks to your network and to connect different subnets within your network. Routers and bridges both serve the same purpose of connecting networks and subnets, but they do so with different techniques. The information in the following sections will help you choose the connection method that best suits your needs.

Bridges

Bridges are used within a network to connect different subnets. A bridge blindly relays all information from one subnet to another without any filtering and is often referred to as a *dumb gateway*. This can be helpful if one subnet in your network is becoming overburdened and you need to lighten the load. A bridge is not very good for connecting to the Internet, however, because it lacks filtering. You really do not want all traffic traveling the Internet to be able to get through to your network.

Routers

Routers can pass data from one network to another, and they allow for filtering of data. Routers are best suited to connect your network to an outside network, such as the Internet. If you have a web server for an internal intranet that you do not want people to access from the Internet, for example, you can use a router's filter to block port 80 from your network. These filters can be used to block specific hosts from accessing the Internet, as well. For these reasons, routers are also called *smart gateways*.

Routers range in complexity and price from an enterprise-grade Cisco brand router that can cost thousands of dollars to consumer brands designed for home or small office use that can cost less than a hundred dollars.

17

Initializing New Network Hardware

All the initial network configuration and hardware initialization for Ubuntu is normally done during installation. At times, however, you could have to reconfigure networking on your system, such as when a host needs to be moved to a different subnet or a different network, or if you replace any of your computer's networking hardware.

Linux creates network interfaces in memory when the kernel recognizes that a NIC or other network device is attached to the system. These interfaces are unlike other Linux interfaces, such as serial communications ports, and do not have a corresponding device file in the /dev directory. Unless support for a particular NIC is built in to your kernel, Linux must be told to load a specific kernel module to support your NIC. More than 100 such modules are located in the /lib/modules/2.6.XX-XX/kernel/net directory (where XX-XX is your version of the kernel).

You can initialize a NIC in several ways when using Linux. When you first install Ubuntu, automatic hardware probing detects and configures your system to use any installed NICs. If you remove the original NIC and replace it with a different make and model, your system will not automatically detect and initialize the device unless you configure Ubuntu to use automatic hardware detection when booting. Ubuntu should detect the absence of the old NIC and the presence of the new NIC at boot time.

If you do not use automatic hardware detection and configuration, you can initialize network hardware by doing the following:

▶ Manually editing the /etc/modprobe.conf file to prompt the system to recognize and support the new hardware upon reboot

▶ Manually loading or unloading the new device's kernel module with the modprobe command

The following sections explain these methods in greater detail.

Editing the /etc/modprobe.conf File

This file may not be present when you first look for it, so you may need to create a blank file in a text editor. You can manually edit the /etc/modprobe.conf file to add a module dependency entry (also known as a *directive*) to support a new NIC or other network device. This entry includes the device's name and its corresponding kernel module. After you add this entry, the Linux kernel recognizes your new networking hardware upon reboot. Ubuntu runs a module dependency check upon booting.

For example, if your system uses a RealTek NIC, you could use an entry like this:

```
alias eth0 8139too
```

The example entry tells the Linux kernel to load the 8139too.o kernel module to support the eth0 network device. On the other hand, if you have an Intel Ethernet Pro NIC installed, you use an entry like this:

```
alias eth0 eepro100
```

Other parameters can be passed to a kernel module using one or more option entries, if need be, to properly configure your NIC. See the modprobe.conf man page for more information about using entries. For more specifics regarding NIC kernel modules, examine the module's source code. (No man pages are yet available [a good opportunity for anyone willing to write the documentation]).

Using modprobe to Manually Load Kernel Modules

You do not have to use an /etc/modprobe.conf entry to initialize kernel support for your new network device. As root (using sudo), you can manually load or unload the device's kernel module using the modprobe command, along with the module's name. For example, use the following command line to enable the example RealTek NIC:

matthew@seymour:~$ sudo modprobe 8139too

After you press Enter, you will see this device reported from the kernel's ring buffer messages, which you can display by using the dmesg command. Here's a portion of that command's output:

matthew@seymour:~$ **dmesg**
...
eth0: RealTek RTL8139 Fast Ethernet at 0xce8ee000, 00:30:1b:0b:07:0d, IRQ 11
eth0: Identified 8139 chip type ORTL-8139C'
eth0: Setting half-duplex based on auto-negotiated partner ability 0000.
...

Note that at this point, an IP address or other settings have not been assigned to the device. Linux can use multiple Ethernet interfaces, and the first Ethernet device is numbered eth0, the second eth1, and so on. Each different Ethernet device recognized by the kernel might have additional or different information reported, depending on its kernel module. For example:

matthew@seymour:~$ **dmesg**
...
eepro100.c:v1.09j-t 9/29/99 Donald Becker http://cesdis.gsfc.nasa.gov/linux/drive
rs/eepro100.html
eepro100.c: $Revision: 1.36 $ 2000/11/17 Modified by Andrey V. Savochkin
Ɣ<saw@saw.sw.com.sg> and others
PCI: Found IRQ 10 for device 00:0d.0
eth0: Intel Corporation 82557 [Ethernet Pro 100], 00:90:27:91:92:B5, IRQ 10.
 Board assembly 721383-007, Physical connectors present: RJ45
 Primary interface chip i82555 PHY #1.
 General self-test: passed.
 Serial sub-system self-test: passed.
 Internal registers self-test: passed.
 ROM checksum self-test: passed (0x04f4518b).
...

In this example, an Intel Ethernet Pro 100 NIC has been recognized. To disable support for a NIC, the kernel module can be unloaded, but usually only after the device is no longer in use. Read the next section to learn how to configure a NIC after it has been recognized by the Linux kernel and how to control its behavior.

Using Network Configuration Tools

If you add or replace networking hardware after your initial installation, you must configure the new hardware. You can do so using either the command line or the graphical configuration tools. To configure a network client host using the command line, you can use a combination of commands or edit specific files under the /etc directory. To configure the hardware through a graphical interface, you can use Ubuntu's graphical tool for X called nm-connection-editor, found at System, Preferences, Network Connections. This section introduces command-line and graphical software tools you can use to configure a network interface and network settings on your Ubuntu system. You'll see how to control your NIC and manage how your system interacts with your network.

Using the command-line configuration tools can seem difficult if you are new to Linux. For anyone new to networking, the nm-connection-editor graphical tool is the way to go. Both manual and graphical methods require super user privileges to work. You should not edit any scripts or settings files used by graphical network administration tools on your system. Your changes will be lost the next time the tool is run. Either use a manual approach all the time and write your own network setup script or stick to using graphical configuration utilities. Don't switch back and forth between the two methods.

Command-Line Network Interface Configuration

You can configure a network interface from the command line using the basic Linux networking utilities. You configure your network client hosts either with commands to change your current settings or by editing a number of system files. Two commands, ifconfig and route, are used for network configuration. The netstat command displays information about the network connections.

/sbin/ifconfig

ifconfig is used to configure your network interface. You can use it to do the following:

▶ Activate or deactivate your NIC or change your NIC's mode.

▶ Change your machine's IP address, netmask, or broadcast address.

▶ Create an IP alias to allow more than one IP address on your NIC.

▶ Set a destination address for a point-to-point connection.

You can change as many or as few of these options as you want with a single command. The basic structure for the command is as follows:

```
ifconfig [network device] options
```

Table 17.1 shows a subset of ifconfig options and examples of their uses.

TABLE 17.1 ifconfig Options

Use	Option	Example
Create alias	[network device]	ifconfig eth0:0_:[number] 10.10.10.10
Change IP address		ifconfig eth0 10.10.10.12
Change the netmask	netmask [netmask]	fconfig eth0 netmask 255.255.255.0
Change the broadcast	broadcast [address]	ifconfig eth0 broadcast 10.10.10.255
Take interface down	down	ifconfig eth0 down
Bring interface up	up (add IP address)	ifconfig eth0 up (ifconfig eth0 10.10.10.10)
Set NIC promiscuous	[-]promisc [ifconfig eth0 - promisc]	ifconfig eth0 promisc mode on [off]
Set multicasting mode	[-]allmulti	ifconfig eth0_on [off] allmulti [ifconfig eth0 -allmulti]
Enable or disable	[-]pointopoint [address] eth0_pointopoint	ifconfig_point-to-point address 10.10.10.20 [ifconfig eth0 pointopoint_10.10.10.20]

The ifconfig man page shows other options that enable your machine to interface with a number of network types such as AppleTalk, Novell, IPv6, and others. Again, read the man page for details on these network types.

NOTE

Promiscuous mode causes the NIC to receive all packets on the network. It is often used to sniff a network. Multicasting mode enables the NIC to receive all multicast traffic on the network.

17

If no argument is given, ifconfig displays the status of active interfaces. For example, the output of ifconfig, without arguments and one active and configured NIC, looks similar to this:

```
matthew@seymour:~$ ifconfig
eth0      Link encap:Ethernet  HWaddr 00:90:f5:8e:52:b5
          UP BROADCAST MULTICAST  MTU:1500  Metric:1
          RX packets:0 errors:0 dropped:0 overruns:0 frame:0
          TX packets:0 errors:0 dropped:0 overruns:0 carrier:0
          collisions:0 txqueuelen:1000
          RX bytes:0 (0.0 B)  TX bytes:0 (0.0 B)
          Interrupt:30 Base address:0xc000
lo        Link encap:Local Loopback
          inet addr:127.0.0.1  Mask:255.0.0.0
          inet6 addr: ::1/128 Scope:Host
          UP LOOPBACK RUNNING  MTU:16436  Metric:1
          RX packets:314 errors:0 dropped:0 overruns:0 frame:0
          TX packets:314 errors:0 dropped:0 overruns:0 carrier:0
          collisions:0 txqueuelen:0
          RX bytes:25204 (25.2 KB)  TX bytes:25204 (25.2 KB)

wlan0     Link encap:Ethernet  HWaddr 00:16:ea:d4:58:88
          inet addr:192.168.1.106  Bcast:192.168.1.255  Mask:255.255.255.0
          inet6 addr: fe80::216:eaff:fed4:5888/64 Scope:Link
          UP BROADCAST RUNNING MULTICAST  MTU:1500  Metric:1
          RX packets:325832 errors:0 dropped:0 overruns:0 frame:0
          TX packets:302754 errors:0 dropped:0 overruns:0 carrier:0
          collisions:0 txqueuelen:1000
          RX bytes:207381807 (207.3 MB)  TX bytes:40442735 (40.4 MB)
```

The output is easily understood. The inet entry displays the IP address for the interface. UP signifies that the interface is ready for use, BROADCAST denotes that the interface is connected to a network that supports broadcast messaging (ethernet), RUNNING means that the interface is operating, and LOOPBACK shows which device (lo) is the loopback address. The *maximum transmission unit (MTU)* on eth0 is 1500 bytes. This determines the size of the largest packet that can be transmitted over this interface (and is sometimes "tuned" to other values for performance enhancement). Metric is a number from 0 to 3 that relates to how much information from the interface is placed in the routing table. The lower the number, the smaller the amount of information.

The ifconfig command can be used to display information about or control a specific interface using commands that are listed in Table 17.1. For example, to deactivate the first Ethernet device on a host, use the ifconfig command, the interface name, and the command down:

```
matthew@seymour:~$ sudo ifconfig eth0 down
```

You can also configure and activate the device by specifying a hostname or IP address and network information. For example, to configure and activate (bring up) the eth0 interface with a specific IP address, use the ifconfig command:

```
matthew@seymour:~$ sudo ifconfig eth0 192.168.2.9 netmask 255.255.255.0 up
```

If you have a host defined in your system's /etc/hosts file (see the section "Network Configuration Files," later in this chapter), you can configure and activate the interface according to the defined hostname, like this:

```
matthew@seymour:~$ sudo ifconfig eth0 dogdog.hudson.com up
```

The next section explains how to configure your system to work with your LAN.

/sbin/route

The second command used to configure your network is the route command. route is used to build the routing tables (in memory) implemented for routing packets and to display the routing information. It is used after ifconfig has initialized the interface. route is normally used to set up static routes to other networks via the gateway or to other hosts. The command configuration is as follows:

```
route [options] [commands] [parameters]
```

To display the routing table, use the route command with no options. The display will look similar to this:

```
matthew@seymour:~$ route
Kernel IP routing table
```

Destination	Gateway	Genmask	Flags	Metric	Ref	Use	Iface
192.168.1.0	*	255.255.255.0	U	2	0	0	wlan0
link-local	*	255.255.0.0	U	1000	0	0	wlan0
default	WirelessAccessPt	0.0.0.0	UG	0	0	0	wlan0

In the first column, Destination is the IP address (or, if the host is in /etc/hosts or /etc/networks, the hostname) of the receiving host. The default entry is the default gateway for this machine. The Gateway column lists the gateway that the packets must go through to reach their destination. An asterisk (*) means that packets go directly to the host. Genmask is the netmask. The Flags column can have several possible entries. In our example, U verifies that the route is enabled and G specifies that Destination requires the use of a gateway. The Metric column displays the distance to the Destination. Some daemons use this to figure the easiest route to the Destination. The Ref column is used by some UNIX flavors to convey the references to the route. It isn't used by Linux. The Use column indicates the number of times this entry has been looked up. Finally, the Iface column is the name of the interface for the corresponding entry.

Using the -n option to the route command will give the same information, substituting IP addresses for names and asterisks (*), and looks like this:

```
matthew@seymour:~$ /sbin/route -n
Kernel IP routing table
 Destination    Gateway         Genmask          Flags   Metric   Ref   Use   Iface

 192.168.1.0    0.0.0.0         255.255.255.0    U       2        0     0     wlan0

 link-local     0.0.0.0         255.255.0.0      U       1000     0     0     wlan0

 0.0.0.0        192.168.1.0     0.0.0.0          UG      0        0     0     wlan0
```

The route command can add to the table using the add option. With the add option, you can specify a host (-host) or a network (-net) as the destination. If no option is used, the route command assumes that you are configuring the host issuing the command. The most common uses for the route command are to add the default gateway for a host, for a host that has lost its routing table, or if the gateway address has changed. For example, to add a gateway with a specific IP address, you could use the following:

```
matthew@seymour:~$ sudo route add default gw 149.112.50.65
```

Note that you could use a hostname rather than an IP address if desired. Another common use is to add the network to the routing table right after using the ifconfig command to configure the interface. Assuming that the 208.59.243.0 entry from the previous examples was missing, replace it using the following command:

```
matthew@seymour:~$ sudo route add -net 208.59.243.0 netmask 255.255.255.0 dev eth0
```

You also can use route to configure a specific host for a direct (point-to-point) connection. For example, suppose that you have a home network of two computers. One of the computers has a modem through which it connects to your business network. You typically work at the other computer. You can use the route command to establish a connection through specific hosts using the following command:

```
matthew@seymour:~$ sudo route add -host 198.135.62.25 gw 149.112.50.65
```

The preceding example makes the computer with the modem the gateway for the computer you are using. This type of command line is useful if you have a gateway or firewall connected to the Internet. There are many additional uses for the route command, such as manipulating the default packet size. See the man page for those uses.

/bin/netstat

The netstat command is used to display the status of your network. It has several parameters that can display as much or as little information as you prefer. The services are listed by *sockets* (application-to-application connections between two computers). You can use netstat to display the information in Table 17.2.

TABLE 17.2 `netstat` Options

Option	Output
`-g`	Displays the multicast groups configured
`-i`	Displays the interfaces configured by `ifconfig`
`-s`	Lists a summary of activity for each protocol
`-v`	Gives verbose output, listing both active and inactive sockets
`-c`	Updates output every second (good for testing and troubleshooting)
`-e`	Gives verbose output for active connections only
`-C`	Displays information from the route cache and is good for looking at past connections

Several other options are available for this command, but they are used less often. As with the `route` command, the man page can give you details about all options and parameters.

Network Configuration Files

As previously stated, five network configuration files can be modified to make changes to basic network interaction of your system:

▶ `/etc/hosts`—A listing of addresses, hostnames, and aliases.

▶ `/etc/services`—Network service and port connections.

▶ `/etc/nsswitch.conf`—Linux network information service configuration.

▶ `/etc/resolv.conf`—*Domain Name Service (DNS)* domain (search) settings.

▶ `/etc/host.conf`—Network information search order (by default, `/etc/hosts` and then DNS).

After these files are modified, the changes are active. As with most configuration files, comments can be added with a hash mark (#) preceding the comment. All these files have man pages, where you can find more information.

Adding Hosts to `/etc/hosts`

The `/etc/hosts` file is a map of IP to hostnames. If you are not using DNS or another naming service and you are connected to a large network, this file can get quite large and can be a real headache to manage. A small `/etc/hosts` file can look something like this:

```
127.0.0.1       localhost
127.0.1.1       optimus


# The following lines are desirable for IPv6 capable hosts
::1      ip6-localhost ip6-loopback
fe00::0 ip6-localnet
```

```
ff00::0 ip6-mcastprefix
ff02::1 ip6-allnodes
ff02::2 ip6-allrouters
ff02::3 ip6-allhosts
```

The first entry is for the loopback entry. The second is for the name of the machine. If no naming service is in use on the network, the only host that myhost will recognize by name is yourhost. (IP addresses on the network can still be used.)

Service Settings in /etc/services

The /etc/services file maps port numbers to services. The first few lines look similar to this. (The /etc/services file can be quite long, more than 500 lines.)

```
# Each line describes one service, and is of the form:
#
# service-name port/protocol [aliases ...]  [# comment]

tcpmux     1/tcp               # TCP port service multiplexer
tcpmux     1/udp               # TCP port service multiplexer
rje        5/tcp               # Remote Job Entry
rje        5/udp               # Remote Job Entry
echo       7/tcp
echo       7/udp
discard    9/tcp       sink null
discard    9/udp       sink null
systat     11/tcp      users
```

Typically, there are two entries for each service because most services can use either TCP or UDP for their transmissions. Usually after /etc/services is initially configured, you do not need to change it.

Using /etc/nsswitch.conf After Changing Naming Services

This file was initially developed by Sun Microsystems to specify the order in which services are accessed on the system. A number of services are listed in the /etc/nsswitch.conf file, but the most commonly modified entry is the hosts entry. A portion of the file can look like this:

```
passwd:         compat
group:          compat
shadow:         compat

hosts:          files dns mdns
networks:       files

protocols:      db files
services:       db files
```

```
ethers:          db files
rpc:             db files

netgroup:        nis
```

This tells services that they should consult standard UNIX/Linux files for passwd, shadow, and group (/etc/passwd, /etc/shadow, /etc/group, respectively) lookups. For host lookups, the system checks /etc/hosts; if there is no entry, it checks DNS. The commented hosts entry lists the possible values for hosts. Edit this file only if your naming service has changed.

Setting a Name Server with /etc/resolv.conf

/etc/resolv.conf is used by DNS, the Domain Name Service. The following is an example of resolv.conf:

```
nameserver 192.172.3.8
nameserver 192.172.3.9
search mydomain.com
```

This sets the nameservers and the order of domains for DNS to use. The contents of this file will be set automatically if you use DHCP (see the section on "Dynamic Host Configuration Protocol," later in this chapter).

Setting DNS Search Order with /etc/host.conf

The /etc/host.conf file lists the order in which your machine will search for hostname resolution. The following is the default /etc/host.conf file:

```
order hosts, bind
```

In this example, the host checks the /etc/hosts file first and then performs a DNS lookup. A couple more options control how the name service is used. The only reason to modify this file is if you use NIS for your name service or you want one of the optional services. The nospoof option can be a good option for system security. It compares a standard DNS lookup to a reverse lookup (host-to-IP then IP-to-host) and fails if the two don't match. The drawback is that often when proxy services are used, the lookup fails, so you want to use this with caution.

Using Graphical Configuration Tools

Ubuntu has made some big improvements to how desktop users may configure networking using graphical configuration tools. For most people, all you need to know is contained in Chapter 2, "Post-Installation Configuration," in the section about Network Manager. For others, you may configure your network connections by right-clicking the networking icon on your top panel and choosing Edit Connections from the menu, as shown in Figure 17.1. From the Network Connections window that opens, you may select from various types of connections to configure, including Wired, Wireless, Mobile

Broadband, VPN, and DSL, as shown in Figure 17.2. By default, each is set to autoconfigure, and most users never need to change the settings available here. If you do need to, just choose the appropriate tab and click the Add button; you can then configure and fine-tune settings as needed, such as in the wireless connection example in Figure 17.3.

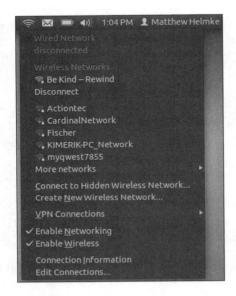

FIGURE 17.1   Use nm-connection-editor to configure your network devices.

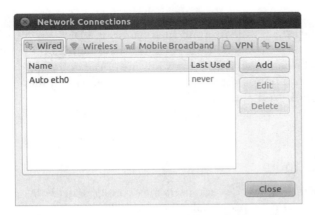

FIGURE 17.2   Choose the connection type to configure from the tabs in Network Connections.

FIGURE 17.3   Assign a static IP address to a network interface.

Dynamic Host Configuration Protocol

As its name implies, *Dynamic Host Configuration Protocol (DHCP)* configures hosts for connection to your network. DHCP allows a network administrator to configure all TCP/IP parameters for each host as he connects to the network after activation of a NIC. These parameters include automatically assigning an IP address to a NIC, setting name server entries in `/etc/resolv.conf`, and configuring default routing and gateway information for a host. This section first describes how to use DHCP to obtain IP address assignment for your NIC, and then how to quickly set up and start a DHCP server using Ubuntu.

> **NOTE**
>
> You can learn more about DHCP by reading RFC 2131, "Dynamic Host Configuration Protocol," at www.ietf.org/rfc/rfc2131.txt.

How DHCP Works

DHCP provides persistent storage of network parameters by holding identifying information for each network client that might connect to the network. The three most common pairs of identifying information are as follows:

▶ **Network subnet/host address**—Used by hosts to connect to the network at will.

▶ **Subnet/hostname**—Enables the specified host to connect to the subnet.

▶ **Subnet/hardware address**—Enables a specific client to connect to the network after getting the hostname from DHCP.

DHCP also allocates to client's temporary or permanent network (IP) addresses. When a temporary assignment, known as a *lease*, elapses, the client can request to have the lease extended, or, if the address is no longer needed, the client can relinquish the address. For hosts that will be permanently connected to a network with adequate addresses available, DHCP allocates infinite leases.

DHCP offers your network some advantages. First, it shifts responsibility for assigning IP addresses from the network administrator (who can accidentally assign duplicate IP addresses) to the DHCP server. Second, DHCP makes better use of limited IP addresses. If a user is away from the office for whatever reason, the user's host can release its IP address for use by other hosts.

Like most things in life, DHCP is not perfect. Servers cannot be configured through DHCP alone because DNS does not know what addresses that DHCP assigns to a host. This means that DNS lookups are not possible on machines configured through DHCP alone; therefore, services cannot be provided. However, DHCP can make assignments based on DNS entries when using subnet/hostname or subnet/hardware address identifiers.

> **NOTE**
>
> The problem of using DHCP to configure servers using registered hostnames is being addressed by Dynamic DNS which, when fully developed, will enable DHCP to register IP addresses with DNS. This will allow you, for example, to register a domain name (such as matthewhelmke.com) and be able to easily access that domain's web server without needing to use static IP addressing of a specific host. The largest hurdle to overcome is the security implication of enabling each host connecting to the system to update DNS. A few companies, such as Dyn.com (www.dyndns.org/), are already offering Dynamic DNS services and have clients for Linux.

Activating DHCP at Installation and Boot Time

Ubuntu automatically defaults your network interfaces to using DHCP, because it is the simplest way of setting up a network interface. With *dynamic*, or DHCP-assigned, IP addressing schemes for your NIC, the broadcast address is set at 255.255.255.255 because dhclient, the DHCP client used for IP configuration, is initially unaware of where the DHCP server is located, so the request must travel every network until a server replies.

The instruction to use DHCP for your NIC can be found under /etc/network/interfaces, with a line that says dhcp.

Other settings specific to obtaining DHCP settings are saved in the file named dhclient. conf under the /etc/dhcp3/dhclient.conf directory and are documented in the dhclient.conf man page. More than 100 options are also documented in the dhcpoptions man page.

However, using DHCP is not that complicated. If you want to use DHCP and know that there is a server on your network, you can quickly configure your NIC by using the dhclient, as follows:

```
matthew@seymour:~$ sudo dhclient
Internet Systems Consortium DHCP Client V3.1.3
Copyright 2004-2009 Internet Systems Consortium.
All rights reserved.
For info, please visit https://www.isc.org/software/dhcp/


Listening on LPF/eth0/00:90:f5:8e:52:b5
Sending on   LPF/eth0/00:90:f5:8e:52:b5
Listening on LPF/virbr0/ee:1a:62:7e:e2:a2
Sending on   LPF/virbr0/ee:1a:62:7e:e2:a2
Listening on LPF/wlan0/00:16:ea:d4:58:88
Sending on   LPF/wlan0/00:16:ea:d4:58:88
Sending on   Socket/fallback
DHCPDISCOVER on eth0 to 255.255.255.255 port 67 interval 7
DHCPDISCOVER on wlan0 to 255.255.255.255 port 67 interval 3
DHCPOFFER of 192.168.1.106 from 192.168.1.1
DHCPREQUEST of 192.168.1.106 on wlan0 to 255.255.255.255 port 67
DHCPACK of 192.168.1.106 from 192.168.1.1
bound to 192.168.1.106 -- renewal in 35959 seconds.
```

In this example, the first Ethernet device, eth0, has been assigned an IP address of 192.168.1.106 from a DHCP server at 192.168.1.1. The renewal will take place in 35959 seconds, or about 10 hours. (Cool tip: Google converts this for you if you search for 35959 seconds in hours.)

DHCP Software Installation and Configuration

Installation of the DHCP client and server is fairly straightforward, mainly because Ubuntu already includes dhclient in a default installation, but also because installing software is easy using synaptic or apt-get.

DHCP dhclient

DHCP is automatically enabled when you install Ubuntu, so you do not need to worry about having to enable it. The DHCP client, dhclient, sends a broadcast message that the DHCP server replies to with networking information for your host. After it has this, you're done.

You can, however, fine-tune how dhclient works and where and how it obtains or looks for DHCP information. You probably will not need to take this additional effort; but if you do, you can create and edit a file named dhclient.conf and save it in the /etc directory with your settings.

CAUTION

You should not just go ahead and overwrite your `dhclient.conf` with any old file, because doing so could lead you to painful networking problems. Instead, copy the file like this:

    matthew@seymour:~$ sudo cp /etc/dhcp3/dhclient.conf/
    etc/dhcp3/dhclient.conf.backup

That way, if anything goes wrong, you can then use the backup to restore the original settings by copying it back to its original location in place of the modified file.

A few of the `dhclient.conf` options include the following:

▶ **timeout time ;**—How long to wait before giving up trying. (The default is 60 seconds.)

▶ **retry time ;**—How long to wait before retrying. (The default is 5 minutes.)

▶ **select-timeout time ;**—How long to wait before selecting a DHCP offer. (The default is 0 seconds.)

▶ **reboot time ;**—How long to wait before trying to get a previously set IP. (The default is 10 seconds.)

▶ **renew date ;**—When to renew an IP lease, where `date` is in the form of `<weekday> <year>/<month>/<day> <hour>:<minute>:<second>`, such as in `3 2010/7/7 22:01:01` for Wednesday, July 7, 2010 at 10:01 p.m.

See the `dhclient.conf` man page for more information on additional settings.

DHCP Server

Again, the easiest way to install the DHCP server on your computer is to use either `synaptic` or `apt-get` to retrieve the `dchp3-server` package. If you are so inclined, you can go to the *Internet Software Consortium (ISC)* website and download and build the source code yourself (www.isc.org/). However, we recommend you stay with the package in the Ubuntu repositories because it will be easy to update if there are security updates.

If you decide to install from a source downloaded from the ISC website, the installation is straightforward. Just unpack your `tar` file, run `./configure` from the root of the source directory, run `make`, and finally, if there are no errors, run `make install`. This puts all the files used by the DHCP daemon in the correct places. If you have the disk space, it is best to leave the source files in place until you are sure that DHCP is running correctly; otherwise, you can delete the source tree.

NOTE

For whichever installation method you choose, be sure that a file called `/etc/dhcp3/dhcpd.leases` is created. The file can be empty, but it does need to exist for dhcpd to start properly.

Using DHCP to Configure Network Hosts

Configuring your network with DHCP can look difficult, but is actually easy if your needs are simple. The server configuration can take a bit more work if your network is more complex and depending on how much you want DHCP to do.

Configuring the server takes some thought and a little bit of work. Luckily, the work involves editing only a single configuration file, /etc/dhcp3/dhcpd.conf. To start the server at boot time, use the service or ntsysv commands.

The /etc/dhcp3/dhcpd.conf file contains all the information needed to run dhcpd. Ubuntu includes a sample dhcpd.conf in /usr/share/doc/dhcp*/dhcpd.conf.sample. The DHCP server source files also contain a sample dhcpd.conf file.

The /etc/dhcp3/dhcpd.conf file can be looked at as a three-part file. The first part contains configurations for DHCP itself. The configurations include the following:

- ▶ **Setting the domain name**—option domain-name "example.org"

- ▶ **Setting DNS servers**—option domain-name-servers ns1.example.org, ns2.example.org (IP addresses can be substituted.)

- ▶ **Setting the default and maximum lease times**—default-lease-time 3600 and max-lease-time 14400

Other settings in the first part include whether the server is the primary (authoritative) server and what type of logging DHCP should use. These settings are considered defaults and can be overridden by the subnet and host portion of the configuration in more complex situations.

> **NOTE**
>
> The dhcpd.conf file requires semicolons (;) after each command statement. If your configuration file has errors or runs improperly, check for this.

The next part of the dhcpd.conf deals with the different subnets that your DHCP server serves; this section is quite straightforward. Each subnet is defined separately and can look like this:

```
subnet 10.5.5.0 netmask 255.255.255.224 {
 range 10.5.5.26 10.5.5.30;
 option domain-name-servers ns1.internal.example.org;
 option domain-name "internal.example.org";
 option routers 10.5.5.1;
 option broadcast-address 10.5.5.31;
 default-lease-time 600;
 max-lease-time 7200;
}
```

17

This defines the IP addressing for the 10.5.5.0 subnet. It defines the IP address ranging from 10.5.5.26 through 10.5.5.30 to be dynamically assigned to hosts that reside on that subnet. This example shows that any TCP/IP option can be set from the subnet portion of the configuration file. It shows which DNS server the subnet will connect to, which can be good for DNS server load balancing, or which can be used to limit the hosts that can be reached through DNS. It defines the domain name, so you can have more than one domain on your network. It can also change the default and maximum lease time.

If you want your server to ignore a specific subnet, you can do so as follows:

```
subnet 10.152.187.0 netmask 255.255.255.0 {
}
```

This defines no options for the 10.152.187.0 subnet; therefore, the DHCP server ignores it.

The last part of your dhcp.conf is for defining hosts. This can be good if you want a computer on your network to have a specific IP address or other information specific to that host. The key to completing the host section is to know the hardware address of the host. As you learned in the "Hardware Devices for Networking" section, earlier in this chapter, the hardware address is used to differentiate the host for configuration. Your hardware address can be obtained by using the ifconfig command as described previously. The hardware address is on the eth0 line labeled Hwaddr.

```
host hopper {
  hardware ethernet 08:00:07:26:c0:a5;
  fixed-address hopper.matthewhelmke.com;
}
```

This example takes the host with the hardware address 08:00:07:26:c0:a5 and does a DNS lookup to assign the IP address for hopper.matthewhelmke.com to the host.

DHCP can also define and configure booting for diskless clients, like this:

```
host bumblebee {
  hardware ethernet 0:0:c0:5d:bd:95;
  filename "vmunix.bumblebee";
  server-name "kernigan.matthewhelmke.com";
}
```

The diskless host bumblebee will get its boot information from server kernigan.matthewhelmke.com and use vmunix.bumblebee kernel. All other TCP/IP configuration can also be included.

CAUTION

Remember, to avoid problems, only one DHCP server should be configured on a local network. Your DHCP might not work correctly on a LAN with hosts running outdated legacy operating systems. Often, Windows NT servers have the Windows DHCP server installed by default. Because there is no configuration file for NT to sort through, that

DHCP server configures your host before the Linux server if both machines are on the same LAN. Check your NT servers for this situation and disable DHCP on the NT server; afterward, your other DHCP-enabled hosts should configure correctly. Also, check to make sure that there are no conflicts if you use a cable or DSL modem, *wireless access point (WAP)*, or other intelligent router on your LAN that can provide DHCP.

Other Uses for DHCP

A whole host of options can be used in dhcpd.conf: Entire books are dedicated to DHCP. The most comprehensive book is *The DHCP Handbook*, available at www.dhcp-handbook. com/. You can define NIS domains, configure NetBIOS, set subnet masks, and define time servers or many other types of servers (to name a few of the DHCP options you can use). The preceding example gets your DHCP server and client up and running.

The DHCP server distribution contains an example of the dhcpd.conf file that you can use as a template for your network. The file shows a basic configuration that can get you started with explanations for the options used.

Wireless Networking

Linux has had support for wireless networking since the first standards were developed in the early 1990s. With computers getting smaller and smaller, the uses for wireless networking increased; meanwhile, the transmission speeds are increasing all the time. There are several ways to create a wireless network. The following sections introduce you to several Linux commands you can use to initialize, configure, and manage wireless networking on your Ubuntu system.

Support for Wireless Networking in Ubuntu

The Linux kernel that ships with Ubuntu provides extensive support for wireless networking. Related wireless tools for configuring, managing, or displaying information about a wireless connection include the following:

▶ **iwconfig**—Sets the network name, encryption, transmission rate, and other features of a wireless network interface.

▶ **iwlist**—Displays information about a wireless interface, such as rate, power level, or frequency used.

▶ **iwpriv**—Used to set optional features, such as roaming, of a wireless network interface.

▶ **iwspy**—Shows wireless statistics of a number of nodes.

Support varies for wireless devices, but most modern (that is, post-2005) wireless devices should work with Ubuntu. In general, Linux wireless device software (usually in the form of a kernel module) support the creation of an Ethernet device that can be managed by

17

traditional interface tools such as ifconfig—with wireless features of the device managed by the various wireless softwares tools.

For example, when a wireless networking device is first recognized and initialized for use, the driver will most likely report a new device:

```
zd1211rw 5-4:1.0: firmware version 4725

zd1211rw 5-4:1.0: zd1211b chip 050d:705c v4810 \
high 00-17-3f AL2230_RF pa0 G--ns

zd1211rw 5-4:1.0: eth2

usbcore: registered new interface driver zd1211rw
```

This output (from the dmesg command) shows that the eth2 device has been reported. If DHCP is in use, the device should automatically join the nearest wireless subnet and be automatically assigned an IP address. If not, the next step is to use a wireless tool such as iwconfig to set various parameters of the wireless device. The iwconfig command, along with the device name (eth2 in this example), shows the status:

```
matthew@seymour:~$ iwconfig eth2
eth2      IEEE 802.11b/g  ESSID:"SKY35120"  Nickname:"zd1211"
          Mode:Managed  Frequency:2.462 GHz  \
Access Point: 00:18:4D:06:8E:2A
          Bit Rate=24 Mb/s
          Encryption key:0EFD-C1AF-5C8D-B2C6-7A89-3790-07A7-AC64-0AB5\
-C36E-D1E9-A230-1DB9-D227-2EB6-D6C8   Security mode:open
          Link Quality=100/100  Signal level=82/100
          Rx invalid nwid:0  Rx invalid crypt:0  Rx invalid frag:0
          Tx excessive retries:0  Invalid misc:0   Missed beacon:0
```

This example shows a 24Mbps connection to a network named SKY35120. To change a parameter, such as the transmission rate, use a command-line option with the iwconfig command, like this:

```
matthew@seymour:~$ sudo iwconfig eth0 rate 11M
```

Other options supported by the iwconfig command include essid, used to set the NIC to connect to a specific network by name; mode, used to enable the NIC to automatically retrieve settings from an access point or connect to another wireless host; and freq, to set a frequency to use for communication. Additional options include channel, frag, enc (for encryption), power, and txpower. Details and examples of these options are in the iwconfig man page.

You can then use the ifconfig command or perhaps a graphical Ubuntu tool to set the device networking parameters, and the interface will work as on a hardwired LAN. One handy output of the iwconfig command is the link quality output, which can be used in shell scripts or other graphical utilities for signal-monitoring purposes.

Advantages of Wireless Networking

Advantages of wireless networking are its mobility and potential range. If you have a large enough antenna network, your network can stretch many miles. This would be an expensive network, but one that would easily break out of the brick-and-mortar confines of the office.

Wireless networking is also a great advantage to college campuses, eliminating the need to tear through walls to install cabling as more and more students expect to have a network connection in their dorm rooms. Wireless networking cards are very reasonable in price and can easily be issued to each student as required.

Home networkers can also benefit from wireless networking. It is a potential solution for those who cannot make wired network modifications to their homes. In addition, wireless networking removes the unsightly wires running along baseboards and ceilings that are required to connect computers in different rooms. With a wireless home network, you are not even confined to inside the house. Depending on the transmit power of your router, you can sit out in your backyard and watch clouds drifting by as you type away.

Choosing the right types of wireless devices is an important decision. The next sections discuss some of the basic differences between current protocols used for wireless networking.

Choosing from Among Available Wireless Protocols

The *Institute of Electrical and Electronics Engineers (IEEE)* started to look seriously at wireless networking in 1990. This is when the 802.11 standard was first introduced by the Wireless Local Area Networks Standards Working Group. The group based the standard roughly around the architecture used in cellular phone networks. The wireless network is controlled by a base station, which can be just a transmitter attached to the network or, more commonly these days, a router.

Larger networks can use more than one base station. Networks with more than one base station are usually referred to as *distribution systems*. A distribution system can be used to increase coverage area and support roaming of wireless hosts. You can also use external omnidirectional antennas to increase coverage area, or if required, you can use point-to-point or directional antennas to connect distant computers or networks. Right now, the least expensive wireless Linux networks are built using devices (such as access points or NICs) supporting 802.11b, although the faster 802.11g devices tend to get more shelf space. Devices are available marketed as N or Pre-N, meaning that they implement a draft standard, while the IEEE carry on debating the full N standard. Significantly more power throughput and range are promised by hardware that supports N, but this specification has yet to be formally agreed on and so implementations are not necessarily standard.

An early standard, 802.11a, offers greater transmission rates than 802.11b, and a number of 802.11a wireless NICs are available. (Some products provide up to 72Mbps, but will not work with 802.11b devices.) Wireless networking devices based on 802.11g, which has the speed improvement of 802.11a and is compatible with 802.11b, are common. Other wireless protocols include Bluetooth, which provides up to 720Kbps data transfers. Bluetooth is intended for short-range device communications (such as for a printer) and supports a typical range of only 10 meters. Bluetooth is unlike IrDA, which requires line of sight (devices that are aimed at each other). Bluetooth use conflicts with 802.11 networks because it also uses the 2.4GHz band. You can find out more at www.bluetooth.com/.

The 802.11 standard specifies that wireless devices use a frequency range of 2400MHz to 2483.5MHz. This is the standard used in North America and Europe. In Japan, however, wireless networks are limited to a frequency range of 2471MHz to 2479MHz because of Japanese regulations. Within these ranges, each network is given up to 79 nonoverlapping frequency channels to use. This reduces the chance of two closely located wireless networks using the same channel at the same time. It also allows for channel hopping, which can be used for security.

Beyond the Network and onto the Internet

Ubuntu supports Internet connections and the use of Internet resources in many different ways. You will find a wealth of Internet-related software included with this book's version of Ubuntu, and you can download hundreds of additional free utilities from a variety of sources. To use them, you must have a working Internet connection.

In this section, you learn how to set up an Internet connection in Ubuntu using a modem and *Point-to-Point Protocol (PPP)* as well as other connection methods, including *digital subscriber line (DSL)* and cable modem services. Just a few years ago, getting a dial-up connection working was difficult—hence, an entire chapter of this book was devoted to it. Today, as long as you have a hardware modem, dial-up configuration is simple. The Ubuntu developers and the wider Linux community have made great progress in making connectivity easier.

Although many experienced Linux users continue to use manual scripts to establish their Internet connectivity, new users and experienced system administrators alike will find Ubuntu's graphical network configuration interface much easier to use. You learn how to use the Internet Connection Wizard in this chapter and how to configure Ubuntu to provide dial-in PPP support. The chapter also describes how to use Roaring Penguin's DSL utilities to manage connectivity through a cable modem connection.

Common Configuration Information

Although Ubuntu enables great flexibility in configuring Internet connections, that flexibility comes at the price of an increase in complexity. To configure Internet connectivity in Ubuntu, you must know more about the details of the connection process than you can learn from the information typically provided by your *Internet service provider (ISP)*. In this section, you learn what to ask about and how to use the information.

Some ISPs are unaware of Linux or unwilling to support its use with their service. Fortunately, that attitude is rapidly changing, and the majority of ISPs offer services using standard protocols that are compatible with Linux, even if they (or their technical support people) aren't aware that their own ISPs are Linux friendly. You just need to press a little for the information you require.

If you are one of the few remaining people using a dial-up modem account (referred to in Linux as *PPP* for the Point-to-Point Protocol it uses), your ISP will provide your computer with a static or dynamic *Internet Protocol (IP)* address. A dynamic IP address changes each time you dial in, whereas a static IP address remains the same. The ISP also might automatically provide your computer with the names of the *Domain Name Service (DNS)* servers. You need to know the telephone number that your computer will dial in to for making the connection; your ISP supplies that number, too. You also need a working modem and need to know the device name of the modem (usually /dev/modem).

NOTE

Most IP addresses are dynamically assigned by ISPs; ISPs have a pool of addresses, and you get whatever address is available. From the ISP's viewpoint, a small number of addresses can serve a large number of people because not everyone will be online at the same time. For most Internet services, a dynamic IP works well because it is the ISP's job to route that information to you, and it sits in the middle—between you and the service you want to use. But a dynamic IP address changes, and if someone needs to find you at the same address (if you run a website or a file transfer site, for example), an IP that changes every time you log on will not work well. For that, you need a static IP. Because your ISP cannot reuse that IP with its other customers, it will likely charge you more for a static IP than for a dynamic IP. Average consumers do not need the benefit of a static IP and so are happy paying less for a dynamically assigned IP. Also, the DNS information can be provided automatically by the ISP by DHCP.

If you are using DSL access or a cable modem, you might have a dynamic IP provided through DHCP, or you might be assigned a static IP. You might automatically be provided with the names of the DNS servers if you use DHCP, or you might have to set up DNS manually (in which case, you have to know the IP addresses of the DNS servers).

In all cases, you have to know your username, your password, and for the configuration of other services, the names of the mail servers and the news server. This information can be obtained from your ISP if you specifically ask for it.

NOTE

The information in this book will help you understand and avoid many connection issues, but you might experience connection problems. Keep the telephone number of the technical help service for your ISP on hand in case you cannot establish a connection. But be aware that few ISPs offer Linux support, and you might need to seek help from a Linux-savvy friend or a Linux user group if your special circumstances cannot be handled from the knowledge you gain from this book. Of course, the best place to look is on the Internet. Use Google's Linux page (www.google.com/linux/) to research the problem and see whether any other users have found fixes or workarounds.

Configuring Digital Subscriber Line Access

Ubuntu also supports the use of a *digital subscriber line (DSL)* service. Although it refers to the different types of DSL available as *xDSL* (which includes ADSL, IDSL, SDSL, and other flavors of DSL service), they can all be configured using the Internet Connection Wizard. DSL service generally provides 256Kbps to 24Mbps transfer speeds and transmits data over copper telephone lines from a central office to individual subscriber sites (such as your home). Many DSL services (technically, cable rather than DSL) provide asymmetric speeds with download speeds greater than upload speeds.

> **NOTE**
>
> DSL service is an "always-on" type of Internet service, although you can turn off the connection under Ubuntu using the network configuration tool found under System, Administration, Network. An always-on connection exposes your computer to malicious abuse from crackers who trawl the Internet attempting to gain access to other computer systems. In addition to the capability to turn off such connections, Ubuntu is preconfigured to not listen on any network ports, which means that any attempts to gain access to your computer will fail because Ubuntu will reject the request. This is the Ubuntu equivalent to surrounding your computer with a 12-foot steel fence.

A DSL connection requires that you have an Ethernet NIC (sometimes a USB interface that is not easily supported in Linux) in your computer or notebook. Many users also configure a gateway, firewall, or other computer with at least two NICs to share a connection with a LAN. We looked at the hardware and protocol issues earlier in this chapter. Advanced configuration of a firewall or router, other than what was addressed during your initial installation of Ubuntu, is beyond the scope of this book.

Understanding PPP over Ethernet

Establishing a DSL connection with an ISP providing a static IP address is easy. Unfortunately, many DSL providers use a type of PPP protocol named *Point-to-Point Protocol over Ethernet (PPPoE)* that provides dynamic IP address assignment and authentication by encapsulating PPP information inside Ethernet frames. Roaring Penguin's rp-pppoe clients are available from the Roaring Penguin site (www.roaringpenguin.com/penguin/pppoe/rp-pppoe-3.8.tar.gz), and these clients make the difficult-to-configure PPPoE connection much easier to deal with. You can download and install newer versions. (See the Roaring Penguin link in the "References" section at the end of this chapter.)

> **NOTE**
>
> When ISPs originally started to roll out ADSL services, they often provided the ADSL modems. Today, however, in much of the world, these modems are optional, which is a good thing because many people choose to purchase a router with an in-built modem to create a dedicated connection. In the United States, these devices are rare, but you

can usually replace the supplied modem with an aftermarket modem if you want to spend the money. Either way, using a router can save many headaches and will enable you to easily connect more than one computer to an Internet connection. Note that if you are using a cable connection, they usually come with an Ethernet cable, in which case you just need a router (which is pretty much how all Internet access works in the United States, because combination modem/router devices are rare in the U.S.). Check with your ISP before buying to ensure that whatever router you do end up with can be supported by them. You might find that your ISP even supplies a router as part of the package.

Configuring a PPPoE Connection Manually

You should only need to use these steps if you are using a modem supplied by your ISP, and not a router. The basic steps involved in manually setting up a DSL connection using Ubuntu involve connecting the proper hardware and then running a simple configuration script if you use rp-pppoe from Roaring Penguin.

First, connect your DSL modem to your telephone line, and then plug in your Ethernet cable from the modem to your computer's NIC. If you plan to share your DSL connection with the rest of your LAN, you need at least two network cards: designated eth0 (for your LAN) and eth1 (for the DSL connection).

The following example assumes that you have more than one computer and will share your DSL connection on a LAN.

First, log in as root, and ensure that your first eth0 device is enabled and up (perhaps using the ifconfig command). Next, bring up the other interface, but assign a null IP address like this:

matthew@seymour:~$ **sudo /sbin/ifconfig eth1 0.0.0.0 up**

Now use the adsl-setup command to set up your system, as follows:

matthew@seymour:~$ **sudo /sbin/adsl-setup**

You are presented with a text script and asked to enter your username and the Ethernet interface used for the connection (such as eth1). You are then asked to use "on-demand" service or have the connection stay up all the time (until brought down by the root operator). You can also set a timeout in seconds, if desired. You are then asked to enter the IP addresses of your ISP's DNS servers if you haven't configured the system's /etc/resolv.conf file.

After that, you are prompted to enter your password two times and must choose the type of firewall and IP masquerading to use. (You learned about IP masquerading in the "Using IP Masquerading in Ubuntu" section, earlier in this chapter.) The actual configuration is done automatically. Using a firewall is essential today, so choose this option unless you intend to craft your own set of firewall rules (a discussion of which is beyond the scope of this book). After you have chosen your firewall and IP masquerading setup, you are asked

17

to confirm, save, and implement your settings. You are also given a choice to allow users to manage the connection, a handy option for home users.

Changes are made to your system's /etc/sysconfig/network-scripts/ifcfg-ppp0, /etc/resolv.conf, /etc/ppp/pap-secrets, and /etc/ppp/chap-secrets files.

After configuration has finished, use the adsl-start command to start a connection and DSL session, like this:

matthew@seymour:~$ **sudo /sbin/adsl-start**

The DSL connection should be nearly instantaneous, but if problems occur, check to make sure that your DSL modem is communicating with the phone company's central office by examining the status LEDs on the modem. Because this varies from modem to modem, consult your modem user's manual.

Make sure all cables are properly attached, that your interfaces are properly configured, and that you have entered the correct information to the setup script.

If IP masquerading is enabled, other computers on your LAN on the same subnet address (such as 192.168.0.XXX) can use the Internet but must have the same /etc/resolv.conf name server entries and a routing entry with the DSL-connected computer as a gateway. For example, if the host computer with the DSL connection has an IP address of 192.168.0.1, and other computers on your LAN use addresses in the 192.168.0.XXX range, use the route command on each computer like this:

matthew@seymour:~$ **sudo /sbin/route add default gw 192.168.0.1**

Note that you can also use a hostname instead if each computer has an /etc/hosts file with hostname and IP address entries for your LAN. To stop your connection, use the adsl-stop command:

matthew@seymour:~$ **sudo /sbin/adsl-stop**

Configuring Dial-Up Internet Access

Most ISPs provide dial-up connections supporting PPP because it is a fast and efficient protocol for using TCP/IP over serial lines. PPP is designed for two-way networking; TCP/IP provides the transport protocol for data. One hurdle faced by new Ubuntu users is how to set up PPP and connect to the Internet. It is not necessary to understand the details of the PPP protocol to use it, and setting up a PPP connection is easy. You can configure the PPP connections manually using the command line or graphically during an X session using Ubuntu's Network Configuration Tool. Each approach produces the same results.

PPP uses several components on your system. The first is a daemon called pppd, which controls the use of PPP. The second is a driver called the *high-level data link control (HDLC)*, which controls the flow of information between two machines. A third component of PPP is a routine called *chat* that dials the other end of the connection for you when you want it to. Although PPP has many "tunable" parameters, the default settings work well for most people.

Ubuntu includes some useful utilities to get your dial-up connection up and running. In this section, we look at two options that will have you on the Internet in no time.

The first way is to configure a connection using `pppconfig`, a command-line utility to help you to configure specific dial-up connection settings.

Enter the following command:

```
matthew@seymour:~$ sudo pppconfig
```

Before you connect for the first time, you need to add yourself to both the `dip` and `dialout` groups by using these commands:

```
matthew@seymour:~$ sudo adduser YOURNAMEHERE dip
matthew@seymour:~$ sudo adduser YOURNAMEHERE dialout
```

After this has been done, it is just a simple matter of issuing the `pon` command to connect and the `poff` command to disconnect. You can create as many different profiles as you need and can launch specific ones by using the command `pon profilename`, again using the `poff` command to disconnect.

CAUTION

Many software modems will not work with Linux because the manufacturers will not release programming information about them or provide Linux drivers. An external serial port modem or ISA bus modem almost always work; USB and PCI modems are still problematic. It is suggested that you do a thorough Google search using your modem's name and model number to see how others have solved problems with that particular modem. Links to software modem compatibility sites appear at the end of this chapter.

Troubleshooting Connection Problems

The Linux Documentation Project at www.tldp.org/ offers many in-depth resources for configuring and troubleshooting these connections. Google is also an invaluable tool for dealing with specific questions about these connections. For many other useful references, see the "References" section at the end of this chapter.

Here are a few troubleshooting tips culled from many years of experience:

▶ If your modem connects and then hangs up, you are probably using the wrong password or dialing the wrong number. If the password and phone number are correct, it is likely an authentication protocol problem.

17

▶ If you get connected but cannot reach websites, it is likely a domain name resolver problem, meaning that DNS is not working. If it worked yesterday and you haven't "adjusted" the associated files, it is probably a problem at the ISP's end. Call and ask.

▶ Always make certain that everything is plugged in. Check again (and again).

▶ If the modem works in Windows but not in Linux no matter what you do, it is probably a software modem, no matter what it said on the box.

▶ If everything just stops working (and you do not see smoke), it is probably a glitch at the ISP or the telephone company. Take a break and give them some time to fix it.

▶ Never configure a network connection when you have had too little sleep or too much caffeine; you will just have to redo it tomorrow.

Related Ubuntu and Linux Commands

You will use these commands when managing network connectivity in your Ubuntu system:

▶ **dhclient**—Automatically acquire, and then set IP info for a NIC.

▶ **ethereal**—GNOME graphical network scanner.

▶ **ufw**—Ubuntu's basic firewalling tool.

▶ **ifconfig**—Displays and manages Linux networking devices.

▶ **iwconfig**—Displays and sets wireless network device parameters.

▶ **route**—Displays and manages Linux kernel routing table.

▶ **ssh**—The OpenSSH remote-login client and preferred replacement for telnet.

▶ **nm-connection-editor**—Ubuntu's GUI for configuring network connections.

References

▶ **https://help.ubuntu.com/10.04/serverguide/C/network-configuration.html**—Official networking help for Ubuntu.

▶ **www.ietf.org/rfc.html**—Go here to search for, or get a list of, *Request For Comments (RFC)*.

▶ **www.oth.net/dyndns.html**—For a list of Dynamic DNS service providers, go to this site.

▶ **www.isc.org/products/DHCP/dhcpv3-README.html**—The DHCP README is available at this site.

▶ **www.ieee.org**—The *Institute of Electrical and Electronics Engineers (IEEE)* website.

▶ Joe Casad, *Sams Teach Yourself TCP/IP Network Administration in 21 Days*, Sams Publishing, ISBN: 0-672-31250-6.

► Craig Hunt and Gigi Estabrook, *TCP/IP Network Administration*, O'Reilly Publishing, ISBN: 1-56592-322-7.

► Frank J. Derfler, Frank Derfler, and Jeff Koch, *Practical Networking*, Que Publishing, ISBN: 0-7897-2252-6.

► Steve Litt, *Samba Unleashed*, Sams Publishing, ISBN: 0-672-31862-8.

► Ralph Droms and Ted Lemon, *The DHCP Handbook*, Sams Publishing, ISBN: 0-672-32327-3.

17

Remote Access with SSH and Telnet

Controlling your system remotely is one of the cooler things you can do with Ubuntu: With just a bit of configuration, you can connect from any Linux box to another computer in a variety of ways. If you just want to check something quickly or if you have limited bandwidth, you have the option of using only the command line, but you can also connect directly to the X server and get full graphical control.

Understanding the selection of tools available is largely a history lesson. For example, Telnet was an earlier way of connecting to another computer through the command line, but that has since been superseded by *Secure Shell (SSH)*. That is not to say that you should ignore Telnet; you need to know how to use it so you have it as a fallback. However, SSH is preferred because it is more secure. We cover both in this chapter.

Setting Up a Telnet Server

Telnet is an older service. The client is part of the default installation, but is not activated by default. The server is not part of the default installation. This is because everything Telnet transmits and receives is in plain text, including passwords and other sensitive information. Telnet is generally not a good choice for communication. However, you may want to install Telnet for certain situations, such as connecting to a piece of equipment that doesn't have SSH available, such as embedded systems where having a small OS footprint is important and more secure methods of communication are not available. In addition, sometimes Telnet is the quickest and easiest way to test newly installed services during configuration, such as a Postfix mail server. You might also want to install Telnet to learn about it and test it, simply because you may run across moments in the real world where no other option exists.

If you decide to install Telnet, use Synaptic or apt to install `telnetd`. This will install the server.

Start by configuring your firewall to allow connections through port 23. If this port is blocked, you cannot use Telnet. See Chapter 19, "Securing Your Machines," for help doing this.

After that is configured, type `telnet` *your IP*. This will test to confirm both the client and server are installed and working by connecting from your terminal using the client back to the server running on your own computer. You are prompted to enter your username and password. The whole conversation should look something like this:

```
matthew@seymour:~$ telnet 192.168.1.102
Trying 192.168.1.102...
Connected to 192.168.1.102 (192.168.1.102)
Escape character is '^]'.

Welcome to babbage
Ubuntu 10.04 LTS

* All access is logged *

login: matthew
Password:
Last login: Sun Jul  4 10:08:34 2010 from seymour
matthew@babbage~$
```

> **TIP**
>
> The server responds with `Welcome to babbage`, `Ubuntu 10.04 LTS`, which is a cus-
> tomized message. Your machine will respond similarly. This may be unsecure: Giving
> away version numbers is never a smart move on a machine that may be accessed from
> outside of a secure network. In fact, even saying `Ubuntu` is questionable. In those
> instances, you can edit the `issue` and `issue.net` files in your `/etc` directory to change
> the message displayed.

To use Telnet to connect to a different computer, use that computer's IP address on the network instead of using your own. You can use Telnet on local networks and across the Internet to connect to any computer running the server on an open port.

Telnet uses port 23, but you can use it with other ports by adding the port to the IP address, as in this example where we use it to connect to port 110 to test a POP3 connection/server:

```
matthew@seymour:~$ telnet 192.168.1.102 110
```

Telnet Versus SSH

Although Telnet is worth keeping around as a fail-safe, last-resort option, SSH is superior in nearly every way. Telnet is fast but also unsecure. As stated earlier, it sends all your text, including your password, in plain text that can be read by anyone with the right tools. SSH, on the other hand, encrypts all your communication and so is more resource intensive but secure—even a government security agency sniffing your packets for some reason would still have a hard time cracking the encryption.

Andy Green, posting to the `fedora-list` mailing list, summed up the Telnet situation perfectly when he said, "As Telnet is universally acknowledged to encourage evil, the service `telnetd` is not enabled by default." It is worthwhile taking the hint: Use Telnet as a last resort only.

Setting Up an SSH Server

If not installed already, the OpenSSH server can be installed through Synaptic by adding the `openssh-server` package. As you might have guessed, `sshd` is the name for the SSH server daemon.

Start by configuring your firewall to allow connections through port 22. If this port is blocked, you cannot use SSH. See Chapter 19 for help doing this.

Two different versions of SSH exist, SSH1 and SSH2. The latter is newer, more secure, comes with more features, and is the default in Ubuntu. Support for SSH1 clients is best left disabled so that older clients cannot connect. This is done by default in the `/etc/ssh/sshd_config` file on this line:

```
Protocol 2
```

If you have no other option and absolutely have to allow an older client to connect, add a new line:

```
Protocol 1
```

SSH Tools

To the surprise of many, OpenSSH actually comprises a suite of tools. We have already seen `ssh`, the Secure Shell command that connects to other machines, and `sshd`, the SSH server daemon that accepts incoming SSH connections. However, there is also `sftp`, a replacement for `ftp`, `scp`, and `rcp`.

You should already be familiar with the `ftp` command because it is the lowest common denominator system for handling FTP file transfers. Like Telnet, though, `ftp` is unsecure: It sends your data in plain text across the network, and anyone can sniff your packets to pick out a username and password. The SSH replacement, `sftp`, puts FTP traffic over an SSH link, thus securing it.

The rcp command might be new to you, largely because it is not used much anymore. Back in its day, rcp was the primary way of copying a single file to another server. As with ftp, scp replaces rcp by simply channeling the data over a secure SSH connection. The difference between sftp and scp is that the former enables you to queue and copy many files simultaneously, whereas the latter is usually used to just send one, although scp can be used with the -r option to send an entire directory at once. See the man page for details.

Using scp to Copy Individual Files Between Machines

The most basic use of the scp command is to copy a file from your current machine to a remote machine. You can do that with the following command:

matthew@seymour:~$ **scp test.txt 192.168.1.102:**

The first parameter is the name of the file you want to send, and the second is the server to which you want to send it. Note that there is a colon (:) at the end of the IP address. This is where you can specify an exact location for the file to be copied. If you have nothing after the colon, as in the previous example, scp copies the file to your /home directory. As with SSH, scp prompts you for your password before copying takes place.

You can rewrite the previous command so that you copy test.txt from the local machine and save it as newtest.txt on the server:

matthew@seymour:~$ **scp test.txt 192.168.1.102:newtest.txt**

Alternatively, if there is a directory where you want the file to be saved, you can specify it like this:

matthew@seymour:~$ **scp test.txt 192.168.1.102:subdir/stuff/newtest.txt**

The three commands so far have all assumed that your username on your local machine is the same as your username on the remote machine. If this is not the case, you need to specify your username before the remote address, as follows:

matthew@seymour:~$ **scp test.txt usernamenewtest.txt**

You can use scp to copy remote files locally, simply by specifying the remote file as the source and the current directory (.) as the destination:

matthew@seymour:~$ **scp 192.168.1.102:remote.txt .**

If you want to copy files from one remote machine to another remote machine using scp, the best method is to first ssh to one of the remote machines and then use scp from that location.

Using `sftp` to Copy Many Files Between Machines

`sftp` is a mix between `ftp` and `scp`. Connecting to the server uses the same syntax as `scp`—you can just specify an IP address to connect using your current username, or you can specify a username using ***username@ipaddress***. *You can optionally add a colon and a directory, as with* `scp`. After you are connected, the commands are the same as `ftp`: `cd`, `put`, `mput`, `get`, `quit`, and so on.

In one of the `scp` examples, we copied a remote file locally. You can do the same thing with `sftp` with the following conversation:

```
matthew@seymour:~$ sftp 192.168.1.102
Connecting to 192.168.1.102...
matthew@192.168.1.102's password:
sftp> get remote.txt
Fetching /home/matthew/remote.txt to remote.txt
/home/matthew/remote.txt          100%  23    0.0KB/s    00:00
sftp> quit
matthew@seymour:~$
```

Although FTP remains prominent because of the number of systems that do not have support for SSH, SFTP is gaining in popularity. Apart from the fact that it secures all communications between client and server, SFTP is popular because the initial connection between the client and server is made over port 22 through the `sshd` daemon. Someone using SFTP connects to the standard `sshd` daemon, verifies himself, and then is handed over to the SFTP server. The advantage to this is that it reduces the attack vectors because the SFTP server cannot be contacted directly and so cannot be attacked as long as the `sshd` daemon is secure.

Using `ssh-keygen` to Enable Key-Based Logins

There is a weak link in the SSH system, and, inevitably, it lies with users. No matter what lengths system administrators go to in training users to be careful with their passwords, monitors around the world have Post-it notes attached to them with pAssw0rd written on them. Sure, it has a mix of letters and numbers, but it can be cracked in less than a second by any brute-force method. *Brute-forcing* is the method of trying every password possibility, starting with likely words (such as *password* and variants, or *god*) and then just trying random letters (for example, *a, aa, ab, ac,* and so on).

Even very strong passwords are no more than about 16 characters; such passwords take a long time to brute-force but can still be cracked. The solution is to use key-based logins, which generate a unique, 1024-bit private and public key pair for your machine. These keys take even the fastest computers a lifetime to crack, and you can back them up with a password to stop others from using them.

18

Creating an SSH key is done through the ssh-keygen command, like this:

```
matthew@seymour:~$ ssh-keygen -t dsa
```

Press Enter when it prompts you where to save your key, and enter a passphrase when it asks you to. This passphrase is just a password used to protect the key. You can leave it blank if you want to, but doing so would allow other people to use your account to connect to remote machines if they manage to log in as you.

After the key is generated, change the directory to .ssh (cd ~/.ssh), which is a hidden directory where your key is stored and also where it keeps a list of safe SSH hosts. Assuming you use the default options, here you see the files id_dsa and id_dsa.pub. The first is your private key and should never be given out. The second is your public key, which is safe for distribution. You need to copy the public key to each server you want to connect to via key-based SSH.

Using scp, you can copy the public key over to your server, like this:

```
matthew@seymour:~$ scp id_dsa.pub 192.186.1.102:
```

This places id_dsa.pub in your /home directory (for an account that uses the same user-name as your local account) on 192.186.1.102. The next step is to ssh into 192.186.1.102 normally and set up that key as an authorized key. So, you can ssh in as yourself:

```
matthew@seymour:~$ ssh 192.168.1.102
```

After logging in normally, type this:

```
matthew@babbage:~$ cat id_dsa.pub >> .ssh/authorized_keys
matthew@babbage:~$ chmod 400 .ssh/authorized_keys
```

The touch command creates the authorized_keys file (if it does not exist already); then you use cat to append the contents of id_dsa.pub to the list of already authorized keys. Finally, chmod is used to make authorized_keys read-only.

With that done, you can type exit to disconnect from the remote machine and return to your local machine. Then you can try running ssh again. If you are prompted for your passphrase, you have successfully configured key-based authentication.

That is the current machine secured, but what about every other machine? It is still possible to log in from another machine using only a password, which means your remote machine is still vulnerable.

The solution to this is to edit the /etc/ssh/sshd_config file. This requires super user privileges. Look for the PasswordAuthentication line and make sure it reads no (and that it is not commented out with a #). Save the file, and run kill -HUP 'cat /var/run/sshd.pid' to have sshd reread its configuration files. With that done, sshd accepts only connections from clients with authorized keys, which stops crackers from brute-forcing their way in.

> **TIP**
>
> For extra security, you are strongly encouraged to set `PermitRootLogin` to no in `/etc/ssh/sshd_config`. When this is set, it becomes impossible to `ssh` into your machine using the root account—you must connect with a normal user account and then use su or sudo to switch to root. This is advantageous because most brute-force attempts take place on the root account because it is the only account that is guaranteed to exist on a server.
>
> Also, even if a cracker knows your user account, she has to guess both your user password and your root password to take control of your system.
>
> Of course, if you don't have a root account enabled on your box, this isn't an issue because it is already impossible to log in directly as root. Hooray for slightly more secure defaults in Ubuntu.

Virtual Network Computing

Everything we have looked at so far has been about remote access using the command line, with no mention so far of how to bring up a *graphical user interface (GUI)*. There are several ways of doing this in Ubuntu, some of which are linked in the "Reference" section later in this chapter. Here we discuss the most popular and the most preferred by the Ubuntu community, which is also the best supported by the developers: *Virtual Network Computing (VNC)*.

VNC is a system for controlling a computer remotely and sharing desktops over a network using a graphical interface. It was created at the Olivetti & Oracle Research Lab, which was acquired by AT&T in 1999 and closed down in 2001. Since then, several of the members of the development team got together to create a free and open-source version of the code (using the GPL), and from that base, many different version have appeared. VNC is widespread in the Linux world and, to a lesser extent, in the Windows world. Its main advantage is its widespread nature: Nearly all Linux distros bundle VNC, and clients are available for a wide selection of platforms.

Start by configuring your firewall to allow connections through port 5900. If this port is blocked, you cannot use VNC. See Chapter 33, "Ubuntu in the Cloud," for help doing this.

To set up VNC on your Ubuntu computer to allow others to access your desktop, you only need to tell Ubuntu who should be allowed to connect to your session. This is done from the menu at System, Preferences, Remote Desktop. By default, your desktop is not shared. Check Allow other users to view your desktop to Share It. Most likely, you also want to check Allow other users to control your desktop; otherwise, people can see what you are doing but not interact with the desktop (which is not very helpful). If you are using this as a remote way to connect to your own desktop or one that is running unattended when you will need access, uncheck You must confirm each access to this machine. If this is not done, when you try to connect from your remote location, Ubuntu pops up a message box

18

on the local machine asking Should This Person Be Allowed to Connect?. Because you are not there to click Yes, the connection will fail. If you want to let someone else remotely connect to your system, keep this box enabled so that you know when people are connecting. You should always enter a password, no matter who it is that will connect. The options suggested are shown in Figure 18.1.

FIGURE 18.1   Remote desktop preferences.

To access a computer that is running VNC from your Ubuntu desktop, in the menu click Applications, Internet, Remote Desktop Viewer. The program starts by searching the local network for shared desktops. If any are found, they are listed. In Figure 18.2, Heather's computer is shown.

From the screen in Figure 18.2, click Connect. You can then select one of the hosts shown in the previous list from a drop box, find others on the network, or enter an IP address of your choosing that correlates to a computer you have already set up somewhere to be accessed using VNC, as in Figure 18.3. Then choose your other options and click Connect to begin.

When you have finished, click Close.

VNC should not be considered secure over the Internet or on untrusted internal networks.

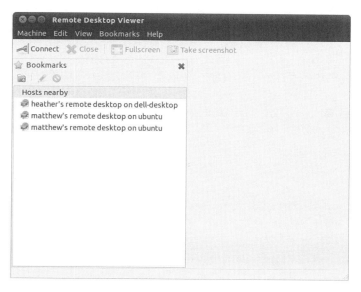

FIGURE 18.2   Remote Desktop Viewer.

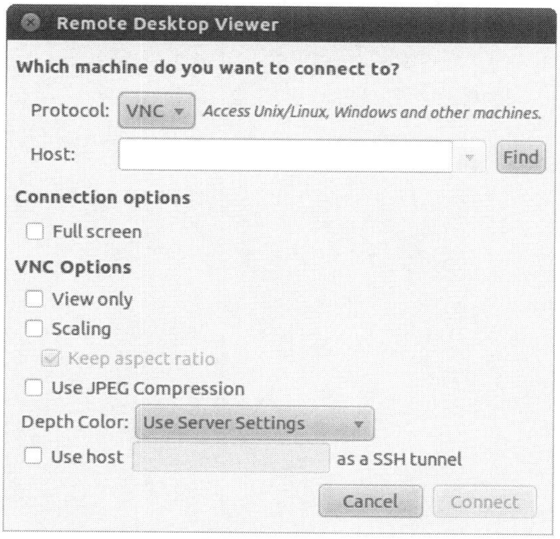

FIGURE 18.3   Choose the machine to which you want to connect.

References

- ▶ www.telnet.org—Telnet's home page.

- ▶ https://help.ubuntu.com/community/SSH—The Ubuntu community documentation for SSH.

- ▶ www.openssh.com—The home page of the OpenSSH implementation of SSH that Ubuntu uses. It is run by the same team as OpenBSD, a secure BSD-based operating system.

- ▶ https://help.ubuntu.com/community/VNC—The Ubuntu community documentation for VNC.

- ▶ www.realvnc.com—The home page of the team that made VNC at AT&T's Cambridge Research Laboratory. It has since started RealVNC Ltd., a company dedicated to developing and supporting VNC.

- ▶ www.tightvnc.com—Here you can find an alternative to VNC called TightVNC that has several key advances over the stock VNC release. The most important feature is that TightVNC can use SSH for encryption, guaranteeing security.

- ▶ https://help.ubuntu.com/community/FreeNX—The Ubuntu community documentation for FreeNX.

- ▶ www.nomachine.com/—Another alternative to VNC is in the pipeline, called NX. The free implementation, FreeNX, is under heavy development at the time of writing but promises to work much faster than VNC.

CHAPTER 19

Securing Your Machines

N‌o computer with a connection to the Internet is 100 percent safe. If this information does not concern you, it should. Although there is no way to guarantee the ability to stop patient, creative, and serious crackers who are intent on getting into your computer or network, there are ways to make it harder for them and to warn you when they do.

In this chapter, we discuss all aspects of securing your Linux machines. You might have wondered why we did not spread this information around the book wherever it was appropriate, but the reason is simple: If you ever have a security problem with Linux, you know you can turn to this page and start reading without having to search or try to remember where you saw a tip. Everything you need is here in this one chapter, and we strongly advise you to read it from start to finish.

Built-In Protection in the Kernel

A number of networking and low-level protective services are built in to the Linux kernel. These services can be enabled, disabled, or displayed using the `sysctl` command, or by echoing a value (usually a 1 or a 0 to turn a service on or off) to a kernel process file under the `/proc` directory.

Understanding Computer Attacks

There are many ways in which computer attacks can be divided for classification. Perhaps the easiest dichotomy is to separate attacks as *internal*, which are computer attacks done by someone with access to a computer on the local network, and *external*, which are attacks by someone with access to a computer through the Internet. This might sound like a trivial separation to make, but it is actually important: Unless you routinely hire talented computer crackers or allow visitors to plug computers into your network, the worst internal attack you are likely encounter is from a disgruntled employee.

Hacker Versus Cracker

In earlier days, there was a distinction made between the words *hacker* and *cracker*. A hacker was someone who used technology to innovate in new or unusual ways, whereas a cracker was someone who used technology to attack another's computers and cause harm. In the original definition, hackers did good or cool things, and crackers did bad things.

This distinction was lost on the general public, so the term *hacker* has now regretfully come to mean the same thing as cracker for most people. However, we recognize the distinction and use the term *cracker* to mean a malicious person using a computer to cause problems for others. In your real-world conversations, realize that most people do not make a distinction, and so be prepared to define your terms if you call yourself a hacker.

Although you should never ignore the internal threat, you should arguably be more concerned with the outside world. The big bad Internet is a security vortex. Machines connected directly to the outside world can be attacked by people across the world, and invariably are, even only a few minutes after having been connected.

This situation is not a result of malicious users lying in wait for your IP address to do something interesting. Instead, canny virus writers have created worms that exploit a vulnerability, take control of a machine, and then spread it to other machines around them. As a result, most attacks today are the result of these autocracking tools; there are only a handful of true clever crackers around, and, to be frank, if one of them ever actually targets you seriously, it will take a mammoth effort to repel the cracker, regardless of which operating system you run.

Autocracking scripts also come in another flavor: prewritten code that exploits a vulnerability and gives its users special privileges on the hacked machine. These scripts are rarely used by their creators; instead, they are posted online and downloaded by wannabe hackers, who then use them to attack vulnerable machines.

So, the external category is itself made up of worms, serious day job crackers, and wannabe crackers (usually called *script kiddies*). Combined, they will assault your Internet-facing servers, and it is your job to make sure your boxes stay up, happily ignoring the firefight around them.

On the internal front, things are somewhat more difficult. Users who sit inside your firewall are already past your primary source of defense and, worse, they might even have physical access to your machines. Anyone with malicious intent and physical access to a machine is nearly impossible to stop unless they are simply inept. The situation is only slightly better if they don't have physical access but do have access to your internal network.

Regardless of the source of the attack, you can follow a five-step checklist to secure your box:

1. Assess your vulnerability. Decide which machines can be attacked, which services they are running, and who has access to them.

2. Configure the server for maximum security. Install only what you need, run only what you must, and configure a local firewall.

3. Secure physical access to the server.

4. Create worst-case-scenario policies.

5. Keep up-to-date with security news.

Each of these is covered in the following sections, and each is as important as the others.

Assessing Your Vulnerability

It is a common mistake for people to assume that switching on a firewall makes them safe. This is not the case and, in fact, has never been the case. Each system has distinct security needs, and taking the time to customize its security layout will give you maximum security and the best performance.

The following list summarizes the most common mistakes:

▶ **Installing every package**—Do you plan to use the machine as a DNS server? If not, why have BIND installed? Go through and ensure that you have only the software you need.

▶ **Enabling unused services**—Do you want to administer the machine remotely? Do you want people to upload files? If not, turn off SSH and FTP because they just add needless attack vectors. This goes for many other services.

▶ **Disabling the local firewall on the grounds that you already have a firewall at the perimeter**—In security, depth is crucial: The more layers someone has to hack through, the higher the likelihood the cracker will give up or get caught.

▶ **Letting your machine give out more information than it needs to**—Many machines are configured to give out software names and version numbers by default, which is just giving crackers a helping hand.

▶ **Placing your server in an unlocked room**—If so, you might as well just turn it off now and save the worry. The exception to this is if all the employees at your company are happy and trustworthy. But why take the risk?

▶ **Plugging your machine into a wireless network**—Unless you need wireless, avoid it, particularly if your machine is a server. Never plug a server into a wireless network because it is just too fraught with security problems.

After you have ruled out these, you are onto the real problem: Which attack vectors are open on your server? In Internet terms, this comes down to which services are Internet-facing and which ports they are running on.

Two tools are often used to determine your vulnerabilities: Nmap and Nessus. Nessus scans your machine, queries the services running, checks their version numbers against its list of vulnerabilities, and reports problems.

Although Nessus sounds clever, it does not work well in many modern distributions (Ubuntu included) because of the way patches are made available to software. For example, if you're running Apache 2.0.52 and a bug is found that's fixed in 2.0.53, Ubuntu backports that patch to 2.0.52. This is done because the new release probably also includes new features that might break your code, so the Ubuntu team takes only what is necessary and copies it into your version. As a result, Nessus will see the version 2.0.52 and think it is vulnerable to a bug that has in fact been backported.

The better solution is to use Nmap, which scans your machine and reports on any open TCP/IP ports it finds. Any service you have installed that responds to Nmap's query is pointed out, which enables you to ensure that you have locked everything down as much as possible.

Nmap is available to install from the Ubuntu software repositories. Although you can use Nmap from a command line, it is easier to use with the front end—at least until you become proficient. To run the front end, open a terminal and run `nmapfe`. If you want to enable all Nmap's options, you must have administrator privileges and run `sudo nmapfe`.

When you run Nmap (click the Scan button), it tests every port on your machine and checks whether it responds. If it does respond, Nmap queries it for version information and then prints its results onscreen.

The output lists the port numbers, service name (what usually occupies that port), and version number for every open port on your system. Hopefully, the information Nmap shows you will not be a surprise. If there is something open that you do not recognize, it could be that a cracker placed a back door on your system to allow easy access, so you should check into it further.

Use the output from Nmap to help you find and eliminate unwanted services. The fewer services that are open to the outside world, the more secure you are. Only use Nmap on systems that you own. It is impolite to scan other people's servers, and you may also be accused of doing so in preparation for illegal activity.

Protecting Your Machine

After you have disabled all the unneeded services on your system, what remains is a core set of connections and programs that you want to keep. However, you are not finished yet: You need to clamp down your wireless network, lock your server physically, and put scanning procedures in place (such as Tripwire and promiscuous mode network monitors).

Securing a Wireless Network

Because wireless networking has some unique security issues, those issues deserve a separate discussion here.

Wireless networking, although convenient, can be very unsecure by its very nature because transmitted data (even encrypted data) can be received by remote devices. Those devices could be in the same room; in the house, apartment, or building next door; or even several blocks away. Extra care must be used to protect the actual frequency used by your network. Great progress has been made in the past couple of years, but the possibility of a security breech is increased when the attacker is in the area and knows the frequency on which to listen. It should also be noted that the encryption method used by more wireless NICs is weaker than other forms of encryption (such as SSH) and should not be considered as part of your security plan.

> **TIP**
>
> Always use OpenSSH-related tools, such as `ssh` or `sftp`, to conduct business on your wireless LAN. Passwords are not transmitted as plain text, and your sessions are encrypted. See Chapter 18, "Remote Access with SSH and Telnet," to see how to connect to remote systems using `ssh`.

The better the physical security is around your network, the more secure it will be. (This applies to wired networks as well.) Keep wireless transmitters (routers, switches, and so on) as close to the center of your building as possible. Note or monitor the range of transmitted signals to determine whether your network is open to mobile network sniffing—now a geek sport known as *war driving*. Wireshark is an example of a program that is useful for analyzing wireless traffic (as well as all network activity) and can be installed from the Ubuntu repositories, with more information at www.wireshark.org/. An occasional walk around your building not only gives you a break from work, but can also give you a chance to notice any people or equipment that should not be in the area.

Keep in mind that it takes only a single rogue wireless access point hooked up to a legitimate network hub to open access to your entire system. These access points can be smaller than a pack of cigarettes, so the only way to spot them is to scan for them with another wireless device.

Passwords and Physical Security

The next step toward better security is to use secure passwords on your network and ensure that users use them as well. For somewhat more physical security, you can force the use of a password with the GRUB bootloader, remove bootable devices such as floppy and CD-ROM drives, or configure a network-booting server for Ubuntu.

Also, keep in mind that some studies show that as many as 90 percent of network break-ins are by current or former employees. If a person no longer requires access to your network, lock out access or, even better, remove the account immediately. A good security policy also dictates that any data associated with the account first be backed up and retained for a set period of time to ensure against loss of important data. If you are able to, remove the terminated employee from the system before the employee leaves the building.

Finally, be aware of physical security. If a potential attacker can get physical access to your system, getting full access becomes trivial. Keep all servers in a locked room and ensure that only authorized personnel are given access to clients.

Configuring and Using Tripwire

Tripwire is a security tool that checks the integrity of normal system binaries and reports any changes to syslog or by email. Tripwire is a good tool for ensuring that your binaries have not been replaced by Trojan horse programs. *Trojan horses* are malicious programs inadvertently installed because of identical filenames to distributed (expected) programs, and they can wreak havoc on a breached system.

There are two versions of Tripwire: an open-source version and a commercial product. The free version of Tripwire is available in the Ubuntu repositories. You can find out about the differences at www.tripwire.org.

To initialize Tripwire, use its --init option, like this:

```
matthew@seymour:~$ sudo tripwire --init

Please enter your local passphrase:
Parsing policy file: /etc/tripwire/tw.pol
Generating the database...
*** Processing Unix File System ***
....
Wrote database file: /var/lib/tripwire/shuttle2.twd
The database was successfully generated.
```

Note that not all the output is shown here. After Tripwire has created its database (which is a snapshot of your file system), it uses this baseline along with the encrypted configuration and policy settings under the /etc/tripwire directory to monitor the status of your system. You should then start Tripwire in its integrity checking mode, using a desired option. (See the tripwire manual page for details.) For example, you can have Tripwire check your system and then generate a report at the command line, like this:

```
matthew@seymour:~$ sudo tripwire -m c
```

No output is shown here, but a report is displayed in this example. The output could be redirected to a file, but a report is saved as /var/lib/tripwire/report/hostname-YYYYMMDD-HHMMSS.twr (in other words, using your host's name, the year, the month, the day, the hour, the minute, and the seconds). This report can be read using the twprint utility, like this:

```
matthew@seymour:~$ sudo twprint --print-report -r \
/var/lib/tripwire/report/shuttle2-20020919-181049.twr | less
```

Other options, such as emailing the report, are supported by Tripwire, which should be run as a scheduled task by your system's scheduling table, /etc/crontab, on off-hours. (It can be resource intensive on less powerful computers.) The Tripwire software package also includes a twadmin utility you can use to fine-tune or change settings or policies or to perform other administrative duties.

Plan to spend some time reading documentation if you want to use Tripwire. It is powerful, but not simple. We recommend starting with the man pages and www.tripwire.com.

Devices

Do not ever advertise that you have set a NIC to promiscuous mode. Promiscuous mode (which can be set on an interface by using ifconfig's promisc option) is good for monitoring traffic across the network and can often allow you to monitor the actions of someone who might have broken into your network. The tcpdump command also sets a designated interface to promiscuous mode while the program runs; unfortunately, the ifconfig command does not report this fact while tcpdump is running!

Remember to use the right tool for the right job. Although a network bridge can be used to connect your network to the Internet, it would not be a good option. Bridges have almost become obsolete because they forward any packet that comes their way, which is not good when a bridge is connected to the Internet. A router enables you to filter which packets are relayed.

Viruses

In the right hands, Linux is every bit as vulnerable to viruses as Windows is. That might come as a surprise to you, particularly if you made the switch to Linux on the basis of its security record. However, the difference between Windows and Linux is that it is much easier to secure against viruses on Linux. Indeed, as long as you are smart and diligent, you need never worry about them. Here is why:

▶ Linux never puts the current directory in your executable path, so typing ls runs /bin/ls rather than any program named ls in the current directory.

▶ A nonroot user can infect only the files that user has write access to, which is usually only the files in the user's home directory. This is one of the most important reasons for never using sudo when you don't need to.

▶ Linux forces you to manually mark files as executable, so you can't accidentally run a file called myfile.txt.exe thinking it is just a text file.

▶ By having more than one common web browser and email client, Linux has strength through diversity: Virus writers cannot target one platform and hit 90 percent of the users.

Despite all that, Linux is susceptible to being a carrier for viruses. If you run a mail server, your Linux box can send virus-infected mails on to Windows boxes. The Linux-based server would be fine, but the Windows client would be taken down by the virus.

In this situation, consider a virus scanner for your machine. You have several to choose from, both free and commercial. The most popular free suite is Clam AV (www.clamav.net), but Central Command, BitDefender, F-Secure, Kaspersky, McAfee, and others all compete to provide commercial solutions. Look around for the best deal before you commit.

Configuring Uncomplicated Firewall

Always use a hardware-based or software-based firewall on computers connected to the Internet. Ubuntu has a firewall application installed by default named *Uncomplicated Firewall (UFW)*. This tool enables you to implement selective or restrictive policies regarding access to your computer or LAN.

UFW is run from the terminal, and you must have administrative privileges to use it. Commands are given like this:

matthew@seymour:~$ **sudo ufw status**

The most useful commands are listed in Table 19.1; for others, the UFW man page. Many are described in greater detail after the table.

TABLE 19.1   Useful Commands for UFW

Usage: UFW COMMAND	
Commands:	
enable	Enables the firewall
disable	Disables the firewall
reload	Reloads the firewall to ensure changes are applied
default allow|deny|reject	Sets default policy
logging on|off	Toggles logging (can also be used to set the level of logging, see manual)
allow ARGS	Adds allow rule
deny ARGS	Adds deny rule
reject ARGS	Adds reject rule
limit ARGS	Adds limit rule
delete RULE	Deletes rule
status shows	Firewall status

`status numbered`	Shows firewall status as numbered list of rules
`status verbose`	Shows verbose firewall status
`show REPORT`	Shows firewall report
`--version`	Displays version information

By default, the UFW or firewall is disabled. To enable the firewall, you run the following command:

`matthew@seymour:~$` **`sudo ufw enable`**

To disable, replace `enabled` with `disabled`.

Next, we want to enable firewall logging. Much like the `enable` command, we run the following command:

`matthew@seymour:~$` **`sudo ufw logging on`**

To enable specific ports on the firewall, you can run the `ufw` command along with the port number to open. For example, if you want to allow port 80 (HTTP) incoming connections to your Ubuntu server, you enter the following:

`matthew@seymour:~$` **`sudo ufw allow 80`**

To remove the firewall rule allowing port 80 connections, run the following command:

`matthew@seymour:~$` **`sudo ufw delete allow 80`**

Many services are already defined in `ufw`. This means you don't have to remember the standard ports those services use, and you can allow, deny, or delete using the service name, like this:

`matthew@seymour:~$` **`sudo ufw allow ssh`**

You can also allow incoming connections from particular IP addresses. For example, if you want to let 192.168.0.1 to connect to your server, you enter the following:

`matthew@seymour:~$` **`sudo ufw allow from 192.168.0.1`**

To remove the firewall rule allowing the previous IP address to connect, run the following command:

`matthew@seymour:~$` **`sudo ufw delete allow from 192.168.0.1`**

There is also a graphical interface that can be installed from the Ubuntu repositories to manage UFW called *GUFW*. If you install it, you can open GUFW at System, Administration, Firewall configuration. The same details apply, but the interface is easier and does not require you to remember as much, as you can see in Figure 19.1, where I have a rule to allow traffic in on port 22 (for the SSH service) and incoming traffic on port 5900 if it uses TCP (for the VNC service).

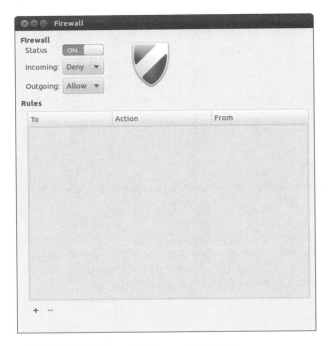

FIGURE 19.1   The GUFW graphical interface.

If you click Add, you can easily add rules for preconfigured services, as shown in Figure 19.2, or you can configure your own rules from the Simple and Advanced tabs.

AppArmor

AppArmor is a *Mandatory Access Control (MAC)* system. It is less complicated than the better known SELinux (www.nsa.gov/research/selinux/), a MAC created by the U.S. *National Security Agency (NSA)*. AppArmor is designed to limit what specific programs can do by restricting them to the use of predetermined resources and only those resources. This is done via profiles, which are loaded into the kernel at boot. It can be run in complain mode, where information is logged about unsecure practices but no action is taken, or in enforce mode where policies and limits are active.

This is a brief introduction to AppArmor. For a fuller introduction, checks the links listed in the "References" section at the end of this chapter.

By default, AppArmor does little. You can install some extra profiles from the Ubuntu repositories by installing the `apparmor-profiles` package. These run in complain mode and log issues in `/var/log/messages`.

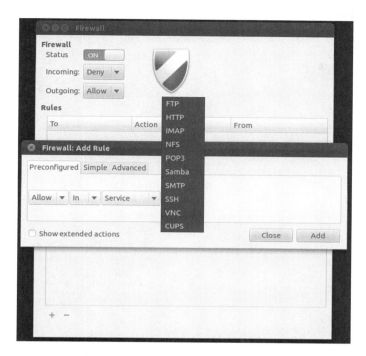

FIGURE 19.2   GUFW preconfigured service options.

To unleash the power of AppArmor, you need to edit or create text files in
/etc/apparmor.d. Profiles are named for the application they restrict, including the full
path to the application in the filesystem. For example, the file sbin.syslogd, shown here,
restricts the system logging daemon:

```
# $Id$
# ----------------------------------------------------------------
#
#     Copyright (C) 2002-2005 Novell/SUSE
#
#     This program is free software; you can redistribute it and/or
#     modify it under the terms of version 2 of the GNU General Public
#     License published by the Free Software Foundation.
#
# ----------------------------------------------------------------


#include <tunables/global>
```

```
/sbin/syslogd flags=(complain) {
  #include <abstractions/base>
  #include <abstractions/nameservice>
  #include <abstractions/consoles>


  capability sys_tty_config,
  capability dac_override,
  capability dac_read_search,
  capability setuid,
  capability setgid,


  /dev/log                    wl,
  /var/lib/*/dev/log          wl,


  /dev/tty*                   w,
  /dev/xconsole               rw,
  /etc/syslog.conf            r,
  /sbin/syslogd               rmix,
  /var/log/**                 rw,
  /var/run/syslogd.pid        krwl,
  /var/run/utmp               rw,
  /var/spool/compaq/nic/messages_fifo rw,
}
```

Even without knowing the syntax, we can see from this file that profiles are simple text files that support the use of comments, that absolute paths and globbing (pattern matching for filenames) are supported, that specific capabilities are allowed or disallowed, and what locations and programs in the filesystem may be accessed or used.

Each access rule specifies specific permissions from this list:

```
r    - read
w    - write
ux   - unconstrained execute
Ux   - unconstrained execute -- scrub the environment
px   - discrete profile execute
Px   - discrete profile execute -- scrub the environment
ix   - inherit execute
m    - allow PROT_EXEC with mmap(2) calls
l    - link
```

These permissions are listed at the end of lines.

Genprof is a program that helps you generate or update a profile. You supply the name of the executable (or the path, if it is not already in the path) and may optionally supply the path to the profiles, as well:

```
matthew@seymour:~$ sudo genprof google-chrome
```

You will be asked to start the program and use it for a bit. After it is complete, you are given an opportunity to choose whether access to each function should be allowed or denied. The program then writes a text file in `/etc/apparmor.d` using the name of the program and its path (in this case, opt.google.chrome.google-chrome, which I installed directly from Google [www.google.com/chrome?platform=linux], so no premade AppArmor profile exists on my system). You may then edit the text file as desired, which you must do if you want to change from complain to enforce mode.

After you have a set of profiles that cover what you need, these are the commands you will use most often:

```
start:
matthew@seymour:~$ sudo service apparmor start

stop:
matthew@seymour:~$ sudo service apparmor stop

reload:
matthew@seymour:~$ sudo service apparmor reload (or restart)

show status:
matthew@seymour:~$ sudo service apparmor status
```

We have just scratched the surface of AppArmor, but hopefully enough to have whetted your appetite to do some further reading. AppArmor is still rather new and is changing. Online documentation is the best way to keep up. A few good places to start are included in the "References" section.

Forming a Disaster Recovery Plan

No one likes planning for the worst, which is why two-thirds of people do not have wills. It is a scary thing to have your systems hacked: One or more criminals has broken through your carefully laid blocks and caused untold damage to the machine. Your boss, if you have one, wants a full report of what happened and why, and your users want their email when they sit down at their desks in the morning. What to do?

If you ever do get hacked, nothing will take the stress away entirely. However, if you take the time to prepare a proper response in advance, you should at least avoid premature aging. Here are some tips to get you started:

▶ **Do not just pull the network cable out**—This acts as an alert that the cracker has been detected, which rules out any opportunities for security experts to monitor for that cracker returning and actually catch him.

▶ **Only inform the people who need to know**—Your boss and other IT people are at the top of the list; other employees are not. Keep in mind that it could be one of the employees behind the attack, and this tips them off.

▶ **If the machine is not required and you do not want to trace the attack, you can safely remove it from the network**—However, do not switch it off because some back doors are enabled only when the system is rebooted.

▶ **Take a copy of all the log files on the system and store them somewhere else**— These might have been tampered with, but they might contain nuggets of information.

▶ **Check the /etc/passwd file and look for users you do not recognize**—Change all the passwords on the system and remove bad users.

▶ **Check the output of ps aux for unusual programs running**—Also check to see whether any cron jobs are set to run.

▶ **Look in /var/www and see whether any web pages are there that should not be.**

▶ **Check the contents of the .bash_history files in the /home directories of your users**—Are there any recent commands for your primary user?

▶ **If you have worked with external security companies previously, call them in for a fresh audit**—Hand over all the logs you have, and explain the situation. They will be able to extract all the information from the logs that is possible.

▶ **Start collating backup tapes from previous weeks and months**—Your system might have been hacked long before you noticed, so you might need to roll back the system more than once to find out when the attack actually succeeded.

▶ **Download and install Rootkit Hunter from www.rootkit.nl/projects/ rootkit_hunter.html**—This searches for (and removes) the types of files that bad guys leave behind for their return.

Keep your disaster recovery plan somewhere safe; saving it as a file on the machine in question is a *very* bad move.

References

▶ **https://help.ubuntu.com/community/InstallingSecurityTools**—Ubuntu community documentation of and suggestions for various security tools.

▶ **www.insecure.org/nmap/**—This site contains information on Nmap.

▶ **www.securityfocus.com/**—The Security Focus website.

▶ **www.tripwire.org**—Information and download links for the open-source version of Tripwire.

▶ **www.ubuntu.com/usn**—The official Ubuntu security notices list; well worth keeping an eye on.

▶ **https://help.ubuntu.com/community/UFW**—Ubuntu community documentation for UFW.

▶ **https://wiki.ubuntu.com/UncomplicatedFirewall**—Ubuntu documentation for UFW.

▶ **https://help.ubuntu.com/community/AppArmor**—Ubuntu community documentation for AppArmor.

▶ **www.novell.com/linux/security/apparmor/**—Novell's excellent introduction to and documentation for AppArmor.

# CHAPTER 20

Performance Tuning

Squeezing extra performance out of your hardware might sound like a pointless task given how cheap commodity upgrades are today. To a certain degree, that is true; for most of us, it is cheaper to buy a new computer than to spend hours fighting to get a 5 percent speed boost. But what if the speed boost were 20 percent? How about if it were 50 percent?

The amount of benefit you can get by optimizing your system varies depending on what kinds of tasks you are running, but there is something for everyone. Over the next few pages, we look at quick ways to optimize the Apache web server, both the KDE and GNOME desktop systems, both MySQL and PostgreSQL database servers, and more.

Before we start, you need to understand that *optimization* is not an absolute term: If we optimize a system, we have improved its performance, but it is still possible it could further be increased. We are not interested in getting 99.999 percent performance out of a system, because optimization suffers from the law of diminishing returns—the basic changes make the biggest differences, but after that it takes increasing amounts of work to obtain decreasing speed improvements.

Hard Disk

Many Linux users love to tinker under the hood to increase the performance of their computers, and Linux gives you some great tools to do that. Whereas Moms tell us, "Don't fix what's not broken," Dads often say, "Fix it until it breaks." In this section, you learn about many of the commands used to tune, or "tweak," your file system.

Before you undertake any under-the-hood work with Linux, however, keep a few points in mind. First, perform a benchmark on your system before you begin. Linux does not offer a well-developed benchmarking application, and availability of what exists changes rapidly. You can search online for the most up-to-date information for benchmarking applications for Linux. If you are a system administrator, you might choose to create your own benchmarking tests. Second, tweak only one thing at a time so you can tell what works, what does not work, and what breaks things. Some of these tweaks might not work or might lock up your machine, but if you are only implementing them one at a time, you will find it much easier to reverse a change that caused a problem.

Always have a working boot disc handy, such as the live Ubuntu CD or DVD. Remember that you are personally assuming all risks for attempting any of these tweaks. If you don't understand what you are doing or are not confident in your ability to revert any changes discussed here, do not attempt any of the suggestions in this chapter. The default settings in Ubuntu work very well for most people and really don't need adjusting—just as most people can use and enjoy their car just as it is. However, some people love taking their cars apart and building hot rods; they enjoy tweaking and breaking and fixing them. This chapter is for that sort of person. If you don't think you can fix it, don't risk breaking it.

Using the BIOS and Kernel to Tune the Disk Drives

One method of tuning involves adjusting the settings in your BIOS. Because the BIOS is not Linux and every BIOS seems different, always read your motherboard manual for better possible settings and make certain that all the drives are detected correctly by the BIOS. Change only one setting at a time.

Linux provides a limited means to interact with BIOS settings during the boot process (mostly overriding them). In this section, you learn about those commands.

Other options are in the following list, and are more fully outlined in the BOOTPROMPT HOWTO and the kernel documentation. These commands can be used to force the IDE controllers and drives to be optimally configured. However, YMMV (your mileage may vary) because these do not work for everyone:

- ▶ `idex=dma`—This forces DMA support to be turned on for the primary IDE bus, where x=0, or the secondary bus, where x=1.

- ▶ `idex=autotune`—This command attempts to tune the interface for optimal performance.

- ▶ `hdx=ide-scsi`—This command enables SCSI emulation of an IDE drive. This is required for some CD-RW drives to work properly in write mode, and it might provide some performance improvements for regular CD-R drives, as well.

- ▶ `idebus=xx`—This can be any number from 20 to 66; autodetection is attempted, but this can set it manually if `dmesg` says that it isn't autodetected correctly or if you have it set in the BIOS to a different value (overclocked). Most PCI controllers are happy with 33.

▶ **pci=biosirq**—Some motherboards might cause Linux to generate an error message saying that you should use this. Look in dmesg for it; if you do not see it, you don't need to use it.

These options can be entered into /etc/lilo.conf or /boot/grub/grub.conf or GRUB2's /boot/grub/grub.cfg in the same way as other options are appended.

The hdparm Command

The hdparm utility can be used by root to set and tune the settings for IDE hard drives. You would do this to tune the drives for optimal performance.

Once a kernel patch and associated support programs, the hdparm program is now included with Ubuntu. You should only experiment with the file systems mounted read-only because some settings can damage some file systems when used improperly. The hdparm command also works with CD-ROM drives and some SCSI drives.

The general format of the command is this:

```
matthew@seymour:~$ hdparm command device
```

This command runs a hard disk test:

```
matthew@seymour:~$ hdparm -tT /dev/hda
```

You must replace /dev/hda with the location of your hard disk. hdparm then runs two tests: cached reads and buffered disk reads. A good IDE hard disk should be getting 400MBps to 500MBps for the first test, and 20MBps to 30MBps for the second. Note your scores, and then try this command:

```
matthew@seymour:~$ hdparm -m16 -d1 -u1 -c1 /dev/hda
```

That enables various performance-enhancing settings. Now try executing the original command again. If you see an increase, you should run this command:

```
matthew@seymour:~$ hdparm -m16 -d1 -u1 -c1 -k1 /dev/hda
```

The extra parameter tells hdparm to write the settings to disk so that they will be used each time you boot, ensuring optimal disk performance in the future.

The man entry for hdparm is extensive and contains useful detailed information, but because the kernel configuration selected by Ubuntu already attempts to optimize the drives, it might be that little can be gained through tweaking. Because not all hardware combinations can be anticipated by Ubuntu or by Linux, and performance gains are always useful, you're encouraged to try.

20

TIP

You can use the `hdparm` command to produce a disk transfer speed result with the following:

    matthew@seymour:~$ **hdparm -tT device**

Be aware, however, that although the resulting numbers appear quantitative, they are subject to several technical qualifications beyond the scope of what is discussed and explained in this chapter. Simply put, do not accept values generated by hdparm as absolute numbers, but only as a relative measure of performance.

File System Tuning

Never content to leave things alone, Linux provides several tools to adjust and customize the file system settings. The belief is that hardware manufacturers and distribution creators tend to select conservative settings that will work well all the time, leaving some of the potential of your system leashed—that's why you have chosen *Ubuntu Unleashed* to help you.

The Linux file system designers have done an excellent job of selecting default values used for file system creation, and the 2.6 version of the Linux kernel now contains code for the IDE subsystem that significantly improves *I/O (input/output)* transfer speeds over older versions, obviating much of the need for special tweaking of the file system and drive parameters if you use IDE disks. Although these values work well for most users, some server applications of Linux benefit from file system tuning. As always, observe and benchmark your changes.

Synchronizing the File System with sync

Because Linux uses buffers when writing to devices, the write will not occur until the buffer is full, until the kernel tells it to, or if you tell it to by using the sync command. Traditionally, the command is given twice, as in the following:

    matthew@seymour:~$ **sync ; sync**

To do it twice is overkill. Still, it can be helpful before the unmounting of certain types of media with slow write speeds (such as some USB hard drives or PCMCIA storage media), but only because it delays the user from attempting to remove the media too soon, not because two syncs are better than one.

The `tune2fs` Command

With `tune2fs`, you can adjust the tunable file system parameters on an `ext2` or `ext3` file system. A few performance-related items of note are as follows:

▶ To disable file system checking, the `-c 0` option sets the maximal mount count to zero.

▶ The interval between forced checks can be adjusted with the `-i` option.

▶ The -m option sets the reserved blocks percentage with a lower value, freeing more space at the expense of fsck having less space to write any recovered files.

▶ Decrease the number of superblocks to save space with the -O sparse_super option. (Modern file systems use this by default.) Always run e2fsck after you change this value.

▶ More space can be freed with the -r option that sets the number of reserved (for root) blocks.

Note that most of these uses of tune2fs free up space on the drive at the expense of the capability of fsck to recover data. Unless you really need the space and can deal with the consequences, just accept the defaults; large drives are now relatively inexpensive.

The e2fsck Command

This utility checks an ext2/ext3 file system. Some useful arguments taken from man e2fsck are as follows:

▶ -c—Checks for bad blocks and then marks them as bad.

▶ -f—Forces checking on a clean file system.

▶ -v—Verbose mode.

The badblocks Command

Although not a performance tuning program per se, the utility badblocks checks an (preferably) unmounted partition for bad blocks. It is not recommended that you run this command by itself, but rather allow it to be called by fsck. It should be used directly only if you specify the block size accurately; don't guess or assume anything.

The options available for badblocks are detailed in the man page. They allow for very low-level manipulation of the file system that is useful for data recovery by file system experts or for file system hacking, but are beyond the scope of this chapter and the average user.

Disabling File Access Time

Whenever Linux reads a file, it changes the last access time (known as the *atime*). This is also true for your web server: If you are getting hit by 50 requests a second, your hard disk will be updating the atime 50 times a second. Do you really need to know the last time a file was accessed? If not, you can disable the atime setting for a directory by typing this:

```
matthew@seymour:~$ chattr -R +A /path/to/directory
```

The chattr command changes file system attributes, of which "don't update atime" is one. To set that attribute, use +A and specify -R so that it is recursively set. /path/to/directory gets changed, and so do all the files and subdirectories it contains.

20

Kernel

As the Linux kernel developed over time, developers sought a way to fine-tune some of the kernel parameters. Before sysctl, those parameters had to be changed in the kernel configuration, and then the kernel had to be recompiled.

The sysctl command can change some parameters of a running kernel. It does this through the /proc file system, which is a "virtual window" into the running kernel. Although it might appear that a group of directories and files exist under /proc, that is only a representation of parts of the kernel. When we're the root user (or using the sudo command), we can read values from and write values to those "files," referred to as *variables*. We can display a list of the variables, as shown in the following. (An annotated list is presented because roughly 250 items, or more, exist in the full list.)

```
matthew@seymour:~$ sysctl -A
net.ipv4.tcp_max_syn_backlog = 1024
net.ipv4.tcp_rfc1337 = 0
net.ipv4.tcp_stdurg = 0
net.ipv4.tcp_abort_on_overflow = 0
net.ipv4.tcp_tw_recycle = 0
net.ipv4.tcp_syncookies = 0
net.ipv4.tcp_fin_timeout = 60
net.ipv4.tcp_retries2 = 15
net.ipv4.tcp_retries1 = 3
net.ipv4.tcp_keepalive_intvl = 75
net.ipv4.tcp_keepalive_probes = 9
net.ipv4.tcp_keepalive_time = 7200
net.ipv4.ipfrag_time = 30
```

The items shown are networking parameters, and tweaking these values is beyond the scope of this book. If we wanted to change a value, however, the -w parameter is used:

```
matthew@seymour:~$ sysctl -w net.ipv4.tcp_retries 2=20
```

This increases the value of that particular kernel parameter.

If you find that a particular setting is useful, you can enter it into the /etc/sysctl.conf file. The format is as follows, using the earlier example:

```
net.ipv4.tcp_retries 2=20
```

Of more interest to kernel hackers than regular users, sysctl is a potentially powerful tool that continues to be developed and documented.

TIP

The kernel does a good job of balancing performance for graphical systems, so there's not a great deal you can do to tweak your desktop to run faster.

Both GNOME and KDE are "heavyweight" desktop systems: They are all-inclusive, all-singing, and all-dancing environments that do far more than browse your file system. The drawback is that their size makes them run slow on older systems. On the flip side, Ubuntu has others available in the repositories like the Xfce and LXDE desktops, which are a great deal slimmer and faster than the other two. If you find GNOME and KDE are struggling just to open a file browser, Xfce or LXDE are likely for you.

Apache

Despite being the most popular web server on the Internet, Apache is by no means the fastest. Part of the "problem" is that Apache has been written to follow every applicable standard to the letter, so much of its development work has been geared toward standards compliancy rather than just serving web pages quickly. However, with a little tweaking, we can convert an inexpensive middle-of-the-road server into something capable of surviving the Slashdot Effect (or "being Slashdotted").

> **NOTE**
>
> Slashdot.org is a popular geek news website that spawned the Slashdot Effect—the result of thousands of geeks descending on an unsuspecting website simultaneously. Although Slashdot is still popular, other sites are newer and have gained great momentum and popularity (we're looking at you, Reddit!). We are not trying to ignore the new sites, but rather honor the original. We freely acknowledge that many other wonderful sources of the effect exist.

The first target for your tuning should be the apache2.conf file in /etc/apache2, as well as the other files in /etc/apache2. The more modules you have loaded, the more load Apache is placing on your server. Take a look through the LoadModule list and comment out (start the line with a #) the ones you do not want. Some of these modules can be uninstalled entirely through the Add or Remove Packages dialog.

As a rough guide, you almost certainly need mod_mime and mod_dir, and probably also mod_log_config. The default Apache configuration in Ubuntu is quite generic, so unless you are willing to sacrifice some functionality, you might also need mod_negotiation (a speed killer if there ever was one), and mod_access (a notorious problem). Both of those modules can and should work with little or no performance decrease, but all too often they get abused and just slow things down.

Whatever you do, when you are disabling modules, you should ensure that you leave either mod_deflate or mod_gzip enabled, depending on your Apache version. Your bottleneck is almost certainly going to be your bandwidth rather than your processing power, and having one of these two compressing your content will usually turn 10KB of HTML into 3KB for supported browsers (most of them).

Next, ensure that keepalives are turned off. Yes, you read that right: Turn keepalives *off*. This adds some latency to people viewing your site because they cannot download multiple files through the same connection. However, it reduces the number of simultaneous open connections and so allows more people to connect.

If you are serving content that does not change, you can take the extreme step of enabling MMAP support. This allows Apache to serve pages directly from RAM without bothering to check whether they have changed, which works wonders for your performance. However, the downside is that when you do change your pages, you need to restart Apache. Look for the `EnableMMAP` directive; it is probably commented out and set to off, so you will need to remove the comment and set it to on.

Finally, if speed is your greatest concern, you should do all you can to ensure that your content is static: Avoid PHP if you can, avoid databases if you can, and so on. If you know you are going to get hit by a rush of visitors, use plain HTML so that Apache is limited only by your bandwidth for how fast it can serve pages.

> **TIP**
>
> Some people, when questioned about optimizing Apache, recommend that you tweak the `HARD_SERVER_LIMIT` in the Apache source code and recompile. Although we agree that compiling your own Apache source code is a great way to get a measurable speed boost if you know what you are doing, you should need to change this directive only if you are hosting a huge site.
>
> The default value, 256, is enough to handle the Slashdot Effect, and if you can handle that, then you can handle most things.

MySQL

Tuning your MySQL server for increased performance is exceptionally easy to do, largely because you can see huge speed increases simply by getting your queries right. However, you can tune various things in the server itself to help it cope with higher loads as long as your system has enough RAM.

The key is understanding its buffers. There are buffers and caches for all sorts of things, and finding out how full they are is crucial to maximizing performance. MySQL performs best when it is making full use of its buffers, which in turn places a heavy demand on system RAM. Unless you have 4GB RAM or more in your machine, you do not have enough capacity to set very high values for all your buffers; you need to pick and choose.

Measuring Key Buffer Usage

When you add indexes to your data, it enables MySQL to find data faster. However, ideally you want to have these indexes stored in RAM for maximum speed, and the variable `key_buffer_size` defines how much RAM MySQL can allocate for index key caching. IfMySQL cannot store its indexes in RAM, you will experience serious performance problems. Fortunately, most databases have relatively small key buffer requirements, but you should measure your usage to see what work needs to be done.

To do this, log in to MySQL and type SHOW STATUS LIKE '%key_read%'; this returns all the status fields that describe the hit rate of your key buffer. You should get two rows back, Key_reads and Key_read_requests, which are the number of keys being read from disk and the number of keys being read from the key buffer. From these two numbers, you can calculate the percentage of requests being filled from RAM and from disk, using this simple equation:

```
100 - ((Key_reads / Key_read_requests) &infin; 100)
```

That is, you divide Key_reads by Key_read_requests, multiply the result by 100, and then subtract the result from 100. For example, if you have Key_reads of 1000 and Key_read_requests of 100000, you divide 1000 by 100000 to get 0.01; then you multiply that by 100 to get 1.0, and subtract that from 100 to get 99. That number is the percentage of key reads being served from RAM, which means 99 percent of your keys are served from RAM.

Most people should be looking to get more than 95 percent served from RAM, although the primary exception is if you update or delete rows very often—MySQL can't cache what keeps changing. If your site is largely read-only, this should be around 98 percent. Lower figures mean you might need to bump up the size of your key buffer.

If you are seeing problems, the next step is to check how much of your current key buffer is being used. Use the SHOW VARIABLES command and look up the value of the key_buffer_size variable. It is probably something like 8388600, which is 8 million bytes, or 8MB. Now, use the SHOW STATUS command and look up the value of Key_blocks_used.

You can determine how much of your key buffer is being used by multiplying Key_blocks_used by 1024, dividing by key_buffer_size, and multiplying by 100. For example, if Key_blocks_used is 8000, multiply that by 1024 to get 8192000; then divide that by your key_buffer_size (8388600) to get 0.97656, and finally multiply that by 100 to get 97.656. Thus, almost 98 percent of your key buffer is being used.

Now, the important part: You have ascertained that you are reading lots of keys from disk, and you also know that the reason for reading from disk is almost certainly because you do not have enough RAM allocated to the key buffer. A general rule is to allocate as much RAM to the key buffer as you can, up to a maximum of 25 percent of system RAM—128MB on a 512MB system is about the ideal for systems that read heavily from keys. Beyond that, you will actually see drastic performance decreases because the system has to use virtual memory for the key buffer.

Open /etc/my.cnf in your text editor and look for the line that contains key_buffer_size. If you do not have one, you need to create a new one. It should be under the line [mysqld]. When you set the new value, do not just pick some arbitrarily high number. Try doubling what is there right now (or try 16MB if there's no line already); then see how it goes. To set 16MB as the key buffer size, you need a line like this:

```
[mysqld]
set-variable = key_buffer_size=16M
datadir=/var/lib/mysql
```

Restart your MySQL server with `service mysqld restart`, and then go back into MySQL and run `SHOW VARIABLES` again to see the `key_buffer_size`. It should be 16773120 if you have set it to 16M. Now, because MySQL just got reset, all its values for key hits and the like will also have been reset. You need to let it run for a while so that you can assess how much has changed. If you have a test system you can run, this is the time to run it.

After your database has been accessed with normal usage for a short while (if you get frequent accesses, this might be only a few minutes), recalculate how much of the key buffer is being used. If you get another high score, double the size again, restart, and retest. You should keep repeating this until your key buffer usage is below 50 percent or you find you don't have enough RAM to increase the buffer further. Remember that you should *never* allocate more than 25 percent of system RAM to the key buffer.

Using the Query Cache

Newer versions of MySQL allow you to cache the results of queries so that, if new queries come in that use the same SQL, the result can be served from RAM. In some ways, the query cache is quite intelligent: If, for example, part of the result changes due to another query, the cached results are thrown away and recalculated next time. However, in other ways, it is very simple. For example, it uses cached results only if the new query is exactly the same as a cached query, even down to the capitalization of the SQL.

The query cache works well in most scenarios. If your site has an equal mix of reading and writing, the query cache does its best but is not optimal. If your site is mostly reading with few writes, more queries are cached (and for longer), thus improving overall performance.

First, you need to find out whether you have the query cache enabled. To do this, use `SHOW VARIABLES` and look up the value of `have_query_cache`. All being well, you should get YES back, meaning that the query cache is enabled. Next, look for the value of `query_cache_size` and `query_cache_limit`. The first is how much RAM in bytes is allocated to the query cache, and the second is the maximum result size that should be cached. A good starting set of values for these two is 8388608 (8MB) and 1048576 (1MB).

Next, type `SHOW STATUS LIKE 'Qcache%';` to see all the status information about the query cache. You should get output like this:

```
mysql> SHOW STATUS LIKE 'Qcache%';
+-------------------------+--------+
| Variable_name           | Value  |
+-------------------------+--------+
| Qcache_free_blocks      | 1      |
| Qcache_free_memory      | 169544 |
| Qcache_hits             | 698    |
| Qcache_inserts          | 38     |
| Qcache_lowmem_prunes    | 20     |
```

```
| Qcache_not_cached      | 0       |
| Qcache_queries_in_cache | 18     |
| Qcache_total_blocks    | 57      |
+------------------------+-------+
8 rows in set (0.00 sec)
```

From that, we can see that only 18 queries are in the cache (`Qcache_queries_in_cache`); we have 169544 bytes of memory free in the cache (`Qcache_free_memory`), 698 queries have been read from the cache (`Qcache_hits`), 38 queries have been inserted into the cache (`Qcache_inserts`), but 20 of them were removed due to lack of memory (`Qcache_lowmem_prunes`), giving the 18 from before. `Qcache_not_cached` is 0, which means 0 queries were not cached—MySQL is caching them all.

From that, we can calculate how many total queries came in—it is the sum of `Qcache_hits`, `Qcache_inserts`, and `Qcache_not_cached`, which is 736. We can also calculate how well the query cache is being used by dividing `Qcache_hits` by that number and multiplying by 100. In this case, 94.84 percent of all queries are being served from the query cache, which is a great number.

In our example, we can see that many queries have been trimmed because there is not enough memory in the query cache. This can be changed by editing your /etc/my.cnf file and adding a line like this one, somewhere in the [mysqld] section:

```
set-variable = query_cache_size=32M
```

An 8MB query cache should be enough for most people, but larger sites might need 16MB or even 32MB if you are storing a particularly large amount of data. Very few sites will need to go beyond a 32MB query cache, but keep an eye on the `Qcache_lowmem_prunes` value to ensure that you have enough RAM allocated.

Using the query cache does not incur much of a performance hit. When MySQL calculates the result of a query normally, it throws it away when the connection closes. With the query cache, it skips the throwing away, and so there is no extra work being done. If your site does have many updates and deletes, be sure to check whether you get any speed boost at all from the query cache.

Miscellaneous Tweaks

If you have tuned your key buffer and optimized your query cache and yet still find your site to be struggling, you can make a handful of smaller changes that will add some more speed.

When reading from tables, MySQL has to open the file that stores the table data. How many files it keeps open at a time is defined by the `table_cache` setting, which is set to 64 by default. You can increase this setting if you have more than 64 tables, but be aware that Ubuntu imposes limits on MySQL about how many files it can have open at a time. Going beyond 256 is not recommended unless you have a particularly DB-heavy site and know exactly what you are doing.

The other thing you can tweak is the size of the read buffer, which is controlled by `read_buffer_size` and `read_buffer_rnd_size`. Both of these are allocated per connection, which means you should be very careful to have large numbers. Whatever you choose, `read_buffer_rnd_size` should be three to four times the size of `read_buffer_size`, so if `read_buffer_size` is 1MB (suitable for very large databases), `read_buffer_rnd_size` should be 4MB.

Query Optimization

The biggest speed-ups can be seen by reprogramming your SQL statements so they are more efficient. If you follow these tips, your server will thank you:

- ▶ Select as little data as possible. Rather than SELECT *, select only the fields you need.
- ▶ If you need only a few rows, use LIMIT to select the number you need.
- ▶ Declare fields as NOT NULL when creating tables to save space and increase speed.
- ▶ Provide default values for fields, and use them where you can.
- ▶ Be very careful with table joins because they are the easiest way to write inefficient queries.
- ▶ If you must use joins, be sure you join on fields that are indexed. They should also preferably be integer fields, because these are faster than strings for comparisons.
- ▶ Find and fix slow queries. Add log-long-format and log-slow-queries = /var/log/slow-queries.log to your /etc/my.cnf file, under [mysqld], and MySQL will tell you the queries that took a long time to complete.
- ▶ Use OPTIMIZE TABLE tablename to defragment tables and refresh the indexes.

References

- ▶ www.coker.com.au/bonnie++/—The home page of bonnie, a disk benchmarking tool. It also contains a link to RAID benchmarking utilities and Postal, a benchmarking utility for SMTP servers.

- ▶ www.phoronix-test-suite.com/—The Phoronix Test Suite was created by a website that does automated performance testing and comparisons and is a quality benchmarking software to consider.

- ▶ http://httpd.apache.org/docs-2.0/misc/perf-tuning.html—The official Apache guide to tuning your web server.

- ▶ http://dev.mysql.com/doc/refman/5.6/en/optimization.html—Learn how to optimize your MySQL server direct from the source, the MySQL manual.

- ▶ One particular MySQL optimization book will really help you get more from your system if you run a large site: *High Performance MySQL*, by Jeremy Zawodny and Derek Balling (O'Reilly), ISBN: 0-596-00306-4.

CHAPTER 21

Kernel and Module Management

A kernel is a complex piece of software that manages the processes and process interactions that take place within an operating system. As a user, you rarely, if ever, interact directly with it. Instead, you work with the applications that the kernel manages.

The Linux kernel is Linux. It is the result of years of cooperative (and sometimes contentious) work by numerous people around the world. There is only one common kernel source tree, but each major Linux distribution massages and patches its version slightly to add features, performance, or options. Each Linux distribution, including Ubuntu, comes with its own precompiled kernel as well as the kernel source code, providing you with absolute authority over the Linux operating system. This chapter covers the kernel and what it does for us and for the operating system.

In this chapter, you also learn how to obtain the kernel sources and how and when to patch the kernel. The chapter leads you through an expert's tour of the kernel architecture and teaches you essential steps in kernel configuration, how to build and install modules, and how to compile drivers in Ubuntu. This chapter also teaches you important aspects of working with GRUB2, the default Ubuntu boot loader. Finally, the chapter's troubleshooting information will help you understand what to do when something goes wrong with your Linux kernel installation or compilation process. As disconcerting as these problems can seem, this chapter shows you some easy fixes for many kernel problems.

Almost all users find that a precompiled Ubuntu kernel suits their needs (and there are several to choose from). At some point, you might need to recompile the kernel to support a specific piece of hardware or add a new feature to the operating system, although the Ubuntu kernel team works very hard to backport or enable any feature possible (as a module), so it is highly unlikely you will ever have a need to do this. They are also approachable and will gladly discuss specific needs and features. Sometimes features are not enabled just because no one has ever asked for or needed them. Occasionally, things are not enabled because of a conflict with another feature. The Ubuntu Kernel Team can help you discover what is going on in those cases (but don't abuse their kindness and availability, they already work quite hard and for long hours).

Really, the main reason today for people compiling their own kernel is because they want to learn to be a kernel developer. If you have heard horror stories about the difficulties of recompiling the Linux kernel, you can relax; this chapter gives you all the information you need to understand how to painlessly work through the process if you are interested in learning a new skill. This is a complex and detail-oriented task, but it is within the grasp of most technical users, even if it is completely unnecessary.

WARNING

Building and using a custom kernel will make it very difficult to get support for your system. Although it is a learning experience to compile your own kernel, you will not be allowed to file bugs in Ubuntu on the custom-built kernel (if you do, they will be rejected without further explanation), and if you have a commercial support contract with Ubuntu/Canonical, this will void the contract.

The Linux Kernel

The Linux kernel is the management part of the operating system that many people call *Linux*. Although many think of the entire distribution as Linux, the only piece that can correctly be called Linux is the kernel. Ubuntu, like many Linux distributions, includes a kernel packaged with add-on software that interacts with the kernel so that the user can interface with the system in a meaningful manner.

The system utilities and user programs enable computers to become valuable tools to a user.

The First Linux Kernel

In 1991, Linus Torvalds released version .99 of the Linux kernel as the result of his desire for a powerful, UNIX-like operating system for his Intel 80386 personal computer. Linus wrote the initial code necessary to create what is now known as the Linux kernel and combined it with Richard Stallman's GNU tools. Indeed, because many of the Linux basic system tools come from the GNU Project, many people refer to the operating system as *GNU/Linux*. Since then, Linux has benefited from thousands of contributors adding their talents and time to the Linux project. Linus still maintains the kernel, deciding on what will and will not make it into the kernel as official releases, known to many as the *vanilla* or *Linus* Linux kernel.

21

Linux Kernel Version Numbers

In 2011, the kernel version numbering system moved to 3.0, mainly because Linus felt it was time for a fresh start with numbering and that doing so would provide a good opportunity to remove some older, no-longer-used parts of the kernel code. Everything in this chapter applies to the latest kernel versions, whether you are using a 2.6 version or a 3.0 version. This edition is being written in advance of the Ubuntu developers' decision of which kernel version to ship with Ubuntu 11.10. Examples in the chapter say 2.6 for maximum flexibility during the transition time, but you can change references to 3.0 where appropriate if you know you have a 3.0 kernel and the information will still apply.

The Linux Source Tree

The source code for the Linux kernel is kept in a group of directories called the *kernel source tree*. The structure of the kernel source tree is important because the process of compiling (building) the kernel is automated; it is controlled by scripts interpreted by the make application. These scripts, known as makefiles, expect to find the pieces of the kernel code in specific places; if they don't find them, they will not work. You learn how to use make to compile a kernel later in this chapter.

It is not necessary for the Linux kernel source code to be installed on your system for the system to run or for you to accomplish typical tasks such as email, web browsing, or word processing. It is necessary that the kernel sources be installed, however, if you want to compile a new kernel. In the next section, you learn how to install the kernel source files and how to set up the special symbolic link required. That link is /usr/src/linux-2.6, and it is how you will refer to the directory of the kernel source tree as we examine the contents of the kernel source tree.

The /usr/src/linux-2.6 directory contains the .config and the Makefile files among others. The .config file is the configuration of your Linux kernel as it was compiled. There is no .config file by default; you must select one from the /configs subdirectory. There, you will find configuration files for each flavor of the kernel Ubuntu provides; simply copy the one appropriate for your system to the default directory and rename it .config.

We have already discussed the contents of the /configs subdirectory, so let's examine the other directories found under /usr/src/linux-2.6. The most useful for us is the Documentation directory. In it and its subdirectories, you will find almost all the documentation concerning every part of the kernel. The file 00-INDEX (each Documentation subdirectory also contains a 00-INDEX file, as well) contains a list of the files in the main directory and a brief explanation of what they are. Many files are written solely for kernel programmers and application writers, but a few are useful to the intermediate or advanced Linux user when attempting to learn about kernel and device driver issues. Some of the more interesting and useful documents are as follows:

▶ **devices.txt**—A list of all possible Linux devices that are represented in the /dev directory, giving major and minor numbers and a short description. If you have ever gotten an error message that mentions char-major-xxx, this file is where that list is kept.

▶ **ide.txt**—If your system uses IDE hard drives, this file discusses how the kernel interacts with them and lists the various kernel commands that can be used to solve IDE-related hardware problems, manually set data transfer modes, and otherwise manually manage your IDE drives. Most of this management is automatic, but if you want to understand how the kernel interacts with IDE devices, this file explains it.

▶ **initrd.txt**—This file provides much more in-depth knowledge of initial RAM disks, giving details on the loopback file system used to create and mount them and explaining how the kernel interacts with them.

▶ **kernel-parameters.txt**—This file is a list of most of the arguments that you can pass at boot time to configure kernel or hardware settings, but it does not appear too useful at first glance because it is just a list. However, knowing that a parameter exists and might relate to something you are looking for can assist you in tracking down more information because now you have terms·to enter into an Internet search engine such as Google.

▶ **sysrq.txt**—If you have ever wondered what that key on your keyboard marked SysRq is used for, this file has the answer. Briefly, it is a key combination hardwired into the kernel that can help you recover from a system lockup. Ubuntu disables this function by default for security reasons. You can re-enable it by entering the command **# echo "1" > /proc/sys/kernel/sysrq**, and disable it by echoing a value of 0 rather than 1.

In the other directories found in Documentation, you will find similar text files that deal with the kernel modules for CD-ROM drivers, file system drivers, game port and joystick drivers, video drivers (not graphics card drivers; those belong to X11R6 and not to the kernel), network drivers, and all the other drivers and systems found in the Linux operating system. Again, these documents are usually written for programmers, but they can also provide useful information to the intermediate and advanced Linux user.

The directory named scripts contains many of the scripts that make uses. It really does not contain anything of interest to anyone who is not a programmer or a kernel developer (also known as a *kernel hacker*).

After a kernel is built, all the compiled files will wind up in the arch directory and its subdirectories. Although you can manually move them to their final location, you learn later in this chapter how the make scripts will do it for you. In the early days of Linux, this post-compilation file relocation was all done by hand; you should be grateful for make.

NOTE

The make utility is a complex program. You can find complete documentation on the structure of make files, as well as the arguments that it can accept, at www.gnu.org/software/make/manual/make.html.

The remaining directories in /usr/src/linux-2.6 contain the source code for the kernel and the kernel drivers. When you install the kernel sources, these files are placed there automatically. When you patch kernel sources, these files are altered automatically. When you compile the kernel, these files are accessed automatically. Although you never need to touch the source code files, they can be useful. The kernel source files are nothing more than text files with special formatting, which means that we can look at them and read the programmer comments. Sometimes, a programmer will write an application but cannot (or often will not) write the documentation. The comments the programmer puts in the source code are often the only documentation that exists for the code.

Small testing programs are even "hidden" in the comments of some of the code, along with comments and references to other information. Because the source code is written in a language that can be read as easily—almost—as English, a nonprogrammer might be able to get an idea of what the application or driver is actually doing (see Chapter 39, "C/C++ Programming Tools for Ubuntu"). This information might be of use to an intermediate to advanced Linux user when the user is confronted by kernel- and driver-related problems.

> **NOTE**
>
> The interaction and control of hardware is handled by a small piece of the kernel called a *device driver*. The driver tells the computer how to interact with a modem, a SCSI card, a keyboard, a mouse, and so on in response to a user prompt. Without the device driver, the kernel does not know how to interact with the associated device.

Types of Kernels

In the early days of Linux, kernels were a single block of code containing all the instructions for the processor, the motherboard, and the other hardware. If you changed hardware, you were required to recompile the kernel code to include what you needed and discard what you did not. Including extra, unneeded code carried a penalty because the kernel became larger and occupied more memory. On older systems that had only 4MB to 8MB of memory, wasting precious memory for unnecessary code was considered unacceptable. Kernel compiling was something of a "black art" as early Linux users attempted to wring the most performance from their computers. These kernels compiled as a single block of code are called *monolithic kernels*.

As the kernel code grew larger and the number of devices that could be added to a computer increased, the requirement to recompile became onerous. A new method of building the kernel was developed to make the task of compiling easier. The part of the kernel's source code that composed the code for the device drivers could be optionally compiled as a module that could be loaded and unloaded into the kernel as required. This is known as the *modular* approach to building the kernel. Now, all the kernel code could be compiled at once, with most of the code compiled into these modules. Only the required modules would be loaded; the kernel could be kept smaller, and adding hardware was much simpler.

The typical Ubuntu kernel has some drivers compiled as part of the kernel itself (called *inline drivers*) and others compiled as modules. Only device drivers compiled inline are available to the kernel during the boot process; modular drivers are available only after the system has been booted.

NOTE

As a common example, drivers for SCSI disk drives must be available to the kernel if you intend to boot from SCSI disks. If the kernel is not compiled with those drivers inline, the system will not boot because it cannot access the disks.

A way around this problem for modular kernels is to use an initial RAM disk (initrd), discussed later in the "Creating an Initial RAM Disk Image" section. The initrd loads a small kernel and the appropriate device driver, which then can access the device to load the actual kernel you want to run.

Some code can be only one or the other (for technical reasons unimportant to the average user), but most code can be compiled either as modular or inline. Depending on the application, some system administrators prefer one way over the other, but with fast modern processors and abundant system memory, the performance differences are of little concern to all but the most ardent Linux hackers.

When compiling a kernel, the step in which you make the selection of modular or inline is part of the make config step detailed later in this chapter. Unless you have a specific reason to do otherwise, select the modular option when given a choice. Because you will be managing kernels more frequently than compiling kernels, the process of managing modules is addressed in the next section.

Managing Modules

When using a modular kernel, special tools are required to manage the modules. Modules must be loaded and unloaded, and it would be nice if that were done as automatically as possible. We also need to be able to pass necessary parameters to modules when we load them, things such as memory addresses and interrupts. (That information varies from module to module, so you need to look at the documentation for your modules to determine what, if any, information needs to be passed to it.) This section covers the tools provided to manage modules and then look at a few examples of using them.

Linux provides the following module management tools for our use. All these commands (and modprobe.conf) have man pages:

▶ **lsmod**—This command lists the loaded modules. It is useful to pipe this through the less command because the listing is usually more than one page long.

▶ **insmod**—This command loads the specified module into the running kernel. If a module name is given without a full path, the default location for the running kernel, /lib/modules/*/, is searched. Several options are offered for this command; the most useful is -f, which forces the module to be loaded.

▶ **rmmod**—This command unloads (removes) the specified module from the running kernel. More than one module at a time can be specified.

▶ **modprobe**—A more sophisticated version of insmod and rmmod, it uses the dependency file created by depmod and automatically handles loading, or with the -r option, removing modules. There is no force option, however. A useful option to modprobe is -t, which causes modprobe to cycle through a set of drivers until it finds one that matches your system. If you are unsure of what module will work for your network card, use this command:

matthew@seymour:~$ **sudo modprobe -t net**

The term net is used because that is the name of the directory (/lib/modules/*/kernel/net) where all the network drivers are kept. It tries each one in turn until it loads one successfully.

▶ **modinfo**—This queries a module's object file and provide a list of the module name, author, license, and any other information that is there. It often is not very useful.

▶ **depmod**—This program creates a dependency file for kernel modules. Some modules need to have other modules loaded first; that is, they "depend" on the other modules. (A lot of the kernel code is like this because it eliminates redundancy in the code base.) During the boot process, one of the startup files contains the command depmod -a and it is run every time you boot to re-create the file /lib/modules/*/modules.dep. If you make changes to the file /etc/modprobe.conf, run depmod -a manually. The depmod command, its list of dependencies, and the /etc/modprobe.conf file enable kernel modules to be automatically loaded as needed.

▶ **/etc/modprobe.conf**—This is not a command, but a file that controls how modprobe and depmod behave; it contains kernel module variables. Although the command syntax can be quite complex, most actual needs are simple. The most common use is to alias a module and then pass it some parameters. For example, in the following code, we alias a device name (from devices.txt) to a more descriptive word and then pass some information to an associated module. The i2c-dev device is used to read the CPU temperature and fan speed on our system. These lines for /etc/modprobe.conf were suggested for our use by the program's documentation. We added them with a text editor:

```
alias char-major-89 i2c-dev
options eeprom ignore=2,0x50,2,0x51,2,0x52
```

A partial listing of lsmod is shown here, piped through the less command, enabling us to view it a page at a time:

```
matthew@seymour:~$ sudo lsmod | less
Module            Size  Used by
parport_pc       19392  1
Module            Size  Used by
parport_pc       19392  1
lp                8236  0
```

```
parport             29640   2 parport_pc,lp
autofs4             10624   0
sunrpc             101064   1
```

The list is actually much longer, but here we see that the input module is being used by the joydev (joystick device) module, but the joystick module is not being used. This computer has a joystick port that was autodetected, but no joystick is connected. A scanner module is also loaded, but because the USB scanner is unplugged, the module is not being used. You use the lsmod command to determine whether a module was loaded and what other modules were using it. If you examine the full list, you will see modules for all the devices attached to your computer.

To remove a module, joydev in this example, use the following:

matthew@seymour:~$ **sudo rmmod joydev**

or

matthew@seymour:~$ **sudo modprobe -r joydev**

The output of lsmod now shows that it is no longer loaded. If we were to remove input, as well, we could then use modprobe to load both input and joydev (one depends on the other, remember) with a simple command, as follows:

matthew@seymour:~$ **sudo modprobe joydev**

If Ubuntu balks at loading a module (because it was compiled using a different kernel version from what you are currently running—for example, the NVIDIA graphics card module), you could force it to load like this:

matthew@seymour:~$ **sudo insmod -f nvidia**

You ignore the complaints (error messages) in this case if the kernel generates any.

When to Recompile

Ubuntu systems use a modified version of the plain-vanilla Linux kernel (a modified version is referred to as a *patched kernel*) with additional drivers and other special features compiled into it.

Ubuntu has quite an intensive testing period for all distribution kernels and regularly distributes updated versions. The supplied Ubuntu kernel is compiled with as many modules as possible to provide as much flexibility as possible. A running kernel can be further tuned with the sysctl program, which enables direct access to a running kernel and permits some kernel parameters to be changed. As a result of this extensive testing, configurability, and modularity, the precompiled Ubuntu kernel does everything most users need it to do. Most users only need to recompile the kernel to do the following:

▶ Accommodate an esoteric piece of new hardware

▶ Conduct a system update when Ubuntu has not yet provided precompiled kernels

▶ Experiment with the system capabilities

Ubuntu supplies precompiled versions of the kernel for 32- and 64-bit processors. For each architecture, they compile a generic kernel that works well for most uses, a server kernel that is optimized for server use, a preempt kernel designed for use in low latency servers, and an `rt` kernel for times when instant response is more important than balanced use (such as in professional audio/visual recording and editing). There is also a special kernel, called *virtual*, available for use in virtual machines. These are all available from the Ubuntu software repositories.

Also available are a series of packages called `linux-backports-modules-`, each with a specific set of kernel modules backported from newer mainline kernels into current version Ubuntu kernels. If you need an updated driver for a piece of hardware, look at the backported modules first.

Kernel Versions

The Linux kernel is in a constant state of development. As new features are added, bugs are fixed, and new technology is incorporated into the code base, it becomes necessary to provide stable releases of the kernel for use in a production environment. It is also important to have separate releases that contain the newest code for developers to test. To keep track of the kernels, version numbers are assigned to them. Programmers enjoy using sequential version numbers that have abstract meaning. Is version 8 twice as advanced as version 4 of the same application? Is version 1 of one application less developed than version 3 of another? The version numbers cannot be used for this kind of qualitative or quantitative comparison. It is entirely possible that higher version numbers can have fewer features and more bugs than older versions. The numbers exist solely to differentiate and organize sequential revisions of software.

For the latest development version of the kernel at the time of writing, for example, the kernel version number from the Linux developers is 3.0.0.0. Ubuntu 11.10 ships with a recent version of 3.0.0 with Ubuntu specific patches applied. It will receive consistent updates throughout the release's life cycle.

The kernel version can be broken down into four sections:

▶ **Major version**—This is the major version number, now at 3.

▶ **Minor version**—This is the minor version number, now at 0.

▶ **Sublevel number**—This number indicates the current iteration of the kernel; here it is number 0.

▶ **Extraversion level**—This is the number representing a collection of patches and additions made to the kernel by the Ubuntu engineers to make the kernel work for them (and you). Each collection is numbered, and the number is indicated here in the kernel name. From our preceding example, it is 0.

Type uname -r at the command prompt to display your current kernel version:

```
matthew@seymour:~$ uname -r
3.0.0-12-generic
```

Obtaining the Kernel Sources

The Linux kernel has always been freely available to anyone who wants it. If you just want to recompile the existing kernel, install the linux-source package from the Ubuntu repositories. To get the very latest vanilla version, which is the commonly used term for the kernel version direct from the main kernel developers and which has not yet been patched or changed by any distribution-specific kernel team, open an FTP connection to ftp.kernel.org using your favorite FTP client and log in as anonymous. Because you are interested in the 3.0 kernel, change directories to /pub/linux/kernel/v3.0. The latest stable kernel as of this writing is 3.0.4.

> **NOTE**
>
> The ftp.kernel.org site receives more than its share of requests for download. It is considered a courtesy to use a mirror site to reduce the traffic that ftp.kernel.org bears. www.kernel.org/mirrors/ has a list of all mirrors around the world. Find one close to your geographic location and substitute that address for ftp.kernel.org.

A number of different entries are on the FTP archive site for each kernel version, but because you are interested only in the full kernel, it is necessary to get the full package of source code (for example, linux-3.0.4.bz2).

The .bz2 extension is applied by the bzip2 utility, which has better compression than gzip.

After it is downloaded, move the package to a directory other than /usr/src and unpack it. The bzip2 unpack command is tar -xjvf linux-3.0.4.tar.bz2. After it is unpacked, the package creates a new directory, linux-3.0.4. Copy it to /usr/src or move it there. Then, create a symbolic link of linux-3.0 to linux-3.0.4. (Otherwise, some scripts will not work.) Here is how to create the symbolic link:

```
matthew@seymour:~$ sudo rm /usr/src/linux-3.0
matthew@seymour:~$ sudo ln -s /usr/src/linux-3.0.4 /usr/src/linux-3.0
```

By creating a symbolic link to /usr/src/linux-3.0, it is possible to allow multiple kernel versions to be compiled and tailored for different functions: You just change the symbolic link to the kernel directory you want to work on.

> **CAUTION**
>
> The correct symbolic link is critical to the operation of `make`. Always have the symbolic link point to the version of the kernel sources you are working with.

Patching the Kernel

It is possible to patch a kernel to the newest Linux kernel version as opposed to downloading the entire source code. This choice can be beneficial for those who are not using a high-speed broadband connection. Whether you are patching existing sources or downloading the full source, the end results are identical.

Patching the kernel is not a mindless task. It requires the user to retrieve all patches from the current version to the version the user wants to upgrade to. For example, if you are currently running 2.6.30 (and have those sources) and want to upgrade to 2.6.35, you must retrieve the 2.6.31 and 2.6.32 patch sets, and so on. After they are downloaded, these patches must be applied in succession to upgrade to 2.6.35. This is more tedious than downloading the entire source, but useful for those who keep up with kernel hacking and want to perform incremental upgrades to keep their Linux kernel as up-to-date as possible.

To patch up to several versions in a single operation, you can use the `patch-kernel` script located in the kernel source directory for the kernel version you currently use. This script applies all necessary version patches to bring your kernel up to the latest version.

The format for using the `patch-kernel` script looks like this:

```
patch-kernel source_dir patch_dir stopversion
```

The source directory defaults to `/usr/src/linux` if none is given, and the `patch_dir` defaults to the current working directory if one is not supplied.

For example, assume that you have a 2.6.33 kernel code tree that needs to be patched to the 2.6.35 version. The 2.6.34 and 2.6.35 patch files have been downloaded from ftp.kernel.org and are placed in the /patch directory in the source tree. You issue the following command in the `/usr/src/linux-2.6` directory:

```
matthew@seymour:~$ sudo scripts/patch-kernel /usr/src/linux-2.6.33 /usr/src/
➥linux-2.6.33/patch
```

Each successive patch file is applied, eventually creating a 2.6.35 code tree. If any errors occur during this operation, files named xxx# or xxx.rej are created, where xxx is the version of patch that failed. You will have to resolve these failed patches manually by examining the errors and looking at the source code and the patch. An inexperienced person will not have any success with this because you need to understand C programming and kernel programming to know what is broken and how to fix it. Because this was a stock 2.6.33 code tree, the patches were all successfully applied without errors. If you are attempting to apply a nonstandard third-party patch, the patch might likely fail.

When you have successfully patched the kernel, you are ready to begin compiling this code tree as if we started with a fresh, stock 2.6.35 kernel tree.

Using the patch Command

If you have a special, nonstandard patch to apply—such as a third-party patch for a commercial product, for example—you can use the patch command rather than the special patch-kernel script that is normally used for kernel source updates. Here are some quick steps and an alternative method of creating patched code and leaving the original code alone:

1. Create a directory in your home directory and name it something meaningful, like mylinux.

2. Copy the pristine Linux source code there with the following:

   cp -ravd /usr/src/linux-2.6/* ~/mylinux

3. Copy the patch file to that same directory, as follows:

   cp patch_filename ~/mylinux

4. Change to the ~/mylinux directory with this command:

   cd ~/mylinux

5. Apply the patch like this:

   -patch -p1 < patch_filename > mypatch.log 2>&1

   (This last bit of code saves the message output to a file so that you can look at it later.)

6. If the patch applies successfully, you are done and have not endangered any of the pristine source code. If the newly patched code does not work, you do not have to reinstall the original, pristine source code.

7. Copy your new code to /usr/src and make that special symbolic link described elsewhere in the chapter.

Compiling the Kernel

If you want to update the kernel from new source code you have downloaded, or you have applied a patch to add new functionality or hardware support, you must compile and install a new kernel to actually use that new functionality. Compiling the kernel involves translating the kernel's contents from human-readable code to binary form. Installing the kernel involves putting all the compiled files where they belong in /boot and /lib and making changes to the boot loader.

The process of compiling the kernel is almost completely automated by the make utility like the process of installing. By providing the necessary arguments and following the steps covered next, you can recompile and install a custom kernel for your use.

Here are the steps to compile and configure the kernel:

1. Do not delete your current kernel, so that you will have a backup that you can use to boot if there is a problem with the one you compile.

2. Apply all patches, if any, so that you have the features you desire. See the previous section for details.

3. Back up the .config file, if it exists, so that you can recover from the inevitable mistake. Use the following cp command:

    matthew@seymour:~$ **sudo cp .config .config.bak**

NOTE

If you are recompiling the Ubuntu default kernel, the /usr/src/linux-2.6/configs directory contains several versions of configuration files for different purposes.

Ubuntu provides a full set of .config files in the subdirectory configs, all named for the type of system they were compiled for. If you want to use one of these default configurations as the basis for a custom kernel, just copy the appropriate file to /usr/src/linux-2.6 and rename it .config.

4. Run the make mrproper directive to prepare the kernel source tree, cleaning out any old files or binaries.

5. Restore the .config file that the command make mrproper deleted, and edit the makefile to change the EXTRAVERSION number.

NOTE

If you want to keep any current version of the kernel that was compiled with the same code tree, manually edit the makefile with your favorite text editor and add some unique string to the EXTRAVERSION variable.

You can use any description you prefer.

6. Modify the kernel configuration file using make config, make menuconfig, or make xconfig; we recommend the last one.

7. Run make dep to create the code dependencies used later in the compilation process.

TIP

If you have a multiprocessor machine, you can use both processors to speed the make process by inserting -jx after the make command, where as a rule of thumb, x is one more than the number of processors you have. You might try a larger number and even try this on a single processor machine (we have used -j8 successfully on an SMP machine); it will only load up your CPU. For example:

    matthew@seymour:~$ **sudo make -j3 bzImage**

All the make processes except make dep work well with this method of parallel compiling.

8. Run `make clean` to prepare the sources for the actual compilation of the kernel.

9. Run `make bzImage` to create a binary image of the kernel.

NOTE

Several choices of directives exist; the most common ones are the following:

- ▶ **zImage**—This directive compiles the kernel, creating an uncompressed file called `zImage`.

- ▶ **bzImage**—This directive creates a compressed kernel image necessary for some systems that require the kernel image to be under a certain size for the BIOS to be able to parse them; otherwise, the new kernel will not boot. It is the most commonly used choice. However, the Ubuntu kernel compiled with `bzImage` is still too large to fit on a floppy, so a smaller version with some modules and features removed is used for the boot floppies. Ubuntu recommends that you boot from the rescue CD-ROM.

- ▶ **bzDisk**—This directive does the same thing as `bzImage`, but it copies the new kernel image to a floppy disk for testing purposes. This is helpful for testing new kernels without writing kernel files to your hard drive. Make sure that you have a floppy disk in the drive because you will not be prompted for one.

---

10. Run `make modules` to compile any modules your new kernel needs.

11. Run `make modules_install` to install the modules in `/lib/modules` and create dependency files.

12. Run `make install` to automatically copy the kernel to `/boot`, create any other files it needs, and modify the boot loader to boot the new kernel by default.

13. Using your favorite text editor, verify the changes made to `/etc/lilo.conf` or `/boot/grub/grub.conf`; fix if necessary and rerun `/sbin/lilo` if needed.

14. Reboot and test the new kernel.

15. Repeat the process if necessary, choosing a configuration interface.

Over time, the process for configuring the Linux kernel has changed. Originally, you configured the kernel by responding to a series of prompts for each configuration parameter; this is the `make config` utility described shortly. Although you can still configure Linux this way, most users find this type of configuration confusing and inconvenient; moving back through the prompts to correct errors, for instance, is impossible.

The `make config` utility is a command-line tool. The utility presents a question about kernel configuration options. The user responds with a Y, N, M, or ?. (It is not case sensitive.) Choosing M configures the option to be compiled as a module. A response of ? displays context help for that specific option, if available. (If you choose ? and no help is available, you can turn to the vast Internet resources to find information.) We recommend that you avoid the `make config` utility.

If you prefer to use a command-line interface, you can use `make menuconfig` to configure the Linux kernel. `menuconfig` provides a graphical wrapper around a text interface. Although it is not as raw as `make config`, `menuconfig` is not a fancy graphical interface either; you cannot use a mouse, but must navigate through it using keyboard commands. The same information presented in `make config` is presented by `make menuconfig`, but it looks a little nicer. Now, at least you can move back and forth in the selection process if you change your mind or make a mistake.

In `make menuconfig`, you use the arrow keys to move the selector up and down and the spacebar to toggle a selection. The Tab key moves the focus at the bottom of the screen to either Select, Exit, or Help.

If a graphical desktop is not available, `menuconfig` is the best you can do. However, both `menuconfig` and `xconfig` (see the following explanation of each) offer an improvement over editing the `.config` file directly. If you want to configure the kernel through a true graphical interface—with mouse support and clickable buttons—`make xconfig` is the best configuration utility option. To use this utility, you must have the X Window System running. The application `xconfig` is really nothing but a Tcl/Tk graphics `widget set` providing borders, menus, dialog boxes, and the like. Its interface is used to wrap around data files that are parsed at execution time.

After loading this utility, you use it by clicking each of the buttons that list the configuration options. Each button you click opens another window that has the detail configuration options for that subsection. Three buttons are at the bottom of each window: Main Menu, Next, and Prev(ious). Clicking the Main Menu button closes the current window and displays the main window. Clicking Next takes you to the next configuration section. When configuring a kernel from scratch, click the button labeled Code Maturity Level Options, and then continue to click the Next button in each subsection window to proceed through all the kernel configuration choices. When you have selected all options, the main menu is again displayed. The buttons on the lower right of the main menu are for saving and loading configurations. Their functions are self-explanatory. If you just want to have a look, go exploring! Nothing will be changed if you elect not to save it.

If you are upgrading kernels from a previous release, it is not necessary to go though the entire configuration from scratch. Instead, you can use the directive `make oldconfig`; it uses the same text interface that `make config` uses, and it is noninteractive. It will just prompt for changes for any new code.

Using `xconfig` to Configure the Kernel

For simplicity's sake, during this brisk walkthrough, this discussion assumes that you are using `make xconfig`, and that prior to this point, you have completed the first five steps in the kernel compilation checklist shown previously.

As you learned in the preceding section, you configure the kernel using `make xconfig` by making choices in several configuration subsection windows. Each subsection window contains specific kernel options. With hundreds of choices, the kernel is daunting to configure. We cannot really offer you detailed descriptions of which options to choose because your configuration will not match your own system and setup.

Table 21.1 provides a brief description of each subsection's options so that you can get an idea of what you might encounter. We recommend that you copy your kernel's `.config` file to `/usr/src/linux-2.6` and run `make xconfig` from there. Explore all the options. As long as you do not save the file, absolutely nothing is changed on your system.

TABLE 21.1   Some Kernel Subsections for Configuration

Name	Description
Code maturity level options	Enables development code to be compiled into the kernel, even if it has been marked as obsolete or as testing code only. This option should be used only by kernel developers or testers because of the possible unusable state of the code during development.
General setup	This section contains several different options covering how the kernel talks to the BIOS, whether it should support PCI or PCMCIA, whether it should use APM or ACPI, and what kind of Linux binary formats will be supported. Contains several options for supporting kernel structures necessary to run binaries compiled for other systems directly without recompiling the program.
Loadable module support	Determines whether the kernel enables drivers and other nonessential code to be compiled as loadable modules that can be loaded and unloaded at runtime. This option keeps the basic kernel small so that it can run and respond more quickly; in that regard, choosing this option is generally a good idea.
Processor type and features	Several options dealing with the architecture that will be running the kernel.
Power management options	Options dealing with ACPI and APM power management features.
Bus options	Configuration options for the PCMCIA bus found in laptops and PCI hotplug devices.
Memory Technology Devices	Options for supporting flash memory devices, such as (MTD) EEPROMS. Generally, these devices are used in embedded systems.
Parallel port support	Several options for configuring how the kernel will support parallel port communications.
Plug-and-play configuration	Options for supporting *plug-and-play (PnP)* PCI, ISA, and PnP BIOS support. Generally, it is a good idea to support PnP for PCI and ISA devices.

TABLE 21.1   Some Kernel Subsections for Configuration

Name	Description
Block devices	Section dealing with devices that communicate with the kernel in blocks of characters instead of streams. This includes IDE and ATAPI devices connected via parallel ports, as well as enabling network devices to communicate as block devices.
ATA/IDE/MFM/RLL support	Large collection of options to configure the kernel to communicate using different types of data communication protocols to talk to mass storage devices, such as hard drives. Note that this section does not cover SCSI.
SCSI device support	Options for configuring the kernel to support Small Computer Systems Interface. This subsection covers drivers for specific cards, chipsets, and tunable parameters for the SCSI protocol.
Old CD-ROM drivers	Configuration options to support obscure, older CD-ROM devices that do not conform to the SCSI or IDE standards. These are typically older CD-ROM drivers that are usually a proprietary type of SCSI (not SCSI, not IDE).
Multidevice support (RAID and LVM)	Options for enabling the kernel to support RAID devices in software emulation and the different levels of RAID. Also contains options for support of a logical volume manager.
Fusion MPT device support	Configures support for LSI's Logic Fusion Message Passing Technology. This technology is for high-performance SCSI and LAN interfaces.
IEEE1394 (firewire) support	Experimental support for FireWire devices.
I2O device support	Options for supporting the Intelligent Input/Output architecture. This architecture enables the hardware driver to be split from the operating system driver, thus enabling a multitude of hardware devices to be compatible with an operating system in one implementation.
Networking support	Several options for the configuration of networking in the kernel. The options are for the types of supported protocols and configurable options of those protocols.
Amateur radio support	Options for configuring support of devices that support the AX25 protocol.
IrDA (infrared) support	Options for configuring support of the infrared Data Association suite of protocols and devices that use these protocols.
Bluetooth support	Support for the Bluetooth wireless protocol. Includes options to support the Bluetooth protocols and hardware devices.

21

TABLE 21.1   Some Kernel Subsections for Configuration

Name	Description
ISDN subsystem	Options to support Integrated Services Digital Networks protocols and devices. ISDN is a method of connection to a large area network digitally over conditioned telephone lines, largely found to connect users to ISPs.
Telephony support	Support for devices that enable the use of regular telephone lines to support VoIP applications. This section does not handle the configuration of modems.
Input device support	Options for configuring *Universal Serial Bus (USB) human interface devices (HID)*, such as keyboards, mice, and joysticks.
Character devices	Configuration options for devices that communicate to the server in sequential characters. This is a large subsection containing the drivers for several motherboard chipsets.
Multimedia devices	Drivers for hardware implementations of video and sound devices, such as video capture boards, TV cards, and AM/FM radio adapter cards.
Graphics support	Configures VGA text console, video mode selection, and support for frame buffer cards.
Sound	Large subsection to configure supported sound card drivers and chipset support for the kernel.
USB support	USB configuration options. Includes configuration for USB devices and vendor-specific versions of USB.
File system	Configuration options for supported file system types.
Additional device driver support	A section for third-party patches.
Profiling support	Profiling kernel behavior to aid in debugging and development.
Kernel hacking	This section determines whether the kernel will contain advanced debugging options. Most users will not want to include this option in their production kernels because it increases the kernel size and slows performance by adding extra routines.
Security options	Determines whether NSA *Security Enhanced Linux (SELinux)* is enabled.
Cryptographic options	Support for cryptography hardware (Ubuntu patches not found in the vanilla kernel sources).
Library routines	Contains `zlib` compression support.

After you select all the options you want, you can save the configuration file and continue with step 7 in the kernel compiling checklist shown earlier.

Creating an Initial RAM Disk Image

If you require special device drivers to be loaded to mount the root file system (for SCSI drives, network cards, or exotic file systems, for example), you must create an initial RAM disk image named /boot/initrd.img. For most users, it is not necessary to create this file, but if you are not certain, it really does not hurt. To create an initrd.img file, use the shell script /sbin/mkinitrd.

The format for the command is the following, where *file_name* is the name of the image file you want created:

```
/sbin/mkinitrd file_name kernel_version
```

mkinitrd looks at /etc/fstab, /etc/modprobe.conf, and /etc/ raidtab to obtain the information it needs to determine which modules should be loaded during boot. For our system, we use the following:

```
matthew@seymour:~$ sudo mkinitrd initrd-2.6.7-1.img 2.6.7-1
```

When Something Goes Wrong

Several things might go wrong during a kernel compile and install, and several clues will point to the true problem. You will see error messages printed to the screen, and some error messages will be printed to the file /var/log/messages, which you can examine with a text editor. If you have followed our directions for patching the kernel, you need to examine a special error log, as well. Do not worry about errors because many problems are easily fixed with some research on your part. Some errors may be unfixable, however, depending on your skill level and the availability of technical information.

Errors During Compile

Although it is rare that the kernel will not compile, there is always a chance that something has slipped though the regression testing. Let's take a look at an example of a problem that might crop up during the compile.

It is possible that the kernel compile will crash and not complete successfully, especially if you attempt to use experimental patches, add untested features, or build newer and perhaps unstable modules on an older system.

At this juncture, you have two options:

▶ Fix the errors and recompile.

▶ Remove the offending module or option and wait for the errors to be fixed by the kernel team.

Most users will be unable to fix some errors because of the complexity of the kernel code, although you should not rule out this option. It is possible that someone else discovered the same error during testing of the kernel and developed a patch for the problem: Check the Linux kernel mailing list archive. If the problem is not mentioned there, a search on Google might turn up something.

The second option, removing the code, is the easiest and is what most people do in cases in which the offending code is not required. In the case of the NTFS module failing, it is almost expected because NTFS support is still considered experimental and subject to errors. This is primarily because the code for the file system is reverse-engineered instead of implemented via documented standards. Read-only support has gotten better in recent kernels; write support is still experimental.

Finally, should you want to take on the task of trying to fix the problem yourself, this is a great opportunity to get involved with the Linux kernel and make a contribution that could help many others.

If you are knowledgeable about coding and kernel matters, you might want to look in the `Maintainers` file in the `/usr/src/linux-2.6/` directory of the kernel source and find the maintainer of the code. The recommended course of action is to contact the maintainer to see if the maintainer is aware of the problems you are having. If nothing has been documented for the specific error, submitting the error to the kernel mailing list is an option. The guidelines for doing this are in the `README` file in the base directory of the kernel source under the section `IF SOMETHING GOES WRONG:`.

Runtime Errors, Boot Loader Problems, and Kernel Oops

Runtime errors occur as the kernel is loading. Error messages are displayed on the screen or written to the `/var/log/messages` file. Boot loader problems display messages to the screen; no log file is produced. Kernel oops are errors in a running kernel, and error messages are written to the `/var/log/messages` file.

Excellent documentation on the Internet exists for troubleshooting just about every type of error that GRUB2 or the kernel could give during boot. The best way to find this documentation is to go to your favorite search engine and type in the keywords of the error you received. Adjust the keywords you use as you focus your search.

If you have GRUB problems, the GRUB manual is online at www.gnu.org/software/grub/manual/, and further information is available at https://help.ubuntu.com/community/Grub2.

TIP

For best results, go to www.google.com/linux to find all things Linux on the Internet. Google has specifically created a Linux area of its database, which should allow faster access to information on Linux than any other search engine.

References

▶ **www.kernel.org/**—Linux Kernel Archives. The source of all development discussion for the Linux kernel.

▶ **www.kerneltraffic.org/kernel-traffic/index.html**—Linux Kernel Traffic. Summarized version and commentary of the Linux Kernel mailing list produced weekly.

▶ **www.gnu.org/**—Free Software Foundation. Source of manuals and software for programs used throughout the kernel compilation process. Tools such as `make` and `gcc` have their official documentation here.

▶ **https://wiki.ubuntu.com/Kernel**—The starting point for anything you want to know about both Ubuntu and its use of the Linux kernel.

▶ **https://wiki.ubuntu.com/Kernel/FAQ**—The Ubuntu Kernel Team answers the most commonly asked questions about Ubuntu's use of Linux kernels.

▶ **www.tldp.org/**—The Linux Documentation Project. The Mecca of all Linux documentation. Excellent source of HOWTO documentation, as well as FAQs and online books, all about Linux.

▶ **www.minix.org/**—The unofficial minix website. It contains a selection of links to information about minix and a link to the actual home page. Although minix is still copyrighted, the owner has granted unlimited rights to everyone. See for yourself the OS used to develop Linux.

21

CHAPTER 22

File and Print

In the early days of computing, file and printer sharing was pretty much impossible because of the lack of good networking standards and interoperability. If you wanted to use a printer connected to another computer, you had to save the file to a floppy disk and walk over. Sometimes people do the same thing today using a USB thumb drive or emailing the file. However, there are better ways.

Both file and printer sharing are important because it is not unusual for someone to own more than one computer. Whether you want to share photographs among various computers or have a central repository available for collaboration, file sharing is an important part of our information age. Alongside this is the need to be able to share printers; after all, people do not want to have to plug and unplug a computer to a printer just so they can print out a quick letter.

Whatever your reasons for needing to share files and printers across a network, you find out how to do both in this chapter. We look at how you can share files using the popular UNIX NFS protocol and the more Windows-friendly Samba system. You also find out how to configure network-attached printers with interfaces such as JetDirect. We look at both graphical and command-line tools, so you should find something to suit the way you work.

> **CAUTION**
>
> By default, Ubuntu ships with all its network ports blocked. That is, it does not listen to any requests on any network ports when it is first installed. To configure the firewall, use *Uncomplicated Firewall (UFW)*, as described in Chapter 19, "Securing Your Machines."

Using the Network File System

Network File System (NFS) is the protocol developed by Sun Microsystems that allows computers to use a remote file system as if it were a real part of the local machine. A common use of NFS is to allow users' /home directories to appear on every local machine they use, thus eliminating the need to have physical home directories. This opens up hot desking and other flexible working arrangements, especially because no matter where the users are their /home directory follows them around.

Another popular use for NFS is to share binary files between similar computers. If you have a new version of a package that you want all machines to have, you have to the upgrade only on the NFS server, and all hosts running the same version of Ubuntu will have the same upgraded package.

Installing and Starting or Stopping NFS

NFS is not installed by default on Ubuntu, so you need to install the nfs-kernel-server package. NFS itself consists of several programs that work together. One is portmap, which maps NFS requests to the correct daemon. Two others are nfsd, which is the NFS daemon, and mountd, which controls the mounting and unmounting of file systems.

Ubuntu automatically adds NFS to the system startup scripts, so it will always be available after you have configured it. To check this, use the command sudo /etc/init.d/nfs-kernel-server status and it will show you that the service is running. If you need to manually start the NFS server, use the following command:

```
matthew@seymour:~$ sudo /etc/init.d/nfs-kernel-server start
 * Exporting directories for NFS kernel daemon:   [ OK ]
Starting NFS kernel daemon:                       [ OK ]
```

In this example, NFS has been started. Use stop to stop the service or restart to restart the server. This approach to controlling NFS proves handy, especially after configuration changes have been made. See the next section on how to configure NFS support on your Ubuntu system.

NFS Server Configuration

You can configure the NFS server by editing the /etc/exports file. This file is similar to the /etc/fstab file in that it is used to set the permissions for the file systems being exported. The entries look like this:

```
/file/system yourhost(options) *.yourdomain.com(options) 192.168.0.0/24(options)
```

This shows three common clients to which to share /file/system. The first, yourhost, shares /file/system to just one host. The second, .yourdomain.com, uses the asterisk (*) as a wildcard to enable all hosts in yourdomain.com to access /file/system. The third share enables all hosts of the Class C network, 192.168.0.0, to access /file/share. For security, it is best not to use shares, such as the last two across the Internet, because all data will be readable by any network the data passes by.

Table 22.1 shows some common options.

TABLE 22.1   /etc/fstab Options

Option	Purpose
rw	Gives read and write access
ro	Gives read-only access
async	Writes data when the server, not the client, feels the need
sync	Writes data as it is received

The following is an example of an /etc/exports file:

```
# /etc/exports: the access control list for filesystems which may be exported
#               to NFS clients.  See exports(5).
/home/matthew 192.168.0.0/24(rw,no_root_squash)
```

This file exports (makes available) /home/matthew to any host in 192.168.0.* and allows users to read from and write to /home/matthew.

After you have finished with the /etc/exports file, the following command exports all the file systems in the /etc/exports file to a list named xtab under the /var/lib/nfs directory, which is used as a guide for mounting when a remote computer asks for a directory to be exported:

```
matthew@seymour:~$ sudo exportfs -a
```

The -r option stands for re-export and tells the command to rereads the entire /etc/exports file and (re)mount all the entries. You can also use the exportfs command to export specific files temporarily. Here's an example using exportfs to export a file system:

```
matthew@seymour:~$ /usr/sbin/exportfs -o async yourhost:/usr/tmp
```

This command exports /usr/tmp to yourhost with the async option.

Be sure to restart the NFS server after making any changes to /etc/exports. If you prefer, you can use Ubuntu's shares-admin graphical client to set up NFS while using the X Window System. Start the client by clicking the System menu and then selecting the Shared Folders menu item from the Administration menu.

After you press Enter, you are prompted for your password. Type in the password and click OK; the main window will then display. Click the Add button to open the Add Share dialog box.

In the Path drop-down box, choose the directory that you want to share; in the Share drop-down box, choose NFS. Click the Add Host button that appears to specify which hosts, IP addresses, or networks are allowed access to the directory. By default, a directory is exported as read/write, but you can choose read-only by ticking the Read-Only option. When finished, click the OK button, click the Apply button, and then use the File menu to quit.

NFS Client Configuration

To configure your host as an NFS client (to acquire remote files or directories), you need to ensure that you have the nfs-common package installed, to be able to access NFS shares. After you've installed this, edit the /etc/fstab file as you would to mount any local file system. However, instead of using a device name to be mounted (such as /dev/sda1), enter the remote hostname and the desired file system to be imported. For example, one entry might look like this:

```
# Device               Mount Point   Type   Options     Freq Pass
yourhost:/home/share   /export/share  none   nfs  0      0
```

> **NOTE**
>
> If you use autofs on your system, you need to use proper autofs entries for your remote NFS mounts. See the Section 5 man page for autofs by entering man 5 autofs at the command line.

You can also use the mount command, as root, to quickly attach a remote directory to a local file system by using a remote host's name and exported directory. For example:

```
matthew@seymour:~$ sudo mount -t nfs 192.168.2.67:/music /music
```

After you press Enter, the entire remote directory appears on your file system. You can verify the imported file system using the df command, as follows:

```
matthew@seymour:~$ df
Filesystem           1k-blocks     Used Available Use% Mounted on
/dev/hda2             18714368  9642600   8121124  55% /
/dev/hda1                46636    13247     30981  30% /boot
none                    120016        0    120016   0% /dev/shm
192.168.2.67:/music  36875376 20895920  14106280  60% /music
```

Make sure that the desired mount point exists before using the mount command. When finished using the directory (perhaps for copying backups), you can use the umount command to remove the remote file system. Note that if you specify the root directory (/) as a mount point, you cannot unmount the NFS directory until you reboot (because Linux complains that the file system is in use).

Putting Samba to Work

Samba uses the *Session Message Block (SMB)* protocol to enable the Windows operating system (or any operating system) to access Linux files. Using Samba, you can make your Ubuntu machine look just like a Windows computer to other Windows computers on your network. You do not need to install Windows on your PC.

Samba is a complex program—the Samba man page (when converted to text) for just the configuration file is 330KB and 7,226 lines long. Although Samba is complex, setting it up and using it does not have to be difficult. There are many options, which accounts for some of Samba's complexity. Depending on what you want, Samba's use can be as easy or as difficult as you would like it to be.

Fortunately, Ubuntu includes a very easy way to access files on a Windows network share by default. To start, click Places, Network from the menu. You will see a Windows Network icon that, when double-clicked, shows you all Windows domains or workgroups found on your network. Just double-click any computer icon there to access shares and files.

To share from your Ubuntu desktop, right-click a folder you own while using the file browser, most likely one in your /home/username directory, and select Sharing Options. You are given a chance to confirm your desire to share the folder and give it a name. Sharing gives others the permission to view, but not necessarily to create or delete files, although those permissions are also available from this menu. If you do not have the Windows sharing service already installed on your computer, Ubuntu prompts you for permission to install it.

> **NOTE**
>
> Most Ubuntu users will not need the information contained in the rest of this section because installing the sharing service also takes care of the configuration and as a result, everything should just work.

The *Samba Web Administration Tool (SWAT)* can be used to configure Samba from a web browser. SWAT provides an easy way to start and stop the Samba server; set up printing services; define remote access permissions; and create Samba usernames, passwords, and shared directories. This section delves into the basics of configuring Samba, and you should first read how to manually configure Samba to get an understanding of how the software works. At the end of this section, you learn how to enable, start, and use SWAT to set up simple file sharing.

Like most of the software that comes with Ubuntu, Samba is licensed under the GPL and is free. Installation is straightforward, and the software is in the Ubuntu repositories. Regardless of which route you take, you should snag the samba and swat packages.

Installing from source code can be more time-consuming. If you do not want to install using Ubuntu's default locations, however, installing from the source code is a more configurable method. Just download the source from www.samba.org/ and unpack the files. Change into the source directory and, as root, run the command, `./configure` along with any changes from the defaults. Then run `make`, `make test` (if you want), followed by `make install` to install Samba in the specified locations.

> **NOTE**
>
> If you haven't done so, you might need to install a meta-package (a single package that provides several related packages) called `build-essential`. This package automatically installs all the `make` tools, plus other development utilities that you will need to compile software from source code.

When you install Samba, it is a good idea to also install the `samba-doc` and `samba-doc-pdf` packages because they contain extensive documentation in text, PDF, and HTML format. After you install it, you can find this documentation in `/usr/share/doc/samba*/doc`. If you install Samba using your Ubuntu disc, you can find a large amount of documentation in the directory tree starting at `/usr/share/doc/samba-doc` or `/usr/share/doc/samba-doc-pdf` in several formats, including PDF, HTML, and text, among others. Altogether, almost 3MB of documentation is included with the source code.

After installing Samba, you can either create the file `/etc/samba/smb.conf` or use the `smb.conf` file supplied with Samba, which is located by default under the `/etc/samba` directory with Ubuntu. You can find nearly a dozen sample configuration files under the `/usr/share/doc/samba*/examples` directory.

> **NOTE**
>
> Depending on your needs, `smb.conf` can be a simple file of fewer than 20 lines or a huge file spanning many pages of text. If your needs are complex, I suggest you browse through The Official Samba HOWTO and Reference Guide, or TOSHARG. You can find this helpful guide at http://samba.org/samba/docs/man/Samba3-HOWTO/.

Manually Configuring Samba with `/etc/samba/smb.conf`

The `/etc/samba/smb.conf` file is broken into sections. Each section is a description of the resource shared (share) and should be titled appropriately. The three special sections are as follows:

▶ **[global]**—Establishes the global configuration settings (defined in detail in the `smb.conf` man page and Samba documentation, found under the `/usr/share/doc/samba/docs` directory).

▶ **[homes]**—Shares users' /home directories and specifies directory paths and permissions.

▶ **[printers]**—Handles printing by defining shared printers and printer access.

Each section in your /etc/samba/smb.conf configuration file should be named for the resource being shared. For example, if the resource /usr/local/programs is being shared, you could call the section [programs]. When Windows sees the share, it is called by whatever you name the section (programs in this example). The easiest and fastest way to set up this share is with the following example from smb.conf:

```
[programs]
path = /usr/local/programs
writeable = true
```

This bit shares the /usr/local/programs directory with any valid user who asks for it and makes that directory writeable. It is the most basic share because it sets no limits on the directory.

Here are some parameters you can set in the sections:

▶ Requiring a user to enter a password before accessing a shared directory

▶ Limiting the hosts allowed to access the shared directory

▶ Altering permissions users are allowed to have on the directory

▶ Limiting the time of day during which the directory is accessible

The possibilities are almost endless. Any parameters set in the individual sections override the parameters set in the [global] section. The following section adds a few restrictions to the [programs] section:

```
[programs]
path = /usr/local/programs
writeable= true
valid users = mhelmke
browseable = yes
create mode = 0700
```

NOTE

You can spell it as writeable or writable—either variant will work. Both spellings are used in this chapter.

The valid users entry limits userid to just mhelmke. All other users can browse the directory because of the browseable = yes entry, but only mhelmke can write to the directory. Any files created by ahudson in the directory give ahudson full permissions, but no one else will have access to the file. This is the same as setting permissions with the chmod command. Again, there are numerous options, so you can be as creative as you want to when developing sections.

Setting Global Samba Behavior with the [global] Section

The [global] section set parameters establishes configuration settings for all of Samba. If a given parameter is not specifically set in another section, Samba uses the default setting in the [global] section. The [global] section also sets the general security configuration for Samba. The [global] section is the only section that does not require the name in brackets.

Samba assumes that anything before the first bracketed section not labeled [global] is part of the global configuration. (Using bracketed headings in /etc/samba/smb.conf makes your configuration file more readable.) The following sections discuss common Samba settings to share directories and printers. You will then see how to test your Samba configuration.

Sharing Home Directories Using the [homes] Section

The [homes] section shares out Ubuntu /home directories for the users. The /home directory is shared automatically when a user's Windows computer connects to the Linux server holding the /home directory. The one problem with using the default configuration is that the users see all the configuration files (such as .profile and others with a leading period in the filename) that they normally wouldn't see when logging on through Linux. One quick way to avoid this is to include a path option in the [homes] section. To use this solution, any users who require a Samba share of their /home directory need a separate "home directory" to act as their Windows /home directory.

For example, this pseudo home directory could be a directory named share in each user's /home directory on your Ubuntu system. You can specify the path option when using SWAT by using the %u option when specifying a path for the default homes shares (see the section, "Configuring Samba Using SWAT," later in this chapter). The complete path setting would be this:

/home/%u/share

This setting specifies that the directory named share under each user's directory is the shared Samba directory. The corresponding manual smb.conf setting to provide a separate "home directory" looks like this:

```
[homes]
        comment = Home Directories
        path = /home/%u/share
        valid users = %S
        read only = No
        create mask = 0664
        directory mask = 0775
        browseable = No
```

If you have a default [homes] section, the share shows up in the user's Network Neighborhood as the user's name. When the user connects, Samba scans the existing sections in smb.conf for a specific instance of the user's /home directory. If there is not one, Samba looks up the username in /etc/passwd. If the correct username and password have been given, the home directory listed in /etc/passwd is shared out at the user's /home directory. Typically, the [homes] section looks like this. (The browseable = no entry prevents other users from being able to browse your /home directory and is a good security practice.)

```
[homes]
browseable = no
writable = yes
```

This example shares out the /home directory and makes it writeable to the user. Here's how you specify a separate Windows /home directory for each user:

```
[homes]
browseable = no
writable= yes
path = /path/to/windows/directories
```

Sharing Printers by Editing the [printers] Section

The [printers] section works much like the [homes] section but defines shared printers for use on your network. If the section exists, users have access to any printer listed in your Ubuntu /etc/printcap file.

Like the [homes] section, when a print request is received, all the sections are scanned for the printer. If no share is found (with careful naming, there should not be unless you create a section for a specific printer), the /etc/printcap file is scanned for the printer name that is then used to send the print request.

For printing to work properly, you must correctly set up printing services on your Ubuntu computer. A typical [printers] section looks like this:

```
[printers]
comment = Ubuntu Printers
browseable = no
printable = yes
path = /var/spool/samba
```

The /var/spool/samba is a spool path set just for Samba printing.

Testing Samba with the `testparm` Command

After you have created your /etc/smb.conf file, you can check it for correctness by using the testparm command. This command parses through your /etc/smb.conf file and checks for any syntax errors. If none are found, your configuration file will probably work correctly. It does not, however, guarantee that the services specified in the file will work. It is merely making sure that the file is correctly written.

As with all configuration files, if you are modifying an existing, working file, it is always prudent to copy the working file to a different location and modify that file. Then, you can check the file with the testparm utility. The command syntax is as follows:

```
matthew@seymour:~$ sudo testparm /path/to/smb.conf.back-up
Load smb config files from smb.conf.back-up
Processing section "[homes]"
Processing section "[printers]"
Loaded services file OK.
```

This output shows that the Samba configuration file is correct, and, as long as all the services are running correctly on your Ubuntu machine, Samba should be working correctly. Now copy your old smb.conf file to a new location, put the new one in its place, and restart Samba with the command /etc/init.d/smbd restart. Your new or modified Samba configuration should now be in place.

Starting, Stopping, and Restarting the `smbd` Daemon

Once your smb.conf file is correctly configured, you may want to start, stop, or restart your Samba server daemon. This can be done with the /usr/sbin/smbd command, which (with no options) starts the Samba server with all the defaults. The most common option you will change in this command is the location of the smb.conf file; you change this option if you don't want to use the default location /etc/smb/smb.conf. The -s option allows you to change the smb.conf file Samba uses; this option is also useful for testing whether a new smb.conf file actually works. Another useful option is the -l option, which specifies the log file Samba uses to store information.

To start, stop, or restart Samba from the command line, use the /etc/init.d/samba script with a proper keyword, such as start, like this:

```
matthew@seymour:~$ sudo /etc/init.d/samba start
```

Using the `smbstatus` Command

The smbstatus command reports on the current status of your Samba connections. The syntax is as follows:

```
/usr/bin/smbstatus [options]
```

Table 22.2 shows some of the available options.

TABLE 22.2 **smbstatus** Options

Option	Result
-b	Brief output
-d	Verbose output
-s /path/to/config	Used if the configuration file used at startup is not the standard one
-u username	Shows the status of a specific user's connection
-p	Lists current smb processes, which can prove to be useful in scripts

Connecting with the `smbclient` Command

The smbclient command allows users on other Linux hosts to access your smb shares. You cannot mount the share on your host, but you can use it in a way that is similar to an FTP client. Several options can be used with the smbclient command. The most frequently used is -I followed by the IP address of the computer to which you are connecting. The smbclient command does not require root access to run:

```
matthew@seymour:~$ smbclient -I 10.10.10.20 -Uusername%password
```

This gives you the following prompt:

```
smb: <current directory on share>
```

From here, the commands are almost identical to the standard UNIX/Linux FTP commands. Note that you can omit a password on the smbclient command line. You are then prompted to enter the Samba share password.

Mounting Samba Shares

There are two ways to mount Samba shares to your Linux host. Mounting a share is the same as mounting an available media partition or remote NFS directory except that the Samba share is accessed using SMB. The first method uses the standard Linux mount command:

```
matthew@seymour:~$ sudo mount -t smbfs //10.10.10.20/homes /mount/point -o
➥username=heather,dmask=777,\ fmask=777
```

> **NOTE**
>
> You can substitute the IP address for hostname if your name service is running or the host is in your /etc/hosts file.

This command mounts heather's /home directory on your host and gives all users full permissions to the mount. The permissions are equal to the permissions on the chmod command.

The second method produces the same results using the smbmount command, as follows:

```
matthew@seymour:~$ sudo smbmount //10.10.10.20/homes /mount/point -o
username=heather,dmask-777,\ fmask=777
```

To unmount the share, use the following standard command:

```
matthew@seymour:~$ sudo umount /mount/point
```

You can also use these mount commands to mount true Windows client shares to your Ubuntu host. Using Samba, you can configure your server to provide any service Windows can serve, and no one but you will ever know.

Configuring Samba Using SWAT

The Samba team of developers has made administering Samba much easier with the *Samba Web Administration Tool (SWAT)*. SWAT is a web-based configuration and maintenance interface that gets as close to a point-and-click Samba environment as possible. This section provides a simple example of how to use SWAT to set up SMB access to a user's /home directory and how to share a directory.

> **NOTE**
>
> You need to enable the root account by giving it a password by using the command sudo passwd root. Not enabling the root account prevents you from using SWAT effectively.

You need to perform a few steps before you can start using SWAT. First, make sure you have the Samba and the swat packages installed. You then enable SWAT access to your system by editing the /etc/inetd.conf file by changing the following lines to remove the #<off># comments if present:

```
#<off># swat   stream  tcp  nowait.400  root\
  /usr/sbin/tcpd  /isr/sbin/swat
```

Save the file, and then restart the openbsd_inetd daemon using the following command:

```
matthew@seymour:~$ sudo /etc/init.d/openbsd-inetd restart
```

Next, start an X session, launch Firefox, and browse to http://localhost:901. You are presented a login prompt. Enter the root username and password, and then click the OK button. The screen clears, and you see the main SWAT page, as shown in Figure 22.1.

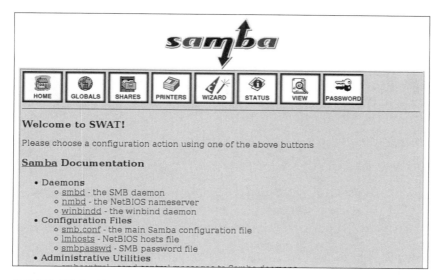

FIGURE 22.1   You can use SWAT to easily configure and administer Samba on your system.

> **TIP**
>
> You can also configure Samba using Ubuntu's `shares-admin` client. Launch the client from the command line of an X terminal window or select the System, Administration, Shared Folders menu item.

First, click the Globals icon in SWAT's main page. You see a page similar to the one shown in Figure 22.2. Many options are in the window, but you can quickly set up access for hosts from your LAN by simply entering one or more IP addresses or a subnet address (such as 192.168.0.—note the trailing period, which allows access for all hosts; in this example, on the 192.168.0 subnet) in the Hosts Allow field under the Security Options section. If you need help on how to format the entry, click the Help link to the left of the field. A new web page appears with the pertinent information.

When finished, click the Commit Changes button to save the global access settings. The next step is to create a Samba user and set the user's password. Click the Password icon on the main SWAT page (refer to Figure 22.1). The Server Password Management page opens, as shown in Figure 22.3. Type a new username in the User Name field; then type a password in the New Password and Retype New Password fields.

> **NOTE**
>
> You must supply a username of an existing system user, but the password used for Samba access does not have to match the existing user's password.

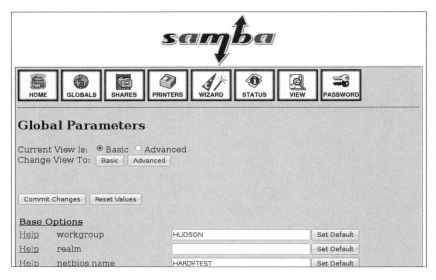

FIGURE 22.2   Configure Samba to allow access from specific hosts or subnets on your LAN.

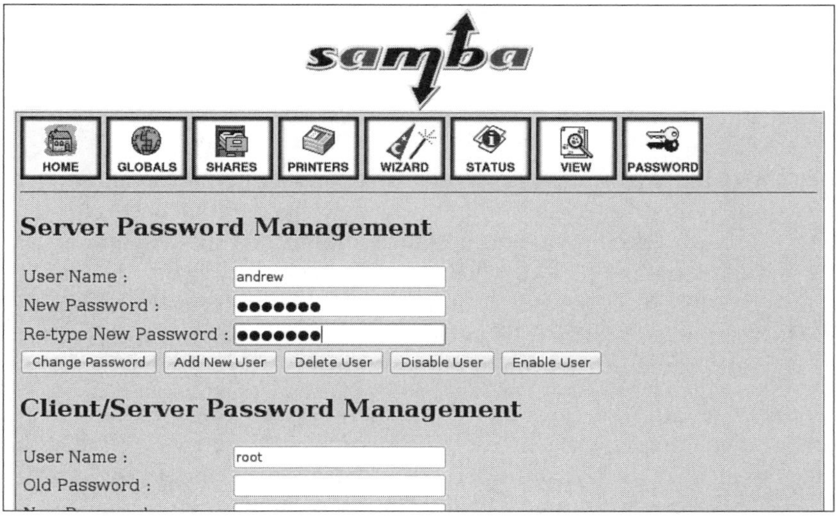

FIGURE 22.3   Enter a Samba username and password in the SWAT Password page.

When finished, click the Add New User button. SWAT then creates the username and password and displays Added user *username* (where *username* is the name you entered). The new Samba user should now be able to gain access to the /home directory from any allowed host if the Samba (smb) server is running.

For example, if you have set up Samba on a host named mini that has a user named andrew, the user can access the /home directory on mini from any remote host (if allowed by the Globals settings), perhaps by using the smbclient command like this:

```
matthew@seymour:~$ smbclient //mini/andrew -U andrew
added interface ip=192.168.0.68 bcast=192.168.0.255 nmask=255.255.255.0
Password:
Domain=[MYGROUP] OS=[Unix] Server=[Samba 3.0.28]
smb: \> pwd
Current directory is \\mini\andrew\
smb: \> quit
```

Click the Status icon to view Samba's status or to start, stop, or restart the server. You can use various buttons on the resulting web page to control the server and view periodic or continuous status updates.

You can also use SWAT to share a Linux directory. First, click the Shares icon in the toolbar at the top of the main Samba page. Then, type a share name in the Create Shares field, and click the Create Shares button. The SWAT Shares page displays the detailed configuration information in a dialog box, as shown in Figure 22.4, providing access to detailed configuration for the new Samba share.

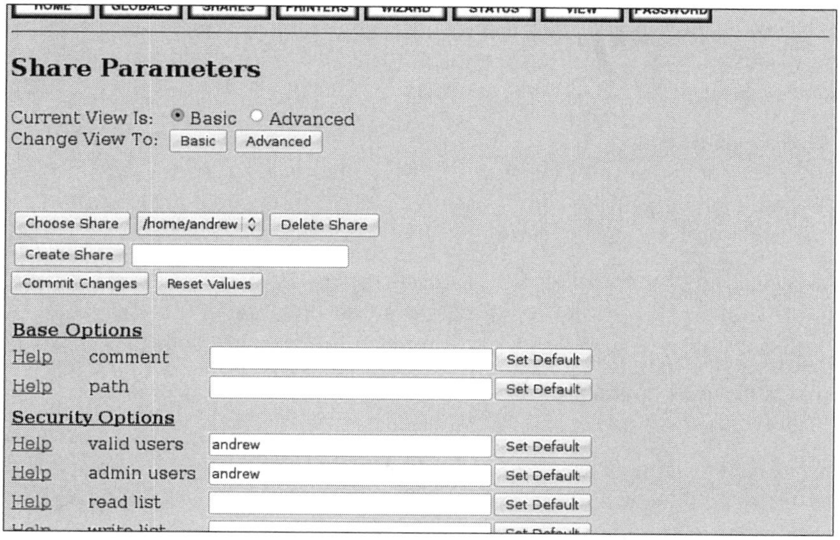

FIGURE 22.4   Use the SWAT Shares page to set up sharing of a portion of your Linux file system.

Type the directory name (such as /music) you want to share in the Path field under the Base options. Select No or Yes in the Read-Only field under Security options to allow or deny read and write access. Select Yes in the Guest OK option to allow access from other users and specify a hostname, IP address, or subnet in the Hosts Allow field to allow access. Click the Commit Changes button when finished. Remote users can then access the shared volume. This is how a Linux server running Samba can easily mimic shared volumes in a mixed computing environment!

Alternatively, use the `shares-admin` client (from the command line or the Server Settings Samba Server menu item on the System Settings menu). Unlock the tool by clicking the Unlock button, use the Add button to create new shares, and use the Properties button to edit the share's access options.

Network and Remote Printing with Ubuntu

Chapter 2, "Post-Installation Configuration," discussed how to set up and configure local printers and the associated print services. This section covers configuring printers for sharing and access across a network.

Offices all over the world benefit from using print servers and shared printers. It is a simple thing to do and can bring real productivity benefits, even in small settings.

Creating Network Printers

Setting up remote printing service involves configuring a print server and then creating a remote printer entry on one or more computers on your network. This section introduces a quick method of enabling printing from one Linux workstation to another Linux computer on a LAN. You also learn about SMB printing using Samba and its utilities. Finally, this section discusses how to configure network-attached printers and use them to print single or multiple documents.

Enabling Network Printing on a LAN

If the computer with an attached printer is using Ubuntu and you want to set up the system for print serving, use the `system-config-printer` client to create a new printer, which is available in the menu at System, Administration, Printing.

First, install any printers you have to the server, as discussed in Chapter 2. (Click Add and wait a moment, and it is likely the printer will be detected automatically; it is probably easy enough that you don't have to look up what is written in the other chapter.)

Next, open Server, Settings and enable Publish Shared Printers Connected to This System. Click OK.

Then, right-click any printer's icon and select Share. That's it. Most users will not need the information in the rest of this section, even to enable access to *Common UNIX Printing System (CUPS)* via the web interface.

To enable sharing manually, edit your /etc/cups/cupsd.conf file. Look for the section that begins with `<Location />` and modify it so that it reads as follows:

```
<Location />
Order Deny,Allow
Deny From All
Allow From 127.0.0.1
```

```
Allow From 192.168.0.*
</Location>
```

This tells CUPS to share your printers across the network `192.168.0.*`, for example. Make sure to change this to match your own network settings.

Next you need to look in the same file for the section that starts:

```
Listen localhost:631
```

Modify it to show this:

```
Listen 631
```

This tells CUPS to listen on port 631 for any printer requests.

Session Message Block Printing

Printing to an SMB printer requires Samba, along with its utilities such as the `smbclient` and associated `smbprint` printing filter. You can use the Samba software included with Ubuntu to print to a shared printer on a Windows network or set up a printer attached to your system as an SMB printer. This section describes how to create a local printer entry to print to a remote shared printer using SMB.

Setting up an SMB or shared printer is usually accomplished under Windows operating systems through configuration settings using the Control Panel's Network device. After enabling print sharing, reboot the computer. In the My Computer, Printers folder, right-click the name or icon of the printer you want to share and select Sharing from the pop-up menu. Set the Shared As item, and then enter a descriptive shared name, such as **HP2100**, and a password.

You must enter a shared name and password to configure the printer when running Linux. You also need to know the printer's workgroup name, IP address, and printer name and have the username and password on hand. To find this information, select Start, Settings, Printers; then right-click the shared printer's listing in the Printers window and select Properties from the pop-up window.

You can use CUPS to configure Samba to use your printers by editing the `smb.conf` file.

In the `[global]` section, enter the following lines, if they are not already there:

```
...
load printers = yes
printing = cups
printcap name = cups
```

This tells Samba to use CUPS to provide printing services. Next, you need to create a new section in the `smb.conf` file at the end of the file, as follows:

```
[printers]
comment = Use this for All Printers
path = /var/spool/samba
```

```
browseable = no
public = yes
guest ok = yes
writable = no
printable = yes
printer admin = root, andrew
```

This publishes your printers to the network and allows others to connect to them via Windows clients.

Make sure you restart the Samba service using the command shown earlier to make Samba pick up the changes to the configuration file.

Using the Common UNIX Printing System GUI

You can use CUPS to create printer queues, get print server information, and manage queues by launching a browser (such as Firefox) and browsing to http://localhost:631. CUPS provide a web-based administration interface, as shown in Figure 22.5.

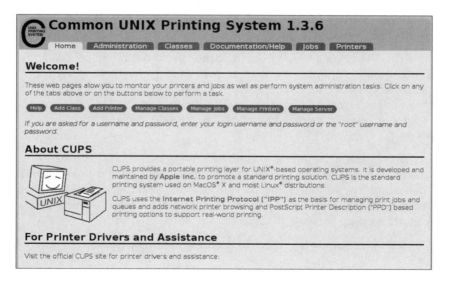

FIGURE 22.5   Use the web-based CUPS administrative interface to configure and manage printing.

If you click the Administration tab in the browser page, you can start configuring your printers, as shown in Figure 22.6.

Creating a CUPS Printer Entry

This section provides a short example of creating a Linux printer entry using CUPS's web-based interface. Use the CUPS interface to create a printer and device queue type (such as local, remote, serial port, or Internet); then you enter a device *uniform resource identifier (URI)*, such as `lpd://192.168.2.35/lp`, which represents the IP address of a remote UNIX print server and the name of the remote print queue on the server. You also need to specify the model or make of printer and its driver. A Printers page link allows you to print a test page, stop the printing service, manage the local print queue, modify the printer entry, or add another printer.

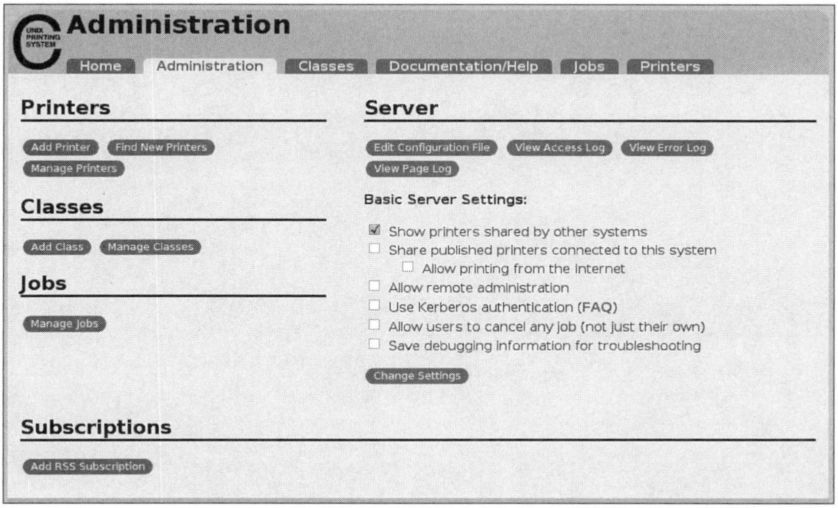

FIGURE 22.6   Enter the root password to perform printer administration with CUPS.

In the Admin page, click the Add Printer button and then enter a printer name in the Name field (such as lp), a physical location of the printer in the Location field, and a short note about the printer (such as its type) in the Description field. Figure 22.7 shows a sample entry for an HP 2100 LaserJet.

Click the Continue button. You can then select the type of printer access (local, remote, serial port, or Internet) in the Device page. For example, to configure printing to a local printer, select LPT1 or, for a remote printer, select the LPD/LPR Host or Printer entry.

Again click Continue and select a printer make, as requested in the dialog box shown in Figure 22.8.

After you click Continue, you then select the driver by choosing the exact model of your printer from the list provided. Finish by clicking the Add Printer button, and you will be prompted for your username and password (make sure you have admin rights linked to your account) before the printer is actually added to the system. After creating the printer, you can then use the Printer page, as shown in Figure 22.9, to print a test page, stop printing service, manage the local print queue, modify the printer entry, or add another printer.

CUPS offers many additional features and, after it is installed, configured, and running, provides transparent traditional UNIX printing support for Ubuntu.

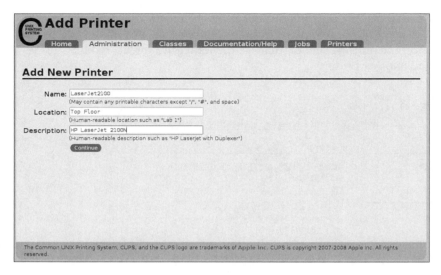

FIGURE 22.7   Use CUPS to create a new printer queue.

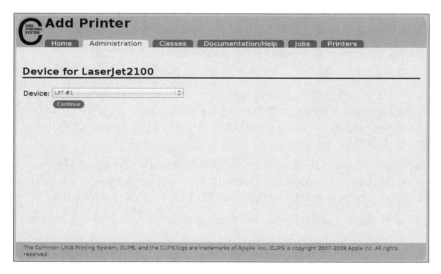

FIGURE 22.8   Select a printer make when creating a new queue.

NOTE

To learn more about CUPS and to get a basic overview of the system, browse to www.cups.org/.

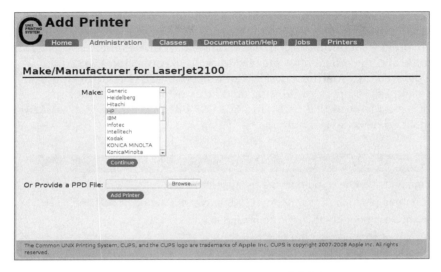

FIGURE 22.9   Manage printers easily using the CUPS Printer page.

Avoiding Printer Support Problems

Troubleshooting printer problems can prove to be frustrating, especially if you find that your new printer is not working properly with Linux. Keep in mind, however, that nearly all printers on the market today work with Linux. However, some vendors have higher batting averages in the game of supporting Linux. If you care to see a scorecard, browse to www.linuxprinting.org/vendors.html.

All-in-One (Print/Fax/Scan) Devices

Problematic printers, or printing devices that might or might not work with Ubuntu, include multifunction (or *all-in-one*) printers that combine scanning, faxing, and printing services. You should research any planned purchase and avoid any vendor unwilling to support Linux with drivers or development information.

One shining star in the field of Linux support for multifunction printers is the HP support of the HP OfficeJet Linux driver project at http://hpoj.sourceforge.net/. Printing and scanning are supported on many models, with fax support in development.

Using USB and Legacy Printers

Other problems can arise because of a lack of a printer's *Universal Serial Bus (USB)* vendor and device ID information—a problem shared by some USB scanners under Linux. For information about USB printer support, check with the Linux printing folks (at the URL in the start of this section) or with the Linux USB project at www.linux-usb.org/.

Although many newer printers require a USB port, excellent support still exists for legacy parallel-port (IEEE-1284) printers with Linux, enabling sites to continue to use older hardware. You can take advantage of Linux workarounds to set up printing even if the host computer does not have a traditional parallel printer port or if you want to use a newer USB printer on an older computer.

For example, to host a parallel-port-based printer on a USB-only computer, attach the printer to the computer using an inexpensive USB-to-parallel converter. USB-to-parallel converters typically provide a Centronics connector; one end of that connector is plugged into the older printer, and the other end is plugged into a USB connector. The USB connector is then plugged into your hub, desktop, or notebook USB port. You can use an add-on PCI card to add USB support for printing (and other devices) if the legacy computer does not have a built-in USB port. Most PCI USB interface cards add at least two ports, and you can chain devices via a hub.

Related Ubuntu and Linux Commands

The following commands can help you manage printing services:

▶ **accept**—Controls print job access to the CUPS server via the command line.

▶ **cancel**—Cancels a print job from the command line.

▶ **disable**—Control printing from the command line.

▶ **enable**—Controls CUPS printers.

▶ **lp**—Sends a specified file to the printer and allows control of the print service.

▶ **lpc**—Displays the status of printers and print service at the console.

▶ **lpq**—Views print queues (pending print jobs) at the console.

▶ **lprm**—Removes print jobs from the print queue via the command line.

▶ **lpstat**—Displays printer and server status.

References

▶ **https://help.ubuntu.com/community/SettingUpNFSHowTo**—Ubuntu community documentation for setting up NFS.

▶ **https://help.ubuntu.com/community/SettingUpSamba**—Ubuntu community documentation for setting up Samba.

▶ **https://help.ubuntu.com/community/Swat**—Ubuntu community documentation for SWAT.

▶ **www.samba.org/**—Base entry point for getting more information about Samba and using the SMB protocol with Linux, UNIX, Mac OS X, and other operating systems.

▶ **www.samba.org/samba/docs/man/Samba-HOWTO-Collection/SWAT.html**—Official Samba documentation for using SWAT.

▶ **www.linuxprinting.org/**—Browse here for specific drivers and information about USB and other types of printers.

▶ **www.cups.org/**—A comprehensive repository of CUPS software and information.

▶ **www.pwg.org/ipp/**—Home page for the Internet Printing Protocol standards.

CHAPTER 23

Apache Web Server Management

This chapter covers the configuration and management of the Apache web server and includes an overview of some of the major components of the server and discussions of text-based and graphical server configuration. In this chapter, you learn how to start, stop, and restart Apache using the command line. The chapter begins with some introductory information and then shows you how to install, configure, and use Apache.

About the Apache Web Server

Apache is the most widely used web server on the Internet today, according to a Netcraft survey of active websites in July 2011, which is shown in Table 23.1 (from http://news.netcraft.com/archives/2011/07/08/july-2011-web-server-survey.html).

Note that these statistics do not reflect use on internal networks, known as *intranets*.

The name *Apache* appeared during the early development of the software because it was "a patchy" server, made up of patches for the freely available source code of the NCSA HTTPd web server. For a while after the NCSA HTTPd project was discontinued, a number of people wrote a variety of patches for the code, to either fix bugs or add features they wanted. A lot of this code was floating around and people were freely sharing it, but it was completely unmanaged.

After a while, Brian Behlendorf and Cliff Skolnick set up a centralized repository of these patches, and the Apache project was born. The project is still composed of a small core group of programmers, but anyone is welcome to submit patches to the group for possible inclusion in the code.

TABLE 23.1   Netcraft Survey Results (July 2011)

Server	Number	Percent Share
Apache	224,484,657	64.88%
Microsoft	58,213,391	16.82%
nginx	22,668,760	6.55%
Google	15,958,106	4.61%

There has been a surge of interest in the Apache project over the past several years, partially buoyed by a new interest in open source on the part of enterprise-level information services. It's also due in part to crippling security flaws found in Microsoft's *Internet Information Services (IIS)*; the existence of malicious web task exploits; and operating system and networking vulnerabilities to the now-infamous Code Red, Blaster, and Nimda worms. IBM made an early commitment to support and use Apache as the basis for its web offerings and has dedicated substantial resources to the project because it makes more sense to use an established, proven web server.

In mid-1999, the Apache Software Foundation was incorporated as a nonprofit company. A board of directors, who are elected on an annual basis by the ASF members, oversees the company. This company provides a foundation for several open-source software development projects, including the Apache Web Server project.

TIP

You'll find an overview of Apache in its FAQs at http://httpd.apache.org/docs/2.2/faq/. In addition to extensive online documentation, you'll find the complete documentation for Apache in the HTML directory of your Apache server. If you have Apache running on your system, you can access this documentation by looking at http://localhost/manual/index.html.

To determine the precise version of Apache included with your system, use the web server's -V command-line option like this:

```
matthew@seymour:~$ /usr/sbin/apache2 -V
```

The output displays the version number, build date and time, platform, and various options used during the build. You can use the -v option to see abbreviated version information.

Installing the Apache Server

You can install Apache through APT or build it yourself from source code. The Apache source builds on just about any UNIX-like operating system and on Win32.

If you are about to install a new version of Apache, shut down the old server. Even if it's unlikely that the old server will interfere with the installation procedure, shutting it down ensures that there will be no problems. If you do not know how to stop Apache, see the "Starting and Stopping Apache" section later in this chapter.

Installing from the Ubuntu Repositories

You can install the apache2 package from the Ubuntu software repositories. Updated packages usually contain important bug and security fixes. When an updated version is released, install it as quickly as possible to keep your system secure.

> **NOTE**
>
> Check the Apache site for security reports. Browse to http://httpd.apache.org/security_report.html for links to security vulnerabilities for Apache 1.3, 2.0, and 2.2. Subscribe to a support list or browse through up-to-date archives of all Apache mailing lists at http://httpd.apache.org/mail/ (for various articles) or http://httpd.apache.org/lists.html (for comprehensive and organized archives).

> **CAUTION**
>
> You should be wary of installing experimental packages, and never install them on production servers (that is, servers used in "real life"). Very carefully test the packages beforehand on a host that is not connected to a network!

For more information about installing software from the Ubuntu repositories, see Chapter 9, "Managing Software."

The Apache package installs files in the following directories:

- ▶ **/etc/apache2**—This directory contains the Apache configuration file, apache2.conf.

- ▶ **/etc/init.d/**—The tree under this directory contains the system startup scripts. The Apache package installs a startup script named apache2 for the web server under the /etc/init.d directory. This script, which you can use to start and stop the server from the command line, also automatically starts and stops the server when the computer is halted, started, or rebooted.

- ▶ **/var/www**—The package installs the default server icons, *Common Gateway Interface (CGI)* programs, and HTML files in this location. If you want to keep web content elsewhere, you can do so by making the appropriate changes in the server configuration files.

▶ **/usr/share**—If you've installed the apache2-doc package, you'll find a copy of the Apache documentation in HTML format here. You can access it with a web browser by going to http://localhost/manual/.

▶ **/usr/share/man**—Ubuntu's Apache package also contains manual pages, which are placed underneath this directory. For example, the apache2 man page is in Section 8 of the man directory.

▶ **/usr/sbin**—The executable programs are placed in this directory. This includes the server executable itself and various utilities.

▶ **/usr/bin**—Some of the utilities from the Apache package are placed here—for example, the htpasswd program, which is used for generating authentication password files.

▶ **/var/log/apache2**—The server log files are placed in this directory. By default, there are two important log files (among several others): access_log and error_log. However, you can define any number of custom logs containing a variety of information. See the section "Logging," later in this chapter, for more detail.

When Apache is being run, it also creates the file apache2.pid, containing the process ID of Apache's parent process in the /var/run/ directory.

> **NOTE**
>
> If you are upgrading to a newer version of Apache, APT does not write over your current configuration files.

Building the Source Yourself

You can download the source directly from www.apache.org/. The latest version at the time of this writing is 2.2.19, although a stable 2.0.64 version is still supported and available. Although many sites continue to use older versions like those in the 1.3 series for script and other compatibility reasons, most sites are migrating to or are starting out using the latest stable version. We strongly recommend you use a currently supported, stable version for your site. The site also has a 2.3 beta available, which you are free to use for testing, but which should not be used on a production server.

After you have the tar file, you must open it in a temporary directory, such as /tmp. Opening this tar file creates a directory called apache_*version_number*, where *version_number* is the version you have downloaded (for example, apache_2.2.19).

There are two ways to compile the source—the old, familiar way (at least, to those of us who have been using Apache for many years) by editing makefile templates, and the new, easy way using a configure script. You will first see how to build Apache from source the easy way. The configure script offers a way to have the source software automatically configured according to your system. However, manually editing the configuration files before building and installing Apache provides more control over where the software is installed and which capabilities or features are built into Apache.

> **TIP**
>
> As with many software packages distributed in source code form for Linux and other UNIX-like operating systems, extracting the source code results in a directory that contains a README and an INSTALL file. Be sure to peruse the INSTALL file before attempting to build and install the software.

Using ./configure to Build Apache

To build Apache the easy way, run the ./configure script in the directory just created. You can provide it with a --prefix argument to install it in a directory other than the default, which is /usr/local/apache/. Use this command:

```
matthew@seymour:~/usr/src/apache2$ sudo ./configure --prefix=/preferred/directory/
```

This generates the Makefile that is used to compile the server code.

Next, type **make** to compile the server code. After the compilation is complete, type **make install** as root to install the server. You can now configure the server via the configuration files. See the "Runtime Server Configuration Settings" section for more information.

> **TIP**
>
> A safer way to install a new version of Apache from source is to use the ln command to create symbolic links of the existing file locations (listed in the "Installing with APT" section earlier in this chapter) to the new locations of the files. This method is safer because the default install locations are different from those used when the package installs the files. Failure to use this installation method could result in your web server process not being started automatically at system startup.
>
> Another safe way to install a new version of Apache is to first back up any important configuration directories and files (such as /etc/apache2) and then use the apt-get command to remove the server. You can then install and test your new version and, if needed, easily restore your original server and settings.
>
> It is strongly recommended that you use Ubuntu's version of Apache until you really know what happens at system startup. No "uninstall" option is available when installing Apache from source!

Apache File Locations After a Build and Install

Files are placed in various subdirectories of /usr/local/apache (or whatever directory you specified with the --prefix parameter) if you build the server from source.

The following is a list of the directories used by Apache, with brief comments on their usage:

▶ **/usr/local/apache/conf**—This contains several subdirectories and the Apache configuration file, httpd.conf. Debian-based systems such as Ubuntu often rename this to apache2.conf, so your mileage may vary. See the section "Editing apache2.conf" later in this chapter to learn more about configuration files.

▶ **/usr/local/apache**—The cgi-bin, icons, and htdocs subdirectories contain the CGI programs, standard icons, and default HTML documents, respectively.

▶ **/usr/local/apache/bin**—The executable programs are placed in this directory.

▶ **/usr/local/apache/logs**—The server log files are placed in this directory. By default, there are two log files—access_log and error_log—but you can define any number of custom logs containing a variety of information (see the "Logging" section later in this chapter). The default location for Apache's logs as installed by Ubuntu is /var/log/apache2.

A Quick Guide to Getting Started with Apache

Setting up, testing a web page, and starting Apache using Ubuntu can be accomplished in just a few steps. First, make sure that Apache is installed on your system. Either select it during installation or install the server, and related package files. (See Chapter 9, "Managing Software," if you need to install the server software.)

Next, set up a home page for your system by editing (as root) the file named index.html under the /var/ www directory on your system. Make a backup copy of the original page or www directory before you begin so you can restore your web server to its default state if necessary.

Start Apache through the Services window (under System, Administration from the menu bar), making sure to enable Web Server.

You can also use the apache2 script under the /etc/init.d/ directory, like this:

    matthew@seymour:~$ **sudo /etc/init.d/apache2 start**

You can then check your home page by running a favorite browser and using localhost, your system's hostname, or its *Internet Protocol (IP)* address in the URL. For example, with the links text browser, use a command line like this:

    matthew@seymour:~$ **links http://localhost/**

For security reasons, you should not start and run Apache as root if your host is connected to the Internet or a company intranet. Fortunately, Apache is set to run as the user and group www-data no matter how it is started (by the User and Group settings in /etc/apache2/apache2.conf). Despite this safe default, Apache should be started and managed by the user named www-data, defined in /etc/passwd as follows:

    www-data:x:33:33:www-data:/var/www:/bin/sh

When you are satisfied with your website, use the Services configuration dialog to ensure that Apache is started.

Starting and Stopping Apache

At this point, you have installed your Apache server with its default configuration. Ubuntu provides a default home page named index.html as a test under the /var/www/ directory. The proper way to run Apache is to set system initialization to have the server run after booting, network configuration, and any firewall configuration. See Chapter 14, "The Boot Process," for more information about how Ubuntu boots.

It is time to start it up for the first time. The following sections show how to either start and stop Apache or configure Ubuntu to start or not start Apache when booting.

Starting the Apache Server Manually

You can start Apache from the command line of a text-based console or X terminal window, and you must have root permission to do so. The server daemon, apache2, recognizes several command-line options you can use to set some defaults, such as specifying where apache2 reads its configuration directives. The Apache apache2 executable also understands other options that enable you to selectively use parts of its configuration file, specify a different location of the actual server and supporting files, use a different configuration file (perhaps for testing), and save startup errors to a specific log. The -v option causes Apache to print its development version and quit. The -V option shows all the settings that were in effect when the server was compiled.

The -h option prints the following usage information for the server:

```
matthew@seymour:~$ apache2 -h
Usage: apache2 [-D name] [-d directory] [-f file]
               [-C "directive"] [-c "directive"]
               [-k start|restart|graceful|stop]
               [-v] [-V] [-h] [-l] [-L] [-t]
Options:
  -D name            : define a name for use in <IfDefine name> directives
  -d directory       : specify an alternate initial ServerRoot
  -f file            : specify an alternate ServerConfigFile
  -C "directive"     : process directive before reading config files
  -c "directive"     : process directive after reading config files
  -e level           : show startup errors of level (see LogLevel)
  -E file            : log startup errors to file
  -v                 : show version number
  -V                 : show compile settings
  -h                 : list available command line options (this page)
  -l                 : list compiled in modules
  -L                 : list available configuration directives
  -t -D DUMP_VHOSTS  : show parsed settings (currently only vhost settings)
  -t                 : run syntax check for config files
```

Other options include listing Apache's *static modules*, or special, built-in independent parts of the server, along with options that can be used with the modules. These options are called *configuration directives* and are commands that control how a static module works. Note that Apache also includes nearly 50 *dynamic modules*, or software portions of the server that can be optionally loaded and used while the server is running.

The -t option is used to check your configuration files. It's a good idea to run this check before restarting your server, especially if you've made changes to your configuration files. Such tests are important because a configuration file error can result in your server shutting down when you try to restart it. There is a bug in the internal username settings for apache2 in Ubuntu that gives you this error if you enter the following:

```
matthew@seymour:~$ sudo apache2 -t
apache2: bad user name ${APACHE_RUN_USER}
```

If this happens to you, enter the command this way to force the command to use the expected username settings and you will get the proper output:

```
matthew@seymour:~$ sudo APACHE_RUN_USER=www-data APACHE_RUN_GROUP=www-data apache2 -t
```

> **NOTE**
>
> When you build and install Apache from source, start the server manually from the command line through sudo (such as when testing). You do this for two reasons:
>
> ▶ The standalone server uses the default HTTP port (port 80), and only the super user can bind to Internet ports that are lower than 1024.
>
> ▶ Only processes owned by root can change their *user* ID (UID) and *group* IP (GID) as specified by Apache's User and Group directives. If you start the server under another UID, it runs with the permissions of the user starting the process.
>
> Note that although some of the following examples show how to start the server through sudo, you should do so only for testing after building and installing Apache.

Using /etc/init.d/apache2

Ubuntu uses the scripts in the /etc/init.d directory to control the startup and shutdown of various services, including the Apache web server. The main script installed for the Apache web server is /etc/init.d/apache2, although the actual work is done by the apache2ctl shell script included with Apache.

> **NOTE**
>
> /etc/init.d/apache2 is a shell script and is not the same as the Apache server located in /usr/sbin. That is, /usr/sbin/apache2 is the program executable file (the server); /etc/init.d/apache2 is a shell script that uses another shell script, apache2ctl, to control the server. See Chapter 13, "Automating Tasks and Shell Scripting," for a description of some service scripts under /etc/init.d and how the scripts are used to manage services such as apache2.

You can use the /etc/init.d/apache2 script to control the web server. Here are some of the most common options to include with the command:

▶ **start**—The system uses this option to start the web server during boot. You, through sudo, can also use this script to start the server.

▶ **stop**—The system uses this option to stop the server gracefully. You should use this script, rather than the `kill` command, to stop the server.

▶ **reload**—You can use this option to send the HUP signal to the apache2 server to have it reread the configuration files after modification.

▶ **restart**—This option is a convenient way to stop and then immediately start the web server. If the apache2 server isn't running, it is started.

▶ **status**—This option indicates whether the server is running; if it is, it provides the *process ID (PID)* for each instance of the server.

For example, to check on the status of your server, use this command:

matthew@seymour:~$ **sudo /etc/init.d/apache2 status**

This prints the following on my machine. Your PIDs differ:

apache2 (pid 4743) is running...

This indicates that the web server is running.

In addition to the previous options, the apache2 script offers these features:

▶ **help**—Prints a list of valid options to the apache2 script (which are passed on to the server as if called from the command line).

▶ **force-reload**—Restarts the server while forcing it to reload configuration files.

TIP

Use the `force-reload` option if you are making many changes to the various server configuration files. This saves time when you are stopping and starting the server by having the system simply reread the configuration files.

Runtime Server Configuration Settings

At this point, the Apache server will run, but perhaps you want to change a behavior, such as the default location of your website's files. This section talks about the basics of configuring the server to work the way you want it to work.

Runtime configurations are stored in just one file—apache2.conf, which is found under the `/etc/apache2` directory. This configuration file can be used to control the default behavior of Apache, such as the web server's base configuration directory (`/etc/apache2`), the name of the server's PID file (`/var/run/apache2.pid`), or its response timeout (300 seconds). Apache reads the data from the configuration file when started (or restarted). You can also cause Apache to reload configuration information with the command

`/etc/init.d/apache2 reload`, which is necessary after making changes to its configuration file. (You learned how to accomplish this in earlier in this chapter, in the "Starting and Stopping Apache" section.)

Runtime Configuration Directives

You perform runtime configuration of your server with configuration directives, which are commands that set options for the `apache2` daemon. The directives are used to tell the server about various options you want to enable, such as the location of files important to the server configuration and operation. Apache supports nearly 300 configuration directives using the following syntax:

```
directive option option...
```

Each directive is specified on a single line. See the following sections for some directive examples and how to use them. Some directives only set a value such as a filename, whereas others enable you to specify various options. Some special directives, called *sections*, look like HTML tags. Section directives are surrounded by angle brackets, such as `<directive>`. Sections usually enclose a group of directives that apply only to the directory specified in the section:

```
<Directory somedir/in/your/tree>
  directive option option
  directive option option
</Directory>
```

All sections are closed with a matching section tag that looks like this: `</directive>`. Note that section tags, like any other directives, are specified one per line.

TIP

Apache is configured with an alias that lets you view the documentation installed in `/usr/share/doc` using your web browser at localhost/manual. After installing and starting Apache, you'll find an index of directives at http://localhost/manual/mod/directives.html.

Editing `apache2.conf`

Most of the default settings in the config file are okay to keep, particularly if you've installed the server in a default location and aren't doing anything unusual on your server. In general, if you do not understand what a particular directive is for, leave it set to the default value.

The following sections describe some of the configuration file settings you *might* want to change concerning operation of your server.

ServerRoot

The `ServerRoot` directive sets the absolute path to your server directory. This directive tells the server where to find all the resources and configuration files. Many of these resources are specified in the configuration files relative to the `ServerRoot` directory.

Your `ServerRoot` directive should be set to `/etc/apache2` if you installed the Ubuntu package or `/usr/local/apache` (or whatever directory you chose when you compiled Apache) if you installed from the source. This is commented out in the file, but `apache2 -V` shows that this default has been compiled into the package.

Listen

The `Listen` directive is actually in a file called `ports.conf` that is included from `apache2.conf` and indicates on which port you want your server to run. By default, this is set to 80, which is the standard HTTP port number. You might want to run your server on another port—for example, when running a test server that you don't want people to find by accident. Do not confuse this with real security! See the "File System Authentication and Access Control" section for more information about how to secure parts of your web server.

User and Group

The `User` and `Group` directives should be set to the UID and GID the server will use to process requests.

In Ubuntu, set these configurations to a user with few or no privileges. In this case, they're set to user `www-data` and group `www-data`—a user defined specifically to run Apache. If you want to use a different UID or GID, be aware that the server will run with the permissions of the user and group set here. That means in the event of a security breach, whether on the server or (more likely) in your own CGI programs, those programs will run with the assigned UID. If the server runs as root or some other privileged user, someone can exploit the security holes and do nasty things to your site. Always think in terms of the specified user running a command such as `rm -rf /` because that would wipe all files from your system. That should convince you that leaving `apache` as a user with no privileges is probably a good thing.

Instead of specifying the `User` and `Group` directives using names, you can specify them using the UID and GID numbers. If you use numbers, be sure that the numbers you specify correspond to the user and group you want and that they're preceded by the pound (#) symbol.

Here's how these directives look if specified by name:

```
User apache
Group apache
```

Here's the same specification by UID and GID:

```
User #48
Group #48
```

TIP

If you find a user on your system (other than root) with a UID and GID of 0, your system has been compromised by a malicious user.

ServerAdmin

The ServerAdmin directive should be set to the address of the webmaster managing the server. This address should be a valid email address or alias, such as webmaster@gnulix.org, because this address is returned to a visitor when a problem occurs on the server.

ServerName

The ServerName directive sets the hostname the server will return. Set it to a *fully qualified domain name (FQDN)*. For example, set it to www.your.domain rather than simply www. This is particularly important if this machine will be accessible from the Internet rather than just on your local network.

You do not need to set this unless you want a name other than the machine's canonical name returned. If this value isn't set, the server will figure out the name by itself and set it to its canonical name. However, you might want the server to return a friendlier address, such as www.your.domain. Whatever you do, ServerName should be a real *Domain Name Service (DNS)* name for your network. If you're administering your own DNS, remember to add an alias for your host. If someone else manages the DNS for you, ask that person to set this name for you.

DocumentRoot

Set this directive to the absolute path of your document tree, which is the top directory from which Apache will serve files. By default, it's set to /var/www/. If you built the source code yourself, DocumentRoot is set to /usr/local/apache/htdocs (if you did not choose another directory when you compiled Apache).

UserDir

The UserDir directive disables or enables and defines the directory (relative to a local user's /home directory) where that user can put public HTML documents. It is relative because each user has her own HTML directory. This setting is disabled by default but can be enabled to store user web content under any directory.

The default setting for this directive, if enabled, is public_html. Each user can create a directory called public_html under her /home directory, and HTML documents placed in that directory are available as http://servername/~username, where *username* is the user-name of the particular user.

DirectoryIndex

The DirectoryIndex directive indicates which file should be served as the index for a directory, such as which file should be served if the URL http://servername/_SomeDirectory/ is requested.

It is often useful to put a list of files here so that if `index.html` (the default value) isn't found, another file can be served instead. The most useful application of this is to have a CGI program run as the default action in a directory. If you have users who make their web pages on Windows, you might want to add `index.htm` as well. In that case, the directive \ looks like `DirectoryIndex index.html index.cgi index.htm`.

Apache Multiprocessing Modules

Apache version 2.0 and later now uses a new internal architecture supporting *multiprocessing modules (MPMs)*. These modules are used by the server for a variety of tasks, such as network and process management, and are compiled into Apache. MPMs enable Apache to work much better on a wider variety of computer platforms, and they can help improve server stability, compatibility, and scalability.

Apache can use only one MPM at any time. These modules are different from the base set included with Apache (see the "Apache Modules" section later in this chapter) but are used to implement settings, limits, or other server actions. Each module in turn supports numerous additional settings, called *directives*, which further refine server operation.

The internal MPM modules relevant for Linux include the following:

- ▶ `mpm_common`—A set of 20 directives common to all MPM modules.

- ▶ `prefork`—A nonthreaded, preforking web server that works similar to earlier (1.3) versions of Apache.

- ▶ `worker`—Provides a hybrid multiprocess multithreaded server.

MPM enables Apache to be used on equipment with fewer resources yet still handle massive numbers of hits and provide stable service. The `worker` module provides directives to control how many simultaneous connections your server can handle.

> **NOTE**
>
> Other MPMs are available for Apache related to other platforms, such as `mpm_netware` for NetWare hosts and `mpm_winnt` for NT platforms. An MPM named `perchild`, which provides user ID assignment to selected daemon processes, is under development. For more information, browse to the Apache Software Foundation's home page at www.apache.org.

Using `.htaccess` Configuration Files

Apache also supports special configuration files, known as `.htaccess` files. Almost any directive that appears in `apache2.conf` can appear in an `.htaccess` file. This file, specified in the `AccessFileName` directive in `apache2.conf`, sets configurations on a per-directory (usually in a user directory) basis. As the system administrator, you can specify both the name of this file and which of the server configurations can be overridden by the contents of this file. This is especially useful for sites in which there are multiple content providers and you want to control what these people can do with their space.

23

To limit which server configurations the .htaccess files can override, use the AllowOverride directive. AllowOverride can be set globally or per directory. For example, in your apache2.conf file, you could use the following:

```
# Each directory to which Apache has access can be configured with respect
# to which services and features are allowed and/or disabled in that
# directory (and its subdirectories).
#
# First, we configure the "default" to be a very restrictive set of
# permissions.
#
<Directory />
    Options FollowSymLinks
    AllowOverride None
</Directory>
```

Options Directives

To configure which configuration options are available to Apache by default, you must use the Options directive. Options can be None; All; or any combination of Indexes, Includes, FollowSymLinks, ExecCGI, and MultiViews. MultiViews are not included in All and must be specified explicitly. These options are explained in Table 23.2.

TABLE 23.2   Switches Used by the **Options** Directive

Switch	Description
None	None of the available options are enabled for this directory.
Indexes	In the absence of an index.html file or another DirectoryIndex file, a listing of the files in the directory is generated as an HTML page for display to the user.
Includes	*Server-side includes (SSIs)* are permitted in this directory. This can also be written as IncludesNoExec if you want to allow includes but don't want to allow the exec option in them. For security reasons, this is usually a good idea in directories over which you don't have complete control, such as UserDir directories.
FollowSymLinks	Allows access to directories that are symbolically linked to a document directory. You should never set this globally for the whole server and only rarely for individual directories. This option is a potential security risk because it allows web users to escape from the document directory and could potentially allow them access to portions of your file system where you really don't want people poking around.
ExecCGI	CGI programs are permitted in this directory, even if it is not a directory defined in the ScriptAlias directive.

TABLE 23.2   Switches Used by the **Options** Directive

Switch	Description
MultiViews	This is part of the mod_negotiation module. When a client requests a document that can't be found, the server tries to figure out which document best suits the client's requirements. See http://localhost/manuals/mod/_mod_negotiation.html for your local copy of the Apache documentation.

NOTE

These directives also affect all subdirectories of the specified directory.

AllowOverrides Directives

The AllowOverrides directives specify which configuration options .htaccess files can override. You can set this directive individually for each directory. For example, you can have different standards about what can be overridden in the main document root and in UserDir directories.

This capability is particularly useful for user directories, where the user does not have access to the main server configuration files.

AllowOverrides can be set to All or any combination of Options, FileInfo, AuthConfig, and Limit. These options are explained in Table 23.3.

TABLE 23.3   Switches Used by the AllowOverrides Directive

Switch	Description
Options	The .htaccess file can add options not listed in the Options directive for this directory.
FileInfo	The .htaccess file can include directives for modifying document type information.
AuthConfig	The .htaccess file might contain authorization directives.
Limit	The .htaccess file might contain allow, deny, and order directives.

File System Authentication and Access Control

You're likely to include material on your website that isn't supposed to be available to the public. You must be able to lock out this material from public access and provide designated users with the means to unlock the material. Apache provides two methods for accomplishing this type of access: authentication and authorization. You can use different criteria to control access to sections of your website, including checking the client's IP address or hostname, or requiring a username and password. This section briefly covers some of these methods.

CAUTION

Allowing individual users to put web content on your server poses several important security risks. If you're operating a web server on the Internet rather than on a private network, read the WWW Security FAQ at www.w3.org/Security/Faq/www-security-faq.html.

Restricting Access with `allow` and `deny`

One of the simplest ways to limit access to website material is to restrict access to a specific group of users, based on IP addresses or hostnames. Apache uses the `allow` and `deny` directives to accomplish this.

Both directives take an address expression as a parameter. The following list provides the possible values and use of the address expression:

▶ All can be used to affect all hosts.

▶ A hostname or domain name, which can either be a partially or a fully qualified domain name; for example, `test.gnulix.org` or `gnulix.org`.

▶ An IP address, which can be either full or partial; for example, `212.85.67` or `212.85.67.66`.

▶ A network/netmask pair, such as `212.85.67.0/255.255.255.0`.

▶ A network address specified in *classless inter-domain routing (CIDR)* format; for example, `212.85.67.0/24`. This is the CIDR notation for the same network and netmask that were used in the previous example.

If you have the choice, it is preferable to base your access control on IP addresses rather than hostnames. Doing so results in faster performance because no name lookup is necessary—the IP address of the client is included with each request.

You also can use `allow` and `deny` to provide or deny access to website material based on the presence or absence of a specific environment variable. For example, the following statement denies access to a request with a context that contains an environment variable named NOACCESS:

```
deny from env=NOACCESS
```

The default behavior of Apache is to apply all the deny directives first and then check the allow directives. If you want to change this order, you can use the order statement. Apache might interpret this statement in three different ways:

▶ **Order deny,allow**—The deny directives are evaluated before the `allow` directives. If a host is not specifically denied access, it is allowed to access the resource. This is the default ordering if nothing else is specified.

▶ **Order allow,deny**—All `allow` directives are evaluated before deny directives. If a host is not specifically allowed access, it is denied access to the resource.

▶ **Order mutual-failure**—Only hosts that are specified in an allow directive and at the same time do not appear in a deny directive are allowed access. If a host does not appear in either directive, it is not granted access.

Consider this example. Suppose you want to allow only persons from within your own domain to access the server-status resource on your web. If your domain were named gnulix.org, you could add these lines to your configuration file:

```
<Location /server-status>
    SetHandler server-status
    Order deny,allow
    Deny from all
    Allow from gnulix.org
</Location>
```

Authentication

Authentication is the process of ensuring that visitors really are who they claim to be. You can configure Apache to allow access to specific areas of web content only to clients who can authenticate their identity. There are several methods of authentication in Apache; Basic Authentication is the most common (and the method discussed in this chapter).

Under Basic Authentication, Apache requires a user to supply a username and a password to access the protected resources. Apache then verifies that the user is allowed to access the resource in question. If the username is acceptable, Apache verifies the password. If the password also checks out, the user is authorized and Apache serves the request.

HTTP is a stateless protocol; each request sent to the server and each response is handled individually, and not in an intelligent fashion. Therefore, the authentication information must be included with each request. That means each request to a password-protected area is larger and therefore somewhat slower. To avoid unnecessary system use and delays, protect only those areas of your website that absolutely need protection.

To use Basic Authentication, you need a file that lists which users are allowed to access the resources. This file is composed of a plain text list containing name and password pairs. It looks very much like the /etc/passwd user file of your Linux system.

CAUTION

Do not use /etc/passwd as a user list for authentication. When you're using Basic Authentication, passwords and usernames are sent as base64-encoded text from the client to the server (which is just as readable as plain text). The username and password are included in each request that is sent to the server. So, anyone who might be snooping on Net traffic would be able to get this information!

23

To create a user file for Apache, use the htpasswd command. This is included with the Apache package. If you installed using the packages, it is in /usr/bin. Running htpasswd without any options produces the following output:

```
Usage:
        htpasswd [-cmdps] passwordfile username
        htpasswd -b[cmdps] passwordfile username password

        htpasswd -n[mdps] username
        htpasswd -nb[mdps] username password
 -c  Create a new file.
 -n  Don't update file; display results on stdout.
 -m  Force MD5 encryption of the password.
 -d  Force CRYPT encryption of the password (default).
 -p  Do not encrypt the password (plaintext).
 -s  Force SHA encryption of the password.
 -b  Use the password from the command line rather than prompting for it.
 -D  Delete the specified user.
On Windows, TPF and NetWare systems the '-m' flag is used by default.
On all other systems, the '-p' flag will probably not work.
```

As you can see, it is not a difficult command to use. For example, to create a new user file named gnulixusers with a user named wsb, you need to do something like this:

matthew@seymour:~$ **sudo htpasswd -c gnulixusers wsb**

You are then prompted for a password for the user. To add more users, repeat the same procedure, only omitting the -c flag.

You can also create user group files. The format of these files is similar to that of /etc/groups. On each line, enter the group name, followed by a colon (:), and then list all users, with each user separated by spaces. For example, an entry in a user group file might look like this:

gnulixusers: wsb pgj jp ajje nadia rkr hak

Now that you know how to create a user file, it's time to look at how Apache might use this to protect web resources.

To point Apache to the user file, use the AuthUserFile directive. AuthUserFile takes the file path to the user file as its parameter. If the file path is not absolute—that is, beginning with a /—it is assumed that the path is relative to the ServerRoot. Using the AuthGroupFile directive, you can specify a group file in the same manner.

Next, use the AuthType directive to set the type of authentication to be used for this resource. Here, the type is set to Basic.

Now you need to decide to which realm the resource will belong. Realms are used to group different resources that will share the same users for authorization. A realm can consist of just about any string. The realm is shown in the Authentication dialog box on the user's web browser. Therefore, you should set the realm string to something informative. The realm is defined with the `AuthName` directive.

Finally, state which type of user is authorized to use the resource. You do this with the `require` directive. The three ways to use this directive are as follows:

▶ If you specify `valid-user` as an option, any user in the user file is allowed to access the resource (that is, provided she also enters the correct password).

▶ You can specify a list of users who are allowed access with the `users` option.

▶ You can specify a list of groups with the `group` option. Entries in the group list, as well as the user list, are separated by a space.

Returning to the `server-status` example you saw earlier, instead of letting users access the `server-status` resource based on hostname, you can require the users to be authenticated to access the resource. You can do so with the following entry in the configuration file:

```
<Location /server-status>
    SetHandler server-status
    AuthType Basic
    AuthName "Server status"
    AuthUserFile "gnulixusers"
    Require valid-user
</Location>
```

Final Words on Access Control

If you have host-based as well as user-based access protection on a resource, the default behavior of Apache is to require the requester to satisfy both controls. But assume that you want to mix host-based and user-based protection and allow access to a resource if either method succeeds. You can do so using the `satisfy` directive. You can set the `satisfy` directive to `All` (this is the default) or `Any`. When set to `All`, all access control methods must be satisfied before the resource is served. If `satisfy` is set to `Any`, the resource is served if any access condition is met.

Here's another access control example, again using the previous `server-status` example. This time, you combine access methods so all users from the `Gnulix` domain are allowed access and those from outside the domain must identify themselves before gaining access. You can do so with the following:

```
<Location /server-status>
    SetHandler server-status
    Order deny,allow
    Deny from all
    Allow from gnulix.org
    AuthType Basic
```

```
    AuthName "Server status"
    AuthUserFile "gnulixusers"
    Require valid-user
    Satisfy Any
</Location>
```

There are more ways to protect material on your web server, but the methods discussed here should get you started and will probably be more than adequate for most circumstances. Look to Apache's online documentation for more examples of how to secure areas of your site.

Apache Modules

The Apache core does relatively little; Apache gains its functionality from modules. Each module solves a well-defined problem by adding necessary features. By adding or removing modules to supply the functionality you want Apache to have, you can tailor Apache server to suit your exact needs.

Nearly 70 core modules are included with the basic Apache server. Many more are available from other developers. The Apache Module Registry is a repository for add-on modules for Apache, and it can be found at http://modules.apache.org/. The modules are stored in the /usr/lib/apache2/modules directory. (Your list might look different.)

httpd.exp	mod_cgi.so	mod_mime_magic.so
mod_actions.so	mod_charset_lite.so	mod_mime.so
mod_alias.so	mod_dav_fs.so	mod_negotiation.so
mod_asis.so	mod_dav_lock.so	mod_proxy_ajp.so
mod_auth_basic.so	mod_dav.so	mod_proxy_balancer.so
mod_auth_digest.so	mod_dbd.so	mod_proxy_connect.so
mod_authn_alias.so	mod_deflate.so	mod_proxy_ftp.so
mod_authn_anon.so	mod_dir.so	mod_proxy_http.so
mod_authn_dbd.so	mod_disk_cache.so	mod_proxy_scgi.so
mod_authn_dbm.so	mod_dumpio.so	mod_proxy.so
mod_authn_default.so	mod_env.so	mod_reqtimeout.so
mod_authn_file.so	mod_expires.so	mod_rewrite.so
mod_authnz_ldap.so	mod_ext_filter.so	mod_setenvif.so
mod_authz_dbm.so	mod_file_cache.so	mod_speling.so
mod_authz_default.so	mod_filter.so	mod_ssl.so
mod_authz_groupfile.so	mod_headers.so	mod_status.so
mod_authz_host.so	mod_ident.so	mod_substitute.so
mod_authz_owner.so	mod_imagemap.so	mod_suexec.so
mod_authz_user.so	mod_include.so	mod_unique_id.so
mod_autoindex.so	mod_info.so	mod_userdir.so
mod_cache.so	mod_ldap.so	mod_usertrack.so
mod_cern_meta.so	mod_log_forensic.so	mod_version.so
mod_cgid.so	mod_mem_cache.so	mod_vhost_alias.so

Each module adds new directives that can be used in your configuration files. As you might guess, there are far too many extra commands, switches, and options to describe them all in this chapter. The following sections briefly describe a subset of those modules available with Ubuntu's Apache installation.

To enable a module, use this command:

```
matthew@seymour:~$ sudo a2enmod module_name
```

To disable a module, use this:

```
matthew@seymour:~$ sudo a2dismod module_name
```

Note that these want the actual name of the module, not the filename; for example, `mod_version.so` is the filename, but `version` is the name of the module. You have to know the name of the module to use either command, but in most cases, it is as simple as the difference in this example. Also, once you run either command, you need to restart apache2 to activate the new configuration:

```
matthew@seymour:~$ sudo /etc/init.d/apache2 restart
```

mod_access

mod_access controls access to areas on your web server based on IP addresses, hostnames, or environment variables. For example, you might want to allow anyone from within your own domain to access certain areas of your web. See the "File System Authentication and Access Control" section for more information.

mod_alias

mod_alias manipulates the URLs of incoming HTTP requests, such as redirecting a client request to another URL. It also can map a part of the file system into your web hierarchy. For example, the following fetches contents from the /home/wsb/graphics directory for any URL that starts with /images/:

```
Alias /images/ /home/wsb/graphics/
```

This is done without the client knowing anything about it. If you use a redirection, the client is instructed to go to another URL to find the requested content. More advanced URL manipulation can be accomplished with mod_rewrite.

mod_asis

mod_asis is used to specify, in fine detail, all the information to be included in a response. This completely bypasses any headers Apache might have otherwise added to the response. All files with an .asis extension are sent straight to the client without any changes.

As a short example of the use of mod_asis, assume you've moved content from one location to another on your site. Now you must inform people who try to access this resource that it has moved, as well as automatically redirect them to the new location. To provide this information and redirection, you can add the following code to a file with a .asis extension:

```
Status: 301 No more old stuff!
Location: http://gnulix.org/newstuff/
Content-type: text/html
```

```
<HTML>
 <HEAD>
  <TITLE>We've moved...</TITLE>
 </HEAD>
 <BODY>
   <P>We've moved the old stuff and now you'll find it at:</P>
   <A HREF="http://gnulix.org/newstuff/">New stuff</A>!.
 </BODY>
</HTML>
```

mod_auth

mod_auth uses a simple user authentication scheme, referred to as Basic Authentication, which is based on storing usernames and encrypted passwords in a text file. This file looks very much like UNIX's /etc/passwd file and is created with the htpasswd command. See the "File System Authentication and Access Control" section earlier in this chapter for more information about this subject.

mod_auth_anon

The mod_auth_anon module provides anonymous authentication similar to that of anonymous FTP. The module enables you to define user IDs of those who are to be handled as guest users. When such a user tries to log on, he is prompted to enter his email address as his password. You can have Apache check the password to ensure that it's a (more or less) proper email address. Basically, it ensures that the password contains an @ character and at least one . character.

mod_auth_dbm

mod_auth_dbm uses Berkeley DB files instead of text for user authentication files.

mod_auth_digest

An extension of the basic mod_auth module, instead of sending the user information in plain text, mod_auth_digest is sent via the *message digest 5 (MD5)* authentication process. This authentication scheme is defined in RFC 2617, "HTTP Authentication: Basic and Digest Access Authentication." Compared to using Basic Authentication, this is a much more secure way of sending user data over the Internet. Unfortunately, not all web browsers support this authentication scheme.

To create password files for use with mod_auth_dbm, you must use the htdigest utility. It has more or less the same functionality as the htpasswd utility. See the man page of htdigest for further information.

mod_autoindex

The mod_autoindex module dynamically creates a file list for directory indexing. The list is rendered in a user-friendly manner similar to those lists provided by FTP's built-in ls command.

mod_cgi

mod_cgi allows execution of CGI programs on your server. CGI programs are executable files residing in the /var/www/cgi-bin directory and are used to dynamically generate data (usually HTML) for the remote browser when requested.

mod_dir and mod_env

The mod_dir module is used to determine which files are returned automatically when a user tries to access a directory. The default is index.html. If you have users who create web pages on Windows systems, you should also include index.htm, like this:

```
DirectoryIndex index.html index.htm
```

mod_env controls how environment variables are passed to CGI and SSI scripts.

mod_expires

mod_expires is used to add an expiration date to content on your site by adding an Expires header to the HTTP response. Web browsers or cache servers won't cache expired content.

mod_headers

mod_headers is used to manipulate the HTTP headers of your server's responses. You can replace, add, merge, or delete headers as you see fit. The module supplies a Header directive for this. Ordering of the Header directive is important. A set followed by an unset for the same HTTP header removes the header altogether. You can place Header directives almost anywhere within your configuration files. These directives are processed in the following order:

1. Core server
2. Virtual host
3. <Directory> and .htaccess files

    <Location>
    <Files>

mod_include

`mod_include` enables the use of server-side includes on your server, which were quite popular before PHP took over this part of the market.

mod_info and mod_log_config

`mod_info` provides comprehensive information about your server's configuration. For example, it displays all the installed modules, as well as all the directives used in its configuration files.

`mod_log_config` defines how your log files should look. See the "Logging" section for further information about this subject.

mod_mime and mod_mime_magic

The `mod_mime` module tries to determine the MIME type of files from their extensions.

The `mod_mime_magic` module tries to determine the MIME type of files by examining portions of their content.

mod_negotiation

Using the `mod_negotiation` module, you can select one of several document versions that best suits the client's capabilities. There are several options to select which criteria to use in the negotiation process. You can, for example, choose among different languages, graphics file formats, and compression methods.

mod_proxy

`mod_proxy` implements proxy and caching capabilities for an Apache server. It can proxy and cache FTP, CONNECT, HTTP/0.9, and HTTP/1.0 requests. This is not an ideal solution for sites that have a large number of users and therefore have high proxy and cache requirements. However, it is more than adequate for a small number of users.

mod_rewrite

`mod_rewrite` is the Swiss army knife of URL manipulation. It enables you to perform any imaginable manipulation of URLs using powerful regular expressions. It provides rewrites, redirection, proxying, and so on. There is little that you cannot accomplish using this module.

TIP

See http://localhost/manual/misc/rewriteguide.html for a cookbook that gives you an in-depth explanation of the `mod_rewrite` module's capabilities.

mod_setenvif

mod_setenvif allows manipulation of environment variables. Using small snippets of text-matching code known as *regular expressions*, you can conditionally change the content of environment variables. The order in which SetEnvIf directives appear in the configuration files is important. Each SetEnvIf directive can reset an earlier SetEnvIf directive when used on the same environment variable. Be sure to keep that in mind when using the directives from this module.

mod_speling

mod_speling is used to enable correction of minor typos in URLs. If no file matches the requested URL, this module builds a list of the files in the requested directory and extracts those files that are the closest matches. It tries to correct only one spelling mistake.

mod_status

You can use mod_status to create a web page containing a plethora of information about a running Apache server. The page contains information about the internal status as well as statistics about the running Apache processes. This can be a great aid when you're trying to configure your server for maximum performance. It's also a good indicator of when something's amiss with your Apache server.

mod_ssl

mod_ssl provides Secure Sockets Layer (versions 2 and 3) and Transport Layer Security (version 1) support for Apache. At least 30 directives exist that deal with options for encryption and client authorization and that can be used with this module.

mod_unique_id

mod_unique_id generates a unique request identifier for every incoming request. This ID is put into the UNIQUE_ID environment variable.

mod_userdir

The mod_userdir module enables mapping of a subdirectory in each user's /home directory into your web tree. The module provides several ways to accomplish this.

mod_usertrack

mod_usertrack is used to generate a cookie for each user session. This can be used to track the user's click stream within your web tree. You must enable a custom log that logs this cookie into a log file.

mod_vhost_alias

mod_vhost_alias supports dynamically configured mass virtual hosting, which is useful for *Internet service providers (ISPs)* with many virtual hosts. However, for the average user, Apache's ordinary virtual hosting support should be more than sufficient.

There are two ways to host virtual hosts on an Apache server. You can have one IP address with multiple CNAMEs, or you can have multiple IP addresses with one name per address. Apache has different sets of directives to handle each of these options. (You learn more about virtual hosting in Apache in the next section of this chapter.)

Again, the available options and features for Apache modules are too numerous to describe completely in this chapter. You can find complete information about the Apache modules in the online documentation for the server included with Ubuntu or at the Apache Group's website.

Virtual Hosting

One of the more popular services to provide with a web server is to host a virtual domain. Also known as a *virtual host*, a virtual domain is a complete website with its own domain name, as if it was a standalone machine, but it's hosted on the same machine as other websites. Apache implements this capability in a simple way with directives in the apache2.conf configuration file.

Apache now can dynamically host virtual servers by using the mod_vhost_alias module you read about in the preceding section of the chapter. The module is primarily intended for ISPs and similar large sites that host a large number of virtual sites. This module is for more advanced users and, as such, it is outside the scope of this introductory chapter. Instead, this section concentrates on the traditional ways of hosting virtual servers.

Address-Based Virtual Hosts

After you've configured your Linux machine with multiple IP addresses, setting up Apache to serve them as different websites is simple. You need only put a VirtualHost directive in your apache2.conf file for each of the addresses you want to make an independent website:

```
<VirtualHost 212.85.67.67>
ServerName gnulix.org
DocumentRoot /home/virtual/gnulix/public_html
TransferLog /home/virtual/gnulix/logs/access_log
ErrorLog /home/virtual/gnulix/logs/error_log
</VirtualHost>
```

Use the IP address, rather than the hostname, in the VirtualHost tag.

You can specify any configuration directives within the <VirtualHost> tags. For example, you might want to set AllowOverrides directives differently for virtual hosts than you do for your main server. Any directives that aren't specified default to the settings for the main server.

Name-Based Virtual Hosts

Name-based virtual hosts enable you to run more than one host on the same IP address. You must add the names to your DNS as CNAMEs of the machine in question. When an HTTP client (web browser) requests a document from your server, it sends with the request a variable indicating the server name from which it's requesting the document. Based on this variable, the server determines from which of the virtual hosts it should serve content.

> **NOTE**
>
> Some older browsers cannot name-based virtual hosts because this is a feature of HTTP 1.1 and the older browsers are strictly HTTP 1.0 compliant. However, many other older browsers are partially HTTP 1.1 compliant, and this is one of the parts of HTTP 1.1 that most browsers have supported for a while.

Name-based virtual hosts require just one step more than IP address-based virtual hosts. You must first indicate which IP address has the multiple DNS names on it. This is done with the `NameVirtualHost` directive:

```
NameVirtualHost 212.85.67.67
```

You must then have a section for each name on that address, setting the configuration for that name. As with IP-based virtual hosts, you need to set only those configurations that must be different for the host. You must set the `ServerName` directive because it is the only thing that distinguishes one host from another:

```
<VirtualHost 212.85.67.67>
ServerName bugserver.gnulix.org
ServerAlias bugserver
DocumentRoot /home/bugserver/htdocs
ScriptAlias /home/bugserver/cgi-bin
TransferLog /home/bugserver/logs/access_log
</VirtualHost>

<VirtualHost 212.85.67.67>
ServerName pts.gnulix.org
ServerAlias pts
DocumentRoot /home/pts/htdocs
ScriptAlias /home/pts/cgi-bin
TransferLog /home/pts/logs/access_log
ErrorLog /home/pts/logs/error_log
</VirtualHost>
```

23

> **TIP**
>
> If you are hosting websites on an intranet or internal network, users will likely use the shortened name of the machine rather than the FQDN. For example, users might type http://bugserver/index.html in their browser location field rather than http://bugserver.gnulix.org/index.html. In that case, Apache would not recognize that those two addresses should go to the same virtual host. You could get around this by setting up VirtualHost directives for both bugserver and bugserver.gnulix.org, but the easy way around it is to use the ServerAlias directive, which lists all valid aliases for the machine:
>
>   ServerAlias bugserver
>
> For more information about VirtualHost, refer to the help system on http://localhost/_manual.

Logging

Apache provides logging for just about any web access information you might be interested in. Logging can help with the following:

▸ System resource management, by tracking usage

▸ Intrusion detection, by documenting bad HTTP requests

▸ Diagnostics, by recording errors in processing requests

Two standard log files are generated when you run your Apache server: access_log and error_log. They are found under the /var/log/apache2 directory. (Others include the SSL logs ssl_access_log, ssl_error_log and ssl_request_log.) All logs except for the error_log (by default, this is just the access_log) are generated in a format specified by the CustomLog and LogFormat directives. These directives appear in your apache2.conf file.

A new log format can be defined with the LogFormat directive:

```
LogFormat "%h %l %u %t \"%r\" %>s %b" common
```

The common log format is a good starting place for creating your own custom log formats. Note that most of the available log analysis tools assume you're using the common log format or the combined log format, both of which are defined in the default configuration files.

The following variables are available for LogFormat statements:

▸ **%a**—Remote IP address.

▸ **%A**—Local IP address.

▸ **%b**—Bytes sent, excluding HTTP headers. This is shown in Apache's *Combined Log Format (CLF)*. For a request without any data content, a - is shown instead of 0.

▸ **%B**—Bytes sent, excluding HTTP headers.

- ▶ **%{VARIABLE}e**—The contents of the environment variable VARIABLE.

- ▶ **%f**—The filename of the output log.

- ▶ **%h**—Remote host.

- ▶ **%H**—Request protocol.

- ▶ **%{HEADER}i**—The contents of HEADER; header lines in the request sent to the server.

- ▶ **%l**—Remote log name (from identd, if supplied).

- ▶ **%m**—Request method.

- ▶ **%{NOTE}n**—The contents of note NOTE from another module.

- ▶ **%{HEADER}o**—The contents of HEADER; header lines in the reply.

- ▶ **%p**—The canonical port of the server serving the request.

- ▶ **%P**—The PID of the child that serviced the request.

- ▶ **%q**—The contents of the query string, prepended with a ? character. If there's no query string, this evaluates to an empty string.

- ▶ **%r**—The first line of request.

- ▶ **%s**—Status. For requests that were internally redirected, this is the status of the original request (%>s for the last).

- ▶ **%t**—The time, in common log time format.

- ▶ **%{format}t**—The time, in the form given by format, which should be in strftime(3) format.

- ▶ **%T**—The seconds taken to serve the request.

- ▶ **%u**—Remote user from auth; this might be bogus if the return status (%s) is 401.

- ▶ **%U**—The URL path requested.

- ▶ **%V**—The server name according to the UseCanonicalName directive.

- ▶ **%v**—The canonical ServerName of the server serving the request.

You can put a conditional in front of each variable to determine whether the variable is displayed. If the variable isn't displayed, - is displayed instead. These conditionals are in the form of a list of numeric return values. For example, %!401u displays the value of REMOTE_USER unless the return code is 401.

You can then specify the location and format of a log file using the CustomLog directive:

```
CustomLog logs/access_log common
```

If it is not specified as an absolute path, the location of the log file is assumed to be relative to the ServerRoot.

References

▶ **http://news.netcraft.com/archives/web_server_survey.html**—A statistical graph of web server usage by millions of servers. The research points out that Apache is by far the most widely used server for Internet sites.

▶ **www.apache.org/**—Extensive documentation and information about Apache are available at The Apache Project website.

▶ **http://modules.apache.org/**—Available add-on modules for Apache can be found at the Apache Module Registry website.

CHAPTER 24

Other HTTP Servers

To determine the best web server for your use, consider the needs of the website you manage. Does it need heavy security (for e-commerce), multimedia (music, video, and pictures), or the capability to download files easily? How much are you willing to spend for the software? Do you need software that is easy to maintain and troubleshoot or that includes tech support? The answers to these questions might steer you to something other than what we covered in Chapter 23, "Apache Web Server Management."

This chapter does not provide a detailed tutorial for these alternatives to Apache, which is by far the most popular web server. Instead, it describes each alternative with enough detail to help you consider whether you may want to investigate it further. All the web servers in this chapter are available in the Ubuntu software repositories.

Nginx

Pronounced "engine-x," this is a lightweight and extremely fast web server. It is free and open source. Some well-known websites such as WordPress, GitHub, and SourceForge use Nginx because it is stable and fast under high-traffic conditions while using fewer resources. It is not as configurable as Apache, nor as well documented in English since it originates from Russia, but for specific use cases, it is an excellent option and is quite easy to set up and use.

The original design of Nginx was created to allow higher numbers of concurrent website requests. Larger websites often have tens of thousands of clients connected simultaneously, each one making HTTP requests that must be responded to. As with many of the web servers described in this chapter, the designers of Nginx heard this problem described as C10K and decided they could write a web server that would be capable of serving at least 10,000 clients simultaneously.

The C10K Problem

The canonical website for learning more about this problem is www.kegel.com/c10k. html. The article linked here is from the early 2000s and describes ideas for configuring operating systems and writing code to solve the problem of serving at least 10,000 simultaneous clients from a web server. Today, this is even more common, and with the continuing maturity of Nginx, lighttpd, and other web servers, many of the largest, highest traffic sites have switched.

Newer versions of the Apache and other modern web servers rely on a concept of threads. *Threads* are kind of like lightweight processes. This deserves some explanation. A process is a specific instance of a computer program running. The process contains both the machine code (the binary, or the compiled version of the program that the computer processor can understand and obey—this is either precompiled, as in C or C++ programs, or may be the output of a just-in-time compilation, as happens with languages like Python or Perl) as well as the current activity of that program, such as the calculations it is performing or the data it stores in memory on which it is operating. Serving an HTTP page by running a complete process each time would be bad because the server's resources would be quickly used up if the site was even moderately popular. Process after process would be started and would fight for attention. A thread is the ordered control of a program: First, do this; then, do that; finally, do this other thing. One process may control many threads. This is good for resource management. By using threads instead of processes, more current versions of Apache and others can serve a large number of client requests using less system resources than a process-based server, like earlier versions of Apache, could.

Most web servers have traditionally been either process based or thread based. There are also examples of hybrid models, where many multithread processes are used. Process-based servers are great because they are stable and the crash of one process does not impact other processes. However, they cannot handle as many clients because the creation and destruction of all of those processes creates a lot of processor overhead and requires a large amount of memory. Thread-based servers are great because requests can share memory, making them more efficient and thereby able to serve more requests more quickly. However, a crash in one thread could bring the entire server down.

What makes Nginx different is that it uses an event-driven architecture to handle requests. Instead of starting a new process or a new thread for each request, in an event-driven architecture, the flow of the program is controlled by events, some form of message sent from another process or thread. Here, you have a process that runs as a "listener" or "event detector" that waits for a request to come in to the server. When the request arrives, instead of a new process starting, the "listener" sends a message to a different part of the server called an "event handler" that then performs a task. The simplified outcome of serving web pages this way is that less processor time and less memory are needed.

There are some significant difficulties inherent in using this method, not the least of which can be greater code complexity, which can make fixing bugs, adding features, and understanding code as a newcomer (or even a returning veteran of the same codebase, but who has been away from it for a little while) more difficult.

Nginx is designed to scale well from one small, low-powered server up to large networks involving many servers.

For configuration, Nginx uses a system of virtual hosts, similar to Apache, using a similar set of configuration files. The differences are semantic and not terribly difficult. You can create URL rewrites in Nginx using a rather different syntax. In addition, there is nothing similar to Apache's rewrite conditions. Occasional blog posts and web tutorials exist to give some workarounds that will handle some of the more common forms, but if this is something you do often, you might not want to use Nginx.

One missing file that many people use and love in Apache is .htaccess. There is nothing similar in Nginx, so if you need the ability to make changes to rewrites or configurations without restarting the server, you are out of luck. This is probably the primary reason that you don't see shared hosting offering Nginx.

Finally, another well-documented option is to use both Apache and Nginx together, where Apache handles any and all dynamic requests and Nginx handles all static requests. This is faster and lighter than using Apache alone, but comes with the burden of added complexity and the increased potential for problems that brings.

lighttpd

Another speedy open-source lightweight server is lighttpd, or "lighty." Like Nginx, lighttpd is designed for high-performance and low resource use. YouTube, Wikipedia, and others are using lighttpd for its scalability and quickness. Also like Nginx, lighttpd uses an event-driven architecture.

One thing that sets lighttpd apart from Nginx is that while Nginx natively handles static content incredibly well, but can require a bit of work to get it functioning as a server for CGI content, such as websites built with PHP. Obviously, because WordPress uses Nginx and is built with PHP, this is not an insurmountable task with Nginx (and web tutorials abound). With lighttpd, this feature is built in, making it quicker to install, configure, and use if this is the sort of site you intend to host.

Configuring lighttpd is again done using a system of configuration files. The syntax is a bit different from either Apache or Nginx, but to anyone familiar with using either, lighttpd will be easy to understand and use.

Rewrite rules are available for lighttpd and can be done using conditionals and regular expressions. However, the syntax for doing this is different and will take a little time to study and use effectively.

lighttpd has a nice website with professional documentation available. Reading through it should give you a good sense of whether lighttpd is suitable for a specific site.

Yaws

Yaws stands for *Yet Another Web Server*. It is written in the Erlang programming language, which is enough to make it unique and interesting for many people. Erlang is primarily designed for and used to build scalable real-time systems that require high availability. It is often found in telephony applications, instant messaging, commerce, and banking and is designed to support concurrency and fault tolerance. Yaws was written from the ground up to be scalable and multithreaded. Like newer versions of Apache, Yaws uses threads—in this case, one thread per request—to serve content. What makes Yaws an interesting alternative is how the underlying language deals with concurrent processes. Because it uses Erlang, Yaws should be significantly faster, even using the same base method for serving content.

Yaws is configured using one configuration file. Virtual servers are the standard, and the syntax of the file is familiar enough that most simple configurations should be quick and easy to set up.

Rewrites are possible in Yaws, but not in the same manner as with Apache. Here is where a major weakness comes in: The documentation available from the Yaws website at the time of this writing was quite sparse, and much of it is outdated (this is acknowledged by the site with a disclaimer). The official site links to a user's blog from 2009 to give information for setting up Yaws to work with WordPress permalinks. This is not unlike past experiences with Nginx, which has greatly improved its official documentation; but be warned, unless you have simple needs, you may get to spend a lot of time trying things out, adjusting, and playing to get your site up and running. On the positive side, if you are looking for a fun experiment, perhaps as a student running a server just to learn rather than to host vital content, Yaws could be exactly what you want. Who knows, because it is an open-source project, you may find yourself studying Erlang and contributing either code or documentation.

Cherokee

The distinguishing feature of Cherokee among the crowd that claims both speed and lightness is its ease of configuration. Cherokee supports all the big features, like virtual hosts, CGI, load balancing, and so on. It also includes a graphical interface for configuration, which makes it unique among all the options in this chapter. The claim is that you can configure Cherokee without ever editing a configuration file.

Setting up Cherokee is as easy as installing it on your system and then opening the Cherokee admin interface by issuing the `cherokee-admin-launcher` command as root. The downside is that this assumes you are running a graphical user interface on the same system as your web server, which is something that most Linux admins do not do. However, fear not. It is possible to use this interface remotely from a system with a web browser and terminal access via `ssh` using the remote system's IP address and a specific port (which is configurable).

The other features of Cherokee are comparable to lighttpd and Nginx. If you like what they offer, but want to use a GUI for your administration tasks, Cherokee is worth a closer look. The end user documentation available from their site is excellent and should get you up and running easily.

Jetty

If you are hosting a personal WordPress site or a few static HTML pages, Jetty is not what you need. Jetty is an Eclipse Foundation project that is written in Java. The Eclipse Foundation exists to provide open source development tools, software frameworks, and more to anyone who wants to use them. Jetty is a web server *and* client. It is a `javax.servlet` container. It supports Web Sockets and many other integrations. All of Jetty's components are open source and freely available, even for commercial use and distribution. Jetty powers frameworks like Google Web Toolkit (code.google.com/webtoolkit/) and Yahoo!'s Hadoop (developer.yahoo.com/hadoop/). It works with Apache Maven (http://maven.apache.org) to provide a way to run a web application locally while in development.

Jetty isn't really a standalone web server in the traditional sense, but rather creates a way to use Java code for web applications. Jetty is complex enough to warrant a book of its own. If you are developing web applications using Java and want a highly configurable network of connectors and handlers at your disposal (and you know what that phrase means), Jetty is a pretty good choice. Jetty components are simple *Plain Old Java Objects (POJOs)*. Jetty has an API that makes using it in Java easy. As the website says, "Jetty provides an HTTP server and Servlet container capable of serving static and dynamic content either from a standalone or embedded instantiations." If you need it, it is great. If you don't, it will be overkill.

thttpd

thttpd is a very light, decidedly not flashy or feature-filled web server. It has not been abandoned, but does not seem to be updated frequently. It is included here for one main reason: It has an interesting feature that makes it unique. First, a general description of the web server.

thttpd is small and simple. It claims to only slightly more than is necessary to support HTTP 1.1. No bells. No whistles. The positive side is that simple code generally has fewer stability issues, fewer security and performance problems, and uses less memory. Virtual hosts can be easily configured in thttpd using a familiar format. Getting CGI type content to run is more complicated than with any of the other servers in this chapter.

Here is the really interesting part: thttpd has a throttling feature that lets you set maximum byte rates on URLs or URL groups. You can limit the speed or use of your site's bandwidth according to the URL being requested by the client. You could use this to host media files and allow them to be accessed while assuring you have plenty of bandwidth available for other users to access your static HTML pages.

thttpd does not to appear to have been updated since sometime in 2005, so it may not be suitable for use on a production server, although there is some evidence that it was once used on a few well-known websites. It seems the world has moved on. However, the throttle-by-requested-URL is an interesting idea, making it worthy of a mention here.

Apache Tomcat

Apache Tomcat is a common and frequently used open source Java servlet container that implements Oracle's Java Servlet and *JavaServer Pages (JSP)* specifications. By doing so, Tomcat provides the means to run Java code in a web server environment. Java programmers love it because they can write web applications in a language they already know. Tomcat can be used as a standalone pure-Java web server, but is often used in conjunction with the regular Apache or another general purpose web server. In those instances, Tomcat serves requests from the other web server.

References

- http://nginx.org/en/—The English version of the main Nginx website.

- http://wiki.nginx.org/Main—The English wiki for Nginx.

- www.lighttpd.net—The main website for lighttpd.

- http://yaws.hyber.org—The main website for Yaws.

- www.cherokee-project.com—The main website for Cherokee.

- http://eclipse.org/jetty/—The main website for Jetty.

- www.acme.com/software/thttpd/—The main website for thttpd.

- http://tomcat.apache.org—The main website for Apache Tomcat.

# CHAPTER 25

Remote File Serving with FTP

*F*ile Transfer Protocol (FTP) was once considered the primary method used to transfer files over a network from computer to computer. FTP is still heavily used today, although many graphical FTP clients now supplement the original text-based interface command. As computers have evolved, so has FTP, and Ubuntu includes many ways with which to use a graphical interface to transfer files over FTP.

This chapter contains an overview of the available FTP software included with Ubuntu, along with some details concerning initial setup, configuration, and use of FTP-specific clients. Ubuntu also includes an FTP server software package named vsftpd, the Very Secure FTP Daemon, and a number of associated programs you can use to serve and transfer files with the FTP protocol.

Choosing an FTP Server

FTP uses a client/server model. As a client, FTP accesses a server, and as a server, FTP provides access to files or storage. Just about every computer platform available has software written to enable a computer to act as an FTP server, but Ubuntu provides the average user with the capability to do this without paying hefty licensing fees and without regard for client usage limitations.

There are two types of FTP servers and access: anonymous and standard. A *standard* FTP server requires an account name and password from anyone trying to access the server. *Anonymous* servers allow anyone to connect to the server to retrieve files. Anonymous servers provide the most flexibility, but they can also present a security risk.

Fortunately, as you will read in this chapter, Ubuntu is set up to use proper file and directory permissions and common-sense default configuration, such as disallowing root to perform an FTP login.

NOTE

Many Linux users now use OpenSSH and its suite of clients, such as the `sftp` command, for a more secure solution when transferring files. The OpenSSH suite provides the `sshd` daemon and enables encrypted remote logins. (See Chapter 18, "Remote Access with SSH and Telnet," for more information.)

Choosing an Authenticated or Anonymous Server

When you are preparing to set up your FTP server, you must first make the decision to install either the authenticated or anonymous service. *Authenticated* service requires the entry of a valid username and password for access. As previously mentioned, *anonymous* service allows the use of the username anonymous and an email address as a password for access.

Authenticated FTP servers are used to provide some measure of secure data transfer for remote users, but will require maintenance of user accounts as usernames and passwords are used. Anonymous FTP servers are used when user authentication is not needed or necessary, and can be helpful in providing an easily accessible platform for customer support or public distribution of documents, software, or other data.

If you use an anonymous FTP server in your home or business Linux system, it is vital that you properly install and configure it to retain a relatively secure environment. Generally, sites that host anonymous FTP servers place them outside the firewall on a dedicated machine. The dedicated machine contains only the FTP server and should not contain data that cannot be restored quickly. This dedicated-machine setup prevents malicious users who compromise the server from obtaining critical or sensitive data. For an additional, but by no means more secure, setup, the FTP portion of the file system can be mounted read-only from a separate hard drive partition or volume, or mounted from read-only media, such as CD-ROM, DVD, or other optical storage.

Ubuntu FTP Server Packages

The Very Secure `vsftpd` server is licensed under the GNU GPL. The server can be used for personal or business purposes and is the FTP server covered in the remainder of this chapter.

Other FTP Servers

One alternative server is NcFTPd, available from www.ncftp.com. This server provides its own optimized daemon. In addition, NcFTPd has the capability to cache directory listings of the FTP server in memory, thereby increasing the speed at which users can obtain a list of available files and directories. Although NcFTPd has many advantages over some other FTP servers, NcFTPd is not GPL-licensed software, and its licensing fees vary according to the maximum number of simultaneous server connections ($199 for 51 or more concurrent users and $129 for up to 50 concurrent users, but free to education institutions with a compliant domain name).

NOTE

Do not confuse the `ncftp` client with `ncftpd`. The `ncftp-3.1` package included with Ubuntu is the client software, a replacement for `ftp-0.17`, and includes the `ncftpget` and `ncftpput` commands for transferring files via the command line or by using a remote file *uniform resource locator (URL)* address. `ncftpd` is the FTP server, which can be downloaded from www.ncftpd.com.

Another FTP server package for Linux is ProFTPD, licensed under the GNU GPL. This server works well with most Linux distributions and has been used by a number of Linux sites, including ftp.kernel.org and ftp.sourceforge.net. ProFTPD is actively maintained and updated for bug fixes and security enhancements. Its developers recommend that you use the latest release (1.3.3e at the time of this writing) to avoid exposure to exploits and vulnerabilities. Browse to www.proftpd.org to download a copy.

Yet another FTP server package is `Bsdftpd-ssl`, which is based on the BSD `ftpd` (and distributed under the BSD license). `Bsdftpd-ssl` offers simultaneous standard and secure access using security extensions; secure access requires a special client. For more details, browse to http://bsdftpd-ssl.sc.ru.

Previously, this book covered an FTP server called `wu-ftp`. We had some concerns about it, such as the fact that when testing it to update this chapter, we discover it runs as root by default and therefore presents a significant security risk. For that reason, and the fact that the package seems to be abandoned and no longer maintained by its authors, we are not covering it in this edition.

Finally, another alternative is to use Apache (and HTTP) for serving files. Using a web server to provide data downloads can reduce the need to monitor and maintain a separate software service (or directories) on your server. This approach to serving files also reduces system resource requirements and gives remote users a bit more flexibility when downloading (such as enabling them to download multiple files at once). See Chapter 23, "Apache Web Server Management," for more information about using Apache.

Installing FTP Software

As part of the standard installation, the client software for FTP is already installed. You can verify that some FTP-related software is installed on your system by using dpkg, grep, and sort commands in this query:

```
matthew@seymour:~$ dpkg --get-selections | grep ftp | sort
ftp                     install
lftp                    install
```

The preceding output is from a fresh installation of Ubuntu 11.10, and what you see are basic FTP clients. These allow you to use FTP to connect to other computers to interact with remote files. You need an FTP server to allow other systems to interact with files on your computer. In this chapter, we discuss one FTP server application: vsftpd.

If vsftpd is not installed, install the package vsftpd from the Ubuntu repositories. For more information about installing packages, see Chapter 9, "Managing Software."

> **NOTE**
>
> If you host an FTP server connected to the Internet, make it a habit to always install security updates and bug fixes for your server software.

The FTP User

Instead of files being uploaded or managed by a current user when anonymous connections are made to your FTP server, an FTP user is created when vsftp is installed. This user is not a normal user per se, but a name for anonymous FTP users. The FTP user entry in /etc/passwd looks like this:

```
ftp:x:116:124:ftp daemon,,,:/srv/ftp:/bin/false
```

The numbers differ on each system because they depend on the number of configured users on the system, but the rest of the information is the same.

> **NOTE**
>
> The FTP user, as discussed here, applies to anonymous FTP configurations and server setup. Our FTP user is configured to use /srv/ftp as the default directory. Other Linux distributions may use a different default directory, such as /usr/local/ftp, for FTP files and anonymous users.

This entry follows the standard /etc/passwd entry: username, password, user ID, group ID, comment field, home directory, and shell. To learn more about /etc/password, see the section "Configuring Your Firewall" in Chapter 19, "Securing Your Machines."

Each of the items in this entry is separated by colons. In the preceding example, you can see that the Ubuntu system hosting the server uses shadowed password (indicated by the X in the traditional password field). The shadow password system is important because it adds an additional level of security to Ubuntu; the shadow password system is normally installed during the Ubuntu installation.

The FTP server software uses this user account to assign permissions to users connecting to the server. By using a default shell of /bin/false for anonymous FTP users versus /bin/bash or some other standard, interactive shell, an anonymous FTP user will be unable to log in as a regular user. /bin/false is not a shell, but a program usually assigned to an account that has been locked. As root inspection of the /etc/shadow file shows (see Listing 25.1), it is not possible to log in to this account, denoted by the * as the password.

LISTING 25.1   Shadow Password File `ftp` User Entry

```
# cat /etc/shadow
bin:*:11899:0:99999:7:::
daemon:*:11899:0:99999:7:::
adm:*:11899:0:99999:7:::
lp:*:11899:0:99999:7:::
...
ftp:*:12276:0:99999:7:::
...
```

The shadow file (only a portion of which is shown in Listing 25.1) contains additional information not found in the standard /etc/passwd file, such as account expiration, password expiration, whether the account is locked, and the encrypted password. The * in the password field indicates that the account is not a standard login account; thus, it does not have a password.

Although shadow passwords are in use on the system, passwords are not transmitted in a secure manner when using FTP. Because FTP was written before the necessity of encryption and security, it does not provide the mechanics necessary to send encrypted passwords. Account information is sent in plain text on FTP servers; anyone with enough technical knowledge and a network sniffer can find the password for the account you connect to on the server. Many sites use an anonymous-only FTP server specifically to prevent normal account passwords from being transmitted over the Internet.

Figure 25.1 shows a portion of a Wireshark capture of an FTP session. The Wireshark client is a graphical browser used to display network traffic in real time, and it can be used to watch packet data, such as an FTP login on a LAN.

Quick and Dirty FTP Service

Conscientious Linux administrators will take the time to carefully install, set up, and configure a production FTP server before offering public service or opening up for business on the Internet. However, you can set up a server very quickly on a secure LAN by completing a few simple steps:

1. Ensure that the FTP server package is installed, networking is enabled, and firewall rules on the server allow FTP access. See Chapter 17, "Networking," to learn about firewalling.

2. If anonymous access to server files is desired, create and populate the /srv/ftp/public directory. Do this by mounting or copying your content, such as directories and files, under this directory. You don't want to use symlinks, however, because a clever anonymous user could easily use that against you to access other parts of your file system. If you are new to this, copy your content into the directory.

3. Edit and then save the appropriate configuration file (such as /etc.vsftpd.conf for vsftpd) to enable access.

4. You must then start or restart the FTP server like this: `sudo service vsftpd restart`.

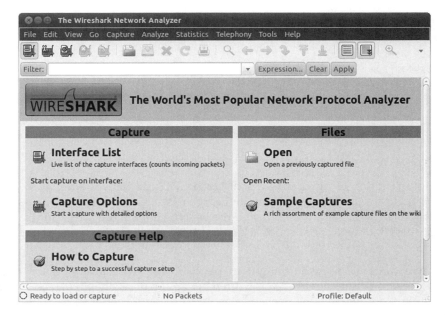

FIGURE 25.1   The Wireshark client can filter and sniff FTP sessions to capture usernames and passwords.

You can use the service to start, stop, restart, and query the vsftpd server. You must have root permission to use the vsftpd script to control the server, but any user can query the server (to see whether it is running and to see its process ID number) using the status keyword, like this:

```
matthew@seymour:~$ sudo service vsftpd status
```

You can also use a shorter version just for finding the status of the FTP daemon, as follows:

```
matthew@seymour:~$ status vsftpd
```

Administrator permissions are not required to use the status command, so we do not need to use sudo.

Configuring the Very Secure FTP Server

The Very Secure FTP server offers simplicity, security, and speed. It has been used by a number of sites, such as ftp.debian.org, ftp.gnu.org, rpmfind.net, and ftp.gimp.org. Note that despite its name, the *Very Secure FTP server* does not enable use of encrypted usernames or passwords.

Its main configuration file is vsftpd.conf, which resides under the /etc directory. The server has a number of features and default policies, but these can be overridden by changing the installed configuration file.

By default, anonymous logins are disabled. Users are not allowed to download or upload files, create new directories, or delete or rename files. The configuration file installed by Ubuntu allows local users (that is, users with a login and shell account) to log in and then access their /home directory. This configuration presents potential security risks because usernames and passwords are passed without encryption over a network. The best policy is to deny your users access to the server from their user accounts. To change these and other settings, edit the well-commented config file at /etc/vsftp.conf. For example, to change these two settings, edit the following lines:

```
# Allow anonymous FTP? (Disabled by default)
anonymous_enable=NO
#
# Uncomment this to allow local users to log in.
local_enable=YES
```

If you want to allow anonymous use of your FTP server, change NO to YES in the first couplet. As you can see in the second couplet, in Ubuntu 10.10, the local user setting was changed by Ubuntu from the default setting that did not allow local users to log in. We suggest commenting the line back out by placing a # at the front if you are going to run an anonymous FTP server. The default settings here work great if you are only allowing one user FTP access on the back end of a web server, for example, which is becoming the more common use for FTP, at least until we can convince the world to move to using SSH. See the "Telnet Versus SSH" section in Chapter 18, and replace *Telnet* with *FTP* for an idea about why this would be a good move.

Controlling Anonymous Access

Toggling anonymous access features for your FTP server is done by editing the vsftpd.conf file and changing related entries to YES or NO in the file. Settings to control how the server works for anonymous logins include the following:

▶ **anonymous_enable**—Disabled by default. Use a setting of YES, and then restart the server to turn on anonymous access.

▶ **anon_mkdir_write_enable**—Allows or disallows creating of new directories.

▶ **anon_other_write_enable**—Allows or disallows deleting or renaming of files and directories.

▶ **anon_upload_enable**—Controls whether anonymous users can upload files (also depends on the global write_enable setting). This is a potential security and liability hazard and should rarely be used; if enabled, consistently monitor any designated upload directory.

▶ **anon_world_readable_only**—Allows only anonymous users to download files with world-readable (444) permission.

After making any changes to your FTP server configuration file, make sure to restart the server; this forces vsftpd to reread its settings.

Other vsftpd Server Configuration Files

You can edit vsftpd.conf to enable, disable, and configure many features and settings of the vsftpd server, such as user access, filtering of bogus passwords, and access logging. Some features might require the creation and configuration of other files, such as the following:

▶ **/etc/vsftpd.user_list**—Used by the userlist_enable and the userlist_deny options; the file contains a list of usernames to be denied access to the server.

▶ **/etc/vsftpd.chroot_list**—Used by the chroot_list_enable and chroot_local_user options, this file contains a list of users who are either allowed or denied access to a home directory. An alternate file can be specified by using the chroot_list_file option.

▶ **/etc/vsftpd.banned_emails**—A list of anonymous password entries used to deny access if the deny_email_enable setting is enabled. An alternative file can be specified by using the banned_email option.

▶ **/var/log/vsftpd.log**—Data transfer information is captured to this file if logging is enabled using the xferlog_enable setting.

TIP

Whenever editing the FTP server files, make a backup file first. Also, it is always a good idea to comment out (using a pound sign, #, at the beginning of a line) what is changed instead of deleting or overwriting entries. Follow these comments with a brief description explaining why the change was made. This leaves a nice audit trail of what was done, by whom, when, and why. If you have any problems with the configuration, these comments and details can help you troubleshoot and return to valid entries if necessary. You can use the dpkg command or other Linux tools (such as mc) to extract a fresh copy of a configuration file from the software's package archive. Be aware, however, that the extracted version will replace the current version and overwrite your configuration changes.

Default vsftpd Behaviors

The contents of a file named .message (if it exists in the current directory) are displayed when a user enters the directory. This feature is enabled in the configuration file. FTP users are not allowed to perform recursive directory listings, which helps reduce bandwidth.

Other default settings are that specific user login controls are not set, but you can configure the controls to deny access to one or more users.

The data transfer rate for anonymous client access is unlimited, but you can set a maximum rate (in bytes per second) by using the anon_max_rate setting in vsftpd.conf. This can be useful for throttling bandwidth use during periods of heavy access, but waiting until heavy use occurs to change the setting could cause problems because you would kill any current connections when you restart the FTP server daemon. If you anticipate heavy FTP usage, change this setting before it happens or during a scheduled maintenance cycle. Another default is that remote clients will be logged out after five minutes of idle activity or a stalled data transfer. You can set idle and stalled connection timeouts by uncommenting idle_session_timeout and setting the time in seconds before idle sessions are disconnected.

Other settings that might be important for managing your system's resources (networking bandwidth or memory) when offering FTP access include the following:

- **dirlist_enable**—Toggles directory listings on or off.

- **dirmessage_enable**—Toggles display of a message when the user enters a directory. A related setting is ls_recurse_enable, which can be used to disallow recursive directory listings.

- **download_enable**—Toggles downloading on or off.

- **max_clients**—Sets a limit on the maximum number of connections.

- **max_per_ip**—Sets a limit on the number of connections from the same IP address.

Using the `ftphosts` File to Allow or Deny FTP Server Connection

You can create a file in /etc called ftphosts to allow or deny specific users or addresses from connecting to the FTP server. The format of the file is the word allow or deny, optionally followed by a username, followed by an IP or a DNS address:

```
allow username address
deny username address
```

Listing 25.2 shows a sample configuration of this file.

LISTING 25.2   ftphosts Configuration File for Allowing or Denying Users

```
# Example host access file
#
# Everything after a '#' is treated as comment,
# empty lines are ignored
allow fatima 208.164.186.1 208.164.186.2 208.164.186.4
deny richard 208.164.186.5
allow jane ubuntuforums.org
```

```
deny john naughtysite.net
allow ahmed 192.168.101.*
allow ahmed *.ubuntu.com
allow ahmed *.matthewhelmke.net
deny anonymous 201.*
```

The * is a wildcard that matches any combination of that address. For example, `allow ahmed *.matthewhelmke.net` allows the user `ahmed` to log in to the FTP server from any address that contains the domain name `matthewhelmke.net`. Similarly, the anonymous user is not allowed to access the FTP if the user is coming from a 201 public Class C IP address. You should set the permissions on this file to `600`.

Changes made to your system's FTP server configuration files only become active after you restart `inetd` because configuration files are only parsed at startup. To restart `inetd` as root, issue the command `/etc/init.d/inetutils-inetd restart`. This makes a call to the same shell script that is called at system startup and shutdown for any runlevel to start or stop the `inet` daemon. `inetd` should report its status as follows:

```
matthew@seymour:~$ sudo /etc/init.d/inetutils-inetd restart
Stopping internet superserver inetd:                            [  OK  ]
Starting internet superserver inetd:                            [  OK  ]
```

After it is restarted, the FTP server is accessible to all incoming requests.

References

▶ **www.cert.org/**—Computer Emergency Response Team.

▶ **www.openssh.com/**—The OpenSSH home page and source for the latest version of OpenSSH and its component clients, such as `sftp`.

▶ **http://vsftpd.beasts.org/**—The home page for the `vsftd` FTP server.

▶ **https://help.ubuntu.com/community/FtpServer**—Ubuntu community documentation for setting up and using an FTP server.

▶ **https://help.ubuntu.com/11.10/serverguide/C/ftp-server.html**—Official Ubuntu documentation for setting up and using `vsftp`.

# CHAPTER 26

Handling Email

Email is still the dominant form of communication over the Internet. It is fast, free, and easy to use. However, much of what goes on behind the scenes is extremely complicated and would appear scary to anyone who does not know much about how email is handled. Ubuntu comes equipped with a number of powerful applications that will help you build anything from a small email server, right through to large servers able to handle thousands of messages.

This chapter shows you how to configure Ubuntu to act as an email server. We look at the options available in Ubuntu and examine the pros and cons of each one. You also learn how mail is handled in Linux and, to a lesser extent, in UNIX.

How Email Is Sent and Received

Email is transmitted as plain text across networks around the world using the *Simple Mail Transfer Protocol (SMTP)*. As the name implies, the protocol itself is fairly basic, and it has been extended to add further authentication and error reporting/messaging to satisfy the growing demands of modern email. *Mail transfer agents (MTAs)* work in the background transferring email from server to server, allowing emails to be sent all over the world. You may have come across such MTA software such as Sendmail, Postfix, Fetchmail, Exim, or Qmail.

SMTP allows each computer that the email passes through to forward it in the right direction to the final destination. When you consider the millions of email servers across the world, you have to marvel at how simple it all seems.

Here is a simplified example of how email is successfully processed and sent to its destination:

1. matthew@seymourcray.net composes and sends an email message to heather@gracehopper.net.

2. The MTA at seymourcray.net receives Matthew's email message and queues it for delivery behind any other messages that are also waiting to go out.

3. The MTA at seymourcray.net contacts the MTA at gracehopper.net on port 24. After gracehopper.net acknowledges the connection, the MTA at seymourcray.net sends the mail message. After gracehopper.net accepts and acknowledges receipt of the message, the connection is closed.

4. The MTA at gracehopper.net places the mail message into Heather's incoming mailbox; Heather is notified that she has new mail the next time she logs on.

However, several things can go wrong during this process. Here are a few examples:

What if Heather does not exist at gracehopper.net? In this case, the MTA at gracehopper. net will reject the email and notify the MTA at seymourcray.net of what the problem is. The MTA at seymourcray.net will then generate an email message and send it to matthew@seymourcray.net, informing him that no Heather exists at gracehopper.net (or perhaps just silently discard the message and give the sender no indication of the problem, depending on how the email server is configured).

What happens if gracehopper.net doesn't respond to seymourcray.net's connection attempts? (Perhaps the server is down for maintenance.) The MTA at seymourcray.net notifies the sender that the initial delivery attempt has failed. Further attempts will be made at intervals decided by the server administrator until the deadline is reached, and the sender will be notified that the mail is undeliverable.

The Mail Transport Agent

Several MTAs are available for Ubuntu, each with its pros and cons. Normally they are hidden under the skin of Ubuntu, silently moving mail between servers all over the world with need for little or no maintenance. Some MTAs are extremely powerful, being able to cope with hundreds of thousands of messages each day, whereas some are geared more toward smaller installations. Other MTAs are perhaps not as powerful, but are packed full with features. In the next section, we take a look at some of the more popular MTAs available for Ubuntu.

Sendmail

Sendmail handles the overwhelming majority of emails transmitted over the Internet today. It is extremely popular across the Linux/UNIX/BSD world and is well supported. A commercial version is available that has a GUI interface for ease of configuration.

As well as being popular, Sendmail is particularly powerful compared to some of the other MTAs. However, it is not without its downsides, and you will find that other MTAs can handle more email per second in a larger environment. The other issue with Sendmail is that it can be extremely complicated to set it up exactly as you want it. A few books are available specifically for Sendmail, but the most popular one has more than a thousand pages, reflecting the complex nature of Sendmail configuration.

We can be thankful, however, that the default configuration for Sendmail works fine for most basic installations out of the box, making further configurations unnecessary. Even if you want to use it as a basic email server, you only need to do some minor tweaks. The level of complexity associated with Sendmail often leads to system administrators replacing it with one of the other alternatives that is easier to configure.

Postfix

Postfix has its origins as the IBM Secure Mailer, but was released to the community by IBM. Compared to Sendmail, it is much easier to administer and has a number of speed advantages. Postfix offers a pain-free replacement for Sendmail, and you are able to literally replace Sendmail with Postfix without the system breaking a sweat. In fact, the applications that rely on Sendmail will automatically use Postfix instead and carry on working correctly (because Postfix uses a Sendmail wrapper, which deceives other programs into thinking that Postfix is Sendmail). This wrapper, or more correctly interface, makes switching to Postfix extremely easy if you are already running Sendmail. Postfix also happens to be the MTA of choice for Ubuntu, so it is this one that we spend more time on later in this chapter.

For enhanced security, many Postfix processes used to use the `chroot` facility (which restricts access to only specific parts of the file system) for improved security, and there are no `setuid` components in Postfix. With the current release of Ubuntu, a `chroot` configuration is *no longer used* and is, in fact, discouraged by the Postfix author. You can manually reconfigure Postfix to a `chroot` configuration, but that is no longer supported by Ubuntu.

If you are starting from scratch, Postfix is considered a better choice than Sendmail.

Qmail and Exim

Qmail is a direct competitor to Postfix but is not provided with Ubuntu. Qmail is designed to be easier to use than Sendmail, as well as faster and more secure. However, Qmail is not a drop-in replacement for Sendmail, so migrating an existing Sendmail installation to Qmail is not quite as simple as migrating from Sendmail to Postfix. Qmail is relatively easy to administer, and it integrates with a number of software add-ons, including web mail systems and POP3 servers. Qmail is available from www.qmail.org/.

Exim is yet another MTA, and it is available at www.exim.org/. Exim is considered faster and more secure than Sendmail or Postfix, but is much different to configure than either of those. Exim and Qmail use the `maildir` format rather than `mbox`, so both are considered "NFS safe" (see the following sidebar).

MDIR Versus Mailbox

Qmail also introduced `maildir`, which is an alternative to the standard UNIX method of storing incoming mail. `maildir` is a more versatile system of handling incoming email, but it requires your email clients to be reconfigured, and it is not compatible with the traditional UNIX way of storing incoming mail. You will need to use mail programs that recognize the `maildir` format. (The modern programs do.)

The traditional mbox format keeps all mail assigned to a folder concatenated as a single file and maintains an index of individual emails. With maildir, each mail folder has three subfolders: /cur, /new, and /tmp. Each email is kept in a separate, unique file. If you are running a mail server for a large number of people, you should select a file system that can efficiently handle a large number of small files.

mbox does offer one major disadvantage. While you are accessing the monolithic mbox file that contains all your email, suppose that some type of corruption occurs, either to the file itself or to the index. Recovery from this problem can prove difficult. The mbox files are especially prone to problems if the files are being accessed over a network and can result in file corruption; one should avoid accessing mbox mail mounted over NFS, the *Network File System*, because file corruption can occur.

Depending on how you access your mail, maildir does permit the simultaneous access of maildir files by multiple applications; mbox does not.

The choice of a *mail user agent (MUA)*, or email client, also affects your choice of mail directory format. For example, the pine program does not cache any directory information and must reread the mail directory any time it accesses it. If you are using pine, maildir is a poor choice. More-advanced email clients perform caching, so maildir might be a good choice, although the email client cache can get out of synchronization. It seems that no perfect choice exists.

Ubuntu provides you with mail alternatives that have both strong and weak points. Be aware of the differences among the alternatives and frequently reevaluate your selection to make certain that it is the best one for your circumstances.

Choosing an MTA

Other MTAs are available for use with Ubuntu, but those discussed in the previous sections are the most popular. Which one should you choose? That depends on what you need to do. Postfix's main strengths is that it scales well and can handle large volumes of email at high speeds, not to mention that it is much easier to configure than the more cryptic Sendmail. However, you may find that there are specific things that you need that only Sendmail can provide. It is easy to switch between MTAs when you need to.

The Mail Delivery Agent

SMTP is a server-to-server protocol that was designed to deliver mail to systems that are always connected to the Internet. Dial-up systems connect only at the user's command; they connect for specific operations, and are frequently disconnected. To accommodate this difference, many mail systems also include a *mail delivery agent (MDA)*. The MDA transfers mail to systems without permanent Internet connections. The MDA is similar to an MTA (see the following note), but does not handle deliveries between systems and does not provide an interface to the user.

> **NOTE**
>
> Procmail or Spamassassin are examples of MDAs; both provide filtering services to the MDA while they store messages locally and then make them available to the MUA or email client for reading by the user.

The MDA uses the *Post Office Protocol version 3 (POP3)* or *Internet Message Access Protocol (IMAP)* for this process. In a manner similar to a post office box at the post office, POP3 and IMAP implement a "store and forward" process that alleviates the need to maintain a local mail server if all you want to do is read your mail. For example, dial-up Internet users can intermittently connect to their ISP's mail server to retrieve mail using Fetchmail—the MDA recommended by Ubuntu (see the section "Using Fetchmail to Retrieve Mail" later in this chapter).

The Mail User Agent

The *mail user agent (MUA)* is another necessary part of the email system. The MUA is a mail client, or mail reader, that allows the user to read and compose email and provides the user interface. (It is the email application itself that most users are familiar with as "email.") Some popular UNIX command-line MUAs are elm, pine, and mutt. Ubuntu also provides modern GUI MUAs: Evolution, Thunderbird, Mozilla Mail, Balsa, Sylpheed, and KMail. For comparison, common non-UNIX MUAs are Microsoft Outlook, Outlook Express, Pegasus Mail, and Apple Inc.'s Mail.

The Microsoft Windows and Macintosh MUAs often include some MTA functionality; UNIX does not. For example, Microsoft Outlook can connect to your Internet provider's mail server to send messages. On the other hand, UNIX MUAs generally rely on an external MTA such as Sendmail. This might seem like a needlessly complicated way to do things, and it is if used to connect a single user to her ISP. For any other situation, however, using an external MTA allows you much greater flexibility because you can use any number of external programs to handle and process your email functions and customize the service. Having the process handled by different applications gives you great control over how you provide email service to users on your network, as well as to individual and *small office/home office (SOHO)* users.

For example, you could do the following:

▶ Use Evolution to read and compose mail.

▶ Use Sendmail to send your mail.

▶ Use xbiff to notify you when you have new mail.

▶ Use Fetchmail to retrieve your mail from a remote mail server.

▶ Use Procmail to automatically sort your incoming mail based on sender, subject, or many other variables.

▶ Use Spamassassin to eliminate the unwanted messages before you read them.

26

Basic Postfix Configuration and Operation

Because Postfix is the Ubuntu-recommended MTA, the following sections provide a brief explanation and examples for configuring and operating your email system. As mentioned earlier, however, Postfix is an extremely complex program with many configuration options. Therefore, this chapter only covers some of the basics.

Postfix is not installed by default. To use it, install the `postfix` package from the Ubuntu software repositories. During installation, you are asked a series of questions to help configure Postfix immediately. Research the settings for your situation before you start; some are merely preferential, but others are based on your hardware, network, and use case. You are asked the following:

```
General type of mail configuration: Internet Site

System mail name: mail.matthewwhelmke.com
Root and postmaster mail recipient: <admin_user_name>
Other destinations for mail: mail.example.com, example.com, localhost.example.com,
localhost
Force synchronous updates on mail queue?: No
Local networks: 127.0.0.0/8

Mailbox size limit (bytes): 0
Local address extension character: +
Internet protocols to use: all
```

If you make a mistake and answer a configuration question incorrectly, you can go back through the process again by entering this from the command line:

```
matthew@seymour:~$ sudo dpkg-reconfigure postfix
```

Postfix configuration is maintained in files in the `/etc/postfix` directory with much of the configuration being handled by the file `main.cf`. You don't have to use the command above to change these settings, but may do so by editing the appropriate files. The syntax of the configuration file, `main.cf`, is fairly easy to read (see the following example):

```
# See /usr/share/postfix/main.cf.dist for a commented, more complete version
# Debian specific:  Specifying a file name will cause the first
# line of that file to be used as the name.  The Debian default
# is /etc/mailname.
#myorigin = /etc/mailname

smtpd_banner = $myhostname ESMTP $mail_name (Ubuntu)
biff = no

# appending .domain is the MUA's job.
append_dot_mydomain = no
```

```
# Uncomment the next line to generate "delayed mail" warnings
#delay_warning_time = 4h

# TLS parameters
smtpd_tls_cert_file=/etc/ssl/certs/ssl-cert-snakeoil.pem
smtpd_tls_key_file=/etc/ssl/private/ssl-cert-snakeoil.key
smtpd_use_tls=yes
smtpd_tls_session_cache_database = btree:${queue_directory}/smtpd_scache
smtp_tls_session_cache_database = btree:${queue_directory}/smtp_scache

# See /usr/share/doc/postfix/TLS_README.gz in the postfix-doc package for
# information on enabling SSL in the smtp client.

myhostname = optimus
alias_maps = hash:/etc/aliases
alias_database = hash:/etc/aliases
mydestination = optimus, localhost.localdomain, , localhost
relayhost =
mynetworks = 127.0.0.0/8
mailbox_size_limit = 0
recipient_delimiter = +
inet_interfaces = all
```

A useful command for configuring Postfix is postconf. It enables you to display and change many configuration settings without editing and saving configuration files. The command's syntax is rather complex, but once learned it becomes a faster way to quickly adjust settings.

If you type the command by itself, it outputs a list of all configuration parameters. This can be quite long, so we recommend either sorting using a pipe and grep or sending the output to a file. See Chapter 11, "Command-Line Master Class," for more on how to do this. This example shows the command piped into grep with a search for hostname:

```
matthew@seymour:~$ postconf | grep hostname
invalid_hostname_reject_code = 501
lmtp_lhlo_name = $myhostname
lmtp_tls_verify_cert_match = hostname
local_transport = local:$myhostname
milter_macro_daemon_name = $myhostname
myhostname = ubuntu
smtp_helo_name = $myhostname
smtp_tls_verify_cert_match = hostname
smtpd_banner = $myhostname ESMTP $mail_name (Ubuntu)
smtpd_proxy_ehlo = $myhostname
unknown_helo_hostname_tempfail_action = $reject_tempfail_action
unknown_hostname_reject_code = 450
```

To show the default parameter settings instead of the current settings, use this:

```
matthew@seymour:~$ postconf -d
```

Use this to discover which parameters have been changed from their defaults and display the current settings:

```
matthew@seymour:~$ postconf -n
```

Setting a parameter requires root privileges. For example, to set the `myhostname` parameter, use the following:

```
matthew@seymour:~$ sudo postconf -e "myhostname=mail.matthewhelmke.com"
myhostname=mail.matthewhelmke.com
```

This works with the parameters listed in the Postfix `main.cf` file:

```
matthew@seymour:~$ sudo postconf -e "smtp_sasl_auth_enable = yes"
myhostname=othername.matthewhelmke.com
```

As you can see, `postconf` is quite convenient. You can learn more about `postconf` from the man page.

You start, stop, and restart Postfix using this command, using the appropriate one of those three action words:

```
matthew@seymour:~$ sudo /etc/init.d/postfix start
```

Complicated email server setup is beyond the scope of this book; consider *Postfix: The Definitive Guide,* by Kyle Dent, for more information. This is a great reference, and rather unusual because it is a complete and useful reference in only 250 pages or so. However, if you want to know something specific about Postfix, this is the book to read.

However, the following five sections address some commonly used advanced options. For more information on Postfix, as well as other MTAs, see the "References" section at the end of this chapter.

Configuring Masquerading

Sometimes you might want to have Postfix masquerade as a host other than the actual hostname of your system. Such a situation could occur if you have a dial-up connection to the Internet, and your ISP handles all your mail for you. In this case, you want Postfix to masquerade as the domain name of your ISP. For example, the following strips any messages that come from `matthew.gracehopper.net` to just `gracehopper.net`:

```
masquerade_domains = gracehopper.net
```

Using Smart Hosts

If you do not have a full-time connection to the Internet, you will probably want to have Postfix send your messages to your ISPs mail server and let it handle delivery for you. Without a full-time Internet connection, you could find it difficult to deliver messages to some locations (such as some underdeveloped areas of the world where email services are unreliable and sporadic). In those situations, you can configure Postfix to function as a smart host by passing email on to another sender instead of attempting to deliver the email directly. You can use a line such as the following in the `main.cf` file to enable a smart host:

```
relayhost = mail.isp.net
```

This line causes Postfix to pass any mail it receives to the server `mail.isp.net` rather than attempt to deliver it directly. Smart hosting will not work for you if your ISP, like many others, blocks any mail relaying. Some ISPs block relaying because it is frequently used to disseminate spam.

Setting Message Delivery Intervals

As mentioned earlier, Postfix typically attempts to deliver messages as soon as it receives them, and again at regular intervals after that. If you have only periodic connections to the Internet, as with a dial-up connection, you likely would prefer Sendmail to hold all messages in the queue and attempt to deliver them whenever you connect to your ISP.

As dialup connections have become the exception rather than the rule and are now quite rare, Ubuntu does not configure them by default and does not include the `pppd` daemon in the default installation. If you need this, install `pppd` from the Ubuntu software repositories. You can then configure Postfix to hold messages for later delivery by adding the following line to `/etc/ppp/peers/ppp0`:

```
/usr/sbin/sendmail -q
```

This line causes Postifix to automatically send all mail when connecting to your ISP.

However, Postfix still attempts to send mail regardless of whether the computer is on or off line, meaning that your computer may dial out just to send email. To disable this, you need to enter the following line into `mail.cf`:

```
defer_transports = smtp
```

This stops any unwanted telephone calls from being placed!

TIP

If you use networking over a modem, there is a configuration file for `pppd` called `ppp0`, which is located in `/etc/ppp/peers`. Any commands in this file automatically run each time the PPP daemon is started. You can add the line `sendmail -q` to this file to have your mail queue automatically processed each time you dial up your Internet connection.

Mail Relaying

By default, Postfix will not relay mail that did not originate from the local domain. This means that if a Postfix installation running at gracehopper.net receives mail intended for seymourcray.net, and that mail did not originate from gracehopper.net, the mail will be rejected and will not be relayed. If you want to allow selected domains to relay through you, add an entry for the domain to the main.cf file like this:

mynetworks = 192.168.2.0/24, 10.0.0.2/24, 127.0.0.0/8

The IP address needs to be specified in *classless inter-domain routing (CIDR)* format. For a handy calculator, head on over to www.subnet-calculator.com/cidr.php. You must restart Postfix for this change to take effect.

> **CAUTION**
>
> You need a good reason to relay mail; otherwise, do not do it. Allowing all domains to relay through you will make you a magnet for spammers who will use your mail server to send spam. This can lead to your site being blacklisted by many other sites, which then will not accept any mail from you or your site's users—even if the mail is legitimate!

Forwarding Email with Aliases

Aliases allow you to have an infinite number of valid recipient addresses on your system, without having to worry about creating accounts or other support files for each address. For example, most systems have "postmaster" defined as a valid recipient, but do not have an actual login account named postmaster. Aliases are configured in the file /etc/aliases. Here is an example of an alias entry:

postmaster: root

This entry forwards any mail received for postmaster to the root user. By default, almost all the aliases listed in the /etc/aliases file forward to root.

> **CAUTION**
>
> Reading email as root is a security hazard; a malicious email message can exploit an email client and cause it to execute arbitrary code as the user running the client. To avoid this danger, you can forward all of root's mail to another account and read it from there. You can choose one of two ways for doing this.
>
> You can add an entry to the /etc/aliases file that sends root's mail to a different account. For example, root: foobar would forward all mail intended for root to the account foobar.
>
> The other way is to create a file named .forward in root's home directory that contains the address that the mail should forward to.

Anytime you make a change to the /etc/aliases file, you must rebuild the aliases database before that change will take effect. This is done with the following:

matthew@seymour:~$ **sudo newaliases**

Using Fetchmail to Retrieve Mail

SMTP is designed to work with systems that have a full-time connection to the Internet. What if you are on a dial-up account? What if you have another system store your email for you and then you log in to pick it up once in a while? (Most users who are not setting up servers will be in this situation.) In this case, you cannot easily receive email using SMTP, and you need to use a protocol, such as POP3 or IMAP, instead.

> **NOTE**
>
> Remember when we said that some mail clients can include some MTA functionality? Microsoft Outlook and Outlook Express can be configured to use SMTP and, if you use a dial-up connection, will offer to start the connection and then use SMTP to send your mail, so a type of MTA functionality is included in those mail clients.

Unfortunately, many MUAs do not know anything about POP3 or IMAP. To eliminate that problem, you can use a program called Fetchmail to contact mail servers using POP3 or IMAP, download mail off the servers, and then inject those messages into the local MTA just as if they had come from a standard SMTP server. The following sections explain how to install, configure, and use the Fetchmail program.

Installing Fetchmail

Similar to other packages, Fetchmail can be installed using either synaptic or apt-get.

You can get the latest version of Fetchmail at www.catb.org/~esr/fetchmail.

Configuring Fetchmail

After you have installed Fetchmail, you must create the file .fetchmailrc in your home directory, which provides the configuration for the Fetchmail program.

You can create and subsequently edit the .fetchmailrc file by using any text editor. The configuration file is straightforward and quite easy to create; the following sections explain the manual method for creating and editing the file. The information presented in the following sections does not discuss all the options available in the .fetchmailrc file, but covers the most common ones needed to get a basic Fetchmail installation up and running. You must use a text editor to create the file to include entries like the ones shown as examples—modified for your personal information, of course. For advanced configuration, see the man page for Fetchmail. The man page is well written and documents all the configuration options in detail.

26

> **CAUTION**
>
> The .fetchmailrc file is divided into three sections: global options, mail server options, and user options. It is important that these sections appear in the order listed. Do not add options to the wrong section. Putting options in the wrong place is one of the most common problems that new users make with Fetchmail configuration files.

Configuring Global Options

The first section of .fetchmailrc contains the global options. These options affect all the mail servers and user accounts that you list later in the configuration file. Some of these global options can be overridden with local configuration options, as you learn later in this section. Here is an example of the options that might appear in the global section of the .fetchmailrc file:

```
set daemon 600
set postmaster foobar
set logfile ./.fetchmail.log
```

The first line in this example tells Fetchmail that it should start in daemon mode and check the mail servers for new mail every 600 seconds, or 10 minutes. Daemon mode means that after Fetchmail starts, it moves itself into the background and continue running. Without this line, Fetchmail checks for mail once when it started and then terminates and never checks again.

The second option tells Fetchmail to use the local account foobar as a last-resort address. In other words, any email that it receives and cannot deliver to a specified account should be sent to foobar.

The third line tells Fetchmail to log its activity to the file ./.fetchmail.log. Alternatively, you can use the line set syslog—in which case, Fetchmail will log through the syslog facility.

Configuring Mail Server Options

The second section of the .fetchmailrc file contains information on each of the mail servers that should be checked for new mail. Here is an example of what the mail section might look like:

```
poll mail.samplenet.org
proto pop3
no dns
```

The first line tells Fetchmail that it should check the mail server mail.samplenet.org at each poll interval that was set in the global options section (which was 600 seconds in our example). Alternatively, the first line can begin with skip. If a mail server line begins with skip, it will not be polled as the poll interval, but will only be polled when it is specifically specified on the Fetchmail command line.

The second line specifies the protocol that should be used when contacting the mail server. In this case, we are using POP3. Other legal options are IMAP, *Authenticated Post Office Protocol (APOP)*, and *Kerberized Post Office Protocol (KPOP)*. You can also use AUTO here, in which case Fetchmail will attempt to automatically determine the correct protocol to use with the mail server.

The third line tells Fetchmail that it should not attempt to do a *Dynamic Name Server (DNS)* lookup. You probably want to include this option if you are running over a dial-up connection.

Configuring User Accounts

The third and final section of .fetchmailrc contains information about the user account on the server specified in the previous section. Here is an example:

```
user foobar
pass secretword
fetchall
no flush
```

The first line, of course, simply specifies the username that is used to log in to the email server, and the second line specifies the password for that user. Many security-conscious people cringe at the thought of putting clear-text passwords in a configuration file, and they should if it is group or world readable. The only protection for this information is to make certain that the file is readable only by the owner; that is, with file permissions of 600.

The third line tells Fetchmail that it should fetch all messages from the server, even if they have already been read.

The fourth line tells Fetchmail that it should delete the messages from the mail server after it has completed downloading them. This is the default, so we would not really have to specify this option. If you want to delete the messages from the server after downloading them, use the option flush.

The configuration options you just inserted configured the entire .fetchmailrc file to look like this:

```
set daemon 600
set postmaster foobar
set logfile ./.fetchmail.log

poll mail.samplenet.org
proto pop3
no dns

user foobar
pass secretword
fetchall
flush
```

This file tells Fetchmail to do the following:

▸ Check the POP3 server `mail.samplenet.org` for new mail every 600 seconds.

▸ Log in using the username foobar and the password secretword.

▸ Download all messages off the server.

▸ Delete the messages from the server after it has finished downloading them.

▸ Send any mail it receives that cannot be delivered to a local user to the account `foobar`.

As mentioned before, many more options can be included in the `.fetchmailrc` file than are listed here. However, these options will get you up and running with a basic configuration.

For additional flexibility, you can define multiple `.fetchmailrc` files to retrieve mail from different remote mail servers while using the same Linux user account. For example, you can define settings for your most-often-used account and save them in the default `.fetchmailrc` file. Mail can then quickly be retrieved like this:

```
matthew@seymour:~$ fetchmail -a
1 message for matthew at mail.matthewhelmke.com (1108 octets).
reading message 1 of 1 (1108 octets) . flushed
```

By using Fetchmail's `-f` option, you can specify an alternative resource file and then easily retrieve mail from another server, as follows:

```
matthew@seymour:~$ fetchmail -f .myothermailrc
2 messages for matthew at matthew.helmke.com (5407 octets).
reading message 1 of 2 (3440 octets) ... flushed
reading message 2 of 2 (1967 octets) . flushed
You have new mail in /var/spool/mail/matthew
```

By using the `-d` option, along with a time interval (in seconds), you can use Fetchmail in its daemon, or background mode. The command will launch as a background process and retrieve mail from a designated remote server at a specified interval. For more-advanced options, see the Fetchmail man page, which is well written and documents all options in detail.

CAUTION

Because the `.fetchmailrc` file contains your mail server password, it should be readable only by you. This means that it should be owned by you and should have permissions no greater than `600`. Fetchmail will complain and refuse to start if the `.fetchmailrc` file has permissions greater than this.

Choosing a Mail Delivery Agent

Because of the modular nature of mail handling, it is possible to use multiple applications to process mail and accomplish more than simply deliver it. Getting mail from the storage area and displaying it to the user is the purpose of the MDA. MDA functionality can be found in some of the mail clients (MUAs), which can cause some confusion to those still unfamiliar with the concept of UNIX mail. As an example, the Procmail MDA provides filtering based on rulesets; KMail and Evolution, both MUAs, provide filtering, but the MUAs `pine`, `mutt`, and Balsa do not. Some MDAs perform simple sorting, and other MDAs are designed to eliminate unwanted emails, such as spam and viruses.

You would choose an MDA based on what you want to do with your mail. We look at five MDAs that offer functions you might find useful in your particular situation. If you have simple needs (just organizing mail by rules), one of the MUAs that offers filtering might be better for your needs. Ubuntu provides the Evolution MUA as the default selection (and it contains some MDA functionality as previously noted), so try that first and see whether it meets your needs. If not, investigate one of the following MDAs provided by Ubuntu.

Unless otherwise noted, all the MDA software is provided in the Ubuntu repositories. Chapter 9, "Managing Software," details the general installation of any software.

Procmail

As a tool for advanced users, the Procmail application acts as a filter for email, as it is retrieved from a mail server. It uses rulesets (known as *recipes*) as it reads each email message. No default configuration is provided; you must manually create a `~/.procmail` file for each user, or users can create their own.

There is no systemwide default configuration file. The creation of the rulesets is not trivial and requires an understanding of the use of regular expressions that is beyond the scope of this chapter. Ubuntu does provide three examples of the files in `/usr/share/doc/procmail/examples`, as well as a fully commented example in the `/usr/share/doc/procmail` directory, which also contains a README and FAQ. Details for the rulesets can be found in the man page for Procmail and in the man pages for `procmailrc`, `procmailsc`, and `procmailex`, which contain examples of Procmail recipes.

Spamassassin

If you have used email for any length of time, you have likely been subjected to *spam*, unwanted email sent to thousands of people at the same time. Ubuntu provides an MDA named *Spamassassin* to assist you in reducing and eliminating unwanted emails. Easily integrated with Procmail and Sendmail, it can be configured for both system-wide and individual use. It uses a combination of rule sets and blacklists (Internet domains known to mail spam).

Enabling Spamassassin is simple. You must first have installed and configured Procmail. The README file found in /usr/share/doc/spamassassin provides details on configuring the .procmail file to process mail through Spamassassin. It will tag probable spam with a unique header; you can then have Procmail filter the mail in any manner you choose. One interesting use of Spamassassin is to use it to tag email received at special email accounts established solely for the purpose of attracting spam. This information is then shared with the Spamassassin site where these "spam trap" generated hits help the authors fine-tune the rulesets.

Squirrelmail

Perhaps you do not want to read your mail in an MUA. If you use your web browser often, it might make sense to read and send your mail via a web interface, such as the one used by Hotmail or Yahoo! Mail. Ubuntu provides Squirrelmail for just that purpose. Squirrelmail is written in PHP and supports IMAP and SMTP. It supports MIME attachments and an address book and folders for segregating email.

You must configure your web server to work with PHP 4. Detailed installation instructions can be found in /usr/share/doc/squirrelmail/INSTALL. After it is configured, point your web browser to the default install location, www.yourdomain.com/squirelmail/, to read and send email.

Virus Scanners

Although the currently held belief is that Linux is immune to email viruses targeted at Microsoft Outlook users, it certainly makes no sense for UNIX mail servers to permit infected email to be sent through them. Although Ubuntu does not provide a virus scanner by default, some of the more popular scanners are available in the Ubuntu repositories. Take a look at ClamAV as the most popular example.

Autoresponders

Autoresponders automatically generate replies to received messages; they are commonly used to notify others that the recipient is out of the office. Mercifully, Ubuntu does not include one by default, but you can find and install an autoresponder like vacation or gnarwl from the Ubuntu software repositories. If you are subscribed to a mailing list, be aware that automatic responses from your account can be very annoying to others on the list. Please unsubscribe from mail lists before you leave the office with your autoresponder activated.

Alternatives to Microsoft Exchange Server

One of the last areas in which a Microsoft product has yet to be usurped by open-source software is a replacement for Microsoft Exchange Server. Many businesses use Microsoft Outlook and Microsoft Exchange Server to access email and to provide calendaring, notes, file sharing, and other collaborative functions. General industry complaints about

Exchange Server center around scalability, administration (backup and restore in particular), and licensing fees.

A "drop-in" alternative needs to have compatibility with Microsoft Outlook because it is intended to replace Exchange Server in an environment in which there are Microsoft desktops in existence using Outlook. A "work-alike" alternative provides similar features to Exchange Server, but does not offer compatibility with the Microsoft Outlook client itself; the latter is typical of many of the open-source alternatives.

Several "drop-in" alternatives exist, none of which are fully open source because some type of proprietary connector is needed to provide the services to Microsoft Outlook clients (or provide Exchange services to the Linux Evolution client). For Outlook compatibility, the key seems to be the realization of a full, open implementation of *MAPI*, the Microsoft *Messaging Application Program Interface*. That goal is going to be difficult to achieve because MAPI is a poorly documented Microsoft protocol. For Linux-only solutions, the missing ingredient for many alternatives is a usable group calendaring/scheduling system similar in function to that provided by Exchange Server/Outlook.

Of course, independent applications for these functions abound in the open-source world, but one characteristic of "groupware" is its central administration; another is that all components can share information.

The following sections examine several of the available servers, beginning with Microsoft Exchange Server itself and moving toward those applications that have increasing incompatibility with it. None of these servers are provided with Ubuntu.

Microsoft Exchange Server/Outlook Client

Exchange Server and Outlook seem to be the industry benchmark because of their widespread deployment. They offer a proprietary server providing email, contacts, scheduling, public folders, task lists, journaling, and notes using Microsoft Outlook as the client and MAPI as the API. If you consider what Microsoft Exchange offers as the "full" set of features, no other replacement offers 100 percent of the features exactly as provided by Microsoft Exchange Server—even those considered drop-in replacements. The home page for the Microsoft Exchange server is www.microsoft.com/exchange/.

CommuniGate Pro

CommuniGate Pro is a proprietary, drop-in alternative to Microsoft Exchange Server, providing, email, webmail, *Lightweight Directory Access Protocol (LDAP)* directories, a web server, file server, contacts, calendaring (third party), Voice over IP, and a list server. The CommuniGate Pro MAPI Connector provides access to the server from Microsoft Outlook and other MAPI-enabled clients. The home page for this server is www.stalker.com/.

Oracle Beehive

Oracle Beehive is probably the closest that you will get to an Exchange replacement, allowing you to collaborate by instant messaging, email, sharing files (workspaces), calendaring, and other tools. Beehive is available for Linux platforms, and its home page is www.oracle.com/us/products/middleware/beehive/index.html.

Bynari

Bynari provides a proprietary group of servers to act as a drop-in replacement for Microsoft Exchange Server for email, calendaring, public folders, scheduling, address book, webmail, and contacts. Although it runs on Linux, it offers no Linux clients, although it can be used with Evolution and Thunderbird, and the connector provides services to Microsoft Outlook only. The home page is www.bynari.net/.

Open-Xchange

Open-Xchange has a great pedigree having been owned and developed by Novell/SUSE until being spun off by itself into its own company. Working with open standards, it provides a number of collaboration options and is firmly based on Linux. It can work with a wide variety of protocols, making it one of the best connected suites available. You can get the open source version at www.open-xchange.com.

phpgroupware

phpgroupware is an open-source application written in PHP (and used with MySQL or postgresql plus a web server and an IMAP mail server). phpgroupware provides a web-based calendar, task list, address book, email, news headlines, and a file manager. Its modular nature enables you to plug in various components (around 50 at the last count) as you need them. The home page is www.phpgroupware.org/.

PHProjekt

PHProjekt is open-source software written in PHP (used with MySQL, PostgreSQL, Oracle, Informix, or Microsoft SQL). PHProjekt provides calendaring, contact manager, time card system, project management, online chat, threaded discussion forum, trouble ticket system, email, public files, notes bookmarks, voting system, task lists, reminders, site search, and integration with the PostNuke news site application. It provides no Exchange/Outlook compatibility whatsoever. The home page is www.PHProjekt.com/.

Horde

Horde is a PHP-based application framework. When combined with an HTTP server (Apache, Microsoft IIS, Netscape) and MySQL database, IMP/Horde offers modules that provide webmail, contact manager, calendar, CVS viewer, file manager, time tracking, email filter rules manager, notes, tasks, chat, newsgroups, forms, bug tracking, FAQ repository, and presentations. The home page is www.horde.org/.

References

- ▶ **www.sendmail.org/**—This is the Sendmail home page. Here you can find configuration information and FAQs regarding the Sendmail MTA.

- ▶ **www.postfix.org/**—This is the Postfix home page. If you are using the Postfix MTA, you can find documentation and sample configurations at this site.

- ▶ **help.ubuntu.com/community/Postfix**—Ubuntu community documentation for Postfix.www.qmail.org/. This is the home page for the Qmail MTA. It contains documentation and links to other resources on Qmail.

- ▶ **https://help.ubuntu.com/community/ClamAV**—Ubuntu community documentation for ClamAV.

- ▶ **www.rfc-editor.org/**—A repository of *Request For Comments (RFCs)*, which define the technical "rules" of modern computer usage.

- ▶ **www.procmail.org/**—The Procmail home page.

- ▶ *Sendmail* **(O'Reilly Publishing)**—This is the de facto standard guide for everything Sendmail. It is loaded with more than 1,000 pages, which gives you an idea of how complicated Sendmail really is.

- ▶ *Postfix* **(Sams Publishing)**—An excellent book from Sams Publishing that covers the Postfix MTA.

- ▶ *Postfix: The Definitive Guide* **(O'Reilly Publishing)**—Another excellent resource for Postfix.

- ▶ *Running Qmail* **(Sams Publishing)**—This is similar to the Postfix book from Sams Publishing except that it covers the Qmail MTA.

26

Proxying and Reverse Proxying

You can never have enough of two things in this world: time and bandwidth. Ubuntu comes with a proxy server—Squid—that enables you to cache web traffic on your server so that websites load faster and users consume less bandwidth.

What Is a Proxy Server?

A *proxy server* lies between client machines—the desktops in your company—and the Internet. As clients request websites, they do not connect directly to the web and send the HTTP request. Instead, they connect to the local proxy server. The proxy then forwards their request on to the Web, retrieves the result, and hands it back to the client. At its simplest, a proxy server really is just an extra layer between client and server, so why bother?

The three main reasons for deploying a proxy server are as follows:

▶ **Content control**—You want to stop people whiling away their work hours reading celebrity news or downloading MP3s.

▶ **Speed**—You want to cache common sites to make the most of your bandwidth.

▶ **Security**—You want to monitor what people are doing.

Squid is capable of all of these and more.

Installing Squid

Squid is easily installed the usual way from the Ubuntu software repositories, where it is called squid. After Squid is installed, it is automatically enabled for each boot. You can check this by running ps aux | grep squid when the machine boots. If for some reason you see nothing there, run /etc/init.d/squid start.

Configuring Clients

Before you configure your new Squid server, set up the local web browser to use it for its web access. Doing so enables you to test your rules as you are working with the configuration file.

To configure Firefox, select Preferences from the Edit menu. From the dialog that appears, select the Advanced settings using the icon in the top row, and within Advanced, select the Network tab. Then click the Settings button next to Configure how Firefox connects to the Internet and select the Manual Proxy Configuration option. Check the box beneath it labeled Use the Same Proxy for All Protocols. Enter 127.0.0.1 as the IP address and 3128 as the port number. See Figure 27.1 for how this should look. If you are configuring a remote client, specify the IP address of the Squid server rather than 127.0.0.1.

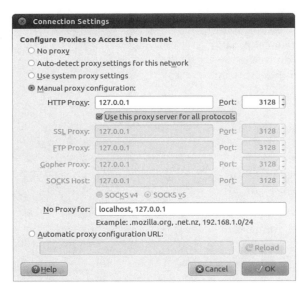

FIGURE 27.1   Setting up Firefox to use 127.0.0.1 routes all its web requests through Squid.

Other web browsers such as Google Chrome, Opera, and so on can be configured similarly. The difference is the labels used and menu locations for the options, so a little digging might be needed to discover where this may be adjusted in a specific browser's settings.

Access Control Lists

The main Squid configuration file is /etc/squid/squid.conf, and the default Ubuntu configuration file is full of comments to help guide you. The default configuration file allows full access to the local machine but denies the rest of your network. This is a secure place to start; we recommend that you try all the rules on yourself (localhost) before rolling them out to other machines.

Before you start, open two terminal windows. In the first, change to the directory /var/log/squid and run this command:

matthew@seymour:~$ **sudo tail -f access.log cache.log**

That reads the last few lines from both files and (thanks to the -f flag) follows them so that any changes appear in there. This allows you to watch what Squid is doing as people access it. We refer to this window as the "log window," so keep it open. In the other window (again, with sudo), bring up the file /etc/squid/squid.conf in your favorite editor. We refer to this window as the "config editor," and you should keep it open, too.

To get started, search for the string acl all; this brings you to the access control section, which is where most of the work needs to be done. You can configure a lot elsewhere, but unless you have unusual requirements, you can leave the defaults in place.

> **NOTE**
>
> The default port for Squid is 3128, but you can change that by editing the http_port line. Alternatively, you can have Squid listen on multiple ports by having multiple http_port lines: 80, 8000, and 8080 are all popular ports for proxy servers.

27

The acl lines make up your *access control lists (ACLs)*. The first 16 or so define the minimum recommended configuration that set up ports to listen to, and so on. You can safely ignore these. If you scroll down further (past another short block of comments), you come to the http_access lines, which are combined with the acl lines to dictate who can do what. You can (and should) mix and match acl and http_access lines to keep your configuration file easy to read.

Just below the first block of http_access lines is a comment like # INSERT YOUR OWN RULE(S) HERE TO ALLOW ACCESS FROM YOUR CLIENTS. This is just what we are going to do. First, though, scroll just a few lines further; you should see these two lines:

```
http_access allow localhost
http_access deny all
```

They are self-explanatory: The first says, "Allow HTTP access to the local computer, but deny everyone else." This is the default rule, as mentioned earlier. Leave that in place for now, and run service squid start to start the server with the default settings. If you have not yet configured the local web browser to use your Squid server, do so now so that you can test the default rules.

In your web browser (Firefox is assumed from here on, because it is the default in a standard Ubuntu install, but it makes little difference), go to the URL www.ubuntulinux.org. You should see it appear as normal in the browser, but in the log window, you should see a lot of messages scroll by as Squid downloads the site for you and stores it in its cache. This is all allowed because the default configuration allows access to the localhost.

Go back to the config editor window and add this before the last two http_access lines:

```
http_access deny localhost
```

So, the last three lines should look like this:

```
http_access deny localhost
http_access allow localhost
http_access deny all
```

Save the file and quit your editor. Then, run this command:

```
matthew@seymour:~$ kill -SIGHUP 'cat /var/run/squid.pid'
```

That looks for the *process ID (PID)* of the squid daemon and then sends the SIGHUP signal to it, which forces it to reread its configuration file while running. You should see a string of messages in the log window as Squid rereads its configuration files. If you now go back to Firefox and enter a new URL, you should see the Squid error page informing you that you do not have access to the requested site.

The reason you are now blocked from the proxy is because Squid reads its ACL lines in sequence, from top to bottom. If it finds a line that conclusively allows or denies a request, it stops reading and takes the appropriate action. So, in the previous lines, localhost is being denied in the first line and then allowed in the second. When Squid sees localhost asking for a site, it reads the deny line first and immediately sends the error page; it does not even get to the allow line. Having a deny all line at the bottom is highly recommended so that only those you explicitly allow are able to use the proxy.

Go back to editing the configuration file and remove the deny localhost and allow localhost lines. This leaves only deny all, which blocks everyone (including the localhost) from accessing the proxy. Now we are going to add some conditional allow statements: We want to allow localhost only if it fits certain criteria.

Defining access criteria is done with the acl lines, so above the deny all line, add this:

```
acl newssites dstdomain news.bbc.co.uk slashdot.org
http_access allow newssites
```

The first line defines an access category called newssites, which contains a list of domains (dstdomain). The domains are news.bbc.co.uk and slashdot.org, so the full line reads, "Create a new access category called newssites that should filter on domain, and contain the two domains listed." It does *not* say whether access should be granted or denied to that category; that comes in the next line. The line `http_access allow newssites` means, "Allow access to the category newssites with no further restrictions." It is not limited to `localhost`, which means that applies to every computer connecting to the proxy server.

Save the configuration file and rerun the `kill -SIGHUP` line from before to restart Squid; then go back to Firefox and try loading www.ubuntu.com. You should see the same error as before because that was not in our `newssites` category. Now try http://news.bbc.co.uk, and it should work. However, if you try www.slashdot.org, it will *not* work, and you might also have noticed that the images did not appear on the BBC News website either. The problem here is that specifying slashdot.org as the website is specific: It means that http://slashdot.org will work, whereas www.slashdot.org will not. The BBC News site stores its images on the site http://newsimg.bbc.co.uk, which is why they do not appear.

Go back to the configuration file and edit the `newssites` ACL to this:

```
acl newssites dstdomain .bbc.co.uk .slashdot.org
```

Putting the period in front of the domains (and in the BBC's case, taking the news off, too) means that Squid will allow any subdomain of the site to work, which is usually what you will want. If you want even more vagueness, you can just specify `.com` to match `*.com` addresses.

Moving on, you can also use time conditions for sites. For example, if you want to allow access to the news sites in the evenings, you can set up a time category using this line:

```
acl freetime time MTWHFAS 18:00-23:59
```

This time, the category is called `freetime` and the condition is `time`, which means we need to specify what time the category should contain. The seven characters following that are the days of the week: Monday, Tuesday, Wednesday, tHursday, Friday, sAturday, and Sunday. Thursday and Saturday use capital *H* and *A* so they do not clash with Tuesday and Sunday.

With that category defined, you can change the `http_access` line to include it, like this:

```
http_access allow newssites freetime
```

For Squid to allow access now, it must match both conditions—the request must be for either `*.bbc.co.uk` or `slashdot.org`, and during the time specified. If either condition does not match, the line is not matched and Squid continues looking for other matching rules beneath it. The times you specify here are inclusive on both sides, which means users in the `freetime` category will be able to surf from 18:00:00 until 23:59:59.

You can add as many rules as you like, although you should be careful to try to order them so that they make sense. Keep in mind that all conditions in a line must be matched for the line to be matched. Here is a more complex example:

▶ You want a category `newssites` that contains serious websites people need for their work.

▶ You want a category `playsites` that contains websites people do not need for their work.

▶ You want a category `worktime` that stretches from 09:00 to 18:00.

▶ You want a category `freetime` that stretches from 18:00 to 20:00, when the office closes.

▶ You want people to be able to access the news sites, but not the play sites, during working hours.

▶ You want people to be able to access both the news sites and the play sites during the free time hours.

To do that, you need the following rules:

```
acl newssites dstdomain .bbc.co.uk .slashdot.org
acl playsites dstdomain .tomshardware.com ubuntulinux.org
acl worktime time MTWHF 9:00-18:00
acl freetime time MTWHF 18:00-20:00
http_access allow newssites worktime
http_access allow newssites freetime
http_access allow playsites freetime
```

NOTE

The letter *D* is equivalent to MTWHF, meaning "all the days of the working week."

Notice that there are two `http_access` lines for the `newssites` category: one for `worktime` and one for `freetime`. This is because all the conditions must be matched for a line to be matched. Alternatively, you can write this:

```
http_access allow newssites worktime freetime
```

However, if you do that and someone visits http://news.bbc.co.uk at 2:30 p.m. (14:30) on a Tuesday, Squid will work like this:

▶ Is the site in the `newssites` category? Yes, continue.

▶ Is the time within the `worktime` category? Yes, continue.

▶ Is the time within the `freetime` category? No; do not match rule, and continue searching for rules.

It is because of this that two lines are needed for the `worktime` category.

One particularly powerful way to filter requests is with the `url_regex` ACL line. This allows you to specify a regular expression that is checked against each request: If the expression matches the request, the condition matches.

For example, if you want to stop people downloading Windows executable files, you use this line:

```
acl noexes url_regex -i exe$
```

The dollar sign ($) means "end of URL," which means it would match www.somesite.com/virus.exe but not www.executable.com/innocent.html. The -i part means "not case sensitive," so the rule will match .exe, .Exe, .EXE, and so on. You can use the caret sign (^) for "start of URL."

For example, you could stop some pornography sites using this ACL:

```
acl noporn url_regex -i sex
```

Do not forget to run the `kill -SIGHUP` command each time you make changes to Squid; otherwise, it will not reread your changes. You can have Squid check your configuration files for errors by running `squid -k parse as root`. If you see no errors, it means your configuration is fine.

> **NOTE**
>
> It is critical that you run the command `kill -SIGHUP` and provide it the PID of your Squid daemon each time you change the configuration; without this, Squid does not reread its configuration files.

Specifying Client IP Addresses

The configuration options so far have been basic, and you can use many more to enhance the proxying system you want.

After you are past deciding which rules work for you locally, it is time to spread them out to other machines. You do so by specifying IP ranges that should be allowed or disallowed access, and you enter these into Squid using more ACL lines.

If you want to, you can specify all the IP addresses on your network, one per line. However, for networks of more than about 20 people or using *Dynamic Host Control Protocol (DHCP)*, that is more work than necessary. A better solution is to use *classless interdomain routing (CIDR)* notation, which allows you to specify addresses like this:

```
192.0.0.0/8
192.168.0.0/16
192.168.0.0/24
```

Each line has an IP address, followed by a slash and then a number. That last number defines the range of addresses you want covered and refers to the number of bits in an IP address. An IP address is a 32-bit number, but we are used to seeing it in dotted-quad notation: A.B.C.D. Each of those quads can be between 0 and 255 (although in practice, some of these are reserved for special purposes), and each is stored as an 8-bit number.

The first line in the previous code covers IP addresses starting from 192.0.0.0; the /8 part means that the first 8 bits (the first quad, 192) is fixed and the rest is flexible. So, Squid treats that as addresses 192.0.0.0, 192.0.0.1, through to 192.0.0.255, then 192.0.1.0, 192.0.1.1, all the way through to 192.255.255.255.

The second line uses /16, which means Squid will allow IP addresses from 192.168.0.0 to 192.168.255.255. The last line has /24, which allows from 192.168.0.0 to 192.168.0.255.

These addresses are placed into Squid using the src ACL line, as follows:

```
acl internal_network src 10.0.0.0/24
```

That line creates a category of addresses from 10.0.0.0 to 10.0.0.255. You can combine multiple address groups together, like this:

```
acl internal_network src 10.0.0.0/24 10.0.3.0/24 10.0.5.0/24 192.168.0.1
```

That example allows 10.0.0.0 through 10.0.0.255, then 10.0.3.0 through 10.0.3.255, and finally the single address 192.168.0.1.

Keep in mind that if you are using the local machine and you have the web browser configured to use the proxy at 127.0.0.1, the client IP address will be 127.0.0.1, too. So, make sure you have rules in place for localhost.

As with other ACL lines, you need to enable them with appropriate http_access allow and http_access deny lines.

Sample Configurations

To help you fully understand how Squid access control works, and to give you a head start developing your own rules, the following are some ACL lines you can try. Each line is preceded with one or more comment lines (starting with a #) explaining what it does:

```
# include the domains news.bbc.co.uk and slashdot.org
# and not newsimg.bbc.co.uk or www.slashdot.org.
acl newssites dstdomain news.bbc.co.uk slashdot.org

# include any subdomains or bbc.co.uk or slashdot.org
acl newssites dstdomain .bbc.co.uk .slashdot.org

# only include sites located in Canada
acl canadasites dstdomain .ca

# only include working hours
acl workhours time MTWHF 9:00-18:00
```

```
# only include lunchtimes
acl lunchtimes time MTWHF 13:00-14:00

# only include weekends
acl weekends time AS 00:00-23:59

# include URLs ending in ".zip". Note: the \ is important,
# because "." has a special meaning otherwise
acl zipfiles url_regex -i \.zip$

# include URLs starting with https
acl httpsurls url_regex -i ^https

# include all URLs that match "hotmail"
url_regex hotmail url_regex -i hotmail

# include three specific IP addresses
acl directors src 10.0.0.14 10.0.0.28 10.0.0.31

# include all IPs from 192.168.0.0 to 192.168.0.255
acl internal src 192.168.0.0/24

# include all IPs from 192.168.0.0 to 192.168.0.255
# and all IPs from 10.0.0.0 to 10.255.255.255
acl internal src 192.168.0.0/24 10.0.0.0/8
```

When you have your ACL lines in place, you can put together appropriate `http_access` lines. For example, you might want to use a multilayered access system so that certain users (for example, company directors) have full access, whereas others are filtered. For example:

```
http_access allow directors
http_access deny hotmail
http_access deny zipfiles
http_access allow internal lunchtimes
http_access deny all
```

Because Squid matches those in order, directors will have full, unfiltered access to the Web. If the client IP address is not in the directors list, the two deny lines are processed so that the user cannot download ZIP files or read online mail at Hotmail. After blocking those two types of requests, the allow on line four allows internal users to access the Web, as long as they do so only at lunchtime. The last line (which is highly recommended) blocks all other users from the proxy.

27

References

▶ **www.squid-cache.org/**—The home page of the Squid web proxy cache.

▶ **www.deckle.co.za/squid-users-guide/**—The home page of *Squid: A User's Guide*, a free online book about Squid.

▶ **https://help.ubuntu.com/community/Squid**—Ubuntu community documentation for setting up Squid.

▶ There are two excellent books on the topic of web caching. The first is *Squid: The Definitive Guide* (O'Reilly) by Duane Wessels, ISBN: 0-596-00162-2. The second is *Web Caching* (O'Reilly) also by Duane Wessels, ISBN: 1-56592-536-X.

Of the two, the former is more practical and covers the Squid server in depth. The latter is more theoretical, discussing how caching is implemented. Wessels is one of the leading developers on Squid, so both books are of impeccable technical accuracy.

# CHAPTER 28

Administering Relational Database Services

This chapter is an introduction to MySQL and PostgreSQL, two database systems that are available in the Ubuntu repositories. In this chapter, you learn what these systems do, how the two programs compare, and how to consider their advantages and disadvantages. This information can help you choose and deploy which one to use for your organization's database needs.

The *database administrator (DBA)* for an organization has several responsibilities, which vary according to the size and operations of the organization, supporting staff, and so on. Depending on the particular organization's structure, if you are the organization's DBA, your responsibilities might include the following:

▶ **Installing and maintaining database servers**—You might install and maintain the database software. Maintenance can involve installing patches as well as upgrading the software at the appropriate times. As DBA, you need to have root access to your system and know how to manage software (see Chapter 9, "Managing Software"). You also need to be aware of kernel, file system, and other security issues.

▶ **Installing and maintaining database clients**—The database client is the program used to access the database (you learn more about that later in this chapter, in the section "Database Clients"), either locally or remotely over a network. Your responsibilities might include installing and maintaining these client programs on users' systems. This chapter discusses how to install and work with the clients from both the Linux command line and through its graphical interface database tools.

▶ **Managing accounts and users**—Account and user management include adding and deleting users from the database, assigning and administering passwords, and so on. In this chapter, you will learn how to grant and revoke user privileges and passwords for MySQL and PostgreSQL.

▶ **Ensuring database security**—To ensure database security, you need to be concerned with things like access control, which ensures that only authorized people can access the database, and permissions, which ensure that people who can access the database cannot do things they should not do. In this chapter, you learn how to manage *Secure Shell (SSH)*, web, and local *graphical user interface (GUI)* client access to the database. Planning and overseeing the regular backup of an organization's database and restoring data from those backups is another critical component of securing the database.

▶ **Ensuring data integrity**—Of all the information stored on a server's hard disk storage, chances are the information in the database is the most critical. Ensuring data integrity involves planning for multiple-user access and ensuring that changes are not lost or duplicated when more than one user is making changes to the database at the same time.

A Brief Review of Database Basics

Database services under Linux that use the software discussed in this chapter are based on a *client/server* model. Database clients are often used to input data and to query or display query results from the server. You can use the command line or a graphical client to access a running server. Databases generally come in two forms: flat file and relational. A *flat file* database can be as simple as a text file with a space, tab, or some other character delimiting different parts of the information. One example of a simple flat file database is the /etc/passwd file. Another example is a simple address book that might look something like this:

```
Doe~John~505 Some Street~Anytown~NY~12345~555-555-1212
```

You can use standard UNIX tools such as grep, awk, and perl to search for and extract information from this primitive database. Although this might work well for a small database such as an address book that only one person uses, flat file databases of this type have several limitations:

▶ **They do not scale well**—Flat file databases cannot perform random access on data. They can only perform sequential access. This means they have to scan each line in the file, one by one, to look for specific information. As the size of the database grows, access times increase and performance decreases.

▶ **Flat file databases are unsuitable for multiuser environments**—Depending on how the database is set up, it either enables only one user to access it at a time or allows two users to make changes simultaneously, and the changes could end up overwriting each other and cause data loss.

These limitations obviously make the flat file database unsuitable for any kind of serious work in even a small business—much less in an enterprise environment. Relational databases—or *relational database management systems (RDBMSs)*, to give them their full name—are good at finding the relationships between individual pieces of data. An RDBMS stores data in tables with fields much like those in spreadsheets, making the data searchable and sortable. RDBMSs are the focus of this chapter.

NoSQL

There is an exception to what was just said. A fairly new category of databases is now in use, usually referred to as *NoSQL* in casual conversation. Unlike typical flat file databases, NoSQL databases are a form of structured storage that is suitable for large and high-traffic uses. These databases have been written and put into use in places where flat files are unsuitable but where relational databases are slower than desired. It is important to note that although NoSQL databases work great when scalability and speed are desirable, you cannot be certain with all NoSQL databases that data is replicated and available instantly across a large installation. It generally is, but there is no guarantee of up-to-the-moment data. This is okay for some applications (web search), but would be disastrous for others (like a financial institution).

There are many forms of NoSQL databases, each with different intents and applications. Some are created and used by big names you will recognize, such as Google's BigTable and Apache's Cassandra. Ubuntu uses Apache's CouchDB for several applications. Other common ones include MongoDB and Berkeley DB. For this chapter, we concentrate on the more traditional relational databases that are used for most applications, but we urge you to keep an eye on what is happening in the NoSQL world. For more information about NoSQL databases, see Chapter 29, "NoSQL Databases."

Oracle, DB2, Microsoft SQL Server, and the freely available PostgreSQL and MySQL are all examples of RDBMSs. The following sections discuss how relational databases work and provide a closer look at some of the basic processes involved in administering and using databases. You also learn about SQL, the standard language used to store, retrieve, and manipulate database data.

How Relational Databases Work

An RDBMS stores data in tables, which you can visualize as spreadsheets. Each column in the table is a field; for example, a column might contain a name or an address. Each row in the table is an individual record. The table itself has a name you use to refer to that table when you want to get data out of it or put data into it. Figure 28.1 shows an example of a simple relational database that stores name and address information.

last_name	first_name	address	city	state	zip	phone
Doe	John	501 Somestreet	Anytown	NY	55011	555-555-1212
Doe	Jane	501 Somestreet	Anytown	NY	55011	555-555-1212
Palmer	John	205 Anystreet	Sometown	NY	55055	123-456-7890
Johnson	Robert	100 Easystreet	Easytown	CT	12345	111-222-3333

FIGURE 28.1   In this visualization of how an RDBMS stores data, the database stores four records (rows) that include name and address information, divided into seven fields (columns) of data.

In the example shown in Figure 28.1, the database contains only a single table. Most RDBMS setups are much more complex than this, with a single database containing multiple tables. Figure 28.2 shows an example of a database named sample_database that contains two tables.

phonebook

last_name	first_name	phone
Doe	John	555-555-1212
Doe	Jane	555-555-1212
Palmer	John	555-123-4567
Johnson	Richard	555-111-4321

cd_collection

id	title	artist	year	rating
1	Mindbomb	The The	1989	4
2	For All You've Done	Hillsong	2004	
3	Trouser Jazz	Mr Scruff	2002	5
4	Natural Elements	Acoustic Alchemy	1988	3
5	Combat Rock	The Clash	1982	4
6	Life for Rent	Dido	2003	5
7	Adiemus 4	Karl Jenkins	2000	4
8	The Two Towers	Howard Shore	2002	5

FIGURE 28.2   A single database can contain two tables—in this case, phonebook and cd_collection.

In the sample_database example, the phonebook table contains four records (rows) and each record hold three fields (columns) of data. The cd_collection table holds eight records, divided into five fields of data.

If you are thinking that there is no logical relationship between the phonebook table and the cd_collection table in the sample_database example, you are correct. In a relational database, users can store multiple tables of data in a single database, even if the data in one table is unrelated to the data in others.

For example, suppose you run a small company that sells widgets and you have a computerized database of customers. In addition to storing each customer's name, address, and phone number, you want to be able to look up outstanding order and invoice information for any of your customers. You could use three related tables in an RDBMS to store and organize customer data for just those purposes. Figure 28.3 shows an example of such a database.

customers

cid	last_name	first_name	shipping_address
1	Doe	John	505 Somestreet
2	Doe	Jane	505 Somestreet
3	Palmer	John	200 Anystreet
4	Johnson	Richard	1000 Another Street

orders

cid	order_num	stock_num	priority	shipped	date
1	1002	100,252,342	3	Y	8/31/01
1	1221	200,352	1	N	10/2/01
3	1223	200,121	2	Y	10/2/01
2	1225	221,152	1	N	10/3/01

overdue

cid	order_num	days_overdue	action
1	1002	32	sent letter

FIGURE 28.3   You can use three related tables to track customers, orders, and outstanding invoices.

In the example in Figure 28.3, we have added a customer ID field to each customer record. This field holds a customer ID number that is the unique piece of information that can be used to link all other information for each customer to track orders and invoices. Each customer is given an ID unique to him; two customers might have the same data in their name fields, but their ID field values will never be the same. The Customer ID field data in the Orders and Overdue tables replaces the Last Name, First Name, and Shipping Address field information from the Customers table. Now, when you want to run a search for any customer's order and invoice data, you can search based on one key rather than multiple keys. You get more accurate results in faster, easier-to-conduct data searches.

Now that you have an idea of how data is stored in an RDBMS and how the RDBMS structure enables you to work with that data, you are ready to learn how to input and output data from the database. This is where SQL comes in.

28

Understanding SQL Basics

SQL (pronounced "S-Q-L" or "sequel" depending on who is talking) is a database query language understood by virtually all RDBMSs available today. You use SQL statements to get data into and retrieve data from a database. As with statements in any language, SQL statements have a defined structure that determines their meanings and functions.

As a DBA, you should understand the basics of SQL, even if you will not be doing any of the actual programming yourself. Fortunately, SQL is similar to standard English, so learning the basics is simple.

Creating Tables

As mentioned previously, an RDBMS stores data in tables that look similar to spreadsheets. Of course, before you can store any data in a database, you need to create the necessary tables and columns to store the data. You do this by using the CREATE statement.

For example, the cd_collection table from Figure 28.2 has five columns, or fields: id, title, artist, year, and rating.

SQL provides several column types for data that define what kind of data will be stored in the column. Some of the available types are INT, FLOAT, CHAR, and VARCHAR. Both CHAR and VARCHAR hold text strings, with the difference being that CHAR holds a fixed-length string, whereas VARCHAR holds a variable-length string.

There are also special column types, such as DATE, that only take data in a date format, and ENUMs (enumerations), which can be used to specify that only certain values are allowed. If, for example, you wanted to record the genre of your CDs, you could use an ENUM column that accepts only the values POP, ROCK, EASY_LISTENING, and so on. You learn more about ENUM later in this chapter.

Looking at the cd_collection table, you can see that three of the columns hold numeric data and the other two hold string data. In addition, the character strings are of variable length. Based on this information, you can discern that the best type to use for the text columns is type VARCHAR, and the best type to use for the others is INT. You should notice something else about the cd_collection table: One of the CDs is missing a rating, perhaps because we have not listened to it yet. This value, therefore, is optional; it starts empty and can be filled in later.

You are now ready to create a table. As mentioned before, you do this by using the CREATE statement, which uses the following syntax:

```
CREATE TABLE table_name (column_name column_type(parameters) options, ...);
```

You should know the following about the CREATE statement:

▶ **SQL commands are not case sensitive**—For example, CREATE TABLE, create table, and Create Table are all valid.

▶ **Whitespace is generally ignored**—This means you should use it to make your SQL commands clearer.

The following example shows how to create the table for the `cd_collection` database:

```
CREATE TABLE cd_collection
(
id INT NOT NULL,
title VARCHAR(50) NOT NULL,
artist VARCHAR(50) NOT NULL,
year VARCHAR(50) NOT NULL,
rating VARCHAR(50) NULL
);
```

Notice that the statement terminates with a semicolon (;). This is how SQL knows you are finished with all the entries in the statement. In some cases, the semicolon can be omitted, and we point out these cases when they arise.

TIP

SQL has a number of reserved keywords that cannot be used in table names or field names. For example, if you keep track of CDs you want to take with you on vacation, you would not be able to use the field name `select` because that is a reserved keyword. Instead, you should either choose a different name (`selected`?) or just prefix the field name with an `f`, such as `fselect`.

Inserting Data into Tables

After you create the tables, you can put data into them. You can insert data manually with the `INSERT` statement, which uses the following syntax:

```
INSERT INTO table_name VALUES('value1', 'value2', 'value3', ...);
```

This statement inserts `value1`, `value2`, and so on into the table `table_name`. The values that are inserted constitute one row, or *record*, in the database. Unless specified otherwise, values are inserted in the order in which the columns are listed in the database table. If, for some reason, you want to insert values in a different order (or if you want to insert only a few values and they are not in sequential order), you can specify which columns you want the data to go in by using the following syntax:

```
INSERT INTO table_name (column1,column4) VALUES('value1', 'value2');
```

You can also fill multiple rows with a single `INSERT` statement, using syntax such as the following:

```
INSERT INTO table_name VALUES('value1', 'value2'),('value3', 'value4');
```

In this statement, value1 and value2 are inserted into the first row, and value3 and value4 are inserted into the second row.

The following example shows how you insert the Nevermind entry into the cd_collection table:

```
INSERT INTO cd_collection VALUES(9, 'Nevermind', ''Nirvana', '1991, ''NULL);
```

MySQL requires the NULL value for the last column (rating) if you do not want to include a rating. PostgreSQL, in contrast, lets you get away with just omitting the last column. Of course, if you had columns in the middle that were null, you would need to explicitly state NULL in the INSERT statement.

Normally, INSERT statements are coded into a front-end program, so users adding data to the database do not have to worry about the SQL statements involved.

Retrieving Data from a Database

Of course, the main reason for storing data in a database is so you can later look up, sort, and generate reports on that data. Basic data retrieval is done with the SELECT statement, which has the following syntax:

```
SELECT column1, column2, column3 FROM table_name WHERE search_criteria;
```

The first two parts of the statement—the SELECT and FROM parts—are required. The WHERE portion of the statement is optional. If it is omitted, all rows in the table table_name are returned.

The column1, column2, column3 syntax indicates the name of the columns you want to see. If you want to see all columns, you can also use the wildcard * to show all the columns that match the search criteria. For example, the following statement displays all columns from the cd_collection table:

```
SELECT * FROM cd_collection;
```

If you wanted to see only the titles of all the CDs in the table, you use a statement such as the following:

```
SELECT title FROM cd_collection;
```

To select the title and year of a CD, you use the following:

```
SELECT title, year FROM cd_collection;
```

If you want something a little fancier, you can use SQL to print the CD title followed by the year in parentheses, as is the convention. Both MySQL and PostgreSQL provide string concatenation functions to handle problems such as this. However, the syntax is different in the two systems.

In MySQL, you can use the CONCAT() function to combine the title and year columns into one output column, along with parentheses. The following statement is an example:

```
SELECT CONCAT(title," (",year, ")") AS TitleYear FROM cd_collection;
```

That statement lists both the title and year under one column that has the label TitleYear. Note that there are two strings in the CONCAT() function along with the fields; these add whitespace and the parentheses.

In PostgreSQL, the string concatenation function is simply a double pipe (||). The following command is the PostgreSQL equivalent of the preceding MySQL command:

```
SELECT (genus||'' ('||species||')') AS TitleYear FROM cd_collection;
```

Note that the parentheses are optional, but they make the statement easier to read. Once again, the strings in the middle and at the end (note the space between the quotes) are used to insert spacing and parentheses between the title and year.

Of course, more often than not, you do not want a list of every single row in the database. Rather, you only want to find rows that match certain characteristics. For this, you add the WHERE statement to the SELECT statement. For example, suppose you want to find all the CDs in the cd_collection table that have a rating of 5. You would use a statement like the following:

```
SELECT * FROM cd_collection WHERE rating = 5;
```

Using the table from Figure 28.2, you can see that this query would return the rows for *Trouser Jazz*, *Life for Rent*, and *The Two Towers*. This is a simple query, and SQL is capable of handling queries much more complex than this. Complex queries can be written using logical AND and logical OR statements. For example, suppose you want to refine the query so it lists only those CDs that were not released in 2003. You use a query like the following:

```
SELECT * FROM cd_collection WHERE rating = 5 AND year != 2003;
```

In SQL, != means "is not equal to." So, once again looking at the table from Figure 28.2, you can see that this query returns the rows for *Trouser Jazz* and *The Two Towers* but does not return the row for *Life for Rent* because it was released in 2003.

So, what if you want to list all the CDs that have a rating of 3 or 4 except those released in the year 2000? This time, you combine logical AND and logical OR statements:

```
SELECT * FROM cd_collection WHERE rating = 3 OR rating = 4 AND year != 2000;
```

This query returns entries for *Mind Bomb, Natural Elements*, and *Combat Rock*. However, it does not return entries for *Adiemus 4* because it was released in 2000.

28

> **TIP**
>
> One of the most common errors among new database programmers is confusing logical AND and logical OR. For example, in everyday speech, you might say, "Find me all CDs released in 2003 and 2004." At first glance, you might think that if you fed this statement to the database in SQL format, it would return the rows for *For All You've Done* and *Life for Rent*. In fact, it would return no rows at all. This is because the database interprets the statement as "Find all rows in which the CD was released in 2003 and was released in 2004." It is, of course, impossible for the same CD to be released twice without requiring a new ISBN and therefore a new database entry, so this statement would never return any rows, no matter how many CDs were stored in the table. The correct way to form this statement is with an OR statement instead of an AND statement.

SQL is capable of far more than is demonstrated here. But as mentioned before, this section is not intended to teach you all there is to know about SQL programming; rather, it teaches you the basics so you can be a more effective DBA.

Choosing a Database: MySQL Versus PostgreSQL

If you are just starting out and learning about using a database with Linux, the first logical step is to research which database will best serve your needs. Many database software packages are available for Linux; some are free, and others cost hundreds of thousands of dollars. Expensive commercial databases, such as Oracle, are beyond the scope of this book. Instead, this chapter focuses on two freely available databases: MySQL and PostgreSQL.

Both of these databases are quite capable, and either one could probably serve your needs. However, each database has a unique set of features and capabilities that might serve your needs better or make developing database applications easier for you.

Note that Oracle recently bought Sun Microsystems, who owned MySQL. In the short term, this might not have any impact, but the database world is watching to see what will happen with MySQL, and at least two groups have forked the code to ensure that the database stays free and open source while still in active development. These groups have released and are working on Drizzle (http://drizzle.org) and MariaDB (http://kb.askmonty. org/v/MariaDB). Although no one really knows yet what will happen, we suggest keeping an eye on these projects and potential replacements for MySQL should the worst fears be realized and Oracle decides that the free MySQL is too much of a competitor to their paid database offerings and kills the project.

Speed

Until recently, the speed choice was simple: If the speed of performing queries was paramount to your application, you used MySQL. MySQL has a reputation for being an extremely fast database. Until recently, PostgreSQL was quite slow by comparison.

Newer versions of PostgreSQL have improved in terms of speed (when it comes to disk access, sorting, and so on). In certain situations, such as periods of heavy simultaneous access, PostgreSQL can be significantly faster than MySQL, as you will see in the next section. However, MySQL is still extremely fast when compared to many other databases.

Data Locking

To prevent data corruption, a database needs to put a lock on data while it is being accessed. As long as the lock is on, no other process can access the data until the first process has released the lock. This means that any other processes trying to access the data have to wait until the current process completes. The next process in line then locks the data until it is finished, and the remaining processes have to wait their turn, and so on.

Of course, operations on a database generally complete quickly, so in environments with a small number of users simultaneously accessing the database, the locks are usually of such short duration that they do not cause any significant delays. However, in environments in which many people are accessing the database simultaneously, locking can create performance problems as people wait their turn to access the database.

Older versions of MySQL lock data at the table level, which can be considered a bottleneck for updates during periods of heavy access. This means that when someone writes a row of data in the table, the entire table is locked so no one else can enter data. If your table has 500,000 rows (or records) in it, all 500,000 rows are locked any time one row is accessed. Once again, in environments with a relatively small number of simultaneous users, this doesn't cause serious performance problems because most operations complete so quickly that the lock time is extremely short. However, in environments in which many people are accessing the data simultaneously, MySQLs table-level locking can be a significant performance bottleneck.

PostgreSQL, in contrast, locks data at the row level. In PostgreSQL, only the row currently being accessed is locked. The rest of the table can be accessed by other users. This row-level locking significantly reduces the performance impact of locking in environments that have a large number of simultaneous users. Therefore, as a general rule, PostgreSQL is better suited for high-load environments than MySQL.

The MySQL release bundled with Ubuntu gives you the choice of using tables with table-level or row-level locking. In MySQL terminology, MyISAM tables use table-level locking and InnoDB tables use row-level locking.

> **NOTE**
>
> MySQL's data locking methods are discussed in more depth at www.mysql.com/doc/en/Internal_locking.html.
>
> You can find more information on PostgreSQL's locking at www.postgresql.org/idocs/index.php?locking-tables.html.

ACID Compliance in Transaction Processing to Protect Data Integrity

Another way MySQL and PostgreSQL differ is in the amount of protection they provide for keeping data from becoming corrupted. The acronym ACID is commonly used to describe several aspects of data protection:

▶ **Atomicity**—This means that several database operations are treated as an indivisible (atomic) unit, often called a *transaction*. In a transaction, either all unit operations are carried out or none of them are. In other words, if any operation in the atomic unit fails, the entire atomic unit is canceled.

▶ **Consistency**—Ensures that no transaction can cause the database to be left in an inconsistent state. Inconsistent states can be caused by database client crashes, network failures, and similar situations. Consistency ensures that, in such a situation, any transaction or partially completed transaction that would cause the database to be left in an inconsistent state is *rolled back*, or undone.

▶ **Isolation**—Ensures that multiple transactions operating on the same data are completely isolated from each other. This prevents data corruption if two users try to write to the same record at the same time. The way isolation is handled can generally be configured by the database programmer. One way that isolation can be handled is through locking, as discussed previously.

▶ **Durability**—Ensures that, after a transaction has been committed to the database, it cannot be lost in the event of a system crash, network failure, or other problem. This is usually accomplished through transaction logs. Durability means, for example, that if the server crashes, the database can examine the logs when it comes back up and it can commit any transactions that were not yet complete into the database.

PostgreSQL is ACID-compliant, but again MySQL gives you the choice of using ACID-compliant tables or not. MyISAM tables are not ACID-compliant, whereas InnoDB tables are. Note that ACID compliancy is no easy task: All the extra precautions incur a performance overhead.

SQL Subqueries

Subqueries allow you to combine several operations into one atomic unit, and they enable those operations to access each other's data. By using SQL subqueries, you can perform some extremely complex operations on a database. In addition, using SQL subqueries eliminates the potential problem of data changing between two operations as a result of another user performing some operation on the same set of data. Both PostgreSQL and MySQL have support for subqueries in this release of Ubuntu, but this was not true in earlier releases.

Procedural Languages and Triggers

A *procedural language* is an external programming language that can be used to write functions and procedures. This allows you to do things that aren't supported by simple SQL. A *trigger* allows you to define an event that will invoke the external function or procedure you have written. For example, a trigger can be used to cause an exception if an INSERT statement containing an unexpected or out-of-range value for a column is given.

For example, in the CD tracking database, you could use a trigger to cause an exception if a user entered data that did not make sense. PostgreSQL has a procedural language called PL/pgSQL. Although MySQL has support for a limited number of built-in procedures and triggers, it does not have any procedural language. It does have a feature called *stored procedures* that is similar, but it doesn't do quite the same thing.

Configuring MySQL

A free and stable version of MySQL is included with Ubuntu. MySQL is also available from www.mysql.com. The software is available in source code, binary, and APT format for Linux. See Chapter 9 for the details on adding (or removing) software.

After you have MySQL installed, you need to initialize the grant tables or permissions to access any or all databases and tables and column data within a database. You can do this by issuing mysql_install_db as root. This command initializes the grant tables and creates a MySQL root user.

> **CAUTION**
>
> The MySQL data directory needs to be owned by the user who owns the MySQL process, most likely mysql (you may need to change the directory's owner using the chown command). In addition, only this user should have any permissions on this directory. (In other words, the permissions should be set to 700 by using chmod.) Setting up the data directory any other way creates a security hole.

Running mysql_install_db should generate output similar to the following:

```
matthew@seymour:~$ sudo mysql_install_db
Preparing db table
Preparing host table
Preparing user table
Preparing func table
Preparing tables_priv table
Preparing columns_priv table
Installing all prepared tables
020916 17:39:05 /usr/libexec/mysqld: Shutdown Complete
...
```

The command prepares MySQL for use on the system and reports helpful information. The next step is to set the password for the MySQL root user, which is discussed in the following section.

> **CAUTION**
>
> By default, the MySQL root user is created with no password. This is one of the first things you must change because the MySQL root user has access to all aspects of the database. The following section explains how to change the password of the user.

Setting a Password for the MySQL Root User

To set a password for the root MySQL user, you need to connect to the MySQL server as the root MySQL user; you can use the command `mysql -u root` to do so. This command connects you to the server with the MySQL client. When you have the MySQL command prompt, issue a command like the following to set a password for the root user:

```
mysql> SET PASSWORD FOR root = PASSWORD("secretword");
```

secretword should be replaced by whatever you want to be the password for the root user. You can use this same command with other usernames to set or change passwords for other database users.

After you enter a password, you can exit the MySQL client by typing `exit` at the command prompt.

Creating a Database in MySQL

In MySQL you create a database by using the CREATE DATABASE statement. To create a database, you connect to the server by typing `mysql -u root -p` and pressing Enter. After you do so, you are connected to the database as the MySQL root user and prompted for a password. After you enter the password, you are placed at the MySQL command prompt. Then you use the CREATE DATABASE command. For example, the following commands create a database called `animals`:

```
matthew@seymour:~$ mysql -u root -p
Enter password:
Welcome to the MySQL monitor. Commands end with ; or \g.
Your MySQL connection id is 1 to server version: 3.23.58

Type 'help;' or '\h' for help. Type '\c' to clear the buffer.

mysql> CREATE DATABASE animals;
Query OK, 1 row affected (0.00 sec)
mysql>
```

Another way to create a database is to use the `mysqladmin` command, as the root user, with the `create` keyword and the name of a new database. For example, to create a new database named `reptiles`, you use a command line like this:

```
matthew@seymour:~$ sudo mysqladmin -u root -p create reptiles
```
Granting and Revoking Privileges in MySQL

You probably want to grant yourself some privileges, and eventually you will probably want to grant privileges to other users. Privileges, also known as *rights*, are granted and revoked on four levels:

▶ **Global level**—These rights allow access to any database on a server.

▶ **Database level**—These rights allow access to all tables in a database.

▶ **Table level**—These rights allow access to all columns within a table in a database.

▶ **Column level**—These rights allow access to a single column within a database's table.

NOTE

Listing all the available privileges is beyond the scope of this chapter. See the MySQL documentation for more information.

To add a user account, you connect to the database by typing `mysql -u root -p` and pressing Enter. You are then connected as the root user and prompted for a password. (You did set a password for the root user, as instructed in the last section, right?) After you enter the root password, you are placed at the MySQL command prompt.

To grant privileges to a user, you use the GRANT statement, which has the following syntax:

```
grant what_to_grant ON where_to_grant TO user_name IDENTIFIED BY 'password';
```

The first option, *what_to_grant*, is the privileges you are granting to the user. These privileges are specified with keywords. For example, the ALL keyword is used to grant global-, database-, table-, and column-level rights for a specified user.

The second option, *where_to_grant*, specifies the resources on which the privileges should be granted. The third option, user_name, is the username to which you want to grant the privileges. Finally, the fourth option, *password*, is a password that should be assigned to this user. If this is an existing user who already has a password and you are modifying permissions, you can omit the *IDENTIFIED BY* portion of the statement.

For example, to grant all privileges on a database named `sampledata` to a user named `foobar`, you could use the following command:

```
GRANT ALL ON animals.* TO foobar IDENTIFIED BY 'secretword';
```

The user `foobar` can now connect to the database `sampledata` by using the password secretword, and `foobar` has all privileges on the database, including the ability to create and destroy tables. For example, the user `foobar` can now log in to the server (by using the current hostname—shuttle2, in this example), and access the database like this:

```
matthew@seymour:~$ mysql -h shuttle2 -u foobar -p animals
Enter password:
Welcome to the MySQL monitor. Commands end with ; or \g.
```

28

```
Your MySQL connection id is 43 to server version: 3.23.58

Type 'help;' or '\h' for help. Type '\c' to clear the buffer.

mysql>
```

NOTE

See the section "The MySQL Command-Line Client" for additional command-line options.

Later, if you need to revoke privileges from `foobar`, you can use the `REVOKE` statement. For example, the following statement revokes all privileges from the user `foobar`:

```
REVOKE ALL ON animals FROM foobar;
```

Advanced database administration, privileges, and security are complex topics that are beyond the scope of this book. See the "References" section at the end of this chapter for links to online documentation. You can also check out Luke Welling's and Laura Thompson's book, *PHP and MySQL Development* from Sams Publishing.

Configuring PostgreSQL

If you do not want to use the version of PostgreSQL bundled with Ubuntu, the latest PostgreSQL binary files and source are available at www.postgresql.org. The PostgreSQL packages are distributed as several files. At a minimum, you want the `postgresql` package. You should see the README file in the FTP directory ftp://ftp.postgresql.org/pub/ to determine whether you need any other packages.

If you are installing from the Ubuntu package files, a necessary `postgres` user account (that is, an account with the name of the user running the server on your system) is created for you automatically:

```
matthew@seymour:~$ fgrep postgres /etc/passwd
postgres:x:26:26:PostgreSQL Server:/var/lib/postgresql:/bin/bash
```

Otherwise, you need to create a user called `postgres` during the installation. This user should not have login privileges because only root should be able to use `su` to become this user and no one will ever log in directly as the user. (See Chapter 12, "Managing Users," for more information on how to add users to an Ubuntu system.) After you have added the user, you can install each of the PostgreSQL packages you downloaded using the standard `dpkg  -i` command for a default installation.

Initializing the Data Directory in PostgreSQL

Installation initializes the database and sets the permissions on the data directory to their correct values.

> **CAUTION**
>
> The initdb program sets the permissions on the data directory to 700. You should not change these permissions to anything else to avoid creating a security hole.

You can start the postmaster program with the following command (make sure you are still the user postgres):

```
matthew@seymour:~$ postmaster -D /usr/local/pgsql/data &
```

If you have decided to use a directory other than /usr/local/pgsql/data as the data directory, you should replace the directory in the postmaster command line with whatever directory you are using.

> **TIP**
>
> By default, Ubuntu makes the PostgreSQL data directory /var/lib/pgsql/data. This is not a very good place to store the data, however, because most people do not have the necessary space in the /var partition for any kind of serious data storage. Note that if you do change the data directory to something else (such as /usr/local/pgsql/data, as in the examples in this section), you need to edit the PostgreSQL startup file (named postgres) located in /etc/init.d to reflect the change.

Creating a Database in PostgreSQL

Creating a database in PostgreSQL is straightforward, but it must be performed by a user who has permissions to create databases in PostgreSQL—for example, initially the user named postgres. You can then simply issue the following command from the shell prompt (not the PSQL client prompt, but a normal shell prompt):

```
matthew@seymour:~# su - postgres
-bash-2.05b$ createdb database
```

where *database* is the name of the database you want to create.

The createdb program is actually a wrapper that makes it easier to create databases without having to log in and use psql. However, you can also create databases from within psql with the CREATE DATABASE statement. Here is an example:

```
CREATE DATABASE database;
```

You need to create at least one database before you can start the pgsql client program. You should create this database while you're logged in as the user postgres. To log in as this user, you need to use su to become root and then use su to become the user postgres. To connect to the new database, you start the psql client program with the name of the new database as a command-line argument, like this:

```
matthew@seymour:~$ psql sampledata
```

If you don't specify the name of a database when you invoke psql, the command attempts to connect to a database that has the same name as the user as which you invoke psql (that is, the default database).

Creating Database Users in PostgreSQL

To create a database user, you use su to become the user postgres from the Linux root account. You can then use the PostgreSQL createuser command to quickly create a user who is allowed to access databases or create new database users, as follows:

```
matthew@seymour:~$ createuser heather
Shall the new user be allowed to create databases? (y/n) y
Shall the new user be allowed to create more new users? (y/n) y
CREATE USER
```

In this example, the new user named phudson is created and allowed to create new databases and database users. (Carefully consider who is allowed to create new databases or additional users.)

You can also use the PostgreSQL command-line client to create a new user by typing psql along with name of the database and then use the CREATE USER command to create a new user. Here is an example:

```
CREATE USER foobar ;
```

> **CAUTION**
>
> PostgreSQL allows you to omit the WITH PASSWORD portion of the statement. However, doing so causes the user to be created with no password. This is a security hole, so you should always use the WITH PASSWORD option when creating users.

> **NOTE**
>
> When you are finished working in the psql command-line client, you can type \q to get out of it and return to the shell prompt.

Deleting Database Users in PostgreSQL

To delete a database user, you use the dropuser command, along with the user's name, and the user's access is removed from the default database, like this:

```
matthew@seymour:~$  dropuser msmith
DROP USER
```

You can also log in to your database by using psql and then use the DROP USER
commands. Here is an example:

```
matthew@seymour:~$ psql demodb
Welcome to psql, the PostgreSQL interactive terminal.

Type: \copyright for distribution terms
 \h for help with SQL commands
 \? for help on internal slash commands
 \g or terminate with semicolon to execute query
 \q to quit

demodb=# DROP USER msmith ;
DROP USER
demodb=# \q
```

Granting and Revoking Privileges in PostgreSQL

As in MySQL, granting and revoking privileges in PostgreSQL is done with the GRANT and
REVOKE statements. The syntax is the same as in MySQL except that PostgreSQL doesn't
use the IDENTIFIED BY portion of the statement because with PostgreSQL, passwords are
assigned when you create the user with the CREATE USER statement, as discussed previously. Here is the syntax of the GRANT statement:

```
GRANT what_to_grant ON where_to_grant TO user_name;
```

The following command, for example, grants all privileges to the user foobar on the database sampledata:

```
GRANT ALL ON sampledata TO foobar;
```

To revoke privileges, you use the REVOKE statement. Here is an example:

```
REVOKE ALL ON sampledata FROM foobar;
```

This command removes all privileges from the user foobar on the database sampledata.

Advanced administration and user configuration are complex topics. This section cannot
begin to cover all the aspects of PostgreSQL administration or of privileges and users. For
more information about administering PostgreSQL, see the PostgreSQL documentation or
consult a book on PostgreSQL, such as *PostgreSQL* (Sams Publishing).

28

Database Clients

Both MySQL and PostgreSQL use a client/server system for accessing databases. In the simplest terms, the database server handles the requests that come into the database and the database client handles getting the requests to the server as well as getting the output from the server to the user.

Users never interact directly with the database server even if it happens to be located on the same machine they are using. All requests to the database server are handled by a database client, which might or might not be running on the same machine as the database server.

Both MySQL and PostgreSQL have command-line clients. A command-line client is a primitive way of interfacing with a database and generally isn't used by end users. As a DBA, however, you use the command-line client to test new queries interactively without having to write front-end programs for that purpose. In later sections of this chapter, you will learn a bit about the MySQL graphical client and the web-based database administration interfaces available for both MySQL and PostgreSQL.

The following sections examine two common methods of accessing a remote database, a method of local access to a database server, and the concept of web access to a database.

> **NOTE**
>
> You should consider access and permission issues when setting up a database. Should users be able to create and destroy databases? Or should they only be able to use existing databases? Will users be able to add records to the database and modify existing records? Or should users be limited to read-only access to the database? And what about the rest of the world? Will the general public need to have any kind of access to your database through the Internet? As DBA, you must determine the answers to these questions.

SSH Access to a Database

Two types of remote database access scenarios are briefly discussed in this section. In the first scenario, the user directly logs in to the database server through *Secure Shell (SSH)* (to take advantage of the security benefits of encrypted sessions) and then starts a program on the server to access the database. In this case, shown in Figure 28.4, the database client is running on the database server itself.

In the other scenario, shown in Figure 28.5, the user logs in to a remote host through SSH and starts a program on it to access the database, but the database is actually running on a different system. Three systems are now involved: the user's workstation, the remote host running the database client, and the remote host running the database server.

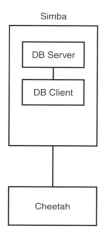

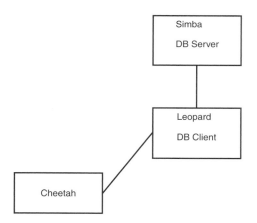

FIGURE 28.4   The user logs in to the database server located on host simba from the workstation (host cheetah). The database client is running on simba.

FIGURE 28.5   The user logs in to the remote host leopard from the workstation (host cheetah) and starts a database client on leopard. The client on leopard then connects to the database server running on host simba. The database client is running on leopard.

The important thing to note in Figure 28.5 is the middleman system leopard. Although the client is no longer running on the database server itself, it isn't running on the user's local workstation, either.

Local GUI Client Access to a Database

A user can log in to the database server by using a graphical client (which could be running on Windows, Macintosh, or a UNIX workstation). The graphical client then connects to the database server. In this case, the client is running on the user's workstation. Figure 28.6 shows an example.

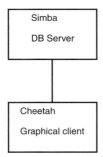

FIGURE 28.6   The user starts a GUI database program on the user's workstation (hostname cheetah). This program, which is the database client, then connects to the database server running on the host simba.

Web Access to a Database

In this section, we look at two basic examples of web access to the database server. In the first example, a user accesses the database through a form located on the World Wide Web. At first glance, it might appear that the client is running on the user's workstation. Of course, in reality it is not; the client is actually running on the web server. The web browser on the user's workstation simply provides a way for each user to enter the data that the user wants to send to the database and a way for the results sent from the database to be displayed to the user. The software that actually handles sending the request to the database is running on the web server in the form of a CGI script; a Java servlet; or embedded scripting such as the PHP or Sun Microsystems, Inc.'s *JavaServer Pages (JSP)*.

Often, the terms *client* and *front end* are used interchangeably when speaking of database structures. However, Figure 28.7 shows an example of a form of access in which the client and the front end are not the same thing at all. In this example, the front end is the form displayed in the user's web browser. In such cases, the client is referred to as *middleware*.

In another possible web access scenario, it could be said that the client is a two-piece application in which part of it is running on the user's workstation and the other part is running on the web server. For example, the database programmer can use JavaScript in the web form to ensure that the user has entered a valid query. In this case, the user's query is partially processed on the user's own workstation and partially on the web server. Error checking is done on the user's own workstation, which helps reduce the load on the server and also helps reduce network traffic because the query is checked for errors before being sent across the network to the server.

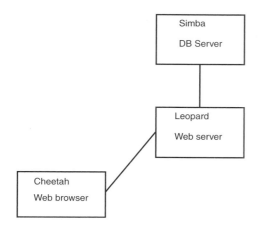

FIGURE 28.7   The user accesses the database through the World Wide Web. The front end is the user's web browser, the client is running on `leopard`, and the server is running on `simba`.

The MySQL Command-Line Client

The MySQL command-line client is `mysql`, and it has the following syntax:

`mysql [options] [database]`

Some of the available options for `mysql` are discussed in Table 28.1. `database` is optional, and if given, it should be the name of the database to which you want to connect.

TABLE 28.1   Command-Line Options to Use When Invoking `mysql`

Option	Action
-h hostname	Connects to the remote host `hostname` (if the database server isn't located on the local system).
-u username	Connects to the database as the user `username`.
-p	Prompts for a password. This option is required if the user you are connecting as needs a password to access the database. Note that this is a lowercase *p*.
-P n	Specifies n as the number of the port that the client should connect to. Note that this is an uppercase *P*.
-?	Displays a help message.

28

More options are available than are listed in Table 28.1, but these are the most common options. See the man page for mysql for more information on the available options.

CAUTION

Although mysql allows you to specify the password on the command line after the -p option, and thus allows you to avoid having to type the password at the prompt, you should never invoke the client this way. Doing so causes your password to display in the process list, and the process list can be accessed by any user on the system. This is a major security hole, so never give your password on the mysql command line.

You can access the MySQL server without specifying a database to use. After you log in, you use the help command to get a list of available commands, like this:

```
mysql> help

MySQL commands:
Note that all text commands must be first on line and end with ';'
help (\h) Display this help.
? (\?) Synonym for 'help'.
clear (\c) Clear command.
connect (\r) Reconnect to the server. Optional arguments are db and host.
edit (\e) Edit command with $EDITOR.
ego (\G) Send command to mysql server, display result vertically.
exit (\q) Exit mysql. Same as quit.
go (\g) Send command to mysql server.
nopager (\n) Disable pager, print to stdout.
notee (\t) Don't write into outfile.
pager (\P) Set PAGER [to_pager]. Print the query results via PAGER.
print (\p) Print current command.
quit (\q) Quit mysql.
rehash (\#) Rebuild completion hash.
source (\.) Execute a SQL script file. Takes a file name as an argument.
status (\s) Get status information from the server.
tee (\T) Set outfile [to_outfile]. Append everything into given outfile.
use (\u) Use another database. Takes database name as argument.
```

You can then access a database by using the use command and the name of a database that has been created (such as animals) and that you are authorized to connect to, as follows:

```
mysql> use animals
Database changed
mysql>
```

The PostgreSQL Command-Line Client

You invoke the PostgreSQL command-line client with the command psql. Like mysql, psql can be invoked with the name of the database to which you would like to connect. Also like mysql, psql can take several options. These options are listed in Table 28.2.

Several more options are available in addition to those listed in Table 28.2. See the psql man page for details on all the available options.

TABLE 28.2   Command-Line Options to Use When Invoking psql

Option	Action
-h hostname	Connects to the remote host hostname (if the database server isn't located on the local system).
-p n	Specifies n as the number of the port that the client should connect to. Note that this is a lowercase *p*.
-U username	Connects to the database as the user username.
-W	Prompts for a password after connecting to the database. In PostgreSQL 7 and later, password prompting is automatic if the server requests a password after a connection has been established.
-?	Displays a help message.

Graphical Clients

If you prefer to interact with a database by using a graphical database client than with the command-line clients discussed in the previous section, you are in luck: A few options are available.

MySQL has an official graphical client called *MySQLGUI*. MySQLGUI is available in both source and binary formats from the MySQL website at www.mysql.com.

Web-based administration interfaces are also available for MySQL and PostgreSQL. phpMyAdmin and phpPgAdmin are two such products. Both of these products are based on the PHP-embedded scripting language and therefore require you to have PHP installed. Of course, you also need to have a web server installed.

28

Related Ubuntu and Database Commands

The following commands are useful for creating and manipulating databases in Ubuntu:

- ▶ **createdb**—Creates a new PostgreSQL database.
- ▶ **createuser**—Creates a new PostgreSQL user account.
- ▶ **dropdb**—Deletes a PostgreSQL database.
- ▶ **dropuser**—Deletes a PostgreSQL user account.
- ▶ **mysql**—Interactively queries the mysqld server.

▶ **mysqladmin**—Administers the mysqld server.

▶ **mysqldump**—Dumps or backs up MySQL data or tables.

▶ **psql**—Accesses PostgreSQL via an interactive terminal.

References

▶ www.mysql.com—This is the official website of the MySQL database server. Here you can find the latest versions as well as up-to-date information and online documentation for MySQL. You can also purchase support contracts here. You might want to look into this if you will be using MySQL in a corporate setting. (Many corporations balk at the idea of using software for which the company has no support contract in place.)

▶ http://radar.oreilly.com/2009/07/oscon-the-saga-of-mysql.html—An interesting article describing the fears of the MySQL community and the creation of forks.

▶ http://drizzle.org/Home.html—The home page for Drizzle, a fork of MySQL.

▶ http://kb.askmonty.org/v/MariaDB—The home page for MariaDB, another fork of MySQL made by one of the founders of MySQL.

▶ www.postgresql.org—This is the official website of the PostgreSQL database server.

CHAPTER 29

NoSQL Databases

If you read Chapter 28, "Administering Relational Database Services," you have already read a brief description of the databases in this chapter. *NoSQL* is a broad term covering a large number of database styles. There are some similarities, but each of these databases was developed for a specific purpose. That means that they are not necessarily interchangeable; although it may be possible to force one to serve a task for which it is not designed, that is rarely a good idea. Also, while there has been a lot of press and hype about NoSQL over the past few years, NoSQL will not and should not be considered as a replacement for relational databases. Rather, this is a new set of databases designed to excel in specific situations, especially in large-scale, high-traffic-volume applications. If you have a need for storing and interacting with specific types of data as is described in one of the following sections, only then do we recommend using a database listed in that section.

Not One Size Fits all

"It's not a one size fits all anymore. One will use multiple technologies. If I were a CTO, I'd want to use NoSQL for scalable high-performance operational data access, lots of reads and writes at high speed, and [for] semi real-time and low latency for end users. And you need another for reporting and BI. These [NoSQL] technologies are not optimal for that. In general, a classic data warehouse is a good solution for those things."

—Dwight Merriman, CEO of MongoDB, at OSCON 2011, as quoted in an article from ZDNet at www.zdnet.com/blog/open-source/mongodb-chief-it-will-be-mixed-sql-nosql-world/9297

There are different definitions and even some controversy over what NoSQL means. Does it mean that the database does not use SQL for interactions? Perhaps, but that is not absolute. Does it mean, as some now suggest, "not only SQL?" Maybe. That is certainly a broader and more accurate description, although it is also a bit misleading as it seems to include all the relational databases that use SQL. Here is a well-known secret: There is no consistent definition of the term. With that said, here is a reasonably accurate set of features that the databases that are generally labeled NoSQL share:

▶ They store structured data (organized in a way that is defined and identifiable).

▶ They do not store data relationally (no tables with rows and columns and relationships between tables).

That's about it.

The advantages to using a NoSQL option instead of a relational database are as follows:

▶ NoSQL databases are designed for really large sets of data and can often handle more than any relational database.

▶ NoSQL databases are designed to scale as needed. That is, instead of buying a bigger database server to handle increased load as you would with a relational model, you can add additional database hosts easily and spread the database out across them. This is designed to work with commodity hardware and transparently.

▶ Commodity hardware is much cheaper than dedicated, professional relational database server hardware, making NoSQL a cheaper option in many cases.

▶ Data models with NoSQL are much more relaxed. Some would call this a disadvantage, but it is included in the advantages list because there are some types of data model that may change frequently. In a relational system, data model changes require taking the database off line to modify the structure. Often, NoSQL databases have very little or even no data model restrictions and can allow quick and dirty changes.

The disadvantages to using a NoSQL database are these:

▶ Support is not as readily available. Most of the NoSQL databases are relatively small open source projects, which is something that should please most readers of this book. However, this also means that, unlike most enterprise-focused relational databases, there is probably not any enterprise support available for businesses. This will frighten many managers.

▶ Most NoSQL projects are fairly new. This also means that they are untested in large enterprises and businesses. It can also mean that it takes longer to set up because of the learning curve; known solutions can be implemented more quickly.

▶ NoSQL is not always ACID (*atomicity, consistency, isolation, durability*) compliant. Instead of guaranteeing that every data transaction is instantly and properly recorded, that only one interaction may occur with a piece of data at any given time, and only the current version is available to the end user, NoSQL databases often work on a system of replication of data across multiple hosts that each get updated eventually. This may happen quickly, but there is no guarantee that at a given moment you will retrieve the most up-to-date data. This matters when dealing with financial transactions, but may not be a concern with web search results where "close enough" may be all that is wanted or necessary.

▶ There is no particular advantage to NoSQL unless you have data that is large enough to benefit from it or your project fits neatly into a specific use case.

▶ It isn't difficult to migrate to NoSQL from traditional relational databases if the need arises. You know the Donald Knuth's saying that "premature optimization is the root of all evil." It may be wiser to design your site or application using known technology and then migrate later if the need arises.

One facet that is sometimes described as an advantage and at other times as a disadvantage relates to administration. Relational databases often require trained staff to administer them. The positive side is that qualified *database administrators (DBAs)* are plentiful, if expensive. NoSQL databases are designed to be created and, at least in theory, require little to no further maintenance. Some pundits claim cost savings, others claim that DBAs will still be needed, but for different tasks and that there are very few people who are trained and available to perform those tasks because of this perspective and the newness of the database style.

An interesting development in the NoSQL world is that specifications are being created for a new database query language called UnQL (pronounced "uncle"), which stands for *Unstructured Query Language* (see http://unqlspec.org). This is being developed as a joint project by two developers: Richard Hipp, the creator of SQLite; and Damien Katz, the creator of CouchDB. They expect more to join them soon. In a nutshell, the language contains some familiar commands, such as SELECT, INSERT, UPDATE, and DELETE. However, it is different from SQL because these commands do not work on tables, but rather on collections of unordered sets of objects that are described using *JavaScript Object Notation (JSON)*. UnQL is not yet ready for use, but the specification is worth keeping an eye on.

The sections that follow group databases by similarities between them, choosing one standout feature as the name of the section. Because NoSQL databases are still fairly new, it is unclear which, if any, will become a long-term standard. For that reason, this chapter gives high-level coverage of a larger number of options rather than deep coverage of a couple of primary options.

Key/Value Stores

Key/value stores are listed first because they are the simplest of the NoSQL databases, at least in the sense of interactions. You have a piece of data of any type; this is your value. You give it a name of some sort; this is your key. Any time you need that specific piece of data, you ask for it using the key. Values may be bits of text, binaries, pretty much anything, and the data type does not need to be defined in advance, or often at all. The database never needs to know what the value object is, just that it is stored using the given key. These databases have no schema. The contents may be vastly different from one another in type, size, domain, and so on. It is the client, the application that uses the database, that is required to know about the value (what it is and the context in which it can be used). The database merely stores it using a key, knows the key/value pair, and serves the value when requested using its key.

Key/value stores are great for things like contents of a website shopping cart, user preference lists, a post in a social media site. Think of things that are not vital, things that may be useful but that will not cause problems if lost. You would not want to use this for credit card information, personal identification, health records, and such. You would want it for high-traffic sites that need to make sure that a local user has quick and accurate access to the information, but where the information can take time to replicate to other database nodes or which might not require replication across nodes at all, where there is heavy access to the database itself, but where users are not necessarily using the same data concurrently.

Berkeley DB

Berkeley DB was originally created at the University of California, Berkeley, to create a disk hash table that worked better than an existing solution while also helping the university clean up its free UNIX version called BSD by removing code inherited from AT&T. Several years later, Netscape asked the developers to add some desired features to make Berkeley DB more useful to them. This resulted in spinning off Berkeley DB from the university to a company founded for this purpose called Sleepycat Software, which headed development for many years. As of the purchase of Sleepycat Software in 2006, Berkeley DB is now owned by Oracle.

Although it is listed under key/value stores, this is not the only way to interact with a Berkeley DB database. Support also exists for using SQL and Java. Interaction is accomplished using an *application programming interface (API)*. Berkeley DB is very fast and very small. As a result, it can be found running on large-scale systems and embedded within applications and even running on mobile devices.

Berkeley DB is easily the most mature database mentioned in this chapter and is most notable for its use within many well known software projects including Subversion, Postfix, OpenLDAP, and was even included as a data storage backend for MySQL prior to MySQL 5.1.

Cassandra

Cassandra was developed by Facebook for their Inbox searching feature. It was released open source when they turned it over to Apache in 2008. Cassandra is a key/value store that runs on a flexible cluster of nodes and is also a wide column store, like HBase discussed later in the "Wide Column Store" section. Nodes may be added and removed from the cluster. Data is replicated across multiple nodes of the cluster. There is no central node, access to data exists from any node; if the node receiving the request does not house the specific data requested, it still services the request by retrieving and sending the data. The main goal of Cassandra is fast retrieval of data with fault tolerance being handled through replication across nodes and speed adjustments via adding additional nodes to create more access points.

One interesting feature is that Cassandra may be tuned to adjust the trade-off between speed of transactions and consistency of data. When data is stored, it is initially stored in memory and gets sent to disk only when specific criteria are met. This makes interaction very quick. In fact, not all data stored in Cassandra is designed to persist over time, and data may not get written to disk at all. This means that not all readers or seekers of data may find a specific piece, but in cases like Facebook's need to store Inbox search data that only has limited time value (like search results, that could be different tomorrow or even ten minutes from now), this may not matter at all. In these cases, both access speed and convenience are more important.

Cassandra is being used by Facebook, Twitter, Reddit, and many others.

Memcached and MemcacheDB

Memcached stores data requested on a system in RAM for a specific period of time to make retrieving that data faster if it is requested again. The time that data persists can be based on a specific setting, memory needs, and other criteria. The goal is to reduce the number of times that data stores must be accessed. Data that is accessed often is held in memory, from where it is much more quickly retrieved. This can alleviate problems such as a page on a blog that has suddenly become popular as a result of the URL being posted on a social networking site. The spike in traffic could be kept manageable because the content of the blog post is being held in memory instead of being requested over and over from the database.

MemcacheDB is an implementation of the Memcached API that uses a key/value format based on Berkeley DB. However, where Memcached is designed as a cache solution to speed up data access from memory, MemcacheDB is designed as a persistent storage engine. Because it uses the same API protocol as Memcached, it is an easy way to add data persistence where caching is already in place with Memcached.

Memcached is used by sites like Twitter, Reddit, YouTube, and Facebook, and is also supported and often used by websites based on content management systems like Drupal and WordPress.

Redis

Initially released in 2009, Redis is intended for applications where performance and flexibility are more important than persistence and absolute data integrity. It is an open-source key/value store written in C. Keys can contain strings, hashes, lists, sets, and stored sets. Redis works in RAM for speed, occasionally dumping to disk. Because actions are performed in memory, they are done faster. Operations include appending to a string, incrementing a hash value, pushing to a list, set computations, and more. Redis is also designed so that master-slave replication is easy to set up.

29

Document Stores

Document stores are designed to store data that is already structured in some form of notation like JSON or XML. They typically focus on one specific type of notation and are intended to allow entire objects, including arrays and hashes, to be stored and retrieved at once.

Many times document stores are implemented as a layer between an application and a relational database to hold the output of certain types of queries. For example, it may be convenient to aggregate information that is typically requested together such as a set of user preferences or name and address information and store it as one object. Requesting and retrieving only one object that is already formatted in an object notation like JSON is faster than making many database queries and supplies per-formatted data for the client application that can be used to both style output and display specific data at the same time.

Data that is stored and served this way does not have to fit database-specific formatting requirements in a NoSQL database. There are no tables to relate and data may be larger or smaller and include more or less information. This is generally called semistructured data. Here is a quick snippet of two sets of user preferences in JSON—one that includes many user-set preferences (see Listing 29.1) and one that includes only one (see Listing 29.2). The client application could be created to assume a set of default preferences that will be used unless specifically overridden by this file.

LISTING 29.1   Heather's Preferences

```
{"userpreferences": {
    "displayName": "Don'tHitOnMe",
    "gender":"DoNotDisplay",
    "siteTheme":"Springtime",
    "postsDisplayed":"25",
    "keepLoggedIn":"True"
    }
}
```

LISTING 29.2   Matthew's Preferences

```
{"userpreferences": {
    "siteTheme":"TieDye",
    }
}
```

CouchDB

CouchDB began in 2005 as a self-funded personal project of Damien Katz. In 2008, it was given to Apache, where development continues. The goal of CouchDB is to provide a database useful for serving web applications. The emphasis is on scalability and fault toler-ance while using commodity hardware (*Couch* is an acronym for cluster of unreliable commodity hardware). This is not an easy task, but when done successfully, it lowers costs.

CouchDB uses a RESTful HTTP API that is designed from the beginning to be used on and for the web. All stored items have a unique *uniform resource identifier (URI)* and full *create, read, update, and delete (CRUD)* functions are available directly using standard HTTP calls, making CouchDB very easy to integrate into web applications. These calls can be made from a browser or from a command line using a tool like cURL, which is available on many typical server platforms, including Ubuntu.

A nice feature of CouchDB is that is designed with the ability to include ACID compli-ance, unlike many NoSQL options. This makes it possible to use CouchDB with more consistency-sensitive data.

CouchDB is written in Erlang, which is a language designed for concurrency. That makes CouchDB even better suited for use in a concurrent distributed system. CouchDB is designed to store JSON document objects.

CouchDB is used by several software and web applications, including many Facebook games and applications, internal use at the BBC, and Ubuntu One, Canonical's cloud storage.

MongoDB

MongoDB is similar to CouchDB in that both are designed as document stores for JSON objects and, like Cassandra, is designed for replication and high-availability. It is created and supported by a company called 10gen and is newer, with its first public release in 2009. A unique feature for this open source database is that the developer offers commer-cial, enterprise-class support, training, and consulting. This has made adoption of MongoDB much faster than is typical for NoSQL products.

MongoDB supports sharding, which automatically partitions data across servers for increased performance and scalability. This produces a form of load and data balancing and also offers a way to add nodes simply. Sharding is also intended to support an auto-matic failover system where node data is replicated allowing no single point of failure.

In addition, MongoDB includes support for indexing in a manner that is more extensive and powerful than most NoSQL solutions.

29

Marketing Hype or Great Design?

MongoDB wasn't designed in a lab. We built MongoDB from our own experiences build-ing large-scale, high-availability, robust systems. We didn't start from scratch; we really tried to figure out what was broken, and tackle that. So, the way I think about MongoDB is that if you take MySQL, and change the data model from relational to document based, you get a lot of great features: embedded docs for speed, manageability, agile development with schema-less databases, easier horizontal scalability because joins aren't as important. There are lots of things that work great in relational databases: indexes, dynamic queries, and updates, to name a few; and we haven't changed much there. For example, the way you design your indexes in MongoDB should be exactly the way you do it in MySql or Oracle; you just have the option of indexing an embedded field.

—Eliot Horowitz, 10gen CTO and co-founder

Obviously, the people behind MongoDB are good at marketing. At the same time, if you listen closely to the crowd, you don't hear many negative comments about MongoDB and they have an impressive list of users including Craigslist, Shutterfly, SourceForge, the *New York Times*, and GitHub. They have quickly garnered great respect and constantly spreading use.

BaseX

BaseX was started by Chrisian Grün at the University of Knostanz in 2005 and was subsequently released using a BSD license in 2007. It is a simple, lightweight database that does not support a lot of features, but which could be just right for specific applications. Rather than using JSON like CouchDB and MongoDB, BaseX is designed to store document objects in XML. It supports standard XML tools like XPath and Xquery and also includes a lightweight GUI.

BaseX creates indexes, supports W3C recommendations and standards, ACID-safe transactions, large documents, and various APIs like REST/JAX-RX and XML:DB. Although not as sexy or well known as other options in this section, perhaps because of the newness and popularity of JSON over XML, BaseX is respected and used by many universities and enterprises.

Wide Column Stores

Wide column stores are often referred to as big table stores, after one of the best-known examples: Google's BigTable. Typically, a relational database reads data from tables using rows. Data is then sorted to find only those contents of a row that are needed. Wide column stores change the system by reading data from tables in columns, selecting the attributes first before reading in data. This is more efficient for input and output read-only queries. This means that wide column stores tend to be very efficient for databases that are mostly used for reading stored data, especially from very large data sets.

Wide column stores use something like tables, with a defined schema for each table. Unlike relational databases, wide column stores do not record relationships between tables. These are not relational databases, but are more like maps that show where data exists across multiple dimensions. They are designed for scalability and as distributed systems.

Two examples of wide column stores are discussed here. One more, Cassandra, was discussed earlier in this chapter as fits into both this category and the earlier key/value stores category.

BigTable

BigTable is a proprietary Google product that is only used by Google. It is designed to work with Google's MapReduce framework, which was created to process huge data sets across large clusters of computing nodes.

BigTable stores the massive sets of data used by many Google programs like Google Reader, My Search History, Google Earth, YouTube, and Gmail. BigTable is not available for use outside of Google.

The papers that describe Google's design for both BigTable and MapReduce are listed in the "References" section of this chapter.

HBase

HBase is the database used by Hadoop. Hadoop is the Apache Project's free software application for processing huge amounts of data across large clusters of compute nodes in a cluster. Hadoop is modeled in part after the information in Google's MapReduce and Google File System papers. HBase is to BigTable what Hadoop is to MapReduce.

The main feature of HBase is its ability to host very large tables, on the scale of billions of rows across millions of columns. It is designed to do so on commodity hardware. HBase provides a RESTful web service interface that supports many formats and encodings and is optimized for real time queries.

Numerous companies are using Hadoop, including some very big names like Amazon, eBay, Facebook, IBM, LinkedIn, Rackspace, and Yahoo!

References

▶ **http://www.oracle.com/us/products/database/berkeley-db/index.html**—The main Berkeley DB website.

▶ **http://cassandra.apache.org/**—The main website for Cassandra.

▶ **http://www.memcached.org/**—The main website for Memcached.

▶ **http://memcachedb.org/**—The main website for MemcacheDB.

▶ **http://redis.io/**—The main website for Redis.

▶ **http://couchdb.apache.org/**—The main website for CouchDB.

▶ **http://mongodb..org/**—The main website for MongoDB.

▶ **http://basex.org/**—The main website for BaseX.

29

▶ **http://labs.google.com/papers/bigtable.html**—The paper describing BigTable.

▶ **http://labs.google.com/papers/mapreduce.html**—The paper describing MapReduce.

▶ **http://hadoop.apache.org/**—The main website for Hadoop.

▶ **http://hbase.apache.org/**—The main website for Hbase, the Hadoop database.

▶ **http://labs.google.com/papers/gfs.html**—The paper describing Google File System.

CHAPTER 30

Lightweight Directory Access Protocol (LDAP)

The *Lightweight Directory Access Protocol* (*LDAP*, pronounced ell-dap) is one of those technologies that, although hidden, forms part of the core infrastructure in enterprise computing. Its job is simple: It stores information about users. However, its power comes from the fact that it can be linked into dozens of other services. LDAP can power login authentication, public key distribution, email routing, and address verification; more recently, it has formed the core of the push toward single sign-on technology.

> **TIP**
>
> Most people find the concept of LDAP easier to grasp when they think of it as a highly specialized form of database server. Behind the scenes, Ubuntu uses a database for storing all its LDAP information; however, LDAP does not offer anything as straightforward as SQL for data manipulation.
>
> OpenLDAP uses Sleepycat Software's *Berkeley DB (BDB)*, and sticking with that default is highly recommended. However, alternatives exist if you have specific needs.

This chapter looks at a relatively basic installation of an LDAP server, including how to host a companywide directory service that contains the names and email addresses of employees. LDAP is a client/server system, meaning that an LDAP server hosts the data and an LDAP client queries it. Ubuntu comes with OpenLDAP as its LDAP server, along with several LDAP-enabled email clients, including Evolution and Mozilla Thunderbird. We cover all three of these applications in this chapter.

Because LDAP data is usually available over the Internet—or at least your local network—it is imperative that you make every effort to secure your server. This chapter gives specific instruction on password configuration for OpenLDAP, and we recommend that you follow the instructions closely.

Configuring the Server

If you have been using LDAP for years, you will be aware of its immense power and flexibility. But, if you are just trying LDAP for the first time, it will seem like the most broken component you could imagine. LDAP has specific configuration requirements, is vastly lacking in graphical tools, and has a large number of acronyms to remember. On the bright side, all the hard work you put in is worth it because when it works, LDAP improves your networking experience immensely. You should read the entire chapter and understand it before you start. Then, read the README file in /etc/ldap/schema before you do anything.

The first step in configuring your LDAP server is to install the client and server applications. Install the slapd and ldap-utils packages from the Ubuntu repositories. Doing so also installs three other packages: odbcinst, odbcinstdebian2, and unixodbc.

By default, Ubuntu configures slapd with the minimum options necessary to run the daemon. We are going to configure everything from that bare-bones installation up to where it will be useful.

Now we need to know the *fully qualified domain name (FQDN)* of your server. In a moment, we will begin to write/modify some configuration files, and this will be a vital part of that process. Let's use matthewhelmke.com. Whenever you see this, change it to your FQDN.

From the FQDN, we acquire our domain component, which is the name of your domain as stored in DNS. This is abbreviated as dc. LDAP considers each part of a domain name (separated by a dot) to be domain components. In our example, there are two dc items: matthewhelmke and com.

OpenLDAP now uses a separate directory containing the cn=config *Directory Information Tree (DIT)* to configure the slapd daemon dynamically. This allows for modifying schema definitions, indexes, and so on without stopping and restarting the service, as was required in earlier versions. Two files are needed for this configuration: a back end that has only a minimal configuration, and a front end that uses a traditional format that is compatible with and accessed by external programs using established standards.

Creating Your Schema

We will start by loading some premade schema files. This makes configuration faster and easier by preloading some settings. If you are building an enterprise server, read the official OpenLDAP documentation and start from scratch so that you know precisely what everything on your server is doing and why. For our example, load these three files into the directory using these commands:

```
matthew@seymour:~$ sudo ldapadd -Y EXTERNAL -H ldapi:/// -f
/etc/ldap/schema/cosine.ldif
matthew@seymour:~$ sudo ldapadd -Y EXTERNAL -H ldapi:/// -f
/etc/ldap/schema/nis.ldif
matthew@seymour:~$ sudo ldapadd -Y EXTERNAL -H ldapi:/// -f
/etc/ldap/schema/inetorgperson.ldif
```

Next, we create a file called backend.matthewhelmke.com.ldif with these contents:

```
# Load dynamic backend modules
dn: cn=module,cn=config
objectClass: olcModuleList
cn: module
olcModulepath: /usr/lib/ldap
olcModuleload: back_hdb

# Database settings
dn: olcDatabase=hdb,cn=config
objectClass: olcDatabaseConfig
objectClass: olcHdbConfig
olcDatabase: {1}hdb
olcSuffix: dc=matthewhelmke,dc=com
olcDbDirectory: /var/lib/ldap
olcRootDN: cn=admin,dc=matthewhelmke,dc=com
olcRootPW: changeMEtoSOMETHINGbetter
olcDbConfig: set_cachesize 0 2097152 0
olcDbConfig: set_lk_max_objects 1500
olcDbConfig: set_lk_max_locks 1500
olcDbConfig: set_lk_max_lockers 1500
olcDbIndex: objectClass eq
olcLastMod: TRUE
olcDbCheckpoint: 512 30
olcAccess: to attrs=userPassword by dn="cn=admin,dc=matthewhelmke,dc=com" write by
anonymous auth by self write by * none
olcAccess: to attrs=shadowLastChange by self write by * read
olcAccess: to dn.base="" by * read
olcAccess: to * by dn="cn=admin,dc=matthewhelmke,dc=com" write by * read
```

Make sure you change all instances of matthewhelmke and com to fit your FQDN and change the entry for olcRootPW to a more secure password of your choosing. Then, add the new file to the directory (I am assuming you are entering this command from the directory where the file was created):

```
$ sudo ldapadd -Y EXTERNAL -H ldapi:/// -f backend.example.com.ldif
```

Populating Your Directory

The back end is ready. Now we need to populate the front-end directory to make this useful. Create another file called `frontend.matthewhelmke.com.ldif` with the following contents:

```
# Create top-level object in domain
dn: dc=matthewhelmke,dc=com
objectClass: top
objectClass: dcObject
objectclass: organization
o: Example Organization
dc: Example
description: LDAP Example

# Admin user.
dn: cn=admin,dc=matthewhelmke,dc=com
objectClass: simpleSecurityObject
objectClass: organizationalRole
cn: admin
description: LDAP administrator
userPassword: changeMEtoSOMETHINGbetter

dn: ou=people,dc=example,dc=com
objectClass: organizationalUnit
ou: people

dn: ou=groups,dc=matthewhelmke,dc=com
objectClass: organizationalUnit
ou: groups

dn: uid=john,ou=people,dc=matthewhelmke,dc=com
objectClass: inetOrgPerson
objectClass: posixAccount
objectClass: shadowAccount
uid: matthew
sn: Helmke
givenName: Matthew
cn: Matthew Helmke
displayName: Matthew Helmke
uidNumber: 1000
gidNumber: 10000
userPassword: changeMEtoSOMETHINGbetter
gecos: Matthew Helmke
```

```
loginShell: /bin/bash
homeDirectory: /home/matthew
shadowExpire: -1
shadowFlag: 0
shadowWarning: 7
shadowMin: 8
shadowMax: 999999
shadowLastChange: 10877
mail: matthew@matthewhelmke.com
postalCode: 85711
l: Tucson
o: Example
mobile: +1 (520) xxx-xxxx
homePhone: +1 (520) xxx-xxxx
title: System Administrator
postalAddress: I'm not putting it in the book.
initials: MH

dn: cn=example,ou=groups,dc=example,dc=com
objectClass: posixGroup
cn: example
gidNumber: 10000
```

Remember to change the details to fit your information. Then, we add this to the LDAP directory:

```
matthew@seymour:~$ sudo ldapadd -x -D cn=admin,dc=example,dc=com -W -f
frontend.example.com.ldif
```

To check that our content has been added to the LDAP directory correctly, we can use ldapsearch, as follows:

```
matthew@seymour:~$ ldapsearch -xLLL -b "dc=example,dc=com" uid=john sn givenName cn

dn: uid=matthew,ou=people,dc=matthewhelmke,dc=com
cn: Matthew Helmke
sn: Helmke
givenName: Matthew
```

In this example, dn stands for distinguished name, uid refers to user identification, ou tells us the organizational unit, dc represents domain component, cn is common name, sn is the family or surname, and many cultures know givenName as your first name.

When you use LDAP, you can organize your data in many ways. You can use a number of currently existing schemas, such as in the previous example using the LDIF files we loaded at the start, or you can write your own. The /etc/ldap/schemas directory has many fine

30

examples in the files with a .schema suffix and a few that have been converted to LDIF format. To be used, the file must be in the *LDAP Data Interchange Format* (*LDIF*, or when used as a file suffix, .ldif). You can convert one of the example schemas or create your own schema.

Configuring Clients

Although Ubuntu comes with a selection of email clients, there is not enough room here to cover them all. So, we discuss the two most frequently used clients: Evolution, the default; and Thunderbird. Both are powerful messaging solutions and so both work well with LDAP. Of the two, Thunderbird seems to be the easier to configure. We have had various problems with Evolution in the past in situations where Thunderbird has worked the first time.

Evolution

To configure Evolution for LDAP, click the arrow next to the New button and select Address Book. A new screen appears; its first option prompts you for the type of address book to create. Select On LDAP Servers.

For Name, just enter **Address book**, and for Server, enter the IP address of your LDAP server (or **127.0.0.1** if you are working on the server), as shown in Figure 30.1. Leave the port as 389, which is the default for slapd. Switch to the Details tab, and set Search Base to be the entire DN for your address book (for example, ou=People,dc=matthewhelmke, dc=com). Set Search Scope to be Sub so that Evolution will perform a comprehensive search. To finish, click Add Address Book.

Thunderbird

Thunderbird is a little easier to configure than Evolution and tends to work better, particularly with entries that have multiple CNs. To enable, go to the Edit menu, click Preferences, and then select Composition from the tabs along the top.

From the Addressing subtab, check the Directory Server box and click the Edit Directories button to its right. From the dialog box that appears, click Add to add a new directory. You can give it any name you want because this is merely for display purposes. As shown in Figure 30.2, set the Hostname field to be the IP address of your LDAP server (or 127.0.0.1 if you are working on the server). Set the Base DN to be the DN for your address book (for instance, ou=People,dc=matthewhelmke,dc=com), and leave the port number as 389. Click OK three times to get back to the main interface.

Administration

After you have your LDAP server and clients set up, they require little maintenance until something changes externally. Specifically, if someone in your directory changes jobs, changes her phone number, gets married (changing her last name [surname]), quits, or so forth, you need to be able to update your directory to reflect the change.

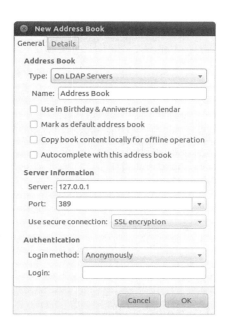

FIGURE 30.1   Configuring Evolution to use LDAP for addresses is easy for anonymous connections.

FIGURE 30.2   Thunderbird's options are buried deeper than Evolution's, but it does allow you to download the LDAP directory for offline use.

We installed some useful utilities with the ldap-utils package earlier. Here are what they do. Each one requires administration privileges, so use sudo:

▶ **ldapsearch**—Opens a connection to an LDAP server and searches its directory for requested information.

▶ **ldapmodify**—Opens a connection to an LDAP server and allows you to add or modify entries.

▶ **ldapadd**—Opens a connection to an LDAP server and allows you to add an entry.

▶ **ldapdelete**—Opens a connection to an LDAP server and allows you to delete one or more entries.

None of these are simple to use, but all come with moderate amounts of documentation in their man pages.

A much smarter option is to use phpLDAPadmin, which is an LDAP administration tool that allows you to add and modify entries entirely through your web browser. The program is available in the Ubuntu software repositories as `phpldapadmin`.

Starting, stopping, or restarting the `slapd` daemon is done in the usual way for system daemons (that do not yet have Upstart methods written for them):

```
sudo /etc/init.d/slapd start/stop/restart
```

References

▶ **www.openldap.org**—The home page of the OpenLDAP project where you can download the latest version of the software and meet other users.

▶ **http://ldap.perl.org/**—The home of the Perl library for interacting with LDAP provides comprehensive documentation to get you started.

▶ **www.ldapguru.com/**—A gigantic portal for LDAP administrators around the world. From forums dedicated to LDAP to jobs specifically for LDAP admins, this site could very well be all you need.

▶ **https://help.ubuntu.com/10.10/serverguide/C/openldap-server.html**—Official Ubuntu Server documentation for OpenLDAP.

▶ **http://phpldapadmin.sourceforge.net/**—The official documentation for phpLDAPadmin.

▶ The definitive book on LDAP is *LDAP System Administration* (O'Reilly), ISBN: 1-56592-491-6. It is an absolute must for the bookshelf of any Linux LDAP administrator. For more general reading, try *LDAP Directories Explained* (Addison-Wesley), ISBN: 0-201-78792-X. It has a much stronger focus on the Microsoft Active Directory LDAP implementation, however.

# CHAPTER 31

Linux Terminal Server Project (LTSP)

The *Linux Terminal Server Project* (LTSP) is an add-on package for Linux that enables you to run multiple thin clients, low-powered terminals, from one main server. A *thin client* is a small, energy-efficient, and generally lower-powered system designed to be used in conjunction with a more powerful server. The thin client will have limited processing power and speed and limited storage, making it very inexpensive. All it is used for is receiving input from a device such as a keyboard or mouse, communicating with a server, and displaying output to a screen.

Processing of information and the actual running of programs are offloaded to the server, meaning the server does all the hard work and is the only system in the network that has strong requirements for processor power and speed, memory, storage, and so on. Thin clients are also generally smaller in size and quieter, which also make them more convenient to use when space and noise are potential issues. Those of us who have been around longer or who have worked in enterprise environments will see an immediate relationship to big metal servers and dumb client terminals, and it is reasonable to think of an LTSP setup this way. In our case, the server isn't as big or as powerful, and the thin clients aren't as dumb and weak, but the idea is the same.

Thin clients are great in places such as classrooms and computer labs where strict control and strong security are desirable, where money for a room of full-powered systems may not be available, and where installing and maintaining core software on one server is preferable to doing so on many systems. For this reason, Edubuntu, a community led official subproject of Ubuntu, is designed for easy LTSP installation and configuration. We focus on using LTSP with standard Ubuntu, but if you want to use LTSP in an education-specific context, or if you just want an additional perspective and more information about LTSP, Edubuntu is worth a closer look. Other common places you are likely to find thin clients in use are libraries for catalog access and searches and in some airports that make courtesy terminals for checking email available for travelers.

Links to several thin client hardware sources are included in the "References" section of this chapter, although they are included to inform and should not be taken as endorsements. (We don't own and have not used equipment from every company listed and can't make any honest recommendations about them.) In addition to those mentioned, you are sure to find others. In fact, computers that often make excellent thin clients are not advertised as such. You can look for compact format systems that use an ARM, VIA, or maybe an Intel Atom processor, for example, and are likely to find that they make wonderful thin clients. You can even recycle older hardware that would otherwise be bound for the trash can and make it useful again as a thin client.

Now that you have a sense of why you might use LTSP and how the network is created, it is a good time to fill you in on some of the details of what LTSP is, what it is not, and how it is designed to work. Armed with this knowledge, you will be able to find documentation to help you decide what you can afford to buy, how you want to configure it, and even whether this is a configuration that is applicable and useful to your situation.

LTSP is add-on software for Linux that creates a server that can be used to boot client computers over a network. It allows them to access and run applications on the server while the client remains responsible for input and display and the server handles processing data and storage. This allows many inexpensive hardware clients to be used to do things that would normally be beyond the capability of the hardware and streamlines administration by placing all the configuration and software on one server. The biggest limitations result from server and networking hardware (for example, switch or hub, 1GB versus 100MB ports, high-end server and storage or less-expensive just-adequate equipment).

Requirements

Our minimum recommended specifications for thin clients are a processor running at 400MHz with 128MB RAM and the ability to boot via PXE (a common network boot protocol). Nearly any system sold today and advertised as a thin client exceeds these requirements by a wide margin. We list them here in case you want to try to reuse old hardware that is otherwise obsolete. Server and other hardware recommendations are listed in the "Installation" section.

Let's start by looking at several wiring schemes to show appropriate methods of using LTSP. The first one, shown in Figure 31.1, is the default install without an Internet connection and is the simplest way to use LTSP.

From the diagram alone, you can see the main pieces of hardware needed: a server, a switch/hub, and a number of thin clients. The switch/hub is the first piece of hardware we discuss.

31

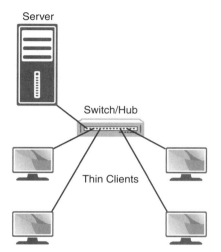

FIGURE 31.1   A default LTSP install without an Internet connection.

For simplicity, we only show four thin clients in each example, but this is not an actual limit. The number of thin clients is limited by your switch/hub, and even an inexpensive hub will support four connections, although it is common for quality enterprise-grade switches to have 48 or more ports. A switch is generally faster and more expensive than a hub and is often preferable for reasons beyond the scope of this chapter, but they both serve the same basic purpose and either can work in an LTSP setting. They are used to control traffic on a network and make sure that communication happens between computers as it is intended.

Ideally, you want a piece of hardware here that will support a GB connection between the server and a switch, with at least 100MB connections between the thin clients and the switch, and enough unused communication ports to make future expansion easy without requiring the addition of another switch or hub and layer of complexity. If money is an issue and ideal performance isn't vital, an inexpensive hub that only had 100MB ports all around and just enough ports to connect everything will certainly work. If you are connecting more than 10 clients to the server, a gigabyte connection to the server is strongly recommended. Life is full of trade-offs and money supplies are not limitless, so use your best judgment and buy the best you can afford.

For the server, recommended specifications depend greatly on the intended use. If every-one will be using the same program on each client, you do not need as much memory and processor speed as you would if everyone is doing different things at the same time. You can easily run LTSP server on a repurposed old machine you have sitting around with 512MB RAM, a 1GHz Celeron processor, and a decent, working hard drive, and it will work, but we don't really recommend that if you are going to have more than a couple of clients doing anything beyond simple and identical tasks.

Our minimum recommendation is the same as the current recommendation for a minimum Ubuntu desktop installation: a 1GHz x 86 processor, 1GB RAM, a 15GB hard drive. At least a 100MB Ethernet card is vital. Ideally, you would bump each category up to the highest level you can afford and expect better performance as a result. Our minimum-if-you-want-a-great-experience recommendation is a current-issue fast-as-you-can-afford multicore 64-bit processor, 4GB RAM, at least two fast hard drives in a RAID array for performance and data backup, and at least one and perhaps two gigabyte Ethernet cards.

Most of the time you use LTSP you will want the network to be connected to the Internet. There are two main ways to do this. Figure 31.2 shows the network with an Internet connection via an Internet router connected to the switch/hub. This is a common method and will work well.

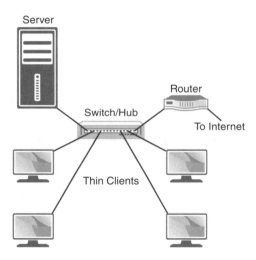

FIGURE 31.2   A typical LTSP install with an Internet connection via an Internet router.

Another common method is to connect the server directly to the Internet router, as in Figure 31.3. This has the benefit of allowing you to easily configure and use the server as a gateway to control thin client access to the Internet. To do this, the server must have two network cards, and we again recommend that the one used to connect to the switch is a 1GB card; all the thin client traffic has to travel between the switch and server over that one connection, so this will cause fewer bottlenecks than if you have multiple clients connecting to a switch at 100MB trying to share a single 100MB connection to a server. The card from the server to the Internet router should be adequate for the Internet connection available, but there is no reason to put anything faster in there. If you have only a 100MB connection with your Internet service provider, using a 1GB card will not give any particular benefit.

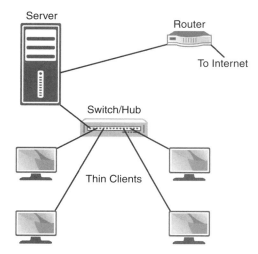

Server

Router

To Internet

Switch/Hub

Thin Clients

FIGURE 31.3 Using a server with two Ethernet cards as a portal to the Internet.

Installation

After you decide how you want to set up your network and connect all the hardware, you can get to the task of installing the software. In Ubuntu, the LTSP software is available for installation in two ways. If you are repurposing a server that already has a current release of Ubuntu installed on it, you install the ltsp-server-standalone and openssh-server packages from the Ubuntu repositories and run the following to set up the environment:

matthew@seymour:~$ **sudo ltsp-build-client**

If your server is a 64-bit system and your thin clients use a different processor architecture, you want to run that command with the −arch option, as follows:

matthew@seymour:~$ **sudo ltsp-build-client --arch i386**

Most people will be installing from scratch and not reusing a system with Ubuntu already installed. This is still quite easy. You must download the alternate install CD from the Ubuntu website at http://releases.ubuntu.com/. From here, find the release version of Ubuntu you want to use for the server. Some will want the current release (at this writing, 11.10), and some will want to use an LTS release like 10.04 LTS. Click the release version you want to use and then find the link for the alternate install CD for your server's processor architecture, either 32-bit or the 64-bit. Download it and burn the image to a CD, as discussed in Chapter 1, "Installing Ubuntu."

Make sure all your thin clients are connected and set to boot from network using PXE, but turned off. Then boot the server using the alternate CD, press F4 for the modes menu, and choose Install an LTSP Server. A regular Ubuntu installation will begin. Near the end of the installation, a message appears that lets you know the thin client system is being built on the server. You are notified that it is being compressed into an image, and when the process is complete, you reboot your server, removing the CD at the appropriate moment in the process.

After the server has rebooted and is running, you may turn on your thin clients and they will boot from the network using the image on the server. Thin clients can run any programs installed on the server.

Using LTSP

When you boot a thin client in an LTSP network, it retrieves the boot image from the LTSP server and uses it to create the environment to be displayed to the user. The process includes using *Dynamic Host Control Protocol (DHCP)* to request from and assign to the client an IP address on the network, downloading the kernel and initial RAM disk from the server, downloading the LTSP configuration and mounting the server-hosted file system, using chroot to use this file system as the client's own root file system, and then finishing the boot using the instructions in that file system. This is a highly configurable process. By default the client boots to a login screen using the *LTSP Display Manager (LDM)* in place of GDM that is used by Ubuntu, KDM that is used by Kubuntu, or others. User accounts are used to limit or control access, and the LDM initializes the details for communication between the server and client, including launching the desktop, mounting storage devices and /home directories, and creating menu items. The entire desktop is run on the server and displayed on the client.

By default, LTSP uses inherent abilities in Linux but has configured them to work together smoothly. Details may be modified to suit your needs. For example, communication between an application server and a client is done by tunneling an X11 session over ssh, making the sharing of a graphical desktop easy and using a standard method while also being a secure method of communicating user credentials.

One really useful feature in LTSP is that you are not limited to using only one server in a network. If your network of thin clients grows to a point where your current server is being taxed, there is an easy way to configure and add a second or multiple servers to the network to share the load. In this case, the server that a thin client uses to boot is not necessarily the same server that a user will log in to. When you add servers, one server is chosen to be the primary server and controls thin client boots, data storage, and runs additional services. Additional, secondary servers can be much simpler because all they do is host desktop sessions and will be configured to use the central services from the primary server for everything else. In a multiple-server network, authentication of users is something that you need to think through and configure because it becomes a little more complex. There are many ways to do this, including the obvious choice: LDAP.

Creating and maintaining an LTSP network is very useful in specific situations and can be a cost-effective way of using administrator time while providing useful functionality to end users. Although the foundation sounds simple in this introductory chapter, it can be a complex task worthy of an entire book. Our intent with this chapter is to give enough information for you to determine whether LTSP is a technology that will suit your needs and is deserving of a closer look. To that end, we offer several useful links in the following section and suggest them as your next step.

References

- ▶ www.ltsp.org/—The official upstream LTSP website.

- ▶ https://help.ubuntu.com/community/UbuntuLTSP—The Ubuntu community documentation page is easily the best resource for LTSP because it includes an organized and up-to-date set of links to information on any aspect you should need.

- ▶ http://edubuntu.com/—The leaders of the Edubuntu community project are very knowledgeable about LTSP and helpful. This site is a great place to start when you are looking for people with experience to help you with questions.

- ▶ https://help.ubuntu.com/community/UbuntuLTSP/Tour—This gives an overview of the differences between a traditional LTSP installation and the Ubuntu community modifications to the process for ease of installation, software updates, and security.

- ▶ https://help.ubuntu.com/community/UbuntuLTSP/ThinClientHowtoNAT/—If you use the network design in Figure 23.3, this tells you how to configure your server so that your thin clients have access to the Internet.

- ▶ http://doc.ubuntu.com/edubuntu/edubuntu/handbook/C/—The Edubuntu Handbook provides one of the most clear and complete guides to setting up and using LTSP.

Here is a sampling of companies advertising thin clients:

- ▶ www.artecgroup.com/thincan

- ▶ www.chippc.com/thin-clients/thin-clients.asp

- ▶ www.devonit.com/hardware

- ▶ www.disklessworkstations.com/

- ▶ http://h10010.www1.hp.com/wwpc/us/en/sm/WF02d/12454-12454-321959.html

- ▶ www.lucidatech.com/

- ▶ www.wyse.com/products/hardware/thinclients/index.asp

# CHAPTER 32

Virtualization on Ubuntu

Virtualization is an important topic today, but it isn't a difficult one to understand, at least conceptually. We cover two distinct use cases in this chapter: server virtualization and virtualization on the desktop. Most of the options covered in this chapter work for either use case. In the sections that follow, this chapter points out specific moments that are focused solely on one use case. There are several scenarios, both large and small, that are helpful to illustrate the potential of virtualization and to give the idea some definition.

For starters, imagine a large corporation or business that processes huge amounts of data. That corporation will have many dedicated computers to assist with the task. In the past, they may have used mainframes, single computers capable of performing multiple tasks concurrently while dealing with large data sets and multiple, concurrent users. Today, the same company may use a server farm, a network of smaller computers that is extensible and which can have specific servers in the network dedicated to precise tasks.

The problem is that some of these servers do not get used to their capacity. Take, for example, a payroll server that may get extensive use at certain times, but which may sit nearly idle at other times. That seems like a waste of resources.

What if a systems administrator could pool the resources of all these machines and then dole out those resources as they are needed? She can by using virtualization.

At other times, there is a need for servers that do not exist and which will not be needed in the long term. A statistics department might have a one-time need for extra processing power for a big project. It would take a long time to set up a dedicated server, and it is hard to justify the effort for a one-time task.

What if a system administrator could easily create and destroy servers for a specific task, making them appear, completely configured, when needed and then disappearing when the need no longer exists, freeing up the physical resources for other uses? He can using by virtualization.

Networks of physical servers can be created using virtualization where the physical resources of each are pooled together and then passed out as designated by an administrator. It is as if, instead of having 10 servers, each with 4 processors, 8GB of RAM, and 100GB of physical disk storage, you now have one huge resource pool with 40 processors, 80GB of RAM, and 1TB of disk space. These resources can then be used by virtual machines.

A *virtual machine (VM)* is a computer that operates on top of a virtualization layer, often called a hypervisor. It isn't real in the sense that it runs on defined, discrete physical resources, but it does all of the same tasks as a "real" computer. The virtualization layer on which the VM runs defines a set of virtual interfaces for the VM, which appear to VM's operating system as if they were real network cards, memory, hard drives, and so on. In a sense, virtualization fools the guest operating system in the VM into thinking it is running on specific physical equipment that is emulated by the virtualization software while the virtualization software takes care of the details of interacting with the actual hardware, which may even change without affecting the VM. This is called *hardware emulation*, sometimes abbreviated to emulation.

Virtual machines are flexible; their allocated resources may be changed, in some cases without any downtime. A VM can be created quickly, as needed, and then removed when it is no longer needed, to make the resources it was using once again available to the pool. Servers that are vital, but generally use few resources can be created using far fewer resources than one of the physical servers in the pool. Others that are needed for larger tasks may be able to take advantage of the resources of many physical servers in the pool.

It is possible for VMs to be created and then have their image saved, so that instead of starting with operating system installation each time a VM is created, the VM starts up with a full operating system and installed programs all configured to work together for a desired task. One neat trick is to run a set of servers locally and then add compute resources from a cloud computing pool like Amazon's EC2, Ubuntu Enterprise Cloud (using Eucalyptus), Ubuntu Cloud Infrastructure (using OpenStack), or OpenStack to start up VMs on their network as needed, using them while paying for the time they are running, then deleting them (see Chapter 33, "Ubuntu in the Cloud"). This saves a lot of time and money.

Some readers may think, "That sounds great, but I run only one machine, and it is my desktop (or laptop)." Virtualization may be useful to you, as well. Have you ever wanted to test out a different operating system than the one you are using? Perhaps you found that you have a need to run a specific program that only runs on Windows, but you have Ubuntu installed on your system. Maybe you want to run the latest development version of Ubuntu to help with testing, but you don't want to use it as your main system operating system. You might want to try out another distribution of Linux or even BSD. In the past, doing these things might involve partitioning your hard drive and installing both operating systems side by side. That worked, but you couldn't easily move data from one to the other, and you couldn't run both operating systems at the same time. Wouldn't it be great if you could run another operating system as a guest on your same machine? You can with virtualization.

There is a trade-off with virtualization, depending on the software used. Some virtualization software runs as an additional layer on top of another operating system. This is great if you want to test something while running on your local desktop machine, but it can add some unwanted and sometimes unacceptable delays when creating a new server. Other virtualization software runs on or near "bare metal," meaning that the virtualization software is either a part of the operating system kernel or runs as the operating system and there are no other software layers between it and the physical resources being used/managed. This method is faster, but not as convenient on the desktop, at least for users who are not as technically advanced.

Virtualization is not new. For example, IBM had useful virtualization running on their mainframes in the 1960s. What has created the recent buzz is that the technology became available to perform the task on much less-expensive x86 hardware.

In November 2005, Intel released its first processors that supported an extension called VT-x, which allows virtualization software access to the processor and other hardware. Before this, virtualization on any x86 platform was slow because it required difficult software workarounds and massaging to get it working. VT-x is available on many of Intel's processors, but not necessarily all of them, as it is one of the ways that Intel differentiates the processors to segment their marketing across various price points. Also, with some motherboards, the extension is not enabled by default but must be enabled in the BIOS before it becomes available.

Following closely behind is AMD, who in May 2006 released virtualization extensions for their processors. Called AMD-V, these extensions are available on many of AMD's processors, but again, not all, as AMD also uses this feature to differentiate their offerings across price points in the market.

KVM

The *Kernel-based Virtual Machine (KVM)* is a part of the Linux kernel. KVM does not perform hardware emulation, but only provides the lower level tasks. It needs a second layer to run in user space. This is much faster than running the entire virtualization process in user space, on top of another operating system. KVM is designed for use on processors that have either the VT-x or AMD-V extension enabled. Managing VMs with KVM in Ubuntu is done using `libvert` and `QEMU`. You can check whether a system has the extensions enabled by installing and running the `kvm-ok` package. It is a simple command-line tool that exits with output `0` if the system is suitable or non-`0` if not.

Start by installing the following packages from the Ubuntu software repositories: qemu-kvm, libvert-bin, virtinst, and bridge-utils:

▶ qemu-kvm is the necessary user-space component of KVM.

▶ libvirt-bin is a binary of a C toolkit to interact with the virtualization capabilities of Linux and currently supports not only KVM, but also XEN, VirtualBox, and more.

▶ virtinst is a set of command line tools for creating VMs.

▶ bridge-utils is a set of utilities for configuring Ethernet connections in Linux.

You may want to add virt-viewer, which provides a nice GUI and VNC interface to VMs, and virt-manager, which provides a nice GUI for managing VMs. If installed, both can be found in the Dash listing of applications.

Log out and back in so that the automatic addition of your user to the libvertd group is certain to be made effective.

By default, any operating system you install as a guest using KVM will have access to network services but will not be visible to other machines on the network. It will be able to download software updates and browse the Web, for example, but cannot run as a server accessible by other systems. By default, VMs receive an IP address in the 10.0.2.0/24 range and hosts are reachable from within a VM using 10.0.2.2. This should be adequate for simple uses such as testing other operating systems, copying files back and forth using scp, or making *virtual private network (VPN)* connections from a host to a guest.

Bridged Networking

If you want to change the network settings to enable the use of a VM as an outside-accessible server, you need bridged networking. This will allow VMs to use a physical interface to connect to the outside network, making them appear to the rest of the network as any other typical server. Note that to do this, you must not use the default Network Manager to control the hardware being bridged. Also, this works only with wired, not wireless, hardware. See Chapter 17, "Networking," if you need help understanding the concepts used here.

To start, install libcap2-bin. Next, you need to grant QEMU the ability to administer networking by setting cap_net_admin. If you have a 64-bit system, use the following:

```
matthew@seymour:~$ sudo setcap cap_net_admin=ei /usr/bin/qemu-system-x86_64
```

And if you have a 32-bit system, use this:

```
matthew@seymour:~$ sudo setcap cap_net_admin=ei /usr/bin/qemu
```

Then, create a bridge interface called br0 in /etc/network/interfaces by adding these lines to use DHCP or your network settings if you want to configure it yourself:

```
auto br0
iface br0 inet dhcp
        bridge_ports eth0
        bridge_stp off
        bridge_fd 0
        bridge_maxwait 0
```

Restart networking by entering this:

```
matthew@seymour:~$ sudo /etc/init.d/networking restart
```

Finally, you need to create guest VMs that use this bridged network. Manually define your guest OS to use the new br0 interface, as you usually would in that operating system.

There are several ways to create VMs for use with KVM. One way is vmbuilder. This is a Python script that is best for servers on which you intend to run Ubuntu JeOS, a specialized, very light Ubuntu server variant that includes a tuned kernel with only the base elements necessary to run as a virtual server, especially under KVM and VMware. Install python-vm-builder to get the package. You run vmbuilder from the command line with two necessary parameters: the virtualization software, and the distribution you will run. However, there are literally tons of useful options and customizations available. Here is an example that builds a VM for KVM from the 11.04 (Natty Narwhal) release of Ubuntu using the virtual flavor (for example, JeOS) in an i386 architecture while overwriting any previous edition of the VM, instructing libvert to inform the local virtualization environment to add the resulting VM to the list of available virtual machines, give the new VM a specific IP address, the hostname lovelace, and to use the br0 bridge interface. Phew! That's a lot in one command:

```
matthew@seymour:~$ sudo vmbuilder kvm ubuntu --suite natty --flavour virtual
➥--arch i386
➥-o --libvirt qemu:///system --ip 192.168.0.100 --hostname lovelace --bridge br0
```

You can learn more from the help file:

```
matthew@seymour:~$ vmbuilder kvm ubuntu --help
```

Because vmbuilder is so specialized, we instead focus here on using the tools from virtinst as they are more likely to appeal to a general audience. However, if you are looking to create server VMs to run on a KVM or VMware installation, you definitely want to explore vmbuilder more fully. However, you might not need to do so. A set of official, prebuilt and Ubuntu-supported VM images are available for download at http://cloud-images.ubuntu.com. These are the exact images that Ubuntu uses in EC2.

NOTE

One of the Ubuntu Server developers, Dustin Kirkland, has a blog post outlining a method for preseeding Ubuntu Server installations, making the process even faster. You can read it at http://blog.dustinkirkland.com/2011/03/ubuntu-server-quick-install-no.html.

virtinst consists of several tools. Here we focus on two: virt-install, to provision new virtual machines; and virt-clone, to clone existing virtual machines.

You can do similar things with virt-install as was done earlier with vmbuilder. The major difference are the options available and that virt-install can also make desktop images that include a GUI, accessible using VNC. See Chapter 18, "Remote Access with SSH and Telnet," for a discussion of VNC.

Here is an example:

```
matthew@seymour:~$ sudo virt-install -n hopper -r 512 --disk
path=/var/lib/libvert/images/hopper.img,size=20 -c /dev/cdrom --accelerate --
connect=qemu:///system --vnc --noautoconsole -v
```

In the preceding example, we find the following options:

▶ -n hopper defines the name of the new VM.

▶ -r 512 specifies the amount of memory the virtual machine will be allotted, in megabytes.

▶ --disk path=... is the path to the virtual disk. It can be a file, a partition, or a logical volume. Here we create a 20GB file named hopper.img in /var/lib/libvert/images.

▶ -c /dev/cdrom is the path to the host's CD-ROM device. You can also use an ISO file.

▶ --accelerate enables use of the kernel's acceleration.

▶ --connect defines the hypervisor to use.

▶ --vnc exports the guest using a VNC virtual console.

▶ --noautoconsole prevents automatic connecting to the virtual machine's console.

▶ -v creates a fully virtualized guest.

To copy a virtual machine, use virt-clone:

```
matthew@seymour:~$ sudo virt-clone -o hopper -n knuth -f
/var/lib/libvert/images/knuth.img -connect=qemu:///system
```

In the preceding example, we find the following options:

▶ -o hopper defines the name of the origin or source VM.

▶ -n knuth defines the name of the new VM.

▶ -f defines the path to the file, partition, or logical volume that the new VM will use.

▶ --connect defines the hypervisor to use.

To start a virtual machine, use the following:

```
matthew@seymour:~$ virsh -c qemu:///system start hopper
```

To stop a virtual machine, use this:

matthew@seymour:~$ **virsh -c qemu:///system shutdown hopper**

Once a VM is installed and running, you can connect to it using the configured IP address and a utility like ssh. You can also use a GUI with the following:

matthew@seymour:~$ **virt-viewer -c qemu:///system hopper**

You may use a GUI to manage your VMs by connecting to the following:

matthew@seymour:~$ **virt-manager -c qemu:///system**

If you are interested in an easy way to use KVM to test Ubuntu development versions, see Chapter 35, "Helping with Ubuntu Testing and QA," and the discussion of Test Drive, which automates this entire process, including the downloading of specific Ubuntu ISO files.

VirtualBox

VirtualBox is much easier to use than KVM, especially if all you want to do is run a second operating system on top of Ubuntu. It was created by innotek GmbH, purchased by Sun Microsystems, and is now owned and developed by Oracle after their purchase of Sun. VirtualBox is installed on top of another operating system, so it isn't ideal for processing intensive activity where every processor cycle counts. However, for testing or for running another operating system because you need specific applications, it is great. VirtualBox will run on top of most UNIX-type operating systems like Linux, BSD, and Mac OS X (as well as on Windows).

There is a version of VirtualBox in the Ubuntu software repositories, but in general, downloading the one from the VirtualBox website is a better idea. Go to www.virtualbox.org/wiki/Downloads. From there, you can download a version for any operating system you are likely to use, including on the Linux page an Ubuntu DEB file that installs using the *Advanced Packing Tool (APT)*, so package management isn't a problem. However, this also gives you quick and easy access to download the extension pack, which isn't available in the Ubuntu repositories, and to get it installed quickly and easily. The extension pack adds a few nice, but proprietary, features that cannot be made available under the GPL used for the main program, such as the ability to connect to the USB port of a host computer from a guest VM in VirtualBox.

Once installed, start VirtualBox at the command line using the following:

matthew@seymour:~$ **virtualbox**

If you want to be able to close your terminal and keep VirtualBox running, run VirtualBox in the background by putting an ampersand (&) after the command, like this:

matthew@seymour:~$ **virtualbox &**

Either way, when you are done, just close the GUI program and VirtualBox will shut down. When you run either, the GUI appears (see Figure 32.1).

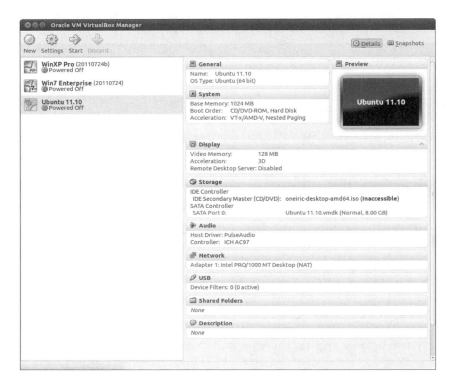

FIGURE 32.1   Oracle VM VirtualBox Manager.

From here, you can create a new VM by selecting New at the top left. Change the settings on any currently installed VM by selecting Settings. Start any installed VM by selecting Start. Delete any VM by selecting Discard. You can see details of the currently selected VM using Details at the upper right or your saved snapshots of existing VMs using Snapshots. Everything is configurable from the GUI. VirtualBox is easy and intuitive to use, even for a complete novice.

From the GUI, you can clone a machine, export it, and import it on another machine running VirtualBox. A command-line interface is available for scripting, focused on VM management activities. You can run VirtualBox headless and access it using *Remote Display Protocol (RDP)*. These activities are beyond the scope of this book but can make VirtualBox a little more interesting to someone who wants to run VMs remotely (although most who are going to go through the trouble would probably go ahead and use KVM and connect to a VM using VNC).

VMware

VMware is an enterprise-focused virtualization platform. They offer a limited-feature version that runs on the desktop for free and sell a full-featured version. It runs well, is easy to use, and has better features than VirtualBox. It also requires buying a new license each year, and the license isn't cheap. Their enterprise server offerings are considered by many to be the most powerful and well-featured in the business. The VMware software runs on bare metal; it is the operating system that gets installed on all the servers in a VMware installation. Then, all the resources are controlled from one central location. VMs can be moved while running from one physical machine to another in the system with no loss of usability and no downtime. This can even be done automatically based on administrator set criteria, such as bandwidth, available memory, or processor load. It is also quite expensive to license. VMware is primarily designed for use by large corporations in enterprise environments. It deserves a mention here, but is not really targeted toward the same audience as this book.

Xen

Xen is a well-known open-source virtualization platform. It is in widespread use by researchers, hobbyists, developers, and others. Web hosting companies that offer virtual servers often use Xen. Generally, Xen installs on bare metal, like VMware. It can be installed on top of another operating system in a host/guest arrangement. However, in 2008, Ubuntu made a decision not to support Xen. Instead, the Ubuntu community has focused its efforts on KVM. This is not a value statement that one is better than the other, but only that KVM seemed to be a better fit for the needs of an Ubuntu developer community that did not have the resources to give quality support to two similar virtualization platforms. It does appear possible to run Xen on Ubuntu, but there are no guarantees. For this reason, many choose to use one of the Linux distributions that use Xen as their primary virtualization platform, like SUSE, Red Hat, or CentOS, if Xen is preferred. At the time this book was being written, rumors began to surface that Ubuntu will once again support Xen in the near future, but no solid news was yet available.

References

- ▶ www.linux-kvm.org—The main page for KVM.

- ▶ www.virtualbox.org—The main page for VirtualBox.

- ▶ www.vmware.com—The main page for VMware.

- ▶ www.xen.org—The main page for Xen.

CHAPTER 33

Ubuntu in the Cloud

Cloud computing enables you to build large, flexible systems for on-demand processing of data. When your requirements are low, you use few resources. As the need arises, your processes scale to use multiple systems with optimized performance according to the requirements of the moment. This is an efficient way to use hardware and minimize waste.

To accomplish this feat of computer engineering, a special network is set up using on-demand virtual systems that consume resources only as needed and release those resources for use by others when they are not in use. Virtualization is the technology that enables this concept. This may be accomplished locally using third-party virtualization platforms such as VMware, VirtualBox, Parallels, and others (see Chapter 32, "Virtualization on Ubuntu"). Ubuntu has another option to offer, the Ubuntu Cloud, which moves virtualization into the cloud and is the main focus of this chapter. Beyond being an outstanding cloud hosting platform, Ubuntu Server is being developed with a strong intent to make it an outstanding cloud guest. Look for the term *Ubuntu Cloud Guest* to become more popular as time goes by.

SysAdmin vs. DevOps

The traditional title for someone who keeps systems up and running is systems *administrator*, or *sysadmin* (sometimes called *ops*, for *operations*). The traditional title for someone who creates the software that runs on those systems is software developer. Over the past few years, a new title has emerged, *DevOps*. *DevOps* combine many of the talents and responsibilities of sysadmins and developers, but often with a cloud computing environment focus and some specific refinements. They aren't purely one or the other and often don't fit neatly into other existing categories like engineer, but they do combine many of the skills of all of these while adding to it a QA-like focus on making sure that new features do not break anything that was working previously. DevOps are the ones who develop large applications to run on cloud resources while simplifying the orchestration of those resources with automation and configuration management. This chapter is not only for DevOps, but the chapter describes the sorts of tools and environments that these folks are likely to love.

Ubuntu Cloud, formerly *Ubuntu Enterprise Cloud (UEC)*, is a stack of applications from Canonical that are included in the Ubuntu Server Edition. These applications make it easy to install and configure an Ubuntu-based cloud. The software is free and open source, but Canonical offers paid technical support.

Ubuntu Cloud was originally based on Eucalyptus. Starting with Ubuntu 11.10, Ubuntu Cloud will be based on OpenStack. Both OpenStack and Eucalyptus are supported by Ubuntu and Canonical, and no plans have been announced to cease supporting Eucalyptus on any of the previous Ubuntu releases like 10.04 LTS, so it can be expected to be supported for several years, at a minimum until those releases reach end of life. However, the energy and buzz have moved to OpenStack. At the time of this writing, if you are going to create cloud deployments for any purpose other than testing or temporary use, you may want to consider doing so using Ubuntu 10.04 LTS for now. It will be supported on servers until April 2015, whereas 11.10 will be supported on servers for only 18 months, which means you will need to upgrade sooner. This chapter covers both Eucalyptus and OpenStack.

> **NOTE**
>
> *Ubuntu Enterprise Cloud (UEC)* is tied to 10.04 LTS and Eucalyptus. With the move to OpenStack starting with 11.10, the name going forward is *Ubuntu Cloud* or *Ubuntu Cloud Infrastructure*.

Why a Cloud?

Businesses and enterprises have built computer networks for years. There are many reasons, but usually networks are built because specific computation or data processing tasks are made easier and faster using more than one computer. The size of the network generally depends on the tasks that need to be done. Building a network usually entails taking a detailed survey of needs, analyzing those requirements, and gathering together the necessary hardware and software to fulfill those needs now, perhaps with a little room for growth if money permits.

Cloud computing is designed to make that easier by providing resources such as computing power and storage as services on the Internet in a way that is easy to access remotely, available on demand, simple to provision and scale, and highly dynamic. In the ideal case, this saves both time and money. Hardware, storage, networks, and software are abstracted as services instead of being manually built and configured and are then accessed locally on demand when the additional resources are required. Sometimes these abstractions are referred to as *infrastructure as a service (IAAS)*, *platform as a service (PAAS)*, and *software as a service (SAAS)*.

Some of the greatest benefits are the ease with which new resources may be added to a cloud, the fault tolerance inherent in the built-in redundancy of a large pool of servers, and the payment schedules that charge for resources only when they are used. There is also a great benefit in abstracting the complexity out of the process; clients perform the tasks they want to perform, and the cloud computing platform takes care of the details of adding resources as needed without the end user being aware of the process. *Virtual machines (VMs)* are created and used when needed and destroyed immediately after they are no longer needed, freeing up system resources for other purposes.

Ubuntu Cloud and Eucalyptus

Ubuntu Cloud on Ubuntu 10.04 LTS is based primarily on Eucalyptus, which is GPL software written to provide cloud computing and cloud storage platforms that are both free (as in freedom and as in beer) and completely compatible with Amazon's EC2 cloud computing and S3 cloud storage platforms. The Eucalyptus services are available through *application programming interfaces (APIs)* that are compatible with EC2/S3, so client tools written for the *Amazon Web Services (AWS)* can also be used with Eucalyptus.

An Ubuntu Enterprise Cloud, based on 10.04 LTS and Eucalyptus, consists of several components. We start with a node, which is a server that is capable of running *Kernel-based Virtual Machine (KVM)* as its hypervisor. A hypervisor is software that allows multiple VMs to run on one piece of hardware by presenting each VM with a virtual platform and monitors each VM for performance, resource use, and needs. This allows multiple operating systems to share hardware resources. Other hypervisors are available, such as Xen, but Ubuntu has chosen KVM as the default.

The next components are the *node controller (NC)* and the *cluster controller (CC)*. The NC runs on each node and controls all VMs running on that node. The NC runs as a layer between the host operating system and the CC above it, serving as a go-between that queries the operating system to discover physical resources available and the state and number of VMs running on the node and reports this information to the CC. The CC then manages the networking for the instances running on that and other nodes and makes sure that the *cloud controller (CLC)* gets that information.

The CLC is the main front end to the whole cloud. It provides the API for client services and deals with all requests and responses, communicating via web services between the client tool and the Ubuntu Cloud components. The CLC also provides a web interface for managing parts of the infrastructure. This is where resource availability is monitored and managed.

Two other controllers are in the interface: the *storage controller (SC)* and the *Walrus storage controller (WS3)*. The SC provides a way to create persistent storage devices similar to Amazon's *elastic block storage (EBS)* devices, which are block storage devices that are created separately from cloud computing instances and are intended to be highly reliable, highly available, and accessible. The WS3 is a simple storage service that uses REST and SOAP APIs that are compatible with Amazon's S3 APIs and that serve to store VM images, snapshots, and store and serve files.

This highly complex system is illustrated in Figure 33.1.

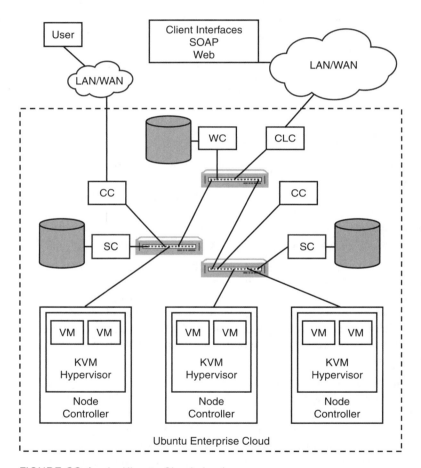

FIGURE 33.1   An Ubuntu Cloud cloud.

Deploy/Install Basics: Public or Private?

There are two ways to deploy Ubuntu Cloud based on Eucalyptus: on a private cloud or on a public cloud. Both have benefits and drawbacks. This section presents the things you need to consider when choosing. We also look at a way to mix the two.

A public Ubuntu Cloud is built on Amazon's EC2. This means your local hardware require-ments are minimal, your startup costs are low, deployment is quick, and growth is easy. This can be useful for testing, but is probably not a great idea for production. The draw-back to working this way is that you do not physically control the hardware on which your cloud is running. For many, this is a benefit, but this may not be suitable for high-security needs. Although you alone control the software and processes on your public cloud, there might be some worry about who has access to the machines. While Amazon would not last long in business if their data centers and machines were not secure, some applications and data are so sensitive you cannot afford to allow *any* outside risk. Legal constraints, such as from the Sarbanes-Oxley Act, sometimes force IT policy decisions in an organization and make the public option impossible. Running Eucalyptus on EC2 has also proven to provide less-than-desirable performance for many people, so again, this is not the best option for anything but light-traffic testing.

A private Ubuntu Cloud is created on hardware you own and control. This requires a large upfront commitment, but you have the security of running everything behind a company firewall and with complete knowledge of who is able to physically access your machines and who is listening on the network.

One thing to consider is the possibility of starting your Ubuntu Cloud as a private cloud and then creating interfaces from there to public services. Perhaps you prefer to keep all your data stored on the private cloud, but you want to use some services and applications on a public cloud. This is an avenue worth exploring if your company has a mixture of "must be secured and held in-house" and "we still want to keep it away from prying eyes, but if something happens it won't be catastrophic" needs. The big issue with this method is moving data between public and private servers; if you have large amounts of data, this can be prohibitive. As always, do your due diligence.

Public

Deploying a public cloud on Amazon's servers is quick and easy. First, go to http://aws. amazon.com/ and sign up for an account. Then, while logged in, go to Your Account, Security Credentials, and define the security settings to manage and access your service.

Next, you need a tool to allow you to start and stop instances. There are several, but we focus on two. One is Euca2ools, which are a set of command-line tools from Eucalyptus for interacting with the Amazon EC2 and S3 services via web services. These are installed by default with Ubuntu Server; you can learn more about using them in the Euca2ools User Guide from the link provided in the "References" section. We cover the basic commands for Euca2ools later in this chapter. The other tool is a paid service from Canonical called Landscape. It provides a web-based *graphical user interface* (GUI) for inter-acting with the Amazon cloud services and for managing your Ubuntu Cloud. It works with both public deployments on Amazon and private installations on your own equip-ment. A link to Canonicals website for Landscape is also in the "References" section.

After your tool is in place, you use it to choose and start your machine instances. You will also use this tool to manage the instances later. Many Ubuntu VM images have already been published to Amazon EC2 and are immediately available for deployment. You can find a list at http://cloud-images.ubuntu.com under the specific Ubuntu release you are interested in using.

The final step is to access your instances to set up the applications you want to provide on your cloud. You will manage your cloud using the tools mentioned earlier.

Private

Installing Ubuntu Cloud on your own machines is more complicated, even though the needs are the same. Much of the complexity is dealt with by Amazon when deploying on its servers. Before you start, check that you have the hardware required. At a minimum, you need two servers. One serves as a front end, and you need one or more nodes.

For the front end, or any system that will run one or more of these—the CLC, the CC, the WS3/SC, the basic requirements shown in Table 33.1 must be met.

TABLE 33.1   Basic Requirements for CLC, CC, WS3, and SC

Hardware	Minimum	Suggested	Notes
CPU	1GHz	2 × 2GHz	For an all-in-one front end, it helps to have at least a dual-core processor.
Memory	2GB	4GB	The Java web front end benefits from lots of available memory.
Disk	5400rpm IDE	7200rpm SATA	Slower disks will work, but will yield much longer instance startup times.
Disk space	40GB	200GB	40GB is enough space for only a single image, cache, and so on. Eucalyptus does not like to run out of disk space.
Networking	100Mbps	1000Mbps	Machine images are hundreds of MB and need to be copied over the network to nodes.

For nodes, which will run the node controller and instances, you need to meet the requirements shown in Table 33.2.

TABLE 33.2   Requirements for the Node Controller and Instances

Hardware	Minimum	Suggested	Notes
CPU	VT extensions	VT, 64-bit, multicore	64-bit can run both i386 and amd64 instances; by default, Eucalyptus will run only 1 VM per CPU core on a node.
Memory	1GB	4GB	Additional memory means more and larger guests.
Disk	5400rpm IDE	7200rpm SATA or SCSI	Eucalyptus nodes are disk intensive; I/O wait will likely be the performance bottleneck.

TABLE 33.2   Requirements for the Node Controller and Instances

Hardware	Minimum	Suggested	Notes
Disk space	40GB	100GB	Images will be cached locally; Eucalyptus does not like to run out of disk space.
Networking	100Mbps	1000Mbps	Machine images are hundreds of MB and need to be copied over the network to nodes.

When you have confirmed that your equipment meets or exceeds the requirements, download the Ubuntu Server installation disk from http://releases.ubuntu.com/ and click the release version you want to use (for example, 10.04 LTS). Make sure you download the server installation CD. Burn it to a disk.

When you boot, select Install Ubuntu Enterprise Cloud. The installer checks and detects whether you have a Eucalyptus cloud controller or other components. Because none are present, you need to install a CLC at a minimum. If this is going to be the only front-end system and will be expected to run all the services, make sure you also tell the installer to include the WS3, CC, and SC components.

You are asked to name your cluster and supply a range of IP addresses on the LAN that Ubuntu Cloud will be able to use and allocate to instances. Typically, this is something like 192.168.1.125 to 192.168.1.240. Allow the installation to complete.

To install node controllers, make sure each system you intend to use as a node is connected to the network on which the CLC is running. Boot each one at a time to the same server installation CD and again select Install Ubuntu Cloud. It should detect the cluster and preselect Node for you. Confirm it and finish the installation as usual. When the node reboots, it is ready to be registered.

Node registration should be automatic and will include servers exchanging public *Secure Shell (SSH)* keys, configuring services properly, services publishing their existence to the rest of the cloud, running the appropriate version of uec-component-listener for components installed, and verifying registration. Instructions for performing these steps manually are available at https://help.ubuntu.com/community/UEC/CDInstall should you discover a failure.

After you install and boot the CLC, users need credentials. These can be retrieved using a web browser or from the command line. From a web browser, open https://<cloud-controller-ip-address>:8443/. You must use a secure connection, but you will receive a security certificate warning. You need to add an exception to view the page. If you do not, you cannot view the Eucalyptus configuration page.

Use the username admin and password admin the first time you log in. Follow the onscreen instructions to change the admin password as required and enter a valid email address for the admin. Click the Credentials tab, and from there, choose Download Credentials. Save the certificates to ~/.euca and unzip.

You may also retrieve your credentials from the command line. Create ~/.euca and enter that directory, and then enter the following:

```
matthew@seymour:~$.euca$ sudo euca_conf --get-credentials mycreds.zip
```

Unzip them and create this link:

```
matthew@seymour:~$.euca$ ln -s ~/.euca/eucarc ~/.eucarc
```

Next, you need to set up the EC2 API and AMI tools on your server. Check that euca2ools package is installed. If it is, you can get the local cluster availability details this way:

```
matthew@seymour:~$.euca/eucarc$ euca-describe-availability-zones verbose
AVAILABILITYZONE    myowncloud                   192.168.1.1
AVAILABILITYZONE    |- vm types              free / max   cpu    ram  disk
AVAILABILITYZONE    |- m1.small              0004 / 0004   1     192    2
AVAILABILITYZONE    |- c1.medium             0004 / 0004   1     256    5
AVAILABILITYZONE    |- m1.large              0002 / 0002   2     512   10
AVAILABILITYZONE    |- m1.xlarge             0002 / 0002   2    1024   20
AVAILABILITYZONE    |- c1.xlarge             0001 / 0001   4    2048   20
```

If everything looks correct, you can start installing images. The easiest way to do this is from the store using the web interface. Access the interface as you did earlier using https://<cloud-controller-ip-address>:8443/ and this time click the Store tab. You will see a list of available images to download and install. Information is also given here about how to run images.

To run an image from the command line, you first need to create a key pair that you can use to log in to that instance as root. Here is an easy way to do that:

```
if [ ! -e ~/.euca/secretkey.priv ]; then
    mkdir -p -m 700 ~/.euca
    touch ~/.euca/secretkey.priv
    chmod 0600 ~/.euca/secretkey.priv
    euca-add-keypair secretkey > ~/.euca/secretkey.priv
fi
```

You can call your key anything you want, and if you forget what keys exist, you can run euca-describe-keypairs to get a list of created keys stored on the system. You then have to allow access to port 22 in each of your instances using the following:

```
matthew@seymour:~$.euca/eucarc$ euca-authorize default -P tcp -p 22 -s 0.0.0.0/0
```

Then you can create instances of your registered image using this:

```
matthew@seymour:~$.euca/eucarc$ euca-run-instances $EMI -k mykey -t m1.small
```

You may have more than one instance of the same image. The first time you run an instance, the system takes a while to start up because it sets up a cache of the image. VM images are quite large. You can watch to see whether it is up by using the following:

```
matthew@seymour:~$.euca/eucarc$ watch -n5 euca-describe-instances
```

When the status changes from pending to running, you want to make a note of the IP address assigned to the instance and connect to it using this:

```
matthew@seymour:~$.euca/eucarc$ IPADDR=$(euca-describe-instances | grep $EMI | grep
running | tail -n1 | awk '{print $4}')
matthew@seymour:~$.euca/eucarc$ ssh -i ~/.euca/mykey.priv ubuntu@$IPADDR
```

When you are done, you can exit your SSH connection and terminate your instance, as follows:

```
matthew@seymour:~$.euca/eucarc$ INSTANCEID=$(euca-describe-instances | grep $EMI |
grep running | tail -n1 | awk '{print $2}')
matthew@seymour:~$.euca/eucarc$ euca-terminate-instances $INSTANCEID
```

A euca2ools Primer

Most uses for cloud computing involve custom tools and software by people who know how to read an API and make their program interact without bothering end users with the details. It is no different with Ubuntu Cloud. For that reason, we list some of the commands from euca2ools without a lot of commentary.

euca2ools contains many commands for managing your resources. Most have numerous configuration options available. After the euca2ools package is installed, the man pages for each command provide valuable information about how to use them. Following is a simple list to help you remember what commands do so that you can look up the details of how to use them:

- ▶ **euca-bundle-image**—Bundles an image for use with Eucalyptus, Ubuntu Cloud, or Amazon EC2.

- ▶ **euca-bundle-vol**—Bundles the local file system of a running instance as a bundled image.

- ▶ **euca-delete-bundle**—Deletes a previously uploaded bundle.

- ▶ **euca-download-bundle**—Downloads a bundled image from a bucket.

- ▶ **euca-unbundle**—Unbundles a previously bundled image.

- ▶ **euca-upload-bundle**—Uploads a previously bundled image to the cloud.

- ▶ **euca-describe-images**—Shows information about machine images.

- ▶ **euca-describe-image-attribute**—Shows image attributes.

- ▶ **euca-register**—Registers a manifest for use with the cloud.

- ▶ **euca-deregister**—Deregisters an image from the cloud.

▶ **euca-describe-instances**—Shows information about instances.

▶ **euca-reboot-instances**—Reboots specified instances.

▶ **euca-run-instances**—Starts instances.

▶ **euca-terminate-instances**—Stops specified instances.

▶ **euca-confirm-product-instance**—Confirms if instance is running with product code supplied.

▶ **euca-attach-volume**—Attaches a volume to an instance.

▶ **euca-create-volume**—Creates a volume in the specified availability zone.

▶ **euca-delete-volume**—Deletes a volume.

▶ **euca-describe-volumes**—Shows information about existing volumes.

▶ **euca-detach-volume**—Detaches a volume from an instance.

▶ **euca-create-snapshot**—Creates a snapshot from an existing volume.

▶ **euca-delete-snapshot**—Deletes a snapshot.

▶ **euca-describe-snapshots**—Shows information about snapshots.

▶ **euca-allocate-address**—Allocates a public IP address.

▶ **euca-associate-address**—Associates an instance with a public IP address.

▶ **euca-describe-addresses**—Shows information about IP addresses.

▶ **euca-disassociate-addresses**—Disassociates a public IP address from an instance.

▶ **euca-release-address**—Releases a public IP address.

▶ **euca-add-group**—Creates a new security group.

▶ **euca-delete-group**—Deletes a security group.

▶ **euca-describe-groups**—Shows information about groups.

▶ **euca-add-keypair**—Creates a new key pair for use with instances.

▶ **euca-delete-keypair**—Deletes a key pair.

▶ **euca-describe-keypairs**—Shows information about key pairs.

▶ **euca-describe-availability-zones**—Shows information about availability zones.

▶ **euca-describe-regions**—Shows information about regions.

▶ **euca-get-console-output**—Prints console output from a running instance.

▶ **euca-modify-image-attribute**—Modifies attributes of an image.

▶ **euca-reset-image-attribute**—Resets attributes for an image.

▶ **euca-revoke**—Revokes a rule for a security group.

▶ **euca-version**—Shows the euca2ools version.

▶ **euca-authorize**—Adds a new rule to a security group.

- **uec-publish-tarball**—Registers an Ubuntu Cloud tarball.

- **uec-registration**—Enables or disables automatic component registration.

- **uec-run-instances**—Same as euca-run-instances.

- **uec-publish-image**—Publishes image to bucket.

- **uec-query-builds**—Finds information about a build.

- **uec-resize-image**—Resizes an Ubuntu Cloud image.

Ubuntu Cloud and OpenStack

OpenStack is an Apache-licensed cloud computing platform. It was founded as a collaboration between NASA and Rackspace. After less than a year, it boasts a worldwide community of developers. Adoption has been swift and already many large corporations, universities, and institutions are using OpenStack for cloud computing.

> **Quick fact**
>
> Both NASA and Ubuntu were early adopters of and participants with Eucalyptus. Both now focus on OpenStack.

OpenStack uses a set of APIs for its services that are compatible with the Amazon EC2/S3 APIs. Client tools written for those can also be used with OpenStack. OpenStack has three main service families: Compute Infrastructure, Storage Infrastructure, and Imaging Service, each described in greater detail in the following subsections.

Compute Infrastructure (Nova)

Nova manages the compute resources, networking, authorization, and scaling for the OpenStack cloud. By itself, it does not perform any virtualization tasks, but rather it uses libvert APIs to interact with supported hypervisors and is the management component of the system. Nova has an Amazon EC2-compatible RESTful API.

Nova consists of several components:

- **nova-api**—The API server provides an interface to enable outside systems to interact with the cloud infrastructure.

- **rabbit-mq**—The message queue server asynchronous calls to communicate with other Nova components, such as the scheduler or the network controller.

- **nova-compute**—The compute nodes' host instances. They carry out operations based on requests received by the message queue. Instances are deployed on available compute nodes based on a scheduling algorithm managed by the scheduler.

▶ **nova-network**—The network controller allocates IP addresses, configures VLANs, configures networks, and implements security groups for compute nodes.

▶ **nova-volume**—The volume worker manage *Logical Volume Manager (LVM)*-based storage volumes. They create and delete volumes, attach and detach volumes from instances, and provide persistent storage for use by instances.

▶ **nova-scheduler**—The scheduler uses an adjustable algorithm to determine which compute, network, or storage volume servers should be used from an available pool of resources. Schedules can be configured based on server loads, availability zones, or random chance.

Storage Infrastructure (Swift)

Swift is an object store. It is scalable up to multiple petabytes and billions of objects. It is elastic. It has built-in redundancy and failover. Swift is designed to store a very large number of objects distributed across a commodity hardware.

Imaging Service (Glance)

Glance is a lookup and retrieval system for VM images. It can use one of three back ends: OpenStack Object Store, S3 storage, or S3 Storage using the OpenStack Object Store as an intermediary.

Installation

We use three physical machines for this simple example. All of the previously mentioned components run on Server 1, except for the compute nodes, which are represented by Server 2. The third machine is Client and is used as the human interface to manage everything. For this example, we use the settings shown in Table 33.3.

TABLE 33.3   Settings for This Basic OpenStack Installation

	Server 1	Server 2	Client
Purpose	Manage all OpenStack components	nova-compute node	client
NICs	eth0 (public net) eth1 (private net)	eth0 (public net) eth1 (private net)	eth0 (public net)
IP address	eth0 10.10.10.2 eth1 192.168.3.1	eth0 10.10.10.3 eth1 192.168.3.2	eth0 10.10.10.4
Hostname	turing.example.com	burroughs.example.com	watson.example.com
DNS	10.10.10.3	10.10.10.3	10.10.10.3
Gateway	10.10.10.1	10.10.10.1	10.10.10.1

Prepare Server 1

Boot the physical machine from a 64-bit Ubuntu 11.10 server CD. Choose Install Ubuntu Server from the menu and proceed with the basic installation, using the specific customizations that follow in this section. We install the Glance and Nova packages later in the process, after we get the basic environment set up.

Choose the option to manually partition the hard drive and create a dedicated partition large enough to host any and all of the storage (via nova-volume) you will need for your network and set the partition type to Linux LVM. Using a dedicated partition for this storage will make it easier to scale by adding additional resources later.

Create the first user with the name localadmin.

You need to know the details for the network on which this installation will exist. Use that information to set up the IP address for the first interface.

In the Packages menu of the installation process, install only openssh-server.

Once the installation is complete, enable the Universe repository in /etc/apt/sources. list, update the package list, and upgrade all your installed packages:

```
localadmin@turing:~$ sudo apt-get update
localadmin@turing:~$ sudo apt-get upgrade
```

Install bridge-utils:

```
localadmin@turing:~$ sudo apt-get install bridge-utils
```

Reboot the server and log in as localadmin.

Replace the contents of /etc/network/interfaces with the following:

```
auto lo
iface lo inet loopback
auto eth0
iface eth0 inet static
address 10.10.10.2
netmask 255.255.255.0
broadcast 10.10.10.255
gateway 10.10.10.1
dns-nameservers 10.10.10.100
auto br100
iface br100 inet static
bridge_ports eth1
bridge_stp off
bridge_maxwait 0
bridge_fd 0
address 192.168.3.1
netmask 255.255.0.0
broadcast 192.168.255.255
```

Restart the network:

```
localadmin@turing:~$ sudo /etc/init.d/networking restart
```

Because this server will act as a *Network Time Protocol (NTP)* server for all the nodes, we want it to sync to official NTP servers. Install NTP server:

```
localadmin@turing:~$ sudo apt-get install ntp
```

Configure it to serve time even when not connected to the Internet by making sure these two lines are in /etc/ntp.conf:

```
server 127.127.1.0
```

```
fudge 127.127.1.0 stratum 10
```

Restart the NTP service so the changes take effect:

```
localadmin@turing:~$ sudo /etc/init.d/ntp restart
```

Install Glance:

```
localadmin@turing:~$ sudo apt-get install glance
```

Install MySQL Server:

```
localadmin@turing:~$ sudo apt-get install -y mysql-server
```

Configure MySQL. First, edit /etc/mysql.my.cnf to change the bind address to the following:

```
bind-address = 0.0.0.0
```

Restart the MySQL server:

```
localadmin@turing:~$ sudo restart mysql
```

Replace secretpassword in these steps with your MySQL password. If you did not set a password during MySQL installation, do so now:

```
localadmin@turing:~$ mysqladmin -u root password secretpassword
```

Create a database named nova:

```
localadmin@turing:~$~$ sudo mysql -uroot -psecretpassword -e 'CREATE DATABASE
➡nova;'
```

Enable root to log in from any IP:

```
localadmin@turing:~$ sudo mysql -uroot -psecretpassword -e "GRANT ALL PRIVILEGES
➡ON *.*
TO 'root'@'%' WITH GRANT OPTION;"
```

Set a MySQL password for root logins from any IP:

```
localadmin@turing:~$ sudo mysql -uroot -psecretpassword -e "SET PASSWORD FOR
➥'root'@'%'
= PASSWORD('secretpassword');"
```

Install Nova components:

```
localadmin@turing:~$ sudo apt-get install -y rabbitmq-server nova-common nova-doc
python-nova nova-api nova-network nova-volume nova-objectstore nova-scheduler nova-
compute
```

Install euca2ools:

```
localadmin@turing:~$ sudo apt-get install -y euca2ools
```

Install unzip:

```
localadmin@turing:~$ sudo apt-get install -y unzip
```

Replace the contents of /etc/nova/nova.conf with the following:

```
--dhcpbridge_flagfile=/etc/nova/nova.conf
--dhcpbridge=/usr/bin/nova-dhcpbridge
--logdir=/var/log/nova
--lock_path=/var/lock/nova
--state_path=/var/lib/nova
--verbose
--s3_host=10.10.10.2
--rabbit_host=192.168.3.1
--cc_host=192.168.3.1
--ec2_url=http://10.10.10.2:8773/services/Cloud
--fixed_range=192.168.0.0/16
--network_size=8
--FAKE_subdomain=ec2
--routing_source_ip=192.168.3.1
--sql_connection=mysql://root:mygreatsecret@10.10.10.2/nova
--glance_host=192.168.3.1
--image_service=nova.image.glance.GlanceImageService
--iscsi_ip_prefix=192.168.
```

Enable iscsitarget:

```
localadmin@turing:~$ sudo sed -i 's/false/true/g' /etc/default/iscsitarget
```

Restart the iscsitarget service:

```
localadmin@turing:~$ sudo service iscsitarget restart
```

Create a physical volume (using the Linux LVM partition created in one of the first steps, here represented by /dev/sda6; your location may differ):

```
localadmin@turing:~$ sudo pvcreate /dev/sda6
```

Create a volume group named nova-volumes:

```
localadmin@turing:~$ sudo vgcreate nova-volumes /dev/sda6
```

Create a group called nova:

```
localadmin@turing:~$ sudo groupadd nova
```

Change the ownership of /etc/nova and the permissions for /etc/nova/nova.conf:

```
localadmin@turing:~$ sudo chown -R root:nova /etc/nova
localadmin@turing:~$ sudo chmod 644 /etc/nova/nova.conf
```

Restart all nova-related services:

```
localadmin@turing:~$ sudo /etc/init.d/libvirt-bin restart; sudo restart
➥nova-network;
sudo restart nova-compute; sudo restart nova-api; sudo restart nova-objectstore; sudo
restart nova-scheduler; sudo restart nova-volume; sudo restart glance-api; sudo
restart glance-registry
```

Create the nova schema in the MySQL database:

```
localadmin@turing:~$ sudo nova-manage db sync
```

Create a list of IPs to be used from the network of fixed IPs set inside nova.conf:

```
localadmin@turing:~$ sudo nova-manage network create 192.168.3.0/24 1 255
```

Allocate 32 public IP addresses for use by the instances, starting from 10.10.10.255:

```
localadmin@turing:~$ sudo nova-manage floating create 10.10.10.2 10.10.10.224/27
```

Create a user with admin rights on nova:

```
localadmin@turing:~$ sudo nova-manage user admin novaadmin
```

Create a project called proj:

```
localadmin@turing:~$ sudo nova-manage project create proj novaadmin
```

Create a directory to download nova credentials and download the ZIP file:

```
localadmin@turing:~$ mkdir /home/localadmin/creds
```

Generate and save the credentials for accessing and managing the nova cloud:

```
localadmin@turing:~$ sudo nova-manage project zipfile proj novaadmin
/home/localadmin/creds/novacreds.zip
```

You will need the novacreds.zip file to use euca2ools. It must be copied to any machine from which you want to run euca2ools commands. Here, we illustrate the process using Server 1, but you will need to copy these credentials and follow the next few steps on any other machine from which you will run euca2ools to manage this cloud.

Enter the creds folder and extract the .zip contents: cacert.pem, cert.pem, novarc, and pk.pem.

```
localadmin@turing:~$ cd /home/localadmin/creds
localadmin@turing:~$ unzip novacreds.zip
localadmin@turing:~$ sudo chown localadmin:localadmin /home/localadmin/creds/ -R
```

The novarc file contains environmental variables that must be recognized before you can use some of the euca2ools commands. Set them by sourcing the file:

```
localadmin@turing:~$ source /home/localadmin/creds/novarc
```

Restart all nova-related services:

```
localadmin@turing:~$ sudo /etc/init.d/libvirt-bin restart; sudo restart
nova-network;
sudo restart nova-compute; sudo restart nova-api; sudo restart nova-objectstore; sudo
restart nova-scheduler; sudo restart nova-volume; sudo restart glance-api; sudo
restart glance-registry
```

Confirm the credentials are applied and nova is properly set up:

```
localadmin@turing:~$ euca-describe-availability-zones verbose
```

Output like this will confirm proper installation:

```
AVAILABILITYZONE   nova available
AVAILABILITYZONE   |- server1
AVAILABILITYZONE   | |- nova-compute enabled : -) 2011-08-13 12:32:50
AVAILABILITYZONE   | |- nova-scheduler enabled : -) 2011- 08-13 12:32:48
AVAILABILITYZONE   | |- nova-network enabled : -) 2011- 08-13 12:32:49
AVAILABILITYZONE   | |- nova-volume enabled : -) 2011- 08-13 12:32:49
```

The final task is to install and set up the Nova/OpenStack dashboard, a web interface for management.

Install Bazaar first, so that the required software may be downloaded from Launchpad:

```
localadmin@turing:~$ sudo apt-get install -y bzr
localadmin@turing:~$ sudo easy-install virtualenv
```

Perform an anonymous checkout of the current OpenStack dashboard code from
Launchpad:

```
localadmin@turing:~$ sudo bzr init-repo .
localadmin@turing:~$ sudo bzr branch lp:openstack-dashboard -r 46 /opt/osdb
localadmin@turing:~$ cd /opt/osdb
localadmin@turing:~$ sudo sh run_tests s.sh
localadmin@turing:~$ cd openstack-dashboard
```

Edit /opt/osdb/openstack-dashboard/local/localsettings.py to include the needed
details for connecting to nova-api. The details for your installation can be found in the
novarc file created earlier and will differ from these, particularly the keys:

```
NOVA_DEFAULT_ENDPOINT = 'http://localhost:8773/services/Cloud'
NOVA_DEFAULT_REGION = 'nova'
NOVA_ACCESS_KEY = 'b6a7e3ca-f894-473b-abca-84329d9829fa:proj'
NOVA_SECRET_KEY = '2d61a361-965a-4ed6-966a-d9f543b42531'
NOVA_ADMIN_USER = 'novaadmin'
NOVA_PROJECT = 'proj'
```

For the dashboard to send notification emails, it requires that a *Simple Mail Transfer
Protocol (SMTP)* server be configured. We do that now.

Edit /opt/osdb/openstack-dashboard/local/localsettings.py further to include the
needed details for connecting to your email server, customizing as appropriate:

```
EMAIL_HOST = 'turing.example.com'

EMAIL_PORT = 25
EMAIL_USER =
EMAIL_PASSWORD =
EMAIL_USE_TLS = 'True'
```

Create a database for the dashboard. When prompted, provide the requested name,
email address, and password for the administrator account that will be created for use
with the dashboard:

```
localadmin@turing:~$ sudo tools/with_venv.sh dashboard/manage.py syncdb
```

Launch the default python-django server, specifying the port on which you want the
dashboard to be available. For this example, we use port 8000:

```
localadmin@turing:~$ sudo tools/with_venv.sh dashboard/manage.py runserver
➥10.10.10.2:8000
```

Using the Django web server is adequate for testing and for this chapter's quick example.
For production, you want to use a web server like Apache, perhaps with the wsgi module
because the dashboard includes a file called /opt/osdb/openstack-dashboard/dashboard/
wsgi/django.wsgi to help set this up. Instructions for doing so are available from http:/
/cloud.ubuntu.com.

Test the installation by opening a web browser and opening this URL:

```
http://10.10.10.2:8000
```

If all is well, you will be able to log in using the credentials you created moments earlier. Others will be able to access the interface to create an account, which must be approved by an existing administrator before access is granted.

By default, the dashboard uses SQLite. Instructions are available from http://cloud.ubuntu.com for using MySQL or PostgreSQL.

Prepare Server 2

Boot the physical server from the same 64-bit Ubuntu 11.10 server CD used for Server 1. Choose Install Ubuntu Server from the menu and proceed with the basic installation, using the specific customizations that follow in this section.

Install `bridge-utils`:

```
localadmin@burroughs:~$ sudo apt-get install bridge-utils
```

Replace the contents of `/etc/network/interfaces` with the following:

```
auto lo
iface lo inet loopback
auto eth0
iface eth0 inet static
address 10.10.10.3
netmask 255.255.255.0
broadcast 10.10.10.255
gateway 10.10.10.1
dns-nameservers 10.10.10.100
auto br100
iface br100 inet static
bridge_ports eth1
bridge_stp off
bridge_maxwait 0
bridge_fd 0
address 192.168.3.2
netmask 255.255.0.0
broadcast 192.168.255.255
```

Restart the network:

```
localadmin@burroughs:~$ sudo /etc/init.d/networking restart
```

Install NTP:@burroughs:~$

```
localadmin sudo apt-get install ntp
```

33

Configure NTP to sync to Server 1 by adding this line to /etc/ntp.conf:

```
server 10.10.10.2
```

Restart NTP:

```
localadmin@burroughs:~$ sudo /etc/init.d/ntp restart
```

This server is being prepared as a compute node, so it only needs the following nova components and dependencies:

```
localadmin@burroughs:~$ sudo apt-get install -y nova-common python-novanova-compute
➥vlan
```

Install euca2ools:

```
localadmin@burroughs:~$ sudo apt-get install -y euca2ools
```

Install unzip:

```
localadmin@burroughs:~$ sudo apt-get install -y unzip
```

Replace the contents of /etc/nova/nova.conf with the following:

```
--dhcpbridge_flagfile=/etc/nova/nova.conf
--dhcpbridge=/usr/bin/nova-dhcpbridge
--logdir=/var/log/nova
--lock_path=/var/lock/nova
--state_path=/var/lib/nova
--verbose
--s3_host=10.10.10.2
--rabbit_host=192.168.3.1
--cc_host=192.168.3.1
--ec2_url=http://10.10.10.2:8773/services/Cloud
--fixed_range=192.168.0.0/16
--network_size=8
--FAKE_subdomain=ec2
--routing_source_ip=192.168.3.2
--sql_connection=mysql://root:mygreatsecret@10.10.10.2/nova
--glance_host=192.168.3.1
--image_service=nova.image.glance.GlanceImageService
```

Prepare Client

A client does not have to be running Ubuntu, but for simplicity (and because this is an Ubuntu book), we describe how to prepare an Ubuntu client.

Install the 64-bit version of Ubuntu 11.10 Desktop.

Configure /etc/network/interfaces as follows:

```
auto lo
iface lo inet loopback
auto eth0
iface eth0 inet static
address 10.10.10.4
netmask 255.255.255.0
broadcast 10.10.10.255
gateway 10.10.10.1
dns-nameservers 10.10.10.100
```

Install NTP:

```
localadmin@watson:~$ sudo apt-get install ntp
```

Configure NTP to sync to Server 1 by adding this line to /etc/ntp.conf:

```
server 10.10.10.2
```

Restart NTP:

```
localadmin@watson:~$ sudo /etc/init.d/ntp restart
```

Install euca2ools:

```
localadmin@watson:~$ sudo apt-get install euca2ools
```

Install qemu-kvm:

```
localadmin@watson:~$ sudo apt-get install qemu-kvm
```

Download the credentials created earlier so that euca2ools may be used from this machine:

```
localadmin@watson:~$ mkdir /home/localadmin/creds
localadmin@watson:~$ cd /home/localadmin/creds
localadmin@watson:~$ scp localadmin/home/localadmin/creds/novacreds.zip
localadmin@watson:~$ unzip creds.zip
```

Source the novarc file and test the connection to the API server:

```
localadmin@watson:~$ source novarc
localadmin@watson:~$ euca-describe-availability-zones verbose
```

The output is similar to when we configured Server 1:

```
AVAILABILITYZONE   nova available
AVAILABILITYZONE   |- server1
AVAILABILITYZONE   | |- nova-compute enabled : -) 2011-08-13 12:32:50
AVAILABILITYZONE   | |- nova-scheduler enabled : -) 2011- 08-13 12:32:48
AVAILABILITYZONE   | |- nova-network enabled : -) 2011- 08-13 12:32:49
AVAILABILITYZONE   | |- nova-volume enabled : -) 2011- 08-13 12:32:49
```

Creating an Image

Create a raw image on Client 1. This represents the main hard drive of the VM, so be sure to give it adequate space:

```
localadmin@watson:~$ kvm-img create -f raw server.img 5G
```

Download the ISO for the OS you want to install. This example uses Ubuntu:

```
localadmin@watson:~$ wget http://releases.ubuntu.com/oneric/
➥ubuntu-11.10-server-amd64.iso
```

Boot a KVM instance using the OS installer ISO to begin installation. The last option here sets up a *Virtual Network Computing (VNC)* display at port 0 that we use to connect to the VM via VNC:

```
localadmin@watson:~$ sudo kvm -m 256 -cdrom ubuntu-11.04-server-amd64.iso -drive
file=server.img,if=scsi,index=0 -boot d -net nic -net user -nographic ~-vnc :0
```

Connect to the VM using VNC. In this case, 10.10.10.4 is the IP for Client:

```
localadmin@watson:~$ vncviewer 10.10.10.4 :0
```

During installation, create a single ext4 partition mounted on /. No swap partition is needed. After installation is complete, relaunch the VM:

```
localadmin@newmachine:~$ sudo kvm -m 256 -drive
➥file=server.img,if=scsi,index=0,boot=on
-boot c -net nic -net user -nographic -vnc :0
```

Add all the packages you want installed. At a minimum, update any default packages and install SSH:

```
localadmin@newmachine:~$ sudo apt-get update
localadmin@newmachine:~$ sudo apt-get upgrade
localadmin@newmachine:~$ sudo apt-get install openssh-server cloud-init
```

Remove the network persistence rules from /etc/udev/rules.d, because they will cause the network interface to come up using a name other than the desired eth0:

```
localadmin@newmachine:~$ sudo rm -rf /etc/udev/rules.d/70-persistent-net.rules
```

Shut down the VM. From Client, we upload the new VM to OpenStack, which needs an ext4 image. We extract that now:

```
localadmin@watson:~$ sudo losetup -f server.img
localadmin@watson:~$ sudo losetup -a
```

This gives you output like this:

```
/dev/loop0: [0801]:16908388 ($filepath)
```

Note the name of the loop device (/dev/loop0 here). Use that name to find the starting sector of the partition:

```
localadmin@watson:~$ sudo fdisk -cul /dev/loop0
```

This gives you output like this:

```
Disk /dev/loop0: 5368 MB, 5368709120 bytes
149 heads, 8 sectors/track, 8796 cylinders, total 10485760 sectors
Units = sectors of 1 * 512 = 512 bytes
Sector size (logical/physical): 512 bytes / 512 bytes
I/O size (minimum/optimal): 512 bytes / 512 bytes
Disk identifier: 0x00072bd4
Device       Boot Start   End       Blocks   Id System
/dev/loop0p1 *   2048      10483711 5240832 83 Linux
```

Note the starting sector of /dev/loop0p1 partition. Multiply this number by 512 to obtain the correct value of the offset in bytes (2048 x 512 = 1048576).

Unmount the loop0 device:

```
localadmin@watson:~$ sudo losetup -d /dev/loop0
```

Now, mount only the loop0p1 partition using the offset value:

```
localadmin@watson:~$ sudo losetup -o 1048576 server.img
localadmin@watson:~$ sudo losetup -a
```

This gives you output like this:

```
/dev/loop0: [0801]:16908388 ($filepath) offset 1048576
```

Note the mount point of the device. Copy the entire partition to a new RAW file:

```
localadmin@watson:~$ sudo dd if=/dev/loop0 of=serverfinal.img
```

This gives us our needed ext4 file system image, serverfinal.img.

Unmount the loop0 device:

```
localadmin@watson:~$ sudo losetup -d /dev/loop0
```

To make this image suitable for use as a cloud instance, we need to tweak /etc/fstab because nova-compute may resize the disk at the time instances are launched based on the type of instance chosen. This can make the *universally unique identifier (UUID)* of the disk invalid. Instead, we use the file system label to identify the partition.

Loop mount serverfinal.img:

```
localadmin@watson:~$ sudo mount -o loop serverfinal.img /mnt
```

33

In `fstab`, you see something like this:

```
UUID=e7f5af8d-5d96-45cc-a0fc-d0d1bde8f31c / ext4 errors=remount-ro 0 1
```

Which needs to be replaced with the following:

```
LABEL-uec-rootfs  /  ext4  defaults  0  0
```

Now, copy the kernel and `initrd` image from `/mnt/boot` to user `/home` directory. These are used when creating and uploading a complete virtual image to OpenStack:

```
localadmin@watson:~$ sudo cp /mnt/boot/vmlinuz-2.6.38-7-server /home/localadmin
```

```
localadmin@watson:~$ sudo cp /mnt/boot/initrd.img-2.6.38-7-server /home/localadmin
```

Unmount the `loop` partition:

```
localadmin@watson:~$ sudo umount loop
```

Change the file system label of `serverfinal.img` to `uec-rootfs`:

```
localadmin@watson:~$ sudo tune2fs -L uec-rootfs serverfinal.img
```

Now we are ready to upload the images to the OpenStack imaging server, Glance:

```
localadmin@watson:~$ uec-publish-image -t image --kernel-file vmlinuz-2.6.38-7-server --ramdisk-file initrd.img -2.6.38-7-server amd64 serverfinal.img bucket1
```

This takes some time, even though the prompt is returned to you almost immediately. You can check the status with this:

```
localadmin@watson:~$ euca-describe-images
```

When images are fully uploaded and ready, they are listed, and the output for each image looks like this:

```
IMAGE aki-ed0ad108 bucket1/vmlinuz-2.6.38-7-server.manifest.xml css available
private x86_64 kernel
```

It is also possible to simplify the process, if you do not want the flexibility of using the same disk image with different kernel and RAM disk images, by creating bootable disk images. In this case, you can skip most of the previous steps that relate to extracting the ext4 image and just use the `server.img` file:

```
localadmin@watson:~$ euca-bundle-image -i server.img
```

```
localadmin@watson:~$ euca-upload-bundle -b mybucket -m /tmp/server.img.manifest.xml
```

```
localadmin@watson:~$ euca-register mybucket/server.img.manifest.xml
```

Instance Management

When you launch an instance of a VM, several things happen. The scheduler allocates resources, the network manager assigns an IP address, the instance is launched and its resources are managed, and eventually it is terminated and shut down. There are many ways to manage this process. One that works for both OpenStack and Eucalyptus instances is euca2ools. Another is the OpenStack dashboard. Because you read about euca2ools in an earlier section, here you get a quick, high-level view of management via the GUI dashboard that we installed earlier in this section. Instance management in the dashboard is accomplished using a series of tabs and menu options. Here it is easy to find where and how to create keys, launch or terminate registered images, or display the console output for a running instance.

Storage Management

Storage management is accomplished using nova-volume. As mentioned earlier, instance storage is not persistent, so a persistent volume is needed if data will be needed longer than the instance will run.

To create a 10GB storage volume, use the following:

```
localadmin@watson:~$ euca-create-volume -s 10 -z nova
```

You get output like this:

```
VOLUME vol-00000002 1 creating (proj, None, None, None) 2011-08-21T11:19:52Z
```

To list all storage volumes, use this:

```
localadmin@watson:~$ euca-describe-volumes
```

You will see output like this:

```
VOLUME vol-00000001 1 nova in-use (proj, None, None, None) 2011-08-21T09:12:42Z
VOLUME vol-00000002 1 nova available (proj, None, None, None) 2011-08-21T11:19:52Z
```

Volumes may only be attached to one running instance at a time. If the listing shows a volume as available, it may be attached to an instance.

To attach a storage volume to a running instance, use the following:

```
localadmin@watson:~$ euca-attach-volume -i i-00000009 -d /dev/vdb vol-00000002
```

The volume appears to the instance as an additional SCSI disk. Log in to the instance and mount the disk normally. If it has not already been done, you must format the disk before use.

To detach a volume, use the following:

```
localadmin@watson:~$ euca-detach-volume vol-00000002
```

Network Management

Network management is done by nova-network, which interacts directly with nova-compute to make sure that running instances are properly configured to communicate, both within the local network and with the wider Internet. Each instance can have two associated IP addresses: one for public communication outside of the local cloud network, and one for private communication within the trusted local network.

Three network management options exist: a flat network, a flat *Dynamic Host Control Protocol (DHCP)* network, and a *virtual local area network (VLAN)*. VLAN is the default. Others may be chosen by modifying the option in nova.conf:

```
--network_manager = nova.network.manager.FlatManager
```

```
--network_manager = nova.network.manager.FlatDHCPManager
```

```
--network_manager = nova.network.manager.VlanManager
```

Regardless of which is used, public and private IPs may be set for use by the instances with these commands:

```
localadmin@watson:~$ sudo nova-manage network create 192.168.3.0/24 1 255
```

```
localadmin@watson:~$ sudo nova-manage floating create 10.10.10.2 10.10.10.224/27
```

Associate an IP with an instance as follows:

```
localadmin@watson:~$ euca-allocate-address 10.10.2.225
```

An OpenStack Commands Primer

The euca2ools primer, earlier in this chapter, listed a large number of commands. Here, we need just one main command, but it has a ton of options. Once Nova packages are installed, the man pages provide valuable information about how to use these options:

- ▶ **nova-manage user**—Can be used to manage users.
- ▶ **nova-manage project**—Can be used to manage projects.
- ▶ **nova-manage role**—Can be used to manage roles.
- ▶ **nova-manage db**—Can be used to manage databases.
- ▶ **nova-manage flavor**—Can be used to manage instance types.
- ▶ **nova-manage service**—Can be used to manage services.

Learning More

Ubuntu Cloud with OpenStack has many more features not discussed here. Some include security using groups to specify roles that may access specific resources and the HybridFox plug-in for Firefox for managing instances. See the official Ubuntu Cloud website for these and more.

Landscape

Landscape, mentioned in Chapter 9, "Managing Software," is an enterprise-focused systems management and monitoring tool that is available from Canonical. It can monitor Ubuntu Cloud servers like the ones discussed in this chapter. Landscape is part of a paid service from Canonical called *Ubuntu Advantage*.

Juju

Although the official documentation at the time of this writing says that Juju is not yet ready for production use, it is interesting and has enough potential to warrant an intro-duction. It is also likely that by the time the book is printed, Juju will be completely ready. Juju has been described as APT for the cloud. APT does an amazing job of installing, configuring, and starting complicated software stacks and services, but only as long as all of that happens on only one system. Juju extends this ability across multiple machines. Often, Linux servers are set up for similar tasks. Multiple physical machines may be deployed with similar configurations to work with one another in a network, perhaps for load distribution or redundancy to prevent downtime in the event of one failing or being overloaded. Systems administrators are masters at creating and orchestrating these networks. However, doing so traditionally requires setting up each machine individually, configuring its software settings and so on.

Tools have appeared over the years to help with this great task, such as Chef and Puppet; see Chapter 9 for a little more about these. Juju works to do for servers what package managers do for individual systems. It enables you to deploy services quickly and easily across multiple servers, simplifying the configuration process, and is particularly designed with cloud servers in mind. As with Chef's recipes, those services are deployed using formulas that standardize communication, for example, and which may have been written by different people.

What makes Juju different from Chef and Puppet is that the Juju formulas, called *charms*, encapsulate services, defining all the ways that services need to expose or consume config-uration data to or from other services. This can be done many ways in the Juju charm, including via shell scripts or using Chef itself in solo mode. Also, Juju orchestrates provi-sioning by tracking its available resources (such as EC2, Eucalyptus, or OpenStack machines) and adding or removing them as appropriate.

As Juju reaches stability, it promises to be a powerful tool. Juju 11.10 is scheduled to be made available via the Ubuntu Universe software repository. Hopefully, it will reach stabil-ity for 12.04 (and if so, expect it to be covered in greater depth in the update PDF mentioned on the back cover of this book and fully in the next edition).

Juju is created to deploy workloads to the cloud. Orchestra is being built to deploy that cloud.

33

Orchestra

The Ubuntu Orchestra Project is a collection of best practices for deploying Ubuntu servers from Ubuntu servers. It is designed to assist with deployments to cloud servers numbering in the dozens, hundreds, or even thousands. The plan is to install Ubuntu Orchestra directly to bare metal on one server, from which all other bare-metal servers are provisioned and set up; an entire data center could be implemented quickly and easily. Once deployed, Orchestra provides automatic federation, and integrated management, monitoring, and logging. It is not yet complete and ready for use, but it is being built quickly and may be available as soon as 12.04. When it is, the initial plan is to include these main pieces and tie them together:

▶ **The Ubuntu Orchestra Provisioning Server**—Based on Cobbler (https://fedora-hosted.org/cobbler/), this automates tasks when provisioning new servers. It adds a `squid-deb-proxy` server to cache local copies of installed packages so that any subsequent installations can occur at LAN speeds and more. The goal is to make network installations operate reliably even when unattended.

▶ **The Ubuntu Orchestra Monitoring Server**—This uses Nagios to monitor all nodes deployed by Orchestra.

▶ **The Ubuntu Orchestra Logging Server**—This uses `rsyslog` to provide comprehensive remote logging.

▶ **The Ubuntu Orchestra Client**—These are the rest of the servers, provisioned using Juju. They all start out as default Ubuntu servers with a few additions: Byobu (see Chapter 11, "Command-Line Master Class"); Capistrano, a tool for running scripts on multiple servers and deploying web applications; Juju; OpenSSH (see Chapter 18, "Remote Access with SSH and Telnet"); Nagios (www.nagios.org); PowerNap, a daemon written by Ubuntu developer Dustin Kirkland that will bring a running system to a lower power state according to a set of configuration preferences; `rsyslog`, a well-known system log daemon; `ntp`, to synchronize time using the Network Time Protocol; and `squid-deb-proxy-client` to take advantage of the `squid-deb-proxy` server installed on the provisioning server.

References

▶ http://cloud.ubuntu.com—The official Ubuntu introduction to cloud computing.

▶ http://eucalyptus.com/resources/overview—Official information resources from Eucalyptus.

▶ http://aws.amazon.com/—The Amazon Web Services main page.

▶ www.linux-kvm.org/page/Main_Page—The main page for KVM, the Kernel-based Virtual Machine.

▶ **http://open.eucalyptus.com/wiki/Euca2oolsGuide_v1.1**—The Euca2ools User Guide.

▶ **www.openstack.org**—The official website for OpenStack.

▶ **www.canonical.com/enterprise-services/ubuntu-advantage/landscape/cloud-management**—Canonical's Landscape is a commercial management tool for Ubuntu Cloud and Amazon EC2 instances.

▶ **http://juju.ubuntu.com**—The official Ubuntu documentation for Juju.

33

CHAPTER 34

Opportunistic Development

There are some among us who love to write program code. Others are able, but do not particularly enjoy doing so. Most of this section of the book (Part V, "Programming Linux") is dedicated to the first group: those who love to code and want to know how to get started using their favorite tools in Ubuntu. However, it also applies to those of us who just want to scratch a specific itch by coding up a quick program to do something useful and make it available to other Ubuntu users, but who are not interested in learning how to become a package maintainer, upload to the official software repositories, and so on. We call this process opportunistic development, where an end user codes up a quick solution to a problem. This is in direct contrast to systematic development with professional planning, requirements gathering, design, processes, and procedures.

We have a couple of links in the "References" section if serious, sustained development and helping with official packaging is your ultimate goal; but to get started, let's look at a ways to help scratch that itch—to get something written and then make it available to others quickly and easily. We start with information about version control systems, and then move on to a short survey of some initiatives in the Ubuntu community to whet your appetite and help you know where to look to get connected and get started if you want to do further work to make your program available to others.

Version Control Systems

It was difficult to decide whether to include this information in this chapter. On one hand, someone who only wants to scratch an itch quickly may not be interested in setting up a version control system. On the other hand, they are not difficult to set up, especially when used with the assistance of a code hosting site like the ones discussed in each section, and they are immensely valuable if code is to have a life outside of your system.

Although make can be used to manage a small software project (see Chapter 39, "C/C++ Programming Tools for Ubuntu"), larger software projects require document management, source code controls, security, and revision tracking as the source code goes through a series of changes during its development. Version control systems provide utilities for this kind of large software project management. Changes to files placed in version control are tracked. Files can be checked out by one developer, changed in their local environment, and tested before those changes are saved in the version control system. Changes that are later discovered to be unwanted can be found and removed from the tracked files. Various version control systems manage projects differently; some use a central repository, others a distributed format where any and every copy could become the master copy.

The next few sections introduce the three most commonly used version control systems at the moment. You have certainly heard of others, and new ones crop up every few years. Each has its strengths and benefits. At the end of the chapter, in the "References" section, you will find a list of resources for learning more about Subversion, Bazaar, Mercurial, and Git to further your knowledge after you peruse this chapter's short and basic introduction to each.

> **NOTE**
>
> Subversion and Mercurial are still in heavy use, but most developers today have switched to Git and Bazaar for new projects. Keep that in mind as you read the next few sections.

Managing Software Projects with Subversion

Subversion was first created in 2000 as a replacement for an older version control system called the *Concurrent Versioning System (CVS)*. At that time, CVS was 10 years old and, although it served its purpose well, lacked some features that developers wanted. It is actively developed and widely used.

In Subversion, you check out a file from a repository in which code is stored in a client/server fashion. Then, changes are tracked over any and all files you check out, including multiple versions of files. Subversion can be used to backtrack or branch off versions of documents inside the scope of a project. It can also be used to prevent or resolve conflicting entries or changes made to source code files by multiple developers. Source code control with Subversion is done from the command line, as shown in the following examples. You first need to install Subversion from the Ubuntu software repositories, where it is called subversion.

You can create a new repository as follows:

```
matthew@seymour:~$ svnadmin create /path/to/your_svn_repo_name
```

To add a new project to the repository, first enter the top directory of the code that is going to be placed into the repository. Then, create three subdirectories: branches, tags, and trunk. Move all of your files into trunk and enter the following:

```
matthew@seymour:~$ svn import project file:///your_svn_repo_name/your_project -m
➥"First Import"
```

To check out code from an existing central repository, use this:

```
matthew@seymour:~$ svn checkout file:///your_svn_repo_name/your_project/trunk
➥your_project
```

To check in code after you have made changes, use the -m flag to add a note, which is a good idea so that others will know what the commit contains:

```
matthew@seymour:~$ svn commit -m "This fixes bug 204982."
```

To update the source code in your local repository from the main repository to make sure you have all the latest changes to the code from other developers, use this:

```
matthew@seymour:~$ svn update
```

To add new files to the repository, use the following:

```
matthew@seymour:~$ svn add file_or_dir_name
```

To delete files from the repository, use this:

```
matthew@seymour:~$ svn delete file_or_dir_name
```

Many open-source projects that use Subversion host their code using SourceForge, which also works with Git and Mercurial. Like the other code-hosting sites discussed in the following sections, SourceForge is a great place to find open-source software projects that may be useful to you or to which you may want to contribute through participation. You can find it at http://sourceforge.net.

Managing Software Projects with Bazaar

Bazaar was created by Canonical and first released 2007 to host all development files for Ubuntu and other projects. It is actively developed and widely used, not only by Canonical and Ubuntu developers, but also by many other open-source projects. Launchpad, covered later in this chapter, uses Bazaar.

Bazaar supports working with or without a central repository. Then, changes are tracked over any and all files you check out, including multiple versions of files. Bazaar does the same sorts of things as Subversion, but is generally considered easier to use. Source code

34

control is done from the command line, as shown in the following examples. You first need to install Bazaar from the Ubuntu software repositories, where it is called bzr.

There are two ways to create a new repository. If you are starting with an empty directory, use the following:

```
matthew@seymour:~$ bzr init your_project_name
```

If you are creating a repository for an existing project, enter the top-level directory for the project and enter the following:

```
matthew@seymour:~$ bzr init
matthew@seymour:~$ bzr add .
```

To check out code from an existing central repository, use this:

```
matthew@seymour:~$ bzr checkout your_project_name
```

To check your changes before you check them in, you can use bzr diff or bzr cdiff. They do the same thing, but bzr cdiff does so with colored output:

```
matthew@seymour:~$ bzr cdiff
```

To check in code after you have made changes, use the -m flag to add a note, which is a good idea so that others will know what the commit contains:

```
matthew@seymour:~$ bzr commit -m "This fixes bug 204982."
```

In Bazaar, a commit does not change the remote files; it only commits the change to your local copy. If you want others to see your changes, you must push the changes to them:

```
matthew@seymour:~$ bzr push sftp://path.to.main/repository
```

To update the source code in your local repository from the main repository to make sure you have all the latest changes to the code from other developers, use the following:

```
matthew@seymour:~$ bzr update
```

Many open-source projects that use Bazaar host their code using Launchpad, which receives more press later in this chapter as it is where Ubuntu development takes place. You can find it at http://launchpad.net.

Managing Software Projects with Mercurial

The Linux kernel used to be hosted using a version control system and code-hosting service that was free to use, but not open source. This was often a source of tension among free software advocates within the Linux community. Then, that service announced it was moving to a for-payment plan and gave some time for transition. Out of that decision, two new version control systems were birthed. Mercurial is one of them; Git is the other. Both were initially written to host the code for the Linux kernel. Git, as it was originally written by the main kernel developer himself, Linus Torvalds (in just two weeks), won out. However, the wider open-source development community was the ultimate winner as two interesting and useful version control systems were birthed.

Mercurial was created by and development is still led by one developer, Matt Mackall. It uses a distributed architecture and is designed to be fast, even when working with large codebases. Its commands are similar to Subversion, which makes transition and initial use quick and easy. One interesting feature is that Mercurial is extensible; extensions may be installed from the project's wiki or written by users to change how things work or to add features without changing the original code. Source code control is done from the command line, as shown in the following examples. You first need to install Mercurial from the Ubuntu software repositories, where it is called mercurial.

> **NOTE**
>
> The chemical symbol for mercury is Hg. This is why Mercurial commands use hg.

To create a new repository, create an empty project directory:

matthew@seymour:~$ **hg init your_project_name**

Then add your files to the directory. cd into the directory if you are not already in it, and enter the following:

matthew@seymour:~$ **hg add**

To check in code the first time or after you have made changes, use the -m flag to add a note, which is a good idea so that others will know what the commit contains:

matthew@seymour:~$ **hg commit -m 'First commit.'**

In Mercurial, a commit does not change the remote files; it only commits the change to your local copy. If you want others to see your changes, you must push the changes to them:

matthew@seymour:~$ **hg push**

To update the source code in your local repository from the main repository to make sure you have all the latest changes to the code from other developers, use this:

matthew@seymour:~$ **hg update**

Many open-source projects that use Mercurial host their code using Bitbucket. You can find it at http://bitbucket.org.

Managing Software Projects with Git

Git was initially created by Linux kernel creator Linus Torvalds and first released in 2005 to host all development files for the Linux kernel. It is now actively developed by a large team of developers led by Junio Hamano and is widely used by many other open-source projects.

Git works without a central repository and works from a different perspective than other version control systems while accomplishing the same goals. Every directory that is tracked by Git acts as an individual repository with full history and source changes for whatever is contained in it. There is no need for central tracking. Source code control is done from the command line, as shown in the following examples. You first need to install Git from the Ubuntu software repositories, where it is called `git`.

To create a new repository, enter the top-level directory for the project and enter the following:

```
matthew@seymour:~$ git init
```

To check out code from an existing central repository, you must first tell Git where that repository is:

```
matthew@seymour:~$ git remote add origin
➥git://path_to_repository/directory/proj.git
```

Then you can pull the code from that repository to your local one:

```
matthew@seymour:~$ git pull git://path_to_repository/directory/proj.git
```

To add new files to the repository, use the following:

```
matthew@seymour:~$ git add file_or_dir_name
```

To delete files from the repository, use this:

```
matthew@seymour:~$ git rm file_or_dir_name
```

To check in code after you have made changes, use the `-m` flag to add a note, which is a good idea so that others will know what the `commit` contains:

```
matthew@seymour:~$ git commit -m 'This fixes bug 204982.'
```

In Git, a `commit` does not change the remote files; it only commits the change to your local copy. If you want others to see your changes, you must push the changes to them:

```
matthew@seymour:~$ git push git://path_to_repository/directory/proj.git
```

Many open-source projects that use Git host their code using GitHub. You can find it at http://github.com.

Introduction to Opportunistic Development

You have an idea for a program that will save time by automating a repetitive task. You plan for it to have a pretty GUI and you think there are probably others out there who would like to use the tool after it is written. The problem is that you work full time, have a family, and already have a ton of side projects that do not get enough attention. You are either not able or not willing to sit down and study how Ubuntu packages programs to get them into the official software repositories. (If you are, see the links in the "References" section.)

It used to be that you had one simple choice at this juncture: Write the program and put it on a website for others to find—and hope that maybe someone would find it useful, make a DEB package, and upload it into either the Debian or Ubuntu repositories. That is no longer the only option if your goal is simply to write your tool and make the software available to Ubuntu users. Now, you need to be technically proficient at writing whatever code you want to write, and you need to be able to understand complex systems, but Ubuntu is lowering the complexity for getting that code written and making it available to the wider community. This allows developers who want only to scratch that one itch to do so without reading tons of documentation about tools they expect to use rarely or only once.

Launchpad

To get started, you need to sign up for an account on Launchpad (see Figure 34.1). Launchpad is an infrastructure created to simplify communication, collaboration, and processes within software development. It was developed and is supported by Canonical, the company that supports the Ubuntu community, but it is used by many software projects, including several that are not a part of the Ubuntu community.

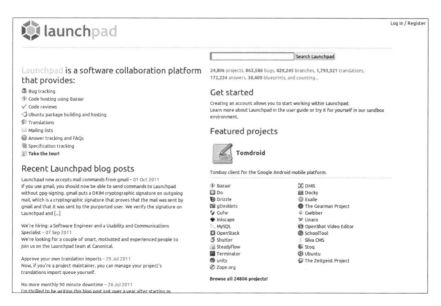

FIGURE 34.1   Launchpad is the place to start for development in Ubuntu.

Launchpad is where Ubuntu development takes place. It integrates Bazaar, the version control system introduced earlier, to make keeping track of changes to software code much simpler and permit those changes to be reverted when necessary while tracking who is performing the actions. Launchpad also incorporates Soyuz, which is a distribution and archive management software that handles the automatic package builds within Launchpad.

For developers using Launchpad, this means that the process became a bit simpler. They can concentrate on writing and editing their code and let Launchpad deal with keeping track of the changes and creating their packages. This is useful for active developers who write and maintain big projects that need source code version control and so on. It also hosts bug reporting and tracking, mailing lists, software interface translation, and much more. Most of this is beyond the scope of this chapter but of great interested to the serious developer.

What is of interest to us is that registered Launchpad users can create a *personal package archive (PPA)*. This is a much simpler way to make programs available. Anyone with a PPA can upload source code to be built in to packages. Those packages will then be made available in an apt repository that may be added to any Ubuntu user's list of source repositories and downloaded or removed using any of the standard package management tools in Ubuntu, such as apt, Ubuntu Software Center, and Synaptic. Instructions are included on the web page for each Launchpad PPA, describing how to add that repository, making this an easy method to share software that may be added and removed by even the most nontechnical end user. Figure 34.2 shows the PPA for the stable version of Google Chromium.

FIGURE 34.2   A Launchpad PPA for the stable version of Google Chromium.

Quickly

Several very knowledgeable and talented Ubuntu developers got together and started talking. These are people who know how to program and who enjoy it. At the same time, they want programming on Linux to be easy and fun and decided that it was not terribly fun for some because it can be so hard to learn. There are so many choices, so many tools, and so much documentation to read and study just to get started. They had a "what if" moment: What if we could write a program that makes some very opinionated choices about tools and templates and make that available to new programmers and people who just want to write a quick application and who are not interested in studying every available option before choosing? Not everyone cares about the benefits of Gtk versus Qt, or even knows what those are. Why force uninterested people to make those choices? Quickly is the result of these discussions and is the solution created by some of those developers.

Quickly is a tool to help you write and package software programs (and other things) quickly. You can select from a set of application templates and use some simple quickly commands to create, edit code and GUI, and publish your software for others to use. Quickly's templates are easy to write. So, if you are a fan of language foo, you can create a foo-project template. Or, if you want to help people making plug-ins for your killer app, you can make a killer-app plug-in template. You can even create a template for managing corporate documents, creating your awesome LaTeX helpers. Better yet, if you do not know what some of that means and you just want to make a useful Python tool with a pretty GUI, you can do that quickly with Quickly.

The most popular template is the ubuntu-application template, which is not surprising because the Ubuntu community wrote Quickly and uses it most often so far. This template uses a specific set of tools that are among the most common used for Linux, and specifically Ubuntu, desktop software. They include the following:

▶ **Python**—An extremely popular, easy-to-learn programming language covered in Chapter 37, "Using Python."

▶ **GTK**—A cross-platform toolkit for creating GUI interfaces that is used extensively in the GNOME desktop environment, making it a good fit for easy integration of new programs into the default desktop used by Ubuntu.

▶ **Glade**—A user interface designer for GTK from the GNOME community. It is powerful and quite easy to use to aggregate all the widgets and windows desired for a project.

▶ **GStreamer**—A media framework used in GNOME for easy integration of audio and video content in desktop applications.

▶ **Desktop Couch**—A database format built on Apache's CouchDB that allows easy integration of powerful database storage, replication, and synchronization in desktop programs. It is used by Ubuntu One and others for cloud storage.

▶ **gedit**—The default text editor in the GNOME desktop environment.

34

Using these very common tools by default eliminates many of the more confusing choices developers need to make when creating a new application. Because each of these choices are common in Ubuntu, in GNOME, and generally throughout the Linux world, an application created using them is almost guaranteed to blend in beautifully with any end user's desktop.

Quickly is in the Ubuntu repositories as quickly. Quickly is run from the command line. After installation, the best way to get going is to run the tutorial and read some basic information:

```
matthew@seymour:~$ quickly tutorial ubuntu-application
```

Some useful commands for Quickly include the following:

```
matthew@seymour:~$ quickly create ubuntu-application matthewsapplication
```

This creates the initial template for an Ubuntu program called matthewsapplication and a subfolder from which you will work on your project, and you'll get feedback with a nice pop-up window (see Figure 34.3).

FIGURE 34.3   Quickly lets you know your application has been successfully created.

To verify that the application has been created, you can change to the new application's directory and list its contents:

```
matthew@seymour:~$ cd matthewsapplication
matthew@seymour:~$ ls -la
```

```
total 44
drwxr-xr-x   6 matt matt 4096 2010-07-31 15:42 .
drwxr-xr-x 125 matt matt 4096 2010-07-31 15:42 ..
-rw-r--r--   1 matt matt   45 2010-07-31 15:42 AUTHORS
drwxr-xr-x   2 matt matt 4096 2010-07-31 15:42 bin
drwxr-xr-x   6 matt matt 4096 2010-07-31 15:42 .bzr
drwxr-xr-x   4 matt matt 4096 2010-07-31 15:42 data
drwxr-xr-x   2 matt matt 4096 2010-07-31 15:42 matthewsapplication
-rw-r--r--   1 matt matt  191 2010-07-31 15:42 matthewsapplication.desktop.in
-rw-r--r--   1 matt matt   76 2010-07-31 15:42 .quickly
-rw-r--r--   1 matt matt 2956 2010-07-31 15:42 setup.py
-rw-r--r--   1 matt matt 2837 2010-07-31 15:42 setup.pyc
```

Start editing the default GUI for your new app using Glade, as follows:

matthew@seymour:~$ **quickly design**

This brings up a beautiful interface to help you create all the actions, containers, widgets, and so on that you need in your application (see Figure 34.4).

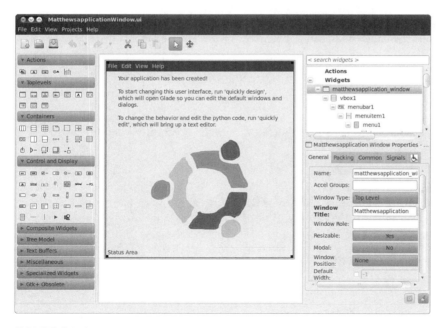

FIGURE 34.4   Quickly uses Glade to help you create your user interface.

Change the application behavior and edit your Python code in gedit (see Figure 34.5):

matthew@seymour:~$ **quickly edit**

FIGURE 34.5   Code files open in adjacent tabs for quick and easy editing in `gedit`.

Test your new application by running it with the following:

```
matthew@seymour:~$ quickly run
```

You can create a package build of your application, which is recommended for testing, using this:

```
matthew@seymour:~$ quickly package
```

One of the most exciting features of Quickly is that it integrates with Launchpad to speed up the process of dealing with PPAs. You will need a Launchpad account. There are two equivalent commands for doing this:

```
matthew@seymour:~$ quickly release
```

and

```
matthew@seymour:~$ quickly share
```

If you have a bit more development experience, you can create templates for Quickly, like the ubuntu-application template, that make specific decisions about programming language and much, much more. Quickly is young and in active development, but is already very usable. Check out the links in the "References" section for more information.

Ground Control

Collaboration on software can be difficult. The bar for entry into that world is set quite high because of the complexity of the tools. Have you ever had a problem with a program and been able to figure out what was wrong—maybe you've even been able to write a quick software patch for it—but not been able to figure out how to submit that patch to the original developer? It happens. Think of the case where someone discovers a misspelled word in a bit of Python code and wants to help save a bit of the developer's time by fixing it.

Ground Control seeks to simplify this and other sorts of collaboration on software projects. It takes the technology and workflows that most developers use and know and makes them available to the Ubuntu desktop where common non-developer end users can use them. It is essentially a version control system built in to the Ubuntu desktop that interacts directly with Launchpad and Bazaar using the standard Ubuntu GNOME file browser. This is also useful when you write the software yourself using Quickly or another method and make it available on Launchpad using a PPA. Then someone comes to you offering a bug fix, someone who may be even less technically proficient with the behind-the-scenes tools.

Install Ground Control (groundcontrol) from the Ubuntu software repositories, from the Ground Control website (https://launchpad.net/groundcontrol), or from the daily build PPA linked from that web page. A program appears in your menu at System, Preferences, Ground Control Configuration, as shown in Figure 34.6, which you need to run to give Ground Control the capability to interact with your Launchpad account. This is also the tool you use to log out when you are done using Ground Control. If you do not have a Launchpad account, Ground Control helps you sign up for one.

FIGURE 34.6   Click Login to Launchpad to get started with Ground Control.

When you sign in, Ground Control gets your Launchpad credentials, including your uploaded ssh key, from Launchpad. An ssh key is a special code needed for secure connections; it identifies you personally so that the systems and others using it can be confident of who uploaded the code. You can use an existing ssh key that you have uploaded to your Launchpad account. If you do not have an ssh key, Ground Control helps you create one. Ground Control then updates your local Bazaar configuration automatically.

Then, when you use the GNOME file browser (a.k.a. Nautilus) to view a directory that is related to a Bazaar branch you have previously used, it gives you tools to interact with it. After you have run the Ground Control Configuration tool the first time, you will discover a new folder in your home folder called Projects. From now on, if you want to log in to Ground Control, you can also do so in that folder by clicking the Identify Yourself button, as shown in Figure 34.7.

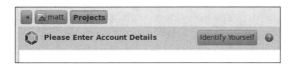

FIGURE 34.7   Identify yourself to Ground Control within the file manager.

After you are logged in, you will see the confirmation box (see Figure 34.8) and notice a change in the file manager. You now have buttons labeled Fix Bug and Fetch Project (see Figure 34.9).

FIGURE 34.8   The confirmation window uses your Launchpad details.

FIGURE 34.9   New capabilities appear in Projects.

If you click Fetch Project, you are taken to a search window. Enter the name of a project you want to find and click Find to begin your search. Figure 34.10 shows the results of a search for "chromium," while looking for the Google open-source browser. Notice that any project with the name you are seeking is returned.

FIGURE 34.10   Searching for the word *chromium*.

When you click to select, a subdirectory for the project is created in your Projects directory. Clicking it enables you to either fix bugs or fetch the Bazaar branch containing the source code for the part of the project that interests you, or all of it if it is a small project (see Figures 34.11 and 34.12). A branch is a version of the code or other items available, such as graphics or documentation.

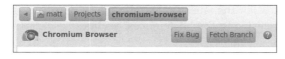

FIGURE 34.11   New options in a new directory.

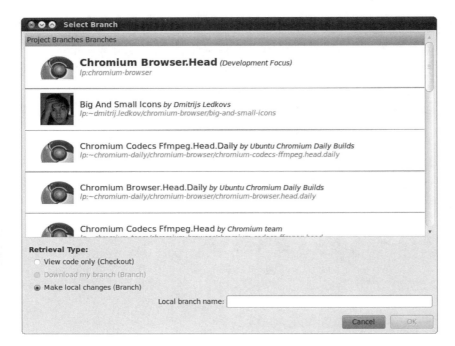

FIGURE 34.12   Selecting which branch from which to download code.

Suppose you want the main development focus branch, which is the first one listed. However, if you were working with someone on a specific part of the code or something else like icons, you could find and download that branch. Select the branch, give it a local branch name in the bottom right, and click OK. Choose a unique name so that when you upload it later with your modifications it will not conflict with anything that currently exists. You must enter your ssh key password, which you created when you created your ssh key, to confirm your identity so that activity on this code can be traced.

This helps prevent, or at least track, sinister activity by people wanting to cause trouble, and it helps track or remove uploaded mistakes. It finds any and all revisions and downloads the code to your computer. You will now find files on your computer.

That should be enough to get you started. Committing your changes works similarly to submitting bug fixes. Ground Control is rather new and in active development that seems to go in spurts, with flurries of activity separated by months of inactivity, which is normal for a small team running a project on the side. For the latest on features and use instructions, check out the Ground Control website, listed in the "References" section.

Bikeshed and Other Tools

Bikeshed was started by Dustin Kirkland in September 2010 as a project to package a series of tools he wrote to scratch some personal itches that he had as an Ubuntu developer working on Canonical's Ubuntu Server Team or that he thought would be useful to others. Every good developer, systems administrator, and DevOps guru eventually writes scripts to perform specific tasks that they find useful. This project began when Dustin gathered his together and made them accessible to the world. The wider Ubuntu community is invited to give suggestions or submit patches to make them better. The project describes itself as "a collection of random useful tools and utilities that either do not quite fit anywhere else, or have not yet been accepted by a more appropriate project. Think of this package as an 'orphanage,' where tools live until they are adopted by loving, accepting parents." The slogan for Bikeshed on the Launchpad project page is "While others debate where some tool should go, we put it in the bikeshed."

To give credit where credit is due, much of the content in this section comes, with permission, from Dustin's blog at http://blog.dustinkirkland.com, from direct communication with him, or from the tool man pages. Dustin also wrote Byobu, a tool that is covered at the end of Chapter 11, "Command-Line Master Class."

The first set of tools in this section are available by installing the bikeshed package from the Ubuntu repositories. Bikeshed sometimes works as an incubator, housing specific tools until they are ready to stand alone as a separate package or until they are accepted into an existing package. All the tools run from the command line, and most have useful man pages. (Others are still being written.)

The current contents of Bikeshed are as follows:

- ▶ apply-patch wraps the patch utility and makes it a little easier to use by automatically detecting the patch strip level.

- ▶ bch determines the files that have been modified in the current Bazaar (bzr) tree, opens debian/changelog for editing, uses dch, and appends a changelog entry for the current list of modified files.

- ▶ bzrp is the same as bzr, except that output is piped to a pager, to make reading easier.

- ▶ col1 splits and prints a given column, where the column to print is the name of the script program you are running (col1 to col9). col2 to col9 are symlinks to col1; their behavior simply changes based on the name called. For example, instead of using awk '{print $5}', you can use col5.

- ▶ dman remotely retrieves man pages from http://manpages.ubuntu.com, but reads them on the local system. This is useful to read the man page for a utility you do not have installed on the local system.

- ▶ pbget retrieves content uploaded to a pastebin by pbput or pbputs.

- ▶ pbput uploads text files, binary files, or entire directory structures to a pastebin. It is similar to pastebinit, covered later, but adds support for binaries and only uses http://pastebin.com.

- ▶ pbputs operates exactly like pbput, except the user is prompted for a passphrase for encrypting the content with gpg before uploading. pbget automatically prompts the user for the preshared passphrase when the file is requested.

- ▶ release-build takes project information for a bzr project in a Launchpad PPA that uses specific parameters and builds the project as an upstream project that can then be released to Ubuntu.

- ▶ release creates a release of a project for Ubuntu.

- ▶ socks-prox establishes an encrypted connection for tunneling traffic through a socks proxy.

- ▶ system-search performs a unified search through a set of system commands, packages, documentation, and files.

- ▶ uquick performs a quick server installation.

- ▶ what-provides determines what package provides a specific binary in your path.

- ▶ wifi-status monitors a wireless interface for connection and associated information.

The contents of Bikeshed are expected to change over time. If you are reading this a year or two after it was written, some of these tools may have graduated to standalone tools or may have been added to more official upstream packages. You can always check the Launchpad page to find a current list of Bikeshed's contents.

The rest of the tools in this section are not an actual part of Bikeshed, but have either graduated from Bikeshed and been spun off as freestanding tools or were developed individually by Dustin or others in the Ubuntu community. All the tools run from the command line and have useful man pages.

Other useful tools that you can find in the Ubuntu repositories and will want to know about include the following:

- ▶ pastebinit is a script to upload a file or the result of a command to the pastebin you want and gives you the URL in return. It was written by another Ubuntu developer, Stéphane Graber, and can be found at https://launchpad.net/pastebinit or from the Ubuntu repositories. By default, it uses http://pastebin.com, but is configurable to use others such as http://paste.ubuntu.com.

- ▶ run-one runs no more than one unique instance of a command with a unique set of arguments. This is often useful with cronjobs, when you want no more than one copy running at a time, but where a cronjob has the potential to run long and not finish before the next scheduled run.

- ▶ run-this-one is exactly like run-one, except that it will use pgrep and kill to find and kill any running processes owned by the user and matching the target commands and arguments. It blocks while trying to kill matching processes, until all matching processes are dead.

- ▶ keep-one-running operates exactly like *run-one*, except that it respawns "COMMAND [ARGS]" any time COMMAND exits (zero or nonzero).

▶ ssh-import-id uses a secure connection to contact a public key server, https:/ /launchpad.net by default, to retrieve one or more user's public keys and append them to the current user's ~/.ssh/authorized_keys file.

▶ bootmail is called by cron to send an email any time a system is rebooted. It reads a list of one or more comma-separated email addresses from /etc/bootmail/recipients, and then loops over a list of whitespace-separated files in /etc/bootmail/logs to construct the email. This is useful to know when remote systems are rebooted.

▶ rootsign cryptographically signs standard input with a public/private keypair only available to the local root user and outputs the result on standard out, suitable for piping to mail. The tool was created to be used by bootmail, but could easily be used by others. It is great for ensuring that mail sent by cronjobs is authentic.

References

▶ http://subversion.apache.org/—The main website for Subversion.

▶ http://bazaar.canonical.com/en/—The main website for Bazaar.

▶ http://mercurial.selenic.com—The main website for Mercurial.

▶ http://git-scm.com/—The main website for Git.

▶ https://launchpad.net/—Launchpad is an open-source website that hosts code, tracks bugs, and helps developers and users collaborate and share.

▶ https://launchpad.net/ubuntu/+ppas—Personal package archives allow source code to be uploaded and built in to .deb packages and made available to others as an apt repository.

▶ https://launchpad.net/quickly and https://wiki.ubuntu.com/Quickly—Quickly makes integrating a graphic toolkit, your code, and the packaging process fast and easy.

▶ www.pygtk.org/, based on http://www.gtk.org/—PyGTK is the toolkit most used by Ubuntu developers when creating GUI interfaces with GTK in Python, which is what Quickly is set to do in the ubuntu-application template.

▶ http://glade.gnome.org/—A user interface designer for GTK.

▶ www.freedesktop.org/wiki/Specifications/desktopcouch, http://couchdb. apache.org/, and https://launchpad.net/desktopcouch—Desktop Couch is a data storage format used by Ubuntu One and many desktop programs for easy integration data storage, replication from one computer to another, and synchronization into programs.

▶ **http://projects.gnome.org/gedit/**—gedit is the default text editor in the GNOME desktop environment.

▶ **https://launchpad.net/groundcontrol and http://ground-control.org/**—Ground Control integrates the power and usefulness of Launchpad into your Ubuntu desktop.

▶ **https://wiki.ubuntu.com/DeveloperStackTour**—This in-progress wiki page is planned to be the first stop for new developers entering the Ubuntu world. Here you will learn about tools and processes.

▶ **https://launchpad.net/bikeshed**—The main page for Bikeshed.

CHAPTER 35

Helping with Ubuntu Testing and QA

There are many ways to help the Ubuntu community create, refine, and promote the operating system. Some are highly technical, like writing code or packaging programs to be included in the software repositories. Some are less technical, such as helping promote Ubuntu locally or through blogging interesting news items from the community. Somewhere in the middle, leaning toward the technical side, is a task that is wide open for greater community involvement.

This is a rather brief and intentionally vague chapter. Testing by volunteers is something that requires more than a casual interest if it is going to be helpful to the developers and not an annoyance. For that reason, this chapter covers the basics of how to get involved and some of the opportunities, but not the precise details. If you are interested, and after reading this chapter we hope you are, the next step is to visit the websites listed at the end of the chapter.

Community Teams

Two community teams would love to see volunteers who can follow directions, be careful and methodical, and who notice details. Both teams work to refine the distribution during the development cycle to help make Ubuntu the best it can be.

The Ubuntu QA Team looks directly at the overall quality of the distribution, trying out default programs and configurations and trying to break things. The goal is to find bugs during the development cycle and make clear reports about them, trying to get them fixed before end users ever know of their existence. The goal here is product improvement and quality control or assurance.

These are big tasks. Even with several Canonical employees working on these full time, it is nearly impossible to test every hardware configuration or use case. It is also impossible to guess what creative ways users will attempt to perform tasks that developers have designed to perform differently. Testing as many of these options as possible is key when the goal is to create a positive experience for as many people as possible. This is why volunteers are both welcome and actively recruited.

These are also exacting tasks. Testing and bug reporting (or fixing) requires careful attention so that problems are reported clearly with steps that can be repeated by developers. This enables them to find where problems lie and more easily fix them. Not everyone is well suited for this sort of thing, but those who are able to be clear and precise and who can follow the directions given in testing plans and procedures are worth their weight in gold. You may not receive public glory for testing, but you will receive honor from those working with you in testing if you can do the job well.

You will notice some crossover in the team descriptions that follow. That is because the teams work together closely. Although each has a main focus, each may perform similar tasks from time to time. Even the individual team's web pages link to the others and offer similar information to help coordinate and direct any interested volunteers to the tasks they feel most equipped to help with.

Ubuntu Testing Team

Members of the Ubuntu Testing Team are probably best known for their work during a release week, when they help validate all of the CD and DVD images. They also operate during the release cycle testing beta releases and release candidates. In addition, they test update packages for stable releases before the packages are pushed out to users. They do this by enabling a new software repository called -proposed and trying out the software there before it ends up in the -updates repository. In addition, they help developers by coordinating communications and actively seeking and connecting additional volunteers when specific testing needs are encountered.

To get started, you need a Launchpad account. Then, join the Ubuntu Testing Team via the team's page in Launchpad at https://launchpad.net/~ubuntu-testing. It is also a good idea to subscribe to the team's email list at https://lists.ubuntu.com/mailman/listinfo/ubuntu-qa. When testers are needed, the Launchpad team list and the mailing list are the initial points of contact for those who are asked to help.

There are many ways to get involved in testing; each has varying requirements on time and technical skill. Some tasks are quick and easy, and others may be more involved. Some of the tests are general in nature, and others involve specific features, applications, and hardware. Some tests are automated and require specific test software to be downloaded and installed. Others are given as a list of instructions. Opportunities exist for many skill levels and most time schedules.

QA Team

The QA Team has a stronger focus on developing and using tools to automate the process. This enables people using the tools to run a large battery of tests against a code base very quickly while ensuring they are probing precisely what is needed. Much of their work is useful for hardware certification, logic testing, and bug discovery. They have developed an Ubuntu developer-focused suite of tools called ubuntu-qa-tools, a library called Mago for the *Linux Desktop Testing Project (LDTP)* to simplify testing of Ubuntu within the wider realm of Linux desktops, a framework called Checkbox that tests and sends test data directly to Launchpad, and more.

Bug Squad

One of the first places people become involved in Ubuntu testing is with Bug Squad. These volunteers are the initial point of contact for most bugs filed with Ubuntu. They read bug reports to see whether the bug seems legitimate (for example, that it isn't something like "Ubuntu doesn't work," but is rather specific and measurable), that it is filed against the appropriate software package, and that adequate information is included with each report for the developers to be able to figure out the problem. If the bug report meets this criteria, the Bug Squad determines which developer or team should be notified. Sometimes during the triage process, they may ask reporters for more information. They attempt to determine the severity of the bug and may assign a priority setting to the report.

Test Drive

One specific tool used by both volunteers and developers that deserves a mention is Test Drive. Dustin Kirkland is an Ubuntu developer on Canonical's Ubuntu Server team. He was looking for an easy way to download and run the latest daily development snapshot of Ubuntu using a virtual machine like KVM or VirtualBox. Like any good developer who doesn't want to repeat tasks unnecessarily, he wrote a tool to automate the process. While creating Test Drive, he made it configurable to use different virtual machines with different settings according to the user's taste. It can even download and run any ISO that may be accessed via a URL, which means it could be used to download and run images from other distributions during their development cycles.

Test Drive is written in a way that enables even a nontechnical Ubuntu user to consistently test Ubuntu development releases. Test Drive is available in the Ubuntu repositories as testdrive. It runs from the command line, although a GUI front end is in active development and may be available by the time this book goes to print.

When you run the program, you are offered a menu:

```
matthew@seymour:~$ testdrive

Welcome to Testdrive!

    1. Ubuntu Desktop (oneiric-amd64)
       +-cache--> [2011-07-24 00:08:09] oneiric-desktop-amd64.iso
    2. Ubuntu Desktop (oneiric-i386)
       +-cache--> [2011-07-24 00:08:09] oneiric-desktop-i386.iso
    3. Ubuntu Alternate (oneiric-amd64)
    4. Ubuntu Alternate (oneiric-i386)
    5. Ubuntu DVD (oneiric-amd64)
    6. Ubuntu DVD (oneiric-i386)
    7. Ubuntu Server (oneiric-amd64)
    8. Ubuntu Server (oneiric-i386)
    9. Other (prompt for ISO URL)

Select an image to testdrive [1]:
```

Type a number to download and run a specific ISO. As you can see, the preceding example is from the development cycle for Oneric Ocelot, which eventually became Ubuntu 11.10.

The Test Drive configuration is stored in a simple text file and is easy to understand and edit (although many using Test Drive will never need to edit it). Test Drive will look in several places for the testdriverc file, including the default location /etc/testdriverc and in the user's /home directory at /home/matthew/.testdriverc and /home/matthew/.config/testdrive/testdriverc.

Here is an example:

```
# This is the global configuration file for the testdrive(1) utility.
[testdrive-common]

# CACHE is the directory to cache the ISOs and disk images
# Default: $HOME/.cache/testdrive
#CACHE = /path/to/your/cache

# CACHE_IMG and CACHE_ISO will default to $CACHE/img and $CACHE/iso, respectively.
# You can set them explicitly if you want (specially interesting if you are
# trying to run the image off /dev/shm.  Make sure you have enough space there!!!
#CACHE_IMG = /dev/shm

# CLEAN_IMG will remove the just-generated image at the end of run. By default the image
# is kept, unless nothing was changed (i.e., the disk image was created, but no installation
# was actually tried).
```

```
# If running the image off /dev/shm, then *by default* the image will be removed (memory is a
# restricted resource, and we should not over-allocate it)
#CLEAN_IMG = False

# VIRT is the type of hypervisor to use
# VIRT can be either 'kvm', 'virtualbox', or 'parallels'
VIRT = kvm
#VIRT = virtualbox
#VIRT = parallels

# MEM is the amount of memory in MB to give to the VM guest
# Default: 384
MEM = 384
#MEM = 512
#MEM = 1024

# SMP is the number of processors to give to the VM guest if
# running in KVM.
# Default is the number of CPUs in the host
#SMP = 1

# DISK_SIZE is the size of the disk image
# Note that this will be a sparse, qcow2 file, so it should not actually
# take that much space on the filesystem.
# Default: 6G
DISK_SIZE = 6G
#DISK_SIZE = 10G

# KVM_ARGS is a string of arbitrary KVM_ARGS to use when launching the VM
# See kvm(1) for a comprehensive list of arguments
KVM_ARGS = -usb -usbdevice tablet -net nic,model=virtio -net user -soundhw es1370 -
vga cirrus

# Uncomment the following line if you want to hardcode the Ubuntu release
# and arch; otherwise, TestDrive will try to determine it dynamically.
#r = maverick
#m = i386
u = rsync://cdimage.ubuntu.com/cdimage

# Section for TestDrive (Command-line) specific variables.
[testdrive]

# DISK_FILE is the full path to the disk image
# Default: $CACHE/$ISO.img
#DISK_FILE = /path/to/foo.img
```

35

```
# The following line determines the default Ubuntu Flavor used by TestDrive.
# Possible flavors are: ubuntu/kubuntu/xubuntu/edubuntu/mythbuntu/ubuntustudio
f = ubuntu

# Section for TestDrive GTK specific variables.
[testdrive-gtk]

# The following line determines the default Ubuntu Flavors used by TestDrive GTK.
# Possible flavors are: ubuntu/kubuntu/xubuntu/edubuntu/mythbuntu/ubuntustudio
f = ubuntu, kubuntu, xubuntu
```

A GUI version of Test Drive is available in the Ubuntu repositories. It is called testdrive-gtk. The back-end software is the same, but the GUI version eliminates the need for new users to interact using the command line.

References

- ▶ **www.ubuntu.com/testing**—An invitation from the Ubuntu website to get involved in testing.

- ▶ **http://qa.ubuntu.com/**—The starting point for understanding and volunteering for QA Testing.

- ▶ **https://wiki.ubuntu.com/BugSquad**—The Ubuntu Bug Squad.

- ▶ **https://launchpad.net/testdrive**—The official location for downloading TestDrive and assisting with its development.

CHAPTER 36
Using Perl

Perl (the *Practical Extraction and Report Language*, or the *Pathologically Eclectic Rubbish Lister*, depending on who you speak to) is a powerful scripting tool that enables you to manage files, create reports, edit text, and perform many other tasks. Perl is included with and installed in Ubuntu by default and could be considered an integral part of the distribution because Ubuntu depends on Perl for many types of software services, logging activities, and software tools.

Perl is not the easiest of programming languages to learn because it is designed for flexibility. This chapter shows how to create and use Perl scripts on your system. You learn what a Perl program looks like, how the language is structured, and where you can find modules of prewritten code to help you write your own Perl scripts. This chapter also includes several examples of Perl used to perform a few common functions on a computer system.

Using Perl with Linux

Although originally designed as a data-extraction and report-generation language, Perl appeals to many Linux system administrators because it can be used to create utilities that fill a gap between the capabilities of shell scripts and compiled C programs (see Chapter 13, "Automating Tasks and Shell Scripting," and Chapter 39, "C/C++ Programming Tools for Ubuntu"). Another advantage of Perl over other UNIX tools is that it can process and extract data from binary files, whereas sed and awk cannot.

> **NOTE**
>
> In Perl, "there is more than one way to do it." This is the unofficial motto of Perl, and it comes up so often that it is usually abbreviated as TIMTOWTDI.

You can use Perl at your shell's command line to execute one-line Perl programs, but most often the programs (usually ending in `.pl`) are run as a command. These programs generally work on any computer platform because Perl has been ported to nearly every operating system.

Perl programs are used to support a number of Ubuntu services, such as system logging. For example, if you install the `logwatch` package, the `logwatch.pl` program is run every morning at 6:25 a.m. by the `crond` (scheduling) daemon on your system. Other Ubuntu services supported by Perl include the following:

▶ Amanda for local and network backups

▶ Fax spooling with the `faxrunqd` program

▶ Printing supported by Perl document-filtering programs

▶ Hardware sensor monitoring setup using the `sensors-detect` Perl program

Perl Versions

As of this writing, the current production version of Perl from the Perl website is 5.14.1 (which is *Perl version 5 point 14, patch level 1*). This is the version that was available at code freeze for the Ubuntu 11.10 release and that is available from the Ubuntu repositories. Perl is installed by default.

You can download the code from www.perl.com and build the newest version from source if you want to, although a stable and quality release of Perl is already installed by default in Ubuntu and most (all?) Linux and UNIX-like distributions, including Mac OS X. Updated versions may appear in the Ubuntu repositories, but generally only security fixes that can be installed by updating your system. See Chapter 9, "Managing Software," to see how to quickly get a list of available updates for Ubuntu.

You can determine what version of Perl you installed by typing `perl -v` at a shell prompt. If you are installing the latest Ubuntu distribution, you should have the latest version of Perl that was available when the software for your Ubuntu release was gathered and finalized.

A Simple Perl Program

This section introduces a very Perl program example to get you started using Perl. Although trivial for experienced Perl hackers, a short example is necessary for new users who want to learn more about Perl.

To introduce you to the absolute basics of Perl programming, Listing 36.1 illustrates a simple Perl program that prints a short message.

LISTING 36.1   A Simple Perl Program

```
#!/usr/bin/perl
print "Look at all the camels!\n";
```

Type that in and save it to a file called `trivial.pl`. Then make the file executable using the `chmod` command (see the following sidebar) and run it at the command prompt.

Command-Line Error

If you get the message `bash: trivial.pl: command not found` or `bash: ./trivial.pl: Permission denied`, you have either typed the command line incorrectly or forgotten to make `trivial.pl` executable (with the `chmod` command):

> `matthew@seymour:~$ chmod +x trivial.pl`

You can force the command to execute in the current directory as follows:

> `matthew@seymour:~$ ./trivial.pl`

Or you can use Perl to run the program like this:

> `matthew@seymour:~$ perl trivial.pl`

The sample program in the listing is a two-line Perl program. Typing in the program and running it (using Perl or making the program executable) shows how to create your first Perl program, a process duplicated by Linux users around the world every day.

36

NOTE

`#!` is often pronounced she-bang, which is short for sharp (the musicians name for the # character), and bang, which is another name for the exclamation point. This notation is also used in shell scripts. See Chapter 13, "Automating Tasks and Shell Scripting," for more information about writing shell scripts.

The `#!` line is technically not part of the Perl code at all. The # character indicates that the rest of the screen line is a comment. The comment is a message to the shell, telling it where it should go to find the executable to run this program. The interpreter ignores the comment line.

Exceptions to this practice include when the # character is in a quoted string and when it is being used as the delimiter in a regular expression. Comments are useful to document your scripts, like this:

```
#!/usr/bin/perl
# a simple example to print a greeting
print "hello there\n";
```

A block of code, such as what might appear inside a loop or a branch of a conditional statement, is indicated with curly braces ({}). For example, here is an infinite loop:

```
#!/usr/bin/perl
# a block of code to print a greeting forever
while (1) {
        print "hello there\n";
};
```

Perl statements are terminated with a semicolon (;). A Perl statement can extend over several screen lines because Perl is not concerned about whitespace.

The second line of the simple program prints the text enclosed in quotation marks. \n is the escape sequence for a newline character.

TIP

Using the perldoc and man commands is an easy way to get more information about the version of Perl installed on your system. To learn how to use the perldoc command, enter the following:

matthew@seymour:~$ **perldoc perldoc**

To get introductory information on Perl, you can use either of these commands:

matthew@seymour:~$ **perldoc perl**
matthew@seymour:~$ **man perl**

For an overview or table of contents of Perl's documentation, use the perldoc command, like this:

matthew@seymour:~$ **perldoc perltoc**

The documentation is extensive and well organized. Perl includes a number of standard Linux manual pages as brief guides to its capabilities, but perhaps the best way to learn more about Perl is to read its perlfunc document, which lists all the available Perl functions and their usage. You can view this document by using the perldoc script and typing perldoc perlfunc at the command line. You can also find this document online at http://perldoc.perl.org/.

Perl Variables and Data Structures

Perl is a *weakly typed* language, meaning that it does not require that you declare a data type, such as a type of value (data) to be stored in a particular variable. C, for example, makes you declare that a particular variable is an integer, a character, a structure, or whatever the case may be. Perl variables are whatever type they need to be, and can change type when you need them to.

Perl Variable Types

Perl has three variable types: *scalars, arrays,* and *hashes.* A different character is used to signify each variable type, so you can have the same name used with each type at the same time.

Scalar variables are indicated with the $ character, as in $penguin. Scalars can be numbers or strings, and they can change type from one to the other as needed. If you treat a number like a string, it becomes a string. If you treat a string like a number, it is translated into a number if it makes sense to do so; otherwise, it usually evaluates to 0. For example, the string "76trombones" evaluates as the number 76 if used in a numeric calculation, but the string "polar bear" evaluates to 0.

Perl arrays are indicated with the @ character, as in @fish. An array is a list of values referenced by index number, starting with the first element numbered 0, just as in C and awk. Each element in the array is a scalar value. Because scalar values are indicated with the $ character, a single element in an array is also indicated with a $ character.

For example, $fish[2] refers to the third element in the @fish array. This tends to throw some people off, but is similar to arrays in C in which the first array element is 0.

Hashes are indicated with the % character, as in %employee. A *hash* is a list of name and value pairs. Individual elements in the hash are referenced by name rather than by index (unlike an array). Again, because the values are scalars, the $ character is used for individual elements.

For example, $employee{name} gives you one value from the hash. Two rather useful functions for dealing with hashes are keys and values. The keys function returns an array containing all the keys of the hash, and values returns an array of the values of the hash. Using this approach, the Perl program in Listing 36.2 displays all the values in your environment, much like typing the bash shell's env command.

LISTING 36.2   Displaying the Contents of the **env** Hash

```perl
#!/usr/bin/perl
foreach $key (keys %ENV)  {
  print "$key = $ENV{$key}\n";
}
```

Special Variables

Perl has a variety of special variables, which usually look like punctuation— $_, $!, and $]—and are all extremely useful for shorthand code. $_ is the default variable, $! is the error message returned by the operating system, and $] is the Perl version number.

$_ is perhaps the most useful of these. You will see that variable used often in this chapter. $_ is the Perl default variable, which is used when no argument is specified. For example, the following two statements are equivalent:

```
chomp;
chomp($_);
```

The following loops are equivalent:

```
for $cow (@cattle) {
        print "$cow says moo.\n";
}
for (@cattle)          {
        print "$_ says moo.\n";
}
```

For a complete listing of the special variables, see the perlvar man page.

Operators

Perl supports a number of operators to perform various operations. There are *comparison* operators (used to compare values, as the name implies), *compound* operators (used to combine operations or multiple comparisons), *arithmetic* operators (to perform math), and special string constants.

Comparison Operators

The comparison operators used by Perl are similar to those used by C, awk, and the csh shells, and are used to specify and compare values (including strings). A comparison operator is most often used within an if statement or loop. Perl has comparison operators for numbers and strings. Table 36.1 shows the numeric comparison operators and their behavior.

TABLE 36.1   Numeric Comparison Operators in Perl

Operator	Meaning
==	Is equal to
<	Less than
>	Greater than
<=	Less than or equal to
>=	Greater than or equal to
<=>	Returns -1 if less than, 0 if equal, and 1 if greater than
!=	Not equal to
..	Range of >= first operand to <= second operand

Table 36.2 shows the string comparison operators and their behaviors.

TABLE 36.2   String Comparison Operators in Perl

Operator	Meaning
eq	Is equal to
lt	Less than
gt	Greater than
le	Less than or equal to
ge	Greater than or equal to
ne	Not equal to
cmp	Returns -1 if less than, 0 if equal, and 1 if greater than
=~	Matched by regular expression
!~	Not matched by regular expression

Compound Operators

Perl uses compound operators, similar to those used by C or awk, which can be used to combine other operations (such as comparisons or arithmetic) into more complex forms of logic. Table 36.3 shows the compound pattern operators and their behavior.

TABLE 36.3   Compound Pattern Operators in Perl

Operator	Meaning
&&	Logical AND
||	Logical OR
!	Logical NOT
( )	Parentheses; used to group compound statements

Arithmetic Operators

Perl supports a variety of math operations. Table 36.4 summarizes these operators.

TABLE 36.4   Perl Arithmetic Operators

Operator	Purpose
x**y	Raises x to the y power (same as x^y)
x%y	Calculates the remainder of x/y
x+y	Adds x to y

TABLE 36.4   Perl Arithmetic Operators

Operator	Purpose
x - y	Subtracts y from x
x*y	Multiplies x times y
x/y	Divides x by y
-y	Negates y (switches the sign of y); also known as the unary minus
++y	Increments y by 1 and uses value (prefix increment)
y++	Uses value of y and then increments by 1 (postfix increment)
-y	Decrements y by 1 and uses value (prefix decrement)
y-	Uses value of y and then decrements by 1 (postfix decrement)
x=y	Assigns value of y to x. Perl also supports operator-assignment operators (+=, -=, *=, /=, %=, **=, and others)

You can also use comparison operators (such as == or <) and compound pattern operators (&&, ||, and !) in arithmetic statements. They evaluate to the value 0 for false and 1 for true.

Other Operators

Perl supports a number of operators that do not fit any of the prior categories. Table 36.5 summarizes these operators.

TABLE 36.5   Other Perl Operators

Operator	Purpose
~x	Bitwise not (changes 0 bits to 1 and 1 bits to 0)
x & y	Bitwise and
x | y	Bitwise or
x ^ y	Bitwise exclusive or (XOR)
x << y	Bitwise shift left (shifts x by y bits)
x >> y	Bitwise shift right (shifts x by y bits)
x . y	Concatenate y onto x
a x b	Repeats string a for b number of times
x, y	Comma operator—evaluates x and then y
x ? y : z	Conditional expression (If x is true, y is evaluated; otherwise, z is evaluated.)

Except for the comma operator and conditional expression, these operators can also be used with the assignment operator, similar to the way addition (+) can be combined with assignment (=), giving +=.

Special String Constants

Perl supports string constants that have special meaning or cannot be entered from the keyboard.

Table 36.6 shows most of the constants supported by Perl.

TABLE 36.6   Perl Special String Constants

Expression	Meaning
\\	The means of including a backslash
\a	The alert or bell character
\b	Backspace
\cC	Control character (like holding the Ctrl key down and pressing the C character)
\e	Escape
\f	Formfeed
\n	Newline
\r	Carriage return
\t	Tab
\xNN	Indicates that NN is a hexadecimal number
\0NNN	Indicates that NNN is an octal (base 8) number

36

Conditional Statements: `if`/`else` and `unless`

Perl offers two conditional statements, `if` and `unless`, which function opposite one another. `if` enables you to execute a block of code only if certain conditions are met so that you can control the flow of logic through your program. Conversely, `unless` performs the statements when certain conditions are not met.

The following sections explain and demonstrate how to use these conditional statements when writing scripts for Linux.

`if`

The syntax of the Perl `if`/`else` structure is as follows:

```
if (condition) {
  statement or block of code
} elsif (condition) {
```

```
  statement or block of code
} else {
  statement or block of code
}
```

condition is a statement that returns a true or false value.

Truth is defined in Perl in a way that might be unfamiliar to you, so be careful. Everything in Perl is true except 0 (the digit zero), "0" (the string containing the number 0), "" (the empty string), and an undefined value. Note that even the string "00" is a true value because it is not one of the four false cases.

The statement or block of code is executed if the test condition returns a true value.

For example, Listing 36.3 uses the if/else structure and shows conditional statements using the eq string comparison operator.

LISTING 36.3   if/elsif/else

```
if  ($favorite eq "chocolate") {
      print "I like chocolate too.\n";
} elsif ($favorite eq "spinach") {
      print "Oh, I do not like spinach.\n";
} else {
      print "Your favorite food is $favorite.\n";
}
```

unless

unless works just like if, only backward. unless performs a statement or block if a condition is false:

```
unless ($name eq "Rich")          {
  print "Go away, you're not allowed in here!\n";
}
```

NOTE

You can restate the preceding example in more natural language, like this:

```
print "Go away!\n" unless $name eq "Rich";
```

Looping

A *loop* is a way to repeat a program action multiple times. A simple example is a countdown timer that performs a task (waiting for one second) 300 times before telling you that your egg is done boiling.

Looping constructs (also known as *control structures*) can be used to iterate a block of code as long as certain conditions apply, or while the code steps through (evaluates) a list of values, perhaps using that list as arguments.

Perl has four looping constructs: `for`, `foreach`, `while`, and `until`.

for

The `for` construct performs a *statement* (block of code) for a set of conditions defined as follows:

```
for (start condition; end condition; increment function) {
  statement(s)
}
```

The `start` condition is set at the beginning of the loop. Each time the loop is executed, the `increment` function is performed until the `end` condition is achieved. This looks much like the traditional `for`/`next` loop. The following code is an example of a `for` loop:

```
for ($i=1; $i<=10; $i++) {
    print "$i\n"
}
```

foreach

The `foreach` construct performs a statement block for each element in a list or array:

```
@names = ("alpha","bravo","charlie");
foreach $name (@names) {
  print "$name sounding off!\n";
}
```

The loop variable (`$name` in the example) is not merely set to the value of the array elements; it is aliased to that element. That means if you modify the loop variable, you're actually modifying the array. If no loop array is specified, the Perl default variable `$_` may be used:

```
@names = ("alpha","bravo","charlie");
foreach (@names) {
  print "$_ sounding off!\n";

}
```

This syntax can be very convenient, but it can also lead to unreadable code. Give a thought to the poor person who'll be maintaining your code. (It will probably be you.)

NOTE

`foreach` is frequently abbreviated as `for`.

while

while performs a block of statements as long as a particular condition is true:

```
while ($x<10) {
    print "$x\n";
    $x++;
}
```

Remember that the condition can be anything that returns a true or false value. For example, it could be a function call:

```
while ( InvalidPassword($user, $password) )        {
        print "You've entered an invalid password. Please try again.\n";
        $password = GetPassword;
}
```

until

until is the exact opposite of the while statement. It performs a block of statements as long as a particular condition is false (or, rather, until it becomes true):

```
until (ValidPassword($user, $password))   {
  print "YSdpgm_m
Sdpgm_m
You have entered an invalid password. Please try again.\n";
Sdpgm_m
  $password = GetPassword;
}
```

last and next

You can force Perl to end a loop early by using a last statement. last is similar to the C break command; the loop is exited. If you decide you need to skip the remaining contents of a loop without ending the loop itself, you can use next, which is similar to the C continue command. Unfortunately, these statements do not work with do ... while.

However, you can use redo to jump to a loop (marked by a label) or inside the loop where called:

```
$a = 100;
while (1) {
  print "start\n";
  TEST: {
    if (($a = $a / 2) > 2) {
      print "$a\n";
      if (--$a < 2) {
        exit;
      }
```

```
    redo TEST;
  }
}
}
```

In this simple example, the variable $a is repeatedly manipulated and tested in an endless loop. The word *start* will be printed only once.

do ... while and do ... until

The while and until loops evaluate the conditional first. The behavior is changed by applying a do block before the conditional. With the do block, the condition is evaluated last, which results in the contents of the block always executing at least once (even if the condition is false). This is similar to the C language do ... while (conditional) statement.

Regular Expressions

Perl's greatest strength is in text and file manipulation, which is accomplished by using the *regular expression (regex)* library. Regexes, which are quite different from the wildcard-handling and filename-expansion capabilities of the shell (see Chapter 13, "Automating Tasks and Shell Scripting"), allow complicated pattern matching and replacement to be done efficiently and easily.

For example, the following line of code replaces every occurrence of the string bob or the string mary with fred in a line of text:

```
$string =~ s/bob|mary/fred/gi;
```

Without going into too many of the details, Table 36.7 explains what the preceding line says.

TABLE 36.7   Explanation of $string =~ s/bob|mary/fred/gi;

Element	Explanation
$string =~	Performs this pattern match on the text found in the variable called $string.
s	Substitute.
/	Begins the text to be matched.
bob|mary	Matches the text bob or mary. You should remember that it is looking for the text mary, not the word mary; that is, it will also match the text mary in the word maryland.
fred	Replaces anything that was matched with the text fred.
/	Ends replace text.
g	Does this substitution globally; that is, replaces the match text wherever in the string you match it (and any number of times).
i	The search text is not case sensitive. It matches bob, Bob, or bOB.
;	Indicates the end of the line of code.

If you are interested in the details, you can get more information using the regex (7) section of the man page by entering man 7 regex from the command line.

Although replacing one string with another might seem a rather trivial task, the code required to do the same thing in another language (for example, C) is rather daunting unless supported by additional subroutines from external libraries.

Access to the Shell

Perl can perform for you any process you might ordinarily perform by typing commands to the shell through the \\ syntax. For example, the code in Listing 36.4 prints a directory listing.

LISTING 36.4   Using Backticks to Access the Shell

```
$curr_dir = 'pwd';
@listing = 'ls -al';
print "Listing for $curr_dir\n";
foreach $file (@listing) {
    print "$file";
}
```

> **NOTE**
>
> The \\ notation uses the backtick found above the Tab key (on most keyboards), not the single quotation mark.

You can also use the Shell module to access the shell. Shell is one of the standard modules that comes with Perl; it allows creation and use of a shell-like command line. Look at the following code for an example:

```
use Shell qw(cp);
cp ("/home/httpd/logs/access.log", "/tmp/httpd.log");
```

This code almost looks like it is importing the command-line functions directly into Perl. Although that is not really happening, you can pretend that the code is similar to a command line and use this approach in your Perl programs.

A third method of accessing the shell is via the system function call:

```
$rc = 0xffff & system('cp /home/httpd/logs/access.log /tmp/httpd.log');
if ($rc == 0) {
  print "system cp succeeded \n";
} else {
  print "system cp failed $rc\n";
}
```

The call can also be used with the or die clause:

```
system('cp /home/httpd/logs/access.log /tmp/httpd.log') == 0
  or die "system cp failed: $?"
```

However, you cannot capture the output of a command executed through the system function.

Modules and CPAN

A great strength of the Perl community (and the Linux community) is the fact that it is an open-source community. This community support is expressed for Perl via the *Comprehensive Perl Archive Network (CPAN)*, which is a network of mirrors of a repository of Perl code.

Most of CPAN is made up of *modules*, which are reusable chunks of code that do useful things, similar to software libraries containing functions for C programmers. These modules help speed development when building Perl programs and free Perl hackers from repeatedly reinventing the wheel when building a bicycle.

Perl comes with a set of standard modules installed. Those modules should contain much of the functionality that you will initially need with Perl. If you need to use a module not installed with Ubuntu, use the CPAN module (which is one of the standard modules) to download and install other modules onto your system. At www.perl.com/CPAN, you will find the CPAN Multiplex Dispatcher, which will attempt to direct you to the CPAN site closest to you.

Typing the following command puts you into an interactive shell that gives you access to CPAN. You can type help at the prompt to get more information on how to use the CPAN program:

```
matthew@seymour:~$ perl -MCPAN -e shell
```

After installing a module from CPAN (or writing one of your own), you can load that module into memory where you can use it with the use function:

```
use Time::CTime;
```

use looks in the directories listed in the variable @INC for the module. In this example, use looks for a directory called Time, which contains a file called CTime.pm, which in turn is assumed to contain a package called Time::CTime. The distribution of each module should contain documentation on using that module.

For a list of all the standard Perl modules (those that come with Perl when you install it), see perlmodlib in the Perl documentation. You can read this document by typing perldoc perlmodlib at the command prompt.

Code Examples

The following sections contain a few examples of things you might want to do with Perl.

Sending Mail

You can get Perl to send email in several ways. One method that you see frequently is opening a pipe to the sendmail command and sending data to it (shown in Listing 36.5). Another method is using the Mail::Sendmail module (available through CPAN), which uses socket connections directly to send mail (as shown in Listing 36.6). The latter method is faster because it does not have to launch an external process. Note that sendmail must be running on your system for the Perl program in Listing 36.5 to work.

LISTING 36.5   Sending Mail Using Sendmail

```
#!/usr/bin/perl
open (MAIL, "| /usr/sbin/sendmail -t"); # Use -t to protect from users
print MAIL <<EndMail;
To: you\
From: me\
```

```
Subject: A Sample Email\nSending email from Perl is easy!\n
.
EndMail
close MAIL;
```

> **NOTE**
>
> The @ sign in the email addresses must be escaped so that Perl does not try to eval-uate an array of that name. That is, dpitts@mk.net will cause a problem, so you need to use dpitts\<indexterm startref="iddle2799" class="endofrange" significance="normal"/>:}]
>
> The syntax used to print the mail message is called a *here document*. The syntax is as follows:
>
>   print <<EndText;
>
>   . . . . .
>
>   EndText
>
> The EndText value must be identical at the beginning and at the end of the block, including any whitespace.

LISTING 36.6   Sending Mail Using the `Mail::Sendmail` Module

```
#!/usr/bin/perl
use Mail::Sendmail;

%mail = ( To => 'you@there.com',
  From => 'me@here.com',
  Subject => 'A Sample Email",
  Message => "This is a very short message"
  );

sendmail(%mail) or die $Mail::Sendmail::error;

print "OK. Log says:\n", $Mail::Sendmail::log;

use Mail::Sendmail;
```

Perl ignores the comma after the last element in the hash. It is convenient to leave it there; if you want to add items to the hash, you do not need to add the comma. This is purely a style decision.

Using Perl to Install a CPAN Module

You can use Perl to interactively download and install a Perl module from the CPAN archives by using the `-M` and `-e` commands. Start the process by using a Perl like this:

```
# perl -MCPAN -e shell
```

When you press Enter, you see some introductory information and are asked to choose an initial automatic or manual configuration, which is required before any download or install takes place. Type no and press Enter to have Perl automatically configure for the download and install process; or if you want, just press Enter to manually configure for downloading and installation. If you use manual configuration, you must answer a series of questions regarding paths, caching, terminal settings, program locations, and so on. Settings are saved in a directory named `.cpan` in current directory.

When finished, you see the CPAN prompt:

```
cpan>
```

To have Perl examine your system and then download and install a large number of modules, use the `install` keyword, specify Bundle at the prompt, and then press Enter, like this:

```
cpan> install Bundle::CPAN
```

To download a desired module (using the example in Listing 36.6), use the `get` keyword like this:

```
cpan> get Mail::Sendmail
```

36

The source for the module will be downloaded into the .cpan directory. You can then build and install the module using the install keyword, like this:

```
cpan> install Mail::Sendmail
```

The entire process of retrieving, building, and installing a module can also be accomplished at the command line by using Perl's -e option, like this:

```
# perl -MCPAN    -e "install Mail::Sendmail"
```

Note also that the @ sign did not need to be escaped within single quotation marks (' '). Perl does not *interpolate* (evaluate variables) within single quotation marks, but does within double quotation marks and here strings (similar to << shell operations).

Purging Logs

Many programs maintain some variety of logs. Often, much of the information in the logs is redundant or just useless. The program shown in Listing 36.7 removes all lines from a file that contain a particular word or phrase, so lines that you know are not important can be purged. For example, you might want to remove all the lines in the Apache error log that originate with your test client machine because you know those error messages were produced during testing.

LISTING 36.7   Purging Log Files

```perl
#!/usr/bin/perl
# Be careful using this program!
# This will remove all lines that contain a given word
# Usage:  remove <word> <file>
$word=@ARGV[0];
$file=@ARGV[1];
if ($file)  {
  # Open file for reading
  open (FILE, "$file") or die "Could not open file: $!";      @lines=<FILE>;
  close FILE;
  # Open file for writing
  open (FILE, ">$file") or die "Could not open file for writing: $!";
  for (@lines)  {
    print FILE unless /$word/;
  } # End for
  close FILE;
} else {
  print "Usage:  remove <word> <file>\n";
}  #  End if...else
```

The code uses a few idiomatic Perl expressions to keep it brief. It reads the file into an array using the <FILE> notation; it then writes the lines back out to the file unless they match the pattern given on the command line.

The die function kills program operation and displays an error message if the open statements fail. $! in the error message, as mentioned in the section on special variables, is the error message returned by the operating system. It will likely be something like 'file not found' or 'permission denied'.

Posting to Usenet

If some portion of your job requires periodic postings to Usenet—a FAQ listing, for example—the following Perl program can automate the process for you. In the code example, the posted text is read in from a text file, but your input can come from anywhere.

The program shown in Listing 36.8 uses the Net::NNTP module, which is a standard part of the Perl distribution. You can find more documentation on the Net::NNTP module by entering 'perldoc Net::NNTP' at the command line.

LISTING 36.8   Posting an Article to Usenet

```perl
#!/usr/bin/perl
# load the post data into @post
open (POST, "post.file");
@post = <POST>;
close POST;
# import the NNTP module
use Net::NNTP;
$NNTPhost = 'news';
# attempt to connect to the remote host;
# print an error message on failure
$nntp = Net::NNTP->new($NNTPhost)
  or die "Cannot contact $NNTPhost: $!";
# $nntp->debug(1);
$nntp->post()
  or die "Could not post article: $!";
# send the header of the post
$nntp->datasend("Newsgroups: news.announce\n");
$nntp->datasend("Subject: FAQ - Frequently Asked Questions\n");
$nntp->datasend("From: ADMIN <root\
$nntp->datasend("\n\n");
# for each line in the @post array, send it
for (@post)     {
  $nntp->datasend($_);
} #  End for
$nntp->quit;
```

One-Liners

One medium in which Perl excels is the one-liner. Folks go to great lengths to reduce tasks to one line of Perl code. Perl has the rather undeserved reputation of being unreadable. The fact is that you can write unreadable code in any language. Perl allows for more than one way to do something, and this leads rather naturally to people trying to find the most arcane way to do things.

Named for Randal Schwartz, a *Schwartzian* transform is a way of sorting an array by something that is not obvious. The sort function sorts arrays alphabetically; that is pretty obvious. What if you want to sort an array of strings alphabetically by the third word? Perhaps you want something more useful, such as sorting a list of files by file size? A Schwartzian transform creates a new list that contains the information that you want to sort by, referencing the first list. You then sort the new list and use it to figure out the order that the first list should be in. Here's a simple example that sorts a list of strings by length:

```
@sorted_by_length =
  map { $_ => [0] }          # Extract original list
  sort { $a=>[1] <=> $b=>[1] } # Sort by the transformed value
  map { [$_, length($_)] }   # Map to a list of element lengths
  @list;
```

Because each operator acts on the thing immediately to the right of it, it helps to read this from right to left (or bottom to top, the way it is written here).

The first thing that acts on the list is the `map` operator. It transforms the list into a hash in which the keys are the list elements and the values are the lengths of each element. This is where you put in your code that does the transformation by which you want to sort.

The next operator is the `sort` function, which sorts the list by the values.

Finally, the hash is transformed back into an array by extracting its keys. The array is now in the desired order.

Command-Line Processing

Perl is great at parsing the output of various programs. This is a task for which many people use tools such as `awk` and `sed`. Perl gives you a larger vocabulary for performing these tasks. The following example is very simple, but illustrates how you might use Perl to chop up some output and do something with it. In the example, Perl is used to list only those files that are larger than 10KB:

```
matthew@seymour:~$ ls -la | perl -nae 'print "$F[8] is $F[4]\n" if $F[4] > 10000;'
```

The `-n` switch indicates that I want the Perl code run for each line of the output. The `-a` switch automatically splits the output into the `@F` array. The `-e` switch indicates that the Perl code is going to follow on the command line.

Related Ubuntu and Linux Commands

You will use these commands and tools when using Perl with Linux:

▶ **a2p**—A filter used to translate awk scripts into Perl.

▶ **find2perl**—A utility used to create Perl code from command lines using the find command.

▶ **perldoc**—A Perl utility used to read Perl documentation.

▶ **s2p**—A filter used to translate sed scripts into Perl.

▶ **vi**—The vi (actually vim) text editor.

References

▶ *Sams Teach Yourself Perl in 21 Days, Second Edition*, by Laura Lemay, Sams Publishing.

▶ *Sams Teach Yourself Perl in 24 Hours, Second Edition*, by Clinton Pierce, Sams Publishing.

▶ *Learning Perl, Third Edition*, by Randal L. Schwartz, Tom Phoenix, O'Reilly & Associates.

▶ *Programming Perl*, Third Edition, by Larry Wall, Tom Christiansen, and Jon Orwant, O'Reilly & Associates.

▶ *Effective Perl Programming: Writing Better Programs with Perl*, by Joseph Hall, Addison-Wesley Publishing Company.

▶ *Mastering Regular Expressions*, by Jeffrey Friedl, O'Reilly & Associates.

▶ **www.perl.com**—This is the place to find all sorts of information about Perl, from its history and culture to helpful tips. This is also the place to download the Perl interpreter for your system.

▶ **http://cpan.perl.org**—CPAN is the place for you to find modules and programs in Perl. If you write something in Perl that you think is particularly useful, you can make it available to the Perl community here.

▶ **http://perldoc.perl.org/index-faq.html**—FAQs index of common Perl queries; this site offers a handy way to quickly search for answers about Perl.

▶ **http://learn.perl.org**—One of the best places to start learning Perl online. If you master Perl, go to http://jobs.perl.org.

▶ **www.pm.org**—The Perl Mongers are local Perl users groups. There might be one in your area. The Perl advocacy site is www.perl.org.

36

Using PHP

This chapter introduces you to the world of PHP programming, from the point of view of using it as a web scripting language and as a command-line tool. PHP originally stood for *personal home page* because it was a collection of Perl scripts designed to ease the creation of guest books, message boards, and other interactive scripts commonly found on home pages. However, since those early days, it has received two major updates (PHP 3 and PHP 4), plus a substantial revision in PHP 5, which is the version bundled with Ubuntu.

Part of the success of PHP has been its powerful integration with databases—its earliest uses nearly always took advantage of a database back end. In PHP 5, two big new data storage mechanisms were introduced: SQLite, which is a powerful and local database system; and SimpleXML, which is an *application programming interface (API)* designed to make *Extensible Markup Language (XML)* parsing and querying easy. As you will see over time, the PHP developers did a great job: Both SQLite and SimpleXML are easy to learn and use.

> **NOTE**
>
> Many packages for PHP are available from the Ubuntu repositories. The basic package is just called php5, but you might also want to add extensions such as php5-ldap, php5-mysql, or php5-pgsql.

Introduction to PHP

In terms of the way it looks, PHP is a cross between Java and Perl, having taken the best aspects of both and merged them successfully into one language. The Java parts include a powerful object-orientation system, the capability to throw program exceptions, and the general style of writing that both languages borrowed from C. Borrowed from Perl is the "it should just work" mentality where ease of use is favored over strictness. As a result, you will find a lot of "there is more than one way to do it" in PHP. This also means that it is possible to accomplish tasks in ways that are less than ideal or without consideration for good security. Many criticize PHP for this, but for simple tasks or if written carefully, it can be a pretty good language and is easy to understand and use, especially for quick website creation.

Entering and Exiting PHP Mode

Unlike PHPs predecessors, you embed your PHP code inside your HTML as opposed to the other way around. Before PHP, many websites had standard HTML pages for most of their content, linking to Perl CGI pages to do back-end processing when needed. With PHP, all your pages are capable of processing and containing HTML. This is a huge factor in PHPs popularity.

Each PHP file is processed by PHP that looks for code to execute. PHP considers all the text it finds to be HTML until it finds one of four things:

- `<?php`

- `<?`

- `<%`

- `<script language="php">`

The first option is the preferred method of entering PHP mode because it is guaranteed to work.

When in PHP mode, you can exit it by using `?>` (for `<?php` and `<?`); `%>` (for `<%`) or `</script>` (for `<script language="php">`). This code example demonstrates entering and exiting PHP mode:

```
In HTML mode
<?php
  echo "In PHP mode";
?>
In HTML mode
In <?php echo "PHP"; ?> mode
```

Variables

All variables in PHP start with a dollar sign ($). Unlike many other languages, PHP does not have different types of variable for integers, floating-point numbers, arrays, or Booleans. They all start with a $, and all are interchangeable. As a result, PHP is a weakly typed language, which means you do not declare a variable as containing a specific type of data; you just use it however you want to.

Save the code in Listing 37.1 into a new file called ubuntu1.php.

LISTING 37.1   Testing Types in PHP

```php
<?php
  $i = 10;
  $j = "10";
  $k = "Hello, world";
  echo $i + $j;
  echo $i + $k;
?>
```

To run that script, bring up a console and browse to where you saved it. Then type this command:

```
matthew@seymour:~$ php ubuntu1.php
```

If PHP is installed correctly, you should see the output 2010, which is really two things. The 20 is the result of 10 + 10 ($i plus $j), and the 10 is the result of adding 10 to the text string Hello, world. Neither of those operations are really straightforward. Whereas $i is set to the number 10, $j is actually set to be the text value "10", which is not the same thing. Adding 10 to 10 gives 20, as you would imagine, but adding 10 to "10" (the string) forces PHP to convert $j to an integer on-the-fly before adding it.

Running $i + $k adds another string to a number, but this time the string is Hello, world and not just a number inside a string. PHP still tries to convert it, though, and converting any non-numeric string into a number converts it to 0. So, the second echo statement ends up saying $i + 0.

As you should have guessed by now, calling echo outputs values to the screen. Right now, that prints directly to your console, but internally PHP has a complex output mechanism that enables you to print to a console, send text through Apache to a web browser, send data over a network, and more.

Now that you have seen how PHP handles variables of different types, it is important that you understand the selection of types available to you, as shown in Table 37.1.

37

TABLE 37.1   PHP Variable Types

Type	Stores
integer	Whole numbers; for example, 1, 9, or 324809873
float	Fractional numbers; for example, 1.1, 9.09, or 3.141592654
string	Characters; for example, "a", "sfdgh", or "Ubuntu Unleashed"
boolean	True or false
array	Several variables of any type
resource	Any external data

The first four can be thought of as simple variables, and the last three as complex variables. Arrays are simply collections of variables. You might have an array of numbers (the ages of all the children in a class); an array of strings (the names of all Wimbledon tennis champions); or even an array of arrays, known as a *multidimensional array*. Arrays are covered in more depth in the next section because they are unique in the way in which they are defined.

Objects are used to define and manipulate a set of variables that belong to a unique entity. Each object has its own personal set of variables, as well as functions that operate on those variables. Objects are commonly used to model real-world things. You might define an object that represents a TV, with variables such as $CurrentChannel (probably an integer), $SupportsHiDef (a Boolean), and so on.

Of all the complex variables, the easiest to grasp are resources. PHP has many extensions available to it that allow you to connect to databases, manipulate graphics, or even make calls to Java programs. Because they are all external systems, they need to have types of data unique to them that PHP cannot represent using any of the six other data types. So, PHP stores their custom data types in resources—data types that are meaningless to PHP but can be used by the external libraries that created them.

Arrays

Arrays are one of our favorite parts of PHP because the syntax is smart and easy to read and yet manages to be as powerful as you could want. You need to know four pieces of jargon to understand arrays:

▶ An array is made up of many *elements*.

▶ Each element has a *key* that defines its place in the array. An array can have only one element with a given key.

▶ Each element also has a *value*, which is the data associated with the key.

▶ Each array has a *cursor*, which points to the current key.

The first three are used regularly; the last one less often. The array cursor is covered later in this chapter in the section "Basic Functions," but we look at the other three now. With PHP, your keys can be almost anything: integers, strings, objects, or other arrays. You can even mix and match the keys so that one key is an array; another is a string, and so on. The one exception to all this is floating-point numbers: You cannot use floating-point numbers as keys in your arrays.

There are two ways of adding values to an array: with the [ ] operator, which is unique to arrays; and with the array() pseudo-function. You should use [ ] when you want to add items to an existing array and use array() to create a new array.

To sum all this up in code, Listing 37.2 shows a script that creates an array without specifying keys, adds various items to it both without keys and with keys of varying types, does a bit of printing, and then clears the array.

LISTING 37.2   Manipulating Arrays

```php
<?php
  $myarr = array(1, 2, 3, 4);

  $myarr[4] = "Hello";
  $myarr[] = "World!";
  $myarr["elephant"] = "Wombat";
  $myarr["foo"] = array(5, 6, 7, 8);

  echo $myarr[2];
  echo $myarr["elephant"];
  echo $myarr["foo"][1];

  $myarr = array();
?>
```

The initial array is created with four elements, to which we assign the values 1, 2, 3, and 4. Because no keys are specified, PHP automatically assigns keys for us starting at 0 and counting upward—giving keys 0, 1, 2, and 3. Then we add a new element with the [ ] operator, specifying 4 as the key and "Hello" as the value. Next, [ ] is used again to add an element with the value "World!" and no key and then again to add an element with the key "elephant" and the value "wombat". The line after that demonstrates using a string key with an array value—an array inside an array (a multidimensional array).

The next three lines demonstrate reading back from an array, first using a numeric key, then using a string key, and then using a string key and a numeric key. Remember, the "foo" element is an array in itself, so that third reading line retrieves the array and then prints the second element (arrays start at 0, remember). The last line blanks the array by simply using array() with no parameters, which creates an array with elements and assigns it to $myarr.

37

The following is an alternative way of using `array()` that allows you to specify keys along with their values:

```
$myarr = array("key1" => "value1", "key2" => "value2",
7 => "foo", 15 => "bar");
```

Which method you choose really depends on whether you want specific keys or want PHP to pick them for you.

Constants

Constants are frequently used in functions that require specific values to be passed in. For example, a popular function is `extract()`, which takes all the values in an array and places them into variables in their own right. You can choose to change the name of the variables as they are extracted using the second parameter—send it a 0 and it overwrites variables with the same names as those being extracted, send it a 1 and it skips variables with the same names, send it a 5 and it prefixes variables only if they exist already, and so on. Of course, no one wants to have to remember a lot of numbers for each function, so you can instead use EXTR_OVERWRITE for 0, EXTR_SKIP for 1, EXTR_PREFIX_IF_EXISTS for 5, and so on, which is much easier.

You can create constants of your own by using the `define()` function. Unlike variables, constants do not start with a dollar sign. Code to define a constant looks like this:

```
<?php
  define("NUM_SQUIRRELS", 10);
  define("PLAYER_NAME", "Jim");
  define("NUM_SQUIRRELS_2", NUM_SQUIRRELS);
  echo NUM_SQUIRRELS_2;
?>
```

That script demonstrates how you can set constants to numbers, strings, or even the value of other constants, although that doesn't really get used much!

References

Using the equal sign (=) copies the value from one variable to another so they both have their own copy of the value. Another option here is to use references, which is where a variable does not have a value of its own; instead, it points to another variable. This enables you to share values and have variables mutually update themselves.

To copy by reference, use the & symbol, as follows:

```
<?php
  $a = 10;
  $b = &$a;
  echo $a . "\n";
  echo $b . "\n";
```

```
  $a = 20;
  echo $a . "\n";
  echo $b . "\n";

  $b = 30;
  echo $a . "\n";
  echo $b . "\n";
?>
```

If you run that script, you will see that updating $a also updates $b, but also that updating $b updates $a.

Comments

Adding short comments to your code is recommended and usually a requirement in larger software houses. In PHP, you have three options for commenting style: //, /* */, and #. The first option (two slashes) instructs PHP to ignore everything until the end of the line. The second (a slash and an asterisk) instructs PHP to ignore everything until it reaches */. The last (a hash symbol) works like // and is included because it is common among shell scripting languages.

This code example demonstrates the difference between // and /* */:

```
<?php
  echo "This is printed!";
  // echo "This is not printed";
  echo "This is printed!";
  /* echo "This is not printed";
  echo "This is not printed either"; */
?>
```

It is generally preferred to use // because it is a known quantity. However, it is easy to introduce coding errors with /* */ by losing track of where a comment starts and ends.

> **NOTE**
>
> Contrary to popular belief, having comments in your PHP script has almost no effect on the speed at which the script executes. What little speed difference exists is wholly removed if you use a code cache.

Escape Sequences

Some characters cannot be typed, and yet you will almost certainly want to use some of them from time to time. For example, you might want to use an ASCII character for new line, but you cannot type it. Instead, you need to use an escape sequence: \n. Similarly,

37

you can print a carriage return character with \r. It is important to know both of these because, on the Windows platform, you need to use \r\n to get a new line. If you do not plan to run your scripts anywhere else, you need not worry about this.

Going back to the first script we wrote, recall that it printed 2010 because we added 10 + 10 and then 10 + 0. We can rewrite that using escape sequences, like this:

```php
<?php
  $i = 10;
  $j = "10";
  $k = "Hello, world";
  echo $i + $j;
  echo "\n";
  echo $i + $k;
  echo "\n";
?>
```

This time, PHP prints a new line after each of the numbers, making it obvious that the output is 20 and 10 rather than 2010. Note that the escape sequences must be used in double quotation marks because they will not work in single quotation marks.

Three common escape sequences are \\, which means "ignore the backslash"; \", which means "ignore the double quote"; and \', which means "ignore the single quote." This is important when strings include quotation marks inside them. If we had a string such as "are you really Conan O'Brien?", which has a single quotation mark in, this code would not work:

```php
<?php
  echo 'Are you really Conan O'Brien?';
?>
```

PHP would see the opening quotation mark, read all the way up to the O in O'Brien, and then see the quotation mark following the O as being the end of the string. The Brien? part would appear to be a fragment of text and would cause an error. You have two options here: You can either surround the string in double quotation marks or escape the single quotation mark with \'.

If you choose the escaping route, it will look like this:

```php
echo 'Are you really Conan O\'Brien?';
```

Although they are a clean solution for small text strings, be careful with overusing escape sequences. HTML is particularly full of quotation marks, and escaping them can get messy:

```php
$mystring = "<img src=\"foo.png\" alt=\"My picture\"
width=\"100\" height=\"200\" />";
```

In that situation, you are better off using single quotation marks to surround the text simply because it is a great deal easier on the eye.

Variable Substitution

PHP allows you to define strings using three methods: single quotation marks, double quotation marks, or heredoc notation. Heredoc is not discussed here because it is fairly rare compared to the other two methods, but single quotation marks and double quotation marks work identically, with one minor exception: variable substitution.

Consider the following code:

```php
<?php
  $age = 25;
  echo "You are ";
  echo $age;
?>
```

That is a particularly clumsy way to print a variable as part of a string. Fortunately, if you put a variable inside a string, PHP performs *variable substitution*, replacing the variable with its value. That means we can rewrite the code like this:

```php
<?php
  $age = 25;
  echo "You are $age";
?>
```

The output is the same. The difference between single quotation marks and double quotation marks is that single-quoted strings do not have their variables substituted. Here's an example:

```php
<?php
  $age = 25;
  echo "You are $age";
  echo 'You are $age';
?>
```

The first echo prints You are 25, but the second one prints You are $age.

Operators

Now that we have data values to work with, we need some operators to use, too. We have already used + to add variables together, but many others in PHP handle arithmetic, comparison, assignment, and other operators. *Operator* is just a fancy word for something that performs an operation, such as addition or subtraction. However, *operand* might be new to you. Consider this operation:

```php
$a = $b + c;
```

In this operation, = and + are operators, and $a, $b, and $c are operands. Along with +, you will also already know – (subtract), * (multiply), and / (divide), but Table 37.2 provides some more.

TABLE 37.2   PHP Operators

Operator	What It Does
=	Assigns the right operand to the left operand.
==	Returns true if the left operand is equal to the right operand.
!=	Returns true if the left operand is not equal to the right operand.
===	Returns true if the left operand is identical to the right operand. This is not the same as ==.
!==	Returns true if the left operand is not identical to the right operand. This is not the same as !=.
<	Returns true if the left operand is smaller than the right operand.
>	Returns true if the left operand is greater than the right operand.
<=	Returns true if the left operand is equal to or smaller than the right operand.
&&	Returns true if both the left operand and the right operand are true.
||	Returns true if either the left operand or the right operand is true.
++	Increments the operand by one.
—	Decrements the operand by one.
+=	Increments the left operand by the right operand.
-=	Decrements the left operand by the right operand.
.	Concatenates the left operand and the right operand (joins them together).
%	Divides the left operand by the right operand and returns the remainder.
|	Performs a bitwise OR operation. It returns a number with bits that are set in either the left operand or the right operand.
&	Performs a bitwise AND operation. It returns a number with bits that are set both in the left operand and the right operand.

At least 10 other operators are not listed; to be fair, however, you're unlikely to use them. Even some of the ones in this list are used infrequently (bitwise AND, for example). Having said that, the bitwise OR operator is used regularly because it allows you to combine values.

Here is a code example demonstrating some of the operators:

```php
<?php
  $i = 100;
  $i++; // $i is now 101
  $i--; // $i is now 100 again
  $i += 10; // $i is 110
  $i = $i / 2; // $i is 55
  $j = $i; // both $j and $i are 55
  $i = $j % 11; // $i is 0
?>
```

The last line uses modulus, which takes some people a little bit of effort to understand. The result of $i % 11 is 0 because $i is set to 55 and modulus works by dividing the left operand (55) by the right operand (11) and returning the remainder. 55 divides by 11 exactly 5 times, and so has the remainder 0.

The concatenation operator, a period (.), sounds scarier than it is: It just joins strings together. For example:

```php
<?php
echo "Hello, " . "world!";
echo "Hello, world!" . "\n";
?>
```

There are two "special" operators in PHP that are not covered here and yet are used frequently. Before we look at them, though, it is important that you see how the comparison operators (such as <, <=, and !=) are used inside conditional statements.

Conditional Statements

In a *conditional statement* you instruct PHP to take different actions depending on the outcome of a test. For example, you might want PHP to check whether a variable is greater than 10 and, if so, print a message. This is all done with the if statement, which looks like this:

```php
if (your condition) {
  // action to take if condition is true
} else {
  // optional action to take otherwise
}
```

The your condition part can be filled with any number of conditions you want PHP to evaluate, and this is where the comparison operators come into their own. For example:

```php
if ($i > 10) {
  echo "11 or higher";
} else {
  echo "10 or lower";
}
```

PHP looks at the condition and compares $i to 10. If it is greater than 10, it replaces the whole operation with 1; otherwise, it replaces it with 0. So, if $i is 20, the result looks like this:

```php
if (1) {
  echo "11 or higher";
} else {
  echo "10 or lower";
}
```

In conditional statements, any number other than 0 is considered to be equivalent to the Boolean value true; so 1 always evaluates to true. There is a similar case for strings: If

37

your string has any characters in, it evaluates to `true`, with empty strings evaluating to `false`. This is important because you can then use that 1 in another condition through `&&` or `||` operators. For example, if you want to check whether `$i` is greater than 10 but less than 40, you could write this:

```
if ($i > 10 && $i < 40) {
  echo "11 or higher";
} else {
  echo "10 or lower";
}
```

If we presume that `$i` is set to 50, the first condition (`$i, 10`) is replaced with 1 and the second condition (`$i < 40`) is replaced with 0. Those two numbers are then used by the `&&` operator, which requires both the left and right operands to be `true`. Whereas 1 is equivalent to `true`, 0 is not, so the `&&` operand is replaced with 0 and the condition fails.

`=`, `==`, `===`, and similar operators are easily confused and often the source of programming errors. The first, a single equal sign, assigns the value of the right operand to the left operand. However, all too often you see code like this:

```
if ($i = 10) {
  echo "The variable is equal to 10!";
} else {
  echo "The variable is not equal to 10";
}
```

That is incorrect. Rather than checking whether `$i` is equal to 10, it assigns 10 to `$i` and returns `true`. What is needed is `==`, which compares two values for equality. In PHP, this is extended so that there is also `===` (three equal signs), which checks whether two values are identical, more than just equal.

The difference is slight but important: If you have a variable with the string value `"10"` and compare it against the number value of 10, they are equal. Thus, PHP converts the type and checks the numbers. However, they are not identical. To be considered identical, the two variables must be equal (that is, have the same value) and be of the same data type (that is, both are strings, both are integers, and so on).

NOTE

It is common practice to put function calls in conditional statements rather than direct comparisons. For example:

```
if (do_something()) {
```

If the `do_something()` function returns `true` (or something equivalent to `true`, such as a nonzero number), the conditional statement evaluates to `true`.

Special Operators

The ternary operator and the execution operator work differently from those we have seen so far. The ternary operator is rarely used in PHP, thankfully, because it is really just a condensed conditional statement. Presumably it arose through someone needing to make a code occupy as little space as possible because it certainly does not make PHP code any easier to read.

The ternary operator works like this:

```
$age_description = ($age < 18) ? "child" : "adult";
```

Without explanation, that code is essentially meaningless; however, it expands into the following five lines of code:

```
if ($age < 18) {
  $age_description = "child";
} else {
  $age_description = "adult";
}
```

The ternary operator is so named because it has three operands: a condition to check ($age < 18 in the previous code), a result if the condition is true ("child"), and a result if the condition is false ("adult"). Although we hope you never have to use the ternary operator, it is at least important to know how it works in case you stumble across it.

The other special operator is the execution operator, which is the backtick symbol, `. The position of the backtick key varies depending on your keyboard, but it is likely to be just to the left of the 1 key (above Tab). The execution operator executes the program inside the backticks, returning any text the program outputs. For example:

```
<?php
  $i = `ls -l`;
  echo $i;
?>
```

That executes the ls program, passing in -l (a lowercase *L*) to get the long format, and stores all its output in $i. You can make the command as long or as complex as you like, including piping to other programs. You can also use PHP variables inside the command.

Switching

Having multiple if statements in one place is ugly, slow, and prone to errors. Consider the code in Listing 37.3.

LISTING 37.3   How Multiple Conditional Statements Lead to Ugly Code

```php
<?php
  $cat_age = 3;

  if ($cat_age == 1) {
    echo "Cat age is 1";
  } else {
    if ($cat_age == 2) {
      echo "Cat age is 2";
    } else {
      if ($cat_age == 3) {
        echo "Cat age is 3";
      } else {
        if ($cat_age == 4) {
          echo "Cat age is 4";
        } else {
          echo "Cat age is unknown";
        }
      }
    }
  }
?>
```

Even though it certainly works, it is a poor solution to the problem. Much better is a switch/case block, which transforms the previous code into what's shown in Listing 37.4.

LISTING 37.4   Using a switch/case Block

```php
<?php
  $cat_age = 3;

  switch ($cat_age) {
    case 1:
      echo "Cat age is 1";
      break;
    case 2:
      echo "Cat age is 2";
      break;
    case 3:
      echo "Cat age is 3";
      break;
    case 4:
      echo "Cat age is 4";
      break;
```

```
    default:
      echo "Cat age is unknown";
  }
?>
```

Although it is only slightly shorter, it is a great deal more readable and much easier to maintain. A switch/case group is made up of a switch() statement in which you provide the variable you want to check, followed by numerous case statements. Notice the break statement at the end of each case. Without that, PHP would execute each case statement beneath the one it matches. Calling break causes PHP to exit the switch/case. Notice also that there is a default case at the end that catches everything that has no matching case.

It is important that you do not use case default: but merely default:. Also, it is the last case label, so it has no need for a break statement because PHP exits the switch/case block there anyway.

Loops

PHP has four ways you can execute a block of code multiple times: while, for, foreach, and do...while. Of the four, only do...while sees little use; the others are popular, and you will certainly encounter them in other people's scripts.

The most basic loop is the while loop, which executes a block of code for as long as a given condition is true. So, we can write an infinite loop—a block of code that continues forever—with this PHP:

```
<?php
  $i = 10;
  while ($i >= 10) {
    $i += 1;
    echo $i;
  }
?>
```

The loop block checks whether $i is greater or equal to 10 and, if that condition is true, adds 1 to $i and prints it. Then it goes back to the loop condition again. Because $i starts at 10 and we only ever add numbers to it, that loop continues forever. With two small changes, we can make the loop count down from 10 to 0:

```
<?php
  $i = 10;
  while ($i >= 0) {
    $i -= 1;
    echo $i;
  }
?>
```

37

So, this time we check whether $i is greater than or equal to 0 and subtract 1 from it with each loop iteration. while loops are typically used when you are unsure of how many times the code needs to loop because while keeps looping until an external factor stops it.

With a for loop, you specify precise limits on its operation by giving it a declaration, a condition, and an action. That is, you specify one or more variables that should be set when the loop first runs (the *declaration*), you set the circumstances that will cause the loop to terminate (the *condition*), and you tell PHP what it should change with each loop iteration (the *action*). That last part is what really sets a for loop apart from a while loop: You usually tell PHP to change the condition variable with each iteration.

We can rewrite the script that counts down from 10 to 0 using a for loop:

```php
<?php
  for($i = 10; $i >= 0; $i -= 1) {
    echo $i;
  }
?>
```

This time we do not need to specify the initial value for $i outside the loop, and neither do we need to change $i inside the loop; it is all part of the for statement. The actual amount of code is really the same, but for this purpose, the for loop is arguably tidier and therefore easier to read. With the while loop, the $i variable was declared outside the loop and so was not explicitly attached to the loop.

The third loop type is foreach, which is specifically for arrays and objects, although it is rarely used for anything other than arrays. A foreach loop iterates through each element in an array (or each variable in an object), optionally providing both the key name and the value.

In its simplest form, a foreach loop looks like this:

```php
<?php
  foreach($myarr as $value) {
    echo $value;
  }
?>
```

This loops through the $myarr array we created earlier, placing each value in the $value variable. We can modify that so we get the keys as well as the values from the array, like this:

```php
<?php
  foreach($myarr as $key => $value) {
    echo "$key is set to $value\n";
  }
?>
```

As you can guess, this time the array keys go in $key and the array values go in $value. One important characteristic of the foreach loop is that it goes from the start of the array to the end and then stops—and by *start*, we mean the first item to be added rather than the lowest index number. This script shows this behavior:

```php
<?php
  $array = array(6 => "Hello", 4 => "World",
                 2 => "Wom", 0 => "Bat");
  foreach($array as $key => $value) {
    echo "$key is set to $value\n";
  }
?>
```

If you try this script, you will see that foreach prints the array in the original order of 6, 4, 2, 0 rather than the numeric order of 0, 2, 4, 6.

The do...while loop works like the while loop, with the exception that the condition appears at the end of the code block. This small syntactical difference means a lot, though, because a do...while loop is always executed at least once. Consider this script:

```php
<?php
  $i = 10;
  do {
    $i -= 1;
    echo $i;
  } while ($i < 10);
?>
```

Without running the script, what do you think it will do? One possibility is that it will do nothing; $i is set to 10, and the condition states that the code must loop only while $i is less than 10. However, a do...while loop always executes once, so what happens is that $i is set to 10 and PHP enters the loop, decrements $i, prints it, and then checks the condition for the first time. At this point, $i is indeed less than 10, so the code loops, $i is decremented again, the condition is rechecked, $i is decremented again, and so on. This is in fact an infinite loop and so should be avoided!

If you ever want to exit a loop before it has finished, you can use the same break statement that we used earlier to exit a switch/case block. This becomes more interesting if you find yourself with *nested* loops (loops inside of loops). This is a common situation to be in. For example, you might want to loop through all the rows in a chessboard and, for each row, loop through each column. Calling break exits only one loop or switch/case, but you can use break 2 to exit two loops or switch/cases, or break 3 to exit three, and so on.

Including Other Files

Unless you are restricting yourself to the simplest programming ventures, you will want to share code among your scripts at some point. The most basic need for this is to have a standard header and footer for your website, with only the body content changing. However, you might also find yourself with a small set of custom functions you use frequently, and it would be an incredibly bad move to simply copy and paste the functions into each of the scripts that use them.

The most common way to include other files is with the `include` keyword. Save this script as `include1.php`:

```php
<?php
  for($i = 10; $i >= 0; $i -= 1) {
    include "echo_i.php";
  }
?>
```

Then save this script as `echo_i.php`:

```php
<?php
  echo $i;
?>
```

If you run `include1.php`, PHP loops from 10 to 0 and includes `echo_i.php` each time. For its part, `echo_i.php` just prints the value of `$i`, which is a crazy way of performing an otherwise simple operation, but it does demonstrate how included files share data. Note that the `include` keyword in `include1.php` is inside a PHP block, but we reopen PHP inside `echo_i.php`. This is important because PHP exits PHP mode for each new file, so you always have a consistent entry point.

Basic Functions

PHP has a vast number of built-in functions that enable you to manipulate strings, connect to databases, and more. There is not room here to cover even 10 percent of the functions; for more detailed coverage of functions, check the "References" section at the end of this chapter.

Strings

Several important functions are used for working with strings, and there are many more less-frequently used ones for which there is not enough space here. We are going to look at the most important here, ordered by difficulty—easiest first!

The easiest function is `strlen()`, which takes a string as its parameter and returns the number of characters in there, like this:

```php
<?php
  $ourstring = "  The Quick Brown Box Jumped Over The Lazy Dog  ";
  echo strlen($ourstring);
?>
```

We will be using that same string in subsequent examples to save space. If you execute that script, it outputs 48 because 48 characters are in the string. Note the two spaces on either side of the text, which pad the 44-character phrase up to 48 characters.

We can fix that padding with the `trim()` function, which takes a string to trim and returns it with all the whitespace removed from either side. This is a commonly used function because all too often, you encounter strings that have an extra new line at the end or a space at the beginning. This cleans it up perfectly.

Using `trim()`, we can turn our 48-character string into a 44-character string (the same thing, without the extra spaces), like this:

```
echo trim($ourstring);
```

Keep in mind that `trim()` returns the trimmed string, so that outputs "`The Quick Brown Box Jumped Over The Lazy Dog`". We can modify that so `trim()` passes its return value to `strlen()` so that the code trims it and then outputs its trimmed length:

```
echo strlen(trim($ourstring));
```

PHP always executes the innermost functions first, so the previous code takes $ourstring, passes it through `trim()`, uses the return value of `trim()` as the parameter for `strlen()`, and prints it.

Of course, everyone knows that boxes do not jump over dogs; the usual phrase is "the quick brown fox." Fortunately, there is a function to fix that problem: `str_replace()`. Note that it has an underscore in it. PHP is inconsistent on this matter, so you really need to memorize the function name.

The `str_replace()` function takes three parameters: the text to search for, the text to replace it with, and the string you want to work with. When working with search functions, people often talk about *needles* and *haystacks*. In this situation, the first parameter is the needle (the thing to find), and the third parameter is the haystack (what you are searching through).

So, we can fix our error and correct *box* to *fox* with this code:

```
echo str_replace("Box", "Fox", $ourstring);
```

There are two little addendums to make here. First, note that we have specified "`Box`" as opposed to "`box`" because that is how it appears in the text. The `str_replace()` function is a *case-sensitive* function, which means it does not consider "`Box`" to be the same as "`box`". If you want to do a non-case-sensitive search and replace, you can use the `stri_replace()` function, which works in the same way.

The second addendum is that because we are actually changing only one character (*B* to *F*), we need not use a function at all. PHP enables you to read (and change) individual characters of a string by specifying the character position inside braces ({ and }). As with arrays, strings are zero based, which means in the $ourstring variable $ourstring{0} is T, $ourstring{1} is h, $ourstring{2} is e, and so on. We could use this instead of `str_replace()`, like this:

37

```php
<?php
  $ourstring = "  The Quick Brown Box Jumped Over The Lazy Dog  ";
  $ourstring{18} = "F";
  echo $ourstring;
?>
```

You can extract part of a string using the substr() function, which takes a string as its first parameter, a start position as its second parameter, and an optional length as its third parameter. Optional parameters are common in PHP. If you do not provide them, PHP assumes a default value. In this case, if you specify only the first two parameters, PHP copies from the start position to the end of the string. If you specify the third parameter, PHP copies that many characters from the start.

We can write a simple script to print "Lazy Dog" by setting the start position to 38, which, remembering that PHP starts counting string positions from 0, copies from the 39th character to the end of the string:

```php
echo substr($ourstring, 38);
```

If we just want to print the word "Lazy," we need to use the optional third parameter to specify the length as 4, like this:

```php
echo substr($ourstring, 38, 4);
```

The substr() function can also be used with negative second and third parameters. If you specify just parameter one and two and provide a negative number for parameter two, substr() counts backward from the end of the string. So, rather than specifying 38 for the second parameter, we can use -10, so it takes the last 10 characters from the string. Using a negative second parameter and positive third parameter counts backward from the end string and then uses a forward length. We can print "Lazy" by counting 10 characters back from the end and then taking the next 4 characters forward:

```php
echo substr($ourstring, -10, 4);
```

Finally, we can use a negative third parameter, too, which also counts back from the end of the string. For example, using "-4" as the third parameter means to take everything except the last four characters. Confused yet? This code example should make it clear:

```php
echo substr($ourstring, -19, -11);
```

That counts 19 characters backward from the end of the string (which places it at the O in Over) and then copies everything from there until 11 characters before the end of the string. That prints Over The. The same thing could be written using -19 and 8, or even 29 and 8; there is more than one way to do it.

Moving on, the strpos() function returns the position of a particular substring inside a string; however, it is most commonly used to answer the question, "Does this string contain a specific substring?" You need to pass it two parameters: a haystack and a needle. (Yes, that's a different order from `str_replace()`.)

In its most basic use, `strpos()` can find the first instance of Box in our phrase, like this:

```
echo strpos($ourstring, "Box");
```

This outputs 18 because that is where the B in Box starts. If `strpos()` cannot find the substring in the parent string, it returns false rather than the position. Much more helpful, though, is the ability to check whether a string contains a substring; a first attempt to check whether our string contains the word The might look like this:

```
<?php
  $ourstring = "The Quick Brown Box Jumped Over The Lazy Dog";
  if (strpos($ourstring, "The")) {
    echo "Found 'The'!\n";
  } else {
    echo "'The' not found!\n";
  }
?>
```

Note that we have temporarily taken out the leading and trailing whitespace from `$ourstring` and we are using the return value of `strpos()` for our conditional statement. This reads, "If the string is found, then print a message; if not, print another message." Or does it?

Run the script, and you will see it print the `"not found"` message. The reason for this is that `strpos()` returns false if the substring is not found and otherwise returns the position where it starts. If you recall, any nonzero number equates to true in PHP, which means that 0 equates to false. With that in mind, what is the string index of the first The in our phrase? Because PHP's strings are zero based and we no longer have the spaces on either side of the string, the The is at position 0, which our conditional statement evaluates to false (hence, the problem).

The solution here is to check for identicality. We know that 0 and false are equal, but they are not identical because 0 is an integer, whereas false is a Boolean. So, we need to rewrite the conditional statement to see whether the return value from `strpos()` is identical to false. If it is, the substring was not found:

```
<?php
  $ourstring = "The Quick Brown Box Jumped Over The Lazy Dog";
  if (strpos($ourstring, "The") !== false) {
    echo "Found 'The'!\n";
  } else {
    echo "'The' not found!\n";
  }
?>
```

37

Arrays

Working with arrays is no easy task, but PHP makes it easier by providing a selection of functions that can sort, shuffle, intersect, and filter them. As with other functions, there is only space here to choose a selection; this is by no means a definitive reference to PHP's array functions.

The easiest function to use is array_unique(), which takes an array as its only parameter and returns the same array with all duplicate values removed. Also in the realm of "so easy you do not need a code example" is the shuffle() function, which takes an array as its parameter and randomizes the order of its elements. Note that shuffle() does not return the randomized array; it uses your parameter as a reference and scrambles it directly. The last too-easy-to-demonstrate function is in_array(), which takes a value as its first parameter and an array as its second and returns true if the value is in the array.

With those out of the way, we can focus on the more interesting functions, two of which are array_keys() and array_values(). They both take an array as their only parameter and return a new array made up of the keys in the array or the values of the array, respectively. The array_values() function is an easy way to create a new array of the same data, just without the keys. This is often used if you have numbered your array keys, deleted several elements, and want to reorder it.

The array_keys() function creates a new array where the values are the keys from the old array, like this:

```php
<?php
  $myarr = array("foo" => "red", "bar" => "blue", "baz" => "green");
  $mykeys = array_keys($myarr);
  foreach($mykeys as $key => $value) {
    echo "$key = $value\n";
  }
?>
```

That prints "0 = foo", "1 = bar", and "2 = baz".

Several functions are used specifically for array sorting, but only two get much use: asort() and ksort(), the first of which sorts the array by its values and the second of which sorts the array by its keys. Given the array $myarr from the previous example, sorting by the values would produce an array with elements in the order bar/blue, baz/green, and foo/red. Sorting by key would give the elements in the order bar/blue, baz/green, and foo/red. As with the shuffle() function, both asort() and ksort() do their work *in place*, meaning they return no value, directly altering the parameter you pass in. For interest's sake, you can also use arsort() and krsort() for reverse value sorting and reverse key sorting, respectively.

This code example reverse sorts the array by value and then prints it as before:

```php
<?php
  $myarr = array("foo" => "red", "bar" => "blue", "baz" => "green");
  arsort($myarr);
```

```
  foreach($myarr as $key => $value) {
    echo "$key = $value\n";
  }
?>
```

Previously when discussing constants, we mentioned the extract() function that converts an array into individual variables; now it is time to start using it for real. You need to provide three variables: the array you want to extract, how you want the variables prefixed, and the prefix you want used. Technically, the last two parameters are optional, but practically, you should always use them to properly namespace your variables and keep them organized.

The second parameter must be one of the following:

▶ **EXTR_OVERWRITE**—If the variable exists already, overwrites it.

▶ **EXTR_SKIP**—If the variable exists already, skips it and moves on to the next variable.

▶ **EXTR_PREFIX_SAME**—If the variable exists already, uses the prefix specified in the third parameter.

▶ **EXTR_PREFIX_ALL**—Prefixes all variables with the prefix in the third parameter, regardless of whether it exists already.

▶ **EXTR_PREFIX_INVALID**—Uses a prefix only if the variable name would be invalid (for example, starting with a number).

▶ **EXTR_IF_EXISTS**—Extracts only variables that already exist. We have never seen this used.

You can also, optionally, use the bitwise OR operator, |, to add in EXTR_REFS to have extract() use references for the extracted variables. In general use, EXTR_PREFIX_ALL is preferred because it guarantees name spacing. EXTR_REFS is required only if you need to be able to change the variables and have those changes reflected in the array.

This next script uses extract() to convert $myarr into individual variables, $arr_foo, $arr_bar, and $arr_baz:

```
<?php
  $myarr = array("foo" => "red", "bar" => "blue", "baz" => "green");
  extract($myarr, EXTR_PREFIX_ALL, 'arr');
?>
```

Note that the array keys are "foo", "bar", and "baz" and that the prefix is "arr", but that the final variables will be $arr_foo, $arr_bar, and $arr_baz. PHP inserts an underscore between the prefix and array key.

Files

As you have learned from elsewhere in the book, the UNIX philosophy is that everything is a file. In PHP, this is also the case: A selection of basic file functions is suitable for

37

opening and manipulating files, but those same functions can also be used for opening and manipulating network sockets. We cover both here.

Two basic read and write functions for files make performing these basic operations easy. They are `file_get_contents()`, which takes a filename as its only parameter and returns the file's contents as a string, and `file_put_contents()`, which takes a filename as its first parameter and the data to write as its second parameter.

Using these two, we can write a script that reads all the text from one file, `filea.txt`, and writes it to another, `fileb.txt`:

```php
<?php
  $text = file_get_contents("filea.txt");
  file_put_contents("fileb.txt", $text);
?>
```

Because PHP enables us to treat network sockets like files, we can also use `file_get_contents()` to read text from a website, like this:

```php
<?php
  $text = file_get_contents("http://www.slashdot.org");
  file_put_contents("fileb.txt", $text);
?>
```

The problem with using `file_get_contents()` is that it loads the whole file into memory at once; that's not practical if you have large files or even smaller files being accessed by many users. An alternative is to load the file piece by piece, which can be accomplished through the following five functions: `fopen()`, `fclose()`, `fread()`, `fwrite()`, and `feof()`. The *f* in those function names stands for *file*, so they open, close, read from, and write to files and sockets. The last function, `feof()`, returns `true` if the end of the file has been reached.

The `fopen()` function takes a bit of learning to use properly, but on the surface it looks straightforward. Its first parameter is the filename you want to open, which is easy enough. However, the second parameter is where you specify how you want to work with the file, and you should specify one of the following:

- ▶ **r**—Read-only; it overwrites the file.

- ▶ **r+**—Reading and writing; it overwrites the file.

- ▶ **w**—Write-only; it erases the existing contents and overwrites the file.

- ▶ **w+**—Reading and writing; it erases the existing content and overwrites the file.

- ▶ **a**—Write-only; it appends to the file.

- ▶ **a+**—Reading and writing; it appends to the file.

- ▶ **x**—Write-only, but only if the file does not exist.

- ▶ **a+**—Reading and writing, but only if the file does not exist.

Optionally, you can also add b (for example, a+b or rb) to switch to binary mode. This is recommended if you want your scripts and the files they write to work smoothly on other platforms.

When you call fopen(), you should store the return value. It is a resource known as a *file handle*, which the other file functions all need to do their jobs. The fread() function, for example, takes the file handle as its first parameter and the number of bytes to read as its second, returning the content in its return value. The fclose() function takes the file handle as its only parameter and frees up the file.

So, we can write a simple loop to open a file, read it piece by piece, print the pieces, and then close the handle:

```php
<?php
  $file = fopen("filea.txt", "rb");
  while (!feof($file)) {
    $content = fread($file, 1024);
    echo $content;
  }
  fclose($file);
?>
```

That only leaves the fwrite() function, which takes the file handle as its first parameter and the string to write as its second. You can also provide an integer as the third parameter, specifying the number of bytes you want to write of the string, but if you exclude this, fwrite() writes the entire string.

If you recall, you can use a as the second parameter to fopen() to append data to a file. So, we can combine that with fwrite() to have a script that adds a line of text to a file each time it is executed:

```php
<?php
  $file = fopen("filea.txt", "ab");
  fwrite($file, "Testing\n");
  fclose($file);
?>
```

To make that script a little more exciting, we can stir in a new function, filesize(), that takes a filename (not a file handle, but an actual filename string) as its only parameter and returns the file's size in bytes. Using that new function brings the script to this:

```php
<?php
  $file = fopen("filea.txt", "ab");
  fwrite($file, "The filesize was" . filesize("filea.txt") . "\n");
  fclose($file);
?>
```

Although PHP automatically cleans up file handles for you, it is still best to use fclose() yourself so that you are always in control.

37

Miscellaneous

Several functions do not fall under the other categories and so are covered here. The first one is isset(), which takes one or more variables as its parameters and returns true if they have been set. It is important to note that a variable with a value set to something that would be evaluated to false—such as 0 or an empty string—still returns true from isset() because it does not check the value of the variable. It merely checks that it is set; hence, the name.

The unset() function also takes one or more variables as its parameters, simply deleting the variable and freeing up the memory. With these two, we can write a script that checks for the existence of a variable and, if it exists, deletes it (see Listing 37.5).

LISTING 37.5   Setting and Unsetting Variables

```php
<?php
  $name = "Ildiko";
  if (isset($name)) {
    echo "Name was set to $name\n";
    unset($name);
  } else {
    echo "Name was not set";
  }

  if (isset($name)) {
    echo "Name was set to $name\n";
    unset($name);
  } else {
    echo "Name was not set";
  }
?>
```

That script runs the same isset() check twice, but it unset()s the variable after the first check. As such, it prints "Name was set to Ildiko" and then "Name was not set".

Perhaps the most frequently used function in PHP is exit, although purists will tell you that it is in fact a language construct rather than a function. exit terminates the processing of the script as soon as it is executed, meaning subsequent lines of code are not executed. That is really all there is to it; it barely deserves an example, but here is one just to make sure:

```php
<?php
  exit;
  echo "Exit is a language construct!\n";
?>
```

That script prints nothing because the exit comes before the echo.

One function we can guarantee you will use a lot is var_dump(), which dumps out information about a variable, including its value, to the screen. This is invaluable for arrays because it prints every value and, if one or more of the elements is an array, it prints all the elements from those, and so on. To use this function, just pass it a variable as its only parameter:

```php
<?php
  $drones = array("Graham", "Julian", "Nick", "Paul");
  var_dump($drones);
?>
```

The output from that script looks like this:

```
array(4) {
  [0]=>
  string(6) "Graham"
  [1]=>
  string(6) "Julian"
  [2]=>
  string(4) "Nick"
  [3]=>
  string(4) "Paul"
}
```

The var_dump() function sees a lot of use as a basic debugging technique because it is the easiest way to print variable data to the screen to verify it.

Finally, we briefly discuss regular expressions; with the emphasis on *briefly* because regular expression syntax is covered elsewhere in this book and the only unique thing relevant to PHP are the functions you will use to run the expressions. You have the choice of either *Perl-Compatible Regular Expressions (PCRE)* or POSIX Extended regular expressions, but there really is little to choose between them in terms of functionality offered. For this chapter, we use the PCRE expressions because, to the best of our knowledge, they see more use by other PHP programmers.

The main PCRE functions are preg_match(), preg_match_all(), preg_replace(), and preg_split(). We start with preg_match() because it provides the most basic functionality by returning true if one string matches a regular expression. The first parameter to preg_match() is the regular expression you want to search for, and the second is the string to match. So, if we wanted to check whether a string had the word Best, Test, rest, zest, or any other word containing est preceded by any letter of either case, we could use this PHP code:

```php
$result = preg_match("/[A-Za-z]est/", "This is a test");
```

Because the test string matches the expression, $result is set to 1 (true). If you change the string to a nonmatching result, you get 0 as the return value.

37

The next function is `preg_match_all()`, which gives you an array of all the matches it found. However, to be most useful, it takes the array to fill with matches as a by-reference parameter and saves its return value for the number of matches that were found.

We suggest you use `preg_match_all()` and `var_dump()` to get a feel for how the function works. This example is a good place to start:

```php
<?php
  $string = "This is the best test in the west";
  $result = preg_match_all("/[A-Za-z]est/", $string, $matches);
  var_dump($matches);
?>
```

That outputs the following:

```
array(1) {
  [0]=>
  array(3) {
    [0]=>
    string(4) "best"
    [1]=>
    string(4) "test"
    [2]=>
    string(4) "west"
  }
}
```

If you notice, the $matches array is actually multidimensional in that it contains one element, which itself is an array containing all the matches to our regular expression. The reason for this is because our expression has no *subexpressions*, meaning no independent matches using parentheses. If we had subexpressions, each would have its own element in the $matches array containing its own array of matches.

Moving on, `preg_replace()` is used to change all substrings that match a regular expression into something else. The basic manner of using this is quite easy: You search for something with a regular expression and provide a replacement for it. However, a more useful variant is *back referencing*, using the match as part of the replacement. For our example, we will imagine you have written a tutorial on PHP but want to process the text so each reference to a function is followed by a link to the PHP manual.

PHP manual page URLs take the form www.php.net/<somefunc> (for example, www.php.net/preg_replace). The string we need to match is a function name, which is a string of alphabetic characters, potentially also mixed with numbers and underscores and terminated with two parentheses, ( ). As a replacement, we will use the match we found, surrounded in HTML emphasis tags (<em></em>), and then with a link to the relevant PHP manual page. Here is how that looks in code:

```php
<?php
  $regex = "/([A-Za-z0-9_]*)\(\)/";
  $replace = "<em>$1</em> (<a href=\"http://www.php.net/$1\">manual</A>)";
  $haystack = "File_get_contents()is easier than using fopen().";
  $result = preg_replace($regex, $replace, $haystack);
  echo $result;
?>
```

The $1 is our back reference; it will be substituted with the results from the first subexpression. The way we have written the regular expression is very exact. The [A-Za-z0-9_]* part, which matches the function name, is marked as a subexpression. After that is \(\), which means the exact symbols (and), not the regular expression meanings of them, which means that $1 in the replacement will contain fopen rather than fopen(), which is how it should be. Of course, anything that is not back referenced in the replacement is removed, so we have to put the () after the first $1 (not in the hyperlink) to repair the function name.

After all that work, the output is perfect:

```
<em>File_get_contents()</em> (<a href="http://www.php.net/
file_get_contents">manual</A>) is easier than using <em>fopen()
</em> (<a href="http://www.php.net/fopen">manual</A>).
```

Handling HTML Forms

Given that PHPs primary role is handling web pages, you might wonder why this section has been left so late in the chapter. It is because handling HTML forms is so central to PHP that it is essentially automatic.

Consider this form:

```html
<form method="POST" action="thispage.php">
User ID: <input type="text" name="UserID" /><br />
Password: <input type="password" name="Password" /><br />
<input type="submit" />
</form>
```

When a visitor clicks Submit, thispage.php is called again, and this time PHP has the variables available to it inside the $_REQUEST array. Given that script, if the user enters 12345 and frosties as her user ID and password, PHP provides you with $_REQUEST ['UserID'] set to 12345 and $_REQUEST['Password'] set to frosties. Note that it is important that you use HTTP post unless you specifically want GET. POST enables you to send a great deal more data and stops people from tampering with your URL to try to find holes in your script.

Is that it? Well, almost. That tells you how to retrieve user data, but you should be sure to sanitize it so users do not try to sneak HTML or JavaScript into your database as something you think is innocuous. PHP gives you the strip_tags() function for this purpose. It takes a string and returns the same string with all HTML tags removed.

Databases

The ease with which PHP can be used to create dynamic, database-driven websites is for the key reason to use it for many people. The stock build of PHP comes with support for MySQL, PostgreSQL, SQLite, Oracle, Microsoft SQL Server, ODBC, plus several other popular databases, so you are sure to find something to work with your data.

If you want to, you can learn all the individual functions for connecting to and manipulating each database PHP supports, but a much smarter, or at least easier, idea is to use PEAR::DB. PEAR::DB is an abstraction layer over the databases that PHP supports, which means you write your code once, and—with the smallest of changes—it will work on every database server.

PEAR is the script repository for PHP and contains numerous tools and prewritten solutions for common problems. PEAR::DB is perhaps the most popular part of the PEAR project, but it is worth checking out the PEAR site to see whether anything else catches your eye.

To get basic use out of PEAR::DB, you need to learn how to connect to a database, run a SQL query, and work with the results. This is not a SQL tutorial, so we have assumed you are already familiar with the language. For the sake of this tutorial, we have also assumed you are working with a database called dentists and a table called patients that contains the following fields:

- ▶ **ID**—The primary key, auto-incrementing integer for storing a number unique to each patient

- ▶ **Name**—A varchar(255) field for storing a patient name

- ▶ **Age**—Integer

- ▶ **Sex**—1 for male, 2 for female

- ▶ **Occupation**—A varchar(255) field for storing a patient occupation

Also for the sake of this tutorial, we use a database server on IP address 10.0.0.1, running MySQL, with username ubuntu and password alm65z. You need to replace these details with your own; use localhost for connecting to the local server.

The first step to using PEAR::DB is to include the standard PEAR::DB file, DB.php. Your PHP will be configured to look inside the PEAR directory for include() files, so you do not need to provide any directory information.

PEAR::DB is object oriented, and you specify your connection details at the same time as you create the initial DB object. This is done using a URL-like system that specifies the database server type, username, password, server, and database name all in one. After you have specified the database server here, everything else is abstracted, meaning you only need to change the connection line to port your code to another database server.

This first script connects to our server and prints a status message (see Listing 37.6).

LISTING 37.6   Connecting to a Database Through PEAR::DB

```php
<?php
  include("DB.php");
  $dsn = "mysql://ubuntu:alm65z@10.0.0.1/dentists";
  $conn = DB::connect($dsn);
  if (DB::isError($conn)) {
    echo $conn->getMessage() . "\n";
  } else {
    echo "Connected successfully!\n";

  }
?>
```

You should be able to see how the connection string breaks down. It is server name first, then a username and password separated by a colon, then an @ symbol followed by the IP address to which to connect, and then a slash and the database name. Notice how the call to connect is DB::connect(), which calls PEAR::DB directly and returns a database connection object for storage in $conn. The variable name $dsn was used for the connection details because it is a common acronym standing for data source name.

If DB::connect() successfully connects to a server, it returns a database object we can use to run SQL queries. If not, we get an error returned that we can query using functions such as getMessage(). In the previous script, we print the error message if we fail to connect, but we also just print a message if we succeed. Next, we change that so we run an SQL query if we have a connection.

Running SQL queries is done through the query() function of our database connection, passing in the SQL we want to execute. This then returns a query result that can be used to get the data. This query result can be thought of as a multidimensional array because it has many rows of data, each with many columns of attributes. This is extracted using the fetchInto() function, which loops through the query result converting one row of data into an array that it sends back as its return value. You need to pass in two parameters to fetchInto() specifying where the data should be stored and how you want it stored. Unless you have unusual needs, specifying DB_FETCHMODE_ASSOC for the second parameter is a smart move.

Listing 37.7 shows the new script.

37

LISTING 37.7   Running a Query Through PEAR::DB

```php
<?php
  include("DB.php");
  $dsn = "mysql://ubuntu:alm65z@10.0.0.1/dentists";
  $conn = DB::connect($dsn);
  if (DB::isError($conn)) {
    echo $conn->getMessage() . "\n";
  } else {
    echo "Connected successfully!\n";
    $result = $conn->query("SELECT ID, Name FROM patients;");
    while ($result->fetchInto($row, DB_FETCHMODE_ASSOC)) {
      extract($row, EXTR_PREFIX_ALL, 'pat');
      echo "$pat_ID is $pat_Name\n";
    }
  }
?>
```

The first half is identical to the previous script, with all the new action happening if we get a successful connection.

Going along with the saying "never leave to PHP what you can clean up yourself," the current script has problems. We do not clean up the query result, and we do not close the database connection. If this code were being used in a longer script that ran for several minutes, this would be a huge waste of resources. Fortunately, we can free up the memory associated with these two by calling $result->free() and $conn->disconnect(). If we add those two function calls to the end of the script, it is complete.

References

▶ **www.php.net**—The best place to look for information is the PHP online manual. It is comprehensive, well written, and updated regularly.

▶ **www.phpbuilder.net**—A large PHP scripts and tutorials site where you can learn new techniques and also chat with other PHP developers.

▶ **www.zend.com**—The home page of a company founded by two of the key developers of PHP. Zend develops and sells proprietary software, including a powerful IDE and a code cache, to aid PHP developers.

▶ **http://pear.php.net/**—The home of the PEAR project contains a large collection of software you can download and try, and it has thorough documentation for it all.

▶ **www.phparch.com/**—There are quite a few good PHP magazines around, but *PHP Architect* probably leads the way. It posts some of its articles online for free, and its forums are good, too.

▶ Quality books on PHP abound, and you are certainly spoiled for choice. For beginning developers, the best available is *PHP and MySQL Web Development* (Sams Publishing). For a concise, to-the-point book covering all aspects of PHP, check out *PHP in a Nutshell* (O'Reilly). Finally, for advanced developers, you can consult *Advanced PHP Programming* (Sams Publishing).

37

CHAPTER 38

Using Python

As PHP has come to dominate the world of web scripting, Python is increasingly dominating the domain of command-line scripting. Python's precise and clean syntax makes it one of the easiest languages to learn, and it allows programmers to code more quickly and spend less time maintaining their code. Although PHP is fundamentally similar to Java and Perl, Python is closer to C and Modula-3, and so it might look unfamiliar at first.

Most of the other languages have a group of developers at their cores, but Python has Guido van Rossum—creator, father, and *benevolent dictator for life (BDFL)*. Although Guido spends less time working on Python now, he still essentially has the right to veto changes to the language, which has enabled it to remain consistent over the many years of its development. The end result is that, in Guido's own words, "Even if you are in fact clueless about language design, you can tell that Python is a very simple language."

This chapter constitutes a "quick-start" tutorial to Python designed to give you all the information you need to put together basic scripts and to point you toward resources that can take you further.

Two supported versions of Python are out in the wild right now. Python version 2.x (the current production release is 2.7) is the backward-compatible status quo, the version that anyone who has already used Python for more than a year or two has learned and the version most likely to have been used in already written code you discover and read. Python 3.x is the newest branch (the current production release is 3.1.4) with lots of shiny newness.

Python 3.x is not backward compatible, and most programs written in or for 2.x need some work to run on 3.x. This should be a factor in any decision you make about using Python: Do you want to run your program on many machines, perhaps including some that have only the older version installed? Does the newer version have all the functionality you want and need, including software libraries, because not all of them have been rewritten for 3.x (like Twisted and Django)? If porting is a nontrivial task, you may want to stick with 2.x for now.

Both versions will be supported for some time, but if you expect you will be using what you write for a very long time, you probably want to try to do so in 3.x, but with a readiness to fall back to 2.x if you discover significant blocking limitations currently in 3.x. The language itself is ready for use, though, and is receiving high marks from people who have used both versions. The official Python website will help you make an informed decision; it contains clear discussion of the advantages and disadvantages of each version at http:/ /wiki.python.org/moin/Python2orPython3.

This chapter is centered on the 2.x version of Python because it is what most people are still using in late 2010 when this was written, as well as in mid 2011 when it was updated, but we try to note places where significant differences exist in 3.x that should be considered. If you are learning Python for the first time, you may want to start with a look at the 3.x series because it is the future and is very likely to already have everything you need. Ubuntu 10.10 comes with Python 2.6.6 installed by default with 2.7 available in the repositories, which is another reason for us to focus this chapter on the 2.x series (although the current 3.x is also available in the repositories and available for easy installation).

NOTE

This chapter is a very elementary introduction to Python. For that reason, nearly everything we cover is identical in both 2.x and 3.x. We mention the differences earlier and in a couple of notes that follow so that readers wanting to learn more will not be surprised later. Unless noted otherwise, you should find what we say in this chapter applies as well to either version.

Python on Linux

Most versions of Linux and UNIX, including Mac OS X, come with Python preinstalled. This is partially for convenience because it is such a popular scripting language—and it saves having to install it later if the user wants to run a script—and partially because many vital or useful programs included in Linux distributions are written in Python. For example, the Ubuntu Software Center is a Python program.

The Python binary is installed into /usr/bin/python (or /usr/bin/python3); if you run that, you enter the Python interactive interpreter where you can type commands and have them executed immediately. Although PHP also has an interactive mode (use php –a to activate it), it is neither as powerful nor as flexible as Python's.

As with Perl, PHP, and other scripting languages, you can also execute Python scripts by adding a shebang line (#!) to the start of your scripts that point to /usr/bin/python and then setting the file to be executable.

The third way to run Python scripts is through mod_python, which is an Apache module that embeds the Python interpreter into the http server, allowing you to use Python to write web applications. You can install from the Ubuntu repositories.

For the purposes of this introduction, we use the interactive Python interpreter because it provides immediate feedback on commands as you type them.

We use the interactive interpreter for this chapter, so it is essential that you become comfortable using it. To get started, open a terminal and run the command python. You should see something like this, perhaps with different version numbers and dates:

```
matthew@seymour:~$ python
Python 2.7.1+ (r271:86832, Apr 11 2011, 18:13:53)
[GCC 4.5.2] on linux2
Type "help", "copyright", "credits" or "license" for more information.
>>>
The >>> is where you type your input, and you can set and get a variable like this:
>>> python = 'great'
>>> python
'great'
>>>
```

On line one, the variable python is set to the text great, and on line two that value is read back from the variable simply by typing the name of the variable you want to read. Line three shows Python printing the variable; on line four, you are back at the prompt to type more commands. Python remembers all the variables you use while in the interactive interpreter, which means you can set a variable to be the value of another variable.

When you are done, press Ctrl+D to exit. At this point, all your variables and commands are forgotten by the interpreter, which is why complex Python programs are always saved in scripts.

38

The Basics of Python

Python is a language wholly unlike most others, and yet it is so logical that most people can pick it up quickly. You have already seen how easily you can assign strings, but in Python, nearly everything is that easy—as long as you remember the syntax.

Numbers

The way Python handles numbers is more precise than some other languages. It has all the normal operators—such as + for addition, - for subtraction, / for division, and * for multiplication—but it adds % for modulus (division remainder), ** for raise to the power, and `//` for floor division. It is also specific about which type of number is being used, as this example shows:

```
>>> a = 5
>>> b = 10
>>> a * b
50
>>> a / b
0
>>> b = 10.0
>>> a / b
0.5
>>> a // b
0.0
```

The first division returns `0` because both a and b are integers (whole numbers), so Python calculates the division as an integer, giving `0`. By converting b to `10.0`, Python considers it to be a floating-point number, and so the division is now calculated as a floating-point value, giving `0.5`. Even with b being a floating point, using `//`—floor division—rounds it down.

Using `**`, you can easily see how Python works with integers:

```
>>> 2 ** 30
1073741824
>>> 2 ** 31
2147483648L
```

The first statement raises 2 to the power of `30` (that is, 2... times 2 times 2 times 2...), and the second raises 2 to the power of `31`. Notice how the second number has a capital L on the end of it—this is Python telling you that it is a long integer. The difference between long integers and normal integers is slight but important: Normal integers can be calculated using simple instructions on the CPU, whereas long integers—because they can be as big as you need them to be—need to be calculated in software and therefore are slower.

When specifying big numbers, you need not put the L at the end—Python figures it out for you. Furthermore, if a number starts off as a normal number and then exceeds its boundaries, Python automatically converts it to a long integer. The same is not true the other way around: If you have a long integer and then divide it by another number so that it could be stored as a normal integer, it remains a long integer:

```
>>> num = 999999999999999999999999999999999L
>>> num = num / 1000000000000000000000000000000000
>>> num
999L
```

You can convert between number types using typecasting, like this:

```
>>> num = 10
>>> int(num)
```

```
10
>>> float(num)
10.0
>>> long(num)
10L
>>> floatnum = 10.0
>>> int(floatnum)
10
>>> float(floatnum)
10.0
>>> long(floatnum)
10L
```

You need not worry whether you are using integers or long integers; Python handles it all for you, so you can concentrate on getting the code right. In the 3.x series, the Python integer type automatically provides extra precision for large numbers, whereas in 2.x, you use a separate long integer type for numbers larger than the normal integer type is designed to handle.

More on Strings

Python stores strings as an immutable sequence of characters—a jargon-filled way of saying that "it is a collection of characters that, once set, cannot be changed without creating a new string." Sequences are important in Python. There are three primary types, of which strings are one, and they share some properties. Mutability makes a lot of sense when you learn about lists in the next section.

As you saw in the previous example, you can assign a value to strings in Python with just an equal sign, like this:

```
>>> mystring = 'hello';
>>> myotherstring = "goodbye";
>>> mystring
'hello'
>>> myotherstring;
'goodbye'
>>> test = "Are you really Bill O'Reilly?"
>>> test
"Are you really Bill O'Reilly?"
```

The first example encapsulates the string in single quotation marks, and the second and third in double quotation marks. However, printing the first and second strings shows them both in single quotation marks because Python does not distinguish between the two. The third example is the exception; it uses double quotation marks because the string itself contains a single quotation mark. Here, Python prints the string with double quotation marks because it knows it contains the single quotation mark.

Because the characters in a string are stored in sequence, you can index into them by specifying the character you are interested in. Like most other languages, these indexes are zero based, which means you need to ask for character 0 to get the first letter in a string. For example:

```
>>> string = "This is a test string"
>>> string
'This is a test string'
>>> string[0]
'T'
>>> string [0], string[3], string [20]
('T', 's', 'g')
```

The last line shows how, with commas, you can ask for several indexes at the same time. You could print the entire first word using this:

```
>>> string[0], string[1], string[2], string[3]
('T', 'h', 'i', 's')
```

However, for that purpose, you can use a different concept: slicing. A *slice* of a sequence draws a selection of indexes. For example, you can pull out the first word like this:

```
>>> string[0:4]
'This'
```

The syntax there means "take everything from position 0 (including 0) and end at position 4 (excluding it)." So, [0:4] copies the items at indexes 0, 1, 2, and 3. You can omit either side of the indexes, and it will copy either from the start or to the end:

```
>>> string [:4]
'This'
>>> string [5:]
'is a test string'
>>> string [11:]
'est string'
```

You can also omit both numbers, and it will give you the entire sequence:

```
>>> string [:]
'This is a test string'
```

Later you learn precisely why you would want to do that, but for now, there are a number of other string intrinsics that will make your life easier. For example, you can use the + and * operators to concatenate (join) and repeat strings, like this:

```
>>> mystring = "Python"
>>> mystring * 4
'PythonPythonPythonPython'
>>> mystring = mystring + " rocks! "
>>> mystring * 2
'Python rocks! Python rocks! '
```

In addition to working with operators, Python strings come with a selection of built-in methods. You can change the case of the letters with `capitalize()` (uppercases the first letter and lowercases the rest), `lower()` (lowercases them all), `title()` (uppercases the first letter in each word), and `upper()` (uppercases them all). You can also check whether strings match certain cases with `islower()`, `istitle()`, and `isupper()`; that also extends to `isalnum()` (returns true if the string is letters and numbers only) and `isdigit()` (returns true if the string is all numbers).

This example demonstrates some of these in action:

```
>>> string
'This is a test string'
>>> string.upper()
'THIS IS A TEST STRING'
>>> string.lower()
'this is a test string'
>>> string.isalnum()
False
>>> string = string.title()
>>> string
'This Is A Test String'
```

Why did `isalnum()` return `false`—our string contains only alphanumeric characters, doesn't it? Well, no. There are spaces in there, which is what is causing the problem. More important, we were calling `upper()` and `lower()` and they were not changing the contents of the string—they just returned the new value. So, to change our string from `This is a test string` to `This Is A Test String`, we have to assign it back to the string variable.

Another really useful and kind of cool thing you can do with strings is triple quoting. This lets you easily create strings that include both double and single quoted strings, as well as strings that span more than one line, without having to escape a bunch of special characters. Here's an example:

```
>>>foo = """
..."foo"
...'bar'
...baz
...blippy
..."""
>>>foo
'\n"foo"\n\'bar\'\nbaz\nblippy\n'
>>>
```

Although this is intended as an introductory guide, the capability to use negative indexes with strings and slices is a pretty neat feature that deserves a mention. Here's an example:

```
>>>bar="news.google.com"
>>>bar[-1]
'm'
```

38

```
>>>bar[-4:]
'.com'
>>>bar[-10:-4]
'google'
>>>
```

One difference between 2.x and 3.x is the introduction of new string types and method calls. That doesn't affect what we share here, but is something to pay attention to as you work with Python.

Lists

Python's built-in list data type is a sequence, like strings. However, they are mutable, which means they can be changed. Lists are like arrays in that they hold a selection of elements in a given order. You can cycle through them, index into them, and slice them:

```
>>> mylist = ["python", "perl", "php"]
>>> mylist
['python', 'perl', 'php']
>>> mylist + ["java"]
['python', 'perl', 'php', 'java']
>>> mylist * 2
['python', 'perl', 'php', 'python', 'perl', 'php']
>>> mylist[1]
'perl'
>>> mylist[1] = "c++"
>>> mylist[1]
'c++'
>>> mylist[1:3]
['c++', 'php']
```

The brackets notation is important: You cannot use parentheses, ((and)) or braces ({ and }) for lists. Using + for lists is different from using + for numbers. Python detects you are working with a list and appends one list to another. This is known as *operator overloading*, and it is one of the reasons Python is so flexible.

Lists can be *nested*, which means you can put a list inside a list. However, this is where mutability starts to matter, and so this might sound complicated. If you recall, the definition of an immutable string sequence is that it is a collection of characters that, once set, cannot be changed without creating a new string. Lists are mutable, as opposed to immutable, which means you can change your list without creating a new list.

This becomes important because Python, by default, copies only a reference to a variable rather than the full variable. For example:

```
>>> list1 = [1, 2, 3]
>>> list2 = [4, list1, 6]
>>> list1
```

```
[1, 2, 3]
>>> list2
[4, [1, 2, 3], 6]
```

Here we have a nested list. list2 contains 4, then list1, then 6. When you print the value of list2, you can see it also contains list1. Now, let's proceed on from that:

```
>>> list1[1] = "Flake"
>>> list2
[4, [1, 'Flake', 3], 6]
```

In line one, we set the second element in list1 (remember, sequences are zero based!) to be Flake rather than 2; then we print the contents of list2. As you can see, when list1 changed, list2 was updated, too. The reason for this is that list2 stores a reference to list1 as opposed to a copy of list1; they share the same value.

We can show that this works both ways by indexing twice into list2, like this:

```
>>> list2[1][1] = "Caramello"
>>> list1
[1, 'Caramello', 3]
```

The first line says, "Get the second element in list2 (list1) and the second element of that list, and set it to be 'Caramello'." Then list1's value is printed, and you can see it has changed. This is the essence of mutability: We are changing our list without creating a new list. However, editing a string creates a new string, leaving the old one unaltered. For example:

```
>>> mystring = "hello"
>>> list3 = [1, mystring, 3]
>>> list3
[1, 'hello', 3]
>>> mystring = "world"
>>> list3
[1, 'hello', 3]
```

Of course, this raises the question of how you copy without references when references are the default. The answer, for lists, is that you use the [:] slice, which we looked at earlier. This slices from the first element to the last, inclusive, essentially copying it without references. Here is how that looks:

```
>>> list4 = ["a", "b", "c"]
>>> list5 = list4[:]
>>> list4 = list4 + ["d"]
>>> list5
['a', 'b', 'c']
>>> list4
['a', 'b', 'c', 'd']
```

Lists have their own collections of built-in methods, such as sort(), append(), and pop(). The latter two add and remove single elements from the end of the list, with pop() also returning the removed element. For example:

```
>>> list5 = ["nick", "paul", "julian", "graham"]
>>> list5.sort()
>>> list5
['graham', 'julian', 'nick', 'paul']
>>> list5.pop()
'paul'
>>> list5
['graham', 'julian', 'nick']

>>> list5.append("Rebecca")
```

In addition, one interesting method of strings returns a list: split(). This takes a character to split by and then gives you a list in which each element is a chunk from the string. For example:

```
>>> string = "This is a test string";
>>> string.split(" ")
['This', 'is', 'a', 'test', 'string']
```

Lists are used extensively in Python, although this is slowly changing as the language matures. The way lists are compared and sorted has changed in 3.x, so be sure to check the latest documentation when you attempt to perform these tasks.

Dictionaries

Unlike lists, dictionaries are collections with no fixed order. Instead, they have a *key* (the name of the element) and a *value* (the content of the element), and Python places them wherever it needs to for maximum performance. When defining dictionaries, you need to use braces ({ }) and colons (:). You start with an opening brace and then give each element a key and a value, separated by a colon, like this:

```
>>> mydict = { "perl" : "a language", "php" : "another language" }
>>> mydict
{'php': 'another language', 'perl': 'a language'}
```

This example has two elements, with keys perl and php. However, when the dictionary is printed, we find that php comes before perl—Python hasn't respected the order in which we entered them. We can index into a dictionary using the normal code:

```
>>> mydict["perl"]
'a language'
```

However, because a dictionary has no fixed sequence, we cannot take a slice, or index by position.

Like lists, dictionaries are mutable and can also be nested; however, unlike lists, you cannot merge two dictionaries by using +. This is because dictionary elements are located using the key. Therefore, having two elements with the same key would cause a clash. Instead, you should use the `update()` method, which merges two arrays by overwriting clashing keys.

You can also use the `keys()` method to return a list of all the keys in a dictionary.

There are subtle differences in how dictionaries are used in 3.x, such as the need to make list calls to produce all values at once so they may be printed. Again, be sure to check the latest documentation as you move ahead, because there are several of these changes in functionality with some tools now behaving differently or even disappearing and other new dictionary tools being added. Some of those features have been backported; for example, Python 2.7 has support for ordered dictionaries, backported from Python 3.1 (see http://docs.python.org/dev/whatsnew/2.7.html#pep-0372).

Conditionals and Looping

So far, we have just been looking at data types, which should show you how powerful Python's data types are. However, you cannot write complex programs without conditional statements and loops.

Python has most of the standard conditional checks, such as > (greater than), <= (less than or equal to), and == (equal), but it also adds some new ones, such as in. For example, we can use in to check whether a string or a list contains a given character/element:

```
>>> mystring = "J Random Hacker"
>>> "r" in mystring
True
>>> "Hacker" in mystring
True
>>> "hacker" in mystring
False
```

The last example demonstrates how it is case sensitive. We can use the operator for lists, too:

```
>>> mylist = ["soldier", "sailor", "tinker", "spy"]
>>> "tailor" in mylist
False
```

Other comparisons on these complex data types are done item by item:

```
>>> list1 = ["alpha", "beta", "gamma"]
>>> list2 = ["alpha", "beta", "delta"]
>>> list1 > list2
True
```

list1's first element (alpha) is compared against list2's first element (alpha) and, because they are equal, the next element is checked. That is equal also, so the third element is checked, which is different. The g in gamma comes after the d in delta in the alphabet, so gamma is considered greater than delta and list1 is considered greater than list2.

Loops come in two types, and both are equally flexible. For example, the `for` loop can iterate through letters in a string or elements in a list:

```
>>> string = "Hello, Python!"
>>> for s in string: print s,
...
H e l l o ,    P y t h o n !
```

The `for` loop takes each letter in a string and assigns it to s. This then is printed to the screen using the `print` command, but note the comma at the end; this tells Python not to insert a line break after each letter. The ellipsis (...) is there because Python allows you to enter more code in the loop; you need to press Enter again here to have the loop execute.

The same construct can be used for lists:

```
>>> mylist = ["andi", "rasmus", "zeev"]
>>> for p in mylist: print p
...
andi
rasmus
zeev
```

Without the comma after the `print` statement, each item is printed on its own line.

The other loop type is the `while` loop, and it looks similar:

```
>> while 1: print "This will loop forever!"
...
This will loop forever!
This will loop forever!
This will loop forever!
This will loop forever!
This will loop forever!
(etc)
Traceback (most recent call last):
  File "<stdin>", line 1, in ?
KeyboardInterrupt
>>>
```

That is an infinite loop (it carries on printing that text forever), so you need to press Ctrl+C to interrupt it and regain control.

If you want to use multiline loops, you need to get ready to use your Tab key: Python handles loop blocks by recording the level of indent used. Some people find this odious; others admire it for forcing clean coding on users. Most of us, though, just get on with programming.

For example:

```
>>> i = 0
>>> while i < 3:
...     j = 0
...     while j < 3:
...         print "Pos: " + str(i) + "," + str(j) + ")"
...         j += 1
...     i += 1
...
Pos: (0,0)
Pos: (0,1)
Pos: (0,2)
Pos: (1,0)
Pos: (1,1)
Pos: (1,2)
Pos: (2,0)
Pos: (2,1)
Pos: (2,2)
```

You can control loops using the break and continue keywords. break exits the loop and continues processing immediately afterward, and continue jumps to the next loop iteration.

Again we find many subtle changes in 3.x. Most conditionals and looping work the same, but because we mention it in this section, we should note that print is no longer a statement in 3.x and is now a function call. That provides a nice segue to our discussion of functions.

Functions

Other languages—such as PHP—read and process an entire file before executing it, which means you can call a function before it is defined because the compiler reads the definition of the function before it tries to call it. Python is different: If the function definition has not been reached by the time you try to call it, you get an error. The reason behind this behavior is that Python actually creates an object for your function, and that in turns means two things. First, you can define the same function several times in a script and have the script pick the right one at runtime. Second, you can assign the function to another name just by using =.

Function definition starts with def, then the function name, then parentheses and a list of parameters, and then a colon. The contents of a function need to be indented at least one level beyond the definition. So, using function assignment and dynamic declaration, you can write a script that prints the right greeting in a roundabout manner:

```
>>> def hello_english(Name):
...     print "Hello, " + Name + "!"
...
```

38

```
>>> def hello_hungarian(Name):
...     print "Szia, " + Name + "!"
...
>>> hello = hello_hungarian
>>> hello("Paul")
Szia, Paul!
>>> hello = hello_english
>>> hello("Paul")
```

Notice that function definitions include no type information. Functions are typeless, as mentioned previously. The upside of this is that you can write one function to do several things:

```
>>> def concat(First, Second):
...     return First + Second
...
>>> concat(["python"], ["perl"])
['python', 'perl']
>>> concat("Hello, ", "world!")
'Hello, world!'
```

That demonstrates how the return statement sends a value back to the caller, but also how a function can do one thing with lists and another thing with strings. The magic here is being accomplished by the objects. We write a function that tells two objects to add themselves together, and the objects intrinsically know how to do that. If they do not—if, perhaps, the user passes in a string and an integer—Python catches the error for us. However, it is this hands-off, "let the objects sort themselves out" attitude that makes functions so flexible. Our concat() function could conceivably concatenate strings, lists, or *zonks*—a data type someone created herself that allows adding. The point is that we do not limit what our function can do. Tacky as it might sound, the only limit is your imagination.

Object Orientation

After having read this far, you should not be surprised to hear that Python's object orientation is flexible and likely to surprise you if you have been using C-like languages for several years.

The best way to learn Python object-oriented programming (OOP) is to just do it. So, here is a basic script that defines a class, creates an object of that class, and calls a function:

```
class Dog(object):
    def bark(self):
        print "Woof!"


fluffy = Dog()
fluffy.bark()
```

Defining a class starts, predictably, with the `class` keyword followed by the name of the class you are defining and a colon. The contents of that class need to be indented one level so that Python knows where it stops. Note that the object inside parentheses is there for object inheritance, which is discussed later. For now, the least you need to know is that if your new class is not based on an existing class, you should put object inside parentheses as shown in the previous code.

Functions inside classes work in much the same way as normal functions do (although they are usually called *methods*); the main difference is that they should all take at least one parameter, usually called `self`. This parameter is filled with the name of the object the function was called on, and you need to use it explicitly.

Creating an instance of a class is done by assignment. You do not need any new keyword, as in some other languages—providing the parentheses makes the creation known. Calling a function of that object is done using a period, the name of the class to call, with any parameters being passed inside parentheses.

Class and Object Variables

Each object has its own set of functions and variables, and you can manipulate those variables independently of objects of the same type. In addition, some class variables are set to a default value for all classes and can be manipulated globally.

This script demonstrates two objects of the dog class being created, each with its own name:

```
class Dog(object):
    name = "Lassie"
    def bark(self):
        print self.name + " says 'Woof!'"
    def set_name(self, name):
        self.name = name
fluffy = Dog()
fluffy.bark()
poppy = Dog()
poppy.set_name("Poppy")
poppy.bark()
```

That outputs the following:

```
Lassie says 'Woof!'
Poppy says 'Woof!'
```

There, each dog starts with the name `Lassie`, but it gets customized. Keep in mind that Python assigns by reference by default, meaning each object has a reference to the class's name variable, and as we assign that with the `set_name()` method, that reference is lost. This means that any references we do not change can be manipulated globally. Thus, if we change a class's variable, it also changes in all instances of that class that have not set their own value for that variable. For example:

```
class Dog(object):
    name = "Lassie"
    color = "brown"
fluffy = Dog()
poppy = Dog()
print fluffy.color
Dog.color = "black"
print poppy.color
fluffy.color = "yellow"
print fluffy.color
print poppy.color
```

So, the default color of dogs is brown—both the fluffy and poppy Dog objects start off as brown. Then, using Dog.color, we set the default color to be black, and because neither of the two objects has set its own color value, they are updated to be black. The third-to-last line uses poppy.color to set a custom color value for the poppy object—poppy becomes yellow, whereas fluffy and the dog class in general remain black.

Constructors and Destructors

To help you automate the creation and deletion of objects, you can easily override two default methods: __init__ and __del__. These are the methods called by Python when a class is being instantiated and freed, known as the *constructor* and *destructor*, respectively.

Having a custom constructor is great for when you need to accept a set of parameters for each object being created. For example, you might want each dog to have its own name on creation, and you could implement that with this code:

```
class Dog(object):
    def __init__(self, name):
        self.name = name
fluffy = Dog("Fluffy")
print fluffy.name
```

If you do not provide a name parameter when creating the Dog object, Python reports an error and stops. You can, of course, ask for as many constructor parameters as you want, although it is usually better to ask only for the ones you need and have other functions to fill in the rest.

On the other side of things is the destructor method, which enables you to have more control over what happens when an object is destroyed. Using the two, we can show the life cycle of an object by printing messages when it is created and deleted:

```
class dog(object):
    def __init__(self, name):
        self.name = name
        print self.name + " is alive!"
    def __del__(self):
        print self.name + " is no more!"
fluffy = Dog("Fluffy")
```

The destructor is there to give you the chance to free up resources allocated to the object, or perhaps log something to a file. Note that although it is possible to override the __del__ method, it is a very dangerous idea because it is not guaranteed that __del__ methods are called for objects that still exist when the interpreter exits. The official Python documentation explains this well at http://docs.python.org/reference/datamodel. html#object.__del__.

Class Inheritance

Python allows you to reuse your code by inheriting one class from one or more others. For example, lions, tigers, and bears are all mammals and so share a number of similar properties. In that scenario, you do not want to have to copy and paste functions between them; it is smarter (and easier) to have a mammal class that defines all the shared functionality and then inherit each animal from that.

Consider the following code:

```
class Car(object):
    color = "black"
    speed = 0
    def accelerate_to(self, speed):
        self.speed = speed
    def set_color(self, color):
        self.color = color
mycar = Car()
print mycar.color
```

That creates a Car class with a default color and provides a set_color() function so that people can change their own colors. Now, what do you drive to work? Is it a car? Sure it is, but chances are it is a Ford, or a Dodge, or a Jeep, or some other make; you do not get cars without a make. On the other hand, you do not want to have to define a class Ford and give it the methods accelerate_to(), set_color(), and however many other methods a basic car has and then do the same thing for Ferrari, Nissan, and so on.

The solution is to use inheritance: Define a car class that contains all the shared functions and variables of all the makes and then inherit from that. In Python, you do this by putting the name of the class from which to inherit inside parentheses in the class declaration, like this:

```
class Car(object):
    color = "black"
    speed = 0
    def accelerate_to(self, speed):
        self.speed = speed
    def set_color(self, color):
        self.color = color
class Ford(Car): pass
class Nissan(Car): pass
mycar = Ford()
print mycar.color
```

38

The pass directive is an empty statement; it means our class contains nothing new. However, because the Ford and Nissan classes inherit from the car class, they get color, speed, accelerate_to(), and set_color() provided by their parent class. Note that we do not need object after the class names for Ford and Nissan because they are inherited from an existing class: car.

By default, Python gives you all the methods the parent class has, but you can override that by providing new implementations for the classes that need them. For example:

```
class Modelt(car):
    def set_color(self, color):
        print "Sorry, Model Ts only come in black!"


myford Ford()
Ford.set_color("green")
mycar = Modelt()
mycar.set_color("green")
```

The first car is created as a Ford, so set_color() will work fine because it uses the method from the car class. However, the second car is created as a Model T, which has its own set_color() method, so the call will fail.

This provides an interesting scenario: What do you do if you have overridden a method and yet want to call the parent's method also? If, for example, changing the color of a Model T were allowed but just cost extra, we would want to print a message saying *"You owe $50 more,"* but then change the color. To do this, we need to use the class object from which our current class is inherited (Car in this case). Here's an example:

```
class Modelt(Car):
    def set_color(self, color):
        print "You owe $50 more"
        Car.set_color(self, color)


mycar = Modelt()
mycar.set_color("green")
print mycar.color
```

That prints the message and then changes the color of the car.

The Standard Library and the Python Package Index

A default Python install includes many modules (blocks of code) that enable you to interact with the operating system, open and manipulate files, parse command-line options, perform data hashing and encryption, and much more. This is one of the reasons most commonly cited when people are asked why they like Python so much: It comes stocked to the gills with functionality you can take advantage of immediately. In fact, the number of modules included in the Standard Library is so high that entire books have been written about them.

For unofficial scripts and add-ons for Python, the recommended starting place is called the *Python Package Index (PyPI)* at http://pypi.python.org/pypi. There you can find well over 10,000 public scripts and code examples for everything from mathematics to games.

References

▶ **www.python.org**—The Python website is packed with information and updated regularly. This should be your first stop, if only to read the latest Python news.

▶ **www.jython.org**—Python also has an excellent Java-based interpreter to allow it to run on other platforms. If you prefer Microsoft .NET, try www.ironpython.com.

▶ **www.pythonline.com**—Guido van Rossum borrowed the name for his language from *Monty Python's Flying Circus*, and as a result, many Python code examples use oblique *Monty Python* references (spam and eggs are quite common, for example). A visit to the official *Monty Python* site to hone your Python knowledge is highly recommended.

▶ **www.zope.org**—The home page of the Zope *content management system (CMS)*, It is one of the most popular CMSes around and, more important, written entirely in Python.

▶ If you want a book, we recommend starting with *Learning Python*, by Mark Lutz (O'Reilly), and for advanced work, move to *Programming Python*, also by Mark Lutz (O'Reilly).

38

If you're looking to learn C or C++ programming, this part of the book isn't the right place to start. Unlike Perl, Python, PHP, or even C#, it takes more than a little dabbling to produce something productive with C, so this chapter is primarily focused on the tools Ubuntu offers you as a C or C++ programmer.

Whether you're looking to compile your own code or someone else's, the *GNU Compiler Collection* (gcc) is there to help. It understands C, C++, Fortran, Pascal, and dozens of other popular languages, which means you can try your hand at whatever interests you. Ubuntu also ships with hundreds of libraries you can link to, from the GUI toolkits behind GNOME and KDE to XML parsing and game coding. Some use C, others C++, and still others offer support for both, meaning you can choose what you're most comfortable with.

Why Use C or C++?

Every language has its benefits and its shortcomings. Some languages make life easier for the programmer, but at the expense of runtime. Languages like Perl and Python and even Java make it hard for the user to guarantee that memory is fetched sequentially or that it fits in cache, due to things such as checks on the bounds on each access. They are useful languages, but they run slower than languages that are harder for the programmer, but faster at runtime like C or Fortran.

For some programs, such as short shell scripts or a quick one-liner in Perl to search text in a file, the difference in the runtime speed is negligible. On a desktop computer, it may not matter that your music player is written in Python, and if it seems slow, then buying a newer, faster desktop system may be an acceptable solution.

There are some applications, however, where the time needed to run your program can make a big difference. For example, using a slow-to-run language to perform calculations on scientific data, especially if you are doing it on *High Performance Computing (HPC)* resources like a supercomputing cluster, is foolish; to take advantage of the platform, it is both time- and cost-effective to use the fastest language available to you, like C.

This idea was reinforced in a conversation between Matthew Helmke and Dan Stanzione, the deputy director of the Texas Advanced Computing Center at the University of Texas at Austin. Stanzione said that HPC computing resources are expensive, so it is often wiser to spend grant money to hire a good C programmer for a year than it is to run a bioinformatics program written in Perl or Python on an HPC system. As he put it, "If your computer costs $2,000, the programmer's time is the dominant cost, and that is what drives software development. If your computer costs $100 million or more, then having a programmer spend an extra month, or year, or decade working on software optimization is well worth it. Toughen up and write in C."

Programming in C with Linux

C is the programming language most frequently associated with UNIX-like operating systems such as Linux or BSD. Since the 1970s, the bulk of the UNIX operating system and its applications have been written in C. Because the C language doesn't directly rely on any specific hardware architecture, UNIX was one of the first portable operating systems. In other words, the majority of the code that makes up UNIX doesn't know and doesn't care which computer it is actually running on. Machine-specific features are isolated in a few modules within the UNIX kernel, which makes it easy for you to modify them when you are porting to different hardware architectures.

C is a *compiled* language, which means that your C source code is first analyzed by the *preprocessor* and then translated into assembly language first and then into machine instructions that are appropriate to the target CPU. An assembler then creates a binary, or *object*, a file from the machine instructions. Finally, the object file is linked to any required external software support by the *linker*. A C program is stored in a text file that ends with a .c extension and always contains at least one routine, or function, such as main(), unless the file is an *include* file (with a .h extension, also known as a *header* file) containing shared variable definitions or other data or declarations. *Functions* are the commands that perform each step of the task that the C program was written to accomplish.

NOTE

The Linux kernel is mostly written in C, which is why Linux works with so many different CPUs. To learn more about building the Linux kernel from source, see Chapter 21, "Kernel and Module Management."

C++ is an object-oriented extension to C. Because C++ is a superset of C, C++ compilers compile C programs correctly, and it is possible to write non-object-oriented code in C++. The reverse is not true: C compilers cannot compile C++ code.

C++ extends the capabilities of C by providing the necessary features for object-oriented design and code. C++ also provides some features, such as the capability to associate functions with data structures that do not require the use of class-based object-oriented techniques. For these reasons, the C++ language enables existing UNIX programs to migrate toward the adoption of object orientation over time.

Support for C++ programming is provided by gcc, which you run with the name g++ when you are compiling C++ code.

Using the C Programming Project Management Tools Provided with Ubuntu

Ubuntu is replete with tools that make your life as a C/C++ programmer easier. There are tools to create programs (editors), compile programs (gcc), create libraries (ar), control the source (Git, Mercurial, Subversion), automate builds (make), debug programs (gdb and ddd), and determine where inefficiencies lie (gprof).

The following sections introduce some of the programming and project management tools included with Ubuntu. If you have some previous UNIX experience, you will be familiar with most of these programs because they are traditional complements to a programmer's suite of software.

Building Programs with make

You use the make command to automatically build and install a C program, and for that use, it is an easy tool. If you want to create your own automated builds, however, you need to learn the special syntax that make uses; the following sections walk you through a basic make setup.

Using Makefiles

The make command automatically builds and updates applications by using a makefile. A *makefile* is a text file that contains instructions about which options to pass on to the compiler preprocessor, the compiler, the assembler, and the linker. The makefile also specifies, among other things, which source code files have to be compiled (and the compiler command line) for a particular code module and which code modules are needed to build the program—a mechanism called *dependency checking*.

The beauty of the make command is its flexibility. You can use make with a simple makefile, or you can write complex makefiles that contain numerous macros, rules, or commands that work in a single directory or traverse your file system recursively to build programs, update your system, and even function as document management systems. The make command works with nearly any program, including text processing systems such as TeX.

You could use make to compile, build, and install a software package, using a simple command like this:

matthew@seymour:~$ **sudo make install**

You can use the default makefile (usually called Makefile, with a capital *M*), or you can use make's -f option to specify any makefile, such as MyMakeFile, like this:

matthew@seymour:~$ **sudo make -f MyMakeFile**

Other options might be available, depending on the contents of your makefile. You may have a source file named hi.c and just run make hi, where make figures out what to do automatically to build the final executable. See make's built-in rules with make -p.

Using Macros and Makefile Targets

Using make with macros can make a program portable. Macros allow users of other operating systems to easily configure a program build by specifying local values, such as the names and locations, or *pathnames*, of any required software tools. In the following example, macros define the name of the compiler (CC), the installer program (INS), where the program should be installed (INSDIR), where the linker should look for required libraries (LIBDIR), the names of required libraries (LIBS), a source code file (SRC), the intermediate object code file (OBJS), and the name of the final program (PROG):

```
# a sample makefile for a skeleton program
CC= gcc
INS= install
INSDIR = /usr/local/bin
LIBDIR= -L/usr/X11R6/lib
LIBS= -lXm -lSM -lICE -lXt -lX11
SRC= skel.c
OBJS= skel.o
PROG= skel

skel:   ${OBJS}
        ${CC} -o ${PROG} ${SRC} ${LIBDIR} ${LIBS}

install: ${PROG}
        ${INS} -g root -o root ${PROG} ${INSDIR}
```

> **NOTE**
>
> The indented lines in the previous example are indented with tabs, not spaces. This is important to remember! It is difficult for a person to see the difference, but make can tell. If make reports confusing errors when you first start building programs under Linux, check your project's makefile for the use of tabs and other proper formatting.

Using the makefile from the preceding example, you can build a program like this:

matthew@seymour:~$ **sudo make**

To build a specified component of a makefile, you can use a target definition on the command line. To build just the program, you use make with the skel target, like this:

matthew@seymour:~$ **sudo make skel**

If you make any changes to any element of a target object, such as a source code file, make rebuilds the target automatically. This feature is part of the convenience of using make to manage a development project. To build and install a program in one step, you can specify the target of install like this:

matthew@seymour:~$ **sudo make install**

Larger software projects might have a number of traditional targets in the makefile, such as the following:

- ▶ **test**—To run specific tests on the final software.
- ▶ **man**—To process an include or a troff document with the man macros.
- ▶ **clean**—To delete any remaining object files.
- ▶ **archive**—To clean up, archive, and compress the entire source code tree.
- ▶ **bugreport**—To automatically collect and then mail a copy of the build or error logs.

Large applications can require hundreds of source code files. Compiling and linking these applications can be a complex and error-prone task. The make utility helps you organize the process of building the executable form of a complex application from many source files.

39

Using the autoconf Utility to Configure Code

The make command is only one of several programming automation utilities included with Ubuntu. There are others, such as pmake (which causes a parallel make), imake (which is a dependency-driven makefile generator that is used for building X11 clients), automake, and one of the newer tools, autoconf, which builds shell scripts that can be used to configure program source code packages.

Building many software packages for Linux that are distributed in source form requires the use of GNU's autoconf utility. This program builds an executable shell script named configure that, when executed, automatically examines and tailors a client's build from source according to software resources, or *dependencies* (such as programming tools, libraries, and associated utilities) that are installed on the target host (your Linux system).

Many Linux commands and graphical clients for X downloaded in source code form include configure scripts. To configure the source package, build the software, and then install the new program, the root user might use the script like this (after uncompressing the source and navigating into the resulting build directory):

```
matthew@seymour:~$ ./configure ; make ; sudo make install
```

The autoconf program uses a file named configure.in that contains a basic *ruleset*, or set of macros. The configure.in file is created with the autoscan command. Building a properly executing configure script also requires a template for the makefile, named Makefile.in. Although creating the dependency-checking configure script can be done manually, you can easily overcome any complex dependencies by using a graphical project development tool such as KDEs KDevelop or GNOME's Glade. (See the "Graphical Development Tools" section, later in this chapter, for more information.)

Debugging Tools

Debugging is both a science and an art. Sometimes, the simplest tool—the code listing—is the best debugging tool. At other times, however, you need to use other debugging tools. Three of these tools are splint, gprof, and gdb.

Using splint to Check Source Code

The splint command is similar to the traditional UNIX lint command: It statically examines source code for possible problems, and it also has many additional features. Even if your C code meets the standards for C and compiles cleanly, it might still contain errors. splint performs many types of checks and can provide extensive error information. For example, this simple program might compile cleanly and even run:

```
matthew@seymour:~$ gcc -o tux tux.c
matthew@seymour:~$ ./tux
```

But the splint command might point out some serious problems with the source:

```
matthew@seymour:~$ splint tux.c
Splint 3.1.2 --- 29 Apr 2009

tux.c: (in function main)
tux.c:2:19: Return value (type int) ignored: putchar(t[++j] -...
  Result returned by function call is not used. If this is intended, can cast
  result to (void) to eliminate message. (Use -retvalint to inhibit warning)
Finished checking --- 1 code warning
```

You can use the splint command's -strict option, like this, to get a more verbose report:

matthew@seymour:~$ **splint -strict tux.c**

gcc also supports diagnostics through the use of extensive warnings (through the -Wall and -pedantic options):

matthew@seymour:~$ **gcc -Wall tux.c**
tux.c:1: warning: return type defaults to 'int'
tux.c: In function 'main':
tux.c:2: warning: implicit declaration of function 'putchar'

Using gprof to Track Function Time

You use the gprof (profile) command to study how a program is spending its time. If a program is compiled and linked with -p as a flag, a mon.out file is created when it executes, with data on how often each function is called and how much time is spent in each function. gprof parses and displays this data. An analysis of the output generated by gprof helps you determine where performance bottlenecks occur. Using an optimizing compiler can speed up a program, but taking the time to use gprof's analysis and revising bottleneck functions significantly improves program performance.

Doing Symbolic Debugging with gdb

The gdb tool is a symbolic debugger. When a program is compiled with the -g flag, the symbol tables are retained and a symbolic debugger can be used to track program bugs. The basic technique is to invoke gdb after a *core dump* (a file containing a snapshot of the memory used by a program that has crashed) and get a stack trace. The stack trace indicates the source line where the core dump occurred and the functions that were called to reach that line. Often, this is enough to identify a problem. It isn't the limit of gdb, though.

gdb also provides an environment for debugging programs interactively. Invoking gdb with a program enables you to set breakpoints, examine the values of variables, and monitor variables. If you suspect a problem near a line of code, you can set a breakpoint at that line and run gdb. When the line is reached, execution is interrupted. You can check variable values, examine the stack trace, and observe the program's environment. You can single-step through the program to check values. You can resume execution at any point. By using breakpoints, you can discover many bugs in code.

A graphical X Window interface to gdb is called the *Data Display Debugger*, or ddd.

Using the GNU C Compiler

If you elected to install the development tools package when you installed Ubuntu (or perhaps later on, using synaptic), you should have the *GNU C compiler* (gcc). Many different options are available for the GNU C compiler, and many of them are similar to those

39

of the C and C++ compilers that are available on other UNIX systems. Look at the man page or information file for gcc for a full list of options and descriptions.

> **NOTE**
>
> The GNU C compiler is a part of the GNU Compiler Collection, which also includes compilers for several other languages.

When you build a C program using gcc, the compilation process takes place in several steps:

1. First, the C preprocessor parses the file. To do so, it sequentially reads the lines, includes header files, and performs macro replacement.

2. The compiler parses the modified code to determine whether the correct syntax is used. In the process, it builds a symbol table and creates an intermediate object format. Most symbols have specific memory addresses assigned, although symbols defined in other modules, such as external variables, do not.

3. The last compilation stage, linking, ties together different files and libraries and then links the files by resolving the symbols that had not previously been resolved.

> **NOTE**
>
> Most C programs compile with a C++ compiler if you follow strict ANSI rules. For example, you can compile the standard hello.c program (everyone's first program) with the GNU C++ compiler. Typically, you name the file something like hello.cc, hello.C, hello.c++, or hello.cxx. The GNU C++ compiler accepts any of these names.

Graphical Development Tools

Ubuntu includes a number of graphical prototyping and development environments for use during X sessions. If you want to build client software for KDE or GNOME, you might find the KDevelop, Qt Designer, and Glade programs to be extremely helpful. You can use each of these programs to build graphical frameworks for interactive windowing clients, and you can use each of them to automatically generate the necessary skeleton of code needed to support a custom interface for your program.

Using the KDevelop Client

You can launch the KDevelop client (shown in Figure 39.1) from the application's menu, or from the command line of a terminal window, like this:

```
matthew@seymour:~$ kdevelop &
```

After you press Enter, the KDevelop Setup Wizard runs, and you are taken through several short wizard dialogs that set up and ensure a stable build environment. You must then run kdevelop again (either from the command line or by clicking its menu item under the desktop panel's Programming menu). You then see the main KDevelop window and can start your project by selecting KDevelop's Project menu and clicking the New menu item.

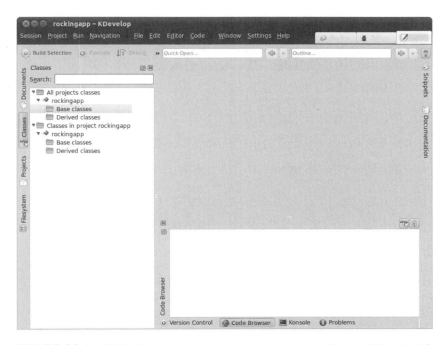

FIGURE 39.1   KDE's Kdevelop is a rapid prototyping and client-building tool for use with Linux.

You can begin building your project by stepping through the wizard dialogs. When you click the Create button, KDevelop automatically generates all the files that are normally found in a KDE client source directory (including the `configure` script, which checks dependencies and builds the client's makefile). To test your client, you can either first click the Build menu's Make menu item (or press F8) or just click the Execute menu item (or press F9), and the client is built automatically. You can use KDevelop to create KDE clients, plug-ins for the `Konqueror` *browser*, KDE `kicker` panel applets, KDE desktop themes, Qt library-based clients, and even programs for GNOME.

The Glade Client for Developing in GNOME

If you prefer to use GNOME and its development tools, the Glade GTK+ GUI builder can help you save time and effort when building a basic skeleton for a program. You launch Glade from the desktop panel's Programming menu.

When you launch Glade, a directory named `Projects` is created in your home directory, and you see a main window, along with two floating Palette and Properties windows (see Figure 39.2, which shows a basic GNOME client with a calendar widget added to its main window). You can use Glade's File menu to save the blank project and then start building your client by clicking and adding user interface elements from the Palette window. For example, you can first click the Palette window's Gnome button and then click to create your new client's main window. A window with a menu and a toolbar appears—the basic framework for a new GNOME client.

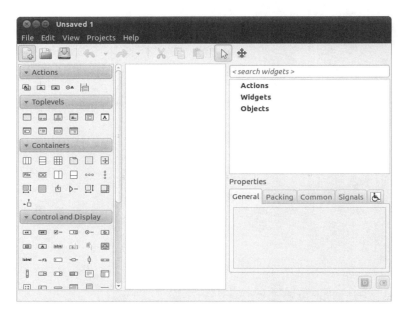

FIGURE 39.2   You can use the GNOME Glade client to build and preview a graphical interface for a custom GNOME program.

References

- ▶ **www.cprogramming.com**—A useful website for learning C and C++.

- ▶ **http://gcc.gnu.org/**—The main website for gcc, the GNU Compiler Collection.

- ▶ **www.gnu.org/software/autoconf/autoconf.html**—More information about the GNU Project's autoconf utility and how to build portable software projects.

- ▶ **http://qt.nokia.com**—The main Qt website.

- ▶ **http://glade.gnome.org**—The home page for the Glade GNOME developer's tool.

- ▶ **www.kdevelop.org**—Site that hosts the KDevelop Project's latest versions of the KDE graphical development environment, KDevelop.

- ▶ *The C Programming Language*, by Brian W. Kernighan and Dennis M. Ritchie, Prentice Hall.

- ▶ *The Annotated C++ Reference Manual*, by Margaret A. Ellis and Bjarne Stroustrup, ANSI Base Document.

- *Programming in ANSI C*, by Stephen G. Kochan, Sams Publishing.

- *Sams Teach Yourself C in 21 Days*, by Peter Aitken and Bradley Jones, Sams Publishing.

- *Sams Teach Yourself C++ for Linux in 21 Days*, by Jesse Liberty and David B. Horvath, Sams Publishing.

- *C How to Program and C++ How to Program*, both by Harvey M. Deitel and Paul J. Deitel, Deitel Associates.

CHAPTER 40

Using Mono

Although Microsoft intended it for Windows, the Microsoft .NET platform has grown to encompass many other operating systems. No, this isn't a rare sign of Microsoft letting customers choose which OS is best for them. Instead, the spread of .NET is because of the Mono project, which is a free re-implementation of .NET available under the GPL license.

Because of the potential for patent complications, it took most distros a long time to incorporate Mono, but it's here now and works just fine. What's more, Mono supports both C# and Visual Basic .NET, as well as the complete .NET 1.0 and 1.1 Frameworks (and much of the 2.0 Framework, too), making it easy to learn and productive to use.

There were some fears that Mono may cease to exist. In early May 2011, Attachmate bought Novell along with its SUSE Linux distribution. Novell headed up the Mono project. One of the first things that Attachmate did after the acquisition was cancel the Mono project. Then they laid off all the Mono developers, about 30 people.

On May 16, 2011, the lead developer of Mono, Miguel de Icaza, announced on his blog the creation of a new company called Xamarin (http://xamarin.com). The new company was created to continue Mono development and to build Mono applications. Many, if not most, of the original developers working on Mono at Novell are now employed by Xamarin, and Mono 2.10 is installed by default in Ubuntu 11.10, along with several default applications that are written in Mono. On July 18, 2011, it was announced by SUSE that an intellectual property agreement and perpetual license had been extended to Xamarin to continue to use and develop Mono as a platform and products that use Mono. No one knows what the future holds for Mono, but at least we know it has not yet been abandoned. In August 2011, Xamarin made its first official Mono release.

Why Use Mono?

Linux already has numerous programming languages available to it, so why bother with Mono and .NET? Here are my top five reasons:

▶ .NET is "compile once, run anywhere"; this means you can compile your code on Linux and run it on Windows, or the reverse.

▶ Mono supports C#, which is a C-like language with many improvements to help make it object-oriented and easier to use.

▶ .NET includes automatic garbage collection to remove the possibility of memory leaks.

▶ .NET uses comes with built-in security checks to ensure that buffer overflows and many types of exploits are a thing of the past. Mono uses a high-performance just-in-time compiler to optimize your code for the platform on which it's running. This lets you compile it on a 32-bit machine, and then run it on a 64-bit machine and have the code dynamically recompiled for maximum 64-bit performance.

At this point, Mono is probably starting to sound like Java, and indeed it shares several properties with it. However, Mono has the following improvements:

▶ The C# language corrects many of the irritations in Java, while keeping its garbage collection.

▶ .NET is designed to let you compile multiple languages down to the same bytecode, including C#, Visual Basic .NET, and many others.

▶ Mono even has a special project (known as IKVM) that compiles Java source code down to .NET code that can be run on Mono.

▶ Mono is completely open source!

Whether you're looking to create command-line programs, graphical user interface apps, or even web pages, Mono has all the power and functionality you need.

Mono is made up of several components, including a C# compiler, the Mono Runtime, the Base Class Library, and the Mono Class Library.

The C# compiler includes all of the features to compile C# 1.0, 2.0, and 3.0 (ECMA) code. The compiler is able to compile itself, is fast, and includes a test suite. The C# compiler gives you your pick of several services that applications may consume, as follows:

▶ `mcs`—References the 1.0-profile libraries and supports C# 1.0 and C# 3.0, minus generics and any features that depend on generics, and is called `mono-cms` in the Ubuntu software repositories.

▶ **gmcs**—References the 2.0-profile libraries and supports the full C# 3.0 language, is called `mono-gcms` in the Ubuntu software repositories, and is installed by default in Ubuntu 10.10.

▶ **smcs**—References the 2.1-profile libraries, supports the full C# 3.0 language, and is used for creating Moonlight (the Mono version of Silverlight) applications. It is not available in the Ubuntu software repositories.

▶ **dmcs**—Targets the C# 4.0 language and is not available in the Ubuntu software repositories.

The first three in that list are all the same compiler, but with different default settings. The last one listed is new and will become the default in Mono 2.8.

The Mono Runtime uses the ECMA *Common Language Infrastructure (CIL)*. This is a runtime similar to the Java Virtual Machine. It provides a *just-in-time (JIT)* compiler, an *ahead-of-time (AOT)* compiler, a library loader, a garbage collector, a threading system, and interoperability functionality. The execution engine, `mono`, can be used as a standalone process. By itself, it runs as a JIT or AOT code generator. With `--full-aot`, it can run in fully static mode with no JIT involvement. You can reuse your existing C and C++ code and extend it with Mono either with scripting or by embedding Mono into applications.

The Mono Base Class Library provides a set of foundational classes that are compatible with Microsoft's .NET Framework. It is extended by the Mono Class Library that provides additional functions that are especially useful when building Linux applications, such as classes for Gtk+, LDAP, and POSIX.

Mono runs on many platforms, not just Linux. It is designed as a free-software implementation of Microsoft's C# and can also run on Windows, Mac OS X, BSD, Solaris, Nintendo Wii, Sony PlayStation 3, and the Apple iPhone. It works on many different types of processors, including the common x86 and x86-64 that Ubuntu targets, and also others such as PowerPC, SPARC, ARM, Alpha, and more. The *Common Language Runtime (CLR)* that comes with Mono allows you to choose other programming languages, write your code using them, and then run the programs in Mono (see http://mono-project.com/Languages).

MonoDevelop

▶ Mono should already be installed on your system, but it is installed only for end users rather than for developers. You need to install a couple more packages to make it usable for programming. Install `mono-complete` and `monodevelop` from the Ubuntu repositories.

▶ These give you the basics to do Mono development.

If you want to do other exciting things with Mono, lots of Mono-enabled libraries are available. Use Synaptic at System, Administration, Synaptic Package Manager to search the Ubuntu software repositories for "sharp" to bring up the list of .NET-enabled libraries that

40

you can use with Mono; the suffix is used because C# is the most popular .NET language, indeed the flagship language in the .NET fleet, written especially for .NET. In this list, you'll see things such as gnome-sharp2 and gtk-sharp2—we recommend you at least install the gtk-sharp2 libraries because these are used to create graphical user interfaces for Mono.

Open MonoDevelop from the menu at Applications, Programming, MonoDevelop.

> **TIP**
>
> You don't have to use MonoDevelop to write your code, but it helps—syntax highlighting, code completion, and drag-and-drop GUI designers are just a few of its features.

When MonoDevelop has loaded, open File, New, Solution. From the left of the window that appears, choose C#, then Console Project. Give it a name and choose a location to save it, as in Figure 40.1. When you're ready, click Forward.

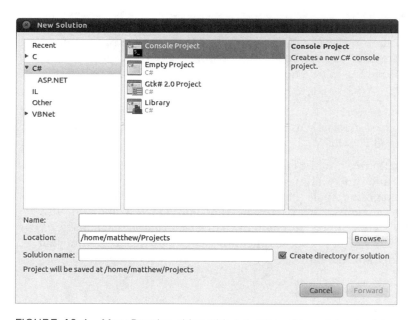

FIGURE 40.1   MonoDevelop ships with a number of templates to get you started, including one for a quick Console Project.

This is a simple command-line project. For our example, select UNIX Integration as the only feature to include in Figure 40.2 and click OK. Notice that this generates a launch script by default and allows you to choose to create a .desktop file if desired. You can also create packaging as an archive of binaries or a tarball and enable support for GTK#. We don't need either of these for our example.

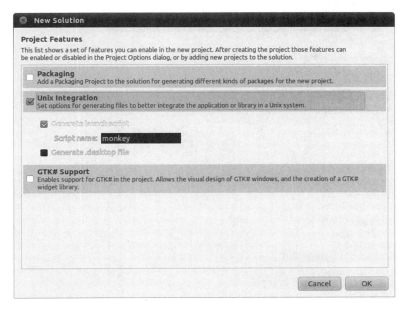

FIGURE 40.2   Choose the project features you want to enable in your project.

The default Console Project template creates a program that prints a simple message to the command line: the oh-so-traditional "Hello World!" Click Build, Build HelloWorld (or F7) to build the project (see Figure 40.3). Click Run, Run (or Ctrl+F5) to run the program. A terminal window will appear to show you the output of your program, as shown in Figure 40.4.

You can also run and debug at the same time using Run, Debug (or F5). If there are errors in the program code, you are notified, as shown in Figure 40.5. I created a simple error by removing a letter from the end of a word. If there are no errors, the program runs as it did when we used Run, Run previously.

The Structure of a C# Program

As you can guess from its name, C# draws heavily on C and C++ for its syntax, but it borrows several ideas from other languages that its creator, Hejlsberg, had experience with, such as Java, Turbo Pascal, Delphi, Python, Icon, Smalltalk, and Modula-2 and 3. C# is object-oriented. In C#, you define a class, which is then instantiated by calling its constructor.

Main() is the default entry point for an executable assembly in MonoDevelop and Visual Studio .NET. To be able to draw on some of the .NET Framework's many libraries, you need to add using statements at the top of your files—by default, only using System; is included, enabling you to access the console to write your Hello World! message.

40

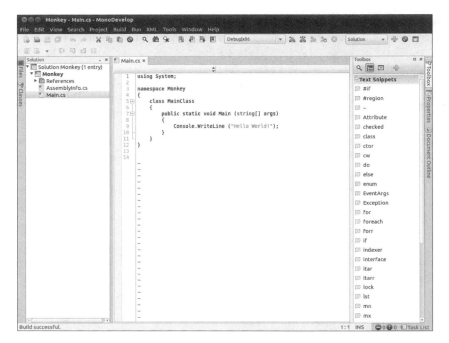

FIGURE 40.3   MonoDevelop with HelloWorld loaded, showing a successful build notice at the bottom.

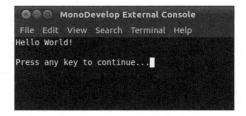

FIGURE 40.4   A successful run of HelloWorld in a terminal.

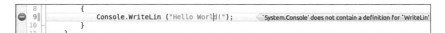

FIGURE 40.5   An error message points out a problem when running in debug mode.

If you have experience with C or C++, you will notice that there are no header files in C#; your class definition and its implementation are all in the same file. You might also have noticed that the Main() method accepts the parameter "string[] args", which means we will be passing arguments from the command line and is C#-speak for "an array of strings." C never had a native "string" data type, whereas C++ acquired it rather late in the game, and so both languages tend to use the antiquated `char*` data type to point to a string of characters. In C#, `"string"` is a data type all its own, and comes with built-in functionality such as the capability to replace substrings, the capability to trim off white-space, and the capability to convert itself to uppercase or lowercase if you want it to. Strings are also Unicode friendly out of the box in .NET, so that's one fewer thing for you to worry about.

The final thing you might have noticed—at least, if you had looked in the directory where MonoDevelop placed your compiled program (usually `/path/to/your/project/bin/ Debug`)—is that Mono uses the Windows-like `.exe` file extension for its programs, because Mono aims to be 100-percent compatible with Microsoft .NET, which means you can take your Hello World program and run it unmodified on a Windows machine and have the same message printed out.

Printing Out the Parameters

We're going to expand this little program by having it print out all the parameters passed to it, one per line. In C#, this is—amazingly—just one line of code. Add this just after the existing `Console.WriteLine()` line in your program:

```
foreach (string arg in args) Console.WriteLine(arg);
```

The `foreach` keyword is a special kind of loop designed to iterate over any collection, in this case an array. The for loop exists in C#, and lets you loop a certain number of times; the `while` loop exists, too, and lets you loop continuously until a conditional is no longer true or a break statement is encountered—the conditional controls the loop and a break statement will allow an exit if desired or included. But the `foreach` loop is designed to loop over a collection from the start to the end. You get each value as a variable of any type you want—the preceding code says `string arg in args`, which means "for each array element in args, give it to me as the variable arg of type string." Because args is already an array consisting of many `strings`, no data type conversion takes place here—but it could if you wanted to convert classes or do anything of the like. One reason you might use a for loop over a `foreach` loop is if you need to determine an index into a collection, as in finding a minimum or maximum value. There is no index available for the current iteration in a `foreach` loop, much like it is not available in a `while` loop.

After you have each individual argument, call `WriteLine()` to print it out. This works whether there's one argument or one hundred arguments—or even if there are no arguments at all (in which case, the loop doesn't execute at all).

Creating Your Own Variables

You can have anonymous variable types and `var` variable declarations in C#. You can also specify variable types with great precision. Most of the time, you can use `int` and leave C# to work out the details. Let's modify our program to accept two parameters, add them together as numbers, and then print the result. This gives you a chance to see variable definitions, conversion, and mathematics, all in one. Edit the `Main()` method to look like this:

```
using System;

namespace AddNumbers
{
        class MainClass
        {
                public static void Main (string[] args)
                 {
                            int num1 = int.Parse(args[0]);
                            int num2 = int.Parse(args[1]);
                            Console.WriteLine("Sum of two parameters is: " + (num1 +
num2)");
                 }
        }
}
```

Run this new code using Run, Run With, Custom Parameter. As you can see, each variable is declared with a type (int) and a name (num1 and num2) so that C# knows how to handle them. The args array contains strings, so we convert the strings to integers with the `int.Parse()` method. Finally, the actual addition of the two strings is done at the end of the method, while they are being printed out. Note how C# is clever enough to have integer + integer be added together (in the case of num + num2), whereas string + integer attaches the integer to the end of the string (in the case of "Sum of two parameters is:" + the result of num1 + num2). This isn't by accident: C# tries to convert data types cleverly, and warns you only if it can't convert a data type without losing some data. For example, if you try to treat a 64-bit integer as a 32-bit integer, it warns you because you might be throwing a lot of data away. You can use `int.TryParse()` to attempt parsing conditionally, and it would also return a Boolean response indicating success or failure. In addition, you can also use checked conversions to perform operations and have the compiler verify that they do not cause overflow (essentially meaning the variable could not represent the value).

Adding Some Error Checking

Right now, your program crashes in a nasty way if users don't provide at least two parameters. The reason for this is that we use `arg[0]` and `arg[1]` (the first and second parameters passed to your program) without even checking whether *any* parameters were passed in. This is easily solved: args is an array, and arrays can reveal their size. If the size doesn't match what you expect, you can bail out.

Add this code at the start of the `Main()` method:

```
if (args.Length != 2) {
   Console.WriteLine("You must provide exactly two parameters!");
   return;
}
```

The new piece of code in there is return, which is a C# keyword that forces it to exit the current method. Because Main() is the only method being called, this has the effect of terminating the program because the user didn't supply two parameters. You could also specify that the Main() method have a return type of int so that an exit code would be returned instead of returning without any feedback. This would be especially helpful if the executable was to be used in a command-line tool chain by another tool that needs feedback after your tool runs.

Using the Length property of args, it is now possible for you to write your own Main() method that does different things, depending on how many parameters are provided. To do this properly, you need to use the else statement and nest multiple if statements, like this:

```
if (args.Length == 2) {
   /// whatever...
} else if (args.Length == 3) {
   /// something else
} else if (args.Length == 4) {
   /// even more
} else {
   /// only executed if none of the others are
}
```

Building on Mono's Libraries

Ubuntu ships with several Mono-built programs, such as Tomboy and gBrainy. It also comes with a fair collection of .NET-enabled libraries, some of which you probably already installed earlier. The nice thing about Mono, like many other object-oriented languages, is that it lets you build on these libraries really easily: You just import them with a using statement and then get started.

To demonstrate how easy it is to build more complicated Mono applications, we're going to produce one using Gtk#, the GUI toolkit that is the standard for GNOME development.

Creating a GUI with Gtk#

Gtk# was included with GNOME by default for the first time in GNOME 2.16, but it had been used for a couple of years before that and so was already mature. MonoDevelop comes with its own GUI designer called GTK# Designer, which lets you drag and drop GUI elements onto your windows to design them.

To get started, in MonoDevelop, go to File, New, Solution, choose C#, and then choose Gtk# 2.0 project. Call it **GtkTest**, and deselect the box asking MonoDevelop to make a separate directory for the solution. Click Forward. In the New Solution Project Features window, all you need is already selected, so click OK.

You'll find that Main.cs contains a little more code this time because it needs to create and run the Gtk# application. However, the actual code to create your GUI is in the User

Interface section in the left pane. If you open that group, you'll see Stock Icons and MainWindow. Double-click MainWindow to bring up MonoDevelop's GUI designer.

Click Toolbox on the left of the screen to drag and drop the different window widgets onto your form to see what properties they have.

For now, drag a button widget onto your form. It automatically takes up all the space on your window. If you don't want this to happen, try placing one of the containers down first, and then putting your button in there. For example, if you want a menu bar at the top, then a calendar, and then a status bar, you ought to drop the VBox pane onto the window first, and then drop each of those widgets into the separate parts of the VPane, the main GUI creation workspace.

Your button displays the text GtkButton and uses the variable name button1 by default. Click to select it, and then click Properties on the right and look for Label in the Button Properties group. Change the label to **Hello**. Just at the top of the Properties pane is a tab saying Properties (where you are right now), and another saying Signals. Signals are the events that happen to your widgets, such as the mouse moving over them, someone typing, or, of interest to us, when your button has been clicked. Look inside the Button Signals group for Clicked and double-click it. MonoDevelop automatically switches you to the code view, with a pre-created method to handle button clicks.

Type this code into the method:

```
button1.Label = "World!";
```

If you want to change the button's variable name, you do so from the same Properties tab using the first entry, Name. Change the Name value, and your variable's name is changed. Press F5 to compile and run, and try clicking the button.

References

- ▶ **www.mono-project.com/**—The home page of the Mono project is packed with information to help you get started. You can also download new Mono versions from here, if there's something you desperately need.

- ▶ **www.monodevelop.com/**—The MonoDevelop project has its own site, which is the best place to look for updates.

- ▶ **www.icsharpcode.net/OpenSource/SD/**—MonoDevelop started life as a port of SharpDevelop. If you happen to dual-boot on Windows, this might prove very useful to you.

- ▶ **http://msdn.microsoft.com/vcsharp/**—We don't print many Microsoft URLs in this book, but this one is important: It's the home page of their C# project, which can be considered the spiritual home of C# itself.

► Jesse Liberty's *Programming C#* (O'Reilly, ISBN 0-596-00699-3) is compact, it's comprehensive, and it's competitively priced.

► If you're very short on time and want the maximum detail (admittedly, with rather limited readability), you should try *The C# Programming Language*, which was co-authored by the creator of C#, Anders Hejlsberg (Addison-Wesley, ISBN: 0-321-33443-4).

► For a more general book on the .NET framework and all the features it provides, you might find *.NET Framework Essentials* (O'Reilly, ISBN: 0-596-00505-9) to be useful.

40

CHAPTER 41

Using Other Popular Programming Languages

This book contains several chapters dedicated to some of the most commonly used programming languages on Ubuntu, but up until this edition has lacked any mention of the wide variety of other languages available. Students and developers who pay attention to either history or current trends are already aware of a vast swath of possibilities that deserve some attention. The goal of this chapter is to introduce many different languages available for you to use—some that are old and some that are new.

This short chapter does not teach you how to use these languages, but rather exposes you to them, making you aware of their existence and giving just enough information about them to help you decide whether each one sounds interesting or useful to you and points to resources to help guide your next steps. The introductions include information for installing and getting started with each language on Ubuntu. Sometimes the version of the language included in the Ubuntu repositories is a little outdated or is a free (as in freedom) version instead of an official, proprietary version. If you discover that you need something more up-to-the-minute current or a version not mentioned, check the "References" section to find links to more information for most languages.

The organization of this chapter was tricky. The original idea was to order the chapter by how well known a language is, but that is problematic. Older languages generally have better name recognition, even though newer ones may be more commonly used. How do we measure popularity and use it to enforce order on a list of programming languages? The people who use them tend to form strong emotional bonds with those they prefer, just as geeks do with text editors (Emacs versus vi), email programs (web based versus Thunderbird versus Mutt), and more important matters like comic book universes (Marvel versus DC). Ultimately, it seemed like an alphabetic order would be best. If your favorite language was not included in this edition, and you think it should be included in future editions, please email your suggestion and reasoning to the author at matthew@matthewhelmke.com for consideration.

Ada

Ada is based on Pascal. It is named after Ada Lovelace (1815–1852), who wrote the first algorithm designed to be processed by a machine, specifically the mechanical computing device created by Charles Babbage.

The language is most known for its use in embedded systems, especially in the aeronautics and avionics realm. Ada is well known as a reliable and efficient real-time language. It is most commonly encountered in aircraft systems, air traffic control and railroad systems, and medical devices. It is also often used as a teaching language for computer science courses.

Language highlights include static typing, concurrency, synchronous message passing, protected objects, modularization, and exception handling. Ada is object oriented, has standard libraries for things like I/O and containers, good interfaces to other languages like C, and works well with distributed systems and numeric processing.

To use Ada on Ubuntu, you write programs in your favorite text editor. To compile, you need the package gnat, which is the *GNU Ada Compiler*. You may want to consider gnat-gps, which installs the Gnat Programming System, an *integrated development environment (IDE)* specifically for Ada and C programming.

Clojure

Clojure is a newer dialect of Lisp that runs on the *Java Virtual Machine (JVM)*. It is intended for general-purpose use. It encourages functional programming and is designed to make writing multithreaded applications easier. Because of the close integration with Java, Clojure applications can be packaged and deployed to JVM environments without adding complexity. It also provides easy access to Java frameworks and Clojure's data structures all implement standard Java interfaces.

Closures are a common in programming, especially in functional programming languages, including Clojure. (The name is rumored to be a mash-up of *closure* and *Java*.) Typically, variables are designed to only work within a defined function. A closure is a way to bend that rule temporarily. A closure starts with a function and allows the value of one or more variables from that function to be available outside of that function while being maintained in the function. Another way to phrase that is to say a closure is a combination of a function and the variables that were in scope at the time that the function was defined;

the function can refer to those variables, even if they are no longer in scope when the function is called. When you are working in a programming language with first-class functions that can be passed around like variables, closures are a convenient way to provide encapsulation without using objects or classes. An example use of a closure is when a function is encapsulated completely within another function but is still able to read the state of a variable that exists in the containing function.

Clojure is unlike most languages in that you don't generally install Clojure itself; it's just a library that's loaded into the JVM. You don't interact with it directly; you use a build tool and editor/IDE integration instead (well, except for when you are interacting using the REPL—in any case, you never run a tool called "clojure" from the command line). That process is a bit beyond the short introduction of this chapter; however, you can get started quickly using one of these two methods:

▶ Install `clojure`. Among other things, this installs a REPL (read-eval-print loop, an interactive programming environment) that can be used by entering `clojure` at the command line. When you install this package, you get what you need for using Clojure in a JVM, but you will need to set up your development environment to use Clojure. See the documentation from each environment for instructions. Note that the most popular, perhaps even the de facto, build tool for Clojure is Leiningen, which adds some really useful functionality, like the ability to manage project dependencies, start a REPL easily, and even install Clojure itself. See https://github.com/technomancy/leiningen#readme for more.

▶ You can try Clojure in a live REPL using www.try-clojure.org.

COBOL

COBOL, *Common Business Oriented Language*, has been around since the 1960s, is one of the oldest programming languages, and is still the dominant language for (legacy) business applications. The majority of big business applications, such as payroll and accounting, were written in COBOL, and most programmers who knew it well have retired. A job market exists for younger programmers willing to learn it and willing to support older applications that are stable and trusted and still running all over the place. This is especially true if you are able to understand the business processes modeled in COBOL and can integrate it with modern technology, which isn't always an easy task.

COBOL's syntax was designed to mimic natural human language. Often a newcomer can read COBOL source code and have a pretty good idea of what it does, even if the reader has little to no programming experience. An interesting feature in early COBOL that is deprecated in more recent versions is self-modifying code, which had the potential to create some interesting situations. COBOL has always been a little controversial, as illustrated by the time that Edsger Dijkstra remarked that "the use of COBOL cripples the mind; its teaching should, therefore, be regarded as a criminal offense."

41

To use COBOL on Ubuntu, you write programs in your favorite text editor. To compile, you need the package open-cobol, which actually translates the programs into C and compiles them using gcc.

Erlang

From the official website, "Erlang is a programming language used to build massively scalable soft real-time systems with requirements on high availability. Some of its uses are in telecoms, banking, e-commerce, computer telephony, and instant messaging. Erlang's runtime system has built-in support for concurrency, distribution, and fault tolerance." Erlang is a declarative, functional language that includes real-time garbage collection and hot-swapping of code. It is primarily designed for distributed applications used in essential applications that require extreme uptime.

Erlang's greatest strength is its ability to create a large number of concurrent processes, each with low overhead, and allow them to communicate with one another using an asynchronous message handling system. In addition, the Erlang developers have a philosophy of development that emphasizes keeping things running, meaning that future stable Erlang updates should not break running code. They like to test extensively and try to break as much as possible in testing to prevent breakage in production systems. One of the technical editors mentioned a neat feature while reading this chapter: Erlang's processes can communicate with each other even if they don't live on the same box. You have to explicitly allow this in your code, but the ability is built in to the language runtime and syntax and is not a third-party library.

To use Erlang on Ubuntu, you write programs in your favorite text editor. To compile, you need the package erlang, which installs the Erlang/OTP runtime, applications, sources, code examples, and the Erlang editing mode for Emacs.

Forth

Forth first appeared in the 1970s. It is an interactive, procedural, imperative language with typeless data that runs as a shell. Sets of instructions can be saved and compiled as bytecode programs. It a very small language by itself and is therefore very useful in boot loaders and embedded systems, and has even been used by NASA in space applications.

On the surface, Forth is a simple language, but it is highly extensible. In essence, a programmer creates a dictionary, beginning with the small set of predefined words. These are combined in new ways to extend the lexicon and create new things that may be done. This is powerful, but it is also dangerous. The lack of standards can lead to less-than-stellar programmers creating unclear sets of vocabulary that make it impossible for anyone else to maintain what they have written. However, thoughtful programmers who are disciplined and organized have created highly complex, yet maintainable programs in Forth that have been used for decades across multiple platforms.

41

Perhaps Forth might be described as a language for experienced programmers who can handle total control over the CPU and want to build sophisticated systems running in extremely limited environments. If you are old enough to remember HP calculators and their "reverse Polish" notation, where the operator is placed after the operands, you will find Forth familiar.

To use Forth on Ubuntu, install the package gforth, which is the GNU implementation of a Forth programming environment.

Fortran

Fortran was developed by IBM in the 1950s for engineering and scientific applications. Its popularity spread quickly in areas of science that are dominated by numeric computation. Today, many of those same Fortran programs are still maintained and in use in fields such as weather modeling and prediction, fluid dynamics, and segments of chemistry and physics. In a published article from 2010, Eugene Loh, an engineer at Oracle, called Fortran the most commonly used and perhaps the ideal language for high-performance computing (http://queue.acm.org/detail.cfm?id=1820518).

Fortran is a terse language in which complex applications may be written with relatively few statements. It is a procedural language with object-oriented abilities. It excels at numeric computation and is often used as the language in which programs are written to test supercomputers for speed.

To use Fortran on Ubuntu, you write programs in your favorite text editor. To compile, you need the package gfortran, the GNU Fortran 95 compiler, which compiles Fortran 95 on platforms supported by the gcc compiler. It uses the gcc back end to generate optimized code.

Groovy

Groovy, like Clojure, is designed for the JVM. It was written to enable features like closures and dynamic typing from popular languages like Python and Ruby to be used by Java developers. It uses a Java-like syntax, making it familiar to those programmers. It can be compiled into standard Java bytecode and used within any Java project. It can also be used dynamically for scripting, templating, or writing unit tests.

To use Groovy on Ubuntu, you must first install a JVM. Then, you need the package groovy. You can then run Groovy code in a shell by entering groovysh at the command line, in an interactive console by entering groovyConsole, or run a specific Groovy script by entering the script file's name at the command line prefaced by groovy, like this:

```
matthew@seymour:~$ groovy scriptname.groovy
```

Haskell

Haskell is a purely functional programming language. It has built-in concurrency and parallelism and good support for integration with other languages. In that sense, it is similar to Erlang. From the beginning in 1990, it has been developed as an open-source project with strong community input and participation. Haskell uses lazy evaluation, meaning that the evaluation of an expression is put off until the last possible moment, until its value is required. This significantly speeds up runtime by avoiding unnecessary or repeated evaluation.

To use Haskell on Ubuntu, install `haskell-platform`, a suite of tools and libraries that contain the most important and best supported components. It is meant to be a starting point for Haskell developers who are looking for libraries to use. To compile, you need the package `ghc`, which is the *Glorious Glasgow Haskell Compilation system (GHC)*, a compiler for Haskell.

Java

Java was created by Sun Microsystems, now owned by Oracle, as a write-once, run-anywhere language. Java programs are compiled to a bytecode that will run on any JVM. A *Java Virtual Machine (JVM)* must exist on a hardware platform for Java code to run, but no recompilation of the program itself is needed for it to run on different hardware platforms. Java is object oriented, and writing program instructions for a virtual machine is generally easier than doing so for a real machine. Java syntax is similar to C and C++, but is a bit simpler and has fewer low-level abilities. It is currently one of the most popular programming languages. Originally, Java technology was proprietary and licensed for use by Sun. In May 2007, several years before being bought by Oracle, Sun finished relicensing and releasing most Java technology under the GNU GPL. (There were parts they could not relicense because they did not own the copyright to the code.)

Java uses automatic garbage collection to remove objects from memory when they are no longer in use. This frees programmers from thinking about memory management. It includes a graphical user interface library called Swing.

Most Java development occurs in an IDE, several of which are available from the Ubuntu repositories. The most popular include Eclipse (www.eclipse.org) and NetBeans (www.netbeans.org). Each of these include plug-ins that help the programmer include and use libraries, compile to bytecode, and do many other tasks quickly and efficiently.

To program in Java on Ubuntu, you write programs in your favorite text editor or IDE. To compile, you need the package `default-jdk`, which installs the Java Development Kit appropriate for the hardware being used.

JavaScript

JavaScript is an object-oriented, functional programming language designed primarily for scripting. It supports closures, dynamic and weak typing, and has a syntax that is influenced by C and Java, even though it is unrelated to either (except for the circumstantial name similarity with Java). JavaScript was designed to be used by the Netscape web browser as a way to run short programs on web clients. The name is a result of a mid-1990s marketing agreement between Netscape and Sun to try to leverage the buzz about Java and make JavaScript the shiny, new programming language for the Web. You will occasionally see JavaScript referred to using its original name, EMCAScript. The JavaScript trademark is now owned by Oracle under a license from the technology creators, including Mozilla, the descendant of Netscape.

JavaScript is easily the most popular scripting language for the Web, widely used in programming web applications. Combined with HTML and CSS, it is used to create interesting, diverse, and powerful websites. JavaScript has spawned tons of extensions and development kits like Node.js and JSP. It is commonly combined with other technologies like XML to create interactive websites using Ajax. Information is often passed using *JavaScript Object Notation*, or JSON, which is rapidly becoming the successor to XML. Whether people love JavaScript or hate it, it is universally acknowledged as a "must know" technology for programmers today.

To use JavaScript on Ubuntu, you write programs in your favorite text editor. Nothing special is needed. Put the script somewhere and open it with your web browser.

Lisp

Lisp is slightly younger than Fortran, making it not-quite the oldest language discussed in this chapter. It was first released in 1958. Clojure, discussed earlier, is a dialect of Lisp. Lisp is designed to process lists. Linked lists are the language's main data structure. It was originally created to be used as a practical mathematical notation for computer programs, but became popular as a program for research in artificial intelligence.

There have been many versions of Lisp over the years, and many dialects. The most commonly used "regular Lisp" in use today is probably ANSI Common Lisp, of which there are also multiple implementations. To use ANSI Common Lisp on Ubuntu, install the package `clisp`. Type `clisp` from the command line to bring up a REPL (from which you may exit by entering `quit`).

Many Lisp programmers prefer to use Emacs as their editor, which was written in a Lisp dialect called elisp. Emacs includes many useful tools for Lisp and has other plug-ins available. From here, it is easy to save code in files, compile it, and enable it to be run as programs rather than from the REPL interface.

Another interesting dialect of Lisp is Scheme, which is also available from the Ubuntu repositories, but not covered in this chapter.

Lua

Lua is a scripting language created in Brazil in the 1990s. It is similar to and based on Scheme. It is a dynamically typed procedural language with memory management and garbage collection. It is small and often used for embedded applications. It can be compiled on any platform that has a C compiler. Lua is also extensible with a reputation for being simple without being simplistic. It was originally designed for extending applications, but is frequently used for standalone and general-purpose needs.

To use Lua on Ubuntu, you write programs in your favorite text editor. To run them, you need the package lua50, which is the Lua interpreter. Run a program by entering lua *programName* at the command line.

Ruby

In Ruby, everything is an object. Every object can be given its own properties and methods. You can use closures (called blocks in Ruby). You do not need to declare variables, and only single inheritance exists. Ruby includes garbage collection, exception handling, and can be extended by writing extensions in C. Ruby was heavily influenced in different ways by Lisp, Perl, Python, and Smalltalk and was originally designed for systems administration-type scripting.

Most Ruby programmers seem to prefer using Ruby in combination with a web application framework called Rails, making what is known as *Ruby on Rails*. This framework is strongly tied to the DRY philosophy, "don't repeat yourself." Every piece of information is stored in a single, unambiguous place. Ruby on Rails runs on top of a web server like Apache or Nginx and is extensible using Ruby Gems (rubygems.org).

To use Ruby on Ubuntu, you write programs in your favorite text editor. To run them, you can install the interpreter package ruby1.8 from the Ubuntu repositories. Because Ruby changes often, the official Ruby documentation recommends *not* using a distribution's package manager, but rather downloading the latest version directly from their website.

Scala

Scala takes its name from "scalable language." It is designed to grow with its users' needs. Scala runs on a JVM. It is suited for both functional and object-oriented programming. Scala programs are bytecode compatible with Java, and you can call either language from the other. Support for the .NET Framework is also available. Scala syntax is much more succinct than Java. Programs are generally shorter to write. Like Ruby, in Scala everything is an object. Types are inferred and do not need to be made explicit. Like Clojure, it suits the desire that many have to perform functional programming on a JVM.

41

To use Scala on Ubuntu, you write programs in your favorite text editor. To compile, you need the package `scala`. To compile, use `scalac` *sourceFile*, and to run using the interpreter, use `scala` *sourceFile*.

Vala

Vala is a very new language. It was designed to make the lives of the developers of GNOME easier by bringing features from modern languages into C for use in GNOME desktop environment development. The syntax is very similar to C#. Vala is a compiled language, but instead of being complied directly to bytecode, Vala is compiled to C, which is then compiled with a C compiler for each specific platform.

In C, a programmer must manually manage reference in memory. In Vala, this is automated if the built-in reference types are used instead of plain pointers. Vala also uses the GNOME GObject system to provide reference counting. For the most part, usage of Vala is primarily by people working on GNOME, which makes sense because this is the reason Vala was developed. Time will tell whether it receives wider interest.

To use Vala on Ubuntu, you write programs in your favorite text editor. To compile, you need the package `valac`, which is the Vala Compiler. You then need to compile the output from that with a C compiler such as the GNU C Compiler described in Chapter 39, "C/C++ Programming Tools for Ubuntu."

References

- http://www.adaic.org/—The main website for the Ada Information Clearinghouse, an excellent resource for learning Ada.

- http://clojure.org/—The main website for Clojure.

- http://www.cobol.com/—The main website for Cobol.

- http://www.erlang.org/—The main website for Erlang.

- http://www.forth.org/—The main website for the Forth Interest Group, a great place to learn more about Forth.

- http://www.jwdt.com/~paysan/gforth.html—The main website for Gforth, the GNU project's implementation of Forth.

- http://gcc.gnu.org/fortran/—The main website for Gfortran.

- http://groovy.codehaus.org/—The main website for Groovy.

- http://haskell.org/—The main website for Haskell.

▶ **http://www.java.com/**—The main website for Java.

▶ **http://www.w3schools.com/js/default.asp**—The W3C Tutorial page for JavaScript. The site is also a great place to learn HTML and CSS.

▶ **http://www.lisp.org/**—The Association of Lisp Users web page.

▶ **http://www.clisp.org/**—The main website for GNU Cisp, an implementation of Common Lisp.

▶ **http://www.lua.org/**—The main website for Lua.

▶ **http://www.ruby-lang.org/en/**—The main website for Ruby.

▶ **http://www.scala-lang.org/**—The main website for Scala.

▶ **http://live.gnome.org/Vala**—The main website for Vala.

CHAPTER 42

Beginning Mobile Development for Android

So many Linux users have embraced not only smart phones, but specifically those based on Android. Android is owned by Google and based on the Linux kernel and is one of the best-selling platforms for smart phones and tablet computers. Android includes the operating system, middleware, and several key applications. Middleware and application examples include an integrated web browser based on WebKit, optimized graphics libraries, media support for most formats, and structured data storage with SQLite. It also includes software for hardware-dependent functions like GSM, Bluetooth, 3G, WiFi, camera, GPS, and more.

Most of the Android source code is freely available and licensed using the Apache License. Google operates an online app store called *Android Market* where anyone with an Android phone or tablet computer can download free and for-payment applications to extend the functionality of their machine. Other third-party sites exist for the same purpose, thereby creating many paths by which one may make their software available to Android users.

This chapter helps you get started writing software for Android on your Ubuntu machine by describing how to find and set up the development tools you need. It discusses the basic details you need to know as you consider whether you want to develop programs for the Android platform, and if so, whether you want to try to get those programs uploaded to and made available via Android Market or a third-party site.

Introduction to Android

Before we get further into the details of development of software for Android, a more detailed introduction to the Android architecture seems appropriate. Our description starts with the hardware and builds layer upon layer from that foundation.

Hardware

While it has been proved possible to run Android on other platforms, the main target platform is ARM. ARM processors are 32-bit *reduced instruction set computer (RISC)* processors. Like other RISC processors, they are designed for speed with the idea that a simpler set of processor instructions creates greater efficiency and throughput. ARM processors are also designed for low power usage, making them ideal for mobile and embedded devices. Indeed, ARM is the dominant processor in these markets.

Linux Kernel

The first layer of software to run in the Android stack is a customized Linux kernel. Most of the customizations take the form of feature enhancements or optimizations to help Android and Linux work together more efficiently. Originally, Google made a point of contributing code they developed, but some of the features were rejected by the mainline Linux kernel developers for inclusion in the standard Linux kernel. This meant that to keep their desired code customizations, Google had to create a fork of the Linux kernel, which is permissible due to the license under which the kernel is released. Chapter21, "Kernel and Module Management," gives an introduction to the Linux kernel.

Libraries

On top of the kernel run a set of software libraries. These are used by the higher-level components of Android and are made available to developers to use when writing Android applications using the Android *software development kit (SDK)*, which is discussed later in this chapter. These libraries include a version of the standard C library (`libc`), libraries for recording and playback of many popular media formats, graphics and web browser engines, font rendering, and more.

Android Runtime

Some of the higher-level components of Android in the Application Layer (described next) interact directly with the libraries just described. Other parts of the Application Layer interact with the libraries via the Android Runtime. Android software is primarily written in Java, using Google-developed and specific Java libraries. That software runs on the Android Runtime, comprised of some additional core libraries running on top of a special virtual machine called Dalvik. The core libraries provide most of the functionality of Java. Dalvik performs *just-in-time (JIT)* compilation and is optimized for mobile devices.

Application Framework

The Application Framework is a set of useful systems and services that top level applications can call. These provide standardized means of accessing system information, using device hardware, creating notifications, and so on. They are the same set that are used by the core applications included in Android, so end user-created applications can have the same look, feel, and interaction style as those provided by Android.

Applications

Android comes with a set of core applications. These include a web browser, programs for text messaging, managing contacts, a calendar, an email client, and more. As noted earlier, Android software is written in Java.

Installing the Android SDK

Android provides a software development kit, which is a set of tools to enable the creation of applications to run on Android. The Android SDK has versions available for Linux, Mac OS X, and Windows.

Install Java

Before you download and install the Android SDK, you need to install the proper dependencies. Start by installing a *Java Runtime Environment (JRE)* or *Java Virtual Machine (JVM)*.

If you are running a 64-bit version of Ubuntu on your machine, you must first install the `ia32-libs` library from the Ubuntu repositories. This is a set of 32-bit runtime libraries configured for use on a 64-bit system that will enable you to develop and test your 32-bit Android programs while using your 64-bit operating system.

You are free to choose either the open-source Open JDK version, `openjdk-6-jre`, or the Sun/Oracle version, `sun-java6-jre`, from the Ubuntu repositories. You must also install the appropriate matching Java SDK, either `openjdk-6-jdk` or `sun-java6-jdk`.

Install Eclipse

Although this step isn't absolutely necessary, the Android SDK includes the *Android Development Tools (ADT)* plug-in for Eclipse that will make development easier and faster. A version of Eclipse is available from the Ubuntu repositories, but it is not the same version that is recommended by Android developers. The version in the Ubuntu repos is actually newer. Search the Eclipse website at www.eclipse.org/downloads/ to find the older 3.3 version that is recommended at the time of this writing at http://developer.android.com/sdk/installing.html. You are also welcome to try your luck with the version in the Ubuntu repositories (called `eclipse`), but you may find it difficult to get support or assistance from Android developers if you do so. Your choice.

Install the SDK

Download the latest version of the Android SDK from the Android Developers website at http://developer.android.com/sdk/index.html. For Ubuntu, you need the Linux version, which is made available as a TGZ archive file. Unpackage the file in the location where you want the development kit to reside (for example, /home/matthew). Doing so creates a new directory called android-sdk-linux_x86. Note where you put this directory; you will need the information later.

Install the ADT Eclipse Plug-In

If you will not be using Eclipse, you can safely skip this section. To install, complete these steps:

1. Start Eclipse. Select Help, Install New Software.

2. Click Add, and in the Add Repository window, enter **ADT Plugin** for Name and this URL for Location: **https://dl-ssl.google.com/android/eclipse/**. Click OK.

3. In the Available Software window, check the box next to Developer Tools and click Next.

4. View the list of tools to be downloaded. Click Next.

5. Read and accept the license agreements. Click Finish.

6. Close and restart Eclipse.

You must configure the plug-in to use the Android SDK by entering the path to the directory in which it was installed in the previous section. To configure the plug-in, in Eclipse do the following:

1. Select Window, Preferences.

2. Choose Android.

3. For SDK Location in the main panel, click Browse and locate the correct directory. Click Apply. Click OK.

Install Other Components

You have installed the SDK starter package, which includes the latest version of the SDK Tools. However, to develop an Android application, you need at least one Android platform and its associated platform tools. You can also add other useful components and platforms at the same time. To do this, you use the Android SDK and AVD Manager.

You can do this in Eclipse from the menu at Window, Android SDK and AVD Manager.

You can do this from the command line by entering the android-sdk-linux_x86/tools directory and entering android.

Either method brings up a *graphical user interface (GUI)* that allows you to browse the online Android SDK repository to select new or updated components. You already have one of the requirements installed: Android SDK Tools.

At a minimum, you should also install the Android SDK Platform-tools package on at least one SDK platform that corresponds to the version of Android for which you want to write applications (for instance, 2.3 or 3.0). Multiple platforms can be installed concurrently.

You should also install Documentation and Samples packages. Next, take a look at the third-party add-ons. If you want to develop an application that uses a Google *application programming interface (API)*, you will also want to install the Google APIs package. If you want to develop for a specific manufacturer's hardware, you will also find their offerings here.

Choose the packages you want to install by marking the appropriate check boxes. Click Install to install the packages.

Install Virtual Devices

Virtual devices are software emulations of hardware that runs Android. These are useful for testing your application to see how it should run on various machines. Select Virtual devices from the panel on the left to begin.

At the right of the Virtual devices window, select New.

In the window that appears, configure your virtual device, as in Figure 42.1. Click Create AVD when ready.

FIGURE 42.1   Create your virtual device with your desired configuration.

To run an *Android Virtual Device (AVD)*, select it from the list and click Start, as in Figure 42.2. The screen is emulated on the left and the hardware buttons on the right. You may use your mouse and keyboard to interact with the AVD. This can take a long time to start, so be patient.

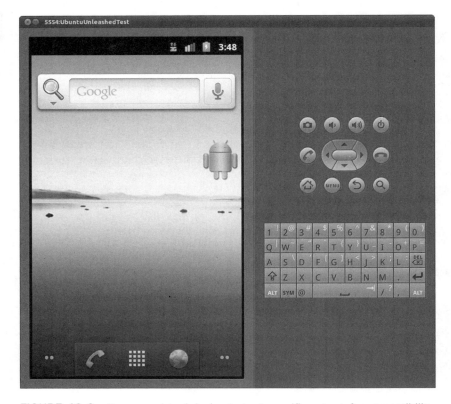

FIGURE 42.2   Run your virtual device to test specific setups for compatibility.

Create Your First Application

Now you are ready to begin. Although it is possible to develop for Android without using Eclipse, the recommended method is to use it. That is what we will use for this brief introduction. This "Hello World" example assumes you have correctly installed and configured the ADT plug-in.

1. Open Eclipse and select File, New, Project.

2. Select Android Project. Click Next.

3. Fill in the project details:

   ▶ Project name: HelloUbuntuWorld—This is the Eclipse project name and the name of the directory that will store the project files.

▶ Application name: `Hello, Ubuntu World!`—This is the title of your application by which it will be known and what will appear on the Android device.

▶ Package name: `com.example.helloubuntuworld`—This follows the same rules as Java package naming. Use a name that is appropriate for your organization or for you individually.

▶ Create Activity: `HelloUbuntuWorld`—This is the name of the class stub that will be created by the plug-in. This is optional.

4. Click Finish.

The project has now been created. You will find it in the Eclipse Package Explorer. Open the `HelloUbuntuWorld.java` file under `HelloUbuntuWorld`, `src`, `com.example.helloubuntuworld` to view the code created for you and begin.

Java development and the details of the Android widgets and other components made available through the SDK are beyond the scope of this chapter, which simply aims to get you started on Ubuntu. Assuming you know how to write in Java and have perused the Android SDK documentation like a good developer, we can safely skip ahead to the final step.

You can run your application for testing in Eclipse. From the menu, select Run, Run. Select Android Application. Eclipse launches an Android emulator. As earlier, the emulator can take a long time to start. Once it has, you see the emulator and your application running in it.

References

▶ **http://developer.android.com/**—The main website for Android development. Most of this chapter could not exist if it were not for this site, which goes into much greater detail than this short introduction and is where this book's author learned most of what he knows on the subject.

▶ **http://developer.android.com/sdk/**—The main web page for the Android SDK.

APPENDIX A

Ubuntu Under the Hood

As with any new thing, it's worthwhile finding out a bit about its history. Ubuntu is no different, and in this appendix, you learn a little more about where Linux (and Ubuntu) came from.

What Is Linux?

Linux is the core, or kernel, of a free operating system first developed and released to the world by Linus Benedict Torvalds in 1991. Torvalds, then a graduate student at the University of Helsinki, Finland, is now a Fellow at the Linux Foundation (www.linuxfoundation.org/). He is an engineer and previously worked for the CPU design and fabrication company Transmeta, Inc. before leaving in 2003 to work for *Open Source Development Labs (ODSL)*, a consortium created by many high-tech companies to support Linux development, which has enabled him to focus on the Linux kernel full time. Fortunately for all Linux users, Torvalds chose to distribute Linux under a free software license named the GNU *General Public License (GPL)*.

> **NOTE**
>
> The free online resource Wikipedia has a great biography of Linus Torvalds that examines his life and notable achievements. You can find it at http://en.wikipedia.org/wiki/Linux_Torvalds.

The GNU GPL is the brainchild of Richard M. Stallman, the founder of the Free Software Foundation. Stallman, the famous author of the Emacs editing environment and GCC compiler system, crafted the GPL to ensure that software that used the GPL for licensing would always be free and available in source-code form. The GPL is the guiding document for Linux and its ownership, distribution, and copyright. Torvalds holds the rights to the Linux trademark, but thanks to a combination of his generosity, the Internet, thousands of programmers around the world, GNU software, and the GNU GPL, Linux will remain forever free and unencumbered by licensing or royalty issues.

Distribution Version and Kernel Numbering Schema

There is a numbering system for Linux kernels, kernel development, and Ubuntu's kernel versions. Note that these numbers bear no relation to the version number of your Ubuntu Linux distribution. Ubuntu distribution version numbers are assigned by the Ubuntu developers, whereas most of the Linux kernel version numbers are assigned by Linus Torvalds and his legion of kernel developers.

To see the date your Linux kernel was compiled, use the uname command with its -v command-line option. To see the version of your Linux kernel, use the -r option. The numbers, such as 2.6.32-24-generic, represent the major version (2), minor version (6), and patch level (32). The final number (24-generic) is the developer patch level and is assigned by the Ubuntu developers.

Even minor numbers are considered "stable" and generally fit for use in production environments. You will find only stable versions of the Linux kernel included with this book. You can choose to download and install a beta (test) version of the kernel, but this is not recommended for a system destined for everyday use. When used, beta kernels are installed by developers to test support of new hardware or operating system features.

Linux, pronounced "lih-nucks," is free software. Combining the Linux kernel with GNU software tools—drivers, utilities, user interfaces, and other software such as the X.Org Foundation's X Window System—creates a Linux distribution. There are many different Linux distributions from different vendors, but many derive from or closely mimic the Debian Linux distribution, on which Ubuntu is founded.

NOTE

To see just how many distributions are based on Debian Linux, go to www.linux.org/, click Distributions, and search for "Debian-based." At the time of writing, 38 distributions owe their existence to Debian.

Why Use Linux?

Millions of clever computer users have been putting Linux to work for more nearly 20 years. Over the past year, many individuals, small office/home office (SOHO) users, businesses and corporations, colleges, nonprofits, and government agencies (local, state, and federal) in a number of countries have incorporated Linux with great success. And, today, Linux is being incorporated into many *information service/information technology (IS/IT)* environments as part of improvements in efficiency, security, and cost savings. Using Linux is a good idea for a number of reasons, including the following:

▶ **Linux provides an excellent return on investment (ROI)**—There is little or no cost on a per-seat basis. Unlike commercial operating systems, Linux has no royalty or licensing fees, and a single Linux distribution on CD-ROM or network shared folder can form the basis of an enterprise-wide software distribution, replete with applications and productivity software. Custom corporate CD-ROMs can be easily crafted or network shares can be created to provide specific installs on enterprise-wide hardware. This feature alone can save hundreds of thousands, if not millions, of dollars in IS/IT costs—all without the threat of a software audit from the commercial software monopoly or the need for licensing accounting and controls of base operating system installations.

▶ **Linux can be put to work on the desktop**—Linux, in conjunction with its supporting graphical networking protocol and interface (the X Window System), has worked well as a consumer UNIX-like desktop operating system since the mid-1990s. The fact that UNIX is ready for the consumer desktop is now confirmed with the introduction, adoption, and rapid maturation of Apple Computer BSD UNIX—based on Mac OS X—supported, according to Apple, by more than 3,000 Mac OS X-specific programs that are known as native applications. This book's disc contains more than 800 software packages, including Internet connection utilities, games, a full office suite, many fonts, and hundreds of graphics applications.

▶ **Linux can be put to work as a server platform**—Linux is fast, secure, stable, scalable, and robust. The latest versions of the Linux kernel easily support multiple-processor computers, large amounts of system memory (up to 64GB RAM), individual file sizes in excess of hundreds of gigabytes, a choice of modern journaling file systems, hundreds of process monitoring and control utilities, and the (theoretical) capability to simultaneously support more than four billion users. IBM, Oracle, and other major database vendors all have versions of their enterprise software available for Linux.

▶ **Linux has a low entry-and-deployment cost barrier**—Maintenance costs can also be reduced because Linux works well on a variety of PCs, including legacy hardware, such as some Intel-based 486 and early Pentium CPUs. Although the best program performance will be realized with newer hardware, because clients can be recompiled and optimized for Pentium-class CPUs, base installs can even be performed on

A

lower-end computers or embedded devices with only 8MB of RAM. This feature provides for a much wider user base; extends the life of older working hardware; and can help save money for home, small business, and corporate users.

▶ **Linux appeals to a wide audience in the hardware and software industry**—Versions of Linux exist for nearly every CPU. Embedded-systems developers now turn to Linux when crafting custom solutions using ARM, MIPS, and other low-power processors. Linux is the first full operating system available for Intel's Itanium CPU, as well as the AMD64 group of CPUs; ports have also been available for HP/Compaq's Alpha and Sun Microsystems SPARC CPUs for some time. PowerPC users regularly use the PPC port of Linux on IBM and Apple hardware.

▶ **Linux provides a royalty-free development platform for cross-platform development**—Because of the open-source development model and availability of free, high-quality development tools, Linux provides a low-cost entry point to budding developers and tech industry start-ups.

▶ **Big-player support in the computer hardware industry from such titans as IBM now lends credibility to Linux as a viable platform**—IBM has enabled Linux on the company's entire line of computers, from low-end laptops through "Big Iron" mainframes. New corporate customers are lining up and using Linux as part of enterprise-level computing solutions. It has been used on some of the world's fastest computers, including IBM's Blue Gene/L. HP also certifies Linux across a large portion of its hardware offering.

Look forward to even more support as usage spreads worldwide throughout all levels of business in search of lower costs, better performance, and stable and secure implementations.

What Is Ubuntu?

Ubuntu is an operating system based on the Linux kernel; created, improved, refined, and distributed by the Ubuntu Community at www.ubuntu.com/. Ubuntu, sponsored by Canonical Software, is an open-source project supported by a worldwide community of software developers.

Ubuntu is one of the newer Linux distributions currently available today, having released its first version in October 2004. It quickly gained a reputation for ease of installation and use, combined with the slightly wacky code names given to each release. However, Ubuntu itself is based on Debian, which is a much older distribution steeped in respect from the wider Linux community. Ubuntu describes Debian as being the rock on which it is founded, and this is a good way to describe the relationship between the two. It is also worth noting that Debian garnered a reputation for infrequent releases. The move from Debian 3.0 to 3.1 took almost three years, during which time many other Linux distros had moved far ahead of Debian.

Sponsored by Canonical Software and with the formidable resources of Mark Shuttleworth, Ubuntu got off to a great start with version 4.10, the Warty Warthog. From the start, Ubuntu specified clear goals: to provide a distribution that was easy to install and use, that did not overly confuse the user, and that came on a single CD (something increasingly rare these days when a distro can occupy four or five CDs). Releasing every six months, Ubuntu made rapid progress into the Linux community and is now one of the most popular Linux distros across the world.

Ubuntu Versions

As mentioned earlier, Ubuntu has chosen a unique numbering scheme and some peculiar code names for their releases since the first launch in October 2004. Doing away with the typical version numbering found elsewhere, Ubuntu decided to take the month and year of release and reverse them. Hence, the first release in October 2004 became 4.10, followed quickly by 5.04 (April 2005), 5.10, 6.06LTS, and so on up to the current 11.10.

The version covered in this book was released in October 2011, and therefore bears the version number 11.10. What's even more special about some releases is that they also carry the *LTS (Long Term Support)* label, meaning that Canonical will support LTS versions for three years on the desktop and a total of five years for the server version after its release. LTS releases come out every two years, and the most recent LTS version was 10.04.

The code names during development are even better: 4.10 was christened the Warty Warthog in recognition that it was a first release, warts and all. The second release, 5.04, was dubbed the Hoary Hedgehog. Things got slightly better with 5.10, code-named the Breezy Badger. 6.06 was announced as the Dapper Drake and was the first Ubuntu distribution to carry the LTS badge. Beyond Dapper, there was the Edgy Eft (6.10) followed by the Feisty Fawn (7.04), and more, up to what was known during development as the Oneric Ocelot (11.10), which is what this book covers. For a full list of development code names, see wiki.ubuntu.com/DevelopmentCodeNames.

Ubuntu for Business

Linux has matured over the years, and features considered essential for use in enterprise-level environments, such as CPU architecture support, file systems, and memory handling, have been added and improved. The addition of virtual memory (the capability to swap portions of RAM to disk) was one of the first necessary ingredients, along with a copyright-free implementation of the TCP/IP stack (mainly due to BSD UNIX being tied up in legal entanglements at the time). Other features quickly followed, such as support for a variety of network protocols.

Ubuntu includes a Linux kernel that can use multiple processors, which allows you to use Ubuntu in more advanced computing environments with greater demands on CPU power. This kernel will support at least 16 CPUs; in reality, however, small business servers typically use only dual-CPU workstations or servers. However, Ubuntu can run Linux on more powerful hardware.

Ubuntu will automatically support your multiple-CPU Intel-based motherboard, and you can take advantage of the benefits of *symmetric multiprocessors (SMPs)* for software development and other operations. The Linux kernels included with Ubuntu can use system RAM sizes up to 64GB, allow individual file sizes in excess of 2GB, and host the demands of— theoretically—billions of users.

Businesses that depend on high-availability, large-scale systems can also be served by Ubuntu, along with the specialist commercial support on offer from hundreds of support partners across the world.

However, Ubuntu can be used in many of these environments by customers with widely disparate computing needs. Some of the applications for Ubuntu include desktop support; small file, print, or mail servers; intranet web servers; and security firewalls deployed at strategic points inside and outside company LANs.

Commercial customers will also benefit from Debian's alliances with several top-tier system builders, including Hewlett-Packard.

Debian itself is also available for multiple architectures, and until recently was developed in tandem on 11 different architectures, from x86 to the older Motorola 680x0 chips (as found in the Commodore Amiga), along with several other architectures.

Small business owners can earn great rewards by stepping off the software licensing and upgrade treadmill and adopting a Linux-based solution. Using Ubuntu not only avoids the need for licensing accounting and the threat of software audits, but also provides viable alternatives to many types of commercial productivity software.

Using Ubuntu in a small business setting makes a lot of sense for other reasons, too, such as not having to invest in cutting-edge hardware to set up a productive shop. Ubuntu easily supports older, or *legacy*, hardware, and savings are compounded over time by avoiding unnecessary hardware upgrades. Additional savings will be realized because software and upgrades are free. New versions of applications can be downloaded and installed at little or no cost, and office suite software is free.

Ubuntu is easy to install on a network and plays well with others, meaning it works well in a mixed-computing situation with other operating systems such as Windows, Mac OS X, and of course, UNIX. A simple Ubuntu server can be put to work as an initial partial solution or made to mimic file, mail, or print servers of other operating systems. Clerical staff should quickly adapt to using familiar Internet and productivity tools, while your business gets the additional benefits of stability, security, and a virus-free computing platform.

By carefully allocating monies spent on server hardware, a productive and efficient multi-user system can be built for much less than the cost of comparable commercial software. Combine these benefits with support for laptops, PDAs, and remote access, and you will find that Ubuntu supports the creation and use of an inexpensive yet efficient work environment.

Ubuntu in Your Home

Ubuntu installs a special set of preselected software packages onto your hard drive; these are suitable for small office/home office (SOHO) users. This option provides a wealth of productivity tools for document management, printing, communication, and personal productivity.

The standard installation requires nearly 2GB of hard drive space but should easily fit onto smaller hard drives in older Pentium-class PCs. The install also contains administrative tools, additional authoring and publishing clients, a variety of editors, a GNOME-based X11 desktop, support for sound, graphics editing programs, and graphical and text-based Internet tools.

64-Bit Ubuntu

Advances in computing saw the introduction of 64-bit x86-compatible CPUs from AMD in the spring of 2003. Intel's EM64T extensions for x86, which largely mirror the advances made by AMD, have further increased the availability of commodity x86-64 hardware.

Ubuntu fully supports AMD64 processors, and you are encouraged to use the 64-bit version of Ubuntu to get the maximum from these advanced processors.

As far as the Intel Itanium architecture goes, unfortunately Ubuntu does not currently support ia64. However, you may want to investigate Debian, which is available for the ia64 platform and several others.

Getting the Most from Ubuntu and Linux Documentation

Nearly all commercial Linux distributions include shrink-wrapped manuals and documentation covering installation and configuration. You will not find official documentation included on the DVD provided with this book. However, you can read or get copies of assorted manuals or topic discussions online at www.ubuntu.com/. There you will find the links to various Ubuntu documentation projects.

Documentation for Ubuntu (and many Linux software packages) is distributed and available in a variety of formats. Some guides are available in PDF and can be read using Adobe's Acrobat Reader for Linux or the evince client. Guides are also available as bundled HTML files for reading with a web browser such as links, KDE's Konqueror, GNOME's Epiphany, or Firefox. Along with these guides, Ubuntu provides various tips, FAQs, and HOWTO documents.

You will find traditional Linux software package documentation, such as manual pages, under the /usr/share/man directory, with documentation for each installed software package under /usr/share/doc.

Linux manual pages are compressed text files containing succinct information about how to use a program. Each manual page generally provides a short summary of a command's use, a synopsis of command-line options, an explanation of the command's purpose, potential caveats or bugs, the name of the author, and a list of related configuration files and programs.

For example, you can learn how to read manual pages by using the man command to display its own manual page, as follows:

```
matthew@seymour:~$ man man
```

After you press Enter, a page of text appears on the screen or in your window on the desktop. You can then scroll through the information using your keyboard's cursor keys, read, and then press the Q key to quit reading.

Many of the software packages also include separate documents known as HOWTOs that contain information regarding specific subjects or software.

If the HOWTO documents are simple text files in compressed form (with filenames ending in .gz), you can easily read the document by using the zless command, which is a text pager that enables you to scroll back and forth through documents. (Use the less command to read plain-text files.) You can start the command by using less, followed by the complete directory specification and name of the file, or *pathname*, like this:

```
matthew@seymour:~$ less /usr/share/doc/httpd-2.0.50/README
```

To read a compressed version of this file, use the zless command in the same way:

```
matthew@seymour:~$ zless /usr/share/doc/attr-2.4.1/CHANGES.gz
```

After you press Enter, you can scroll through the document using your cursor keys. Press the Q key to quit.

If the HOWTO document is in HTML format, you can simply read the information using a web browser, such as Firefox. Or if you are reading from a console, you can use the links or lynx text-only web browsers, like this:

```
matthew@seymour:~$ links /usr/share/doc/stunnel-4.0.5/stunnel.html
```

The links browser offers drop-down menus, accessed by clicking at the top of the screen. You can also press the Q key to quit.

If the documentation is in PostScript format (with filenames ending in .ps), you can use the gv client to read or view the document like this:

```
matthew@seymour:~$ gv /usr/share/doc/iproute-2.4.7/ip-crefs.ps
```

Finally, if you want to read a document in Portable Document Format (with a filename ending in .pdf), use the evince client, as follows:

```
matthew@seymour:~$ evince /usr/share/doc/xfig/xfig-howto.pdf
```

> **NOTE**
>
> This book was developed and written using the standard Ubuntu CD. You can use the disc included with this book for your install or download your own copy, available as ISO9660 images (with filenames ending in `.iso`), and burn it onto a 700MB CD-R or a DVD. You can also order prepressed CDs directly from Ubuntu at http://shipit.ubuntu.com.
>
> Along with the full distribution, you get access to the complete source code to the Linux kernel and source for all software in the distribution—more than 55 million lines of C and nearly 5 million lines of C++ code. Browse to www.ubuntu.com/download/ to get started.

A

Ubuntu Developers and Documentation

If you are interested in helping with Ubuntu, you can assist in the effort by testing beta releases (known as preview releases, and usually named after the animal chosen for the release name), writing documentation, and contributing software for the core or contributed software repositories. You should have some experience in installing Linux distributions, a desire to help with translation of documentation into different languages, or be able to use various software project management systems, such as CVS.

Mailing lists are also available as an outlet or forum for discussions about Ubuntu. The lists are categorized. For example, general users of Ubuntu discuss issues on the ubuntu-users mailing list—beta testers and developers via the ubuntu-devel, and documentation contributors via the ubuntu-doc mailing list. You can subscribe to mailing lists by selecting the ones you are interested in at http://lists.ubuntu.com/mailman/listinfo/. Be warned, however: Some of the mailing lists have in excess of 200 to 300 emails per day.

References

- ▶ **www-1.ibm.com/linux/**—Information from IBM regarding its efforts and offerings of Linux hardware, software, and services.

- ▶ **www.ubuntu.com/**—Home page for Ubuntu, sponsored by Canonical Software, and your starting point for learning more about Ubuntu.

- ▶ **http://help.ubuntu.com/**—Web page with links to current Ubuntu documentation and release notes.

- ▶ **www.tldp.org/**—The definitive starting point for the latest updates to generic Linux FAQs, guides, and HOWTO documents.

- ▶ **www.justlinux.com/**—One site to which new Linux users can browse to learn more about Linux.

- ▶ **www.ubuntuforums.org/**—A popular site that allows users to communicate and support each other with questions and problems.

Ubuntu and Linux Internet Resources

Ubuntu enjoys a wealth of Internet support in the form of websites with technical information, specific program documentation, targeted white papers, bug fixes, user experiences, third-party commercial technical support, and even free versions of specialized, fine-tuned clone distributions.

This appendix lists many of the supporting websites, FTP repositories, Usenet newsgroups, and electronic mailing lists that you can use to get more information and help with your copy of Ubuntu.

If You Need Help 24/7

Whether you are an individual, small business, corporate, or enterprise-level Ubuntu user, don't forget that you can always turn to the source, Canonical, or third-party companies who supply Ubuntu support for commercial technical support on a 24/7 onsite basis, by phone, by email, or even on a per-incident basis. Canonical Software offers a spectrum of support options for its software products. You can read more about support options from the Ubuntu website: http://www.ubuntu.com/support.

The appendix is divided into the following sections:

▶ Websites with Linux information arranged by category

▶ Usenet newsgroups pertaining to Linux

▶ Mailing lists providing Linux user and developer discussions

▶ Internet Relay Chat groups for Linux information

This appendix also lists websites that might be of general interest when using Ubuntu or specific components such as Xorg. Every effort has been made to ensure the accuracy of the URLs, but keep in mind that the Internet is always in flux!

Keep Up-to-Date

Keeping informed about bug fixes, security updates, and other errata is critical to the success and health of an Ubuntu system. To keep abreast of the most important developments when using Ubuntu, be sure to register with the Ubuntu Announcements mailing list. From there, you will learn which updates have been issued and what has been fixed as a result. Go to https://lists.ubuntu.com/mailman/listinfo/ubuntu-security-announce to register for this mailing list. To keep up with bug fixes, new software packages, and security updates, also keep an eye out for Update Manager notifications.

Websites and Search Engines

Literally thousands of websites exist with information about Linux and Ubuntu. The key to getting the answers you need right away involves using the best search engines and techniques. Knowing how to search can mean the difference between frustration and success when troubleshooting problems. This section provides some Internet search tips and lists Ubuntu- and Linux-related sites sorted by various topics. The lists are not comprehensive, but they have been checked and were available at the time of this writing.

Web Search Tips

Troubleshooting problems with Linux by searching the Web can be an efficient and productive way to get answers to vexing problems. One of the most basic rules for conducting productive searches is to use specific search terms to find specific answers. For example, if you simply search for "Ubuntu Linux," you will end up with too many links and too much information. If you search for "Ubuntu sound," however, you are more likely to find the information you need. If you've received an error message, use it; otherwise, use the Linux kernel diagnostic message as your search criterion.

Other effective techniques include the following:

▶ Using symbols in the search string, such as the plus sign (+) to force matches of web pages containing both strings (if such features are supported by the search engine used by web search site)

▶ Searching within returned results

▶ Sorting results (usually by date to get the latest information)

▶ Searching for related information

▶ Stemming searches; for example, specifying returns for not only "link" but also "linking" and "linked"

Invest some time and experiment with your favorite search engine's features—the result will be more productive searches. In addition to sharpening your search skills, also take the time to choose the best search engine for your needs.

Google Is Your Friend

Some of the fastest and most comprehensive search engines on the Web are powered by Linux, so it makes sense to use the best available resources. Out of the myriad number of websites with search engines, http://google.com stands out from the crowd, with millions of users per month. The site uses advanced hardware and software to bring speed and efficiency to your searches. If you are looking for specific Linux answers, take advantage of Google's Linux page at http://google.com/linux.

Why is Google (named after a math number) so powerful? You can get a quick overview from the Google folks at www.google.com/corporate/tech. Part of its success is because of great algorithms, good programming, and simple interface design; but most users really seem to appreciate Google's uncanny capability to provide links to what you are looking for in the first page of a search return. Google's early success was also assured because the site ran its search engine on clusters of thousands of PCs running a version of Red Hat Linux. It is also rumored that an Ubuntu-based distribution is in use on desktops at Google, with the informal moniker of Goobuntu.

Google has the largest database size of any search engine on the Web, with many billions of web pages searched and indexed. The database size is important because empty search results are useless to online users, and the capability to return hits on esoteric subjects can make the difference between success and failure or satisfaction and frustration.

To get a better idea of what Google can offer you, browse to www.google.com/options/. You will find links to many services and tools covering specialized searches, databases, information links, translators, and other helpful browsing tools.

Ubuntu Package Listings

You can quickly and easily view a list of the installed packages on your Ubuntu system, along with a short description of each package, by using the Ubuntu Software Center or Synaptic. Each also shows you descriptions of each package so you can decide whether you want it installed. For more information see Chapter 9, "Managing Software."

Certification

Linux certification courses are part of the rapidly growing information technology training industry. Hundreds of different vendors now offer courses about and testing of Linux skill sets. However, because Linux is open-source software, no formal rules or mandates dictate the knowledge or level of expertise required for certification. If you are interested in certification and want to pursue a career or obtain employment with a company using Linux, you really should seek training. You can find a good list of companies that can provide training at www.ubuntu.com/support/training/, along with other resources.

Commercial Support

Commercial support for Ubuntu is an essential ingredient to the success of Linux in the corporate and business community. Although hundreds, if not thousands, of consultants well versed in Linux and UNIX are available on call for a fee, here is a short list of the best-known Linux support providers:

▶ **www.ubuntu.com/support/services**—Go straight to the source for a range of support options. You can get help on Ubuntu direct from Canonical software, or from a local support provider.

▶ **www.hp.com/linux**—HP offers a comprehensive package of Linux services and hardware that cover almost everything that you would want to do, including consultancy, business solutions, and hardware specification and implementation.

▶ **www.ibm.com/linux/**—Linux services offered by IBM include e-business solutions, open-source consulting, database migration, clustering, servers, and support.

In addition to service-oriented support companies, nearly every commercial distributor of Linux has some form of easily purchased commercial support. There are various ways in which to take advantage of support services (such as remote management, onsite consulting, device driver development, and so on), but needs will vary according to customer circumstances and installations.

The Benefits of Joining a Linux User Group

Join a local Linux Users Group (LUG). Joining and participating in a local LUG has many benefits. You will be able to get help, trade information, and learn many new and wonderful things about Linux. Most LUGs do not have membership dues, and many often sponsor regular lectures and discussions from leading Linux, GNU, and open-source experts. For one great place to start, browse to www.tux.org/luglist.html. For Ubuntu-specific groups, check out Ubuntu Local Community, or LoCo Teams at http://loco.ubuntu.com/.

Documentation

Nearly all Linux distributions include thousands of pages of documentation in the form of manual pages, HOWTO documents (in various formats, such as text and HTML), mini-HOWTO documents, or software package documentation (usually found under the /usr/share/doc/ directory). However, the definitive site for reading the latest versions of these documents is the Linux Documentation Project, found at www.tldp.org.

Linux Guides

If you are looking for more extensive and detailed information concerning a Linux subject, try reading one of the many Linux guides. These guides, available for a number of subjects, dwell on technical topics in more detail and at a more leisurely pace than a HOWTO. You can find copies of the following:

- ▶ "Advanced Bash-Scripting Guide," by Mendel Cooper; a guide to shell scripting using bash

- ▶ "LDP Author Guide," by Mark F. Komarinski; how to write LDP documentation

- ▶ "Linux Administration Made Easy," by Steve Frampton

- ▶ "Linux Consultants Guide," by Joshua Drake; a worldwide listing of commercial Linux consultants

- ▶ "Linux from Scratch," by Gerard Beekmans; creating a Linux distribution from software

- ▶ "Linux Kernel Module Programming Guide," by Peter J Salzman, Michael Burian, and Ori Pomerantz; a good guide to building 2.4 and 2.6 series modules

- ▶ "Securing and Optimizing Linux," by Gerhard Mourani

- ▶ Linux certification guides

- ▶ "The Linux Network Administrator's Guide, Second Edition," by Olaf Kirch and Terry Dawson; a comprehensive Net admin guide

Ubuntu

The best place to start for Ubuntu-specific information is at Ubuntu-focused websites. Where better to start than the main website for the distribution and the official web forums? Although these are not the only official Ubuntu resources, they are the most likely to be immediately useful. You can easily find others under the Support tab on the Ubuntu.com website:

- ▶ **www.ubuntu.com**—Home page for Ubuntu, Canonical's community-based free Linux distribution. Ubuntu is the main release of this Linux distribution and includes thousands of software packages that form the core of an up-to-date, cutting-edge Linux-based desktop. You can also find links to the other *buntus, such as Kubuntu, Xubuntu, and EdUbuntu.

- ▶ **www.ubuntuforums.org**—A good place to go if you need specific Ubuntu support.

Mini-CD Linux Distributions

Mini-CD Linux distributions are used for many purposes. Some distributions are used to boot to a read-only firewall configuration, some are used to provide as complete a rescue environment as possible, and others are used to either install or help jumpstart an install of a full distribution. Mini-CDs are available in a variety of sizes, such as 3CD-Rs (or CD-RW) with sizes ranging from 185MB to 210MB. You can also download an ISO image and create a Linux bootable business card, typically fitting on a 40MB or 50MB credit card-size CD-R. (Consider using a mini–CD-RW, especially if you want to upgrade your distribution often.) Here are some links to these distributions:

▶ **www.lnx-bbc.com**—Home page for the Linux BBC, a 40MB image hosting a rather complete live Linux session with X, a web browser, and a host of networking tools.

▶ **http://crux.nu/**—Home page of the CRUX i686-optimized Linux distribution.

▶ **www.smoothwall.org**—The 69MB SmoothWall distribution is used to install a web-administered firewall, router, or gateway with SSH, HTTP, and other services.

Various Intel-Based Linux Distributions

Choosing a Linux *distribution (distro)* for an Intel-based PC is generally a matter of personal preference or need. Many Linux users prefer Red Hat's distro because of its excellent support, commercial support options, and widespread use around the world. However, many different Linux distributions are available for download. One of the best places to start looking for a new distro or new version of your favorite distro is at www.distrowatch. com:

▶ **www.debian.org**—The Debian Linux distribution, consisting only of software distributed under the GNU GPL license. Ubuntu, itself, is based on Debian.

▶ **www.slackware.com**—Home page for download of the newest version of one of the oldest Linux distributions, Slackware.

▶ **www.opensuse.org**—Home page for SUSE Linux.

▶ **http://fedoraproject.org/**—A popular distribution closely related to Red Hat.

▶ **www.redhat.com/**—One of the most used distributions in the corporate and server world.

PowerPC-Based Linux Distributions

PowerPC processors were created by an alliance between Apple, IBM, and Motorola. They have been used extensively in video game consoles, embedded applications, and were the processors used in Apple's Macintosh computers from 1994 to 2006:

▶ **http://penguinppc.org/**—Home page for the PowerPC GNU/Linux distribution.

▶ **www.yellowdoglinux.com**—Home page for Terra Soft Solutions's Yellow Dog Linux for the PowerPC, which is based on Fedora.

Linux on Laptops and PDAs

One of the definitive sites for getting information about running Linux on your laptop is Kenneth Harker's Linux Laptop site. Although not as actively updated as in the past, this site (www.linux-laptop.net) still contains the world's largest collection of Linux and laptop information, with links to user experiences and details concerning specific laptop models.

Another site to check is Werner Heuser's Tuxmobil-Mobile UNIX website at www.tuxmobil.org. You will find links to information such as IrDA, Linux PDAs, and cell phones. Linux Zaurus PDA users can browse to www.openzaurus.org to download a complete open-source replacement operating system for the Zaurus 5000 and 5500 models.

The X Window System

Although much technical information is available on the Internet regarding the X Window System, finding answers to specific questions when troubleshooting can prove to be problematic. If you are having a problem using X, first try to determine whether the problem is software or hardware related. When searching or asking for help (such as on Usenet's `comp.os.linux.x` newsgroup, which you can access through Google's Groups link; see the next section for other helpful Linux newsgroups), try to be as specific as possible. Critical factors or information required to adequately assess a problem include the Linux distribution in use; the kernel version used; the version of X used; the brand, name, and model of your video card; the names, brands, and models of your monitor and other related hardware.

Definitive technical information regarding X is available from www.X.org.

Usenet Newsgroups

Linux-related Usenet newsgroups are another good source of information if you're having trouble using Linux. If your ISP does not offer a comprehensive selection of Linux newsgroups, you can browse to http://groups.google.com/.

The primary Linux and Linux-related newsgroups are as follows:

- ▶ **`alt.os.linux.dial-up`**—Using PPP for dial-up
- ▶ **`alt.os.linux.mandriva`**—All about Mandriva Linux
- ▶ **`alt.os.linux.slackware`**—Using Slackware Linux
- ▶ **`alt.os.linux.ubuntu`**—Using Ubuntu Linux
- ▶ **`comp.os.linux.advocacy`**—Heated discussions about Linux and other related issues
- ▶ **`comp.os.linux.alpha`**—Using Linux on the Alpha CPU
- ▶ **`comp.os.linux.announce`**—General Linux announcements

▶ **comp.os.linux.answers**—Releases of new Linux FAQs and other information

▶ **comp.os.linux.development.apps**—Using Linux development tools

▶ **comp.os.linux.development.system**—Building the Linux kernel

▶ **comp.os.linux.embedded**—Linux embedded device development

▶ **comp.os.linux.hardware**—Configuring Linux for various hardware devices

▶ **comp.os.linux.m68k**—Linux on Motorola's 68K-family CPUs

▶ **comp.os.linux.misc**—Miscellaneous Linux topics

▶ **comp.os.linux.networking**—Networking and Linux

▶ **comp.os.linux.portable**—Using Linux on laptops

▶ **comp.os.linux.powerpc**—Using PPC Linux

▶ **comp.os.linux.security**—Linux security issues

▶ **comp.os.linux.setup**—Linux installation topics

▶ **comp.os.linux.x**—Linux and the X Window System

▶ **comp.windows.x.apps**—Using X-based clients

▶ **comp.windows.x.i386unix**—X for UNIX PCs

▶ **comp.windows.x.intrinsics**—X Toolkit library topics

▶ **comp.windows.x.kde**—Using KDE and X discussions

▶ **comp.windows.x.motif**—All about Motif programming

▶ **comp.windows.x**—Discussions about X

▶ **linux.admin.***—Two newsgroups for Linux administrators

▶ **linux.debian.***—30 newsgroups about Debian

▶ **linux.dev.***—25 or more Linux development newsgroups

▶ **linux.help**—Get help with Linux

▶ **linux.kernel**—The Linux kernel

Mailing Lists

Mailing lists are interactive or digest-form electronic discussions about nearly any topic. To use a mailing list, you must generally send an email request to be subscribed to the list, and then verify the subscription with a return message from the master list mailer. After you subscribe to an interactive form of list, each message sent to the list will appear in your email inbox. However, many lists provide a digest form of subscription in which a single- or half-day's traffic is condensed in a single message. The digest form is generally preferred unless you have set up email filtering.

The main Ubuntu mailing lists are detailed here, but there are quite a few Linux-related lists. You can search for nearly all online mailing lists by using a typical mailing list search web page, such as the one at www.lsoft.com/lists/list_q.html.

GNOME and KDE Mailing Lists

GNOME users and developers should know that more than two dozen mailing lists are available through http://mail.gnome.org/. KDE users will also benefit by perusing the KDE-related mailing lists at www.kde.org/mailinglists.html.

Ubuntu Project Mailing Lists

The Ubuntu Project is always expanding, as many new users continue to find Ubuntu for the first time. You will find many other knowledgeable users with answers to your questions by participating in one of Ubuntu's mailing lists. The lists are focused on using, testing, and developing and participating in Ubuntu's development:

▶ **http://lists.ubuntu.com/mailman/listinfo/ubuntu-security-announce**—Security announcements from the Ubuntu developers.

▶ **http://lists.ubuntu.com/mailman/listinfo/ubuntu-announce**—Announcements concerning Ubuntu.

▶ **http://lists.ubuntu.com/mailman/listinfo/ubuntu-users**—Discussions among users of Ubuntu releases.

▶ **http://lists.ubuntu.com/mailman/listinfo/ubuntu-devel**—Queries and reports from developers and testers of Ubuntu test releases.

Internet Relay Chat

Internet Relay Chat (IRC) is a popular form and forum of communication for many Linux developers and users because it allows an interactive, real-time exchange of information and ideas. To use IRC, you must have an IRC client and the address of a network and server hosting the desired chat channel for your discussions.

You can use the `irc.freenode.net` IRC server, or one listed at www.freenode.net/ to chat with other Ubuntu users. Some current channels are as follows:

▶ **#Ubuntu**—General chat about Ubuntu.

▶ **#edubuntu**—General chat about Edubuntu.

▶ **#xubuntu**—General chat about Xubuntu.

▶ **#kubuntu**—General chat about Kubuntu.

For more channels to look at, head over to https://help.ubuntu.com/community/ InternetRelayChat for an exhaustive list of "official" channels.

However, Google can help you find other channels to explore. Enter the distro name and IRC into the search options to retrieve information on any IRC channels relevant to your requirements. To get help with getting started with IRC, browse to www.irchelp.org/. Among channels you might find interesting are the following:

▶ **#linux**—General discussions about Linux.

▶ **#linuxhelp**—A help chat discussion for new users.

Most IRC networks provide one or more Linux channels, although some providers require signup and registration before you can access any chat channel.

Index

Symbols

A

B

C

How can we make this index more useful? Email us at indexes@samspublishing.com

G

How can we make this index more useful? Email us at indexes@samspublishing.com

U

Related Linux and Open Source Titles

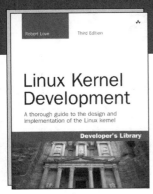

Linux Kernel Development

Robert Love

ISBN-13: 9780672329463

The Official Ubuntu Book

**Benjamin Hill
Matthew Helmke
Corey Burger**

ISBN-13: 9780137081301

A Practical Guide to Fedora and Red Hat Enterprise Linux

Mark G. Sobell

ISBN-13: 9780132757270

A Practical Guide to Linux Commands, Editors, and Shell Programming

Mark G. Sobell

ISBN-13: 9780131367364

Addison Wesley

SAMS

PRENTICE HALL

informit.com/opensource

Books are available at most retail and online bookstores. For more information or to order direct, visit our online bookstore at **informit.com**

Online editions of all titles are available by subscription from Safari Books Online at **safari.informit.com**

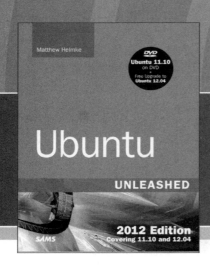

FREE Online Edition

Your purchase of **Ubuntu Unleashed** includes access to a free online edition for 45 days through the **Safari Books Online** subscription service. Nearly every Sams book is available online through **Safari Books Online**, along with thousands of books and videos from publishers such as Addison-Wesley Professional, Cisco Press, Exam Cram, IBM Press, O'Reilly Media, Prentice Hall, Que, and VMware Press.

Safari Books Online is a digital library providing searchable, on-demand access to thousands of technology, digital media, and professional development books and videos from leading publishers. With one monthly or yearly subscription price, you get unlimited access to learning tools and information on topics including mobile app and software development, tips and tricks on using your favorite gadgets, networking, project management, graphic design, and much more.

Activate your FREE Online Edition at
informit.com/safarifree

STEP 1: Enter the coupon code: MCDHHFH.

STEP 2: New Safari users, complete the brief registration form.
Safari subscribers, just log in.

If you have difficulty registering on Safari or accessing the online edition,
please e-mail customer-service@safaribooksonline.com